OLD TESTAMENT SURVEY

Old Testament

The Message, Form, and Background

by

with contributions by
Leslie C. Allen
John E. Hartley
John E. McKenna

WILLIAM B. EERDMANS PUBLISHING COMPANY

Survey

of the Old Testament

SECOND EDITION

William Sanford LaSor†
David Allan Hubbard†
Frederic Wm. Bush

James R. Battenfield
Robert L. Hubbard, Jr.
William B. Nelson, Jr.

GRAND RAPIDS, MICHIGAN / CAMBRIDGE, U.K.

© 1982, 1996 Wm. B. Eerdmans Publishing Co.
255 Jefferson Ave. S.E., Grand Rapids, Michigan 49503 /
P.O. Box 163, Cambridge CB3 9PU U.K.

First edition 1982
Second edition 1996

Printed in the United States of America

01 00   7 6 5

Library of Congress Cataloging-in-Publication Data

LaSor, William Sanford.
    Old Testament survey: the message, form, and background of the
  Old Testament / William Sanford LaSor, David Allan Hubbard,
  Frederic Wm. Bush; with contributions by Leslie C. Allen . . . [et al.].
  — Second ed.
      p.   cm.
  Includes bibliographical references and indexes.
  ISBN 0-8028-3788-3 (cloth: alk. paper)
    1. Bible. O.T. — Introductions. I. Hubbard, David Allan.
  II. Bush, Frederic William. III. Allen, Leslie C. IV. Title.
BS1140.2.L25   1996
221.6'1 — dc20   96-14385
                                  CIP

Contents

Acknowledgments for the Second Edition

To take advantage of the most recent biblical scholarship and the carefully crafted inclusive language where human beings are the subject, we have used the *New Revised Standard Version (NRSV)*, unless otherwise indicated. Special thanks go to the Word Processing team at Fuller Theological Seminary who prepared the disks and the hard copy for these chapters. Marilyn Marshall, who served as a member of David A. Hubbard's staff at Fuller and continued to assist him in his emeritus years, deserves much credit for the coordination of the project. Special mention is due Katherine Jeffrey for her accurate and sensitive editing work. Allen Myers has carried the burden of the seemingly endless task on behalf of the group at Eerdmans who have seen our efforts through to a happy conclusion.

Acknowledgments for the First Edition

Unless otherwise stated, scripture quotations are from the Revised Standard Version of the Bible, copyrighted 1946, 1952 © 1971, 1973 by the Division of Christian Education of the National Council of the Churches of Christ in the U.S.A., and used by permission.

Special thanks for help goes to our graduate assistants Eugene Carpenter, Ph.D., Edward M. Cook, Marianne Meye Thompson, and Marguerite Schuster, Ph.D. Inez T. Smith coordinated the typing and collating of the various drafts. Phyllis Jarvis of Wm. B. Eerdmans Publishing Co. retyped the entire edited manuscript, which was revised for style and checked for accuracy by Allen Myers.

Preface to the Second Edition

The steady and widespread use of *The Old Testament Survey* since its publication in 1982 has encouraged us to make it even more serviceable in this revised form. Several aims have shaped our efforts in the updating of the volume. First, we have tried to make the text more congenial to the thousands of college and university students who use it annually. Simpler style, gender-sensitive language, shorter sentences, a more congenial look to the pages, additional charts, illustrations, and maps — these and other devices have been employed to that end. Furthermore, we have transferred a number of chapters from the beginning to the end of the book to offer teachers the choice of plunging immediately into the biblical writings.

Second, we have sought to include in the text as well as in the endnotes and bibliographies material as current as possible, especially in those instances where new interpretative options have arisen or the scholarly consensus has changed. Third, we have added a new chapter on Archaeology and have included more data from recent archaeological research in the other chapters.

Our hope is that the revisions will enhance the use of the book for its intended readership: college and seminary students and their teachers, as well as pastors, Bible students, and interested laypersons. The cordial participation of a team of colleagues in the task means that the work has undergone a breadth and depth of scrutiny that will enhance both its clarity and its quality. We are honored by the appearance of their names on the title page.

The sudden death in 1991 of our senior colleague, Bill LaSor, meant that we were deprived of his keen eye and ready pen during much of the process. He did, however, leave mounds of materials behind him with perceptive suggestions and pointed queries that have reminded us of his commitment to the task and his competence through six decades of indefatigable labor in biblical and Semitic studies.

May 1996   DAVID ALLAN HUBBARD
                                                FREDERIC WM. BUSH

                              *   *   *

On June 7, 1996, as this revision of *Old Testament Survey* was in its final stages, David Allan Hubbard died of a heart attack at his home in Santa Barbara, California. He was born to John and Helena Hubbard on April 8, 1928, in Stockton, California. He is survived by his wife of 46 years, Ruth; their daughter, Mary Given; son-in-law Dean Given; grandsons David and Jeffrey; brothers John and Robert, and a sister, Laura Smith, and their families.

David graduated from Westmont College, Santa Barbara, and completed his M.Div. and M.Th. degrees at Fuller Seminary in 1954, subsequently being ordained as a minister in the American Baptist Churches of the USA. He earned a Ph.D. degree in Old Testament studies at St. Andrew's University in Scotland in 1957, whereupon he joined the faculty of Westmont College.

In 1963, at the age of 35, he was called to be the third president of Fuller Theological Seminary, at which post he served until his retirement in 1993. Under his leadership, Fuller grew to be the largest independent, fully accredited theological seminary in the world, and, largely due to his creative vision and administrative skill, came to include not only the School of Theology but a School of Psychology and a School of World Mission as well. In addition to his heavy administrative duties as president, David regularly carried a half-time load of teaching in the Old Testament department, always packing the classroom as a gifted and charismatic teacher. And the heritage of his parents, both of whom served as ministers, was not only realized in the warm and vibrant faith which marked him, but also in his service as the host and speaker of "The Joyful Sound" international radio broadcast from 1969 to 1980.

In addition to his administrative and teaching responsibilities, David continued an active scholarly and publishing career, producing 36 books, including four commentaries on the Old Testament. He was both the instigator and catalyst for the first edition of *Old Testament Survey,* with great skill enabling the three of us both to make progress toward its completion and to find consensus on its contents (no mean task!); and he carried the complete editorial responsibility for this revised edition. Without his skill and dedication neither edition would have seen the light of day. He was also serving as the editor of the Word Biblical Commentary series at the time of his death.

He served for two years as president of the Association for Theological Schools in the United States and Canada, and later in the month in which he died was to have received a lifetime achievement award from the Association. But his contributions were not limited to the theological world. He chaired the Pasadena Urban Coalition from 1968 to 1971, and, at the invitation of the governor of California, served as a member of the California State Board of Education from 1972 to 1975.

But David Hubbard was more than seminary president and scholar. He was an accomplished musician and an inveterate lover of baseball: at almost any time of the season he could give you the batting averages of not only the leaders of both leagues but most of the rest as well! He especially enjoyed taking his grandsons to the game. And at the memorial service held for him at Fuller Seminary on June 20, 1996, those who spoke testified time and again that it was not just the dignity and elegance that marked all that he did nor his many accomplishments which most endeared him to their memory, but the warm and unconditional loving friendship which he bestowed upon all of us in lavish measure. To me he was a mentor, colleague, and co-author but most of all a warm, accepting friend.

The encomium in the order of service at his memorial at Fuller Seminary concluded as follows: "In the 'Mission Beyond the Mission' he wrote to the Fuller community: 'Call the Church of Christ to renewal; work for the moral health of society; seek peace and justice in the world; uphold the truth of God's revelation." David Allan Hubbard did just that. And in so doing he left a legacy of blessing to us all."

FREDERIC WM. BUSH

Preface to the First Edition

This book has been in the making for some years. The plan for it developed when one of us taught Old Testament survey courses at the collegiate level and was frustrated by the lack of an adequate text. Though teachers of Scripture have been blessed amply with specialized works like histories, theologies, and introductions, no one volume was available that combined those elements in a framework whose theological and scholarly approaches we found congenial. For more than fifteen years now the three of us have taught together as a team at Fuller Theological Seminary, sharing the Old Testament core courses and testing these chapters with hundreds of students along the way. Their suggestions and criticisms we have tried to incorporate into the various drafts, and their fingerprints are on every page.

We have approached our materials with both college and seminary students in mind. Our aim has been to pitch the text at a level that most college students can handle and then to meet some of the more technical needs of seminary instruction with the footnotes and bibliographies. (Works cited in the annotated chapter bibliographies — labeled "For Further Reading" — are representative studies chosen to supplement those cited in the chapter notes. For more comprehensive works see the General Bibliography.) Though each of us has drafted certain chapters, we have all read, reviewed, and revised each other's work so thoroughly that the book is a joint effort in every sense.

Our purpose is straightforward: to introduce the reader to the background, content, literary quality, and message of the Old Testament as a whole and of its various books. To do this we have not followed a rigid outline for each biblical book but have sought to let the contents and style of each book dictate the way we have studied it. The basic sequence of the later prophets has been altered to fit our understanding of their approximate chronological order. In no way is our design to substitute for the Bible. What book can? Our hope is that it will be read as a guide and supplement to the biblical text itself and that, as such, it will enhance the devotion and obedience of its readers to Scripture and to Scripture's Lord.

We venture to state succinctly here what we have tried to make apparent throughout the book: we are committed to the inspiration and the authority of the Bible, including every part of the Old Testament, and seek to honor it as Holy Scripture in all we say about it. Beyond that, we have written of the Old Testament as those who understand that its fulfillment is in the New Testament and in Jesus of Nazareth, whom we believe to be the Messiah and the incarnation of the living God. Though at every point we have sought to approach the Old Testament text from the vantage of Israel's sons and daughters to whom it was first given, yet we have been constrained not to stop there but to suggest the relationships of the Old Testament themes to the New Testament, the creedal affirmations of the early Church, and the evangelical confessions of the Reformation — all of which govern and express what we believe and teach.

Out of that commitment to the reality and authority of divine revelation flows a concern to take with full seriousness the historical, cultural, and social setting of Scripture together with the literary and linguistic means by which it was recorded. That concern necessarily entails the reverent use of the tools of textual, literary, and form criticism in order to hear the nuances with which God spoke to the first hearers of his word. We do the Bible no honor to revere it without making every effort, with every available scholarly means, to understand it. Obedience to God and worship of his holy name are our ultimate aim as God's people. Such obedience and worship will be best informed where we have grasped the how, why, when, where, and by whom of his sacred revelations. Both piety and study are essential to sound discipleship. To combine them has been the goal of our ministries and of this book.

September 1981   WILLIAM SANFORD LASOR
                                                         DAVID ALLAN HUBBARD
                                                         FREDERIC WM. BUSH

Contributors

LESLIE C. ALLEN
> Professor of Old Testament, Fuller Theological Seminary
>
> *The Former Prophets; Micah; Ezekiel; Jonah; The Writings; Psalms; The Chronicler's Perspective; Revelation and Inspiration; Canon*

JAMES R. BATTENFIELD
> Formerly Lecturer, California State University, Long Beach
>
> *Archaeology*

JOHN E. HARTLEY
> Professor of Old Testament, Azusa-Pacific University
>
> *The Pentateuch; Genesis: Primeval Prologue; Genesis: Patriarchal History; Exodus: Historical Background; Exodus: Contents and Theology; Leviticus; Job; Geography*

ROBERT L. HUBBARD, JR.
> Professor of Old Testament, North Park Theological Seminary
>
> *Divided Monarchy; Judah Alone; Hebrew Poetry; Jeremiah; Ruth; Lamentations; Esther; Ezra-Nehemiah*

JOHN E. MCKENNA

Minister in the American Baptist Churches, Pasadena, California

Joshua; Judges; Amos; Isaiah: Background; Isaiah: Message; Daniel; Messianic Prophecy

WILLIAM B. NELSON, JR.

Associate Professor of Old Testament, Westmont College

Haggai; Zechariah; Malachi; Formation of the Old Testament

All other chapters were revised by David A. Hubbard and Frederic Wm. Bush, who also bear responsibility for the final form of the whole book.

Maps

PART ONE

THE TORAH

CHAPTER 1

The Pentateuch

The "Pentateuch" is made up of the first five books of the Old Testament — Genesis, Exodus, Leviticus, Numbers, and Deuteronomy. This word derives from Gk. *pentateuchos*, "five-volume (book)." Jews call these books the "Torah" (i.e., "instruction"), often rendered in English as "Law" (so Matt. 5:17; Luke 16:17; Acts 7:53; 1 Cor. 9:8). The Jews assign to the Torah a greater authority and sanctity than the rest of Scripture.

> So they read from the book, from the law (Torah) of God, with interpretation. They (the Levites) gave the sense, so that the people understood the reading. Neh. 8:8

Unity

The Pentateuch contains a wide variety of material — stories, incidents, laws, rituals, regulations, ceremonies, calendars, exhortations. It is nevertheless united by a historical narrative. The vital importance of this historical narrative is proven by its usage in the New Testament as the background and preparation for God's work in Christ. The New Testament writers especially draw on the sequence of divine acts from Abraham's call through the kingship of David.

A vivid example is Paul's address to the Jews in the synagogue at Antioch of Pisidia (Acts 13:17-41). He begins (vv. 17-23) with a confessional summary of what God has done from Abraham through David, after which he moves directly to Jesus Christ. Paul implies that the stream of history from the patriarchs to David is the most significant part of the Old Testament story. He affirms that Christ is the culmination and fulfillment of God's redemptive purposes begun there.

There are similar summaries in the Old Testament, especially the confession prescribed for the ritual of firstfruits (Deut. 26:5-10; which has been called "the Pentateuch in a nut-shell"; compare Deut. 6:20-24 and Josh. 24:2-13). These recitals contain the same basic details of God's saving acts:

(1) God chose Abraham and his descendants (Acts 13:17; Josh. 24:3) and promised them the land of Canaan (Deut. 6:23).
(2) Israel went down into Egypt (Acts 13:17; Josh. 24:4) and fell into slavery (Deut. 6:21; 26:5), from which the Lord delivered them (Acts 13:17; Josh. 24:5-7; Deut. 6:21f.; 26:8).
(3) God brought Israel into Canaan as promised (Acts 13:19; Josh. 24:11-13; Deut. 6:23; 26:9).

> The building blocks of the Pentateuch, then, are *promise, election, deliverance, covenant, law,* and *land.*

The element central to these confessions of faith is the Exodus, for it represents both Yahweh's deliverance of Israel from slavery and their election as his people. Yahweh's pivotal saving deed in Israel's history, the Exodus serves as the model for other saving acts (cf. Amos 2:4-10; 3:1f.; Jer. 2:2-7; Pss. 77:13-19 [MT 14-20]; 78:12-55). This is the plot of the narrative of the Pentateuch: Yahweh *chose* the people he delivered dramatically at the Red Sea as "his treasured possession out of all the peoples" (Exod. 19:5). Then he bound them to himself in his *covenant* as their God. His gracious, unmerited *deliverance* is thus the grounds for the covenant. For their constitution Yahweh gave to his people the *law.* This story is recorded in Exodus through Deuteronomy. Gen. 12–50, the patriarchal prologue, sets forth the *promise* which the *deliverance* from Egypt, the granting of the *covenant*, and giving of the *land* fulfills.

The *promise* element of this plot structure is primary and fundamental. It is set forth in its most succinct form in God's words to Abraham in Gen. 12:1-2:

> Now the LORD said to Abraham, "Go from your country and your kindred and you father's house to the land that I will show you. I will make of you a great nation, and I will bless you, and make your name great, so that you will be a blessing."

4

As this passage reveals, this promise is threefold. It consists of land, of nationhood, and of blessing. In other formulations of the promise, however, the third element, the promise of blessing, is stated in other ways: "I will make my covenant between me and you, and your offspring after you" (Gen. 17:7a, 19); "I will be with you" (Gen. 26:3, 24; 28:15; 46:3; Exod. 3:12); "I will be your God, and you shall be my people" (Gen. 17:7c; Exod. 6:7; Lev. 26:12); "I am the God of your father" (Gen. 26:24; 46:3; Exod. 3:6, 15). All of these different statements can be most helpfully and insightfully summed up under the heading of "the promise of a relationship with God."[1] This promise, then, a promise whose fulfillment is only partially realized within the Pentateuch itself, includes posterity (peoplehood, community), a divine-human relationship, and land.

This threefold theme is repeated in the stories about Abraham (cf. Gen. 13:14-17; 15:2-5, 18-21; 17:7f., 15-19). It is renewed with each patriarchal generation: Isaac (Gen. 26:2-4), Jacob/Israel (28:13; 35:11-13), and Joseph and his sons (48:1-6). Its fulfillment is promised in the deliverance begun at the Exodus (Exod. 6:6-8; Deut. 34:1-4).

The whole story is given special theological meaning by its relationship to the preface, the primeval prologue (Gen. 1–11).[2] In contrast to the narrow focus on promise and election which is central from Gen. 12 to Deut. 34, the focus of Gen. 1–11 is universal. It looks back to the creation itself. It sets in view the way that man and woman came to be at enmity with themselves, alienated and separated from God and their fellows. Their plight involves social disharmony as well as individual alienation.

In light of this deep human alienation, the author of Gen. 1–11 addresses the fundamental question of God's future relationship to the creation. Is God's patient endurance exhausted? Has God dismissed the nations with unending wrath? In response to these questions the election and blessing of Abraham carry great significance for all humanity.

The contrast, then, between Gen. 1–11 and the particularistic history of promise, election, deliverance, and covenant that occupies the rest of the Pentateuch is striking. In God's special dealings with Abraham and his descendants lies the answer to the anguish of the whole human family. The Pentateuch thus has two major divisions: Gen. 1–11 and Gen. 12–Deut. 34. The relation between them is one of question and answer, problem and solution; the clue is Gen. 12:3:

I will bless those who bless you and the one who curses you I will curse; and in you all the families of the earth shall be blessed.

5

This structure not only makes clear the binding unity of the Pentateuch; it also reveals that the structure begun here stretches far beyond the Pentateuch itself. For all three elements of the promise are only partially fulfilled in the Pentateuch. At the close of Deuteronomy Israel as the covenant people of God in the land of promise still lies in the future. Indeed, not only does the full realization of God's plan lie beyond Deut. 34, it lies beyond the whole Old Testament! Nowhere does the Old Testament set forth a final solution to the universal problem which Gen. 1–11 so poignantly portrays.

> When the Old Testament ends, Israel still is looking for the final consummation when hope shall be fulfilled and promise become fact.

This consummation is found in the Son of Abraham (Matt. 1:1), who draws all people to him (John 12:32). He thus ends the alienation of humanity from God and of individuals from one another which is so penetratingly portrayed in the primeval prologue.

Complexity

The Pentateuch reveals, beside a definite unity of purpose and plan, a diversity that is equally amazing. This complexity has given rise to varied theories about its origin. Many of these theories, unfortunately, offer views of its origin, date, and authorship which evaluate negatively its historical and theological worth. Since the Pentateuch is regarded as originating many centuries later than the Mosaic period, it is sometimes thought to preserve little genuine historical information. The religious ideas and practices recorded are said to be those held centuries later. For example, J. Wellhausen, an eloquent proponent of these theories, viewed the Pentateuch as the product of the exilic and postexilic periods and thus as the starting-point for the history of Judaism only, not that of ancient Israel.[3]

Although the Wellhausenian view has now been so modified as to be almost unrecognizable, this shift has not resulted in a more sympathetic evaluation of the Pentateuch. In fact, according to a very important school of Old Testament thought, represented by scholars like Martin Noth, hardly a single positive historical statement can be made on the basis of the Pentateuchal traditions. Noth holds that it is erroneous to view Moses as the founder of a religion, or even to speak of a Mosaic religion at all. As we have seen, however, the Pentateuch is united in the affirmation that God has acted in history for the sake of the entire human family in the events of the patriarchal and Mosaic story. Views like those of Noth attack the very heart and core of the biblical proclamation.

Reaction against such extreme criticism is the only possible approach for those committed to the truth of the Bible. Error must be combatted. However, conservative scholars have reacted all too often by going to the other extreme, without producing a thorough introduction to the Pentateuch — one that takes seriously both the evidence for the Law's basic unity and the diversity on which negative theories are based.

Literary Evidence for Complexity. As soon as one begins to wrestle with the literary character of the Pentateuch, one is struck with the mixture of law and history. No other law code, ancient or modern, is anything like it. The historical narrative constantly cuts across and interrupts the legislation. This dual nature must be recognized in seeking the origin of the Pentateuch. God did not just promulgate a law code or redeem a people through a special series of saving acts. God did both. He chose a people whom he bound to himself by a law. The Pentateuch then has an intentional twofold character: blocks of legal material integrally tied to a narrative.[4]

Other literary complexities also become obvious upon careful analysis of the text.

(1) Both the narrative and legal division have a striking lack of continuity and order in subject matter. For example, there is no sequence between Gen. 4:26 and 5:1; in fact, Gen. 2:4b–4:26 breaks the thread of the account of 1:1–2:4a; 5:1ff. Again, there is a definite discontinuity between Gen. 19:38 and 20:1, as between Exod. 19:25 and 20:1. In fact, the decalogue found in 20:1-17 is disjunctive to the narrative of its literary setting (19:1-25; 20:18-21). Further, the legal codes themselves are not grouped in any logical arrangement.

(2) Given the diversity of the material, it is not surprising to find significant differences in vocabulary, syntax, and style and general composition of the various sections of the work. Such differences, for example, are manifest in comparing the law codes of Leviticus and Deuteronomy.

(3) Further evidence of literary complexity is the variable use of the divine names Yahweh ("Lord") and Elohim ("God") from Genesis 1 through Exodus 6. Even though these names often occur without any evident reason for the choice, several chapters, or sections of chapters, especially in Genesis, use exclusively or predominantly one name or the other. A correlation exists between the name chosen and the theological concepts in a given passage.

(4) Duplications and triplications of material occur in the Pentateuch. Of concern is not the simple repetition of identical material, but repetition of

the same basic subject matter, replete with common features, yet with certain marked divergences. While zealous exponents of the documentary source theory have identified as doublets passages that are far more easily explained in other ways,[5] the fact remains that a number of such duplications cannot be readily resolved. For example:

In two accounts, Abraham risks Sarah's honor by passing her off as his sister (Gen. 12; 20; compare Isaac's surprisingly similar episode, 26:6-11). The name Beersheba ("Well of the Oath") commemorates not only a covenant between Abraham and Abimelech (Gen. 21:22-31), but also an agreement between Isaac and Abimelech (26:26-33). The passage on the clean and the unclean in Lev. 11:1-47 is duplicated by Deut. 14:3-21; and the passage on slaves occurs in triplicate (Exod. 21:1-11; Lev. 25:39-55; Deut. 15:12-18).

The evidence suggests a long history of transmission and development. A striking number of terms, facts, and remarks require an age later than that of Moses. Statements such as "at that time the Canaanites were in the land" (Gen. 12:6; 13:7) and "the people of Israel ate the manna . . . till they came to the border of the land of Canaan" (Exod. 16:35) imply that Israel already occupied Canaan. Gen. 14:14 indicates that Abram pursued Lot's captors as far as Dan, yet the place did not receive this name until the Danites captured it following the Conquest (Josh. 19:47; Judg. 18:29).

Positive Evidence for Authorship and Origin. The Pentateuch is an anonymous work. Moses is not mentioned as its author nor is anyone else. Such anonymity is in keeping with Old Testament practice in particular and with ancient literary works in general. In the ancient Middle East, an "author" was primarily a preserver of the past and was bound by traditional material and methodology. "Literature" was far more community than individual property.[6]

Nevertheless, the Pentateuch does give indications of literary activity by its principal figure, Moses. He is described, in passing, as ordered to write or actually writing historical facts (Exod. 17:14; Num. 33:2), laws or sections of law codes (Exod. 24:4; 34:27f.), and one poem (Deut. 31:22). However, his contribution need not be limited strictly to the portions of the Pentateuch specifically attributed to him.

Moses' literary activity is corroborated by scattered but significant references in the rest of the preexilic literature. The exilic and postexilic references are far more numerous. In fact, careful examination yields a striking pattern:[7]

(1) Postexilic books (Chronicles, Ezra, Nehemiah, Daniel, etc.) refer quite frequently to the Pentateuch as a written text with authority; they draw on all the codes of the Pentateuch. Here the expression "book of Moses" occurs for the first time.

(2) Middle books (i.e., the preexilic historical books, Joshua, 1-2 Samuel, 1-2 Kings) refer very rarely to Moses' literary activity. All such references are to Deuteronomy.

(3) Earlier books (i.e., the preexilic prophets) have no such references. This evidence indicates that the tradition is a growing one. The connection to Moses is extended from some laws, to all laws, then to the whole Pentateuch.[8] The tradition's continued growth is further seen in the frequent New Testament references to the whole Pentateuch as the "law" or "book of Moses" (Mark 12:26; Luke 2:22; Acts 13:39) or simply "Moses" (Luke 24:27), and to the whole Old Testament as "Moses and the prophets" (16:29).

Implications of These Facts. What conclusions can be drawn from these data? Here, one must be radically biblical, letting the Bible speak and not imposing on it arbitrary concepts of the kind of literature it must be. At the same time theories of its origin and development must be recognized as theories. Thus they must be held tentatively, with an openness to change and modification as more understanding is gained.

Two facts need to be stressed. First, the biblical sources and various streams of tradition concur that Moses wrote narrative, legislative, and poetic literature. Abundant evidence now exists that such diverse abilities in one author were by no means unique to the ancient Near East even centuries earlier than Moses. Hence Moses' role in the production of the Pentateuch must be affirmed as highly formative although it is unlikely that Moses wrote the Pentateuch *as it exists in its final form.* The core of both the narrative framework and legislative material goes back to his literary instigation and authentically reflects both the circumstances and events there related.

Second, the complexities of the text and the distribution and growth of the evidence for its origin must be taken into account. These literary phenomena reveal that the Pentateuch is a complex, composite work with a long and involved history of transmission and growth. Faith affirms that this development was superintended by the same Spirit of God that prompted Moses to act and write in the first place. Although this process is difficult to detail with certainty, its main outlines are reasonably sure. The narratives of the patriarchs were preserved, primarily by oral means, during the period of slavery in Egypt. They probably were first put into writing in the Mosaic period.[9] To these were added the poetic and prose accounts of the Exodus and wanderings, possibly in the early Davidic period. In light of the new shape of society as a monarchy, the preservation of the events and meaning of Israel's formative period would have had prime importance. Gathered in various compilations, the documents of the Mosaic age may have been finally formed into a single collection by Ezra in the period of restoration after the Exile (fifth century). This suggestion is based on the following considerations. The biblical text itself presents Ezra as scribe par excellence, learned in the law of Moses (Ezra 7:6, 11ff.). His task was to teach the Torah and regulate its observance in Judah and Jerusalem (vv. 14, 25f.). Jewish tradition unites in attributing to him the final inscripturation of the Torah.[10] Finally, whatever the details of this process, one must affirm with W. F. Albright:

The contents of our Pentateuch are, in general, very much older than the date at which they were finally edited; new discoveries continue to confirm the historical accuracy of the literary antiquity of detail after detail in it. Even when it is necessary to assume later additions to the original nucleus of Mosaic tradition, these additions reflect the normal growth of ancient institutions and practices, or the effort made by later scribes to save as much as possible of extant traditions about Moses. It is, accordingly, sheer hyper-criticism to deny the substantially Mosaic character of the Pentateuchal tradition.[11]

To explain the implications of these literary complexities, some Old Testament scholars have developed the "documentary theory." This is a hypothesis which seeks to separate out the various "sources" behind the present text of the Pentateuch.[12]

This theory identifies four main documents as the sources behind the present text of the Pentateuch. It does this by identifying strata within the text that may be separated by subject matter, the use of the divine names Yahweh and Elohim, and the duplication of material. From these findings it seeks to identify large bodies of material that are marked by similarity of vocabulary and style and by uniformity of theological outlook. In the typical analysis, four "sources" have been detected and described:

J (because of the German spelling *Jahweh*) is the Yahwist narrative that runs from Gen. 2 through Num. 22–24 (Wolff). Others assign the death of Moses reported in Deut. 34 to J. J was put together in Judah between 950 and 850 B.C. This source emphasizes God's nearness, often in anthropomorphic language, where God is described in human terms. It underscores the continuity of God's purpose from creation through the patriarchs to Israel's role as his people. This continuity leads to the establishment of the monarchy under David.

E is a narrative of Israel's (the northern kingdom's) tradition that parallels J. It stresses God's transcendence. It prefers Elohim as the name for God until the revelation of his name Yahweh to Moses (Exod. 3; 6); afterwards it employs either name for God. At first scholars thought E began with Gen. 15, but they have settled on Gen. 20. Most scholars locate its setting in northern Israel, for it gives special attention to Bethel, Shechem, and the Joseph tribes, Ephraim and Manasseh. It is dated around 750-700 B.C. The surviving portions of this document are very fragmented. Noth accounts for this phenomenon by postulating that a redactor supplied J with material found in E. From this perspective it is almost hopeless to recover the E source.

JE is the sigla used either for texts in which it is virtually impossible to unravel the two sources (note Yahweh Elohim, LORD God, in Gen. 2:4b–3:24) or in discussion of a text from these two sources over against material from the priestly source. These sources were brought together a century after E's origin.

D refers to the core material that makes up the book of Deuteronomy. The style of this book is very distinctive: prosaic, wordy, parenetic (full of advice or counsel, "preachy"), and dotted with stereotyped phrases. Wherever this style appears in the Old Testament it is called deuteronomistic. To the deuteronomist(s) is attributed the shaping of the historical narrative from Joshua through 2 Kings (see Ch. 9). Overall this source may be considered preaching on the law (von Rad). It emphasizes purity of worship at a central shrine, and it exhorts the people to serve God from a heart filled with love. Several scholars have postulated that the core was collected and composed in the early seventh century B.C. This core was found during the renovation of the temple under Josiah (2 Kgs. 22); it then gave practical direction to that reform. The core was later expanded and eventually joined to JE.

P is a historical narrative which has been expanded with legal texts and other material. Concerned with the origin and regulation of institutions in Israel, P focuses on genealogies, cultic laws, covenants, high days like the sabbath, blueprints of cultic buildings, and procedures for sacrifices and ceremonies. It emphasizes God's holiness, sovereignty, and transcendence along with the establishment of the true worship of Yahweh led by the priests. It places Israel's worship within the context of creation (Gen. 1). Older material such as the sacrificial rituals (Lev. 1–7) and the laws of holiness (Lev. 17–26) were grafted into this document. The ground source of P is often dated to the middle of the Exile (ca. 550 B.C.); and its final compilation sometime before the end of the fourth century B.C.

Advocates of the documentary hypothesis have proposed a wide variety of views on its various details. Certain scholars, for example, have divided J into two sources; e.g., Eissfeldt identified one of them as L (lay, in contrast to priestly, source), but Fohrer called it N for its nomadic character. The origin of P is also a subject of debate. Some scholars like Cross have argued that P never had an independent existence; rather, it was a stage in the redaction of the earlier traditions.[13] Y. Kaufmann, on the other hand, has strongly argued for the priority of P over D in that P does not presuppose the material in D.[14]

His position is significant in that a number of Jewish scholars continue to pursue his approach.

Accepting the documentary framework, H. Gunkel gave new impetus to critical studies *ca.* 1900 by introducing *Formgeschichte* (study of literary forms) or *Gattungsgeschichte* (study of literary genres).[15] Not concerned to analyze the text by grouping basic units into larger literary collections or sources, this method isolates the literary units to determine their genre. It then seeks to identify the social setting *(Sitz im Leben)* from which each unit arose. This approach has sometimes resulted in radical views. Nevertheless, when followed judiciously, it aids greatly in understanding the variety of texts in the Pentateuch.

Applying *traditions criticism* ("criticism" here means an attempt to recognize and appreciate, as in music- or art-criticism) to the Pentateuch, von Rad looked for its theological message, not so much in the various sources, but in the identifiable complexes of the tradition. He named five primary traditions: the primal tradition, patriarchal history, exodus tradition, Sinai tradition, and settlement tradition. To deal with the last element von Rad expanded the narrative to include Joshua and thus formed a "Hexateuch."

While von Rad accepted the basic framework of the documentary hypothesis, Rendtorff has demonstrated that von Rad's work and that of other form critics has in fact unraveled the account of the origin of the Pentateuch as presented in the documentary hypothesis.[16] In Rendtorff's judgment the Pentateuch consists of several individual units of tradition. These units were collected and then shaped according to key themes and perspectives. For example, the theme of promise has been used to unite the narratives about the different patriarchs, each of which has a distinctive form. The material in Exodus-Numbers has been joined under "overarching patterns of tradition" involving the tent, the ark, the cloud and the pillar of fire, and the leadership of Moses. The final collection was arranged by members of the Deuteronomic school, since the formulaic expressions cherished by this school have been stamped on the material. In addition, several texts bear the marks of priestly language and style, a fact which suggests that these underwent a priestly revision. Rendtorff calls for further study on the relationship of this revision to that of the Deuteronomists. Nevertheless, in his judgment the latter group gave the self-standing shape to the five books of the Pentateuch.

It is doubtful that the documentary hypothesis will survive the critical labors of contemporary scholarship. What new hypothesis will receive wide acclaim is far from clear. Certainly, the Pentateuch is an anthology of a wide variety of literature, accounts, laws, rituals, exhortations, sermons, and instructions. How were these texts preserved before they were canonized? How did an ancient text address a later audience? These questions are crucial to understanding the complexity of the Pentateuch. They lead one to conclude that it was not written by one person in a given decade. Rather it is the product of the believing community through many centuries. Of much more importance for interpretation is the final result of this long process, produced by the inspired authors, editors, and tradition-bearers of God's chosen people.

Paramount Importance of Structural Unity

Although the Pentateuch is a complex literary production, the fact that it has a structural unity is of greater significance. Whatever the process of its transmission and growth or the date at which it finally reached its present form, the final creation bears the paramount importance. An overarching unity is powerfully present in its component parts. This unity transcends the existence of whatever sources its complexities may imply. The real danger of literary criticism is that biblical scholarship can become preoccupied with it to the exclusion of more comprehensive considerations. Such a focus reduces the Pentateuch to unrelated fragments and results in the draining of power from its message.

Recent trends in Old Testament scholarship admit to this imbalance. There is considerable recognition that Old Testament study has devoted itself too heavily to the reconstruction of the origin of the literary text and the process of its transmission, rather than to the interpretation of the text. Increasingly, Old Testament research is treating the text as an end in itself, not just as a means to ascertain its genetic history. One such approach is "canonical criticism," which studies the form and function of the text in the shape which the community of faith gave to it.[17] Some who support this method focus on intertextual interpretation or inner-biblical exegesis, the ways that authors use each other's material in Scripture. This field of study argues for a "post-critical alternative"[18] which, while taking seriously the results of historical scholarship, seeks to determine the role that the canonical form of the text played in Israel's faith. In this view the

> . . . formation of a Pentateuch established the parameters of Israel's understanding of its faith as Torah. For the biblical editors the first five books constituted the grounds of Israel's life under God and provided a critical norm of how the Mosaic tradition was to be understood by the covenant people.[19]

The basic procedure in this volume will be to allow the Pentateuch to stand as it is, the essential witness to how God brought the nation of Israel into existence and made its people into his people through the leadership of Moses.

CHAPTER 2

Genesis: Primeval Prologue

"Well begun is half done." So goes an ancient Greek proverb. Its point applies aptly to the first book of the Bible. Creation by the divine word, rebellion by the human family, judgment and grace from the covenant Lord, election of Abraham's family and especially Jacob's descendants to embody and convey the message of salvation — all these basic biblical themes are sounded boldly and clearly in the pages of Genesis.

Name

Genesis is well named. It is a transliteration from the Greek of the LXX; it means "source, origin." The Hebrew name comes from the book's first word, $b^e r \bar{e}' \check{s} \hat{\imath} t$ — "in the beginning." Both names are appropriate, for Genesis sets the stage for a full understanding of biblical faith.

Structure

The book has two distinct sections: chs. 1–11, the primeval history, and chs. 12–50, the patriarchal history (technically 1:1–11:26 and 11:27–50:26). Gen. 1–11 is a preface to salvation history, addressing the origin of the world, of humankind, and of sin. Gen. 12–50 recounts the origins of redemptive history in God's election of the patriarchs with the promises of land, posterity, and relationship.

> And the Lord God planted a garden in Eden, in the east, and there he put the man whom he had formed. Out of the ground the Lord God made to grow every tree that is pleasant to the sight and good for food, the tree of life also in the midst of the garden, and the tree of the knowledge of good and evil. Gen. 2:8-9

> Then the Lord God said, "See, the man has become like one of us, knowing good and evil; and now he might reach out his hand and take also from the tree of life, and eat, and live forever" — therefore the Lord God sent him forth from the garden of Eden, to till the ground from which he was taken. Gen. 3:22-23

On the basis of literary structure the book divides into ten sections. The clue to these sections is the "*toledoth* formula": "And these are (this is) the descendants (or story; Heb. *tôledôt*) of . . . [.]" *Toledoth* is not just a boundary marker in the book. Since its Hebrew root *yld* has to do with birth, it is also a signal of the survival and continuity of God's plan for creation despite the ravages of human sin. The contents are set forth in the Table.

Contents

The first five sections, each punctuated by *toledoth*, shape the structure of the primeval prologue. Ch. 1 is closed by 2:4a. The next unit (2:4b–4:26) — concerning the origin and execution of sin — is concluded by 5:1, which introduces the roll of Adam's descendants. In 6:9 the formula prepares for the narrative of the Flood, separating the story of the sons of God and the daughters of men (6:1-4) and the sketch of human sin (vv. 5-8). These two short pieces describe the terrible corruption that moved God to bring on the Flood.

Contents of Genesis

	I. PRIMEVAL PROLOGUE					II. PATRIARCHAL HISTORY		
Subject	Creation	Eden and the Fall	Patriarchs before the Flood	The Flood and Its Aftermath	Patriarchs after the Flood	Abraham and His Family	Jacob and His Sons	Joseph and His Brothers
Division:	1:1–2:4a	2:4b–4:26	5:1-32	6:1–11:9	11:10-26	11:27–25:18	25:19–37:1	37:2–50:26
Clue:			*" . . . . These are the descendants/story (toledoth) of . . . . "*					
Genealogies:			5:1 Adam and his descendants	10:1 Sons of Noah	11:10 Shem and his descendants	25:12 Ishmael and his descendants	36:1, 9 Esau and his descendants	
Narratives:	2:4a the heavens and the earth			6:9 Noah and the Flood		11:27 Terah and his family (Abraham)	25:19 Isaac and his family (Jacob and Esau)	37:2 Jacob and his family (Joseph and his brothers)

Gen. 10:1 begins with the Table of Nations, emphasizing the repeopling of the earth after the Flood (6:9–9:29). Ch. 11:10 concludes the Tower of Babel story (11:1-9) and prepares for the sagas of the patriarchs after the Flood. These, then, are the divisions of the primeval prologue in the text itself. (See chart on p. 17.)

Literary Genre

To discern the intent of this section, we shall look at (1) the literary nature of Gen. 1–11, (2) the ancient Near Eastern materials from which Israel drew to tell the primeval story, and (3) implications for Gen. 1–11.

Literary Nature. First, these chapters are strongly characterized by literary artifices of two markedly different types. One set of texts (including chs. 1; 5; 10; 11:10-26) is distinguished by a schematic character and careful logical arrangement.

For example, ch. 1 consists of a highly structured series of succinct, almost formulaic, sentences. Each creative command consists of the following components:

- an introductory word of announcement,
  "God said . . ." (1:3, 6, 9, 11, 14, 20, 24, 26).
- a creative word of command,
  "let there be" (1:3, 6, 9, 11, 14-15, 20, 24, 25).
- a summary word of accomplishment,
  "and it was so" (1:3, 7, 9, 11, 15, 24, 30).
- a descriptive word of accomplishment,
  "God made . . . ," "the earth brought forth . . ." (1:4, 7, 12, 16-18, 21, 25, 27).
- a descriptive word of naming or blessing,
  "God called . . . ," "God blessed . . ." (1:5, 8, 10, 22, 28-30).
- an evaluative word of approval,
  "God saw that it was good" (1:4, 10, 12, 18, 21, 25, 31).
- a concluding word of temporal framework,
  "It was evening and it was morning, day . . ." (1:5, 8, 13, 19, 23, 31).

This uniform style is not wooden because the order, length, and presentation of these components are varied. The arrangement of the commands follows a strict temporal order, consciously separated into two periods: (1) the creation and separation of the elements of the cosmos, moving from the general to the particular (first four commands, vv. 1-13); (2) the adornment of the cosmos, from the imperfect to the perfect (second four commands, vv. 14-31). The account rises to a crescendo in the eighth command, the creation of human beings. The whole chapter reads less like a story than a carefully constructed report of a series of commands.

Similarly, ch. 5 and 11:10-32 are genealogies shaped to repeat the same structure for each generation. Again, ch. 10, an ethno-geographical list, is marked by a similar schematic character.

The second set of passages (chs. 2–3; 4; 6–9; 11:1-9) is very different. Here the story form is used. For example, in chs. 2–3 we hear an exquisite, literary narrative, almost a drama. Each scene is drawn with a few bold strokes and a host of images. The author revels in naive, but expressive, anthropomorphisms, describing God in human terms. Yahweh, one of the *dramatis personae*, appears as potter (2:7, 19), gardener (v. 8), surgeon (v. 21), and peaceful landowner (3:8).[1]

The names used are literary devices. They correspond to the person's function or role: Adam means "humankind"[2] and Eve is "(she who gives) life";[3] Cain means "forger (of metals)"; Enoch is connected with "dedication, consecration" (4:17; 5:18), and Jubal with horn and trumpet (4:21). Cain, condemned to be a *nad*, "wanderer," goes to live in the land of *Nod*, "the land of wandering"! This style suggests that the author is a skilled storyteller. The interpreter, then, must endeavor to discern what the literary devices mean.

Ancient Near Eastern Background. The inspired author(s) of the primeval prologue drew on the manner of speaking about origins that was part of their culture and literary traditions. Ch. 1 needs to be read in light of creation accounts from Mesopotamia. Although detailed comparisons are relatively few, three basic parallels exist: the picture of the primeval state as a watery chaos, the basic order of creation, and the divine rest at the end of creation.[4]

Although the storyline involving the first sin has no ancient Near Eastern parallel, there are similarities to Mesopotamian literature in individual elements, symbols, and conceptions.

These parallels even extend to technical terminology. The *'ēd* in 2:6, usually translated "mist," may be understood as an Akkadian loanword meaning "flow of water from underground." The geographical term "in Eden" (2:8) may be borrowed from Sumerian, later Akkadian, *edinu* "plain," which quite fits the context.[5] The literal meanings of these terms are not indigenous to Palestine.

The most striking resemblances between Mesopotamian literature and the primeval prologue occur in accounts of the Flood. Beyond basic similarities there are detailed correspondences. The hero is instructed by divine agency to build an unusual boat and caulk it with pitch. He is to take animals along to preserve them from a universal catastrophe. The entire population is destroyed.

Fragments of Enuma Elish, the Assyrian creation epic. *(British Museum)*

After the flood waters abate, the hero releases birds to determine if there is any dry land. Eventually the ship comes to rest on a mountain. On leaving the ark, the hero offers sacrifice, and the gods happily smell the sweet odor.[6]

The clearest connection to Mesopotamia is the account of the Tower of Babel (11:1-9), for it is set in Babylon (v. 2). True to this locale, the building material is mud brick. This setting explains the scornful comment made about this building material (v. 3). The tower is most likely a reference to a ziggurat, a temple constructed as a stepped mountain and made out of clay (v. 4). The name of the city, Babel, reflects the Babylonian name *Bâbili* "the Gate of God" (v. 9).

These resemblances prove nothing beyond a genetic relationship between the biblical and Mesopotamian accounts. The Genesis stories in their present form do not go back to the Babylonian traditions. The evidence, even that of the close ties between the Flood stories, merely suggests a diffuse influence of a common cultural heritage. The inspired authors of the primeval account drew on the manner of speaking about origins that was part of a common literary tradition.

Implications for Gen. 1–11. Identifying the genre of Gen. 1–11 is difficult because of its uniqueness. None of these accounts belongs to the genre "myth." Nor is any of them "history" in the modern sense of eyewitness, objective reporting. Rather, they convey theological truths about events, portrayed in a

The main stairway of the ziggurat at Ur. *(Jack Finegan)*

largely symbolic, pictorial literary style. This is not to say that Gen. 1–11 conveys historical falsehood. That conclusion would follow only if the material claimed to contain objective descriptions. From the above discussion it is certain that such was not the intent. On the other hand, the view that the truths taught in these chapters have no objective basis is mistaken. Fundamental truths are declared: creation of all by God, special divine intervention in the origin of the first man and woman, the unity of the human race, the pristine goodness of the created world, including humanity, the entrance of sin through the disobedience of the first pair, the rampant spread of sin after this initial act of disobedience. These truths are all based on facts. Their certainty implies the reality of the facts.[7]

Emphasizing solely the similarities to other ancient literature produces a misleading impression that they are the most distinctive features of the material in Genesis. The situation is just the opposite. The reader is first impressed with the unique features of the biblical accounts. Only a trained eye discovers the similarities.

In contrast to the exalted monotheism of Gen. 1–11, the Mesopotamian accounts present gods which are embodiments of natural forces. They know no moral principle. They lie, steal, fornicate, and kill. Moreover, humans enjoy no special dignity in these accounts. They are the lowly servants of the gods, being made to provide them with food and offerings.

The biblical narratives present the true, holy, and omnipotent God. The

21

Creator exists before the creation and is independent of the world. God speaks and the elements come into being. The divine work is good, just, and whole. After the human family rebels, God tempers his judgment with mercy. Even when an account shares common elements with the thought forms of nearby cultures, the distinctive nature of the Creator shines through the narrative.

How then is the unique literary genre of Gen. 1–11 to be understood? One may suppose that the author, inspired by God's revelation, employed current literary traditions to teach the true theological import of humanity's primeval history. The book's purpose was not to provide a biological and geological description of origins. Rather, it was intended to explain the unique nature and dignity of human beings by virtue of their divine origin. They have been made by the Creator in the divine image, yet marred materially by the sin that so soon disfigured God's good work.

Theology

Having determined that the primary purpose of this material is theological, we give attention to its teaching. Four major theological themes stand out: (1) God is Creator; (2) the entrance of sin into the created order radically alters the original creation; (3) God's judgment meets human sin at each point; (4) God sustains both the creation and humans by his preserving grace.

God as Creator. The opening chapter beautifully reveals that all of creation came forth at the free and sovereign command of God. The world view out of which and to which the account spoke was radically different from today's. The ancients personalized the forces of nature as divine beings. Natural phenomena were conceived in terms of human experience. Today we regard the phenomenal world as an "it," but the ancients responded to it as a "thou." For them the variety of forces were personified as gods.[8] Therefore, the divine was multipersonal, usually ordered and in balance but at times capricious, unstable, and fearful.

The text of ch. 1 combats such a view of deity. It pictures nature as coming forth at the simple command of God, who is prior to and independent of it. The sun, moon, stars, and planets, which were regarded as gods by other peoples, are not even named. They are referred to simply as lights (vv. 16-18). The sea and the earth are not primeval deities which procreate other gods. Rather they are natural objects (v. 10). The description demythologizes the cosmos, the deification of which had led to polytheism.[9]

Greek thought also broke away from this polytheistic conception. Greek philosophers conceived of the primacy of the rational and speculative over the intuitional and inarticulate. They thereby raised the processes of reason to autonomy. Replacing the gods is *nature,* manifested in the various realities of the world. As a result, God becomes removed from nature and disappears from the horizon of reality altogether. To this world view Genesis speaks by affirming that God is the Creator. All creation is dependent on God; all creation will give answer before God. Biblical Hebrew contains no word for "nature." It speaks only of "creation."

Heb. *bārā'* "to create" is a key word, being used six or seven times in the creation account. This word has God as its only subject in the Old Testament, and no mention is made of the material out of which an object is created. It describes a way of acting that has no human analogy. Only God creates, as only God saves.

A major refrain in ch. 1 is the affirmation that what God creates is good (vv. 4, 10, 12, 18, 21, 25, 31). The final declaration (v. 31), "And God saw everything that he had made, and indeed it was very good," stands out from the terse, calm language of the chapter. No evil was laid on the world by God's hand. The value of the world comes solely from the fact that God made it. This teaching of the pristine goodness of creation, humans included, bears great theological weight: (1) it prepares the way for discussion of the cause that disrupted this good order — sin; (2) it sets the stage for the unquenchable hope of the world's complete renewal (Rev. 21:1).

The conscious apex of creation is humanity (Gen. 1:26-28). The monotone of formulas of command is broken as the creation of humankind is announced in terms of a divine *resolution,* "Let us make humanity." Only here does the text exchange the use of repetitive, carefully framed prose for the beauty and power of the parallelism of Hebrew poetry:

> So God created humankind in his own image,
> > In the image of God he created them,
> > Male and female he created them. (v. 27)

The threefold use of *bārā'* "to create" and the inverted structure signal that here the account reaches the climax toward which it has moved in ever ascending stages.

The unique relationship of humans to God is captured by the deliberately ambiguous phrase "the image of God." The reason for the choice of these words lies in the uniform Old Testament abhorrence of the representation of God in any form. This phrase raises humans above the rest of creation by placing them alongside God. The term *ṣelem* "image" is explained more precisely by *dᵉmût* "similarity" (1:26). The two words together mean "according to a similar but not identical representation." This description is to be distinguished from the ancient Near Eastern tradition in which a deity formed humanity in divine shape.

23

Yet we need to avoid connecting the "image" too exclusively to the "spiritual" side or moral capacity of mankind. The point of these terms is far more functional than conceptual. It touches what the likeness entails rather than its precise nature. The likeness is dynamic in that human beings (*'āḏām*) become God's representatives on earth. They have the natural right to explore, subdue, and partake of the creation as the words "and let them have dominion over . . ." convey. Being in God's image, man and woman are to rule the world in God's name. The picture is that of an emperor appointing administrators over his domain and erecting his own statue so that the inhabitants may know whose will it is that rules them. Inherent in this command to rule in God's stead is the God-given capacity to know, worship, and enjoy the Creator.

In chs. 2–3 we find a story of great theological truth in beautiful word pictures, full of symbol and imagery. Sometimes the differences in the accounts of ch. 1 and ch. 2 are pressed, as though these reflected two separate "creation accounts," somewhat in contradiction. This opinion ignores the differences in their genre as well as the fact that ch. 2 does not purport to be a "creation account." It is not an independent literary unit but sets the stage for the drama in ch. 3.

The essential fact is that both accounts employ symbol and style to communicate that humankind is the apex of God's creation. This is accomplished in ch. 1 by making man and woman the climax of God's creative activity. The same goal is achieved in ch. 2 by speaking of their creation first. In this graphic story, Yahweh is the potter who "fashions" *'āḏām* out of "dust" from the ground. This choice of words involves a play on the common expression for "to die," namely, "to return to the dust" (3:19; cf. Job 10:9; 34:15; Ps. 104:29). The imagery stresses the bond between humans and the earth and also underlines our frailty, especially our mortality.

Into this lifeless form that he has shaped, Yahweh breathes the "breath of life." Man then becomes a "living being." The word "breath" is literal. The text thus says that man is "body and life," not "body and soul."[10] A person has a two-part nature. One is of the earth, earthy. The other is a life principle that comes from God. This composite nature does not by itself set man and woman apart from the animals. They are also identified as "living beings" (1:20; 2:19) and as having the breath of life (6:17; 7:22). These vivid word pictures, however, stress that humans are the object of God's special attention. God's relationship to humankind is personal and immediate. Humanity, fresh from the Creator's hand, is a pictograph of "the image of God." The emphasis here, though, falls on the frailty, mortality, and utter dependence of humanity on God. Only in this light can one see how unmerited was *'āḏām*'s privileged position in Eden and how monstrous the desire to be like God.

In Gen. 2:18-25 the focus is on the creation of woman. The story prepares for her creation by emphasizing the essential corporate nature of humanity —

his sociability: "It is not good that man should be alone" (v. 18). True human life is life together. Therefore, a life of isolation from human fellowship — male and female — would be a perversion of human nature as divinely created. God's answer to man's aloneness is to make for him a "help as one over against him." This new creature is to be his "counterpart," one who corresponds to him and is suitable to him.

Before making woman, God brings the animals to Adam. Adam names them, showing his insight into their essence. He does not, however, find among them any "helper as his partner" (NRSV). To the ancient Israelites, surrounded by religions which had exalted the animal world to divine status, this verdict proclaims that no animal is the equal of man, let alone his superior.

God, therefore, fashions woman out of a part of the man's body. He brings her to Adam, and he shouts joyfully, "At last!" (v. 23). He thus recognizes her to be of his own essence. He indicates the fullness of their correspondence in his choice of a name for her: to capture this correspondence the names are related by similar sound ʾîš "man" and ʾiššâ "woman."

This intimate bond between a man and a woman explains why a man severs the close tie to his parents to become "one flesh" with his wife (v. 24). "Flesh" or better "body" refers to the tangible side of humanity. Thus the physical side of marriage comes into its own (2:25; cf. Eph. 5:31).

This narrative (chs. 2–3) opens by defining the place of humans in God's creation. The picture is one of wholesomeness, completeness and good order.

Problem of Sin. After the refrain of Gen. 1: "God saw that it was good," the way has been prepared to tell what corrupted that world. Chs. 2–3 address the question of why things exist in a ruined condition.[11] Why are humans subject to physical and moral evil? This corruption is a fact of experience, painfully driven home as one matures. Everyone wrestles with the evil present in the world: the inhumanity of human behavior as well as the personal duplicity in one's own breast. The certainty and fear of death also haunt our short span on earth.

How can such evil be reconciled with God's goodness and with the truth that everything originates from God? There is evidently a vast chasm between the way God created the world and the way we experience it. The drama in chs. 2–3 discloses how humans become sinners and corrupt the created order by willful disobedience. As a consequence of their action, the world of human experience becomes fractured and broken, alienated and chaotic. The drama insists that humankind, not God, is to blame for the corruption of God's world.

At the beginning (2:8-17), the man lives in a well-watered garden of trees and marvelous fruitfulness in Eden. All is in complete harmony, from the highest forms of life to the lowest. Although there are tasks to perform (v. 15), the man does not have to struggle in pain to wrest a living from a recalcitrant earth. Thorns and thistles do not grow. Only plants are used for food. For the modern reader there is a certain unreality about Eden, for such a world lies far beyond human experience. Indeed, life in Eden is ideal. These pictures highlight the peaceful fellowship our first parents shared with God. There is no evil, either physical or moral, in that garden. Nor is there any distress in human experience. Sin does not yet exist.

In the midst of the garden are two trees, the tree of life and the tree of the knowledge of good and evil. The meaning of the second tree is uncertain. The text is deliberately vague. From its usage (2:16f.; 3:3-7, 22), the tree symbolizes the freedom of choice over good and evil. By eating of the tree, the first human pair aspires to be "as God" (3:5, 22). They seek to determine for themselves what is good and bad and thus usurp the divine authority.

The first sign of moral anarchy is declared through the serpent's obviously malevolent machinations. His subtle wiles induce the woman to doubt first God's word (3:1) and then God's goodness (vv. 4f.). Seeing the tree in an entirely different light (v. 6), she takes of its fruit and eats. The man follows suit. So simple the act: "she took . . . and she ate." So drastic the results. Humanity lost its state of innocence forever. So hard the undoing. God himself will taste poverty and death before "take and eat" become verbs of salvation.[12]

In the sequel the altered relationship of humans with God is vividly pictured. The pair became ashamed of their own nakedness (v. 7; cf. 2:25). Moreover, they flee in fear from the presence of God (v. 8). The unity between the couple disintegrates. The new togetherness in sin does not unite but divides. The man seeks to clear himself by placing the guilt first on the woman and then on God (v. 12). The woman, in turn, blames the serpent. Through proud ambition, Adam and Eve have become sinners and lost open fellowship with God. They must now wrestle with evil at all levels of their existence.

In the narratives that follow (chs. 4, 6, 11), the author piles story upon story to show the radical seriousness of sin by the sheer volume of the evidence. Once introduced into the world, sin rapidly reaches avalanche proportions. Humanity's second generation experiences fratricide, and the account of the succeeding generations ends with Lamech's brutal "Song of the Sword" (4:23f.).

These two passages differ widely in literary form. Gen. 4:1-16 adopts the story form of chs. 2–3 to continue the narrative of Eden and the Fall, playing upon themes and ideas familiar from those chapters. On the other hand, 4:17-24 is basically a genealogical tree. It is modified with annotations and comments that communicate the intent. Its primary interest is not who Cain's descendants were, but the nature of their life. This information is given both at the beginning of the seven-member genealogy (v. 17) and the end, where it broadens into three branches and, indeed, is hardly a genealogy at all.

Cain and Abel bring offerings to the Lord. Without any explanation the Lord accepts Abel's and not Cain's. Then in a jealous rage Cain kills his brother, even though forewarned by God (4:3-8). God immediately comes on the scene as interrogator. Now the question to the guilty man is not "Where are you?" as in the garden (3:9), but "Where is your brother?" Cain responds with an impertinent witticism: "Am I my brother's keeper?" Sin not only moves in ever widening circles; its manifestation grows more blatant and heinous. Cain goes on to become the first builder of a city (v. 17), with its organized community life. Thus the rise of civilization is noted in terms of a shameful posterity.

With Lamech and his sons comes the rise of arts and crafts, metalwork and music, together with animal husbandry (vv. 19-22). The author sketches humankind's cultural history in bold brush strokes, uncluttered by detail. His purpose is to get to the Song of the Sword (vv. 23f.). This is a new literary element, a lyric poem. It is a savage song of vengeance, a "boasting song." Having murdered (or intending to murder, depending on how the Heb. tense is read) a youth for striking him, Lamech boasts to his wives, who presumably are to honor his cruel and barbaric valor. This scene uncovers the brazen attitude that leads to intimidating neighbors. Such an attitude accompanies the rise of culture. First the Fall, then fratricide, now extravagant bloody vengeance becomes a cause for boasting! These accounts of the dark side of sin anticipate God's coming judgment that "the wickedness of humans was great in the earth, and . . . every inclination of the thoughts of their hearts was only evil continually" (6:5).

The same theme appears in the account of the sons of God and daughters of men (6:1-4). The interpretation of this obscure passage is problematical. Three main views concerning the term "sons of God" have been adopted since antiquity: (1) it refers in an ethical sense to the pious descendants of Seth's line, in opposition to the ungodly descendants of Cain ("the daughters of men"); (2) it denotes angelic beings; (3) it describes noblemen, whether kings, rulers, or judges.[13] As one scholar puts it, "if the second view defies the normalities of experience, the first defies those of language."[14] The usual meaning of "sons of God" is angels, though it refers to judges in Ps. 82, while the singular applies to the king in 2 Sam. 7:14 and Ps. 2:7. There is no clue in the text that "daughters" and "men" have a different sense in v. 2 than in v. 1. In this light, the sin is that God's decrees separating the divine and human worlds have been overstepped. As a result demonic powers are now loose that humanity cannot control. The third interpretation has ancient roots in rabbinic traditions. It has recently been combined with the second possibility that sons of God here may include "*both* divine beings and ante-diluvian [pre-flood] rulers."[15] In any case, whether the account reports that the descendants of Seth have become corrupt or that something demonic has entered the world and perhaps snatched the scepters of leadership, a new level has been reached in the rampant spread of evil.

This account is reinforced by the introduction to the Flood story (6:5-8).

27

That introduction is very different in origin and form from the previous passages where the book has drawn on existing traditions, freely adapting, modifying, and transforming them. In 6:5-8, under divine inspiration, the narrator presents a theological judgment from God himself about the sordid and sinful state of the world. This passage points out that human sin has become so heinous that God has no recourse but to wipe out his creatures. He must begin again his program of revelation and redemption with Noah, alone in his generation a man of integrity.

The final story in the primeval prologue is the account of the Tower of Babel (11:1-9). Human beings are no longer migratory. They are now living in a civilized state. Motivated by a lust for fame and power, they build a city and a tower. They express their ambition in the words, "Let us make a name for ourselves, otherwise we shall be scattered abroad upon the face of the whole earth" (v. 4). God recognizes that he needs to block the tremendous evil propensities in human society (vv. 6-7). Sin not only radically corrupts the individual, but it invades corporate structures and entities, which strive for mastery without regard for justice. Therefore, God confuses the people's common language and scatters them throughout the earth.

The primary theme woven through Gen. 1–11 is the corrupting power of sin. From the beginning of humankind's rebellion, sin has marred and stained God's good work.

God's Judgment on Human Sin. In each episode God meets human sin with judgment. In Eden, he first judges the serpent (3:14f.), then the woman (v. 16), and finally the man (vv. 17-24). The judgment for each is the new state in which he or she must live in a world now characterized by sin and alienation. The serpent becomes the despicable, crawling creature that people fear and shun. The age-long battle between a person and a reptile (v. 15) mirrors the relentless struggle between humanity and the subtle but wanton force of evil. The first line of v. 15 places the serpent over against the woman; the second line places the serpent's descendants over against the woman's descendants. Then the final two lines place her descendants, viewed collectively in the pronoun "he," in opposition to the serpent itself, not its descendants. Thus, the real antagonist of humanity is this primeval serpent. The power it symbolizes remains in the world as a spiritual force in opposition to all the woman's descendants.

In turn, the woman's descendants will struggle ceaselessly against this enslaving, spiritual force. One day the victory will be theirs. This victory will come about through an individual who represents humanity. While this detail is not expressly stated, it is there potentially in the collective designation of the descendants by the pronoun "he." Christians rightly interpret this unformulated hope as having been realized in Christ's victory over sin and death (cf. Luke 10:17-20).

An important point should be noted about the judgments on the man and the woman. The woman and man are penalized, but not cursed. Only the serpent is cursed. Their judgment involves the sources of their survival, bearing children and producing food. Woman is to bear children in pain and yet be drawn in desire to her husband, her master. Man must wrest bread by toil and sweat from a begrudging earth. In the end he returns to the soil from which he was taken. These judgments are on the same level, for the Hebrew term "pain" is the same for both the woman and man. Furthermore they reflect the social milieu and institutions of ancient Israel through which, under divine inspiration, they were formulated. This is the case especially with regard to the status of the woman, who often was little more than her husband's chattel in the ancient world. In this light one should no more argue on the basis of v. 16 that the wife slavishly should be subject to her husband than, on the basis of vv. 17-19, that man should scrap his air-conditioned tractors, grub the earth with a hoe, and sweat profusely!

As a further judgment, God expels both the man and the woman from the garden. He then bars the way to their ever returning (v. 24).

The judgment God pronounces on Cain is severe indeed (ch. 4). Since at his hand the soil has drunk his brother's blood, it will no longer yield to Cain its produce. He is doomed to be a fugitive in the earth. He leaves the Lord's presence to live in the land of ceaseless wandering (Nod) in the distant East.

The account of the Flood reveals the excruciating lengths to which God's judgment may go. The path to understanding the Flood is strewn with the stumbling blocks of familiarity, depriving the story of its full force. Most people, as children, hear the story told as a delightful tale of ancient adventure — a tale of the venerable and good-hearted Noah; boat building on the colossal scale; lighthearted and quick-footed animals of all shapes and sizes gaily tripping over a gangplank into a cavernous interior, two by two; the bursting of the fountains of the deep and the opening of the windows of heaven; the ark and its comic contents bobbing about in safety on wild waters while Noah's nasty neighbors (with whom one never identifies) sink from view.

The original setting, however, is far removed from that of a bedtime story. For the peoples of the ancient Levant, the story was concerned with nature, i.e., the forces of reality that so deeply affected their very life. As noted earlier these forces were personalized as divine beings. Nature was not an "it" but a whole series of divine "thous." The biblical view of God, however, cuts diametrically across this view of nature. The God of Israel stands outside nature and its forces. As their Creator, God uses them as instruments of his purpose. Nature is, nonetheless, of a personal order, throbbing with the mysterious, powerful presence of the Lord. Viewed against this background, the awesome terror of the cataclysmic destruction of the Flood is raised to almost unutterable proportions as the expression of God's judgment on human sin. Here was the appropriate judgment of God that came on humanity when "every inclination of the thoughts of their hearts was only evil continually" (6:5).

So, too, God's judgment confronts the sin of corporate humanity at the Tower of Babel. To meet the threat of the evil propensities inherent in collective existence, God scatters humankind by confusing their language. They become divided into countless tribes and states. At the end of the primeval prologue, humankind finds itself in an alienated state; persons are separated from God and from one another in a hostile world. Individual is pitted against individual, social element against social element, nation against nation.

God's Sustaining Grace. A fourth theological theme that gently blows through the primeval prologue is that of God's sustaining grace. That grace is present in and along with each judgment except the last. In the Eden story, the penalty prescribed for eating the forbidden fruit is death that very day (2:17). Yet God shows his forbearance in the fact that death, though certain, is postponed to an unspecified time (3:19). Further, God himself clothes the guilty pair, enabling them to cope with their shame (v. 20). Moreover, the guilty Cain is merely left to despair before his punishment. In unmerited mercy, God responds to his bitter complaint by decreeing a sevenfold vengeance on anyone who takes Cain's life. He places a mark on him to make this protective relationship obvious to all (4:15).

The Flood story, although the supreme example of God's judgment on human sin, also subtly reflects his preserving grace. At its end there is a word from the Lord that is not found in other ancient traditions (Gen. 8:21f.). This word offers a glimpse into God's own heart. The Flood is seen as a measure of the grace of the living God as well as of his judgment. This stark paradox pervades the whole Bible. The very same condition which affords the grounds for God's terrible judgment ("every inclination of the thoughts of their hearts was only evil continually," 6:5) is also the grounds for his grace ("for the inclination of the human heart is evil from his youth," 8:21). The measure of God's supporting grace exceeds all expectations. Incomprehensibly the natural order continues to sustain humans despite their cruel sinning. The language turns poetic to trumpet this promise:

> "As long as earth endures,
> seedtime and harvest, cold and heat,
> summer and winter, day and night,
> shall not cease." (v. 22)

Although human corruption is unchanged God transfers humanity to a newly ordered world whose natural course of events is solemnly guaranteed to endure.

The ethnic and political significance of that endurance is paraded in the Table of Nations (ch. 10). Placed strategically *before* not *after* the Tower of Babel episode, it serves as the fulfillment of God's command to people the earth (9:1; cf. 1:28). It also depicts God's blessing on the nations and his work of recreation after the uncreation of the Flood.[16]

This theme of God's sustaining grace is muted, however, at one point in the account — the very end, where the bleaker side of God's relationship to the human family is depicted:

> The story about the Tower of Babel concludes with God's judgment on mankind; there is no word of grace. The whole primeval history, therefore, seems to break off in shrill dissonance, and the question . . . now arises even more urgently: Is God's relationship to the nations now finally broken; is God's gracious forbearance now exhausted; has God rejected the nations in wrath forever? That is the burdensome question which no thoughtful reader of ch. 11 can avoid; indeed, one can say that our narrator intended by means of the whole plan of his primeval history to raise precisely this question and to pose it in all its severity. Only then is the reader properly prepared to take up the strangely new thing that now follows the comfortless story about the building of the tower: the election and blessing of Abraham. We stand here, therefore, at the point where primeval history and sacred history dovetail, and thus at one of the most important places in the entire Old Testament.[17]

The genealogy of Noah's son Shem (11:10-27) serves as a bridge between the judgment of Babel and the divine promises to Abraham. The list of generations does not sing the words of God's grace with the full vigor of covenant announcements such as 8:20–9:17. But it does hum the tune. As do the earlier genealogies in 4:17-26 and 5:1-32, it catches the rhythm and melody of the march of God's program. Death, the penalty of sin, is offset by the birth of generations following. Childbirth carries the pain of judgment (3:16), but divine mercy makes survival and continuity possible.

> The primeval prologue prepares the way for the history of redemption. The relationship is that of problem and solution. Its chapters carry utmost importance for understanding all of Scripture. The desperate problem of human sin so poignantly portrayed in Gen. 1–11 is solved by God's gracious initiative, already intimated in the prologue, but sounded strongly in the promise of land and posterity to Abraham.

The redemptive history that begins here, however, will not come to fruition until its consummation in the Son of Abraham (Matt. 1:1), whose death and resurrection will provide the ultimate victory over the sin and death that so soon disfigured God's good work.

31

CHAPTER 3

Genesis: Patriarchal History

The last line of the primal history names Abram and his brothers (11:26). The earlier stories spotlighted Adam and Noah as key figures whose lives were pivotal to the divine plan and its human consequences. Now the central player in the drama is Abram. His personal and family story saturates the remaining chapters of Genesis and forms a stream that carries through the whole Bible.

> Now the LORD said to Abram, "Go from your country and your kindred and your father's house to the land that I will show you. I will make of you a great nation, and I will bless you, and make your name great, so that you will be a blessing. I will bless those who bless you, and the one who curses you I will curse; and in you all the families of the earth shall be blessed." Gen. 12:1-3

Contents of Genesis 11:27–50:26

Like the primal history, the patriarchal history (Gen. 11:27–50:26) is divided into five sections by the *toledoth* formula (p. 16). In three instances this literary

32

structure corresponds with major divisions based on content: stories about Abraham (11:27–25:18), about Jacob (25:19–37:1) and the long narrative about Joseph (37:2–50:26).[1] The remaining *toledoth* formulas introduce short genealogical sections following the first two major divisions: Ishmael at the end of the Abraham cycle (25:12, 18) and Esau at the end of the Jacob cycle (36:1, 43). This device relegates Isaac's role to a secondary importance.

Historical Background

The call of Abraham initiates a radical new development. God acts in history to set in motion a series of events that will ultimately heal the breach that sin has placed between God and the world.

Through two centuries of higher criticism, with its attempts to decipher clues to the background, authorship, sources, and literary forms of Genesis, some scholars have come to view the patriarchal narratives as having little historical worth. The narratives are said to reflect the beliefs of the time in which they were written — either the early Monarchy (ninth-eighth centuries B.C.) or the postexilic period (sixth-fifth centuries, see ch. 1). The patriarchs themselves are regarded as figures of Canaanite deities, heroes drawn from pre-Israelite folklore, or personifications of tribes whose history is reflected in their movements and relationships. When these views were first developed, the history and culture of the third and second millennia were virtually unknown. Since then a wealth of material has been discovered. Numerous sites in Palestine, Syria, and Mesopotamia have been excavated. Hundreds of thousands of texts have been found.[2] This material permits a much fuller reconstruction of early Near Eastern history, at least for the major centers of civilization, Egypt and Mesopotamia. Although many gaps and many questions remain, these discoveries have so transformed knowledge of the period that it is no longer a dark age. A brief outline of the major events of the period follows.[3]

Prehistoric Period. History in the proper sense began shortly after 3000 in the ancient Near East. A sophisticated culture had already arisen in the great river valleys of both Mesopotamia and Egypt. In Mesopotamia agriculture was advanced, with elaborate drainage and irrigation. Cities were founded and organized into city-states. They cooperated to develop large irrigation projects. These city-states had a complex administrative system. Writing had already been developed. The same was true in Egypt. The numerous local districts in Egypt had formed two large kingdoms, one in the northern delta region and the other in the south. A strong pharaoh then united Egypt but it was always known as the two lands. Hieroglyphic script had already advanced beyond primitive stages. By the Fourth Dynasty (*ca.* 2600), both administrative structure and technological knowledge enabled the building of the great pyramids at Giza. Furthermore, Egypt and Mesopotamia were already engaged in significant cultural interchange. This took place some 1500 years before Israel was to appear.

Ancient Near East, Third Millennium. (1) Mesopotamia. The Sumerians were the creators of Mesopotamian civilization. The origin of their civilization cannot be traced. Politically it consisted of independent city-states (Early Dynastic Age, *ca.* 2800-2360).[4] Sumerian life was organized around the temple; religious and political authority were closely integrated. The temple scribes had already invented cuneiform writing, and most of the epics and myths of later Assyrian and Babylonian literature were written first in this period. Trade, commerce, and economic life flourished.

Among the dominant Sumerians, Semites inhabited lower Mesopotamia in this period. They were called Akkadians after the city-state of Akkad, where they first gained ascendancy. Deeply influenced by Sumerian culture and religion, they adapted the cuneiform syllabic script to their own language. Eventually a Semitic ruler, Sargon I, seized power and founded an empire that lasted for 180 years (2360-2180). His dynasty controlled all Mesopotamia. His domain at times extended to Elam in the east and the Mediterranean in the west.[5]

This Akkadian empire was ended by barbarian tribes called the Guti. They swept in from the Zagros mountains to the east *ca.* 2180. Very little is known about the following century, but *ca.* 2050 the Sumerian city-states of the south broke the Gutian power. Under the third dynasty of the city of Ur (Ur III, 2060-1950), Sumerian civilization experienced a last glorious revival.

West-Semitic (Amorite or "Asian") caravan, from tomb painting (ca. 1890 B.C.) at Beni Hasan, Egypt. *(Oriental Institute, University of Chicago)*

Ur-nammu, the founder of that dynasty, is noted for his law code. Sumerians and Akkadians lived side by side in racial and cultural harmony. Akkadian language and culture slowly replaced Sumerian. Sumerian language continued only as a sacred and traditional medium in the scribal schools.

By the time God called Abraham from Ur of the Chaldees, Sumerian civilization had emerged, flowered, and faded from the scene. Ur III collapsed shortly after 2000. It had been weakened by the influx of new peoples, notably the Amorites, who were to shape the history of Mesopotamia, south and north, for the next several hundred years.

(2) Egypt. After unification, strong central rule in Egypt continued for some seven hundred years. This era is called the Old Kingdom (*ca.* 2900-2200). The most impressive remains of this remarkable civilization are the pyramids, massive monuments to its cult of the dead Pharaohs. Egypt reached its golden age under the Third and Fourth Dynasties (*ca.* 2700-2500). During this period the characteristic features of Egypt's unique culture were firmly established. By accident of discovery, the work of the pharaohs of the Fifth and Sixth Dynasties are better known. But these are pale reflections of the glories of the Third and Fourth Dynasties, in which, for example, the walls of the pyramids were covered with carefully carved and painted magic spells and hymns — the Pyramid texts, the oldest known religious compositions.

In the twenty-third century the central government disintegrated before rival provincial governors. Egypt fell into a period of social chaos and economic ruin known as the First Intermediate Period (*ca.* 2200-2000). The literature of the period strongly reflects the difficulty of life during the national malaise.[6] Finally, in the mid-twenty-first century, a dynasty from Thebes, the Eleventh, reunited the land and ushered in the Middle Kingdom. This was Egypt's second period of greatness. Long before Abraham, Egypt had experienced a millennium of progressive civilization.[7]

(3) Syria-Palestine. Knowledge of Syria and Palestine in the third millennium is shrouded by the mists of prehistory. The discovery in 1975-76 of nearly twenty thousand fragments of clay tablets at Tell Mardikh (Ebla), near modern Aleppo, has led scholars to believe that a vast empire was centered here in the mid-third millennium.[8] This empire had vassal cities as far away as Cyprus, Sinai, Anatolia, and the Mesopotamian highlands. Study of these cuneiform texts has not progressed extensively enough to permit adequate interpretation of this Early Bronze Age civilization.

In the early third millennium Palestine itself was characterized by the development of small but well-built and heavily fortified cities, including Jericho, Megiddo, Beth-shean, and Lachish. The inhabitants are usually known as Canaanites, from the name of this region in later texts. Late in the third millennium, every known Canaanite city underwent a vast destruction, bringing to an end the Early Bronze Age civilization. The agents of this destruction are not known. Frequently it is speculated that they belonged to the Amorite groups, whose dynamic presence in Mesopotamia and northeast Syria is well documented.[9] The Old Testament counts them among the people of Canaan at the time of Israel's settlement in the land (Josh. 2:10; Amos 2:9).

Patriarchal Age, ca. 2000–ca. 1500. (1) Mesopotamia. Around 1950 Ur III was falling from power under pressure from the influx of West Semitic peoples, the Amorites. The city-states of Lower Mesopotamia became rivals. At the end of this period every city-state in Upper and Lower Mesopotamia was ruled by an Amorite dynasty. Although the basic population in southern Mesopotamia remained Akkadian, in the northwest the Amorites completely displaced them. This period, however chaotic in political and economic terms, was not a dark age. Two law codes have been found, one in Akkadian from Eshnunna, the other from Isin, codified by Lipit-Ishtar. Both evidence considerable similarities to the Covenant Code (Exod. 21–23).

Assyria and Babylonia first played roles of historical significance in this period. About 1900 Assyria, ruled by an Akkadian dynasty, established a commercial colony far to the northwest at the ancient Anatolian town of Kanish (modern Kültepe near Turkish Kayseri). This colony is known from the Cappadocian texts — several thousand tablets discovered at Kanish. This Akkadian dynasty continued in power until *ca.* 1750. It was replaced by an Amorite dynasty founded by Shamshi-adad. He briefly dominated Upper Mesopotamia, his principal rival being the city of Mari (on the west bank of the Euphrates). That city threw off the Assyrian yoke *ca.* 1730 and became a major power for a short period.

Extensive excavations at Mari have brought to light a brilliant civilization. It is documented by more than twenty thousand tablets which have great importance for patriarchal backgrounds.

Babylon under Hammurabi (*ca.* 1728-1686) was the city that emerged victorious. He faced not only Mari and Assyria but also Larsa which, under an Elamite dynasty (centered in Susa in southwest Persia), ruled all Mesopotamia south of Babylon. In a series of brilliant campaigns Hammurabi defeated his rivals. He came to rule a modest empire from Nineveh (on the northern end of the Tigris) to the Persian gulf. Babylon developed into the greatest cultural center of the day. A wealth of texts reveals a level of learning seldom achieved in ancient times. Most important is Hammurabi's law code. It is based on a legal tradition stretching back centuries (as the codes of Ur-nammu, Lipit-Ishtar, and Eshnunna show). In the code there are numerous and striking parallels with the laws of the Pentateuch. Hammurabi's empire, however, ended with him. Under his immediate successors most tributary states broke away. Babylon particularly struggled for its existence against the Kassites, a new people sweeping in from the Zagros mountains to the east.

Part of the reason for Babylon's decline was a virtual flood of new peoples into the area, especially from the north. The ethnic movements were so disruptive that for almost two centuries events were not documented. New states and empires emerged, most important being the Hurrians. They were non-Semites who had settled in northwestern Mesopotamia since the late third millennium. They now moved in force into the area. When documentary evidence resumes *ca.* 1500, the Hurrians control the empire of Mitanni, stretching from Alalakh to the foothills of the Zagros, across the Tigris to the east. The proud state of Assyria lies under their control. For a time in the early fifteenth century the Hurrians vied with Egypt for world empire. Moving with the Hurrians, but in far smaller numbers, were Indo-Europeans, who seem to have been mostly a ruling aristocracy. Most names of kings of the Mitanni empire are Indo-European.

In Asia Minor the Hittites came to prominence. They spoke an Indo-European language, though they used a cuneiform system to write it. During the late third millennium they had moved into central Asia Minor and began to gain ascendancy among the city-states. By *ca.* 1550 they had created a kingdom in central and eastern Asia Minor, with the capital at Hattusas (modern Boghazköy). They soon came into conflict with the Hurrian kingdom of Mitanni. It was indeed a sign of things to come that the end of the First Dynasty of Babylon in 1530 came, not from a Mesopotamian power, but from a lightning-like raid of Mursilis I, an early ruler of the Hittite Old Kingdom. However, the Hittites were not able to take the path of empire for another century. Thus, shortly after 1500, Mesopotamia was just emerging from a period of disruption. A new political alignment was taking shape that would soon bring a struggle for world empire.

(2) Egypt. The Middle Kingdom, lasting for nearly three hundred years, was Egypt's second period of cultural growth (*ca.* 2100-1800). It reached its zenith with the Twelfth Dynasty. The capital was once more at Memphis (Heb. Noph, Isa. 19:13; Moph, Hos. 9:6), the political center between north and south and the revered home of the Old Kingdom pharaohs. This was a period of great prosperity. Literature and the arts reached heights seldom achieved again, with wisdom literature and narrative tales abounding. From this era come the Execration texts, fragments of broken bowls on which were written the names of Egypt's enemies. To effect a curse the names of enemies were written on bowls; the bowls were turned upside down and smashed. The shattering of the names written on the bowl sympathetically cursed the people of that name. These names indicate that Egypt exercised loose control over most of Canaan.

In the latter half of the eighteenth century, the Middle Kingdom declined under rival dynasties. With the country weakened, foreign peoples from Canaan (later called Palestine) and southern Syria infiltrated and eventually seized power. Named Hyksos, an Egyptian term meaning "foreign chiefs," their exact identity is still much debated. The majority were certainly West Semites

(Canaanites or Amorites). They placed their capital at Avaris in the north-eastern Delta region. For about a century (*ca.* 1650-1540), during the Second Intermediate period, they ruled Egypt and parts of Canaan. It is not unlikely that during this time Joseph and his brothers came down into Egypt.

The struggle for Egyptian independence from this foreign control began in the south, in Upper Egypt. Ahmosis, founder of the Eighteenth Dynasty, took Avaris and pursued the Hyksos into Palestine. He captured Sharuhen in southwest Palestine (Josh. 19:6), their main center there, after a three-year siege. Free again, Egypt determined that the best defense was a good offense and embarked on the path of empire in Asia for the first time. This strategy led to direct conflict with the new powers already centered there, precipitating a struggle for world empire.

(3) Syria-Palestine. By comparison with the evidence for this period in the major cultural centers of Egypt and Mesopotamia, that for the area of Syria-Palestine is minuscule. Part of the reason for this is the accidents of discovery, but much of it is due to the inherent nature of the history and physical culture of Palestine itself. As W. G. Dever puts it:

> Now that we have a more representative view of Palestine in the context of the entire ancient Near East, it is clear that the country was always a cultural backwater, impoverished artistically as well as economically. Furthermore, its stormy political history has led to frequent pillage, destruction, and rebuilding by a long succession of peoples of various cultures. This has rendered the stratification of its mounds complex and has left its material remains in a poor state of preservation. Finally, the damp climate of central Palestine and the choice of papyrus and parchment as writing materials have combined to rob us of all but a handful of epigraphic remains (the Bible being a notable exception). Even if we are fortunate enough to turn up literary remains, they are usually so fragmentary as to be enigmatic, and thus their correlation with the artifactual remains often poses severe difficulties. In short, in contrast to neighboring cultures, much of the archaeology of Palestine before the Israelite era is really "prehistory."[10]

Consequently, a history of Palestine in this period cannot really be written at all. A few very general statements must suffice.

After an obscure interim period at the end of the third millennium, usually known as Middle Bronze (MB I),[11] a new cultural synthesis took place that produced an increasingly developed and urban civilization. For lack of written materials, this civilization is better referred to by its archaeological designation, Middle Bronze II. This period is divided on the basis of pottery styles into two subperiods, MB II A (dated 2000/1950-1800), the formative phase of the culture, and MB II B-C[12] (1800, 1550/1500[13]). This last period, representing a continuous development from MB II A, saw the full flowering of the "Canaanite" civilization which produced the prosperous city-states of Syria-Palestine found in the later part of the period, after 1600: Carchemish, Aleppo, Hazor, Megiddo, Jerusalem, to name some. On the basis of the archaeological data scholars have concluded that Palestine in this period forms a cultural continuum with greater Syria. There is now little doubt that this urban civilization contributed the major portion of the so-called Hyksos peoples who controlled Egypt during the Second Intermediate Period. It also forged the major opposition to the creation of the Egyptian empire in Asia under the Eighteenth-Dynasty Pharaohs at the end of the Hyksos interlude.

Since no texts from Palestine are available from this period, the identity of the people who created this culture remains an open question. However, basing their conclusions on the apparent similarity between the pottery of this culture and that of contemporaneous Syria, most scholars attribute the MB II culture in Palestine to the arrival of the Amorites. Also many make a connection between the personal names from Palestine occurring in the Egyptian Execration texts (see above, p. 37) and the Amorite names found in contemporary texts from Syria and Mesopotamia. They go on to posit a large-scale ethnic migration from north-central Syria into Palestine.[14] This general conclusion is not warranted by the evidence available.[15] First, the archaeological evidence is, by its very nature, mute. It is quite possible that the pottery styles that appear so suddenly in Palestine in MB II A and seem to have such close connections with Syria arose because of the borrowing of pottery styles through trade and other contacts, that is, by cultural diffusion, rather than ethnic migration.

Secondly, the alleged similarity of the names from Palestine to those of the Amorites from Mesopotamia is far from conclusive.[16] Even if this basic correlation could be established, it would not demonstrate an ethnic migration from Mesopotamia to Palestine. There is good evidence that early West Semites were present in Palestine and Phoenicia long before they penetrated Syria.[17] No data at present can be construed to support the hypothesis of a large-scale ethnic migration of Amorites from north-central Syria. Further, if the hypothesis of a migration of West Semites to Palestine should be required by the data, it is far more likely that they would have come either from the regions of southwest Syria to the immediate north[18] or the Syrian steppe-land to the northeast.

Finally, toward the end of the era of MB II, Hurrian and Indo-European names appear in texts from the area. It is referred to as "Hurru land" by the Egyptians of the Eighteenth and Nineteenth Dynasties. This means that Palestine was influenced by the same movement of these ethnic groups that was described above in connection with northwest Mesopotamia. How deeply this influence was felt is still disputed. It seems very unlikely that the date could have preceded the fifteenth century.[19]

Date and Historicity of the Patriarchal Narratives

The voices of all the Old Testament traditions are unanimous in placing the patriarchal era prior to the exodus from Egypt.[20] The patriarchal history describes a group whose lifestyle was, in all probability, that of pastoral nomads. Because this material is family history no data relates either the persons or events to the political history of contemporary states and peoples. The only exception is the account of the attack of the four kings in Gen. 14. This episode has thus far defied attempts to relate it to extrabiblical events. Almost all the events of the patriarchal narratives take place within Palestine itself, but knowledge of that area in this period is exceedingly limited (and by the nature of the evidence likely to remain so). As a result, the struggle of scholars to locate the patriarchs in a specific historical time has been long and complicated.

Because of the advance in knowledge of the Near East in the second millennium, many scholars have come to attach greater historical value to the patriarchal narratives than they enjoyed at the beginning of this century (see p. 33 above). The ablest exponent of this newer view was W. F. Albright,[21] while the most complete formulation of it has been that of J. Bright.[22] Albright's conclusion is reflective of a dominant position:[23]

> . . . as a whole the picture in Genesis is historical, and there is no reason to doubt the general accuracy of the biographical details and the sketches of personality which make the Patriarchs come alive with a vividness unknown to a single extrabiblical character in the whole vast literature of the ancient Near East.[24]

Albright situated the patriarchs in the Middle Bronze I period.[25] The majority of scholars, however, have placed them early in the general era of MB II (i.e., the early centuries of the second millennium) in connection with the presumed Amorite migration.[26] This is the view persuasively argued by R. de Vaux.[27] It has, however, in recent years, faced many challenges. Almost every line of evidence and argumentation used to establish this consensus has been seriously questioned,[28] and an increasing number of scholars regard the view as no longer valid. In spite of the skeptical approach there is still more than sufficient evidence from the Bible and extrabiblical texts to indicate historicity as a warrantable conclusion.

First, a literary study of the patriarchal narratives reveals their historiographical nature.[29] Their primary message is theological. They have come down through a long, complex process of oral and written transmission. As a result neither in basic message nor form are they history in the modern sense (see below).[30] Nevertheless, they stand closest in literary type to historically based narratives.[31] Two separate traditions place the patriarchs some four

The name Israel, mentioned in a hymn of victory on the Merneptah stele (ca. 1220 B.C.). *(Egyptian Museum, Cairo)*

hundred years before the Exodus.[32] Since the Merneptah stele (see below, p. 56) dates Israel's presence in Palestine *ca.* 1220,[33] the end of the patriarchal period must be *ca.* 1700 at the latest.[34]

Second, there is significant evidence that the patriarchal narratives reflect authentically the conditions of the early second millennium. The main lines of evidence are as follows:

(1) The kinds of names the patriarchs bore are abundantly exemplified among the Amorite population of the period.[35] The names can be identified as Early West Semitic, i.e., as belonging to the languages of the West Semitic family extant in the second millennium.[36] Yet these names are exceedingly rare among the Canaanite peoples of the first millennium. Thus the chronological distribution of names in various texts argues strongly that the patriarchal period is to be dated to the second millennium.[37]

(2) Abraham's journey from Haran in northwest Mesopotamia to Canaan (Gen. 12:4-6) accords well with conditions known to pertain during MB II A (2000/1950-1800). This era knew a stable, peaceful, and prosperous way of life. In particular, the roads were open between Canaan and northwest Mesopotamia. In this period most of the cities mentioned in the patriarchal narratives were in existence, e.g., Shechem, Bethel, Hebron, Dothan, and Jerusalem (if it is the Salem of Gen. 14). A major problem, though, is lack of

evidence that the Negeb, one of the major areas of Abraham's travel, was occupied in MB II. However, it was extensively occupied in MB I.[38]

This view does not assume an ethnic migration of Amorites from northwest Mesopotamia to Canaan in either MB I or MB II as a historical context for Abraham's migration from Haran to Canaan. The description of Abraham's journey does not require a massive migration of peoples. His move is not even that of a tribe (let alone a people!) but of one family.[39]

(3) The nomadic lifestyle of the patriarchs fits the cultural milieu of the early second millennium. Understanding of nomadism in the ancient Near East has been radically transformed by recent anthropological studies. No longer can one uncritically adopt as a model the pattern of life of the much later camel-mounted Arab Bedouin, with their ceaseless raids on the sedentary peoples of the civilized lands.[40] On the contrary, pastoral "nomads" of the semi-arid steppe zone between the desert and the cultivable land[41] were in constant contact with village farming areas. Thus was formed a dual society in which villagers and pastoralists were mutually dependent and integrated parts of the same tribal community.[42] Movement back and forth between the lifestyle of the settled agricultural community and that of the pastoralists who roamed seasonally into steppes seeking pasturage was endemic. Its timing and extent depended on the rainfall in the semi-arid steppe zone. Such nagging conflict as existed was not so much between pastoralist and villager as between the organized city-states with their powerful urban centers and these autonomous tribal chiefdoms.

Detailed comparison of this concept of nomadism with the biblical texts remains to be done. But the patriarchal lifestyle seems to reflect this same "dimorphic" society.[43] The patriarchs camp in the vicinity of towns (e.g., Gen. 12:6-9; 33:18-20) and even live as "resident aliens" in certain towns (e.g., 20:1ff.). They sporadically practice agriculture (26:12f.); Lot settles "among the towns of the plain, . . . on the outskirts of Sodom" (13:12); and the contrasting vocations of Jacob and Esau (25:27-34) possibly reflect this same dichotomy. Yet the patriarchs are sheepbreeders, moving with their flocks over considerable distances; e.g., Jacob, while residing at Hebron, sends Joseph to visit his brothers at Shechem, and he finds them further north at Dothan (37:12, 17). Parallel technical vocabulary has been observed in the usage of both the Mari society and Israel in the areas of tribal kinship terms and pastoral encampments.[44] It is clear that the patriarchal mode of life has similarities to the pastoral nomadism of the Mari texts and that their mode of life fits well in the cultural context of the early second millennium.

(4) Various social and legal customs occurring in the patriarchal narratives can be compared with a wide range of socio-juridical customs from both the second and first millennia. These parallels, particularly those drawn from the Nuzi texts, must be interpreted with great care. The customs, when they

have been valid, have been shown to be insufficiently precise chronologically to be used for dating purposes. It is hard to establish dates in this way, for socio-juridical customs in the ancient Near East were most often of long duration. A case in point is the alleged connection between the patriarchal narratives and a specifically Hurrian socio-juridical milieu based on the Nuzi texts. This connection often loomed large in the argument for the historicity of the patriarchs. We now know this argument to be heavily flawed.[45] The Nuzi customs used for comparison were drawn from only a half dozen of the approximately three hundred family law texts found at the site, so they can hardly be said to be representative even of Nuzi society.[46] The Nuzi customs, moreover, show much greater similarity to the socio-juridical practices of the Mesopotamian world at large than originally thought. Consequently the whole question of a specifically Hurrian pattern of family law is suspect. Nevertheless, a sufficient number of valid parallels between patriarchal customs and those of the ancient Near East have been established to show that the patriarchal narratives accurately reflect the social and historical setting in which the Bible places them.[47]

(5) The general picture of patriarchal religion reflects an early era. God is the personal God of the patriarchal father and his clan (rather than a God of places and sanctuaries as among the Canaanites). He grants a unilateral covenant and promises of divine protection. Patriarchal religion is clearly not a retrojection into the past of later Israelite belief. Several features — the regular use of the divine name El instead of Yahweh; the absence of the name Baal; the directness of the relationship between God and the patriarch without the mediation of priest, prophet, or cultus; the lack of reference to Jerusalem — indicate this.

What has been presented is sufficient to permit the conclusion that the patriarchs are indeed historical figures.[48] It is unlikely that specific references to any of them will be attested in other sources, because the patriarchal narratives are family history. The patriarchs themselves were chiefs of semi-nomadic clans, who, in their lifetimes, affected few outside their own family circle.[49]

Literary Genre of the Patriarchal Narratives

Although rediscovery of the ancient world has demonstrated that the patriarchal narratives authentically reflect the period in which the Bible places them, does this mean that they are "history" in the modern sense? Behind all historical writing lie the actual events in space and time. Two major problems interpose themselves between these events and what is called "history." The first is the problem of *knowledge*. What are the facts and how have they been preserved? If the historian possesses documentary evidence, what is the interval between the event and when it was recorded? If this interval was spanned by oral tradition, did conditions exist to preserve the facts faithfully, such as a cohesive social group with historical continuity? Much will depend upon how historians come to know about the events they record.

The second problem is *significance*. To record all that happened is impossible. Furthermore, many events are insignificant for particular purposes. To the political historian a marriage contract between common people is of little interest, whereas to the social historian it is primary. History writing is much more than the bare chronicling of events. It involves a selecting of events, relating them to one another, and determining cause and effect. Therefore, the question of the writers' purposes, on the basis of which they select their data, becomes of paramount importance.

The biblical writers were not exempt from either of these considerations. Their writing under divine inspiration (see below, ch. 45) does not imply anything different about their human, material knowledge of the past. Inspiration did not give them new information or make the obscure clear. They frequently mention sources (Num. 21:14; Josh. 10:12f.; 1 Kgs. 14:19). A comparison of passages reveals vast differences in their knowledge of the past.

The aims of the biblical authors are largely theological, so they select events and incidents in keeping with their primary interest in God's actions in bringing about his purpose. They recount what God has done to inspire faith. They do not falsify history, but they are highly selective in light of their purposes. This is especially true in Genesis, in which several centuries are covered.[50]

In this light, what can be said about the historical genre of the patriarchal narratives? First, they are family history, handed down primarily through oral tradition. Pastoral nomads normally do not keep written records. There is little interest in relating their story to contemporary events. The narratives are grouped in three "cycles" (stemming from three of the patriarchal generations), marked off by the *toledoth* formula. They give only the most general indications of chronological relationship. If the chronology is pressed, difficult problems result. For instance, in Gen. 21:14 Abraham is said to have placed Ishmael on Hagar's shoulder and sent her off into the desert. Based on the chronology of the sequence of chapters, Ishmael was 16 years old (16:16; 21:5). Again, Jacob was born when Isaac was 60 (25:26), and Isaac died at 180 (35:28). A similar reading finds that Rebekah was deeply disturbed about a wife for Jacob (27:46) when he is between 80 and 100 years old!

Some traditions are difficult to harmonize with history. Both Midian and Ishmael are Joseph's great-uncles, yet the Midianites and Ishmaelites appear in his boyhood as caravan merchants plying their trade between Transjordan and Egypt (37:26-28). Amalek is the grandson of Esau (36:12), Abraham's grandson, yet in Abraham's day the Amalekites were settled in southern Palestine (14:7).

These facts are problematic only if these cycles are interpreted as history in a modern sense. Their primary purpose is to show the unfolding of Abraham's call. With that call God makes definitive promises to Abraham (12:1-3). The succeeding chapters show how God brought these promises to pass in spite of Abraham's lack of an heir (see below, p. 47). This kind of "history writing" must be recognized as the "remembered past" — the folk memory of a people. The distinction between this style and that of the historical writing in the time of Israel's monarchy is not in the historical reality of the events but in the manner of their presentation. The centuries have been bridged by oral tradition.[51] In primitive societies, oral tradition is far more precise than can be imagined by the modern western reader.[52] The patriarchal culture provided an ideal environment for the accurate transmission of tradition: it was characterized by a closed social sphere bound by ties of blood and religion. These narratives, then, are vital traditions which were kept alive by the collective memory of the tribe.

Religion of the Patriarchs

It is not possible to gather from the narratives of Gen. 12–50 a complete picture of the religious life of the patriarchs. Nonetheless, enough information can be gathered to give a general description and set their religion in its cultural context. This picture can be augmented by the archaeological rediscoveries from the patriarchal age.

Abraham was a polytheist at the time of God's call:

> Long ago your ancestors — Terah, and his sons Abraham and Nahor — lived beyond the Euphrates and served other gods. (Josh. 24:2f.)

(Cf. also Josh. 24:14; Gen. 31:19-35, 53; 35:2.) What type of cult he followed is unknown. In obeying God's call, Abraham left Haran for Canaan. He abandoned his old religious ways in order to follow God with single-minded devotion. This same God appeared to each of the patriarchs, chose them, and promised to be with them (12:1-3; 15:1-6, 17; 28:11-15). Each in turn chose this God as the family's patron. They identified this God in relation to the family: "the God of Abraham," "the God of Isaac," and "the God of Jacob"

(24:12; 28:13; 31:42, 53; cf. Exod. 3:6), and, as well, "the God of Nahor" (31:53). He is called also "the Kinsman" (see NJB; most versions translate "Fear of Isaac"; 31:42, 53) and "the Mighty one of Jacob" (49:24). This close personal tie is revealed by the title "the God of my/your father" (26:24; 31:42, 53; 32:9; 49:25; and esp. Exod. 3:6). This terminology has close parallels in the Cappadocian and Mari texts[53] as well as in Arabic and Aramean texts from the early Christian centuries.[54] This God of the clan blesses the patriarchs (12:1-3; 26:3f.) with the promise of the land of Canaan and innumerable descendants (12:2, 7; 13:14-17; 15:4f., 18; 26:3f.; 28:13f.). He protects and saves (19:29). He can be called on by name and petitioned (18:22-33). He punishes evil (38:7) but has regard for the just (18:25).

God sealed the relationship with the one elected through a covenant. He first made a covenant with Abraham (ch. 15).[55] It was ratified in a solemn, mysterious ceremony (vv. 7-21). God placed himself under oath by passing between the halves of the animals which Abraham had slaughtered in the form of a firebrand and smoking furnace, ominous symbols of the divine presence. God symbolically placed himself under a curse should he violate the promise.

This account reveals God to be a personal God, desiring to associate with persons. The Canaanite gods, by contrast, were primarily associated with places. The patriarchs understood that there was one God. Isaac worshipped the God of his father (26:23ff.), as did Jacob (31:5, 42, 53). This God is unique, without colleagues or consort. Therefore, Jacob's family had to put away the strange gods they brought from Mesopotamia (35:2).

The texts give only sparse information about the worship of the patriarchs. They prayed (25:21), often prostrating themselves in the common Near Eastern manner (17:3; 24:52). They built altars and made sacrifices (12:7; 22:9; 35:1). However, there was no special location for such rites and no official priesthood. Worship was conceived primarily in terms not of ceremony but of a relationship between God and human beings. The distinctiveness of the patriarchs' faith resided in their conception of God and in their close personal relationship with him.

Theology of the Narratives

Patriarchal history begins with the election of Abraham in 12:1-3. His call comes dramatically and definitively. It catches Abraham in mid-course. This sudden new beginning throws the summons itself into relief. It provides a model by which all of patriarchal history is to be interpreted.

Yahweh said to Abram:
"Go forth from your native land
    And from your father's home
To a land that I will show you.
I will make of you a great nation,
    Bless you, and make great your name.
So be a blessing.
I will bless those who bless you,
    And curse him who curses you;
And through you shall bless themselves
    All the communities on earth." (12:1-3, lit.)[56]

This universal promise provides the word of grace for the disobedience and judgment of the primeval prologue. It answers the disturbing questions about God's relationship to his scattered humanity. The choice of Abraham and the unconditional promises of land and nationhood have as their ultimate goal the blessing of all the earth's communities. The beginning of redemptive history offers a word about its end. The salvation promised Abraham will ultimately embrace all humankind. God has not dismissed the human family in wrath forever, but now acts to mend the breach that sin has placed between him and his world. This promise stands as a key to understanding all of Scripture.

Election and Promises of God. The promises to Abraham come in conflict with his real life journey. He is to be a great nation (12:2), but Sarah is barren (11:30). The land belongs to his descendants (12:7), but the Canaanites occupy it (v. 6). At the beginning the narrator consciously juxtaposes God's promise and Abraham's circumstances. This problem is the overarching, all-consuming interest of chs. 12–21. The promise is stated in the most extravagant way — Abraham's descendants are to be "as the dust of the earth" (13:16) and as numerous as the stars in heaven (15:5). To implement this promise, Abraham, childless, follows stratagem after stratagem. He adopts a slave born in his own house (15:2f.). Sarah, to protect her position as his wife, provides her maid Hagar as a secondary wife, through which union Ishmael is born (ch. 16). But neither attempt fulfills God's pledge of a son through Sarah (15:4; 17:18f.). Finally, when old age makes the promise seem impossible in human terms, "the LORD dealt with Sarah as he had said, and the LORD did for Sarah as he had promised" (21:1). Isaac is born.

The same promise is reaffirmed to each of the patriarchs: to Isaac (26:2-4); to Jacob at Bethel as he leaves Canaan for fear of Esau (28:13f.); again to Jacob at Bethel upon his return (35:11f.); and to Joseph and his sons (48:1-6).

Later, this overarching promise is seen as fulfilled in God's deliverance of Israel from Egypt:

> I also established my covenant with them [the patriarchs], to give them the land of Canaan, . . . and I have remembered my covenant. I will redeem you with an outstretched arm. . . . And I will bring you into the land which I swore to give to Abraham, to Isaac, and to Jacob. Exod. 6:4-8

In the patriarchal period, redemptive history is God's election of Abraham and his line. Fulfillment of that promise seems strangely postponed, however, for the land was possessed by the Canaanites.[57] All that Abraham ever possessed was the cave of Machpelah (Gen. 23). Abraham (25:7-10), Isaac (35:27-29), and Jacob (49:29-31) were buried there with their wives. Only in death did they cease to be sojourners. At the end of the patriarchal period, the descendants of Abraham were no longer even sojourners in the land, but had removed to Egypt.

The story of Joseph provides the first stage in the transition from a patriarchal family to an independent nation, in keeping with the divine promise. The favorite son, badly spoiled, is hated by his brothers, sold into slavery, and taken to Egypt. There his virtue, wisdom, and grace quickly establish him in leadership. A foreigner, he is maligned and imprisoned (chs. 37–39). A God-given ability to interpret dreams brings Joseph to Pharaoh's attention. When he interprets the dreams that trouble Pharaoh, Pharaoh is impressed by his great wisdom and appoints him to high administrative office (chs. 40–41). This position, in turn, opens the way for Joseph to provide for his own family during the harsh famine by bringing them to Egypt (chs. 42–47). This story, recounted in form so different from that of the Abraham and Jacob stories, is one long lesson: God's providence brings human plots to naught and turns their evil intent to his own ends (50:20). Further, God protects and provides for those who follow him.

The result of Joseph's betrayal is an important step in the creation of the chosen people. The "children of Israel" became for a time an isolated and protected community, dwelling in the land of Goshen (generally identified as the northeastern Nile delta). This theme of "salvation" (the "survival of a numerous people," 50:20) looks forward to the Exodus (and ultimately to God's final deliverance through Christ). But now Israel is in the setting to increase greatly in number while retaining its identity. The promise of land and nationhood must wait to be fulfilled specifically through God's dramatic redemption from slavery in Egypt and the taking of Canaan under Joshua.

These accounts teach many theological truths. Two of the more important are touched on here.

Faith and Righteousness. In the stories of Abraham, the promise of innumerable descendants narrows to the absorbing question of one son. The fulfillment is strangely, almost perversely it seems, postponed. The point of the stories is Abraham's faith, as seen in the account of his call. The summons to Abraham is radical. He is to abandon all his roots — land, kindred, and immediate family (12:1)[58] — for an uncertain destination, "a land that I will show you." After the call, the narrator presents Abraham's response in terse and utter simplicity: "So Abraham went, as the LORD told him" (v. 4). Abraham is presented as a paradigm of faith. His obedience and trust in the God who has called him are exemplary. That the author wrestles with the question of faith (and its relationship to righteousness) is seen in 15:6: "And he [Abraham] believed the LORD; and he reckoned it to him as righteousness." The importance of this verse is signaled in that it is not part of the narrative of what happened between God and Abraham (vv. 1-5). Instead it is the narrator's own summarizing word that Abraham's righteousness consisted in his trusting — having faith in — God's promise.

The highest test of Abraham's faith consisted in God's command to sacrifice Isaac (ch. 22). Jewish tradition thrusts Isaac into the foreground by naming the episode "The Binding of Isaac" (Gen. 22:9). But "the testing of Abraham" is what the narrator himself calls it (v. 1). It is a haunting and mysterious story of a situation which demands of Abraham incredible trust. He is called to an obedience which jeopardizes the very promise that drove him from Haran. The reader is cast back and forth between Abraham the loving father, who faces unspeakable tragedy, and Abraham, the obedient sacrificer who raises the knife over Isaac's bound and prostrate form.[59] Abraham can meet the test in only one way — total and complete faith in the God who promised him Isaac and fulfilled the promise when it was beyond human means. Abraham meets the test. So does God, by providing a ram. Abraham, thus, becomes the model of the faith that God asks of his people. And the God of all grace shows his faithfulness — as "the LORD who will provide" — to those who fear him (vv. 12, 14).

Abraham's righteousness resided in his faith in God's gracious promise. If righteousness is conceived, as in modern western society, as conformity to an abstract moral code, this equation is indeed hard to understand. However, righteousness in the Bible is not a norm-prescribing ethics, but faithfulness to a relationship. The righteous person is loyal to the claims of all personal relationships.[60] Therefore, a person's righteousness in relation to God is fulfilled when that relationship is characterized by faith (see Rom. 1:16f.; 4; Gal. 3:6-9).

The transition from election to becoming God's covenant people is not simple, historically or theologically. Tensions arise out of the nature of humankind vis-à-vis the character of the sovereign God. These tensions are most dramatic in the life of Jacob. If Abraham is pictured as a man of faith scaling the heights of trust in God, Jacob appears as a very "worldly" character — a model of guile and self-reliance. From birth, he is a crafty, scheming individual (25:26; 27:5-17, 41-45). His twenty-year service with his uncle Laban is a continual struggle between two crafty men, each scheming to get the better of the other. Finally, on his return to Canaan at the Jabbok, Jacob meets his match when he wrestles with someone whom he later recognizes as divine. Only by God's direct action, elsewhere hidden in these stories in the "unedifying manifestations of human nature,"[61] does Jacob the Supplanter become Israel the Prevailer (32:28).

After that encounter Jacob's story is a series of vignettes of a life mastered by God:[62] reconciled with Esau (33:1-11), chagrined by his sons' behavior (34:30), revealed as faithful by the discarding of the idols (35:2-5), heartbroken at the loss of his favorite son, Joseph (37:33-35), and finally, obtaining the Lord's permission to go down into Egypt (46:1-5). At his death he requests (49:29-32) that his body be buried in the cave of Machpelah. Jacob clearly places himself within the promise God made to Abraham.

Covenant. Another element of great theological importance in Gen. 12–50 is the covenant God makes with Abraham (chs. 15 and 17). Covenant is a central theme in all of Scripture. It forms a bond that did not exist by normal ties of blood or social requirements. Covenant, then, is the establishment of a particular relationship or the commitment to a particular course of action, not naturally existing, which is sanctioned by an oath normally sworn in a solemn ceremony of ratification.[63] God condescends to place himself symbolically under a curse in order to affirm to Abraham the certainty of his promises (15:7-17). It is God who takes the oath; nothing is required of Abraham (except the rite of circumcision [ch. 17] as a sign of the covenant). In this way the covenant with Abraham differs from that with Moses (see below, pp. 72-75). In the Abrahamic covenant only God lays himself under obligation. In the Mosaic covenant, Israel takes the oath and places the nation under the stringent stipulations of the covenant. These two covenants, therefore, are very different in their results. Since God solemnly commits himself by an oath to provide land and nationhood to Abraham's descendants, this covenant of promise depends only on the unchangeable character of the One who makes it.[64]

In Gen. 12–50 are presented the basic elements of the beginning of redemptive history. God has freely chosen one man and his descendants through whom "all the families of the earth shall find blessing" (12:3). How this promise is to be effected and in what terms it will come, however, waits to be disclosed. It is clear, though, that those who live by the covenant are to live a life of trust and faith in him who calls.

God's masterful surprises are part of his pattern of fulfilling his promises: overcoming barrenness of the patriarchal marriages and overriding the traditional rights of the firstborn to the greater blessing. God will see that covenant redemption takes place, but in God's own time and on God's own terms. The book ends with the scene set for the next act in the drama of redemption, deliverance from slavery in Egypt.

CHAPTER 4

Exodus: Historical Background

The Exodus is the primary event of redemption in the Old Testament. God delivered his people from slavery in Egypt, made a covenant with them at Sinai, and eventually brought them into the land of promise. Nevertheless, fixing the time and place of the Exodus is a difficult task. The book itself never names the Pharaoh with whom Moses contended, nor is any other person or event recorded to connect it with certainty to the known history of Egypt and Palestine.

> When the horses of Pharaoh with his chariots and his chariot drivers went into the sea, the LORD brought back the waters of the sea upon them; but the Israelites walked through the sea on dry ground. Exod. 15:19

Historical Background of the Period

The Exodus took place some time during the heyday of the Egyptian empire. The following historical sketch covers the end of the "patriarchal age," *ca.* 1550 B.C., to *ca.* 1200, when Israel had settled in Palestine. This time span coincides roughly with the Late Bronze Age in Palestine (see Ch. 50). During that age

Egypt dominated the ancient world, and Palestine lay within the bounds of its sovereignty.

Rise of the Egyptian Empire. In the middle of the second millennium, several new states and empires were developing in the ancient Near East (see Ch. 3). By *ca.* 1550 the Hurrian state of Mitanni lay stretched across northwest Mesopotamia, from western Syria to the foothills of the Zagros mountains in the east. These Hurrian peoples were ruled by Indo-Europeans. This alliance revolutionized ancient warfare with the invention of the chariot and the composite bow, made of laminated wood, horn, and sinew. Northwest of Mitanni, in the eastern reaches of Asia Minor, were the Hittites, slowly recovering from the period of weakness into which they had fallen after a raid on Babylon (*ca.* 1560). East of Mitanni lay Assyria, totally under its control. The nation about to become prominent was Egypt, just emerging from the dominance of the Hyksos, Asian invaders who held sway in Egypt *ca.* 1700-1550. Under Ahmosis Egypt threw off the Hyksos yoke with a determination to secure its northeastern borders by defeating the enemy in its own territory of Asia.

Thutmosis I, a Pharaoh of the great Eighteenth Dynasty, even reached the Euphrates. Egypt's presence in Asia at first, though, was mostly limited to punitive expeditions. The Pharaohs did not control any Asian territory. The main focus of the early Eighteenth Dynasty was on the subjugation of Nubia and the Sudan in the south. Later, however, Thutmosis III (1490-1436), one of Egypt's ablest rulers, directed his attention to Asia. In a famous battle at Megiddo, *ca.* 1468, he defeated the Hyksos, whose center was at Kadesh on the Orontes in southern Syria. In later campaigns he extended the empire as far north as Aleppo. Inevitably this expansion brought Egypt into conflict with Mitanni over control of Syria. War between these two states continued intermittently for nearly fifty years. However, under Thutmosis IV (*ca.* 1412-1403), a treaty between them was concluded. Both sides were motivated to make peace in order to deal with the resurgent Hittites, now pressing into northern Syria.

For some fifty years the agreement between them worked well, particularly for Egypt, now at the zenith of its power. Experiencing no military threat, Amenophis III (1403-1364) pursued a life of pleasure and luxury. He engaged in an unprecedented building program aimed at self-glorification. In Egypt an age of imperial magnificence ensued.

A remarkable revolution in Egyptian worship occurred under Amenophis IV (1364-1317). The Pharaoh began to worship the Aten (the Solar Disk), whom he proclaimed the only god. The Aten cult, though not strict monotheism, seems to have approached it. To advance the new worship the Pharaoh changed his name to Akhenaten ("the Splendor of Aten"), left Thebes, the center of the powerful priests of Amon, Egypt's main god, and built a new capital, Akhetaten, modern Tell el-Amarna. At this site the Amarna letters were found in 1887. These letters are part of the official court archives apparently

"Look on my works, ye Mighty, and despair" (Shelley, "Ozymandias," 1817).
Monumental head of Rameses II (1290-1213), regarded as pharaoh of the
Exodus, in the Rameseum at Thebes. *(Neal and Joel Bierling)*

brought from Thebes to the new capital. The tablets include letters to Amenophis III and IV from most of the important states of the day, including Babylon, Assyria, Mitanni, and the Hittites. The correspondence is principally from
Egyptian vassals in Palestine, including Byblos, Megiddo, Shechem, and Jerusalem. These letters throw brilliant light on the history and society of the
"Amarna Age." They reveal that Palestine was organized into administrative
districts with resident commissioners in garrison towns, such as Gaza. These
towns served as centers of provisions and supplies for the Egyptian troops.
They, nevertheless, were allowed considerable local control and autonomy. By
the mid-fourteenth century, Palestine could be controlled by small garrisons
of Egyptian soldiers stationed in the administrative centers.

Egypto-Hittite War. Amenophis III's opulence and Akhenaten's religious
innovations boded ill for the Egyptian empire in Asia. Because of these Pha-

raohs' lack of attention to the empire, Palestine fell into virtual anarchy, as the Amarna letters show. Some Palestinian rulers were vying for power and were often in open revolt against Egyptian authority. Loyal vassals appealed eloquently to Pharaoh for aid, but apparently in vain. Egyptian control in Syria ceased altogether. About 1375, Suppiluliuma came to the Hittite throne and proceeded to carve out an empire in Syria. With Egypt's weakness, Mitanni was left to face the resurgent Hittites alone. In a lightning attack Suppiluliuma crossed the Euphrates and totally defeated the Hurrian state and put a vassal on the throne. Assyria, now revived under Assur-uballit I (*ca.* 1356-1321), took the northeastern part of the empire. His army inflicted harsh vengeance on the Hurrian cities. By 1350 Mitanni was no more. The Hittites began directly to threaten Egyptian territory in southern Syria.

The once powerful Eighteenth Dynasty was ineffective before these forces. Egypt's control over Asia virtually ceased. But before the Hittites could consolidate their control of Syria, they became concerned about a resurgent Assyria with ambitions toward the west. Consequently, under the new Nineteenth Dynasty, Egypt was able to recuperate. This dynasty was led by Rameses I, a descendant of the old Hyksos kings. For quick access to Asia he located his capital at Avaris in the northeastern delta. His son Seti I set out to recoup Egypt's losses in Asia, quickly gaining control of Palestine. On his fourth campaign he claimed to defeat a Hittite army under Muwattalis. Although this victory probably represents only a skirmish, full-scale war between these empires broke out under Seti's son Rameses II, who reigned for sixty-seven years (1290-1224).

In his fifth year Rameses II mounted a major attack on the Hittites. They ambushed him near Kadesh on the Orontes, forcing him to retreat. The Hittites went on to reach Damascus. Consequently revolts against Egyptian rule flared as far south as Ashkelon. It took Rameses five years to restore order and regain control of northern Palestine. Thereafter he occasionally made raids into territory under Hittite control, but he never again seriously menaced Syria. After Hattusilis III (1275-1250) ascended the Hittite throne, the two nations entered into a peace treaty. Fostered in part by exhaustion from the long strife, the treaty was also motivated by the external problems each faced. The Hittites were being menaced by Assyria from the east and the Indo-European peoples from the west. Egypt faced continuous pressure from the Peoples of the Sea, i.e., Aegeo-Cretan tribes that had begun moving in from the west in the early years of Rameses II. These migrations being faced by both empires were undoubtedly related.

In the main, though, Rameses II's concluding years comprised an era of peace and colossal building activity. He spent much of his time in the various palaces he built in the northeast delta. His favorite was Per-Rameses, "the House of Rameses," identified either with Tanis or Qanṭir a few miles south (cf. Exod. 1:11).

55

Peoples of the Sea. At the major battle of Kadesh, both the Egyptians and Hittites employed as mercenary troops some of the same Aegeo-Cretan "Peoples of the Sea." These groups were forerunners of a vast movement soon to inundate the coast of Asia Minor, Palestine, and Egypt. Eventually, both the Hittites and the Nineteenth Dynasty in Egypt were to be swamped by it.

After Rameses II died, his thirteenth son Merneptah succeeded him. In his fifth year, *ca.* 1220, Merneptah faced a horde of Peoples of the Sea who, together with Libyans, moved on Egypt from the west, along the coast of North Africa. In a fierce battle he defeated them and commemorated the event with a Hymn of Victory inscribed on a stele. This hymn contains the first extrabiblical mention of Israel, stating, "Israel is laid waste, her seed is not." Merneptah died in 1211, and the Nineteenth Dynasty disintegrated in internal chaos and disunity. Apparently Egypt was even controlled by a Syrian usurper for a time. Egyptian control of Palestine had come to an end.

While Egypt struggled for its life, the Hittites met complete disaster. During the last decades of the thirteenth century, the Peoples of the Sea poured across Asia Minor and shortly after 1200 erased the Hittites from the pages of history.[1] From Asia Minor they pushed by land and sea in wave after wave down the Palestinian coast to threaten once again Egypt's very existence. Egypt's decline at the end of the Nineteenth Dynasty was reversed by Sethnakht and his son Rameses III (*ca.* 1183-1152). The latter inaugurated the Twentieth Dynasty. Early in his reign Rameses III regained control of Palestine, at least as far as Beth-shean (also called Beth-shan) at the eastern end of the Jezreel Valley. Between his fifth and eleventh years, he faced a massive onslaught of Sea Peoples, who came overland through Palestine. He barely managed to keep Egypt from being overwhelmed. Exhausted by war and racked by internal dissension, the Egyptian empire came to an end under the successors of Rameses III.

Repelled by Egypt, elements of the Sea Peoples fell back to Palestine. There they occupied large areas of the coastal plain. According to Egyptian sources, these included the *Peleset,* i.e., the Philistines.[2] Thus the nation that was to mount a major threat to Israel's existence arrived in Palestine at approximately the same time as Israel. Although the arrival of the Peoples of the Sea introduced ethnic groups into Canaan, it did not alter materially the culture or socio-political structures. Canaan continued to be organized in small city-states. The majority were located on the coastal plain and in the valley of Jezreel. The heavily forested, mountainous interior was sparsely populated. The chief ethnic group was the Canaanites, indigenous to the area since at least the third millennium.

Some notable features of this complex historical scene should be stressed. First, Israel moved into a very advanced and cosmopolitan world. During the period of the Egyptian empire, unprecedented and extensive international contacts occurred in the whole of the ancient Near East. These produced the cultural diffusion and cross-fertilization that J. H. Breasted termed the "First Internationalism." In the Amarna letters Egyptians corresponded with Babylonians, Assyrians, Mitannians, Hittites, Arzawans (inhabitants of a kingdom in Western Anatolia), Cypriots, and Canaanites, primarily in an international Akkadian dialect that was the *lingua franca* of the time. This correspondence bears witness to a highly organized system of embassies and a keenly trained scribal class, able to function in several languages.

The power politics of the day called for international alliances and an elaborate system of treaties to maintain them. For the first time the principle of law was extended beyond the boundaries of a nation or empire into the sphere of international relations. It was also a period of extensive identification of a nation's gods with similar deities in foreign pantheons. The Sumero-Akkadian gods were adopted into the pantheons of Hurrians, Hittites, Amorites, and Canaanites. The grain god Dagon originated in northwestern Mesopotamia among the Amorites, yet appears in the Bible as the principal god of the Philistines in southwestern Palestine.[3]

Next, literary diffusion was remarkable. Akkadian myths and epics were translated into Hurrian and Hittite. They appear as school texts among the Amarna tablets, having been used by Egyptian scribes for instruction in Akkadian. The Hurrians were especially active in spreading Akkadian literature to Asia Minor and Syria-Palestine.[4] A Hurrian hymn to the goddess Nikkal has been found in Ugaritic. In the Amarna tablets from Tyre two Egyptian poems are translated into Akkadian. In addition, the Canaanite myth of Astarte and the Sea is found in Egyptian hieroglyphics.[5] At Ugarit West Semitic scribes wrote religious texts in Hurrian for a Hurrian clientele. Thus, Israel entered a world that had produced a cross-fertilization and synthesis of culture hitherto unknown.

A striking achievement of this cultural situation is the appearance of alphabetic writing among the Canaanites of Syria-Palestine. Although writing developed before 3000 in both Mesopotamia and Egypt, the cumbersome syllabic and ideographic cuneiform and hieroglyphic systems, burdened with hundreds of signs, failed to become simplified. Although culturally dependent and less advanced, the Canaanites nevertheless developed an alphabet with fewer than thirty symbols. The economy of writing in an alphabet made literacy possible on a wider scale. The earliest alphabetic script thus far known is the "proto-Sinaitic." It was developed by West Semitic tribes drafted into service by Egyptian mining expeditions to Sinai. Closely related scripts have been found in isolated discoveries in Palestine, e.g., at Gezer, Lachish, Shechem, and Megiddo. The forms of the letters were influenced by Egyptian hieroglyphics. These scripts date from *ca.* 1700 to 1200, with the largest and most important collection, the Sinai inscriptions, dating to 1550-1450.[6]

The outstanding texts from this period are tablets from the city-state of Ugarit, modern Ras Shamra, on the North Syrian coast opposite Cyprus, dating to *ca.* 1300. The Ugaritians were Northwest Semites, closely related to their Canaanite neighbors to the south. These texts are also alphabetic, written on clay in a cuneiform script. Although deeply influenced by the writing techniques of the dominant culture — Egypt for the proto-Sinaitic alphabet and Mesopotamia for Ugarit — both Ugaritians and Canaanites broke amazing new ground in adapting them to an alphabetic principle.

The Ugaritic texts preserve a rich religious and epic literature (as well as letters and administrative texts) whose contents indicate many parallels with Israelite culture and institutions. They are of utmost importance for documenting the Canaanite religion and culture of Palestine at the time when Israel entered the land. Indeed, Israel appeared at the right time and place to inherit the highest cultural legacy the ancient world had yet attained.

Finally, the struggle for world empire in the third quarter of the second millennium ended in the exhaustion of all the combatants. Assyria loomed large briefly in the late thirteenth century but soon slipped into a period of weakness. That period was prolonged in the second millennium by incursions of the Aramean peoples, who flooded Syria and northwest Mesopotamia. This course of events was advantageous for the settlement in Canaan of God's new people. Another world dominion would not emerge until the Neo-Assyrian empire under Tiglath-pileser III in mid-eighth century. During this interval Israel grew into a nation-state free from the threat of any dominant power.

Does the eye of faith see too much when it views Israel's emergence precisely at this time of grand cultural synthesis and flowering as God's providential guidance of the forces of world history for the sake of redemptive history? It surely would seem not.

Evidence for the Exodus

Placing the Exodus historically within the general period just outlined is exceedingly difficult. A review of the problems is beyond the scope of this work; a presentation of the more important facts and conclusions must suffice.[7]

First, while there is no direct historical evidence for either the oppression in Egypt or the escape,[8] the conviction that Israel became a nation at the Exodus is deeply rooted in the Israelite tradition (e.g., Hos. 2:15; 11:1; Isa. 43:3). The indirect evidence is supportive.[9] The story of Joseph authentically reflects Egyptian life, customs, and literature (especially in the northeast delta region).[10] This correspondence lends historical credence to the sojourn in

Egypt. It is also known that the Egyptian court employed large numbers of Semitic peoples as state slaves on building projects near Thebes in the Eighteenth Dynasty and in the northeast delta during the Nineteenth Dynasty.[11] In addition, several Israelite names of the period, especially in Moses' family, are authentically Egyptian.[12] The escape of subject peoples from a major state is not without analogy in the ancient world.[13] From the perspective of social psychology, it is doubtful that a people would invent a story about being slaves to a foreign power. Indeed, this story is unique in literature that has survived from the ancient Near East. The most viable explanation of these facts is that God did indeed intervene to save his people.

Date of the Exodus

Even though the Exodus was certainly the central event of Israel's history, no solution is yet available to explain the complex chronological and geographical problems involved.[14] Exactly when and where the Exodus took place cannot be stated with certitude. However, the general period that best fits most of the biblical and extrabiblical evidence is the first half of the thirteenth century. The main arguments are as follows:

(1) In the "Israel stele" Merneptah claims to have subdued several entities in Canaan, including Israel, in his fifth year, *ca.* 1209. The Exodus, then, must have taken place a few years earlier.[15]

(2) According to Exod. 1:11, Israelite slaves built the store cities of Pithom and Raamses. Although some question remains as to the exact location of these cities in the northeast delta,[16] Raamses is most likely Pi-Rameses built by Rameses II sometime in the mid-thirteenth century B.C. The Exodus, then, must have taken place after his ascension to the throne, *ca.* 1300.[17]

(3) Archaeological findings, at best, paint a very complex picture of the transition from Canaanite culture to Israelite.[18] Evidence of an Israelite settlement being established on a destroyed Canaanite site is clear at Bethel and possibly at Tell Beit Mirsim,[19] Tel Zeror, and Beth Shemesh.[20] Also the sudden destruction of Hazor in the thirteenth century B.C. may reflect the time of Joshua-Judges.[21] Evidence from other sites is far from conclusive. Furthermore, the fact that several Canaanite cities experienced destruction over a span of two centuries rather than at the same time makes it harder to argue for a unified conquest. Complicating the picture are some cities which were left abandoned and others which were reoccupied by peoples of a similar culture. During the transition from Late Bronze to Iron I there was a surge of population by pastoral peoples.[22] These settlements were regional in nature (cf.

Judg. 1:27-36). It can be argued that this increase coincides with the biblical claim that Israel began to settle this region around this time.[23] As more information comes to light from excavations and surveys, it will be necessary both to reinterpret the biblical evidence and to reevaluate the current theories of the Israelite settlement (see Chapter 10: Joshua).

(4) Contemporary Egyptian documents provide historical parallels. Texts from the time of Merneptah and Rameses II illustrate the use of Semites as slaves (using the Egyptian term for ůApiru) in their building projects.[24] Another text deals with permission for nomadic groups of Shasu Bedouin from Edom to cross the line of border fortresses to the pools at Pithom (Eg. *Pr-Itm*).

(5) This date accords well with the view that the most likely setting for the descent into Egypt of Joseph and his brothers is the Hyksos period. According to Gen. 15:13, the time spent in Egypt, viewed in prospect, would be 400 years,[25] or according to Exod. 12:40 in retrospect, 430 years. In light of this position the descent into Egypt would have taken place during the first half of the seventeenth century — in the Hyksos period.

The principal objection to this date on biblical grounds is that it does not fit the 480 years between the Exodus and the foundation of Solomon's temple *ca.* 970 given in 1 Kgs. 6:1. This calculation places the Exodus in the mid-fifteenth century. However, the Old Testament, an ancient Near Eastern book, often uses numbers quite differently from a modern chronology. Thus, the 480 years may be understood as an "aggregate" or "symbolic number." It was probably based on the total of twelve generations of 40 years each.[26] The writer is more concerned with delimiting epochs than establishing exact time frames.

Many conservative scholars have concluded that a date of 1300-1250 suits the majority of evidence better than any other.[27] By this reckoning the Pharaohs of the oppression would be Seti I (1305-1290) and Rameses II (1290-1213). The Exodus then took place under the latter Pharaoh. Nonetheless, present information cannot determine with certainty that the Exodus took place during this period.

Route of the Exodus

No more certain is the route of the Exodus or the location of Mt. Sinai.[28] With increased knowledge of the topography of the northeast delta, a few of the sites mentioned in Exod. 12:37; 13:17–14:4; and Num. 33:5-8 can be located with some certainty (see Map, p. 62). Raamses, the starting point, is to be located in the vicinity of Qanṭîr. Succoth, the next stopping point, is usually identified with Eg. *Tjeku,* modern Tell el-Maskhuta in the Wâdî Tumilat, the valley forming the main route to the east from the Nile area. It is about 22 mi. NW of Pi-Rameses. This area is usually equated with Goshen, where the Israelites settled in Joseph's day. The next three sites, Etham, Pi-Hahiroth, and Migdol, are quite uncertain.[29] The name usually translated "Red Sea" means literally "Sea of Reeds"[30] and doubtless refers to one of the reed-filled, sweet-water marshes between and around Lake Menzaleh and the Bitter Lakes to the south, along the present Suez Canal. The fourth site, Baal-zephon, is often identified with Tell Defneh on the western shore of Lake Menzaleh about 5 mi. west of modern Qantara,[31] well within the area where the Sea of Reeds must be located.

Two plausible locations for the crossing of the Sea of Reeds may then be proposed. One is in the south near the Bitter Lakes. In that case the Israelites moved directly west or southwest from Succoth (Wâdî Tumilat), crossing a marshy lake, into the Sinai Desert.[32] The other location is in the north, near Tell Defneh (Baal-zephon). Then the Israelites doubled back from Succoth (14:1), crossing an arm of Lake Menzaleh, turning south into Sinai.[33] It is not possible, however, to establish the exact route.

It is certain that the Israelites did not take the normal route from Egypt to Canaan, known later as "the way of the Philistines" (Exod. 13:17). This road paralleled the coast, reaching Canaan at Gaza (see Map, p. 62). Since this route was controlled by Egyptian forts and supply stations, the Israelites would have had to face Egyptian troops (v. 17b). They therefore chose to go by the "Way of the Wilderness" (v. 18). After crossing the Sea of Reeds, they entered the "Wilderness of Shur" (15:22; Num. 33:8) in the northwest Sinai Peninsula (cf. 1 Sam. 15:7; 27:8), east of the region between Lake Timsah and Lake Menzaleh. From there they proceeded by various stations to Mt. Sinai.

Direct evidence for the location of Sinai and Israelite presence there may never be forthcoming. That presence was, historically speaking, ephemeral. The Israelite tribes left behind no sedentary population to perpetuate the names of places they visited. In fact, Sinai itself has never had a sedentary population, so names have been attached to few sites with any permanence. Hence scarcely any names from the Mosaic period are likely to have survived in the Arabic nomenclature of the area. However, the awesome granite mountains near the traditional site of Jebel Musa (Arab. "Mountain of Moses") and the Monastery of St. Catherine (see Map) remain the most plausible site for Mt. Sinai (Horeb, in some passages). The identification in Christian tradition reaches back at least to the fourth century A.D. when monks from Egypt settled there. The Bible makes clear that Mt. Sinai was far south of Kadesh-barnea. Deut. 1:2 depicts the journey from Kadesh-barnea to Mt. Sinai as eleven days, and Elijah took "forty days and forty nights" (meaning a very long journey) to reach Sinai from Beersheba (1 Kgs. 19:8).

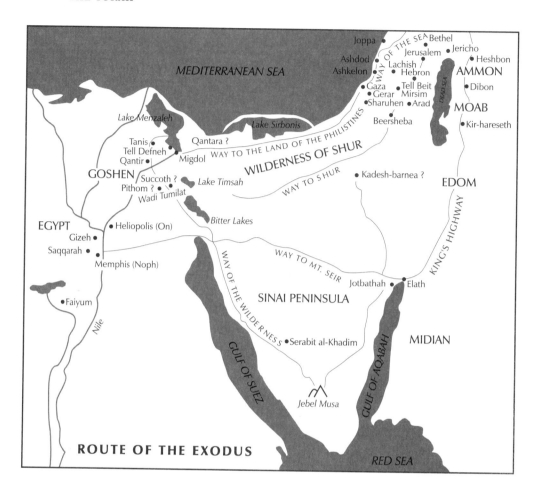

ROUTE OF THE EXODUS

CHAPTER 5

Exodus: Message

The story that began brightly with Adam and Eve living in a garden ended gloomily with Joseph lying in a coffin in Egypt (Gen. 50:26). God's promises to the patriarchs needed new expression and fresh action to implement them. The book of Exodus conveys that expression and action.

> I am the LORD your God, who brought you out of the land of Egypt, out of the house of slavery; you shall have no other gods before me. Exod. 20:2

Name and Contents

"Exodus" is derived from its name in the LXX, *exodos* "departure" (Exod. 19:1). It is an excellent name, for this book recounts the formative event in Israel's history, the "departure from Egypt" (1:1–15:21). In the Hebrew Bible the book is known from its first two words, *we'ēlleh šᵉmôt*, "these are the names" (often just *šᵉmôt*, "Names").

The book centers on two crucial divine acts in Israel's history: God mightily delivered his people from slavery in Egypt (1:1–18:26), and he entered into covenant with them at Mt. Sinai (19:1–40:38). The term "Exodus" sometimes has a broad meaning, encompassing the whole complex of events from the deliverance to entry into the promised land (cf. 3:7-10). As such, it forms the high point of Old Testament redemptive history.

The contents of the book can be outlined as follows:

Deliverance from Egypt and journey to Sinai (1:1–18:27)
    Oppression of Hebrews in Egypt (1:1-22)
    Birth and early life of Moses: his call and mission
        to Pharaoh (2:1–6:27)
    Plagues and Passover (6:28–13:16)
    Exodus from Egypt and deliverance at Sea of Reeds (13:17–15:21)
    Journey to Sinai (15:22–18:27)
Covenant at Sinai (19:1–24:18)
    Theophany on Sinai (19:1-25)
    Granting of covenant (20:1-21)
    Book of the Covenant (20:22–23:33)
    Ratification of covenant (24:1-18)
Instructions for tabernacle and cultus (25:1–31:18)
    Tabernacle and furnishings (25:1–27:21; 29:36–30:38)
    Priests and consecration (28:1–29:35)
    Craftsmen of tabernacle (31:1-11)
    Observance of Sabbath (31:12-18)
Breach and renewal of covenant (32:1–34:35)
    Golden calf (32:1-35)
    God's presence with Moses and people (33:1-23)
    Renewal of covenant (34:1-35)
Building of tabernacle (35:1–40:38)
    Freewill offering (35:1-29)
    Appointment of craftsmen (35:30–36:1)
    Building of tabernacle and furnishings (36:2–39:43)
    Completion and dedication of tabernacle (40:1-38)

Role of Moses

Moses is the key figure in the Pentateuchal narratives, from Exodus through Deuteronomy. Throughout the Old Testament he is regarded as the founder of Israel's religion, promulgator of the law, organizer of the tribes in work and worship, and their charismatic leader. Consequently those who would regard him as unhistorical or a later addition to the Pentateuch[1] render inexplicable the religion and even the very existence of Israel.[2]

Name, Parentage, and Early Life. The book opens with the account of the great population increase of the Hebrews in Egypt. God's promise to Abraham of plentiful posterity (Gen. 12:2) was being fulfilled but at high cost. Their numbers had become so large that the Pharaoh began to fear for the security of his nation. This situation may have developed after the Hyksos period, when Palestinian Semites did seize power. To fortify the northeast frontier, where the Hyksos entered Egypt, Pharaoh reduced the Hebrews to state slaves. He put them to work on many building projects in the delta, notably the cities of Pithom and Raamses. When his stratagem to limit their increase failed (1:15-21), he decreed that all males born to the Hebrews were to be drowned in the Nile.

In these circumstances Moses was born. After a time his mother hid him in a basket and placed him in the reeds along the Nile, hoping that he might somehow survive. A daughter of Pharaoh found the child and adopted him. His sister, who was watching the basket from a distance, saw the daughter of Pharaoh rescue her brother. She then went up to her and secured the employment of his own mother as nurse. The sister, Miriam, reappears at the end of the Exodus rescue as one of its featured celebrants (15:20-21). The God of surprises uses her both to initiate and to culminate this story of deliverance.

Although no details are given, Moses apparently grew up in the Egyptian court, receiving an education for royalty (cf. Acts 7:22; Heb. 11:23-28). He was certainly trained in reading, writing, archery, and administration. These skills equipped him for posts of confidence and responsibility in government administration.[3]

The daughter of Pharaoh named him Moses, "because I drew him out of the water" (2:10). This constitutes a wordplay between the Hebrew name *Mōšeh* and the verb *māšâ* "to draw out." Most scholars feel the name is actually Egyptian, and related to the names of Pharaohs of the Eighteenth Dynasty such as Thutmosis or Ahmosis. If so, the explanation in 2:10 must be regarded as popular etymology,[4] in which words are connected because of similarity of sound.

In the introduction to the story of Moses (ch. 2) neither his father or mother are named; both of them were from the tribe of Levi. The four-member genealogy in 6:16-20 then is probably best understood as tribe (Levi), clan (Kohath), and family group (Amram by Jochebed). Then came Moses and Aaron, several generations later.[5] The next time Moses is mentioned, he is an adult.

Moses in Midian. Seeing a Hebrew being beaten, Moses came to his defense and slew the Egyptian bully. This incident demonstrates that he was aware of his origin and race. Fearing for his life, he fled Egypt and took refuge in Midian.[6] There Moses settled with Jethro, priest of Midian, and married his daughter Zipporah. She bore him two sons.

The narrative next reports that the Pharaoh who sought Moses had died (2:23-25). It also states that God had heard the cries of his people in Egypt and remembered his covenant with Abraham, Isaac, and Jacob. This statement indicates that God was about to set in motion the deliverance of the people from Egyptian slavery.

Call of Moses. While pasturing Jethro's sheep near Horeb, "the mountain of God," Moses came upon a strange sight. A bush was burning, yet not consumed (3:2). Turning aside to investigate, he was addressed by God, who introduced himself as "the God of your father, the God of Abraham, the God of Isaac, and the God of Jacob" (v. 6a). Moses knew immediately who was speaking to him and hid his face, "for he was afraid to look at God" (v. 6b). After stating his intention to deliver his people from their hard lot (vv. 7-9), God commissioned his messenger: "So come, I will send you to Pharaoh to bring my people, the Israelites, out of Egypt" (v. 10).

Suddenly, all was transformed: the shepherd was to become the deliverer. Indeed, so radical was the call that Moses raised a series of objections, to which God patiently responded (3:11–4:17). In this dialogue, material of great theological import is set forth:

(1) Revelation of the divine name. Moses objected, because of the contrast between his humble status as an exiled shepherd and the loftiness of his mission: "Who am I that I should go to Pharaoh . . . ?" God replied with the great, unconditional promise that he himself would be with Moses (3:11f.). Moses, however, remained unpersuaded, apprehensive that the people would question his commission:

> "*If* I go to the people of Israel and say to them, 'The God of your fathers has sent me to you,' and they ask me, 'What is his name?' what shall I say to them?" (v. 13)

God responded with a revelation of the divine name. That revelation is reiterated three times in slightly different forms for emphasis:

> "I Am who I Am. . . . Thus you shall say to the Israelites, 'I Am has sent me to you. . . . Yahweh, the God of your ancestors, the God of Abraham, the God of Isaac, and the God of Jacob, has sent me to you':
>
>> This is my name forever,
>> and this my title for all generations." (vv. 14f.)

To grasp the force of Moses' question, we must understand that a name in ancient times was bound closely with that person's essence.[7] It expressed one's character. To learn a person's name was to have access to a person's very character.[8] Moses is really asking "What is God's relationship to the people?

66

He has been the 'God of the ancestors.' Who is he now?" The force of God's name can be seen in 33:18f. There Moses asks to see God's glory. When God passes by Moses and manifests his glory (vv. 22f.), he proclaims his name, stressing his grace and mercy (34:5-7).

God's response, usually translated "I am who I am," sounds evasive. Can it be a refusal to answer?[9] No, for in 3:15 God does reveal his name — Yahweh. Thus the words of v. 14 explain the name Yahweh. "I am who I am" reflects a Hebrew idiom in which something is defined in terms of itself. It can indicate something undetermined, but can also express totality or intensity.[10] For example, "I will be gracious to whom I will be gracious, and will show mercy on whom I will show mercy" (33:19) means "I am indeed he who is gracious and shows mercy."[11] Taken with that force, "I am who I am" means "I am indeed he who is."[12] Further, this statement is not philosophical. Rather it has an efficacious sense: "I am he who is there (for you) — really and truly present, ready to help and to act." This interpretation is strongly supported by the need of the people of Israel for God's powerful presence to overcome their hopeless situation. By revealing his personal name, God has made himself accessible to his people in fellowship and in saving power.

The name *YHWH* is sometimes referred to as the "tetragrammaton."[13] The interpretation given in v. 14 takes the name to be the third person form of the verb *hāyâ* "to be," i.e., "he is." God, in speaking of himself, does not say "he is" but "I am." Thus only God himself can say "I am." Others must say "he is." From the period of the second (postexilic) temple on, the Jewish community refrained from pronouncing this name out of their high reverence for God. The difficulty of translating such a name, combined with respect for the Jewish community, leads most modern translators to follow the KJV in rendering it LORD (usually in small capital letters to distinguish it from the ordinary Heb. *'adōnay* "lord").

(2) Moses, the prophet. Even after the revelation of God's name, Moses continued to object to his call. In 4:10ff. he complained that he was not eloquent but slow of speech and tongue. God countered with the promise to be "with his mouth," teaching him what to speak. God kept after Moses, forcing him to decide. Moses couched his refusal in the desperate plea that God send someone else (v. 13). Still, God would not bypass his stubborn messenger. But he made a concession: Aaron was commissioned as Moses' spokesman. Moses would play the role of God, and Aaron would be his prophet (vv. 14-16; see also 7:1-2). Finally conceding to God's call (4:8), Moses was commissioned in characteristic prophetic fashion. We note the "messenger formula" by which the prophetic word was authorized as the word of God: "Thus says the Lord." Although prophecy did not reach its fullest development until the period of the Monarchy, its form emerged full-blown in the call, commission, and task of Moses, prophet of God par excellence (Deut. 18:15-20; Hos. 12:13).[14]

Plagues and the Passover

When Moses confronted Pharaoh, insisting that he let the Hebrews go, he received in reply an unqualified "no":

> "Who is the LORD, that I should heed him and let Israel go? I do not know the LORD, and I will not let Israel go." (5:2)

As a result a battle was about to take place between Yahweh and Pharaoh, whom the Egyptians viewed as an incarnate deity. God made his power and authority evident in a series of ten catastrophes or "plagues" (9:14) that devastated Egypt. Through these plagues the Lord defeated the Egyptian gods, including Pharaoh. Pharaoh ultimately allowed Israel to leave (7:8–13:16).

Plagues. The first nine plagues are a continuous series (7:8–10:29), set apart from the tenth, the death of the firstborn. The nine are structured by a literary device that groups them into three sets of three plagues. In the first plague in each set Moses is commanded to appear before Pharaoh at the river. In the second he is to "come before Pharaoh" at his palace. In the third he is to make a gesture which brings the plague without warning to Pharaoh.

First Set	Second Set	Third Set	Structure
1. Water turns to blood	4. Land swarms with flies	7. Hail destroys crops	Moses appears before Pharaoh in morning at river
2. Frogs leave water, cover land	5. Cattle in field die of plague	8. Locusts devour all that is left	Moses "comes before" Pharaoh
3. Land fills with mosquitoes or gnats	6. Boils cover man and beast	9. Thick darkness covers land	Moses and Aaron do not appear before Pharaoh but use a symbolic gesture

This pattern and other elements of literary structure[15] show that this account had a long history of transmission before reaching its current form. This has led some interpreters to conclude that the narratives were not his-

The fertile land of Goshen in the eastern Nile Delta, given as grazing land to the descendants of Jacob. *(Neal and Joel Bierling)*

torical but rather "piously decorated accounts" whose actual value was "symbolic."[16] But a recognition that an account has long, complex transmission need not prejudice its historical worth. Its historical value can be decided only by determining how closely the received account fits the background of the time and place of its origin.

An important study shows that the nine plagues fit precisely the natural phenomena of Egypt.[17] In this study all the plagues (except the *hail*) form a sequence of severe natural events which exhibit a cause-and-effect relationship in the very order of their happening. The plagues begin with an abnormally high inundation of the Nile. These extremely high waters would have washed down large quantities of bright red earth of the Ethiopian plateau. This soil plus reddish-colored microorganisms called flagellates, turned the Nile blood red and foul, killing the fish (first plague). The decomposing fish caused the frogs to desert the river banks (second plague) and infected them with the disease organism *Bacillus anthracis*, which in turn caused the frogs' sudden death. The third and fourth plagues are mosquitoes and the *Stomoxys calcitrans* fly, both of which breed freely in the conditions created by the stagnant waters of the retreating Nile flood. The cattle disease (fifth plague) was anthrax, caused by the contaminated dead frogs. The boils on men and cattle (sixth plague) would be skin anthrax, principally transmitted by the bite of the fly of the fourth plague. Hail and thunderstorms (seventh plague) would destroy flax and barley but leave the wheat and spelt for the locusts (eighth plague), whose immense numbers (10:6) would be favored by the same Abyssinian rains that had caused the initial flood. Finally, the thick darkness (ninth plague; v. 21) aptly describes an unusually strong *ḥamsîn*,[18] made far worse by the thick layer of fine red dust from the mud deposit of the inundation. In this interpretation the miraculous elements consist both in the unusual severity of the events[19] and in their timing. God uses the created order for his own ends.

However, the tenth plague — the death of the firstborn children — has no "natural" explanation.[20] This catastrophe is described in a very complex section (12:1–13:16) that also narrates and gives regulations for the Passover meal, feast of Unleavened Bread *(maṣṣôt)*, and redemption of the firstborn.

Passover. In the Passover meal (12:1-14) a year-old male animal from the flock (i.e., sheep or goat) was sacrificed and roasted. The Israelites ate it with their "loins girded. . . . sandals on [their] feet, and . . . staff in . . . hand" (v. 11), ready for an immediate journey. Some blood of the sacrifice was placed on the lintel and two doorposts to mark the houses of the Israelites. When God saw the blood, he passed over that house, sparing the firstborn.

With the lamb the Israelites ate unleavened bread and bitter herbs. On leaving Egypt, they took the still unleavened dough (v. 34). When they arrived at Succoth, they baked cakes with it. This whole sequence following the night of Passover is to be memorialized by the Feast of Unleavened Bread, described in vv. 15-20. This feast signified the haste with which they left Egypt.

The original meaning of Heb. *pesaḥ* "passover" (Gk. *pascha,* hence Eng. "paschal") is much disputed. The verbal form *(pāsaḥ)* occurs only in vv. 13, 23, and 27. In vv. 13 and 27, the verb clearly means "to pass over, to spare."[21] When in vv. 21ff. Moses carries out God's instructions given in vv. 1-14, he tells the Israelites to "kill the Passover lamb," without defining the term. Many believe that Moses was speaking of something already known, perhaps a spring festival customary to a shepherd people. Similarly, the Feast of Unleavened Bread originally may have been a spring agricultural festival.[22] Evidence for the origin of these festivals prior to Moses and the Exodus is highly suggestive. If such was the case, the meaning of these feasts was reinterpreted radically as a result of the dramatic deliverance from Egypt.[23]

As Israel's circumstances have changed, so have the specific rites of the Passover celebration. After the settlement in Canaan, it probably continued as a home celebration, as in Egypt. At some stage it became a pilgrim festival, with the slaughter of the lamb taking place in the temple (see Deut. 16:5-6). By New Testament times the communal meal was eaten in private, though part of the ritual took place in the temple. After the destruction of the temple in A.D. 70, Passover again became a home festival, a family celebration of God's rescue of his people from slavery. It has played a crucial role in preserving the identity of the Jews in the diaspora.

The Last Supper, which Jesus celebrated with his disciples in the upper room was certainly patterned after a passover meal, if not the Passover itself.[24] Through this event the Passover was transformed in Christian observance into the Lord's Supper. That meal commemorates the death of Jesus the Messiah, through whom all that the Passover and old covenant anticipated has been brought to full fruition.[25]

Deliverance at the Sea of Reeds

In his confrontation with Pharaoh, Moses acted primarily as a prophet, a messenger. His message, "Thus says the LORD . . . 'Let my people go . . .' " (5:1), was repeated and reinforced by the plagues. After the death of the firstborn, Pharaoh finally acceded to this demand (12:29-32). The Israelites, fortified and united by the solemn Passover meal, departed from Egypt (vv. 37-42). Although their exact route is not known (see pp. 60-61), they eventually arrived beside the "Sea of Reeds." This body of water was a natural barrier to entering Sinai. True to his character, Pharaoh had a change of heart. He mustered his chariotry and troops to overtake the escaping Israelites. The Israelites, trapped between the onrushing Egyptians and the sea, feared for their lives. The people complained. Moses spoke to them an oracle of salvation (14:13-14). Then God told him to lift up his rod so that the people might cross the sea on dry ground. God sent a strong easterly wind all night that drove back the waters (14:21), and the Israelites crossed to the other side. The pursuing Egyptians, however, got their chariot wheels mired in the soft ground. When the waters returned, they were engulfed.

> That day, Yahweh rescued Israel from the clutches of the Egyptians, and Israel saw the Egyptians lying dead on the seashore. When Israel saw the mighty deed that Yahweh had performed against the Egyptians, the people revered Yahweh and put their faith in Yahweh and in Moses, his servant. (vv. 30f., NJB)

In response Moses composed a song of victory and praise (15:1-18). The song expressed the people's faith in Yahweh.[26] It is so exclusively focused on God that Moses is not even mentioned. This presents a sharp contrast to the literature of Israel's neighbors which lauded their heroes.[27]

The opening of the song brims with faith and joy as it looks back on the Genesis stories:

> Yahweh is my strength and my song,
>   and he has become my salvation;
> this is my God, and I will praise him,
>   my father's God, and I will exalt him. (15:2)

Yahweh revealed at the bush and the sea, is identified with the "God of the fathers." The poem closes by looking ahead to the end of their journey, picturing the dismay of those in Canaan (see Joshua), and the ultimate presence of the Lord among his people in the hill country of Palestine (v. 7, see Judges).

Throughout their history, Israelites recalled this great deliverance as the constitutive event by which they became the people of God. The Psalms, particularly Ps. 78, dwell on the Exodus in praise of God for his mighty deeds. The prophets again and again extol Yahweh as the One who brought Israel out of Egypt, led them through the wilderness, and gave them the law (cf. Isa. 43:16f.; Jer. 16:14; 31:32; Ezek. 20:6ff.; Hos. 2:15; 11:1; Amos 2:10; 3:1f.). The Exodus becomes the standard of divine redemption. It would be exceeded only by that greater deliverance which God accomplished by the death of his Son on Calvary. Luke connects the two redemptive events by calling Jesus' death an "exodus" (departure, NRSV; Lk. 9:31).

Covenant and Law at Sinai

After the deliverance at the sea, Israel traveled to Mt. Sinai (see pp. 60-61), a journey of over two months (19:1). The text recounts a few episodes that demonstrate Yahweh's ability to sustain his new people (15:22–18:27). These episodes include the provision of water at Marah (15:22-25) and at Rephidim, where Moses struck the rock (17:1-7); the sending of food, both quails and manna (16:1-36);[28] and the Israelites' victory over the Amalekites (17:8-16).

On arrival at Mt. Sinai, the people camped before the mountain. Moses ascended the mountain to meet with God. There God informed him that he was going to enter into covenant with Israel that they might become God's own possession among all peoples. The condition was "if you obey my voice and keep my covenant" (19:5). In a three-day period of consecration the people were to wash their clothes and make themselves ready (vv. 9-15). At the foot of the mountain (v. 17), the momentous event began. God manifested himself in awe-inspiring majesty:

Now at daybreak two days later, there were peals of thunder and flashes of lightning, dense cloud on the mountain, and a very loud trumpet blast. . . . Mount Sinai was entirely wrapped in smoke, because Yahweh had descended on it in the form of fire. The smoke rose like smoke from a furnace and the whole mountain shook violently. (vv. 16-18, NJB)

In the midst of this terrifying appearance,[29] God summoned Moses and delivered the Ten Commandments (20:1-17).

The immense significance of the Ten Commandments has been made clear by the awesome setting in which they were given. By obeying them Israel will become and remain the people of God. Moses' recounting of the event in Deut. 5 makes this abundantly clear:

". . . The LORD our God made a covenant with us at Horeb. Not with our ancestors did the LORD make this covenant, but with us, who are all of us here alive today. . . . He said: 'I am the LORD your God, who brought you out of the land of Egypt. . . .'" (vv. 1-6)

A covenant is a means of establishing a relationship (not naturally existing), which is sanctioned by an oath sworn in a ceremony of ratification. All the elements that make up a covenant are present at Sinai. In Exod. 19:3-8 Israel is summoned to a special relationship with God, described by three phrases: a special possession among all peoples, a kingdom of priests, a holy nation. Israel is to be set apart from other nations for God's service just as priests were set apart from other men. As priests they had to have a quality of life commensurate with the holiness of their covenant God.[30] Israel accepts the invitation to enter into covenant with Yahweh with the solemn affirmation: "All that the LORD has spoken we will do" (v. 8). In 20:1-17 the covenant demands are set forth, and in 24:3-8 the covenant is ratified by a solemn ceremony. Here the oath is reaffirmed and given sanction by the sacrifice and the sprinkling of the blood, a reminder of the life-and-death importance of the covenant.

This covenant relationship differs from the Abrahamic covenant only in the party to the covenant that is bound by oath. This change, however, produces covenants that differ in both form and function. In the Abrahamic covenant God places himself under oath, bound by irrevocable promises to Abraham and his posterity. In the Sinai covenant Israel takes the oath, and the obligation is obedience to the covenant stipulations.[31]

Recently the specific cultural background of the Sinai covenant has become clear. The covenant follows very closely the structure of the international treaty of the ancient Near East between an overlord (or suzerain) and his subject people (vassals).[32] The form was widely known and used during the second millennium. The largest number of examples of the suzerain-vassal treaty — and the most complete — are to be found in the fourteenth- and thirteenth-century Hittite texts from Boghazköy. Most of the elements of this form[33] may be found in the texts that deal with the Mosaic covenant, especially 20:1-17:

(1) Preamble (identifying the author and giving his titles): "I am Yahweh, your God" (v. 21). God needs no further titles, after the recent dramatic revelation of his name.

(2) Historical prologue (setting forth the previous relations between the parties and emphasizing the suzerain's kind deeds to the vassal; these acts are the grounds for the vassal's gratitude and future loyalty): "who brought you out of the land of Egypt, out of the house of slavery" (v. 2b). The historical survey here is brief and basic, since Israel's memory of God's dramatic deliverance is recent and fresh. In the covenant renewal ceremony at Shechem (Josh. 24), the historical prologue is long and detailed (vv. 2-13).

(3) Stipulations of the treaty, consisting of:
   (a) the basic demand for allegiance: "You shall have no other gods before me" (20:3).

Sun-dried mud brick tempered with straw, inscribed with the cartouche of Rameses II (nineteenth dynasty). *(Oriental Institute, University of Chicago)*

74

(b) specific stipulations: in treaty use, normalizing relationships within the empire (vv. 4-17).

(4) Provisions for:

(a) deposition of the text (treaties were kept in the temple): the tablets containing vv. 1-17 were placed in the ark of the covenant (25:16; Deut. 10:1-5).

(b) periodic public reading (Deut. 31:10-13).

(5) Curses and blessings: invoked upon the vassal for breaking or keeping the covenant (Deut. 28:1-14 [blessings], 15-68 [curses]).

Also, provision was made for a formal ratification ceremony by which the vassal pledged obedience, often with blood sacrifices (cf. Exod. 24). The treaty was written in very personal terms, using an "I-Thou" dialogue pattern.

These close parallels show that the suzerain-vassal treaty form was adapted to serve the theological needs of this special relationship. Thus the Ten Commandments were never intended to institute a system of legal observances by which one could earn God's acceptance. Rather they are the stipulations of a covenant relationship anchored in grace. The prologue to the covenant looks back to God's gracious deliverance and so forms a kerygma, a proclamation of good news. Redemption already has been accomplished.

But the covenant carries a dire threat. It offers Israel not only blessing for obedience, but curse for disobedience. Note the conditions posed in Exod. 19:5: "If you obey my voice and keep my covenant, you among all the peoples shall be my own possession." The covenant stipulations are not only the Lord's will for a redeemed people; they are threats of his wrath should the people fail to keep them. Under the Mosaic covenant, Israel lived in the tension between these two affirmations. Their history is only understandable in light of this covenant. Over time Israel broke the covenant so often that God had to invoke the curses. He sent the prophets to warn the people of the danger they were in. Without repentence, they would suffer the ultimate curse of exile.

The Ten Commandments, then, are not law in the modern sense, for they are not carefully defined and contain no penalties. They are rather "legal policy," a basic statement of that kind of behavior which the covenant community is willing to sustain by force.[34] When Israel accepted the covenant, the need arose to place them in a form more suitable to "law." This development is found in the "Book of the Covenant" (20:23–23:33). Careful examination shows that most of the stipulations of 20:1-17 are repeated in that section as specific laws.[35]

The Tabernacle

Two long passages in Exodus describe the tabernacle and its furnishings.[36] In chs. 25–31 God reveals to Moses the plan, materials, and designs for making it. In chs. 35–40, Moses carries out God's commands, to the minutest detail.[37]

The tabernacle was a portable shrine, consisting of a square latticework frame of acacia wood covered by two large linen curtains. One of the curtains formed the main hall, the Holy Place, while the second covered the Holy of Holies (i.e., the "Most Holy Place"), a smaller room at the back of the main hall and separated by a special curtain. The Holy Place was 30 feet long by 15 feet wide by 15 feet high, while the Holy of Holies was 15 feet on each side. Inside the Holy of Holies was housed only the ark, a wooden chest containing the tablets of the Ten Commandments. On top of the ark was the mercy seat, the place where blood on the Day of Atonement was sprinkled. Above the mercy seat were the two cherubim, over which Yahweh was invisibly enthroned. In the Holy Place were the altar of incense, the lampstand, and a table with the "bread of the Presence." The tabernacle was placed in a court 150 feet by 75 feet, screened off from the rest of the camp by white curtains 15 feet high. In the court before the tabernacle stood the altar of burnt offering, and between it and the tabernacle stood the laver.

The tabernacle was of great importance to Israel, as the double description of it suggests. In 25:8 God says: "Have them make me a sanctuary, so that I may dwell among them." The tabernacle, then, was the localization of God's presence with his people, a visible symbol that he was their God.[38] Here Israel was to worship and to make atonement for breaches of the covenant stipulations.[39] The tabernacle with its imagery and sacrificial system was the means by which the holy, transcendent, infinite God could yet be present with his people — "tabernacling" or "tenting" among them. And it was the means by which a sinful people could maintain fellowship with their holy Lord. As the symbol of God's presence, it looks forward to the time when God in the person of his Son would be visibly present with his people: "the Word became flesh and 'tabernacled' among us,[40] full of grace and truth" (John 1:14).

The Golden Calf

The episodes in Exod. 32–34 separate the instructions for building the tabernacle (Exod. 25–31) from the record of the completion of those instructions (Exod. 35–40).[41] These three chapters report Israel's violation of the covenant by worshipping the golden calf (ch. 32), Moses' interchange with God about the divine presence (ch. 33), and the renewal of the covenant (ch. 34).

This section opens with the people pressuring Aaron to make gods for them because they felt leaderless during Moses' long absence (32:1-6). Aaron responded by instructing them to present their gold jewelry. From these gifts he had a calf made and overlaid with gold. Then he built an altar and set it before the calf. The people proclaimed a feast which turned into a frenzied celebration. They were brazenly breaking the second commandment (20:4-6).

On the mountain Yahweh informed Moses of the people's rebellion (32:7-14), expressing his angry intent to punish them. Moses pleaded with Yahweh not to blot out his people. In response, Yahweh restrained his wrath.[42]

Moses descended the mountain with the two tablets of the covenant (32:15-29). When he arrived at the camp and saw the wild dancing before the calf, he smashed the tablets to convey to the people that they had broken the covenant. Moses then had the calf burned and ground to powder. He scattered the powder on water and made the people drink it. It is implied that those who were most zealous for the golden calf became deathly ill from drinking this solution as punishment for their sin. The measures Moses had taken caused a riot in the camp.[43] Moses gave an impassioned plea for people to separate themselves from the crowd and identify with Yahweh. The Levites answered the call and helped Moses restore order. Their response guaranteed them a permanent place in the priesthood.

Moses ascended the mountain again (32:30–33:6). There he continued to intercede, asking Yahweh to forgive the people. He won a reprieve from Yahweh. Yahweh said he would still give the land to the people, but he no longer dwelt among them in their journey. Instead he would send his messenger. This divine pronouncement caused heavy mourning among the people.

At this place there is a comment inserted in the text (33:7-11); it reports that Moses was accustomed to set up a tent of meeting outside the camp. Anyone who wished to receive direction from Yahweh would go out to that tent. Moses would also leave the camp and go to the tent. The cloud would descend, and Moses would converse with God face to face, i.e., without a mediator.[44] This report, which has the marks of being very ancient, bears witness to the people's full acceptance of Moses' leadership. There is no further explanation about this special tent of meeting in Scripture. Certainly there is no connection between it and the ark of the covenant. Even though two tents have this same name, the tent outside the camp is to be distinguished from the Tent of Meeting, which was yet to be erected in the center of the camp. Both tents have in common the tradition that there Yahweh manifested his presence, but the one in this account was a special tent connected to Moses' unique leadership through direct communication with Yahweh.

Moses continued to intercede with Yahweh, pleading that his Presence accompany them on the journey to the promised land (33:12-17). Yahweh finally conceded to Moses' unrelenting entreaty. This amazing narrative reveals the power inherent in intercessory prayer. It also suggests that Yahweh may invite the leaders of his people to share in the making of decisions about their destiny.

Though Yahweh agreed to go with Israel, the essential difficulty raised by Israel's apostasy remained: How may Yahweh be present among a "stiff-necked" (i.e., stubbornly sinful) people (33:3, 5) without destroying them? So Moses pressed his intercession to its conclusion and asked to see Yahweh's "glory," i.e., the very Person of God (33:18). God responded to this incredible request primarily by proclaiming his name (v. 19). After instructing Moses to prepare for the renewal of the covenant (34:1-3), God descended to Mount Sinai and proclaimed his name (i.e., his identity):

> "The LORD, the LORD,
>   a God merciful and gracious, slow to anger,
>   and abounding in steadfast love and faithfulness,
>   keeping steadfast love for the thousandth generation,
>   forgiving iniquity and transgression and sin,
>   yet by no means clearing the guilty,
>   but visiting the iniquity of the parents
>   upon the children and the children's children,
>   to the third and the fourth generation." Exod. 34:6-7

With this revelation of God's identity, Moses pressed for full restoration and forgiveness: "I pray, let the LORD go with us. Although this is a stiff-necked people, pardon our iniquity and our sin, and take us for your inheritance." (34:9). The renewal of the covenant that follows in 34:10-28 indicates unmistakably that God has indeed forgiven Israel. Here we have a theology of grace unsurpassed in the Old Testament. Though God's judgment is not swallowed up in his mercy, nevertheless the emphasis is all on his grace. For, despite the people's grievous sin against the covenant, it has not come to an end. What is the basis for this remarkable forgiveness? According to 33:18–34:9 its grounds lie entirely in the character of God as merciful and gracious.[45]

This self-description of Yahweh occurs several times in the Old Testament in a variety of forms.[46] It stresses Yahweh's grace and love to forgive sins and to fellowship with his people. At the same time it warns that over time Yahweh will become angry if his people persist in their sinful ways.

After this revelation Yahweh renewed the covenant (34:10-28). He promised to do marvels among his people that would enable them to possess the promised land (vv. 10-11). Then Yahweh gave a series of laws, ethical and cultic (vv. 12-26). Some have identified this list of commandments as a "ritual decalogue" in contrast to the "eternal decalogue" in 20:2-17. It is very difficult, however, to number *ten* commandments in this list without major alteration to the text. This list is more like a small law book. These laws guard against and prohibit the worship of foreign gods on entering Canaan (vv. 12-17), instruct on keeping the feasts to honor Yahweh throughout the year (vv. 18-24), and regulate some details about worship (vv. 25-26). The themes in these laws point both to the Decalogue (20:2-17) and to the Book of the Covenant (20:22–23:33). They stress loyalty to Yahweh and faithfulness in observing proper worship in order to guard against a recurrence of the false worship. The context in which these laws have been placed strongly suggests an act of covenant renewal.[47]

In strong contrast to the elaborate inaugural ceremony for sealing the first covenant (Exod. 24), this covenant is renewed on Mt. Sinai between Moses, acting as covenant mediator, and Yahweh.[48] The tangible sign that the covenant had been renewed was the new set of tablets containing the Decalogue to replace those Moses broke before the golden calf.

This account of the golden calf and covenant renewal stands as a pattern of Israel's history. Israel began with great zeal for Yahweh. When they became discouraged, often over a small matter, they turned to other gods. After the euphoria of the new religion wore off and they languished under a curse for breaking the covenant, an intercessor arose to plead with God for the restoration of the covenant. On the grounds of his character as gracious and merciful, God restored his people time and again. The book of Judges and Ps. 106 particularly witness to the many repetitions of this scenario. More specifically this account sheds light on and condemns the two calves set up at Dan and Bethel by Jeroboam I (1 Kgs. 12:25-33).

The account of Israel's idolatry ends with the full recognition of Moses' definitive role as leader (34:29-35). It was the people's rejection of his leadership that led to the making of the calf (32:1ff.). Therefore, Yahweh reestablished his authority by a visible sign that magnified the divine Presence.[49] On descending from Sinai, his face shone, reflecting the glory of God. This demonstrated that Moses, by reason of his close relationship with Yahweh, was the mediator of Yahweh's word to his people. "There is conveyed in *Moses' own body* something of the nature of the divine communication to the community."[50] From Exodus through Numbers numerous sections have a heading something like this: "And Yahweh said to Moses, 'Say to the Israelites.'" This account of Moses' ordination by Yahweh endows these many speeches with revelatory authority.

79

CHAPTER 6

Leviticus

Since Exod. 19:1, the Israelites had been encamped in the shadow of Mt. Sinai. They had experienced the great redemptive act of Yahweh — the deliverance from Egyptian bondage — that would remain central to their faith for all generations. They had seen and heard the thunder and lightning on the holy mountain (Exod. 19:16-19), and Yahweh had given his commandments (20:1-17). He had declared that he was their God and they were his people.

But how was this relationship to be maintained? The Israelites could not dwell forever at Mt. Sinai. They were to settle in a land where they could experience the benefits of being his people. Moreover, they were to become the source of blessing to all nations (Gen. 12:3), communicating their faith to other peoples. Not the wilderness of Sinai but Canaan was to be the land of the promise. In that land, however, they would be confronted by Canaanite cultic practices.[1] To resist them they needed to learn the proper ways to worship Yahweh. The location for this worship, the tabernacle or Tent of Meeting, had been described to Moses by God in Exod. 25–31. The details of worship are given in Leviticus, the book that stands at the heart of the Pentateuch.

> "You shall be holy to me, for I the LORD am holy, and I have separated you from the other peoples to be mine." Lev. 20:26

Name and Contents

The English name of this book comes from the Vulgate, which took over the title found in the LXX. "Leviticus" is an adjective for "the levitical (book)" or "the book pertaining to the Levites." The name is ambiguous, since "Levites" may describe either (1) members of Levi's tribe, like the house of Aaron whose priestly offspring play a major role in the book; or (2) the lesser officials whose role was to serve the priests.[2] In the Hebrew Bible this book receives its name from the first word *wayyiqra'* "and he [the LORD] called," a title which rightly spotlights God's authority and initiative in issuing the rules for acceptable worship.

Purpose

Leviticus is part of a large section of instructions and regulations that runs from Exod. 25:1 to Num. 10:10. Yet, those who put the Pentateuch together gave it a distinct heading (1:1-2) and a conclusion (26:45). The last chapter (27) serves as an appendix, with a summary statement closing the chapter and the whole book: "These are the commandments that the LORD gave to Moses for the people of Israel on Mount Sinai."

Exodus through Numbers is a narrative about the origins of Israel as the people of God.

One function of this narrative is to fulfill the promise made to the Patriarchs that God would enter into a special *relationship* to them. As Gen. 12–50 centered on the pledge of *posterity* and as Num. 10:11–Deut. 34:12 focuses on the gift of land, so Exod. 1:1–Num. 10:10 highlights in its narrative the nature and terms of the covenant relationship. Woven into this narrative are the instructions for the people's worship of God. This material is not a haphazard mixture of story and law. Rather, it is the account of God's bringing a nation to birth, a story embellished with rules for worship and civil order. Both story and law are essential to the creation of a new nation. In Leviticus the narrative comes to the forefront only in a few specific sections (chs. 8–10; 16; 24). The laws are set in speeches that Yahweh gave Moses to deliver to the congregation. The material thus is designed for oral instruction. The occasions for using it must have been the great feasts, when all the tribes assembled before Yahweh at the central sanctuary.[3]

Is Leviticus primarily a handbook for the *priests?* No. Numerous details and directions that the priests would have needed in order to carry out the sacrifices and to officiate at the high days are missing: (1) there is no description of the instruments required for slaughtering, skinning, and cutting up an animal; (2) nothing informs a priest where to stand while performing the sacrificial rites; (3) no liturgy is provided for a priest to speak during the sacrifice. Such details would hardly have been omitted from an official manual.

This book, then, was compiled for the instruction of the *congregation* in matters pertaining to the cult, i.e., the correct procedures for making sacrifices, for observing the high times in the calendar, and for living as a holy people. This knowledge enabled the people both to perform their worship acceptably to God and to monitor the accuracy of the priests' handling of the law. In addition, it guarded the priests from gaining improper control over the people by holding as secret knowledge the basic operation of the sanctuary.

Contents

Leviticus has six major divisions:

Division I, which contains the regulations for offering the various kinds of sacrifices, has two sections. The first section (chs. 1–5) gives basic teaching on the sacrifices, while the second section (chs. 6–7) describes administrative details.[4] In the first section the sacrifices fall into two groups: (1) sacrifices that offer a soothing aroma to Yahweh, namely, the whole burnt offering (ch. 1),[5] the grain offering (ch. 2), and the offering of well-being or the peace offering (ch. 3); and (2) sacrifices that provide expiation and forgiveness — the sin offering and the guilt offering (chs. 4–5). Though a grain offering could stand alone, it usually accompanied an animal offering to make a meal of bread and meat. Any of these sacrifices could be offered spontaneously by any Israelite. Also, the calendar required the presentation of whole burnt offerings with attending grain offerings every morning, possibly every evening, and on high days.

Here is a summary of the offerings described in Division I (1:1–7:38):

Name of Offering	Purpose	Kind of Offering	Nature of Offering	Actions of Offerer	Actions of Priest
ʿôlâ Holocaust or whole burnt offering 1:3-17 6:8-13	To atone for basic human sinfulness	A male without blemish from herd or flock of two birds	Completely burned	Brings offering Places hand on head Slays, skins, cuts in pieces	Accepts offering Throws blood against altar Places pieces on fire Washes entrails, legs
ḥaṭṭāt Purification or sin offering 4:1-5, 13 6:24-30	To atone for a specific unwitting sin	Priest: bull Congregation: young bull Ruler: male goat One of people: female goat or sheep Poor person: two birds; very poor: flour	Fatty portions burned Remainder eaten	Brings offering (Elders do so for congregation)	Accepts offering Throws blood against altar Burns fat, etc., eats meat If own sin is included, burns portion outside camp
ʾāšām Guilt, trespass, or reparation offering 5:14–6:7 7:1-10	To atone for a sin requiring restitution or a breach of faith	Like purification offering (plus specified restitution)	Like purification offering	Like purification offering (plus specified restitution)	Like purification offering (plus specified restitution)
minḥâ Grain or cereal offering 2:1-16 6:14-23	To secure or retain good will	Fine flour or cakes or wafers or firstfruits with oil, frankincense, salt, but no leaven or honey Usually accompanied by animal sacrifice	Token (ʾaskārâ) burned	Brings offering Takes handful	Burns handful Priests and sons eat remainder
šelāmîn Peace offerings or offerings of well-being 3:1-17 7:11-21, 28-36	To render praise to Yahweh . . .	Male or female from herd or flock without blemish	Fatty portions burned Remainder eaten	Brings offering Places hand on head Slays, skins, cuts in pieces Eats of remainder* (same day or next)	Accepts, Throws blood on altar Burns fatty portions Eats of remainder* (same day)
tôḏâ Praise offering	For a blessing received				
neḏer Vow offering	In fulfillment of a vow				
neḏāḇâ Freewill offering	Spontaneously from a glad heart				

[*Note that these offerings are expressions of *communion* among people, priests, and God.]

Limestone horned altars from Megiddo (ca. tenth century B.C.), on which the
Israelites could offer "a pleasing odor to the LORD" (Lev. 2:2).
(Oriental Institute, University of Chicago)

Since an offering of well-being was usually presented in praise of God,
larger portions of the sacrificial animal were returned to the worshiper. The
meat became the basis for a celebrative meal with one's clan. Given the joyful
nature of this sacrifice, the law permitted the use of an animal with a blemish
as a freewill offering (22:23).

A look at the sacrificial ritual for presenting a bull as a whole burnt
offering offers some insight into the procedure for making a sacrifice in ancient
Israel (1:3-9):

1. Presentation of a bull by a citizen (v. 3); an offering was to be of superior
   quality, such as a male without blemish, semolina (cereal ground from
   hard wheat), and the best of firstfruits.[6]
2. The citizen's laying a hand on the animal's head (v. 4a). With this gesture
   the offerer identified the animal as his own. Thus rich persons or high

officials could not present sacrifices by having another person stand in for them. We may assume the citizen spoke some words, identifying the purpose of the offering, confessing any sin, and affirming faith in Yahweh.

3. Slaughter of the animal by the citizen (v. 5a).
4. The priest's dashing the blood against the altar (v. 5b).
5. The citizen's skinning the animal and then his cutting it (v. 6).
6. Arrangement of the animal and preparation of the fire by the priest (vv. 7-8).
7. The citizen's washing of the innards and legs (v. 9a).
8. The priest's burning of the fat (v. 9b).[7]

This ritual is ordered so that the activity alternated between the priest and the citizen. The key role of the citizen indicates that this ritual is quite ancient. Later, as the population grew and the cult became more formalized, the priests took over the duties after the presenter had laid hands on the animal's head (cf. 2 Chr. 29:34; Ezek. 44:11).

The second section (chs. 4–5) presents the regulations for the two major expiating sacrifices: the "sin offering," which has been better termed the "purification offering," and the "guilt offering," also called the "reparation offering." *Expiation (kipper)* is the key term that unites these two sacrifices. Anyone who sinned had to present one of these sacrifices to remain in fellowship with Yahweh as a member of the covenant community. The sins expiated in this sacrifice were *unintentional* and *ignorant* failures to keep the commandments. High-handed sins, i.e., sins done with premeditation, were for the most part beyond the power of the sacrificial system to expiate (cf. Num. 15:27-31; Ps. 51:16-17).

The regulations for the *purification* offering were ordered according to the status of the person or group that sinned. The greater purification offering was prescribed for the high priest and the covenant community (4:2-21). None of this offering could be eaten. The lesser purification offering (4:22-36) was for a prince, i.e., a tribal leader, and an individual. A portion of this offering became the priests' and they were to eat it in a holy place (6:25-29). In eating it they participated in the removal of the sin (10:17). One explanation for this distinction is that the higher the standing of the one who had sinned the more potent the pollution released by that sin, empowering it to penetrate deeper into the sanctuary.[8] Thus the ritual for the greater purification offering included special rites for the cleansing of the inner sanctuary, whereas the cleansing rites for the lesser purification offering were performed outside the sanctuaries at the main altar. The fact that the greater offering was for the high priest and the congregation bears witness that this element of law regarded Israel as a theocracy, a people directly accountable to the sovereign God.

The *reparation* offering was to be presented for either a sin for which restitution or compensation could be made or for the violation of "holy things," including vessels, incense, garments, portions of sacrifice that have been dedicated to the Lord (5:14–6:7). The regulations do not make precise the distinctions between these two expiating sacrifices. Nevertheless, we have good reason to believe that these offerings are distinct. One suggestive interpretation is that the person who had committed a premeditated sin could reduce the offense to an inadvertent sin through repentance.[9] Then such a person was able to make expiation for that sin by presenting a reparation offering. There is support for this interpretation in latter rabbinic writings. Furthermore, this procedure would allow the sacrificial system to deal with serious ("high-handed") sins.

The regulations make concessions for the poor with respect to required offerings, except for a reparation offering. In case of a purification offering, a person who could not afford an offering from the flock could bring two pigeons or doves or even a specified amount of flour (5:7-12). In case of a whole burnt offering a person could present two birds (1:14).

Division II of the book (chs. 8–10) recounts the ordination of Aaron and his sons as priests (ch. 8) and the offering of the first sacrifices at the newly erected sanctuary (ch. 9). Moses officiated over an elaborate ordination ceremony. Several sacrifices, including an ordination offering, were presented. After the ceremony the priests remained at the sanctuary in the presence of God for a week as part of their ordination. At the end of the week they presented the first sacrifices on behalf of themselves and the congregation on the new altar. God honored this day with the appearance of his Glory, from which fire went out and consumed the sacrifices (9:23-24). While this narrative recounts the first ordination service in Israel, it also provides the protocol for the ordination of Aaron's successors.

This high occasion was marred by a tragic incident (10:1-7). Nadab and Abihu, Aaron's two younger sons, became so caught up in their enthusiasm that they presented fire before Yahweh that he had not authorized. At once fire came forth from Yahweh's presence in the Glory, consuming these two men. The brevity of the account omits mention of the exact nature of the transgression. The use of the term "strange" or "illicit" points to the possibility that they sought to carry out a pagan rite in the very sanctuary of Yahweh, perhaps seeking to enter the very Holy of Holies. Certainly Yahweh saw the need to prevent such impure practice at the inception of worship at the new sanctuary. This strange incident has a remarkable parallel in the first days of the Christian church in the death of Ananias and Sapphira (Acts 5:1-11).

Division III (chs. 11–15) presents a series of laws regulating *ritual purity*:

(1) clean and unclean foods and animals (ch. 11);
(2) the giving of birth (ch. 12);

(3) leprous growths on people, contaminated garments and houses (chs. 13–14);

(4) discharges from the genitals (ch. 15).

Since God is holy, it is crucial that his people prepare themselves to enter his presence. This is the essential reason for the complex and seemingly harsh rules of ritual purity. Nevertheless, we need to be mindful that there are numerous customs and laws in modern countries that regulate all sorts of issues in regard to purity, from the handling of food in stores and restaurants to the disposal of waste.

The most famous purity laws set up categories in the animal realm. These laws are central to a *kosher* practice which orthodox Jews continue to keep as they avoid not only eating but even touching non-kosher meats.

Anyone who became unclean by violating any law of purity was forbidden to approach the sanctuary for fear of death. The danger in becoming unclean was not from the uncleanness itself, but from the holy; by entering the holy place in an unclean state one would encounter the consuming power of the holy. Except for an enduring case of uncleanness, becoming unclean was not a serious matter as long as one took the appropriate steps to remove the uncleanness at the earliest time. Mild uncleanness, such as contact with the carcass of an unclean animal (11:28), was removed by waiting until evening. More serious uncleanness — such as childbirth (ch. 12) — required ritual washing plus waiting for a period of time. The strongest uncleanness caused by a grievous skin disease (ch. 13) required the one suffering to live outside the community as long as the disease was present. Once recovered, the person could rejoin the community after an elaborate "rite of aggregation" — a term used by anthropologists to describe a ritual that allows a person to rejoin a group from which he has been excluded — that took place over a week (14:1-20). It is important to underscore the fact that rituals for restoration were provided. But anyone who defiantly remained unclean was barred from the community (cf. 17:16). These laws of ritual purity taught all Israelites to prepare themselves for entering Yahweh's presence at the sanctuary. They kept before the people the wide gulf separating the human family from the holy God.

Furthermore, the laws of ritual purity separated Israel from the worship practices and customs of their neighbors, particularly those associated with witchcraft. It is hard to worship with people with whom you cannot eat. According to Mary Douglas these laws taught the people about the wholeness and completeness of the holy. They provided numerous symbols or illustrations for the people about the wholeness, purity, perfection, and unity of God.[10] Only perfect members of their species, whole, free from defect, were acceptable in the worship of the holy God.

Building on this interpretation, another scholar argues that the center of gravity for these laws is the relative virtues of nature (animals) vs. culture (human beings).[11] Animals that invade and threaten culture are those that are taboo. Also, animals that live in desolate and forsaken habitations outside of civilized areas are taboo. The center of power for witchcraft lies in the arena of death, darkness, confusion, and chaos. Thus these laws help establish a barrier in ancient Israel against the forces of the demonic. The unclean becomes associated with death. Death is the opposite of the holy things and of God, for God is the living God (Deut. 5:26; 30:20; Josh. 3:10; Jer. 10:10), the author of life. Keeping the laws of ritual purity promotes and honors life, health, and holiness; the unclean, conversely, coincides with illness, pollution, and death.

These laws had a profound impact on the moral fiber of ancient Israel. Observing them promoted solidarity among the Israelites and encouraged their spiritual development.[12] In both Testaments clean and unclean become symbols for moral purity or impurity (e.g., Isa. 1:16; 35:8; 52:1; 59:3; Pss. 24:4; 51:2; Matt. 5:8; Acts 15:8-9; 2 Cor. 7:1; 1 Tim. 1:5; 3:9; 1 John 1:7, 9; Rev. 21:27). Jesus, however, put an end to the laws of ritual purity, calling his followers to a purity not of dress or diet but of heart (Mark 7:14-23; Matt. 15:17-20; Rom. 14:14; Eph. 2:11-21; Tit. 1:15).

Division IV (ch. 16) presents the regulations for the *Day of Atonement.* It includes an elaborate description of the ritual for securing atonement for the whole nation. The Day of Atonement (Yom Kippur), the most solemn day in Israel's calendar, even today, takes place on the tenth day (7 + 3) of the seventh month (late September) in keeping with the great significance of the number seven to ancient Israel.

On this day the high priest entered alone into the very Holy of Holies. Given the austerity of the day, he wore simple linen clothing, not his regal garments. He presented purification offerings, first for himself, and then for the congregation. For each of these two rites of purification he entered into the Holy of Holies, where Yahweh was enthroned over the cherubim on top of the ark of the covenant. There he sprinkled blood on the Atonement Slate (mercy seat). Afterwards he sprinkled blood on the main altar in the courtyard to cleanse it.

Integral to the day was the offering of the live goat to Azazel. The identity of Azazel remains obscure. This term has often been translated "scapegoat." But given that "for Azazel" stands parallel with "for Yahweh" in vv. 9-10, the name probably refers to a place or a demon that inhabited the desert. Ancients would not have made a major distinction between a place and its most noteworthy inhabitants.

Before sending out the goat, the high priest laid both of his hands on its head and confessed the people's sins, thus transferring them to the goat. Then

88

the goat was released into the desert, viewed as the abode of demons. Hence, the congregation's sins were returned to the place of their origin. The intent of this ritual was to remove the power of sin from the congregation. The ritual foreshadowed the work of Christ, for he not only secured forgiveness of sin for all who believe in him; he also broke the power that sin has in the lives of those who believe.

Division V (chs. 17–26) has been called the Holiness Code (H). Scholars have suggested that it was an ancient collection of laws that had circulated independently before being placed in its present location in Leviticus. Eventually it was worked into the priestly material. This material is distinguished by certain terms and phrases: "I am Yahweh" (18:5, 6, 21; 19:12, 14, 16, 18, etc.), "I am Yahweh, your God" (e.g., 18:2, 4, 30; 19:3, 4, 10, 25, etc.),[13] and the admonition "you shall be holy, for I, Yahweh your God am holy" (19:2; cf. 20:7, 26; 21:8; 11:44-45).

This division consists of:

A.	Laws restricting animal sacrifice to the Tent of Meeting (tabernacle) and forbidding the eating of blood.	17:1-16
B.	Admonitions and laws for family life, especially sexual relations.	18:1-30
C.	Admonitions to holy living with cultic, moral, and civic laws.	19:1-37
D.	Penalties for sacrifice to Molech, sorcery, and sexual offences.	20:1-27
E.	Laws regulating the lives of the priests.	21:1–22:16
F.	Laws governing animals for sacrifice.	22:17-33
G.	The calendar of feasts and holy days.	23:1-44
H.	Commands regarding oil for the lampstand and bread for the table of the Presence.	24:1-9
I.	A case of the punishment of blasphemy, followed by laws on personal injury.	24:10-23
J.	The calendar for seven-year cycles concluded by blessings and curses.	25:1–26:46

Despite the similarities in some phraseology cited above, the variety of topics is so heterogeneous that the material may never have had an existence as an independent body of law.[14]

Ethical and civic issues hold center stage in ch. 19. Here Israel is called to be holy, as God is holy (v. 2). This call is explained in a mixture of cultic (religious) and moral laws. This mixture shows that there was not as wide a gap between these two classes of laws for the ancient Israelites as there is for modern readers. Faithful worship supports holy living, and a moral life finds fulfillment in worship. Specific laws give content to this principle: a master is not to hold back the wages of a day laborer, causing him hardship (v. 13), nor is one to put a stumbling block in the path of a blind person (v. 14). In short, one is not to prey on the vulnerability of the disadvantaged to enhance one's own gain. It is no surprise then, that the great commandment to love a neighbor as oneself comes here (v. 18). Behavior governed by love is at the heart of holy living.

Israel's God was Lord of *time* as well as of moral life. He set the calendar that determined the seasons of worship (ch. 23). On three occasions during the year all Israelites were to present themselves before the Lord: in the spring (1) the feast of Passover, followed immediately by the feast of Unleavened Bread, and (2) the feast of Weeks; and in the fall (3) the joyful feast of Booths. Added to this calendar in the fall are two high days in the seventh month: a sacred assembly to be held on the first day (vv. 23-25) and another on the tenth day (vv. 26-32). (See chart, pp. 92-93.)

The regulations for the Sabbatical Year and the Year of Jubilee were essential to ancient Israel's calendar (ch. 25). Every seventh year the people were to let their land lie fallow. At the end of seven sabbatical years came the Year of Jubilee. Observance of these years taught the people not to be in bondage to endless work or to greed. Yahweh wanted them both to enjoy the results of their labors and at the same time to trust him for sustenance (vv. 18-22). During these years of rest, not only the land but the animals and the people had a chance to rest.

While this legislation is often interpreted as an ideal not actually put into practice, there is evidence to suggest that the Israelites observed the sabbatical years sporadically, though not universally.[15] The legislation for the Year of Jubilee is hard to account for. There is little evidence of its existence outside of this text (27:16-25; Num. 36:4), and none of its observance. We wonder how, if the ancient Israelites had spent two successive years without crops, they could have escaped financial ruin, if not starvation. Yet the laws on inalienable land and the kinsman-redeemer, tied to the Year of Jubilee, are too central to the theology of the Old Testament for us to relegate this legislation to the realm of utopian thought. The Jubilee contributed to the eschatological vision (Isa. 61:1-3; Ezek. 46:16-18; Dan. 9:24-27), giving evidence that the people's awareness of this year inspired hope.

It is possible that the Year of Jubilee did not occupy an entire calendar year. It could have been a time added into the calendar that marked the end of the seventh sabbatical year. It might have coincided with every seventh sabbatical year. Or it might have been a period of several days added into the calendar like a leap year; since Israel used a lunar calendar, days had to be entered at various times to bring it into phase with the solar year.

Closely tied to the Jubilee are the laws regulating the sale of land and houses in Israel. A tribal inheritance was inalienable; it could not be bought or sold. If a person fell into debt, that one could sell the harvests on the family's patrimony until the next Jubilee. Then the land reverted to the original owner. These laws are tightly connected to the laws of the kinsman-redeemer[16] and of slavery. While Israelites could own slaves, they were not to hold their own people as slaves (25:44-46; Jer. 34:8-20). Should an Israelite fall into debt, he could sell himself into servitude until the next year of release (25:39-41). In another law code, if a slave married while in servitude and his wife bore children, he could go free but not with his wife (Exod. 21:4). He also had the option of binding himself to his master as a permanent slave. The year of Jubilee, however, was a time when all Israelite slaves were to be released. In the meantime a slave could purchase his own freedom, or one who was next of kin could intervene and secure the freedom of a relative (25:47-53). In the case of selling part of one's patrimony, the next of kin could buy it back for his fellow kinsman (25:25). This role of the kinsman was vital to Israel's understanding of God. Yahweh is called Israel's Redeemer (Isa. 41:14; 43:14; 47:4; 48:17; 54:5), especially in delivering his people from Egypt (Pss. 74:2; 106:10; Exod. 6:6; 15:13; cf. Isa. 51:10).

Message of Leviticus

Leviticus is a picture window into ancient Israel's worship. From it we learn about the holiness of God. It unfolds the relationship between holiness and ethics, and even more it provides background for grasping the significance of Christ's sacrificial death.

God Is Holy. His very name is holy (20:3; 22:32), and in the Old Testament, as we have seen, a name depicts one's essence. The Glory of God is the external manifestation of the divine holiness. God's appearance is so awesome that it causes nature to break forth in fear and joy. The mountains melt, the lightning flashes, the thunder rumbles, the earth quakes (Mic. 1:3-4; Job 9:5-10). Fire, which is the symbol of God's holiness (Deut. 4:24), issues from the Glory and consumes both the sacrifices on the altar (9:23-24) and Nadab and Abihu for their violation of the holy things (10:1-2). Therefore, to protect those who seek his presence God wraps himself in clouds and thick darkness (Ps. 97:2-3). The beauty inherent in the Glory draws one to God, but with deep feelings of apprehensive awe.

As the Holy One, God is jealous (Deut. 4:24). This jealous zeal protects the integrity of his holy character. Above all God cannot tolerate worship of any other god (Exod. 20:3-6). Since there are no other gods, worship of them

Old Testament Feasts and Other Sacred Days

(Source: *NIV Study Bible.* © 1990. Used by permission of Zondervan Bible Publishers)

Name	OT References	OT Time	Modern Equivalent
Sabbath	Ex 20:8-11; 31:12-17 Lev 23:3; Dt 5:12-15	7th day	Same
Sabbath Year	Ex 23:10-11; Lev 25:1-7	7th year	Same
Year of Jubilee	Lev 25:8-55; 27:17-24; Nu 36:4	50th year	Same
Passover	Ex 12:1-14; Lev 23:5; Nu 9:1-14; 28:16; Dt 16:1-3a, 4b-7	1st month (Abib) 14	Mar.-Apr.
Unleavened Bread	Ex 12:15-20; 13:3-10; 23:15; 34:18; Lev 23:6-8; Nu 28:17-25; Dt 16:3b, 4a, 8	1st month (Abib) 15-21	Mar.-Apr.
Firstfruits	Lev 23:9-14	1st month (Abib) 16	Mar.-Apr.
Weeks (Pentecost) (Harvest)	Ex 23:16a; 34:22a; Lev 23:15-21; Nu 28:26-31; Dt 16:9-12	3rd month (Sivan) 6	May-June
Trumpets (Later: Rosh Hashanah– New Year's Day)	Lev 23:23-25; Nu 29:1-6	7th month (Tishri) 1	Sept.-Oct.
Day of Atonement (Yom Kippur)	Lev 16; 23:26-32; Nu 29:7-11	7th month (Tishri) 10	Sept.-Oct.
Tabernacles (Booths) (Ingathering)	Ex 23:16b; 34:22b; Lev 23:33-36a, 39-43; Nu 29:12-34; Dt 16:13-15; Zec 14:16-19	7th month (Tishri) 15-21	Sept.-Oct.
Sacred Assembly	Lev 23:36b; Nu 29:35-38	7th month (Tishri) 22	Sept.-Oct.
Purim	Est 9:18-32	12th month (Adar) 14, 15	Feb.-Mar.

On Kislev 25 (mid-December) Hanukkah, the feast of dedication or festival of lights, commemorated the purification of the temple and altar in the Maccabean period (165/4 B.C). This feast is mentioned in Jn 10:22. In addition, new moons were often special feast days (Nu 10:10; 1 Ch 23:31; Ezr 3:5; Ne 10:33; Ps 81:3; Isa 1:13-14; 66:23; Hos 5:7; Am 8:5; Col 2:16).

Description	Purpose	NT References
Day of rest; no work	Rest for people and animals	Mt 12:1-14; 28:1; Lk 4:16; Jn 5:9; Ac 13:42; Col 2:16; Heb 4:1-11
Year of rest; fallow fields	Rest for land	
Canceled debts; liberation of slaves and indentured servants; land returned to original family owner	Help for poor; stabilize society	
Slaying and eating a lamb, together with bitter herbs and bread made without yeast, in every household	Remember Israel's deliverance from Egypt	Mt 26:17; Mk 14:12-26; Jn 2:13; 11:55; 1 Co 5:7; Heb 11:28
Eating bread made without yeast; holding several assemblies; making designated offerings	Remember how the Lord brought the Israelites out of Egypt in haste	Mk 14:1, 12; Ac 12:3; 1 Co 5:6-8
Presenting a sheaf of the first of the barley harvest as a wave offering; making a burnt offering and a grain offering	Recognize the Lord's bounty in the land	Ro 8:23; 1 Co 15:20-23
A festival of joy; mandatory and voluntary offerings, including the firstfruits of the wheat harvest	Show joy and thankfulness for the Lord's blessing of harvest	Ac 2:1-4; 20:16; 1 Co 16:8
An assembly on a day of rest commemorated with trumpet blasts and sacrifices	Present Israel before the Lord for his favor	
A day of rest, fasting and sacrifices of atonement for priests and people and atonement for the tabernacle and altar	Cleanse priests and people from their sins and purify the Holy Place	Ro. 3:24-26; Heb 9:7; 10:3, 19-22
A week of celebration for the harvest; living in booths and offering sacrifices	Memorialize the journey from Egypt to Canaan; give thanks for the productivity of Canaan	Jn 7:2, 37
A day of convocation, rest and offering sacrifices	Commemorate the closing of the cycle of feasts	
A day of joy and feasting and giving presents	Remind the Israelites of their national deliverance in the time of Esther	

93

is false and destructive (19:4; 26:1). Furthermore, none among his people may misuse his personal name (19:12; 24:10-23; Exod. 20:7). Speaking the name of God in vain is an attempt to use God for one's own selfish purpose. In so doing a person exalts the self above God.

Whatever else is holy is holy by reason of its relationship to God. Spatial gradation in Israel's camp witnesses to the fact that there are degrees of holiness. For Israelites two factors determined the space one could enter: (1) the status of a person's role in the cult, and (2) the state of a person's ritual purity.[17]

SPACE	PERSON
the sanctuary	priests
the camp	people
outside the camp	those temporarily unclean
wilderness	unclean spirits

The closer something is to God the more holy it becomes. There are degrees of holiness within the sanctuary itself:

SPACE	PERSON
the inner court	Levites
the holy place	priests
the holy of holies	high priest

Only the holiest person in the congregation, the high priest, was permitted to enter the Holy of Holies, and that permission became limited to specific occasions.

The laws of ritual purity, regulating the clean/unclean and the holy/common, ordered the daily lives of the Israelites. These laws kept the people conscious of the holy. They also protected a person from the danger of entering a sacred area in a state of ritual impurity. To leave the common area in order to enter the courtyard of the sanctuary, the people had to prepare themselves. They had to make sure that they were ritually clean. This activity implied that they were to examine their hearts, that is, their inner motives, to make sure that they also were pure (Pss. 15:2; 24:3-4). The insistence on cleanness reminded all persons that they were to take responsibility for their daily lives, following the procedures for restoring cleanness whenever they became unclean.

The polarity of life/death coincides with the polarity of clean/unclean.[18] Death was utterly defiling. Touching a carcass rendered one unclean (11:24-25, 39-40). Contact with a human corpse was so defiling that the law required an elaborate purification ritual extended over a seven-day period (Num. 19:11-

19). Priests were forbidden to come into contact with the corpse of anyone except a close relative (21:1-4); the high priest could not contact any corpse save possibly that of his wife (21:10-12). Death is the opposite of holiness. The Holy, then, is the source of life. This is visible in the confession that God is the living God (Deut. 5:23-26; Josh. 3:10). The holiness of God, furthermore, prompts God to redeem. It is the grounds of his desire to liberate his people from Egypt (11:45; 19:36; 22:33, etc.).

The backbone of holiness is justice. Justice seeks to establish equity among people. It is founded on the principle of *lex talionis* (the law where the punishment precisely fits the crime), "tooth for tooth" (24:20). Save in the case of life for life, it is a mistake to assume that this principle was applied literally in ancient Israel. Rather it served as a guide for setting the penalty for a personal injury. Its introduction into the law codes was, in fact, a great advantage for the people, for it raised personal injury from a civil tort to a criminal act and it forbade excessive retaliation (Gen. 4:23-24). In this way it elevated the worth of persons. In court the judge was to decide a case impartially, not favoring the poor or the rich (19:15).

While holiness in itself is a spiritual trait, beyond morality, in Yahweh the interconnection of justice and holiness means that any expression of holiness must exemplify justice. Yahweh's moral integrity is inseparable from his holiness. This explains why Yahweh's demand that the people of his covenant be holy was always bound up with the law. Biblically speaking, holiness came to have the derived meaning of moral excellence, though the pursuit of holiness requires more than a high moral lifestyle.

God expresses his holiness both in loving his people (Deut. 7:7-10) and in calling them to love the Lord their God (Deut. 6:5). Those who love God are exhorted, "Love your companion who is a person like you" (19:18; cf. 19:34). This principle becomes tangible in several laws that address a variety of relationships. The call to express love in human relationships counters uttering slander (19:16), bearing a grudge, or seeking vengeance (19:18). It urges the kind of compassion which leaves some grain standing for the poor to glean (19:9-10).

Love causes divine justice to be tempered with mercy.

Sin and Sacrifice. Given the fact that human beings continually sin, fellowship with the holy God, the very purpose of the covenant, required a means of access to God. That means was atonement through the presentation of sacrifices. Sin produces profound consequences: responsibility for the tangible damages caused by a sin; alienation of the sinner from the one sinned against and from God, alienation within the individual sinner, and release of a pollution that defiles the altar and the tabernacle.

> To correct the alienating and polluting force of sin, God gave the sacrificial system.

Specific sacrifices addressed the human need of overcoming the effects of sin. In fact, the requirement of making a sacrifice etches in the sinner the reality that death is the penalty for sin. In addition, the rituals of the Day of Atonement broke the power of sin in the community, purged the sanctuary of the pollution of sin, and made expiation for the priest and the people as a whole. Given human proneness to sin, whole burnt offerings for the whole community had to be presented every morning.

How does a sacrifice counter the harm caused by a sin? Leviticus does not address this issue directly. Insights have to be gleaned from sparse clues in the text.

The key term is *kipper*. Does it mean "expiate" or "propitiate"?[19] While the term stands for the cooling of God's wrath (propitiate) in a few texts (e.g., Num. 25:13; Gen. 32:20 [MT 21] uses the word to describe Jacob's hope of appeasing Esau's wrath), in the sacrificial legislation the action of the *kipper* is the actual removal of the sin (expiation). A person who had sinned was to present the appropriate sacrifice soon after having sinned, that is, before God's wrath was ignited. God's wrath was normally kindled by a person's persistent refusal to make amends for sinning rather than by a single blunder. Furthermore, the usage of this term suggests that what was done by the action of *kipper* was done on behalf of the person rather than to the person. Therefore, *kipper* addressed the multiple damage caused by a sin. The action of *kipper* removed both the pollution released by the sin and the guilt or blame. Thus the achievement of expiation through making a sacrifice provided God a just basis for granting forgiveness.

The key text for the significance of the use of blood in the sacrificial system is Lev. 17:11: "For the life of an animal resides in the blood: I have assigned it to you to make expiation on the altar, for your lives, because it is the blood that makes expiation by the life."[20] In this verse a play is made on the term life or person (*nepeš*).[21] The life source is the blood.[22] When an animal's blood is poured out in sacrifice, that animal gives its life for the person who had sinned. The life of the animal is poured out in death, which is the penalty for sin, so that the presenter might continue to live. There is thus an element of substitution in the dynamics of sacrifice. The principle is life for life, meaning that expiation is achieved on a solid, just foundation. The guilt or blame for having sinned is thereby satisfied. Furthermore, the sprinkling of the blood cleanses the altar from the sin's pollution. Blood has this cleansing power because it was the locus of the animal's life.

When a sacrifice, therefore, is presented in a way that is acceptable to God, it works expiation (1:4). As a result a person is forgiven (4:20, 26). The implied subject of the passive "forgiven" is God. This grammatical construction indicates that the initiative to grant forgiveness resides with God. Following a ritual does not automatically ensure forgiveness. It is implied that God assesses the person's reasons and attitudes in making the sacrifice before granting forgiveness. Thus, no magical concept of sacrifice is taught in the Old Testament. The presenter relies on the mercy of Yahweh for acceptance and forgiveness.

Leviticus and the New Testament

The sacrificial legislation recorded in Leviticus provides the basis for understanding the death of Christ as a sacrifice (1 Cor. 5:7). Through familiarity with Old Testament sacrifice the believer is better able to understand the uniqueness and the finality of Christ's sacrificial death (Heb. 7:27; 9:23-28). The book of Hebrews sheds light on the role of Christ as the superior high priest (Heb. 2:17; 3:1; 7:26-28). The New Testament as a whole continues to call the people of God to be holy (1 Pet. 1:15-16; Matt. 5:48), and to reinforce the insights of Leviticus into the nature and importance of holiness. Lessons for worshiping the holy God and for maintaining God's presence in the community of the faithful are abundant throughout the New Testament, which also offers perspectives on the priestly role of all believers (1 Pet. 2:5, 9).

Law and Grace. It is sometimes stated that salvation under the old covenant was gained by performing works of law, whereas under the new covenant people are saved by faith in Christ alone. This view is based largely on a somewhat distorted understanding of Paul's teachings. Careful study of the Torah as well as the rest of the Old Testament shows that people are never saved by their own efforts — but only by the grace of God. Everyone deserves condemnation and death for having sinned. God is graciously willing to accept a person on the basis of faith, having provided the means for redemption. Paul understood the covenant with Abraham in this way and declared that it was not annulled by the law given to Moses (Gal. 3:6-18). The author of Hebrews, discussing the Old Testament cultic acts, stated it succinctly: "For it is impossible for the blood of bulls and goats to take away sin" (10:4).

Likewise, many Jews understood salvation to be by God's sovereign grace:

> Rabbi Jochanan said: "Hence you may learn that man has no claim upon God; for Moses, the greatest of the prophets, came before God only with an appeal for grace." (*Deut. Rab. wa'eth/anan* 2:1)
>
> It was not for their works that the Israelites were delivered from Egypt, or for their fathers' works, and not by their works that the Red Sea was cloven in sunder, but to make God a name. . . . So Moses told the Israelites, "Not through your works were you redeemed, but so that you might praise God, and declare His renown among the nations." (*Midr. Ps.* 44:1)

Many Jewish prayers express dependence on God for salvation:

> "Sovereign of all worlds! Not in reliance upon our righteous deeds do we lay our supplications before thee, but by reason of thine abundant mercies. . . . Our Father, our King, though we be void of righteousness and virtuous deeds, remember unto us the covenant with our fathers, and our daily testimony to thy Eternal Unity."[23]

Hebrews. The Letter to the Hebrews frequently quotes or cites Leviticus, especially the Day of Atonement passage (ch. 16). Especially noteworthy are chapters 6–10. They provide insight into the community to whom Hebrews was written, and give the New Testament (and therefore Christian canonical) significance of the levitical ritual. The sacrifice of Christ is the "true form of these realities," and, therefore, it need never be repeated. Therefore, the ritual of the Mosaic law is no longer necessary; in fact, "what is obsolete and growing old will soon disappear" (8:13).

CHAPTER 7

Numbers

The Israelites had departed from Egypt on the fifteenth day of the first month (Num. 33:3; cf. Exod. 12:2-5) and reached the wilderness of Sinai on the first day (new moon) of the third month (Exod. 19:1). On the third day, God revealed himself on the mountain (v. 16). The tabernacle was erected on the first day of the first month of the second year (40:17). The book of Numbers opens with Yahweh's command to Moses dated the first day of the second month of the second year. On the twentieth day of that month "the cloud lifted from over the tabernacle of the covenant. Then the Israelites set out by stages from the wilderness of Sinai" (Num. 10:11f.). Deuteronomy opens with a reference to the first day of the eleventh month of the fortieth year, or about thirty-eight years, eight months, and ten days after the departure from Sinai. Numbers, then, covers a span of thirty-eight years and nine months, the period of "wilderness wanderings."[1]

An obvious purpose of the book is to record the period from the encounter with God at Sinai to the preparations in Moab to enter the promised land. However, far more than this is involved. The journey from Sinai to Kadesh-barnea by way of the Gulf of Aqaba would normally have taken only eleven days (Deut. 1:2).[2] The direct route would consume a few days less, and by way of Edom and Moab hardly more than a couple of weeks.[3] The narrative makes clear that the thirty-eight year period was punishment for lack of faith: none of the unbelieving generation was allowed to enter the land (Num. 14:20-45; cf. Deut. 1:35f.). Numbers, therefore, is not a mere bit of ancient history but another recital of the acts of Yahweh. It is a complex story of unfaithfulness, rebellion, apostasy, and frustration, set against the background of God's faithfulness, presence, provision, and forbearance.

> At the command of the LORD they would camp, and at the command of the LORD they would set out. They kept the charge of the LORD, at the command of the LORD by Moses. Num. 9:23.

Contents

Name. Originally, the book had no title. The translators of the LXX gave it the name "Numbers" because of its census lists; that title was passed on through the Vulgate to the European and English versions. Its name in the Hebrew Bible, taken from the words in the first verse, is "In the wilderness of [Sinai]." This title suited the setting of chs. 1–10. An earlier title, coined by rabbis, called it "The one-fifth [of the Torah] dealing with the Mustered," again featuring the census lists (chs. 1–4; 26).

Outline. The book divides into three main portions, each centered in a geographical setting to mark the main stages of the wilderness march. The first two sections conclude with a description of the journey to the next stage. The third section does not do that, since the march from Moab to Canaan is not recounted until the book of Joshua. Instead, the Moab portion concludes by retracing the whole itinerary and laying down some geographical, political, and social ground rules for life in the new land.

Kadesh   in the wilderness of Paran (13:1–20:13)
   Spies' mission and report (13:1-33)
   People's decision and God's judgment (14:1-45)
   Miscellaneous laws (15:1-41)
   Korah's rebellion (16:1-50)
   Story of Aaron's rod (17:1-13)
   Priestly duties and portions (18:1-32)
   Purification of the unclean (19:1-22)
   Closing events at Kadesh (20:1-13)
  Conclusion: Journey from Kadesh to the Plains
  of Moab (20:14–22:1)
   Edom's opposition (20:14, 21)
   Death of Aaron; victory over opponents (20:22–22:1)

Moab: Preparations for Canaan (22:2–32:42)
   Balaam and Balak (22:2–24:25)
   Apostasy at Peor and the plague (25:1-18)
   Second census (26:1-65)
   Daughters of Zelophehad, women's rights (27:1-11)
   Joshua as successor to Moses (27:12-23)
   Offerings at the feasts (28:1–29:40)
   Vows of women (30:1-16)
   Vengeance on Midian (31:1-54)
   Portions of the Transjordan tribes (32:1-42)
  Conclusion: a backward and forward look (33:1–36:13)
   Review of the journey from Egypt (33:1-56)
   Boundaries of Israel in the land (34:1-29)
   Cities of the Levites (35:1-34)
   Daughters of Zelophehad and women's inheritance
   (36:1-13)

Critical Problem. At one time it was generally believed that Numbers, like the rest of the Pentateuch, was written entirely by Moses. With the rise of historical and literary analysis of the Bible came a variety of challenges to this theory, with some scholars denying any historical validity to the book. Today, on the contrary, considerable support exists for the view that Numbers incorporates much historical material, although handed down in various forms and substantially edited and revised. These are some of the elements of the problem:

(1) No mention is made of the book's author. Num. 33:2 indicates that "Moses wrote down their starting places, stage by stage, by command of the LORD," but this is the only reference to Moses' literary activity.

Throughout the book, he is described in the third person. It could be argued (and, indeed, has been) that Moses, like Caesar, could write of himself in the third person.[4] In Deuteronomy, by contrast, we find Moses as a central *speaker*. In Numbers, he is certainly the central actor, and much of the material may have come from notes kept by Moses or one of his contemporaries, possibly Joshua.

(2) Considerable early material is found in Numbers. At the same time, several problems exist in harmonizing the material, particularly certain laws, ordinances, and cultic practices. In some cases, scholars conclude that later practices are reflected.[5] Yet there is hardly a consensus:

> ... although these institutions had a basic form already in the days of Moses, and although they preserved the spirit and the essential elements of the early forms, there were modifications at various times during the centuries of use, and ... the form set out in Numbers represents the usage at the time of the final compilation of the source materials.[6]

The early material demonstrates intimate knowledge of the wilderness, the Israelite people, and their constant complainings and disparagement of Moses, as well as much descriptive material about Moses himself. Recent studies of lists of place names in Egyptian texts from the Late Bronze Age (the probable period of the Exodus) confirm the accuracy of the itinerary listed in Num. 33:44-49. The validity of this list had previously been questioned for lack of archaeological evidence of the cities listed.[7] Ancient rites, the practice or significance of which seems later to have disappeared, are preserved in 5:11-22 and 19:1-22. Quotations from "The Book of the Wars of Yahweh" (21:14f., 17f., 27-30) also appear to be from an old source. In particular, several poetic passages (such as the utterances of Balaam in chs. 23–24) are written in very ancient Hebrew, i.e., thirteenth to tenth century B.C. Details of geography and historical allusions in these poems, notably 24:23f., may point to the time of the invasion of the Sea Peoples, *ca.* 1190. Even the so-called "priestly" sections of Numbers frequently dated after the Exile (*ca.* 500 B.C.), are now seen to be replete with terms, customs, and institutions from Israel's history, which passed from view or had their meaning changed in the Exile or after. A recent survey has listed several dozen such examples based on Hebrew usage or Egyptian, Hittite, and Akkadian parallels from the middle of the second millennium B.C. to the early centuries of the first millennium.[8]

Like many other biblical books, Numbers, as we have it, seems to be the end product of a lengthy process of composition. We do well to look at it in terms of *three horizons* of interpretation. First, it spoke to the Jews of their *past* history. It explained why Moses, Aaron, and their generation, redeemed in the Exodus and commissioned by God at Sinai, did not themselves inherit the promised land. At the same time, it testified to God's patient and provident presence with his pilgrim people.

Second, it spoke to them of their *present* history during and immediately after the Exile. In fact, Numbers was probably recast in its final form during that turbulent period of disorientation. For many Jews, Nebuchadnezzar's Babylon was Egypt revisited. A new Exodus was yearned for, but another wilderness had to be crossed. The idea of returning to Palestine left many Jews perplexed. They longed for their homeland but they feared the pains of return: an arduous journey, a farewell to the Babylonia that for decades had been their abode, an uncertain future in what had become a Persian province, an uneasy reception at the hands of fellow citizens and less than friendly strangers. Exodus would become their story once again: God's provision and forbearance would see them through.

The third horizon spoke to the Jews of their *future* history. There is a strong word of warning: "Do not disobey God's covenant commands nor forget his promise of faithfulness. Twice God has led you through the wilderness to the land of plenty. Remain loyal through the generations, and the land that is God's gift you will continue to enjoy."

Numbers in Numbers. According to 1:45f., "the whole number of the Israelites, by their ancestral houses, from twenty years old and upward, every one able to go to war in Israel," totalled 603,550. This was at the first census, taken at Sinai on the "first day of the second month, in the second year after they had come out of the land of Egypt" (v. 1).[9] If the men of military age are estimated as between 20 and 25 percent of the population — based on records of other peoples — the total of all Israelites would have been 2.5 to 3 million persons. By any reckoning, the number can hardly be reduced below 2 million.

This number is extremely large, and the problems it raises are many and varied. If the Hebrews took with them "livestock in great numbers, both flocks and herds" (Exod. 12:38), how could such a multitude have been kept in any kind of discipline during the departure from Egypt? How could the wilderness, with little pasture and water, have supported them? And how could the original seventy Israelites who went down to Egypt have multiplied to more than two million in four or seven, or even ten, generations?[10]

There are four basic approaches to the problem of the numbers:

(1) The numbers may be taken literally.[11] "But the Israelites were fruitful and increased greatly . . . so that the land was filled with them" (Exod. 1:7). This population explosion gave Pharaoh such concern (vv. 9-12) that he issued the order to kill all male Hebrew babies (v. 22). As for the journey, the Israelites were organized into smaller groups, which tribal leadership could handle. Food and water were miraculously provided as necessary; some suggest that the wilderness was more fertile then, hence capable of supporting more people and flocks.

103

Census Figures in Numbers 1 and 26

Tribe	Cited	Figures	"A"[a]	"M"[b]	Cited	Figures	"A"[a]	"M"[b]
Reuben	1:20f.	46,500	46	500	26:5ff.	43,730	43	730
Simeon	1:22f.	59,300	59	300	26:12ff.	22,200	22	200
Gad	1:24f.	45,650	45	650	26:15ff.	40,500	40	500
Judah	1:26f.	74,600	74	600	26:19ff.	76,500	76	500
Issachar	1:28f.	54,400	54	400	26:23ff.	64,300	64	300
Zebulun	1:30f.	57,400	57	400	26:26f.	60,500	60	500
Ephraim	1:32f.	40,500	40	500	26:35ff.	32,500	32	500
Manasseh	1:34f.	32,200	32	200	26:28ff.	52,700	52	700
Benjamin	1:36f.	35,400	35	400	26:38ff.	45,600	45	600
Dan	1:38f.	62,700	62	700	26:42f.	64,400	64	400
Asher	1:40f.	41,500	41	500	26:44ff.	53,400	53	400
Naphtali	1:42f.	53,400	53	400	26:48ff.	45,400	45	400
Totals		603,550	598	5,500		601,730	596	5,730
Average		50,296	49.8	462.5		50,144	49.7	477.5
High		74,600	74	700		76,500	76	730
Low		32,200	32	200		22,200	22	200

Greatest increase: Manasseh (20,500)
Greatest decrease: Simeon (37,100)

[a]"A" = ʾelāpîm "thousands, clans"
[b]"M" = mēʾôt "hundreds"
This table includes the censuses of Num. 1 and 26. The figures are given as commonly translated in the biblical texts: the following elements are broken down into the "thousands" (clans, chieftains) and "hundreds" (possibly the actual totals).

However, this approach does not deal with all of the problem, nor does it include all the biblical data. The peoples of Canaan were described as "seven nations mightier and more numerous than you" (Deut. 7:1). Yahweh said: "It was not because you were more numerous than any other people that the LORD set his heart upon you and chose you — for you were the fewest of all peoples" (Deut. 7:7, 9). If the data in Numbers are interpreted to mean that there were 2.5 million Hebrews, one is forced to conclude that they numbered almost as many as are found in the same area (Israel and the other parts of Cisjordan) at present — yet this multitude would have been less numerous than the population of each of the other nations already in the land. Such a condition is highly unlikely.

Some figures from antiquity may be used for comparison. For example, the Assyrian king Shalmaneser III was opposed by a coalition of nations at the battle of Qarqar (853), including Hadadezer of Damascus, Irhuleni of Hamath,

Ahab the Israelite, and eight other kingdoms. According to Shalmaneser's inscription, Ahab contributed 2000 chariots and 10,000 soldiers,[12] out of a total of about 3000 chariots and 70,000 fighting men — and this was at the height of the ten northern tribes. Since nothing less than the survival of his kingdom was at stake, presumably Ahab would not have spared part of his forces. When Sargon II captured Samaria, he reported that he "led away as booty 27,290 inhabitants of it" (presumably the city of Samaria) along with fifty chariots.[13] When Sennacherib invaded Judah (701), shutting up Hezekiah "like a bird in a cage," he besieged forty-six cities, and drove out 200,150 people, "young and old, male and female."[14] Added to these estimates, we have evidence from archaeology. Most cities that have been excavated cover sites of a few acres that could have housed a few thousand people at the most. At no time would Palestine have had more than a few dozen towns of any significant size. Every bit of available evidence, biblical, extrabiblical, and archaeological, seems to discourage interpreting the numbers in Numbers literally.

(2) The figures in Numbers represent a "misplaced" census list from the time of the Monarchy.[15] This hypothesis does not really deal with the basic problem, but simply shifts it to a later period. It does, however, remove such problems as the rapid multiplication of the Israelites, and the ability of the wilderness to sustain so great a number of people and animals.

(3) The word translated "thousands" also can be translated "tribes," or, with slightly different vocalization, "chieftains."[16] This attempt to solve the problem without doing violence to the biblical text was suggested by a pioneer archaeologist[17] and more recently revised somewhat in the light of further archaeological discoveries.[18]

This theory is attractive: (1) it can be carried over to deal with similar problems of great numbers during the Monarchy and divided kingdoms (e.g., 1 Sam. 6:19; 1 Kgs. 20:30; 2 Chr. 17:14-18); (2) it requires minimum emendation of the Hebrew text.[19] However, it is not without problems. There seems to be no relation between the number of "tribes, clans" and the total in each group.[20] Furthermore, it is strange that a census dealing with numbers never greater than seven hundred would supply figures primarily in even hundreds.[21] Another possible problem is the relationship between the number of "thousands" and the fighting men in each — generally less than ten in each thousand, which (using the ratio of 1:5) would indicate a total population of only about fifty persons in each "clan."

The most serious difficulty lies in numbering the firstborn males of Israel. According to Num. 3:43, the total was 22,273. The Levites, not required to supply fighting men, were to serve as surrogates for the firstborn (vv. 44f.). The Levites are numbered at 22,000. This can be meaningful only if 22,000 is a numerical figure, not a grouping of twenty-two "thousands."[22]

(4) The numbers are part of the epic style of narrative, intended to

105

express the majesty and miracle of the deliverance from Egypt. In this view, they are "not meant to be understood either strictly literally or as extant in a corrupt textual form."[23] One scholar is content to say: "The census lists represent an ancient tradition of tribal quotas of men available for war, so that the terms in question signify military units of some kind. . . . The exact numerical value of the terms is unknown."[24] To some students of the Bible, this is no solution, but rather an evasion of the problem. To others, it is an admission that we can not presume to answer all the problems with the limited knowledge available.[25]

Theology

Presence. In some way too marvelous for comprehension, the Lord made his presence with the Israelites visually known:

> On the day the tabernacle was set up, the cloud covered the tabernacle, the tent of the covenant; and from evening until morning it was over the tabernacle, having the appearance of fire. It was always so: the cloud covered it by day, and the appearance of fire by night. (9:15f.)

When the cloud was taken up, the people set out; and when it settled down, they encamped. As long as the cloud rested over the tabernacle, the people remained in camp (vv. 17-23).

Once, when Miriam and Aaron became exasperated with their brother Moses "because of the Cushite [Nubian or Ethiopian] woman whom he had married" (12:1), the Lord called a meeting of the three at the "tent of meeting" (v. 4). "In a pillar of cloud," he appeared and uttered these solemn words:

> When there are prophets among you,
>   I the LORD make myself known to them in visions;
>   I speak to them in dreams.
> Not so with my servant Moses;
>   he is entrusted with all my house.
> With him I speak face to face — clearly, not in riddles;
>   and he beholds the form of the LORD.

In these and other ways, the Lord made his presence known. The stories of his continual presence throughout the wilderness period must have been told and retold for generations, for this theme recurs centuries later in the message of the prophets (Hos. 2:14-15; Jer. 2:1-3).[26]

The Providence of Yahweh. The wilderness period was a constant demonstration of the Lord's provision for the people's needs. Numbers highlights this care in three ways: (1) the stories of guidance, protection, and material supplies (10:11–14:45; chs. 16–17; 20-25; 27:12-23; 31:1–33:49); (2) the instructions in God's law (1:1–10:10; ch. 15; chs. 18–19; 26:1–27:11; chs. 28–30; 33:50–36:13); (3) the institution of effective patterns of leadership (11:1–14:45; 16:1-35; 27:12-23).

God provided "manna" for the people to eat; and when they tired of this vegetarian diet, he sent quails (Exod. 16). This story is elaborated in Num. 11. There the Lord's providential care is seen against the background of the people's murmurings and complaints. The provision of quails was apparently temporary; the manna, however, continued throughout the journey, ceasing only when the Israelites entered Canaan (Josh. 5:12).[27] When Moses recounted the wilderness experiences, he mentioned more than the marvelous provision of food (Deut. 8:3): "The clothes on your back did not wear out and your feet did not swell these forty years" (v. 4). When the people lacked water and complained to Moses, God told Moses and Aaron to assemble the congregation and "command the rock before their eyes to yield its water" (Num. 20:8). Moses was irritated by the unreasonable complaints of the people and, in a moment of anger, struck the rock twice (v. 11). For this he was told he would not enter Canaan (v. 12). Throughout the Old Testament there are many reminders of God's providential care, often illustrated by reminiscences of the wilderness period of Israel's history (Hos. 9:10; 13:4-5).

Jebel Nebī Harun, traditionally identified with Mt. Hor where Aaron died and was buried (Num. 20:2). *(Neal and Joel Bierling)*

107

The legal provisions outlined in Numbers shaped Israel's worship and judged their disobedience on the journey; they also prepared the people for possession of the land, which was the destination in view in Numbers. The organizational structure as tribes, clans, and families (chs. 1–4); the ceremonies of confession and restitution (ch. 5); the regulations for sacrifices and offerings, including Passover, and Pentecost [weeks], the Day of Atonement, and Festival of Booths (chs. 7–10; 15–19; 28); the guidelines for dividing the land and reserving cities for the Levites (chs. 32–35) — these all were instruments of God's grace to enable them to live in community as God's people on the march and in the settlement.

As for *leadership* and its necessary authority, we can point first to *Moses* on whom God laid both special charges (chs. 12; 16), and stern rebuke (20:12). In response to Moses' plea for a leader to succeed him, Yahweh named *Joshua* (27:12-23); "a man in whom is the spirit" (v. 18). The strong role of the *priests* in the community, whether traveling or settled, is evident in the stories of Aaron and his sons (2:1; 3:1-4), especially the high priest *Eleazer*, who looms large in the account of Joshua's commissioning (27:12-23). The *Levites* (chs. 3–4; 18; 35) are regularly featured throughout the book as guardians and caretakers of the Tent of the Covenant. Not to be omitted are the *Nazirites*, whose special dedication provided a living lesson of God's indescribable holiness and the wholehearted commitment which it merited (6:1-21).

Patience. A cardinal assertion of Israelite theology is that the Lord is long-suffering. Numbers recounts several incidents on which this belief was founded. God was patient with Moses, both at the call in Sinai, when Moses tried to get out of the task, and later in the wilderness. (Moses himself was likewise usually patient with the people; his striking the rock at Meribah was quite out of character [20:9-13].)

Numbers is filled with accounts of the Israelites' grumbling. They complained about their misfortunes (11:1). They longed for the fish, cucumbers, melons, leeks, onions, and garlic of Egypt (v. 5), as if they had forgotten the terrible hardships of slavery. When the Lord sent them quails, they complained (v. 33; cf. Exod. 16). Miriam and Aaron grumbled about Moses' wife (12:1), and their anger spilled over into jealousy of Moses (v. 2). When the spies returned from Canaan with tales of giants and walled cities, the people were ready to choose a captain and head back to Egypt (14:4). The Lord's patience wore thin at that point, and he declared that none of that generation would enter the land except Caleb and Joshua, the two spies who had encouraged the people to go in and possess the land (ch. 13; 26:65). But even in that situation, God persisted in his great redemptive plan, and he extended his promise to include the children of those who refused to trust him. And in spite of the rebellions (chs. 14; 16; 25), he continued to provide food and water.

Intercession. In the book of Leviticus, Yahweh's holiness prompts the question: "How can a sinful people have fellowship with a holy God?" The biblical answer includes someone to intercede between them. The priesthood and sacrificial system provided one means of intercession. Numbers also contains several examples of personal intercession.

In one such instance, God is portrayed in human terms.[28] The incident involves Miriam's and Aaron's jealousy toward their brother Moses, as a result of which "the anger of the LORD was kindled against them, and he departed." Miriam was stricken with leprosy, and Aaron cried to Moses: "Oh, my lord, do not punish us for a sin that we have so foolishly committed." Moses then interceded: "O God, please heal her." God did heal her, but only after a token punishment of seven days' banishment from the camp (12:9-15).

When the people rebelled at the report of the returning spies, God threatened to smite them with pestilence and disinherit them (14:4-12). Moses argued that the Egyptians might hear of it and say: "It is because the LORD was not able to bring this people into the land he swore to give them, that he has slaughtered them in the wilderness" (vv. 13-16). Arguing from his faith that the Lord is "slow to anger, and abounding in steadfast love, forgiving iniquity and transgression," Moses prayed that God would pardon the iniquity of the people. The Lord did, but refused to let that faithless generation enter Canaan (vv. 20-23). From such experiences, the Israelites gained a strong belief in the power of a righteous person to intercede on behalf of sinners. Such intercession was not reserved to the priestly office, but was part of Moses' ministry as prophet (cf. Gen. 20:7; Amos 7:2-5).

Yahweh and the Nations. The conviction that the Lord was ruler of all nations is not fully expressed until the latter part of Isaiah. Like other aspects of Old Testament theology, it was built on experience. The Lord had demonstrated in the Exodus that he was stronger than the gods of the Egyptians. When the people refused to accept the report of Joshua and Caleb, they were prevented from learning that Yahweh was more than a match for the gods of Canaan.

Probably the most graphic lesson, however, is found in the story of Balak and Balaam. The Israelites had been forbidden to march through Edom, so they had bypassed it (21:4). They had to cross Amorite territory and requested permission to do so peaceably. Sihon, king of the Amorites, refused. The Israelites defeated him and his people and took his land (vv. 21-25). Then they entered Moab, the last region to be traversed on their way to Canaan. To hinder their march, Balak, king of Moab, sought aid from Balaam, a Mesopotamian prophet renowned for his power to pronounce effective curses (22:6). But Yahweh persuaded Balaam not to curse Israel. When Balak put pressure on the prophet, God warned Balaam to say only what God told him to say. Balaam saddled his ass and rode off with the princes of Moab. The angel of the Lord blocked the road, and when Balaam struck his donkey for refusing to go further, the donkey spoke to him. The angel then prevailed upon Balaam to go with the Moabites but, instead of cursing Israel, to bless them. Balaam did so, three times to attest the completeness of the blessing. The story is delightfully told, and must have been a great favorite in the tents and around the campfires. But this memorable story of a talking donkey contains a deep truth: Israel's Lord is the one who is in charge; even a Mesopotamian prophet, confronted by Yahweh, can speak only what the Lord puts in his mouth.

There is a sequel to the story. Balaam, called "Balaam son of Beor" in both accounts (22:5; 31:8), apparently joined himself to the Midianites and enticed Israelites to commit abominable sin against Yahweh by worshiping Baal of Peor (31:16; cf. 25:1-3). This likely involved ritual prostitution (25:6) and was the beginning of the harlotries — both spiritual and physical — that infested Israel[29] throughout the time of the prophets up to the Exile. The Lord commanded Moses to punish the Midianites; and in the brief war, Balaam was slain (31:8).

Star-and-Scepter Prophecy. After Balaam had blessed Israel the second time, the Spirit of God came upon him:

> The oracle of Balaam son of Beor,
>> the oracle of the man whose eye is clear,
> the oracle of one who hears the words of God,
>> and knows the knowledge of the Most High,
> who sees the vision of the Almighty,
>> who falls down, but with his eyes uncovered;
> I see him, but not now;
>> I behold him, but not near —
> a star shall come out of Jacob,
>> and a scepter shall rise out of Israel;
> it shall crush the borderlands of Moab,
>> and the territory of all the Shethites.
> Edom will become a possession,
>> Seir a possession of its enemies,
>> while Israel does valiantly.
> One out of Jacob shall rule,
>> and destroy the survivors of Ir. (24:15-19)

The prophecy is remarkable for its reference to the dominion of Jacob, but most frequently quoted is that passage which speaks of the star and scepter (v. 17). Many have taken it as a messianic prophecy. It was understood in some such sense at Qumran, where it is quoted in the Dead Sea Scrolls.[30] In its context, the prophecy says nothing about a Messiah, and there is not even a vague suggestion of the beginning of the messianic age. "Star" (Gen. 37:9f.) and especially "scepter" are symbolic of rule (Gen. 49:10; Ps. 45:6), so the prophecy speaks of a ruler that shall come forth from Israel to vanquish their nearby enemies. This small spark helped kindle the burning fire of hope in a Messiah who would rule all nations with righteousness and peace.[31]

CHAPTER 8

Deuteronomy

For thirty-eight years after they had balked at entering Canaan, the Israelites were restrained in the wilderness of Paran and at Kadesh-barnea. Only when the old generation had died off, were they permitted to resume their journey. God led them in a long detour up the east side of Edom. Then they were ordered to camp in Moab, awaiting final instructions to cross the Jordan river and possess the promised land. It was an awesome moment.

Moses, mindful that he was barred from the new land (Deut. 1:37), took this occasion to give three lengthy speeches to the people of Israel. The substance of these farewell addresses is found in Deuteronomy. The first was delivered "beyond the Jordan, in the land of Moab" (1:5). The second — if the words of 4:44-49 are intended as a heading for the second portion and not as a summary of the first — was given "beyond the Jordan in the valley opposite Beth-peor, in the land of Sihon the king of the Amorites" (v. 46). The third was simply "in the land of Moab" (29:1). Quite possibly the same location is intended for all three messages.

The almost unbroken chain of speeches shows the aptness of the Hebrew name for Deuteronomy: "These are the words" (Heb. *'ēlleh haddebārîm*), or simply "words." Only the account of Moses' death (ch. 34) can be called a "narrative." The rest, except for the handful of introductory notes, is a flow of passionate words. The Greek name that has carried over into the European languages, *Deuteronomion*, "second law book" or "second telling of the law," acknowledges the ties with Exodus, where the law occurs first in the Torah.

111

> Today you have obtained the LORD's agreement: to be your God; and for you to walk in his ways, to keep his statutes, his commandments, and his ordinances, and to obey him. Today the LORD has obtained your agreement: to be his treasured people, as he promised you, and to keep his commandments; for him to set you high above all nations that he has made, in praise and in fame and in honor, and for you to be a people holy to the LORD your God, as he promised. Deut. 26:17-19

Outline and Contents

Outline and Genre. Most efforts to analyze Deuteronomy begin with its obvious divisions — the three *speeches*. The book's hortatory or sermonic style has often been noted: the three addresses consist of four, twenty-four, and two chapters, respectively. The seemingly disproportionate distribution can be explained by viewing the second address as the heart and core of the book and the other two as frames to introduce it and describe its consequences. "The "speaker is endeavoring to move from specifically legal formulations toward pastoral exhortation and encouragement."[1] But *speeches* alone as a label may not be adequate to describe the movement, order, and intent of the book. Its wide range of legal concerns lend it a *constitutional* tone. To some, it sounds like an extended *exposition* of the Decalogue. These descriptions of genre point to Deuteronomy's character as a *document* rather than merely a collection of speeches: "the document prepared by Moses as a witness to the dynamic covenant which the Lord gave to Israel on the Plains of Moab."[2]

The flow of the outline of Deuteronomy seems to follow that of the suzerain-vassal treaty.[3] Hittite and Akkadian (both Assyrian and Babylonian) forms of these treaties have survived to shed light on the nature of God's royal authority over Israel, his servant people (see pp. 73-75 above). An alternate suggestion points to Egyptian labor agreements or covenants as a possible backdrop for Deuteronomy.[4] The book does, however, far exceed in length any such treaty published to date. Whether Deuteronomy was prepared in the form of such a treaty or not, that structure is a good starting place. The basic outline is as follows:

Introduction (1:1, 5)
First Address: Acts of Yahweh (1:6–4:43)

Whether originally presented orally as three addresses or written as a farewell document, the book sets forth the theme of God's covenant with Israel:

> So now, O Israel, what does the LORD your God require of you? Only to fear the LORD your God, to walk in all his ways, to love him, to serve the LORD your God with all your heart and with all your soul, and to keep the commandments and statutes of the LORD your God and his decrees, which I am

> commanding you this day, for your own well-being. Deut.
> 10:12f.; see also vv. 14-22

Composition and Interpretation

The book of Deuteronomy is often called the keystone of the entire documentary hypothesis of the Pentateuch (see Ch. 1). The date of its composition has been set forth as one of the "assured results" of modern scholarship. However, in recent years the theory as originally presented has undergone substantial and complicated revision. Therefore a survey of the critical views of the book's composition may be useful.

Classical Documentary Hypothesis. In the Graf-Wellhausen theory of the composition of the Pentateuch, the four documentary sources were J, E, D, and P. The D document was the major portion of Deuteronomy (chs. 12–26). In the eighteenth year of King Josiah of Judah (621 B.C.), workmen repairing the house of the Lord found "the book of the law." When it was read to the king, he tore his clothing, remorseful that his people had been disobeying the words of this book. His penitence kindled a religious revival (2 Kgs. 22–23). As early as Jerome (fourth century A.D.), it was believed that the book found was Deuteronomy. In 1805, W. M. L. de Wette sought to show that Deuteronomy came from a source not found in the first four books of the Pentateuch. He proposed a date in the seventh century, later than J and E. Toward the end of the nineteenth century, J. Wellhausen was convinced that Josiah's reforms were sparked by contemporary religious leaders who had composed "the book of the Law" and planted it in the temple. Subsequently, it was "discovered," and, since it purported to date from the time of Moses, gave great support to the reforms.[5] Some scholars have claimed that "the book of the law" consisted of Deut. 12–26; others suggest that it was chs. 5–26.

Deuteronomic Historian. A host of scholars once dated "the book of the law," according to a theory that it was composed just prior to discovery in 621. This approach has not stood up to scholarly scrutiny in the twentieth century. Some have pushed the date of Deuteronomy back to the days of Manasseh or Hezekiah or Amos, or even as early as Samuel. Others set the work after the Exile, in the time of Haggai and Zechariah or later. Meanwhile, some scholars have noted that Deuteronomy has at least as much in common with Samuel-Kings as with the first four books of the Pentateuch.

Hammurabi stele (ca. 1700 B.C.) containing 282 laws, which suggest
interesting comparisons in form and detail with the laws of the Pentateuch
(e.g., Deut. 19:21). *(Louvre)*

As a result of these varied conclusions, the term "Deuteronomist" came to the fore, and scholars began speaking of the "Tetrateuch" (Genesis-Numbers) and "Deuteronomic history" (Deuteronomy, Joshua, Judges, Samuel, and Kings);[6] scholars who had followed the Wellhausenian theory had insisted that the major purpose of the D document was to establish Jerusalem's claim as the sole sanctuary, even though the city was mentioned nowhere in Deuteronomy. Furthermore, this theory seemed at odds with the command to erect an altar on Mt. Ebal (Deut. 27:4-8).[7] Some authors pointed out that Deuteronomy has some points in common with Hosea and concluded that rather than a product of the southern kingdom, it was a northern composition.[8] It is addressed to Israel as a whole, rather than Judah, Zion, and the Davidic line.[9] The main purpose of the book, as a German wordplay succinctly captures it, was not *Kulteinheit* (unity of worship, i.e., at the central sanctuary) but *Kultreinheit* (purity of worship).[10] Some concluded that Deuteronomy was the result, not the cause, of the Josianic reforms.[11] Obviously the same data were leading scholars in quite opposite directions.

Present Status. No scholarly consensus exists at present. Form-critical studies have led more and more scholars to recognize quite early elements in Deuteronomy. The possibility that the book is structured like the second-millennium suzerainty treaties (see above), rather than those of the mid-first millennium, would point to an earlier date. The hortatory style convinces some modern scholars that the book rests on a tradition going back to Moses himself.[12] Others put the tradition in the early Monarchy.

The book as we have it, like many Old Testament works, appears to have undergone a lengthy process of composition. The process entails updating and modification to fit the changing needs of Israel's life through the centuries. The collections of miscellaneous laws in the central speech may reflect this process of updating. Yet the end product as analyzed by recent stylistic techniques reveals a remarkable unity despite its apparent diversity in its forms of speech.[13]

As to the influences that shaped the book during its development at least four have been noted: (1) the writings of prophets, especially Hosea, with his emphasis on Yahweh's covenant love and the hazards of rebelling against it; (2) Levitical priests, who treasured the sacred legal and cultic traditions present in the book; (3) court scribes steeped in the Wisdom traditions of Israel, who fostered the emphases on righteousness and its rewards, as well as the fear of Yahweh and its fruit in humane treatment of persons and animals;[14] (4) Levitical singers, who for generations chanted the text in public worship.[15]

If one removes apparently late glosses and possibly some material in the final chapters, little remains in Deuteronomy that could not have come from the time of Moses. It is certainly more likely that Deuteronomy greatly influenced the prophets than that the prophets produced it. None of the major points of contemporary tension in the prophets, such as Baal worship or specific types of idolatry, are found in Deuteronomy. Moses, not the prophets after him, established the great principles of Israelite religion; the prophets developed those principles and applied them to the spiritual and moral problems of their day. Hosea himself saluted Moses' role in Israel's beginnings: "By a prophet the LORD brought Israel up from Egypt, and by a prophet [perhaps Samuel] he was guarded" (Hos. 12:13). After two centuries of critical scholarship, the evidence would seem to indicate that if Deuteronomy is not a record of the actual words of Moses, it is at least a tradition that accurately represents him and faithfully reflects his application of the covenantal laws and statutes of Yahweh to the needs of the Israelites about to enter Canaan.[16]

Horizons of Interpretation

Under God's provident guidance, Deuteronomy had special significance in three eras of Israel's life. First was the *period of its original setting* on the plains of Moab when the people were poised to cross the Jordan without Moses as their leader. It was a time of covenant renewal, a reaffirmation and amplification of what God had commanded at Sinai, a generation earlier. All the changes the conquest and settlement called for were laid out in detail. The transition from a pilgrim community encamped in wilderness venues to a scattered coalition of tribes, clans, and families was drastic. Deuteronomy, like a national constitution, took this transition seriously and anticipated the dozens of major adjustments that were required. In Moses' farewell sermons especially, the people were warned against the enticements in a land where pagan influences abounded. The tribes were about to *gain the land* and had to know all that it promised, for good and ill.

The second horizon occurred during the *period of the late monarchy*. The traditions safeguarded in the book certainly contributed to the reforms of Josiah begun in 621 B.C. Earlier, they may also have fueled Hezekiah's zeal to purge the pagan practices denounced in 2 Kings 15. A further contribution of the book may have occurred during these decades at the end of the era of Assyrian dominance and the beginning of the Babylonian period: the patterns of judgment and grace may have been systematically applied to the histories of Israel and Judah recorded in Samuel and Kings. The term Deuteronomistic is used to describe these works along with Joshua and Judges, suggesting that their final core position was shaped in part by the great themes of Deuteronomy (see Ch. 9). At stake was whether Judah could remain the elect of God and *retain the land* which had been the physical expression of that election.

Though the series of books that comprise the spine of biblical history were not completed until the Exile, the understanding of God's dealings with the people featured in Deuteronomy gained new importance during Judah's last decades of political independence.

The Exile did nothing to dwarf Deuteronomy's importance. The entire Pentateuch took on greater significance than ever under the ministries of Ezra and Nehemiah. The books became the badge of Israel's uniqueness, once divine judgment had taught its lessons. The third horizon is *the return to Palestine* where the covenant community had to survive without kings or princes. The law and the priests that taught it loomed larger than before. For the humbled and chastened Jews, Deuteronomy again became the handbook to guide them in their land. More than any other document it told their story — past, present, future. It reminded them of the divine grace by which they had first gained the land, the grievous sin by which they failed to retain the land, and the covenant love which alone explained how they had *regained the land.*[17]

Theology

Deuteronomy is a treasure chest of theological concepts that have influenced the religious thought and life of ancient Israelites, Jews, and Christians. Its basic ideas are credited to Moses. Expanded and adapted by the Spirit's nurture, they influenced the prophets who were responsible for the "Deuteronomic history" — the "Former Prophets" — as well as the "Latter" writing prophets. No wonder Bible students have yearned to understand the theological ideas of Deuteronomy. Its antiquity, its centrality in Old Testament thought, and its influence on the New Testament church all testify to an importance that cannot be exaggerated.

Creed. Deut. 6:4f. is the "Creed" of Israel, or, to use the opening word which has become its Jewish name, the "Shema":

> Hear, O Israel: The LORD is our God, the LORD alone (or "is one"). You shall love the LORD your God with all your heart, and with all your soul, and with all your might.

These words were to be upon the hearts of the Israelites, they were to teach them urgently to their children. The words were to be bound "as a sign" on the hand and "as frontlets" between the eyes. They were to be written on the doorposts of the house and on the gates. These instructions, immediately following the Shema, are essentials in the Jews' daily religious rituals. Jesus took the words of v. 5 as the first and greatest commandment (Matt. 22:37).

The creed sets forth the unity and uniqueness of Yahweh the God of Israel specifically in the relationship established between him and his people. The word used for "one" is the numeral — literally, "The LORD our God, the LORD, one."[18] If this passage specifically taught monotheism, another Hebrew word could have been used, hence, "The LORD our God is the only God."[19] At the same time, Deut. 6:4f. does exclude any concept of polytheism, for God is not many but one. Above all, there is an exclusiveness about Yahweh which demands total love (loyalty, commitment, dedication) from his people. The creed does not set forth monotheism as a philosophical idea. But it certainly sets forth the Lord as the only God the Israelite could love. To love him with all the heart and soul and might leaves no place for devotion to another god. Furthermore, it lifts allegiance to God above all human loyalties.

The name "monolatry" (worship of one god) is sometimes given to the early Israelite view, since it does not explicitly deny the existence of other gods. However, both monotheism and monolatry are philosophical concepts, and the Israelites do not appear to have been speculative philosophers. They did not conjecture about God. They knew him from their experiences with him. God had delivered them from Egypt and, consequently, demanded their complete devotion. Their faith was the result of experience and not the conclusion of abstract logic.

God Who Acts. The picture of Yahweh as one who enters into activities with selected human beings is not presented for the first time in Deuteronomy. It was an essential part of the creation story, the Flood narrative, and certainly the Abrahamic covenant. It was illustrated supremely in Yahweh's double victory over Pharaoh, crushing both his refusal to release the Israelites and his efforts to recapture the escaped slaves.

In Deuteronomy, however, the historical acts of Yahweh became a basic part of the book's viewpoint: these acts related to the claims Yahweh made on the Israelites both before and after they entered the land of promise. Moses reminded them "what Yahweh did with regard to the Baal of Peor" (4:3). His purpose was to instruct their future behavior in the promised land (v. 5). "What other great nation is there that has a god so near to it as Yahweh our God is whenever we call to him?" asks Moses (v. 7) in a driving rhetorical question that insists the answer be "None." The events which engendered such faith are to be made known "to your children and your children's children" (v. 9).

The doctrine that God is invisible and the commandment against making any images to represent God are both drawn from the Horeb experience (vv. 15f.). "And when you look up to the heavens, and see the sun and the moon and the stars, all the host of heaven, do not be led astray and bow down to them and serve them, things which the LORD your God has allotted to all the peoples under heaven," Moses goes on to say. "But the LORD has taken you,

119

and brought you forth out of the iron-smelter, out of Egypt, to become a people of his very own possession . . ." (vv. 19f.). The sun, moon, and stars belong to everyone — by God's decree — but the deliverance from Egypt was his action on behalf of Israel alone, designed to make them his own people.

If Israel forgets these experiences and their meaning, Yahweh will certainly punish them, drive them out of the land and scatter them among the nations. On the other hand, if Israel returns to Yahweh and obeys his voice, God is merciful and will not forget the covenant he swore to their fathers (vv. 25-31).

> For ask now about former ages, long before your own, ever since the day that God created human beings upon the earth; ask from one end of heaven to the other: has anything so great as this ever happened or has its like ever been heard of? Has any people ever heard the voice of a god speaking out of the midst of the fire as you have heard, and [still] lived? Or has any god ever attempted to go and take a nation for himself from the midst of another nation, by trials, by signs and wonders, by war, by a mighty hand and an outstretched arm, and by terrifying displays of power, as the LORD your God did for you in Egypt before your very eyes? To you it was shown, so that you would acknowledge that the Lord is God; there is no other besides him. (vv. 32-35)

In Moses' final address, he declares: "you have seen all that the LORD did before your eyes in the land of Egypt . . . but to this day the LORD has not given you a mind to understand, or eyes to see, or ears to hear" (29:2-4). Again the fact that Yahweh had led them through the wilderness and provided for their needs is featured. Then Moses remarks that this was so "he may establish you today as his people and that he may be your God, as he promised you and as he swore to your ancestors, to Abraham, to Isaac, and to Jacob" (vv. 12f.).

Election of Israel. The concept that Yahweh has chosen Israel to be his possession is called "election." The basis of the doctrine is found in the call of Abraham (Gen. 12:1-3; 15:1-6), where God's promise is directed to the "seed" or descendants of Abraham. This idea is thrust into the forefront of God's call to Moses (Exod. 3:6). It is found in the revelation of the law at Sinai (cf. 20:2, 12) and in the sacrificial system set forth in Leviticus (cf. Lev. 18:1-5, 24-30). The reference to the promise is found in the account of sending the spies into Canaan (Num. 13:2) and in the minority report of Joshua and Caleb (14:8). But election is *the* pervasive idea in Deuteronomy.

The word most often used to express the concept of election is the verb "to choose."[19] But the idea of election — that God had selected Israel to be his people — is expressed also in many other ways. It is often implied when no explicit word is used (cf. 4:32-35). We should remember that God's choice of Israel was effected by his creating it as a new people. Divine election is not an arbitrary act, as though God picked an already existing nation while snubbing others. God's new work of redemption called for a new people, hence the call to Abraham and the formation of a new nation from Abraham's family.

"For you are a people holy to the LORD your God," says Moses; "the LORD your God has chosen you out of all the peoples on earth to be his people, his treasured possession" (7:6). The choice was made not because of the numerical superiority of Israel (v. 7), but "because the LORD loved you, and kept the oath that he swore to your ancestors . . ." (v. 8). Because of this election, Israel was to destroy the nations in the land of Canaan "seven nations mightier and more numerous than you" (vv. 1f.). Israel was to make no treaties with them and to show no mercy to them. There was to be no intermarriage between Israelites and the peoples of the land. This could only turn the Israelites from Yahweh to serve other gods (vv. 3f.). Above all, they were to destroy all religious symbols of the Canaanites (v. 5). These seem to be harsh obligations. Since Yahweh is equally the God of all nations, and, therefore, all people are equally his creatures, why these stern restrictions? They must be put in their proper perspective, against the background of election. Yahweh has chosen Israel and is the God of Israel. God makes no specific commitment to other nations except as it involved his covenant with Israel. This basic idea of election lies behind the exclusivist portions of the New Testament, such as the difference between the followers of Christ and the "world" (cf. John 1:10-13; 8:23; 15:18f.; 1 John 2:15).

But there is another side to this concept of election. God's choice of Abraham and his descendants had a purpose: "in you all the families of the earth shall be blessed" (Gen. 12:3). God's jealousy for Israel does not stem from his indifference to other peoples; rather, it arises from his concern that Israel transmit God's truth to other peoples. If Israel is not careful to guard the truth which Yahweh has revealed in words and acts, the truth will never reach the rest of the world.

Accordingly, Deuteronomy stresses that the Israelites are to do all that the Lord commanded, once they enter Canaan. This is the reason behind the law of the "single sanctuary" (Deut. 12:1-14). The injunction forbade Israel to worship at any of "the places where the nations whom you are about to dispossess served their gods" (v. 2). "But you shall seek the place that the Lord your God will choose . . ." (v. 5). That place, wherever it might be — Ebal, Shechem, Shiloh, and finally Jerusalem — was to be the exclusive place of worship for the chosen people. Only thus could the faith remain uncontaminated by Canaanite religion: only thus could there be a clear witness to the nations.

The purpose of election — witness to the nations that were to be blessed because of Israel's election — is not stressed in Deuteronomy. Moses' central concern was to place before the Israelites the dangers of corrupting their faith, of losing the truth revealed to them, in their new land.[20]

Covenant Relationship. The word "covenant" crops up frequently in the Old Testament.[21] Although sometimes described as a "contract" or "agreement," the biblical covenant is something different. A contract has a *quid pro quo* ("something for something"): "for value received I agree to pay. . . ." If either party fails to keep its side, the other is freed from obligation. Even the suzerainty treaty is not quite the same as the biblical covenant, although it seems a closer parallel. Here, the ruler has conquered the vassal people, and therefore demands certain obligations of them. In turn, he promises to provide appropriate benefits. In contrast, the biblical covenant, God's relation to the chosen people, originates neither in a *quid pro quo,* nor in conquest. It begins with love: "because the LORD loved you . . ." (7:8). Therefore, even though the people fail to keep their part of the obligation — as they certainly did in the wilderness and throughout much of their history — God will not break his covenant (4:31).

For the prophets, the covenant relationship becomes the cornerstone of their hope. There were three basic elements to that hope: (1) formation of the people God had chosen, (2) their inheritance of the land he had promised the patriarchs and their descendants, and (3) establishment of the throne he had pledged to David and his posterity (2 Sam. 7). Because their Lord is a God who keeps covenant promises, the prophets knew that ultimately God must redeem the people, restore them to the land, and establish the king on the throne. The elements of this hope are present already in Deuteronomy. In setting forth his convictions, Moses is truly the archetypal prophet (cf. 9:26-29; 17:14-20; 18:15-18).

We must not suppose, however, that no obligations were laid upon Israel. In fact, the law given on Sinai, in Exodus, which Moses reiterates in Deuteronomy with sermonic applications, is composed of the obligations of the covenant relationship. We must not miss the fine distinction between a contract and a covenant. If the relationship between Israel and Yahweh had been the kind conveyed in a modern contract, Yahweh's commitment would have been contingent upon Israel's keeping of its obligations. In the covenant relationship, Yahweh honors his part (the promises) because of his love and because he is God. The Lord may punish Israel for disobedience, and may even chasten whole generations for stubborn disbelief. But the covenant remains in force — simply because of God's nature.

Israel, on the other hand, is honor-bound to keep the covenantal requirements — not to put Yahweh in debt to Israel, but because Israel is Yahweh's people and so should behave accordingly. Moses appeals to the foundational principle laid down in Leviticus — "You shall be holy; for I the LORD your God am holy" (Lev. 19:2) — as he repeats the law:

The entire commandment which I command you today you must diligently observe, so that you may live and increase, and go in and occupy the land that the LORD promised on oath to your ancestors. Remember the long way that the Lord your God has led you these forty years in the wilderness. . . . Know then in your heart that as a parent disciplines a child so the LORD your God disciplines you. Therefore, keep the commandments of the LORD your God, by walking in his ways and by fearing him. (Deut. 8:1-6)

Concept of Sin. The basis of the biblical doctrine of sin is set forth in the story of the Fall (Gen. 3) and illustrated in the subsequent chapters, culminating in the Flood (Gen. 4–9). In Numbers, the sin of Israel is depicted in several events of murmuring and rebellion. In Deuteronomy, it is seen against the backlight of the covenant relationship.

The obligation of the Israelites to keep and do God's ordinances stemmed from the fact that in the Exodus, God had chosen them to be his possession (7:6). When they claimed the land, they were to remember these facts and obey God's commandments (8:1-10). However, they were in constant danger of turning to other gods (vv. 11-18), a death-dealing act (v. 19). Loving God and keeping his commandments are set side by side (11:1, 13). Blessing in the land is the fruit of such obedience (vv. 8-12).

The gravity of sin is made dramatically clear in Deuteronomy. A central feature of the book is the series of instructions about ceremonies of blessings and curses to be observed as soon as the people set foot on the new land (chs. 27–28). The tribes were to divide into two groups. Six tribes were to climb Mt. Gerizim for a ritual of blessing; six, Mt. Ebal for a ritual of curse.

The liturgy of twelve curses (27:11-26) covers a range of spiritual, social, and sexual crimes similar to but broader than those in the Decalogue. The lengthy list of blessings (28:1-19) embraces the whole range of God's gracious gifts to the people politically, agriculturally, militarily. Conversely, the even longer series of curses (28:15-68) threatens everything the Israelites hold dear, from freedom to health, from prosperity to loss of the land. The apostle's assertion, "The wages of sin is death" (Rom. 6:23) is an apt summation of these bleak and bitter curses. To trifle with or rebel against God's covenant claims was to turn the Savior into the Judge. These ancient covenant curses rang in the words of Israel's great prophets as they delivered their doom-laden threats of judgment to Israel and Judah.

Apostasy or idolatry was the most damning sin of all. Deuteronomy left no doubt about that:

It may be that there is among you a man or a woman, or a family or tribe, whose heart is already turning away from the LORD our God to serve the gods of those nations. . . . the LORD will be unwilling to pardon them, for the LORD's anger and passion will smoke against them. All the curses written

123

in this book will descend on them, and the LORD will blot out their names from under heaven. (29:18-20)

So serious is the sin of idolatry that the Israelites were commanded to kill a brother, son or daughter, wife, or friend who sought to lure them to serve other gods: "You must not yield to or heed any such persons. Show them no pity or compassion and do not shield them. But you shall surely kill them; . . . Stone them to death for trying to turn you away from the LORD your God, who brought you out of the land of Egypt . . ." (13:8-10). If the inhabitants of a city were to try to entice Israelites away from Yahweh, that city with everything in it was to be destroyed (13:15f.).

Despite the humanitarian nature of many of the laws set forth in Deut. 15–26, the penalties for idolatry were terribly severe. The only explanation that can be derived from Deuteronomy, or any other portion of the Bible, is the sanctity of the covenant relationship. As a general rule, the Bible does not enjoin the people of God to slaughter unbelievers. The only such instances are in connection with the Israelite conquest of Canaan. As Joshua and Judges make clear, the covenantal purpose of the promised land underlies the requirements for Israel to remove the Canaanites. The ancients knew little of the tolerance that modern, pluralistic societies have developed. The typical Middle Eastern nation — like tribal peoples today — had a uniform culture and religious belief adhered to by all who lived within their region. Uniqueness was best preserved by intolerance of other cultures. As Israel's later history demonstrated, failure to obey Yahweh's command to destroy the Canaanites led to gross idolatry. The tragic outcome was the destruction of the kingdom and exile from their land.

Like the marriage covenant, the relationship between Yahweh and the people is a covenant of mutual love and trust. Like adultery, apostasy breaks the relationship by despising the love on which it is based, violating the trust, and treating the person as unworthy of total commitment. The covenant relationship is impossible under such conditions, as argued at length in the prophets, especially Hosea and Jeremiah. The person who turns from God to serve other gods faces grave consequences. But the sin of attempting to lead someone else into idolatry is greater still; its penalty is death.

The concept of progressive revelation (see below, Ch. 47) applies here. One type of law was necessary at the time the Israelite nation was becoming established in Canaan. Rampant idolatry at that point could have destroyed completely the means of conveying God's redemptive revelation to future generations. Gross idolatry several centuries later brought the nation to defeat and destruction. Only by God's grace was a remnant spared. God's revelation through Jesus Christ and his apostles brought a gentler law.

God in History. The concept that God has actually entered into history is a unique biblical doctrine. The consistency and sovereignty of God's grace and judgment are unmatched in the literature of any other religion. In Deuteronomy this biblical theme is set forth in a unique way which greatly influences the later writings, especially the "Deuteronomic history."

To cite chapter and verse is largely superfluous; the entire book is a recital of God's acts on behalf of the people: how God led Israel out of Egypt, gave them the law at Sinai, patiently endured their stubborn unbelief in the wilderness, and brought them to the verge of the Jordan. This sequence of events is summarized in chs. 6–12, several portions of which are quoted above.

The Bible's second account of the Ten Commandments (or Decalogue) is found in ch. 5; the first is in Exod. 20:1-17. The implications of these injunctions are set forth in the chapters that follow. The story moves back and forth between Israel's future obligations in Canaan, and Israel's past experiences of Yahweh's words and deeds. This interplay of past and future gives rise to a "prophetic" view of history, in which the past not only provides lessons for the future but also becomes the source of movements that influence the future. When God acted in the past — in the time of Abraham, for example — he said or did things which can be lessons for today or give hope for tomorrow. More than that, God revealed the nature of his ongoing activity, by which he will fulfill his redemptive purpose. So Moses, the prophets, and the New Testament writers understood the history of God's activity.

The biblical view is neither that of Kismet, the fatalism of Islam, nor that of Karma, the deterministic cause-and-effect of Hinduism and Buddhism. The human actors always behave as if free in their choices and therefore responsible for them. Yahweh often is portrayed as if angered or frustrated by human activities, but in the end, his purpose prevails. God bought Israel out of Egypt despite the power and cunning of Pharaoh. God brought Israel through the wilderness despite the unbelief of the majority. God gave them victory over the kings and nations who sought to bar their way. God turned the curses of Balaam into blessings. And despite their utter disbelief that they could enter the land of Canaan, God had brought them to the shore of the Jordan and was giving instructions for the time when they would enter the land.

This same concept of history — sometimes called *Heilsgeschichte*, the history of salvation — can be seen in the prophets. In the Former Prophets it is applied primarily to the contemporary situation; in the Latter Prophets, to the future as well. It pervades the works of the psalmist. It sustains the people of God in the Exile and afterwards, times that otherwise would have left them helpless. It is even intertwined with the events set forth in Esther — where the name of God does not appear at all. To God's people, history becomes "his story."

Mt. Gerizim, overlooking Shechem, where the Israelite tribes recited the blessings of the covenant (Josh. 8:33). *(Neal and Joel Bierling)*

Influence of Deuteronomy

How can the influence of a book be measured? One yardstick is the number of books written about it or that quote it. Another indication would be some great achievement that can be traced directly to motivation which the book supplied. Of course, we can never calculate the individual decisions influenced by reading the book or the persons who received hope from it.

Bible students see the influence of Deuteronomy on Samuel and Elijah, on Hosea and Jeremiah, and on Jesus. The number of quotations or citations of Deuteronomy in the New Testament mark it as one of the most influential sources.[22] Deuteronomy was one of the most valued works at Qumran, among the more than twenty fragments are found quotations or sections from every chapter of the book.[23] Jesus thrice found strength in Deuteronomy to turn back Satan's temptation (Matt. 4:1-11; cf. Deut. 8:3; 6:13, 16). When asked which commandment was greatest, he quoted Deut. 6:5 in reply.

But this is only the peak of the iceberg. How many times was Deuteronomy quoted in the home of Joseph and Mary, that Jesus came to know it so well? In how many Jewish homes, where the Shema (6:4f.) is recited several times a day, has the book brought faith and inspiration? How many Christians have found help and strength in these pages? Every indication points to the conclusion that Deuteronomy is one of the most significant books in the Old Testament. In any generation it deserves careful study.

PART TWO

THE PROPHETS

CHAPTER 9

The Former Prophets

The books called "Law" (or Pentateuch) have carried the account of God's actions from creation to the borders of the promised land. That story is continued in the second main division of the Hebrew Bible: the "Prophets," which is subdivided into "Former Prophets" and "Latter Prophets." The Former Prophets consist of four books: Joshua, Judges, Samuel (later divided into 1-2 Samuel), and Kings (later divided into 1-2 Kings). Their record of divine activity spans nearly seven centuries from Joshua's call to Jehoiachin's release.

> The LORD spoke to Joshua . . . saying, "My servant Moses is dead. Now proceed to cross the Jordan, you and all this people, into the land that I am giving to them. . . ." Josh. 1:1-2

> In the thirty-seventh year of the exile of King Jehoiachin of Judah . . . King Evil-Merodach of Babylon . . . released King Jehoiachin of Judah from prison. 2 Kgs. 25:27

Classification

"Prophets" or "History"? In the English Bible, these six books (counting Samuel and Kings as four books) are included in the "historical" division along with Ruth, 1-2 Chronicles, Ezra, Nehemiah, and Esther. Why did the arrangers of the Hebrew canon call these books "Prophets"? And why are they now considered as "history"?[1]

The question of what constitutes "history" is complicated, and scholars have come to various conclusions. Behind any history lie the brute facts — what actually happened. An attempt to record every fact would hardly be possible, yet a record of only the principal events interposes, between the events and the reader, the person making the record. Such a record is a chronicle rather than history. It makes no attempt to relate the events to one another, or to relate the events of one chronicle to those of another chronicle from another region or period.

The books of Kings contain many references to "the Annals of the Kings of Israel" or "of Judah" and similar titles.[2] These were used as source materials in the composition of 1-2 Kings. They were probably daybooks (diaries) in which principal events were recorded, perhaps in an edited form. The annals of several Assyrian kings likewise represent a kind of chronicle. History writing could be defined as the product of selecting incidents from such chronicles and arranging them editorially to tell a story, whether a history of painting or of the rise and fall of the German Third Reich.

The individual books that comprise the Former Prophets are not a history as defined by the modern historian. Joshua tells the story of the settlement of Israel in Canaan; but as a record of events, the account is not all of the same detailed character. The crossing of the Jordan, the religious rites at Gilgal, the capture of Jericho and of Ai are all given with considerable detail. Yet the conquest of southern Canaan is told very succinctly, and that of the north even more briefly. In some cases, the peoples involved or cities taken are not indicated.

Judges is even more tantalizing — comprising a series of stories apparently from various parts of the country and various times. There is a high degree of theological interpretation. The purpose of Judges was not to give a continuous account of the new nation's development, but to lay out the pattern of God's dealings with his people in judgment and grace during that period.

The books of Samuel look more satisfactory as history, for they do give a good picture of the monarchy being established and of the first kings. 1-2 Kings is a rather full chronological account, complicated somewhat because the histories of the northern and southern kingdoms are interwoven. Even here kings are evaluated more by their religious practices than their political significance.

Throughout the Former Prophets, the religious viewpoint dominates. This, then, is not history as modern historians might write it. Rather it is history from a prophetic point of view: (1) There is a focus on prophetic messengers, especially Samuel, Nathan, Elijah, and Elisha and their role in history. (2) There is an anti-establishment perspective, like that of the preexilic prophets in the Latter Prophets. Failure and shortcomings in the leadership of Israelite society are continually exposed. (3) Events are analyzed in the light of the prophetic truth that Yahweh is sovereign in history, both foretelling and fulfilling his prophetic word.

Historical Significance. To make such a statement, however, is not to denigrate the historical value of the biblical books. All historical writing is selective and written with a conscious purpose in mind. The degree of "purposeful" shaping of materials may vary. There is a great difference, for example, between the strongly biased annals of the Assyrian kings and the histories of Herodotus and Josephus[3] — even if the historical worth of many statements in Herodotus or Josephus may be questioned. But historians always have a purpose in the selection of materials.[4] What may look like invention or falsification to those with differing purposes is often the presentation of genuine historical facts in line with the overarching purpose of the writer. The Former Prophets contain historical data chosen from a prophetic viewpoint.

It will usually be conceded today that the Old Testament contains more historical material than any other single book before Herodotus, the "father of history."[5] Archaeological discoveries have frequently demonstrated its high degree of historical accuracy.[6] Nonetheless, the historical element in the Former Prophets — or throughout the Old Testament — is bound up with their spiritual message. The Former Prophets took their cue from the prophetic movement and interpreted events in the light of God's prophetic will.

Former and Latter Prophets. The two sets of books differ in the periods of time they cover. The Former Prophets give most attention to the period of settlement in Canaan and to the early Monarchy, even though they continue the story to the Exile. The Latter Prophets are concerned with the closing centuries of the two kingdoms and with the later history of Judah. A more fundamental difference is that the Former Prophets consist of narratives. They selectively tell a continuous story of the events in Israel's history. From Joshua through 2 Kings one can reconstruct — in outline form, at least, and in some cases with considerable detail — the sequence of Israel's history from the entrance into Canaan until the Exile, roughly 1250-586 B.C. This is why these books are called "historical" in the English canon.

In contrast, only a vague outline of history can be reconstructed from the Latter Prophets. Historical persons and events are mentioned, but there is no sequence of events. The Latter Prophets focus on the preaching message of the prophets and relegate narrative to a minor role.

133

Probably the most extensive "prophetic" writing in the Former Prophets is the Elijah cycle (1 Kgs. 16–2 Kgs. 1). Yet even these chapters and the Elisha cycle that follows (2 Kgs. 2–9) are nothing like a "prophecy of Elijah (or Elisha)" as we have, for example, in the books of Micah or Zephaniah. The Former Prophets give a continuous history of Israel, but mainly from a prophetic perspective. When Chronicles looks back to the books of Kings as a source, it often gives them prophetic titles.[7]

Date and Composition

Source Theories. In a previous generation, the documentary hypothesis that found four sources (J, E, D, P) in the Pentateuch was applied also to the Former Prophets. It was common to include Joshua with the preceding books as a sixth component, thus forming a "Hexateuch." More recently, Deuteronomy has been separated from the first four books (the "Tetrateuch") and included with the Former Prophets to form the "Deuteronomistic history."[8] The approach taken here follows Jewish tradition in including Deuteronomy in the Pentateuch and beginning the Deuteronomic history with Joshua.

Within the Former Prophets, account must be taken of certain literary techniques. First would be the apparent "doublets." One of the most notable of these is David's first introduction to Saul (1) as a musician who could bring therapy to the king (1 Sam. 16:14-22), and (2) in the contest with Goliath (17:12-54, particularly vv. 55-58). Second would be the citation of sources like "the Book of Jasher" in Josh. 10:13. Older materials appear to have been combined and edited into a larger whole.

The Evidence of Kings. Several different types of writing occur in the books of Kings. Any theory of composition of these books must take these into account.

In some instances sources can be identified behind the recorded accounts. For example, the "Solomon cycle," the series of stories about Solomon, from his proclamation as king until his death, is told in 1 Kgs. 1:1–11:40. Following these stories is the statement, "Now the rest of the acts of Solomon, all that he did as well as his wisdom, are they not written in the Book of the Acts of Solomon?" (11:41). Similarly, after the account of Solomon's son Rehoboam, reference is made to "the Book of the Annals of the Kings of Judah" (14:29). Again, following the brief account of Baasha king of Israel, the source is mentioned: "the Book of the Annals of the Kings of Israel" (16:5).[9] Many such references occur in the books of Kings.

Also included are stories about prophets, especially the Elijah cycle (1

Kgs. 17:1–19:21; 22:41–2 Kgs. 1:18) and the Elisha cycle (2:1–10:36). Some of these stories are interwoven with other accounts. Among the shorter ones is the account of Ahijah the Shilonite and Jeroboam (1 Kgs. 11:29-39). In 2 Chr. 13:22 we read of a prophetic narrative: "The rest of the acts of Abijah, his behavior and his deeds, are written in the story of the prophet Iddo."

Prophetic oracles are often interwoven with the story about the prophet. Ahijah's oracle to Jeroboam (1 Kgs. 11:31-39) occupies most of the story. Shorter oracles are contained in the long story of Elijah, for instance, the oracle to Ahab (21:20-24). Similar to the prophetic oracle is the revelation to the prophet found in the words of Yahweh to Elijah in 19:15-18.

Prophetic evaluations are particularly noticeable in the accounts of the kings of Israel and Judah. In introducing the reign of Jehoash or Joash, the writer says: "Jehoash did what was right in the sight of the LORD all his days, because the priest Jehoiada instructed him" (2 Kgs. 12:2). On the other hand, the account of Jehoahaz of Israel comments: "He did what was evil in the sight of the LORD, and followed the sins of Jeroboam the son of Nebat . . ." (13:2).

It is possible to construct a theory of inspiration that explains the various types of literature as the result of direct revelation. However, such an approach is not biblically derived, and never has been the historical position of the Church. The details should be considered as clues to the process by which God brought the Scriptures into existence. There must have been a storehouse of traditions, preserved at court, in the temple, and among prophetic groups. Either at different stages of history or after the latest recorded event — the release from prison of King Jehoiachin in 562 (2 Kgs. 25:27-30) — authors or editors must have woven together the various accounts to form the basic structure of Kings.

Deuteronomistic History. The relating of historical events into a purposeful sequence as the acts of Yahweh is apparently a concept unique to the Bible. True, certain events are attributed to the actions of deities in other ancient Near Eastern literature. Nowhere else, however, is the idea consistently carried through a historical period, nor are all events related to one deity alone.

The origin of this concept has been the subject of debate. Recent scholarship has attributed it to a seventh-century "Deuteronomistic historian."[10] Perhaps the most sustained illustration of the concept is in Judges. There we find a major theme: sin brings punishment in the form of oppression by a foreign nation, while repentance causes Yahweh to raise up a deliverer (see below, Ch. 11). The same understanding of history is found in evaluations of the kings of Judah and Israel throughout 1-2 Kings.

This concept is evidently indigenous to Israel. It was carried through with a unique consistency, and is completely different from anything found in any other ancient literature. It requires at least a superior religious insight — the kind that basically comes from divine revelation to minds capable of comprehending the revelation. Did the originator of this concept of history live in the days of Josiah, when the kingdom was rapidly drawing to a close? Certainly the best time to develop an understanding of a period is at its end, rather than its beginning. Only after looking back over the great deeds of God can it be said: "God meant it for good" (Gen. 50:20). Along the way, one may question God's fairness or wisdom. The time of Jeremiah and Josiah seems a fitting period to frame a theological understanding of God's work in Israel's history.

If certain statements in Deuteronomy are taken at face value, the bulk of that work presents an interpretation of history in terms of the great works of Yahweh. According to many scholars, "the book of the law" discovered by Hilkiah in the temple in the days of Josiah (2 Kgs. 22:8-13) was the book of Deuteronomy in some form. It appears to be a Judean version of an older book preserved in the northern kingdom and probably brought to Judah by refugees when Samaria fell in 721 B.C. Deuteronomy in its final stage of composition must lie behind the completed version of the Former Prophets. It provides one of the keys to interpreting the history of the two kingdoms. Most of the theological tenets of Joshua-Kings are derived from Deuteronomy: the struggle against pagan idolatry, the centralization of worship, the saving events of the Exodus and the related themes of covenant and election, a firm belief in monotheism, observance of the Torah as evidence of covenant loyalty, the land as God's gift, retribution and material motivation for human conduct, the fulfillment of prophecy and the role of the king.[11] In Samuel and Kings this last theme is developed in terms of the election of the Davidic dynasty.

Message

This literary epic was built on the foundation of the law and the prophets. Deuteronomy contributed a sense of God's grace and a call for exclusive obedience. The preexilic prophets supplied insights to divine judgment on Israel and Judah for religious disloyalty and social wrongdoing. While the book of Joshua introduces all the people, having left Egypt, inspiring fear in the Canaanites, Kings ends with a tragic reversal. In 2 Kgs. 25:26 "all the people . . . went to Egypt; for they were afraid of the Chaldeans."[12] "Why the exile?" is the basic question this epic seeks to answer (see 1 Kgs. 9:8-9).

> Its overall purpose is "not . . . primarily to offer an explanation of the past but to function as scripture for the new

> generation of Israel who are instructed from the past for the sake of the future."[13]

On this reckoning, the book of Joshua serves not only to describe an ideal soon lost, but provides a model for restoration after the exile. Was the epic designed to provoke repentance and confession of sins, in the hope that Yahweh would be moved to deliver from exile? So its interest in repentance suggests (Judg. 10:10; 1 Sam. 7:3; 12:10; 1 Kgs. 8:33-53).[14] In the light of 1 Kgs. 8:50, the postscript of Jehoiakim's release in 2 Kgs. 25:27-30 offers hope for a renewal of God's grace to the dynasty of David and, thereby, to all of Israel.

CHAPTER 10

Joshua

The death of Moses marks the transition from Deuteronomy to Joshua. At the end of Deuteronomy, the Israelites were encamped in the Plains of Moab, awaiting the Lord's command to go over and possess Canaan. Moses, who had led them thus far, was not to enter the land (Deut. 3:23-27; 32:48-52). God had instructed Moses to turn over the leadership to Joshua (3:28; 31:23). Shortly after he had done so, Moses died (34:5). We are told,

> Joshua son of Nun was full of the spirit of wisdom, because Moses had laid his hands on him; and the Israelites obeyed him, doing as the LORD had commanded Moses. (v. 9)

The book of Joshua resumes the story at this point:

> After the death of Moses the servant of the LORD, the LORD spoke to Joshua son of Nun, Moses' assistant, saying, "My servant Moses is dead. Now proceed to cross the Jordan, you and all this people, into the land that I am giving to them, to the Israelites. Every place that the sole of your foot will tread upon I have given to you, as I promised to Moses. From the wilderness and the Lebanon as far as the great river, the river Euphrates, all the land of the Hittites, to the Great Sea in the west shall be your territory. No one shall be able to stand against you all the days of your life. As I was with Moses, so I will be with you; I will not fail you or forsake you." Josh. 1:1-5

Contents

The account of Israel's conquest of the land is given in two approximately equal parts: a survey of the conquest and a record of the division of the land among the twelve tribes. The book's purpose is not merely to give information about the taking of the land. Though it contains a great deal of historical data, its intention is to be more than a history book. For very good reasons, the Jewish Bible lists it among the works of the prophets (see Chapter 9): (1) it carries a prophetic message; (2) its final compilation was the work of persons who saw Israel's story through the eyes of the prophets; (3) its lessons were couched in terms that gave hope and instruction to a people threatened by Assyrian, Babylonian, and Persian conquerors reminding them of God's provision of leadership and God's requirement of loyalty.

Joshua's first address — warnings and farewell (23:1-16)
Joshua's second address — the covenant at Shechem (24:1-28)
Burials of Joshua, Joseph's bones, and Eleazar (vv. 29-33)

When Joshua prepared to cross the Jordan, one of the first obstacles he would face was the ancient city of Jericho, a few miles from the river. Joshua sent two spies to reconnoiter the land and city. They were protected by an innkeeper, the harlot Rahab (2:1-24). The crossing of the Jordan, which was in flood,[1] was made possible by the damming-up of the waters a dozen miles or so north, so Israel might pass over on dry ground. Then, according to the well-known account, Jericho was taken by the intervention of Yahweh. The Israelite army is said to have marched around the city for seven days, with seven priests blowing rams' horns. Jericho's walls fell and the army overwhelmed the city, a victory attributed to the command of God over his people.

But the campaign to take the area at the ancient ruins of Ai (the Hebrew word means "the ruins") resulted in a setback. When Joshua sought a reason for the defeat, the Lord answered: "Israel has sinned; they[2] have transgressed my covenant . . ." (7:11) — by secretly keeping spoils of battle, which should have been "devoted"[3] to Yahweh. The guilty party was determined by casting lots, which the people of the Old Testament believed were guided by Yahweh. By the process of elimination, the tribe of Judah, the clan of the Zerahites, the family of Zabdi, and finally Achan were singled out. Achan confessed his sin in taking a beautiful mantle, a quantity of silver, and a gold bar. He and his entire household, his sons, daughters, large and small cattle, and his tent, as well as the booty, were destroyed by stoning and fire. It was only then that Ai could be conquered (7:16–9:17).

Then Joshua planned to move his forces to the top of the central mountain range, probably to begin the campaign in the south of the land. Gibeonites there met him, dressed as though they had just come on a long journey. They persuaded Joshua to enter a covenant (or treaty) with them (9:15). Without seeking the Lord's direction, Joshua agreed, only to learn that they were inhabitants of the cities he was supposed to capture to unify the land. Because of his treaty, sworn by solemn oath, Joshua did not destroy the Gibeonites and "devote" their cities to the Lord. He thus permitted the first of the Canaanite enclaves (small cities and villages occupied by non-Israelites), in the midst of the land. Later, this coalition of Gibeonite cities astride the main north-south route would become a factor in preventing the unification of the tribes of Israel in the land. Ultimately, this would contribute to the division of Israel into northern and southern kingdoms (1 Kgs. 12).

Also, five Amorite kings of the city-states south and southwest of Gibeon received news of the conquest of Ai, and hastened to confront the Israelites. Once again Yahweh gave them victory, and the enemy fled past Beth-horon

Aerial view of Ai (et-Tell) and Wâdī el-Jaya, thought to be the ravine
mentioned in the account of Joshua's capture of the city (Josh. 8:11).
(Joseph A. Callaway)

toward the maritime plain to the west. Yahweh had sent a storm with large
hailstones and then stayed the sun (10:6-14) on this "long day of Joshua," when
the Amorites were routed into the land.

The further conquest of the south, including the Negeb and Shephelah
(10:1-43), is told very briefly, without detailed accounts of the battles (vv.
28-43). This is followed by a similarly brief account of the advance to the north,
including a battle by the waters of Merom (11:7) and the conquest of Hazor
(v. 10). Evidently, Jericho, Ai, Gibeonites, and Amorites are the main concerns
of the account.

The style changes markedly in the second half of the book, with recount-
ings of the division of the land among the tribes. Perhaps most interesting is
the detailed story of the altar which the Transjordanian tribes erected by the
Jordan as they returned to their lands. The purpose of the altar was misunderstood by the Cisjordanian tribes (those in Canaan). Only a prompt explanation that it was intended to witness to the unity rather than some division

prevented a serious breach between the tribes on the two sides of the river (22:21-29).

How Complete Was the Victory? A casual reading of Joshua, with no attempt to consider the implications of the data in the book of Judges, might suggest that the Israelite victory over the Canaanites was quick, easy, and complete. Several statements could easily foster such a conclusion: "Joshua defeated the whole land" (10:40); "Joshua took all that land" (11:16); "they put to the sword all who were in it, utterly destroying them; there was none left who breathed" (v. 11); "there was not a town that made peace with the Israelites, except the Hivites, the inhabitants of Gibeon; all were taken in battle" (v. 19).

The misunderstanding doubtless arises from failure to interpret the terms "all" and "every" in Hebrew (as in other languages) appropriately in the context of the stories. For instance, in the story of the plagues in Egypt, where the hail "struck down everything that was in the open field throughout all the land of Egypt" (Exod. 9:25), there was still enough vegetation left for the locusts to destroy "all that the hail had left" (10:12). The viewpoints of the later editors also may have played a part in the shaping of the stories. Joshua's conquest was seen as the trigger of a process that led ultimately to the possession of the whole land, and the narrative anticipated the final result.

The account does note the fact that "very much of the land still remains to be possessed," in the midst of Joshua's successes (13:1-7).[4] The Philistine territory and some land north of Palestine was yet to be captured. Much of the land in fact remained unconquered, particularly in the Canaanite enclaves, where Canaanite altars and high places later seduced the Israelites from obeying the God with whom they were in covenant.

The Man Joshua

The leading character of the book is obviously Joshua[5] ben Nun, an Israelite of the tribe of Joseph (the "half-tribe" of Ephraim). He was born in Egypt and was a young man at the time of the Exodus (Exod. 33:11). He was named "Hoshea" ("salvation"; cf. Num. 13:8), but Moses called him "Jehoshua" or "Joshua" ("Yahweh is salvation"; v. 16). Joshua (Greek, *Iēsous* "Jesus") was chosen by Moses to be his "minister" — probably his personal attendant (NRSV: "assistant") — and was present on the mountain when Moses received the law (Exod. 24:13ff.). He was also guardian of the tent of meeting when Moses met with Yahweh (33:11).

Moses gave Joshua charge of a detachment of Israelites to repel an

Amalekite attack at Rephidim in the Sinai wilderness (Exod. 17:9). Later, he was one of the twelve sent to spy out Canaan (Num. 13:8). With Caleb, he submitted the minority report urging the people to go in and take the land. As a result, he and Caleb were permitted to enter Canaan (14:30). Finally, we have already noted that he was commissioned by Yahweh to become leader when Moses died (Deut. 31:14f., 23). His strategy as a general of an army in setting up a base at Gilgal, effectively cutting the land in two and enabling him to take first the south and then the north, has impressed military experts. From the biblical point of view, however, the success of the Conquest should not be attributed simply to his superior military genius. Yahweh fought in the battles he waged (cf. Josh. 5:13-15). It was Yahweh that gave the Israelites victory. Joshua was only God's servant.

But Joshua's role was not limited to his military career. He had experienced the deliverance from Egypt, the giving of the law at Sinai, the terrible frustrations and sufferings of the wilderness, and the tremendous leadership of Moses. It is entirely inconsistent with the whole thread of the story to suppose, as did scholars of a previous generation, that various strands of stories involving the gradual migration of Hebrews in Canaan over perhaps two or three centuries were woven into the story, and that only then was Joshua attached to the narrative as its hero. Joshua must be understood as a servant whose faithfulness is continuous with the history of Israel's deliverance from Egypt and her reception of Yahweh's Torah. To separate the history from the theology of this servant is to divide fact from meaning and to divorce personal reality from the intent of the accounts.

Joshua's character is part of the theological message of the book. He is pictured both as a second Moses leading the people to victory in Yahweh's name and power and as a prototype of ideal kingship in Israel. In righteousness, wisdom, and loyalty to the Lord he is seen to embody the traits necessary to all servant leaders. He stands alone in the Old Testament as a political and military hero whose story is untainted.

Composition and Authenticity

In the nineteenth century, many scholars were convinced that the same sources that had been discovered for the Pentateuch could be traced in Joshua (see p. 134, above). On this view, chs. 1–12 were composed almost entirely by JE and D, and chs. 13–24 were almost entirely the work of P. According to this theory, the first twelve chapters include etiological tales, stories made up in earlier times to explain certain facts or answer questions such as "Where did the

Israelites come from?" or "Why are the Gibeonites menial servants (hewers of wood and drawers of water)?" (9:27).

More recently this view has been abandoned. Increasing stress has been placed on Deuteronomy's connections with Joshua, Judges, 1-2 Samuel, and 1-2 Kings and less on the supposed J, E, and P elements of the books which preceded it. To the earlier material compiled by a Deuteronomistic editor (see Ch. 9, above) in chs. 1–12 were added later materials such as lists of towns and border descriptions, probably dating from the time of the Monarchy, the tenth century b.c.[6] Shortly afterward a "Deuteronomistic" section (chs. 13–21) was appended,[7] and other additions were made later.[8]

Authenticity. Some material in Joshua, particularly chs. 5–7, possesses the quality of an eyewitness account. In addition, quite a few details in later chapters suggest that these accounts were either contemporary or nearly contemporary with Joshua.[9] However, glosses, such as the phrase "to this day," clearly suggest a time somewhat later than the event itself. Therefore, it appears that the work consists of material (oral or written) from the time of Joshua, some of it reworked, as well as some clearly later material.[10] The "Deuteronomistic" editing must have been a lengthy process beginning in the early monarchy and continuing sporadically until the Exile.

In addition to a considerable body of material in Joshua which clearly reflects historical events, significant archaeological evidence must be considered. Some important Canaanite cities are judged to have been destroyed in the thirteenth century, suggesting an invasion of the land. Excavations at such widely separated places as Beitin (Bethel), and Tell el-Duweir (Lachish), Tell el-Ḥeṣi (Eglon?), Tell Beit Mirsim (Anshan?), and Tell el-Qedah (Hazor) indicate that this invasion was widespread, leaving its effects in the south, center, and north of Canaan. The extent of the damage, which left thick layers of ash and, in some cases, almost complete destruction, indicates that the warfare was severe. As a result, several modern scholars have expressed confidence in the historical reliability of the pertinent portions of Joshua.

Many problems, however, remain to be solved. The conclusions drawn from J. Garstang's 1929-1936 excavations,[11] that Jericho gave evidence of conquest as described in Joshua and indeed in the fifteenth and early fourteenth centuries, have been severely challenged. (1) Erosion has made reconstruction of the Late Bronze Age city plan impossible. (2) The Late Bronze Age town was small (no walls have been found) and was destroyed earlier than the date usually ascribed to Joshua's invasion (*ca.* 1250 b.c.). (3) No evidence indicates resettlement until the earlier ninth century.[12] Excavations at et-Tell (Ai; chs. 7–8) indicate that the city was destroyed *ca.* 2200 and not rebuilt until about 1200 in Iron Age I.[13] In addition, literary and textual problems both in Joshua itself and in its connections to other Old Testament writings remain to be solved.

Perhaps the most important problem arises from numerous indications that certain Hebrew peoples (it is uncertain whether they were "Israelites" or specific Israelite tribes) entered Canaan at periods both before and after the invasion by Joshua.[14] Indeed, the question has been asked whether there was an actual invasion of Canaan, led by Joshua, in the days immediately following Moses. According to some scholars,[15] nothing took place that could be called a "conquest of Canaan." Some Hebrew peoples, probably to be identified in part with the "Habiru" of the Amarna letters (see p. 147), entered Canaan over a period that stretched from Abraham to the Monarchy.[16] The variant forms of this view find little material of historical value in Joshua.[17] Other scholars conclude that there were two invasions of Canaan, and possibly even two emigrations from Egypt. The first invasion would have been in the Amarna age (fifteenth century), and the Hebrews again would be identified with the Habiru of the Amarna letters. This exodus would be connected with Moses. The second invasion of Canaan would have been led by Joshua in the thirteenth century, when Israelite tribes were already in the land.[18]

Archaeological evidence does not seem to support a fifteenth-century invasion, nor does the picture of the Habiru obtained from the many references in ancient Near Eastern literature agree with the biblical picture of the Israelite invaders. Further, the entire range of biblical material, from Moses to Malachi, knows of only one exodus from Egypt, in which all twelve tribes participated in one entrance into Canaan. This is the picture presented in Joshua, and some archaeological evidence can be understood to support it. However, the prophetic and religious purposes of the book have prompted a stylizing of the materials to put across major theological lessons for God's people: (1) the land is a gift of Yahweh's covenant grace; (2) that gift embraces the whole land and provides living space for every Israelite tribe and clan; (3) the gift of the land is conditional on Israel's faithfulness to Yahweh and her rejection of Canaanite religious and social practices.

An alternate explanation of the settlement period is found in G. E. Mendenhall's theory that Israel's historical existence in Canaan found its roots in a rebellion of nomads and peasants who were already in or near the land. These rebels overthrew, then, the oppressive power of the urban, Canaanite overlords.[19] This theory has been expanded from a sociological viewpoint and coupled with an interpretation of class struggle in a massive study by N. K. Gottwald.[20] While there is no way in which such theories can completely dislodge the role of the historic Exodus and Conquest, they can serve as a reminder that the formation of Israel's tribes and their settlement in Canaan may have been more complex than has yet been fully grasped. We are still far from working out the relationships between texts, history, and theological significance. But, however we learn to resolve the complexities in these relationships, we cannot divorce God's revelation from real history and its record in the texts.[21]

Historical Scene

Date of Joshua's Invasion. As seen in Chapter 4, the biblical data point to two different dates for the Exodus. On the one hand, according to 1 Kgs. 6:1, it was in the 480th year after the people of Israel came out of Egypt that Solomon commenced building the temple. Since this is dated in the fourth year of his reign (probably 967), the date of the Exodus would be 1446. On the other hand, the Hebrew slaves built the store cities Pithom and Raamses (Exod. 1:11); and since the name Raamses (or Ramses, or Rameses) has not been found prior to Rameses I, and building operations in the eastern delta were not carried out to any extent before Seti I (1305-1290) and Rameses II (*ca.* 1290-1224), the Exodus would be dated *ca.* 1290.[22]

The account of Moses' dealings with Pharaoh (Exod. 7–12) strongly implies that Pharaoh's residence was not far from the Hebrews, in other words, in the Delta region. In the fifteenth century, the Pharaohs were located at Thebes in Upper Egypt, about five hundred miles south. Given the forty years of testing in the wilderness (Numbers), the invasion of Canaan would have taken place *ca.* 1250.

International Scene. The powerful Eighteenth Dynasty in Egypt had ended. Located at Thebes, it had controlled Palestine and Syria and waged campaigns even to the Euphrates. However, it had been weakened by the revolt of Amenophis IV (Akhenaten; 1369-1352) against the Amon priesthood. His relocation of the capital at Akhetaten (Tell el-Amarna)[23] marked the decline of the dynasty. Its end was brought about by a military takeover in the late fourteenth century. At the beginning of the Nineteenth Dynasty, Seti I began building a capital at Avaris (Tanis) or at Qanṭîr, 30 km. south in the eastern Delta. Rameses II continued this work on a grand scale. Egyptian control of Palestine had begun to fade in the Amarna period, as the Amarna letters clearly show. Rameses II attempted to hold back the Hittites, who were pushing down into Syria. He was evidently forced to sign a treaty with Hattusilis III (*ca.* 1275-1250),[24] confirmed by a marriage alliance between Hattusilis' daughter and Rameses. The agreement marked the Orontes river as the limit of Egypt's northern influence.[25] Both the Hittite and Egyptian empires were weakened by the long struggle. The Hittite capital was destroyed, and the Hittite empire fell to the Sea Peoples *ca.* 1200. Egyptian power and influence in Palestine faded and the Nineteenth Dynasty fell *ca.* 1197. The Assyrian empire did not arise until *ca.* 1100. It was into this "power vacuum" in Palestine that the young nation of Israel began to flourish.

Amarna Letters and the Ḥabiru. The discovery at el-Amarna in 1887 of the diplomatic correspondence of Amenhotep III and Amenhotep IV and their allies and vassals in the nearer parts of Asia provides us with many details concerning Palestine *ca.* 1400-1350.[26]

The letters were written by kings of city-states in Palestine and Syria, appealing for help against armies spoiling the lands of the Egyptian king and warning that, unless aid was sent quickly, his lands were lost. Scholars favoring a date of 1446 for the Exodus and 1400 for Joshua's invasion of Canaan have suggested that the Amarna correspondence may actually reflect conditions resulting from this invasion. It sometimes has been claimed that the name Joshua occurs in these letters.[27]

Quite often the Amarna letters mention a people or class denoted by the Sumerian word SA.GAZ and Akkadian ha-bi-ru, both taken as the same people.[28] Since *ŭpr* occurs in both Egyptian and Ugaritic and the Akkadian can be read *ha-pî-ru,* the word is Anglicized as both "Ḫabiru" and "Ḫapiru." The earliest mention of the SA.GAZ or Ḫabiru occurs in a text from the Third Dynasty of Ur (*ca.* 2050); if the *ŭpr* and Ḫabiru are the same — which is not at all firmly established — references to the Ḫabiru can be found in Assyrian, Babylonian, Ugaritic, Egyptian, and Hittite texts for the next seven or eight hundred years.

Identification of the Ḫabiru with the Hebrews is tempting. However, it is impossible to interpret most references to the Ḫabiru as indicating the Hebrews. Moreover, the Ḫabiru are described as warriors, mercenaries, marauders, and caravaneers all over the ancient Near East — which does not fit the biblical picture of the Hebrews. If the Exodus was in 1446, then the Hebrews were in the wilderness of Sinai when Amenhotep II (1438-1412) was reporting from his campaign in Syria and Palestine the capture of 89,600 prisoners, among them 3,000 ŭApiru.[29] If it was in 1290, then the Hebrews were still slaves in Egypt at the time of Amenhotep. Neither case permits an easy identification.

The problem of the Ḫabiru cannot be solved here.[30] The important point is that identification of the Ḫabiru with the Hebrews is far from justified.[31]

Ḥerem, or Killing in the Name of Yahweh. According to the biblical narrative, when the Israelites captured Jericho, they burned the city, including all inhabitants except Rahab and her family (Josh. 6:24f.). They did the same at Ai (8:24, 29) and elsewhere. The word for this total destruction is *ḥerem* "devotion," and the verb may be translated "utterly destroyed" (cf. 6:17 "devoted to the LORD for destruction").

If the biblical presentation of this subject were couched in language implying that such "devotion" was practiced because the Israelites only thought the Lord wanted it (but God nowhere asked them to do it), the idea would still be disturbing. But it is stated several times explicitly that Joshua acted "as the LORD God of Israel commanded" or "as Moses the servant of the LORD had commanded" (10:40; 11:12; cf. Deut. 7:24).

The suggestion that God could command anyone to kill another or require the complete extermination of every living being in a city seems offensive or even outrageous. To dodge the problem some have proposed that the God (Yahweh) of the Old Testament cannot be the same as the Father of Jesus Christ of the New Testament. This, of course, runs counter to the teachings of Christ and the apostles, who clearly identify their God with the God of Abraham and Isaac and Jacob, and with the God who revealed himself to Moses and the prophets.

A partial answer to this puzzle is the fact that religious "devotion" was a part of the culture of the day. Ancient Near Eastern peoples "devoted" persons and possessions and captives to their gods. That such action was customary does not, of course, make it right, but it does help explain why the Israelites did not think it necessarily wrong. God takes the people where they are, and leads them step by step until at last they will be where God is. Divine revelation is progressive. At this point, the Israelites did not have as their Torah the Sermon on the Mount ("love your enemies"). This understanding of love had to wait for the New Joshua (Jesus) to make it known in his life and death.

But this is not the whole answer. The biblical position regarding the Canaanites is not simply "Exterminate them!" There is good reason behind the command. In Yahweh's eyes, the Canaanites with their culture and religion were exceedingly evil sinners, who not only committed abominations against God but also sought to entice Israel to join them in these "religious" acts. The discovery of Ugaritic documents at Ras Shamra in Syria has opened up detailed information about Canaanite religious practices. Religious prostitution, child sacrifice, and other features of this religion plagued Israel for centuries, as the books of Kings and of the early prophets bear witness.[32]

Yahweh, the Israelites were often reminded, is holy, a God who does not tolerate such abominable practices, especially in the name of serving a deity. This was idolatry against both creation and Creator. The Canaanites merited punishment. Further, the purity of Israelite religion had to be preserved. The sensual attractions of Canaanite religion (as at Baal-peor; Num. 25:1) posed a serious threat to Yahwistic life. A surgeon does not hesitate to remove an arm or a leg, or even a vital organ, when life is at stake. The very existence of Israel — and ultimately the salvation of the world — depended upon Yahweh's blessing.

Admittedly, this is only an interpretation and a partial attempt to justify the difficult biblical position. But there is the verdict of history. The Israelites, sickened by slaughter or seduced by sensual religious rites, ceased exterminating Canaanites, and Canaanite religious practices gradually pervaded Israelite religion. The punishment this brought upon Israel was terrible. Yahweh inflicted on them foreign oppression, invasion, destruction of Israelite cities, and the destruction of Jerusalem and exile from the promised land.

To repeat, Yahweh did not order the Israelites to exterminate all Gentiles but only the Canaanites. This policy was not a permanent or eternal principle.

It was intended for an immediate situation, when the Israelites were occupying the land God had promised their fathers. Later, the moral and ethical teachings of prophets such as Amos, Micah, and Isaiah would be presented just as stridently to Israel as the word of Yahweh. Still later Jesus Christ would claim that he came to fulfill the law and prophets. The "devotion" of the Canaanites in the land must be seen against all these factors.

Did Joshua Make the Sun Stand Still? Josh. 10:12f. reads:

On the day when the LORD gave the Amorites over to the Israelites, Joshua spoke to the LORD; and he said in the sight of Israel,

"Sun, stand still at Gibeon,
and Moon, in the valley of Aijalon."
And the sun stood still, and the moon stopped,
until the nation took vengeance on their enemies.

Is this not written in the Book of Jashar? The sun stopped in mid-heaven, and did not hurry to set for about a whole day.

At face value, the text says that the sun and moon stopped their movement across the sky for approximately an entire day. In folklore throughout the world, there are many legends of a day when the sun did not set. The question, though, is whether the occurrence of such a day is what the biblical passage actually signifies.

It is important for belief to be open to the possibility of miracles. We raise no doubt of God's ability to perform supernatural wonders. We ask the question of whether this passage teaches actually that the sun stood still.

The key clauses are poetry. In poetry, literal meanings often are replaced by figures of speech. Moreover, the translation quoted above is not precise. Words are added to make the language pleasing. Literally, it reads:

Sun on Gibeon be still,
And moon in the valley of Aijalon!
And the sun was still, and the moon stood. . . .

The verb translated "be still," as in English, can mean either "remain motionless" or "be quiet." Therefore it is an open question whether Joshua was asking the sun to "stand still" or "be still" (not shine forth its brilliant light and so expose the position of the Israelite troops). The words that follow in v. 13 ("The sun stopped in mid-heaven, and did not hurry to set for about a whole day") tend to support the meaning "stand still."[33]

Secondly, reference is made to "the Book of Jashar" (2 Sam. 1:18). Just what this was, who wrote it, and even how much of the passage in Joshua is taken from it, are unresolved questions. If this reference is to the words that

Excavations at Jericho, a city "devoted to the Lord for destruction" (Josh. 6:17).
(*Jericho Excavation Fund, photo Kathleen M. Kenyon*)

follow, then support for the interpretation "stand still" must be attributed to the Book of Jashar, a reminder that Joshua's book itself bears testimony to use of earlier sources by editors who were not themselves eyewitnesses.

Perhaps most to the point is the application of the principle that the Bible draws a moral relationship between the nature of miracle and the purpose for which it occurs. God does not perform miracles arbitrarily, but purposefully — to deliver his people, sustain them with food and water, heal them from the bites of serpents, or deliver them from their enemies. As a general observation, a relationship also exists between the magnitude of the miracle and its purpose. A miracle of cosmic proportion would be necessary to change the relationship between the earth and the sun in a twenty-four-hour period. Was such a tremendous and mysterious effort required to give Joshua the victory that day?

Not all scholars arrive at the same answer. But there is considerable agreement on a number of issues: (1) the context is "holy war," when Yahweh's power and might enable victory over outlandish odds; note the huge hailstones in the preceding verse (10:11); (2) Joshua's prayer was addressed to the Lord, not to sun and moon directly, which would have had the pagan overtones of acknowledging the celestial bodies as deities; (3) the call — quoted from the Book of Jashar with its poetic exuberance — was for prolonged relief either from the sun's heat or its illumination in order to assure Israel's opportunity for victory; (4) the call was answered with astonishing effectiveness — whether by another hailstorm, a heavy cloud cover, a partial eclipse or some other divinely ordered method.[34] Whatever happened — and something must have occurred — the faith of the Israelites was greatly strengthened with a victory that showed them clearly God was keeping with them his ancient promise.

Theological Insights in Joshua

The Promise-Keeping God. Centuries before, Yahweh had entered into a covenant with Abraham to give the land of Canaan to his descendants. This promise had been repeated to Isaac and Jacob, renewed to Moses, repeated to the Israelites in the wilderness, and again when Joshua was commissioned to lead them across the Jordan. Yahweh fought for Israel and gave them victory. When at last Joshua began to describe the boundaries of the tribal possessions, it was the fulfillment — in part — of Yahweh's promise. A considerable amount of land remained unconquered, but Yahweh promised to drive out the inhabitants before the people of Israel (13:2-7). As for the land already taken, he said: "Allot the land to Israel for an inheritance."

The concept of promise and fulfillment plays a large part in the story of Israel's faith. The story of how Yahweh delivered the Israelites from Egyptian slavery, sustained them in the wilderness, and gave them Canaan is remembered many times as the prophets seek to call the people back to their God.

The Covenantal Idea. The concept of the relationship between Yahweh and Israel as a covenant has been presented in preceding chapters. In Joshua the concept is worked out largely through the conquest of the land: "Thus the LORD gave to Israel all the land which he swore to give to their fathers" (21:43); "Not one of all the good promises that the LORD had made to the house of Israel had failed; all came to pass" (v. 45).[35]

Throughout the Old Testament, the land is a fundamental element in the character of the covenant. The Israelites were to obey the words of Yahweh that their days might be long in the land, and that there might be prosperity in the land. When idolatry and apostasy became serious problems, the prophets declared that, unless they repented, the people or seed would be driven out of the land. Then the word was given through the prophets that, because of his promise, Yahweh would cause a remnant to return. He would reestablish them in the land. During the Exile, this promise of restoration to the land was the basis for hope.   *devotion*

Likewise, the *ḥerem* (pp. 147, 776 n. 28) must be viewed within the context of Israel's prophetic outlook. Yahweh acted for Israel and against Israel's enemies because of his covenant promise with the fathers. In fact, this makes the idea of total destruction an understandable item in biblical religion, for the covenant's ultimate purpose is to provide for all the nations of the earth the knowledge of Yahweh and the covenant blessings. Anything or any person that would prevent the working out of this redemptive purpose for all peoples must be removed as an enemy of Yahweh.

The Achievement of Rest. One of the great concepts expressed in the book of Joshua, often embraced in the hymns of the Church, is that of the *rest,* from the pangs of slavery, the hardships of the wilderness, and the rigors of war (e.g., 1:13; 11:23). Israel was to live as God's own nation, a witness to the other nations, once they were established in Canaan. Israel failed in this when they were unable to rest in the God who had redeemed and created them for a new world. The prophets of the eighth century testify to Israel's breaches of the covenant relationship.

> Nevertheless, there is a rest for the people of God. This basic truth develops into a rich doctrine of future hope and blessing (e.g., 2 Sam. 7:1), with a heavenly place of rest from the rigors of the earthly pilgrimage. Jesus, the New Joshua, offered such rest to all who come to him (Matt. 11:28).

The author of Hebrews can speak of this "rest of the people of God" and draw his imagery from the wilderness experience and the settlement in the land of Canaan (Heb. 3:7–4:11) as it is narrated in the book of Joshua.

CHAPTER 11

Judges

With Joshua, the tribes of Israel occupy the land Yahweh had promised to the patriarchs. They subdue some of their enemies in the land, but not all. The struggle with their enemies will lead them to become a nation among the nations with a king among kings. But this will take two hundred years or more. The interval, when the tribes are learning to live together and to meet the problems of living with Canaanite cities in their midst and hostile nations on their borders, is known as "the period of the judges." The story is told in the book of Judges.

After an introductory portion (Judg. 1), which gives a sketchy summary of the conquest of Canaan and notes the portions still not conquered,[1] the story is resumed where it ended in Joshua:

> When Joshua dismissed the people, the Israelites all went to their own inheritances to take possession of the land. The people worshiped the LORD all the days of Joshua, and all the days of the elders who outlived Joshua, who had seen all the great work that the LORD had done for Israel. . . . Moreover, that whole generation was gathered to their ancestors, and another generation grew up after them, who did not know the LORD or the work that he had done for Israel . . . and they abandoned the LORD, the God of their ancestors, . . . they followed other gods, from among the gods of the peoples who were all around them, and bowed down to them. . . . Judg. 2:6-12

A central problem is immediately clear — the Israelites' forgetfulness of God's great acts for them and their forsaking of Yahweh for the gods of the Canaanites.

Central Concept

A common definition of what is called the "Deuteronomistic history" is not crucial at this point. What is important for our understanding of the Former Prophets is the fact that a definite concept of history was developing in the writing of Israel's story. According to this concept, what happened to Israel was specifically determined by Yahweh's response to Israel's faithfulness or lack of it. The words from 2:6-12 provide the background for this history in Judges.

Yahweh Tests Israel. Canaanites were left in the land. Joshua makes that clear, and Judges even more so. Why? The reason is given in a few words. Yahweh had brought his people from Egypt to fulfill the covenant. Part of this covenant is expressed by the "angel of the Lord": "You shall make no covenant with the inhabitants of this land; you shall break down their altars" (2:2); but Israel had disobeyed the Lord. Joshua's story of the conquest stresses the victories. But it is evident here also that many cities were not conquered and many altars were left standing. Thus, the angel of the Lord continues: "I will not drive them out before you; but they shall become adversaries to you and their gods shall be a snare to you" (2:3). The disobedience of the Israelites becomes then the means by which God brings his people to a deeper understanding of his covenant relationship to Israel. The testing (see 3:1, 4) will demonstrate clearly the twofold truth that Yahweh is faithful even though his people are not and that, when they call upon him he will save them from the curses that their disobedience has warranted (Deut. 27–29).

What Is a "Judge"? The book takes its name from the eleven or twelve persons in its pages who "judged" Israel. Having read the account of the giving of the law on Sinai, one might easily conclude that the judges were officials appointed to try the people for violating that law. But these persons, except on rare occasions, do not at all resemble the modern concept of a judge; their main task was not to hear complaints or make legal decisions. The elders or family heads usually did so in the social sphere, while priests were the final interpreters of religious law. The Judges with whom we have to do here were leaders or military deliverers.[2]

Ch. 3 furnishes a useful paradigm (pattern or model) for understanding succeeding accounts of the Judges. Israelites are seen dwelling among the peoples of the land. They intermarry with the outsiders, and then serve their pagan gods (vv. 5f.). This evil intermingling kindles Yahweh's anger against the people. He brings against them Cushan-rishathaim, a ruler from northeast

Syria, who presses them into his service for eight years (vv. 7f.). Then the Israelites cry to Yahweh, who raises up for them a Judge or "deliverer," Othniel, brother of Caleb. "The Spirit of the LORD came upon him and he judged Israel; he went out to war, and the LORD gave Cushan-rishathaim king of Aram (Syria) into his hand" (vv. 9f.). Then the land "had rest" (v. 11). This pattern is followed in the stories of other Judges:

> The people "do evil" by serving other gods.
> Yahweh sends a nation to oppress them.
> The people cry to Yahweh.
> He raises up a deliverer.
> The oppressor is defeated.
> The people have rest.

Not all parts of this pattern are mentioned in every Judges story, but the pattern is about the same each time (cf. vv. 12-30; 4:1-24; 5:31b).

The Judge was a charismatic leader, not selected officially by the people but raised up by Yahweh. God's Spirit came to empower the Judge to deal with a particular situation. He was not a king and did not establish a dynasty or ruling family. The Judge was the person — man or woman (Deborah was one of them; chs. 4–5) — chosen by Yahweh to drive out the oppressor and give rest to the land and people.

Outline

Summary of the conquest of Canaan (1:1–2:5)
    Judah and Simeon (1:1-21)
    House of Joseph and Bethel (vv. 22-26)
    Canaanite enclaves (vv. 27-36)
    Angel of Yahweh at Bochim (2:1-5)
Israel in the period of the Judges, to the death of Gideon (2:6–8:35)
    Death of Joshua; the new generation (2:6-10)
    Reason for Judges (vv. 11-19)
    Reason for leaving Canaanites in the land (2:20–3:6)
    Oppression by Cushan-rishathaim; deliverance by Othniel (3:7-11)
    Oppression by Eglon; deliverance by Ehud (vv. 12-30)

Historical Background

A political vacuum had resulted from the long struggle between the Egyptians and the Hittites (Chapter 10, above). Other features may be noted in our efforts to understand this pivotal period.

Migration of Peoples. In the latter part of the second millennium, population movements in southeastern Europe and southwestern Asia seriously disturbed the distribution of peoples that had prevailed for centuries. The Minoan and Mycenean culture of Crete and the Peloponnesus was brought to an end. Invaders in Asia Minor destroyed the Hittite capital and pushed the Hittites[3] eastward into Syria.

Key players in the drama were the Sea Peoples. They left their coastal homes in Greece, Asia Minor, and the Aegean islands (notably Crete, biblical Caphtor), and flooded the southeastern coast of the Mediterranean in a series of invasions.

They also contributed to the collapse of the Hittite and Ugaritic kingdoms. Although Rameses III was able to repel their raid on the Egyptian coast during the eighth year of his reign (*ca.* 1188), they met no similar resistance in Canaan. The Philistines from Caphtor (cf. Amos 9:7) settled on the southern end of the maritime plain in Palestine. These non-Semitic invaders rapidly established five strongholds: Gaza, Ashkelon, Ashdod, Gath, and Ekron — names found many times in Judges and Samuel. This league of cities, "the Philistine pentapolis," represented a united threat with which the loosely knit Israelite tribes were unable to cope. The "Samson cycle" (13:1–16:31) features the Philistines.[4]

The migrations in southeastern Europe and the eastern Mediterranean involved mainly Indo-European peoples, though from time to time there were incursions of Semites from the Arabian desert. Available evidence suggests an invasion of the Transjordanian region in the thirteenth century, resulting in the establishment of Edom, Moab, and Ammon. The Israelites, in journeying from Kadesh-barnea to Moab under Moses, had problems with the Edomites and Moabites; and in the period of the Judges they were oppressed by the Moabites and Ammonites. The Midianites were in the area earlier and appear to have been tolerated by the Moabites — indeed, the Moabite king solicited their cooperation against the Israelites (Num. 22:4); later the camel-borne Midianites engaged in a protracted series of raids on Israel (Judg. 6:1-6). They were likely a nomadic people from east of the Gulf of Aqaba, who roamed the region, as do Bedouin today.[5]

Introduction of the Iron Age. The Iron Age in the Middle East begins *ca.* 1200. Widespread application of the newly discovered means of refining iron ore and manufacturing iron tools and weapons brought an end to the preceding Bronze Age (bronze being a mixture of copper and tin). The Hebrew word for iron *(barzel)* is apparently borrowed from Hittite; iron metallurgy seems to have been introduced in the district of Kizzuwatna, in the eastern Hittite empire. Probably as early as 1400 (prior to the Hittite conquest of the Mitanni *ca.* 1370), Mitannian kings sent presents of iron objects to Egyptian pharaohs. The early references to iron in the Old Testament include the iron bedstead (or sarcophagus) of Og, king of Bashan (Deut. 3:11, if properly interpreted), the iron-rimmed chariot-wheels of the Canaanites (Josh. 17:16) and of Sisera (Judg. 4:3), and the Philistine monopoly of iron metallurgy (1 Sam. 13:19, 22). However, the monopoly enjoyed by the Hittites and later the Philistines was soon broken. By the twelfth century, iron was a commodity in the Middle East.[6]

Canaan and Its Peoples. Largely a land of mountains and valleys (see pp. 620-28), Palestine was better suited to house a large number of small city-states than an integrated people, for it engendered isolation rather than communication. Among the nations left in the land to test the Israelites were "the Canaanites, the Hittites, the Amorites, the Perizzites, the Hivites, and the Jebusites" (3:5). What is really known about these peoples?

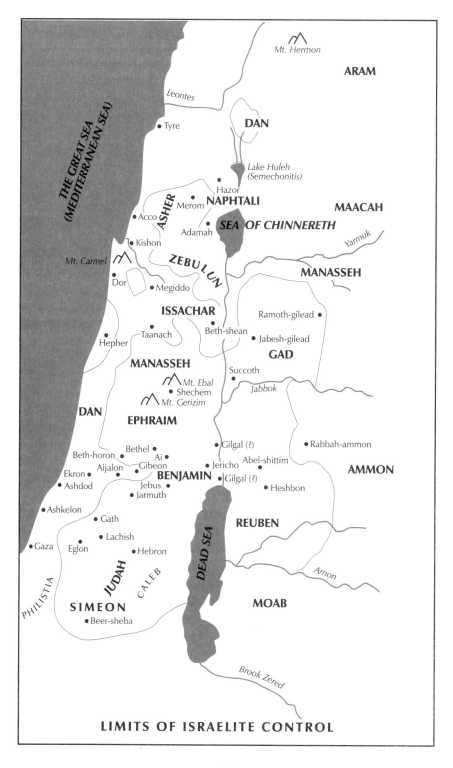

LIMITS OF ISRAELITE CONTROL

"Canaanite" is an imprecise term, used sometimes in the larger sense of all who lived in Canaan, and sometimes with reference to a particular people (compare Josh. 7:9 and 11:3). When finally the Israelites became dominant in Palestine, the center of Canaanite population shifted to what is now Lebanon, and the term "Phoenician" came to be applied to them.[7] It has been credibly suggested that an amalgamation of Amorite nomads with the previously existing culture in the region around Byblos resulted in the people known as Canaanites; they migrated to Palestine *ca.* 2300.[8]

As for the "Amorites," Babylonian sources refer to a people with the same name who came from the land of Amurru, whose capital was at Mari on the Euphrates. They invaded southern Mesopotamia very early in the second millennium and founded an Amorite dynasty at Isin and Larsa. Hammurabi, whose name shows Amorite connections, conquered Mari, and soon thereafter the Hittites brought an end to the Amorite dynasty. Amorites occupied city-states in Syria, according to the Amarna letters. They were in both Palestine and Transjordan (Judg. 10:8; 11:19ff.).[9]

Still fewer data exist for the other peoples. The Jebusites were the inhabitants of Jerusalem (1:21). The Perizzites are mentioned many times, but nothing is known about them. Possibly the name meant those who did not live in walled cities. The Hivites settled at Mt. Lebanon (3:3), Mt. Hermon (Josh. 11:3), along the route from Sidon to Beersheba (2 Sam. 24:7), and in the Gibeonite cities (Josh. 9:7; 11:19). Many times, confusion of the Hivites with the Horites occurs within accounts or between the Hebrew and Greek texts; sometimes these terms are also confused with "Hittites." The three words are quite similar in Hebrew writing.

The Hittites are mentioned in the Old Testament as early as patriarchal times, but no record exists of Hittite movements into Syria until about the twelfth century. The term "Hittite," however, needs definition. The original Hittites (Hatti or Proto-Hittites) and the later "Hittites" who invaded the land of the Hatti (*ca.* 2000) were not the same people. Furthermore, the Hyksos penetration of Egypt (*ca.* 1700) was accomplished by a mixture of peoples, some of whom were Indo-Europeans (as were the Hittites). When the Hyksos were expelled from Egypt (*ca.* 1570), it is not unlikely that some settled in Palestine. Some of the peoples mentioned in the biblical account as inhabitants of Canaan may have been there as a result of this Indo-European movement through the land.[10]

Centrifugal Situation in Israel. Putting together these various elements helps to clarify the picture of Israel in the time of the Judges. The geography, continuing struggles with the other inhabitants, and internal tensions between strong personalities all tended to segregate the tribes. The loosely related tribes were comprised of groupings of villages, each occupied by several clans that, in turn, were composed of extended and nuclear families. The closest ties were based on kinship, and the social structures were more egalitarian than hierarchical. There was no national structure in any modern sense. Archaeological evidence from the early Iron Age suggests that "highland villages reflect the essential social structure of early Israel — almost precisely as the book of Judges . . . has faithfully preserved it in the written record."[11]

Some scholars have applied the Greek concept of "amphictyony"[12] to Israel. The term describes a very loose association of twelve tribes unified only by the single sanctuary located at Shiloh. Use of the term "amphictyony" is questionable, for the ark and its palladium (tent-shrine) at Shiloh play little if any part in Judges. The unifying factor, rather, is the concept that Yahweh, who made a covenant with his people, was willing whenever they turned to him to act repeatedly on their behalf by raising up judges or deliverers.

Chronology of Judges. The book of Judges contains references to numerous periods of time. For example, after the deliverance from Cushan-rishathaim (3:10), the land had "rest" for 40 years (v. 11). Then the people sinned again and were delivered into the hand of Eglon, king of Moab, for 18 years (v. 14). The Israelites cried to the Lord, who delivered them by sending Ehud, and the land had rest for 80 years (v. 30). The references to time in Judges total 410 years. Adding to this the years for the invasion of the land and the years between the end of Samson's judgeship and the beginning of Solomon's temple yields a figure close to the dates obtained on the basis of 1 Kgs. 6:1 — *ca.* 1440 for the Exodus and *ca.* 1400 for the entrance into Canaan.[13]

There are, as previously noted, serious obstacles to accepting these dates (see Ch. 4). If the entrance into Canaan took place *ca.* 1250, what is to be done with the figures in Judges? Two different approaches have been attempted. In one, the figures are taken as "round numbers," since 40, 80, and 20 occur several times. Interspersed with them, however, are others — 18, 8, 7, 3, 6. Moreover, even "round" numbers must mean something; 410 hardly can be reduced to about 200 and numbers still be taken seriously.[14]

A second approach is to look upon the periods of oppression and the judgeships as local and overlapping. The nations that oppressed Israel were situated on various sides or in different parts of Canaan. Jabin "king of Canaan" ruled Hazor in the north; the conflict was in the Plain of Esdraelon (4:2-4) and only a few northern tribes were involved (vv. 6-10). The Midianite attacks came from the east (6:3), and, although their raiding extended to Gaza (v. 4), the conflict took place in the valley of Jezreel (Esdraelon) and involved northern tribes (vv. 34f.). The Ammonite oppression was in Gilead in Transjordan; it then extended into central Palestine (10:8f.), but Jephthah was from Gilead (11:1), and the conflict was in Transjordan (vv. 29-33). The oppression of the Philistines, when Samson was judge, was localized in the southwest. The judges were raised up to meet more or less regional situations; if so, the period of "rest" in one region overlapped the "oppression" in another.

Authorship and Composition

Author. Nowhere does the book give any indication of its author. According to Jewish tradition, it was written by Samuel. As with Joshua, there are both earlier and later elements in Judges.[15] Scholars agree that the Song of Deborah is among the earliest portions of the Old Testament,[16] but after this there is considerable debate over the redactional processes in the book.[17]

Composition. It is often assumed that a period in which the stories of the Judges were told by word of mouth (twelfth to tenth centuries) was followed by a time when some or most were put in written form (tenth and ninth centuries). To these were added editorial comments (e.g., "in those days there was no king") and further stories not always in the same form or location in the Greek version (e.g., the story of Shamgar). Editing may have continued through the eighth and seventh centuries. As part of the "Deuteronomistic history," Judges, along with Joshua, Samuel, and Kings, probably was put in final form about the sixth century.[18]

Careful study of Judges points up different styles; compare the Gideon story, for example, with the Samson cycle. These evident differences tend to support the theory that the stories were composed by different authors and transmitted in different forms; the final "author" or "editor" made no substantial effort to conform them to a uniform style.

Religious Questions

Deceit and Treachery. Several stories contain elements that may be taken as morally offensive. Ehud carries tribute to Eglon king of Moab, then sends the bearers away, saying: "I have a secret message for you, O king." Since Ehud is left-handed, he can hide his sword under his garment on his right thigh, where it will not be detected. He seizes it suddenly, attacks the king, and escapes (3:15-25).

When Sisera is fleeing Deborah and Barak, Jael gives him refuge in her tent; she gives him milk and covers him with a rug. After asking her to stand watch, he takes a nap. Jael thereupon takes a tent peg and mallet and drives the peg through his skull (4:17-21).

Only when the biblical characters are viewed as being "on our side" can such incidents be rationalized. Nothing is to be gained by attempting to justify such behavior. As God recognized, these people were doing what they thought was right (Judg. 21:25). But obviously they had much to learn, and through the prophets and apostles God has freely displayed a willingness to continue to teach his people.

Mt. Tabor, where Barak gathered the forces of Zebulun
and Naphtali to fight Sisera. *(Neal and Joel Bierling)*

Jephthah and His Daughter. When Jephthah is called upon to deliver Gilead
from the Ammonites, he makes a vow to Yahweh: "If you will give the Ammonites into my hand, then whoever comes out of the doors of my house to
meet me, when I return victorious from the Ammonites, shall be the Lord's,
to be offered up by me as a burnt offering" (11:30f.). Upon his return his
daughter, his only child, comes out to meet him. He fulfills his vow (vv. 34-39).

Although he may be judged by modern standards, Jephthah was not
brought up under those standards. He was a Gileadite, and the non-Israelites
in that region in that day followed Chemosh, whose worship included the
sacrifice of children as burnt offerings (2 Kgs. 3:27). According to our understanding of progressive revelation, God takes people where they are and leads
them to a more complete knowledge of his person and will. It is difficult for
us to understand how Jephthah could be a worshipper of Yahweh — even
more, a deliverer raised up by Yahweh — and still practice what is later described as an "abominable act." Yahweh had not asked him to make such a
vow, or any vow at all, according to the biblical account. It was an impulsive
act on Jephthah's part, made with good intention. The significant fact is that
even though the Israelites came to regard child sacrifice as an abomination in
Yahweh's eyes, they did not remove this story from their sacred Scriptures.
Lessons can be learned even from well-intentioned mistakes.

162

Samson's Exploits. What is to be made of a man who cavorted with Philistine women and finally let the woman who had betrayed him three times know the secret of his strength (ch. 16)? Can the story be dismissed as a "solar myth," as some have done, or Samson's deeds compared with the legendary labors of Hercules?[19]

The story of Samson's birth is somewhat similar to that of Samuel (1 Sam. 1). It comes as the result of the prayer and faith of his parents. At birth he is dedicated as a Nazirite (cf. Num. 6), specifically bound to the instruction that no razor should come upon his head (Judg. 13:5; 16:17). Yahweh blesses the child, and the Spirit is in him (13:24f.). After that, the story becomes somewhat bizarre. Samson demands that his father arrange a marriage with a Philistine girl. ("His father and mother did not know that this was from the LORD; for he was seeking a pretext to act against the Philistines" [14:4].) Before the ceremony is over, the wedding gives way to the first of his personal campaigns against the Philistines (vv. 10-20). Following several other exploits, the story of Samson and Delilah presents the tragic end of Samson. By Delilah's deceit and collusion with the Philistine "lords"[20] and by Samson's folly or stupidity, the secret of his great strength is discovered. His hair is cut while he sleeps. His strength gone, the Philistines are able to bind Samson, put out his eyes, and imprison him. But they unwisely let his hair grow, and, in a final burst of strength accompanied by a cry to Yahweh, Samson collapses a Philistine temple by pulling away the pillars that support the roof, killing himself and a large number of Philistines (16:18-31).

The story of Samson certainly illustrates no New Testament ethic! But Samson, too, is a child of his day. Moreover, he was selfish and showed little or no control of his passions. One author describes him as "a negative religious hero — an example of what God's charismatic individual should not be."[21] But aspects of Samson's life and ministry should be viewed positively as well. For instance, Samson trusts in Yahweh and is put in such situations precisely for the purpose of punishing the Philistines. In the book of Hebrews Samson is named as one of the great heroes of faith (11:32ff.). Again, the contingency of history and the freedom of God's place in its development does not allow us either to idealize its character or conceive of it as absolutely free from God's command.

Theological Contributions

God Is the Savior. Though the judges are called "savior," obviously in the mind of the authors of the book God is the Savior. (Cf. the view presented in Isaiah, pp. 303-4.) Yahweh hears the cry of the people, and on each occasion endows a judge with the Holy Spirit in order to deliver the people from their enemies.

One lesson from the lives of the judges is that those who are dedicated to Yahweh can be used by Yahweh. Elements in their lives may not be in keeping with the Lord's will. Their methods may not stand up as exemplary. But these matters can be resolved by later revelation of Yahweh's person and will. Something to censure can be found in almost everyone mentioned in Heb. 11, or, for that matter, in the Old Testament — and certainly in Judges. Nonetheless, because of their dedication, Yahweh, the Savior, could use them to deliver Israel from its oppressors and to keep the tribal federation alive until Israel was ready for the next stage in his redemptive purpose.

View of History. The work of the "Deuteronomistic historian"[22] in Judges is often identified with the following pattern: sin brings punishment, but repentance brings deliverance and peace.

> The basic assumption of this pattern, which the longer stories in Judges seem to follow, is that Yahweh is sovereign. He uses non-Israelite peoples in Palestine and surrounding areas to punish the Israelites for their idolatry and concomitant practices. He raises up deliverers when his people turn to him, and endues them with the Spirit's power, so they can overcome the enemy and find peace in the land once more.

The lessons are positive, but begin from the negative position of unbelief and idolatry. The stories are told to arm Israel against apostasy, explain why Israel's enemies sometimes triumph, and create prophetic hope in Israel.

Monarchy. Is the book of Judges a low-key apology for the Davidic monarchy? The statement "there was no king in Israel in those days" (17:6; 18:1; 19:1; 21:25) links the writing to a time when there was a king and contrasts the days under the Monarchy with those prior to it. Perhaps this prepares for understanding the Monarchy in its unique role whereby the central shrine is perpetuated where Israel may come and do what is right in God's eyes. There, Yahweh's covenant with his people may be repeatedly emphasized and renewed. It is out of the spiritual and social chaos in the period of judges, then, that we may begin to understand the responsibility of Israel's kings and of the Messiah, who would come after them: "He shall judge the people with equity" (Ps. 72:2; Isa. 11:4).

164

CHAPTER 12

Birth of the Monarchy
(1 Sam. 1:1–2 Sam. 5:10)

Introduction

The period of Israel's history described in 1-2 Samuel and 1 Kgs. 1–11 displays sweeping changes in political, social, and religious life. Beginning in the arid era of the judges when there was no king in Israel, the period ends with Solomon's empire in full bloom. Israel begins as a loose, flexible coalition of tribes unified by certain ethnic and social ties but even more strongly by a common faith in Yahweh. By the close of the period Israel is the strongest nation in western Asia. In 1 Samuel, people make pilgrimages to the simple shrine of Eli at Shiloh. By 1 Kgs. 11 they hold their feasts in an elaborately designed royal temple whose construction and maintenance have sorely taxed their resources and good will. The record of these startling changes centers in the story of four people: Samuel, Saul, David, and Solomon. The spotlight shines most brightly on David. The accounts of Samuel and Saul are prologue and those of Solomon's feats and follies are epilogue. It is David's rise to the throne and his struggle to keep it that dominates the plot.

Originally one book, 1-2 Samuel was probably divided early in the Christian era; perhaps the division was first made in the LXX, which treats Samuel and Kings as parts of a unified work called the book of Kingdoms.[1] The tragic death of Saul marks the division between 1-2 Samuel. The division is clearly arbitrary since David's response is recorded in 2 Sam. 1. The division between 2 Samuel and 1 Kings also is artificial: the story of Solomon's rise to power and David's last days in 1 Kgs. 1–2 is linked in style and contents to 2 Sam.

> The LORD! His adversaries shall be shattered;
>   the Most High will thunder in heaven.
> The LORD will judge the ends of the earth;
>   he will give strength to his king,
>   and exalt the power of his anointed. 1 Sam. 2:10

9–24. As with the Pentateuch, size seems to have prompted the divisions between some of the books.

Jewish tradition names Samuel as author of these books,[2] but they more likely bear his name because of his dominant role in the first twenty-five chapters. He may have been responsible for some of the material in 1 Samuel, especially the early history of David, as 1 Chr. 29:29f. suggests:

> Now the acts of King David, from first to last, are written in the records of the seer Samuel and in the records of the prophet Nathan and in the records of the seer Gad, with accounts of all his rule and his might and of the events that befell him and Israel and all the kingdoms of the earth.

This passage is a reminder that the ancient editors had several sources at their disposal.[3]

Many attempts have been made to trace the influence of the Yahwist and the Elohist in 1-2 Samuel,[4] but the difficulties inherent in the documentary hypothesis are even more impressive here. Recent studies of Samuel have therefore tended to stress the background and origin of various sections of the book rather than to look for parallel strands dovetailed by an editor.[5] Stories of events in the lives of Samuel, Saul, and David as well as accounts that feature the Ark of the Covenant have been woven into cycles or sections that carry forward the narrative from the time of the Judges to the establishment of David's kingdom.

A typical summary of the stages and components of the narrative goes like this:

- Early stories of Samuel (1 Sam. 1:1–4:1a)
- Ark as centerpiece of Israelite life (4:1b–7:2)
- Beginnings of monarchy featuring Saul (7:3–15:35)
- David's entrance and rise to power (1 Sam. 16–2 Sam. 5:10)
- David's power and dynasty consolidated (2 Sam. 5:11–8:18)
- David's struggles to maintain power; his personal failure and family opposition (chs. 9–20)

- Epilogue: David's successes and failures;[6] God's judgment and pardon (chs. 21–24)

1-2 Samuel refer to sources, although so cryptically as to be of little help. 1 Sam. 10:25 depicts the kingmaker Samuel recording the rights and duties of kingship in a book, while 2 Sam. 1:18 cites the book of Jashar, familiar from Josh. 10. When these stories were combined is a moot question, and the editor's identity is just as vexing. In contrast with Judges and especially Kings, the editorial framework is scarcely discernible, with a maximum of straightforward narration and a minimum of interpreting or exhorting.[7] Because the final author rarely intruded his own observations, the stories frequently have a remarkable firsthand freshness and often the unblurred perspective of an eyewitness. Apart from minor alterations, the cycles seem to date close to the end of David's reign.[8] They may, however, have been recast under prophetic influence after the failure of monarchic rule became more clear. As with Judges and Kings, the compiler and editor was strongly influenced by a prophetic view of history and selected and shaped his material so as to highlight the role of Samuel and Nathan in dealing with Saul and David. In so doing he showed that the kings of Israel were obligated to be sensitive to the prophets, who interpreted the covenant for the nation.[9]

The debate that dominates current discussions of Samuel turns on the appropriate methods for investigating the books.[10] Crucial to the discussion is whether the work is to be treated as historical record of actual events or literary account of traditional memories and reconstructions. Several major recent commentaries have paid close attention to archaeological, linguistic, and cultural clues that argue for a strong historical basis for the stories.[11] Other approaches have focused on the literary characteristic of the narrative, with separate analyses of the stories of Samuel, Saul, and David.[12] One scholar, at least, has named *entertainment* as the narrator's chief purpose.[13] Both the historical and the literary approaches have benefited measurably from interaction with sociology and anthropology. These disciplines have shed light on clan and tribal structures, political practices, and in general the social world reflected in the documents.[14] Happily we do not have to choose any of these methods to the neglect of the others. We can acknowledge that we are dealing with documents that combine solid historical memory and even written records contemporary with the events with skilled literary artistry and accurate reflections of the social worlds both of the events themselves and the later periods when the documents were being compiled.

Samuel — Priest, Prophet, Judge (1 Sam. 1–7)

Perhaps the greatest Old Testament figure since Moses, Samuel played a pivotal role in the crucial transition from tribal coalition to monarchy. He was the last of the judges and the guiding light in the establishment of the kingship. A true charismatic leader, he embodied the great offices of his time. Nothing that happened among the tribes was beyond his concern. Acting in a variety of capacities, he served the tribes faithfully when the external pressures brought upon Israel by the Philistines called for far-reaching social and political changes. To his credit, Samuel was able to shape Israel's future while still clinging to and insisting on their ancient covenant practices.

Samuel's Childhood (1:1–3:21). (1) Pious Hannah (1:1–2:11). Judges gives a picture of almost unrelieved darkness. Apart from sporadic revivals in times of invasion and oppression, the scene was gloomy. Yet Israel's historic ideals were not completely neglected. The book of Ruth and the account of Samson's parents (Judg. 13) show that piety and family loyalty were not altogether absent. Hannah's story gives an even clearer look at the brighter side of this bleak time.

Among the annual pilgrims to the central shrine at Shiloh[15] in central Palestine, about midway between Shechem and Bethel, were Elkanah of Ephraim and his wives, Hannah and Peninnah. There seems to be ample evidence of a central sanctuary at Shiloh from the time of settlement until its destruction by the Philistines in Samuel's day. Although the feast which drew Elkanah and his wives is not identified, it was most likely the autumn harvest celebration, the feast of Booths (or Tabernacles; Lev. 23:33-36; Deut. 16:13, 15).[16] The festivals during this period do not appear elaborate. An atmosphere of simplicity hangs over the whole story: no bustling temple complex, but a modest shrine managed by a priest, Eli, and his two sons, Hophni and Phinehas. Hannah had ready access to the chief priest, and he took personal interest in her circumstances.

Many interpreters read this simplicity as evidence that Exodus, Leviticus, and Numbers picture much later developments, namely postexilic religious patterns.[17] Another possibility is that this simplicity reflects the general degradation of a period when there was almost no central authority to enforce the laws. In such times the pious of the land did their best to preserve the spirit if not the letter of the law.

The story focuses on Hannah's distress at not being able to obey the "imperative of fruitfulness," distress compounded by her rival's scornful chidings. Her plight resembles Sarah's (Gen. 16:1ff.; 21:9ff.) but was even more vexing; whereas Hagar was a slave wife, Peninnah had full marital status. As was customary for Israelites in desperate need, Hannah made a strong vow to the Lord (1 Sam. 1:11). She may have considered her husband's sacrifice as a votive offering (cf. Lev. 7:11ff.). If so, Elkanah's sacrifice was a festive occasion, accompanied by eating and drinking (v. 9).[18] Hannah's pledge seems to indicate her intention to consecrate her son as a Nazirite: "He shall drink neither wine nor intoxicants, and no razor shall touch his head."[19]

This vow is an appropriate introduction to Samuel, who stood firmly throughout his life for Israel's historic standards in the face of compromise and indifference. To be a Nazirite meant to maintain the ancient way, favoring the semi-nomadic simplicity of earlier generations over the sophisticated influence of Canaan.[20] Amos (2:11f.) may have had Samuel in mind when he mentioned Nazirites as messengers from God who were nonetheless unheeded by the people.

Hannah's silent praying caught Eli's eye (1 Sam. 1:12ff.). The Israelites, like most Orientals, typically prayed aloud regardless of the circumstances ("I cry aloud to the LORD"; Ps. 3:4; "Hear my voice, O God"; 64:1). Israelite worship must have been quite exuberant, but Hannah was in no such mood. Eli's rebuke for what he interpreted to be drunkenness may indicate either the rarity of silent prayer or the frequent drunken excesses of these ceremonies. The Canaanites regularly turned ritual into orgy, and the Israelites were prone to do the same, as prophets like Hosea (e.g., 4:11, 17f.) indicate.

When Hannah's prayer was answered by Samuel's birth,[21] she made no pilgrimage to Shiloh until she had weaned him, probably at age three.[22] Then she brought him to Eli and dedicated him to the service of the Lord with what was probably a thank offering (Lev. 7:11ff.).

The power and beauty of Hannah's prayer (1 Sam. 2:1-10) has evoked praise. The prayer shows that devout Israelites did not necessarily compose their own prayers but used established patterns, which they may have altered to suit their needs. Hannah's prayer is based on a song of thanksgiving for success in battle (cf. "the bows of the mighty," v. 4; destruction of adversaries, v. 10). So great was her victory over Peninnah and others who mocked her barrenness that she expressed strong jubilation and derided those who had made fun of her. By mentioning the anointed king (v. 10) the author gives a clear hint of Samuel's future role in the formation of the monarchy.

(2) Eli's wicked sons (2:12-36). Representative of the toll Canaanite corruption had taken on Israel's values were Phinehas and Hophni, the sons of Eli. They flaunted the laws limiting the priests' share of the sacrifice (vv. 13-17), even demanding pieces of meat before the sacrificer offered it. Furthermore, they fornicated with the female attendants at the shrine. Whether or not this was sacred prostitution, such conduct was repulsive to pilgrims who brought the abominable news to Eli (vv. 22-25).

The doom of Eli's sons was announced to him by a nameless prophet, "a man of God" (vv. 27ff.), perhaps one of the itinerant prophets active during this period (e.g., 10:5ff.).

169

This section is connected with the preceding by the mention of Hannah's annual visits, her loving ministries to Samuel, and continued fruitfulness in bearing children (vv. 18-21). It anticipates the following section by noting Samuel's faithfulness before the Lord (vv. 18, 21, 26),[23] in marked contrast to the depravity of Eli's sons.

(3) Samuel's call (3:1-21). The prophetic influence discernible in parts of 1-2 Samuel stands out in the emphasis on the Lord's call (vv. 1, 7, 19, 21). Samuel was dedicated to priestly service by his mother, in keeping with Israel's custom of consecrating the firstborn to the Lord in memory of the rescue of the firstborn in Egypt (Exod. 13:2, 15). Perhaps to make the practice easier to keep, the Mosaic laws substituted the tribe of Levi for the firstborn of all the tribes (cf. Num. 3:11ff.). Hannah, however, felt so keenly her obligation to God that she conformed to the tradition literally.[24] This chapter announces the expansion of Samuel's ministry from mere priestly apprenticeship to full prophetic office. The story of the voice which Samuel mistook for Eli's shows that Samuel had a direct call from God to be a prophet.[25] This experience, which ushered in a new era of prophetic activity, may be compared with Moses' burning bush or the visions of Isaiah, Jeremiah, and Ezekiel. Samuel had heard the voice of God. He was never the same afterward, and Israel knew it (v. 20).

The Philistines and the Ark (4:1–7:17). (1) Capture of the ark (4:1–7:2). Much of the Philistine strength lay in their skill in metallurgy. Whether iron or bronze, their weaponry proved more than a match for Israel's.[26] The conflict between the two peoples was spasmodic for a century or more. By the time of Samuel (*ca.* 1050 B.C.) the invaders had mustered sufficient strength to indulge their lust for conquest. Though probably not numerous themselves, they incorporated numbers of Canaanites into their disciplined, well-equipped fighting units. For these Canaanites, the Philistine invasion had not meant the loss of liberty. Rather, it marked a transfer of allegiance from the Egyptian pharaohs of the Eighteenth through Twentieth Dynasties.

When the Philistines finally attacked Israel, they were not to be denied. The Israelites lost the initial skirmish and four thousand troops (4:1-4). They then called for the spiritual support of the ark of the covenant. They did this perhaps to remind Yahweh, who allowed if not caused their defeat (v. 3), of his covenant loyalty to them. But the ark served more to spark the Philistines to fever pitch than to bolster the sagging hopes of Israel. Israel lost thirty thousand men, Phinehas and Hophni (whose death the man of God had predicted), and the ark (vv. 5-11). The news overwhelmed the aged Eli, who died when he heard it (vv. 12-18). Phinehas' widow wrote the epitaph for Israel's faded hopes after this stunning defeat when she named her son Ichabod — "No glory"; for the glory of God departed when the ark fell into Philistine hands (vv. 19-22).

The Philistines, however, got more than they had bargained for. When their idol Dagon collapsed before the ark, their cities refused to welcome the ark (5:1-10).[27] An epidemic, apparently bubonic plague, followed. The chastened Philistines prepared a guilt offering of five golden objects shaped like tumors and five golden mice and dispatched the ark to Beth-shemesh in Israelite territory (5:11–6:21). Probably the mice and the tumors, suggestive of the plague, are to be connected with sympathetic magic, in which persons craft a representation of the curse they want to avoid or the blessing they want to attain.

This section (4:1–7:1a) along with 2 Sam. 6 may have originally circulated as an independent set of stories about the importance of Yahweh's ark. If so it has now been artfully woven in the Samuel-Saul narrative.[28]

(2) Judgeship of Samuel (7:3-17). Though no record exists in Samuel, Shiloh was probably destroyed in a Philistine raid and its shrine demolished. Parts of the town were rebuilt and survived into the sixth century,[29] but remnants of the destruction were known to Jeremiah, who used it to warn against false trust in the security afforded by the Jerusalem temple (7:12; 26:6;

Ein Gedi, where the outlaw David sought refuge from the pursuit of King Saul.
(Neal and Joel Bierling)

171

cf. Ps. 78:60). That the ark, after seven months among the Philistines (1 Sam. 6:1), remained for twenty years (7:2) at Kiriath-jearim (where it had been brought from Beth-shemesh) may be added testimony that the shrine at Shiloh had been leveled.[30]

It was after these crushing defeats from the Philistines that Samuel came into his own as a judge. Like his noble predecessors, Deborah, Barak, Gideon, and Shamgar, he rallied the people to repentance (vv. 3-9). The Lord routed the Philistines at Mizpah, apparently by sending a thunderstorm to confuse their troops; the Israelites then recovered confidence in their God and both held the Philistines at bay and recaptured much of their lost territory. This passage (vv. 3-17), which reads like an episode in Judges, is the last glimpse of the old order. Clamor for a king was growing.

Samuel and Saul — Time of Transition (1 Sam. 8:1–15:35)

The pressure of Philistine opposition called for a new tactic from Israel. Neither the aging Samuel nor his irresponsible sons could provide the leadership the times demanded. The threat of the highly organized Philistine communities could be answered only in kind. Israel needed a king.[31]

Quest for a King (8.1–12:25). (1) Monarchy versus theocracy. The request of Israel's elders for a king was greeted with mixed emotions. Some passages seem to oppose the idea (8:1-22; 10:17-19; 12:1-25), others favor it (9:1–10:16; 10:20–11:15). One explanation holds that two documents with contrasting attitudes toward kingship have been combined by an editor who made no attempt to smooth out the apparent contradictions.[32]

Such an approach runs like this:

> It seems more probable that the two opinions [for and against calling a king] were in fact alive at the same time. The two opinions reflect a genuine dispute and a genuine probe of a serious issue upon which the theological answers were not yet clear.[33]

Monarchy was necessary for Israel's survival, but, like every turning point in the nation's history, it carried great risk. How could Israel have a king like its neighbors (8:5) without the loss of freedom inherent in such centralization (vv. 10-18)? The old order was obviously passé, but what would the new order bring? These and other questions troubled Samuel and other advocates of Israel's covenant tradition (see Deut. 17:14-20).[34]

The absolutist tendencies of ancient oriental monarchies are widely documented. We can see how their patterns threatened both Israel's tradition of personal freedom and the conviction that Yahweh was the true king. As the Psalms attest, Israel's tradition of sacral kingship (as opposed to secular kingship) did not elevate the king to divine status, as that of their neighbors frequently did.[35] Rather, it viewed him as God's representative charged with the responsibilities of enforcing (and embodying) the covenant. Far from a dictator, he was, ideally at least, a servant of his people.[36]

1-2 Samuel reflect accurately both the necessity of kingship and its hazards. God's use of the kingship as part of the preparation for the King of Kings validates the monarchy in Israel. That the vast majority of Israel's kings failed to fulfill their ordained role is testimony to kingship's intrinsic dangers.[37] The truly successful pattern of government for Israel was a delicate balance — not theocracy or monarchy but theocracy through monarchy. If Israel was to be God's people God had to be acknowledged as the true ruler. Nonetheless, God could rule through a human king. Amidst this tension, Saul proceeded to the chieftancy of the tribes.

(2) Long live the king! According to 1 Sam. 9–13, Saul's ascent was accomplished in stages, each of which increased his stature with the people. First, he was anointed by Samuel (in response to God's command [9:16]) after the two had met while Saul was tracking his father's stray asses. Later, at Mizpah he was singled out by lot from the clan of Matrites of the tribe of Benjamin (10:21). As Saul himself suggested, Benjamin's political insignificance ("least of the tribes of Israel"; 9:21) minimized the threat for the other tribes in choosing a king from one tribe to rule over all the others. Saul's modesty also showed at Mizpah when he hid behind the baggage as Samuel attempted to introduce him (10:20-24). A striking figure, Saul gained a good deal of popular support despite the opposition of some rabble-rousers (vv. 25-27).

Finally, an Ammonite invasion put Saul's charismatic gifts to the test (11:1-15). Though privately anointed leader and publicly hailed as such, he was still farming in Gibeah when he learned of the Ammonite raid on Jabesh-gilead. The tribes were mustered and the Ammonite forces ravaged or routed. Saul seems still to have regarded Samuel as coregent or fellow judge (cf. v. 7). Saul's success quelled any opposition to his regency; and once again, at Gilgal, Samuel proclaimed him king.[38] These stories of Saul's rise to power need not be viewed as separate and independent accounts, but perhaps as stages in the transition from judgeship to monarchy.[39] Indeed, their variety speaks for their authenticity. The times required several public proclamations and the display of charismatic gifts before Saul could be accepted uniformly both by the tribes and by the local city-states that had not previously deemed themselves part of Israel. Galilee and most of Judah seem not to have been folded into Saul's domain.[40]

The hero's acclaim given Saul seemed to sharpen Samuel's awareness of the monarchy's potential menace to Israel's life and faith. Perhaps he, like Saul

173

himself (11:13), resented the new king's being given the credit due to God for the victory. Samuel's farewell address (ch. 12) divides the accounts of Saul's career into good (chs. 9–11) and bad (chs. 13–15) phases. He seized the occasion to defend the integrity of his ministry as judge, to recount the mighty acts of God in the Exodus and the theocratic confederacy, and to admonish the people concerning the implications of the quest for a king (12:1-18). Samuel's speech summarizes his attitude and that of his prophetic successors (including the Deuteronomistic historians) toward the kingship: ". . . if both you and the king who reigns over you will follow the LORD your God, it will be well; but if you will not heed the voice of the LORD, but rebel against the commandment of the LORD, then the hand of the LORD will be against you and your king" (vv. 14f.).

(3) Is Saul among the prophets? (10:9-13). 1-2 Samuel offer glimpses of prophetic activity before the golden age of prophecy, the eighth century. In this early period the moral and ethical ministry of the prophets, though not altogether absent, as Samuel's speeches indicate, was not always prominent. Their messages sometimes concerned religious protocol, as in the indictment of Eli's sons for failure to honor God in the sacrifices. At other times they were like diviners with access to special knowledge, often of a very practical nature, such as the location of Saul's lost asses (9:3-20). Such information generally required payment or a gift.

Ecstatic behavior — dancing or chanting to music, uttering oracles in a trancelike state (note Balaam in Num. 24:4) — seems to have been characteristic of some prophets of this period. The band of prophets, bearing harp, tambourine, flute, and lyre, among whom Saul prophesied was typical (10:3ff.).[41] Their connection with the high places, established centers of worship, should not be overlooked. Samuel probably was not alone in performing both priestly and prophetic functions.

Prophecy during this period is described curiously: "for the one who is now called a prophet was formerly called a seer" (9:9). The simplest explanation seems to be that in Israel's early days, there were two offices, seer (here Heb. rô'eh, not hôzeh; Amos 7:12) and prophet, which later were merged under the title "prophet." The distinction between the terms was not hard and fast. Were they separate offices (2 Kgs. 17:13)? Some would define the seer's original function as looking into the future to give guidance concerning it, and assign the prophet a wider ministry often including a predictive element.[42]

Saul's Military Exploits (13:1–14:52). The Philistines put constant pressure on the young monarchy. They monopolized the metal industry (13:19, 22) and took advantage of their superior chariotry (v. 5) where the terrain permitted. They were thus able to maintain a distinct military advantage over the Israelites. Prior to the time of Saul the tribes had no standing army but in times of emergency depended on volunteers. When Saul or his son Jonathan defeated a Philistine garrison (e.g., at Geba; 13:3), raids of reprisal were sure to follow (cf. vv. 17f.). In a lightning attack, the crafty and courageous Jonathan and his armor-bearer inflicted such losses on the Philistines that Israel's courage was kindled (14:1-15). By clearing them out of the hill country of Ephraim, Saul gained respite from the relentless Philistine pressure. This enabled him to wage war against other neighbors, including Moab, Ammon, Edom, and Amalek (see vv. 47f.).[43]

Though Saul did little to change the old political order and made almost no attempt at centralization, he did sense the necessity of a trained military leadership. Since so much of the fighting remained in the hands of volunteers from the tribes, a corps of highly skilled recruits was essential for Saul's daring raids (v. 52).

Saul's Fatal Choice (15:1-35). Saul's rise to power was gradual; so was his descent. His daring and brashness made him mighty in battle. They also made him dangerously unpredictable in dealing with his people, particularly with conservative religious leaders like Samuel. His explosive disposition caused trouble more than once with both his subjects and the prophet. His rash vows, although fulfilling the need of the hour, can scarcely have endeared him to his countrymen (11:7; 14:24). Jonathan's protest (vv. 29f.) may have reflected a widespread attitude.

Saul's flagrant disobedience of Samuel caused his final rejection. Two episodes are recounted. First, Saul waited seven days at Gilgal for Samuel to arrive and supervise the prebattle sacrifice which prepared the Israelites for further combat with the outraged Philistines (13:8ff.). The impatient Saul presumptuously usurped Samuel's priestly rights by sacrificing the animals himself. Saul's insensitivity to the limits of his office suggested to Samuel that his first experiment in monarchy was doomed to fail.

When the king ignored the command to put to the sword all the Amalekites, their livestock, and their goods, Samuel's suspicion was confirmed (1 Sam. 15:1-3). Like Achan (Josh. 7:1ff.), Saul had not taken the holy war seriously. This was no mere foray to restock depleted supplies or capture troops for slave labor. It was to be vengeance in the name of God. Saul's casualness toward the divine directive was viewed by Samuel as rebellion. The stern prophet remained resolute despite Saul's pleadings (vv. 24-31). The lesson had to be made clear, regardless of the cost: for king and commoner alike, obedience was better than sacrifice (v. 22).

David — Shepherd, Warrior, King-Elect (1 Sam. 16:1–2 Sam. 5:10)

In a sense, the narrative of Samuel and Saul (chs. 1–15) can be read as prologue to the compelling account of David's rise to the throne.[44] The books of Samuel and Kings are about David and his family, just as the sequence of stories in Gen. 11:26–Exod. 19:25 are about Abraham and his family. The account of David's life is told in three sections:

- David's ascent to kingship — 1 Sam. 16:1–2 Sam 5:10
- David's exercise of kingship — 2 Sam. 5:11–24:25
- David's transfer of kingship — 1 Kgs. 1:1–2:46.

Saul and David — Struggle for Power (16:1–31:13). The search for a new king had to begin. In spite of Saul's abject failure, the option of returning to the loose tribal and regional coalition was never considered. The factors which called the monarchy into being still existed. The call was not for a change of government but for a new king. In response to God's command Samuel went to Bethlehem to find him.

The account of the selection of David — the name means "beloved," probably a shortened form of "beloved of Yahweh" (16:6-13)[45] — suggests a familiar biblical pattern: younger brothers are chosen over elder — Isaac over Ishmael, Jacob over Esau, Joseph over the other ten. This pattern highlights these events as turning points in God's redemptive program. The choices are based not on the laws of authority or inheritance but on God's sovereign will and power. Consequently the mighty accomplishments of these persons are not their own. God is their source.

(1) David, Court Favorite (16:1–20:42). The anointing of David was followed by the departure of charismatic power from Saul (16:14). Instead of the Spirit of the Lord, an evil spirit had come upon him. That this spirit is said to be from the Lord suggests that its coming is part of God's judgment on Saul and that the Israelites viewed all reality as under God's control. Saul apparently began to experience spells of acute depression which could be relieved only by music. It is this curious circumstance that caused Saul's and David's paths to cross (vv. 18, 23). Saul's servant gives as good a description of the future king's varied talents as the narrative contains: ". . . skillful in playing, a man of valor, a warrior, prudent in speech, and a man of good presence; and the LORD is with him" (v. 18).

The story of the slaying of Goliath (17:1–18:5) originally may have been a separate account incorporated by an editor during the compilation of the books of Samuel. It introduces David again (v. 12), although he is already well known from the preceding chapter. Perhaps this story had been circulated separately as one of David's mighty acts and then found its place in the text without much alteration.[46]

Goliath's challenge to the Israelites (vv. 4-16) is an instance of representative warfare or single combat, a custom attested in antiquity. The battle was to be decided by a contest between a representative of each side. Perhaps a concept of corporate personality, in which the power of a tribe or family could be summed up in one member, helped foster this practice.

David's victory over Goliath elevated him to a position of responsibility in Saul's army. More than that, it endeared him to Saul's son Jonathan (18:1-5). When David's popular appeal began to exceed Saul's, the king became jealous and suspicious and tried to kill him (vv. 6-11). Though David still had access to the court, his acceptance by Saul faded as the king's behavior became increasingly turbulent.

Saul's offers of his daughters, Merab (vv. 17-19) and Michal (vv. 20-29), to David were double-edged. Taken at face value, they would have supported David's claim to the throne. The monarchy, particularly in Judah, had a strong matriarchal tinge: queen mothers were always to be reckoned with. To be married to the king's daughter would have given David considerable leverage. However, when Saul asked for the foreskins of one hundred Philistines as marriage price, his strategy was betrayed: he really hoped that David would be killed.[47] The plan miscarried when David and his band slew twice the required number without hurt to David.

More than once, only Jonathan stood between David and death (19:1ff.; 20:1ff.; 20:30ff.). The two had formed a pact of friendship, solemnized by a covenant ritual. As Abraham had given animals to Abimelech (Gen. 21:27ff.) in pledge of his faith, so Jonathan gave David his robe and armor. This did more than bind them as equals; it symbolized Jonathan's support of David's right to the throne. The sincerity of this relationship is shown by its frequent mention (1 Sam. 18:3; 20:16, 42; 23:18). Jonathan's grave vow — "the LORD do so to Jonathan, and more also" (20:13; see David's vow in 25:22) — is a stern reminder that death was the judgment upon one who broke such a covenant. Such vows may have been accompanied by a gesture, such as feigning to cut one's own throat.

(2) David, Hunted Refugee (21:1–27:12). Even Jonathan's intervention could not protect David permanently. With exile or death his only alternatives, David fled (21:10). Later, others of his clan, doubtless fearing retaliation, joined him in exile. With his motley band of about four hundred fellow fugitives (22:2), David frequently hid by day and traveled by night to escape Saul. The Philistine borders, southern hill country of Judah, the Negeb, Edom, and Moab were laced with the tracks of his bandit raiders. At times he attacked the Philistines (23:1ff.); at other times his dread of Saul forced him to sojourn among them (at Gath; 27:1ff.).

177

David's capital on the Ophel ridge, captured from the Jebusites.
(Neal and Joel Bierling)

David's tactics with Saul were defensive, not aggressive. Twice he could have taken the king's life handily but refused (24:4ff.; 26:6ff.). His attitude toward Saul remained one of respect and reverence for Yahweh's anointed leader. Even when he craftily cut off a piece of Saul's skirt, he regretted the insult against his ruler (24:5f.).

Saul, by contrast, was relentless in stalking David. Despite the constant Philistine threat, Saul compulsively pursued David and his outlaw band to the neglect of other royal responsibilities. Saul's unbalanced mental state became increasingly apparent: (1) he butchered Ahimelech, who had given aid and comfort to David (21:1ff.); (2) he slaughtered a priestly company of more than eighty together with their families (22:11ff.). This latest in a series of outrages against the priests' authority highlights the contrast between Saul's and David's attitude. From the outset, David had enlisted the priests' support and was sensitive to their religious leadership. Indeed, Ahimelech's son Abiathar escaped Saul's bloody coup and found asylum in David's exiled company (22:20ff.).

David's willingness to consult the Lord is evidence of his concern for the priestly ministry. The narrative records this immediately after the arrival of Abiathar. The suggestion is that it was through Abiathar that David determined

God's will for his journeys and battles (23:1ff.). The ephod (a priestly garment to which a pouch was attached) which the fleeing priest clutched probably contained lots or other forms of oracles for divining (see 23:6). In contrast with David's ready access to Yahweh's will, Saul tried desperately but unsuccessfully to discern it by dreams, Urim (sacred lot?),[48] and prophetic activity (28:6).

Not surprisingly, Samuel's death draws scant notice (25:1), for the aged kingmaker had been upstaged for some time by David and Saul. More prominent is David's encounter with the ill-tempered Nabal and his gracious wife Abigail (25:2ff.). Nabal's failure to receive David and his men with the courtesies demanded by custom would have cost him dearly had his wife not intervened. David's rough-and-ready life as a fugitive is amply documented in this episode. He took food where he could find it and was willing to spill the blood of any who refused him. He wooed the widowed Abigail and married Ahinoam as well (25:43). These were days of dash and daring. And David was equal to them.

(3) Decline and Death of Saul (28:1–31:13). It was a desperate Saul who faced a Philistine onslaught from the north and could find no word from God for guidance. He had zealously banned all wizards and mediums (28:3), yet in his panic he consulted one (28:8ff.). The mysterious scene shows Saul frantically begging for advice from the prophet he had disobeyed consistently in life. Samuel is shown to be as dauntless in the afterlife as in the days of his flesh, bringing from the underworld only a more trenchant version of what he had announced at Gilgal (15:17ff.): Saul's disobedience had cost him the crown.

If the scene at Endor was fraught with mystery, that at Gilboa was charged with tragedy (31:1ff.). Giving no quarter, the Philistines forced the battle against Saul and his sons. The younger men fell first, and the wounded Saul pleaded for the *coup de grâce*. When his armor-bearer refused, Saul fell on his own sword. The Philistines customarily looted their dead enemies. They severed Saul's head and took his armor as trophy of their triumph over one who had dogged them for a decade or more. The Philistines rejoiced at Saul's death and Israel's vulnerability. But they had yet to reckon with David.

David's Double Anointing (2 Sam. 1:1–5:10)

The death of Saul left Israel leaderless and subject to Philistine threat. But with firm steps David marched to the throne of Judah and all Israel, more than filling the vacuum. Saul's urge to destroy David had left the land vulnerable to Philistine attack. David's dedication to enlarging Israel's borders drove him to subdue the Philistines and bring all of Israel's near neighbors under his sway.

(1) King over Judah at Hebron (1:1–4:12). David's respite from Saul's persecution and his return from exile among the Philistines were clouded by his remorse at the slaughter on Mt. Gilboa (2 Sam. 1:1-27). His grief over the death of his king and his beloved Jonathan was compounded by his concern for Israel, now in need of firm shepherding. The fate of the Amalekite opportunist who sought David's favor by reporting the king's death and claiming a hand in it displays the depth of David's emotions.

Further proof is his moving lament punctuated with "How the mighty have fallen!" (vv. 19, 25, 27). Using dramatic contrast (in which past glories of the heroes are recited to sharpen feeling for their present humiliation) and the short, sobbing lines of the funeral dirge, David invokes all Israel, including the mountains of Gilboa which witnessed the tragic scene, to lament their great loss — the king and his son.[49]

David's triumphal return from his sojourn in Ziklag resulted in his acclamation as king of Judah in Hebron (2:1-4). This ancient town, rich with memories of Abraham's day, was his capital for seven and a half years (5:5). Meanwhile, Saul's family was still to be contended with. At the instigation of Abner, the crafty general, Saul's son Ishbosheth[50] had been made king of the other tribes, including those fragments of the nation dwelling in Transjordan. Nothing indicates that Ishbosheth's government gained extensive popular support. Its capital was in Transjordan, and that greatly curtailed its influence among the tribes, who looked increasingly to David as leader.

After several years of skirmishes between the two contestants for the throne (2:10; 3:1), Ishbosheth angered Abner by accusing him of intimacy with Saul's concubine (vv. 6-11). Such a liaison, if indeed it had taken place, probably would suggest that Abner was himself ambitious for the crown, since sexual union with one of Saul's partners would have been interpreted as a credential for kingship. This break with Ishbosheth forced Abner to make overtures to David (vv. 12-16). The king-elect responded by demanding that Saul's daughter Michal be restored to him as wife. The political reason behind this request (granted by Ishbosheth) is apparent: a son by Michal would help consolidate under David those factions loyal to Saul.[51] The turncoat Abner spearheaded David's drive to unify the nation by traveling through the land to confer with the tribal elders (vv. 17-19). Apparently jealousy and desire for revenge goaded David's general, Joab, to slay his rival who, overtly at least, had become his ally. Abner's death grieved David (note his brief lament, vv. 33f.). It also dismayed Ishbosheth, who himself was soon assassinated by two cutthroats that had previously served Saul (4:2f.). This did not please David, and he summarily slew the murderers who had sought to impress him by their deed.

(2) King over All Israel at Jerusalem (5:1-10). The rival gone, David was hailed at Hebron as king of all Israel (5:1-5). The house of Judah, which at this time included Simeonites, Calebites, Othnielites, Jerahmeelites, and Kenites (1 Sam. 27:10; 30:29), was united with the northern tribes ("Israel"),[52] whose elders journeyed to Hebron and completed David's rise to sovereign by anointing him as their king as well as Judah's. The lad who tended Jesse's sheep in Bethlehem had been acclaimed by Yahweh as "shepherd of my people Israel" (5:2). That the northern tribes never wholeheartedly accepted Judean kingship is proved by the readiness with which the kingdom split at the time of David's grandson Rehoboam (1 Kgs. 12).

The united kingdom needed a capital centrally located and closely identified with the new king. The Canaanite stronghold of Jerusalem had remained outside Israel's control during their two-and-a-half-century occupation of the land. An ancient city (cf. Gen. 14:18),[53] Jerusalem was ideally situated to be David's capital.[54] Lying between the two halves of his kingdom in territory to which no tribe could lay claim, it was sufficiently neutral to serve as a unifying factor. The details of David's conquest are obscure, but his men may have crept through a water shaft (5:8).[55] David's enmity toward the Jebusites and the tactic he used in whipping his men to battle pitch are shown in his sneering of the enemy soldiers as "the lame and the blind." This derision apparently recalled Jebusite mockery of him (v. 8). Such taunts were a common tactic in ancient warfare. David's capture of the new capital made it literally his — "the city of David."

The detailed, complex account of David's rise to kingship closes at this point. Its conclusion is marked by the editor's summary (v. 10):

And David became greater and greater, for the LORD, the God of hosts, was with him.

Of this whole section (1 Sam. 16:1–2 Sam. 5:10) it has been aptly noted: "Each step of the way is authorized by the will of Yahweh that David should become king. . . . The most interesting interpretive question is the way in which the hidden purpose of Yahweh is worked out through the awkward and raw events of historical interaction."[56]

CHAPTER 13

Israel's Golden Age: David and Solomon (2 Sam. 5:11–1 Kgs. 11:43)

Introduction

The seventy-five years or so outlined in this section saw an almost total transformation in Israel's political and economic life. David and his son forged Judah and Israel into a military entity able to dominate its neighbors, and into a mercantile enterprise bringing unprecedented wealth and fame. The loose-knit tribes were welded together by a strong monarchy that set the style for almost four centuries. It was indeed Israel's golden era, if politics and economics are the coinage of value. If the characters of the kings are the index of worth, the evaluation of this period is more complex.

> So David reigned over all Israel and David administered justice and equity to all his people. 2 Sam. 8:15

> When David's time to die drew near, he charged his son Solomon, saying: . . . Be strong, be courageous, and keep the charge of the LORD your God, walking in his ways and keeping his statutes, his commandments, his ordinances, and his testimonies . . . so that you may prosper in all that you do and wherever you turn. 1 Kgs. 2:1-3

> Then the LORD was angry with Solomon, because his heart had turned away from the LORD, the God of Israel, who had . . . commanded him . . . , that he should not follow other gods; but he did not observe what the LORD commanded. 1 Kgs. 11:9-10

David's Exercise of Kingship (2 Sam. 5:11–24:25)

The landscape of these chapters is a panorama of peaks and valleys. With candor, vigor, and pathos, David's years in Jerusalem are recounted as a series of lofty successes and profound failures. Two major questions dominate the scene: (1) How will the monarchy fare? (2) Who will succeed the celebrated king?

David's consolidation of his gains (5:11–8:18)

(1) Buildings and Battles (5:11-25). David set out immediately to fortify and beautify his capital. David's new house brought a tone of luxury which Saul's best days had not known. The size of David's family alone (see 3:2-5; 5:13-16) suggests an extensive court. Israel's pattern of life was changing, and David was spearheading the change. Jerusalem was his own city, taken with his private troops instead of a tribal army. It was the spoil of his victory, and he treated it accordingly. Almost immediately he set out to do what Saul had failed to do: to rid the land of the Philistines. Well-versed in Philistine tactics and blessed with Yahweh's guidance, David was able both to win decisive victories and to control and confine the enemy to their own borders (5:17-25) for the first time in 150 years.[1]

183

(2) Religious Reforms (6:1–7:29). One of Saul's basic mistakes had been his insensitivity to Israel's religious institutions, particularly the central shrine and priesthood. But David grasped the importance of Israel's spiritual heritage and sought to perpetuate and promote it. Israel could not have been truly united unless its political head was also its religious leader. Saul had long neglected the ark of the covenant. David brought it to Jerusalem and thereby made his city the religious as well as political capital. This master stroke greatly enhanced his people's loyalty to him. His uninhibited participation in the ceremonies of dedication offended his decorous wife Michal (6:20), but his enthusiasm marked him off as one who revered Israel's God and fostered the faith, a reputation he well deserved and never lost.

Saul's rise to power had produced misgivings in the prophet Samuel, but David's had Nathan's full support (7:1-3). The prophet, at divine command, announced to David the unique relationship the king and his seed were to enjoy with God. The terms were reminiscent of the Abrahamic covenant (Gen. 12; 15; 17). Nathan promised him "a great name" (a lofty and well-earned reputation); stability for his people in the land; an everlasting dynasty; and an intimate relationship between God and David's successors. David was forbidden to build a permanent temple; instead, he was assured that his son would build the "house" God really wanted, a permanent line of kings on whom God's steadfast love would remain (7:11-16).

The importance of this covenant can scarcely be exaggerated.[2] Prophetic expectation of a Davidic king to reign in future glory over Israel (Isa. 9:6ff.; 11:1ff.) hinges on this promise. So does the prophets' rejection of the non-Davidic kings of the northern kingdom. New Testament faith traces Christ's right to rule to his descent from David (Matt. 1:1; Luke 1:32).

The numerous details of public worship called for meticulous administration. David appointed as priests Zadok and Ahimelech (8:17). Ahimelech's father Abiathar was apparently still active (15:24), perhaps as a "priest emeritus." The families of both priests seem to have had roots that go back to the sanctuary at Shiloh and beyond that to Aaron, founder of the priestly line.[3] But not all priests were descendants of Aaron, for David's own sons were numbered among them (8:18). While the description of official religion is sketchy in 2 Samuel, the Chronicler spares no effort to give a full account (1 Chr. 23:1–29:30). His record is testimony to David's strategic role in shaping the transition from the simplicity of the shrine at Shiloh to the elaborate cultic activities of Solomon and his successors.

(3) Unparalleled Military Success (8:1-14). An impressive list of David's military achievements is summarized here. Details are sometimes given in succeeding passages (e.g., his conflict with the Ammonites and their Syrian allies, ch. 10). When the dust of the various battles had settled, the Philistines as well as the Edomites, Moabites, Ammonites, and the great city-states of Syria

like Damascus, Zobah, and even Hamath were either in David's control or subject to him.

Two decades earlier, the Israelites had been trying to avoid strangulation by the Philistines. But the Philistine pentapolis had been broken, and David had greatly enlarged the areas of Israel's influence. Now indeed the most powerful kingdom in western Asia, Israel's borders stretched from the desert to the Mediterranean, and from the Gulf of Aqaba to the outskirts of Hamath on the Orontes.

(4) Political Centralization (8:15-18; see 20:23-26). David's religious reforms, military outreach, and political and social reorganization called for sweeping changes in administrative structure. How elaborate this structure became is hard to calculate. The two lists of David's chief officials include a commander-in-chief of the Israelite troops (Joab); leader of the Philistine mercenaries (Cherethites and Pelethites);[4] the two priests mentioned above; two officers responsible for official records, documents of state, and administrative details; and for part of the time at least, a superintendent of the corvée, who apparently managed the foreign labor force. These officials had no independent authority, but were closely supervised by the king, whose judgment was final in every area, military, religious, or political.[5]

The prophets' strong opposition to David's census in ch. 24 probably stems from objections to its purpose. This was no mere counting of the people, but an attempt to determine the strength of the various tribes in order to levy taxes and recruit troops. In spite of a move toward internal taxation, David's chief sources of revenue were undoubtedly the spoils of war and the tribute of conquered or fearful nations around him. More secure from outward attack under David, the citizens had less personal freedom. This transition from tribal coalition to centralized monarchy was hard, and subsequent history reveals that the Israelites never did adjust to it.

This painful transition may be telegraphed in the chiastic structure of 5:13–8:18:[6]

1 List of family (5:13-16)	3′ Nathan's oracle as symbol of new way (7:1-20)
2 Battles with Philistines (5:17-25)	2′ Battle with two nations (8:1-14)
3 Ark as sign of old ways (6:1-20)	1′ List of officials (8:15-18)

David's compassion and cruelty (9:1–12:31)

The transition from charismatic to dynastic leadership was not resolved by David's ascent to the throne. Saul's son Eshbaal had made a thwarted attempt

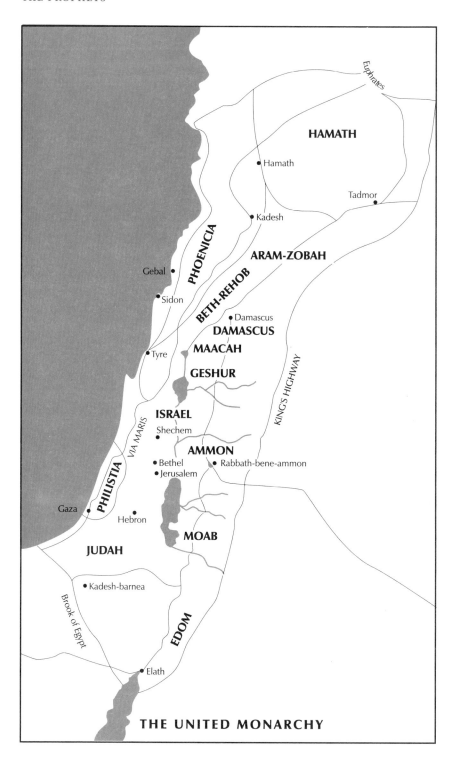

THE UNITED MONARCHY

at succession. Later the Benjaminite Sheba would seek to rally Israel against David (20:1-22). But, tragically, not all competition for the throne came from without. David, who handled international and national affairs so readily, had trouble in his own household. At least three sons desired the throne. Theirs is a tragic human story of intrigue and counter intrigue, love and blood, shining success and wretched failure.

These chapters introduce what is sometimes considered the finest piece of history writing in antiquity — the Court History of David (2 Sam. 9–20; 1 Kgs. 1–2):

> Its author has equal command of the art of the dramatic construction of a tale and of the realistic characterization of the persons whom he presents true to life and unadorned. He keeps himself in the background, and yet quite a number of indications (. . . 11:27; 12:24; 17:14) reveal the fact that he regards even the ultimate relationships in history to be between earthly events and divine dispensation.[7]

The detailed knowledge of court life and language point to a member of the court as author — among the candidates are Ahimaaz, Solomon's son-in-law, and Abiathar, priest to David.

(1) Display of Mercy (9:1-13). The picture of David's kindness to the house of Saul and his profound regard for Jonathan, sketched throughout the narrative, is enhanced by his mercy to Jonathan's son Mephibosheth.[8] The pointed mention of the lameness highlights the king's condescension: (1) such infirmities were often considered divine judgments (see John 9:1f.). (2) A lame lad could pose no threat to David's rule. The kindly treatment of a member of the rival's household is all the more remarkable in view of the frequent oriental custom of doing away with the male line of the opposing royal family. David kept his pledge to Jonathan and spared his line (see 1 Sam. 20:14-17). His loyalty to that covenant was tested again when revenge had to be taken for Saul's outrage against the Gibeonites (2 Sam. 21:1-6). Apparently, Mephibosheth responded to David's kindness and remained loyal to the end, although his guardian and servant, Ziba, turned traitor during Absalom's revolt and tried to undermine David's confidence in Mephibosheth (16:1-4).

(2) Abuse of Power (11:1–12:31). An episode during the Ammonite war (11:1-27) showed another side of David. Invading armies, especially the Assyrians, usually timed their campaigns between the latter rains in March and the grain harvest in May and June. Roads were dry enough to be passable, and the soldiers could sustain themselves on their enemies' ripening crops and newborn lambs and calves. But while his armies were on the march, David remained in the capital, and his illicit encounter with the lovely Bathsheba then occurred. By his desperate plot to get rid of her husband Uriah, David added

187

murder to adultery. Nathan's parable, a subtle yet forceful rebuke of David, is convincing evidence of the great prophets' crucial role in Israel's life (12:1-15).

The king, whose chief obligation was to enforce the terms of the covenant and insure justice at every level of society, had himself grossly violated the covenant. He had used his power for cruel purposes. David crumbled before the righteous indictment of the stern prophet. God's mercy was his only hope; and although his sin had such dire effects as the death of Bathsheba's baby (12:15-19) and the loosening of the moral fibers of David's sons (e.g., Amnon; 13:1-39), that mercy spared him.[9] The remarkable honesty of the Old Testament is apparent here, for no attempt is made to hide or excuse the great king's glaring moral lapses. We do well to see chs. 11–12 as turning points in David's biography: they mark the reasons for the chaos that defined his final years.

Turmoil in the court (13:1–18:33)

David's wars had taken a toll on the morale of the troops levied from Israel. They were forced to bear arms for extended periods, along with David's private army of mercenaries. Within the court itself scheming and conniving increased — particularly among David's wives — as the question of David's successor was raised.

Open conflict for the crown was triggered when Amnon, David's oldest son (3:2), took unfair advantage of his half-sister, Tamar, then cruelly rejected her, even though he could have asked her hand in marriage (13:1-19). Absalom, the third son (3:2), undoubtedly with mixed motives, set out to avenge his sister's honor and also to remove a rival for the throne. Absalom seethed bitterly over his father's failure to punish Amnon. Then after two years, he had Amnon slain, and fled to the Aramean state of Geshur, his mother's home (vv. 20-39).

Joab, David's general, was also a powerful political figure. His cunning attempt to effect reconciliation between David and Absalom was discovered by the king. Yet he succeeded in getting the king to allow Absalom's return to Jerusalem. For two years the young man had no access to his father's court (14:1-33). Absalom's personal grace and beauty were coupled with an irresponsible opportunism. He stirred discontent among litigants in the gate by saying he would judge in their favor were he in charge of Israel's affairs. This charm and malice made him a serious threat to David's security (15:1-6). Surreptitious plot became open rebellion when Absalom had himself proclaimed king at Hebron (vv. 7-12). David's earlier abuse of power (chs. 11–12) was more than matched by Absalom's.[10]

Support for Absalom's coup grew stronger. David mustered his band of loyal Philistine mercenaries and fled Jerusalem. The picture of the beaten king trudging barefoot up the Mount of Olives, head covered in mourning, cheeks wet with tears, is as touching as any in the Old Testament. Particularly grievous to David was the report that his wise counselor and friend, Ahithophel, joined the rebels (15:30f.; 16:15-23). One of the few bright spots was the loyalty of Hushai, whom David commissioned to stay in Jerusalem to spy on Absalom (15:32-37; 16:16-19). Hushai succeeded in thwarting the advice of Ahithophel, who recommended immediate pursuit of David (ch. 17).[11] So crushed was Ahithophel that he took his own life.

After consolidating his forces in Transjordan, David, probably joined by groups of loyal citizens, sent three armies to battle Absalom. They smashed decisively the rebel troops. Absalom himself was killed, in defiance of his father's orders, by Joab. The general knew that peace was impossible while Absalom lived (17:24–18:33).

Restoration to power (19:1–24:21)

Absalom's death left David in double distress. Any relief he took in the downfall of the rebels was swamped by his tears of sorrow for his dead son (18:33–19:4). Coupled with a father's bereftness was a king's sense of abandonment. The leaders he counted on to welcome him back from exile were intolerably slow in issuing an invitation for David to return (19:8b-13).

(1) More Displays of Mercy (19:18:b-43). In the chemistry of divine providence, the double grief seems to have produced renewed compassion in the king's heart. Three incidents illustrate that change of spirit. The first beneficiary was Shimei, a man of Benjamin, who had cursed David at the time Absalom usurped the throne (16:5). He met the king at the Jordan along with a large welcoming delegation finally sent to escort David to Jerusalem. Shimei cast himself on the king's mercy and the king sealed his promise of clemency with an oath (19:16-23). Mephibosheth, Jonathan's son, also made the journey to the Jordan to meet David (19:24-30). The lame lad had been in a virtual state of mourning during the king's absence. He had fully intended to accompany David into exile, but had been tricked by his servant who lied to the king. Ziba told David that Mephibosheth had remained in Jerusalem in the hope of gaining his grandfather's throne (16:3). David heard Mephibosheth's explanation and sensed its credibility in the young man's contrition. The king compassionately revoked the rash promise in which he had earlier disinherited Mephibosheth. David's third act of mercy was toward Barzillai, an elderly man, who had provided food for David during his sojourn in Transjordan (19:31-40). Though David begged Barzillai to make his home in the Jerusalem palace, the old man refused. In token of their valued friendship Barzillai offered his choice servant to David, and the king responded by offering the servant all the court privileges which Barzillai's faithful hospitality deserved.

(2) Another Instance of Revolt (20:1-26). This final section of David's

court history reprises at least three themes found earlier in the books of Samuel. First, the rivalry between Judah and the northern tribes had in no way abated during Absalom's revolt and David's exile. David's return sparked a tug-of-war between the two parts of the realm, with the king used as the rope: Judah claiming a privileged hold on him through tribal kinship; Israel countered with a double defense of their right to David's blessing — their tenfold advantage in number of tribes and their initiative in persuading the king to return (19:39-43).

Second, members of Benjamin, Saul's tribe, notably one Sheba, tried to rally the northerners against David. Keenly aware of the enmity the supporters of the house of Saul carried against him, the king lost no time in sending Amasa to crush the revolt. The final victory, however, was credited to Joab, who treacherously killed Amasa and took control of his troops (20:1-26). That Joab was not put in charge of the chase at the outset probably reflects David's strong disapproval of his slaying of Absalom (18:14f.).

Third, the list of military leaders, court officials, and priests (20:23-25) serves as the closing bookend to the section of court history that began with an almost identical list in 8:15-18. The repetition of several names signals the continuity between the beginning and the later years of David's reign. The absence of a note about David's sons serving as priests (8:18) and the inclusion of Adoram as administrator of the "forced labor" (20:24) may speak volumes about the failure of David's family and the need for tighter control of the non-military laborers.[12]

(3) Closing Stories and Prayers (21:1–24:25). These chapters are both a summary of David's reign — in victory and failure — and an expression of his total gratitude to Yahweh for unfailing faithfulness. The literary pattern blends artistry with intentional message:

> A Story of Saul's sinful act and its expiation (21:1-14)
>   B List of heroes and their deeds (21:15-22)
>   C Song of thanksgiving: David to Yahweh (22:1-51)
>   C′ Oracle of trust: Yahweh through David (23:1-7)
>   B′ List of heroes and their deeds (23:8-39)
> A′ Story of David's sinful act and its expiation (24:1-25)[13]

The arch-like form of this section conveys the authors' understandings of the connections and contrasts between Saul (A) and David (A′). It honors the exploits of the warriors who contributed to David's defense and expansion of his kingdom (B, B′). Above all, its keystone is the praise of Israel's Lord, who is the true Warrior, Judge, and Shepherd of the people and their king (C, C′).

Though chs. 21–24 are often called an *appendix*, they are shaped to combine with 1 Sam. 1–3 in a frame for the book of Samuel:

A Predicament and prayer — Hannah's (1 Sam. 1)
  B Divine deliverance (1 Sam. 1:19)
    C Psalm of praise — Hannah's (1 Sam. 2:1-10)
    C′ Psalm of praise — David's (2 Sam. 22)
  B′ Divine deliverance (2 Sam. 24:25)
A′ Predicament and prayer — David's (2 Sam. 24)[14]

Pivotal to the structure and movement of the book are 2 Sam. 11–12. David's double sin of murder and adultery mark a major shift in the narrative from blessing to judgment, from triumph to tragedy, from a narrative that features David's public ministry to one that focuses on his inner person — vulnerable, sensitive, compassionate, humble before God.

The skill and scope of the book's composers are praiseworthy indeed. They have achieved with uncommon effectiveness their aim: "presenting the character of David as the bearer of Israel's historical possibility and as the vehicle for God's purposes in Israel."[15]

David's Transfer of Kingship (1 Kgs. 1:1–2:46)

This section sharpens the question which has been lurking beneath the surface of the story since Solomon's birth (2 Sam. 12:24-25) and Absalom's revolt (2 Sam. 15): Whom will David name as his successor? Despite the obvious instability of the land and the people's apprehension concerning the future, David took no definite steps to make this decision until the close of his life. As 1 Kings begins, advancing age and decreasing vitality give urgency to the choice.

Adonijah, his oldest surviving son (2 Sam. 3:4), made a strong bid for the throne by enlisting the support of Abiathar and Joab, David's priest and general. The report reached Jerusalem that Adonijah had actually held a coronation feast at En-rogel. In response, Nathan the prophet and Bathsheba, mother of Solomon, pressured the king to name Solomon. Affirming the request of his favorite wife, David sealed Solomon's appointment with an oath. The king then gave concrete evidence by turning over to Solomon his private army of Philistine mercenaries. With Zadok as priest, Nathan as prophet, and Benaiah, son of Jehoiada, as general, Solomon was crowned at Gihon, while Adonijah's festivities turned to mourning (1 Kgs. 1:1-53).

Adonijah, fearful of his life, had taken sanctuary at the altar, where Solomon spared him. Finally and foolishly, he made one more desperate attempt to unseat Solomon: he asked for David's consort, Abishag, as wife after his father's death. Solomon, sensing the political implications of his brother's

Six-chambered gate and casemate wall at Hazor, representative of Solomon's
extensive building activity throughout his kingdom (1 Kgs. 9:15).
(*Lawrence T. Geraty*)

request (cannily made through the influential Bathsheba), executed Adonijah.[16] The new king banished Abiathar to Anathoth (cf. Jer. 1:1) and slew Joab
to fulfill David's dying request for vengeance upon the murderer of Absalom
and Amasa. At last Solomon reigned without rival upon the throne of Judah
and Israel (1 Kgs. 2:1-46). Dynastic rule had been established. For almost four
centuries the kings in Jerusalem would be sons of David.

David, despite his moral lapses, high-handed policies, and failure to
order his own household, gave Israel some of its finest moments. All future
kings were measured by their likeness to him. In fact, recent archaeological
evidence indicates that foreigners used the phrase "house of David" for the
Judean kings who reigned in Jerusalem. The names occur in parallel with "king
of Israel" in an Aramaic inscription found at Tel Dan. The text apparently
marks the victory of an Aramean king over the combined forces of the king
of Israel and the king of the "house of David." It is noteworthy that Israel's
monarchy is labeled after the nation, while Judah's king bears the dynastic title
of his celebrated ancestor. This is the earliest appearance of "Israel" in Semitic
script yet discovered and the first mention of King David's name in any
inscription outside the Hebrew Bible.[17]

Solomon in All His Glory (3:1–11:43)

Solomon's stony path to the throne was followed by an era of unparalleled economic and political prosperity. His forty-year reign (*ca.* 971-931) saw Israel rise to splendid heights in peaceful pursuits, just as his father's long rule had witnessed unprecedented military success. Originally named Jedidiah ("beloved of the LORD") by Nathan (2 Sam. 12:24f.), Solomon (probably his regnal name) stands in the background in the biblical account until the last days of David. When others like Amnon, Absalom, and Adonijah had been set aside, Solomon stepped to the throne and enhanced its power and prestige.

Authorship and Composition of Kings. Solomon's story dominates the first eleven chapters of Kings. The admirable Court History of David ends at 1 Kgs. 2:46. The account of David's successors in Judah and their northern counterparts in Israel (1 Kgs. 3–2 Kgs. 25) is the work of a gifted and inspired compiler who gave the books their uniform theological outlook and highly stylized presentation of Israel's history. He probably lived at the close of Judah's history (*ca.* 590).[18] The emphasis on Elijah, Elisha, and other prophets, together with the editor's general prophetic outlook, has led many to attribute 1-2 Kings to Jeremiah. Indeed, the unknown author did view Israel's history from a perspective akin to Jeremiah's and wrote under many of the same influences. Here, as in 1-2 Samuel, the mere chronicling of events has given way to a subjective approach. The historian is not a court apologist whose aim is to celebrate the exploits of the king — as was common among ancient peoples (the Hittites are probably an exception). Instead, he evaluates and frequently criticizes the rulers, comparing each with David, the great royal prototype.

The compiler of Kings has given some clues as to his sources. Probably most of the material concerning Solomon in 1 Kgs. 3–11 was drawn from the book of the Acts of Solomon (11:41),[19] while many of the other stories were found in the book of the Chronicles of the Kings of Israel and its counterpart for Judah. The LXX suggests that 8:12f. (LXX 8:53) was taken from the book of Jashar (cf. Josh. 10:13; 2 Sam. 1:18). The deeds of Elijah and Elisha may have been transmitted orally among the schools of the prophets.

All of these materials have been skillfully formed into a synchronized historical narrative. Chronicles of the two kingdoms, originally separate, have been painstakingly combined and interwoven with the editor's own prophetic comments.[20] The result is that

> the Book is a history written with a religious and a practical aim. . . . The remarkable note is that when all was lost, someone found the history of that tragic period worth recording as a lesson of God's discipline of His people.[21]

Solomon — the Master Sage. As Israel's first dynastic ruler, Solomon took office with no obvious charismatic powers. In the report of the vision he had at Gibeon, however, God offered him his choice of gifts (1 Kgs. 3:5-14). Solomon, aware of his wide and weighty responsibilities, requested a wise and discerning mind.[22] He took full advantage of his international contacts, wealth, and respite from war to dedicate himself to literary pursuits. His collections of wise sayings, his repertoire of riddles, his encyclopedic knowledge of nature, earned for him a reputation beyond that of his Egyptian, Arabian, Canaanite, and Edomite contemporaries (4:29-34) and made him the great patron of Israel's wisdom literature. Solomon's specific role in Old Testament literature will be discussed in connection with Proverbs, Ecclesiastes, and Song of Solomon.

Solomon not only attained heroic status in Israel but also captured the imagination of many peoples in widespread areas. No figure of antiquity (with the possible exception of Alexander the Great) is so widely celebrated in folk literature among Jews, Arabs, and Ethiopians.

Solomon — Merchant and Statesman. David had bequeathed to his son a substantial empire. Solomon's task was to control it and strengthen the centralized government to maintain the empire. Disregarding to some extent the traditional tribal boundaries, Solomon set up administrative districts, each responsible for providing support to the court one month during the year (4:7-19), a formidable task (vv. 22f.).

Another unpopular policy was Solomon's drafting of laborers from the tribes. The 30,000 Israelites engaged in public projects (5:13-18) were not technically slave laborers as were the Canaanite workers (9:15-22). Yet they relished their freedom too much to submit without complaint. The assassination of Adoniram (or Adoram), superintendent of the labor crews (4:6; 5:14; 12:18), indicates the strong feelings toward Solomon's rigid policies.

The most lasting and influential legacy of Solomon's era was the temple at Jerusalem. Only during this period did Israel have the combination of wealth, centralized government, and relief from enemy attack necessary to complete a project of this scale. The resources of Solomon's kingdom and the ties of friendship with Phoenicia (5:1) were fully exploited to provide a house of worship. Foreign artisans were indispensable: (1) the pastoral life of the Israelites did not stimulate craftsmanship; (2) the prohibition against making any replica of the deity (Exod. 20:4) tended to curtail artistic activity.

Archaeological discoveries in Canaan together with the fairly detailed biblical descriptions (1 Kgs. 5–8) permit reasonable reconstruction of the temple and its furnishings. However, nothing of the temple itself[23] remains, and no tenth-century Phoenician temple has yet been discovered. The ninth-century shrine of Tainat in Syria contains the same tripartite division — porch, nave (holy place), and inner sanctuary (holy of holies).[24]

194

Solomon's foreign policy was based mainly on friendly alliances, sometimes sealed by marriage, and maintenance of a formidable army. Among his wives was Pharaoh's daughter, for whom he built a special wing on his palace (3:1; 7:8). This profitable alliance is testimony both to Solomon's prestige and Egypt's weakness, for, although Egyptian kings frequently wed foreign princesses, they rarely married their daughters to non-Egyptians. For a dowry, Pharaoh (perhaps Siamun, one of the last of the feeble Twenty-first Dynasty) gave Solomon the border city of Gezer (9:16).[25]

Solomon's alliance with Hiram of Tyre was also profitable (5:1-12). The Phoenicians[26] were just entering the heyday of their colonial expansion. They supplied architectural skill and many materials, especially Lebanese timber, for the temple and palaces. They built and manned his ships and provided a market for Israel's wheat and olive oil. This tie proved especially lucrative when Hiram extended to Solomon a substantial loan (9:11).

Solomon was the first Israelite to use chariotry effectively. Quartered in a ring of fortified border cities (vv. 15-19), his militia included 4,000 stalls for horses,[27] 1,400 chariots, and 12,000 horsemen (4:26). Recent excavations at Hazor, Eglon, and Gezer have yielded Solomonic remains.[28]

Trading was Solomon's forte. Eager to control the land bridge between Asia and Egypt, he governed the chief north-south caravan routes. Merchant ships carried his cargoes from ports like Ezion-geber to harbors in Asia and Africa. The famed visit of the queen of Sheba (10:1-13) may have had a commercial purpose. Her people, the Sabeans in southwest Arabia, were apparently in danger of economic suppression by Solomon's tight hold on their caravan routes. Though the queen's journey was successful, she probably had to share her profits with Solomon.[29] He was also middleman between the Hittites and Arameans in the north and the Egyptians, who sold chariots to these northerners. The king held a similar monopoly on the horse-trading enterprises of Cilicia, biblical Kue (10:28f.). Solomon's commercial enterprises brought fabulous wealth to Jerusalem. Unfortunately, this wealth did not benefit all classes in Israel. Nor did it relieve the severe taxation necessary to support the massive building enterprises. The commoner, in fact, may have been less comfortable under Solomon than under David and Saul. The tendency toward centralization of wealth which angered the great prophets of the eighth century began in Solomon's golden reign.[30]

Restiveness among Israel's neighbors revealed that Solomon was losing his grip on the empire. Hadad led a revolt in Edom. More formidably, Rezon seized Damascus, jeopardizing Solomon's hold on the Aramean city-states (11:14-25). The author of Kings interpreted these events as tokens of divine judgment for Solomon's serious religious compromises. Note the warning of this possibility in Solomon's second vision (9:1-9). The book does not chide Solomon for his sensuality or amoral living but for disobedience to Israel's monotheistic ideal. Embracing the religions of his wives, Solomon forsook his Israelite heritage and shirked his royal responsibilities as guardian of the faith.

> Like Saul's and David's reigns before him, Solomon's is divided into two phases: "good king" and "bad king."[31] Judgment had to come, if not in Solomon's lifetime (he was spared for David's sake), then afterward. And come it did.

CHAPTER 14

Divided Monarchy (1 Kgs. 12:1–2 Kgs. 18:12)

For the editors of Kings, the two centuries that followed Solomon were as gloomy as Solomon's era was glorious. Historically significant acts of divine judgment open and close the period, with increasing apostasy in between. Literarily, prophetic stories, especially ones involving Elijah and Elisha, dominate the account. Thematically, the editors stress how the idolatry of the northern kingdom earned it Yahweh's terrible judgment.

> The people of Israel continued in all the sins that Jeroboam committed; they did not depart from them until the LORD removed Israel out of his sight, as he had foretold through all his servants the prophets. So Israel was exiled from their own land to Assyria until this day. 2 Kgs. 17:22-23

Rehoboam and Jeroboam — The Kingdom Torn in Two (1 Kgs. 12:1–14:31)

Because Solomon had tolerated idolatry, disastrous divine judgment inaugurated the reign of Rehoboam, Solomon's son and successor. The prophet

Ahijah prophesied that Jeroboam, an able young Ephraimite whom Solomon had appointed to supervise northern work gangs in Jerusalem (11:28), would lead the northern tribes to independence.[1] The oracle evidently made Jeroboam's rebellion public, so he fled to Egypt to escape Solomon's wrath (vv. 26-40), returning when Solomon died.

Rehoboam's Drastic Policy (12:1-24). The showdown with Jeroboam took place at ancient Shechem, site of many historic Israelite convocations (cf. Josh. 24). Rehoboam wanted the northern tribes to recognize him as king, but they sought relief from Solomon's oppressive policies.[2] Poorly advised by ambitious friends, the brash Rehoboam announced that his policies would be even harsher than his father's. So, led by Jeroboam, the Israelites declared independence by invoking an old northern political slogan:

> What share do we have in David?
> We have no inheritance in the son of Jesse.
> To your tents, O Israel!
> Look now to your own house, O David. (v. 16; cf. 2 Sam. 20:1)

Rehoboam's attempts to enforce his demands failed. The Israelites assassinated his taskmaster Adoram, and prophetic intervention kept his troops from marching north. Only Judah remained loyal (v. 20), although Benjamin formed part of Rehoboam's army (cf. vv. 21-24). God used Rehoboam's miscalculation to bring long overdue judgment on Judah for Solomon's idolatry and oppression — judgment in the form of Jeroboam's insurrection.

Jeroboam's Rival Religion (12:25–14:20). The editors of Kings remember Jeroboam mainly for two things — his founding of a rival form of Yahwism in the north and his condemnation by prophets.[3] Afraid that pilgrimages to Jerusalem might sabotage his kingdom, Jeroboam outlawed trips to the Solomonic temple and set up alternative shrines at Dan and Bethel. He not only staffed these "high places" with priests and attendants who did not stem from Levi but also equipped them with golden calves like those Israel worshiped at Sinai (Exod. 32:1ff.). Archaeology suggests that these calves probably were only pedestals which the invisible Yahweh was thought to mount.[4] But common people undoubtedly identified them with the images of the Canaanite fertility cult and began to merge the worship of Yahweh and Baal. This syncretism explains the prophetic rebuke of Jeroboam and his shrines (e.g., from the man of God, 13:1-32; from Ahijah, 14:14-16).[5] Jeroboam even changed the date for the nation's main feast, probably the feast of Tabernacles (cf. Num. 29:12-39).

Struggles Inside and Outside (14:21–15:34). Under Rehoboam the religious apostasy that had characterized Solomon's reign became more blatant. Yahwism struggled with Canaanite religion, as the mention of Asherim (NRSV "sacred poles") and male cult prostitutes indicates (vv. 23f.).[6] Rehoboam also struggled to steer Judah's ship of state through stormy political seas. Judah's army continued to spar militarily with their northern rival, neither nation getting the upper hand (v. 30; cf. 15:6). Worse, the powerful Libyan-Egyptian, Sheshonk (biblical Shishak), invaded Judah (*ca.* 926 B.C.) and exacted heavy tribute, even plundering Solomon's gold shields (vv. 25-28).[7] Sheshonk's inscriptions in the temple at Karnak in Egypt confirm the bloody swath cut by his campaign: Egyptian troops ravaged more than 150 places throughout Palestine and Edom. Only political instability in Egypt kept Sheshonk from wreaking even greater devastation. Rehoboam's replacement of the lost gold shields with shields of bronze signaled that Judah's golden age was gone (vv. 26f.). The editors of Kings read the entire episode as God's judgment on the people of Judah for their apostasy.

After the brief, uneventful reign of Abijam (15:1-8; called Abijah in 2 Chr. 13:1), Kings introduces the lengthy rule of Asa (*ca.* 911-870) with its typical formula for rulers of Judah. Specifically, it (1) synchronizes the king's accession to the throne with the rule of the northern king; (2) states the length of his rule; (3) gives his mother's name;[8] and (4) evaluates his reign, usually in comparison with David's pious devotion (vv. 9-11).[9] Asa is one of the few kings of Judah to whom the editors give a favorable evaluation. Thematically, he represents Judah's first religious reformer — the forerunner of Hezekiah and Josiah.[10] His pious devotion also highlights how apostate the northern kingdom had become under Jeroboam's rival religion.

Divine judgment on Jeroboam's infamous dynasty soon fell, as the prophets had predicted. In a violent coup, Baasha, of Issachar, took the throne from Jeroboam's son Nadab, annihilating Jeroboam's whole family (vv. 27-30). By providing the north with an alternate cult to Jerusalem's, Jeroboam had outraged the editors of Kings. They constantly remind their readers that Jeroboam led Israel into open and flagrant sin (e.g., 16:26; 22:52) and condemn him for failing to protect Israel against religious compromise.[11] So, Jeroboam's kingdom, formed to bring judgment on Judah, itself fell victim to God's judgment. Significantly, because of apostasy Baasha's brief dynasty (i.e., he and his son Elah) suffered the same prophetic condemnation and humiliating judgment as Jeroboam's (15:33–16:14).

House of Omri — Building the Northern Capital (16:1-34)

The northern kingdom never established a stable royal dynasty. Jeroboam's son Nadab ruled only two years before Baasha murdered him and his family

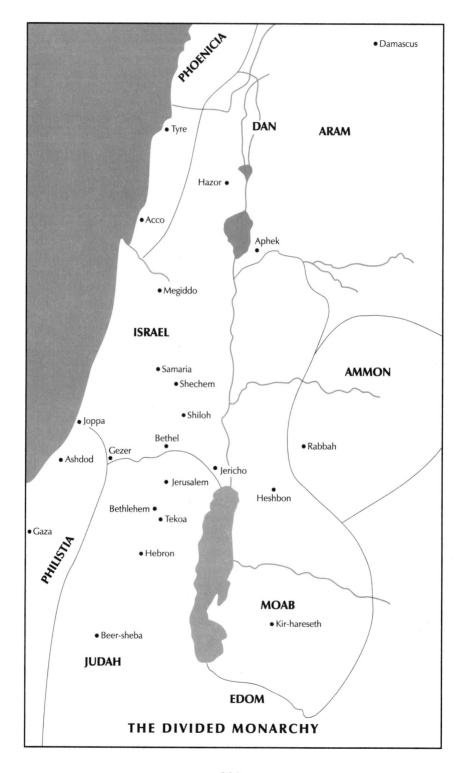

THE DIVIDED MONARCHY

(15:27-30). Baasha's son Elah suffered the same fate at the hands of Zimri, a military commander (16:8-14). But Zimri reigned only seven days before another general, Omri, besieged his capital at Tirzah. Zimri's death divided the people's loyalty between Omri and Tibni, but eventually Omri's forces prevailed.

To his credit, Omri finally stabilized the northern kingdom politically. He gave it a permanent capital, Samaria, an admirable site near Shechem. He bought it legally, so like David's Jerusalem it was his city. It remained the capital until Assyria destroyed it 150 years later, a tribute to Omri's skill as architect and builder. As one modern archaeologist observes, "Samaria lies athwart the main north-south route, watchful of any advance up from Judah and in easy contact with Phoenicia. . . . It was equally important for him [Omri] to have easy communication to the west, where lay the richest lands of his kingdom. On all accounts, Samaria was a much better focus than Tell el Far'ah [Tirzah]."[12]

Excavations have laid bare Omri's lavish building enterprises, projects continued by his son Ahab. The luxury Amos denounced a century later began under Omri.[13] Probably Omri's shrewdest political move was his alliance with prosperous Phoenician Tyre, a pact sealed by the marriage of his son Ahab to Jezebel, daughter of the king of Tyre (16:41).[14] The alliance gave Omri a ready market for Israel's agricultural products and enough military strength to keep the Arameans of Damascus from invading his large territory in Transjordan. But for the editors of Kings the alliance had a disastrous drawback which completely outweighed its benefits. It eventually brought to power Ahab and Jezebel, who used their royal position and resources to promote Baal worship in Israel. Fortunately, God provided Israel a powerful witness, Elijah the prophet, to oppose that policy and to promote the true faith.[15] Omri's dynasty is given about one-third of the space in the account of the houses of Kings, even though it occupies only one-tenth of the 400 years embraced in the narrative. By the length, detail, and centrality of their account, the authors of Kings were making clear that the contest between Yahweh and Baal was the centerpiece of their understanding of Israel's history.[16]

Elijah versus Ahab and Jezebel — Israel at the Crossroads (17:1–22:53)

The clashes between Elijah and Ahab drive the plot of 1 Kings 17–22.[17] As their major theme, the conflicts detail where Israel went wrong and describe the coming divine judgment on those responsible. These chapters present "an

Remains of a large, columned building at Megiddo, formerly identified as
Solomon's stables but now dated to the reign of the Omride dynasty and
probably built by Ahab. *(Oriental Institute, University of Chicago)*

epic, . . . which recounts the mighty battle that determined for all times the
fate of the entire nation."[18]

Canaanite Religion. Israel found the worship of Baal attractive. The idols
of the Canaanite fertility god offered them something tangible to worship, and
Baal's festive occasions fed Israelite passions for wine and immorality. Baal was
lord of the vine and god of fertility, so Baalism taught heavy drinking and
sexual license as religious duty. Baal worshipers believed that sexual intercourse
in worship with cultic prostitutes (both male and female) promoted fertility.
The practice was thought to encourage Baal to enjoy intercourse with his
consort, thus ensuring fertility in the land.

Furthermore, though worshipped in local forms, Baal had become for
the Canaanites a universal god. Jezebel's god was Baal Melqart (or simply
Melqart; also spelled Milqart), the form of Baal revered in her home city, Tyre.
But Ugaritic texts imply that Baal's title Melqart (lit., "king of the city")
branded him lord of the underworld and his authority was not limited to any
one geographical area.[19] That is why the editors of Kings regard Baalism as
such a threat. By denying Yahweh's exclusive sovereignty, it cut at the heart of
Israel's faith.

The Showdown (1 Kgs. 17–19). This carefully crafted literary unit presents "a Battle of the Gods" in which Yahweh takes on the forces of Baal.[20] The prophet Elijah fired the opening salvo by aiming a startling announcement point-blank at Ahab: "As the LORD the God of Israel lives, . . . there shall be neither dew nor rain these years, except by my word" (17:1). Since Canaanite religion worshipped Baal as the god of life and fertility, the decree implied that, if Baal failed to overcome the drought imposed by Yahweh, Israel should draw two conclusions: (1) that only Yahweh, and not Baal, is God, and (2) that Elijah, not the prophets of Baal, is God's true messenger. Subsequent episodes in chs. 17–18 serve to confirm those truths. Though involving human characters, they amount to skirmishes between Yahweh and Baal which refute point-by-point popular beliefs about Baal.[21]

For example, while Israel gradually dried up without rain, Yahweh provided Elijah food and water at the Wadi Cherith east of the Jordan River (17:2-6). Similarly, throughout the drought Yahweh kept Elijah, the widow of Zarephath (a coastal town south of Sidon), and her son alive (vv. 7-16), even raising the boy from the dead (vv. 17-24). The incidents demonstrated that Yahweh, not Baal, controlled both fertility and life itself.[22] The demonstration is all the more persuasive because the skirmish takes place in Phoenicia, Baal's home territory. At the end, the widow voices one of the chapter's main themes when she affirms that Elijah, not other prophets, truly speaks on Yahweh's behalf (v. 24).

The warring deities and their prophets fought the decisive battle at Mt. Carmel (1 Kgs. 18). Once again, as if taunting his divine opponent, Yahweh fired the first shot by announcing through Elijah that he would soon send rain (v. 1). Later on Mt. Carmel Elijah, Yahweh's lone representative, dramatically confronted Baal's 450 prophets (vv. 20-40).[23] Boldly, Elijah called Israel to worship either Yahweh or Baal, depending on which god would send fire on the prepared sacrifice (vv. 21, 24).[24] But when a full morning of shouting and ritual dancing produced nothing from Baal (v. 26), Elijah needled his frenzied opponents with hilarious sarcasm (v. 27): "Shout louder! . . . Surely he is a god! Perhaps he is deep in thought, or busy, or traveling. Maybe he is sleeping and must be awakened." Or maybe there is no Baal!

When Elijah's turn came, he moved with a striking simplicity. His prayer was short, direct, and devoid of frantic display: "Answer me, O LORD, answer me, so that this people will know that you, O LORD, are God . . ." (v. 37). Immediately, fire fell from heaven, consuming his sacrifice and the altar itself (v. 38). The stunning sight so shook Israel that they acknowledged Yahweh as the only God (v. 39). Elijah had the prophets of Baal executed (v. 40), and Yahweh confirmed that he alone was God by sending the rain he had announced earlier. The deluge almost overtook Ahab before the king, urged by Elijah, reached safety in his palace at Jezreel (vv. 41-46). The painful drought was over! If the previous chapter cast doubt on the divine claims of Baal, this episode questioned his very existence. For Israel, the choice was between Yahweh and pure delusion.

But ch. 19 shows that Baal's forces fought on. Threatened with death by Jezebel (v. 2), Elijah fled for his life into the desert south of Beersheba (vv. 3-5a). There Yahweh fed the depressed prophet (cf. ch. 17), guided him farther south to Mt. Horeb, and appeared to him in "a sound of sheer silence" (vv. 5b-18).[25] The theophany scene echoes Yahweh's appearance to Moses on Mt. Horeb (Exod. 19; 32–34) and portrays Elijah as a kind of second Moses.[26]

Yahweh sent Elijah back to Israel to anoint three leaders who would violently purge Israel of Baal worship: Hazael, king of Syria; Jehu, king of Israel; and Elisha, Elijah's successor (vv. 15-18). But of the three Elijah actually anointed only Elisha (vv. 19-21; for the rest see 2 Kgs. 8–10). This partial completion of the mission signals that the bitter contest with Baal would not be a quick, decisive *Blitzkrieg* as on Mt. Carmel but a long and bloody struggle.[27]

The End of Ahab (1 Kgs. 20–22). The rest of 1 Kings details the gravity of Ahab's sin, pronounces his sentence, and reports his execution. Ahab's two heroic victories over Ben-hadad of Syria (20:1-34) surprisingly turn sour when an unnamed prophet announces the king's death for the first time (vv. 35-43). The reason given is that Yahweh wanted Ben-hadad killed but Ahab set him free.[28] The cold-blooded scheme by Jezebel and Ahab to murder Naboth to acquire his vineyard further confirms Ahab's guilt (ch. 21). Small wonder that Elijah expounds upon the death sentences of the wicked king and his savage queen in the strongest terms (vv. 20-24). Finally, condemned again by Micaiah ben-Imlah, Ahab dies in battle — struck, ironically, by an arrow shot at random (ch. 22).[29] The editors of Kings regarded his death as the well-deserved punishment predicted by the prophets.[30]

Exploits of Elisha (2 Kgs. 1:1–8:29)

Though Ahab was dead, 2 Kgs. 1 shows that Canaanite religion was very much alive. When Ahab's successor, Ahaziah (*ca.* 853-852), suffered an injury, he sent messengers to priests or prophets of Baal-zebub, god of the Philistine city of Ekron, to find out if he would heal. The mission implied that Baal, not Yahweh, was lord of Israel and shaper of its future. Ever Baal's staunch opponent, Elijah intercepted Ahaziah's emissaries, held off three military attempts to capture him, and announced that Ahaziah would not recover (1:2-16). The prophecy came true, and Ahaziah's brother Jehoram (or Joram) ruled Israel until about 841. Ahaziah's death and succession by a brother, not a son, hinted that Ahab's dynasty was on its last leg, just as Elijah had prophesied.

Elisha Succeeds Elijah. To signal the transition from Elijah to Elisha, 2 Kings reports their "farewell visit" with Elijah's "sons" — i.e., his apprentice-prophets or followers (2:1-5). When a dramatic yet mysterious event took Elijah from him, Elisha cried out: "My father, my father! the chariots of Israel and its horsemen!" (2:12). Some years later King Joash voiced the same tragic lament over Elisha as the prophet lay dying (13:14). In a sense, this expression sets literary bookends around the life of Elisha. It suggests that godly leaders, not mighty armies, gave Israel strength; their prophets were their true defense.

As heir to Elijah's ministry, Elisha begged also to inherit his power (2:9). The request for a double share of Elijah's spirit is not a presumptuous request for twice what Elijah had. Rather it seeks two portions as an inheritance just as the firstborn son was entitled to a double share of the estate (cf. Deut. 21:17).[31] The episode recalls the transition of power from Moses to Joshua, portraying Elisha as a new Joshua destined to win decisive new victories for Israel. Two inaugural miracles (2:19-22, 23-25) confirmed that God's power was indeed with Elisha as it had been with Elijah.

Elisha and Jehoram (ca. 852-841). As Elijah had troubled Ahab, so Elisha harried Jehoram — and for good reason! Outside of token reforms such as tearing down Ahab's pillar to Baal, Jehoram made little effort to undo the damage wrought by his parents (3:1-4). The editors of Kings include several stories to show that he shared their cavalier attitude toward the ethical and religious demands of covenant faith. The same neglect of social justice found in the story of Naboth's vineyard underlies the appeal by a prophet's widow to Elisha to rescue her from the creditor who threatened to enslave her two sons (4:1-7; cf. 1 Kgs. 21). Still, the Elisha stories offer more evidence of the seven thousand that had not bowed to Baal than does 1 Kings (cf. 1 Kgs. 19:18). Despite the young delinquents who mocked the bald-headed prophet (2:23f.),[32] the Shunammite woman proved devout and generous (4:8-37).

Resisting the temptation to consult pagan oracles (1:2, 6, 16), active bands of prophets loyal to Yahweh responded to the leadership of Elisha (2:15-18; 3:4-8; 6:1-7).[33] And although infiltration of foreign religions was a hazard to Israel's faith, Israel itself was involved in some missionary outreach. For example, it was a captive Israelite young woman who pointed her master, Naaman, commander of the Syrian army, to the prophet of the true and living God to find healing (5:1-27).[34]

Two episodes marked the politics of Jehoram's reign. First, Mesha, king of Moab, whom Omri and Ahab had forced to pay heavy tribute in sheep and wool, revolted against Israel (3:4-8). Initial military setbacks against Jehoram and his ally, Jehoshaphat of Judah, drove Mesha to desperate measures.[35] He sacrificed his eldest son, his successor, to Chemosh, the Moabites' deity, as a burnt offering upon the wall. This appalling sight apparently caused Israel's troops to panic. The meaning of the words "And a great wrath came upon

Israel" is unclear (v. 27). Perhaps God used this bizarre sight to confuse them so that the Moabites could defeat them. Or perhaps some of Israel's superstitious soldiers (not all had the insight of Elijah or Elisha!) feared the wrath of Chemosh in the land where he, not Yahweh, was thought to rule.[36]

The second noteworthy event was the series of skirmishes between Israel and Syria. In 5:2 and 6:8 there are hints that raiding Israel, especially Transjordan, may have been standard Syrian practice. Elisha doubtlessly viewed the wars of Israel as holy wars and was consulted frequently before battle by the king (e.g., 3:13-19; 6:9ff.). If he was an aid to the king of Israel, Elisha was a thorn in the side of the king of Syria. The prophet always seemed to know the king's battle strategy before he himself did, so it is no surprise that the king took drastic but vain action to rid his land of Elisha (6:8-23). The episode plays on the literary motif of blindness versus sight and sounds a significant theme: Yahweh preserves his people because, being sovereign, he revises the plans of nations.[37]

Elisha and the Syrians. Elisha had a finger in Syrian affairs on other occasions. One striking story from this period concerns a Syrian siege of Samaria which almost starved the city. The king of Israel blamed Elisha for the disaster (6:31), perhaps because the prophet had recommended clemency for captured Syrian raiders (vv. 20-33). Or, the king might have known that Elisha had predicted the defeat in an unrecorded prophecy. Calmly weathering the king's fury, Elisha prophesied the end of the famine the very next day (7:1f.). The prophecy came true when the Syrians, panicked by strange noises they took to be an attacking army, fled, leaving their equipment and rations (vv. 3-20). Ironically, lowly lepers rather than royal scouts discovered the defeat and broke the news. The episode conveys the message that God faithfully fulfills his prophetic word, often through the unwitting help of his humble followers.[38]

On a journey to Damascus, Elisha learned that the aged Ben-hadad, ruler of Damascus and head of the league of Aramean city-states for about forty years, was ailing (8:7-9). Desperate to discover his fate, Ben-hadad sent gifts to Elisha by his trusted steward Hazael. Elisha's response was puzzling: "Go, say to him, 'You shall certainly recover'; but the LORD has shown me that he shall certainly die" (v. 10). The apparent answer to Ben-hadad was that the illness would not be fatal. Elisha knew, however, that Hazael would plot against the king, and this would cause Ben-hadad's death.[39] The firm gaze which the prophet fixed on Hazael was prompted by his knowledge of both the pending assassination and the suffering that subsequently would befall Israel (v. 12). When Hazael smothered Ben-hadad with a wet bedsheet, the throne of Damascus was his.[40] Thus, Elisha carried out the second part of the commission God gave Elijah at Mt. Horeb (1 Kgs. 19:15).[41]

While the Syrians plagued Jehoram of Israel throughout his reign, Jehoram of Judah (*ca.* 853-841), Ahaziah's father, had troubles of his own (vv. 20-24). Edom followed Moab (3:3-8) in revolting against its masters. This show of independence underscores the weakness of the southern kingdom, no longer able to hold their southern neighbors in check.[42]

With amazing courage and vitality, Elisha ministered throughout the land to commoner and aristocrat, Israelite and foreigner. More than once he drew the fire of kings, both Israelite and Syrian. Yet when either wanted word of the future, he called upon Elisha. Clad in Elijah's rude mantle of haircloth (1:8; 2:13), he soothed a widow's anxiety, helped a servant recover an axe head (6:5-7), baffled Ben-hadad, and infuriated Jehoram. Moreover, he initiated the plan which toppled the wicked and compromising dynasty of Omri, fulfilling Elijah's dire prophecies against Ahab and Jezebel. In the end, Elisha lived up to his name, for through him "God saved" Israel.

Jehu and His House — Trouble in Israel (9:1–14:29)

To bring down the house of Omri, Elisha elected Jehu, a hard-driving, swash-buckling officer in Jehoram's army, assigned to guard against a Syrian coun-terattack at Ramoth-gilead (9:1-37). In the ancient charismatic manner — as when Samuel elected Saul and David — Elisha's representative anointed Jehu, and Jehu's soldiers acclaimed him king. With this mandate Jehu led a bloody purge that claimed a host of victims: Jehoram of Israel (9:24), his ally Ahaziah of Judah (vv. 27f.), Jezebel (vv. 30, 37), the male descendants and associates of Ahab (10:1-11), forty-two members of Ahaziah's clan (vv. 13f.), and all the worshippers of Baal in Samaria (vv. 18, 27). Yahweh rewarded Jehu's obedience by promising him a dynasty of four generations (v. 30). Jehu's purge brought about the doom which Elijah had predicted for Ahab's dynasty (vv. 1, 17, 30; 1 Kgs. 20:21-22). It also evidenced Yahweh's continuing mastery over Baal and the political machine that had long promoted Baal worship in Israel.

But Jehu's brutality carried dire consequences (see Hos. 1:4). On his famous Black Obelisk, the Assyrian Shalmaneser III records that he took tribute from Jehu of the house of Omri (*ca.* 841).[43] Ahab had joined with Damascus against Shalmaneser at Qarqar (*ca.* 853), but Jehu decided to pay tribute to Assyria instead. He refused to join forces with Hazael of Syria against Assyria, so Hazael raided and ravaged Israel, chipping away at Israel's holdings in Transjordan (10:32f.). The editors of Kings interpreted this event as the hand of Yahweh beginning to reduce the size and power of Israel.

Jehu's death only encouraged the Syrians to take greater liberties. And the reign of Jehu's son Jehoahaz brought Israel to the brink of disaster. The

Black Obelisk of Shalmaneser III (841 B.C.) depicting "Jehu, son of Omri" bowing in tribute before the Assyrian king. *(British Museum)*

cryptic note in 13:7 shows the impotence which Hazael's attacks had produced: "For there was not left to Jehoahaz an army of more than fifty horsemen and ten chariots. . . ." (A half-century earlier Ahab had fielded two thousand chariots at the battle of Qarqar!) Looking back on those dark days, the authors of Kings had no other explanation for Israel's survival than the covenant loyalty of God who had pledged to be faithful to the patriarchs (vv. 22f.).[44]

Athaliah and Joash (ca. 841-835; ca. 835-796). When Jehu killed Ahaziah, he plunged Judah into a monarchical crisis. Ahaziah's ambitious mother, Athaliah, occupied his throne and used her power to further the worship of Baal Melqart. By saving the boy Joash (also spelled Jehoash), the priest Jehoiada foiled her plot to destroy all competitors for the throne (11:1-3). Later Jehoiada, who had reared Joash, secretly engineered the lad's enthronement as king and the execution of Athaliah (11:4-21). The chief accomplishment of Joash was the refurbishing of the temple, probably neglected and desecrated under the influence of Athaliah (12:1-21). But after doing so much for Joash, the priests evidently resented his attempts to control them. Perhaps the palace conspiracy which took his life resulted from his high-handed policies in regard to the temple project. Also, by paying tribute to Hazael during the Syrians' campaign to Philistine Gath, Joash may have become unpopular with the more warlike elements of his people (vv. 17-18).

Jehu's savagery had another long-term consequence: it soured relations between Israel and Judah during the reign of Jehu's grandson Jehoash (*ca.* 798-782). Flushed with success against Edom (14:7), Judah's king Amaziah (*ca.* 796-767) sent a brash challenge to Jehoash of Israel. The northern king's reply is typical of the sage expressions in which the ancient kings and wise men took pride: "A thorn bush on Lebanon sent to a cedar on Lebanon, saying, 'Give your daughter to my son for a wife'; but a wild animal of Lebanon passed by and trampled down the thorn bush" (v. 9).[45] When Amaziah persisted, Jehoash crushed his forces at Beth-shemesh. Pursuing Judah's routed army, Israel stormed Jerusalem, smashed a portion of her wall, and looted the temple and royal treasury (vv. 11-14).[46]

Jeroboam II (ca. 793-753). While Joash's son Amaziah ruled Judah, the skillful administrator and soldier Jeroboam II enjoyed in Israel a long, prosperous reign. With Syria and Assyria weak, Jeroboam expanded Israel's territorial holdings just as Jonah ben Amittai had prophesied (14:23-29). He pushed Israel's borders north to the vicinity of Hamath in northern Syria and south to the Dead Sea. Undoubtedly, he also incorporated substantial areas of Transjordan, perhaps as far south as Ammon and Moab. The editors of Kings regarded Jeroboam as a savior mercifully sent by Yahweh to wrest the nation from the edge of ruin (vv. 26f.). But in Israel's empty ritual and in routine oppression of the poor, Amos the prophet saw grounds for full-scale judgment. It seems that Jeroboam gave Israel respite from judgment at the outset of his reign only to ripen it for judgment after its close.

Last Days of Israel (15:1–18:12)

After Jeroboam, the northern kingdom moved steadily and unknowingly toward the historical storm which would eventually shatter it. The leading edge of that storm could be seen in two momentous developments. First, Israel suffered serious internal instability — a series of violent coups like those that had leveled the dynasties of Jeroboam I, Baasha, and Omri. Just as Hosea predicted (1:4), Jehu's dynasty collapsed when Shallum killed Zechariah (*ca.* 753-752), son of Jeroboam II (2 Kgs. 15:8-12). Only a month later (*ca.* 752), ruthless Menahem in turn assassinated Shallum (vv. 13-16). Menahem ruled about a decade and apparently died a natural death, the only one of the last half dozen kings of Israel to do so.[47] Pekahiah (*ca.* 742), Menahem's son, was slain by his officer, Pekah, who occupied the throne until *ca.* 732 when Hoshea (*ca.* 732-722) conspired against him and gained the crown. The prophet Hosea, an eyewitness, described this relentless pattern of intrigue and counterintrigue:

> All of them are hot as an oven,
>   and they devour their rulers,
> All their kings have fallen;
>   and none of them calls upon me. (7:7; see 8:4)

Second, under Tiglath-pileser III (*ca.* 745-727) and his successors, the threat of Assyrian attack once again pressured Israel externally. Menahem (*ca.* 752-742), Pekah (*ca.* 742-732), and Hoshea (*ca.* 732-722), the three most important Israelite kings of this final period, had to reckon seriously with Assyrian invaders, whether in paying tribute or being ravaged (15:19f., 29; 17:3-6).[48]

Uzziah, Jotham, Ahaz (ca. 790-715). Meanwhile, Judah enjoyed relatively smooth sailing. Its kings generally followed a program of appeasement of Assyria and, after the coup against Joash (12:20), an unbroken succession of Davidic kings ruled Judah from Jerusalem. Judah greatly benefited from the practice of establishing coregencies: a son was placed on the throne by his father to identify him clearly as heir apparent well before the old king's death. This prevented the difficulties experienced at the death of David (1 Kgs. 1). However, after the long, prosperous reign of Uzziah (also called Azariah),[49] Judah was forced to struggle for survival against an alliance between Pekah of Israel and Rezin of Damascus (*ca.* 750-732), whose primary aim was opposition to Assyria (15:37).[50]

Uzziah's son Jotham (*ca.* 750-731) refused to join this coalition and incurred their wrath. His son Ahaz (*ca.* 735-715) faced an even more serious threat when the two kings laid siege to Jerusalem (16:5). Though the invasion failed, apparently Ahaz lost his port and industries at Elath (Ezion-geber)[51] on the Gulf of Aqaba to Rezin (v. 6).[52] Tiglath-pileser's invasions of Syria and Israel brought relief to Judah, although at a high price: agreeing to become an Assyrian vassal, Ahaz had to deplete the treasuries and partially to strip the temple to pay the required tribute (2 Kgs. 16:5-9, 17-20). This expedient served Judah well in political terms, deferring an Assyrian attack on Judah for a few decades. But the editors of Kings especially single out one act of Ahaz — his replacement of Solomon's altar with one of Syrian design (vv. 10-16) — to show Ahaz to be as apostate as the kings of the northern kingdom (cf. v. 3). The episode is read as a tragic turning point for Judah — the day it chose the rebellious path which ended, generations later, in its national demise.

The End of Israel: Hoshea (ca. 732-722). To underscore its significance, the editors of Kings recounted the end of the northern kingdom at great length

(17:1–18:12). During Pekah's reign, Tiglath-pileser had pared away huge portions of Israel, leaving intact only the core around Samaria (15:29). So, when Hoshea seized the throne (*ca.* 732), he had no choice but to yield to Tiglath-pileser's demands for tribute. Sometime after Shalmaneser V (*ca.* 727-722) succeeded Tiglath-pileser, Hoshea defied his Assyrian lord and courted Egypt's support against him (17:4). But Egypt was too weak to help when Shalmaneser swept into Israel and stormed Samaria. The fortress capital held out for a couple of years, during which time Shalmaneser died. His successor, Sargon II (*ca.* 722-705), finished the task with a vengeance (*ca.* 721).[53] Israel's proud kingdom had fallen, no more to rise (vv. 1-6; Amos 5:2).

> Here the authors pause to survey the rubble of this once lofty realm and to interpret its demise (2 Kgs. 17:7-23; cf. 18:12). In true prophetic fashion they view the Assyrians as mere instruments of a God who had to judge Israel's unbridled profligacy and unrelieved spiritual depravity. Their contempt for the covenant, say the authors, fired God's fury, leaving no alternative but judgment.

That judgment was compounded by the deporting of much of the surviving Israelite remnant and the importing of pagan hordes, who contributed to the delinquency of the land with their alien religions. Such a mixture of populations was standard Assyrian practice, intended to curb revolt by thinning the warm blood of patriotism. The ethnic and religious syncretism of the Samaritans (17:41) as well as their opposition to the restoration in Judah (recorded by Ezra and Nehemiah) helps explain hostile attitudes toward them in New Testament times (e.g., John 4).

CHAPTER 15

Judah Alone (2 Kgs. 18–25)

Hezekiah's Reforms (2 Kgs. 18:1–20:21)

After Israel's demise, questions arise about Judah. Will it survive? Will God's next move be judgment or grace? Will Judah renew its loyalty to the covenant? The closing chapters of Kings give the answers by telling the story of two heroes whose reigns were separated by that of one villain. Their lives explain why Judah followed Israel's lead and suffered Israel's fate.

> Indeed, Jerusalem and Judah so angered the LORD that he expelled them from his presence. 2 Kgs. 24:20

Rebellion against Assyria. Hezekiah, the first hero, was coregent of Judah with his father, Ahaz, from *ca.* 729 B.C. Then he ruled alone from *ca.* 716 to 687. He learned important lessons from Israel's collapse. Spurred on by the prophet Isaiah, Hezekiah pursued two commendable goals. First, he tried to break Assyria's political dominance in the west. Second, he attempted to purify Judah's covenant faith by abolishing the worship of Canaanite and Assyrian gods. The two tasks were related. In the ancient Near East, suzerains normally required vassal states to practice their masters' religions along with their own.

Troubles at home kept Sargon preoccupied in Assyria. For nearly a decade (720-711), he battled his northern neighbors, particularly Armenia (Urartu). Free of Assyrian invasions, Hezekiah slackened his ties with Nineveh and awaited the right moment to rebel. Probably about 711, he joined Philistine Ashdod and the kingdoms of Edom and Moab in revolting against Sargon (18:7). The Nubians may have promised help, but their hold on the throne in Egypt was still too shaky, since they had just conquered the Nile valley and established the Twenty-fifth Dynasty (715-663). Sargon easily put down the rebellion and set up an Assyrian governor in Ashdod.

Ancient vassal kings knew that their best chance for revolt came when the dominant nation changed rulers. In 705, Sargon died, leaving the Assyrian throne to his son Sennacherib.[1] Hezekiah chose that moment openly to rebel again.

Intrigue with Egypt. Hezekiah was not alone in his will to revolt. Egypt, too, was itching to break with Assyria. This worried Isaiah, who knew that revolt would not solve Judah's problems. Rebellion would actually cost Judah in two ways: an Assyrian invasion would ravage Judah, and the influence of their pagan allies would compromise Judah's covenant faith. In a dire oracle of woe, Isaiah warned that God's wrath would cause Judah's plan to backfire:

> "Oh rebellious children," says the LORD,
>   "who carry out a plan, but not mine;
> and who make an alliance, but against my will,
>   adding sin to sin;
> who set out to go down to Egypt,
>   without asking for my counsel,
> to take refuge in the protection of Pharaoh,
>   and to seek shelter in the shadow of Egypt;
> Therefore the protection of
>   Pharaoh shall become your shame,
> and the shelter in the shadow of
>   Egypt your humiliation." (Isa. 30:1-3)

The prophets hated foreign military alliances, especially those with Egypt. These amounted to rejections of the Exodus. Israel's Lord had proved himself master of Pharaoh and his army in the plagues and at the Red Sea. To trust Egypt for help showed that the people of Judah had lost confidence in their once-victorious covenant God.

Overtures from Babylon. The Babylonian ruler, Merodach-baladan, shared Egypt's hunger for freedom. He sent an emissary to Jerusalem, supposedly because of Hezekiah's illness, but actually to talk revolt (20:12-19). Banished from Babylon by Sargon, Merodach-baladan had recovered his kingdom in 709. His wearisome quarrel with Assyria had honed to a fine edge his desire to revolt. Longtime vassals of Assyria, the Babylonians wanted to see whether Hezekiah would make a stout ally against Sennacherib. Hezekiah showed them the royal wealth, supplies, and military equipment. That gave Isaiah the opportunity for a frightful prediction. Any treaty with Babylon would have the direst of consequences. It would prove a trap which catches the hunter instead of the prey. A century later Isaiah's words came true. Three times the Babylonian army attacked Judah and their neighbors. They left Jerusalem's walls and temple in ruins and brought to a bitter end the reign of Hezekiah's line (ch. 25).

Hezekiah followed the counsel of his pro-Egyptian political advisers rather than heeding the advice of Isaiah. The king fortified Jerusalem for the inevitable siege. The authors of Kings singled out especially his steps to assure an adequate water supply: ". . . he made the pool and the conduit and brought water into the city . . ." (20:20). The "pool" is the pool of Siloam inside Jerusalem. The "conduit" describes a remarkable feat of engineering, a tunnel which still survives today. More than 1,700 feet long, it carried water from the spring of Gihon (1 Kgs. 1:33) outside the walls in the Valley of Kidron to the pool inside.[2] Isaiah, however, read these preparations as arrogant self-reliance, where trust in God was needed (Isa. 22:8-11).

Invasion by Sennacherib. Sennacherib soon noticed the defiance of Hezekiah and his allies. He amply outfitted his army, defeated Merodach-baladan, and set an Assyrian prince over Babylon. Then he marched west,

Sennacherib's attack on Lachish (701 B.C.), depicted on relief
from his palace at Nineveh. *(British Museum)*

crushing the coastal rebellion of Tyre, Acco, Joppa, and Ashkelon. Near Ekron in Philistine territory, he defeated an Egyptian army that had marched north to support the rebels.

Then he turned on Judah and confirmed Isaiah's worst fears.[3] The account in Kings is brief: "In the fourteenth year of King Hezekiah [701] Sennacherib king of Assyria came up against all the fortified cities of Judah and captured them" (2 Kgs. 18:13). Sennacherib's own descriptions better convey the awful mayhem: forty-six fortified towns captured, and 200,150 prisoners, plus innumerable animals of all kinds. Vividly the king details his tactics: he piled earthen ramps against city walls, pounded the gates with battering rams, and tunneled under the brick walls.

As for Jerusalem, Sennacherib's account describes a siege: "He himself [Hezekiah, the Jew] I shut up like a caged bird within Jerusalem, his royal city. I put watchposts strictly around it and turned back to his disaster any who went out of its city gate."[4] Sennacherib is silent about Jerusalem's fall, but Kings supplies the explanation: the angel of the Lord annihilated the Assyrian army, perhaps by a terrible epidemic of bubonic plague.[5] Twenty years later (681), Sennacherib's sons killed him.

Archaeological testimony also documents the events at Lachish (Tell ed-Duweir) outlined in 18:17-37. A relief on the palace wall at Nineveh shows Sennacherib seated on his portable throne outside Lachish receiving homage from defeated inhabitants of Judah.[6] Apparently, Lachish was Sennacherib's headquarters before the assault on Jerusalem. After Lachish fell, the Assyrian king sent three high officials and a sizable force to persuade Hezekiah to surrender Jerusalem.[7] The Assyrian delegation did its best to intimidate the city's leaders. They denounced Judah's Egyptian allies and ridiculed Hezekiah's leadership. They mocked Hezekiah's reliance on Yahweh to rescue the city, jeering at the failure of local gods to save Hamath and Samaria. Such cajoling and sarcasm apparently were standard ploys of ancient diplomacy.

Heartened by Isaiah (19:6f.), Hezekiah refused to surrender. Sennacherib reminded him by letter of the chain of victories with which he had enslaved Syria and Palestine. Once more Isaiah encouraged the king. In the Lord's name, the prophet denounced the Assyrians' arrogance and specifically promised the relief of Jerusalem: "He shall not come into this city, shoot an arrow there, come before it with a shield, or cast up a siege mound against it" (v. 32).

Theological Themes. The writers of Kings contrast the apostasy of Israel with the firm faith of Hezekiah. Against long odds, the king trusted Yahweh to deliver Judah — and Yahweh delivered! Further, they portray the Assyrian invasion as a confrontation between Yahweh and Assyria.[8] Yahweh, not Assyria, emerged victorious, even striking down Sennacherib in his own home temple! Sadly, the miraculous deliverance caused problems for later prophets like Jeremiah. People interpreted the rescue as evidence that Zion, with its Davidic palace and Solomonic temple, would never fall. They used Judah's victory as an excuse for complacency and compromise. Finally, the references to Babylon anticipate its future role in Judah's demise. Later the authors of Kings, who have told the story of miraculous preservation, will have the sad task of telling the tragic story of Jerusalem's collapse (ch. 25).[9]

Manasseh's Rebellion (21:1-26)

Manasseh, the villain of Judah's last days, drastically reversed the policy of Hezekiah. Ironically, though Judah's most apostate king, he reigned longer than any of his predecessors — fifty-five years (696-642).

Compromise with Assyria. Manasseh was as bent upon collaboration with the Assyrians as Hezekiah was upon resisting them. A startling reversion to pagan practices accompanied that collaboration.[10] High places, altars, and images were erected, including an image of the Canaanite Asherah in Solomon's temple. Judah came to celebrate the Assyrian astrological cult and to practice all kinds of magic and fortunetelling. Once, probably in some national emergency, Manasseh sacrificed his own son. He brutally crushed any opposition, even that of the prophets. The authors of Kings appraised his reign with horror: ". . . Manasseh misled them to do more evil than the nations had done that the LORD destroyed before the people of Israel" (21:9); "Moreover, Manasseh shed very much innocent blood, until he had filled Jerusalem from one end to another . . ." (v. 16).[11] He combined the worst qualities of Jeroboam I and Ahab.

Conflict with the Prophets. Eventually Manasseh collided head-on with the prophets. Their theme was judgment: "I will wipe Jerusalem as one wipes a dish, wiping it and turning it upside down" (v. 13). Unlike Isaiah in the days of Sennacherib, they could no longer promise rescue for Jerusalem and the temple. A later prophet, Zephaniah, aptly describes the vicious legacy which Manasseh left Jerusalem: capitulation to foreign cults and compromise with foreign fashions (see Zeph. 1:1-9).

The short, ill-fated reign of Manasseh's son Amon (642-640) also featured idolatry. Unhappiness with the pro-Assyrian policies in which he imitated his father probably led to his assassination by political underlings ("servants," 2 Kgs. 21:23). Fearing Assyrian reprisals for revolt, the "people of the land," who may have been landed gentry, killed the assassins.[12]

Theological Themes. The writers of Kings can hardly contain their diatribe against Manasseh. In their view, his abominable reign made divine judgment on Judah inevitable. Judah would join Israel in exile — and for the same reason, apostasy. At the same time, Kings again reminds readers and hearers to take Yahweh's prophets seriously. They, not the popular false prophets, speak for God. So, the downward trend had been set. The narrative in Kings moves relentlessly toward its disastrous denouement. Even Josiah's splendid attempts to revive covenant faith cannot measurably alter the plot.

Josiah's Revival (22:1–23:30)[13]

In some ways the reign of Josiah (639-609), Judah's final hero, paralleled that of Hezekiah.[14] Again military and political pressures kept Assyria close to home. This time, however, Assyria would not recover. By the time of Josiah's tragic death, the dire prophecies of Nahum about Nineveh's demise had already come true.

Three events aided Josiah's desire to reform the faith. In 626 Ashurbanipal, Assyria's last great ruler, died and Nabopolassar led the Babylonians in a successful revolt against Assyria.[15] More important, in 621 construction workers discovered the book of the law in the temple (22:2-20).[16]

Book of the Law. The surprising discovery came during a major temple renovation sponsored by Josiah. The repairs probably reflect the king's sincere personal piety and emerging independent political policy. But the law stirred him to sponsor even more radical measures. He personally led a dramatic ceremony renewing Israel's covenant with Yahweh (23:1-3). He also sought to undo much of Manasseh's damage (23:4-20). Across the land, he deposed idolatrous priests and defiled pagan shrines. The defilement meant they could not be used again. He purged the temple of pagan vessels and presided over the first Passover celebration in more than 400 years (23:21-23). Undoubtedly, prophets like Jeremiah and Zephaniah supported him.

Battle with Neco.[17] Good king Josiah was the first to suffer the judgment which Judah deserved (23:28-30). His tragic death was the leading edge of the storm which would soon overwhelm Judah. In the end, Josiah fell victim to an ironic twist in Egyptian policy. For centuries, Egypt had contested Assyrian domination of the Mediterranean coast. Now Pharaoh Neco marched his army northward to prop up the shaky Assyrians against the Babylonians and Medes, a group of tribes settled in northwestern Persia (Iran).[18] Apparently, Neco preferred a sickly Assyria to a robust Babylonia.

Josiah probably saw the invasion as a threat to his hopes of ruling the territory of the old northern kingdom (vv. 19f.). Boldly, he marched his army to Megiddo to cut off the Egyptian advance toward the Euphrates. He was killed in action, and a stunned Jerusalem greeted the chariot bearing his body home. His death fulfilled Huldah's prophecy, though not as expected (22:20). Josiah had not lived to see judgment fall on Jerusalem, but his demise was certainly a harbinger of it.

Theological Themes. For the writers of Kings, Josiah's career shows that Judah's judgment was inescapable. Not even his sweeping reforms could soothe the Lord's wrath over Manasseh's outrageous reign (23:26f.). At the same time, the writers stress that certain doom did not eliminate all hope of God's grace. Repentant Josiah enjoyed Yahweh's favor despite the coming judgment. Finally, Josiah's death symbolizes the often puzzling ways of divine sovereignty. God reserves the right to deviate from his own patterns: wicked Manasseh lived to a ripe age; righteous Josiah was cut off in his prime.

Jerusalem's Fall (23:31–25:30)

With Josiah gone, the fall of Jerusalem became inevitable. During Judah's last twenty years, Josiah's successors ruled only on terms set by their Egyptian and Babylonian overlords.

Egypt's Dominance. Jehoahaz, Josiah's oldest son, ruled just three months. Though Neco had apparently failed to save Assyria, his victory over Josiah made Judah a tributary. The Pharaoh summoned Jehoahaz to his camp at Riblah in northern Syria, removed him from power and exacted massive tribute. Neco then appointed Eliakim, another son of Josiah, as puppet king (608-597). He gave him the regnal name Jehoiakim (23:34f.) and goaded him to tax Judah severely to pay the tribute.

Babylon's Conquests. Neco soon met his own military match. At Carchemish in 605, Nebuchadnezzar (sometimes spelled Nebuchadrezzer) defeated him. The defeat ended four years of Egyptian control of Palestine (609-605). It also crowned the Babylonians as unrivaled masters of the Middle East. Jehoiakim (*ca.* 603) had to pledge allegiance to Nebuchadnezzar (24:1) but later rebelled — despite Jeremiah's stern warnings. He had misread Babylon's failure to defeat Egypt in battle (601) as a symptom of weakness. But in 598, Nebuchadnezzar marched west again, a move which may have led to Jehoiakim's death. Most likely, citizens of Judah hoping to win Babylonian clemency assassinated the rebel king (vv. 2-7). Judah's defeat was made more painful because its traditional neighbors and relatives — Syria, Moab, and Ammon — aided Nechadnezzar in the siege.

Jehoiachin, Jehoiakim's eighteen-year-old son, mounted the throne (vv. 6-9). But three months later Nebuchadnezzar took the young king, his family, and other nobles hostage to Babylon (597). To forestall further revolt, the

Babylonians also deported Judah's finest leaders and craftsmen. Judah had neither will nor ability to rebel for another decade (vv. 10-16).

Zedekiah's Rebellions.[19] Like Neco, Nebuchadnezzar installed a puppet king in Jerusalem, Mattaniah, Josiah's youngest son and Jehoiachin's uncle. He also gave him the throne name Zedekiah. As if plagued by a death wish, Judah made rebellion against Babylon the dominant drive of Zedekiah's reign (597-586). Two circumstances made the king's rule especially difficult. First, many influential leaders pushed for Judah's independence to boost economic prosperity. Second, some citizens still recognized Jehoiachin, alive in Babylon, as Judah's true king. Jeremiah urged Zedekiah to rule sensibly, but the king lacked the ability to do so.

In 593 Judah resisted the suicidal urge to rebel when it did not join a brewing regional revolt. But a few years later blind ambition and misguided confidence in promises of Egyptian help prevailed. The political juggernaut crushed Jeremiah's opposition and quelled Zedekiah's uncertainty. Judah's arrogance, revealed in the refusal to pay tribute to Babylon, left Nebuchadnezzar no choice. Early in 588 his armies surrounded Jerusalem and besieged it for two years. Judah's foolish leaders waited in vain for the angel of the Lord to help as in Hezekiah's day. Meanwhile, hunger and fatigue weakened and unnerved the populace. The Babylonians intercepted Zedekiah's desperate bolt for freedom and exacted a heavy price for his rebellion. They made him witness the murder of his sons, blinded him, and carted him to Babylon. Thus, history closed the curtain on the tattered remnant of David's ancient glory (25:1-7). One line inscribes the nation's sad epitaph: "So Judah went into exile out of its land" (25:21).

The last smoldering sparks of rebellion consumed even the puppet governor, Gedaliah. Ishmael, a member of the royal family, assassinated him, probably out of spite for the Babylonian conquerors. The assassins fled to Egypt for safety, tragically taking Jeremiah with them (25:22-26).

Jehoiachin's Release. Jehoiachin had lived thirty-seven years in captivity. When Evil-merodach succeeded Nebuchadnezzar in Babylon (562), he freed him and accorded him royal treatment (vv. 27-30).[20] This passage indicates that the authors finished 2 Kings late in the Exile. Only then did they see the full implications of the events.

Theological Themes. The authors of Kings describe Jerusalem's suffering in great detail (as does Lamentations in poetic form). The savage sacking and burning, spoiling and looting document the long-expected divine judgment for Manasseh's crimes. In the end, Judah suffered the same fate as Israel — exile. At the same time, the writers of 1-2 Kings end on a more hopeful note. The necessary judgment, warned against in the Torah (Lev. 26; Deut. 28), introduced in Judges, long promised by the prophets, and so ruthlessly executed by the Babylonians, had done its work. Jehoiachin, whose captivity was the first chapter of the Exile, lived to see the last chapter begin. God had sent the dove to signal the end of the Flood. That same God prompted the sacred writers to depict Jehoiachin, free of chains and dining at the king's table. The storm was past; a better day had dawned. That story, however, belongs not to Kings but to Ezra and Nehemiah.[21]

CHAPTER 16

Prophets and Prophecy

In popular usage, a "prophet" is someone who can foretell the future, and "prophecy" means predictions of things to come. Although containing elements of truth, these popular definitions are by no means adequate for the biblical terms. Before studying the prophets we call "Major" and "Minor" (i.e., whose books are longer and shorter) we want to understand the biblical meaning of "prophets" and "prophecy."[1]

> I will raise up for them a prophet like you [Moses] from among their own people; I will put my words in the mouth of the prophet, who shall speak to them everything that I command. Deut. 18:18

Names Used for the Prophet

Prophet. The most common term for the person and office is "prophet" from Greek *prophētēs*. It means, basically, "one who speaks for a god and interprets his will to man."[2] The word is composed of two elements, the second of which means "to speak." The first can mean "for, forth" and "beforehand,"[3] so the word can mean either "to speak for, proclaim," or "to speak beforehand, foretell." A prophet, then, is a "*forthteller*" as well as a "*foreteller*"; both meanings are implicit, and both usages are found in the Bible.

The Hebrew term, which the Greek attempts to translate, is *nābî'*. The derivation and basic meaning, long debated, now seem well established. The root *nb'* means "to call," and its vowel-pattern supports the meaning, "one called."[4] The prophet, then, was one called by God, and as seen in the Old Testament, called to speak for God. Thus the Greek term accurately describes the prophet even if it does not precisely translate the Hebrew.

Biblical usage is best illustrated in God's message to Moses, where Moses is likened to "God" and Aaron is described as his "mouth" (Exod. 4:15f.), and Moses is described as "God to Pharaoh" and Aaron is his "prophet" (7:1f.). The prophet is pictured here as God's mouth.[5] This meaning is reinforced in the formulas frequently used to introduce or close speeches in the prophetic books: (1) the *messenger formula*, "Thus says (said) the LORD," links the prophet's words to Yahweh's in the same way that a message carries a dispatch verbatim from a king to a battle commander in the field; (2) the *message reception formula*, "the word of the LORD came unto me," stresses the divine source of the message and the consequent authority of the prophet; (3) the *oracle formula*, "says the LORD" (lit. "uttered of the LORD"; Heb. *neûm yhwh*), has the same force.

"Seer" and Other Terms. The prophet also was called a "seer," meaning "one who sees in a vision." Two different Hebrew words are so translated and, it seems, are completely interchangeable. One passage (1 Sam. 9:9) indicates that the term "seer" was earlier and came to be replaced by "prophet," but if there was ever any clear-cut difference, it had become indistinct by Old Testament times.[6]

Other terms for the prophets include "man of God," "watchman," "messenger of Yahweh," and "man of the Spirit." These terms are actually descriptions of the prophet's activities, although at times they seem to have become titles. They add significant aspects to an understanding of the prophet.

Characteristics of the Prophet

Ecstasy. According to one widely held view, the prophets' major characteristic was ecstatic behavior:

> We can now call before our minds a picture of the prophet's activity in public. He might be mingling with the crowd, sometimes on ordinary days, sometimes on special occasions. Suddenly something would happen to him.

His eye would become fixed, strange convulsions would seize upon his limbs, the form of his speech would change. Men would recognize that the Spirit had fallen upon him. The fit would pass, and he would tell to those who stood around the things which he had seen and had heard.[7]

In a few instances in the Old Testament a person was seized by sudden ecstasy. When King Saul was grasped by the Spirit, the people asked: "Is Saul also among the prophets?" (1 Sam. 10:11). But there are many more examples of prophets who exhibit normal behavior. One classic study has summarized prophecy like this: God "speaks to His prophets, not in magical processes or through the visions of poor phrenetics, but by a clear intelligible word addressed to the intellect and the heart. The characteristic of the true prophet is that he retains his consciousness and self-control under revelation."[8] How revelation actually took place is a mystery. The forms vary from external and internal hearing to seeing objects that became catchwords like Jeremiah's almond branch and Amos' basket of fruit, to fantastic visions like Ezekiel's wheels and living creatures and Zechariah's flying scroll. What are more important than the means of revelation are the results: a prophet captured by God's word and compelled to declare it to God's people.

Call. The biblical prophets were certain not only that God had spoken to them, but also that they were called to speak God's message.[9] In some instances, the call is described in considerable detail, and each account has distinctive elements not found in the others. Thus the call was an individual event, not a stereotyped formula used by prophets to validate their activity. Isaiah seems to have accepted his call willingly, while Jeremiah was reluctant and contended with Yahweh. Amos seems to have had a single call, while Ezekiel cites the day, month, and year of several occasions when the Lord called him and gave him a message.[10] Any purely humanistic explanation that would interpret the experience of a call as merely a convergence of events or a subjective psychological experience is not consonant with the biblical data. Yet, God did use historical situations and personal circumstances in communicating with the prophets.

The descriptions of the call have at least two roles in the prophetic books. First, they validate the authority of the prophet as distinct from that glibly claimed by the false prophets. Second, they contain summaries of the main themes of the prophets' ministries.

Character. Peter, referring to prophecy, said: "Moved by the Holy Spirit saints of God spoke."[11] While biblical statements about the holiness of the prophets are rare, it is generally accepted that God would only use holy people as his prophets. One might argue that God saw fit to use those whose moral behavior was not always above reproach in other offices, such as Moses the lawgiver, Aaron the high priest, or David the king. But it is difficult to think that Nathan would have had any effective word of reproach for David if he himself had been a man of unbridled passions. Still, it is closer to the biblical data to stress the prophet's wholehearted dedication to Yahweh and to the obedience of the covenant rather than his or her moral excellence.

Chronology of the Prophets

Before Samuel. Samuel sometimes is called "the last of the judges and the first of the prophets" (see Acts 3:24; 13:20). However, the term *prophet* is used also of a number of persons prior to Samuel. About all that can be deduced from the material may be summarized as follows: (1) the concept of revelation from God to a chosen servant (the basic element of prophecy) was familiar prior to Samuel; (2) since Moses is taken as the prototype of the prophet (see Deut. 18:18), his prophetic ministry should be taken into account in defining the prophetic task; (3) the idea that prophecy had diminished and then resumed with Samuel is implicit in Eli's reaction to Samuel's call (1 Sam. 3:7-9). The implications are quite significant, for studies of prophecy cannot begin with the prophetic writings of the Old Testament, or even the prophetic sayings of Samuel, Nathan, Elijah, and Elisha. They certainly must include the prophetic ministry of Moses, and, probably, the prophetic elements in the patriarchs. Hosea seems to highlight the ministries of Moses and Samuel in this description of the historic role of Israel's prophets:

> By a prophet the LORD brought Israel up from Egypt,
> and by a prophet he was guarded. (Hos. 12:13)

Prophets

Prior to Samuel
Enoch (Jude 14)
"Holy prophets from the beginning" (Luke 1:70; Acts 3:21; Heb. 1:1)
Abraham (Gen. 20:7; cf. Ps. 105:14f.)
Moses (Num. 12:1-8; Deut. 34:10; Hos. 12:13)
Miriam (prophetess; Exod. 15:20)
Eldad, Medad, and the Seventy (Num. 11:24-29)
Deborah (prophetess; Judg. 4:4)

"Man of God" (13:6ff.)

Prophetic vision rare in the days of Eli (1 Sam. 3:1)

Monarchy [*ca.* 1075-931]

Samuel (1 Sam. 3:1) [time of Saul and David]

Gad (2 Sam. 22:5) [Saul and David]

Nathan (12:1) [David]

Ahijah (1 Kgs. 12:22) [Rehoboam and Jeroboam I]

Saul, David, Solomon; experiences with prophetic characteristics

Asaph, Heman, and Jeduthun (Ethan) (1 Chr. 25:1)

Iddo (seer; 2 Chr. 9:29) [Solomon, Rehoboam, and Ahijah]

From division of the Monarchy to the Assyrian period [931–*ca.* 800]

Shemaiah (1 Kgs. 12:22) [Rehoboam]

Ahijah, Iddo (see above)

Hanani (seer; 2 Chr. 16:7) [Asa]

Jehu son of Hanani (1 Kgs. 16:1) [Asa and Jehoshaphat]

Elijah (17:1) [Ahab and Ahaziah of Israel]

Elisha (19:16) [Ahab-Jehoash of Israel (860–*ca.* 795)]

Micaiah ben Imlah (22:4) [Ahab]

Jehaziel and Eliezer (2 Chr. 20:14, 37) [Jehoshaphat of Judah]

Zechariah (24:19) [Joash]

Unnamed prophet (1 Kgs. 20:13) [Ahab]

Unnamed prophet (2 Kgs. 9:4) who anointed Jehu

"Sons of the prophets" (1 Kgs. 19:10)

"False" prophets (ch. 13; etc.)

Eighth-century [*ca.* 800-*ca.* 675]

Jonah son of Amittai [Jeroboam II; 2 Kgs. 14:25]

Amos [Uzziah of Judah and Jeroboam II]

Hosea [before fall of Jehu's dynasty]

Micah [Jotham, Ahaz, and Hezekiah]

Isaiah [Uzziah, Jotham, Ahaz, and Hezekiah]

Oded (2 Chr. 28:9)

Seventh-century [*ca.* 675-597]

Zephaniah [Josiah]

Nahum [between 663 and 612]

Huldah [prophetess in Josiah's day; 2 Kgs. 22:14-20]

Habakkuk [perhaps shortly after 605]

Jeremiah [626-586]

Sixth-century [*ca.* 597-538]

Obadiah

Ezekiel [592-572 (or 570)]

(Daniel [605-538, or considerably later])

Isaiah 40–66 [*ca.* 550-538 (possibly later)]

Postexilic (*ca.* 538-*ca.* 450)
Haggai [520]
Zechariah 1–8 [520 and 518]
Joel
Malachi [between *ca.* 486 and 450]
Zechariah 9–14
Jonah

(Note: problems of dating and authorship of Jonah, Joel, and portions of Isaiah and Zechariah are discussed under the individual prophets.)

Tenth and Ninth Centuries.[12] With the call of Samuel, a new period of prophetism begins in the biblical account. Since it coincides with the inauguration of the Monarchy one may conclude that the prophet was specifically intended to serve as the voice of God to the king. The fact that the end of the prophetic activity of the Old Testament is approximately contemporary with the end of the Israelite kingdom would seem to support this view. The books of Samuel and Kings contain numerous pictures of kings consulting with prophets on battle plans and other political decisions, as well as of prophets confronting kings about their behavior and its consequences.[13]

The prophets of the Monarchy and early Divided Kingdom are sometimes called the "oral" or "nonwriting" prophets. This means that the Bible has no books which are solely the products of individual prophets of this period, such as a "prophecy according to Elijah." In contrast, the prophets of the later period of the Divided Kingdom are called "literary" or "writing" prophets. These terms are unfortunate, for they fail to elucidate the facts as derived from the Scriptures. On the one hand, one book (or two) bears the name of Samuel. (Whether he wrote it or not is beside the point.) On the other hand, one should not assume that the "writing" prophets set out to write books of prophecy. The evidence in the book that bears Jeremiah's name indicates that he was for the most part an "oral" prophet, and that the writing down of his prophecy was largely the work of Baruch (Jer. 36:4, 32). It is clear from their contents that most of the prophetic books were first spoken messages, written down later, perhaps by the prophet himself, perhaps by his disciples.[14]

Eighth and Seventh Centuries. Prophecy changed markedly in the eighth century. In general, the prophets of the tenth and ninth centuries were "advisors to the kings." They may have had prophetic messages for the people, but most evidence indicates that they counseled the kings, helping them discern the will of God, encouraging them to walk in the way of Yahweh or, more often, rebuking them for failing to do so. In the eighth century, the prophets, following Amos' example, turned their attention more to the people, the nation, or in some cases foreign nations. It seems unlikely that prophetic messages addressed to Edom, Tyre, Egypt, etc., were actually intended to be delivered to and heard by the rulers of those nations and, if so, that they would have had any effect. More likely, they were intended for Israel, the people of God, in the contemporary generation, and even more, in future generations. The speeches to the nations served to teach their hearers lessons of Yahweh's universal sovereignty which showed itself both in judgment and salvation.

Along with this change of the object of address came the introduction of written prophecies. True, earlier prophetic speeches survive, such as Samuel's words to Saul and David, Nathan's rebuke of David, and the words of Elijah to Ahab or Jezebel. But with the eighth-century prophets came longer messages and collections that constitute books bearing the prophets' names. At the same time, the "sons of the prophets" were less prominent, perhaps having developed into a state-supported institution. They may have become the targets of the true prophets' criticism of "false" prophets (Mic. 3:5-8; Jer. 23:16-22).

A crisis had gripped Israel and Judah by the throat.[15] Within the century, indeed within the lifetime of the eighth-century prophets and in some cases during their prophetic ministry, the northern kingdom would be brought to an end. God's judgment was about to be poured out upon the kingdom of Israel. The kings and the leaders were so enmeshed in sin that there was no hope of rescue. The prophets, therefore, sounded clear warnings, seeking to move the people to repentance. Inscripturation of the prophecies seemed to be a way to get the message to a wider audience, as well as to a future generation.

What had happened to Israel in the eighth century was used as an illustration to Judah, whose end would come at the close of the seventh and beginning of the sixth century (for example, Ezek. 23). The seventh-century prophets therefore shared a more urgent sense of judgment and issued a strengthened plea for repentance. At the same time, the element of hope for the remnant was sounded ever more clearly.

Exile and Postexilic Period. With the end of the southern kingdom and the destruction of Jerusalem (586 B.C.), the old way of life had come to an end. Many of the people were in captivity, needing hope and encouragement to begin again. They had to be reminded that Yahweh's covenant was still in force, and that he would complete his redemptive purpose in the world. Accordingly, these themes abound in the prophets of the sixth and fifth centuries.

At the same time, Israel's basic beliefs had to be enlarged so Yahweh could be seen as God of all nations, not of Israel alone. The revelation of his purpose, originally expressed in the covenant with Abraham (e.g. Gen. 12:2-3; 18:18), had to be made clear. Israel was to continue to be distinct from the nations (or Gentiles). Nevertheless, Yahweh's purpose was to bring the nations to worship him and learn his laws from Israel. As this became clearer, more references were made to the "latter days" or "those days." The study of events leading up to and following the "end" of the age (eschatology) began to assume greater prominence.

Specifically, postexilic prophets encouraged rebuilding the temple, reestablishing the kingdom and throne of David, and resuming the formal worship that helped preserve Israel's separate identity. But even this would not be the ultimate achievement of God's redemptive program. Troubles, persecution, and even another destruction of Jerusalem lay beyond the immediate future. The temple was nothing like the previous temple in its splendor, and the nation was only a tolerated and insignificant bit of a vast Persian empire. These were not the glory-filled "latter days" that had been foretold. Accordingly, prophetic hope looked to still-future blessings. Apocalyptic elements were introduced, claiming that God himself would intervene to destroy Israel's enemies and set up his king on Zion. There would be a time of judgment that would be a refining fire for Israel. Then would come an age of righteousness and peace. Having sounded that note, the prophets became silent.

This chronological sequence is reflected in the order of chapters in the *Survey*. It is important to try to grasp the message of each prophet in the context of his life. At the same time, we recognize that the books of the prophets have gone through a process of editing and revision that may have extended over decades or even centuries. In the long run, it is wise to put more emphasis

"Let justice roll down like waters, and righteousness like an everflowing stream" (Amos 5:24); waterfall at Banias. *(Neal and Joel Bierling)*

228

on the books themselves than on the persons or experiences of the prophets. We know very little about the lives of the majority of them. But we treasure and ponder the results of their ministry as the community of believers, led by God's Spirit, has preserved them for us in the books that bear the prophets' names.

Prophecy

In general, there are two simplistic approaches to prophecy, one stressing the predictive element, the other featuring the message as applied to the contemporary situation. In biblical prophecy, both elements are present.

God's Message to the Present Situation. By simply picking verses from the prophets and pasting them together to give "prophecies that prove the Bible" or "Jesus Christ in prophecy," one creates the impression that prophecy is "history written in advance." However, when one studies the prophets, this glamorous concept suddenly disappears. It is necessary to plow through chapters that have nothing to do with the future in order to find a single verse, or even part of a verse, that is "prophecy" in this sense.

A careful study of the prophets and their messages reveals that they are deeply involved in the life and death of their own nation. They speak about the king and his idolatrous practices, prophets who say what they are paid to say, priests who fail to instruct the people in Yahweh's law, merchants who use false balances, judges who favor the rich and give no justice to the poor, greedy women who drive their husbands to evil practices so they can bask in luxury. All this is prophecy in the biblical sense. The shadow of Mt. Sinai, with its covenant law, tinges everything the prophets say. A prophecy is God's message to the people and the leaders who rule them in God's place. It is a message of judgment because God's people are constantly in need of correction. At the same time, it is a message of hope, for Yahweh has not broken his covenant and will complete his redemptive task when the inescapable judgment has run its course.

God's Message concerning the Future. God is never concerned with the present simply for the sake of that moment. Ever since creation, he has been working out his plan for humankind. And God never forgets where he is going and what he is doing. The prophets are let in on that purpose (Amos 3:7). Prophecy, therefore, is not simply God's message to the present situation, but is designed also to show how that situation fits into the larger plan, how God will use it to judge and refine or comfort and encourage the people. Prophecy is God's message to the present in the light of the ongoing redemptive mission.

On exceptional occasions, he gives rather precise details about what he is going to do. Yet even in "predictive prophecy," the prediction is almost always attached to the present situation. The prophet speaks about what has meaning for his listeners. He does not suddenly forget them and utter a detached "prophecy of things to come." Rather, he takes them from that moment into the sweep of divine redemptive activity and centers on a truth that will become a beacon to God's people.

> Since God's redeeming purpose culminates in Jesus Christ, all prophecy somehow must point to Christ. In that sense Christ "fulfills" prophecy, or, rather, prophecy is fulfilled in him. While this may not be what is commonly understood by "fulfillment of prophecy," it is the definition properly derived from the biblical evidence.

Prophecy is a window that God has opened for his people by his servants the prophets. Through it one can see more of God's purpose in his redemptive work than would be possible otherwise. It gives a better understanding of what he has done for and with and through his people in the past, and a clearer comprehension of his purpose in the present. And, while it may never satisfy insatiable demands for specific details of the future, it nevertheless gives a clear view of where God's grace is taking humanity and what obligations therefore are laid upon his people.

CHAPTER 17

Hebrew Poetry

The Old Testament contains a great deal of poetry. In any language, poetry features tightly structured lines and highly emotive word pictures.[1] It appeals more to human imagination and emotion than to reason. Since the form of poetry controls the message to some extent, the reader must seriously reckon with its form to understand its content. Also, scholars frequently suggest that a passage be emended or deleted "for the sake of meter."[2] Occasionally, the poetic structure will help restore a broken text or understand a difficult one.[3] Thus, one should know enough about Hebrew poetry to assess the value and limitations of such emendations. Since many characteristics of poetry are common to most languages, our survey focuses primarily on features unique to Hebrew poetry.[4]

> Pleasant words are like a honeycomb,
>   sweetness to the soul and health to the body. Prov. 16:24

Characteristics

Parallelism of Members. Parallelism is the most prominent characteristic of ancient Semitic poetry including that in Hebrew.[5]

Parallelism is "the repetition of the same or related semantic content and/or grammatical structure in consecutive lines or verses."[6] In other words, it has to do with the relationship or correspondence between successive poetic lines. Scholars disagree on exactly what kind of relationship links them, but the most common descriptions suggest that the lines "match," "intensify," or "second" each other.[7] The effect produced by parallel lines has been summarized insightfully:

> Parallelism focuses the message on itself but its vision is binocular. Like human vision it superimposes two slightly different views of the same object and from their convergence it produces a sense of depth.[8]

How does parallelism work? The dynamic of parallelism seems to derive from several factors.[9] Its *grammatical aspect* has to do with items of grammar like verb tenses and the cases of nouns. Parallel lines may differ in grammatical form rather than simply repeat the same grammar. For example, in Gen. 27:29 observe how the verbs differ (imperative vs. jussive) and how the subject of one line becomes the direct object of its parallel:

Be lord over your brothers,
and may your mother's sons bow down to you.

Such grammatical elements provide parallelism its basic structural skeleton.

The other aspects give parallelism its flesh and blood. The *lexical aspect* focuses on the relationship between specific parallel words. For example, one might observe a poet's use of word pairs, words commonly associated together (e.g., day/night; eat/drink), as well as creative, unexpected word juxtapositions. The *semantic aspect* concerns the relationship between the meaning of entire parallel lines. Though now thought to be inadequate, the traditional categories of parallelism (i.e., synonymous, antithetical, synthetic) illustrate this aspect. Finally, the *phonological aspect* touches on the use of words of similar sounds for poetic effect.

Hebrew poetry uses parallelism in a variety of ways. The following sample is intended to sensitize the reader to some of them rather than to offer a comprehensive catalog.[10]

(1) In *synonymous parallelism,* each poetic line (*stich* or *colon*) expresses the same thought in equivalent language. Consider this affirmation of God's mercy:

a	b
He does not deal with us	according to our sins,
a´	b´
Nor repay us	according to our iniquities. (Ps. 103:10)

The statement consists of two stichs, each a sentence with a verb, direct object, and prepositional phrase.[11] The first words of each line parallel each other (deal with us/repay us) and so do the concluding phrases (according to our sins/according to our iniquities). One may describe the first line as *ab,* the second as *a′b′* (read "a prime, b prime"), and the complete pair as *ab/a′b′*.[12] As a whole, the distich expresses a single thought: human sinfulness does not determine how the Lord treats his people.

In longer stichs, an *ellipsis* may occur when the second line omits an element from the first but is lengthened to compensate for the loss. This is sometimes called "incomplete parallelism":

	a	b	c
	And I will turn	your feasts	into mourning,
		B′	c′
		and all your songs	into lamentation.

(Amos 8:10)

The parallel elements are obvious (feasts/songs; mourning/lamentation), but the second line assumes the repetition of the missing verb (I will turn). Additional words (and all) compensate for its absence, so both lines have about the same length. To indicate that one unit of the second stich is somewhat longer than its parallel, the longer unit is called *B′* ("heavy-*b* prime"). As a whole, the distich says that Yahweh will turn Israel's joyful parties into dismal wakes.

(2) In *antithetical parallelism,* the second line restates the first as a contrast:[13]

	a	b	c	d
	A-child	wise	gladdens	a-father,
	-a	-b	-c	-d
but	a-child	foolish	grieves	his/her mother.

(Prov. 10:1)

In this example, the first unit is a noun and adjective (a + b), while the parallel stich has its opposite (indicated by a minus sign, "-"). Likewise, the verbs (gladdens/grieves) and direct objects (father/mother) are opposites, although one could render the latter as "parents."[14] Paraphrased, the proverb says, "A wise child makes his parents happy, but a foolish child gives them grief." This statement does not mean that a wise child gladdens only its father, whereas a foolish child grieves only its mother. Clearly, the distich contrasts the effect which a wise or foolish child has on its parents. Of course, though framed antithetically, the proverb actually seeks to promote wise conduct among children.

(3) In the *parallelism of specification,* succeeding lines give the specifics of their predecessor(s). For example, observe in the following example how Isaiah develops his message from a basic principle to specific examples:

	-a	-b
The principle	Cease	the-evil
	a	b
	Learn	the-good.
	c	d
The examples	Seek	justice;
	c′	-d
	Set-straight	oppression.
	e	f
	Vindicate	the-orphan;
	e′	f′
	Litigate-for	a-widow. (Isa. 1:16c-17)

The examples specify what it means to do good rather than evil, i.e., to stand up for the orphan and widow.

Often parallelism specifies the result which follows the initial action described. Amos provides an illuminating example:

a	b	c
And-I-will-send	fire	on-the-way-of Gaza
d		e
and-it-shall-devour		her palaces. (Amos 1:7)

The verb "shall devour" is not truly parallel to "fire," but is rather the effect of the fire. "The-wall-of-Gaza" and "her palaces" are complementary statements, implying the entire city. The rest of the passage illustrates synonymous parallelism:

a	b	c
And-I-will-cut-off	inhabitant	from Ashdod,
	B′	c′
	and-holder-of-scepter	from Ashkelon,
D		c″
And-I-will-turn-my-hand		against Ekron,
e		C‴
And-they-shall-perish		the-remnant-of-the-Philistines, said LORD Yahweh.

(v. 8)

Once again, "and-they-shall-perish" is the result of "and-I-will-cut-off." The Philistine cities (Gaza, Ashkelon, Ekron) are parallel with "the-remnant-of-the-Philistines." The entire passage, then, has three distichs (verses of two stichs each), voicing one message against the Philistines. The words, "said LORD Yahweh," form a "prose cliché," and one should always set such lines outside the poem's poetic structure (as in Ugaritic poetry; see below). Thus, despite a common practice of some scholars, there is no good reason to delete such statements "for the sake of meter" *(metri causa),* i.e., to conform to poetic meter.

(4) Hebrew poetry evidences both external and internal parallelism. *External parallelism* describes the correspondence between distichs and is a supplement to *internal parallelism,* the correspondence within a distich. Consider this example:

Internal			External
a	b		
Hear-ye	the-word-of-Yahweh,		A
c		d	
Rulers-of		Sodom;	B
a′	b′		
Give-ear-to	the-Torah-of-our-God,		A′
c′		d′	
People-of		Gomorrah.	B′

(Isa. 1:10)

In this instance, the capital letters represent the stichs, "A" consisting of *a b,* etc. Clearly, the units of the first stich parallel those of the third, as those of the second do those of the fourth. Alternatively, one could analyze the passage as two distichs, each having a verb, object, and vocative: *a b c : a′ b′ c′.* In the following illustration, such reduction is impossible:

a	b		c	
Knows	the-ox		his-owner,	
	b′		C′	
	and-the-ass		the-crib-of his lord;	
d		-A		
Israel	(negative)	knows		
d′		-A′		
My-people	(negative)	understand.		

(Isa. 1:3)

Both the first and second distichs clearly show synonymous parallelism, as the schematization a b c : b′ C′ and d -A : d′ -A′ indicates. But the first distich stands in antithetical parallelism with the second, hence -A and -A´ balance, albeit negatively, the "knows" of the first stich. Also, observe how short the lines of the final distich (Israel . . ./My-people . . .) are compared to the two preceding ones. Literally, the short lines underscore the simple, sad truth of Israel's spiritual dullness.

In conclusion, Hebrew poetry evidences an almost endless variety of parallelism. Readers would do well to analyze enough examples to develop a sensitivity to Hebrew poetry and the meaning of each verse.

Rhyme, Rhythm, and Meter. Unlike English poetry, *rhyme* is not a fundamental element of Hebrew poetry. Occasionally, Israelite poets use rhyming words very effectively, but the rhyme may fall anywhere in a line rather than only at the end.[15] As for *rhythm* and *meter,* decades of lively discussion have produced no agreement as to whether or not Hebrew poetry has them.[16] To date, every proposed metrical system ends up manipulating the poetry so it fits a preconceived pattern.[17] Thus, it seems best to assume that Hebrew follows a *flexible pattern of free rhythm* which uses two to four accented syllables in a line.[18] Scholars use a simple numerical device to describe the number of such accents in parallel lines. For example, if each line has three stresses, the rhythm of that pair would be 3:3; but if the second line has four accents, its rhythm would be 3:4. Obviously, a careful reader would seek to explain the poetic effect of the rhythm, especially when parallel lines differ significantly (e.g., 4:2).

The study of poetry from Ugarit confirms that Hebrew poetry lacks regular patterns of either rhythm or meter.[19] The following examples, again translated literally, show how remarkably Old Testament poetry resembles the Ugaritic materials:

a	b	c
And-depart,	O-king,	from-my-house
a´	b´	c´
Be-distant,	O-Keret	from-my-court

(Krt. 131f.)

a	b	c
Departed	Kothat	from-his-tents
b´	a	c´
Hayum	departed	from-his-tabernacles.

(2 Aqht V.31)

a	b	c	
Lo,	your-enemies,	O-Baal;	
a	b		d
Lo,	your-enemies		you-shall-strike;

a	d		b
Lo,	thou-shalt-vanquish		your foes.

(68:9; cf. Ps. 92:9 [MT 8])

a	b	c
I-shall give	her-field	for-a-vineyard,
	B′	c′
	the-field-of-her-love	for-an-orchard.

(77:22)

a	b	c
They-shout,	Athirat	and-her-sons,
	b′	c′
	The-goddess	and-the-band-of-her-kin.

(Anat V.44)

a	b	c		
She-washes	her-hands,	the-virgin-Anat,		
	b′	C′		
	her-fingers,	the-sister-in-law-of-nations,		
a	b		d	e
She-washes	her-hands		in-the-blood-of	soldiers,
	b′		d′	e′
	her-fingers		in-the-gore-of	troops

(Anat II.32)

Significantly, outside the parallelism, prose clichés similar to "thus said Yahweh" appear in every column. As noted above, this suggests that one should be cautious in emending poetic texts because a phrase supposedly violates expectations of parallelism.

Other Devices. The structural device called *chiasm* commonly appears in Hebrew poetry. In chiasm, the parallel stich reverses the order of units found in the initial stich. If connected with lines, the parallel members would form an *X* or Gk. *chi*, hence the name "chiasm."

A	B
Thou-shalt-break-them	with-a-rod-of-iron;
B′	A′
Like-a-vessel-of-a-potter	Thou-shalt-crush-them.

(Ps. 2:9)

237

a	b	c	d
In-the-wilderness	prepare	the way	of Yahweh,
b′	a′	c′	d′
Make-straight	in-the-desert	a-highway	for-our-God.

(Isa. 40:3)

In both illustrations, the chiasm (crossing) is obvious. In the second example, its present form makes it apparent, but it would have been less obvious if arranged as a tetrastich:

a	b
c	d
b′	a′
c′	d′

Though chiasm is a very common element in Hebrew poetry, both internally and externally, it is not always readily recognizable. In Ps. 2:9, above, it is external, for if set down as a tetrastich, it would look like this:

a + b	A
c d	B
e f	B′
a′ + b′	A′

Even so, this is not obvious, for "with a rod of iron" and "like a potter's vessel" are not exact parallels. The verse's basic thought is: "Thou shalt break and crush them like a potter smashing a pot with an iron hand."

The discussion, above, of the lexical aspect of parallelism briefly mentioned the stylistic device of *word pairs*. The languages of the ancient Near East had many such fixed pairs of synonyms. The following are noteworthy: hear//listen to; silver//gold; gold//fine gold; voice//speech; gift//present; wine//strong drink (or beer, *škr*); serve//bow down; fashion//create//make; people//nation; reside//dwell; count//number; hand//right hand; thousands//ten-thousand(s); earth//dust (or soil). The following Ugaritic and biblical citations illustrate how poets built parallelism around such word pairs:[20]

> We have planted thy foes in the *earth*
> > In the *dust* those who rise against thy brother. (76 II 24-25)

> Their *land* shall be soaked with blood,
> > their *soil* made rich with fat. (Isa. 34:7b; cf. v. 9)

[Let her place] a cup in my *hand*,
    A goblet in my *right hand*. (1 Aqht 215-16)

Your *hand* will find out all your enemies;
    your *right hand* will find out those who hate you.

                            (Ps. 21:8 [MT 9]; cf. 26:10)

He cast *silver* by *thousands*,
    Gold he casts by *ten-thousands*.   (51 I 28-29)

A *thousand* may fall at your side,
    ten thousand at your right hand. . . .   (Ps. 91:7, cf. Deut. 32:30;
                            Mic. 6:7; Dan. 7:10 [Aramaic])

One final poetic device is the use of *graded numbers* or the "x, x + 1" pattern:

Once God has spoken,
    twice have I heard this. . . .   (Ps. 62:11 [MT 12])

For three transgressions of Damascus,
    and for four I will not revoke the punishment. . . .   (Amos 1:3)

There are six things that the LORD hates,
    seven that are an abomination to him. . . .   (Prov. 6:16)

We will raise against them seven shepherds
    and eight installed as rulers.   (Mic. 5:5)

The literary effect of the device is to spotlight one specific, crucial item among a list — as it were, the "straw that broke the camel's back" or the "deciding factor."

The "x, x + 1" form is also found in Ugaritic literature. There it has other, more complex patterns not found in the Hebrew Bible: "10x + x, 10(x + 1) + (x + 1)" (e.g., sixty-six//seventy-seven; seventy-seven//eighty-eight), and "10x, 10(x + 1)" (e.g., eighty/ninety).

Interpreting Hebrew Poetry

The parallelisms of a poem help to shape its message. Thus, one must study both the contribution of poetic elements to a passage as well as the *total* passage itself.

Analyzing the Passage. The first step is to analyze the passage to determine its poetic components, as illustrated above. Whether one uses schematic arrangements, such as *a b c : a´ b´ c´*, is unimportant, but the ability to recognize the elements is essential. For example, Amos 1:8 clearly deals with the Philistines. Therefore, component parts must help illuminate the message about the Philistines. Likewise, Prov. 10:1 deals with the effects of a child's behavior on the parents, so its components must contribute to that meaning.

Analysis, but Not Fragmentation. One must keep the total message of a poem in view. To conclude, for example, from Prov. 10:1 that a wise child brings joy only to its father, while a foolish child grieves only its mother, is to miss the whole point. The proverb in no way suggests that the mother has no joy in a wise child or the father no grief over a foolish one. Likewise, to conclude from Amos 1:8 that the Lord will cut off the inhabitants of Ashdod but not the other Philistine cities is to misunderstand what the poetry says. Often, the poetry's component parts compose an important larger lesson. Isa. 1:16b-20, quoted above, gives a fairly comprehensive picture of "doing good," particularly toward vulnerable people such as the orphan and widow.

Recognizing Poetic Figures of Speech. Poetic language differs from prosaic wording. Expressions like "the trees clap their hands" or "the little hills skip like lambs" are poetic, not botanical or geological descriptions. Similarly, when Isaiah addresses the "rulers of Sodom" and the "people of Gomorrah" (1:10; see above), one must pay careful attention to what he means. By his time, Sodom and Gomorrah had long since disappeared. In using this form of address, Isaiah was comparing his Israelite audience with the greatest sinners the land had ever seen. When Amos parallels "the pastures of the shepherds" with "the head of Carmel" (1:2), he is probably using a device called *merismus.* Merismus juxtaposes opposite extremes in order to include everything in between.[21] Thus, the topographical extremes — mountain top ("head") and valley ("pastures") — stand for the entire land.

In sum, the Bible uses many figures of speech, especially in poetic passages. One must learn to recognize and interpret them as the author intended.[22]

Stylistic Devices. Authors often use stylistic devices to catch the reader's attention or impress their message upon the reader.[23] In poetry, play on the sounds of language is particularly striking. With *alliteration,* words or syllables begin with the same or similar sounds. *Assonance* uses the same or similar sounds (usually vowels) within words. *Paronomasia* (pun) plays on words with the same or similar sounds but different meanings. *Onomatopoeia* is the use of words that sound

Dead Sea Isaiah scroll (1QIsaᵃ), containing oracles againsts rebellious
Jerusalem (Isa. 2:21–3:22). *(Israel Department of Antiquities)*

similar to or suggest the activity they describe. Unfortunately, these devices can
rarely be carried over in translation. For example, when God asks Amos: "What
do you see?" and Amos answers: "A basket of summer fruit" (8:1f.), the Hebrew
word for "summer fruit" sounds almost like that for "end." This similarity of
words prepares Amos for God's statement, "The end has come upon my people
Israel." But the pun is lost in the translation.

241

Retaining the Beauty of Expression. Most readers recognize the beauty of poetic expression. When translating the word of God, it is particularly important to preserve every appealing feature, including the poetry. The New Testament has poetry in the teaching of Jesus, snatches of hymns (Phil. 2:6-11), fragments of creeds (1 Tim. 3:16), and bursts of song (Rev. 4:11; 5:9f.). So, sensitivity to poetry in the Old Testament will enhance one's ability to understand the New. Translators struggle for hours with a single verse, striving to find words and phrasing that convey the meaning with the same beauty as the original. Perhaps the main quality that made the KJV so beloved was its beauty of language. When dealing with poetry, ideally one should work in the original languages. Alternatively, one should at least compare several recent English translations, testing each for both beauty and accuracy. God is the author of beauty. To convey the beauty of the word honors and glorifies God.

Summary

Two methods are available to speak about God: negation and analogy. By negation, one describes him as "infinite" (not finite), "immaterial" (not matter), "invisible" (not subject to human sight), and "unchangeable" (not changing). This method derives from Western rationalism, shaped largely by Greek philosophical methods. By analogy, however, one compares God to something familiar in everyday life. Here one enters the imagery and symbolism of the biblical world, especially that of its poetry. Poetic imagery compares the Unseen to something readers have already seen, helping them to know God better. Ultimately God is known most fully in the incarnate image, the Son. Without denying the value of philosophy, we can say that the biblical approach is superior in many ways to the philosophical. People learn far more through the senses than through speculation. The poetry of the Bible has universal appeal. Its structure and imagery are not lost in translation. It speaks to "every nation and kindred and people and tongue."

Likewise, there is no better way to express devotion to God than through song. Much of the poetry of the Old Testament was originally performed as music. Rather than a source of theological doctrines, it was the expression of deep faith, whether that of the individual singer or of the community. It has maintained its appeal through centuries because the believing community can join in the song to express its own faith and devotion. Today, the musical score has been lost, but the potent poetic words still provide not only a way to know God, but even more, a way to voice praise for God who alone is worthy of it.

CHAPTER 18

Amos

"Come to Bethel — and transgress," said Amos, with sharp irony in bitter confrontation with Israel (4:4). "Go back home, you seer!" said Amaziah, priest of Bethel. "Prophesy there but never again prophesy at Bethel, for it is the king's sanctuary" (7:12f.). This encounter between the prophet of Yahweh and the priest of a famous shrine in the northern kingdom well introduces the study of the prophets. The early prophets proclaimed Yahweh's words in continual conflict with the rulers, priests, and others who would not heed these utterances. This struggle lies at the heart of their passions. For Amos, the transcendent God of the universe was immanently present in Israel as their Judge and Savior, towering over and against all who opposed him.

> "I saw the LORD standing beside the altar. . . ." Amos 9:1

Amos and His Preaching

Prophet. When Amaziah warned Amos to return to Judah and "earn your bread there, do your prophesying there" (7:12, JB), he was implying that Amos was a professional prophet. To his words of contempt, Amos replied: "I (was) no prophet; I (was) no son of a prophet, but I (was) a herdsman[1] and a dresser of sycamore trees, and the LORD took me from following the flock, and the LORD said to me, 'Go, prophesy to my people Israel'" (7:14f.).

Amos was a sheep-raiser of Tekoa (1:1; the same Hebrew word describes King Mesha of Moab in 2 Kgs. 3:4), a village on the edge of the wilderness of Judah about six miles (10 km.) south of Bethlehem, in the southern kingdom of Judah. In addition to breeding sheep, he pierced (or pinched) sycamore figs, a fruit that must be punctured or slit shortly before ripening to be edible.[2] Since figs are not found in Tekoa, Amos may have garnered food for his flocks with seasonal work in the lowlands of western Judah, where such trees were found (see 1 Kgs. 10:27).

His statement, "I not a prophet" (lit.), has elicited continuing debate. In such a verbless clause the tense must be supplied from context. To some, the present tense appears most appropriate: "I *am* not a prophet." Following this interpretation, scholars have argued that Amos disclaimed any connection with a prophetic office and in fact was repudiating it as an instrument of Yahweh's revelation. Other scholars feel this is contradicted by what follows: "Go, prophesy to my people Israel."[3] How could Amos say, "I am not a prophet," and then immediately say that God had commanded him to be just that? Thus these scholars suggest that the clause be understood as indicating past tense: "I *was* no prophet."

Likewise the next segment would read: "I (was) no son of a prophet." The "sons of the prophets" were members of the prophetic guild training to be professional prophets. In the days of Elijah and Elisha, they were apparently highly regarded (see 2 Kgs. 2:3-19), but there were also professional prophets and their young trainees who prostituted their services, saying merely what the rulers wanted (see 1 Kgs. 22:6-23). Without judging the prophetic office, Amos simply declared that he had not been a prophet, but that the Lord called him suddenly to prophesy to the northern kingdom.[4]

Nothing further is known about Amos. Presumably, after delivering the Lord's words he went south to Tekoa and edited his messages. Then he wrote them substantially as we have them today. Another possibility is that disciples followed him about and later recorded his words. In any case, the Lord had raised up this pioneer prophet in order both to preach and to leave a written legacy.

Times. Without doubt Amos' words were delivered in the days of Jeroboam ben Joash (Jeroboam II), who ruled Israel 793-753,[5] for the clash between Amos and Amaziah (7:10-17) is to be understood as an integral part of the message. Since v. 10 therefore is to be accepted as authentic, there can be no basic objection to the claim that 1:1 also is accurate. Now, since the reigns of Uzziah of Judah and Jeroboam II of Israel overlapped for the period 767-753[6] (removing the portions of each reign that were coregencies with the previous kings), Amos' prophecy can be placed within that period, *ca.* 760.

Amos indicates that the revelation was given "two years before the earthquake" (1:1). This event must have been a very severe seismic phenomenon. It was remembered well over two centuries later as "the earthquake in the days of Uzziah" (Zech. 14:5). Physical evidence of it has been posited in the archaeological descriptions of a mid-eighth-century stratum at Hazor, an ancient town north of the Sea of Galilee.[7] However, it does not help us date the prophecy any more precisely. It simply suggests that Amos' ministry was shorter than that of other prophets.

The Assyrian King Adad-nirari III (811-784), in a series of campaigns against the Aramean city-states (805-802), had broken the power of Damascus and removed for a time the Syrian threat to Israel. The succeeding kings of Assyria were checked by the advances of Urartu,[8] while the Aramean (Syrian) city-states of Hamath and Damascus battled each other for supremacy.[9] As a result, Uzziah of Judah and Jeroboam II of Israel could extend their boundaries almost to those of David and Solomon (see Map).[10] Jeroboam's northern border was at the entrance of Hamath, and for a while he ruled both Hamath and Damascus (2 Kgs. 14:25).

Such successes inspired national pride in Yahweh's favor of Israel. The development of international trade made the merchants rich. But wealth brought injustice and greed. The poor were neglected, then actively persecuted. Religion became routine, almost mechanical, and alienated from Yahweh's real presence.

Message. This is the picture of society Amos painted so vividly. Two classes had developed: rich and poor (Amos 5:10f., 15; 6:4f.). The poor were oppressed (2:6f.; 5:11; 6:3-6) and even sold into slavery (2:6-8). The rich had summer and winter palaces crammed with of ivory-inlaid art and furniture (3:15),[11] great vineyards for choice wines, and precious oils for hygiene and perfume (5:11; 6:4-6). The women, fat and pampered "cows of Bashan," drove their husbands to injustice so they might live in luxury (4:1). Justice was a commodity to be purchased, even in the towns that housed the sacred shrines, such as Bethel and Gilgal, but where Yahweh was no longer present (5:4f.). The God of Israel had come to despise their rituals (vv. 21-24).

The Israelites were serving another god who could not help them (8:14). Their religion desperately needed reform (3:14; 7:9; 9:1-4). Yahweh abhorred the "pride (self-sufficiency) of Jacob" (6:1-8) and planned to unmask its absurdity (6:9-14). Israel must come to see its God for who he truly is.

Ivory carving of a sphinx from Megiddo, typical of the wealth and luxury
assailed by Amos (3:15; 6:4). *(Israel Department of Antiquities)*

Amos and His Prophecy

Its Nature. Obviously, Amos did not sit down in Tekoa of Judah and write a
prophecy against Israel. The confrontation with Amaziah at Bethel and the
report Amaziah sent to Jeroboam indicate clearly that Amos had gone to the
northern kingdom and preached with such power and persistence that Amaziah could write, "the land is not able to bear all his words" (7:10). Thus, Amos

246

must have given his prophetic messages orally, probably at Samaria and other places as well as Bethel. His message for the northern kingdom was summarized with these words:

> Jeroboam shall die by the sword,
> and Israel must go into exile away from his land. (7:11)

His prophecy, in its written form, is tightly and gracefully structured. Scholars agree that it was not delivered orally in this form. Some think they can see smaller units that were probably the original messages, while others think certain key words ("locusts," "plumb-line," "basket of summer fruit," etc.) were symbols Amos used in his brief messages, and the expanded form was written later. It is unlikely that such questions will ever be answered. Like the preaching of Jesus, the message of Amos was probably delivered in both shorter and longer forms on various occasions. The written text of his prophecy ought to be understood as a summary of the structure and substance of his prophetic ministry in Israel — as a summary which possesses great precision and beauty.

Its Structure. We may trace the flow of the book as in the chart on page 248.[12] It is important to grasp the scope and movement of this structure if the biting irony of the prophet's rhetoric is fully to be appreciated.

A few comments on the major sections may help to clarify their emphasis. (1) The oracles against six surrounding nations as well as Judah list blatant sins of each along with appropriate threats of punishment. Each begins with the formula, "For three transgressions of . . . , and for four, I will not revoke the punishment" (1:3, 6, 9, etc.). This is the "x, x + 1 pattern."[13] Here it probably indicates that the nations had sinned "enough and more than enough" to warrant God's judgment. The list includes nations bordering Israel and Judah, three of which (Edom, Ammon, and Moab) were related to Israel by blood. The accusations of the neighbors were based on crimes against humanity. Judah was indicted "because they have rejected the law of the Lord, and have not kept his statutes" (2:4). If the nations that did not call Yahweh their God were accountable to him, how much more were his covenant people? This series sets a trap for the Israelites, who would have rejoiced in the doom of the border states. Even more, by linking Israel with the nations in the formula, Amos negated "the whole history of salvation and . . . upset the foundations of communal identity."[14] This ironic reversal of Israel's relation to Yahweh becomes crystal clear in 3:1-2.

(2) The initial shock Israel felt in hearing their name in the roll-call of the guilty was heightened, not eased, in the sections that followed (2:6–6:14). These judgment speeches and woe oracles are freighted with a damning list of

The Structure of Amos

Introduction: Title and Theme	(1:1-2)
Seven Judgment Speeches against the Nations	(1:3–2:5)
"Thus says the LORD"	
"For three transgressions of ——— and for four,	
I will not revoke the punishment"	
"because" (specific indictment)	
"So I will send a fire" (specific threat)	
Transitional Judgment Speech against Israel	(2:6-16)
Three Judgment Speeches against Israel	(3:1–5:17)
"Hear this word" — introduction to indictment	(3:1; 4:1; 5:1)
"Therefore" — introduction to threat	(3:11; 4:12; 5:16)
Two Woe Oracles against Israel	(5:18–6:14)
Misguided interpretation of Day of Yahweh	(5:18-27)
Misdirected sense of material security	(6:1-14)
Five Judgment Visions against Israel	(7:1–9:10)
Locusts, fire, plumb-line	(7:13; 7:4-6; 7:7-9)
Report of Amos' encounter with Amaziah	(7:10-17)
Basket of summer fruit	(8:1-10)
Vision	(8:1-2)
Interpretative oracles	(8:3-10)
The Lord above the altar	(9:1-10)
Two Salvation Promises	(9:11-15)
Restoration of David's realm	(9:11-12)
Return of material prosperity	(9:13-15)

the sins of the royalty, nobility, and priesthood. Each section contains the usual elements of prophetic denunciations — messenger formula ("Thus says the LORD"), indictment of sin, note of transition ("therefore" or "behold"), and threats of judgment where the punishment suits the crime. The overwhelming emphasis, however, is on the crimes themselves, which are described in painful detail. The announcements of judgment are sketched in a handful of sentences (2:13-16; 3:12-15; 4:12; 5:16-17, 27; 6:7-11, 14).

(3) With the vision reports (7:1–9:10), the ratio shifts, and judgment not indictment dominates. This change of tone turns the entire book into a lengthy judgment speech, beginning with multi-faceted descriptions of sin and ending with arguments for and accounts of the inescapable punishment.

248

(4) Yet salvation, not punishment, is God's last word to Israel (9:11-15). Not salvation *instead of* punishment but salvation *after* punishment. The future holds a double blessing as Yahweh fulfills the covenant both to David (2 Sam. 7) and to Abraham and his family: David's realm will be restored (9:11-12); the land's prosperity will be renewed (9:13-15). The Israelites, purged of their sins by the sword of judgment, will hear their Lord once again call them "my people."

Significant Questions

Ethical Monotheism. In a former generation it was a common belief that Amos introduced ethical monotheism — the concept that there was only one God, who demanded ethical behavior.[15] Many scholars now reject the idea that the prophets were introducing a religion, holding rather that they based their words on the covenant tradition.[16] Amos certainly meant to uphold the covenant relationship between God and Israel, often referring to an earlier tradition,[17] and frequently using the covenant name "Yahweh."[18] The prophet's demands for social justice are mostly a restatement of the ancient covenant laws, not simply applied to individuals, but understood as deciding even national destiny.[19] He was more a reformer than an innovator. The idea that Yahweh is God of all nations, after all, only extends the Abrahamic covenant to all the families of the earth (Gen. 12:3; 18:18; 22:18). That Yahweh will punish other nations is not a new idea but rather an expansion of the Exodus tradition in which Yahweh punished Egypt and its gods. That Yahweh was passionately concerned for justice in both Israel and among the nations is inherent in the meaning of the covenant with God.

The charge that the "social gospel" is "another gospel" (see Gal. 1:8) and is therefore contrary to the true gospel of salvation by the grace of God will not stand biblical scrutiny. True, erroneous emphases have sometimes been placed on the biblical doctrine of social justice, both in the pre-Reformation period and in recent decades. The stress on social responsibility (or "good works") has sometimes become a legalistic system opposed to the biblical doctrine of salvation. Human interpretations should not distort the wholeness of the teachings of Scripture. Amos was not the first to stress social justice — nor the last. Responsibility to other persons is part of biblical religion — from the story of Cain and Abel to the closing chapters of Revelation.[20]

Judgment and Hope. A former generation also held that the eighth-century prophets were mainly "prophets of doom and gloom." The elements of hope in the book must on this account be excised as later insertions. This view is commonly rejected today, but some still question whether Amos 9:11-15 is part of the original work. The principal objection is that it is inconsistent with Amos' constant announcements of judgment. It is held therefore to be inconceivable that he would sound a hopeful note to close his prophecy.[21]

However, at least two questions must be answered. First, is Amos really ever devoid of hope? On two occasions, when given visions of judgment, Amos interceded for "Jacob" (7:2, 5). If Yahweh would listen to such intercession — and he did (see vv. 3, 6) — was it too much to believe that Yahweh would restore the nation *after* he had punished it? The second question is more fundamental, for it begins not with the prophet but with covenant theology. Since Amos was building on God's revelation in the light of the covenantal relationship, is it not axiomatic that ultimate restoration is necessary to fulfill Yahweh's purpose? Admittedly, not all Israelites would perceive this truth, but would not Yahweh's prophets? How could Yahweh fulfill his covenants with Abraham and David if total and final destruction of Israel were to be the end of the matter?

A further objection to the authenticity of 9:11-15 is based on the reference to the "booth of David that is fallen" (v. 11). Such a statement apparently requires a date subsequent to the fall of Jerusalem. However, this view relies on English translation rather than the Hebrew text. The passage says "the booth of David (which is) falling" — a participial form. It also could be translated "the falling booth of David." The house of David, presumably as the "booth," already had begun to fall when the kingdom was divided following the death of Solomon (931), and the northern kingdom viewed the Davidic dynasty as ending. In the apostasy of the northern kingdom, and certainly since Ahab and Jezebel (874-853), the kingdom of Israel was also "falling." This demise was experienced in the loss of land to the Assyrians and the payment of tribute to Assyria by Jehu. And beyond doubt, the punishment revealed by Yahweh to Amos foretold the fall of Samaria as well as Judah. God as Judge was for the prophet also the Savior of all Israel's history. Therefore, there seems no valid argument against the use by Amos himself of the language of 9:11.[22] It is even possible that we ought to understand this hope as fundamental to the proclamation of judgment upon the people of God.

Prophet and Cult? Several statements in Amos seem to belittle Israel's religious practices (see 4:4f.; 5:21-24, and esp. v. 25). It has been suggested, therefore, that he opposed the cult. In fact, scholars have often posited a fundamental rivalry between the prophets and priests. They hold that the cultic ideas in the Old Testament developed when the priests triumphed over the prophets after the Exile.[23] This problem, again, is in no way limited to Amos.

However, Amos actually utters no statement against the principle of sacrifice or against the sanctuary. His criticism is directed against specific sins in the northern kingdom. The people of this sinful nation had violated the sanctity of the house of their God (2:8), and Yahweh's servants, both Nazirites and prophets, had been forced into disobedient acts (v. 12). Punishment of the altars of Bethel is pronounced because of Israel's transgression (3:14). The religious ritual of 4:4f. is empty because it is out of phase with the greed and inhumanity of the people. Certainly the passionate statements in Amos are reactions against meaningless ritual which is remote from Yahweh's true presence:

> I hate, I despise your festivals,
> and I take no delight in your solemn assemblies.
> Even though you offer me your burnt offerings and grain offerings,
> I will not accept them;
> and the offerings of well-being of your fatted animals
> I will not look upon.
> Take away from me the noise of your songs;
> I will not listen to the melody of your harps.
> But let justice roll down like waters,
> and righteousness like an ever flowing stream. (5:21-24)

Theological Insights

Yahweh the Supreme God. So consumed is Amos with the call for justice that it is easy to overlook his profound insights into the character of God and, as did scholars of the early twentieth century, reduce Amos to a prophet of social concern. In fact, Amos' cry for justice arose from his recognition of the very nature of God in relationship to the world.

Yahweh judges all nations. This is implicit in the opening cycle of indictments against the surrounding nations (chs. 1–2). He is free to go everywhere he chooses (9:2) and sovereign over all natural phenomena (9:5f.). He made the Pleiades and Orion (5:8). He forms the mountains and creates the wind (4:13). Yahweh not only brought up Israel from Egypt, but also the Philistines from Caphtor and the Syrians from Kir (9:7). This God, who rules heaven and earth, is the God with whom all nations must deal.

Yahweh is a God of moral perfection, who requires moral behavior of all people. God gives life to all, and all will be held accountable for their actions in the world. Amos speaks of Damascus as threshing Gilead (1:3) — literally driving threshing sleds with pieces of iron or flint imbedded in their underside over the wounded and dying bodies of the conquered. Gaza sold a people into slavery to Edom (v. 6), as did Tyre. These acts of inhumanity are sins against the God who made all people. Yahweh sits in judgment especially upon Israel for similar sins of oppression.

Yahweh the God of Israel. Israel, however, is not just another nation among nations. Rather, Israel stands in a special relationship. "You only have I known of all the families of the earth," says Yahweh (see 3:2). The essence of the Old Testament covenantal religion is that Yahweh chose Israel to be his people.

This is shown by constant use of the covenant name Yahweh (see p. 249, above), first intimately associated with Israel in the Exodus account. But the name does not merely identify God with Israel. It speaks of the redemptive purpose of Yahweh as the one who delivers his people from bondage (see 2:10), destroys their enemies (see v. 9), and raises up their sons for prophets (see v. 11), all for the purpose that he might be known in the world. Yahweh is the revealing God (3:7f.).

The relationship between Yahweh and Israel is brought out especially in the judgments pronounced because of the nature of covenant relationship. God finds Israel guilty precisely because "You only have I known of all the families of the earth; therefore I will punish you for all your iniquities" (v. 2). Yahweh used famine, rain, blight, mildew, and pestilence to turn Israel back to him, but to no avail (4:6-11).[24] God must now proceed to punishment (v. 12). One of the most noteworthy judicial acts is the sending of a famine — not of material but of spiritual bread, of hearing the words of Yahweh (8:11). God is free not only to reveal himself but to withhold revelation, especially when his prophetic word is not heeded. Yahweh is free to speak to and free to hide himself from the people he called into being.

Election Responsibility. The close relationship between the covenant name of the Lord and the judgment upon the people for their sins — whether religious, political, or social — underscores a much neglected Old Testament truth: election by Yahweh carries with its freedoms the responsibility of the elect to live according to the revealed will. This was stressed when the law was given at Sinai (see Chapter 5, above), and reiterated often in Numbers, Deuteronomy, and Joshua. It is the basic theme underlying many of the prophetic utterances. It is God himself in his holy love for creation and its creatures who is the substance of prophecy in Israel.

In Amos, the people's sins are related to the law of Yahweh. This is not readily apparent, for Amos does not cite chapter and verse nor quote exact words. Nonetheless, the elements of the law are present, including care of the poor and needy, administration of justice, use of just weights in commerce, and, above all, the obligation to worship Yahweh alone. Even more significantly, Amos repeatedly cites past historical situations and associates them with the name Yahweh.[25]

Yet there is another aspect to the responsibility of election. Since Yahweh has chosen Israel, he has a special commitment to them. Sinful Israel cannot count on any special leniency to spare their judgment (see 9:7f.). Indeed, Israel will be held to a standard of moral accountability above that of the other nations. Yahweh, nevertheless, will not completely destroy the house of Jacob. Only the sinners among his people will die (vv. 8-10). Something of a remnant will survive. Since Amos already has stressed that Yahweh repeatedly tried to cause his people to return to him, certainly implying the possibility of forgiveness, the "sinners" he now speaks about must be those who sin presumptuously and persistently. They presume that, because they are Israelites, Yahweh will accept any kind of behavior.

Amos ends, however, on a far more hopeful note than that regarding a disobedient people and their punishment. He foresees clearly that Yahweh's covenant has not been destroyed. On the contrary, when the judgment is complete, the promise will be kept. The "tottering hut of David" (v. 11, JB) will be repaired, raised up, rebuilt "as in the days of old." But Yahweh does not simply patch up the nation. He promises for the future something far more glorious in prosperity, stability, and security.

> "The time is surely coming," says the LORD,
>   "when the one who plows shall overtake
>   the one who reaps,
>   and the treader of grapes the one who sows the seed;
> the mountains shall drip sweet wine,
>   and all the hills shall flow with it.
> I will restore the fortunes of my people Israel,
>   and they shall rebuild the ruined cities and inhabit them;
> they shall plant vineyards and drink their wine,
>   and they shall make gardens and eat their fruit.
> I will plant them upon their land,
>   and they shall never again be plucked up
>   out of the land that I have given them,"
>   says the LORD your God. Amos 9:13-15

The God who is free to be the Judge of Israel is also gloriously free to be its Savior. This is the vision of God the prophecy of Amos would proclaim.

CHAPTER 19

Hosea

A decade or so after Amos came north to denounce Jeroboam's court, the Lord called Hosea, a son of the northern kingdom, to the prophetic ministry. His message, proclaimed over many years, resounds with God's grace and judgment.

Hosea's book was chosen to head the collection of Minor Prophets, all of which were written on one scroll, called "the Book of the Twelve." He was among the earliest of the writing prophets, and his book, which is the longest of the preexilic prophetic works, contains the major prophetic themes of doom and hope.

> And I will take you for my wife forever; I will take you for my wife in righteousness and in justice, in steadfast love, and in mercy. I will take you for my wife in faithfulness; and you shall know the LORD. Hos. 2:19-20

Introduction

Prophet. We know nothing of Hosea's life or upbringing. The book's focus is on one event: his tragic marriage.

Hosea's compassionate tone is remarkable; the frequent comparisons

Eighth-Century Prophets and Their World

	Prophet	Judah	Israel	Syria	Assyria	Egypt
					Adad-nirari III 810-783	
800						
790	I S A I A H (?) / M I C A H / H O S E A / A M O S	Amaziah 796-767 Azariah (Uzziah) *790-740	Jehoash 798-782 Jeroboam II *793-753			
780					Shalmaneser IV 782-772	
770					Ashur-dan III 771-754	
760						Sheshonk IV 763-727
750		Jotham *751-732	Zechariah 753 (6 months) Shallum 752 (1 month) Menahem 752-742	Rezin 750-732	Ashur-nirari V 753-744 Tiglath-pileser 747-727	
740			Pekahiah 741-740			
730		Ahaz *735-716 Hezekiah *728-687	Pekah ♦752-732 Hoshea 731-722 Fall of Samaria 722	Fall of Damascus 732	Shalmaneser V 727-722 Sargon II 722-705	Osorkon IV 727-716
720						
710						Shabako 715-702
700		Manasseh *696-642			Sennacherib 705-681	Shabataka 702-690
690						Tirhaqa 690-664

*Coregency   ♦Rival claim to throne

255

with Jeremiah in the Old Testament and John in the New are appropriate. Overwhelmed by God's boundless love (see 11:8f.), he reached out in concern for his countrymen. Unlike Amos, he was preaching to his own people. Though at times unsparing in his indictments, he was never cold or heartless. What contributed most to Hosea's empathy was his own suffering and rejection. Like Jeremiah, he had felt something of God's own heartbreak and was stamped with an imprint of divine compassion.

We are told nothing of his station before his call. Some number him among the *priests* because of his intimate knowledge of religious affairs in the northern kingdom and his grave concern for the corruption of the priesthood (e.g., 4:5-9). Others link him with the official *prophets* because he quotes a frequent jibe: "The prophet is a fool, the man of the spirit is mad!" (9:7). Neither view can be held with certainty.

This much can be said: his outstanding knowledge of both the political tensions of his own day and the major events of Israel's past mark him as an unusual prophet. Like Isaiah, he was sensitive to political currents and analyzed their implications shrewdly. His outstanding literary gifts, particularly his figures of speech, are additional evidence that he was probably from the upper classes.[1]

Date. The introductory verse (1:1) places Hosea's ministry in the reigns of Uzziah, Jotham, Ahaz, and Hezekiah of Judah and Jeroboam II of Israel. Its minimum length was twenty-five years, since Jeroboam II died *ca.* 753 and Hezekiah began a coregency *ca.* 728 and ascended the throne *ca.* 715. The book itself gives no evidence that Hosea continued to preach after the fall of Samaria in 721.

When the prophet's first son was born, Jehu's dynasty still reigned: the Lord specifies that Jehu's house was yet to be punished (1:4). It is not certain whether the ruler then was Jeroboam II or his ill-fated son, Zechariah, assassinated by Shallum *ca.* 752. If his ministry began at the close of Jeroboam's reign, the bulk of it took place during the hectic days of Menahem (*ca.* 752-742), Pekahiah (*ca.* 741-740), Pekah (*ca.* 740-732), and Hoshea (*ca.* 732-722). These were desperate times, when Assyrian armies thrust westward repeatedly and the Israelites sought vainly, both by war and appeasement, to preserve their independence.

Hosea's ministry coincided closely with the reign of Tiglath-pileser III (*ca.* 745-727), who brought unprecedented vigor to the throne of Assyria. Both biblical history (2 Kgs. 15:19) and Assyrian records report that Menahem paid heavy tribute to Tiglath-pileser (called here Pul, after the Babylonian form of his name). Menahem hoped to use Assyrian support to bolster his tottering throne, which he had seized from Shallum. He raised the funds for tribute by taxing wealthy Israelites. Hosea makes veiled references to this courting of Assyrian favor:

Israel is swallowed up;
> now they are among the nations as a useless vessel.
For they have gone up to Assyria,
> a wild ass wandering alone;
> Ephraim has bargained for lovers (allies). (8:8-9)

They multiply falsehood and violence;
> they make a treaty with Assyria,
> and oil is carried to Egypt. (12:1)

Threatened without by Assyria, Israel was unsettled within by political intrigue. An instability that failed to maintain a ruling dynasty for any length of time was a characteristic of this period. Hosea voiced God's grief at the situation:

All their kings have fallen;
> none of them calls upon me. (7:7)

They made kings, but not through me;
> they set up princes, but without my knowledge. (8:4)

The references to Egypt may relate to the second half of King Hoshea's reign. After a time of playing vassal to Assyria, he sought Egyptian support for his opposition to Shalmaneser V, who succeeded Tiglath-pileser in 727. Hosea aptly pictured the rapid and fickle fluctuations in foreign policy:

Ephraim has become like a dove,
> silly and without sense;
they call to Egypt, they go to Assyria.[2] (7:11)

Throughout the troubled third quarter of the eighth century (*ca.* 750-725), Hosea's lot was to watch Israel's last illness. All attempted cures came to naught. Neither a quelling of internal revolt nor aid from allies like Egypt could stay Israel's demise. Judgment had to come. We do not know whether Hosea lived to see the end. But the word from God and the prophet's own understanding of the times convinced him of its certainty. That certainty he faithfully proclaimed but cannot have rejoiced in.

Hosea's Marriage (1:2–3:5)

God's demand of Hosea is unique:

> "Go, take for yourself a wife of whoredom and have children of whoredom,
> for the land commits great whoredom by forsaking the LORD." (1:2)

The details are few; the account is condensed. But the questions about the story's meaning are not merely academic. The command to marry is the foundation of Hosea's ministry. A clear understanding of the marriage is essential to a clear grasp of the message.

Problems of Interpretation. Are the narratives of chs. 1 and 3 the prophet's actual experience (history) or a story he composed to convey a spiritual truth (allegory)? They will be treated here as history : (1) the book itself does not suggest that it be taken other than at face value; (2) certain details do not fit an allegorical pattern: no suitable meaning for Gomer's name has been found; no purpose is apparent in references to the weaning of Not-pitied (1:8) or in the order of the children's births; (3) the traditional reason for reading the story as allegory is to avoid the stigma on the morality of God and the prophet which the command to marry a harlot apparently involves. However, does what is morally doubtful as history become any less questionable when viewed as allegory?

A second main question is the relationship between chs. 1 and 3. The approach here is that the two chapters are not two parallel accounts of the same incident — Hosea's taking of Gomer as wife.[3] Rather, ch. 3 is the sequel to ch. 1. Not only does this seem more natural, but certain details support it. Ch. 3 says nothing of the children, so prominent in ch. 1. Again, ch. 3 strongly suggests that the woman is barred for some time from any contact with a man, including her husband, as a disciplinary measure, just as Israel is to be chastened by exile (3:3f.). But ch. 1 implies that Gomer conceived her first child shortly after marriage (1:3). Furthermore, ch. 3 is intended quite clearly to symbolize Israel's return to God, her first husband, as prophesied in 2:7:

> She shall pursue her lovers,
> but not overtake them;
> and she shall seek them,
> but shall not find them.
> Then she shall say, "I will go and return to my first husband,
> for it was better with me then than now."

Several scholars have held that the woman in ch. 3 is not Gomer but a second wife. Although the wording of v. 1 — "love a woman who has a lover" — is strange, it is unlikely the prophet would marry two women if his marriages are to symbolize God's relationship with one nation, Israel:

> Therefore, I will now allure her,
> and bring her into the wilderness,

258

and speak tenderly to her.

. . . . . .

And there she shall respond as in the days of her youth,
as at the time when she came out of the land of Egypt. (2:14f.)

Another problem of interpretation is the kind of woman Gomer was. What is the meaning of God's command (1:2): "Go, take for yourself a wife of *whoredom*"? Some view this harlotry as religious fornication, i.e., idolatry. Gomer, then, would not be a sexually immoral woman but a member of an idolatrous people. This would fit most citizens of the northern kingdom, dedicated as it was to calf worship. The desire to protect Gomer's reputation stems, in part, from the alleged moral problem in God's command and Hosea's response.

Many have held that Gomer was not wicked when Hosea married her but turned to evil later. The command in v. 2 is taken to represent not God's actual call but Hosea's interpretation in retrospect. Hosea realized that the call came when he took his wife, who proved as unfaithful to him as Israel had to God. If Gomer was evil when they married, her husband knew nothing about it. But if this approach affords an acceptable interpretation for ch. 1, what about ch. 3? Here Hosea knows full well what kind of woman he is taking. To an Israelite, reconciliation with an adulteress would be scarcely less repugnant than marrying one in the first place, since stoning was the customary penalty for adultery (Lev. 20:10; Deut. 22:22; John 8:5).

Another interpretation is that Gomer, like many Israelite virgins, had participated in a Canaanite ritual of sexual initiation with a stranger prior to her marriage.[4] The purpose was to assure fertility of the marriage. This theory suffers from lack of Old Testament evidence for this practice.[5]

Some scholars have considered Gomer a cult prostitute, but the technical form for religious harlot (*qᵉdēšâ*) is nowhere used of her. Further, Hosea scathingly denounced cult prostitution. It is unlikely, therefore, that marriage to such a person would have been any less distasteful to Hosea than marriage to an ordinary harlot. We know so little about cult prostitutes in Israel that it is hazardous to guess how Hosea's marriage to one would have been viewed.

Character and Meaning of the Marriage. Hosea connected his prophetic call with his marriage to Gomer, but the relation between the two is puzzling. Was he called before the marriage, or did his call grow out of his experience with Gomer? If 1:2 is taken at face value, his call came immediately before he married. His prophetic naming of his first son Jezreel is evidence that he was already a prophet at his marriage. No doubt, however, his tragic experiences with Gomer had a profound influence, refining his character and enriching his ministry. In a sense, his call was continuous, beginning when he took Gomer and deepening through his pain.

(1) Gomer and her children. Israel's drastic situation called for drastic measures. The corruption and luxury that marked Jeroboam's lengthy reign had brought the nation to spiritual and moral bankruptcy. Baal worship, introduced officially by Ahab's queen Jezebel (1 Kgs. 16:29-33), was still rampant despite Jehu's drastic measures to wipe it out. In turning to the Baals Israel had played false with her first love, Yahweh. To illustrate memorably this spiritual adultery, God commanded Hosea to marry a woman whose reputation was to become evil. Their relationship may have been pure at first, as Israel's relationship with God was pure in the Exodus experiences:

Metal pendant from Ugarit depicting the Canaanite
fertility goddess Ashtoreth, for whom Israel
"played the harlot" (Hos. 2:5). *(Louvre)*

I remember the devotion of your youth,
>   your love as a bride,
how you followed me in the wilderness,
>   in a land not sown.

Israel was holy to the LORD,
>   the first fruits of his harvest. (Jer. 2:2f.)

The main point of Hosea's marriage, however, was not to recapitulate God's dealings with Israel but to thrust into sharp relief Israel's present degeneracy. This was done effectively and dramatically by the story of marriage between a prophet and a woman who unexpectedly turned to wickedness.[6]

The three children symbolize aspects of God's dealing with his people. The name God gave to the firstborn, Jezreel, was a prophecy of judgment upon the house of Jehu, whose vicious purges began with the murders of Joram and Jezebel at Jezreel (2 Kgs. 9:16-37). The threat ("I will break the bow of Israel in the valley of Jezreel," v. 5) was probably fulfilled in the assassination of Jeroboam's son Zechariah, the last of Jehu's dynasty (2 Kgs. 15:8-12). Jezreel's name is aptly chosen: it not only speaks of judgment for Jehu's act at Jezreel but also suggests subsequent restoration (Hos. 2:22f.), since it means "God will sow."

The second child is a daughter, Not-pitied (Lō'-ruḥāmâ), who symbolizes a reversal in God's attitude toward Israel. Mercy has been spurned; trust in divine deliverance has been replaced by confidence in arms and alliances. God has little choice but to withdraw his mercy and let Israel suffer the consequences of their faithlessness (1:6f.). The third child, a son, is called Not-my-people (Lō'-'ammî) to symbolize the broken covenant. God does not reject Israel; rather, Israel had rejected God and refused to be his people (vv. 8f.).

The relationship between Hosea and these two children is not clear. The text does not state specifically that Gomer bore them to him as it does in Jezreel's case. To some, the tone of ch. 2 suggests that they are children of Gomer's adultery:

Plead with your mother, plead —
>   for she is not my wife,
>   and I am not her husband —
that she put away her whoring from her face,
>   and her adultery from between her breasts,

>   . . . . . .

Upon her children also I will have no pity,
>   because they are children of whoredom. (2:2, 4)

Ch. 2 is an extended commentary on 1:2. It begins with Gomer and her children and then shifts to the infidelity of the Israelites. They courted the

Baals without realizing that it was Yahweh, not Baal, who had blessed them abundantly (2:8).

(2) God's forgiveness and Hosea's. Following the threat of judgment (vv. 9-13), to Israel who had forgotten Yahweh, the tone in ch. 2 changes abruptly: Israel will not return to God so he himself will fetch his people back (vv. 14-23). The very names of Baal are to be erased from their memory and a new marriage is to take place: "And I will take you for my wife forever" (v. 19). Israel, scattered in judgment, will be sown in the land ("Jezreel" in the positive sense), pity will be poured out on Not-pitied, and Not-my-people will again be God's people. God's grace will reverse the judgment and bring restoration (vv. 21-23).

Then God commanded Hosea to follow the divine example and restore Gomer as his wife (3:1-5). The order is important. God pledged forgiveness to Israel, and Hosea followed suit. The sequence of chs. 2 and 3 is theologically profound. Forgiveness does not come naturally; those who have felt God's forgiveness learn thereby to forgive (cf. Eph. 4:32).

Hosea bought Gomer for the price of a slave and took her back. The degrading state into which she had fallen is itself emblematic of the wages which sin pays. Rebellion against God issues in slavery to something else. God's forgiveness does not mean that he treats sin lightly. God's love for Israel involved exile as well as exodus, and Hosea disciplined Gomer to demonstrate both the seriousness of her sin and God's chastening of Israel in captivity (3:3f.). But discipline is not the last word: "Afterward the children of Israel shall return (or repent) and seek the LORD their God . . . and they shall come in awe to the LORD . . . in the latter days" (v. 5).

A remarkable story, this! A prophet is called to bear a cross, to experience both the suffering heart and the redeeming love of God. With unflinching obedience Hosea drank a bitter cup. His home was his Gethsemane. In bending to a will not his own, he not only left a poignant illustration of divine love but prepared the way for One who perfectly embodied this love.[7]

Hosea's Message (4:1–14:9)

In two distinct sections — 4:1–11:11 and 11:12–14:9 — the book lays bare the sins of Israel with shocking detail. These chapters unpack the meaning of the accusation: "the land commits great whoredom by forsaking the LORD" (1:2).

Whereas the outline of Amos' prophecy jumps out at us, for Hosea's we have to search closely. What we find for the first and longest section of speeches is something like this:

In these chapters Hosea shows himself a gifted poet as well as an insightful prophet. Indeed, his are among the most moving poems of the Bible. He has rhetorical gifts, particularly in his use of figures of speech, that few Old Testament poets match. How better, for instance, could the weakening effects of Israel's foreign alliances be described?

> Ephraim mixes himself with the peoples;
>   Ephraim is a cake not turned (half-baked).
> Foreigners devour his strength,
>   but he knows it not (7:8f.).

Hosea's metaphors are frequently rural, such as in God's complaint over Israel's failure to fulfill their destiny:

> Ephraim was a trained heifer
> > that loved to thresh,
> > and I spared her fair neck;
> but I will make Ephraim break the ground;
> > Judah must plow;
> > Jacob must harrow for himself.
> Sow for yourselves righteousness;
> > reap steadfast love;
> > break up your fallow ground;
> for it is time to seek the Lord,
> > that he may come and rain righteousness upon you. (10:11f.)

The final set of messages — 11:12–14:9 — anticipates Samaria's imminent fall to the greedy forces of Assyria. Ephraim, the kingdom named for one of Joseph's proud sons, has been reduced to a tiny enclave in the hills around Samaria. In a speech both puzzling and poignant (ch. 12) Ephraim's treacherous idolatry and foolish self-reliance are compared to the dishonest ambition of Jacob, Ephraim's famous ancestor. Such behavior is viewed by the prophet as a family trait which has persisted despite God's continuing acts of rescue in the Exodus and through the prophets (vv. 9-10, 13). Ephraim's inevitable tragic fall (13:1-3) will be followed by ferocious judgment (13:4-8) to which he is totally vulnerable (13:9-11). In fact, his stubborn folly issues in both a failure to repent and a bent to rebel which sign and seal the death warrant of the northern kingdom (13:12-16).

Yet as was his custom, Hosea looked forward to a hope beyond judgment, a restoration that God had burned into his being with the command,

> "Go, love a woman . . . just as the Lord loves the people of Israel, though they turn to other gods . . ." (3:1).

That note of hope brightens the first series of messages, with a promise of return from exile:

> "They shall go after the Lord
> > who roars like a lion;
> when he roars,
> > his children shall come trembling from the west.
> They shall come trembling like doves from
> the land of Assyria;
> And I will return them to their homes,
> > says the Lord." (11:10-11)

Hosea's final words of hope reach new poetic heights in a poignant and powerful love song, which recalls the Song of Solomon:

I will heal their disloyalty;
   I will love them freely,
   for my anger has turned from them.
   . . . . . .
They shall again live beneath my shadow,
   they shall flourish as a garden;
they shall blossom like the vine,
   their fragrance shall be like the wine of Lebanon. (14:4, 7)

Hosea's Theological Contributions

A brief look at Hosea's more important emphases will illustrate the tone and the dramatic power of the messages in chs. 4–14.

Knowledge of God. Repeatedly Hosea traces Israel's spiritual and moral problems to lack of knowledge of God:

Hear the word of the LORD, O people of Israel;
   for the LORD has an indictment against the inhabitants of the land.[8]
There is no faithfulness or loyalty,[9]
   and no knowledge of God in the land;
there is swearing, lying, and murder, and stealing and committing
   adultery;
they break all bounds and murder follows murder. (4:1f.)

My people are destroyed for lack of knowledge;
   because you [the priest] have rejected knowledge,
   I reject you from being a priest to me.
And since you have forgotten the law of your God,
   I also will forget your children. (v. 6)

Knowledge of God is not merely knowing about God; it is being properly related to him in love and obedience. Israel did not need more information about God but a stronger desire for fellowship with God. "In the Old Testament knowledge is living in a close relationship with something or somebody . . . a relationship . . . called communion."[10]

In response to what God had done in the Exodus and after, Israel pledged loyalty to God's will as revealed in the law. In refusing to respond, Israel broke fellowship with God as Gomer had with Hosea.[11] Sin shattered the communion, and only repentance could restore it:

> Their deeds do not permit them
>> to return to their God.
> For the spirit of whoredom is within them,
>> and they do not know the LORD. (5:4)

Empty ritual cannot substitute for cordial communion:

> For I desire steadfast love and not sacrifice,
>> the knowledge of God rather than burnt offerings. (6:6)

Against the present apostasy, Hosea sees a brighter day, when God in grace will again take Israel to wife. The consummation will be renewed communion:

> I will take you for my wife in faithfulness;
>> and you shall know the LORD. (2:20)

In depicting Israel's relationship with God in the way he does, Hosea prepares for Jeremiah (e.g., Jer. 4:22) and the New Testament. His teachings provide rich background for certain statements of Christ: "All things have been handed over to me by my Father; and no one knows the Son except the Father, and no one knows the Father except the Son and anyone to whom the Son chooses to reveal him" (Matt. 11:27). And especially, "And this is eternal life, that they know you, the only true God, and Jesus Christ whom you have sent" (John 17:3; see also 1 John 2:3-6).

Folly of Ingratitude. As much as any other prophet, Hosea recalls Israel's past as he speaks to the present.[12] Beginning with the Exodus, he traces God's care for his people and their rebellion against him. History, according to Hosea, is the story of God's graciousness and Israel's ingratitude.

> Like grapes in the wilderness,
>> I found Israel.
> . . . . .
> But they came to Baal-peor (cf. Num. 25:1-3),
>> and consecrated themselves to a thing of shame,
>> and became detestable like the thing they loved. (9:10; see 12:13f.)

Israel's present conduct scarcely matches God's blessing upon them. Having spurned his grace in both past and present, God's people are ripe for judgment.

> It was I who fed you in the wilderness,
>> in the land of drought.
> When I fed them,
>> they were satisfied; and their heart was proud;
>>> therefore they forgot me.

. . . . .
So I will fall upon them like a bear robbed of her cubs. (13:5-8)

Israel gave the Baals credit for what God had done (2:8). Indeed, the more abundantly God blessed Israel, the more they chased after idols.

Israel is a luxuriant vine
    that yields its fruit.
The more his fruit increased
    the more altars he built;
as his country improved,
    he improved his pillars. (10:1)

Hosea's sketch is not unlike Paul's picture of pagan practices in Rom. 1:21: "for although they knew God, they did not honor him as God or give thanks to him. . . ." To fail to thank God means to attribute blessings incorrectly to some other source or even to oneself. This constitutes a denial of God's sovereignty and grace.

Futility of Mere Religion. When Israel's religious structure served its true purpose in celebrating the mighty acts of God and reminding the people of their present obligation and future expectations, the prophets gave it full support.[13] But in Hosea's day the cult failed miserably to fulfill its purpose. The people were intensely religious. Feasts were kept judiciously (2:11, 13), sacrifices and offerings were burnt continually (5:6; 6:6), altars were built in abundance (10:1). This outward show, however, masked an inward corruption of the worst kind.

The priests were a special target of Hosea's ire. They were as corrupt as the people they should have been helping (4:9). Having neglected their duty to teach the law, with its demands of righteousness and justice, they were chiefly responsible for Israel's defection (4:4-9; 5:1f.).

Pagan practices were observed alongside divinely established forms of worship. Israel's faith, grounded in the redemption of the Exodus, had degenerated to a fertility cult. The Baals were thanked for the spring crops (2:11f.), and immorality was practiced as a religious celebration (4:12-14). The people did not seek Yahweh's word, but were content to discern the future by magic (v. 12). Canaanite ritualistic orgies were performed by the Israelites, who wailed and gashed themselves, just as the prophets of Baal had done in contesting with Elijah's God on Mt. Carmel, to gain answers to their prayers (7:14; cf. 1 Kgs. 18:28). The drunken revelries (4:11) and criminal outbursts (v. 2; 6:7-9; 7:1) add to a grim picture of religious failure.

"People are kissing calves!" (13:2) was Hosea's graphic summary of the abysmal depths to which God's covenant people descended when they poured out their love to metal images.

God's Changeless Compassion. Yet God's love for Israel is greater than their sin (11:1-9). Hosea first pictures God complaining of Israel's failure to be grateful:

> When Israel was a child, I loved him,
>   and out of Egypt I called my son.
> The more I called them,
>   the more they went from me;
> they kept sacrificing to the Baals,
>   and offering incense to idols.
> Yet it was I who taught Ephraim to walk,
>   I took them up in my arms;
>   but they did not know that I healed them. (11:1-3)

The passage then shows how God's unquenchable compassion triumphs over Ephraim's inconstancy:

> How can I give you up, Ephraim?
>   How can I hand you over, O Israel?
>   . . . . . .
> My heart recoils within me;
>   my compassion grows warm and tender.
>   . . . . . .
> I will not execute my fierce anger;
>   I will not again destroy Ephraim;
> for I am God and no mortal,
>   the Holy One in your midst,
>   and I will not come in wrath.[14]

"I am God and no mortal" — this is the secret of divine righteousness and love. God does not stoop to the level of human sin or corruption and so is not fickle or inconstant. God's love abides despite rebellion and hostility. Of all the prophets, Hosea knew what it was to love, be sinned against, and go on loving; he was the best equipped to proclaim "the quite irrational power of love as the ultimate basis of the covenant relationship."[15]

Hosea took a certain risk in couching the relationship between Yahweh and his people in terms of love. The Canaanite nature cult put great stress on the erotic nature of the divine-human relationship and the role of physical love in maintaining the order of the universe. Hosea guarded against misunderstanding by his insistence that God's love is best understood not in sexual terms, or in the cycles of fertility each spring, but in the redemptive acts of the Exodus. More than passion is involved; there is the deliberate activity of God's will throughout Israel's history, itself a continuity of divine instruction and discipline.[16]

For Hosea the covenant religion can never be reduced to purely legal terms but involves a personal fellowship, a family tie, between God and Israel. Rather than opposing or criticizing the law, Hosea says much in its support (e.g., 4:6ff.; 8:12f.). He shows that behind and beneath the law lies love. Israel's response to God can never be merely formal obedience because God's overture came first not by law but by love. For Amos sin was represented in terms of the breaking of the covenant, but for Gomer's husband, Hosea, sin is represented in terms of the spurning of God's love.

This love, in Hosea, is never reduced to mere sentiment. His view of the holiness of God guards against this.

> Wrath and love, or "the wrath of love,"[17] are expressed clearly in God's willingness to woo his wicked wife Israel and yet punish the nation's wickedness. He loves and judges them simultaneously.[18]

Revelation comes in many and strange ways. None of them is more mysterious than this picture of God's intense feeling toward his people through a prophet's conflicting emotions toward a faithless yet beloved wife. This is enacted prophecy[19] at its highest Old Testament level. Through Hosea's life the word became flesh.

CHAPTER 20

Micah

Micah was a contemporary of Isaiah. Both prophets were convinced that Judah was headed for disaster because of the oppressive and idolatrous lifestyle of its leaders. They were certain too that, beyond the disaster, God had a brighter future in store. Micah's accusations have the same intensity as those of Amos. Indeed, few passages from the prophets can match the fiery fury of his denunciations of Jerusalem's leaders in chs. 2 and 3.

> "Hear this, you rulers of the house of Jacob
>   and chiefs of the house of Israel,
>   who abhor justice
>   and pervert all equity,
>   who build Zion with blood
>   and Jerusalem with wrong!" Mic. 3:9-10

Introduction

The Prophet. Micah offers hardly any direct information about himself. Most of what is known about his life and background must be inferred from the contents and tone of his writings. His name is an abbreviation of *Mîkāyāhû* "who is like Yahweh?" Moresheth, his hometown, is Moresheth-gath (1:14), a village about twenty-five miles southwest of Jerusalem in the Judean foothills. Several lines of evidence mark him as a country man, perhaps a peasant farmer. He attacks the crime and corruption of Jerusalem and Samaria as one not really at home in either capital (1:1, 5-9; 3:1-4, 12). He focuses on the effect of the impending judgment on the villages and towns of his home region (1:10-16). His protests against oppression of the underprivileged reflect his own identification with their lot.

Isaiah and Micah are an interesting pair: one is an aristocrat, confidant of kings and statesmen, and the other a peasant farmer or landowner, whose visits to the capital confirmed reports heard back home. While the two differ in background and breeding, they share common courage and convictions. Both staunchly uphold the covenant and champion Israel's historic faith.

Like Amos (Amos 7:14f.), Micah was probably not a professional prophet. He criticizes the prophets who "give oracles for money" (Mic. 3:11) or tailor their messages according to their clients' generosity (3:5). His credentials are divine inspiration and his unflinching stand for moral truth (3:8). His strong sense of call is vindicated in virtually every line. Fervently yet concisely he speaks to the issues of his day in terms of Israel's covenant obligations. Behind the covenant, in spite of Israel's failure to maintain that bond, is the God of the covenant who yet will lead his people to future glory.

Basic Date. The book's title (1:1) places Micah in the reigns of Jotham, Ahaz, and Hezekiah, roughly 735-700 B.C. The message in 1:2-9 was given before the destruction of Samaria in 721. The appeal of Jeremiah's supporters to the prophecy of Micah confirms his connection with Hezekiah:

> And some of the elders of the land arose and said to all the assembled people, "Micah of Moresheth prophesied during the days of Hezekiah king of Judah. . . ." (Jer. 26:17f.)

The judgment on Judah depicted in 1:10-16 seems to be linked with Assyrian campaigns against the Philistines in 720 or 714-711. The reference to human sacrifice (6:7) is often taken to reflect Manasseh's terrifying reign when the rite was common, but 2 Kgs. 16:3 attributes it to Ahaz as well. So the tradition that Micah, like Isaiah, prophesied just before and after the fall of the northern kingdom finds internal support. The threat of doom hanging over Jerusalem (see 3:12) and the references to Assyria as the prime national enemy (5:5f.) suggest the period between the fall of Samaria in 721 and the withdrawal of Sennacherib's army from blockading Jerusalem in 701. The affinities to Isaiah in theme and emphasis support this conclusion.

Unity. While the oracles of judgment in chs. 1–3 have generally been accepted as Micah's, considerable question has arisen over dating the oracles of chs. 4–7.[1] The major role of the preexilic prophets was to give a negative critique of conditions in the nation and to announce the judgment that must follow. So scholars look very carefully at messages of hope. They ask whether they came from the prophet who gave his name to the book or from later prophets. Certainly the final, canonical edition of the book gives the impression of coming from early postexilic times. The liturgical poem in 7:8-20 may presuppose that judgment has fallen on Judah and lay claim to the fulfillment of the messages of hope. Most of the messages of hope can be credited to Micah,[2] but often their general content hinders reconstruction of a specific historical setting. What is important is the spiritual message of these prophetic texts rather than their precise historical origin.

Structure

The double note of judgment and hope gives Micah its basic structure. The book divides into three sections, the editorial clue being an initial "hear" (or "listen") in 1:2; 3:1; 6:1. The first and last sections are symmetrical: a series of negative messages, capped by a shorter, positive message (1:2–2:11 + 2:12-13; 6:1–7:7 + 7:8-20). The middle section is more complex. Its beginning and end mirror those of the whole book, on a smaller scale. Judgment oracles in ch. 3 are followed by a brief message of hope in 4:1-5. The same pattern reappears in a single piece, in 5:10-14 + 15. The intervening material of 4:6–5:9 begins and ends with hope for the remnant of God's people (4:6-8; 5:7-9). Its middle part mingles notes of distress and hope, gradually altering the proportion in favor of hope (4:9-10, 11-13; 5:1-6). This literary architecture suggests a deliberate attempt to underscore the twofold nature of Micah's prophetic tradition, as both bad news and good news. The good news highlighted the concept of the remnant and gives central place to the sure hope of messianic deliverance (5:1-6).

Message

We read the canonical book through the eyes of the postexilic community of faith, who come to the fore in 7:8-20. So it is best to start there and then look back. This final word of hope is a liturgy of prayer, assurance and praise, most probably used in worship after public reading of Micah. It plays on Micah's name (v. 18, "Who is a God like you?") and reiterates four of Micah's themes: sin and transgression, the remnant, God's shepherd role, and his overthrow of the oppressing nations.

In 7:8-10 the community, through its spokesperson ("I"), laments over the judgment that eventually fell on Jerusalem, and confesses the sin that caused it. Now the same community looks forward to the salvation also predicted in the book. In vv. 11-13 a prophet gives assurance of coming restoration. Next (vv. 14-17) the congregation pleads that their prayers may be answered, with language echoing that of Micah. Finally, in vv. 18-20 they sing a hymn of praise to Yahweh, claiming by his faith divine forgiveness and covenant faithfulness.

This liturgical pattern attests the importance of Israel's worship. The preexilic prophets denounced public worship (e.g., Amos 5:21-24) only because they believed that, to be valid, it must be accompanied by social and moral commitment to the covenant. This pattern of confession, prayer, hymn, and prophetic response in ch. 7 affords an "Amen" to that prophetic perspective. It indicates that Micah's message influenced the form and content of Israel's worship and contributed to its renewal.

First Messages of Doom (1:2–2:11). Catastrophe lay ahead for the northern kingdom (1:2-9). Yahweh was to visit the world as judge, and Samaria was to be his first stop. The southern kingdom was also to fall (vv. 10-16). The impact of enemy invasion on the towns and villages of Micah's home area is described in concise, almost telegraphic, phrases. A series of wordplays, which English translations cannot possibly transmit, and (now cryptic) allusions to the various towns evoke a mood of grief and despair.[3] The coming attack will pose a threat to the southern capital, Jerusalem.

Next Micah, employing a "woe" oracle (seee Amos 6:1), furiously attacks the sins that have made the judgment necessary. In 2:1-5 he expresses Yahweh's anger at the buying up of land by a new moneyed class. These actions have denied the sacred right of land tenure that celebrated God's gift to the people (cf. 1 Kgs. 21; Isa. 5:8-10). In 2:6-11 Micah attacks both the heartless land grabbers and those self-proclaimed prophets who supported them.

First Hint of Hope (2:12f.). This oracle of salvation relieves the darkness with a glimmer of light. Like Isaiah's promise in Isa. 37:32, it probably announces the relief of blockaded Jerusalem in 701 B.C., but to later readers it was a portent of eschatological hope. Micah did not preach doom and hope simultaneously — which would only have confused his audience. Those who preserved and edited his utterances wanted to stress that judgment was never Yahweh's last word for the covenant people. The divine Shepherd would care for the flock.

Second Message of Doom (ch. 3). Another reason for judgment was the complete collapse of Judah's leadership. Micah charges in vv. 1-4 that human

273

Micah invokes God's care as shepherd of his people (Mic. 7:14).
Sheep on the hills of Jotbathah (Jotbah). *(Neal and Joel Bierling)*

rights have been suppressed in the law courts. Using graphic images of butchery and cannibalism to denounce their savage abuse of the people, he predicts that they will find little mercy when they have to answer to a higher court. In vv. 5-8 Micah, as God's true messenger, singles out rival prophets who have succumbed to materialism, losing all sense of true mission. Reaffirming his own credentials, Micah forecasts the loss of their prophetic gifts. In vv. 9-12 we hear a general indictment of the established order. The assumption that God's presence in the temple makes the city invulnerable is false security, he chides. Jerusalem will fall, temple and all. Eventually, in 586 B.C., this did happen, but for now Micah's preaching, and his hearers' repentance, avert immediate disaster (see Jer. 26:17-19).

Second Message of Hope (4:1-5). The bleak landscape of religious and social degeneracy was to be succeeded by a brighter future. This oracle of salvation occurs in a shorter form in Isa. 2:2-5. Out of Jerusalem's ashes would rise a new Jerusalem, a center of worship for all nations of the world. Like Israelite pilgrims, Gentiles would stream to Jerusalem, seeking God's will, and then return home to put it into practice. A fine hope, but what of the present? Israel was to model the dream and show now how pilgrims should live.

Oracles of Hope in Times of Distress (4:6–5:9). Two positive messages about the "remnant" are given in 4:6-8 and 5:7-9. They frame three present/fu-

274

ture contrasts in 4:9-10, 11-13; 5:1-6. Notice the term "now" in 4:9, 11; 5:1. The last of the three is well known as a messianic promise (see Matt. 2:6). Like Isaiah, Micah reaffirmed ancient promises associated with the Davidic covenant (2 Sam. 7:8-16), and celebrated in the royal psalms (see Ps. 2). Hezekiah's weakness during the Assyrian blockade of Jerusalem was to be followed by a new era of power and peace under a true son of David. Bethlehem is mentioned (v. 2) to stress the humble origin of both David and his future successor, who would be a true shepherd of the people (v. 4). In its context the oracle prophesies not the birth of the coming king, but the continuity of the line of David.

The oracle of 5:7-15 describes Judah's besetting sins of militarism and pagan religious practices. Yahweh must wrench them away. Only God can give the victory Judah has been seeking by the wrong means.

Third Message of Doom (6:1–7:7). A lawsuit is conducted in 6:1-8. The mountains are called as witnesses to the dispute between Yahweh and his people.[4] God complains of breach of contract. In proof of his own goodwill, he adduces the Exodus and the gift of the land. Micah puts a protest on the people's lips, offering any religious response God cared to ask for. The prophet's reply in v. 8 shows that they had missed the point. It is not displays of worship but a righteous way of life that validates a healthy relationship with God.

> The LORD has told you mortals what is good,
>   and what it is that the LORD requires of you:
> only to act justly, to love loyalty,
>   to walk humbly with your God. Mic. 6:8, REB

God's indictment becomes specific in 6:9-16. Violence, deception, and crooked business practices were rampant. They would bring desolation and destruction to the land. The reference to Omri and Ahab indicates that the same kinds of corruption that destroyed the northern kingdom had now spread to Judah.

The picture of treachery and oppression concludes in 7:1-7, actually a psalm of individual complaint. Micah was distressed by the moral degradation of his society, and vexed by the total collapse of personal and social values. He looked to God to vindicate the stand he had taken.

In the closing response Micah's later hearers take his messages to heart. His descriptions of sin became a mirror in which they check their lives. His words of hope gave them new heart to live as God's people in a darkened world.

CHAPTER 21

Isaiah: Background

Isaiah is noteworthy in the biblical canon for several reasons. In length, it ranks second only to Psalms. Its influence is clear in its contribution to the Qumran community whose Dead Sea Scrolls have preserved at least fifteen manuscripts or fragments thereof and especially in its impact on the New Testament which contains more than 400 quotations and echoes of Isaiah's language.[1] More striking than such statistics, however, is the sheer grandeur of the book. The majesty of its dramatic language, the range of its theological themes, the power of its historical perspective — these all combine to justify the superlative language with which scholars, preachers, and poets have described this sixty-six-chapter legacy that without exaggeration may be called the centerpiece of prophetic literature.

> In the year that King Uzziah died, I saw the Lord sitting on a throne, high and lofty; and the hem of his robe filled the temple. Seraphs were in attendance above him; each had six wings: with two they covered their faces, and with two they covered their feet, and with two they flew. And one called to another and said:
>
> "Holy, holy, holy is the LORD of hosts;
> the whole earth is full of his glory." Isa. 6:1-3

Siloam tunnel inscription recounting the completion of the water tunnel
constructed by Hezekiah, during whose reign Micah prophesied.
(Israel Department of Antiquities)

The Prophet

Isaiah ben Amoz (to be distinguished from the prophet Amos) was a Judean,
probably a Jerusalemite. His ministry may have begun in the final years of Uzziah's
reign. It certainly extended from the year of Uzziah's death (740 B.C.; cf. 6:1)
through the regimes of Jotham, Ahaz, and Hezekiah (at least to 701). According
to tradition, which finds some support in the prophecy itself, it may have continued into the reign of Manasseh (696-642). Tradition also records that Isaiah was
a cousin of Uzziah or a nephew of Amaziah (Talmud *Meg.* 10b), born in or near
Jerusalem. Modern scholars regard this attribution as "simply a guess,"[2] but
Isaiah's ready access to both king (7:3) and priest (8:2) lends support to the
tradition. He was married to a prophetess and had two sons (7:3; 8:3); according
to Jewish tradition, the second son was born of a second marriage to a "virgin"
(see 7:14; NRSV "young woman"). Another tradition reports that Isaiah was
martyred in Manasseh's day by being sawed in two (*Assumption of Isaiah*, which
is possibly the basis for Heb. 11:37). Isaiah's ministry thus extended over a period
of at least forty years (740-701), and possibly more, since Hezekiah's death did
not occur until 687 and it is doubtful that the coregent Manasseh would have
dared to martyr Isaiah while Hezekiah was still alive.

The Vision. The prophet clearly gained a sense of mission from his divine encounter with Yahweh. This momentous event was probably not an initial call but a recommissioning for the specific task of heralding judgment. We should read chs. 1–5 as both a brief overview of the entire message and a summary of the themes that Isaiah preached during Uzziah's final years. Included are the indictment of the people for their stupor and rebellious sin (1:1-26) and the promise of redemption for those who will turn to their God (vv. 27-31); a vision of the glory of the latter days (2:1-4) and of the judgment of the proud, haughty, and idolatrous (vv. 6-10); another alternation, this time in reverse order, of the judgment (3:1–4:1) and the glory to come (4:2-6); and the beautiful "song of the vineyard" (ch. 5). Two visions are indicated (1:1; 2:1), possibly combined with several separate messages to shape the introductory argument.

The vision of Yahweh (ch. 6) is dated "in the year that King Uzziah died" (740 B.C.). Before this event, Isaiah saw the glories and splendor of Uzziah's earthly court, but when the king died, God gave Isaiah a vision of the heavenly court. The vision contains a revelation of the thrice-holy (i.e., incomparably holy) One (vv. 1-3), seated on a throne "high and lifted up," clad in a robe whose hem fills the temple. Angels called *seraphim* serve to guard the throne, worship the Lord, and minister to Isaiah in his sinful need (v. 7). Isaiah also has a vision of himself — a sinner dwelling in the midst of sinners (v. 6), in need of mercy because his eyes have "seen the King, the Lord of Hosts" (v. 5). At this point Isaiah receives the revelation of his appointed ministry (vv. 8-13).

The Mission. Isaiah's was an agonizing ministry part of whose impact was to make it impossible for the people of God to see and hear God's truth. God's judgment upon them would be made very real and virtually total. Yet a remnant of Judah — of whom the forgiven and cleansed Isaiah (v. 7) was the forerunner — would survive, as a felled tree may take fresh root (v. 13). The names the prophet gave his sons — Shear-jashub (7:3) "a remnant will return" and particularly that of the younger, Maher-shalal-hash-baz (8:1-4) "speed spoil, hasten prey"[3] — are indicative of his twofold message. The first son's name speaks of Assyrian conquests that leave only a remnant of survivors.[4] The second describes the Assyrian looting of Damascus and Samaria whose greedy coalition had threatened Judah's King Ahaz. The vision declares both God's freedom to make himself known and the forgiveness of sin for his prophet and the faithful people.

Isaiah's assignment is complex. At first glance, it seems to entail a message of the rejection of both Israel and Judah. Yahweh tells Isaiah that he is to make it impossible for the people to repent (6:10). The Pharaoh-Moses confrontation may be a parallel: Pharaoh first hardens his own heart, and then Yahweh seals the process (see Exod. 7:3, 14). In Isaiah, however, a redeeming feature is found in the words "the holy seed is its stump" (Isa. 6:13). This horticultural picture of future hope becomes part of the prophetic imagery of messianic promise (Jer. 23:5-6; 33:15; Zech. 3:8; 6:12). Several scholars have rejected this final line of ch. 6 as non-Isaianic, on the assumption that Isaiah's commission was to announce doom alone. We need not remove this element of redeeming significance, since it is already anticipated in the gift of forgiveness to Isaiah (v. 7).[5] Both judgment and hope are inherent in the relationship we see between God and Israel.

According to 2 Chr. 26:22, Isaiah ben Amoz had written the "acts" of Uzziah, implying that the prophet was a scribe or keeper of the official chronicle of that king. The prophecy implies that Isaiah moved easily in official circles and was close to the kings (see 7:3; 8:2; 36:1–38:8, 21f.; par. 2 Kgs. 18:3–20:19). Such a position would satisfactorily explain Isaiah's knowledge of world affairs.[6] Indeed, his perception of God's sovereign use of the nations in carrying out covenant blessings and judgments was one of his profound contributions to Israel's understanding of its place in God's program of history.

The Times

The chapters on 2 Kings, Amos, Hosea, and Micah have shown us something of the national and international situation of Isaiah's time. For at least part of his ministry Isaiah was contemporary with these prophets. Although his recommissioning (ch. 6) came in the year that Uzziah died, we may assume from 2 Chr. 26:22 that he had been active in the court for at least a few years prior to that event. Indeed, chs. 1–5 may date from Uzziah's last years. If the record of Sennacherib's death (Isa. 37:38) comes from Isaiah's pen, his court life and prophetic ministry extended from ca. 745 to ca. 680. Even if this period were shortened to "the last four and a half decades of the eighth century" as some have suggested, we would have to agree that they "were filled with the most momentous events, more so than almost any other period of Israelite history."[7] Isaiah's times were nothing less than a watershed in the history of the people of God.

Tiglath-pileser came to the Assyrian throne in 745, and, free from his concerns about Mesopotamia and Urartu, had conquered by 740 all of northern Syria. In 738 he subjugated the Aramean city-state of Hamath and forced other small kingdoms to pay tribute to escape the same fate. Included in this group were Israel under Menahem (2 Kgs. 15:19f.), and one Azriyau of Ya'udi, taken by some to be Azariah (Uzziah) of Judah.[8] In 734 Tiglath-pileser led an expedition to the Philistine territory and set up a base of operations at the River of Egypt (Wâdi el-'Arîsh). Several small states allied against him in the so-called Syro-Ephraimite war (733). Israel under Pekah participated in this war, but Judah under Ahaz refused. The coalition then turned against Ahaz, hoping to overthrow the Davidic dynasty and put someone on the throne who would join their alliance (2 Kgs. 15:37; 16:5; Isa. 7:1). Rejecting Isaiah's advice, Ahaz turned to Assyria for help (2 Kgs. 16:7-9). Tiglath-pileser invaded the upper Jordan region, took Gilead and Galilee, and carried off many of the Israelites to Assyria. The people of Israel were displaced (2 Kgs. 15:29). Assyria was eying the borders of Judah.

About this time Pekah of Israel was overthrown, and his successor Hoshea paid tribute to Tiglath-pileser after the Assyrian king had inflicted horrible devastation on Damascus (732). When Tiglath-pileser died in 727, Hoshea refused to pay tribute to his successor, Shalmaneser V. Instead, Hoshea courted Egypt as an ally (2 Kgs. 17:4). Assyria moved against Israel and seized the king and his land, but was unable to take Samaria, the capital. After a three-year siege, Samaria fell (721) either to Shalmaneser or his successor Sargon II (who claimed the victory). A host of Israelites were then carried into captivity. The land was resettled by captives from other lands, including Babylonians (v. 24), which may partly explain Isaiah's intimate knowledge of Babylon. With the fall of the northern kingdom, Assyria extended its empire to the northern boundary of Judah. It is this crisis which provides the backdrop for the messages of judgment and hope in chs. 7–14.

In 720 some of the city-states in Syria and Palestine rebelled, but were immediately suppressed. Gaza tried to revolt with the help of Sib'u of Egypt. In the battle that ensued, Assyrian forces drove the Egyptians back into their own land, leaving Judah practically an island. Ahaz died in 715, and Hezekiah (who had acted as coregent for twelve years) succeeded him.[9] In 714 the Twenty-fifth (Ethiopian) Dynasty came into power in Egypt (possibly reflected in Isa. 18:1-6). In 713-711 an anti-Assyrian uprising occurred at Ashdod, in which Edom, Moab, and Judah participated. Sargon of Assyria sent his Turtan ("second") to Ashdod (ch. 20), and Ashdod and Gath became an Assyrian province. Judah was becoming increasingly vulnerable.

Sargon died in 705, setting off an immediate rash of revolts against Assyria, including Hezekiah's effort (2 Kgs. 18:4-8), which was doubtless encouraged by Egypt (cf. Isa. 30:1-5; 31:1-3). Merodach-baladan led an uprising in Babylon, and most likely sent envoys to Hezekiah to lay the groundwork for a two-pronged revolt or attack (2 Kgs. 20:12-19; Isa. 39:1-4). Sennacherib of Assyria was busy stamping out revolts and could not focus on Judah until 701. In that campaign he crushed Sidon, and caused Ashdod, Ammon, Moab, and Edom to pay tribute. He also subjugated Ashkelon and Ekron and was victorious over Egyptian forces under Tirhakah at Eltekeh.[10] Lachish was besieged, Hezekiah was "shut up like a bird in a cage"[11] and forced to pay tribute to Sennacherib (2 Kgs. 18:13-16). More of his land was taken, at least temporarily, and given to Philistine kings. The history of these times is so interwoven with Isaiah's prophecy that the prophecy cannot be understood without a knowledge of the events.[12]

The Authorship

The traditional view that Isaiah wrote the entire book is held today by exceedingly few scholars. Many critics today accept two books (1–39 and 40–66), usually called "First" and "Second" (or "Deutero") Isaiah.[13] Further refinement finds three books — 1–39; 40–55; 56–66 — the last section of which is named "Third" (or "Trito") Isaiah. Extreme positions find four or more authors, and in some cases no identifiable authors at all; the work is seen as the progressive compilation of unknown members of the believing community (see Chapter 17, above).[14]

Arguments for Plural Authorship. Three major arguments have been given for dividing the prophecy of Isaiah among two or more authors responsible for chs. 1–39 and 40–66: the historical perspective, including the mention of Cyrus, king of Persia from 559-530 B.C. (45:1); the style; and the theological themes. The lines of argument run like this, although the refinements brought to them in recent decades are legion:[15] (1) Internal evidence suggests that the prophecy of chs. 40–66 points not to Judah's contacts with Assyria as does the prophecy of chs. 1–39 but to the period of Babylonian captivity, a century and a half later. Jerusalem is ruined and deserted (44:26; 58:12; 61:4; 63:18; 64:10). The prophet is addressing exiles in Babylonia (40:21, 26, 28; 43:10; 48:8; 50:10f.; 51:6, 12f.). (2) The literary style of chs. 40–66 is held to be different from that of chs. 1–39, employing repetition of words for emphasis, references to cities as though they were persons, dramatic pictures of the fate of nations and persons.[16] Some points are discussed that cannot be specifically illustrated, such as an apparent contrast between the terse, compact style of Isaiah himself and the lengthy development of an idea in Second Isaiah or between the grave, restrained rhetoric of Isaiah and the warm and impassioned rhetoric of Second Isaiah. (3) The theological ideas of 40–66, it is contended, differ too remarkably from those which appear in 1–39 to be identified with Isaiah. The author of the second part of the book "moves *in a different region of thought* from Isaiah; he apprehends and emphasizes different aspects of Divine truth."[17] The differences in theological emphases will be surveyed in Chapter 22, below.

Arguments for a Third Isaiah (Trito-Isaiah; chs. 56–66) have been summarized thus:[18] (1) "The nation is living in Palestine; Jerusalem is built up again." (2) "The subject-matter . . . is no longer the great longing for deliverance and for the return home, but miserable conditions, details and quarrels in the life of the community" (56:9ff.; 57:3ff.; 65:1ff.; 66:3ff.). (3) "The expectations of salvation bear a marked worldly and materialistic colouring." (4) "The conception of God is not as lofty as that of Deutero-Isaiah and his strong trustful optimism will be sought in vain." It has been noted that in chs. 60–62, sayings of Deutero-Isaiah are frequently employed and quoted, but with their original meaning distorted. This perspective sees a "deep gulf" between Deutero- and Trito-Isaiah.[19]

Many recent works no longer give any reasons for accepting the notion of two or three Isaiahs. The authors state as solid fact that chs. 1–39 were written by "Isaiah of Jerusalem" and 40–66 (or 40–55) by "an unknown prophet of the Exile." It is fair to say, however, that the break between chs. 39 and 40 is much clearer than that between chs. 55 and 56.

Discussion of Arguments for Multiple Authorship. Even with the view of inspiration stated in Chapter 45 below, it is no more difficult to accept the concept of "an unknown prophet of the Exile" as the author of chs. 40–66 or 40–55 than that of an unknown author of the epistle to the Hebrews. One could concede that the religious values of "Second" or "Third" Isaiah are equally great, assuming their divine inspiration. A person's position concerning Isaianic authorship should not be made a test of orthodoxy. Nevertheless, it is as much a violation of critical principles to say without further explanation that "Isa. 40–66 was written by an unknown prophet of the Exile" as it is to say "Isaiah wrote the entire book." We need continually to attempt to grasp the significance of the book as it has been given to us and leave as an open question the process of its composition.

(1) Cyrus. Is the argument based on the mention of Cyrus a refusal to admit the possibility of a divinely revealed look at the future? If so, it is dangerous, since a biblical worldview must be based on the reality of God's supernatural presence and activity. There are, however, thoroughgoing theists who believe that Cyrus' name indicates an exilic date for chs. 40ff. They point out that it is contrary to the nature of prophecy, as illustrated everywhere else in the prophetic literature of the Bible, to announce the names of individuals in advance. (One exception is the specific mention of Josiah in 1 Kgs. 13:1f., more than three centuries before he came on the scene, though "Josiah" here is often taken as an insertion of a Deuteronomistic editor.)[20] But consider the startling statement made by G. von Rad in another context: "In fact, Deutero-Isaiah puts in bold relief the question of who is the controller of world-history, and the answer he gives almost takes one's breath away — the Lord of history is he who can allow the future to be told in advance."[21] Some scholars, who hold to a single authorship of Isaiah, believe that the name "Cyrus" in 44:28 and 45:1 is an addition to the text.[22] On the other hand, it has been pointed out that Cyrus is the subject of the entire context (from ch. 41 on) and that

the name cannot be excised without destroying the literary structure of the passage.[23]

Therefore, the argument for multiple authorship from the mention of Cyrus is not entirely compelling: (a) it can be accommodated by those who hold to a single author; (b) the two-author view does not and cannot actually depend on it alone.

(2) Style. All scholars admit that any argument based on style is precarious. An author's style may vary according to purpose, audience, mood, age, and other factors. In fact, scholars who hold to multiple authorship often admit that the "unknown author" of chs. 40–66 deliberately sought to imitate the style of Isaiah of Jerusalem: "Relationships in vocabulary and in thought make us conclude that Second Isaiah not only knew the oracles of Isaiah of Jerusalem, but also that he thought of himself as the continuation of Isaiah of Jerusalem."[24] Several dozen parallels in wording, concepts, and literary images have been identified to demonstrate the linkage between the two halves of the book.[25]

Likewise, style is not a decisive factor in Trito-Isaiah. Typically, scholars find that "the style for the most part is inferior,"[26] yet they may acknowledge that "the style of these chapters closely resembles that of Deutero-Isaiah, but it is not uniform throughout, that of some passages being much inferior to that of others.[27] Style alone can be used to argue for a unity between one Isaiah and the second Isaiah.[28] In fact, on the basis of style alone, scholars find no compelling agreement in their results, whether for the book of Isaiah or any other part of the Old Testament.

(3) The argument based on the geographical and historical situation cannot be disposed of in quite so summary a fashion. One cannot dispute that the viewpoint of chs. 40–66, in general, does not anticipate the Exile, but rather stands within the Exile. An accepted principle of the grammatico-historical hermeneutic holds that prophecy always arises from the historical situation[29] and speaks to people of that situation (see Ch. 16, above). For prophecy to be given exclusively in advance of a situation is a violation of this principle — i.e., while it may refer to a future time, it must do so from within the present situation, for otherwise it would have no relevance to people of its own day.

Although this principle is acceptable in general, it must not be taken to exclude predictive prophecy. Predictive prophecy, as a rule, indicates its own historical setting. For example, in the Olivet discourse (Mark 13; Matt. 24–25), Jesus clearly is sitting on the Mount of Olives with his disciples not long before the Crucifixion, talking about the future. But in Isa. 40–66 there is nowhere any indication that Isaiah of Jerusalem is in the Jerusalem of his own time talking to contemporaries about a future exile. Rather, numerous indications show that the author is living within the Exile, talking to people who are living under exilic conditions.[30]

However, the argument is not quite so simple. If it were, all scholars might be among the disciples of B. Duhm[31] and his approach to Deutero-Isaiah. For even chs. 1–39 contain segments (chs. 13; 24–27; 32–35, and according to some scholars many more) which do not have the eighth-century viewpoint of Isaiah. Therefore, most scholars deny their Isaianic authorship. Chs. 56–66 contain so many references that do not have a Babylonjan *Sitz im Leben* (setting) that many scholars insist that these were delivered in Jerusalem — after the Exile, of course.[32] But the details of the Jerusalem or Palestinian passages in chs. 56–66 are frequently not at all in harmony with the postexilic period. The idolatry, high places, and related sins (see 57:3-13) are characteristic of the period before the Exile, but not after. Scholars of Old Testament history and religion have long contended that the Exile cured Israel of its ancient idolatry: ". . . the problem of idolatry continued through much of Israel's history. It was only after the Babylonian Exile that the problem was effectively eradicated."[33]

The kinds of sin mentioned in 59:1-8 sound much more like those in Amos, Micah, and the original Isaiah, than like those in Haggai, Zechariah, Malachi, or Ezra-Nehemiah. A reading of the postexilic prophets alongside Isa. 56–66 will suggest at least as many contrasts as similarities. Chs. 40–55 have points in common with both the earlier and the later chapters of Isaiah. In fact, scholars have been so puzzled by the complexity of the data that some have tended to fragmentize the book of Isaiah into numerous sources, possibly as many as ten, stretching over a period from 740 to the second century B.C. As to the geography, numerous minor details are given about Jerusalem, but no details about Babylonia. (Compare this with Ezekiel or Daniel, which include a host of details about Babylonia.) If "Deutero-Isaiah" ("Isaiah of Babylon") wrote from Babylon, he left us little concrete evidence of his whereabouts.

We may well ask whether the viewpoints expressed in the book of Isaiah would have been as far removed from the experience of the eighth-century Judeans, as the various scholarly theories suggest. In 722 the people of the northern kingdom had been taken into captivity. Deportees from Babylon were relocated in Israel. Many of the northerners had fled south, doubtless with tales to tell, so talk about exile would be quite relevant. Would not references to Babylonia have been plentiful? The visit of envoys of Merodach-baladan, the Babylonian revolutionary, in the days of Hezekiah (*ca.* 701; see 2 Kgs. 20:12; Isa. 39:1) must have raised the possibility of alliance with Babylon in an attempt to overthrow Assyria. Isaiah opposed that position. With divine revelation (or even without it) he might indeed have foreseen that the future would bring divine retribution upon Judah at the hands of Babylon — a message certainly not irrelevant to his day.

Moreover, Isaiah indicates clearly that his message is intended not for his own day alone, but for a future time. Just after the account of Ahaz's refusal to heed Isaiah's advice (ch. 7), and just before the promise of the coming Davidic ruler (9:2-7 [MT 1-6], accepted as Isaianic by many critics), Isaiah speaks of binding up the testimony and sealing the teaching among his disciples (8:16). The passage is not without linguistic difficulties,[34] but the intent is clear: Isaiah, whether by command from Yahweh or by personal decision, is looking to a distant time when his message will be more completely relevant.[35]

A reasonable possibility is that Isaiah's messages were collected and preserved by his disciples[36] and later edited and put into written form. This would be sufficient to account for the introduction of a later viewpoint resonating with its origins. What Isaiah said with immediate relevance, as well as with reference to the future, was put into language that was more meaningful later, at the time of writing. Isaiah's immediate disciples (born, perhaps, no

Deportees from Ekron with Assyrian escort, depicted on seventh-century relief from Nineveh. *(Louvre, photo William Sanford LaSor)*

285

later than 700) could hardly have lived until the capture of Jerusalem (597), much less the return from exile (537 or later). But, of course, his disciples could, in turn, have passed the traditions on to their disciples. Uncertainty about the process makes it the better part of wisdom to keep an open mind on the subject.

The influence of Isaiah of Jerusalem on the whole work should not be underestimated. His is the only name listed as a prophet in the sixty-six chapters. His themes set the tone for the entire work. The sections that may have been added later were woven into the fabric that plainly came from his hand. His successors apparently saw themselves as heirs of his ministry. And whoever did the final editing, under the Spirit's guidance, viewed the book as a unified whole, not a collection of prophetic materials parallel to the obvious liturgical and sapiential collections of Psalms and Proverbs.

(4) The theological ideas in Isaiah and the argument that those in Deutero-Isaiah are much advanced beyond those of Proto-Isaiah will be discussed in the following chapter. Here, we note only that in some respects this is a circular argument. Some scholars seek to determine what the level of theological thought must have been in the eighth century. Then they proceed to excise from the texts of Amos, Micah, Hosea, Isaiah, or the Deuteronomic history what does not fit that assumption. Then, on the basis of the emended texts, they offer proof for the original thesis. Such logic fails to carry conviction, and is finally unconvincing.

There can be no question concerning the development of ideas in the book of Isaiah. A notable difference can be seen between chs. 1–39 and 40–66, as even a perusal of the outline (pp. 290-92 below) will show. Furthermore, it is exceedingly difficult, even impossible, to reconstruct the process whereby original utterances of the prophet and the final inscripturated form are connected. Taking the book at face value, one must assume that various prophecies were remembered, possibly written down, and preserved beginning *ca.* 740 and continuing through the Exile and return, until the canonical shape of the book was achieved. No one should attempt this reconstruction without a profound sense of our need to understand the theological dimension of the vision.[37]

Therefore, although there must be some degree of flexibility in considering various suggestions, no reason suffices to reject the view that Isaiah of Jerusalem was the dominant personality whose influence shines through the entire prophecy. The presence of later additions and explanatory glosses is not only a possibility but a demonstrable fact. The theory of the activity of Isaiah's disciples is not unreasonable. It is suggested by the text itself. The Gospels parallel this development. They are essentially the teachings of Jesus Christ, although he did not write a word of them. The Gospel of Mark is very likely the preaching of Peter or the catechetical instruction that accompanied Peter's preaching, even though the literary form and structure are almost certainly Mark's. The Torah is essentially Mosaic, although how much of it actually was written down by Moses is not at all clear. Here, then, are three different types of transmission of the teachings of religious leaders, and doubtless others can be found within the Scriptures. Any similar process is acceptable when one says, "Isaiah was responsible for the entire prophecy."

What ought to be rejected is any view that leaves only a microscopic Isaiah of Jerusalem and a gigantic anonymous figure of the Exile. More promising are the recent commentaries that root Isaiah's ministry in the history of his times; make him an important player in the reigns of Uzziah, Ahaz, and Hezekiah; and credit most of chs. 1–39 to his prophetic activity.[38]

Authority. More significant than the discussion of authorship is the question of authority. What does the prophecy of Isaiah say to the believing community? Without debate, the critical division of Isaiah, as B. S. Childs has pointed out, resulted in the loss of much of the message:

> First of all, critical scholarship has atomized the book of Isaiah into a myriad of fragments, sources, and redactions which were written by different authors at a variety of historical moments. To speak of the message of the book as a whole has been seriously called into question, and even such relatively conservative scholars as W. Eichrodt have been forced to isolate a small number of "genuine" or "central" passages from which to interpret the rest of the book. Again, critical exegesis now rests upon a very hypothetical and tentative basis of historical reconstructions. Since it is no longer possible to determine precisely the historical background of large sections of Isaiah, hypotheses increase along with the disagreement among the experts. Finally, the more the book of Isaiah has come into historical focus and has been anchored to its original setting, the more difficult it has become to move from the ancient world into a contemporary religious appropriation of the message.[39]

The question that must be asked first is not, "What value has this work for the church today?" but rather, "What value did this work have to the believing community that caused it to be preserved, revered, and considered as sacred Scripture?" The snips and patches identified by critical analysis would long ago have disappeared without something compelling in the characterization of the relation between God and Israel. The solution proffered by Childs, namely the canonical process, while of great merit, will not satisfy everyone. According to his view, First Isaiah underwent "theological redaction . . . to assure that its message was interpreted in the light of Second Isaiah."[40] But why was First Isaiah preserved for 150 years or more? Childs notes: "In the light of the present shape of the book of Isaiah the question must be seriously raised if the material of Second Isaiah in fact ever circulated in Israel apart from its being connected to an earlier form of

First Isaiah."[41] His answer, which delays production of the canonical Isaiah for two centuries or more, does not speak to the prior question concerning First Isaiah. The element of hope of future redemption must have been ignited in Isaiah's disciples, and it must have burned so fiercely that the destruction of the temple, exile of the nation, and disappointments of the return, all combined, could not quench it. We have no evidence that Second Isaiah and Third, and as many other "Isaiahs" as critical scholars may identify, ever circulated without First Isaiah. The hypothetical book contains no heading, no date formula, no statement indicating "The vision of 'Second Isaiah' which he saw in the days of Zerubbabel" such as is found in every other prophetic work. As far as can be ascertained, only one prophecy of Isaiah existed, however scholars finally may succeed in getting from the prophet Isaiah of Jerusalem to the canonical book that bears his name.

The authority of the book, then, is the message of the entire book. It combines judgment and deliverance, despair and hope. To study the prophecy of Isaiah in the light of the above analysis is not to claim that Isaiah plotted his work in outline and then wrote it. Rather, the entire process may be attributed to the action of God's Spirit, as the ultimate Author, both on the prophet Isaiah and on his "disciples," whoever they were and whenever and however they put the work in its final canonical form.

This leads us to consider the hermeneutical principle that must guide every effort to grasp the message of Isaiah. One must seek, as always, to know the situation to which "the prophet" spoke. But in this case, the *Sitz im Leben* extends from preexilic Israel facing the awful judgment of the Lord, whom they had rejected, to the exiles, who need to know that their experience of divine judgment has been completed and to hear words of comfort.

> This is one reason for the greatness of the prophecy of Isaiah: it stands astride two worlds. It speaks to the sinners who face an angry God (1:21-26) and also to the remnant who are to receive salvation from that same God (40:1f.), revealed for them as Father and Redeemer (63:16). From this perspective, Isaiah's prophecy speaks with authority to every person of every age.

Like Israel, all humankind has sinned repeatedly, in thought, word, and deed. Like Israel all are in need of salvation. The Book of Isaiah proclaims that salvation is provided by the God who is in full control of this world with its nations, strong or weak, and who can reveal to his prophets what is to take place in the future.

CHAPTER 22

Isaiah: Message

Appreciation of the grandeur of Isaiah's message does not depend on an accurate analysis of the book's origins. We can be left breathless by the majesty of the Alps or the Tetons without a technical grasp of the geology that shaped them. For two and a half millennia the words of this magnificent vision have brought rebuke and encouragement to God's people. We should ponder the process of the composition and weigh each new contribution with discerning delight. But we do not gain what Isaiah has to give by being enlightened spectators. We want with believers through the ages to become participants in the vision, players in the drama of hope and salvation, worshippers of the One whose glory fills the whole earth (6:3).

> Let me sing for my beloved my love-song
>   concerning his vineyard:
> My beloved had a vineyard
>   on a very fertile hill.
> He dug it and cleared it of stones
>   and planted it with choice vines;
> he built a watchtower in the midst of it,
>   and hewed out a wine vat in it;
> he expected it to yield grapes,
>   but it yielded wild grapes. Isa. 5:1-2

> For the vineyard of the LORD of Hosts
> is the house of Israel,
> and the people of Judah
> are his pleasant planting;
> he expected justice, but saw bloodshed;
> righteousness, but heard a cry! Isa. 5:7

Structure

No ancient manuscript or version gives any indication that the book of Isaiah existed in two or more parts. The LXX (third century B.C.) gives no hint of a "First" or "Second" Isaiah, although it does divide other books (e.g., Samuel, Kings, Chronicles). The complete Isaiah manuscript found among the Dead Sea scrolls (1QIsaᵃ) makes not the slightest break at the end of ch. 39. Rather, 40:1 is the very last line of the thirty-second column, with no indentation or any unusual space at the end of the preceding line. There is a linebreak which separates ch. 33 from 34 (bottom of col. 27). In the Jewish listing of canonical books, Isaiah was always counted as one book. Therefore, the book needs to be studied as a single work, in spite of the countless ways in which it may be analyzed in its various parts.

On the basis of style and content, the book breaks into two distinct parts, which can be further subdivided. Some find an "historical interlude" dividing the two.

Part One: Judgment with Promise (chs. 1–35)

Judah's sins (chs. 1–12)
  Arraignment (ch. 1)
  Jerusalem: Yahweh's and Israel's contrasted (chs. 2–4)
  Song of the Vineyard (ch. 5) with woes of judgment
  Isaiah's vision and special commission (ch. 6)
  Immanuel: the sign of Ahaz (chs. 7–8)
  Prince of Peace (9:1-7 [MT 8:23–9:6])
  Yahweh's anger; Assyria his rod (9:8 [MT 9:7]–10:34)
  Future hope: the Branch (ch. 11)
  Song of thanksgiving (ch. 12)

"Burdens" of judgment (chs. 13–23)
    Burden concerning Babylon (13:1–14:27)
    Burdens concerning Philistia, Moab, Damascus, Cush, Egypt,
        the wilderness of the west, and Tyre (14:28–23:18)
Yahweh's purpose in future judgment (chs. 24–27)
    Judgment on the nations (ch. 24)
    Salvation of Yahweh's people (ch. 25)
    Song of trust (ch. 26)
    Deliverance of Israel (ch. 27)
Warning against humanistic efforts to save (chs. 28–35)
    Ephraim — a warning to Jerusalem (ch. 28)
    Hypocrisy of Zion (ch. 29)
    Reliance on Egypt of no avail (chs. 30–32)
    Salvation from Yahweh (ch. 33)
    Yahweh's day of vengeance (ch. 34)
    Zion's blessed future (ch. 35)
Historical interlude (ch. 36–39)
    Sennacherib's invasion and failure (36:1–37:20)
    Isaiah's message (37:21-38)
    Hezekiah's illness (ch. 38)
    Envoys from the king of Babylon (ch. 39)

Part Two: Comfort with Judgment (chs. 40–66)

Deliverance (chs. 40–48)
    Comfort from Yahweh by return from Exile (chs. 40–41)
    Yahweh's servant (ch. 42)
    Yahweh the divine redeemer (ch. 43)
    Idols no gods (ch. 44)
    Cyrus, Yahweh's anointed, but Yahweh supreme (ch. 45)
    Judgment on Babylon (chs. 46–47)
    Israel's lack of faith rebuked (ch. 48)
Expiation (chs. 49–59)
    Yahweh's servant a light to the nations (ch. 49)
    Opposition to Yahweh's servant (ch. 50)
    Yahweh's comfort of Zion (51:1–52:12)
    Yahweh's servant a redeemer of the people (52:13–53:12)
    Heritage of Yahweh's servants (ch. 54)
    Mercy freely offered (ch. 55)
    Righteousness and wickedness contrasted (chs. 56–58)
    Confession of the nation's transgressions (ch. 59)
Glory (chs. 60–66)

Future glory of Zion (ch. 60)
Good tidings to the afflicted (ch. 61)
Vindication of Zion (ch. 62)
Yahweh's wrath on the nations (ch. 63)
Prayer for mercy (ch. 64)
Rebellious punished (65:1-16)
New heavens and new earth (65:17–66:24)

We would note that the closing verses (66:15-24) are reminiscent of the opening verses (1:1-26). The two passages intentionally form a frame which highlights the cosmic consequences — "heavens and earth" — of Yahweh's judgment and salvation.

Basing his analysis on a two-part division which may have been indicated by the three-line break in the Dead Sea Scroll 1QIsa[a], R. K. Harrison takes a slightly different approach. He sees an "overlapping." The first half ends with the hope of restoration of the Davidic regime (chs. 32–33), and the second half (34–66) opens with a renewal of the note of judgment (34–35).[1] While acknowledging the complex nature of the book's development, J. D. W. Watts has attempted most recently to treat the vision as a unity revealing twelve acts of God rehearsed as repertory drama.[2] For all of the evident complexity in shaping of the book, efforts to grasp the entire prophecy as the eighth-century vision of Isaiah will certainly continue.[3]

Perspectives

In addition to the survey of the book's overall structure, we need to look at Isaiah in two other ways, if we are to catch its message. We have already seen the tug-of-war between those interpreters who feature its unity and those who are so impressed by its diversity that they hear two or three separate prophetic voices in its pages. The unity and diversity are both present. To get at the diversity we need to look at the three main divisions (chs. 1–39; 40–55; 56–66) and see their theological, historical, and literary perspective. That task can then be followed by a sketch of the great themes that give the work its remarkable unity of tone, spirit, and subject.

Isaiah 1–39. Geographically, these chapters center in Judah and especially in Jerusalem, its capital. Key personalities include: the kings of Judah — Uzziah, Ahaz, Hezekiah; the king of Israel — Pekah; the ruler of Damascus — Rezin; and the prophet Isaiah with his two sons — Shear-jashub (7:3) and Maher-shalal-hash-baz (8:1).

The Lord's vineyard, Judah, has yielded "wild grapes" and must face judgment (Isa. 5:1-7). Vineyard near Lachish. *(Neal and Joel Bierling)*

Two historical events dominate the story and help shape the speeches: the westward marches of the Assyrian army under Tiglath-pileser III (745-727 B.C.) and the ravaging of Judah by the later Assyrian king Sennacherib in 701 B.C. Chs. 7–10 reflect the earlier threat, and chs. 36–39, the later. Isaiah uses these invasions and Judah's reaction to them as occasions for teaching basic lessons about Yahweh's will and ways.

First, the prophet observes that Judah and its ancient capital are full of crimes of all sorts: rebellion, meaningless religious ritualism, outright idolatry, flagrant injustice, self-satisfied arrogance, drunken carousing. Judgment is called for, and God will implement it by means of foreign invaders whose speed and viciousness will swamp the land like a tidal wave (chs. 1–5). It will be Isaiah's lot to proclaim this judgment till Judah's hills and valleys are a patch-work of scorched earth (ch. 6).

Second, Isaiah sets up a contrast between the two kings who are faced with the Assyrian threat. Ahaz is pictured as wavering between God's command to "stand firm in faith" (7:9) and his own fear of the evil plots of the kings of Israel and Damascus who are badgering him to join them in resisting Tiglath-pileser's conquests (7:1-2). Hezekiah, however, does not waver in his approach to Sennacherib's threat. Instead, he pleads with the Lord, "Save us from his hand, so that all the kingdoms of the earth may know that you alone are the

293

Lord" (37:20). In turn, he hears the Lord's promise: "For I will defend this city to save it, for my own sake and for the sake of my servant David" (37:35). These two narratives — Ahaz's and Hezekiah's — anchor the first half of the book, demonstrating the importance of trust. It was the king's part to depend on the God of the covenant, God's sovereign use of foreign nations to work his will, and the divine concern for Jerusalem and the family of David who occupy its throne.[4]

Third, this divine concern is often described as the "Zion tradition" in the Old Testament. It has its roots in David's conquest of the old Jebusite city which did not become part of Judah in the conquest of Joshua and the judges (2 Sam. 5–6). The central fortress called Zion (2 Sam. 5:7) lent its name as a poetic description both to the city and its inhabitants settled on Jerusalem's mountains. It spoke of their commitment to the worship of Yahweh who had chosen their ruling dynasty, established a dwelling place among them, and preserved them from their enemies.[5] Isaiah shows clearly that Yahweh's care for Jerusalem is two-edged. Both protection and cleansing are divine purposes for the holy city. The Lord uses the foreign aggressors — first Assyria and then Babylonia, whose devastating invasion is anticipated in ch. 39 — to purify the people. But the divine hand sets limits to their mayhem and preserves a remnant to carry on the covenant relation and ultimately become a light to all the nations.

Because Zion belongs primarily to Yahweh and only secondarily to the people, God exercises full freedom in dealing with its crimes within and its military threats without. This freedom sets up the rhythm of judgment and hope that dominates chs. 1–39. A prominent beat in that rhythm is the judgment of the nations that sets the context for judgment of Judah and Jerusalem. These were the nations whose religious and social practices God's people were tempted to imitate. They were also the nations who participated in or gloated over Judah's misfortunes: Babylon (13:1–14:23; 21:6-10), Assyria (14:24-27), Philistia (14:28-32), Moab (15:1–16:14), Damascus (17:1-14), Ethiopia (18:1-7; 20:1-6), Egypt (19:1–20:6), Edom (21:11-12), Arabia (21:13-17), and Tyre (23:1-18). Most of these had also felt to a milder degree the pain of Assyrian conquest, whether under Tiglath-pileser III, Shalmaneser V, Sargon II (20:1), or Sennacherib. The large space given to them in the book signaled clear messages to Judah: (1) their Lord was Ruler of the nations that did not yet call on his name; (2) those nations would be judged by Yahweh for their pagan worship, brazen pride, and inhumane treatment of their enemies; (3) yet they would also be used as part of God's process of purging his people of their transgressions of his will; (4) so sovereign was the Lord of Judah and Israel that they were to trust him, and not alien powers, for their military and political security, nor even rely on their horses and weapons; (5) above all, the empty worship, vain self-glory, and savage cruelty of the nations was to be deplored, not adopted by the covenant people.

Fourth, Judah needed to learn a lesson from Israel's (or Ephraim's) calamitous fall ending with the collapse of Samaria in 721 B.C. (chs. 28–33). Foreign alliances were no safeguard when the leadership — kings, nobles, prophets, priests — failed to keep their covenant with Yahweh and instead made a "covenant with death" (28:15, 18, see chs. 30–31).

Fifth, the prophet's eyes were lifted beyond the specifics of the present situation, with Assyria on center-stage and Babylonia waiting in the wings. He saw that universal accountability to the Creator called for universal judgment on the nations and ultimate salvation for the chosen people (chs. 24–27; 34–35). Sometimes called Isaiah's Apocalypse, these chapters do not bear the marks of true apocalyptic literature such as Daniel or Revelation, with their high symbolism, their dramatic conflicts between good and evil, and their angelic interpreters. They are rather, lofty prophetic visions that catch the larger, future implications of the judgment and deliverance that Yahweh is presently accomplishing.

Finally, we should note the patterns of prayer and praise that punctuate the book's first section: (1) the rescue from the threats of Tiglath-pileser and the Syro-Ephraimite coalition is celebrated in a hymn of thanksgiving (ch. 12); (2) the promise of full deliverance in the day when the whole earth is judged sparks a song of praise in place of the cries of oppression — a song that culminates in the striking "The song of the ruthless was stilled" (25:5); (3) the land of Judah will one day ring with a paean of victory that heralds the indispensable role of faith:

> Those of steadfast mind you keep in peace —
> In peace because they trust in you (26:3);

(4) The communal plea for salvation from trouble, familiar in the Psalms (e.g., 44; 74; 79; 80), is answered by the assurance that Jerusalem will survive the Assyrian crisis (33:2-6, 17-24); (5) Hezekiah's prayer (37:16-20), phrased like the complaints of the psalmists, reveals the urgency of the situation and the firmness of the king's trust in Yahweh. History on the move, nations on the march, life-shaking decisions in the making — these are all viewed by the prophet as occasions for prayer. Prayer becomes central to the prophetic drama because it demonstrates what Yahweh wants of his people and it anticipates the hope and victory that lie beyond the judgment.

Isaiah 40–55. When we turn the page from ch. 39 to ch. 40 we seem to be carried to a different time, place, and situation. The judgment threatened in chs. 1–39 has taken place (42:21-25; 50:1); announcements of it are described by God as "the former things I declared long ago" (48:3). The Babylonian havoc of which God warned Hezekiah (39:5-7) has resulted in a long period of bitter exile in Mesopotamia, an exile orchestrated by the Lord's own hand (42:21-25). Cyrus, the leader of the powerful Persian empire, has been chosen by that hand to spearhead the fall of Babylon (ch. 47), resettle God's people in their land, and rebuild Jerusalem and its temple (44:28–45:7). Between Hezekiah's reception of Babylonian envoys (ch. 39) and the rise of Cyrus on the international horizon, more than a century and a half has elapsed.

The chief burden of these chapters is to announce the end of God's punishment (40:1-2), God's glorious intervention on behalf of the exiles (40:3-5), and the promise of restoration based on the divine word which always accomplishes its purposes (40:6-8; 55:10-11).[6] This redemption is seen as no longer a future reality but a present one:

> "But *now* . . . do not fear,
>   for I have redeemed you;
> I have called you by name,
>   you are mine." (43:1)

That imminent redemption did not have as its cause Israel's repentance so much as Yahweh's gracious forgiveness:

> "I, I am He
>   who blots out your transgressions
>   for my own sake,
>   and I will not remember your sins." (43:25)

The prophet's repeated calls to return (48:20-22) and promises of joy (55:12-13) speak to two impediments in the hearts of the exiles: fear of Babylonian recrimination and a history of compromise with Babylonian religion. To deal with these impediments virtually every tool in the prophet's kit was put to use.

Fear of the Babylonians was met with a cluster of arguments: (1) It was the Lord, not the Babylonian armies alone, who accounted for their initial captivity (42:24-25); the suffering God had brought, he was now ready to relieve. (2) Cyrus was God's instrument chosen to bring the Babylonians to their knees; their intimidating might would be short-lived (ch. 47). (3) The power that spoke the creation into being (Gen. 1–2) was ready to do a new thing in transforming the life and destiny of the people; that power is irresistible (40:21-31; 42:5-9; 44:24-28). (4) The God of the Exodus was ready to do it all again — swamp the armies of hostile kings (43:17; 45:1), dry up the sea and the rivers (43:16; 44:27; 50:2), and tame the desert into a safe highway (41:17-20; 43:19-21).

The objections to return based upon religious compromise were met with similar cogency: (1) Israel's suffering was not due to God's neglect, as some had complained, but to God's activity; divine forgetfulness was a contradition in terms (49:14-17). Judah's judgment was not a rash, whimsical act — like divorcing a wife or selling a slave — but a measured, reasonable response to the people's rebellion (50:1-2). (2) Religious compromise, especially the worship of idols, was the height of stupidity; the prophet makes this clear in language of sarcasm so fierce that it sears the scroll on which it is recorded (44:9-20; 45:20-21; 46:1-7). (3) The sarcasm is balanced by indescribable tenderness. Yahweh invites the people, whose sin had forced a painful but temporary separation, to a new marriage, marked by God's everlasting love and compassion (54:4-8).[7]

The literary forms that convey and support these arguments are noteworthy: (1) *Salvation promises* or announcements[8] head the list. They feature commands to rejoice or fear not (41:10; 43:1); guarantees of divine help, "I will" (41:10; 43:5; 55:3); declarations of the results of God's activity (41:11-12, 15-16a; 43:2; 44:3-5; 54:4); and, at times, statements of God's basic aim in all this — "you shall rejoice in the LORD" (41:16); "so that they might declare my praise" (43:21); "this one will say, 'I am the LORD's' " (44:5). (2) *Hymns* celebrate both the salvation promised and the Savior who makes the promises; they feature calls to praise, usually followed by lines that give reasons for the praise (42:10-13; 44:23; 49:13). Another form of hymn uses relative clauses (participles in Heb.) to describe God's activities as Creator and Redeemer:

> Thus says the LORD,
> who makes a way in the sea . . .
> who brings out chariot and horse. . . .　　　　(43:16-17; see 42:5;
> 　　　　　　　　　　　　　　　　　　　　　　　　43:1; 44:2; 45:18)

The Lord, who brooks no comparison with anything or anyone in the universe, celebrates his own glory in hymnlike self-introductions:

> I, I am the LORD,
> and besides me there is no savior.　(43:11; see 42:8; 43:10-13; 44:24-28;
> 　　　　　　　　　　　　　　　　　　　　　　45:5-7; 46:9-10; 48:12-13; 51:15)

(3) *Courtroom settings* seem to influence the style of a number of passages where the argument centers in proving the worthiness of Yahweh and the worthlessness of other gods:

> Set forth your case, says the LORD;
> bring your proofs, says the King of Jacob.
> . . . .
> Tell us what is to come hereafter,
> that we may know you are gods;

do good, or do harm,
    that we may be afraid and terrified.
You, indeed, are nothing
    and your work is nothing at all;
        whoever chooses you is an abomination.   (41:21, 23-24; see 41:1-5;
                                                        43:8-13; 44:6-8, 21-22; 45:20-25)

(4) In *disputations* the arguer is usually the prophet, not Yahweh. A number of examples are featured in chs. 40–55. They are frequently based on analogies and use what is generally agreed to make affirmations of God's sovereignty and trustworthiness. Their mood is often interrogative, with the question leading the hearer to the appropriate answer (40:12-17, 18-26, 27-31; 45:9-13; 55:8-11; see also 46:9-11; 48:1-11, 12-16).[9]

Certain forms and features of chs. 1–39 play almost no part in chs. 40–55. There are no narratives like the Ahaz and Hezekiah stories that serve as bookends to Isaiah's message (chs. 7–8; 36–39). The emphasis on the new Exodus and the new creation replaces the hope of a son of David to rule in righteousness. No human leader besides Cyrus is mentioned. The prophetic voice in chs. 40–55 is nameless. Biographical details are nonexistent whereas Isaiah is mentioned by name about twenty times in the first part of the book. The absence of human heroes spotlights the work of the Creator-Redeemer whose glories are lauded, whose promises are sounded, whose call is to be heeded. Nothing in the text is allowed to divert our attention from the incomparable Lord of creation and covenant. The Sovereign-Savior is on the march. His cadence determines what we see and hear in these visions, speeches, and hymns.

Isaiah 56–66. Of the book's three sections, the perspective of these chapters is the hardest to discern. The person of the prophet is glimpsed in a couple of places only and there with the simple use of the pronouns *I* or *me* (61:1; 62:1, 6). The geographical locale is Jerusalem and more specifically the temple (56:7; 60:10, 13; 61:3-4; 62:1, 6, 12; 64:10-11; 65:18ff; 66:6). The judgment of chs. 1–39 has apparently taken place. Both the pictures of desolation (63:18; 64:10-11) and the promises of salvation (chs. 60–62; 65:17-25) suggest this. But the actual time in view is impossible to pin-point. We are left to guess whether or not the destroyed temple has been rebuilt (as it was in 515 B.C.). We cannot be sure whether the period in view is that of Haggai, Zechariah, and Zerubbabel or the days of Ezra, Nehemiah, and Malachi some fifty to seventy years later. This obscurity results from the lack of specific information in the text but even more so from our ignorance of life in Judah during and immediately after the Exile. Given the uncertainty, it is wiser to deal with chs. 56–66 as a thematic section and to unpack its various emphases without tying them too closely to a specific historic situation.

The centerpiece of this section seems to be the salvation speeches of chs. 60–62. They highlight the close of the Exile and the return of the dispersed members of the covenant community from their widely scattered dwelling places. The return is marked by the participation of the nations, the exaltation of the captives, the bounty of the economy, the reign of peace and righteousness, and the unquenchable light of God's presence (ch. 60). The restoration includes reversals of status and disposition, rebuilding of devastated cities, recovery of a priestly role among the other nations, and retribution for injustices suffered during captivity (ch. 61). So radical is this transformation that nothing less than a shower of new names (62:2) can describe it: the land called "Forsaken" and "Desolate" will be known as "My Delight Is in Her" and "Married" (62:4); the people will become "The Holy People, the Redeemed of the Lord" and Jerusalem, "Sought Out, a City Not Forsaken" (62:12). (For other salvation speeches, see 57:14-20; 60:6-16; 65:16-25.)

On either side of this centerpiece are complaints of the community that despair of the absence of God's light (59:9-10) and God's forgiveness (vv. 11-15), while pleading for God, their only father, to make his revealing, redeeming presence known (63:15–64:12). The recognition of sin (64:6-9) is interwoven with signs of economic distress (60:17; 62:8-9), foreign domination (60:18), and the consequent loss of face (61:7; 62:4). In both the pleas of salvation and the hope-filled answers to them, all Israel is in view — not just Judah. Only one entity is pictured; the days of a divided kingdom are past history.

The community whose redemption is at hand is in need of strong instruction. First, the covenant demands of righteousness and justice must be upheld: the sabbath must be kept (56:1-2; 58:13-14); the needs of the oppressed and destitute must be attended to (58:6-12); greed and dishonesty in the lawcourts must be quelled (59:1-8); profane acts in worship must be purged (65:1-7). The oracles of chs. 56–66 have passionate concern for restoring holiness to Zion (62:1), a concern that corresponds to a chief element in the perspective of chs. 1–39. The zeal for the house of God together with the heavy use of liturgical language in the complaints and oracles points to a close connection between these speeches and the actual practice of worship in Jerusalem.

A second didactic emphasis shows that these ties to religious activity did not make for narrowness or exclusivity in the prophet's picture of the future. To the contrary, the themes of God's Lordship over the nations and his exclusive claim to the worship of all peoples are sounded as clearly in the final section of Isaiah as in the first two (60:1-4, 9; 61:9; 66:12). Access to the temple will not be restricted by physical maiming or foreign birth (56:1-8; see Deut. 23:1-6), "for my house shall be called a house of prayer for all peoples" (v. 7).

The strong promises of salvation came in a context that was not all peace and light. Factions within the community are hinted at. A group Yahweh called "rebellious" (65:2) seems to be distinguished from "my servants" in conduct and in destiny (65:8-16). The sins of the rebellious seem to center in corrupt worship (vv. 1-7). So illicit was their conduct that it evoked judgment-speeches reminiscent of Isa. 1–5 and Mic. 2–3 (Isa. 56:9–57:13). The precise nature of the conflict cannot be reconstructed with any confidence. The evidence is too thin. But the sins of the past were apparently not eradicated by the Exile, and stern warnings to both leaders (56:9-12) and people (57:13) were necessary even in an era that promised transformation and restoration.[10]

The pictures used to describe God's new day are somewhat different from the prophecies of the first two sections of Isaiah. No overt mention of the Davidic dynasty (see chs. 9; 11) is heard (see 55:3-4 for a reference to David's rule). Nor does the language of the Exodus (chs. 40ff.) play a significant part, though it is recalled in 63:7-14. Akin to the themes of chs. 40–55 is the anticipation of a new creation (65:17-25) marked by joy, good health, longevity, prosperity, harmony with all God's creatures, and especially by universal adoration of God's holy name (66:22-23). Family language is featured to point up the intimacy of God's loving relationship with the people: the Lord will delight in them as a bridegroom in a bride (62:4-5), coddle them as a mother does a child (66:13), protect them as the One responsible for their very being (63:16; 64:8).

Two things may be said about the fulfillment of these prophecies. First, the return from exile brought frustration as well as relief. The glory and blessing promised in chs. 1–39 and 40–55 were realized only in part by the returnees. As Haggai, Zechariah, and Malachi witness, the splendor hoped for fell short in at least three ways: the lack of political independence, the paucity of material prosperity, and the compromises in covenant loyalty. The community often felt a strong discrepancy between what it had expected and what it experienced. The last pages of the Old Testament are marked by a yearning for what was yet to come. Second, the obedience of the chosen people was important, along with the wisdom that had been gained from their chastisement and the knowledge of God brightened by their rescue from pagan captivity. But permanent changes could be effected only by further divine intervention. Hence the emphasis on a transformation so radical, so total, that it could only be understood as a new creation. The exuberant, indeed, superlative language of the ideal future prepares the way for the revelation of God in Jesus Christ in whom the true relief from oppression was to be achieved (61:1-7; Luke 4:18). The startling imagery of a universe made new set the tone for the ultimate consummation of God's covenant program as the prophets and apostles of the early church saw it:

But, in accordance with his promise, we wait for new heavens and a new earth, where righteousness is at home. (2 Pet. 3:13)

And the one who was seated on the throne said, "See, I am making all things new." (Rev. 21:5)

Themes

The Lord's Character. In some respects Isaiah is *the* theological textbook of the Old Testament. Here appear not only the elements for a doctrine of God, but — particularly in the latter portion — expressions of faith that are in essence very well developed formulations of the doctrine (see 11:1-5; 48:12f.; 63:15-17). This very fact (as seen in Ch. 21 above) has been used to argue for the late date of such passages. The theology, it is claimed, is too well developed for the eighth century. But true theological statements come, humanly speaking, from great individual minds able to comprehend extensive data and compress it into a form useful to the believing community. The elements of theology come from an appreciation and assimilation of the acts of God. Israel's history was the result of many acts of God, and formulating the theological significance of those acts was, indeed, the work of Moses and the prophets, including Isaiah. All of the elements for Isaiah's theology are found implicitly, at least, in the eighth-century vision of these acts.

(1) The Holy One of Israel. It is appropriate that Isaiah, whose temple vision was a revelation of the thrice-holy Yahweh, should stress the holiness of God. "The Holy One of Israel," is referred to twenty-five times in the book (twelve times in chs. 1–39, eleven in chs. 40–55, and twice in chs. 56–66).[11] In the rest of the Old Testament, it occurs only six times (2 Kgs. 19:22; Jer. 50:29; 51:5; Pss. 71:22; 78:41; 89:18 [MT 19]). It cannot be demonstrated that the expression was used either before Isaiah's time or long after Jeremiah's time.

The root *qdš* carries the idea of "separate, set apart." It may mean "set apart to" rather than "set apart from," and may concern the suprahuman world.[12] Thus, when Moses received his call in Sinai at the burning bush, he was told "the place on which you are standing is holy ground" (Exod. 3:5). Upon this ground Yahweh named himself and sent Moses to his people.

Although no moral or ethical quality is implied in the earliest uses of the word "holy," certainly by the Mosaic period a moral or ethical connotation was intended. At Sinai Yahweh said to Moses: "You [Israel] shall be to me a kingdom of priests and a holy nation" (Exod. 19:6). This relationship required fidelity to Yahweh their God and obedience to his moral code as specified in the covenant. Israel's holiness, then, implied being separated to Yahweh in belief and action.

Isaiah, however, is the one who actually points up the moral nature of holiness, citing "uncleanness" (Heb. *ṭāmēʾ*) rather than "profaneness" as the characteristic of sinfulness. He stresses the moral or behavioral substance of holiness more than its ritual significance. In the wilderness and the post-Mosaic periods, holiness was bound up with the cult of Yahweh,[13] one purpose of which was to inculcate the Torah. The elaborate details of the sacrificial system were designed to impress upon the Israelites that disobedience to the revealed law alienated them from Yahweh, and required atonement or reconciliation. But the cult had become an empty form. The term "unclean" came to be used more with reference to ceremonial or ritual uncleanness than to immoral behavior or disobedience of the precepts of Torah.[14] The prophets sought to reestablish the relationship between worship and obedience.[15] In the temple vision, Isaiah was confronted by Yahweh's moral perfection over against Israel's "uncleanness" in which the prophet himself shared (6:5). Yahweh confirmed the accuracy of Isaiah's perception by sending a seraph to cleanse his lips with a burning coal from the altar, saying: "Your guilt is taken away, and your sin forgiven" (v. 7). This action is not to be understood as anticultic. Indeed, the entire episode takes place in the temple, the center of the cult.

The sin of the people to whom Isaiah was sent — supposedly a holy nation — was a refusal to hear the word of Yahweh (6:9f.; see 1:2-6, 10-17). Without obedience the elements of worship were meaningless (vv. 11-15; cf. Amos 5:21-24). What Yahweh wanted from his people was proper behavior (vv. 16f.). The once-faithful city had lost its essential moral qualities — justice and righteousness (vv. 21f., see below)[16] — consistent with its relationship with a holy God, and had become a harlot (*zônâ*, 1:21).

Isaiah stresses the relationship of the Holy One to his redemptive activity, especially in chs. 40–55 (41:14; 43:3, 14; 47:4; 48:17; 49:7; 54:5).[17] The punishment of the nation was due to uncleanness, a violation of Yahweh's holiness. Restoration requires the cleansing involved in salvation and redemption. To present the indictment of uncleanness without the remedy of divine salvation would be of no help, and to speak of salvation without making clear the reason for such divine activity would verge on nonsense. Isaiah's own experience, the recognition of his own sin and the acceptance of God's cleansing, became the basis of Isaiah's message to Israel:

> Come now, let us argue it out,
>   says the Lord:
> though your sins are like scarlet,
>   they shall be like snow;

> though they are red like crimson,
> > they shall become like wool. (1:18)

(2) Yahweh as Savior. Isaiah's name (Heb. *yᵉšāʿyāhû*) means "Yahweh will save" or possibly "Yahweh is salvation," which may partly explain the prophet's great interest in salvation.[18] In chs. 1–39, Yahweh is "the God of your salvation" (17:10), which has special reference to deliverance from Assyria (see 11:11-16; 12:1). Salvation is personal ("my salvation," 12:2; "the LORD will save me," 38:20), but it also refers to the city (37:35) and the people who cry to the Lord (19:20). Salvation is mentioned in connection with "stability of your times," and is joined with "wisdom," "knowledge," and "the fear of the LORD" (33:6). It is deliverance in the time of trouble (v. 2), but also has reference to "that day" for which the people of God have waited (25:9), which in context appears to be a future time of blessing.

In chs. 40–55 salvation is also deliverance from foes and oppressors (45:17; 49:25). The idea of ransom is connected with salvation, for Yahweh gave Egypt, Ethiopia, and Seba in exchange for Israel's salvation (43:3). Yahweh is the only Savior (vv. 11f.). Idols are unable to save (46:7); so are sorcerers and astrologers (47:13). In Isa. 40–55, the idea of righteousness — God does

Wadi in the region of the Dead Sea, a dry brook which, with heavy rainfall, might become a "river in the desert" (Isa. 43:19f.; cf. 30:25; 32:2).
(L. K. Smith)

303

what is right for his covenant people — is connected with salvation (45:8, 21). Moreover, righteousness is to be extended to the ends of the earth (v. 22; 49:6), and, as a result of the rule of Yahweh, is to continue forever (51:5f.).

In chs. 56–66, salvation calls for a response of doing justice and righteousness (56:1). The parallel to righteousness is found also in 59:17 and 61:10, and to justice in 59:11. Righteousness, justice, salvation, vengeance, and fury are all combined as the garments of the Lord when he comes in judgment (v. 17). Salvation is wrought with reward and recompense (62:11). "Victory" (59:16) is sometimes used to translate forms of *yš'*, because it is a result of salvation.

Since Isaiah's idea of salvation is connected with the concepts of redemption, deliverance, righteousness, and justice, it is necessary to take up these ideas also to get a complete picture of what the prophet meant by the words "save," "savior,"[19] and "salvation."

(3) Yahweh as Redeemer. The verb *gā'al*, "redeem," and its participle *gô'ēl*, "redeemer," are also brought into prominence in Isaiah.[20] The basic idea of *g'l* is to recover property (including persons) no longer held by the original owner. In Lev. 25:47-49 the "near kinsman" *(gô'ēl)* could redeem a person who had had to sell himself into slavery. In Ruth, the "near kinsman" had the privilege and responsibility of marrying Ruth and raising up progeny in the name of the dead relative, to protect the inheritance of the deceased.[21] Isaiah's *gô'ēl* kinsman-redeemer is presented without detailed explanation. The basic idea is clear: "For thus says the LORD: 'You were sold for nothing, and you shall be redeemed without money'" (52:3). In an extended passage about the redemption of Israel (ch. 43, esp. vv. 1, 14), Yahweh says: "I give Egypt as your ransom, Ethiopia and Seba in exchange for you" (v. 3).

Chs. 1–39 do not contribute to the study of the word. However, the very unusual word *ge'ûlîm*, "redeemed (ones)," occurs in 35:9; 51:10; 62:12; 63:4 (i.e., all three sections), and elsewhere only in Ps. 107:2.

We find the most productive study of the root in chs. 40–55. "Your Redeemer is the Holy One of Israel," says Yahweh (41:14; cf. 43:14; 47:4; 48:17; 54:5). Clearly Isaiah uses the word primarily with reference to redemption from captivity (43:14, cf. 47:4 and its context; 52:3-9). However, the contexts also show that this redemptive activity is not an end in itself, but part of a process moving on toward something greater. This Redeemer will make his people victorious, and they shall rejoice in Yahweh (41:14-16). The redemption reveals the truth that Yahweh is the first and the last; beside him there is no god (44:6f.; cf. vv. 24-28), a lesson that Babylon will learn with pain (47:3ff.), yet is at the same time instructive both to his people (48:17) and to the kings of the earth (49:7). Yahweh's redemptive activity results in his glorification (44:23).

The crowning touch is added in chs. 56–66:

In his love and in his pity he redeemed them;
> he lifted them up and carried them all the days of old. (63:9)

Therefore they say, and all the redeemed with them:

"You, O Lᴏʀᴅ, are our Father,
> our Redeemer from of old is your name." (v. 16)

To this add the words of Isa. 35:

No lion shall be there,
> nor shall any ravenous beast come up on it;
they shall not be found there,
> but the redeemed shall walk there.
And the ransomed of the Lord shall return,
> and come to Zion with singing;
> everlasting joy shall be upon their heads;
they shall obtain joy and gladness,
> and sorrow and sighing shall flee away. (35:9f.)[22]

(4) Yahweh as Supreme and Only Ruler. One of Isaiah's greatest theological contributions is his absolute monotheism. Yahweh's glory is the whole earth (6:3), therefore the other gods are nothing (2:8, 18, 20f.): "They were no gods, but the work of human hands — wood and stone" (37:19).

Some scholars have insisted that this concept is too advanced for the eighth century (but see Amos 1–2; 9). According to one view the Israelites finally came to this realization when Babylon was about to be taken by the advancing Persian forces, and the Babylonians were scurrying about trying to save their gods (see Pss. 115:3-8; 135:15-18). That the experiences of the Exile made deep theological impressions on the Jews cannot be doubted, but were these experiences sufficient to make them monotheists? Many other peoples lived in exile, even at the same time the Israelites did; yet only the worshippers of Yahweh became monotheists. Was it not the God of this true worship that Yahweh's prophets — like Amos, Hosea, Micah, and Isaiah — saw as the cause of the Exile? The Lord's method was always to tell his people through the prophets what he was going to do and why, to carry out that activity, and to explain to his people what he had done and why. He is not only "the God who acts." He is the "God who reveals" to his servants the prophets the reasons for these acts.

When the great superpowers developed, beginning with the Assyrian period, and first Israel and then Judah were swallowed up by foreign empires, the people of Yahweh faced the frightening question of whether Yahweh was weaker than the gods of Assyria or Babylonia. The practice of the nations was to carry off the gods from the temples of the peoples they conquered, symbolizing the supposedly greater strength of their gods. But Isaiah looked at the situation and proclaimed that Assyria was only a rod in Yahweh's hand (10:5) to punish Israel. Yet God himself would soon enough punish Assyria for its arrogance and pride (vv. 12f.). Even though deep darkness was to come upon the land, because of the zeal of Yahweh, light would come to dispel that darkness (cf. 8:21–9:2, 7 [MT 9:1, 6]).[23] It was in this light that Isaiah sought for his people to believe and walk (2:6; 7:9).

In the second part of Isaiah, however, is found the most sustained presentation of the universal nature and power of God's rule. Reading chs. 40–49 from beginning to end, one cannot help but feel the cogency of the presentation. Yahweh is not only the protector and sustainer of his people Israel, but the controller of all nations (40:11, 13-17). The One who gives power to the faint is the Creator of the ends of the earth (vv. 28f.). Yahweh stirred up one leader from the east (41:2) and one from the north (v. 25) — and "declared it from the beginning, that we might know" (v. 26; cf. 44:6-8). Yahweh, who created heavens and earth (42:5), called his servant Israel in righteousness, intending it to be a light to the nations (v. 6; cf. 41:8), even though his servant was blind and deaf (42:19). Even in the inevitable chastisement (43:2), Yahweh is with his people as their Redeemer. This One will deliver them (vv. 6f.), break down the bars of Babylon (v. 14), make a way in the wilderness and rivers in the desert (v. 19), and blot out the transgressions of his chosen people (v. 25; cf. 44:1).

Yahweh forms light and creates darkness; he makes weal and creates woe (45:7). The Maker of Israel (44:21), Creator of the earth and the heavens (v. 24) is also Maker of Cyrus, his "shepherd" (v. 28), who shall rebuild his city and free his exiles (45:13). Bel and Nebo, who must be carried on beasts, will themselves go into captivity; Yahweh, who has borne and will continue to carry Israel, is the only true God (46:1-9). Babylon will be reduced to shame (ch. 47), but Yahweh will ease his anger toward the house of Jacob for his name's sake (48:1-11).

The same doctrine of God is found in chs. 56–66, with the added promise: "For behold, I create new heavens and a new earth; and the former things shall not be remembered or come into mind" (65:17). "For as the new heavens and the new earth which I will make shall remain before me, . . . so shall your descendants and your name remain" (66:22).

(5) Spirit of Yahweh. Isaiah has more to say about the Spirit than any other Old Testament writer. In spite of the difficulties inherent in determining a doctrine of the Spirit,[24] a strong and clear teaching is evident in all parts of Isaiah. The key passage is 11:2, in a context that promises the advent of "a shoot from the stump of Jesse" (v. 1). The "Spirit of Yahweh" will rest upon this "shoot," and is described further as "the spirit of wisdom and understanding, the spirit of counsel and might, the spirit of knowledge and the fear

of the LORD." The description "comprises intellectual, practical and spiritual gifts."[25] Christians who find fulfillment of the messianic promise in Jesus may connect this passage to the time of the baptism (Matt. 3:16 and par.). To the degree that the Church is an extension of Christ's Incarnation ("the body of Christ") the description of the Spirit in Isa. 11:2 may be understood in terms of the "gifts" and "fruit" of the Spirit in the New Testament (see 1 Cor. 12:4-11; Gal. 5:22f.).

In the day of desolation the people of Yahweh will wait "until the Spirit is poured upon us from on high" (32:15), bringing justice and righteousness; the result will be peace, quietness, and trust forever (vv. 16-18). In 34:16 the Spirit is mentioned in parallel with "the mouth of the LORD," but since the stichs are in the nature of action-result ("synthetic parallelism"), it is not clear that the two should be equated. A possible interpretation would be that Yahweh commanded and his Spirit carried out the action.

Is the prophet speaking of "Spirit" or "wind" in 40:7 ("The grass withers, the flower fades, when *rûaḥ yhwh* blows upon it")? The reference to "the word of our God" (v. 8) favors "Spirit." In v. 13 the divine Spirit seems clearly intended, but to insist that this is the "third person" of a triune being goes beyond the teaching of the passage. In 42:1 Yahweh says he has put his *rûaḥ* upon his servant, that he might bring forth justice to the nations; interpretation of this passage is further complicated by making it a messianic promise.[26] In 44:3 "I will pour my Spirit (spirit?) upon your descendants" is parallel with "and my blessing on your offspring." "And now the Lord GOD has sent me and his spirit" (48:16) seems to be an introductory statement to what follows (vv. 17-22): the spirit has inspired the prophet to proclaim the Lord's message.

The prophet is clearly speaking of the spirit (not the *wind;* see 59:19) of Yahweh in 61:1 (lit., "the spirit of the Lord Yahweh is upon me, because Yahweh has anointed me; he has sent me to bring good news to the oppressed, to bind up the brokenhearted . . ."). Jesus used this passage in the synagogue at Nazareth, and said that it was fulfilled "this day," "in your hearing" (Luke 4:18-21).[27] The term "holy spirit" is used twice in Isa. 63:10f., and "the spirit of Yahweh" in v. 14.

Obviously Isaiah contains nothing like the fullness of the New Testament doctrine of the Spirit, but this should not be expected. Scripture was revealed "at various times and in various ways" (*polymerōs kai polytropōs,* Heb. 1:1), and the revelation was not complete until its completion in the Son. Nonetheless, Isaiah represents a marked advance in the revelation concerning the Spirit over what had been given previously, even if Joel is accepted as antedating Isaiah.

The Lord's Requirements

(1) Righteousness. Heb. ṣedeq and ṣᵉdāqâ "righteousness" occur 273 times in the Old Testament. Isaiah uses the word 58 times, and all the other prophets combined, 12 times. The bulk of the occurrences is in Psalms.

The original meaning may have been "straightness," hence "that which is, or ought to be, firmly established, successful and enduring in human affairs."[28] Perhaps a simpler definition of the basic meaning is conformity with accepted standards.[29] Conformity with a divinely revealed law is a later biblical definition. This can be illustrated by the story of Judah and Tamar (Gen. 38). Measured by custom, Judah was out of step for having failed to provide for the widow of his dead son; Tamar, who was trying to eke out a living by playing the harlot and thereby tricking Judah into fulfilling his responsibility, actually was "more righteous" (v. 26).[30]

In the Prophets, however, particularly Isaiah, "righteousness" means conformity to God's ways, especially as set forth in God's Torah. Usually this involves ethical behavior, but it is not mere ethics.[31] "God's ṣᵉdāqā or ṣedeq is his keeping of the law in accordance with the terms of the covenant."[32] Isaiah gives a "picture of the conduct of the Prince of Peace, who establishes his kingdom with judgment and righteousness (Isa. 9:7), and puts an end to all violence and oppression, so that his people are united in the harmony of a purpose in keeping with the nature of their God (Isa. 11:3-5, 9)."[33] This righteousness is not the result of independent human effort but rather is the gift of God. Only such righteousness "can lead to that conduct which is truly in keeping with the covenant."[34] Accordingly, "righteousness" and "mercy" often are found in parallelism in the Psalms. As a result of this stress on God's mercy, the term "righteousness" comes to be used of human benevolence, for if people act in God's way, they will be merciful. This is the sense in which New Testament *dikaiosynē* sometimes means "deeds of righteousness, religious duties."[35]

Isaiah reports that in Jerusalem righteousness had been replaced by murder (1:21) and bloodshed (5:7), but when God's redemptive work was finished, it would be called the city of righteousness (1:26). Righteousness rained down from heaven and brought forth righteousness on earth (45:8). Righteousness and justice frequently are mentioned in poetic parallel (e.g., 1:27; 16:5; 28:17). Righteousness is sometimes seen as judicial (cf. 10:22), and is learned from God's judgments (26:9f.). Righteousness is an attribute of the messianic figure who is to arise from the stump of Jesse and it governs his acts (11:3-5). One result of righteousness is peace (32:17). The redeemed Israelites rejoice and exult in Yahweh because God has covered them with the robe of righteousness (61:10).

English translations present a problem in studying the concept of "righteousness." The RSV often translates Heb. *ṣedeq* and *ṣᵉdāqâ* as "deliverance," sometimes "victory," and occasionally "vindication." The result of Yahweh's righteousness with reference to his covenant people is deliverance or victory and therefore vindication from the taunts of their enemies (see 41:2, 10; 51:1, 5, 7; 54:17). Hence, righteousness in Isaiah may be defined as a quality of Yahweh, his actions in accordance with that quality, particularly with reference to his covenant people; and results of those righteous acts not only for his people but for the entire earth (see Ps. 71:15f., 24).[36]

(2) Justice. Heb. *mišpāṭ* "judgment" occurs some 420 times in the Old Testament and is translated 29 different ways in the KJV (239 times as "judgment"). It is used throughout the Old Testament, but principally in Psalms (65 times), Isaiah (40), Deuteronomy, Ezekiel (37 each), and Jeremiah (31). In about 18 of the passages in which the word occurs in Isaiah, it is either parallel or in close proximity to the word *ṣedeq* or *ṣᵉdāqâ* "righteous(ness)."

The root meaning seems to have suggested something like "judge," and therefore developed into such meanings as "to judge, govern," "justice, decision," "manner, custom, the way of living under the judgments that have been made," "vindication or condemnation, the judgment issued," "to enter into judgment" (43:26), and the like. The only practical way to study this word is to observe its usages in their contexts.

"Neither this word, nor its early companion *torah* (later 'The Law') can ever wholly be separated from God. For us, 'justice' means either the demands of some moral law, or, more often, the king's justice. To the Hebrew it meant the demands of God's law, and God's justice."[37] Human judgment ideally considered, therefore, is judgment in conformity with God's judgment. "But no judge, whether priest or prophet, could give any other judgements than those which are regarded as being the veritable word of God. It is necessary therefore to think of 'doing mishpat' (Micah vi. 8) as meaning 'doing God's will as it has been made clear in past experience' "[38] — or, perhaps preferably, as has been made clear in past revelation.[39]

Isaiah sees the breakdown of Israel to be due, at least in part, to the collapse of judgment. "How the faithful city has become a harlot! She that was full of *mišpāṭ*. *Ṣedeq* lodged in her, and now murderers" (1:21; cf. 5:7). He also sees redemption to be accomplished by judgment, but whether this means the action of Yahweh or of the people is perhaps not clear; in 1:27b we hear that it is by the action of the people: "Zion shall be redeemed by *mišpāṭ*, and those in her who repent by *ṣᵉdāqâ*." The judicial act of Yahweh certainly is not absent, for the day of holiness comes "once Yahweh has washed away the filth of the daughters of Zion and cleansed the bloodstains of Jerusalem from its midst by a spirit of judgment and by a spirit of burning" (4:4). Yahweh enters into judgment with the elders and princes of his people (3:14). Yahweh is a God of judgment (or justice), exalted in justice (5:16; 30:18). "Ah, you who make iniquitous decrees" refuse to grant justice to the needy (10:1-2). But the child who is to be born will uphold his kingdom with justice and righteousness (9:7 [MT 6]; cf. 16:5). The Lord Yahweh says that he is laying a cornerstone in Zion and "will make justice the line and righteousness the plummet" (28:17). The servant of Yahweh receives the Lord's spirit in order to bring forth justice to the nations, and "he will not grow faint or be crushed till he has established justice in the earth" (42:1-4). The Lord says: "I . . . love justice, I hate robbery and wrong" (61:8), and tells his people: "Maintain justice, and do what is right, for soon my salvation will come, and my deliverance (ṣᵉdāqâ) be revealed" (56:1).

For Isaiah, then, mišpāṭ is a complex idea involving Yahweh, his nature and acts, and his requirements of all his creatures, but especially of his covenant people. He manifests good judgment, and in that judgment brings justice. He longs for the same in his people. In his judgment he will establish mišpāṭ in the earth through his servant.

The Lord's Servant. A most significant figure in Isaiah is "the servant of Yahweh." More than a century ago, B. Duhm separated certain passages, namely 42:1-4; 49:1-6; 50:4-9; and 52:13–53:12, from the rest of chs. 40–55, and designated them as the "Servant Songs," or songs of 'ebed yhwh.[40] Since that time, it has been almost an axiom to consider these passages as independent poems.[41] However, scholars are not in complete agreement over the extent of the poems, and while some scholars count five Servant Songs, others count six or even seven.[42] According to some, the poems existed before "Second Isaiah" and were used by him; others say they were written later and inserted into "Deutero-Isaiah" by a redactor. A few scholars have rejected the independent existence of the Servant Songs.[43]

Attempts to identify the Servant of Yahweh have been equally confused and confusing. Is the Servant Israel, the prophet himself, Cyrus, or someone else? Christians, on the basis of Acts 8:35, contend that the Servant is Jesus, but neither that reference nor Isa. 53 requires such a conclusion on the basis of pure exegesis. That Jesus used the term "servant" with reference to himself is clear, and that the early Church called him "servant of God" *(pais theou)* is also clear. By seeking a fuller or deeper meaning in the Servant passages in Isaiah, it is possible to find "fulfillment" in Jesus. But first of all, the Isaianic text must be considered exegetically.

At the outset, Israel is the servant (41:8f.). The purpose of a servant is to do the will of the master, and Israel was chosen to do Yahweh's will, to "bring forth justice to the nations" (42:1), to be "a light to the nations" (v. 6). But Israel was a blind, deaf servant (v. 19) and therefore had to be punished (v. 24). Some interpreters detect two persons in dialogue in this portion: Israel the nation and a righteous individual or remnant in Israel. All admit that interpretation is difficult. Some believe that Cyrus of Persia is Yahweh's servant (and some even claim that this entire portion of Isaiah is about him). This identification is based on the passages in 44:28, where Cyrus is called "my shepherd," and 45:1, where he is called "his (Yahweh's) anointed (or messiah)." There is no doubt that Cyrus is called upon to serve Yahweh, and that the portion seems to extend at least to v. 13 ("he shall build my city and set my exiles free"). However, careful reading will indicate that Israel is still the servant (44:1f.; cf. v. 21). But most important, the text clearly states that the calling of Cyrus was "for the sake of my servant Jacob, and Israel my chosen" (45:4). Only by detaching the Servant Songs from the context can such a conclusion be avoided. Cyrus is servant in concert with Yahweh's purposes for Israel.

In 48:1 the house of Jacob is still being addressed, but in 49:1-6 it becomes clearer that two persons are in view: Jacob and "my servant, Israel" (v. 3). The latter was "formed from the womb" to be Yahweh's servant, "to bring Jacob back to him, and that Israel might be gathered to him" (v. 5). This seems to be the prophet himself, whose task — and a very difficult one — is to "raise up the tribes of Jacob" (v. 6). Ch. 50 describes some of the sufferings and persecutions that this servant had to undergo (see vv. 5-7). Ch. 51 reads at times like the preaching of the prophet, yet at others it seems that God himself is speaking to the people.

> In the great passage in 52:13–53:12, however, the prophet now joins himself with the people in looking at another servant: "All we like sheep have gone astray . . . and the LORD has laid on him the iniquity of us all" (53:6). The personal pronouns — "we, our, us" on the one hand, and "he, his, him" on the other — require the interpretation that the servant is neither the blind and deaf nation Israel, nor the righteous remnant or prophet called "Israel," but the true Israel, the obedient servant.[44]

The Servant of the Lord imagery can be represented by a triangle or cone.

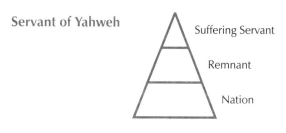

311

The bottom represents the entire nation, thus the servant of chs. 41–48. The middle portion represents the more faithful servant, whether interpreted as the righteous remnant or the prophet himself (or even someone else). The apex represents the servant who perfectly serves his Lord, having "borne our infirmities and carried our diseases" (53:4). He is the one who made himself an offering for sin (v. 10) and made many to be accounted righteous (v. 11). He is the true Israel, who fulfills to the utmost the will of Yahweh and the purpose which Yahweh had in mind when he first chose Israel. "Accordingly, the fuller meaning of the servant passages has to do with the perfect Servant, and the Christian rightly identifies this Servant with the one who came in the form of a servant and who was obedient even unto death (cf. Phil. 2:7-8)."[45]

In ch. 14 the satanic servant (the one who became an adversary to the Lord) is portrayed as fallen from heaven, cast away, nevermore to be named (vv. 4-21). In ch. 53 the obedient servant is portrayed as the sin bearer, who will have his portion with the great (v. 12). Yahweh uses a satanic servant as a "rod" by which to lead his rebellious people into captivity. He uses his "shepherd," Cyrus, to bring his people back to their land — but that is not the end of sin. Yahweh uses the suffering servant to bring his ransomed people into the kingdom of righteousness and justice, the eternal realm of peace.

CHAPTER 23

Zephaniah, Nahum, and Habakkuk

Three books of the Minor Prophets are contemporary with Jeremiah's ministry, especially its early years. Zephaniah, Nahum, and Habakkuk reflect the
circumstances and outlook in Judah during Josiah's reign (640-609) and the
days immediately following his death. They depict the imminent rise of Babylon and the subsequent collapse of Assyria. Above all, they set in bold relief
the justice of God at work in Judah and the world. They discern the divine
hand in the changing of the guard internationally, they call attention to the
need for reform internally, and they anticipate divine reckoning with persistent
rebellion where reform is rejected.

Zephaniah

If the prophetic books were placed in chronological order, Zephaniah would
fit between Isaiah and Jeremiah. It was probably Zephaniah who broke the
half-century of prophetic silence in Judah during Manasseh's violent reign. He
applied the major themes of the eighth-century prophets to the turbulent
international and domestic scene of the late seventh century. His preaching
lent support to Jeremiah, as together they helped spark Josiah's reforms.

Personal Background. Nothing is known about Zephaniah except what is
found in his writing. In the introduction (1:1) his family history is traced
through four generations to Hezekiah. Two factors may account for this
lengthy genealogy: Zephaniah's lineage is linked to Judah's great king (1) to

> Seek the LORD, all you humble of the land,
>   who do his commands;
> Seek righteousness, seek humility;
>   perhaps you may be hidden on the day
>   of the LORD's wrath. Zeph. 2:3

substantiate his intimate knowledge of the sins of Jerusalem's leaders (see vv. 11-13; 3:3-5) and/or (2) to authenticate his Jewish origin and to counter questions raised by his father's name, Cushi ("Ethiopian").

The mention of Josiah's reign (1:1) provides the rough limits of Zephaniah's ministry (*ca.* 640-609 B.C.). The shocking pictures of idolatrous practices in Judah and Jerusalem offer clues that the prophecy dates from before Josiah's reforms and thus coincides approximately with the time of Jeremiah's call (*ca.* 626).

Jerusalem lies at the heart of Zephaniah's concern. He indicts the city's religious degradation and social apathy (1:4-13; 3:1-7) and predicts its ultimate salvation (3:14-20). Combining concern with firsthand knowledge, Zephaniah describes the capital in detail (1:10f.): the Fish Gate, probably in the northern wall near the Tyropoeon valley; the Second Quarter (Mishneh), apparently the northern section immediately west of the temple area; the Mortar (Maktesh), a natural basin (perhaps part of the Tyropoeon valley) just south of the Mishneh, used for a marketplace.[1] Zephaniah focuses on the northern sector because steep embankments on the other three sides encouraged attack from the north.

Some scholars have been even more specific in reconstructing Zephaniah's ministry, linking him with the temple prophets.[2] Indeed, both Isaiah and Jeremiah paid a good deal of attention to the temple. Joel is vitally concerned with the priests and their daily round of sacrifices. But saying that a prophet shows interest in the religious life of his temple is not the same as claiming that he was a temple prophet, a member of the temple staff whose task was to declare the word of God in connection with stated religious functions such as feast days. "All committed Yahwists, especially one called by God as a prophet to his people, would be attracted to and concerned for the Temple as the earthly abode of their heavenly king."[3]

Historical and Religious Background. Judah never recovered from Manasseh's infamous half-century of rule. Hezekiah's son, despite token attempts at reformation (2 Chr. 33:12-19), left indelible blots on the nation's character. When Amon reverted to his father's worst traits, Judah's fate was sealed. Zephaniah shattered the prophetic silence not with hope but with impending doom:

> The great day of the Lord is near . . .
>> the sound of the day of the Lord is bitter. . . .
> That day will be a day of wrath,
>> a day of distress and anguish,
> a day of ruin and devastation,
>> a day of darkness and gloom,
> a day of clouds and thick darkness,
>> a day of trumpet blast and battle cry. . . .[4] (1:14f.)

What nation did Zephaniah see as God's whip to drive Judah to its knees? Some have found a clue in Herodotus' description of the Scythian hordes that swept down from their mountain homes into western Asia and even as far as Egypt.[5] But this identification lacks sufficient support from other ancient records. More likely Zephaniah has a sense of foreboding of Assyria's imminent collapse and is aware of ominous rumblings from Babylon, seeking to recover its ancient splendor. Within two decades after Zephaniah's prophecy, proud Nineveh had been humbled (cf. 2:13-15) and Josiah killed at Megiddo (2 Kgs. 23:29), Nebuchadnezzar had whipped the Egyptians at Carchemish, and Syria and Palestine were his. Within four decades Judah had been ravaged, and the cry and wail had risen from the Fish Gate, Second Quarter, and Mortar. It was a day of wrath indeed!

Message. Two themes dominate this brief book: the threat of imminent judgment (1:2–3:7) and the hope of ultimate deliverance (3:8-20).

Apart from a brief call to repentance (2:1-3), 1:2–3:7 is unrelieved in its stress on God's wrath. The universal scope of God's judgment will have effects as cataclysmic as the flood in Noah's day (see Gen. 6):

> I will utterly sweep away everything
>> from the face of the earth. . . .
> I will sweep away humans and animals. . . . (1:2f.)

The prophet first focuses on his own land and city (1:4–2:3), whose religious and social sins have made them objects of divine ire. They have sold themselves to the worship of Baal, the Canaanite fertility god; the sun, moon, and stars; and Milcom, king god of their Ammonite neighbors to the east. They formed debilitating alliances with pagan nations, particularly Assyria. And they aped foreign fashions which tended to compromise their identity as God's special people. The social unsettledness hinted at in 1:9[6] is amplified in 3:1-7, where the blame is placed squarely on the leaders. These sins, coupled with the spiritual and moral apathy of Jerusalem's citizenry, merit the fiercest kind of judgment, and Zephaniah describes God's wrath with a white-hot fury almost unparalleled in Scripture. Whether offered by Yahweh or by the prophet, who seem to take turns in a drama-like manner, the oracles are intense and graphic in their poetic power.[7] The variety of Zephaniah's literary forms is impressive: judgment speeches (1:2-3, 4-6, 8-9, 10-13, 17-18; 2:4-15), calls to respond (1:7; 2:1-3; 3:8), hymn with a call to praise (3:14-18a), salvation speeches (3:4-13, 18b-20).[8]

In the finest prophetic tradition (see Isa. 13–23; Jer. 46–51; Ezek. 25–32; Amos 1–2), Zephaniah also includes oracles against Judah's neighbors (2:4-15). The Philistine coastal area, hotbed of opposition to Judah since the days of the judges, receives special attention, with four key cities — Gaza, Ashkelon, Ashdod, Ekron — marked for judgment (vv. 4-7).[9] This territory, long accustomed to military activity, felt the conqueror's boot before Judah: Nebuchadnezzar ravaged Ashkelon in 604 and used Philistia as a launching site for his abortive invasion of Egypt in 601. So blatant was the Philistines' paganism and so patent their opposition to God's purposes in Israel that the prophet felt no need to cite grounds for their judgment.

As for Israel's kinsmen, Moab and Ammon (see Gen. 19:36-38), familiarity apparently had bred contempt (vv. 8-11). Smarting for centuries from defeats at the hands of David (2 Sam. 8:2; 10:1-14) and Jehoshaphat (2 Chr. 20:22-30), they had goaded the Israelites and their God with barbed taunts. Moab and Ammon were absorbed into Nebuchadnezzar's network of nations and used to subdue Judah at the time of Jehoiakim's revolt, a task which they no doubt relished (2 Kgs. 24:2). Mention of the Ethiopians (2:12) demonstrates the geographical extent of God's sovereignty (see 3:10).[10] Assyria and

Moab, traditional enemy of Israel, would be laid waste (Zeph. 2:8-11).
(J. R. Kautz)

316

its proud capital, Nineveh, were earmarked for special judgment (2:13-15), which the ruthless coalition of Medes, Babylonians, and Scythians (?) unwittingly brought to pass in 612. It is worth remembering that these oracles were intended not for a foreign audience but for Judah alone. The people frequently needed to be reminded that, though they belonged exclusively to God, God did not belong exclusively to them.

The indictments of Jerusalem (3:1-7) are more specific than those of the pagan nations: the city's greater privilege carried greater responsibility. All normal channels for bringing God's instruction to the people — "rulers, prophets, priests" — were clogged with vice and greed (see Mic. 3). Even the tragic example of the northern kingdom could not brake Judah's race to self-destruction. The more God warned, the faster they plummeted toward calamity (Zeph. 3:6f.).

Turning from a theme of wrath to one of restoration, the prophet makes clear that God's judgment is not only punitive but corrective. When the nations have been chastened, they will call on the Lord with "a pure speech" and serve him cordially (vv. 8-10). A lowly yet faithful remnant will survive in Judah to replace the leaders whose pride was their snare. Above all, God will dwell among his people and right past wrongs: he will give prominence to the humble and renown to the lame and outcast (vv. 17-20), a theme at the heart of the Christian gospel (note the Magnificat sung by Mary in Luke 1:46-55).[11]

Theological Insights. Zephaniah elaborates on Amos' outline of the day of the Lord (cf. Amos 5:18-20), showing just how dark that "day of darkness not light" (v. 18) will be (see also Isa. 2:9-22). In a startlingly unique metaphor, the day is likened to a banquet in which those who expect to be guests become victims (1:7f.; cf. the story of Isaac, Gen. 22:7). The point is clear. The people of Judah have assumed that God would vindicate them before the nations. But his constant aim was to vindicate, on a universal scale (1:18; 2:4-15), his own righteousness, even though this proved costly to Judah, their neighbors, and their enemies.[12] As interpreter of the covenant, Zephaniah saw that God's judgment of Judah was drastic but not final. Through restoration of the remnant his covenant love would triumph. This restoration is the positive, creative side of judgment, without which the purified remnant could not arise. If God's judgment means destruction of the wicked, it also means vindication of the righteous, who, refined by suffering, can render purer service.[13] Following earlier prophecies (Amos 3:12; Isa. 4:2f.; Mic. 5:7f.), Zephaniah views the remnant as the ruler over God's enemies (2:7), his humble, honest, sincere servant (3:12f.), and the victorious army whose success springs from trust in the Lord (v. 17), not military prowess.

Like Isaiah, Zephaniah had seen God's greatness and was transformed by it. He saw that God cannot brook haughtiness and that the people's only hope lay in recognizing their own frailty. Pride is a problem rooted in human nature, and neither Judah (2:3), Ammon, Moab (v. 10), nor Nineveh is exempt. Nineveh epitomizes insolence, boasting "I am and there is no one else" (v. 15). Such rebellion, the declaration of spiritual independence from God, is the most heinous of sins. Those who escape God's fury are those who humbly "seek refuge in the name of the LORD" (3:12).

Picturing the Lord with lamp in hand searching Jerusalem and finding "people who rest complacently on their dregs," he gives stern warning about the perils of apathy (1:12f.). These citizens are sluggish and lifeless, like wine which has settled (see Jer. 48:11f.). Doubting God's love and refusing both to advance God's program and to stem their own corruption, they share the punishment of the more active rebels.

> The great causes of God and Humanity are not defeated by the hot assaults of the Devil, but by the slow, crushing, glacierlike masses of thousands and thousands of indifferent nobodies. God's causes are never destroyed by being blown up, but by being sat upon.[14]

Nahum

What we can know of Nahum's (the name means "comforted"; a longer form may have meant "comforted by Yahweh") background is limited to the dating of his prophecy between two events to which he alludes: the fall of the Egyptian city of Thebes in 663 B.C. to the Assyrian armies of Ashurbanipal (3:8-10) and the destruction of Nineveh in 612 (1:1; 2:8 [MT 9]; 3:7).[15] The tone of imminence throughout the book suggests a date shortly before the collapse of the Assyrian capital — perhaps *ca.* 615 when the coalition of Babylonians and Medes that toppled the city was being formed. Reasons have been given for dating the work before Zephaniah's, though we have not found them compelling.

More than a century of archaeological research has uncovered something of Nineveh's splendor from the heyday of the empire under Sennacherib (*ca.* 705-681), Esarhaddon (*ca.* 681-669), and Ashurbanipal (*ca.* 669-633).[16] Discoveries include the massive wall eight miles in circumference built by Sennacherib, his water system (including one of the most ancient aqueducts) and palace, and Ashurbanipal's palace and royal library which held more than

> Your shepherds are asleep, O king of Assyria;
>   your nobles slumber.
> Your people are scattered on the mountains
>   with no one to gather them.
> There is no assuaging your hurt, your wound is mortal.
> All who hear the news about you clap their hands over you.
> For who has ever escaped your endless cruelty?
>
> Nah. 3:18-19

20,000 clay tablets, including the creation (Enuma Elish) and flood (Gilgamesh) epics.

The Babylonian Chronicle of the Fall of Nineveh,[17] a concise record of Nabopolassar's campaigns from 616 to 609, recounts the circumstances of Assyria's demise. Nabopolassar gained decisive victories over the Assyrians by joining forces with Cyaxares, king of the Medes. Together they laid siege to Nineveh for about two months, apparently aided by the flooding river which ran through the city:

> The river gates are opened,
>   the palace trembles. (2:6)

Assyria did not vanish immediately. But shorn of the fortress capital and the provinces which had lent support, the nation was in its death throes. Attempts by Egyptian Pharaoh Neco II to rally the Egyptian-Assyrian alliance against Cyaxares and Nabopolassar miscarried. Assyria could postpone the inevitable only until shortly after 609.

Literary Qualities. As a literary craftsman Nahum has no superior and few peers among the Old Testament poets. His sense of the dramatic is felt throughout the book. In ch. 1, for instance, he simulates a court scene in which God as judge directs alternating verdicts to Judah (1:12f., 15 [MT 2:1]; 2:2 [MT 3]) and Assyria (1:9-11, 14; 2:1 [MT 2]). Judah is comforted by the thought of imminent release after more than a century under the Assyrian yoke (1:9-11, 14). Nahum imaginatively uses two audiences whom God addresses in turn — with judgment speeches to Assyria interleaved with salvation oracles to Judah. Whether the intent is liturgical or merely dramatic is not certain.[18] Some scholars contend that the book was first composed as a New Year's liturgy for the autumn festival in 612, immediately after Nineveh's fall.[19]

As vividly as an eyewitness, Nahum describes, whether by vision or imagination, the siege and frenzied activity of Nineveh's troops as they try in vain to halt the invaders:

> The crack of whip and rumble of wheel,
> > galloping horse and bounding chariot!
> Horsemen charging,
> > flashing sword and glittering spear,
> piles of dead,
> > heaps of corpses,
> dead bodies without end —
> > they stumble over the bodies! (3:2f.; cf. 2:3f.)

No war correspondent ever reported more graphically than Nahum does by prophetic foresight. Moreover, through his poetic genius he becomes a participant in the defense of Nineveh and, with subtle irony, barks battle commands to the defenders:

> Guard the ramparts;
> > watch the road;
> gird your loins;
> > collect all your strength. (2:1)

And, even more powerfully:

> Draw water for the siege,
> > strengthen your forts;
> trample the clay,
> > tread the mortar,
> take hold of the brick mold! (3:14)[20]

Linked to this flair for the dramatic is Nahum's gift for scintillating imagery. He sings of God's majesty in a hymn which celebrates his coming to judge the nations (a theophany like Judg. 5:4f.; Ps. 18:7-15 [MT 8-16]; Hab. 3:3-15):

> His way is in whirlwind and storm,
> > and the clouds are the dust of his feet. (1:3)

He uses numerous metaphors or similes which are both apt and brief — palace maidens "moaning like doves, and beating their breasts" (2:7); Assyrian fortresses likened to trees laden with ripe figs: "if shaken they fall into the mouth of the eater" (3:12).[21] Nahum also employs at least two extended figures of speech: (1) Nineveh, dependent on foreign booty, is compared to a lair where the lioness and her whelps wait restively for the lion to return with the prey (2:11f.), and (2) No longer the seductive harlot who lured nations to their doom by her charm, naked Nineveh is pelted with garbage by passersby, and no one cares (3:4-7).[22]

Yet for all its literary vitality, a prophecy of destruction of an enemy capital cannot match the lofty themes of relationship between God and humanity which dominate Job, Habakkuk, and Isaiah (esp. ch. 40). But part of the beauty and strength of the Scriptures is that the various books augment and complement each other. Both Amos' note of God's universal sovereignty and Nahum's word of God's special care for Judah are uniquely valuable.

Theological Significance. The prophecy of Nahum, absorbed as it is with the destruction of Israel's ancient enemy, presents some theological questions. Why, for instance, is the book silent about the sins of God's people and their need for repentance? Only Nahum and Obadiah, who also directs his ire at a hostile nation, omit that message of reform which lies at the heart of true prophetism. Yet, though loyal to Judah, these prophets are not narrow nationalists.[23] Nahum, particularly, senses the smarting wounds of many outraged nations, while acknowledging that Judah's afflictions also come from God's hand (1:12). Like Amos (ch. 1) before and Habakkuk (ch. 1) after, he is incensed at human inhumanity. To have swerved from his central theme in order to censure Judah would have dissipated his attack and spoiled the unity of his message. Perhaps more significantly, Nahum's date seems to coincide with the reforms of Josiah (2 Kgs. 22:8–23:25), from which the king and some of the prophets took great hope.[24]

How can Nahum's vindictive, taunting lines be reconciled with the compassion and forgiveness in Hosea and Jonah, and especially in Christ's teachings (e.g., Matt. 5:43f.)? Herein lies a more general Old Testament problem — the place of imprecatory (curse-filled) writings in sacred Scripture. Both psalmists and prophets were at times relentless in insisting that God judge their enemies. This passion for retribution was part of the Hebrew (and general Semitic) emphasis on lex talionis, "an eye for an eye" — the punishment must suit the crime.

Far from a savage call for blood, Nahum's prophecy testifies to his firm belief in the righteousness of God. The beginning hymn which describes God's character and action in judgment surely is the fount which waters the seeds of destruction sown in Nahum's speeches. "It has been our failure to let Nahum be a book about God that has distorted the value of the prophecy in our eyes."[25]

The ruthlessness of the Assyrians was notorious: their policy of deporting masses of their victims — on what were, actually, brutal death marches — and their genocidal treatment of nations reckless enough to rebel against their iron yoke were well known. Only a shriveled soul would remain dispassionate in the face of such atrocities. As C. S. Lewis has forcefully demonstrated, the Jews cursed their enemies bitterly because they took right and wrong seriously.[26] Moreover, the Assyrians' imperialism offended the righteousness of God himself. If God is God, Nahum and his fellows held, he cannot allow unbridled wickedness to flourish indefinitely. God can be Warrior as well as Shepherd

(2:13).[27] Assyria, God's "razor" (Isa. 7:20), had eagerly shorn its neighbors, including Israel and Judah, and it was time for the razor to be broken: instruments of God's judgment are not, themselves, exempt from judgment. The absence of a well-developed view of afterlife in this period forced the prophet to demand a temporal and public vindication of God's righteousness.

If some prophets seem to relish the prospect of annihilation of their ancient enemies, it is because the suffering of their people has been acute. Their enthusiasm for such punishment may seem to outrun the bounds of propriety, for although they knew the law of neighbor love (Lev. 19:17f.), they had not seen it spelled out clearly in Christ. But the Christian revelation also has confirmed what the members of the old covenant knew well: love has its sterner side. Its fires can sear as well as warm:

> A man who is deeply and truly religious is always a man of wrath. Because he loves God and his fellow men, he hates and despises inhumanity, cruelty and wickedness. Every good man sometimes prophesies like Nahum.[28]

In a sense Nineveh's doom epitomizes the fate of all nations whose ultimate trust is, as Kipling put it, "in reeking tube and iron shard." Military might does not preclude obligations of righteousness and justice. The crumbling rubble of the arrogant city is a grim reminder that only those nations who rely on the God who is the source of true peace will see "on the mountains the feet of him who brings good tidings, who proclaims peace" (1:15 [MT 2:1]; see Isa. 52:7 and the New Testament applications in Acts 10:36; Rom. 10:15).

Habakkuk

The absence of information concerning Habakkuk's personal background has provided ample opportunity for speculation concerning his message and times.[29] Dates ranging from 700 to 300 have been suggested, and enemies from the cohorts of Sennacherib to the phalanxes of Alexander have been identified in his writing. Current opinion, however, places the writer in the last quarter of the seventh century, roughly contemporary with Zephaniah, Jeremiah, and Nahum. The outstanding clue to his date is the reference to the imminent Chaldean (Babylonian) invasion of Judah (1:6). The earliest date would be *ca.*

625, when Nabopolassar seized the Babylonian throne and triggered the rise of the Neo-Babylonian kingdom; the latest date would be *ca.* 598, just before Nebuchadnezzar's retaliatory attack on Judah in the days of Jehoiakim (*ca.* 609-598). The graphic descriptions of the Chaldean military exploits (vv. 6-11) may point to a date after 605, when at the battle of Carchemish Nebuchadnezzar's forces proved their power and prowess by routing the Egyptians.

> But the LORD is in his holy temple;
> let all the earth keep silence before him! Hab. 2:20

Message. Like Haggai and Zechariah, Habakkuk is called "the prophet," possibly a technical title designating an official position in the religious community,[30] or perhaps merely indicating that this writing was worthy to be included among the canonical prophetic books. The close connection between prophetic vision and spoken message is expressed in the phrase "the oracle (KJV burden) which Habakkuk the prophet saw" (1:1), meaning that the prophets uttered what God showed them. "Oracle" (Heb. *maśśā'*) may be further defined as a pronouncement "that attempts to explain the manner in which God's intention will be manifested in human affairs."[31] Inspired by a revelatory experience, the prophet responds to specific historical events (see Isa. 13:1; 15:1; 17:1; 19:1; 21:1; 22:1; 23:1; Nah. 1:1; Zech. 9:1; 12:1; Mal. 1:1.)[32]

(1) Problem: God has not judged Judah's wickedness (1:2-4). God, not the people, is the first object of Habakkuk's censure. Judah's sin has become so flagrant and heinous that God's reputation is jeopardized by his reluctance to judge. Habakkuk's complaint about God's righteousness shapes the style of his book, a summary of his conversations with God. The judgment for which he pleads is twofold: vengeance on the wicked and vindication of the righteous.

The background of the violence, oppression, and lawlessness under which the prophet chafes seems to be the reign of the wretched Jehoiakim, who so vexed Jeremiah (Jer. 22:13-23).[33] Habakkuk, theologian as well as prophet, was baffled by the seemingly interminable delay in judgment, while whatever vitality remained in Judah from Josiah's reform was being sapped by the corruption of the national leaders.[34]

(2) God's answer: The Babylonians will judge Judah (1:5-11). Habakkuk did not have to wait long for God's response. The plural form of "you" indicates that God's words are directed to a larger audience than just the prophet. The divine response rings with surprise. Ordinarily a complaint would be answered by a promise of deliverance, a salvation speech,[35] but here "deliverance" comes in the form of the Babylonian army ("Chaldeans," [v. 6] an Aramaic tribe that

came to prominence in lower Mesopotamia and a few centuries later joined other Babylonian groups in the coalition that Nabopolassar shaped into the Neo-Babylonian empire). The vivid description of their speed, maneuverability, and might captures something of the terror which Nebuchadnezzar's troops must have fired in their victims. No fortress could withstand their battering rams, inclined planes, and sapping (tunneling under the walls), as the Ninevites had discovered; no king was clever enough to outmaneuver them in open warfare, as Neco had learned at Carchemish. God was to employ this unholy alliance of skill and savagery to impose judgment on Judah.

(3) Problem: Can a righteous God use the wicked to punish those more righteous (1:12-17)? God's response poses an even more vexing question, again in the form of a complaint:

> Your eyes are too pure to behold evil,
>   and you cannot look on wrongdoing;
> why do you look on the treacherous,
>   and are silent when the wicked swallow
>   those more righteous than they? (v. 13)

Habakkuk was well aware of Judah's faults, but by any standards his countrymen, particularly the righteous nucleus, were no match for the wickedness of the Babylonians. Apparently the fate of Babylon's enemies was common knowledge, and Habakkuk recoils at the thought that the Babylonians would ruthlessly ravage Judah and Jerusalem. The sustained figure of speech (1:14-17), which compares the invaders to an unconscionable angler who fishes for the delight of killing the catch, is as impassioned a plea against inhumanity as the Old Testament contains.[36] Habakkuk did not doubt God's sovereignty over the enemy nation, but this sharpened the problem. How could a righteous God refrain from intervening?

(4) God's answer (ch. 2). Habakkuk's motive in posing these questions was neither idle curiosity nor a desire to dabble in divine affairs. He was an honest and devout seeker after truth, and God honored his quest. His watchtower (v. 1) was probably a place of solitude where he as one of God's watchmen (cf. Isa. 21:8; Ezek. 33:7-9) could await the divine vision and voice without distraction.

The first part of God's answer, introduced by an announcement of a vision (vv. 2f.), allays the prophet's fears about God's judgment: the righteous remnant will be preserved (vv. 4f.). The precise meaning of these verses is difficult, but the basic thought is clear — the sharp contrast between the faithful righteous and the proud, debauched, and bloodthirsty Babylonians. The conduct of each group determines its fate: the Babylonians fail; the righteous live. "Faith" (Heb. 'mûnâ) in v. 4 connotes faithfulness and dependability. The righteous rely on God, and, in turn, God can rely on them.

324

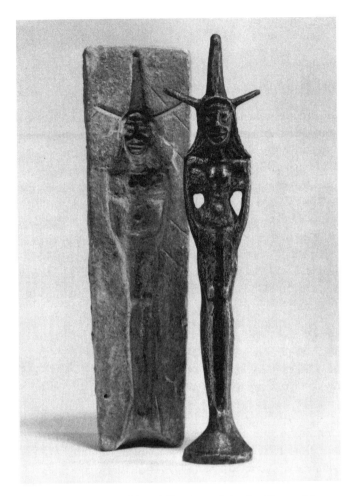

Bronze casting mold and figurine of the fertility goddess
Astarte — "a cast image, a teacher or lies" (Hab. 2:18).
(Israel Department of Antiquities, photo David Harris)

The answer continues in the form of a taunt song with which the oppressed peoples will mock their oppressors (vv. 6-19). Five woes ("alas," NRSV; vv. 6, 9, 12, 15, 19) punctuate this direful message: Babylon's doom is sealed.[37] Particular stress is given to God's law of retribution; the Babylonians are to be repaid measure for measure (vv. 6-8, 15-17). *Woe* oracles are compared to boomerangs: what the wicked hurl at their victims circles back to strike the hurler. God is not mocked, and the Babylonians are not exempt from the law of sowing and reaping (Gal. 6:7). The poetic irony is remarkable, especially in the speech against the enemy's idolatry:

325

> Woe to him who says to a wooden thing, Awake;
>> to a dumb stone, Arise!
>> Can this give revelation?
> Behold it is overlaid with gold and silver,
>> and there is no breath at all in it. (v. 19, *RSV*)[38]

Babylon's cause is doomed not only because it was wicked but also because its gods are powerless. In contrast, the Lord of Israel rules the earth from the temple (whether heavenly or earthly) and bids all to stand in silence before him (v. 20). Perhaps this verse brought both comfort and rebuke to Habakkuk: comfort, as he was confronted personally by the sovereign of the universe; rebuke, because he, the protesting prophet, was included in "all the earth" which must yield to God's lordship.

(5) Habakkuk's response (ch. 3). The revelation of God's program to save a righteous remnant and to send trouble ("woe") to wicked oppressors silences the complaints. Like Job, Habakkuk responded to God's answer, including the personal revelation of God's sovereignty, by a confession of confidence in God's power to rescue.[39]

> O Lord, I have heard of your renown,
>> and I stand in awe, O Lord, of your work.
> In our own time revive it;
>> in our own time make it known;
>> in wrath may you remember mercy. (v. 2)

The prophet seems to stand between the times — looking back to the Exodus and ahead to the day of the Lord. But neither past nor future intervention will ease his problem: he longs for a display of God's power in his present circumstances. This prayer leads to vivid recital of the mighty acts of God (theophany; cf. Pss. 77:16-20 [MT 17-21]; 78:9-16). Using an array of literary techniques including hyperbole (v. 6), irony (v. 8), personification (v. 10), and simile (v. 14), this hymn merges the various events into a highly stylized, emotion-charged description of God's redemptive activity which suggests cinematographic montage. Episode mounts upon episode — God's journey from the Sinai peninsula (vv. 3f.), the plagues (v. 5), wilderness march (v. 6), crossing of the Sea and Jordan (vv. 8-10), Joshua's long day (v. 11) — as the Exodus and Conquest are recreated before the prophet's eyes. God's ability to wage war outstrips the might of the Babylonian troops. The hymn of ch. 3 counters the threat of ch. 1.

This fresh look at God's saving acts sparks Habakkuk's courage as he awaits the enemy's attack. Invasion may mean devastation and deprivation, yet the prophet's staunch faith is untouched. Like Paul, he has learned the experience of divine contentment in any state (Phil. 4:11), for he has seen the living

God. He ends his book by confessing confidence in the God of the covenant, but with an enthusiasm sparked by the theophanic vision:

> Though the fig tree does not blossom,
>   and no fruit is on the vines,
> though the produce of the olive fails
>   and the fields yield no food;
> though the flock is cut off from the fold
>   and there is no herd in the stalls,
> yet I will rejoice in the LORD,
>   I will exult in the God of my salvation. (vv. 17f.)

Theological Insights. (1) Life for the faithful. God showed Habakkuk that the judgment of Judah, though sweeping, would not be total. He reaffirmed the promise that a remnant would be spared to carry on the redemptive mission and to serve as foundation for the renewed nation. Habakkuk's despair over the fate of the righteous (1:13) evoked God's promise that they would survive the awful day (2:4). The basis of their survival was their faithfulness, their total dependence and dependability.

This principle became the seed plot for Paul's key doctrine of justification by faith. The apostle's drastic reinterpretation of the Old Testament in the light of his own conversion caused him to focus on two passages: Gen. 15:6 and Hab. 2:4. The translation of Heb. *'emûnâ* "faithfulness" by Gk. *pistis* "faith" or "faithfulness" formed a useful bridge between Habakkuk's view of "life through faithfulness" and Paul's doctrine. What Habakkuk learned to be God's principle of operation in the Babylonian invasion, Paul with inspired insight saw to be God's universal principle of salvation. Habakkuk's message gave strategic preparation for the New Testament evangel (see Rom. 1:17; Gal. 3:11; Heb. 10:38f.).

(2) Understanding through honest doubt. Honest doubt may be a more acceptable religious attitude than superficial belief.

Like Job, Habakkuk used his questions neither to shield himself from moral responsibilities nor to shun God's claims upon his life. He was genuinely perplexed by the unpredictable nature of God's dealings. He raised his protests because he hungered and thirsted to see God's righteousness vindicated. God's self-revelation laid to rest the ghost of the prophet's doubts and gave birth to a finer faith. The redeeming God had used the questions as a means of grace to fortify Habakkuk's faith.

CHAPTER 24

Jeremiah

When God shapes momentous events he often sends someone to interpret them. So, during the most momentous period in Judah's long history, God sent Jeremiah, a prophet of remarkable insight and literary skill. Through four turbulent decades, Jeremiah declared the word of God to king and common people alike at great personal cost. His book recounts both his life and message and presents the paradigm for all true prophecy.[1]

> Thus says the LORD:
>   Stand at the crossroads, and look,
> and ask for the ancient paths,
>   where the good way lies; and walk in it,
> and find rest for your souls.
>   But they said, "We will not walk in it."
>   . . . . . .
>   Therefore, hear, O nations, . . .
> what will happen to them.
>   . . . I am going to bring disaster
> on this people, the fruit of their schemes,
>   because they have not given heed to my words;
> and as for my teaching, they have rejected it. Jer. 6:16, 18

The Prophet

His Background. The biographical and autobiographical sections of his book make Jeremiah better known than any other writing prophet. He was born in the village of Anathoth, north of Jerusalem (1:1; 11:21, 23; 29:27; 32:7-9), the son of Hilkiah, a priest. Probably his family descended from Abiathar, the priest whom Solomon banished to Anathoth for his part in Adonijah's play for the throne (1 Kgs. 2:26). If so, Jeremiah's priestly roots ran back to Moses and Aaron through Eli, priest at the earlier sanctuary at Shiloh (see 1 Sam. 1–4). Jeremiah's heritage may explain his emphasis on the Mosaic covenant and past history at Shiloh (see Jer. 2:1-3; 7:12-14; 15:1).[2] On the other hand, despite that heritage, his brothers, close relatives, and neighbors attacked him vigorously, probably because he supported Josiah's reforms (see 11:21; 12:6). By abolishing shrines outside of Jerusalem, Josiah's sweeping reforms may have deprived Hilkiah's family of the right to practice their priestly profession.

Josiah and Jeremiah seem to have been about the same age. The prophet calls himself a youth when God first spoke to him in the thirteenth year of Josiah's reign, *ca.* 627 B.C. (1:2).[3] This was five years before the discovery of the book of the law gave Josiah's reform an added boost (622 B.C.; 2 Kgs. 22:8ff.). Thus, Jeremiah probably was born shortly after 650. Most of the written prophecies concern events after Josiah's tragic death in 609. In all, Jeremiah's ministry spans more than forty years (until after 586 when Jerusalem fell to Nebuchadnezzar) and embraces the reigns of Josiah's four successors, the last kings of Judah.

His Call. Jeremiah's call marked him as a true prophet and set the tone for his ministry:

> Then the LORD put out his hand and touched my mouth;
> and the LORD said to me,
> "Now I have put my words in your mouth.
> See, today I appoint you over nations and over kingdoms,
> to pluck up and to pull down,
> to destroy and to overthrow,
> to build and to plant." (1:9f.; cf. Deut. 18:18)

Like Moses, Jeremiah felt inadequate for the job. He believed his youth would hamper his delivering this word of gloom to a hostile audience. Certainly, such preaching was not popular! So, the prophet needed the guarantee implicit in the vision of the almond rod, that God would see that his word came about (see 1:11-12; 20:7-18, Heb. wordplay uses *šāqēd*, almond branch, as a signal that God is *šōqēd*, "watching" over Jeremiah). Hosea suffered shame and reproach because of a wicked wife, but by God's command Jeremiah never married or had children. Such celibacy was rare among Jews and undoubtedly reinforced people's suspicions about his emotional health. But like Hosea's marriage, Jeremiah's singleness served a prophetic purpose: to symbolize the barrenness of a land under judgment (16:1-13).

Because of his preaching, serious threats on his life stalked Jeremiah repeatedly. Besides the opposition from his own family, a coalition of priests and prophets charged him with blasphemy for predicting the temple's destruction (26:1, 6). Fortunately, he escaped death because someone recalled that Micah had made a similar prediction without being punished and because Ahikam, an influential Jew, protected him (26:24). Jeremiah had two more brushes with death: when Pashhur the priest beat him and put him in stocks (20:1-6), and when the princes of Judah left him to die in a mire-filled cistern (38:6-13). Further, he had to endure the fury of King Jehoiakim, enraged by Jeremiah's indictments of Judah's sins and announcements of his country's doom (36:1-7). Only divine protection kept both Jeremiah and his faithful secretary Baruch safe from royal wrath.

Worst of all, other prophets in Jerusalem — people more attuned to popular whims than to God's word — opposed Jeremiah. These false prophets contradicted Jeremiah's message, preaching peace and security instead of judgment. They were themselves so deeply implicated in the sins of their fellow Jews that they could not cry against them:

> But in the prophets of Jerusalem
> I have seen a more shocking thing:
> they commit adultery and walk in lies;
> they strengthen the hands of evildoers,
> so that no one turns from wickedness. . . . (23:14)

They claimed to know the word of the Lord, but their claim was empty:

> I did not send the prophets,
> yet they ran;
> I did not speak to them,
> yet they prophesied.
> But if they had stood in my council,
> then they would have proclaimed my words to my people,
> and they would have turned them from their evil way,
> and from the evil of their doings. (vv. 21f.)

Jeremiah's dramatic conflict with the prophet Hananiah symbolizes the struggle between true and false prophets (28:1-17). Claiming divine inspiration, Hananiah contradicted Jeremiah's message that Judah and her neighbor nations should submit to Babylon rather than rebel. He announced that cap-

Carchemish • Haran
Lake Van
• Nineveh
Lake Urmia
Aleppo • Asshur •
Euphrates
Tigris
Babylon • Nippur • Susa
Erech •
Ur •
• Tema

ASSYRIA AND BABYLONIA

tured Jews, including King Jehoiachin, would return from Babylon within two years (28:2-5). It takes little imagination to feel how such opposition rankled Jeremiah's righteous soul.

His Character. The book's abundance of autobiography and biography shows us what kind of person Jeremiah was. Five characteristics stand out:[4]

(1) Jeremiah was personally honest, especially in his relationship with God. Unlike the false prophets, he gave his hearers no glib answers, but wrestled with God to be certain he really understood God's word. At times this frankness sounds like insubordination or even blasphemy:[5]

> I did not sit in the company of merrymakers,
>   nor did I rejoice;
> under the weight of your hand I sat alone,
>   for you had filled me with indignation.
> Why is my pain unceasing,
>   my wound incurable, refusing to be healed?
> Truly, you are to me like a deceitful brook,
>   like waters that fail. (15:17f.)

And again:

> O LORD, you have enticed me,
>   and I was enticed;
> you have overpowered me,
>   and you have prevailed.
> I have become a laughingstock all day long;
>   everyone mocks me. (20:7)

Jeremiah readily admitted that his ministry was distasteful at times. He felt trapped, unable to escape God's call, with the word burning inside him like a fire. Yet when he preached, God made him look foolish by delaying fulfillment of the prophecy (20:8-10). But Jeremiah trusted God so much that his directness was an asset. Like Habakkuk he wanted to believe, and cried out for help in his unbelief. His personal fellowship with God gave him the strength to go on despite questions and fears, for God himself gave assurance:

> If you turn back, I will take you back,
>   and you shall stand before me.
> If you utter what is precious, and not what is worthless,
>   you shall serve as my mouth.
> It is they who will turn to you,
>   not you who will turn to them.
> And I will make you to this people
>   a fortified wall of bronze;

they will fight against you,
>   but they shall not prevail over you,
for I am with you
>   to save you and deliver you,
says the LORD. (15:19f.)

(2) Jeremiah was courageous in living out his convictions. None of his suffering — threats from family, royalty, or priesthood — caused him to back away from his message. He knew what he had to do, and he did it — not always happily, but always faithfully and courageously.

(3) Jeremiah was passionate in his hatred of immoral or unspiritual conduct. In righteous indignation he hurled fiery blasts against idolatry (e.g., chs. 2–5), social injustice (e.g., 5:26-29), and false prophecy (e.g., vv. 30f.). He believed so strongly that Judah deserved judgment that his prayers for vindication at times became pleas for vengeance on his enemies:

Remember how I stood before you
>   to speak good for them,
>   to turn away your wrath from them.
Therefore give their children over to famine;
>   hurl them out to the power of the sword,
let their wives become childless and widowed.
>   May their men meet death by pestilence,
their youths be slain by the sword in battle. (18:20f.)

Such strong statements reflect Jeremiah's greatness, not weakness. He took sin seriously because he took God's righteousness seriously. A later Sufferer would show how to hate transgression, and yet make intercession for the transgressors.

(4) Jeremiah combined a sensitivity to his people's suffering and a gracious humanity. His role as a prophet of doom often clashed with his love for his people and land.[6] Judah's refusal to repent and indifference to imminent judgment put a knife through Jeremiah's heart:

Let my eyes run down with tears night and day,
>   and let them not cease,
for the virgin daughter — my people — is struck down
>   with a crushing blow,
>   with a very grievous wound. (14:17)

Jeremiah's call demanded that he be serious, but he was not morbid. He found joy in his close communion with God and his friendship with loyal friends like Baruch. Despite his prophetic austerity, Jeremiah seems to have had warm relationships with others. Zephaniah the priest appeared responsive

Demonstrating his confidence in the future of Judah, Jeremiah purchased
a field at Anathoth and preserved the deed in an earthenware jar.
(Neal and Joel Bierling)

to his message (29:29), and King Zedekiah was secretly receptive to him (chs. 37–38). Ahikam, a prince of Judah, dared to protect him (26:24), and the Ethiopian steward Ebed-melech saved him from possible death (38:7-13).

(5) Besides his relentless preaching of doom, Jeremiah also saw hope for the future. That hope rested not in the glib optimism of his prophetic peers but in God's sovereignty over history and his loyalty to Israel. In Judah's final days, Jeremiah demonstrated his confidence by buying family property in Anathoth. The purchase testified to his expectation that, after Judah's purification by judgment, God would resettle his people in their land (32:1-44).

Literary Qualities

No Old Testament prophet used a wider variety of literary forms or showed more artistic skill than Jeremiah. And because Jeremiah used them in fresh and striking ways, his oracles have a vitality, vividness, and urgency unsurpassed in the Bible. The following samples illustrate his creative skill in addressing a host of situations.

Poetry. More than in most prophetic writings, prose and poetry are interleaved in Jeremiah. In the poetry we hear the prophet's voice speaking directly in these forms:

(1) The judgment speech is frequent, but much more varied in form than in Amos. The indictment, for instance, may take the form of an admonition:

> Beware of your neighbors,
>> and put no trust in any of your kin;
> for all your kin are supplanters,
>> and every neighbor goes around like a slanderer. (9:4)

The threat of judgment may be a rhetorical question:

> Shall I not punish them for these things? says the LORD;
>> and shall I not bring retribution on a nation such as this?
>>>> (v. 9; cf. 5:9, 29)

The oracles against the nations (chs. 46–51) sometimes contain only the threat of judgment with no specific indictment of sin (46:1-12; 47:1, 7). However, the speech against the Ammonites includes:

(a) an indictment:

> Has Israel no sons?
>> Has he no heir?
> Why then has Milcom[7] dispossessed Gad,
>> and his people settled in its towns? (49:1)

(b) a threat of judgment introduced by "therefore":

> Therefore, the time is surely coming, says the LORD,
>> when I will sound the battle alarm against Rabbah[8] of the Ammonites;
> it shall become a desolate mound. . . . (v. 2)

(c) a promise of restoration:

> But afterward I will restore the fortunes of the Ammonites, says the LORD.
> (v. 6)

(2) The "Book of Comfort" (chs. 30–33) contains salvation speeches, promises of hope and deliverance for Judah (30:12-17, 18-22; 31:1-14, 15-22). Their form tends to be less stereotyped than that of the judgment speech. Sometimes Judah's plight is described in order to contrast what is and what will be:

> For thus says the LORD:
> Your hurt is incurable,
> > your wound is grievous.
> There is no one to uphold your cause,
> > no medicine for your wound,
> > no healing for you.
>
> . . . . . .
>
> For I will restore health to you,
> > and your wounds I will heal, says the LORD. . . . (30:12f., 17)

Frequently, a salvation speech contains elaborate descriptions of the restoration: rebuilding of cities, renewed fertility of crops, abundance of children, and a reestablished monarchy (vv. 18-21). The promise may include the destruction of enemies that have inflicted the suffering, usually in the form of a lex talionis, an exact equivalent of their crime:

> Therefore all who devour you shall be devoured,
> > and all your foes, everyone of them, shall go into captivity;
> those who plunder you shall be plundered,
> > and all who prey on you I will make a prey. (v. 16)

A possible climax may be the renewal of the covenant, phrased in the language of wedding vows:

> And you shall be my people,
> > and I will be your God. (v. 22)[9]

Portions of hymns may be included, as God not only proclaims deliverance but invites the people to sing about it:

> For thus says the LORD:
> > Sing aloud with gladness for Jacob,
> and raise shouts for the chief of the nations;
> > proclaim, give praise, and say,
> "Save, O LORD, your people,
> > the remnant of Israel." (31:7)

Prose. The prose takes several forms:
(1) Prose sermons are not uncommon (7:1–8:3; 11:1-17; 17:19-27; 18:1-

12; 23:1-8).[10] Most are forms of judgment speech: indictment of sins, threat of judgment (often introduced by "therefore"), and messenger formula. A call to repentance or a command to act righteously may be inserted (7:5-7; 22:1-4). Frequently the oracle begins with a divine commission about where, when, and to whom the word is to be given (7:1f.). A poetic section may be included (e.g., 22:1-8, where vv. 6b-7 is poetry).

(2) One of Jeremiah's most famous salvation speeches is in prose — the prophecy of the "new covenant." The basic message is the contrast between the old covenant made at the Exodus and the new covenant to be written on the heart of God's people (31:31-34).

(3) Symbolic acts of prophecy usually are described in prose (13:1-11; 16:1-18; 19:1-15; 27:1-15). Ordinarily, these accounts follow this form: the Lord commands the prophet to perform an act, the prophet does so, and then the Lord interprets it. These enacted prophecies are more than illustrative; they unleash divine power to accomplish what they symbolize.

(4) Autobiographical and biographical narratives form a large part of the book. The account of the prophet's call, told in the first person, is autobiographical narrative, even though some of God's words are poetic (1:4-19). The story of Jeremiah's suffering at the hands of Pashhur the priest is biographical narrative (20:1-6), as is the description of Jehoiakim's burning of Baruch's scroll (36:1-32). The distinction between prose biography and prose oracle is often blurred, because judgment speeches and other prophecies sometimes occur within a narrative section (e.g., 35:1-19, where vv. 13-17 is a prose judgment speech).

(5) Historical narratives, which tell not Jeremiah's personal story but Judah's history, occur in 39:1-18 (fall of Jerusalem) and 52:1-34 (destruction of the temple and subsequent details of the Exile; cf. 2 Kgs. 24:18–25:30).

Literary Techniques. The following exemplify some of Jeremiah's literary techniques:

(1) He uses pungent figures of speech, as, for example, in his description of Judah's sexual corruption:

> They were well-fed lusty stallions,
>   each neighing for his neighbor's wife. (5:8)

or his picture of the selfish greed of Judah's wealthy:

> For scoundrels are found among my people;
>   they take over the goods of others.
> Like fowlers they set a trap;
>   they catch human beings.
> Like a cage full of birds,
>   their houses are full of treachery. . . . (vv. 26f.)

337

(2) Rhetorical questions are favorite devices. Jeremiah uses questions where the answer should be obvious, yet the people seem to disregard what they know to be right. The dispute put in question form may be drawn

from common custom:

> Can a girl forget her ornaments,
>   or a bride her attire?
> Yet my people have forgotten me,
>   days without number. (2:32)

from the law:

> If a man divorces his wife
>   and she goes from him,
> and becomes another man's wife,
>   will he return to her?
> Would not such a land be greatly polluted?
>   You have played the whore with many lovers;
> and would you return to me? says the LORD. (3:1)

from nature:

> Does the snow of Lebanon leave the crags of Sirion?
>   Do the mountain waters run dry, the cold flowing streams?
> But my people have forgotten me,
>   they burn offerings to a delusion. . . . (18:14f.)

or from history:

> Has Israel no sons?
> . . . Why then has Milcom dispossessed Gad. . . . (49:1)

These questions employ a method of entrapment: they cause their audience to condemn themselves. By giving the obvious answer, the hearers acknowledge that the proper line of conduct is equally obvious and yet they have done just the opposite.

(3) Like Isaiah and Amos, Jeremiah used literary forms usually associated with wisdom literature. Consider this illustration from nature:

> Even the stork in the heavens knows its times;
>   and the turtledove, swallow, and crane observe the time of their coming;
> but my people do not know the ordinance of the LORD. (8:7; cf. Isa. 1:3)

In addition, the judgment speech in 13:12-23 uses popular proverbs (vv.

12f., 23),[11] while 17:5-8 has the blessing-cursing pattern with an emphasis akin to Ps. 1.

(4) Psalmlike complaints are typical of Jeremiah's confessions. The "why" and "how long" of 12:1-4 and the ardent pleas for deliverance of 17:14-18; 18:19-23; 20:7-12 are examples of the complaint form.

(5) Jeremiah enriched his message with ingredients from many areas of Israel's life. The courts of justice in the town gates furnished the form for the powerful indictment in 2:1-13, where the Lord argues his case against Judah. The watchtower, where guards sounded the alert of impending battle, supplied these words:

> Flee for safety, O children of Benjamin,
>   from the midst of Jerusalem!
> Blow the trumpet in Tekoa,
>   and raise a signal on Beth-haccerem;[12]
> for evil looms out of the north,
>   and great destruction. (6:1)

From the battlefield come these commands which signal an invasion of Egypt:

> Prepare buckler and shield,
>   and advance for battle!
> Harness the horses;
>   mount the steeds!
> Take your stations with your helmets,
>   whet your lances,
>   put on your coats of mail! (46:3f.)

This sampling shows the imaginative way in which Jeremiah employed familiar forms to stir his fellow citizens to respond to God's word.[13]

The Book

As the above literary survey shows, the book of Jeremiah is an anthology of diverse materials relating to the prophet Jeremiah (e.g., poetic oracles, prose narratives, etc.). It seems to be organized primarily in a thematic and literary rather than chronological fashion.[14] Our aim here is to survey the finished book as a piece of literature.

Composition. Few biblical books have stirred up as much discussion concerning their origin as has Jeremiah.[15] Without doubt the process of composition was a complex one whose stages we probably can never retrace. On the other hand, the book itself provides clues about how some of it came into being.

Ch. 36 reports that, as Jeremiah dictated, Baruch wrote down on a scroll all the prophet's preaching up to that time (Jehoiakim's fourth year, i.e., 605). Apparently, the idea of writing down prophecy was exceptional since God specifically commanded it; before then it probably existed only in oral form. When Jehoiakim brazenly burned the first scroll, Jeremiah dictated a second, even longer scroll which probably contained much of the poetry of chs. 1–6. It centered on the dire fate awaiting Judah and Jerusalem for their deep moral and spiritual corruption. Many portions of chs. 1–6 are written in the first person (e.g., 1:4; 2:1; 3:6; 5:4f.), perhaps a reflection either of their dictation by Jeremiah or their preservation as originally preached.

Chs. 26–51 use the third person and contain much more prose than poetry. They consist primarily of episodes in Jeremiah's life during the reigns of Jehoiakim and Zedekiah and after the fall of Jerusalem.[16] As Jeremiah's close friend and associate, Baruch probably wrote these semi-biographical narratives and appended them to the second scroll.[17] Also, ch. 51 ends with the line "Thus far are the words of Jeremiah" (v. 64) as if it may have closed a collection (cf. 48:47). This remark implies that someone other than Jeremiah appended ch. 52 (which closely resembles 2 Kgs. 24:18–25:30) to material already compiled by Jeremiah, Baruch, or someone else.[18]

One phenomenon unique to the book — the prose sermons — has long puzzled scholars. Throughout the book, there occur oracles reportedly given by Jeremiah in prose rather than poetry (e.g., 7:1–8:3; 11:1-17; 17:19-27). Strikingly, their style and theology sound like that of Deuteronomy (D) and the so-called "Deuteronomistic History" (DtH; i.e., Joshua–2 Kings).[19] For that reason, several generations of scholars theorized that exilic or postexilic writers ("Deuteronomists") composed them and even edited the finished book.[20]

Today, however, many scholars argue that the prose sermons have more in common with the book's poetry (usually conceded to be from Jeremiah himself) than with D or DtH. This approach suggests that, if not written by Jeremiah or Baruch, the prose sermons convey, at least, the voice of Jeremiah or a "Jeremianic tradition" rather than that of later Deuteronomists. Further, two other explanations for the style of the prose sermons seem reasonable: they may reflect either a rhetorical style typical of that period, or Jeremiah's conscious imitation of the book of Deuteronomy in his preaching.[21]

One other problem clouds the issue of composition even more: the Hebrew and Greek texts of the book differ significantly. The LXX text is one-seventh shorter than the MT and also has the oracles against the nations in the middle (between 25:13 and 15) rather than at the end (chs. 46–51). Evidence from Qumran suggests that LXX was translated from a short Hebrew original different from that behind MT.[22] Given how greatly LXX and MT diverge, the final book may once have existed in more than one form, or both MT and LXX may ultimately derive from a common Hebrew original.[23] As for the order of the oracles, while most scholars favor the priority of the LXX arrangement, a good case can be made that the MT's order came first.[24]

In sum, the editorial and textual history which gave us the present book (and *most* OT books!) remains a mystery. Our ignorance of that past, however, in no way lessens the profit which the book affords its readers.

Literary Structure and Themes. However it came to be, the finished book shows a fairly discernible structure.[25] A brief narrative introduction (1:1-3) presents the whole as the "legacy" of Jeremiah and sets the chronological boundaries of his ministry.[26] Its reference to "the captivity of Jerusalem in the fifth month" (v. 3) also forms a nice literary inclusion with the Historical Appendix about that event (ch. 52). In between, the book offers the content of Jeremiah's legacy (1:4–ch. 51) in three main sections (chs. 2–25; 26–45; 46–51). Ch. 1 sets out to establish Jeremiah's credibility by detailing his call (vv. 4-10) and his commission to speak as a prophet (v. 17). "It is clear that the book has been constructed to allow the voice of Jeremiah to dominate the beginning, end, and core of the text."[27]

The first chapter also introduces two of the book's main themes: Judah's flagrant idolatry and its consequent punishment by an invasion from the north. Two collections primarily of poetic oracles fire the first rhetorical salvos. The so-called "harlotry cycle" (chs. 2–3) indicts Judah as a spiritual whore who has abandoned her faithful husband, Yahweh:[28]

> I remember the devotion of your youth,
> your love as a bride,
> how you followed me in the wilderness,
> in a land not sown.
> Israel was holy to the LORD,
> the first fruits of his harvest.
> All who ate of it were held guilty;[29]
> disaster came upon them, says the LORD. (2:2f.)

Further, Judah's forsaking of Yahweh for other gods was particularly shocking on two accounts. The action was unparalleled even among Judah's pagan neighbors, and in the end Judah was far worse off than before:

> Has a nation changed its gods,
> even though they are no gods?
> But my people have changed their glory
> for something that does not profit.
> . . . . . .

for my people have committed two evils:
  they have forsaken me,
the fountain of living water,
  and dug out cisterns for themselves,
cracked cisterns
  that can hold no water. (vv. 11, 13)

Worse yet, Judah deliberately ignored the clear example of Israel, who suffered national disaster for similar sins:

She saw that for all the adulteries of that faithless one, Israel, I had sent her away with a decree of divorce; yet her false sister Judah did not fear, but she too went and played the whore. (3:8)[30]

The second poetic collection, the so-called "foe cycle" (chs. 4–10), details the doom of Zion, the great city of God, by invaders from the north. For example:

See, a people is coming from the land of the north,
  a great nation is stirring from the farthest parts of the earth.
They grasp the bow and the javelin,
  they are cruel and have no mercy,
  their sound is like the roaring seas;
they ride on horses,
  equipped like a warrior for battle,
  against you, O daughter of Zion! (6:22f.; cf. 5:15-17)[31]

Even more shockingly, in his "Temple Sermon" Jeremiah predicts the destruction of the temple and the exile of Judah:

And now, because you have done all these things, says the LORD, and when I spoke to you persistently, you did not listen . . . , therefore I will do to the house that is called by my name, in which you trust, . . . just what I did to Shiloh.[32] And I will cast you out of my sight, just as I cast out all your kinsfolk, all the offspring of Ephraim. (7:13ff.)

Two final subsections round out chs. 2–25 and advance earlier themes. The "Confessions of Jeremiah" (chs. 11–20) consist of psalmlike complaints in which Jeremiah prays for divine deliverance from suffering. They incorporate something unprecedented in the prophetic books — startling, blunt conversations between Jeremiah and Yahweh (see 15:17f. and 20:7, quoted above). They convey Jeremiah's deep personal despair, particularly over Judah's rejection of his preaching. It seems likely that Jeremiah wrote the Confessions and shared them privately with his disciples.[33]

Late Bronze Age cistern at Jerusalem (cf. Jer. 38:6).
(Israel Department of Antiquities)

In the book, they underscore four themes: (1) Jeremiah's agony mirrors the agony of Yahweh at his rejection by Judah; (2) by rejecting Jeremiah's message, Judah confirms its guilt and justifies the coming national judgment;[34] (3) Jeremiah's escalating pleas for vengeance anticipate the events of judgment in chs. 37–39; (4) God's reassurances of Jeremiah and announcements of restoration (e.g., 15:20f.; 16:14f.; 17:7; cf. 20:13) prepare the reader for the book's oracles of hope later (e.g., chs. 30–31).[35]

Finally, chs. 21–25 combine narratives and poetry on a single theme — the inevitability of judgment. When Zedekiah asked Jeremiah whether Yahweh might save Jerusalem from Nebuchadnezzar, Yahweh gave the king a fateful choice — to surrender or die:

> See, I am setting before you the way of life and the way of death. Those who stay in this city shall die by the sword, by famine, and by pestilence; but those who go out and surrender to the Chaldeans . . . shall have their lives as a prize of war. For I have set my face against this city for evil and not for good, says the LORD: it shall be given into the hands of the king of Babylon, and he shall burn it with fire. (21:8-10; cf. Deut. 30:19)

The book reserves the severest punishment for Jeremiah's bitterest opponents, the Davidic monarchy and the Jerusalem clergy. Despite his royalty, Jehoiakim will receive neither a proper state funeral nor a decent burial:

> They shall not lament for him,
>   saying, "Alas, lord!" or "Alas, his majesty!"
> With the burial of a donkey he shall be buried —
>   dragged off and thrown out beyond the gates of Jerusalem (22:18f.)

Worst of all, the death of his exiled brother Jehoiachin (called Coniah and Jeconiah) spells the end of the Davidic dynasty (v. 30; cf. vv. 24f.). As for the clergy who serve the temple, their condemnation is certain and severe:

> Both prophet and priest are ungodly;
>   even in my house I have found their wickedness,
>   says the LORD.
> Therefore their way shall be to them
>   like slippery paths in the darkness,
>   into which they shall be driven and fall;
> for I will bring disaster upon them
>   in the year of their punishment, says the LORD. (23:11f.)

Indeed, in a vision (ch. 24) Jeremiah learned how little regard Yahweh had for the people left in Jerusalem: they were like a basket of rotten figs — worthless and destined to be thrown away.

At the same time, chs. 21–25 also interweave two threads of hope. First, though pruning and discarding David's last descendants, Yahweh would send him another descendant:

> The days are surely coming, says the LORD, when I will raise up for David a righteous Branch, and he shall reign as king and deal wisely, and shall execute justice and righteousness in the land. In his days Judah will be saved and Israel will live in safety. And this is the name by which he will be called: "The LORD is our righteousness." (23:5-6; cf. 33:14-16)[36]

Second, Jeremiah announced a seventy-year exile — a far longer period than Jeremiah's opponents foresaw, yet with an end:

> This whole land shall become a ruin and a waste, and these nations shall serve the king of Babylon seventy years. Then after seventy years are completed, I will punish the king of Babylon and . . . the land of the Chaldeans, for their iniquity, says the LORD, making the land an everlasting waste. (25:11f.)

The vision of ch. 24 describes the exiles as a basket of good figs: they would be brought back to the land and restored to covenant relationship.

(2) Chs. 26–45 comprise the second major section of Jeremiah's legacy. Structurally, narratives (chs. 26–29; 34–45) surround the "Book of Comfort" (chs. 30–33). In chs. 26–29, two dramatic scenes underscore a common theme: the rejection by the prophets of the word of God through Jeremiah. In the first (ch. 26), the priests and prophets show their rejection of Jeremiah's message by putting him on trial for blasphemy, i.e., for his Temple Sermon (7:1-15). Jeremiah rebuts the charge simply by claiming that Yahweh has sent him (vv. 12, 15), while his defenders quote Micah's similar prophecy against the temple (v. 18; cf. Mic. 3:12). That Jeremiah escaped execution does not mean acceptance of his message, however, for 26:20-23 reports how Jehoiakim cruelly executed Uriah, another prophet of the day, for a similar message.

The second scene, the dramatic confrontation between Jeremiah and the prophet Hananiah in the temple (ch. 28), also stresses the rejection of Jeremiah's message by the Jerusalem clergy. In ch. 27, Jeremiah had symbolically worn a yoke to urge Judah and their neighbors to submit to the rule of Babylon. But, claiming the same divine authority (i.e., "Thus says the LORD of hosts," v. 2), Hananiah boldly contradicted Jeremiah. He announced that the exiles and the temple vessels would return from Babylon within two years (vv. 3-4). Significantly, two months later, the prophet Hananiah was dead — the precise penalty Jeremiah had predicted for his false prophecy (vv. 15f.).

Both these scenes represent more than just conflicts between clergy. Here the religious leadership exemplifies the stubbornness of heart which Jeremiah saw as typical of the people of Judah (e.g., 5:23; 16:12; 23:17) and which made them unable to repent.

In the Book of Comfort (chs. 30–33), poetry and narratives dovetail into a common theme: Jeremiah's message of restoration. These chapters expound how Yahweh will bring his people back to the land from exile and "restore [their] fortunes" (for the latter phrase, see 30:3, 18; 31:23; 32:44; 33:26). To buttress such hope, Jeremiah had to answer a theological problem: the people of Judah had such a stubborn heart — how could they ever obey Yahweh? For Jeremiah, the fate of the future hung not on Judah's self-reformation but on a new act of Yahweh himself — the gift of a new covenant. As a follow-up to 24:7 ("I will give them a heart to know that I am the LORD"), this new covenant would overcome the people's stubbornness by being written on their heart:

> The days are surely coming, says the LORD, when I will make a new covenant with the house of Israel and the house of Judah. It will not be like the covenant that I made with their ancestors when I took them by the hand to bring them out of the land of Egypt. . . . But this is the covenant that I will make with the house of Israel . . . says the LORD: I will put my law within them, and I will write it on their hearts; and I will be their God, and they shall be my people. (31:31ff.)

To confirm the certainty of Judah's hope, ch. 32 relates God's command that Jeremiah purchase some family property in Anathoth from his uncle. Even though he obeyed (vv. 6ff.), the prophet was mystified by this order since at that moment Babylon had already surrounded Jerusalem (vv. 24f.). In reply, God reiterated his plan to bring the people of Judah back to the land after the Exile, to make an everlasting covenant with them, and to do them good (vv. 36ff.).

If chs. 26–29 recount the rejection of the prophetic word by priests and prophets, chs. 34–36 portray its rejection by the kings. In ch. 34, Zedekiah led Judah to release its slaves as the covenant demanded (Exod. 21:2) but failed to keep Judah from backtracking and reclaiming them (ch. 34). In reply, God granted Judah a release — "a release to the sword, to pestilence, and to famine . . ." (v. 17) — and promised to hand Zedekiah and his officials over to the brutal Babylonians. Ch. 36 details the ultimate royal rejection of prophecy when Jehoiakim burns the scroll of Jeremiah's early oracles. The episode echoes the discovery of the law book during Josiah's reign (2 Kgs. 22), subtly contrasting Josiah's acceptance of God's word with Jehoiakim's rejection of it. By rejecting Yahweh's word, the kings (and Judah) again confirmed their guilt and their worthiness of judgment. They also signaled that, if Judah was to have any future hope, it must somehow make a new beginning.

The closing narratives (chs. 37–45) relate the tragic consequences of that rejection — the fall of Judah and destruction of Jerusalem. Chs. 37–39 track the nation's increasing desperation as the Babylonian army tightens the noose around the capital. Three times Zedekiah seeks an eleventh-hour reprieve from Yahweh through Jeremiah (37:3, 17; 38:14), but each time the answer is denied. For example:

> If you [Zedekiah] will only surrender to the officials of the king of Babylon, then your life shall be spared, and this city shall not be burned with fire, and you and your house shall live. But if you do not surrender . . . , then this city shall be handed over to the Chaldeans, and they shall burn it with fire, and you yourself shall not escape from their hand. (38:17f.)

Meanwhile, branding Jeremiah as a traitor, angry Judean officials kept him either under house arrest or in prison (37:11ff.; 38:1ff.). To the bitter end, when Jerusalem fell and Judah was lost (ch. 39), they doggedly rejected God's word through the prophet.

Subsequent episodes (chs. 40–44) show that, even amid the ashes of defeat, Judah still refused to submit to Babylon as Yahweh commanded. Rebels assassinated Gedaliah, whom the Babylonians had appointed governor (chs. 40–41). Terrified of Babylonian reprisals, the people asked Jeremiah to seek Yahweh's guidance about what to do. But when Yahweh advised them to stay in the land, they rejected his word and migrated to Egypt, taking Jeremiah with them against his will (chs. 42–43). So, through Jeremiah, Yahweh announced that Egypt was no refuge against his wrath (44:11ff.). And one last time, Judah rejected God's word, sinking instead to the level of begging help from an idol, the queen of heaven (vv. 17f.).

At the same time, the closing narratives follow up the hope offered by the Book of Comfort. They intentionally interweave reports of Judah's gathering gloom with brief glimpses of personal survival. For example, in ch. 35 God promises the family of Rechab, who had obeyed the command of their human ancestor for centuries, that they "shall not lack a descendant to stand before me for all time" (v. 19). More importantly, after the fall of Jerusalem, the book stresses that the Babylonians honored Jeremiah by sparing him the pangs of exile (39:11-14). Apparently, the editor viewed Jeremiah's survival as a symbol of Judah's future restoration as foreseen by the prophet.[37]

(3) The Oracles (mostly poetic) against the Nations (chs. 46–51) represent the climax of the book.[38] The book had already led readers to expect them: it introduced Jeremiah as a prophet "to the nations" (1:5, 10) and thematically anticipated his prophecies against them (e.g., 25:13). Oracles against Egypt open the section, linking it to the preceding narratives about Egypt (chs. 43–45) and following up the judgment pronounced earlier on Egypt (e.g., 43:8ff.; 44:30).

The lengthy oracles against Babylon — the enemy responsible for Judah's demise — bring the section to a crescendo.[39] In battle scenes reminiscent of Nahum, Jeremiah describes Yahweh's vengeance on Babylon:

> Raise a standard against the walls of Babylon;
>> make the watch strong;
> post sentinels;
>> prepare the ambushes;
> for the LORD has both planned and done
>> what he spoke concerning the inhabitants of Babylon.
> . . . . . .
> Babylon must fall for the slain of Israel,
>> as the slain of all the earth have fallen because of Babylon. (51:12, 49)

To dramatize Babylon's doom, chs. 46–51 conclude with Jeremiah commissioning Baruch's brother, Seraiah, to perform a prophetic symbolic action. During a visit to Babylon (594), he is to read Jeremiah's prophecies against that nation from a scroll, then sink the scroll in the Euphrates, to symbolize Babylon's future collapse.

The Oracles against the Nations are intended to encourage Judah to look forward to restoration. They reinforce Jeremiah's statements about Yahweh's sovereignty, remind Judah of the awesome power of their oppressor, and renew hope that all their enemies will ultimately fail. The disaster of their neighbors means Judah may return soon from exile. Indeed, the book takes pains to reassure its originally exilic readers:

> But as for you, have no fear, my servant Jacob,
>> and do not be dismayed, O Israel;
> for I am going to save you from far away,
>> and your offspring from the land of their captivity.   (46:27; see also
>>>>>>> 50:17-20, 28, 33-34; 51:9-10, 45-46, 50-51)

The book's Historical Appendix (ch. 52) offers a literary postscript. Its graphic recounting of Jerusalem's fall confirms that Jeremiah's prophecies have been fulfilled literally. This in turn authenticates Jeremiah as a true prophet, implicitly coaxing the reader to take Jeremiah's legacy with utmost seriousness. The book closes with a flickering yet captivating glimmer of hope — the release of exiled King Jehoiachin from prison (52:31-34). The seventy-year exile prophesied by Jeremiah (25:11f.; 29:10) is half over.

Main Theme. Ultimately, the book of Jeremiah is about hope. Structurally, the book signals this in two ways. First, it offers the Book of Comfort in the middle (chs. 30–33), as if to say that hope lies at the center of Jeremiah's message. Second, while concentrated in chs. 30–33, glimpses of hope also appear throughout the book (e.g. 1:10; 3:15ff.; 12:15f.; 52:31ff.). Thus, while warning God's people of his judgment for their unfaithfulness, the completed book of Jeremiah points to future restoration, the gracious gift of Israel's sovereign Lord.

The Theological Contribution

The keystone of Jeremiah's theological insight is his emphasis on the Exodus as Israel's foundational spiritual experience. This experience includes the deliverance from slavery in Egypt, the Sinai covenant with its detailed list of obligations, and the settlement in Canaan by Yahweh's guidance and power. Most of the prophet's other themes depend, in varying degrees, on the Exodus.

Yahweh's Sovereignty in History. Certain monumental events shaped Israel's view of history. Her birth as a nation, Egypt's failure to prevent the Exodus, and Canaan's surrender to Joshua are all read as acts of direct divine intervention. Thus, Israel saw history as the arena where the Lord of Abraham, Isaac, and Jacob makes himself known.

Jeremiah affirmed that view of history. Events in Judah, Egypt, and Babylon resulted much more from divine sovereignty than from human politics. Human politics could succeed only when they agreed with God's will. Jeremiah pressed this point with Jehoiakim and Zedekiah. Nebuchadnezzar's success was due not so much to political prowess or military strength as to God's command (cf. 27:6). Yahweh's sovereignty in history showed itself in his using of nations to do his will.

This sovereign Lord also reserved the right to change his plans. In the midst of God's great act of grace, Israel wandered in the wilderness for forty years in judgment.[40] But Judah failed to remember this stern lesson, complacently assuming that the God of covenant grace would forever defend the nation and its capital from attack. But God's sovereignty is not limited, as Jeremiah learned:

> At one moment I may declare concerning a nation or a kingdom, that I will pluck up and break down and destroy it, but if that nation, concerning which I have spoken, turns from its evil, I will change my mind about the disaster that I intended to bring on it. And at another moment I may declare concerning a nation or a kingdom that I will build and plant it, but if it does evil in my sight, not listening to my voice, then I will change my mind about the good that I had intended to do to it. (18:7-10)

Here Jeremiah takes the principle of blessing or judgment applied to Israel in Deut. 27–28 and extends it to cover God's freedom in dealing with nations in general.

As Jeremiah's oracles against foreign powers (chs. 46–51) make clear, God shows his sovereignty in history by judging nations directly. Time and again they picture judgment falling with no human agent responsible. This is not to say that these events involved only divine acts such as earthquake, famine, plague, or flood; usually the judgment came through military assault (cf. 51:1-4). But God claimed that he sent the armies just as he had breached the walls of Jericho (Josh. 6) and routed the troops of Midian (Judg. 6–7).

Old Torah and New. The Exodus also illumines Jeremiah's indictments of Judah's sin and his high hopes for future restoration. In the light of God's magnificent rescue of his people from Egyptian slavery, the idolatry so blatant in Manasseh's day (2 Kgs. 21) looked all the more appalling. In a telling argument God cites his early relationship with Israel, then asks the condemning question:

> What wrong did your ancestors find in me
>   that they went far from me,
> and went after worthless things,[41]
>   and became worthless themselves? (2:5)

Israel's defection was out of keeping with the actions even of pagan nations:

> Has a nation changed its gods,
>   even though they are no gods? (v. 11)

Israel's defection was also out of keeping with its own past:

> Yet I planted you as a choice vine,
>   from the purest stock.
> How then did you turn degenerate
>   and become a wild vine? (v. 21)

Jeremiah sees both personal and national sins as violations of covenant law, law which should have disciplined life as a yoke does an ox:

> "Let me go to the rich
>   and speak to them;
> surely they know the way of the LORD,
>   the law of their God."
> But they all alike had broken the yoke,
>   they had burst the bonds. (5:5)

From commoner to leader, the people had flaunted God's covenant with their ancestors. Perhaps Jeremiah's greatest theological contribution was his insight into the human heart. Only sin — as indelibly stamped in human lives as a leopard's spots or an Ethiopian's dark skin (13:23) — explains Israel's ungrateful rebellion. Jeremiah observes that the human heart — center of intellectual and moral decision — is deceitful and corrupt (17:9). He is not speaking about human nature theoretically but practically — from years of observing his fellow Israelites. He has personally watched them despise their covenant heritage while at the same time justifying their wicked conduct.

No superficial solution — not even Josiah's sweeping reforms — will remedy the flagrant idolatry and open corruption. Only a New Covenant — a binding relationship between a sovereign God and Israel his people — will do: "and I will be their God, and they shall be my people" (31:33).[42] Like the Old Covenant, the New is initiated by the Lord (v. 31), an expression of his sovereignty.

The New Covenant aims to meet the specific needs that made it necessary: (1) it is more personal than the marital contract which Israel so flagrantly violated ("a covenant that they broke, though I was their husband" [v. 32]); (2) it is written on the hearts of the people, the seedbed of their iniquity, not on stone tablets (v. 33); (3) it results in the true knowledge of God — the New Torah of full obedience and rich fellowship without need of human teaching (v. 34); (4) it carries full forgiveness of the sins that have earned judgment (v. 34).[43]

This hope of total transformation through the law written on the heart shapes Jeremiah's view of the future. He expresses it more in spiritual and personal terms than in political ones. One would expect that of a prophet who witnessed the tragic failure of Judah's political system and sensed that no superficial reformation could provide a lasting remedy.

But Jeremiah was not silent concerning the political future. True, he had given up all hope that David's city and household would be spared. Yet he foresaw the rise of a "righteous Branch," a legitimate heir to David's throne. His reign would bring justice within Israel's borders and security outside them (23:5f.), all as a gift of God's intervening grace. The name of the promised king proclaimed it: "The Lord is our righteousness," the One who looks out for the rights of his people.

The New Covenant, with its New Torah and New King combine to shape the prophet's picture of the future: a binding personal relationship with God and a bright national destiny.[44]

Strength of Personal Faith. This bright hope is further evidence of Jeremiah's deep dedication to God's will and strong confidence in his power. Only his solid faith in the covenant Lord could prompt such optimism in the face of the political and religious disaster of his day.

In a sense his whole ministry had been spiritual preparation for his role as comforter as well as critic. His call and commissioning had assured him of God's personal interest: "Before I formed you in the womb I knew you," and

"I am with you to deliver you" (vv. 5, 8; cf. 19). The encounter with God's word through the decades of his ministry must have convinced Jeremiah of the Lord's persistence and power to carry out his plans.

The word of God was "something like a burning fire shut up in my bones" (20:9), so Jeremiah's only option was to declare it and watch it work.[45] The relentless drive of that word assured him that God's future was certain.

Neither the persecution of political enemies nor the misunderstanding of familiar friends could shake Jeremiah's trust in God. Even his severe complaints about God's will seemed eventually to strengthen his faith, as did the doubts of false prophets like Hananiah (ch. 28).

> One cannot separate Jeremiah's personal experiences from his message. God's gracious, firm guidance of his own life nurtured his confidence in the grace of God to transform Israel's future. Jeremiah's own pilgrimage of judgment and grace became a paradigm which conveyed the character and will of the living God to Israel and beyond.[46] If total obedience to the Lord of covenant grace is the major lesson of Scripture, no one in the Old Testament taught it better than Jeremiah.

Dating of Jeremiah's Prophecies and Experiences

The dating of much of Jeremiah's material is controversial, so one must regard the table below as only a tentative suggestion. An asterisk (*) indicates passages which name the king or contain a chronological reference.[47]

Dating of Jeremiah's Prophecies and Experiences

King	Year(s)	Reference	Summary
Josiah	627 B.C.	1:1-19*	Jeremiah's call
	627-621	2:1–6:30	Indictments of Judah's sin; appeals to repentance; threats of judgment by invasion from north
	627-621	8:4–9:24 [MT 25]	Indictments of Judah's sin; Jeremiah's grief over Judah's failure to repent and his anticipation of their laments when judgment comes
	621	11:1-14	Jeremiah's support of Josiah's reform based on Book of the Covenant
	621	13:1-11	Symbolic act of burying waistcloth by Euphrates to show folly of dependence on other gods
	621	16:1-9	Lord commands Jeremiah not to marry in light of pending calamities
	621	30:1–31:40	Book of Consolation, which culminates in promise of New Covenant
Jehoahaz	609	22:10-12*	Jeremiah exhorts people to lament not Josiah's death but Jehoahaz' exile
Jehoiakim	608-605	7:1–8:3; 11:15-17; ch. 26*	Prophecies of temple's destruction
	608-605	22:13-19*	Jeremiah indicts Jehoiakim for valuing splendor above righteousness
	608-605	17:1-27	Jeremiah chides Judah for idolatry and failure to keep sabbath, and laments his own suffering
	608-605	21:11–22:9	King commanded to execute justice
	608-605	11:18–12:6; 5:10-21; 18:18-23; 20:7-18	Complaints of Jeremiah both at his opposition and God's delay in promised judgment
	605	25:1-26*	Summary of Jeremiah's message plus some oracles of judgment
	605	46:1–49:33*	Judgment speeches against Egypt and Judah's other neighbors
	605	19:1–20:6	Jeremiah's prophecies of doom provoke harsh retaliation from Pashhur the priest

	605	45:1-5*	Lord promises to spare life of Baruch, Jeremiah's secretary
	601	12:7-17	Jeremiah laments ravages to Judah by invaders
	601-598	35:1-19*	Jeremiah brings Rechabites to temple to illustrate the obedience which the Lord had expected from Judah
	601-598	18:1-11	Jeremiah's visit to potter's house
Jehoiachin	598	15:5-9; 9:10-11, 17-22 [MT 9-10, 16-21]	Lament over Nebuchadnezzar's attack on Jerusalem
	598	10:17-24; 16:16-18	Jeremiah commands people to prepare for exile
	598	22:24-30*; 13:18-19	Lord promises judgment to Jehoiachin
Zedekiah	597	24:1-10*	Vision of good and bad figs, symbols of those God spares in exile and those he judges in Judah
	597	49:34-39*	Prophecy against Elam
	597	29:1-29*	Jeremiah's letter encouraging exiles to plan for long stay in Babylonia
	594	51:59-64*	Symbolic act of throwing scroll into Euphrates to prophesy destruction of Babylon
	594	27:1–28:16	Jeremiah wears symbolic yoke of slavery and confronts opposition from prophet Hananiah
	595-590	23:1-40	Jeremiah's indictment of Judah's leaders (esp. the prophets) and his prophecy of David's Righteous Branch
	589	34:1-22*	Prophecy of Jerusalem's fall and indictment of Judah's aristocracy for failure to free their slaves
	588	21:1-10*	Jeremiah urges Zedekiah to surrender to Nebuchadnezzar
	588	37:1–38:28*	Siege of Jerusalem, Jeremiah's imprisonments, and his counsel that Zedekiah surrender
	588	32:1-44*	Jeremiah buys field at Anathoth as symbol of hope for return from exile
	586	33:1-26*	Jeremiah assured that God will restore Judah's fortunes after exile

	586	39:1-18*	Fall of Jerusalem, capture of Zedekiah, sparing of Jeremiah's life
	586	52:1-30*	Fall of Jerusalem, looting of temple, and total number of Nebuchadnezzar's captives
Gedaliah (Governor appointed by Babylon)	586	40:1-16	Jeremiah released to custody of Gedaliah, whom Nebuchadnezzar appointed governor of Judah
	586	41:1-18*	Assassination of Gedaliah; political confusion that followed
Johanan (Leader of Judean remnant)	586	42:1-22*	Jeremiah counsels Judah's remnant to stay in land and not seek asylum in Egypt
	585	43:1-13*	Judean remnant flees to Egypt to escape Nebuchadnezzar's wrath, takes Jeremiah along against his will
	585	44:1-30*	Jeremiah's last speech to Jews in Egypt, reviewing their sins and promising judgment even in Egypt
	560	52:31-34*	Evil-merodach succeeds Nebuchadnezzar, grants mercy to Jehoiachin after thirty-seven years in captivity

CHAPTER 25

Ezekiel

Ezekiel is a prophecy from the Exile. According to the book itself, the prophet's message came from Yahweh during the first part of the Exile, between 593 and 571 B.C. Ezekiel therefore marks a distinct phase in Israelite prophecy, and its form and characteristics differ somewhat from the prophecies studied thus far.

> Then he brought me to the gate, the gate facing east. And there the glory of the LORD of Israel was coming from the east; the sound was like the sound of mighty waters; and the earth shone with his glory. The vision I saw was like the vision that I had seen when he came to destroy the city, and like the vision that I had seen by the river Chebar; and I fell on my face. Ezek. 43:1-3

Ezekiel and His Times

The Prophet. Ezekiel ben Buzi came from a priestly family (1:3). He grew up in Palestine, probably in Jerusalem, and was taken into exile in 597 (see 33:21; 2 Kgs. 24:11-16). He was probably twenty-five years old at the time, for five years later, at thirty (see 1:1),[1] he was called to the prophetic office.

Ezekiel was happily married (24:16), and the sudden death of his wife, announced to him in advance by Yahweh, was treated as an ominous sign to warn Israel (vv. 15-24). He lived in his own house in exile, at Tel Abib near the Chebar Canal (3:15; cf. 1:1), which was in the vicinity of Nippur in Babylonia. Elders came to Ezekiel's home for counsel (8:1), which agrees with the statement that he was "among the exiles" (1:1), living in a settlement of Judean prisoners of war. He dates certain revelations by the particular year of the exile of King Jehoiachin. His prophetic call came in year 5 (593), and the last recorded date is year 27 (571), indicating a ministry of at least twenty-three years.

Because of his recorded visions, his strange behavior in acting out certain prophecies, the record of being transported from Babylon to Jerusalem and back (8:3; 11:24), and other details, Ezekiel has sometimes been called psychotic, and schizophrenic.[2] Indeed, his manner of prophesying strikes the reader as a strange conglomeration of styles but his unique exilic context goes a long way toward explaining, or at least accounting for, these peculiarities.

The Times. The Exile (597-538) was almost coterminous with the Babylonian empire (612-539).[3] The captivity of a select group of Judeans in 597 was followed by a more general exile in 586.

Physical conditions in exile apparently were acceptable to many Jews. The Babylonians were not bent on punishing conquered people, but merely took steps to ward off revolutions. The more cruel Assyrians carried out a policy of displacing populations, breaking up and scattering them, and leaving them to lose their national identity through intermarriage and other forms of absorption. By contrast, the Babylonians deported peoples in small groups and allowed them to preserve their national identities. (Hence the Judeans were permitted to return from exile, whereas most of the members of the ten "lost tribes" of the northern kingdom had become absorbed.) Jeremiah advised a policy of "business as usual" in captivity (Jer. 29:4-7), and this apparently was followed by the exiles. Before long, Jews were found in mercantile ventures. When the opportunity came to return to Jerusalem, many preferred to stay in Babylonia. Their choice marked the beginning of the Jewish center that later produced the Babylonian Talmud, a massive compendium of Jewish law completed in the sixth century A.D.

Religious conditions in exile were mixed. Basing his conclusions in part on what he regarded as exilic additions to the preexilic prophecies, and to that extent not textually supported but essentially correct, one scholar has observed:

> It would be a great mistake to conclude from Isaiah's prophecies about the remnant, or Jeremiah's vision of the good figs, that those Jews who were deported to Babylonia were the moral elite of the Jewish people. The Babylonians did not select them for religious and moral reasons. As for the

Isaianic idea of the remnant, its implication was simply that a part of the people would be saved from the general ruin and then turn to Yahweh.[4]

Nevertheless, the Exile was a period of testing ideas about God. Was the divine presence limited to Palestine? Was God impotent against the gods of Babylon? Could Yahweh be worshipped in a strange land? The theology of Ezekiel was suited to this new situation.

Canonical and Critical Questions

Canonicity. Obviously, Ezekiel was included in the canon. But proof of the book's canonicity lies mainly in a second fact: a lengthy discussion over whether it should be removed (or "hidden"). "The question was not, is this book sacred, or inspired, Scripture? but, assuming its prophetic authorship and inspiration, is it expedient to withdraw the book from public use lest the unlearned or the half-learned be stumbled by the apparent discrepancies between it and the Law?"[5] Hananiah ben Hezekiah of the school of Shammai (an influential rabbi who lived about the time of Jesus) burned three hundred jars of oil in his study while harmonizing the seeming conflicts between Ezekiel and the Pentateuch. Then, even though the prophecy was retained as canonical, reading of ch. 1 was not permitted in the synagogue, and private reading of the prophecy was forbidden to anyone under thirty.[6]

Criticism. In 1913, the learned opinion was expressed: "No critical question arises in connexion with the authorship of the book, the whole from beginning to end bearing unmistakably the stamp of a single mind."[7] This widespread scholarly assessment subsequently changed when, in 1924, a student of the prophets stated that Ezekiel had too long escaped the critic's knife; of the 1,273 verses in Ezekiel, he claimed 1,103 were additions to the original work.[8] Since then the academic camp has been split into diverse groups. W. Zimmerli has won a large following in seeking to understand the book, not just dissect it, with a theory of *Nachinterpretation,* a process by which Ezekiel's original message influenced a succeeding "school" which has contributed new levels of understanding in its additions to the book.[9] M. Greenberg has advocated a "holistic" reading of the book, whereby the book in its present form is the primary object of study, and most of it is credited to Ezekiel himself.[10] Both Zimmerli and Greenberg understand Ezekiel not only as an oral prophet but as a literary editor. The difference between them lies in how much material is assigned to Ezekiel and in literary perspective. Greenberg has a synchronic approach, which inclines him to engage in analyses of the structure of literary units in order to demonstrate their overall unity. On the other hand, Zimmerli has a diachronic understanding of literary units and so envisions a piecemeal development of the text, with sometimes tenuous links between its various parts. The book seems to have been intended for exilic readers or hearers. It looks back at Ezekiel's pre-586 oracles of judgment and his post-586 oracles of salvation.

The Form of the Book

Analysis. The prophecy basically consists of messages given at Yahweh's command, delivered orally (3:10-11; 14:4; 20:27; 24:1-3; 43:10), and presumably gathered by the prophet and/or editors at a later time. Thirteen dates are given, each connected with a revelation from Yahweh.

		yr.	mo.	day	(1 = 597/6)[11]
1:2	Opening vision	5	4	5	July 31, 593
8:1	Vision in the temple	6	6	5	Sept. 17, 592
20:1	Message to the elders	7	5	10	Aug. 14, 591
24:1	Report of the siege of Jerusalem	9	10	10	Jan. 15, 588
26:1	Prophecy against Tyre	11	(1)	1	Apr. 23, 587
*29:1	Prophecy against Pharaoh	10	10	12	Jan. 7, 587
*29:17	Prophecy to Babylon about Egypt	27	1	1	Apr. 26, 571
30:20	Prophecy against Pharaoh	11	1	7	Apr. 29, 587
31:1	Prophecy to Pharaoh	11	3	1	June 21, 587
*32:1	Lamentation over Pharaoh	12	12	1	March 3, 585
32:17	Lamentation over Egypt	12	1	15	Apr. 27, 586
33:21	Report of Jerusalem's fall	12	10	5	Jan. 8, 585
40:1	Vision of restored temple	25	1	10	Apr. 28, 573

*Obviously not in chronological sequence

The prophecy divides into three parts:

Judgment on Israel (chs. 1–24)
    Ezekiel's call as prophet of judgment (1:1–3:21)
    Signs of judgment (3:22–5:17)

359

Oracles of judgment (6:1–7:27)
Visions of judgment (chs. 8–11)
Signs and oracles of judgment (chs. 12–19)
Oracles of judgment (chs. 20–24)
Judgment on the other nations (chs. 25–32)
  [Ammon, Moab, Edom, Philistia, Tyre, Sidon, Egypt]
Restoration of Israel (chs. 33–48)
  Oracles of salvation (chs. 33–36)
  Vision of new life (37:1-14)
  Sign of a royal scepter (37:15-28)
  Victory over Gog (chs. 38–39)
  Visions of the new temple and the repossessed land (chs. 40–48)

Features of Ezekiel's Prophesying

Allegories and Sign Acts. The book of Ezekiel includes a number of allegories: Jerusalem as a vine (ch. 15) and Yahweh's wife (16:1-43), imperial eagles (17:1-21), the Davidic dynasty as a lioness (19:1-9) and a vineyard (19:10-14), the sword of judgment (21:1-17), Oholah and Oholibah representing the two corrupt capitals, Samaria and Jerusalem (23:1-35), and the caldron of destruction (24:1-14).

The prophecy also includes a series of symbolic or dramatic actions (sometimes called "enacted prophecy"); see the chart on page 361.

Allegories were a constant feature of Ezekiel's prophesying, to which the exiles once objected (20:49). They were an attempt to represent in a "theatrical" form the plain truth of the coming fall of Jerusalem and the end of the nation of Judah. His hearers were not inclined to listen: only the hope of imminent return kept them going. To break through this natural resistance, the prophet resorted to picture after picture. The sign acts had the same purpose. The coming catastrophe was acted out in dramatic form, to reinforce the oracles of judgment. In 37:15-23 the message of restoration and reunion of the divided kingdom was dramatized by a sign act, in which two sticks were permanently joined as one.

"Son of Man." This title, rendered "Mortal" in the NRSV, is used some ninety times in Ezekiel, always by Yahweh when addressing Ezekiel. As a form of address it appears elsewhere in the Old Testament only in Dan. 8:17.[12] The phrase occurs throughout Ezekiel, often preceded by the formula for receiving a message, "The word of the LORD came to me." It occurs in commissioning contexts (e.g., 2:3: "Son of man, I send you to the people of Israel . . ."; cf. 2:1;

Text	Ezekiel's Action	Meaning
4:1-3	Sketches Jerusalem on a brick	The city will be put to siege
4:4-8	Lies on left side for 390 days, on right side for 40	The years of iniquity and punishment for Judah
4:9-17	Eats exile's rations	Jerusalem's starvation diet when siege occurs
5:1-12	Shaves his head with a sword, weighs and divides the hair, burning a portion of it, smiting a second portion with a sword and scattering the third portion to the winds	The smallness of the escaping remnant amidst the thoroughness of the judgment
12:1-12	Digs his way through a wall and takes an exile's baggage with him	Exile is an inescapable reality for which the people must be prepared
21:18-23	Marks out a route for the Babylonian army with a crossroads that forces the king to cast lots to decide which road to take	God will determine the itinerary of the Babylonian troops and it will lead inevitably to Jerusalem
25:15-24	Loses his wife in death	The chosen people, the delight of Yahweh's eyes, will be lost in death or exile

3:4). It is unlikely that the title "son of man" in Ezekiel is to be compared with the same title used by Jesus of himself (used for him elsewhere only by Stephen; Acts 7:56). It is questionable, also, that it has any relationship to the phrase "one like a human being" in Dan. 7:13 (Aram. *kᵉbar ᵉnāš*, "like a son of man"). More likely the title was used to stress the human nature of the agent over against the divine source of the message. The title frequently precedes the messenger formula, "Thus says the Lord God." Over against the transcendent divine Lord, Ezekiel is assigned a humble role, as a mere mortal.

"*Set Your Face Against.*" On nine occasions Ezekiel's oracles are introduced by the instruction, "Set your face against . . ." This appears to be an echo of an archaic practice of staring at the object of a prophecy (Num. 24:1; 2 Kgs. 8:11). Such a prophetic stare is a physical reinforcement of the focus of the divine message. (One may also compare the notion of exiles praying in the direction of the temple in 1 Kgs. 8:48 [cf. Dan. 6:10]).

This formula is used with messages to the mountains of Israel (6:2), false

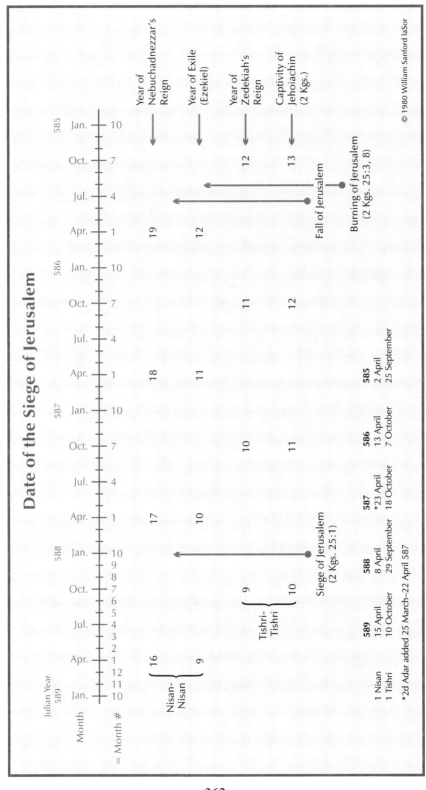

Date of the Siege of Jerusalem

© 1980 William Sanford laSor

women prophets (13:17), the south (20:46), Jerusalem (21:2), the Ammonites 25:2), Sidon (28:21), Pharaoh, king of Egypt (29:2), Mt. Seir (35:2), and Gog (38:2). Where distant places or people are involved, such a formula does not imply that Ezekiel traveled to deliver his oracles. Rather, as in the rhetorical address to the Pharaoh in 31:2; 32:2, such oracles were evidently meant for the exiles' ears and delivered in their hearing.

"I Am Yahweh." This formula of self-designation occurs many times in Ezekiel, and may be considered a hallmark of the book. The same expression appears in Leviticus (18:2, 4-6, 21, 30; etc.). The purpose or result intended in Ezekiel's messages is often expressed in the "recognition" formula: "Then you/they shall know that I am the LORD" (6:7, 14; 7:4, 27; 11:10, etc.). The defeat and exile of the chosen people created an aching need for Yahweh to be vindicated and for his true character and will to be made clear to Israel and to the world.

Visions of God. As recorded in ch. 1, Ezekiel saw a theophany or earthly manifestation of Yahweh before he heard a commission to function as a prophet of judgment. The theophany presented God arriving in a fiery storm and seated on a throne of judgment. The throne rested on a platform or firmament (NRSV "dome"), which was supported by "living creatures" whose wings bore the structure to earth. Beneath it were wheels, invisibly controlled by the creatures, for travel on the earth. This complicated vision fused ancient Israelite conceptions with other, Near Eastern representations evidently known to the exiles.[13] It presented to them a powerful image of the transcendent and awesome character of the God who had come to judge his people.[14]

The supernatural chariot-like contrivance of ch. 1 reappears in chs. 8–11, in a vision of the destruction of Jerusalem and its citizens. It comes to rest in the temple court (10:3). The fire that burns at its base (1:13) supplies coals to set the city ablaze (10:2, 6-17). Its "living creatures" are now called "cherubim" (10:1-3). The new designation is meant to invite comparison with the static representation of the divine presence inside the temple, the ark with its cherubim (9:3). Yahweh abandons the temple, mounts the mobile throne, and departs from the city (10:18-19; 11:22-23), leaving Jerusalem to its fate.

In the vision of the new temple in chs. 40ff., the contrivance, described as the divine "glory," comes to take up residence (43:2, 4-5; 44:4). The new Jerusalem is fittingly renamed "The LORD is There" (48:35). The restored divine presence is to be the guarantee of blessing for the exiles after their return to the land.

Judah's Sins. The basis of God's punishment is given in Lev. 26:14-33: it will be inflicted "if you will not obey me, and do not observe all these commandments" (v. 14). Ezekiel builds on this theme, echoing Lev. 26 especially in chs. 4–6. The prophet attacks the unorthodox worship at the high places, or local shrines, throughout Judah (ch. 6). He finds the very area of the temple to be the scene of gross acts of idolatry (8:4-16). Moreover, he denounces the social sins rampant in Judah and Jerusalem (7:23; 9:9; 22:6-13, 25-29). The capital is characterized as unfaithful to Yahweh, its patron, both in hosting pagan forms of worship, especially child sacrifice, and in its political recourse to foreign alliances (16:15-29; 23:11-21, 36-45). The sins of the present generation of the covenant people are the climax of a long history of rebellion (2:3, 4). Jerusalem is not the glorious city of God that Zion theology, espoused by its leaders, claimed: its sins are an expression of its pagan origins (16:3). Israel's rottenness goes back to the time of its redemption from Egypt: the people had regularly responded truculently to divine grace (20:5-31).

A Program of Moral Renewal. Both Jeremiah and Ezekiel quote what was probably a current proverb: "The parents have eaten sour grapes, and the children's teeth are set on edge" (Jer. 31:29; Ezek. 18:2). It blames the present situation of exile on the older generation, and bespeaks the fatalism of the "children" of the Exile. In a post-586 oracle, Ezekiel sets forth in reply a double principle: "It is only the person who sins that shall die," but "one [who] is righteous . . . shall surely live" (18:4-9). God's promise of eschatological life and restoration to the land (cf. 37:14) is to be the motivation for living a morally good life even now, in exile. The exiles are accused of having lived in transgression of God's traditional commands (18:10-13), which still constitute God's will for the people (18:5-9). Is it too late to change? By no means. Yahweh invites the wicked to repent (18:21-23), and to inherit the life promised to his obedient people (18:30-32). Ezekiel thus infuses the demoralized exiles with something to live for and challenges them to face up to spiritual reality.

The Setting of Chs. 1–24

Chs. 1–24 fall into three primary parts, which begin with chs. 1; 8; and 20 respectively. The first and second parts both consist of a dated vision, sign acts, and oracles of judgment. The date that opens the second part relates not only to a vision but also to consultation among the exilic elders, which marks communal acceptance of Ezekiel as a prophet. This latter feature recurs at the beginning of the third part, in 20:1, while its oracles include two sign acts, in 21:6-23.

This primary material all relates to the radical judgment that actually befell Judah and Jerusalem in 586. Why did readers of the book need to be reminded of it? For three reasons. First, it provided meaning to Israel's chaotic history, in terms of national sin and divine punishment. Two of Ezekiel's post-586 oracles look back and explain in God's name the necessity for such radical judgment (22:23-31; 36:16-23). Second, the exhortations to the exiles to take their past judgment seriously and let it influence their present way of life (16:54; 36:31; 39:26) give a good reason for their continuing to read or listen to the judgment oracles. A third reason emerges from the collection of oracles that introduce Ezekiel's messages of salvation, in 33:1–34:24. It looks back to the radical judgment of 586 and, even as it speaks of salvation to come, warns too of a discriminating judgment ahead which will befall apostates and oppressors among the Judean exiles. They will be barred from returning home and enjoying God's new era of blessing.

This theme of mingled assurance and challenge finds a dominant place in chs. 1–24. The pre-586 oracles of judgment function as powerful flashbacks. They are tied into counterparts of Ezekiel's post-586 message of 33:1–34:24 at several points. These are 3:17-21; 11:14-21, the blocks of oracles in 12:21–14:11 and in chs. 17–19, and also 20:32-44. In 3:17-21 Ezekiel's mission to prepare the exiles for life and protect them from death is presented with the imagery of the sentinel drawn from 33:1-7. In 11:14-41 the assurance of return to the land is given, with a stinging threat to apostates among the exiles (11:21). The block of messages in 12:21–14:11 builds on Ezekiel's accuracy in predicting the national judgment of 586 in order to present his later announcements of a lighter, but no less certain, judgment for abuses being perpetuated among

"O dry bones, hear the word of the LORD" (Ezek. 37:4). First temple period tombs adjacent to the École Biblique, Jerusalem. *(Neal and Joel Bierling)*

the exiles. In chs. 17–19 oracles about the downfall of the Davidic dynasty, which by now have been fulfilled, are capped at the center with an oracle of messianic promise (17:22-24). This hope is given a contemporary moral application in ch. 18. The message of salvation in 20:32-44 is the plainest example of modified assurance. It presents the certain hope of return home along with a warning of judgment for "the rebels among" the exiles (20:38).

The lesson of all these barbed assurances is that the exiles' hope for the future must be matched by moral responsibility in the present. God wants to be their savior, but they have to make even now an ethical choice for or against God and between future life or death.

> As I live, says the Lord GoD, I have no pleasure in the death of the wicked, but that the wicked turn from their ways and live; turn back, turn back from your evil ways; for why will you die, O house of Israel? 33:11

The Oracles against the Nations

Like the other major prophetic books, Ezekiel includes a collection of messages against foreign nations (cf. Isa. 13–23; Jer. 45–51). Most of the oracles are directed against Tyre (26:1–28:19) and Egypt (chs. 29–32). Ch. 25 is concerned with Palestinian states — Ammon, Moab, Edom, Philistia. The block falls into two parts. Chs. 25–28 speak of divine judgment against Israel's enemies, as part of a program of vindication and restoration for Yahweh's own people (cf. 25:3, 8, 12, 15; 26:2). Chs. 29–32, on the other hand, denounce Judah's hoped-for ally, Egypt, and find in its coming destruction the end of Judah's misplaced confidence: "The Egyptians shall never again be the reliance of the house of Israel" (29:16). Egypt was to fall, as an extension of divine judgment against Judah. Egypt's attempt to relieve the siege of Jerusalem was a failure, as Ezekiel predicted in his pre-586 oracles. It was expected that Egypt itself would fall to Nebuchadnezzar (30:10, 25). The Babylonian campaign against Egypt in 568 did not accomplish this. It was only in the reign of the Persian king Cambyses, in 525, that Egypt was conquered.

There is an increasing emphasis on death and the underworld in this series of judgment speeches (26:19-21; 28:8; 31:14-18; 32:18-22). It functions as a negative foil to the positive promise of life for Israel, beginning in ch. 33.

The Message of Restoration

After the mingled notes of hope and challenge with which Israel's future is treated in 33:1–34:24, the ensuing oracles express pure hope. The best known of these is the vision of revived bones in 37:1-14. It provides an answer to the exiles' lament concerning their hopeless and virtually deathlike state (37:11). The vision initially says amen to the lament, but promises a divine miracle of renewal and restoration to the homeland. The sign act of the royal scepter in 37:15-23 goes on to promise a reunited kingdom under a restored Davidic monarchy. This message is repeated in 34:23-24, while in the rest of ch. 34 an earlier motif of Israel as God's flock, abused by its exploitive rulers ("shepherds"), is developed in terms of renewed occupation of the land. The promised land also comes to the fore in 35:1–36:15. Although the Edomites have overrun the southern part of Judah during the Exile, their expulsion and Israel's reoccupation are promised.

Earlier in the book the issue of Israel's future obedience is resolved by the divine gift of "a heart of flesh" that would be responsive to Yahweh's will (11:19). This promise is repeated in 36:26, in the context of forgiveness of the sins that had caused expulsion from the land, and of renewed blessing in the land. The most powerful argument that exile would give way to restoration was the theological need to vindicate Yahweh's holy name or reputation, after the fact of exile had compromised it among the nations (36:22-23).

The message about the invasion and defeat of Gog is an assurance of security in the land (38:8, 11, 14; 39:26; cf. 34:25-28). It envisions a worst case scenario of foreign invasion yet argues that the exiles have no need for anxiety: God's security system will prove more than adequate.

The visions and accompanying oracles in chs. 40–48 probably functioned in an earlier version of the book as an expansion of 37:25-28. Temple, land, king, and people are its themes. The new temple is conceived as a divine creation, a building not made with hands.[15] Yahweh's holy transcendence was to be reflected in its design and also in its maintenance. After Ezekiel's visionary tour of the temple in chs. 40–42, chs. 43–46 begin and end with fresh visionary descriptions. But they mainly consist of regulations concerning three topics: the two-tier system of temple personnel — (1) Levites who function as caretakers and (2) levitical priests, descendants of Zadok who serve Yahweh in the inner court (44:6-31), the economic maintenance of personnel and offerings (45:1-17), and the procedures of rites and offerings (45:18–46:18).

Finally, an exotic picture of a river of life, flowing from the temple down into the Dead Sea and transforming it, takes the reader from the temple to the land. Its frontiers and the tribal allotments of territory are painstakingly described.

367

In chs. 44–48 a key role is assigned to the "prince," as the Davidic monarch is called to emphasize his subordination to the divine King. He represents the people in worship and is assigned extensive estates in the land. There seems to be a desire to affirm the hope which earlier prophets held of a monarchy that would live up to God's ancient promises. This hope is intended to counter the exiles' opposition to the restoration of a ruling dynasty after years of preexilic royal oppression. Accordingly, assurances are given that misappropriation of land will no longer occur in the new age (45:8-9; 46:16-18).

> Ezekiel and his book provided an invaluable service to the Judean exiles, in interpreting the situation that engulfed them and pointing them to a responsible hope. In the light of this book, and also of Isa. 40–55, the return from exile that started in 538 must be regarded as the beginning of a new, eschatological work of God.[16]

However, the experiences of postexilic Judah fell tragically short of the hopes held out in the book of Ezekiel. For example, they had to be content with a temple made with human hands. Whether we in our day are meant to understand its promises as delayed to a still future age (cf. Luke 21:24; Acts 1:6-7) is a question that defies an absolute answer. For the Christian reader, the cultural trappings associated with the original setting of the book may fall away, while the hope remains, a hope that purifies (1 John 3:3), as we await the appearance of the King of Kings.

We can be grateful for three miniature presentations of Ezekiel's overall message: 28:25-26; 37:25-28; and 39:23-29. They reflect an awareness of the complexity of the book and a need to help readers grasp its essential themes. The last and longest of these summaries may serve as a fitting conclusion to this survey of the work of this extraordinary prophet of the Exile:

> And the nations shall know that the house of Israel went into captivity for their iniquity, because they dealt treacherously with me. So I hid my face from them and gave them into the hand of their adversaries, and they all fell by the sword. I dealt with them according to their uncleanness and their transgressions, and hid my face from them.

Therefore thus says the Lord GOD: Now I will restore the fortunes of Jacob, and have mercy on the whole house of Israel; and I will be jealous for my holy name. They shall forget their shame, and all the treachery they have practiced against me, when they live securely in their land with no one to make them afraid, when I have brought them back from the peoples and gathered them from their enemies' lands, and through them have displayed my holiness in the sight of many nations. Then they shall know that I am the LORD their God because I sent them into exile among the nations, and then gathered them into their own land. I will leave none of them behind; and I will never again hide my face from them, when I pour out my spirit upon the house of Israel, says the Lord GOD. Ezek. 39:23-29

CHAPTER 26

Obadiah and Joel

Judgment fell on Judah. Ezekiel's prophecies, with those of Micah, Isaiah, Zephaniah, Habakkuk, and Jeremiah, were fulfilled. Nebuchadnezzar's Babylonian armies ravaged the land, captured the king, leveled the temple, and took thousands of the people into exile. The pain of Judah's loss and dislocation was aggravated by the behavior of her neighbors. That aggravation is a major theme of two books among the Twelve: Obadiah and Joel. As deserved as Judah's judgment may have been, the opportunistic greed and cruelty of the surrounding nations was outrageous and unforgettable. Joel remembered particularly the mayhem wrought by Egypt, Edom, and the cities of Phoenicia and Philistia (Joel 3:1-8, 19). Obadiah's burden is the crime of the Edomites.

Obadiah

Obadiah is the shortest book in the Old Testament canon. Next to nothing is known about its author. Its date and historical setting have been subject to much debate.

Nevertheless, Obadiah makes its contribution to our hearing of the Word of God. The believing community found this prophecy to be divinely authoritative and included it in the canonical prophets with good reason and firm hope. The believing community has through the centuries, therefore, sought to hear God as he speaks through this prophet.

> Though you soar aloft like the eagles, though your nest is set among the stars, from there I will bring you down, says the LORD. Obad. 4

The Prophet and the Prophecy

Obadiah is believed to be from Judah, but the ascription (v. 1) names neither the prophet's family nor his home region. The tradition that he was the steward of King Ahab (Talmud *Sanh*. 39b; see 1 Kgs. 18:1-16) has no supporting evidence. Obadiah ("Yahweh's servant or worshiper") was a common Hebrew name, used of a dozen persons in the Old Testament and found in Hebrew inscriptions.[1]

The "vision" (see Isa. 1:1; Nah. 1) concerns Edom (v. 1), Israel's ancient enemy, especially despised for its treatment of Judah during the fall of Jerusalem. Analysis of the prophecy indicates two main parts:

> Vision concerning Edom (vv. 1-14)
> > Edom's fall announced (vv. 1-4)
> > Edom's destruction as complete as its pride was high (vv. 5-9)
> > Reason: Cruelty against "brother" Judah (vv. 10-14)
> Description of Day of Yahweh (vv. 15-21)
> > Judgment on the nations (vv. 15f.)
> > Deliverance of Judah (vv. 17-20)
> > Kingdom of Yahweh (v. 21)

Striking parallels exist between the book of Obadiah and Jer. 49:7-22, as well as between Obadiah and Joel.[2] The likely explanation is that both accounts quote an earlier tradition.[3] The animosity between Judah and Edom was a fact of life throughout the entire monarchy. Judah's ability to keep Edom in check was viewed by the biblical sources as a test of the relative strength of Judah's kings.

Obadiah's words against Edom call to mind other speeches common among the prophets of Yahweh (see Isa. 34; 63:1-6; Ezek. 25:12-14; 35; Amos 1:11f.; Mal. 1:2-5). Some scholars see such prophecies as extreme forms of nationalism, markedly inferior to other oracles in the classical prophets (see below). Much ink has been spilt in an effort to condemn or condone these nationalistic interests. But Obadiah clearly claimed that Israel would be restored for purposes quite beyond any mere nationalism. The restoration belonged to a day when all the nations would know the justice and righteousness of God (v. 15).

The combination of themes in Obadiah probably accounts for its position in the Hebrew canon. The centrality of the Day of Yahweh links it to Joel and Amos. So does the spotlight which it places on Edom (Joel 3:19; Amos 9:12). It is possible that Jonah was placed after Obadiah as an example of the "messenger . . . sent among the nations" (Obad. 1).[4]

Dates from 889 to 312 B.C. have been presented and defended by various scholars for the prophecy's final written form. Reference to the tension between Esau (Edom) and Jacob (Israel) appears at several points in the Old Testament, beginning with Gen. 25:23; 27:39f. During the Monarchy, Edom was often controlled by kings of Israel and Judah. Sporadic wars are recorded (note 2 Sam. 8:13f., reading 'dm for 'rm; 1 Kgs. 11:14-17; 2 Kgs. 14:10; 16:5f.). When the Babylonians invaded the region, Edom quickly surrendered and assisted in the destruction of Jerusalem (Lam. 4:21; Ezek. 25:12; 35:10). The oracle in Obad. 11-14 almost certainly refers to this event. Hence, a date within a few years after 586 B.C. seems likely. When later the Edomites were pushed out of their territory by the Nabateans, and occupied the Negeb and Judah as far north as Hebron, they became known by the Greek equivalent, "Idumeans," the people of whom Herod the Great was an illustrious member.

Geographical Details. Mt. Esau (v. 19) is one of the highest mountains south-southeast of the Dead Sea, possibly Umm el-Bayyârah near Petra (Sela; cf. "the clefts of the rock," v. 3; RSV mg. "Sela"). Teman (v. 9) defies specific identification. It may describe a city, a region in southern Edom, or be synonymous with Edom itself. In both biblical and extrabiblical sources it was viewed as one of Yahweh's dwelling places.[5] Halah (v. 20, NRSV, but Heb. *ḥēl* "army") may be a region of Assyria to which Israelites were taken (2 Kgs. 17:6; 18:11). Sepharad (v. 20) is traditionally taken to be "Spain," but other identifications are Sardis (in western Asia Minor; however, no "exiles" were located there) and Shaparda in southwest Media (cf. 2 Kgs. 18:11). "Exiles" (v. 20) has been used to support a postexilic date.

Message and Relevance

According to at least one scholar, "Obadiah is of little theological interest and its presence in the canon can easily be explained as a result of the anti-Idumaean polemic which was in full flood at the beginning of the first century A.D."[6] This negative evaluation cannot account for the preservation of

Territory of the Edomites, "who live in the clefts of the rock" (Obad. 3).
(William Sanford LaSor)

this book or any other anti-Edomite prophecies. In Obadiah, as in Esther and other similar books, we are not dealing with narrow nationalism. Something deeper and more significant theologically must be found to account for the canonization and preservation of the work.

Edom. Oracles and prophecies against Edom, like those against other nations, were addressed primarily to Israel. The prophets did not travel to Edom to deliver their taunt songs, for who would have listened to them? Edom epitomized national pride, self-sufficiency, trust in human wisdom and might. All of this turned into greed and cruelty in the face of Judah's calamity. Opportunism crowded out compassion. Edom's pending calamity became a warning to Judah of the dangers of national arrogance. What the prophets said about Edom was heard by Israel, evaluated, cherished, safeguarded, and canonized as the Word of God.

Day of Yahweh. Israel also heard Obadiah's speeches as promises that

Yahweh would set matters right. Three points most frequently revealed by Yahweh through the prophets are pertinent here:

(1) Yahweh is a God who demands righteousness. Although long-suffering, compassionate, and gracious, the Lord will not always tolerate behavior contrary to his holy will. Since Israel is his particular people, whose destiny is to teach all nations of Yahweh and the Torah, God requires of them a covenant loyalty that obligates them to a high level of righteousness. When the nation proves disloyal to the task, God determines to punish its disobedience. The Lord will, however, spare some, and with this remnant accomplish his will. Although not spelled out in the prophecy, it is this background with which Obadiah is implicated (see vv. 10-12, 17-21; also Amos 1–2).

(2) Yahweh is Ruler of heaven and earth, God of all the nations. This is a strong undercurrent in the prophetic hope. If Yahweh were only the God of Israel, how could he punish the Edomites or even expect them to listen to his word? How could God hold Edom accountable for violence done to his brother Jacob? Far from a late idea in Israel, this assumption underlies the initial prophecies in Amos and recurs in nearly all of the prophets. It is basic to the Abrahamic covenant that Yahweh's blessing comes to the nations of the world through the elect Abraham and his descendants. Yahweh is not only the redeemer of Israel, but the creator of all things. We cannot understand the prophetic hope without reckoning with this One.

(3) But if Yahweh is the Holy One and demands holiness of his people, how can he permit the evil deeds of the nations of the world? Obadiah answers first by citing the evil that Edom has done, and second by announcing the coming of the Day of Yahweh: "As you have done, it shall be done to you; your deeds shall return on your own head" (v. 15). After this judgment upon all nations in the day of the Lord, then will come the hoped-for restitution and restoration. "Saviors," like those in the early days (Judg. 3:9, 15), ascend Mt. Zion and rule Mt. Esau. The result: "the kingdom shall be Yahweh's" (v. 21). That is the point of the prophecy. It is Yahweh, not nationalism, that dominates the prophetic view.

Relevance. Of what value today is a discourse on the family strife between Jacob and Esau? Must this message be relegated to a past or future time only — the "time of Jacob's trouble" (Jer. 30:7) — or can it be applied today? As part of the eternal Word of God, it must have relevance in all generations, across all times, despite its special importance in certain times and under certain conditions. Since the message is addressed primarily to Israel and not to Edom, those of the household of faith today will properly consider its words to them. It speaks of enemies of God's people. It rehearses the cruel and inhuman treatment they have carried out. But judgment begins at the house of God. What can we expect if we treat family (v. 10) and neighbor as the Edomites treated Judah? Is not such behavior pagan?

The wisdom of the Edomites was proverbial (cf. Jer. 49:7). The message against Edom was in part a condemnation of their wisdom (v. 8) and pride (v. 3).

> But the prophetic message thus becomes a judgment on all merely human wisdom; even the "foolishness" of God is wiser than human wisdom (1 Cor. 1:25), while "the wisdom of this world is foolishness with God" (3:19).

May not this be especially important for us to hear today, when secular humanism, in the pride and haughtiness of its accomplishments, threatens to set itself up against the Word of God?

People still chafe under injustices in this world, and yearn for a day when things will be "as they should be." Human intervention, crucial though it is, is not the ultimate answer to this cry for justice. Hearing the One who promises that his Day will come is crucial, however. And when it does, all will indeed know the One who rights all wrongs, restores the just possessions (v. 19f.), and performs his will on earth as it is now done in heaven.

Joel

Even less is known about Joel as a person than about Obadiah. Apart from mentioning his father, Pethuel, this book reveals nothing of his personal history. The avid interest in Jerusalem, particularly the temple and its ceremonies (1:9, 13f., 16; 2:14-17, 32 [MT 3:5]; 3 [MT 4]:1, 6, 16f.), suggests that he was a temple prophet or at least a prophet who valued and frequented the temple.

The first two chapters may have been used liturgically either during disasters like Joel's locust plague, or in commemorating anniversaries of deliverance from them (see below on Lamentations). Summons to witness to the events recorded (1:3), calls to lament or complaint (vv. 5, 8, 11, 13f.), individual complaint (vv. 19f.), invitation to repentance (2:12-14), call to assemble in the temple (vv. 15-17a), a fragment of a communal complaint (v. 17), and divine response promising salvation (vv. 18-27) all suggest possible liturgical use. If so, this is again evidence of the process which shaped the canon. God's people not only heard the prophet's word but used it in worship through the centuries.

> You shall know that I am in the midst of Israel, and that I,
> the LORD, am your God and there is no other. And my people
> shall never again be put to shame. Joel 2:27

Date. The thorny question of date traditionally has been solved either by assigning the book to the period of the minority of Jehoash (Joash; *ca.* 835-796)[7] or by dating the prophet long after the return from exile, near the end of the fifth century or even later.[8] More recently, arguments have been posed for a date just before or shortly after the Exile. They tend to be based on (1) absence of mention of a king, (2) parallels to the works of Zephaniah, Jeremiah, Ezekiel, and Obadiah, (3) prominence of the "Day of the LORD," (4) havoc wrought against Judah and total disruption of life that is best explained by a recent exile, (5) pictures of the activity of the temple, whose rebuilding was completed in 515 B.C.[9]

Happily, Joel's message does not hinge on the date. The prophet's words are salient despite our current inability to reconstruct his historical background with accuracy.[10]

Problem of Interpretation. Just as troublesome as Joel's date have been the locusts in 1:4; 2:25. Three major lines of interpretation have been proposed. First, many Christian interpreters have followed the Jewish Targum in viewing them as *foreign armies* which ravaged Judah in successive waves.[11] This interpretation reads the description of 2:4-11 as a literal military invasion of which the locusts in ch. 1 are a metaphor. Most modern commentators have found this approach too subjective. If the locusts are foreign armies, which foreign armies do they represent? Furthermore, it is unlikely that the locust waves actually *are* armies since they are *compared* to armies in ch. 2:4-7.

Second, the descriptions in 2:4-11 are read figuratively in apocalyptic fashion which views the insects as unearthly creatures who will wreak havoc at the day of the Lord (cf. Rev. 9:3, 7-11).[12] Regular use of the past tense, however, and the fact that the narrator seems to have been an eyewitness (see Joel 1:16) suggest that Joel is not forecasting the future but depicting divine judgment that has already taken place. This is not to overlook such apocalyptic features as the description of heavenly portents (2:30f. [MT 3:3f.]).

Third, a more literal approach sees the catastrophe in Joel as a series of locust invasions which strip the vegetation of Judah, bringing unprecedented damage.[13] This devastation is conveyed powerfully by the chainlike poetic structure of 1:4:

> What the cutting locust left,
> the swarming locust has eaten.

What the swarming locust left,
   the hopping locust has eaten.
And what the hopping locust left,
   the destroying locust has eaten.

The emphasis is not so much on the various types of locusts as on the thoroughness of their destruction. Judah's plight was made even worse because this marauding spanned more than one year (2:25). In powerful poetry sometimes approaching hyperbole the locusts are likened to a looting army, so relentless is their plundering, so terrible their sound and appearance (2:1-11). In the far-flung and all-encompassing judgment which they bring on Judah, the prophet cannot help but see a prototype of the day of Yahweh (1:15; 2:11).

Message. Joel consists of two almost equal parts: the locust plague and day of the Lord (1:1–2:17) and the victory to come (2:18–3:21 [MT 4:21]). In the first section the prophet speaks; in the second, the Lord. The turning point is 2:18 where the Lord, perhaps through a temple prophet, responds to the penitent overtures of his people and brings deliverance.

After stressing the unprecedented and unique nature of the calamity (1:2-4), the prophet surveys various groups drastically affected by the plague

Hellenistic tomb (second-first century B.C.) popularly called the pillar of Absalom in the Kidron valley, traditional location of the valley of Jehoshaphat (Joel 3:2; cf. vv. 12, 14). *(Neal and Joel Bierling)*

— drunkards (vv. 5-7), farmers (vv. 11f.), and priests (vv. 13f.) — and calls each to lament the tragedy. Particularly desperate is the plight of the priests, who cannot maintain the daily round of sacrifices. The severity of God's judgment is sharpened by his destruction of his people's means of access to him. In the face of such death-dealing devastation, they have only one hope: to assemble in the temple and cry to the Lord (v. 14).

To Joel a disaster of such magnitude can mean only that the day of the Lord, God's final reckoning with his people and the nations, is near (1:15-20). In the insect invasions and drought (see vv. 19f.) which followed, the prophet sees the harbinger of the dreaded day of darkness forecast by Amos (5:18-20; 7:1-6), Zephaniah (1:7, 14-18), and Obadiah (v. 15). In order to sense this connection, one must remember that the Hebrews were able to see the general in the particular. Each instance of God's judgment contained the facets of all judgment, including the final one:

> ... the prophet can move freely from the threat of a past historical event to the coming eschatological judgment because he sees both as sharing the selfsame reality. To posit two totally separate and distinct historical events recorded in these two chapters not only misses the subtle literary manner of shifting from past to future but seriously threatens the theological understanding of prophetic eschatology which spans temporal differences.[14]

Thought of the day of the Lord prompts a more vivid picture of the plague. Advancing like a relentless army the locusts besiege the land and terrorize its citizens (2:1-11). Their sound is like rumbling chariots or crackling flames. In huge clouds they hang shroudlike over the land and obscure the sun and moon. The literary form itself — a call to alarm (v. 1) followed by the description of destruction (vv. 2-10) — reinforces the military metaphors employed.

The situation is dire but not hopeless. The one way out is wholehearted repentance of the entire nation (2:12-17). Joel features the contemporary religious system more than do Amos, Hosea, and Jeremiah. But he certainly has no interest in ritual for ritual's sake. His ultimate appeal is to the gracious nature of the God of the covenant (vv. 13, 17).

Unlike most of Israel's great prophets, Joel makes no explicit mention of the sins which precipitated the calamity. Where they look forward to impending doom, Joel stands in the midst of it. Solution, not cause, is the pressing problem. Moreover, Joel more than hints at a major crisis that may have triggered the judgment: confusion and compromise in Judah's understanding of Yahweh's uniqueness. True knowledge of God was apparently lacking (2:27; 3:17 [MT 4:17]). That the Lord did answer his people's plea (2:18ff.) may indicate that in this case God's judgment brought the desired results: Judah turned to the true God from corrupt, misguided worship.

Judah's repentance is more than matched by God's full-scale restorations, announced in an extended oracle of salvation:[15] staple crops are restored (2:19, 22); insects and drought are withdrawn (vv. 20, 23); and the losses of the blighted years are repaid (vv. 24f.). On a larger scale, God's act of redemption becomes a pattern of the final deliverance of the people: (1) both spiritual and material blessings are lavished on the remnant of Judah (2:28 [MT 3:1]–3 [MT 4]:1, 16-18, 20f.); and (2) the nations (3 [MT 4]:2-15, 19), overripe for judgment because of their cruelty to God's people, are threshed in the valley of Jehoshaphat ("the LORD has judged").

As in the case of judgment, the Hebrews see here also the general in the particular: any single act of deliverance may have huge ramifications as it symbolizes God's power and willingness to perform full-scale redemption.[16] Deliverance from the plague damage (2:18-27) anticipates God's end-time rescue of the covenant people (2:28–3:21 [MT 3:1–4:21]).

Theological Importance. In addition to striking portrayals both of the day of the Lord and of the compassionate nature of God, Joel teaches some valuable lessons about God's complete control of nature.[17] Nowhere does Joel hint that anyone or anything else is responsible for the locusts: they are God's army (2:11), dispatched and withdrawn by him (v. 20).[18] No dualism which would seek to attribute calamities to forces outside God's authority and no pantheism which would identify God with the creation find a place here. God is Lord over all and yet active in all.

For the Hebrews, God's creating and sustaining activity gave both unity and meaning to the reality around them. Shaped by God's touch and infused with divine power, the creation is both good and vital. Though appointed master over creation, humankind was not completely separated from it but enjoyed a certain kinship, for both were creatures of God. The sharp distinctions between animal and human, inanimate and animate were not rigidly maintained by the Hebrews. Thus a poet like Joel could describe the plights of thirsty fields and famished animals in quasi-human terms (see 1:10, 18-20; 2:21f.). This sense of the coherence and interrelatedness within creation means that judgment for human sin takes its toll on nature, while repentance and restoration bring not only forgiveness but prosperity and fertility (3:18 [MT 4:18]; see Amos 4:6-10; 9:13-15).

Joel's picture of Israel's hopeful future contains an element of responsibility as well as privilege. The outpouring of God's spirit upon the people will lay upon the redeemed remnant the weighty obligations of the prophetic office. None will be exempt — young or old, slave or free, male or female. 2:28f. (MT 3:f.)

This prophecy looks forward to fulfillment of Moses' ancient yearning:

> Would that all the LORD's people were prophets, that the Lord would put his spirit upon them! (Num. 11:29)

The Israelites are to pledge themselves to the covenant in unswerving obedience (cf. Jer. 31:31-34; Ezek. 36:27) and to embody and proclaim God's sovereign love (cf. Isa. 61:1).

Under the inspiration of the Spirit, Peter found in the miracle of Pentecost God's announcement that what Joel had foreseen was coming to pass in the infant Church (Acts 2:17-21). The messianic age discerned by Joel and others was at hand. The Church has been recruited to carry on the prophetic ministry and longs for the restoration of Jews to that service (see Rom. 11:24). Then Joel's and Obadiah's faith will have become sight, and the mission of both Israel and the Church fulfilled, when "the kingdom shall be the LORD's" (Obad. 21).

CHAPTER 27

Jonah

Every other prophetic book presents Yahweh's messages through the prophet to Israel.[1] The book of Jonah is unique in that it is an account of what happened to a prophet and not a collection of his messages. Since this book was placed in the canon among the prophets, we may conclude that the story of Jonah's experiences and reactions is the message. And the story involves much more than being swallowed by a fish.

> Who knows? God may relent and change his mind; he may turn from his fierce anger so that we do not perish. Jon. 3:9

Story of Jonah

Divine Command and Its Consequences. Jonah ben Amittai (Jon. 1:1) was a prophet who predicted the expansion of the northern kingdom in the reign of Jeroboam II, about 780 B.C. (2 Kgs. 14:25).[2] The book of Jonah tells nothing of his prophetic activity in Israel. It simply begins with the command of Yahweh to prophesy against wicked Nineveh. Instead of going east toward Assyria, Jonah boarded a ship bound for Tarshish — in the opposite direction,[3] "away from the presence of the LORD" (v. 3), as far away as the ancient mind could imagine.

Yahweh stirred up a storm that threatened shipwreck. The pagan sailors reacted by praying to their gods. The captain woke up sleeping Jonah and urged him to pray to his God. The sailors cast lots to determine the blame for the angry sea, and the lot pointed to Jonah. He confessed he was trying to get away from Yahweh, "who made the sea and the dry land" (v. 9), and urged them to throw him into the sea. They tried to row back to land, but finally agreed to throw Jonah overboard. The storm stopped, and they sacrificed to Yahweh and praised him. Yahweh "provided a large fish to swallow up Jonah" (v. 17). After "three days and three nights," during which Jonah sang a psalm of thanksgiving to God for saving him from drowning, the fish reached land, "and it spewed Jonah out" (2:10).

Second Command and Its Results. Yahweh gave Jonah a second chance, again commissioning him to go to Nineveh. This time Jonah went. The only words of his prophetic message recorded are these: "Forty days more, and Nineveh shall be overthrown!" (3:4). Surprisingly, "the people of Nineveh believed God" (v. 5). They and "the king of Nineveh" (v. 6) engaged in fasting, prayer, and repentance, to avert their doom. Yahweh duly relented.

Jonah was upset and angry. "Is this not what I said while I was still in my own country?" he complained to Yahweh. "That is why I fled to Tarshish at the beginning; for I knew that you are a gracious God and merciful, slow to anger, and abounding in steadfast love, and ready to relent from punishing" (4:2).[4] Then Jonah set up a shelter outside the city, sitting out the forty days. Yahweh appointed a plant, probably the castor bean (v. 6, NRSV mg.), which grew rapidly and protected Jonah from the sun. But the next day God sent a worm to kill the plant, and then a hot east wind that made Jonah wish he were dead. Yahweh drew the moral, contrasting Jonah's selfish concern for the plant and his own compassion for his creatures in Nineveh, "more than a hundred and twenty thousand persons who do not know their right hand from their left, and also many animals" (v. 11).[5]

Interpretation

History or story? That is the first question most readers pose. Former generations tended to understand the story of Jonah's book in a literal or historical sense. Modern scholarship, for a variety of reasons, has been more inclined to treat the story not as history but as some form of fiction.

The teaching value of a story does not necessarily depend on its historicity. Whether or not the details of the parable of the Good Samaritan (Luke 10:30-35) are historically accurate, or the event itself historical, the parable

Assyrian trading vessels transporting logs in a sea inhabited by serpents and
other creatures; alabaster relief from Khorsabad (721-695 B.C.).
(CNMHS/ARS, NT/SPADEM)

makes its point. Likewise, the story of Jonah could have been told simply to illustrate a lesson. Other factors must be examined to determine whether it was intended as a historical account.[6]

Historical Interpretation. The surface indications of the story lead naturally to the historical interpretation. Jonah ben Amittai actually lived in the days of Jeroboam II. The story is introduced in the standard message reception formula: "Now the word of the LORD came to Jonah . . ." (Jon. 1:1). The presentation is not in the form of a dream or a vision, but in a situation requiring Jonah to get up and go to Nineveh. The account of the storm, the sailors' reactions, their pagan practices, and even their surprising cries and sacrifices to Yahweh are told as historical events.

The incident of the "large fish" brings an exceptional feature into the story. Jesus spotlighted the story of Jonah in the belly of the fish for three days and nights as a "sign" of his own burial and (by implication) resurrection (Matt. 12:39f.). Those who hold to the historical interpretation of Jonah have argued that (1) Jesus placed this story on the same historical level as his own resurrection and (2) if the Jonah story is not true, then the resurrection of Jesus cannot be defended.

Again, Jonah's visit to Nineveh must be related to the words of Jesus: "The people of Nineveh will rise up at the judgment with this generation and condemn it, because they repented at the proclamation of Jonah, and see, something greater than Jonah is here!" (Matt. 12:41). In the same context, does not his mention of the visit of the queen of Sheba to Solomon suggest that the preaching of Jonah in Nineveh was on the same historical footing (Matt. 12:41f.; cf. Luke 11:29-32)?

Those who question the historical interpretation find several bases for challenging this position. First, exception has been taken to the incident of the "large fish." It has been debated whether a whale can swallow a human being. Could Jonah have survived for three days in the belly of the fish, without oxygen and exposed to gastric fluids?[7] If Jonah had been swallowed, would he have composed a psalm while in the fish's belly (2:1-9)?

According to 3:3, Nineveh was "an exceedingly large city," about sixty miles in diameter.[8] The location of Nineveh is known, and the walls have been partially excavated; it is not nearly that large. So some expositors have interpreted the passage as referring to "Greater Nineveh," including surrounding cities. It is more significant that Nineveh did not become a royal city until 700 B.C., when Sennacherib made it the capital of Assyria. Moreover, the story presupposes the Assyrian empire, which hardly impacted Israel between 800 B.C. and the 730s. The explicit verb used, "Now Nineveh *was*[9] an exceedingly large city," implies that the city no longer existed. If Jonah lived in the days of Jeroboam II (786-746), it is highly unlikely that he was still living to tell this story after the fall of Nineveh (612 B.C.).

It has also been argued that the details of Nineveh's repentance have no historical verification. In what language did Jonah preach? Had he learned Akkadian, did the people understand Hebrew, or did he use Aramaic, which was the language of trade and politics? There is no evidence outside the Bible that Nineveh ever underwent such religious conversion. So far as we know, the king of Assyria was never called "king of Nineveh" (3:6). For such reasons, the historical nature of the account is strongly challenged. Those who defend the historical character of the book have answered such objections point by point, with varying degrees of success.[10]

Mythological, Allegorical, and Parabolic Interpretations. Grouping these interpretations is not to suggest that they are the same, but rather that they view the general intent of the book as something other than historical.

(1) Myth. Myth seeks to present truth about human experience or natural origins (usually involving the gods) in a form that purports to be historical. In ancient myths, the struggle of humanity against nature, or even of nature itself with its seasons of seedtime and harvest, may be portrayed as a contest with a god or between gods. In Canaanite texts, Yamm (the Sea) was such a god, and a sea monster (here a large fish, but elsewhere Leviathan in Hebrew or *Lītān* in Ugaritic) was a hostile force. The name "Nineveh" also has been compared with the word for "fish" (cuneiform *Ninā*). Jonah's fish, however, was a rescuer, not an enemy. However, while elements in the story might be associated with mythic language, there is no clearly recognizable mythic plot. This view has fallen out of favor.

(2) Allegory. In allegory, a story is told to convey a message and most details contribute to the whole. Thus in Jesus' parable of the wheat and weeds (Matt. 13:37-43), the sower, seed, field, wheat, weeds, enemy, harvest, and reapers all have symbolic meaning. So here the name Jonah means "dove," a metaphor for Israel (Hos. 11:11; Ps. 74:19). Israel was disobedient and did not preach the truth to the gentile nations, symbolized by the attempt to sail to Tarshish; therefore Yahweh punished Israel with exile, illustrated by the swallowing up of Jonah. In the postexilic period, Israel only reluctantly witnessed to the gentiles, and never really understood the heart of Yahweh for the "Ninevites."

(3) Parable. A parable is a lifelike short story which embodies a moral or spiritual truth. Unlike the allegory it does not have meaning attached to every part. "All parables resemble a record of historical events. It is impossible to argue from the form of the book of Jonah that it must have been meant as a record of historical events."[11] A parable sometimes includes extraordinary features to encourage the hearer to listen to the message. The contrast between debts of ten thousand talents and a hundred denarii (Matt. 18:23-35) is an example. A parable may refer to a historical person. The nobleman in the parable of the pounds (Luke 19:11-27) was Archelaus, who went to Rome to get his succession to Herod confirmed.

Is the book of Jonah a similar "what if?" story? Then the book, taken as a parable (what the Hebrews might have called *māšāl;* see Proverbs), sets forth the unwillingness of "Jonah" — whether a person, the people of Israel, or any other group hearing the story — to see "Nineveh" spared, and his inability to understand the heart of Yahweh. Election by Yahweh had been selfishly interpreted as an end rather than a means, and the divine purpose, stated by Yahweh to Abraham, "that in you all the families of the earth shall be blessed" (Gen. 12:3), had been forgotten. The basic similarity of the allegorical and parabolic interpretations is obvious. The parabolic interpretation, since it is not forced to find a meaning for each detail, is preferable.

Which Interpretation Is Correct? No simple solution exists. The larger issue of our understanding of biblical inspiration will vitally affect our decision. Those who adopt the historical interpretation must recognize that fully satisfactory answers to the questions raised are not available. Selection of parabolic or religious-fiction interpretation necessitates coming to grips both with the extraordinary encounter with the fish (not a common episode as we usually find in parables) and with Jesus' use of Jonah in the Gospels. Those who subscribe to the authority of the Lord's words must study them carefully. They involve a reinterpretation of the basic story. Jonah was swallowed by the fish in order to rescue him from drowning and to bring him back to land. Jesus was playing off the contemporary Jewish understanding in giving it a negative force.[12] Was he echoing a popular story, as a preacher might by referring to an incident from *Pilgrim's Progress?*

The motivation for one's choice of interpretation is important. If one decides on the parabolic or symbolic interpretation solely because the miraculous element is offensive, then the decision is based on a modern a priori conclusion which, contrary to the biblical position, rejects God's supernatural intervention in history. Yet it is entirely possible to decide on grounds of literary form and content that the book is intended as a sort of parable.

A firm principle in biblical study is that, even in a clearly historical passage, the theological message is more important than historical details. The Bible was not written to satisfy curiosity about peoples and events in the ancient Near East. It was inspired by God's Spirit, with doctrinal, spiritual, and moral intent. As part of the biblical canon, Jonah must be studied with primary attention to the theological message. At this point the historical and parabolic interpretations come together, for either approach yields the same lesson: Yahweh is concerned about pagan peoples and commands his servants to proclaim his message to the nations.

Dating

There are some indications that the book in its present form emanates from the postexilic period. This dating does not rule out use of an older historical tradition and literary adaptation of it. The references to Nineveh and the presupposition of an Assyrian empire have been mentioned above. Nineveh's "wickedness" (1:2) features in the seventh-century book of Nahum, in 3:19 (NRSV "cruelty"). There seem to be deliberate echoes of Jeremiah and Joel in the book (see below). "Steadfast love" is normally a feature of Yahweh's covenant with Israel, but in 4:2 it is used to speak of his universal love for his creatures, as in psalms sometimes regarded as late (Pss. 33:5; 119:64; 145:9).

Structure

I. 1:1–2:10		A Hebrew sinner saved
A. 1:1-3		Jonah's disobedience
B. 1:4-16		Jonah's punishment and the pagan sailors' worship of Yahweh
C. 1:17–2:10		Jonah's rescue by Yahweh
	1:17	God's grace
	2:1-9	Jonah's praise
	2:10	God's last word
II. 3:1–4:11		Pagan sinners saved
D. 3:1-4		Jonah's obedience
E. 3:5-9		Nineveh's repentance
F. 3:10–4:11		Jonah's rebuke of Yahweh
	3:10	God's grace
	4:1-3	Jonah's complaint
	4:4-11	God's last word

The book falls into two parts. Their correspondence is shown in the outline above. The first and fourth (A./D.) of the six main episodes deal with Jonah's response to God's call. The second and fifth (B./E.) describe a social situation in which a pagan group under their leader appeal to God for help. In the third and sixth (C./F.) episodes Jonah is by himself and speaks with God.

The first half of the book has a preparatory role, to set up expectations for the reader which the second half will put to the test. It reveals God's grace to the disobedient prophet, which raises the possibility of grace for the sinful people of Nineveh. It also shows the pagan sailors in a good light, which predisposes the reader to accept the repentance of the Ninevites. Jonah, on the other hand, appears in a bad light in the first two episodes (A./B.), which encourages the reader to side against him in the second half of the story. The third and sixth episodes (C./F.) begin in the same way, "he prayed to the LORD" (2:1; 4:2), and shockingly parallel a song of thanksgiving with a disgruntled complaint.

Key words and phrases run through the book. "Nineveh, that great city" opens both halves of the book (1:2; 3:2), and occurs in a surprising climax at the end (4:11). Jonah's cry *(qārā')* of judgment for the Ninevites in the first and fourth episodes (A./D.; 1:2; 3:2, 4) is answered by their cries (*qārā'* again) in the fifth (E.; 3:5, 8), which are anticipated in the second episode (B; 1:6, 14). Nineveh's badness ("wickedness," 1:2) and bad ("evil") ways (3:8, 10) should logically lead to a bad end ("calamity," 3:10), but repentance averts it (3:8, 10), just as prayer averted the sailors' bad experience ("calamity," 1:7, 8). Jonah, however, takes this illogical development badly (finding it "displeasing," 4:1).

Message

Jonah makes two doctrinal statements about Yahweh, in 1:9 and 4:2. The first identifies Yahweh as the creator of the world, and several incidents in the book underline his power over creation. In the second he quotes a traditional proposition concerning God's love and mercy to the covenant people, in the form it takes in Joel 2:13, but he reapplies it to non-Israelites. The book is concerned with Yahweh's relationship to humanity (and animals, 4:11), beyond the people of Israel.

A strange feature for a prophetic narrative is the poor estimate it fosters of the prophet. He is an anti-hero, at cross purposes with Yahweh who sent him. His name conjures up animosity. He was a nationalistic prophet who foresaw expansion for the realm of wicked Jeroboam II (2 Kgs. 14:24-25), whereas Amos had nothing but criticism for his kingdom. In his tantrum he talks like Elijah (4:3; cf. 1 Kgs. 19:4), but lacks his greatness. So readers are conditioned to dislike Jonah's narrow views and enlarge their own theological horizon.

A context for the book may be provided by the eschatological, almost apocalyptic, prophetic literature, such as the book of Joel, which spoke of the destruction of the nations.[13] The book of Jonah accepts the validity of such prophecies, but argues from Jer. 18:1-11 (Jer. 18:8 is echoed in 3:10) that

Yahweh is not obliged to carry them out. The factor of openness to God, so important for Israel in Joel 2:14 (echoed in Jonah 3:9; cf. 1:14, 16), could hold off the judgment of the nations.

From the perspective of creation theology (1:9) the book urges a balanced view of the nations and their destiny. John 3:16 starts here: God so loves the world.

Coming Around

And Jonah stalked
    to his shaded seat
    and waited for God
      to come around
      to his way of thinking.

And God is still waiting
    for a host of Jonahs
    to come around
    to his way of loving.[14]

CHAPTER 28

Haggai

On 12 October 539 B.C., the army of Cyrus the Great entered Babylon and brought the Babylonian empire to an end. World dominion thus passed from East to West,[1] from the Semitic Babylonian empire to the Indo-European Medo-Persian empire. Just as the Israelites testified that their God, Yahweh, helped them win battles during the conquest, Cyrus claimed in his victory cylinder to have the patron god of Babylon on his side. "Without any battle [Marduk] made [Cyrus] enter his town Babylon, sparing Babylon any calamity."[2] The Nabonidus chronicle likewise records a conflict-free takeover: "On the sixteenth day . . . the troops of Cyrus without fighting entered Babylon."[3] Since the last Babylonian kings had been oppressive and since Cyrus had a reputation for being more benevolent, the people did not resist his invasion. Rather they welcomed him joyously.[4]

One of the more unpopular acts of Nabonidus, the last Babylonian king, had been to bring the gods of Sumer and Akkad to the capital. Cyrus quickly returned them "to dwell in peace in their habitations."[5] Consistent with this policy of restoring gods to their homes, in 538 Cyrus allowed the Jews to return to their land to rebuild the Jerusalem temple with Persian funds, so that their God, Yahweh, would once again have a house in which to live (see Ezra 1:1-4; 6:3-5).[6]

Historical Situation

The Return. One might suppose that the Jews, who had been in exile in Babylonia for fifty years or more (from 605 or 597 or 586 to 538), would be more than anxious to return "home." However, following Jeremiah's advice, they had settled in Babylonia, built houses, planted gardens, married, and raised families (Jer. 29:4-9). Some became very successful in business. Children born in exile were now more than fifty years old, with children and grandchildren of their own. Not all wanted to tear up established roots and go back to a land they had never known. Yet some fifty thousand did return initially (Ezra 2:64; Neh. 7:66), and others followed under Zerubbabel (520?; see note 11), Ezra (458),[7] and Nehemiah (445). A sizable Jewish community remained in Babylon for centuries, becoming a center of Jewish scholarship and producing, among other things, the Babylonian Talmud, a collection of Jewish religious instruction. Therefore the return in 538 included only a fraction of the exiles.

A New "Exodus"? Although the books of the prophets (especially Isaiah's) had spoken of a deliverance by the Lord in terms reminiscent of the Exodus, the regathering of the exiles was quite different. No miracles attended their emigration such as plagues or the splitting of a sea. As far as we know they were not fed with manna from heaven or supplied supernaturally with water. Sheshbazzar, the descendant of David who led them back, was no Moses with divine might. The land had been ravaged; Jerusalem still lay in ruins, little

Darius I (521-486 B.C.), seated, with Crown Prince Xerxes behind him; relief from Persepolis. *(Oriental Institute, University of Chicago)*

having been done to restore it. As a result, glorious expectations were frustrated by a harsh reality.[8]

Sheshbazzar and Zerubbabel. The first band of exiles was led by Sheshbazzar son of Jehoiachin,[9] who was the last Judean monarch.[10] Cyrus appointed Sheshbazzar governor of Judah and allowed him to return the temple vessels which Nebuchadnezzar had removed (Ezra 1:7). When he and his band of Jews, including leaders from Judah and Benjamin, priests, and Levites (Ezra 1:5), reached Jerusalem sometime in 538, they did not succeed in their objective. They attempted to rebuild the temple but accomplished little more than laying the foundation (Ezra 6:16). That is all we know about the first return. Our sources are silent about Sheshbazzar's fate and about events which followed.

A second wave of exiles arrived in Judah under the leadership of Zerubbabel.[11] He was also a Davidide (grandson of Jehoiachin and nephew of Sheshbazzar)[12] and governor of Judah. Joshua (sometimes spelled "Jeshua") son of Jehozadak was the high priest. In this crucial time, God raised up two prophets: Haggai and Zechariah (Ezra 5:1). It was largely through their work that the temple was rebuilt.

Haggai and His Message

> And the LORD stirred up the spirit of Zerubbabel son of Shealtiel, governor of Judah, and the spirit of Joshua son of Jehozadak the high priest and the spirit of all the remnant of the people. And they came and worked on the house of the LORD of hosts, their God. Hag. 1:14

The Prophet. Very little is known about Haggai. On the basis of Hag. 2:3 some have supposed that Haggai had seen the former temple, but the verse will not support this interpretation. His name comes from Heb. *ḥag,* meaning "festival" (note the Latin name *Festus*). The presence of priestly teaching in 2:11-14 does not prove that the prophet was also a priest.

The Chronology. The book of Haggai contains six date formulae. Four are attached to prophecies while two (1:15a and 2:18) are connected to temple construction. The book of Zechariah (see Ch. 29 below) has three dates. Since the two prophets were contemporaries, the following table includes dates for both with the modern equivalents.[13]

Reference	Day	Month	Year of Darius	Julian Calendar
Hag. 1:1	1	6	2	29 Aug. 520
Hag. 1:15a	24	6	—	21 Sept. [520]
Hag 1:15b–2:1	21	7	2	17 Oct. 520
Zech. 1:1	—	8	2	Oct./Nov. 520
Hag. 2:10	24	9	2	18 Dec. 520
Hag. 2:18	24	9	—	18 Dec. [520]
Hag. 2:20	24	9	—	18 Dec. [520]
Zech. 1:7	24	11	2	15 Feb. 519
Zech. 7:1	4	9	4	7 Dec. 518

Editorial Considerations. All of the above dates head up prophetic sections except Hag. 1:15a and 2:18. For this reason some scholars argue that 1:15a once introduced oracular material which has been lost. Others claim that it has not been lost, only moved by a redactor to a later position. Commentators remark that Hag. 2:15-19 does not provide a logical conclusion to 2:10-14. Because it mentions the laying of the temple's foundation, and because the inception of rebuilding activity comes immediately before 1:15a, it (2:15-19) should be transposed after 1:15a. In addition, those who rearrange the text this way usually identify "this people" and "this nation," whose sacrifices are unclean 2:14, with the Samaritans. Ezra 4:1-5 is cited as corroborating witness. There the local population, thought by some to be the progenitors of the Samaritans,[14] are rejected from assisting in the construction of Yahweh's house. Finally, to make everything consistent, 2:18 must be dropped or emended to "the twenty-fourth day of the *sixth* [not ninth] month" to force agreement with 1:15a.[15]

However, such reconstructions are unnecessary, for the text of Haggai makes better sense in its present order. Hag. 1:15a forms a proper finish to 1:12-14, revealing how quickly the people responded; there is no reason why a date must *introduce* a message. Hag. 2:15-19 supplies an apt conclusion to the preceding priestly teaching (2:10-14; see following comments on the third message). The term "this people" in 1:2 refers to the Jews; so also in 2:14. Lastly, if 2:15-19 is left where it is, the date in 2:18 agrees with 2:10 and therefore needs no correction.

The First Message. The first message (1:1-11) was addressed to Zerubbabel, the governor, and to Joshua, the high priest. It was a call to finish building the temple. Work on Yahweh's house, which began under Sheshbazzar, had by now ceased. The people's excuse was that it was not yet time to engage in temple construction. They were busy building their own "paneled houses" (1:4). Suffering drought and economic hardship (1:6, 10-11), they felt they needed to care for themselves first. Haggai rebuked them for their wrong priorities, crediting their crop failures to their disregard for Yahweh's house. The prophet was challenging the people to put God first by building his house before their own and thus to regain God's blessing. The Lord filled them with hope, promising to "appear in his glory" (NRSV, "be honored"; 1:8) and to be with them (1:13). The message was instantly obeyed by Zerubbabel, Joshua, and the remnant of the people (1:12). They made preparations, gathered materials, and resumed work on the temple three weeks later. Within another week they had erected an altar and restored the sacrificial worship, although the temple's foundation was not yet laid (Ezra 3:1-6).[16]

The Second Message. The second oracle (Hag. 2:1-9) came about a month later to encourage them. It, too, was addressed to the governor, the high priest, and the remnant (2:2). Disappointment had set in as some compared their simple structure with the glory of the former temple (2:3; cf. Ezra 3:12 and Zech. 4:10). In words reminiscent of God's charge to Joshua the son of Nun before the conquest (Josh. 1:5-7), the "new" Joshua (the son of Jehozadak), Zerubbabel, and the people are told to take courage because of the divine presence, reminiscent of that in the Exodus (Hag. 2:4-5; Exod. 33:14). The message climaxes in an eschatological promise: I will shake the heavens and the earth. . . . I will shake all the nations, and the treasures[17] of all the nations will come in, and I will fill this house with glory, says the LORD of Hosts"[18] (2:6-7, NAB). Yahweh reminds his hearers that the silver and gold are his, and promises that "the glory of the present house will exceed that of the former house" (2:9, NIV).

The Third Message. Before Haggai gave his next prophecy, Zechariah delivered his first (Zech. 1:1-6), in November or December, calling the people to repentance. Haggai's third message (2:10-19), a month or so later, underscored this need (2:17). Questioning the priests, one of whose tasks was to answer questions on the specific interpretation of the law, Haggai draws out the truth that uncleanness is more contagious than holiness. A garment carrying holy meat will not sanctify things it touches, while people defiled by contact with a dead body will contaminate things they touch. Haggai concludes from this that although animal sacrifice had been restored, the people and the sacrifices they had been offering were unclean (2:14). Apparently the sin of the people was so strong that it actually polluted the sacrifice rather than being removed by it. What was their sin? They had failed to lay the foundation of the temple (2:15). For this reason, Yahweh had been afflicting the land with diminished produce (2:16-17). Repentance, literally "return," was required (2:17; cf. Amos 4:17 for a similar indictment). Fortunately, Haggai's message coincided with the day the foundation was laid (2:18),[19] which explains why it ends on a positive note from the Lord: "From this day on I will bless you" (2:19).

Dated Events of the Years 539-515

12 Oct.	539 (16 Teshritu)	Fall of Babylon; accession year of Cyrus
24 Mar.	538 (1 Nisanu)	First year of reign of Cyrus (Dan. 5:31?)
	538	Edict permitting Jews to return to Jerusalem (Ezra 1:1)
? May	538	Departure of Sheshbazzar and group for Jerusalem[22]
Sept.	538 (7th month)	Arrival at Jerusalem (3:1)
10 Apr.	537 (2/-/YC 2)	Work begun on altar (v. 8)
	537 (?)	Work on temple halted until days of Darius (4:5)
16 Jan.	535 (1/24/YC 3)	Daniel's vision (Dan. 10:1)
29 Aug.	520 (6/1/YD 2)	First message to Haggai (Hag. 1:1)
21 Sept.	520 (6/24/YD 2)	Work resumed on temple (v. 15)
17 Oct.	520 (7/21/YD 2)	Second message to Haggai (2:1)
27 Oct.	520 (8/1?/YD 2)	Message to Zechariah (Zech. 1:1)
18 Dec.	520 (9/24/YD 2)	Third, fourth messages to Haggai (Hag. 2:10, 20)
15 Feb.	519 (24 Shebat)	Message to Zechariah (Zech. 1:7)
7 Dec.	518 (9/4/YD 4)	Message to Zechariah (7:1)
12 Mar.	515 (3 Adar/YD 6)	Temple is finished (Ezra 6:15)
21 Apr.	515 (14 Nisan/YD 6)	Passover is held (v. 19)

(YC = Year of Cyrus; YD = Year of Darius)

The Fourth Message. Haggai addressed his final oracle (2:20-23) to Zerubbabel (v. 21) on the same day as his third. The fourth message is similar to the second with its promise that the Lord will "shake the heavens and the earth" (2:6, 21). However, here Yahweh amplifies it: "I am about to . . . overthrow the thrones of kingdoms" (2:21-22); such language concerns the end time. He also focuses it on the Davidide line: "I will take you, O Zerubbabel my servant, . . . and make you like a signet ring; for I have chosen you" (2:23). This language is clearly messianic.[20] The term "signet ring" particularly symbolizes royal authority. Jeremiah had used it to condemn Jehoiachin and his descendants (Jer. 22:24-30). Now through Haggai, God offered hope to Zerubbabel, a descendant of Jehoiachin, that the negative word was to be overturned. The prophecy of Zechariah provided further support for burgeoning messianic expectations, especially for those who looked to Zerubbabel, a branch from David's tree (Isa. 11:1; Zech. 3:8; 6:12).

Besides stimulating this hope, the greater effect of the prophecies of Haggai and Zechariah was to encourage the nation, its governor, its high priest, and the remnant of the people to finish rebuilding the temple. They accomplished their task in 515 (Ezra 6:14-15). Known in Jewish terminology as "the Second Temple," this one was never replaced by a third.[21]

Relevance for Other Times

The Problem. The Old Testament is considered part of the Christian scriptures. Yet how can Haggai, with its emphasis on rebuilding the Jerusalem temple, speak to the church worldwide? Indeed, how can it concern any generation other than the one engaged in the reconstruction? After it was built, certainly no other generation of Jews needed encouragement to build it. Although it was destroyed again in A.D. 70, there is no reason to rebuild it again in the light of the teachings in the epistle to the Hebrews (see esp. 9:11–10:22). How can one draw a lesson from Haggai that is relevant today?

Some Possible Applications. Haggai testifies to the importance of worshiping God in ways God himself ordains. In Old Testament times, Yahweh gave the people a sacrificial system of worship. It provided them with atonement for sin and fellowship with God. The preexilic prophets who denounced the temple did not contradict that fact; they appear not to have been opposed to the cult *per se* but to its misuse and corruption.[23] The book of Haggai should not be devalued because its teaching is bound up with a building. The temple was where God especially chose to meet with his people. Ezekiel described its rebuilding (chs. 40–48), and Haggai announced the appropriate time. God required that his people approach him in the temple with the blood of animals; he now requires that we draw near through the blood of Christ (Heb. 10:19-23). Obedience is not optional.

Haggai taught also the importance of putting God first. For Haggai that involved physical activity, producing something material: the temple. But it was also a spiritual activity, for the Lord had stirred up those who participated (1:14). God promised that they would prosper who put him first. While the kingdom of God cannot be identified with a material building, still those who pursue it may at times find themselves involved in construction projects. The book of Haggai is a reminder that God sometimes used material things such as buildings for spiritual ends. More importantly, Jesus taught, like the prophet, that those who put God's kingdom and righteousness before their own material needs, will find those goods supplied as well (Matt. 6:25-33).

Toward the end of the Old Testament period, prophetic activity dimin-

Exilic and Postexilic Prophets and Their World

	Prophet	Judah	Babylonia	Egypt	Persia	Notable Events
600	Jeremiah	Jehoiakim 608-597	Nebuchadnezzar 605-562	Neco II 610-595		Fall of Jerusalem 15/16 Mar. 597
	Ezekiel	Jehoiachin				Ration tablets of
595		597		Psamtik 11		Jehoiachin, 10th-
	Daniel	Zedekiah		595-589		35th yrs of
590		597-586		Apries (Hophra) 589-570		Nebuchadnezzar Pharaoh failed to help Judah
585						Destruction of Jerusalem
580						12 Aug. 586
575						
570				Amasis 570-525		
565			Evil-merodach 562-560			
560			Neriglissar 560-556 Labashi-Marduk Nabonidus		Cyrus king of Anshan 559	Jehoiachin set free
555			556-539			
550						
545						
540			Last king of			Fall of Babylon
		Sheshbazzar returns 538	Babylon		Cyrus 539-530	Cyrus enters Babylon 12 Oct. 539, "Year 1" Rebuilding temple begins 537
535						
530				Psamtik III	Cambyses	
525				Cambyses	530-522	
520	Haggai Zechariah			Darius I	Darius I 522-486	Work on temple resumed
515						Completed 10 Mar. 516
510						
500	Joel(?)					
480				Xerxes I	Xerxes I 480-465	
465				Artaxerxes I	Artaxerxes I 464-423	
	Malachi					
458		Ezra				
445		Nehemiah 445-423				

ished, but faith did not die. In fact, there was fervent hope that the Lord would fulfill the promises he had made through the prophets. Jewish authors produced a number of apocalyptic writings, and several Jewish sects (like the Qumran community) arose which had distinctive messianic hopes and interpretations. At the time of Jesus' birth, according to the New Testament, devout Jews were looking for the Messiah, and some believed that the infant Jesus was this hoped-for One. Haggai, along with Zechariah and Malachi, was to some degree responsible for this messianic expectation. The language of Haggai makes clear that the rebuilding was in some way to be related to the promise of the coming Redeemer. Some Jews of that period doubtless read more into Haggai's words than unfolding history would support: Zerubbabel was not the Messiah.[24] In fact, for reasons unknown, he fades from the biblical record after the completion of the temple (except for the mention in Jesus' genealogy; Matt. 1:12-13; Luke 3:27). Yet the rebuilding of the temple was a reminder of God's promised redemption and a sign of the people's faith in that promise.[25] Haggai, then, has meaning for today and every age, until all biblical hopes are realized.[26]

The Second Temple Period

Political Scene. Under the Persians (539-331), Judah was part of the satrapy known as "Beyond the River," i.e., the region beyond the Euphrates (from the Persian vantage point). Standard Persian policy was to grant considerable home rule. Therefore, the Jews were allowed their own local governor (but not a king), responsible to the high Satrap, the provincial Persian governor. With the conquest of Persia by Alexander the Great and the subsequent division of his empire among his successors (the *Diadochoi* in Greek), Palestine came first under Egyptian (Ptolemeian) rule and then under the Seleucid dynasty, which was centered in Syria. During this period the Near East was considerably Hellenized, and Judah was not exempt. Certain Seleucid rulers were zealous to extend this influence, and under Antiochus IV Epiphanes (175-164) to destroy the Jewish religion by polluting the temple. Reaction was swift, led by the Hasmonean family (the Maccabees), and for about eighty years the Jews had "independence" under Hasmonean rule (142-63), until Pompey (106-48) claimed Palestine for Rome. A nominal Jewish kingdom was permitted by the Romans under Herod the Great (37-4), and to a greatly limited extent under other Herodian rulers. With the Jewish revolt and the destruction of the temple in A.D. 70, followed by the Bar Kochba revolt in 132-135,[27] the end came to Jerusalem Judaism.

Jewish Developments. During the second temple period, Jews lived not only in Judah but in the Diaspora, or dispersion: Babylon, Egypt, and quite likely other places. Jeremiah refers to the Jews in Egypt (Jer. 44:1), and the Aramaic papyri from Elephantine (on the Nile near the Aswan dam) indicate a sizable community there. Alexandria became especially important as a Jewish center. From there came the Greek translation of the Old Testament (the LXX). Synagogues developed as places of prayer, religious training, and worship for Jews who no longer had access to the Jerusalem temple.[28] However, by New Testament times they were located in Palestine, including Jerusalem itself, even though the temple was available.

Jewish sects, notably the Sadducees, Pharisees, and Essenes (among others), also emerged at this time. Of course, Judaism was never monolithic. Christianity itself began as a Jewish sect. Even today, Judaism is diverse and complex. However, the party that most shaped its development after the destruction of the second temple was the Pharisees, hence the term "Pharisaic Judaism," which is sometimes called "Rabbinic Judaism," or "Normative Judaism."[29] Their teachings were preserved mainly in the Mishnah.[30] Other sectarian literature can be found in editions of the "Apocrypha"[31] and "Pseudepigrapha,"[32] and the Qumran writings.[33] As for the Old Testament canon, it probably achieved its final shape sometime in the first century A.D.

Summary of the Period. Haggai was the prophet to open this period of the foundations of Judaism, although others — the prophets Zechariah and Malachi, the scribe Ezra, and Nehemiah, the governor — made valuable contributions. The Jews returned to their homeland, but things were different from what they had been in earlier Old Testament history. On the one hand, the offices of priest and scribe were enhanced as a greater need arose for teaching and copying the law. On the other hand, the prophetic office grew weaker, and hopes of a Davidic king, for the most part, either disappeared or were projected to the future in apocalyptic fashion. The community survived the political and sociological pressures of the Second Commonwealth by centering itself on the temple and the Torah, not the monarchy. In the words of Hosea, Israel indeed dwelled "many days without king or prince" (Hos. 3:4).

CHAPTER 29

Zechariah

The return from exile in Babylonia sparked joy in the hearts of the Israelites. But it also prompted anxiety. Would they be safe in their own land or would enemies old and new harass them again? Had God really forgiven them or would he continue their punishment? Would they remain faithful to God or fall back into the sins of their ancestors? What kind of leadership would they have now that their monarchy had been obliterated? How were they to live godly lives in circumstances so drastically changed from what they had known before the Exile? What would God's ultimate future hold for his people and the other nations? To these and other gnawing questions God raised up Zechariah to give answers.

The dates given in Zechariah's prophecy[1] show it to be contemporary with Haggai (for historical background, see the closing section of Ch. 28). The book is a product of the postexilic era, distinctly different from preexilic prophetic works. These points are essential to a reliable picture of the historical nature of this revelatory work.

> Thus says the LORD of hosts: Here is a man whose name is Branch: for he shall branch out in his place, and he shall build the temple of the LORD. It is he that shall build the temple of the LORD; he shall bear royal honor, and shall sit and rule on his throne. There shall be a priest by his throne, with peaceful understanding between the two of them. Zech. 6:12-13

Introduction

The Prophet. Zechariah's name means "Yah[weh] remembers" or "Yah[weh] has remembered." Was he "the son of Iddo" as recorded in Ezra (5:1; 6:14) or "the son of Berechiah, the son of Iddo" as in Zechariah (1:1)? It may be that the prophet Zechariah became confused with Zechariah the son of Jeberechiah of Isa. 8:2 with shortening of the name from Jeberechiah to Berechiah.[2] In that case we might follow Ezra — he was the son of Iddo. However, the Hebrew word "son" can mean "descendant." This would remove the difficulty: Zechariah was indeed the son, i.e., grandson, of Iddo (Ezra 5:1; 6:14) but his father was Berechiah (Zech. 1:1). Nehemiah also lists a priest named Zechariah from the family of Iddo (Neh. 12:16). If this is the same Zechariah, he was probably a priest as well as a prophet — but we cannot be sure. Beyond these few bits of information, little else is known. One thing is certain: Zechariah played a key role, along with Haggai, in rousing the elders under Zerubbabel the governor and Joshua the high priest to complete the rebuilding of the temple (Ezra 5:1-2; 6:14).

Problems of Authorship. The book divides clearly into two parts. Chs. 1–8 are dated prophecies, largely in the form of visions along with some oracles. They are situated in the Persian period and concerned with the rebuilding of the temple under the leadership of Joshua and Zerubbabel. In contrast, chs. 9–14 contain no dated prophecies or "night visions" and exhibit a markedly different style. Nothing is said about the rebuilding of the temple. As for leadership, instead of Joshua and Zerubbabel who are in divine favor, we find anonymous "shepherds" who fall under God's judgment. It seems that the two parts should probably be distinguished,[3] and may come from different hands and periods.[4] Of the first eight chapters it has been said: "There is every reason to believe that basically these are the authentic words of the prophet, possibly arranged in their present order by Zechariah himself, but more probably collected and edited shortly after his day."[5] The remainder of the book is more puzzling.

Historically, some have considered chs. 9–14 to be preexilic. This idea may have originated because Zech. 11:12-13 is quoted in Matt. 27:9-10 as a prophecy of Jeremiah. For this reason some in times past have attributed part or all of Zech. 9–14 to Jeremiah. The prediction of Israel's return from exile, the mention of Assyria and Egypt as its enemies, and the mention of the continued existence of Ephraim, the northern Israelite kingdom, also suggest a preexilic date. However, the book gives no indication that Jeremiah contributed anything, and the historical references are so general that they can be fitted into almost any period. Therefore, the preexilic theory enjoys little support today.[6]

More common is the view that chs. 9–14 are postexilic. Some assign these chapters to a single anonymous author, "Deutero-Zechariah" or "Second Zechariah,"[7] while others divide the collection, attributing parts to two or more authors. Dating ranges from the sixth to the second centuries. Some who divide it may date different sections to different centuries. A few point to the Hellenistic era because of the mention of the Greeks in 9:13, but the Greeks were present in the ancient Near East long before the fourth century.[8]

The biblical text yields some evidence as to how it was compiled. Three times the word *maśśa'*, "oracle," heads up a section at the end of the Book of the Twelve (Minor Prophets): Zech. 9:1; 12:1; Mal. 1:1. Since "Malachi" means "my messenger" and may be a title, not a proper name, the book may be anonymous. If so, there are three anonymous collections of prophecies found together (Zech. 9–11; 12–14; Malachi). Perhaps they circulated independently at one time, only to be later brought together and added to the end of the prophetic corpus. Ultimately, the first two of the collections were added to the book of Zechariah while the last was left to stand on its own.

Why was this done? First of all "Malachi" came to be construed as a proper name. Secondly, it was desirable to have a total of twelve prophetic works because of the twelve tribes of Israel. Finally, whereas the first two collections are tied together by some common themes, the author of Malachi is "a person characteristically different from 'Deutero-Zechariah.'"[9] While this sketch of development is not certain, what scholarship has demonstrated with reasonable certainty is the difficulty of holding to a single author.[10]

Zech. 1–8

Structure. These chapters exhibit an elaborate design. Clearly they were fashioned by a skillful literary artisan (see chart, pp. 404-5). First, we notice that there are three parts, each introduced by a date formula.[11] Part I is simple and brief, recording a call to repentance and the obedient response of the people.

Part II is more complex. It comprises eight visions intertwined with various oracles. The First and Eighth Visions are connected by the common theme of patrolling the earth (horses of four colors/four chariots). The Second and Seventh are similar because both visions have two symbols which are interpreted (four horns and four smiths/an ephah and a woman inside it). The Third and Sixth have in common a formal element: an attached concluding oracle (Yahweh will be Jerusalem's walls/Yahweh will send forth the scroll). The Fourth and Fifth Visions are united by the theme of the two chosen leaders,

Joshua and Zerubbabel.[12] There are also correspondences between the Second and Third visions; and the Sixth and Seventh Visions. The former pair share a concern for Jerusalem (casting down its enemies/repopulating and defending it). The latter are joined by the theme of purification (punishing sinners/removing sin). There is also movement within the progression of visions from the whole earth (1st) to the nations, Judah, and Jerusalem (2nd and 3rd) to the two leaders (4th and 5th) and back again to the whole land (6th and 7th) and ultimately to the whole earth (8th).[13] The oracles all focus on Jerusalem and are an integral part of the structure.

Part III contains four sections. Each is introduced by the "message-reception formula" (with some variations) "the word of Yahweh of hosts came to me saying." This section of the book opens with a question regarding fasting. Sections 1 and 4 are tied together by that theme while Sections 2 and 3 both contain exhortations to keep the law.

Finally, each part moves to a climactic conclusion: (1) repentance (1:6); (2) the dispersed Jews return to rebuild the temple (6:15); (3) foreign people join in the Jerusalem worship (8:20-23). This represents a widening of God's grace from the Jews nearby to the Jews far off and at last to Gentiles.

Interpretation. Part I (Zech. 1:1-6). Chs. 1–8 begin in Jerusalem in 520, with the problems of rebuilding the temple. Through the prophet Haggai, the Lord had already stirred up the people to begin construction (Hag. 1:14-15). That was in the sixth month of Darius' second year. In the seventh month the people seemed to experience some discouragement. Comparisons with the former temple were disheartening (Hag. 2:3; Zech. 4:10). Both prophets responded. In the eighth month Zechariah pled for repentance (Zech. 1:1-6). In the ninth month, Haggai urged them to return to the Lord by performing the ceremony for laying the foundation (Hag. 2:10-19).[14]

Part II. Zechariah's visions (Zech. 1:7–6:15) are dated to the eleventh month. The First Vision (see outline, above) notes that the earth is at rest. This probably refers to the period after Darius consolidated his power by quelling various revolts throughout the Persian empire. The First Oracle raises the question about Yahweh's seventy-year indignation over Jerusalem and Judah (1:12). God expresses anger with the nations because they "made the disaster worse" (v. 15) and determines to deal with Jerusalem in compassion by seeing the temple and city rebuilt (1:16-17). The mentions of anger at the Gentiles, blessing on Jerusalem, and a measuring line (1:16) anticipate the next two visions.

The "four horns" of the Second Vision are nations that "scattered Judah, Israel, and Jerusalem" (v. 19 [MT 2:2]). The "four smiths" are avengers who will cast down those nations (v. 21 [MT 2:4]). In the Third Vision Zechariah sees a man with a measuring line. However, it is unnecessary to measure Jerusalem for walls. Yahweh will repopulate the city and protect it. The Second Oracle entreats the exiles to come home while continuing the themes of

The Structure of Zechariah 1–8

Part I 1:1-6

Date Formula	"In the eighth month, in the second year of Darius" (1:1)
Oracle	1:2-6 call to repentance
Climax:	1:6 They repented and accepted what God had done

Part II 1:7–6:15

Date Formula	"On the twenty-fourth day of the eleventh month, the month of Shebat, in the second year of Darius" (1:7)
First Vision	1:8-11 patrolling horses of four colors; earth is at rest
First Oracle	1:12-17 anger at nations; temple to be rebuilt; measuring line stretched over Jerusalem; cities prosperous; Jerusalem comforted and chosen
Second Vision	1:18-21 (a) four horns = nations which have scattered Judah, Israel, and Jerusalem; (b) four smiths = those who will terrify and cast down the horns/nations
Third Vision	2:1-4 man with measuring line to measure Jerusalem; Oracle within: 2:5 Jerusalem will be abundantly inhabited; no walls needed: Yahweh will be a wall of fire without and glory within
Second Oracle	2:6-13 call to return to the land from the north, from the four winds; Jews will plunder enemies; many nations will join; Jerusalem chosen
Fourth Vision	3:1-10 The Satan accuses; Joshua the high priest cleansed; God will bring his servant the Branch (Zerubbabel); guilt removed in a day; peace and prosperity
Fifth Vision	4:1-6a, 10b-14 two anointed ones (Joshua and Zerubbabel?)
Third Oracle	4:6b-10a Zerubbabel will complete the temple
Sixth Vision	5:1-3 flying scroll = curse over whole earth (or all the land): thieves and false swearers cut off; Oracle within: 5:4 Yahweh will send it forth
Seventh Vision	5:5-11 a. ephah going forth = iniquity; b. woman inside = wickedness; two women with wings take woman in ephah to Shinar (Babylon) where they build a temple for it and set it on its base
Eighth Vision	6:1-8 four patrolling chariots and horses; spirit of angel (God?) at rest in north
Fourth Oracle	6:9-14 crowns, Joshua crowned, Branch who will build temple will rule on a throne next to priest; crowns in temple
Climax:	6:15 Far off ones will come to build the temple, if there is obedience

Part III   7:1–8:23

Date Formula	"In the fourth year of King Darius, the word of Yahweh came to Zechariah on the fourth day of the ninth month, which is Chislev" (7:1)
Introduction	7:2-3 question regarding fasting
Section 1	7:4-7 Oracle Formula 7:4 "Then the word of Yahweh of hosts came to me";
	7:5-7 fasting motive questioned
Section 2	7:8-14 Oracle Formula 7:8 "The word of Yahweh came to Zechariah, saying"
	7:9-14 they should keep the law; the Exile came as a result of breaking the law
Section 3	8:1-17 Oracle Formula 8:1 "The word of Yahweh of hosts came to me, saying"
	8:2-17 God will bring his people back from exile to Jerusalem and will prosper it again; therefore they should keep the law
Section 4	8:18-23 Oracle Formula 8:18 "The word of Yahweh of hosts came to me, saying"
	8:18-19 fasts of 4th, 5th, 7th, and 10th months will become feasts of joy and gladness
Climax:	8:20-23 Many people from many nations will come to seek Yahweh in Jerusalem, acknowledging that God is with the Jews

comfort for the Jews and punishment on the nations. But there is something new: the promise that foreigners will one day be numbered among Yahweh's people (2:11).

In the Fourth Vision Joshua the high priest appears with the Angel of Yahweh. "The Satan" ("The Adversary"; NRSV note) is present also. The use of the definite article shows that "Satan" is not understood as a proper name yet but as a title. His role is that of a prosecuting attorney before the heavenly court, in this instance accusing Joshua. Since he is rebuked by God, he is clearly not understood as a good force. However, neither is he the thoroughly evil creature found in later biblical writings. Joshua is purified. Next Yahweh's servant "the Branch" is introduced (3:8). The Branch symbolizes a Davidic descendant who will bring salvation (Jer. 23:5; 33:15; Isa. 4:2; 11:1).[15] Since Zech. 6:12 indicates that the Branch will build the temple and since we know from history and from Zech. 4:9 that Zerubbabel, a descendant of David (Davidide), accomplished that, Zerubbabel must have been in view. The stone (3:9) must be connected with the building of the temple in some way. Removal of guilt (3:9) anticipates the Sixth and Seventh Visions. This Fourth Vision

Tripod lampstand, an image
related to Zerubbabel's
completion of the temple
in Zechariah's fifth
vision (4:1-14).
*(Oriental Institute,
University of Chicago)*

shows how carefully the leaders of the return were following the prophecies of Ezekiel (37:24-28; 44:1-31; 45:1-6) and Jeremiah (33:14-18). Both prophets agree that in the restoration the government should be a dyarchy (two leaders) headed by a Zadokite priest and a Davidide.

The Fifth Vision of the lampstand and olive trees is interrupted by the Third Oracle dealing with Zerubbabel's completion of the temple (4:6b-10a), including the divine word: "not by might, nor by power, but by my Spirit" (4:6). The future establishment of Jerusalem is not the fruit of human effort alone. The two olive trees are the two "anointed ones" who stand by the Lord (4:14).[16] From the context, this could hardly indicate any two other than Joshua and Zerubbabel.

The next two visions are connected to the earlier promise that guilt would be removed (3:9). The flying scroll (5:1) of the Sixth Vision represents a curse which is to be pronounced on the thief and on the one who swears falsely (5:3-4). In the Seventh Vision the ephah symbolizes iniquity (5:6) and the woman inside symbolizes wickedness (5:8). These will be transferred to "the land of Shinar" (5:11), which is Babylonia, as a purification of Israel and corruption of Babylonia.[17]

Finally, the four chariots and horses (6:1-8) go forth to patrol the earth in the Eighth Vision.[18] It is the black ones who head north and "set my Spirit at rest in the north country" (6:8). Since in the previous prophets the "north country" is the source of invasions into Israel and Judah, this figure may imply that the patrols had made an end to such aggression and set God's Spirit at rest. More specifically, it explains why Persia, the current northern power, allowed the Jews to rebuild Yahweh's house.[19] The Lord had decreed it.

This vision is followed by the Fourth Oracle. Crowns[20] are fashioned, yet only Joshua is crowned. The Branch is mentioned, again signifying Zerubbabel, but this time with lofty imagery: "he shall bear royal honor, and shall sit and rule on his throne" (6:13). The dyarchy is highlighted to emphasize the "peaceful understanding" between priest and Davidide (6:13). Curiously, Zerubbabel is not crowned. The crowns are to be held ready in the temple (6:14). Some scholars have suggested that the text once had the name "Zerubbabel" in 6:11. When he turned out not to be the Messiah, Joshua's name was substituted.[21] Another, more likely view, given the dyarchic model and the fact that the text mentions crowns (pl.), is that in the original text both Joshua and Zerubbabel were to be crowned.[22] When royal aspirations for Zerubbabel were not realized, the text was edited to reflect reality. While this is plausible, there is no manuscript support for it.[23]

Doubtless there were those who wished to restore the monarchy after the return. But the point of this oracle, in its final form, is that the time had not yet come. Both Joshua and Zerubbabel exercised royal functions of leadership as priest and governor. However, Joshua's crowning shows that power was to shift to the priesthood (although the image is figurative, for the priests were not crowned kings). The hope of a Davidic deliverer who would defeat the nations and bring in an everlasting kingdom of righteousness was to be put on hold. This is exactly what happened in history. After Zerubbabel disappeared, the priestly aristocracy provided direction to the struggling community throughout the rest of the Persian era and also through the Hellenistic period (down to 63 B.C.).[24] Messianic hopes were not abandoned but were projected to the future.

Part III. The third part of Zechariah (chs. 7–8), dated two years later (4th year of Darius [518 B.C.], 9th month), begins with a question for the priests: should mourning and fasting to commemorate the destruction of the temple continue? (We are reminded of Hag. 2:10-13 where the priests were consulted on a matter of holiness.) Four sections follow this introduction: (1) Zech. 7:4-7 calls into question the people's motivation, implying that they fast and eat for selfish reasons (Isa. 58 develops this theme of the proper fast in more detail); (2) Zech. 7:8-14 underlines the importance of obedience and compassion for the poor; the earlier generation endured exile for neglecting these; (3) Zech. 8:1-17 is filled with glorious promises for Jerusalem: the return of God's presence, the renewal of the covenant (Zech. 8:8), and economic prosperity. These are the result of the laying of the temple foundation (Zech. 8:9-12) and are conditional upon obedience to God's laws (Zech. 8:14-17; cf. Hag. 2:15-19); (4) Zech. 8:18-23 reverts to the opening theme: fasting. Mournful fasts will be transformed into feasts of rejoicing, and not just for Jews. People from many nations will come to Jerusalem to worship Yahweh.

Conclusion. The *inclusio* or envelope construction is used to demarcate

Zech. 1–8 as a unit. At the outset is the theme of the fathers' disobedience and punishment contrasted with the present generation's need to repent and inherit blessings (Zech. 1:4-6). Toward the conclusion the same theme recurs (Zech. 8:14-15). It is also clear that Haggai and Zech. 1–8 are intended to be read together. This is indicated by the overlapping dates[25] and similar themes. Both prophets emphatically teach that the rebuilding of the temple is prerequisite to the receiving of the blessings of God; both highlight the key role Zerubbabel is to play; both magnify the priestly office in their examples of consulting the priests on difficult questions.

Zech. 9–14

> Then the LORD will go forth and fight against those nations. . . . On that day his feet shall stand on the Mount of Olives. . . . Then the LORD my God will come, and all the holy ones with him. . . . And the LORD will become king over all the earth. . . . Then all who survive of the nations that have come against Jerusalem shall go up year after year to worship the King, the LORD of hosts, and to keep the feast of booths. Zech. 14:3, 4, 5, 9, 16

Structure. Chs. 9–14 divide naturally into two parts, marked by the heading "An Oracle" (Heb. *maśśā'*) in 9:1 and 12:1 (also Mal. 1:1). In contrast to Zech. 1–8, these chapters do not display a carefully organized structure.[26] Sometimes small units are loosely connected to each other by common or "catch" words. For example, the first unit, 9:1-8, may have attracted or "caught" the second unit, 9:9-10, because of the word "king" (9:5; 9:9). A different word in the second unit, "bow" (9:10), could have led to the addition of the third unit, 9:11-13, where this word also occurs (9:11). Similarly, "arrow" is common to 9:11-13 (v. 13) and 9:14-15 (v. 14); "wine" is found in 9:14-15 (v. 14) and 9:16-17 (v. 17). An important structural element in the second set of oracles (chs. 12–14) is the frequent use of "on that day" (the day of Yahweh). The reader should not think, however, that the arrangement of chs. 9–14 was completely haphazard. One finds repetition of themes (e.g., the shepherd) and movement toward a peak in the final chapter. Nor has the second part of Zechariah (chs. 9–14) been carelessly appended to the first (chs. 1–8). There are connections, such as the covenant formula (8:8; 13:9), the divine protection of Jerusalem (2:5, 8-10; 14:11), and the return of the exiles (8:7; 10:9-12). Most importantly, the climax of the second part of Zechariah is similar to that of the first: the inclusion of gentiles in the Jerusalem worship of Yahweh (8:20-22; 14:16-19).

Content. See the chart on pages 410-11 for the segments with summaries of their contents.

Interpretation

Apocalyptic. Apocalyptic is a literary genre typified by certain distinct features. Divine revelations about the future, especially the end of time, are given to a prophet in the form of visions or dreams. Occasionally, the recipient views heavenly events or is taken up into heaven. Frequently, an angel is present as mediator or interpreter. Symbolic imagery is common, for instance visions of animals and horns. Oftentimes the symbols are transparent but sometimes they are obscure. Other features are: periodization of history, a final battle, the establishment of the kingdom of God, resurrection of the dead, an end-time judgment, and paradisaical supernatural phenomena (e.g., eternal day, living water, tree of life). Usually apocalyptic arises in order to comfort God's people who are enduring distress or persecution.[27] Only one book in the Old Testament is categorized as fully developed apocalyptic: Daniel (corresponding to Revelation in the New Testament; see Ch. 43). However, apocalyptic elements are found in other books or parts of books, such as Ezek. 38–39; 47; Isa. 24–27; 56–66; Joel 3; and Zechariah.

A number of these elements are present in Zech. 1–8. The prophet is given a series of eight "night visions" (1:7–6:15). The "angel of Yahweh" explains the visions, acting as mediator (1:13-17). The visions and oracles are oriented to the future (e.g. 6:11-13; 8:20-23). One finds symbolic images of horses, chariots, an ephah, and a measuring line. The reference to Joshua standing before the angel of the Lord with the Satan "at his right hand to accuse him" (3:1) suggests a heavenly scene (cf. Job 1:6-12). The returning Jews were struggling with resistance from the local populace and with economic hardship; Zechariah's visions and oracles came to encourage those who were rebuilding.

Although symbolic visions and angels are absent from Zech. 9–14, the second part of Zechariah also contains apocalyptic elements. Because of the severe oppression of the leaders ("shepherds"), comfort is even more dominant here. The "sheep" can rejoice, knowing that Yahweh will send a king who

The Structure of Zechariah 9–14

First Collection (chs. 9–11)

9:1-8   Judgment on Syria, Phoenicia, and Philistia, with Philistia becoming a clan in Judah; no more oppression for God's people.

9:9-10   Jerusalem's king is coming on a donkey, ushering in an age of peace with his universal dominion.

9:11-13   Yahweh will free his people and use them as weapons against Greece.

9:14-15   Yahweh will give his people victory in a bloody battle (v. 15; cf. 14:12).

9:16-17   Fertility of the land will be restored.

10:1-2   Command to seek fertility from Yahweh; divination is forbidden.

10:3-12   Yahweh will punish the "shepherds" (rulers) but will give military success to his people and will bring them back from exile.

11:1-3   Punishment of Lebanon (Phoenicia), forests, and "shepherds" (rulers)

11:4-14   The prophet is commissioned to become the shepherd, although the flock is destined for destruction. He destroys three shepherds but is despised. He breaks Favor, his staff, signifying the end of the covenant with all the peoples (11:10). He is paid thirty pieces of silver, which he casts into the temple treasury (11:12-13). Finally, he breaks Unity, his second staff, signifying the end of the union between Judah and Israel (11:14; cf. Ezek. 37:15-28).

11:15-17   The prophet is told to take the implements of a worthless shepherd, signifying the kind of leader that Yahweh will allow to come to power over his people.

11:17   A woe oracle against the worthless shepherd.

Second Collection (chs. 12–14)

12:1-9   The siege of Jerusalem; Judah and Jerusalem will win; David's house (family) will be like God; and Yahweh will seek the destruction of the hostile nations.

12:10–13:1 David's house and Jerusalem (a) will mourn over the one they pierced; and (b) will be purified from sin and uncleanness.

13:2-6   Idols will be destroyed; prophecy will cease.

13:7-9   Yahweh's shepherd will be struck, resulting in a scattering of the sheep; the small remnant of people will be refined by fire (cf. Isa. 6:13); the covenant will be renewed (cf. Exod. 6:7; Hos. 1:9; 2:23; Jer. 31:33; Ezek. 11:20; 36:28).

> 14:1-21   The Day of Yahweh: all the nations will gather for battle against Jerusalem (v. 2). Yahweh (a) will fight against the nations (v. 3); (b) will stand on the Mount of Olives, splitting it in two (v. 4); (c) will bring all his holy ones with him (v. 5). Miracles will abound: no more cold; no more night; living waters will flow east and west (vv. 6-8; cf. Ezek. 47:1-12). Yahweh will reign (v. 9). Jerusalem will be exalted and secure (vv. 10-11). Plagues will come on the enemies (v. 12; cf. v. 15). The wealth of nations will be gathered (v. 14). All nations will come to Jerusalem to worship Yahweh and to observe the feast of Booths (vv. 16-19). Even horses and pots will become sacred to Yahweh in Jerusalem (vv. 20-21).

will defeat all enemies and establish peace (9:9-10). In fact, Yahweh himself will bring his kingdom to earth after winning the final battle (14:1-11). When this happens miraculous signs will attend: the Mount of Olives will be split in two; cold and night will be banished, yielding to everlasting day; and living water will flow out of Jerusalem (14:4-8).

Prophetic vs. Apocalyptic Eschatology. Eschatology deals with "the end." The preexilic prophets had an eschatology but it was within history. Amos and Hosea, for example, predicted the end of Israel; Jeremiah predicted the end of Judah. Yet time and history continued after these events were fulfilled. Apocalyptists, on the other hand, posited a radical break between time and eternity; between this world and the next. Here, then, is a key distinction: whereas prophetic eschatology looks for an end within history, apocalyptic eschatology looks for the end of history.[28]

The earlier prophets also looked for a deliverer. Normally, this was a Davidic descendant who would defeat sin and reign in righteousness (cf. Isa. 9:6-7; 11:1-5). Again, this was a figure from within history, a human rather than a supernatural being. As time went on people despaired of finding such a king. When kings and other leaders failed to conquer their enemies and continued to be oppressive and corrupt, people began to look for deliverance from heaven rather than from earth. Prophetic eschatology, then, expects the kingdom of God to emerge from below while apocalyptic eschatology anticipates its descent from above (e.g., Dan. 7:13-18).

Here we see a distinct difference between the two parts of Zechariah. In Zech. 1–8 as well as in Haggai, expectations are still fixed on the human Davidide, Zerubbabel. Even if Haggai and Zechariah themselves had some intuition that Zerubbabel was only a type of the one to come, still their words fed the hope that Zerubbabel would usher in the kingdom of God. In Zech.

9–14, this is not so. Without clear historical referents it is difficult to date these chapters. Nevertheless, they are probably from a later time because human leaders are mostly cast in a negative light.[29] Anticipation of a human king is not absent (Zech. 9:9-10) but the image of the heavenly king is much brighter by reason of its climatic position (Zech. 14). Both have an eschaton, an end time, but there is more continuity with what preceded in Haggai and Zech. 1–8: temple worship, a high priest, and a human king.[30] By way of contrast, Zech. 9–14 describes the cataclysmic day of Yahweh, the breaking in of the kingdom of God from heaven, and revolutionary changes, with overtones of paradise. Therefore, Zech. 1–8, though more developed than Hosea, Amos, or Isaiah, still constitutes prophetic eschatology; Zech. 9–14, on the other hand, is closer to apocalyptic eschatology.

Zechariah in the New Testament. Some seventy-one quotations of Zechariah appear in the New Testament (31 from chs. 1–8, 40 from chs. 9–14). Most are found in Revelation (a total of 31; 20 from chs. 1–8, 11 from chs. 9–14). Another twenty-seven are found in the Gospels (14 in Matthew, 7 in Mark, 3 each in Luke and John), twenty-two of which are from chs. 9–14. Many of these are found in the record of the last week of Jesus' ministry.

The more familiar quotations are from Zech. 9–14. Christians find fulfillment of the advent of the triumphant yet humble king (Zech. 9:9)[31] in Jesus' Palm Sunday entry into Jerusalem (Matt. 21:5; John 12:14-15).[32] When Judas betrayed the Lord for thirty pieces of silver (Matt. 26:14-16) and then threw the pieces into the temple (Matt. 27:3-5), the Gospel writer readily made a connection with Zech. 11:12-13.[33] The disciples forsook Christ and fled after he was arrested (Matt. 26:31, 56), in order to fulfill the saying, "Strike the shepherd, that the sheep may be scattered" (Zech. 13:7). Following his death, a soldier pierced his side (John 19:34-37), in keeping with Zech. 12:10, which says that the inhabitants of Jerusalem will mourn when they look on the one they pierced. This passage is alluded to again in Rev. 1:7; in the second coming of the Messiah, all will see the one they pierced and will wail. Jesus ascended to heaven from the Mount of Olives (Luke 24:50; Acts 1:12) and will come again as he left (Zech. 14:4; Acts 1:11). When he returns he will bring all the angels with him (Zech. 14:5; Matt. 25:31). In the new world there will be continual daylight and a miraculous river (Rev. 21:25; 22:1,5; Zech. 14:7-8).

Modern Relevance. Both parts of Zechariah pave the way for the gospel by including the Gentiles in God's plan of salvation. Like Haggai, Zech. 1–8 is concerned with right worship, seeking God's kingdom first, and messianic hope. Haggai witnesses to the sovereignty of God by looking to the shaking of the nations; Zechariah, by giving God the glory for the rebuilt temple. Although Zerubbabel will be instrumental, it will take place "not by might, nor by power, but by my spirit, says the Lord of hosts" (Zech. 4:6). More than Haggai, Zechariah calls for obedience to God's laws and compassion for the poor.

Zech. 9–14 speaks of both a human king (9:9-10) and a divine king (14:1-17). It also witnesses to a figure whose suffering results in redemption (12:10–13:1; cf. 13:7 and the Suffering Servant of Isa. 53). The people of Old Testament times were given these pieces of a puzzle but did not know how to bring them together. Only in the Incarnation were these disparate images integrated into one person. As the son of David, Jesus could claim the human throne. As God in human form, Jesus fulfills the prophecies of the heavenly king who comes to earth (although some events await the second advent). In his first appearing he suffered for the sins of the world, bringing forgiveness. When he returns, he will bring his kingdom to earth.

The final section of Zechariah thus provides comfort and hope for all who are suffering under oppressive "shepherds." Both voices in this prophetic masterpiece must be heard: the pragmatic voice which encourages us to be involved in building this world into a better place; and the visionary voice which encourages us to renounce this world, to lift up our heads in anticipation of our redemption (Luke 21:28), and to look for a better world with "foundations, whose architect and builder is God" (Heb. 11:10).

Zech. 1–8 affirms the importance of this world. Just as it was important for Zerubbabel to build Yahweh's temple, we need to build structures today through which God can work. They may be actual buildings, such as churches and hospitals or societal structures, such as missionary organizations and humanitarian agencies. Zech. 9–14 reminds us that all things human will pass away. Worse still, there is radical evil in the world which must be destroyed. For this reason we should not be embarrassed by the war imagery here, or by the representation of God as warrior. One day God will powerfully replace this fallen world with a perfect one.

413

CHAPTER 30

Malachi

Malachi is the best window we have through which to survey the spiritual and social needs of God's people in Judah and Jerusalem during the early fifth century B.C. It is the closing section of the Hebrew Book of the Twelve and in the English Bible the last Old Testament book. Most scholars consider it to be substantially a unity. It conveys God's word first to the Jews living in the second temple era and beyond them to all believers in all times.

> Then those who revered the LORD spoke with one another. The LORD took note and listened, and a book of remembrance was written before him of those who revered the LORD and thought on his name. Mal. 3:16

Title

"Oracle, the word of Yahweh" (Heb. *maśśā' debar yhwh*) is the phrase with which Zech. 9:1; 12:1; and Mal. 1:1 all begin. The similarity in introduction suggests that the three passages originally belonged together. Perhaps they were from separate hands and some editor linked them by the common superscription.[1] These probably once comprised three anonymous appendices to the prophetic corpus. At some point in time, however, two of them were attached to the book of Zechariah (Zech. 9–11 and 12–14) while the last was left to stand on its own as a separate work. Two main factors may account for the rearrangement. First, the two blocks incorporated into Zechariah have themes in common with each other and with the prophecy of that book. Second, by removing two oracles and leaving one, the collection of minor prophets was reduced from fourteen to twelve — a significant number, perhaps symbolizing the twelve tribes of Israel.

Composition

Authorship. The last block is now called the book of Malachi. It may be that "Malachi" (Heb. *mal'ākî*, Mal. 1:1), which means "my messenger," is not a personal name. In Mal. 3:1 the same word is translated "my messenger." There it describes the anonymous agent who will be sent to prepare the way for God's future coming. Furthermore, Mal. 2:7 refers to priests as Yahweh's *messengers.* The Targum adds a phrase in Mal. 1:1 to read: "by the hand of my messenger whose name is called Ezra the scribe."[2] There is no solid evidence for attributing the book to Ezra: "If Ezra's name was originally associated with the book, it would hardly have been dropped by the collectors of the prophetic Canon."[3] This reading, nevertheless, does show that Jews in antiquity did not uniformly consider *mal'ākî* to be a proper name. The LXX has *angelou autou*, "his messenger," an indication that the Jews who translated the Bible into Greek did not construe "malachi" as a proper name either (the change from "my" to "his" is probably a Greek corruption). Some have attempted to create a proper name by adding *-yā(h)*, thus *mal'ākîyâ*, meaning "my messenger (or angel) is Yahweh" or "messenger of Yahweh." However, the former makes no sense and the latter is unattested.

It is unlikely, therefore, that this book was written by a prophet named Malachi. But these observations do not shed any light on who did write it. Since it is convenient to have a name for the book and for the author when discussing the content, many modern scholars continue to use the name "Malachi" for that purpose. We shall do the same.

Date. There is broad scholarly consensus as to "Malachi's" date. The word *peḥâ* is found in Mal. 1:8. Since this was the term employed for "governor" in the Persian period, it indicates a postexilic time frame. Furthermore, the date must be later than 515 B.C. because the temple had been rebuilt. We can judge it to be a number of years later because sacrificial worship had declined in quality (Mal. 1:7-14). Many scholars attempt to set the date more specifically before Ezra's arrival in 458 B.C. They read Mal. 2:11 ("Judah . . . has married the daughter of a foreign god") as a polemic against Jews who divorced their Jewish wives to marry foreign ones. Ezra's opposition to such mixed marriages is well known (Ezra 9:1–10:15). It is argued that if there were Jews marrying Gentiles then it must have been before Ezra arrived to put a stop to the practice. Malachi is therefore commonly dated to the first half of the fifth century.

However, Mal. 2:10-16 is somewhat obscure. Nowhere does it indicate that Jewish wives were divorced. It is possible that Mal. 2:11 is attacking worship of foreign gods rather than marriage to foreign women.[4] Malachi may in fact be criticizing Ezra's program of divorcing foreign wives (Ezra 10:10-11, 19, 44). The first verse in the section affirms that there is one God over all (2:10).[5] Along with earlier passages in the book (Mal. 1:11, 14) this indicates an openness to foreigners, as an expression of Yahweh's universal kingship.[6] Further, Malachi unequivocally states that Yahweh hates divorce (2:16). Such observations may indicate his conviction that even if one has married a non-Jew, a man should be faithful to the wife of his youth. In this case, Malachi might be contemporary with Ezra or later.[7]

The conditions described imply that the return from exile had not brought anything like the messianic age. The people had lost heart, questioning God's love (Mal. 1:2) and justice (Mal. 2:17). Cynicism reigned (Mal. 3:14-15), breaking of the commandments and oppression of the underprivileged were rampant (3:5), and organized religion was held in contempt (1:7-14; 3:7-12). A new revelation from God was necessary if his people were to walk in his ways.

The Prophecy

Apart from the introductory verse and two appendices at the end, the outline is characterized by a question-and-answer format sometimes called a *disputation style*. The book can be analyzed as shown in the chart on page 417.

Malachi's dialectical style points out the people's hostility. They had the audacity to accuse God; he responded to their complaints by correcting their faulty thinking. Furthermore, the divine judge brought his own indictments against them. They questioned Yahweh's love, which had been proved in Israel's election (1:2-5). They did not give him the respect due either a father or a master (1:6). The priests neglected the requirement (e.g., Lev. 1:10) that only the best of the flock be presented as offerings (Mal. 1:7-14). The people profaned the covenant of the fathers by divorcing the wives of their youth (2:14-16). They had "robbed God" (3:8) by failing to pay their tithes and

Superscription (1:1) An oracle of Yahweh by my messenger.

First Dispute (1:2-5) Yahweh loves Israel.
Yahweh: I have loved you.
The people: How have you loved us?
Yahweh: By choosing Jacob (Israel) over Esau (Edom).

Second Dispute (1:6–2:9) Israel's Father deserves honor.
Yahweh: Why do you priests despise my name?
Priests: How have we despised your name?
Yahweh: By offering polluted sacrifices.
Priests: How have we done that?
Yahweh: By offering blemished, lame, or sick animals.

Third Dispute (2:10-16) Yahweh hates divorce.
Prophet: Yahweh will not accept your offerings.
People: Why?
Prophet: Because you have broken your marriage covenant
                with the wife of your youth.

Fourth Dispute (2:17–3:5) God is just. Part 1.
Prophet: You have wearied Yahweh.
People: How?
Prophet: By questioning his justice, thinking that evildoers
                will prosper. God will punish the wicked.

Fifth Dispute (3:6-12) Tithing is evidence of repentance.
Prophet: Return to Yahweh.
People: How?
Prophet: You are robbing God.
People: How?
Prophet: By withholding tithes and offerings.

Sixth Dispute (3:13–4:3 [MT 3:13–3:21]) God is just. Part 2.
Yahweh: You have spoken against me.
People: How?
Yahweh: By saying it is vain to serve God. He will punish
                the wicked and reward the faithful.

First Epilogue (4:4 [MT 3:22]) Keep the law of Moses.
Second Epilogue (4:5-6 [MT 3:23-24]) Elijah will come
        before the day of Yahweh.

offerings. They had become arrogant, believing that evildoers who test God both prosper and escape punishment (2:17–3:5, 14) while those who fear God enjoy no benefits (3:14). Both priests and people had fallen away and needed the message of Malachi to call them back to repentance.

Theology

Yahweh of Hosts. The most common name of God in Malachi is Yahweh Sabaoth *(yahweh ṣeḇā'ôt),* which is difficult to explain, both as to formation and significance. It is often rendered "Yahweh of Hosts," but that is contrary to Hebrew grammar.[8] Objecting to the standard translation, some suggest that "Yahweh-Sabaoth" is a compound name.[9] Others think that the name is a shortened form of an original yahweh *'elôhê ṣeḇā'ôt* "Yahweh, God of hosts."[10] However, it is more likely that the short form, which is less grammatical, was expanded into the long form to make it conform to the rules. If so, it may be construed as an elliptical phrase "Yahweh (the God) of Hosts," equivalent to the later expanded expression.[11]

Another strong possibility is that it originated in the patriarchal period when God was known by the name El. In this view "yhwh" would still retain its verbal force, meaning "he causes to be" or "creates." The full expression would have been *'ēl zū yahwê ṣaba'ōt* "El, he who creates the hosts." Once the name Yahweh was introduced, it would have replaced El in the above: *yahwê zū yahwê ṣaba'ōt* "Yahweh, he who creates the hosts." Finally, it would have been shortened to *yahweh ṣaba'ōt.*[12]

Besides the problem of its origin is the question of the term's meaning.[13] Because the term is found in connection with the ark and its (limited) use in battle, some suggest that "Lord of hosts" means "Lord of the armies (of Israel)," or something like "warrior God." However, this view fails to take into account the sacral nature of war in ancient Israel, especially in the conquest. Joshua was the commander of the earthly host when Israel entered Canaan, but there was a corresponding commander of the heavenly host (Josh. 5:14). Therefore, *ṣeḇā'ôt* must refer to the heavenly hosts of Yahweh's army: angels, cherubim, seraphim, and the heavenly bodies (sun, moon, and stars).[14]

Covenant. Malachi mentions several covenants: the covenant with Levi (2:4, 5, 8); the covenant with the fathers (2:10); and the marriage covenant (2:14).[15] In addition, he predicts that the one who comes to prepare for the coming of the Lord is "the messenger of the covenant" (3:1).

Divine Love. God reminds his people that he loved Jacob but hated Esau (1:2-3). This is not to be taken absolutely but relatively, i.e., God preferred, or chose Jacob. Neither are Jacob and Esau to be understood exclusively as individuals but as nations: Israel and Edom. God's love, then, primarily has to do with election and covenant. God formed a covenant relationship with the Israelites, so that they were the special objects of his love. Nevertheless, Gentiles are not completely excluded. The creator and father of all people (2:10) is cognizant that there are those who fear him in every nation (1:11, 14).

Apocalyptic. Daniel is the only apocalypse in the Old Testament. Never-

Bronze offering stand, showing worshiper or priest bringing gift to seated deity; Megiddo, tenth century B.C. *(Oriental Institute, University of Chicago)*

theless, there are other books, such as Malachi, which have apocalyptic elements in them. Malachi shows one stage along the way in the development between classical prophecy and apocalyptic prophecy.

(1) Sociological analysis. When the Jews returned from Babylon to rebuild the temple, they followed the restoration plan of Ezekiel regarding cult officials: the Zadokite priests were the only ones who could offer sacrifice, while the Levites were relegated to subordinate positions as minor clergy (Ezek. 44:9-31). This exclusivity — here expressed toward temple functionaries —

419

was evident in other ways, too. Those in power were unwilling to allow local people to assist in rebuilding, even though these people desired to help, professed to worship the same God, and may have been partly descended from the northern Israelite tribes (Ezra 4:1-3).[16] Another manifestation of this closed attitude can be seen in the way that foreigners, especially Moabites and Ammonites, were excluded from the community (Ezra 9:1-2; 10:2, 10-11, 19, 44; Neh. 13:1, 23-31; cf. Deut. 23:3-5). Ezra even forced Jews to divorce their foreign wives (Ezra 10). Malachi takes the side of the outcasts. He excoriates the priests (Mal. 2:1-3) while affirming the covenant that God made with the Levites (Mal. 2:4-6), predicting that in the future God will restore them once again to their rightful place at the altar (Mal. 3:3). Malachi also is surprisingly accepting of foreigners, acknowledging that God is father of all and that there are those who fear God among all the nations (Mal. 1:11, 14; 2:10). Finally, Malachi roundly condemns divorce (Mal. 2:16).

The two attitudes of exclusiveness and inclusiveness were found in the postexilic Jewish community and are represented in various books of the Bible. The more closed attitude is evident in Ezra, Nehemiah, and partly in Haggai and Zech. 1–8, while the more open view is found in Malachi, Isa. 56–66, Ruth, and Jonah. While the two are in tension, they are not irreconcilable. Both are God's word, but to two different groups. Those in power needed to be vigilant to protect the purity of Yahweh's worship. Syncretism — the mixing of Yahwism with foreign religious practices — was what caused them to go into exile. It was necessary to be wary of foreigners lest the faithful Jews be corrupted by pagan cults once again. Those who were excluded, who were on the fringes of society, who found no help from the structures of power, looked to God in hope of a better future. From this hope apocalyptic was born.[17] God revealed to the outcasts that he was the God of all people whether Jew or Gentile, priest or Levite, and that one day he would vindicate those who had been ostracized unfairly.

(2) The day of Yahweh. This is the day of vindication sorely longed for, especially by the oppressed. This notion becomes very important in apocalyptic eschatology. It figures in prophetic eschatology too, in Amos, Joel, and Zephaniah, as well as in Malachi. Yahweh will come on his day to right all wrongs, punishing the wicked and rewarding the righteous. "The Lord . . . will suddenly come to his temple" (Mal. 3:1). "But who can endure the day of his coming . . . ?" (Mal. 3:2). Like a refiner's fire he will refine and purify the Levites (Mal. 3:2-3), and judge the sorcerers, adulterers, false witnesses, and oppressors of the poor — in short, all who do not fear God (Mal. 3:5).

But the day is not all darkness and fire. Malachi alone informs us that the Lord has a "book of remembrance" in which are written the names of those who do fear Yahweh. "They shall be mine, says the Lord of hosts, my special possession on the day when I act" (Mal. 3:17). The distinction will be made between the "righteous" and the "wicked," between one who serves God and one who does not (Mal. 3:18). The day comes burning like an oven, "but for you who revere my name, the sun of righteousness shall rise, with healing in its wings" (4:2 [MT 3:20]).

The Forerunner. Unique to Malachi is this doctrine concerning "Elijah the prophet" (Mal. 4:5 [MT 3:23]). Isaiah had spoken of the "voice" that cries: "In the wilderness prepare the way of the LORD" (Isa. 40:3). The slightly vague idea that someone is to precede the messianic king and prepare for his coming develops into a rather full doctrine in the intertestamental period. It is found at Qumran and in the New Testament. Malachi identifies this forerunner as Yahweh's messenger (Mal. 3:1) and then, more specifically as "Elijah" (Mal. 4:5 [MT 3:23]), an idea taken over in Judaism.[18] In the New Testament, John the Baptist is recognized as the one who fulfills the prophecies of Isaiah and Malachi, serving as forerunner and messenger (Matt. 11:7-15; Mark 1:2-8; Luke 7:24-30); Jesus even uses the name Elijah for John (Matt. 11:14).[19]

Message for Today. Just as God chose Jacob (Mal. 1:2-3), he chooses people today. Those within the covenant must avoid the sin of pride (Rom. 11:18-21), remembering that they did not choose; rather they were chosen (John 15:16). Furthermore, Malachi was tender toward non-Israelites but harsh toward the priests (1:6-14). We must remember that God is parent of all (2:10) and "to whom much has been given . . . much will be required" (Luke 12:48), meaning that more is expected from those who receive more revelation. Therefore, God's elect must respond to him with humble gratitude and obedient worship. And they must show kindness and humility toward outsiders (Mal. 3:5).

Although we do not worship God with animal sacrifices, Malachi teaches us the importance of offering the best of what we have to God (1:6-14). He also stresses tithing (3:8-12), which is overemphasized in some pulpits today and neglected by others. An unbalanced emphasis on this passage can lead to legalism. Especially because of the promised blessing, some have misused Malachi to encourage the notion that we can barter with God. On the other hand, it is a mistake to neglect instruction on regular and sacrificial giving, which the New Testament also affirms (Luke 6:38; 1 Cor. 16:2; 2 Cor. 9:7).

Two other themes from Malachi find confirmation in the New Testament. One is fidelity to the marriage covenant (Mal. 2:14-16; Matt. 19:1-12; Mark 10:2-12). The other is the concern which God has for those on the fringe of society: the hireling, the widow, the orphan, and the resident alien (Mal. 3:5; Matt. 25:31-46; Jas. 1:27).

Conclusion. In the Hebrew canon, the Writings follow Malachi.[20] However, Malachi closes the English Old Testament. This arrangement is appropriate since the prophecies of the preparing messenger, and of the subsequent coming of the Lord, provide links with Matthew, anticipating the coming of John the Baptist and of Jesus.

> Clearly Malachi's message says "Unfinished." The rebuilding of the temple in the postexilic period did not usher in the kingdom of God. But Malachi heightened Jewish expectations by engendering a fear of judgment and a hope of healing.

Christians believe that fulfillment of these expectations comes in at least two stages: the First Advent of Christ, providing salvation for all who believe in him; and the Second Advent, bringing the final judgment and ultimate salvation. Malachi, like the other prophets, does not make this distinction. Rather, he sees the near and the distant in a single view. Further uncovering of God's plan had to await the new revelation of God in Christ, as heralded and interpreted in the writings of the New Testament.

PART THREE

THE WRITINGS

CHAPTER 31

Introduction to the Writings

Name

The third section of the Jewish canon is the Writings (Heb. $k^e t \hat{u} \underline{b} \hat{i} m$). The Church Fathers minted the Greek term *hagiographa* "sacred writings" to describe this part of the Old Testament.

Although a date for the completion of the Writings cannot be attested before *ca.* A.D. 100, ample evidence of a third section of the canon (in addition to the Law and the Prophets) does appear as early as 180 B.C., when Ben Sirach's grandson noted in the prologue to Ecclesiasticus that his distinguished grandfather "devoted himself especially to the reading of the Law and the Prophets, and the other books of our ancestors." Jesus' words underscore such a tripartite canon: ". . . that everything written about me in the law of Moses, the prophets and the psalms must be fulfilled" (Luke 24:44). Most likely, "psalms" here is shorthand for all the Writings, since that book was the most significant liturgical work and may have stood first in the collection.

Uncertainty about the precise contents of the Writings in the pre-Christian period should not suggest that the canon was in a complete state of flux. That Ben Sirach and the Wisdom of Solomon were not included must show that fairly clear boundaries had been drawn by at least 50 B.C. Furthermore, heated debates among the rabbis about the canonicity of Esther, the Song of Solomon, and Ecclesiastes[1] indicate that these books had been well accepted by at least a strong sector of Judaism. It is doubtful that the scriptures known to Jesus and the apostles varied at all in contents from the present Hebrew Bible.

Order

The order presently followed in the Hebrew Bible probably is no earlier than the twelfth century A.D.: Psalms, Job, Proverbs, Ruth, the Song of Solomon, Ecclesiastes, Lamentations, Esther, Daniel, Ezra, Nehemiah, 1-2 Chronicles.[2] Earlier Jewish traditions vary in the location of Chronicles — sometimes at the beginning, sometimes at the end of the collection — and in the order of Job and Proverbs.[3] The five scrolls (Heb. *m^egillôt*) used for the feasts and fasts, have appeared together since about the sixth century A.D. However, the present order, which parallels approximately the liturgical events assigned, did not take shape until the twelfth century: the Song of Solomon (eighth day of Passover), Ruth (second day of Weeks, or Pentecost), Lamentations (ninth day of Ab, in mourning for the destruction of Solomon's temple), Ecclesiastes (third day of Tabernacles), Esther (Purim).

Date and Purpose

The date of the collection (300 B.C.–A.D. 100) must be distinguished from the dates of the individual books. As a collection, the Writings were preceded by the Pentateuch and the Prophets, although parts of Psalms and Proverbs undoubtedly were composed centuries before either of the earlier sections reached final form.

Consequently, other factors along with the historical process of collection caused these books to be grouped together as the Writings, although several (Ezra, Nehemiah, Chronicles, Esther, Song of Solomon, and Ecclesiastes) undoubtedly were composed, in their present form at least, after the time of Malachi, the last writing prophet. The unique character of the books has as much to do with their inclusion as does the date of composition or collection.[4]

The books that make up the Writings have a rainbow-like variety. They fall into four groups: wisdom literature, the five scrolls, Daniel, and the complex of Ezra-Nehemiah and Chronicles. The collection of the scrolls reflects their use in public worship. The core of wisdom literature, Job and Proverbs, has been left together. The book of Psalms that precedes them has been preserved in a wisdom edition, as the introductory Ps. 1 attests, so that its position beside the core wisdom books is fitting. Ecclesiastes, a literary member of the wisdom group, has been moved into the group of the scrolls. The Song of Solomon also previously belonged to the wisdom group. It doubtless owes its canonicity to being included under the umbrella of wisdom teaching, as an expression of proper sexuality.

Thematically, Ruth belongs with Chronicles in its indirect celebration of David, who stood both for the glory of the past and as a symbol of eschatological promise. A sweep of history, which gave self-understanding to the people of God, is provided by Chronicles, Lamentations, Ezra-Nehemiah, Daniel, and Esther. The last two books grapple from different perspectives with the concerns of the diaspora community, while Ezra-Nehemiah and Chronicles celebrate return from exile and the resettlement of Israel around the Jerusalem temple. The book of Daniel also trumpets the survival of God's people and their distinctive temple worship, after the second-century B.C. threat to both, and testifies to the eschatological hope of Israel. Chronicles is given final place: (1) it establishes a framework for the Old Testament by its echoing of Adam and the patriarchs in 1 Chr. 1:1–2:2; (2) it presents perennial ideals for the ongoing people of God to live up to; and (3) it ends with a ringing note of hope in Cyrus's decree of the possibility of return to Jerusalem — "Let him go up."

Though the Writings do not contain specific commands of God as does the Law or verbatim oracles as do the Prophets, they are nonetheless essential for the edification of God's people: they give indispensable patterns for prayer and praise; they offer insight into God's work in history; they alert the reader to the lessons to be drawn from creation and the human social environment; they reflect the anxious and angry responses of believing people to the mystery of God's ways; and they model the courage and devotion God's people are to maintain despite human frailty and hostile opposition.

The Writings analyze from different angles the rich and rewarding theme of human life in relation to God. Life is celebrated in the sexuality of the Song of Songs, in the exuberant gratitude of the hymns and thanksgiving songs of the Psalms, and in the down-to-earth enjoyment advocated in parts of Ecclesiastes. Life under threat is portrayed from a national perspective in Lamentations, Esther, Daniel, and the communal complaints of the Psalms, and from an individual perspective in Job, Ruth, and the personal complaints in the Psalms. Lessons in how to live a full and good life are taught in Proverbs and Ecclesiastes. Life in community is presented in Ezra-Nehemiah and Chronicles.

> The Psalms, the wisdom literature, the Chronicler's history, the songs of love and lamentation, the visions of comfort — these all give dynamic expression to the depths of faith which God expects of his people. The impact of law, prophecy, and history on succeeding generations would have been less powerful if God had not also inspired and preserved the emotions, the instructions, even the frustrations represented in the Writings.

They are an essential part of "all Scripture . . . inspired by God and . . . useful for teaching, for reproof, for correction, and for training in righteousness" (2 Tim. 3:16).

CHAPTER 32

Psalms

As we embrace the Psalms, we join a vast company of persons who for nearly thirty centuries have grounded their praises and prayers in these ancient words. Kings and peasants, prophets and priests, apostles and martyrs, nuns and reformers, executives and housekeepers, professors and folk singers — for all of them and a host of others the Psalms have been spiritual life and breath.

> Happy are those whose help is the God of Jacob,
>   whose hope is in the LORD their God,
>   who made heaven and earth, the sea,
>   and all that is in them;
>   who keeps faith forever;
>   who executes justice for the oppressed;
>   who gives food to the hungry.
> The LORD sets the prisoners free;
>   the LORD opens the eyes of the blind.
> The LORD lifts up those who are bowed down;
>   the LORD loves the righteous.
> The LORD watches over the strangers;
>   he upholds the orphan and the widow,
>   but the way of the wicked he brings to ruin.
> The LORD will reign forever,
>   your God, O Zion, for all generations.
> Praise the LORD! Ps. 146:5-10

Name

The title "Psalms" reflects the book's name in the LXX *(Psalmoi)*. The alternate Greek title, *Psalterion*, is frequently used in its anglicized form, Psalter. Both terms entered English versions through the Latin Vulgate, which transliterated the Greek. The Greek words, from *psallō* "to pluck," were used first for the playing of a stringed instrument or for the instrument itself. Later they were used to describe the song *(psalmos)* or collection of songs *(psaltērion)*. Luke used the full Greek title "Book of Psalms" (Luke 20:42; Acts 1:20).

Although the closest Hebrew word to "psalm" would be *mizmôr* "a song sung to musical accompaniment," the actual Hebrew title is *tᵉhillîm* "praises" or "songs of praise." The singular form *(tᵉhillâ)* is used in the title of Ps. 145 in the sense of a hymn and occurs more than twenty times in various psalms (e.g., 9:14; 22:25; 33:1; 34:1).[1]

In the Hebrew Bible, Psalms stands at the beginning of the Writings.[2] Rabbinic custom placed it before Proverbs and the rest of the wisdom literature, assuming that David's collection should precede that of his son, Solomon. The LXX puts Psalms at the beginning of the books of poetry. The Latin and English order, where Job precedes Psalms, is probably based on the supposed antiquity of Job.

Structure of the Canonical Psalter

The Psalter in its final form has been divided into five books: Pss. 1–41; 42–72; 73–89; 90–106; 107–150. The division probably follows the pattern of the Pentateuch. Indeed, the number of psalms (150) follows closely the number of sections into which the Pentateuch is divided for reading in the synagogue (153). Synagogue practice in the postbiblical period may have called for using a psalm with each reading from the Pentateuch.[3] Each of the books ends with a doxology: 41:13; 72:18f.; 89:52; 106:48; and 150, which serves as a concluding doxology for the whole collection as well. The intent of the doxologies is to give praise for what has been revealed about God in each book. This emphasis on praise agrees with the Hebrew title for the whole book, "praises." It also matches a switch from lament in the first half of the Psalter to praise in the second half. Whereas particular psalms focus on human concerns in relation to God, the intent of the book as a whole is to concentrate on God.

The LXX contains a Ps. 151, purportedly related to David's combat with Goliath, but describes the poem as "outside the number [the traditional 150]."[4]

Though both the Greek and the Hebrew contain 150 psalms in the received collection, the actual numbering differs: the LXX combines Pss. 9 and 10 and divides Ps. 147 into 146 and 147. Thus, in the LXX all psalms from 10–147 are one number lower than their Masoretic counterparts.

Collections

Behind the editorial division of books there lies a process of historical development involving the combination of different collections of psalms. Two are attributed to David (Pss. 3–41; 51–71). Others are assigned to the levitical choirs of the sons of Korah (Pss. 42–49; 84–85; 87–88) and Asaph (Pss. 50; 73–83), and presumably represent their repertoires. The Songs of Ascents (Pss. 120–134) were probably a collection of pilgrim songs sung while processing through Jerusalem to the temple. Pss. 146–150 are a collections of psalms that use the rubric "Hallelujah."

Literary Types

The Psalter contains a range of literary types which suggest different functions in Israel's private and public worship. Comparison of these forms makes possible a better grasp of both their meaning and their use.

The task of understanding a given psalm begins with certain questions: (1) What is happening in the psalm: complaint, praise, thanksgiving, instruction? (2) Who is speaking: an individual or the community? If an individual, is he a spokesperson for a group, such as a king, a priest, or a prophet, or an individual complaining of suffering or giving thanks for deliverance? Are both singular and plural pronouns used, as though an individual and the congregation were both involved? (3) Is the king mentioned? Do words like "anointed," "son," or "shield" denote his relationship to God and Israel?

Only within the current century has the importance of such questions been learned. Until the early decades of the century, the standard scholarly approach to Psalms and other books was historical criticism, which "sought to understand the books of the Bible by a critical analysis of their composition, their authorship, date, provenance, purpose, and sources."[5] For the Psalms, this method had proved highly inadequate due to lack of specific data to help with dates and historical settings of the various poems. Even where a possible background is given in the titles of psalms (e.g., 7; 18; 30; 34; 51–52; 54; 56–57; 59–60; 63), neither the reliability of the tradition that produced the titles nor the psalm's use in the worship of Israel is certain. Invasions and battles may be mentioned, but nothing specific is said. Enemies loom large, but they are almost always nameless. Comparative study of the great nineteenth-century commentaries indicates no strong consensus as to the background, date, or use of the various psalms.

A new approach was needed, and Herrmann Gunkel (1862-1932) more than anyone else provided it. This approach, called form criticism (German *Formgeschichte*), is based on three main premises: (1) Since the Bible contains religious literature, which by nature tends to resist change and maintain established patterns, literary materials may be categorized (German *Gattungen* "categories") according to formal similarities. (2) Similarity of form probably

David playing the harp in a fragment of a sixth-century A.D. mosaic from Gaza. *(Israel Department of Antiquities)*

432

means similarity of use; presumably, therefore, similar forms were used in the religious life setting (German *Sitz im Leben*). (3) Since similarities are found in forms of worship and liturgy among Israel and their neighbors, religious texts from other Near Eastern cultures may help in understanding the use and meaning of Israel's literary forms. In other words, comparative literature and comparative religion can be useful in understanding the Old Testament.[6]

With Gunkel the emphasis in Psalm studies shifted from an attempt to pinpoint the historical setting of a given psalm's composition to an endeavor to trace the psalm's use in public worship or private devotion. Concentration on authorship gave way to investigation of the religious setting in which the psalm may have arisen and of its oral transmission in living worship.[7]

Gunkel's analysis of literary categories remains the backbone of contemporary approaches to the Psalms, though more emphasis is now given to their individuality. The following list represents Gunkel's outline, as modified by later research:[8]

Hymns. The hymns or psalms of praise ring with the enthusiasm of worshippers who sense that they are face to face with God. The hymns frequently contain three elements:

(1) A call to worship, where a leader urges the congregation to praise the Lord:

> O give thanks to the LORD,
>   call on his name. . . . (105:1)

Often the worshippers are called by name:

> O offspring of his servant Abraham,
>   children of Jacob, his chosen ones. (v. 6)

The exhortations are in the plural, indicating that the whole congregation or a substantial group within it is involved.

(2) A description of God's acts or attributes, usually forming the body of the hymn, giving the motivation for praise:

> He is the LORD our God;
>   his judgments are in all the earth. (v. 7)

> So he brought his people out with joy,
>   his chosen ones with singing. (v. 43)[9]

(3) A conclusion, calling for fresh praise or obedience:

> Praise the LORD! (v. 45c)

Psalms which contain, in one way or another, most of these elements are 8; 19; 29; 33; 104–105; 111; 113–114; 117; 135–136; 145–150.

The life situations in which hymns were used and within which they developed must have been numerous: victory after battle, thanks for harvest, relief from drought and plague, commemoration of the Exodus, and the seasonal feasts.

A number of subcategories have been identified which seem to cluster around special events:

(1) Victory songs (e.g., Ps. 68) were patterned after the stirring hymn raised by Miriam:

> Sing to the LORD, for he has triumphed gloriously;
> > horse and rider he has thrown into the sea. (Exod. 15:21)

(2) Processional hymns describe the longings and expectations of pilgrims and worshippers as they approach the temple. Some reflect the ardors of the journey as well as the anticipation of blessing (Pss. 84; 122). Others preserve an "entrance liturgy," part of a ceremony by which pilgrims passed a test of loyalty to God before admittance to the temple court (15; 24). Songs like Pss. 132; 68:24-27 capture the processions of worshippers on the move, perhaps accompanied by the ark of the covenant, not unlike 2 Sam. 6:1-11, where David first brought the ark to Jerusalem. Descriptions of the glorious walls and buildings of the holy city are frequent (e.g., Ps. 87).

(3) Songs of Zion (Pss. 46; 48; 76) praise the Lord for his majestic presence in Zion:

> His abode has been established in Salem,
> his dwelling place in Zion. (76:2)

(4) Enthronement songs (47; 93; 96–99) celebrate the reign of God as Lord of the nations. Two components are characteristic: an exhortation in the plural, rhetorically calling the nations and creation to praise Yahweh, and the reasons for the praise, such as God's saving deeds to Israel (99:6f.), strength (97:4), glory (96:6), justice (99:4), and victory (47:3). Some of these songs have an eschatological focus, celebrating God's final coming to make all things right (e.g., 96:13; 98:9).

Sigmund Mowinckel focused attention on these psalms by reconstructing a feast of Yahweh's enthronement. This alleged festival was connected with the autumn harvest and new year activities usually called the feast of Booths or Tabernacles (Lev. 23:33-36). Purportedly established early in the monarchy, this festival enacted the enthronement of Yahweh as king of all creation and relived his victories over chaos at the first creation and his conquest of Pharaoh and others in the Exodus. It also reconsecrated the temple, and commemorated

David's sovereignty over Israel and his settlement in Jerusalem. So important was this festival to Israel's cultic life that Mowinckel attached to it many psalms that are not strictly enthronement psalms (e.g., 68; 81; 95; 132).[10]

A major challenge to Mowinckel's reconstruction has come from H.-J. Kraus, who questioned Mowinckel's interpretation (1) grammatically: Kraus argued against the translation of *yhwh mālak* as "Yahweh has become king," a pillar in Mowinckel's structure, by showing that the reference is to a state, not an act; thus "Yahweh is king";[11] (2) cultically: How could God have been elevated to the throne when there was no image or representation as in the Babylonian and Canaanite cults from which Mowinckel drew his pattern? (3) theologically: Israel's view of the "living God" could not assume any mythic rhythm in which Yahweh dies annually or is weakened during the summer drought like pagan fertility gods; (4) exegetically: Kraus cites "the way in which the unchangeable and eternal kingship of Yahweh is extolled" in Ps. 93:2 as "subject to no variations."[12]

Both Mowinckel and Kraus note that the enthronement psalms have historical (remembering God's past deliverance) and eschatological (anticipating God's future victory) dimensions. Kraus stresses both their historical and eschatological character, while Mowinckel's chief concern is their use in the cult to express the present reality of God's exaltation as king.[13]

Complaints of the People.[14] Psalms like 12; 44; 60; 74; 79–80; 83; 85; 90; and 126 are prayers by the congregation in times of national emergency, such as plague, drought, invasion, or defeat (44; 60; 74; 79–80; cf. Lam. 5). Among the literary components in most psalms of communal complaint are:

(1) An address to God and a preliminary cry for help:

O God, why do you cast us off forever? (74:1)

(2) A reference to God's past work of salvation:

Remember your congregation, which you acquired long ago,
which you redeemed to be the tribe of your heritage. (74:2)

(3) A description of the people's suffering, usually in highly figurative terms. This often focuses on the three parties involved — (a) the enemies, (b) the people themselves, and (c) Yahweh:

(a) Your foes have roared within your holy place; (v. 4)
(b) We do not see our emblems;
there is no longer any prophet,
and there is no one among us who knows how long. (v. 9)
(c) Why do you hold back your hand,
why do you keep your right hand in your bosom? (v. 11)

435

(4) An affirmation of trust, frequently based on God's past deeds:

Yet God my King is from of old,
    working salvation in the earth. (v. 12)

(5) A series of petitions for rescue:

Do not deliver the soul of your dove to the wild animals;
    do not forget the life of your poor forever. (v. 19)

Do not forget the clamor of your foes,
    the uproar of your adversaries that goes up continually. (v. 23)

(6) A double wish relating to the people and their enemies:

Let the groans of the prisoners come before you . . .
Return sevenfold into the bosom of our neighbors
    the taunts with which they taunted you, O Lord! (79:11-12)

(7) A vow of praise in which the sufferers promise to celebrate their rescue with public praises:

Then we your people, the flock of your pasture,
will give thanks to you forever;
from generation to generation we will recount your praise. (79:13; cf. 74:21)[15]

The use of these complaints is clear. Solomon's dedicatory prayer included detailed descriptions of those occasions when God's people would gather at the temple and pray for his deliverance (1 Kgs. 8:33-40). More dramatically, the prophet Joel summoned the people to fast and to assemble with the priests to beg God to spare his people from the dreadful locusts (2:15-17).

The complaint in Joel is followed by an oracle of salvation, the promise of deliverance uttered in Yahweh's own words (vv. 19-29). Such speeches, delivered by a priest or temple prophet, appear to have accompanied or interrupted the complaints and assured the people that their prayers had been answered (cf. 2 Chr. 20:13-17).

A few psalms may be prayers of the people even though in the "I form." In the royal complaint of Ps. 89 the king served as spokesperson for the community.[16] Even psalms where the "we" form predominates sometimes use "I" or "my," when the spokesperson intervenes (44:6, 15; 74:12; 83:13).

Complaints of the Individual. More psalms fall into this category than any other.[17] The components of the individual complaints are virtually identical to those of the communal form, though the appeal to God's past salvation of the nation and the double wish are no longer standard elements.

(1) An address to God and cry for help:

My God, my God, why have you forsaken me? (22:1)

(2) A highly poetic, stylized description of the crisis, often referring to (a) the psalmist's enemies, (b) the psalmist, and (c) God:

(a)   Many bulls circle me,
        strong bulls of Bashan surround me; (v. 12)
(b)   I am poured out like water,
        and all my bones are out of joint; (v. 14)
(c)   You lay me in the dust of death. (v. 15c)

(3) An affirmation of trust:

In you our ancestors trusted;
    they trusted, and you delivered them. (v. 4)

(4) A series of petitions, sometimes expressed as a wish ("May the LORD . . ."), more frequently in the imperative:

But you, O LORD, do not be far away!
    O my help, come quickly to my aid!
Deliver my soul from the sword,
    my life from the power of the dog! (vv. 19f.)

(5) An additional argument, such as an appeal to God's special care, a description of the rejoicing of God's enemies, a prayer of confession (51:3-5), or a protest of innocence (26:3-8).[18]

Yet it was you who took me from the womb;
you kept me safe on my mother's breast. (22:9)

(6) A vow of praise, promising public testimony and a thank offering (Lev. 7:11-18):

I will tell of your name to my brothers and sisters;
in the midst of the congregation I will praise you. (22:22; cf. vv. 25f.)

(7) An assurance of being heard, where the sufferer expresses in advance his confidence in God's answer:

The righteous will surround me,
    for you will deal bountifully with me. (142:7)

Two types of circumstances seem to have prompted prayers of individual complaint: (1) social persecution, often manifested in unjust accusations of wrongdoing (e.g., 3; 5; 7; 17; 25; 27; 56; 69) and (2) illness (e.g., 38; 39; 62; 88). Sometimes both elements are combined in the same prayer (e.g., 6; 31; 88). Whether the persecution made the sufferer ill or illness led to charges of sin, the sufferer is both racked with pain and abandoned by friends.

Thanksgiving Songs of the Individual. These are closely related to the individual complaints. They were meant to be used when the crisis had been resolved and the complaint had been answered. Among the thanksgiving songs are 30; 32; 34; 40:1-10; 66; 116; 138. The structural elements frequently found in these psalms include the following:

(1) A resolve to give thanks:

I love the LORD . . .
I will call on him as long as I live. (116:1-2)

(2) An introductory summary:

. . . because he has heard my voice and my supplications. (v. 1; cf. v. 2)

(3) A poetic recollection of the time of need:

The snares of death encompassed me. (v. 3)

(4) A report of the petition and rescue:

Then I called on the name of the LORD:
    "O LORD, I pray, save my life!" (v. 4)

(5) Generalized teaching:

Gracious is the LORD, and righteous;
    our God is merciful.
The LORD protects the simple. (vv. 5-6)

(6) Renewed thanksgiving:

I will pay my vows to the LORD
    in the presence of all his people. (v. 14)

The thanksgiving song was normally recited at a service of thanksgiving, both as a prayer of thanksgiving and as a testimony to God's help spoken to the congregation. It was associated with the sacrifice of the thank offering, whose meat was later eaten at a sacred meal with family members and friends. Pss. 107 and 116 refer to this religious event.[19]

The story of Jonah illustrates a non-cultic use of the thanksgiving song: Jonah, safe within the large fish, gave thanks for deliverance from drowning (Jon. 2:1-9). The gap between this non-cultic setting and the normal temple setting of the thanksgiving psalms is bridged by Jonah's vow to participate in a formal service of thanksgiving (v. 9).

Royal Psalms. Though not designating strictly a literary type, this term is often used for a group of psalms that center on Israel's king. They illustrate the role of the preexilic king in Israel's worship and the expectations and obligations which the covenant laid upon the sons of David.

Content and literary form permit reconstructions of occasions when these royal psalms would have been used in public worship:

(1) Weddings. Ps. 45 celebrates the marriage of the king to a foreign princess, presumably to seal a political treaty. The wedding gave opportunity to stress the king's role as military leader and champion of justice, anointed by God himself (v. 7).

(2) Coronations. It is not certain whether psalms such as 2; 21; 72; and 110 were used at installation services, anniversaries of royal accession, or both. The fragmentary knowledge about such ceremonies comes from brief accounts of Solomon's hasty anointing (1 Kgs. 1:32-40) or Jehoash's bloody enthronement (2 Kgs. 11:9-21), and portions of psalms that hark back to installation rites (e.g., Ps. 89:19-37).

(3) Prayers before or after battle. Ps. 20 was used to petition Yahweh for blessing and victory in battle. The king, as military leader, is mentioned specifically. An assurance of victory may at times have been uttered by an inspired priest or prophet during these prayers (cf. 2 Chr. 20:14-17). In Ps. 20 this seems to be the role of the triumphant exclamation:

> Now I know that the LORD will help his anointed;
>> he will answer him from his holy heaven
>> with mighty victories by his right hand. (v. 6)

Ps. 89 takes the form of an individual complaint reminding Yahweh of past promises and his present absence. Ps. 18 (found also as 2 Sam. 22) is a royal thanksgiving for a military victory. Of special interest is the poetic description of the divine intervention in terms of a theophany.

All of these psalms reflect a unique tie between Yahweh and the king, although its precise nature is not readily discerned. Scholars have suggested several possibilities: (1) divine kingship (the king is an incarnation of God); (2) sacral kingship (the king mediates divine blessing); (3) charismatic kingship (the king rules by virtue of divine gift); (4) sacerdotal kingship (the king performs priestly functions); and (5) divinely appointed kingship (the king reigns by God's authority). Most emphasis should be put on the last suggestion.

Israel's kings received their authority by divine sanction bestowed in the ceremony of anointing and endorsed by communal acclamation. The biblical narratives are as mindful of the human factors as of the divine in the making of a king.[20]

In the postexilic period the royal psalms, under the influence of prophetic royal oracles, such as Isa. 9:2-7 and Mic. 5:2-6, became implicit prayers for restoration of the Davidic monarchy, and so acquired a messianic tone. The early church inherited this tradition and identified the hoped-for king with Jesus.[21]

Wisdom Psalms. A number of psalms use the language and style of the wisdom literature of the Old Testament: Proverbs, Job, and Ecclesiastes.

To fit this category, a psalm should: (1) reflect the literary techniques of wisdom, such as the use of proverbs, acrostics, numerical series, comparisons beginning with "better," admonitions addressed to sons, the commendation formula beginning with *'ašrê* "happy is/are . . . ," figures of speech drawn from nature; (2) have an obvious intent to teach by direct instruction (e.g., Pss. 1; 127; 128) or by grappling with a problem like the prosperity of the wicked (e.g., 37; 49; 73); (3) contain themes characteristic of wisdom, such as the doctrine of the two ways, the contrast between righteous and wicked, right speech, work, use of wealth, and fitting into the social structure.

By applying these tests and examining the use of "wisdom" vocabulary, one scholar has identified three subtypes of wisdom psalms: (1) sentence wisdom psalms (127; 128; 133), which describe exemplary conduct and its results, using expanded proverbs and similes; (2) acrostic wisdom psalms (34; 37; 112), in which verses or lines begin with succeeding letters of the Hebrew alphabet; (3) and integrative wisdom psalms (1; 32; 49), carefully planned compositions that center on significant wisdom themes, namely the relationship between wisdom and Torah (1), the certainty of just, if delayed, retribution (49), and the lessons to be learned from divine forgiveness (32).[22]

In addition to these wisdom psalms, others contain verses or stanzas that reflect the influence of wisdom literature: Pss. 25:8-10, 12-14; 31:23f.; 39:4f.; 40:4f.; 62:8, 10; 92:6-8; 94:8-15.[23] That such ingredients are found in psalms of complaint and thanksgiving may indicate close links, especially during later periods of psalm collecting (500 B.C. and after), between the temple and the wisdom movement.

One must discriminate between psalms that combine wisdom features with a cultic background, such as Pss. 32; 34; and 73, and compositions designed for use in the wisdom schools (Pss. 37; 49; 112; and 127). The presence of the latter texts in the Psalter suggests that the canonical edition of the book represents a collection of temple songs that have been edited by wisdom teachers. Ps. 1, with its commendation of *tôrâ* or written revelation forms a fitting introduction to this edition.[24]

Partially unrolled Thanksgiving scroll (1QH) from Qumran. *(Israel Museum)*

The Psalms and Israel's Worship

The Jerusalem temple must have been a busy place. The laws prescribed daily services (Exod. 29:38-42; Num. 28:2-8) in the morning and at twilight, sabbath rituals with extra sacrifices (Num. 28:9f.) and a greater number of participants (2 Kgs. 11:5-8), and special burnt offerings at the new moon (the beginning of each lunar month; Num. 28:11-15; cf. Hos. 2:11). In addition, those with ready access may have used the temple to commemorate special family occasions. Public events were also observed in the temple: the coronation of the king, a victory in battle, relief from drought or plague, and experiences of national disaster.

Annual feasts lasted for several days and drew to Jerusalem pilgrims from throughout the land: Unleavened Bread and Passover, a combined feast in early spring (Exod. 23:15; Lev. 23:5); Weeks (a harvest festival in late spring, called Pentecost in the New Testament; Exod. 23:16; 34:22; Num. 28:26; Acts 2:1); and Tabernacles in early fall (also called Booths or Ingathering; Exod. 23:16;

441

34:22; Deut. 16:16). Tabernacles, celebrating completion of the summer harvest as well as recalling Israel's wilderness days, apparently became the preeminent religious event of the year, though its precise role has been warmly debated.[25] The variety of festive activities and the lack of specific mention of feasts in the Psalter should caution us against theories that try to integrate the Psalms around a particular feast. Just as criticism has been leveled against Mowinckel's reconstruction of an enthronement or new year festival, Arthur Weiser's theory of a feast of covenant renewal coinciding with Tabernacles[26] likewise has drawn fire. His focus has several drawbacks: (1) he assumes a closer link between the account of God's theophany on Sinai and the theophanies of the Psalter than can be maintained; (2) in highlighting the covenant ceremonies from the days of the judges, he gives insufficient attention to the role of the Davidic covenant in the Psalms; (3) like Mowinckel, he neglects "the complexity of Israel's tradition and cultic life, sacrificing historical differentiation for an all-embracing 'lump' theory."[27]

Kraus's summary of the background of Israel's cult is broader and more balanced: (1) a tent festival commemorating the Exodus and wilderness wanderings was later incorporated in the harvest feast of Tabernacles; (2) a covenant renewal ceremony, perhaps originally observed at Shechem (Josh. 24), also came to be part of the Tabernacles ritual; (3) David's election as king and Jerusalem's capture were remembered at Tabernacles along with the entry of the ark into the holy city (2 Sam. 6).[28]

This approach shows ways in which earlier and later elements were combined, and it gives equal weight to wilderness/settlement components and later events of the monarchy. Above all Kraus, with Weiser, has grounded Israel's public worship soundly in the events of its own history rather than in the myths and ceremonies of its neighbors, as Mowinckel does.

Kraus's picture of a temple festival is worth noting, especially with regard to Tabernacles, the most important of the annual feasts before Passover (2 Kgs. 23:21-23), which had assumed substantial importance by the time of Josiah (639-609). Possible components of the festival include:

(1) the pilgrimage to Zion, anticipated with joy (Ps. 42:1f.), pursued with patience (84:6), and achieved with exultation (122:1f.);

(2) the ascent of the ark (perhaps from an area south of David's city), accompanied by hymns with a summons to enter the temple (95:1-6; 100), by memories of the recovery of the ark at Kiriath-jearim (132:6), and by recital of God's covenant with David (vv. 11f.);

(3) the entrance torah (15; 24:1-6), which posed questions about the qualifications of true worshippers and gave a priestly answer of a list of qualities, such as loyalty to God and integrity toward one's neighbor;

(4) the entrance liturgy (24:7-10), with antiphony between priests in the

procession who beg for entry and priests within the temple who ask for a confession of faith in "Yahweh of hosts" as the password (v. 10);

(5) the adoration of Yahweh in the temple courts, expressed in hymns and musical accompaniment (150), punctuated with reminders of God's glorious deeds in creation (104) and history (105; 136), and climaxed, perhaps, in the expectation of a theophany (50:1-3; 80:1-3), a special manifestation of God's presence and glory, though God was always present in the temple (46:5);

(6) the blessing of departure (91; 118:26; 121), assuring the pilgrims of God's protection and provision even though they could not, like the priests, stay permanently in the sanctuary (84:10).[29]

In their feasts and fasts, their daily worship, and their special celebrations, the people of Israel remembered and relived God's past victories, committed themselves to present obedience of the covenant laws, which called for full loyalty to Yahweh, and anticipated future triumphs, especially the ultimate defeat of Yahweh's foes.

> Thanksgiving for the past, rededication for the present, and expectation for the future were the all-embracing components of Israel's worship as voiced in the Psalms — a worship rooted in the healing, compelling, and hopeful revelation of God in their history.

The description of the Psalter as the hymnbook of the Second Temple (Zerubbabel's temple, rebuilt in 516) has been extended in recent years to include Solomon's temple. At least three factors have contributed to the recognition that very many of the psalms were composed and used before the Exile. (1) Psalm forms were well known to prophets like Jeremiah (a hymn in 10:12-16; complaints in 15:15-18; 17:14-18). (2) The royal psalms together with their clues to the king's role in public worship were composed during the monarchy. (3) Frequent parallels in vocabulary, grammar, and poetic structure between psalms and Ugaritic epic poetry (fourteenth century B.C.) are too numerous and striking to be accounted for unless the psalms stem from the earlier as well as later periods.[30]

Titles and Technical Terms

No area of Psalm studies has produced more dispute than attempts to decipher the titles and notes attached to individual poems. These cannot be defined or even dated with confidence. Though headings and notations of authorship are found in Mesopotamian and Egyptian psalms from well before David, evidence suggests that most biblical headings were added at a very late stage.

The notes have been divided into five categories.[31]

Collections, Compilers, or Authors. The most common notation is "Of David" (*l^edāwîd*, 73 times), meaning, perhaps, (1) "authored by David," whose musicianship is well attested (1 Sam. 16:17-23; 18:10; 2 Sam. 1:17-27; 3:33f.; 23:1-7; Amos 6:5), (2) "on behalf of David" (Ps. 20, a prayer for the Davidic king on the eve of battle), or (3) "belonging to David," part of a royal collection, perhaps including David's compositions.

Some psalms are attributed to "the Sons of Korah" (11 times), and to "Asaph" (12 times). Other individuals are named in psalms headings: "Moses" (Ps. 90); "Solomon" (Pss. 72; 127); heads of choir families, Heman the Ezrahite (88), Ethan the Ezrahite (Ps. 89), and "Jeduthun" (39; 62; 77).

Psalm Types. The most frequent designation is "psalm" *(mizmôr)*, used more than fifty times in the Psalter and nowhere else in the Old Testament. It refers to a cultic song accompanied by musical instruments. Thirty psalms are called "song" *(šîr)*, presumably referring to a composition sung a capella. Several psalms (65; 75–76; 92) bear both titles, denoting different traditions of their use. Heb. *miktām* describes six psalms (16; 56–60); there is no firm agreement as to its meaning. "Prayer" *(t^epillâ)* denotes a psalm of complaint (17; 86; 90; 102; 142). *Maśkîl*, used with thirteen psalms (e.g., 32; 42; 44), may mean "instruction" or "contemplation," though its precise sense is unknown. The title Song of Ascents (120–136) probably indicates that these psalms were used in the processional ascent to the temple. Ps. 145 is called "praise" *(t^ehillā)*, meaning a hymn, from which comes the Hebrew title for the Psalter. Ps. 45 is fittingly called "a love song" *(šîr y^edîdōt)*. The meaning of *šiggāyôn* (7) is unknown.

Liturgical Purposes and Usage. A few terms indicate the occasion for use: *tôdâ* (100) refers to a hymn used at the thanksgiving service; *hazkîr* (Pss. 38; 70) has been variously explained as a psalm "for the memorial offering" (NRSV; *'azkārâ*, Lev. 24:7) or to invoke Yahweh in "a petition" (NIV). Ps. 30 is labeled "A Song of the dedication of the temple"; *l^elammēd* (60) probably means "for instruction." The notation to Ps. 92 calls it "A Song for the Sabbath Day"; the meaning of *l^e'annōt* (88) is uncertain, perhaps signifying "for singing."

Technical Musical Expressions. Words like *bin^eginōt* "with stringed instruments" (4; 6; 54–55; 67; 76; and probably 61) and ʾel-hanneḥîlôt (5) "for the flutes," specifying the kind of accompaniment, are reasonably clear. However, terms like higgāyôn (9:16), haššᵉmînît (6; 12), haggittît (8; 81; 84), and ʿalāmôt (46), šôšannîm ("lilies"; 45; 69; 80), māhᵃlat (53), and ʾal-tašḥēt (58–59; 75) await further study. Suggestions include names of tunes, instructions for accompaniment, or notes for use in temple rituals.

The term lamᵉnaṣṣēaḥ, used fifty-five times in the Psalter (cf. Hab. 3:19) and often rendered "to the choirmaster," may alternatively designate a collection of psalms. Selah (selâ), used more than seventy times, appears to refer to a musical interlude, though its sectional placing may not always have been correctly preserved.

Historical Notes. The chief value of the notes that link a psalm (e.g., 3; 7; 18; 34; 51–52; 54; 56–57; 59–60; 63; 142) to a historical event is their clues as to how postexilic interpreters understood the texts. Most of these headings are later additions and do not afford accurate information about the origin of the poems. These historicizing notes reflect an exegetical enterprise that regarded David as a spiritual role model.[32]

Contributions to Biblical Theology

Like the windows and carvings of medieval cathedrals, the Psalms were pictures of biblical faith for a people who had no copies of the Scriptures in their homes and could not have read them. They present a compendium of Old Testament faith. Summaries of history (e.g., Pss. 78; 105–106; 136), instructions in piety (e.g., 1; 119), celebrations of creation (8; 19; 104), acknowledgment of God's judgment (37; 49; 73), assurances of his constant care (103), and awareness of his sovereignty over all nations (2; 110) were built into the bone and marrow of Israel's faith through the sustenance of the Psalter.

More than anything, the psalms were declarations of relationship between the people and their Lord. They assumed his covenant with them and its obligations of provision, protection, and preservation. Their songs of adoration, confessions of sin, protests of innocence, complaints about suffering, pleas for deliverance, assurances of being heard, petitions before battle, and thanksgivings afterwards were all expressions of their unique relationship to the one true God.

Awe and intimacy combined in Israel's appreciation of that relationship. They stood in awe of God's power and glory, his majesty and sovereignty. At the same time, they pleaded before him, arguing with his decisions and begging for his intervention. They revered him as Lord, and recognized him as Father.

This sense of special relationship best accounts for the psalms that curse Israel's enemies. The covenant was so binding that any foe of Israel was a foe of God, and vice versa. Moreover, Israel's relationship with God was expressed in a fierce hatred of evil that called for a judgment as severe as the crime (109; 137:7-9). Even that call for judgment was a product of the covenant, a conviction that the righteous Lord would protect his people and punish those who disdained his worship or his law. The judgment apparently would take place in the lifetime of the wicked. Jesus' teachings about love for enemies (Matt. 5:43-48) may have made these psalms difficult for Christians to pray, but Christians must not lose the hatred of sin or the zeal for God's holiness that prompted them.[33]

G. von Rad subtitles the section of his *Old Testament Theology* on the Psalms and wisdom literature as "Israel's Answer."[34] The Psalms are indeed responses of the priests and people to God's acts of deliverance and revelation in their history. Yet they are revelation as well as response. Through them one learns what God's salvation in its varied fullness means to God's people, as well as the heights of adoration and the lengths of obedience at which they must aim. No wonder the Psalms, along with Isaiah, was the book most frequently cited by Jesus and his apostles. The early Christians, like their Jewish forebears, heard God's word in these hymns, complaints, and instructions and made them a foundation for life and worship.

CHAPTER 33

Wisdom Literature

Biblical wisdom literature is part of a vast body of written and oral sayings with roots deep in antiquity. This literature is marked by sage observations about life set down in memorable form. It specializes in rules for success and happiness. It had existed for more than a millennium before Israel began to make its own distinctive contribution. The Egyptian Instructions of the Vizier Ptah-hotep were written about 2450 B.C., and Instruction for King Meri-ka-re[1] about 2180. Ancient Mesopotamia had a wealth and diversity of wisdom writings well before the time of Abraham. S. N. Kramer has distinguished five categories of Sumerian wisdom: proverbs; miniature essays; instructions and precepts; essays concerned with the Mesopotamian school and scribe; and disputes and debates.[2] Recent research has called attention to the deposit left in Ugaritic documents by Canaanite sages and scribes.[3]

Biblical wisdom literature had its formal beginnings in the tenth century, when it began to codify the sage advice and observations on life that had been passed orally from generation to generation. Since in form, if not always in content, biblical wisdom writings resemble their non-Israelite counterparts, it is worth noting some of the main themes and forms of nonbiblical wisdom literature.

> God gave Solomon very great wisdom, discernment, and breadth of understanding as vast as the sand on the seashore, so that Solomon's wisdom surpassed the wisdom of all the people of the east, and all the wisdom of Egypt. 1 Kgs. 4:29-30

Types of Wisdom Literature

Two main types of wisdom writings can be distinguished: (1) proverbial wisdom — short, pithy sayings which state rules for personal happiness and welfare or condense the wisdom of experience and make acute observations about life; and (2) contemplative or speculative wisdom — monologues, dialogues, essays, or stories which delve into basic problems of human existence such as the meaning of life, the path to success, and the problem of suffering. One should not read either mysticism or philosophy into the terms "contemplative" or "speculative." The sages did not deal in theory but in practice; they focused not on abstract problems but concrete examples: "There was a man in the land of Uz whose name was Job."

Proverbial Wisdom. From time immemorial people of wit and wisdom have coined and collected sage sayings about life. These wise men and women used these sayings as pegs on which to hang lessons for their children and other pupils and as pointers for those who sought advice and counsel. One hallmark of a great person, especially a king, was the ability to dispense wisdom in proverbial form or to outwit a foe with clever sayings: "One who puts on armor should not brag like one who takes it off" (1 Kgs. 20:11). For other examples see Goliath's questions to David (1 Sam. 17:43) and Joash's rebuff of Amaziah (2 Kgs. 14:9).

The origin of the proverb is lost in the preliterary fog of antiquity, but many factors must have contributed to its development. The earliest sayings were designed for oral transmission, and much wisdom writing reflects this oral character (cf. "hear" in Prov. 1:8; 4:1). From earliest times wisdom sayings, especially in Mesopotamia, seem to have been connected with religious and magical practices. In Babylon, rather than having a moral content, "generally 'wisdom' refers to skill in cult and magic lore, and the wiseman is the initiate,"[4] the one who can get what he wants from the gods. Some trace the beginnings of wisdom sayings to cultic practices almost exclusively, but other spheres of life such as child-training, trade, agriculture, commerce, and politics seem to have contributed to its development as well.[5] Indeed, it seems to be a common human trait to attempt systematic observations about life and to pass them on to others.

The earliest literary documents reveal highly sophisticated forms of didactic sayings, especially in Egypt where the sages tended to use paragraphs dealing with one theme rather than brief, mutually independent and often metaphorical statements. Note the Instructions of Vizier Ptah-hotep:

> Let not thy heart be puffed-up because of thy knowledge; be not confident because thou art a wise man. Take counsel with the ignorant as well as the wise. The (full) limits of skill cannot be attained, and there is no skilled man

equipped to his (full) advantage. Good speech is more hidden than the emerald, but it may be found with maidservants at the grindstones. . . .[6]

A Babylonian counterpart, from the Kassite period (1500-1100), is the *Counsels of Wisdom,* which advises on subjects like avoidance of bad companions, kindness to those in need, the undesirability of marrying a slave girl, and the duties and benefits of religion:[7]

> Let your mouth be controlled and your speech guarded:
> Therein is a man's wealth — let your lips be very precious.
> Let insolence and blasphemy be your abomination;
> Speak nothing profane nor any untrue report.
> A talebearer is accursed.
>
> . . . . . .
> Do not return evil to the man who disputes with you;
> Requite with kindness your evil-doer,
> Maintain justice to your enemy,
> Smile on your adversary.
>
> . . . . . .
> The house which a slave girl rules, she disrupts.
>
> . . . . . .
> Every day worship your god.
> Sacrifice and benediction are the proper accompaniment of incense.
> Present your free-will offering to your god.
> For this is proper toward the gods.[8]

These excerpts illustrate the practical, ethical, and religious tone of Near Eastern wisdom literature. To an extent they suggest the didactic essays in Prov. 1–9, and issue a warning against dating those longer and more unified chapters later than other parts of the book.

Brief, independent proverbs and popular sayings are found in lavish measure in Sumerian, Babylonian, and Assyrian texts. The popular sayings circulated among the common people and sometimes were designed more for entertainment than moral instruction. Many, apparently from the late Assyrian period (*ca.* 700), resemble fables, centered in the activity and conversation of animals and insects. For example:

> The spider spun a web for a fly.
> A lizard was caught
> On the web, to the spider's disadvantage![9]
>
> . . . . . .
> A *mosquito,* as it settled on an elephant,
> Said, "Brother, did I press your side? I will make [off] at the
>   watering-place."

> The elephant replied to the *mosquito,*
> "I do not care whether you get on — what is it to have you? —
> Nor do I care whether you get off."[10]

A longer, more highly developed Akkadian fable involves the debate between the date palm and tamarisk (an evergreen shrub). Each claims to be more useful to the king: the palm for shade and fruit, the tamarisk for wood and foliage.[11]

The distinction between popular saying and proverb is not easy. Both may use observations from nature and contain an admonition or moral. "Proverbs," as used here, refers to brief, crisp maxims, usually found in a series, yet mutually independent. In Mesopotamian literature proverbs are usually in bilingual form, written in parallel columns in Sumerian and Akkadian. For example:

> Whom you love — you bear (his) yoke.
> . . . . . .
> Seeing you have done evil to your friend,
>   what will you do to your enemy?[12]
> . . . . . .
> A people without a king (is like) sheep without a shepherd.[13]
> . . . . . .
> Would you place a lump of clay in the hand of him who throws?[14]
> . . . . . .
> Has she become pregnant without intercourse? Has she become fat without eating?[15]
> . . . . . .
> Last year I ate garlic; this year my inside burns.[16]

These sayings from ancient Mesopotamia illustrate the concrete nature of Oriental thought. Observations about life are made in terms of down-to-earth objects, creatures, and experiences, with little abstraction or theorizing. The proverbs and popular sayings have an immediacy and vitality which drive their message home with vigor and directness. To illustrate this, contrast the English proverb "in union is strength" with the Arabic proverb "two dogs killed a lion," or "familiarity breeds contempt" with the Jewish saying "the poor man hungers and knows it not."[17] "Pretty is as pretty does" pales beside the much more pungent observation:

> A good wife is the crown of her husband,
>   but she who brings shame is like rottenness in his bones. (Prov. 12:4)

or

> Like a gold ring in a pig's snout
>   is a beautiful woman without good sense. (11:22)

450

Egyptian scribe; Egyptian Museum, Cairo.
(Neal and Joel Bierling)

The Hebrew equivalent of "a word to the wise is sufficient" is "a rebuke strikes deeper into a discerning person than a hundred blows into a fool!" (17:10). English proverbs may be concrete ("a bird in the hand is worth two in the bush"; "people who live in glass houses should not throw stones"), but Hebrew and Semitic proverbs almost always are.

Why are some sayings cherished through the centuries and others cast aside? We may list several conditions for an effective proverb: (1) brevity —

bulky sayings will not lodge well in the memory, and proverbs must be memorable; (2) intelligibility — the meaning must be grasped readily; (3) flavor — only the pungent maxim will stick in people's minds; and (4) popularity — even a good saying will die if not repeated frequently and passed along through the generations.[18]

Speculative Wisdom. The ancients were as vexed by some of the pressing problems of life as are modern people. From the Kassite period in Mesopotamia comes a *monologue* of a sufferer who feels that all of life has turned in on him. The text is named from its opening lines Ludlul Bel Nemeqi ("I will praise the Lord of wisdom" — Marduk, chief god of Babylon). When the text first becomes legible the narrator complains of being forsaken by his gods:[19]

> My god has forsaken me and disappeared,
> My goddess has failed me and keeps at a distance.
> The benevolent angel who (walked) beside [me] has departed,
> My protecting spirit has taken to flight, and is seeking someone else.
> My strength is gone; my appearance has become gloomy;
> My dignity has flown away, my protection made off. (1.43-48)

Divine rejection is followed by the apathy or enmity of his friends, admirers, and slaves:

> I, who strode along as a noble, have learned to slip by unnoticed.
> Though a dignitary, I have become a slave.
> To my many relations I am like a recluse.
> If I walk the street, ears are pricked;
> If I enter the palace, eyes blink.
> . . . . . .
> My friend has become foe,
> My companion has become a wretch and a devil.
> . . . . . .
> My intimate friend has brought my life into danger;
> My slave has publicly cursed me in the assembly.[20] (1.77-81, 84f., 88f.)

Rejected by those he trusted both in heaven and on earth, the sufferer is further plagued by a host of physical ailments. None of the traditional ritual or magic cures provides relief, and he wonders why the gods have treated him like a wrongdoer:

> The diviner with his inspection has not got to the root of the matter,
> Nor has the dream priest with his libation elucidated my case.
> I sought the favour of the *zaqiqu*-spirit, but he did not enlighten me;
> And the incantation priest with his ritual did not appease the divine
> wrath against me.

. . . . . .
Who knows the will of the gods in heaven?
Who understands the plans of the underworld gods?
Where have mortals learnt the way of a god?

He who was alive yesterday is dead today.
For a minute he was dejected, suddenly he is exuberant.

One moment people are singing in exaltation,
Another they groan like professional mourners.
. . . . . .
As for me, the exhausted one, a tempest is driving me!
Debilitating Disease is let loose upon me:
. . . . . .
My lofty stature they destroyed like a wall,
My robust figure they laid down like a bulrush,
I am thrown down like a bog plant and cast on my face. (2.6-9, 36, 42,
49f., 68-70)

The text concludes with a series of dreams which reverse the sufferer's tragic
condition and show that Marduk's wrath has been appeased:

His hand was heavy upon me, I could not bear it.
My dread of him was alarming. . . .
. . . . . .
A third time I saw a dream,
And in my night dream which I saw —
. . . a young woman of shining countenance,
A queen of . . . , equal to a god.
. . . . . .
She said, "Be delivered from your very wretched state,
Whoever has seen a vision in the night time."
. . . . . .
After the mind of my Lord had quietened
And the heart of the merciful Marduk was appeased,
. . . . . .
He made the wind bear away my offenses. (3.1f., 29-32, 37f., 50f., 60)

Although this work has often been called the "Babylonian Job," its author
makes little attempt to delve into why the righteous suffer. Furthermore, the
cultic and magical emphases, the stress on demons as instruments of affliction,
and the visionary messengers of healing are all a far cry from Job, where God
assumes full responsibility for both the suffering and its relief. Job is finally
confronted by the living God and thus learns to accept his plight. The author

453

of Ludlul, however, describes at great length the stages of his healing. His actual relationship with Marduk is left unexplored, while the relationship between God and Job stands at the heart of the biblical work.

Ancient wisdom writings sometimes occur in *dialogue* form. An example is the Babylonian Theodicy, an acrostic poem of twenty-seven stanzas with eleven lines each. Dated by Lambert *ca.* 1000, this poem is a conversation between two friends: (1) a sufferer who complains of social injustice and (2) a comrade who tries to harmonize the experience of suffering with traditional views of divine justice.[21]

Orphaned at an early age, the sufferer wonders why the gods did not protect him as they did his parents' firstborn. The friend responds that piety will bring prosperity:

> He who waits on his god has a protecting angel,
> The humble man who fears his goddess accumulates wealth.

The sufferer counters with examples from both society and nature of violations of this principle. But the friend is convinced that all abuses of justice will be corrected and urges the sufferer to maintain piety and patience. The sufferer continues his plea of injustice, even blaming his dire condition on religious devotion:

> I have looked around society, but the evidence is contrary.
> The god does not impede the way of a devil.
> A father drags a boat along the canal,
> While his first-born lies in bed.
> . . . . . .
> The heir stalks along the road like a bully,
> The younger son will give food to the destitute.
>
> How have I profited that I have bowed down to my god?
> I have to bow beneath the base fellow that meets me;
> The dregs of humanity, like the rich and opulent, treat me with contempt. (243-46, 249-253)

The friend, now somewhat impressed by these arguments, takes refuge in the thought that the ways of the gods are past knowing:

> The divine mind, like the centre of the heavens, is remote;
> Knowledge of it is difficult; the masses do not know it. (256f.)

Finally, both friend and sufferer seem to agree that the gods are ultimately responsible for human injustice, since they fashioned people with a bent in this direction. The friend acknowledges that the deities

Gave perverse speech to the human race.
With lies, and not truth, they endowed them forever.

Solemnly they speak in favour of a rich man,
"He is a king," they say, "riches go at his side."

But they harm a poor man like a thief,
They lavish slander upon him and plot his murder,

Making him suffer every evil like a criminal, because he has no *protection*.
Terrifyingly they bring him to his end, and extinguish him like a flame.
(279-286)

The sufferer concludes by reaffirming his plight and pleading for respite.

The dialogue ends by begging the question. Responsibility for people's evil conduct is placed squarely on the gods. But some important points are glossed over. Is the ultimate answer that the gods are unjust? If so, what responsibilities are people to take for their actions? The differences from Job's approach to the problem of suffering or injustice are apparent. In the biblical account God's intervention provides the solution, and though God's righteousness may be questioned, it is sustained at the end of the story.

From a later period (1000-500 B.C.) comes the Babylonian Dialogue of Pessimism. This conversation between a master and his slave follows a simple pattern: a nobleman tells his slave of his plans to enjoy a certain recreation or pleasure. The slave replies by outlining the merits of that proposition. Then abruptly the master decides not to carry out his plans. Promptly and dutifully the slave gives cogent reasons for not following the plan:[22]

"Slave, listen to me." "Here I am, sir, here I am."
"Quickly, fetch me the chariot and hitch it up so that I can drive to the open country."
"Drive, sir, drive. A hunter gets his belly filled.
The hunting dogs will break the (prey's) bones,
The hunter's falcon will settle down,
And the fleeting wild ass . . . (.)"
"No, slave, I will by no means [drive] to the open country."
"Do not drive, sir, do not drive.
The hunter's luck changes:
The hunting dog's teeth will get broken,
The home of the hunter's falcon is in [. . .] wall,
And the fleeting wild ass has the uplands for its lair." (17-28)
. . . . . .
"Slave, listen to me." "Here I am, sir, here I am."
"I am going to love a woman." "So love, sir, love.

455

The man who loves a woman forgets sorrow and fear."
"No, slave, I will by no means love a woman."
["Do not] love, sir, do not love.
Woman is a pitfall — a pitfall, a hole, a ditch.
Woman is a sharp iron dagger that cuts a man's throat." (46-52)

As in Ecclesiastes, various possibilities for pleasure and public service are suggested and then discarded. None seems worthwhile to the master, who has lost his appetite for life. The conclusion, however, is poles apart from that of the critical Old Testament Preacher:

"Slave, listen to me," "Here I am, sir, here I am."
"What, then, is good?"
"To have my neck and your neck broken
And to be thrown into the river is good."
"Who is so tall as to ascend to the heavens?
Who is so broad as to compass the underworld?"
"No, slave, I will kill you and send you first."
"And my master would certainly not outlive me by even three days."

(79-86)

Scope of Biblical Wisdom Literature

Role of the Wise Man. Like their Babylonian, Canaanite, Edomite, and Egyptian neighbors, Israel had, from the beginnings of national consciousness, people famed for wisdom. Such skills were not limited to men. Early in Israel's history we find several references to wise women. The Song of Deborah mentions the answer of the "wisest ladies" on whom Sisera's mother depended for advice (Judg. 5:29). Similarly, 2 Sam. 14:2-20 cites the "wise woman" of Tekoa, who was apparently more than a professional mourner. Her words in v. 14 suggest that she was familiar with the proverbial sayings of the wisdom circles: "We must all die, we are like water spilled on the ground, which cannot be gathered up." Other early examples include David's counselor, Ahithophel: "Now in those days the counsel which Ahithophel gave was as if one consulted the oracle of God; so all the counsel of Ahithophel was esteemed, both by David and by Absalom" (2 Sam. 16:23); and the wise woman of Abel (a place famous for its wise counsel), who "went to all the people with her wise plan" (20:22).[23]

Israel's wisdom movement undoubtedly began in clan life, where it was used to prepare each generation to assume responsibilities of family, land, and social leadership.[24] However, wisdom took on new significance under Solomon, whose court offered support and prestige. The literary aspects are rooted in this period, when Solomon's wealth, international contacts, and cultural pursuits combined to launch the movement that produced the biblical wisdom writings.[25] Solomon's stellar role in the development of this official wisdom is attested in 1 Kgs. 4:32-34 (MT 5:12-14):

> He composed three thousand proverbs, and his songs numbered a thousand and five. . . . People came from all the nations to hear the wisdom of Solomon; they came from all the kings of the earth who had heard of his wisdom. (See also Prov. 1:1; 10:1; 25:1.)

The precise setting within which the movement flourished is a matter of question. The general consensus is that Solomon and his successors established schools, modeled after those in Egypt, to train administrators, scribes, and other officials for the tasks of the centralized government. Though plausible, this supposition lacks specific biblical support. The first actual mention of a school in Jewish literature is in the time of Sirach (*ca.* 180 B.C.; Sir. 51:23). Thus, despite the traditional interpretation of Jer. 18:18, which seems to point to the existence of three offices — prophet, priest, wise man — ongoing debate grapples with two basic questions: (1) did the wise in Israel occupy a special office or constitute a separate class? (2) were there schools for sages and scribes attached to temple or court?[26]

Prov. 25:1 indicates that Hezekiah served as a second royal patron of the sages. By the time of Jeremiah (*ca.* 600) the wise men, on occasion, could be compared in prestige and influence to the prophets and priests. Like other religious leaders, the sages drew the prophet's fire for failing to discharge their duties in obedience to God and his word:

> The wise shall be put to shame,
>   they shall be dismayed and taken;
> since they have rejected the word of the LORD,
>   what wisdom is in them? (Jer. 8:9)

Again, Jeremiah's enemies acknowledge the prominence of the wise men when they seek to refute Jeremiah's prophecy that the law would perish from the priest, counsel from the wise, and the word from the prophet (18:18). Perhaps the clearest testimony to the prestigious position of sages during this period is the extent to which the prophets used wisdom sayings and techniques in their writings. Amos' writings are laced with wisdom motifs, e.g., the three-four pattern of chs. 1–2 (see Prov. 30:15, 18, 21, 29; cf. Job 5:19) and disputation questions of 3:3-8; 6:12. Prophetic use of wisdom forms (see Isaiah, Hosea, Habakkuk, Jeremiah) also indicates that divisions of office should not be considered ironclad.[27]

The wise were obligated to counsel people who faced difficult decisions or needed advice as to the proper course of action, including leaders of government.[28] Much of this advice was probably dispensed in proverbial form. The truly wise person had ready access to sayings which would speak pungently and clearly to an inquirer's problem (note Eccl. 12.9: "Besides being wise, the Teacher also taught the people knowledge, weighing and studying and arranging many proverbs"; also v. 11: "The sayings of the wise are like goads, and like nails firmly fixed are the collected sayings that are given by one shepherd"). Also, the sages were to contemplate the perplexing issues of life and make appropriate pronouncements or observations. Job and Ecclesiastes are the most notable examples. This phase of wisdom is as close as the Hebrews came to what the Greeks called "Philosophy," though the differences are marked.

Characteristics of Biblical Wisdom. In garnering their wise sayings, the sages knew no limitations of culture or nationality. In fact, one distinctive of wisdom literature is its international character. Proverbs of one society are freely borrowed by another, because their very character as observations based on study or reflection upon life gives them a universality not always found in epic or historical writings.

Accordingly, wisdom in the ancient Orient and the Old Testament tends to emphasize the success and well-being of individuals, their families, and their community. This individualism contrasts with the prophets' marked emphasis on national and corporate religious life. The great themes of Israel's faith — election from Egypt, the covenant with Yahweh, public worship, the day of the Lord — play little part in wisdom writings. Further, almost no references to Israel's history are found. This, however, should not be interpreted as meaning that wisdom in Israel was a secular matter or that Israel's wisdom writings did not differ from those of their neighbors. Far from it! No one can read Job, Proverbs, or Ecclesiastes without hearing overtones of Israel's distinctive faith.[29] For the true Israelite all wisdom stemmed from God and was available to human beings only because they were creatures of God, capable of receiving divine revelation. But more than this, only the devout worshipper, who feared God, could really begin to be wise.

> Wisdom based on human skill or ingenuity was a gift of God, part of his order in creation. But without awe of God and obedience to him, wisdom was doomed to defeat because of pride and presumption. Part of the fear of God for Israel's wise teachers was their reverence for the divine order in creation that governed all of life, rewarding sound judgment and behavior and inflicting harmful consequences on foolishness.[30]

Biblical Wisdom Writings. In the broadest sense of "wisdom" as "didactic or instructive literature," Job, Proverbs, and Ecclesiastes are clearly the three great contributions of Israel's sages to the Old Testament. In addition, certain psalms reflect wisdom themes (see 1; 32; 34; 37; 49; 73; 112; 127–28; 133; see above, Ch. 32, p. 440). They either contain precepts or admonitions (rather than hymns or prayers) or deal with perplexing questions such as the prosperity of the wicked and adversity suffered by the righteous. Both Song of Solomon and Lamentations reflect considerable wisdom influence in their graphic figures of speech and highly stylized forms, particularly the acrostic patterns of Lamentations. Moreover, both Job and Ecclesiastes, though examples of speculative wisdom, contain numerous proverbs.

In the New Testament the wisdom school is reflected in many of Christ's teachings. Notable are his proverbs and parables drawn from nature, and his ability to pose and solve puzzling questions. As one "greater than Solomon" (Matt. 12:42), Christ was the master sage, fulfilling this Old Testament office as well as those of prophet, priest, and king. The epistle of James, which stresses the wisdom from above (3:15) and uses analogies from nature and proverbs, is an outstanding example of New Testament wisdom literature.[31]

CHAPTER 34

Proverbs

Purpose

Hebrew wisdom is the art of success, and Proverbs is a guidebook for successful living. By citing both negative and positive rules of life, Proverbs clarifies right and wrong conduct in a host of situations. The absence of allusions to Israel's history and to great prophetic themes like the *covenant* does not mean that the wisdom authors were unaware of them. Rather, their aim was to apply the principles of Israel's covenant faith to everyday attitudes, activities, and relationships. The laws of love (Lev. 19:18; Deut. 6:5; cf. Mark 12:29-31) are central Old Testament emphases. Proverbs serves as an extended commentary on them. God's people were bound to view God's law as an inescapable duty demanding total obedience. Proverbs calls this obedience "the fear of the Lord" (Prov. 1:7; 2:5; 9:10; Job 28:28; Ps. 111:10). This obligation, akin to the knowledge of God as stressed in the prophetic books (Hos. 4:1; 6:6), entails reverence, gratitude, and commitment to do God's will in all circumstances. The prime mission of Proverbs is to spell out strikingly, memorably, and concisely just what it means to be fully at God's disposal.

> The fear of the Lord is the beginning of knowledge;
> fools despise wisdom and instruction. 1:7

Contents

The variety of literary forms in Proverbs illustrates the wide range of the Hebrew *māšāl* which in the plural form *m^ešālîm* gives the book its name. *Māšāl* is apparently derived from a root meaning "to be like" or "compared with." Thus, a proverb originally may have been a comparison of a type found in the Old Testament:

> Pleasant words are like a honeycomb,
> sweetness to the soul and health to the body. (Prov. 16:24)

or:

> Better is a dinner of vegetables where love is
> than a fatted ox and hatred with it. (15:17)

Frequently, however, no comparison appears even in the oldest proverbs (e.g., "Out of the wicked comes forth wickedness"; 1 Sam. 24:13). Rather, these sayings comprise pithy, succinct phrases which condense the wisdom of experience.[1] In Prov. 1–9 *māšāl* also describes the longer, sermonlike passages which are not strictly proverbs (cf. Job's speeches, 27:1; 29:1). Elsewhere it may denote a byword (Deut. 28:37; Jer. 24:9; Ezek. 14:8) or a taunt song (Isa. 14:4ff.), in which the sufferer becomes an example held up to ridicule.[2]

Proverbs seems to contain eight separate collections, distinguishable by either an introductory subtitle or a striking change in literary style. Prov. 1:1-6 is a general introduction or superscription, clarifying both the book's purpose and its connection with Solomon, Israel's master sage. This introduction sets Proverbs in the international context of wisdom which Solomon represented (1 Kgs. 4:29-34; 10:1-29). It also anchors the wisdom movement to the beginnings of the Monarchy rather than the postexilic period.[3]

Importance of Wisdom (1:7–9:18). This section illustrates the techniques of wisdom. The teacher addresses the pupil as his son (e.g., 1:8; 2:1; 3:1) and maintains a parental tone throughout. Oral instruction dominates, as the frequent references to hearing and memorizing indicate; writing is scarcely mentioned. These chapters contain numerous figures of speech and graphic expressions which aid the hearer's memory. Constant use of parallelism, the basis of Semitic poetry, was itself a help in memorizing.

The writer's purpose here is to draw the strongest possible contrast between the results of seeking and finding wisdom and those of pursuing a life of folly. Both wisdom and folly are intensely religious and extremely practical concepts. Wisdom begins with the fear of God and moves out into the whole range of life. Folly is not ignorance, but the deliberate disdain of

461

moral and godly principles. The combination of moral depravity, spiritual irresponsibility, and social insensitivity described in Isa. 32:6 is an apt summary of Proverbs' view of the fool (see Jesus' warning in Matt. 5:22):

> For fools speak folly, and their minds plot iniquity:
> to practice ungodliness, to utter error concerning the LORD,
> to leave the craving of the hungry unsatisfied,
> and to deprive the thirsty of drink.

Although they convey some specific instructions, chs. 1–9 seek mainly to clarify the consequences of choosing wisdom or folly, righteousness or wickedness. While praising the virtues of true wisdom, the teacher sternly warns the pupil against certain prevalent temptations: crimes of violence (1:10-19; 4:14-19), hasty pledges (6:1-5), laziness (vv. 6-11), dishonesty (vv. 12-15), and especially sexual immorality (2:16-19; 5:3-20; 6:23-35; 7:4-27; 9:13-18). The vivid descriptions of the lurid charms of wanton women may refer not only to the dangers of physical unchastity but also to the menace of spiritual impurity — worship of false gods, often described by the prophets (particularly Hosea: 1:2; 2:13; 4:12-15; and Jeremiah: 3:1-13; 5:7f.) as adultery or harlotry. Because the Canaanite and other Near Eastern religions involved cult prostitution, the sage could issue both warnings at once. The profoundly religious character of these chapters (e.g., 1:7; 3:5-12), their moral and social concern, and the sermonlike style are reminiscent of the speeches in Deuteronomy.[4]

The personification of wisdom in ch. 8 is of special importance. As in Prov. 1:20-33, Wisdom is pictured as a woman calling the human family to follow her instruction and find the meaning of life. This personalization peaks in 8:22-36, where Wisdom claims to have been created before all else, even suggesting that she playfully applauded God at creation (v. 30; cf. 3:19). These claims are more practical than theological: Wisdom presents her credentials so as to attract the hearer's allegiance (8:32-36). She remains a creature of God, not an independent deity or even a *hypostasis,* an attribute of God that takes on an existence of its own. The Hebrews thought and wrote in concrete, not theoretical, terms. This often led their poets to treat inanimate objects or ideas as though they had personality.[5]

This personification, which became even more intense during the intertestamental period (e.g., Sir. 24:1-34; Wisd. of Sol. 6:12-16; 7:22–8:18), contributed significantly to New Testament teachings about Christ. The doctrine of the Logos "Word" in John 1:1-14 is based, at least in part, on Prov. 8: both wisdom and the Logos exist from the beginning (8:22; John 1:1); are active in creation (8:30; John 1:3); and have a life-giving influence (8:35; John 1:4).[6] Similarly, Paul's description of the lordship of Christ in Col. 1:15-20 contains overtones of Prov. 8, and the specific references to Christ as the source of true wisdom (1 Cor. 1:24-30) are deeply rooted in Proverbs.[7]

The author of these chapters will never be identified conclusively. The superscription (1:1-6) seems to credit the entire book to Solomon. Since he is mentioned again specifically as author of the collection which begins at 10:1, chs. 1–9 are probably the product of anonymous sages. Usually considered among the latest sections of the book, these essays may have been included as late as 600 B.C., although much of the material seems to stem from an earlier age. The parallels in thought and structure between this section (especially chs. 8–9) and Ugaritic and Phoenician literature, suggest that "it is entirely possible that aphorisms and even longer sections go back into the Bronze Age in substantially their present form."[8] In sharp contrast to the tendency of some studies to date wisdom materials by their length, placing shorter sayings earlier and longer speeches later,[9] the existence of longer wisdom speeches in Egypt and Mesopotamia well before Solomon's time witnesses to the antiquity of this literary form. "Length can therefore no longer be regarded as a criterion for dating the various parts of the book."[10]

Proverbs of Solomon (10:1–22:16). This section of some 375 proverbs is generally considered the oldest in the book. Increased understanding of ancient Near Eastern wisdom literature and fresh light on the splendors of Solomon's reign have brought renewed appreciation for his role as patron of Israel's wisdom movement. He enjoyed intimate contacts with the Egyptian court, access to foreign learning afforded by a far-flung empire, and comparative peace in his reign. His administrative innovations called for a highly trained bureaucracy, and his fabulous wealth could support companies of scribes and recorders on a scale impossible for his heirs. Coupled with his God-given wisdom (1 Kgs. 3:9-28), these factors strongly support biblical claims concerning his activities as a wise man (1 Kgs. 4:29ff. [MT 5:9ff.]; Prov. 1:1; 10:1; 25:1). Failure to apply his wisdom, however, led ultimately to the division of Solomon's kingdom (1 Kgs. 12).

These proverbs usually consist of two stichs (lines). In chs. 10–15 the poetic structure is largely antithetic: the second line of the parallelism states an idea opposite to that of the first:

> A child who gathers in summer is prudent,
> but a child who sleeps in harvest brings shame. (10:5)

or:

> The memory of the righteous is a blessing,
> but the name of the wicked will rot. (v. 7)

This structure is admirably suited to wisdom teaching because it makes clear both the negative and positive courses of attitude or conduct. Furthermore, it depicts in graphic form the conviction of the sages that ultimately people have only two ways to walk — the way of the righteous (wise) or that of the wicked (foolish), of blessing or dire judgment (cf. Ps. 1).

Chs. 16–22 use antithetic parallelism sparingly. The predominant patterns are synthetic parallelism, in which the second line completes the first:

> The LORD has made everything for its purpose,
>> even the wicked for the day of trouble. (16:4)

and synonymous parallelism, in which the second line restates and reinforces the first:

> Pride goes before destruction,
>> and a haughty spirit before a fall. (v. 18)

The sayings in chs. 10–22 show little continuity, and scholars are still groping to discern reasons for their sequence in the text.[11] All but a handful are classified as statements or affirmations (German *Aussagen*), with verbs in the indicative mood. They contain concisely summarized observations from experience:

> A friend loves at all times,
>> and kinfolk are born to share adversity. (17:17)

or:

> A cheerful heart is a good medicine,
>> but a downcast spirit dries up the bones. (v. 22)

The lesson in each is implied; no direct exhortation is given to the student. This type of saying is "self-confirming, commending itself to empirical validation or to disconfirmation."[12]

An alternate form is the "better" proverb:

> Better is a little with righteousness
>> than large income with injustice. (16:8; cf. 12:9; 15:16f.; 16:19; 17:1)

This comparison values righteousness as so infinitely preferable to injustice that no amount of wealth can compensate for its absence.

Another form of comparison is based on "like" or "as":

> Like vinegar to the teeth, and smoke to the eyes,
>> so are the lazy to their employers. (10:26; cf. 11:22; 16:24; 17:8)

At times the comparison is implied, with no connecting word:

> The crucible is for silver, and the furnace is for gold,
> but the LORD tests hearts. (17:3)

Such comparisons demonstrate the Hebrew belief in "visible connections which point to an all-embracing order in which both phenomena [in the comparison] are linked with each other."[13] This order is what the wise sought to understand and express in their proverbs.

Despite some religious emphasis (see 15:3, 8, 9, 11; 16:1-9), most of these proverbs are not related explicitly to Israel's faith; they are based on practical observations of everyday life. Their point is intensely practical, frequently stressing the rewards of wise living (see 11:18, 25-31). Some scholars, believing that pure religion should involve worship of God for what God is and not for what God gives, have criticized this concern: "In their obviousness the [religion-ethical] principles render God necessary only as the guardian of the system."[14] But since God had not yet revealed the mystery of life after death or the role of suffering in his redemptive program, how could a practical scribe have made his point without highlighting the blessings of the wise and the pitfalls of the fool?[15] Those who would discount the importance of Proverbs have been rightly criticized: "Only the man who has allowed his senses to be dulled in his dealing with the materials or who does not know the real purpose of this poetic wisdom can be deceived as to the magnitude of the intellectual achievement of our wisdom teachers."[16]

Words of the Wise (22:17–24:22). The title of this section has been concealed in 22:17 by the Masoretic text and English versions:

> Incline your ear, and hear the words of the wise,
> and apply your mind to my knowledge. (RSV)

The more obvious heading, "These also are sayings of the wise" (24:23), implies that this is a separate collection from a group of unknown sages. They may have been royal scribes commissioned to build a collection of useful maxims and apt observations, like Hezekiah's men (25:1).

These proverbs, in contrast with those in the previous section, are generally longer (many being two or more verses in length), more closely related, and sustained in theme. Antithetic parallelism is rare (see 24:16), while synonymous and, especially, synthetic parallelism are frequent. The topics show considerable variety: concern for the poor (22:22, 27); respect for the king (23:1-3; 24:21f.); discipline of children (23:13f.); moderation in drinking (vv. 19-21, 29-35); obedience to parents (vv. 22-25); and sexual purity (vv. 26-28). Here also a religious note (22:19, 23; 24:18, 21) is sounded, although the influence of Israel's faith is implicit rather than explicit.

The characteristic form of proverb here is the admonition or exhortation

Wisdom of Amenemope, Egyptian proverbs which bear resemblance
to Prov. 22:17–23:11. *(British Museum)*

(German *Mahnwort*). The verbs are imperative or jussive (a third-person
command, usually translated with "Let . . ."), either negative or positive:

> Listen to your father who begot you,
> and do not despise your mother when she is old. (23:22)

The exhortations carry the authority of the teachers and their experiences; but
they frequently are reinforced by clauses which state the reason or motivation
for the command:

> Do not be among winebibbers, or among gluttonous eaters of meat;
> for the drunkard and the glutton will come to poverty,
> and drowsiness will clothe them with rags. (vv. 20f.)

In these admonitions also, the idea of a divine order which governs the outcome of obedience and disobedience is implicit.

The sayings of 22:17–23:11 bear remarkable resemblance to a section of
the Egyptian proverbs of Amenemope (Amenophis), probably *ca.* 1000 or
somewhat earlier. The resemblance is reinforced if "thirty sayings" (NRSV) is
read instead of "excellent things" (AV). The change makes a connection with
Amenemope's thirty chapters and entails no emendation of the Hebrew consonants. For decades scholars have debated as to which collection influenced
the other, although widespread agreement now favors Amenemope as the

466

original.[17] Whatever their source, these proverbs have been shaped and molded by Israelite sages in terms of Israel's historic faith, and thus have become part of God's inspired message. For instance, Amenemope warns:

> Guard thyself against robbing the oppressed
> And against overbearing the disabled. (ch. 11)

while Proverbs adds a significant reason for abstaining from such robbery:

> Do not rob the poor, because he is poor,
> or crush the afflicted at the gate;
> for the Lord will plead their cause. . . . (22:22f.)

The following passages illustrate parallels between Proverbs and the Instruction of Amenemope:[18]

Amenemope	Proverbs (RSV)
Give thy ears, hear what is said, Give thy heart to understand them. To put them in thy heart is worth while. . . . (ch. 1)	Incline your ear, and hear the words of the wise, and apply your mind to my knowledge; for it will be pleasant if you keep them within you. . . . (22:17f.)
Do not carry off the landmark at the boundaries of the arable land, Nor disturb the position of the measuring-cord; Be not greedy after a cubit of land, Nor encroach upon the boundaries of a widow. (ch. 6)	Do not remove an ancient landmark or enter the fields of the fatherless; (23:10)
. . . they [riches] have made themselves wings like geese And are flown away to the heavens. (ch. 8)	For suddenly it takes to itself wings, flying like an eagle toward heaven. (23:5b)
Do not eat bread before a noble, Nor lay on thy mouth at first. If thou art satisfied with false chewings, They are a pastime for thy spittle. Look at the cup which is before thee, And let it serve thy needs. (ch. 23)	When you sit down to eat with a ruler, observe carefully what is before you; and put a knife to your throat if you are a man given to appetite. Do not desire his delicacies, for they are deceptive food. (23:1, 3)

Additional Sayings (24:23-34). This brief collection contains both concise proverbs (v. 26) and longer maxims (vv. 30-34; cf. 6:6-11). The keen sense of moral and social responsibility characteristic of Proverbs is much in evidence here (24:28f.), although with little stress on religion. This section also is the product of an anonymous company of sages.

Proverbs of Solomon Copied by Hezekiah's Men (25:1–29:27). Both in style and content this section bears a number of similarities to 10:1–22:16 (e.g., compare 25:24 with 21:9; 26:13 with 22:13; 26:15 with 19:24). However, the proverbs here tend to vary in length. Antithetic parallelism is less frequent (although chs. 28–29 contain numerous examples), while comparison appears repeatedly here (25:3, 11-14, 18-20).

As with the proverbs in 10:1–22:16, there is no reason to doubt the Solomonic origin of this collection. The Jewish tradition (Talmud *B. Bat.* 15a) that Hezekiah and his company wrote Proverbs is based on 25:1. Hezekiah's interest in Psalms (2 Chr. 29:25-30) and his concern for the Hebrew prophets (see Isa. 37) may well have been paralleled by his patronage of Israel's wisdom movement. Perhaps his scribes copied the proverbs in these chapters from an older manuscript specifically for this collection. Or they may have written down maxims which had been preserved in oral form from the early days of the Monarchy. While it is not impossible that something of the turbulence of the eighth century is reflected here, most of the allusions to kings or officials are general enough to fit the Solomonic period as well.

Words of Agur (30:1-33). Both Agur and his father Jakeh defy identification. They were probably from the tribe of Massa (translating the Heb. 30:1 as a proper name, not as "oracle" or "prophecy" as do AV and ASV), descendants of Ishmael who settled in northern Arabia (Gen. 25:14; 1 Chr. 1:30). If Agur and Lemuel (ch. 31) are Massaites, their collections of maxims are further examples of the international character of Hebrew wisdom, adopted and molded to the Israelites' covenant ideals.

The precise thought of vv. 2-4 is difficult to discern. A slight sarcasm is detectable: the writer apparently quotes a skeptic who claims that little can be known about God, especially his role in the universe. The doubter chides the wise man to tell him about his God. The sage shuns argument and affirms the truthfulness of God's word and the security to be found in God (vv. 5f.; cf. Job 38–40, where Job is silenced when confronted personally by the Lord of the universe). Agur concludes this section by a brief but moving prayer that God supply only his real needs, lest either in poverty or self-sufficiency he be tempted to sin (vv. 7-9).

The remainder of the chapter consists largely of observations from nature or social relationships which contain implicit lessons for successful living. Featured is the use of numerical patterns in the organization of the statements, particularly the x, x + 1 pattern ("three things . . . four . . .") well attested in the Old Testament (Amos 1–2; Mic. 5:5) and Semitic (esp. Ugaritic)[19] literature. In wisdom literature this pattern creates a feeling of anticipation by building to a climax and is an aid to the hearer's memory. At times the numerical proverbs exhibit a gamelike quality which may bear some ancient connection to the riddle.[20]

Words of Lemuel (31:1-9). Like Agur, this king of Massa is unknown. His brief collection consists of sage advice by his mother to prepare him for office. She warns him to avoid excess with women and wine and encourages him to protect the rights of the poor and underprivileged.

Description of an Excellent Women (31:10-31). Even though it has no separate title, this carefully polished anonymous poem seems to be separated from the sayings of Lemuel by its alphabetical acrostic form. The highly self-conscious techniques involved in this form (see Ps. 119) were an aid to memorization. More importantly, they served to affirm the sense of wholeness embodied in this picture of the perfect wife and mother. This portrait of an industrious, competent, conscientious, pious woman is a conclusion well suited to a book which teaches the nature and importance of a life lived in obedience to God in every detail.

Limits of Wisdom. In seeking to interpret the various proverbs and apply them to life, one must bear in mind that they are generalizations. Though stated as absolutes — as their literary form requires — they are meant to be applied in specific situations and not indiscriminately. Knowing the right time to use a proverb was part of being wise:

> A word fitly spoken
> is like apples of gold in a setting of silver. (25:11)

Implicit, then, to a correct understanding of wisdom was the awareness of its limits.[21] As effective as the proverbs were as a guide to success, they could be misleading if viewed as magical sayings which would always and automatically bring results. The best among the sages warned against such presumptive self-confidence and made room for God to work some sovereign surprises:

> The human mind plans the way,
> but the Lord directs the steps. (16:9; cf. vv. 1f.; 21:31)

In part at least, the failure of the wisdom circles to follow their own convictions about these limits led to the sharp reactions of Job and Ecclesiastes.

Date of the Collection

It is clear from Prov. 25:1 that the book could not have been completed before Hezekiah's time (*ca.* 715-686). The last two chapters may well have been added during or shortly after the Exile (*ca.* 500). Most likely chs. 10–29 were edited during Hezekiah's time and the introductory and concluding chapters were added during the two following centuries. The fifth century is a reasonable date for the final editing, although most of the contents are much earlier, with most individual proverbs and even longer speeches stemming from long before the Exile.

Attempts to date various sayings within the book as later than others because they are overtly religious[22] should be disregarded. The entire background of the sayings so clearly implies a faith in Yahweh that no distinction can be made in dating between verses that mention God's work and those that do not.

> The Lord's presence in the order which he created and sustains is presumed in every saying: "The experiences of the world were for [Israel] always divine experiences as well, and the experiences of God were for her experiences of the world."[23]

Proverbs and the New Testament

New Testament writers have drawn freely from Proverbs to support their teachings. For instance, a number of quotations and allusions are embedded in the New Testament: e.g., 3:7a, Rom. 12:16; 3:11f., Heb. 12:5f.; 3:34, Jas. 4:6 and 1 Pet. 5:5b; 4:26, Heb. 12:13a; 10:12, Jas. 5:20 and 1 Pet. 4:8; 25:21f., Rom. 12:20; 26:11, 2 Pet. 2:22. The Christ who came to fulfill the law and the prophets (Matt. 5:17) also fulfilled the wisdom writings by revealing the fullness of God's wisdom (Matt. 12:42; 1 Cor. 1:24, 30; Col. 2:3). He used the techniques of the sages — proverbs, parables, illustrations from nature, puzzling questions — to fix his words in his hearers' hearts.[24] Proverbs is an extensive commentary on the law of love. It is, therefore, part of the Old Testament preparation for the coming of the One in whom divine love took on human form.

CHAPTER 35

Job

"Have you considered my servant Job?" — the pointed question that Yahweh put to Satan (1:8; 2:3) — triggered the forty-two chapters of suffering, complaint, argument, and response that comprise the book of Job. Few stories in the literature of human experience have such power to stretch minds, tax consciences, and expand visions as does Job's. All who witness the disaster in the land of Uz, eavesdrop on the conversations in Yahweh's court, arbitrate the debate between Job and his friends, or shiver at the voice from the whirlwind will have their basic beliefs challenged. One's view of divine sovereignty and freedom as well as one's picture of human suffering and arrogance and integrity will be altered. This is both the danger and the blessing of the book.

> Where then does wisdom come from?
>   And where is the place of understanding?
> It is hidden from the eyes of all living,
>   and concealed from the birds of the air.
> Abaddon and Death say,
>   "We have heard a rumor of it with our ears."
> God understands the way to it,
>   and he knows its place.
> For he looks to the ends of the earth,
>   and sees everything under the heavens. Job 28:20-24

Name and Place in Canon

The name Job (Heb. *'iyyôb*) has been variously interpreted. One suggestion is "Where is (my) Father?" Another reading takes the name from the root *'yb* "be an enemy." It may be read as either an active form (opponent of Yahweh) or a passive form (one whom Yahweh has treated as an enemy). There may be play on this meaning when Job laments that he is "an enemy" *('ôyēb)* of God (13:24). In any case the name is well attested in the second millennium, appearing in both an Amarna letter (*ca.* 1350 B.C.) and the Egyptian Execration texts (*ca.* 2000).[1] In both cases it is applied to tribal leaders in Palestine and its environs. These instances lend weight to the view that the book recorded the ancient experience of an actual sufferer whose story was given its present setting by a later poet. However, the value of the story does not rest on a possible historical basis.

The book's presence in the canon has not been debated, but its location within that canon has. In the Hebrew traditions, Psalms, Job, and Proverbs almost always were linked, with Psalms first and the order of Job and Proverbs varying. The Greek versions differed widely in the placement of Job — one text put it at the end of the Old Testament, following Ecclesiastes. The Latin translations established an order which the English tradition has followed: Job, Psalms, Proverbs. Because of the story's alleged patriarchal setting and the belief that Moses was the author, the Syriac Bible inserts the book between the Pentateuch and Joshua. Uncertainty as to both date and literary genre accounts for these differences in placement.

Background

Date. There is no consensus either among ancient rabbis or modern scholars about the date of Job. The marks of antiquity are apparent in the prose prologue (1:1–2:13) and epilogue (42:7-17): (1) Without priesthood or shrine, Job performed his own sacrifices (1:5). (2) His possessions, like Abraham's and Jacob's, were measured in sheep, camels, oxen, asses, and servants (1:3; cf. Gen. 12:16; 32:5). (3) His land was subject to raids of pillaging tribes (1:15-17). (4) Job's life span of 140 years is matched only in the Pentateuch (42:16). (5) The epic character of the prose story has its closest parallels in Genesis and Ugaritic literature. (6) An ancient, righteous hero named Job is cited by Ezekiel in connection with Noah and Daniel[2] (Ezek. 14:14, 20). Most likely the prose story was ancient and handed down from an original setting before 1000.[3]

The poetic sections (3:1–42:6) come from a latter period, for there are numerous affinities between lines in the book of Job and other Old Testament texts; e.g., compare 3:3-26 to Jer. 20:14-18; 7:17f. to Ps. 8:5f. [MT 6f.]; 9:8, 9 to Amos 4:13 and 5:8; and 15:7f. to Prov. 8:22, 25. Many themes in Job appear in Isa. 40–55 and there is a special affinity between Job and Isaiah's portrait of the suffering servant.[4] It is possible to argue for a seventh century or later date for Job based on these comparisons, since the author of Job is commenting on the received tradition. Many scholars postulate an exilic or postexilic date. But their reasons are not compelling, particularly if we take the position that the book concerns personal, not national, suffering. It does not address the nature and limits of divine retribution toward Israel as do Lamentations and Habakkuk. Its debate with conventional wisdom does not require that the book of Proverbs had been completed; the points under discussion were prevalent long before the final collection of Proverbs. All in all, a date between 700 and 600 seems reasonable for the completion of the work.

Near Eastern Parallels. Additional support for a preexilic date comes from other ancient stories of righteous sufferers. Such tales belong "to the category of higher Wisdom, which was speculative in temper, unconventional in approach, and concerned with ultimate issues."[5] None of these stories (see Chapter 33, above) is a true parallel to Job. At most they show that, from the dawn of literature, people have been puzzled at the ways of the gods, especially when these entailed human suffering. Job's puzzlement, then, has a lengthy chain of precedent but no sign of direct ancestry:[6]

> Job stands far above its nearest competitors, in the coherence of its sustained treatment of the theme of human misery, in the scope of its many-sided examination of the problem, in the strength and clarity of its defiant moral monotheism, in the characterization of its protagonists, in the heights of its lyrical poetry, in its dramatic impact, and in the intellectual integrity with which it faces the "unintelligible burden" of human existence.[7]

Authorship. The name of the author of Job is lost forever. Rarely has history left such a literary genius unnamed and unknown as to his circumstances or motive for composing such a magnificent work.

All that can be learned about the author must be read back from the book. (1) He must have suffered excruciatingly, for his empathy for Job is so genuine. (2) He too may have found insight into his suffering and release from his pain in an encounter with God (38:1–41:34 [MT 26]; cf. Ps. 73:17). (3) He had been thoroughly trained in the wisdom tradition, as both the theme and the variety of literary devices attest. (4) His experience of suffering must have set him at odds with the teaching of conventional wisdom about absolute patterns of divine retribution — blessing is always the fruit of righteousness, suffering ever the wage of sin. (5) He was surely an Israelite, as his view of divine sovereignty, call for divine justice, and impeccable code of ethical be-havior (31:1-40) intimate. (6) He probably used the non-Israelite setting of Uz (whether south in Edom or east in Gilead) both because it was the source of the ancient story and because such suffering is a universal human woe. (7) In good Hebrew fashion, he wanted to share his insight to fortify friends and students against future suffering. In this effort he joined and expanded the efforts of those who composed Pss. 37; 49; and 73.

Structure

Movement of the Book. While debate continues about the unity of Job (see below), the thrust of the work in its finished form will be investigated here. One can draw an analogy between the development of such a masterwork and the construction, often over centuries, of medieval cathedrals. Those massive sanctuaries arouse deep appreciation in their final architectural form, to which each stage contributed; "to restore the original plans . . . would be an act of barbarism."[8] Dissecting the book of Job into its component parts actually may diminish one's understanding of its message.

I. Prologue (prose)	chs. 1–2
II. Body of Speeches (poetry)	chs. 3–42:6
A. Dialogue	chs. 3–28
1. Job's opening lament	ch. 3
2. Dialogue between Job and Friends in three cycles:	chs. 4–27
Eliphaz [Job replies to each]	chs. 4–5; 15; 22
Bildad	chs. 8; 18; 25
Zophar	chs. 11; 20
3. Poem on Wisdom	ch. 28
B. Series of Speeches from one Person	chs. 29–41
1. Job's avowal of innocence	chs. 29–31
2. Elihu's speeches	chs. 32–37
3. Yahweh's speeches with Job's response	chs. 38–42:6
III. Epilogue (prose) 42:7-17	

The overall form is A-B-A (prose-poetry-prose). The *prologue* consists of six scenes. It opens with the introduction of Job and closes with the intro-duction of the three comforters. In the middle there is a twofold interchange between a scene in heaven and Job's trial on earth. The *dialogue*, which is composed of three cycles, is framed by Job's opening lament (ch. 3) and the

Hymn to Wisdom (ch. 28). Next, there are a *series of speeches* from three speakers, Job, Elihu, and Yahweh. Job's last speech has three parts (chs. 29–31). This pattern balances the threefold pattern of the dialogue. Elihu delivers four unanswered speeches. Delivering one more speech than the friends do raises his stature above theirs. Afterwards there are two long speeches from Yahweh, each followed by a short reply from Job. The total of four speeches balances the four speeches of Elihu. The *epilogue* has two distinct parts, matching the use of pairs in the prologue.

A more detailed look at the role of each section and its relation to the whole shows:

(1) *A drama on a double stage: Job's prosperity and Yahweh's test* (prose prologue, chs. 1–2). The narrative alternates between the land of Uz, where Job lives with integrity and piety, in prosperity (1:1-5) or in disaster (vv. 13-22; 1:7-13), and the court of Yahweh, where the Satan (see below) challenges Yahweh to test Job (1:6-12; 2:1-6). Tragic reversal sharpens the pathos and spotlights Job's plight: the radical change from life with an ideal family and vast possessions to poverty, pain, and loneliness (1:1-5; 2:7f.). Repetition, subtle yet powerful, deepens the poignancy and increases the suspense: the standard description of Job's uprightness (1:1, 8; 2:3), the stereotyped account of Satan's coming and going and his terse conversations with Yahweh (1:6-8; 2:1-6; cf. 1:12b; 2:7a), the tragic report of the messenger (1:16f., 19), and the summary of Job's passing of the test (1:22; 2:10b).

The prologue sets the stage for all the speeches that follow. It enables the audience to have confidence in Job, while at the same time it keeps all the characters in the debate in darkness about the real nature of Job's plight. Job never knows that God trusts him or that his faith is being tested. Nor does Job know that God's honor is on the line with his own. God's interest lies more in Job's response of trust than in his personal comfort. The prologue depicts God's sovereignty over the Satan, who can not harm Job beyond God's limits (1:12; 2:6), and sets up a deliberate tension with the conversations that follow by honoring Job's strong trust in Yahweh (1:21f.; 2:9f.). It introduces the three friends as sympathetic comforters, a touch of irony to set up the sharp conflict that ensues.

(2) *A fate worse than death: Job's despair and Yahweh's silence* (poetic lament, ch. 3). With a despair matched only by Jeremiah's shorter lament (Jer. 20:14-18), Job both curses the day of his birth (Job 3:1-10) and wails his complaint (vv. 11-26). The contrast with his controlled piety in the prologue is startling and deliberate. The author refuses to soften the shock with explanation or transition. Using characteristic Semitic hyperbole (emphasis by over-statement), he lays bare Job's full humanity. The initial trauma of loss has given way to the full horror of his plight. Job sees his life stripped of all signs of divine blessing and, therefore, all sources of joy.

Implicitly God has become his enemy. Who else is responsible for the very survival which he questions? Job's attack on God's creative power, timing, and providence sets the tone for the dialogue that follows. No comfort is found in Israel's cult or history — realities on which the author is consciously silent: "it is in an existence totally without community or saving history that Job in steely isolation carries on his struggle with God."9

(3a) *A comfort more painful than censure: three accusers and one defender* (poetic dialogue, chs. 4–27). Here the author's literary genius shines through both in detail and overall execution. The conversational form, with each friend speaking three times save for Zophar, enriches the debate both through repetition and variety. Each friend speaks from a different perspective — Eliphaz as a gentle, confident mystic (chs. 4–5; 15; 27; esp. 4:12-21), Bildad as a firm traditionalist (chs. 8; 18; 25; esp. 8:8-10), Zophar as a rash dogmatist (chs. 11; 20; esp. 11:5f.). The basic message of each is the same: a call for Job to repent of the sin that must have caused his suffering (Eliphaz, 5:8; 15:12-16; 22:21-30; Bildad, 8:3-7; Zophar, 11:13-15). In so doing the comforters end up tempting Job to seek God for personal gain rather than for God himself.

The speeches of the friends consist of many genres. Eliphaz, the most compassionate, opens with words of consolation (4:2-6). Bildad and Zophar, however, begin with an accusation (8:2-4; 11:2-6). The body of the friends' speeches includes wisdom instruction (4:7-11; 8:8-10), description of the fate of the wicked (5:1-7; 8:11-19) as well as the fate of the upright (5:17-28; 8:20-22), hymnic lines in praise of God (5:9-16; 11:7-11[12]), and exhortations to seek God (5:8, 27; 8:5-7; 11:13-20). Eliphaz alone underscores the positions he espouses with his own personal observations. Distinctive also is his amazing encounter with a spirit in which he received a revelation (4:12-21). This is the only vision report by a wise person in Scripture. Some prophetic visions also contain an audition, but they lack any mention of an apparition and of physical response on the part of the prophet. The description shows that the wise were not restricted to natural observations but were open to mystical experiences as well.

In the second cycle the friends suspect that Job has done something wrong. Their position is reflected in their speeches which consist essentially of two elements: accusations (15:2-6; 18:2-4; 20:2-3) and implied threats in descriptions of the fate of the wicked (15:17-35; 18:5-21; 20:4-29). Only Eliphaz adds a wisdom instruction (15:7-16). They recount in detail the fate of the wicked as a means of badgering Job to repent.

In the third cycle only Eliphaz's speech is definitely intact (see p. 484). It consists of an accusation (22:2-11), a couplet in praise of God (22:12), a disputation (22:13-20), and an eloquent call to repentance (22:21-30). He pointedly accuses Job of breaking the patriarchal standard of morality, and makes a passionate plea for Job to repent. As the text now stands there is only a brief speech from Bildad. It is a hymn in praise of God (25:2-6). Since the friends agree that Job is guilty of some serious, hidden wrongdoing, the gulf between him and them has widened considerably. Despite the rounds of repetition and the intensified attacks of the friends, they only come to tempt Job to seek the wrong solution.

(3b) *Job's speeches likewise are composed of many genres.* At this point it is important to mention two characteristics of the dialogue: (1) Job tends to speak to the friends as a group; and (2) his responses are not always directed at the preceding speech. They may reach back to earlier questions or arguments; e.g., in 9:3f., 15-24, Job is actually answering Eliphaz's question "Can a mortal man be righteous before God?" (4:17)[10] rather than speaking to issues raised by Bildad.

Job begins by venting his total despair of life (ch. 3). In this opening lament he utters an incantation to remove from the calendar the day of his birth and the night of his conception so that his existence may be erased (3:3-10). Since this is impossible, he longs for God to let him die to enjoy the rest in Sheol (3:11-26; 6:8-10; 7:15-16). Afterwards he laments his plight more realistically. He pours out his heart against the ruthlessness of God's affliction. He pictures God using him for target practice or attacking him as though he were a mighty fortress (16:6-14; 19:8-12). Within his complaints Job mourns the hardship of human life in general, establishing a bond between his experience and that of others (7:1-2; 14:1-12).[11] He also petitions God to ease his suffering (7:7-10, 16-21; 10:20-22; 14:13-17; 17:3-4). He chides his comforters for heartlessness and treachery (6:14-23) and pleads that they listen to what he is really saying (12:3; 13:5-6; 21:2-3). If they would listen, they might be able to instruct him with compassion and bring some ease to his pain (6:24-27; 19:21-22). Although Job is at odds with his friends' dogma, his more substantial quarrel is with God, who he knows is ultimately responsible for his misery (e.g., 9:15-35; 13:23-28; 16:6-17). With God his protest is not that he is sinless, but that his suffering far exceeds any sin he may have committed.

The use of the complaint as a basic component in most of Job's speeches has several purposes. It allows him to describe his suffering in powerful, figurative poetry (e.g., 16:6-17). The vivid, poignant imagery of Job's lamenting, though it hovers near total despondency, keeps Job from falling into the abyss of despair. It enables him to gain some control over his distressed thoughts as it opens his mind to the hope of recovery. In addition, it keeps the book from being a didactic discourse on the reasons for suffering.

Like the friends, Job recounts hymnic lines in praise of God (9:5-13; 10:8-12; 12:13-25; 23:8-9, 13-14; 26:5-14). These thoughts direct him to look to God for a resolution, the very God whom he fears is capriciously afflicting him.

Without forcing the text, it is possible to see the steps Job takes to cope with his suffering. There is movement in the book, though not all its students agree. Amidst his complaining Job gropes for some way to prove his innocence (6:29; 16:17; 23:10-12; 27:2-6; cf. 9:15, 20f.). At first he wildly conjectures what would happen if he could hold God accountable in court for afflicting him so harshly (9:14-24). Fearful of God's awesome power, he sees no way for a mere mortal to win a dispute with God (9:2-4, 14-16, 32). The only hope for a person would be if there were an umpire to restrain God from using his terrifying rod (9:33-34), but no such arbiter exists.

Nevertheless, Job decides that he will take God to court (13:3, 13-27). Because he is convinced that his suffering has turned his very body into a false witness against his words, he draws on language of the court to press his craving for vindication. Job goes on to postulate that at the heavenly court there is a celestial witness who will testify in his defense (16:18-21). The identity of that witness is not clear. Is it the heavens themselves, for they along with the earth hear cases tried before the divine tribunal (Mic. 6:1-2)? Is it a third party in heaven, one who has the opposite role of the prosecuting Satan?[12] Elihu will speak of such a mediating angel (33:23-25). Certainly the witness is more than the umpire wished for earlier (9:33).

In his next speech Job's faith grows stronger. He says with conviction:

> For I know that my Redeemer lives,
>   and that at the last he will stand upon the earth;
> and after my skin has been thus destroyed,
>   then in my flesh I shall see God. (19:25-26)

Some think that this kinsman is God himself. It seems absurd that God would speak against himself on behalf of his servant. But this dialectic is the very essence of redemption. Jesus, the Son of God, likewise is forsaken by God in his effort to be the redeemer of sinful humans and win their reconciliation with God the Father (Matt. 27:46). Job is convinced that his redeemer will come to his defense, make sure he has a fair trial, and enable him to win a favorable verdict.

Having gained some mental control over his suffering, Job moves beyond concern for himself to lament the lack of justice on earth. He delivers two long discourses in which he recounts the success of the wicked as a challenge to the standard doctrine of retribution as defended by the friends (21:2-33; 24:1-17). This evidence refutes the tenacious claims that the doctrine of retribution is universally and mechanistically implemented. It calls also for a clearer under-standing of how a just God rules the world (see the Yahweh speeches).

In the third cycle Job comes to the conviction that an upright person could win acquittal before the divine judgment seat (23:4-7). The problem, though, is that he cannot find God in order to have the trial held (23:3, 8-9). Nevertheless, in faith Job states that at the end of this testing his character will be proven to be as pure as gold (23:10-12). Job brings the dialogue to an end with two oaths and an assertion of innocence (27:2-6). His boldness is evident in a brazen accusation: the very God by whom he swears is making his life bitter and denying him justice. Job vows that he will never contrive lies of repentance to win God's favor, despite the badgering of friends. He will not yield to their pressure; to do so would cost him his integrity. According to ancient custom the silence of the friends determines Job to be winner of the debate.

In the dialogue Job has moved from utter despair that indulges in wishful thinking to a firm resolution to defend his honor. His free and bold venting of anguish enables him to cope with his pain without yielding to a solution that would compromise his integrity. Job's pain has not lessened in the course of his speeches. Rather he has been able to get a sufficient grip on it to place his personal integrity above any coveted solution. Confronting God outweighs finding relief. No false confession to God, no manipulation of God, no bargaining with God, not even by using the means of grace — by eschewing these options he disproves Satan's snide quip that humans always compromise their standards on the basis of skin for skin (2:4). Thus God's confidence in him is fully vindicated.

(4) *An interlude with a message: musings on the mystery of wisdom* (poetic paean, ch. 28). This magnificent description of the wonders of wisdom and its inaccessibility to human enterprise seems to be an intervention of the author. If part of Job's speech which began in 27:1, it probably is to be interpreted ironically. Job had feared God (28:28; cf. 1:1, 8; 2:3), but to no avail![13] If this is a purposeful interlude, it should be credited to the final author, who uses it to bring one phase of the book to a close and prepare for the next. As though reflecting on the stalemate to which the windy dialogue has led, he muses on the human inability to discover, buy, or discern true wisdom without divine help. Indeed, that is his summary of the book thus far: neither Job nor the friends have found the key. By pointing to the need for divine help ("God understands the way to [wisdom], and he knows its place," 28:23), he quickens anticipation for the speeches from the whirlwind (ch. 38).

The hymn has four parts: (1) Human genius develops the technology that enables humans to mine gems from the earth. Human brilliance, however, does not approach wisdom (vv. 1-11). (2) Wisdom cannot be purchased, not even by the total sum of human wealth (vv. 12-19). (3) God alone has access to wisdom. God employed it when he created (vv. 20-27). Mortals catch a glimpse of this wisdom in the wonders of creation. (4) Divine wisdom is beyond human reach. Nevertheless, one may begin to gain wisdom by fearing God and turning from evil (v. 28). This practical wisdom resembles God's, but it falls far short of the glory of divine wisdom.

(5) *A protest against heaven: Job's calamitous fall and demonstrated inno-*

Job's camels were symbolic of the stature he lost and would regain.
Herd in Negeb region. *(Neal and Joel Bierling)*

cence (poetic complaint and oath, chs. 29–31). Skillfully prolonging the suspense, the author allows Job to summarize his argument before resting his case. First, he reviews the scenes in the land of Uz by recounting his tragic reversal from blessing and prestige (ch. 29) to mockery and anguish (ch. 30). Next, he swears an oath of innocence. He lists numerous sins, both of act and thought, that he has not committed (31:1-34). This statement expresses a high standard of biblical ethics surpassed only by the Sermon on the Mount.[14] Finally, he restates his demand for a hearing with God. He seals that demand with a curse that he would be ready to endure suffering if his guilt were proven (vv. 35-40). Job reaffirms his driving theme: he has done nothing to warrant his suffering. Job rests his case with an oath of innocence. And the next move is God's — either to vindicate Job or destroy him. If God remains silent, Job will be vindicated.

(6) *A rebuke and a lesson: Elihu attempts to correct both Job and his friends in four unanswered speeches* (poetic discourse, chs. 32–37, with prose introduction, 32:1-5). Elihu's speeches sound disconnected from the rest of the book. Yet his message is integral to it. Only Elihu is an Israelite. Only he is introduced by a lineage. What a lineage! The names of his ancestors are tied directly to the patriarchs (see Buz in Gen. 22:21). Furthermore, the young Elihu is bombastically wordy, though boasting deep inspiration for his speeches (32:18-20).

Elihu presents new ideas about suffering and prepares Job for the appearing of Yahweh.[15] His first speech, the most original (chs. 32–33), teaches that God is gracious to those who serve him, ever seeking to turn them from the error of their ways. God uses two primary means: dreams and disciplinary suffering. He differs from Eliphaz, who held that suffering is preliminary punishment for some wrong done. For Elihu it is a preventative discipline to keep a person from doing wrong. In addition, God provides a mediating angel to rescue a person who is approaching the grave (33:23-25). In the Old Testament the identity of the angel is veiled, only to be revealed in the New.

In the next two speeches (chs. 34–35) Elihu drives home the truth that righteousness is the foundation of God's rule. He rejects Job's complaint that God does not rule justly all the time. Job, moreover, must drop his complaint that God has dealt with him unjustly, lest he be handed a greater penalty. Unlike the other friends, Elihu locates Job's sin in his rhetoric rather than in some unknown wrong. In his third speech (ch. 35), he lays bare the presumptuous tone of Job's argument. Elihu, like the others, overstates his case. Yet he does plant the idea in Job's mind that he will have to drop his claim of innocence before finding reconciliation with God. In his fourth speech (chs. 36–37) Elihu recounts the theme of disciplinary suffering and then in powerful poetry describes the glory of God's appearing in a thunderstorm. Is it possible that he sees the signs that portend Yahweh's coming (37:21-24)?

(7) *A voice that silences debate: Yahweh appears and interrogates Job about the structure and maintenance of the world* (38:4-24; 38:25–39:30) — both the natural world (38:25-38) and the animal world (38:39–39:30). This unfolding of the glories of the universe becomes a kind of hymn of praise. The use of questions is reminiscent of a lawsuit in which a defendant is examined. The overall style, though, is closer to a disputation (or argument) than to a court case. The content of God's speeches seems to miss the issues raised by Job, especially his avowal of innocence. Yet Yahweh does not reprove Job's complaints to bring him back to an orthodox way of thinking, as the friends imagined God would do. Nor does he immediately vindicate Job as Job himself expected.

The Yahweh speeches, nevertheless, serve many functions. Yahweh both establishes rapprochement with Job by asking him questions and gives him a mild reprimand by questioning him in a way that he can not answer. (Jesus, in his sojourn on earth, will pose questions in a similar vein.) Yahweh shows respect for Job by entering into conversation with him, while the irony embedded within the questions may be intended to ease, with a touch of humor, the bitterness of Job's complaint.

Yahweh observes that he brought forth the sea and fixed a limit for it (38:8-11). Since the sea came to symbolize forces hostile to God, this section implies that what was deemed evil has its source in God and that it is confined behind set boundaries. This picture recalls the restraints placed on the Satan (chs. 1 and 2). In addition, the morning light drives the wicked into hiding. Yahweh thus concedes that there is evil on the earth — evil that God limits and controls for good purposes.

Yahweh next recounts the human inability to visit God's far recesses of the world: the depths, the horizon, the heights (38:16-24). How then can finite humans frame a sound theory to explain how Yahweh governs the world justly and wisely?

Yahweh's further questions show that he maintains the creation wisely. He sends rain to the desolate places (38:25-38). Today we are just beginning to get an inkling of God's providence in this respect, how vital is the ecology of the remote inaccessible places of the planet for the well-being of all. Next Yahweh sets before Job a series of animal portraits. In each portrait a trait is praised, and a hardship is mentioned. Yahweh is drumming home a lesson: the benefits a particular creature enjoys are worth far more than the hardship it endures. A wild ass, for example, survives on a skimpy food supply, but unlike the tamed donkey it never has to hear a master's loud shouts (39:5-8). The ostrich is large and awkward and cannot fly, but amazingly it can outrace the majestic steed (39:13-18). These strange truths of nature tell Job that his pain and loss are not of ultimate consequence. His integrity, freedom, and trust in God far exceed the weight of his suffering.

Yahweh pauses to give Job a chance to answer. Job speaks only a few words (40:3-5). Their gist, briefly put, is that he will not renounce his avowal of innocence.

God wants to prevent Job from clutching his claim so doggedly that he places his innocence above God's moral purity. That sin would be *hubris,* unbridled arrogance. Persistently, Yahweh takes up a second speech (40:6–41:34). He questions Job's ability to cope with the stratagems of the proud and the wicked (40:6-14). Can Job even tame the two super animals: Behemoth (40:15-24) and Leviathan (41:1-34)? The portraits of these two creatures, unlike those in Yahweh's first speech, are lengthy and tinged with mythical elements. Behemoth is often identified as the hippopotamus, and Leviathan as a crocodile. Yahweh describes these creatures as more than ordinary animals to highlight the cosmic dimensions of Job's suffering. Nowhere does Job learn of the contest in heaven reported in the prologue; yet here Yahweh addresses the supernatural aspects of his trial through the imagery of these two beasts. This imagery is an ironic means of breaking down Job's defenses in order that he may see how his suffering fits in the broader scheme of Yahweh's universal rule.

If Job's complaints against God are valid, Job should be able to don royal robes and rule every proud foe. If Job cannot order the world better than God, he will have to abandon his complaint. The contest is between two wills: Job's challenge to God (ch. 31) and God's counter challenge to him. Who will win?

In this light it is possible to understand the extensive and tedious detail in Leviathan's portrait. Yahweh is dragging out his speech, patiently laboring to move Job to seek his favor and abandon his trust in his own innocence.

Job's brief speech (42:1-6) says volumes. He affirms that Yahweh governs supremely and his purpose prevails. Who can know enough to challenge God's just rule? Job's vision of God leaves him abased, recanting in dust and ashes. "Recant" is often rendered in English translations "repent." But it is the same Hebrew word that often has Yahweh "repent" (e.g., Amos 7:3, 6). The word suggests taking a different course of action after being strongly impelled to do so. Job did not repent of any sin. But he abandoned his powerful oath of innocence, dropped his court case against God. No longer are the two opponents. Job steps back from the brink of hubris. Reconciliation lies ahead.

(8) *A vindication scarcely needed: God restores Job's reputation, wealth, and family* (prose epilogue, 42:7-17). For Job to recognize the vast difference between God's wisdom and power and his own ignorance and frailty is God's intention. The test has been passed. The wager with the Satan is won — but only after monumental struggle and massive pain. Job's faith, strong at the beginning, has been refined like gold through the fires of doubt, adversity, and misunderstanding.

In the epilogue the author lets that golden character glisten in the light of God's blessings. Job's vindication begins with the repeated rebuke of the three friends (vv. 7f.), a rebuke ringing with irony: God brands as "folly" the friends' view of the very essence of pious wisdom (v. 8). Moreover, God assigns to Job the priestly role in intercession, reminiscent of his dutiful service to his children (v. 8; cf. 1:5). This vindication is a magnanimous display of grace: God forgives the friends, restores Job's possessions and family (42:10, 12-15),[16] prolongs his life, and multiplies his posterity (vv. 16f).[17] Job, in turn, emulates God's grace by praying for the friends whose arguments had bludgeoned him (v. 10) and by his generosity to his daughters (v. 15).

The vindication is affirmed in the honor and sympathy accorded by Job's kin, who come to fulfill the role intended for the friends (compare v. 11 with 2:11). It completes the book's movement by describing God's restoration of Job's possessions even beyond their initial state. This restoration preserves God's integrity: Job has passed the test. It disproves the friends' contention: Job's deprivation was not due to his sin. The restoration shows that poverty is not necessarily a more righteous state than prosperity. It shouts its word of grace in both its setting and its content. Yahweh leaves the courts of heaven and comes to the ash heap of Uz. There he forgives the doctrinaire sages and restores the fortunes of the beleaguered Job, whom he affectionately calls his servant (vv. 7f; cf. 1:8; 2:3).

Unity. The story's movement argues for the unity of the book. Some brief comment, nevertheless, may help point up some problems in the book's composition and their possible solutions.

(1) The relationship of the prose prologue and epilogue to the poetic sections has been explained in a number of ways. Most scholars reject the idea that the poem was written first and the prose sections added later. The dialogues are hard to understand without the story as their setting, and lead nowhere without the epilogue to complete them. More likely, the author adapted the prose story by recounting his own theological and, perhaps, personal struggle in the poetic sections.

Though some aspects of the prologue and epilogue seem in conflict with the tone of the poetry, this need not mar the book's integrity: (a) the semi-nomadic life depicted in the prologue can be reconciled with the agricultural (31:8, 38-40) or even urban setting (19:15; 29:7) if Job's social setting is dimorphic (see Genesis: Patriarchal History);[18] (b) the difference in Job's mood and response between the prologue and dialogue may reflect both the passage of time and the sharp aggravation at his friends' easy answers.

(2) The third cycle of the dialogue (chs. 22–27) is incomplete: Bildad's speech is unexpectedly short (25:1-6); part of Job's response sounds more like Bildad (26:5-14); and the final verses of Job's response, describing the terrible fate of a wealthy wicked person and his family (27:13-23), may originally have belonged to Bildad. It seems that the poet intentionally did not compose a third speech for Zophar: (1) Of the three friends only Zophar's second speech is longer than his first. (2) What little there is of Bildad's third speech sounds like a quotation from Eliphaz. If 27:13-23 belongs to his third speech, he seems to be citing Zophar. Thus Bildad's last speech is basically a summation of the position of the three friends.[19] It can be said with conviction that the composition of the third cycle offers further testimony that the argument of the three friends is itself sterile and uncompelling.

(3) The poem on wisdom (ch. 28) has often been identified as a later addition.[20] The present text assigns it to Job. Yet its contemplative mood is in stark contrast to Job's passionate words. It seems best therefore, to read the poem as the author's interlude, a bridge between the dialogue and the final series of speeches that are to come from Job, Elihu, and Yahweh. The poem is intricately composed for this location: (1) Its emphasis on fear of the Lord as wisdom ties directly to the description of Job in the prologue, to Eliphaz's emphasis on fear of the Lord (chs. 4; 15; 22), and points both to the conclusion of Elihu's speeches and Job's response to Yahweh's words (42:2-6). (2) Its teaching that wisdom is beyond human finding issues a strong judgment on the friends' speeches in their brash claims to know true wisdom.

(4) Yahweh's second speech (40:15–41:34 [MT 26]) has been considered a later addition. It supposedly lacks brilliance, is redundant, and concentrates on just two animals. In defense of the unity of the two speeches of Yahweh

and their role in the book, it can be argued that the first speech (chs. 38–39) is designed deliberately to speak to the first section of Job's final avowal (chs. 29–30), while the second speech (40:7–41:26) is calculated in content and length to overmatch the second section of Job's monologue (ch. 31).[21] Further evidence of the unity of these speeches is grounded in the descriptions of the hippopotamus and the crocodile: God delights in them despite their repulsiveness to humans: "the universe and its Maker cannot be judged by man in anthropocentric terms."[22] The increasing length of the animals' descriptions (horse, 39:19-25; hippopotamus, 40:15-24; crocodile, 41:1-34 [MT 40:25–41:26]) is part of the artistry. The multiplication of details is designed to overwhelm Job and evoke the desired surrender, absent from Job's first response (40:3-5).

(5) The speeches of Elihu (32:1–37:24) have provoked more controversy than any other portion of Job: "The speeches violently disturb the artistic structure of the original book."[23] Among the arguments usually adduced in support of such a verdict is the observation that Elihu is not mentioned in the prologue or prior to his appearance.[24] Two explanations of this omission are possible: (1) as part of the comforters' retinue or one of their pupils, he was not singled out for special mention;[25] or (2) mention is delayed deliberately to enhance the surprise and increase the suspense which these speeches produce.

Given his insight and intensity it is remarkable that Elihu's intervention is not mentioned in the epilogue. Perhaps because Elihu was God's forerunner, the ancient author felt no need for God to censure him or even mention him. Elihu's speeches may have been added by the author at a later date without harmonizing the details by adding his name to the epilogue.

The style of Elihu is said to differ significantly from that of the dialogue. Arguments based on the use of divine names (e.g., El, Yahweh, Eloah, El Shaddai) or the alleged presence of Aramaic words are noteworthy, but not conclusive. Different subjects and circumstances can call for different wording even from the same author. One major shift in style from the other speakers is Elihu's treating Job's position as a basis for his own remarks (e.g., 33:8-11; 34:5f; cf. 42:3-4a). This may spotlight one of the author's purposes: to summarize and restate key aspects of Job's stance in preparation for Yahweh's speeches.

Discussion of the unity and integrity of the book of Job will persist. Increasingly, however, scholars have concluded that the book is best understood not when dissected into separate parts, each with its own history, but when its final form is studied to grasp the message as it now stands: "The book thus emerges [from the various stages of the author's work] as a superbly structured unity, the work of a single author of transcendental genius, both as a literary artist and as a religious thinker, with few peers, if any, in the history of mankind."[26]

Literary Considerations

Genre. What kind of book is Job? The question has defied conclusive answer, as shown in a sampling of proposed genres:

(1) "Complaint and reconciliation" has sometimes been identified as a distinct genre, with the following components (as in the Babylonian Ludlul Bel Nemeqi): account of suffering; lamentation; divine intervention to heal the sufferer.[27] This suggestion falters in not accounting for the heart of the present book — the controversy with the friends.

(2) Other scholars have thought the psalmlike laments (complaints) to be the backbone of Job.[28] This theory contends that Job's discussion of suffering is more poignant and personal than that found in typical wisdom discourse.[29] Such studies have rendered yeoman service in stressing the numerous parallels between Job's speeches and psalms of individual complaint. At the same time, the role of the prologue and epilogue as well as the friends' counsel distinguish the book of Job markedly from the simpler, more stereotyped psalm forms.[30]

(3) Legal disputation is held by some to be the key to the book's form:

> Formally it cannot be better understood than as the record of the proceedings of a *rib* [legal controversy or indictment] between Job and God Almighty in which Job is the plaintiff and prosecutor, the friends of Job are witnesses as well as co-defendants and judges, while God is the accused and defendant, but in the background and finally the ultimate judge of both Job and his friends.[31]

This insight into possible legal innuendoes and terms is useful, but a disputation category is insufficient to describe the structure and thrust of the work as a whole.

(4) Understood as a school lecture, the book pictures a master teacher striving to cope with students' questions about "God's supervision of the righteous and the wicked."[32] This approach seems more appropriate to the didactic style of Ps. 37 than the spirited debate of Job. Moreover, so little direct evidence exists for Israel's schools that this view builds one theory on the unsure foundation of another theory.

(5) As a philosophic debate, Job could be a Semitic model of the dialogue form developed much more fully by Plato,[33] but the subtle reasonings and theoretical arguments of the Greek symposium are a continent away from the intense personal and theological debate of the ash heap in Uz.

(6) Tragedy in the Greek pattern, though occasionally suggested,[34] is implausible on two counts: (1) the virtual absence of any dramatic presentation in worship or entertainment in Jewish life before the second century B.C.; (2) vast differences in content between the malicious fates and moral flaws that

comprise Greek tragedy and the tension of God's freedom with Job's integrity that governs the book of Job.

(7) Job can be defined as a comedy in light of "its perception of incongruity and irony; and . . . its basic plot line that leads ultimately to the happiness of the hero."[35] Though this view is attractive, it remains to be proven that such comedic components were prevalent in the Middle East during the first millennium.

(8) Parable form (Heb. *māšāl)* was suggested as early as Rabbi Simeon ben-Laqish (second century A.D.), who believed that Job was a fictional story, written to convey a spiritual lesson.[36] Indeed, Job's speeches sometimes are called *māšāl* (27:1–29:1), and his experiences are obviously intended as spiritual instruction.[37] Parable, however, may be a misleading term for such a complicated story as Job's, because it is generally associated with brief stories with one specific point to make.

(9) Epic history is another frequent suggestion. Andersen likens Job to the stories of the patriarchs, Moses, David, or Ruth, and assigns to it four characteristics: economy in relating facts; objectivity in describing the characters' actions without plumbing their emotions; restraint by the author in making moral judgments; and focus on the speeches which reveal the plight and faith of the characters.[38] But none of these other "epics" contains speeches of the length, power, and intensity of those in Job.

Each of these approaches may have something to contribute to an understanding of Job. The matter of genre is more than an item of intellectual curiosity; it is an essential clue to the book's meaning. Form and content are inextricably intertwined.

So important, in fact, is this book's genre that it must not be fit into any preconceived mold. It does weep with complaint, argue with disputation, teach with didactic authority, excite with comedy, sting with irony, and relate human experience with epic majesty. But above all, Job is unique — the literary gift of an inspired genius.[39]

Literary Characteristics. Students of literature lavish superlatives on the artistry of Job. For example, the varieties of poetic parallelism, including the exquisite use of complete triplets and even longer units, reveal remarkable literary prowess. The present survey must be content with a brief look at the metaphors and similes, the vivid descriptions of the creation, and the quotations which are hallmarks of the author's style:

(1) Metaphors and similes abound in startling numbers and masterful quality. For example:

My days are swifter than a weaver's shuttle. (7:6)

My days are swifter than a runner;
    they flee away, they see no good.

They go by like skiffs of reed,
  like an eagle swooping on the prey. (9:25f.)

He breaks me down on every side,
  and I am gone,
he has uprooted my hope like a tree. (19:10)

They waited for me as for the rain;
  and they opened their mouths as for the spring rain. (29:23)

Even more impressive are the extended metaphors, so intricately detailed that they border on allegory:

My companions are treacherous like a torrent-bed,
  Like freshets that pass away,
that run dark with ice,
  turbid with melting snow.
In time of heat they disappear;
  when it is hot, they vanish from their place.
The caravans turn aside from their course;
  they go up into the waste, and perish.
The caravans of Tema look,
  the travelers of Sheba hope.
They are disappointed because they were confident;
  they come there and are confounded.
Such you have now become to me;
  you see my calamity, and are afraid. (6:15-21)

(2) Descriptions of the creation are virtually unrivaled in poetic power:

Has the rain a father,
  or who has begotten the drops of dew?
From whose womb did the ice come forth,
  and who has given birth to the hoarfrost of heaven? (38:28f.)

Do you give the horse its might?
  Do you clothe its neck with strength?
Do you make it leap like a locust?
  Its majestic snorting is terrible.
. . . . . .
It laughs at fear, and is not dismayed;
  it does not turn back from the sword.
Upon it rattle the quiver,
  the flashing spear and the javelin. (39:19f., 22f.)

488

(3) Quotations play a significant role in the argument, though they are sometimes hard to identify. They can be divided into a number of categories:[40]

Citations from folk wisdom: "Then Satan answered the Lord, 'Skin for skin![41] All that a man has he will give for his life'" (2:4). Proverbs may also be quoted in 11:12; 17:5.

Direct quotations of the speaker's thoughts:

> When I lie down, I ask, "When shall I arise?"
>   But the night is long, and I say,
> "I have had my fill of tossing till daybreak." (7:4)[42]

Quotation of a speaker's previous viewpoint:

> I have made a covenant with my eyes;
>   how then could I look upon a virgin?
> What would be my portion from God above,
>   and my heritage from the Almighty on high? (31:1f.)

We can capture the full meaning of v. 2 by adding an introductory line to clarify its relationship to v. 1: "For I thought, if I sinned [by that lustful look], What would be my portion from God above . . . ?"[43]

Quotation of a proverb as a text:

> I am young in years,
>   and you are aged;
> therefore I was timid and afraid
>   to declare my opinion to you.
> I said, "Let days speak,
>   and many years teach wisdom."
> But truly it is the spirit in a mortal,
>   the breath of the Almighty,
>   that makes for understanding. (32:6-8)

Elihu used the proverb in order to refute it and justify his right to intervene, despite his youth.

Quotation of a proverb to correct a proverb:

> Is wisdom with the aged,
>   and understanding in length of days?
> With God are wisdom and strength;
>   he has counsel and understanding. (12:12f.)

Adding "You say" to the first verse and "But I say" to the second[44] clarifies the debate.

Quotations of another person's views:

> You say, "God stores up their iniquity for their sons."
>   Let it be paid back to them, so that they may know it. (21:19)

The NRSV rightly adds "You say" as Job summarizes views expressed by the friends in 5:4; 18:19; 20:10, 26.

The following quotation, which should be introduced by "You say," seems to summarize the argument of the comforters that God's ways are incomprehensible (4:17; 11:7, 12; 15:8, 14):

> Will any teach God knowledge,
>   seeing that he judges those that are on high? (21:22)

Job answers that question in vv. 23-26.

Sometimes the text itself uses an introductory phrase to make clear that what follows is a quotation:

> For you say, "Where is the house of the prince?
>   Where is the tent in which the wicked dwelt?" (v. 28)[45]

Forms. "The book of Job is an astonishing mixture of almost every kind of literature to be found in the Old Testament."[46] Indeed, its forty-two chapters are a gold mine for the study of form criticism. With incredible ingenuity the author has woven several dozen readily distinguishable literary forms into the texture of the work:

(1) The prose narrative (1:1–2:13; 32:1-5; 42:7-17) tells the basic story, serves as a setting for the poem, and introduces Elihu. Most of the characteristics have been discussed above (pp. 484-85).

(2) The laments of his birth (ch. 3; cf. 10:18f.) represent the strongest literary form available to Job to express the depths of his depression (cf. Jer. 20:14-18). Actually two kindred forms are combined here: (a) an incantation against his birthday — a wish that he had never been born and had thus been spared such anguish (3:3-10); and (b) complaining questions, which begin with "why" and call for no specific answer but introduce explanatory descriptions of suffering (vv. 11-26; cf. 10:18f., where the question is followed by a wish that he had been born dead). The author intends to picture Job in the depths of defeat in order to set the stage for the friends' counsel and Job's response.

(3) The complaint form is that which Job himself most frequently employs (chs. 6–7; 9:25–10:22; 13:23–14:22; 16:6–17:9; ch. 23; 29:1–31:37). It embraces other components such as implied pleas for rescue (13:24f.) and oaths of innocence (31:3-40). It can be directed to the friends whom Job now counts as enemies (e.g., 6:14-23), or to God (e.g., 10:2-22), leaving room for

all three participants in a complaint — God, foes, and sufferer. It hovers above total despair, implying confidence in God's willingness to hear and his ability to rescue (e.g., 19:23-29).

(4) Proverbs are abundant throughout Job. Both Job (e.g., 6:14, 25a; 12:5f., 12; 13:28; 17:5) and his friends (Eliphaz, 5:2, 6f.; 22:2, 21f.; Zophar, 20:5; Elihu, 32:7) cite them liberally. Most are descriptive sayings. The hearers are left to make their own applications:

> Surely vexation kills the fool,
>> and jealousy slays the simple. (5:2)

> For misery does not come from the earth,
>> nor does trouble sprout from the ground;
> but human beings are born to trouble
>> Just as sparks fly upward. (vv. 6f.)

Job may use a proverb and then refute it:

> How forceful are honest words! (proverb)
>> But your reproof, what does it reprove? (6:25).

He may even counter a proverb with a proverb (12:12f.), as does Qoheleth (see below, pp. 503, 505). Admonition, a form familiar from Proverbs, with imperative verbs and a reason given for the command, is also found:

> Agree with God, and be at peace;
>> in this way good will come to you.
> Receive instruction from his mouth,
>> and lay up his words in your heart. (22:21f.)

This was a standard form of instruction, implying that the teacher had the right by experience and authority to issue these admonitions. Inclusion of a reason indicated that the teacher's authority was not arbitrary but was backed by sound evidence.

(5) Rhetorical questions (sometimes called disputation-questions) are a handy tool in the kit of the wise. Each participant uses them with skill: Eliphaz, 4:7; 15:2f., 7-9, 11-14; Bildad, 8:3, 11; 18:4; Zophar, 11:2f., 7f., 10f.; Job, 6:5f., 11f., 22f.; 7:12; 9:12; 12:9; 13:7-9; Elihu, 34:13, 17-19, 31-33; 36:19, 22f. Scarcely any literary form is more useful in debate, because the questioners can determine the answer by the way they cast the question. The listeners are lured into debate because they have to answer. Usually the required answer is "No!" or "By no means!" or "Of course not!" or "No one!":

> Should a multitude of words go unanswered,
>> and should one full of talk be vindicated? (Zophar, 11:2)

Is my strength the strength of stones,
  or is my flesh bronze? (Job, 6:12)

Who gave him charge over the earth
  and who laid on him the whole world? (Elihu, 34:13)

The bite of the question is sharpened by the poetic parallelism — in these cases synonymous — which rephrases the question and doubles the intensity.

The question forms in the divine speeches need special mention. They may call for the answer "I do not know" or "I was not there":

Where were you when I laid the
  foundation of the earth?
Who determined its measurements —
  surely you know!
Or who stretched the line upon it? (38:4a, 5)

or for the answer "No!" as in the rhetorical question:

Have the gates of death been revealed to you,
  or have you seen the gates of deep darkness? (v. 17)

or for an admission of weakness, "No, I cannot!"

Can you lift up your voice
  so that a flood of waters may cover you? (v. 34)

Designed to force Job to admit his ignorance ("I do not know!") and powerlessness ("Of course, I cannot!"), these questions are reinforced in at least two ways: (a) by the injection of imperatives needling Job to respond — "Tell me, if you have understanding" (38:4b), "Declare, if you know all this" (v. 18); and (b) by the use of irony in which God chides Job as sharply as Job chided the friends: "You know, for you were born then, and the number of your days is great!" (v. 21; cf. 12:2). The questions, thus fortified, weigh on Job like a leaden mantle until he sinks to his knees in speechless humility.

(6) Onomastica, catalogues or encyclopaedias containing organized lists of natural phenomena, may furnish material that fills out the speeches from the whirlwind.[47] Scientific lists of stars, constellations, types of precipitation, and other data were compiled both in Egypt and Israel as a means of training students to understand the realities around them. Such lists may also have influenced other biblical passages (see Ps. 148, which names a catalogue of natural entities and urges them to praise Yahweh). Solomon may have used such onomastica to organize his vast knowledge of God's creatures, so admired by his biographer (1 Kgs. 4:33).[48] The question form which dominates Job 38

also has Egyptian parallels in the thirteenth-century Papyrus Anasti I, in which a scribe, Hori, attacks with a barrage of questions the alleged ignorance of another scribe, Amenemope.[49] Job 38 may follow an earlier form, perhaps pioneered in Egypt, in which such lists were couched in questions and used either for instruction or debate. These parallels in form do not, of course, account for the theological power of the whirlwind speeches. The magnificent questions about creation (vv. 4-11) have no Egyptian parallel.

(7) A number of characteristic wisdom forms deserve mention: (a) the 'ašrê ("blessed" or "happy"; cf. Ps. 1:1) formula, which spells out the pattern of life that leads to happiness (5:17-27); (b) the numerical proverb (here combined with the 'ašrê saying, 5:19-22), which highlights a series of threats from which God will deliver the happy person whom he reproves (see Prov. 30 for the x, x + 1 pattern); (c) the summary appraisal, which concludes a statement with a summation of its significance (8:13; 18:21; 20:29):

> Such you have now become to me;
>   you see my calamity, and are afraid; (6:21)[50]

(d) sarcastic overstatement (6:27; 11:12; 12:2; 15:7; 26:2-4), which was often used in ancient contests (e.g., Goliath, 1 Sam. 17:43; Jehoash, 2 Kgs. 14:9); and (e) parody, which is close to sarcasm, as Job's rendition of Ps. 8:4 (MT 5) suggests:

> What are human beings, that you make so much of them,
>   that you set your mind on them,
> visit them every morning,
>   test them every moment? (7:17f.)

Theological Contribution

All biblical books must be studied as a whole, with their parts seen in relationship to the author's overall intent. This is particularly true of Job. Its full message cannot be discerned short of the final page.[51] The tracing of the book's movement has been an exposition of its message.

The story is the message. Its parts must not be snatched from the whole, nor its main emphasis hardened into rigid principles or fine-tuned into narrow propositions. To do this would violate what the book teaches about the mysteries of God's workings in human lives.

Freedom of God. This, if any, doctrine should be singled out. Both Job and his friends were utterly baffled by God's freedom. The friends assumed that suffering was always and only the sign of God's retribution. Job could imagine no worthy divine purpose to his unmerited suffering.

To the bearers of conventional wisdom, the book introduces a God who is free to work his surprises, correct human distortions, and revise the books written about him. God is free to enter into the Satan's test and tell none of the participants about it. He sets the time for his intervention and determines its agenda. God is free not to answer Job's goading questions nor agree with the friends' high-sounding doctrines. Above all, he is free to care enough to confront Job and to forgive the friends.

As with the whole of Scripture, Job's author pictures God as neither bound by human concerns nor beholden to human concepts of him. What God does springs freely from his own will. There are no guidelines to which he must conform. He chose to create and sustain the universe, to inaugurate and govern the march of history. God may work by the order and pattern spelled out in Deuteronomy and Proverbs or transcend those bounds in Job. A lesson in this is that people find their freedom only to the degree that they acknowledge God's. Nothing is more frustrating and restricting than to set up rules for God and then wonder why he does not follow them.

Testing of the Satan. One of the earliest Old Testament references to this adversary is his appearance in the prologue (cf. 1 Chr. 21:1; Zech. 3:1). The Satan has access to the presence of Yahweh, yet is governed by his sovereignty. Nothing suggests that the Satan is anything other than God's creature; the biblical doctrine of creation rules out any true form of dualism. Yet every indication is that the Satan's intentions are harmful. He represents conflict and ill-will. His purposes are contrary to God's aims and hostile to Job's welfare.

The absence of the Satan from the epilogue is not "to be regretted as a flaw in the harmony of the prologue and epilogue."[52] It is a deliberate factor in the book's message. God, not the Satan, is sovereign. The test has been passed. The story points to Job's future, not his past. The Satan is but an interloper in the relationship of God and Job as depicted in the book's beginning and ending.

The role of the Satan in Job anticipates his role in the rest of the Bible. He is a creature of God, yet an enemy of God's will (cf. Matt. 4:1-11; Luke 4:1-13). He seeks to plague God's people both physically (2 Cor. 12:7) and spiritually (11:14). He has been defeated by Christ's obedience and will disappear from the story at the end (Rev. 20:2, 7, 10).

The thrust of the Satan's strategy was not to lure Job into acts of sin such as immorality, dishonesty, or violence but to tempt him to *the* sin — disloyalty to God. Loyalty, trust, and allegiance are the essence of biblical piety, the roots from which stem all fruits of righteousness. The Satan, as is ever his pattern, sought the root of the matter: Job's relationship to God. Job passed this test of loyalty and earned full marks, despite his protests, doubts, and challenges.

Retribution and Justice. Job's message reshapes the understanding of the doctrine of divine retribution. The general pattern of just retribution remains operative: good deeds bring benefits and bad deeds bring harm. This principle, however, is not absolute. Forces and powers, earthly and heavenly, interrupt the cause-effect sequence. Some wicked may prosper and live a long life; some righteous may suffer chronic agony (ch. 21; 24:1-17). Only God's final judgment will bring justice to all.

Furthermore, Job's story warns against applying this principle to all individual situations. Since the righteous may suffer and the wicked prosper, it is dangerous to brand a sufferer as guilty of secret sin or to praise the prosperous as righteous. The moral design of the universe is far too complex to yield to this simple principle. Pain, hardship, tragedy do not require those who have been serving God faithfully either to bear guilt or to doubt their relationship with God.

The Yahweh speeches teach that God restricts the movement of the wicked and promotes the general good of every dimension of the creation — the desert and the garden, the wild and the domesticated. God seeks balance and freedom within creation, not just strict application of retribution. In his governance there is grace and tolerance. God promotes the welfare of those who seek him earnestly, though he chooses the time and the location. Job's abundant prosperity after his encounter with God was in principle a gift of God's grace. It was not a *reward* earned for having endured suffering.

Job's experience demonstrates that a person may serve God with resolve in adversity as well as in affluence. The highest human virtue is to see God, as Job confessed in his response to Yahweh's second speech (42:5). God's presence and acceptance far exceed the burden of any temporal suffering, even the worst possible situation.

Job clung to his faith and integrity throughout his trial. He prevailed over undeserved suffering and prepared the way for Isaiah's portrait of the suffering servant, who, though righteous, suffers on behalf of others (49:1-7; 50:4-9; 52:13–53:12). Job's harsh lot has made it possible to believe that Jesus, the Messiah, was truly righteous even though he endured an excruciating death among criminals.

Strength for Suffering. Not every life will bear afflictions of the magnitude of Job's. Yet suffering, intense and prolonged, will be the lot of virtually every human being. Surely one of Job's purposes is to help us bear such adversity.

The book does this by preparing the reader to accept God's freedom. Job shatters idols in people's minds and leaves a realistic picture of God. The view of the free God opens people to mysterious purposes, to righteous goals in the suffering that he may allow. God is seen as mighty but not mean, victorious but not vindictive. The reader can believe that God will work good through suffering, even though one rightly may hate every bit of the pain.

Job also teaches the importance of friendship in suffering. Especially condemned are simplistic advice, naive counsel, or false comfort. They do damage even when motivated by a desire to defend God in the face of caustic words from one who is in pain. The greatest tragedy of the book may be that of failed friendship, aggravated by plausible theology badly applied.

Job did not suffer in silence, but argued with his friends and complained to God. In the end, God overrode those complaints, but he did not judge Job for them. Whatever else a biblical relationship with God includes, it surely has room for an honesty built on trust in God and the security of his love. Some of the Bible's noblest — Jeremiah, the psalmists, Habakkuk, even Jesus Christ (Mark 14:36; 15:34) — complained of their lot and thus found respite in suffering.

A final lesson about dealing with suffering comes from Job's sense of loyalty to God. Job's conscience was clear. His pain, though excruciating, was not aggravated by the burden of guilt. Open rebellion, flagrant disloyalty, refusal of forgiveness can all make suffering unbearable for anyone. To the pain they add the worry of blame. But Job knew that his commitment to God was clear, and he trusted in that commitment to sustain him until death and beyond (19:23-29).[53]

"Have you considered my servant Job?" (1:8; 2:3) is a fitting question for all. James uses Job as an example of those who learn happiness in the school of suffering: "Indeed, we call blessed those who showed endurance. You have heard of the endurance of Job and you have seen the purpose of the Lord, how the Lord is compassionate and merciful" (Jas. 5:11). Is there a better summary of the book's message — a steadfast sufferer held in the arms of the God of purpose and compassion?

CHAPTER 36

Ecclesiastes

Few biblical writings have sparked such an array of opinions as to what they mean as Ecclesiastes. Trying to figure out the gist of its message is as tantalizing and frustrating as it is important. The book presents us with a chest full of puzzles. Each time we open it we have to cope again with its style, track down its arguments, decode its imagery. And when we do we sense God at work, we see our human problems laid bare, we find warnings against our simple solutions. We sharpen our longings for the One whose cross and resurrection are windows on the fullness of what God wants human life to be.

> He has made everything suitable for its time; moreover, he has put a sense of past and future into their minds, yet they cannot find out what God has done from the beginning to the end. Eccl. 3:11

Name

Ecclesiastes is a Greek translation of Heb. *qôhelet* "one who convenes a congregation," presumably to preach to it.[1] "Preacher," then, is not an inaccurate translation of either the Greek or Hebrew. However, Qoheleth (sometimes spelled Koheleth) would hardly parallel the Christian meaning, since his texts were taken more from his own observations of life than from the Law or the Prophets.

Place in Canon

Some Hebrew traditions placed Qoheleth among the five scrolls (Megilloth) used on official festive occasions, assigning it to Tabernacles. Other Hebrew groupings link Qoheleth to Proverbs and the Song of Solomon, as do our English versions. The reasons are clear: the implied references to Solomon in Eccl. 1:1, 12, 16; and the obvious connections of the three books as examples of wisdom literature attached to Solomon's name.[2] This group was placed after Psalms because it was thought that the Solomonic writings should follow those credited to his father, David.

The tie between Solomon and Qoheleth probably helped the book find its way into the Scriptures, but with some difficulty. The rabbis and early Christian sages were aware both of the book's seeming contradictions and its humanistic, almost skeptical, perspective. The positive verdict of Hillel (*ca.* 15 B.C.) about the book's inspiration triumphed over the negative opinion of Shammai. Doubts about authority survived among Christians at least until the time of Theodore of Mopsuestia (*ca.* A.D. 400); that influential exegete of Antioch questioned Qoheleth's right to stand among the holy books.

Author and Date

Protestant scholars since Luther's time have tended to date Qoheleth much later than Solomon. The rabbis' view of Solomon's authorship was based on their literal interpretation of 1:1 and their tendency to tie Solomon's name to all wisdom literature: he was viewed as master sage just as his father was associated with the Psalter as master singer.

A variety of evidence exists for a date much later than the tenth century. Solomon's name is not mentioned in the text, where only cryptic references occur ("the son of David, king in Jerusalem," 1:1; "king over Israel in Jerusalem," v. 12; "surpassing all who were over Jerusalem before me," v. 16; cf. 2:9). Even these cryptic references disappear after ch. 2, and some later statements do not fit well in a king's mouth (e.g., 4:13; 7:19; 8:2-4; 9:14f.; 10:4-7). Furthermore, much of what Qoheleth says presupposes the highly developed wisdom movement reflected in Proverbs. This movement, in Israel, began with Solomon but reached its height only after Hezekiah's time (seventh century; Prov. 25:1). The serious questioning of the beliefs and values of ancient Israel points to a time when prophetic activity had decreased and vital hope in God's active presence and power had waned. Finally, both vocabulary and sentence structure are postexilic, more closely akin to Mishnaic style than any other Old Testament book.[3]

For a century or more now this linguistic argument has been the most cogent line of evidence for a date between 400 and 200.[4] A date later than 200 is ruled out, both by Ecclesiasticus (Sirach; *ca.* 180), which refers to Qoheleth, and by fragments of Qoheleth among the Qumran scrolls.[5]

Efforts to buttress this dating with parallels to Greek philosophy have not proved fruitful. Despite superficial resemblances to Aristotle, Theogonis, Epicureans, and Stoics, Qoheleth was a Semitic wise man, not a Greek philosopher. His mood and approach reflect a different world. Suggestions of similarities to the thought and style of Egyptian and Mesopotamian wisdom writings have not been especially fruitful.[6] In fact, it is clear that Qoheleth did not consciously borrow from foreign sources. Rather, he continued an ancient

Pool of Solomon, south of Bethlehem, "from which to water the forest of growing trees" (Eccl. 2:6). *(Neal and Joel Bierling)*

499

trait of wisdom writers in questioning his colleagues' conclusions. Because he and they were Israelites steeped in Israel's peculiar faith and culture, the book is unique and ought not to be seen as the literary offspring of Egyptian or Mesopotamian parents.

It is easier to say that King Solomon did not write Ecclesiastes than to say who did. The author was a wise man eager to challenge the opinions and values of other wise men. But who he was or where he lived is unknown. Suggestions that he was a Phoenician or Alexandrian Jew have not received wide acceptance.[7] Qoheleth's reference to Jerusalem, the hub of political and commercial activities, should be taken at face value.

If Solomon is not the actual author, why does Qoheleth seek to link himself with the famous king? The simplest answer is for literary effect. The words of the head of Israel's wisdom movement would carry weight with the sages whom Qoheleth aimed to correct. Moreover, Solomon himself could serve as a model of the life Qoheleth was striving to evaluate. Wisdom, pleasure, wealth, influence, accomplishment were attributes touted by the wise men. The author could offer no better illustration of their limitations than Solomon's own case.[8]

The author does not pretend to be Solomon to deceive his audience. His literary intent is plain. He does not mention Solomon nor carry the disguise beyond the first two chapters. His strategies are to capture his readers' attention and to use the circumstances of Solomon to probe ironically the weaknesses in his fellow sages' teachings. He then sets aside Solomon's garb and presses his arguments home. He uses the master's personage to judge those who claim to be Solomon's followers.

Theme and Contents

The mention of Solomon and the sages who counted him their mentor gets to the heart of Qoheleth's purpose and theme. He sought to use traditional tools of wisdom to refute and revise its traditional conclusions. Like Job, he protested against the easy generalizations with which his fellow teachers taught their pupils to be successful. They had oversimplified life and its rules so as to mislead and frustrate their followers. Their observations seemed superficial and their counsel thin in a world beset by toil, injustice, and death.

Theme. For Qoheleth, conventional wisdom was not only inadequate, but close to blasphemous. At stake was the difference between God and humankind. The sages trespassed on territory belonging to God when they tried to predict infallibly the outcome of the conduct of both wise and foolish. The freedom of God and the mystery of God's ways were realities that Qoheleth understood better than his compatriots, who did not always recognize the limits that divine sovereignty has placed on human understanding. Two of his main emphases speak to this point:

> For who knows what is good for mortals while they live the few days of their vain life, which they pass like a shadow? For who can tell them what will be after them under the sun? (6:12)

These rhetorical questions point out the vast gulf between what God knows and what human beings can know.[9]

Failure to reckon with that gulf has caused humankind to overvalue its accomplishments in wisdom, pleasure, prestige, wealth, and justice. This false confidence is what Qoheleth attacks:

> Vanity of vanities, says the Teacher,
>   vanity of vanities! All is vanity. (1:2)

The literary form adds to the intensity: (1) the pattern "x of x" is a superlative (as in "King of Kings" or "Song of Songs"), meaning the vainest vanity, the most futile futility; (2) repetition of the phrase is a standard Hebrew means of emphasis; (3) the conclusion "All is vanity" makes the point as sweeping as possible. "Vanity" (Heb. *hebel*) may mean "breath" or "vapor" (Isa. 57:13), thus meaning something without substance. The list of suggested translations is staggering: "nothingness," "emptiness," "futility," "temporariness," "absurdity," "unfathomableness," "enigma." The last two terms capture best for us the Preacher's meaning: (1) our human inability to grasp life's mysteries; (2) our impotence to change life's realities.[10]

The bulk of the Preacher's words demonstrate and explain this theme. He begins with his conclusion and then spends twelve chapters to show how he reached it. "All is vanity" is only the negative half of his conclusion. He continues to drive it home (1:14; 2:11, 17, 19, 21, 23, 26; 4:4, 7f., 16; 5:10[MT 9]; 6:9; 8:14; 12:8) because his brashly optimistic countrymen need to hear it. But interwoven with it is his positive conclusion about what is good and meaningful in life:

> There is nothing better for mortals than to eat and drink, and find enjoyment in their toil. This also, I saw, is from the hand of God. (2:24)

This point is reaffirmed periodically (3:12f., 22; 5:18-20 [MT 17-19]; 8:15; 9:7-10) and underscored in the conclusion: "Fear God, and keep his commandments" (12:13), meaning not the laws of Moses but the counsels of Qoheleth to enjoy the simple things of life as God gives them.

Structure. Qoheleth's unique method of argumentation makes a coherent outline of this work almost impossible. It seems to be more a collection of separate thoughts than a unified argument which can be systematically followed from beginning to end. Part of the problem may be in imposing a modern definition of a "book" as "a unified, logically argued and constructed whole."[11]

Of the many ways in which the book has been analyzed, the form chosen here recognizes two essential points in Qoheleth's method. The first is the repetitive nature of his arguments to demonstrate his theme, a typically Semitic device. The second is the use of clusters of proverbs, "words of advice" to clarify or reinforce the argument. This technique is particularly telling in light of Qoheleth's desire to correct the more conventional wise men.[12]

Introduction (1:1-13)
   Title (v. 1)
   Theme (vv. 2f.)
Theme demonstrated — I (1:4–2:26)
   by the constancy of creation (1:4-11)
   by knowledge (vv. 12-18)
   by pleasure (2:1-11)
   by fate of all persons (vv. 12-17)
   by human toil (vv. 18-23)
     Conclusion: Enjoy life now as God gives it (vv. 24-26)
Theme demonstrated — II (3:1–4:16)
   by God's control of all events (3:1-11)
     Conclusion: Enjoy life now as God gives it (vv. 12-15)
   by the lack of immortality (vv. 16-21)
     Conclusion: Enjoy life now as God gives it (v. 22)
   by evil oppression (4:1-3)
   by work (vv. 4-6)
   by miserly hoarding of wealth (vv. 7-12)
   by the transient nature of popularity (vv. 13-16)
Words of Advice — A (5:1-12 [MT 4:17–5:11])
   Honor God in your worship (5:1-3 [MT 4:17–5:2])
   Pay your vows (vv. 4-7 [MT 3-6])
   Expect injustice in government (5:5f. [MT 7f.])
   Do not overvalue wealth (5:10-12 [MT 9-11])
Theme demonstrated — III (5:13–6:12 [MT 5:12–6:12])
   by wealth lost in business (5:13-17 [MT 12-16])
     Conclusion: Enjoy life now as God gives it (vv. 18-20 [MT 17-19])
   by wealth that cannot be enjoyed (6:1-9)
   by the fixity of fate (6:10-12)
Words of Advice — B (7:1–8:9)

Honor is better than luxury (7:1)
Sobriety is better than levity (vv. 2-7)
Caution is better than rashness (vv. 8-10)
Wisdom with wealth is better than wisdom alone (vv. 11f.)
Resignation is better than indignation (vv. 13f.)
Integrity is better than pretentiousness (vv. 15-22)
Facing limitations is better than claiming achievements (vv. 23-29)
Compromise is sometimes better than being right (8:1-9)
Theme demonstrated — IV (8:10–9:12)
by the inconsistencies in justice (8:10-14)
Conclusion: Enjoy life now as God gives it (v. 15)
by the mystery of God's ways (vv. 16f.)
by death, common fate of wise and foolish alike (9:1-6)
Conclusion: Enjoy life now as God gives it (vv. 7-10)
by the uncertainty of life (vv. 11f.)
Words of Advice — C (9:13–12:8)
Introduction: a story on the value of wisdom (9:13-16)
Wisdom and folly (9:17–10:15)
Rule of kings (vv. 16-20)
Sound business practices (11:1-8)
Enjoying life before old age comes (11:9–12:8)
Epilogue
Aim of the Preacher (12:9f.)
Commendation of his teachings (vv. 11f.)
Conclusion of the matter (vv. 13f.)[13]

Unity. The outline above presumes a unity to Qoheleth's work that was seriously questioned earlier in our century. Approaches were in vogue that credited more positive wisdom sayings to "an editor deeply interested in Wisdom Literature" or to a more pious later editor "imbued with the spirit of the Pharisees" and supportive of "the orthodox doctrines of the time."[14]

A fresh understanding of Semitic literature has bolstered the recent emphasis on the unity of Qoheleth.[15] Especially helpful have been parallels between Babylonian and Egyptian wisdom literature and Qoheleth in the tendency to combine conventional and unconventional wisdom and to imbed traditional proverbs in original material. Further, scholars now view many apparent contradictions (recognized by the rabbis who debated the book's canonicity) as the results of the author's own struggle with life's complexities, not an editor's attempts at patchwork.[16]

Other apparent contradictions can be readily resolved when it is seen that Qoheleth often quoted material in order to refute it. For example, the comment on work in 4:5 ("Fools fold their hands, and consume their own flesh") is a piece of conventional wisdom aimed to condemn laziness. To point out its inadequacy, Qoheleth cites his own proverb: "Better is a handful with quiet than two handfuls with toil and a chasing after wind" (v. 6).

Undoubtedly the strongest argument against multiple authorship is the question of motive. If Qoheleth caused so many problems to the wise and pious among the Jews, why did they bother to rework the text with a multitude of glosses? Would it not have made more sense simply to scrap the book?

Generally, it is recognized that the title (1:1) and epilogue (12:9-14) may have been added by a disciple of Qoheleth, speaking of his master in the third person. But the work itself remains intact with all its puzzling perplexities.

Form-critical studies during the past fifty years have divided the book into segments of various lengths and number. A growing tendency is to view the book "as a *cahier* or notebook," rather than a debate, dialogue, or philosophical treatise.[17] Of the unity of these notes von Rad remarks:

> There is, to be precise, an inner unity which can find expression otherwise than through a linear development of thought or through a logical progression in the thought process, namely through the unity of style and topic and theme, a unity which can make a work of literature into a whole and which can in fact give it the rank of a self-contained work of art.[18]

Literary Characteristics

Reflections. The backbone of Qoheleth's literary style is a series of first-person prose narratives in which the Preacher relates his observations about the futility of life. These reflections (Zimmerli calls them "confessions")[19] begin with such phrases as: "And I applied my mind" (1:13, 17), "I have seen everything" (v. 14), "I said to myself" (v. 16; 2:1), "Moreover I saw" (3:16), "Again I saw" (4:1, 7; 9:11). The role of observation is key, reflected by repeated use of the verb "to see," which may mean both "observe" and "reflect on." J. G. Williams, following Zimmerli, found in this "confession style" a "departure from the security and self-certainty of the wise."[20] Questioning whether clear-cut conclusions about the human place in God's cosmos can be affirmed, as other wise men taught, Qoheleth can only rehearse what he has searched, seen, and concluded. The reflective literary form matches precisely his understanding of reality: empirical yet rational and personal.

Frequently these reflections summarize their conclusion, usually in one closing sentence: "I perceived that this also is but a chasing after wind" (1:17);

"Then I considered all that my hands had done . . . and again, all was vanity and a chasing after wind" (2:11; cf. 2:26; 4:4, 16; 6:9).[21]

Proverbs. Qoheleth used proverbs in both conventional and nonconventional ways. Like his fellow sages, he used two main types: (1) statements (called "truth sayings" by Ellermeier) that simply affirm what reality is like: "The lover of money will not be satisfied with money; nor the lover of wealth, with gain" (5:10 [MT 9]); (2) admonitions (or "counsels") that consist of commands with motivations. Those are sometimes positive: "Send out your bread upon the waters, for after many days you will get it back" (11:1); sometimes negative: "Do not be quick to anger, for anger lodges in the bosom of fools" (7:9).

A favorite form is the comparison of two forms of conduct, one "better" than the other (4:6, 9, 13; 5:5 [MT 4]; 7:1-3, 5, 8; 9:17f.). The literary form is a hedge against pessimism and nihilism: things may not be all good or bad; but some are surely better than others. It is also used to turn conventional wisdom topsy-turvy, by calling good what is usually deemed bad (e.g., ch. 7).

The proverbs (see the tribute paid Qoheleth's skill in 12:9) occur at two main points: (1) imbedded in the reflections, where they reinforce or summarize the conclusions (1:15, 18; 4:5f.; vv. 9-12 act almost as a numerical proverb such as Prov. 30:5, 18, 21, 24, 29); and (2) clustered in the "words of advice" sections (5:1-12 [MT 4:17–5:11]; 7:1–8:9; 9:13–12:8).

Most important is their role in the argument: Qoheleth uses proverbs to help his hearers cope with life's difficulties. Such proverbs become a commentary on his positive conclusion calling his followers to enjoy life now as God gives it. The "words of advice" in 5:1-12 [MT 4:17–5:11]; 9:13–12:8 are filled with sound counsel on how to make the best of life.

Qoheleth quotes other proverbs so he can argue against them. He cites conventional wisdom, then rebuts it with his own statements (2:14; 4:5f.). In 9:18, the first line represents the traditional value put on wisdom: "Wisdom is better than weapons of war." This may be true, Qoheleth says, but it should not be overvalued because "one bungler destroys much good."[22]

A clever device is the Preacher's use of antiproverbs, sayings coined in wisdom style but with a message opposite to that found in the tradition:

> For in much wisdom is much vexation,
>   and those who increase knowledge increase sorrow. (1:18)

The contrast between these statements and the happiness promised by wisdom in passages such as Prov. 2:10; 3:13; 8:34-36 is striking and must have cut Qoheleth's wise opponents to the quick.

Rhetorical Questions. To draw his audience into his argument and force a "yes" to his vanity verdict, Qoheleth frequently uses rhetorical questions.

505

Since they often occur toward the end of a section, they are a clue to his point: "What do mortals get from all the toil and strain with which they toil under the sun?" (2:22); "What gain have the workers from their toil?" (3:9).[23]

Descriptive Language. "Enjoy life now as God gives it" is the Preacher's positive conclusion. At the end of the book, he reinforces it with a series of graphic pictures (12:2-7). His main point, made in an admonition ("Remember your Creator in the days of your youth"; v. 1), is driven home in images of the frailties of old age, death, and a funeral. An estate is immobilized by the death of one of its members: darkness shrouds the place (v. 2); all work on the plantation grinds to a halt as the employees inside and out are gripped by grief or cease their labors to attend the funeral (v. 3); shut doors protect the grieving, almost empty household; the voice of a bird signals life in the presence of the "daughters of song" who keen their chants of mourning (v. 4); the blossoming almond tree likewise heralds life to the gloomy cortege (v. 5); silver cord, golden bowl, pitcher, and wheel are all figures of life-functions snapped at death (v. 6). The pictorial language is introduced by a proverb to make its meaning and purpose clear; similarly, it closes with a literal description of death (v. 7) that eliminates the need for speculation as to its general thrust, even though interpretation of the details may vary.[24]

Contributions to Biblical Theology

Freedom of God and Limits of Wisdom. Far from a mere skeptic or pessimist, Qoheleth sought to contribute positively to his contemporaries' relationship to God. He did so by stressing the limits to human understanding and ability. Thus, he would have considered even his verdict about the vanity of human endeavor a positive contribution.

(1) People are limited by the way in which God has determined the events of their lives. They have little power to change the course of history:

> What is crooked cannot be made straight,
> and what is lacking cannot be counted. (1:15)

That antiproverb is echoed in the rhetorical questions:

> Consider the work of God;
> who can make straight what he has made crooked? (7:13)

Even the times for life's experiences are set in place in such a way that human toil cannot alter them (3:1-9).[25]

"Under the sun"[26] is an almost nagging reminder of the earthbound life of perplexed humanity. At base, it means that people are in the world, not in heaven where God dwells. In many contexts, it

> suggests also that the sun relentlessly makes *labour* and *toil* hard, as relentlessly exposes everything to view, showing how "empty" it is, and just as relentlessly measures the passages of ceaseless days and nights.[27]

(2) Human creatures are limited by their inability to discover God's ways. Though they may understand that their lives are determined by God's sovereignty, they cannot understand how or why. This was especially vexing to Israel's wise men, who sought to know the proper time for each of life's tasks:

> To make an apt answer is a joy to anyone,
>   and a word in season [lit. "in its time"], how good it is! (Prov. 15:23)[28]

The problem is not God's, but humankind's:

> He has made everything suitable for its time; moreover he has put a sense of past and future[29] into their mind, yet they cannot find out what God has done from the beginning to the end. (3:11)

The phrases "not find out" ("who can find out?") or "do not know" ("no knowledge") dominate chs. 7–11.[30] No wonder Qoheleth counsels against rashness in prayer: ". . . for God is in heaven, and you upon earth; therefore let your words be few" (5:2 [MT 1]).

The wise men of Proverbs recognized the limits of human wisdom and the sovereignty of God's ways:

> The human mind plans the way,
>   but the Lord directs the steps. (Prov. 16:9)

> The human mind may devise many plans,
>   but it is the purpose of the Lord that will be established. (19:21)

But Qoheleth's neighbors apparently had underplayed these truths. They felt overconfident about their ability to effect their own destinies. Why did Qoheleth choose to stress those limitations?

Was it due to a loss of trust in God, accompanied by a radical desire to find more systematic order in life and to discern the future more clearly than the older wise men dared?[31] Was Qoheleth a "frontier guard" who refused to allow the sages to claim an all-embracing skill in controlling life? Qoheleth knew that a true "fear of God never allows a human person in his 'art of directing' to hold the helm in his own hands."[32] Was Qoheleth's silence about Israel's election a negative reminder that a doctrine of creation by itself is

507

incomplete until "it dares to believe that the creator is the God who in free goodness promised Himself to His people?"[33]

Facing Life's Realities. (1) Grace. Though Qoheleth indicates no concern for Israel's experience of covenant or redemption, he was certainly aware of God's grace. For him, grace showed itself in God's provision of the good things of creation. His positive conclusion ("There is nothing better for mortals than to eat and drink, and find enjoyment in their toil") is rooted in God's goodness: "This also . . . is from the hand of God; for apart from him who can eat or who can have enjoyment?" (2:24f.). Elsewhere (3:13), this is all described as "God's gift." A dozen times the root *nātan* "give" is used with God as subject.

> Whatever else may have baffled him about the inscrutable ways of God, Qoheleth had no doubt that this grace appears daily in provisions of the Creator who "has made everything suitable for its time." 3:11

The realities of grace and human limitation converge in Qoheleth's use of "portion" (Heb. *hēleq*; 2:10, 21; 3:22; 5:18f. [MT 17f.]; 9:6, 9). Translated "lot" "reward," or "all" (2:21), the term signifies the partial, and limited, nature of God's gifts. He does not give mortals everything, yet these simple pleasures are gifts, to be used gratefully. "Portion" is contrasted with "profit" or "gain" (*yitrôn*), another favorite word (1:3; 2:11, 13; 3:9; 5:9, 16 [MT 8, 15]; 7:12; 10:10f.; cf. the related word *môtar* "advantage," 3:19). Profit describes the surplus that human labor can generate; portion depicts the lot which God's grace bestows. Humankind can earn nothing; God sees that they have enough.[34]

(2) Death. Death's coming is sure, but its timing is not. It is the one fate that comes to all — wise and foolish (2:14f.; 9:2f.), person and beast (3:19). Death confronts people most drastically with their limitations, reminding them continually that the future is beyond their control. It strips them naked, whether they have toiled with wisdom only to leave their goods to the undeserving (2:21) or whether they have wanted to bequeath them to an heir but lost them first (5:13-17 [MT 12-16]). Qoheleth's description of death seems based on the creation narrative of Gen. 2, where divine breath and earthly dust combined to make the human self. In death the process seems reversed: "and the dust returns to the earth as it was, and the same spirit (NRSV "breath") returns to God who gave it" (12:7), although Qoheleth questions just how dogmatic one can be (3:20f.). For him, death was the great discourager of false optimism.[35]

(3) Enjoyment. If "toil" (Heb. *ûāmāl*) dominated Qoheleth's view of the rigors of life,[36] so he used "joy" or "enjoyment" (from *śmḥ*) frequently, especially in stating his positive conclusion.[37] As grim as are life's painful present and precarious future, joy is possible when sought in the right place: gratitude for and appreciation of God's simple gifts of food, drink, work, and love. Writing to a society preoccupied with the need to succeed, achieve, produce, control,[38] Qoheleth warned of the joylessness and futility of such endeavors. Joy was not to be found in human achievement, as elusive as chasing the wind (2:11, 17, etc.), but in the everyday gifts apportioned by the Creator.[39]

Preparation for the Gospel. Though Qoheleth contains no recognizable prophetic or typological material, it does prepare for the Christian gospel. This does not mean that this was the book's central purpose or its role in the canon. As a critique of the extremes of the wisdom school, a window on the tragedies and injustices of life, and a pointer to the joys of existence, it stands on its own as a word from God to all humankind.[40]

Yet its Christian value should not be ignored. Its realism in depicting the ironies of suffering and death helps explain the crucial importance of Jesus' crucifixion and resurrection.

> Qoheleth's insistence on the inscrutability of God's ways underscores the magnificent breakthrough in divine and human communication which the Incarnation effected.

His dreary pictures of wearying toil paved the way for the Master's call from taxing labor to gracious rest (Matt. 11:28-30). His command to enjoy God's simple gifts without anxiety found echo in Jesus' exhortations to trust the God of the lily and the sparrow (6:25-33). His verdict of "vanity" set the stage for Paul's comprehensive evaluation: "for the creation was subjected to futility" (Rom. 8:20).

With burning eye and biting pen, Qoheleth challenged the overconfidence of the older wisdom and its misapplication in his culture. Thereby, he prepared for the one "greater than Solomon," "in whom are hid all the treasures of wisdom and knowledge" (12:42; Col. 2:3).[41]

CHAPTER 37

The Song of Songs

Lovers have always sensed that *song* alone was a fit expression for strong feelings, high delight, deep commitment. Overcome by desire to give themselves to another and to gain the unaskable from that other, they do not derive a formula, concoct a recipe, write a ritual, draw a map, chart a graph. They sing a song. In Holy Writ, they find the best song possible.

It takes its name from 1:1, "The Song of Songs [i.e., the finest song], which is Solomon's." (An alternate name, Canticles, is derived from the Vulgate.) The Song is placed first among the five scrolls (Megilloth) in the Jewish canon used on festive occasions; it is assigned to be read at Passover.

> Many waters cannot quench love,
>   neither can floods drown it.
> If one offered for love all the wealth of his house,
>   it would be utterly scorned. Song of Sol. 8:7

Canonicity

Acceptance in the Jewish canon did not come easily, as the Mishnah more than hints. Rabbi Akiba's strong affirmation (*ca.* A.D. 100) undoubtedly was calculated to quell opposition and assure the book's place in Scripture: "The whole world is not worth the day on which the Song of Songs was given to Israel; all the Writings are holy, and the Song of Songs is the holy of holies."[1] Without doubt the erotic nature of the Song prompted questions. Eventually the objections were overcome (1) by the poem's connection with Solomon, (2) by rabbinic and Christian allegorical interpretations, which helped to mitigate the sensual tone, (3) and possibly by Jewish realization that "it celebrated the mysteries of human love expressed in the marriage festival."[2]

Authorship and Date

Traditional Solomonic authorship is based on references to the king throughout the book (1:5; 3:7, 9, 11), especially in the title (1:1). "To Solomon," Heb. *lišlōmōh* (1:1), may indicate authorship. Yet other interpretations are possible: "for" or "in the style of Solomon." Solomon's skill as a songwriter is known from 1 Kgs. 4:32 (cf. Pss. 72; 127), but his relationship to these love poems is obscure.[3] Attempts to fit the love and loyalty expressed here into Solomon's patterns of political marriage and concubinage (see 1 Kgs. 11) are hard to justify.

Alleged Persian and Greek loanwords,[4] almost uniform use of the relative pronoun form characteristic of later Hebrew,[5] and words and phrases reflecting Aramaic influence[6] hint but do not prove that the final editing, if not the actual composition, was later than Solomon. However, the book need not be dated in the Hellenistic period (after 330). Ample evidence exists both for commerce between Ionia and Canaan and for Aramaic impact on Hebrew literature from the early centuries of the Monarchy.[7]

The lack of historical references in the Song makes dating difficult. Some scholars argue for the Persian period, more precisely between Nehemiah's time and 350, on the basis of linguistic arguments and geographical data. They find in the descriptions of Solomon's fabulous glory reflections of "the pomp and circumstances of the Persian Empire and the luxurious palaces of the Great King at Susa (Shushan) and Persepolis."[8] But the witness of archaeology to Solomon's splendid reign seems to render Persian influence unnecessary. The Song's lavish setting accurately reflects Solomon's glory, just as the luxury, wealth, and wisdom of Ecclesiastes carefully recall his regal circumstances.

Though Solomon himself probably was not the author, much of the setting and tone reflect his age. As with Proverbs, the nucleus or core of Canticles may have been transmitted (perhaps orally), added to, and then given its present setting by a nameless, inspired editor, who, around the time of the Exile, organized and collected what were traditional Israelite love songs.[9]

"Like Lebanon, choice as the cedars" is the beloved in the
Song of Songs (Cant. 5:15). *(Robert Smith)*

Literary Qualities

Strictly speaking, the Song should not be classified as wisdom literature, since its dominant form is love poetry, not instruction or debate. But because it is connected with Solomon and probably was copied, preserved, and published in the wisdom circles, it can be studied alongside that corpus.[10] Moreover, by celebrating the glories of marriage as a gift of the Creator and a norm for human life, its poets are close kin to the wise men (see Prov. 5:15-19).[11]

Most of the Song is stylized conversation between the lover and beloved (e.g., 1:9ff.; 4:1ff.; 6:2ff.), though much may be imagined speech, uttered when the partner was absent. Various forms of love poetry have been identified.[12]

Descriptive Songs. This is an ancient form, well attested in Babylonian, Egyptian, and modern Arabic (where it is called *wasf*) literature. Each lover describes the other's beauty in highly figurative language (he describes her, 4:1-7; 6:4-7; 7:1-9 [MT 2-10]; she describes him, 5:10-16). These descriptions salute the partner, while stimulating both for love (see 1:15f., where each in turn admires the other's beauty).

Self-Descriptions. Only the woman used this form, usually to disclaim modestly the beauty ascribed to her (1:5f.; 2:1). Her self-description in 8:10 seems to take pride in her virginity and maturity; she has passed her brothers' test (vv. 8f.).

Songs of Admiration. This form differs from the descriptive song in calling attention to the loved one's dress or ornamentation (e.g., the jewelry in 1:9-11; 4:9-11). Cant. 7:7-9 shows the passion that such admiration aroused.

Songs of Yearning. The lovers' ardent desire, especially when apart, is voiced in such songs (e.g., 1:2-4; 2:5f.; 8:1-4, 6f.). The characteristic form is a wish for love or a call to love, a reminder that absence can make the heart grow fonder.

Search Narratives. Twice the woman recounts her impassioned searches for her lover. Unable to sleep, she wanders through the city looking for him, once with satisfaction (3:1-4), once with frustration (5:2-7). These narratives show her willingness to take initiative in love.

Game of Love. The second search narrative begins a "game" between the woman and her friends, the "daughters of Jerusalem":

She:	search narrative (unsuccessful)	5:2-7
She:	oath placed on friends to help find the lover	v. 8
Friends:	teasing question about lover's worth	v. 9
She:	answer-song describing his beauty	vv. 10-16
Friends:	teasing question about accompanying her to find him	6:1
She:	erotic account of where he is; formula of belonging (indicates that she will not share him)	(cf. 2:16; 7:10a) 6:2f.

This game displays the playfulness which was part of ancient wisdom. Even more, it is a reminder of the exclusive, covenantal relationship that the partners enjoyed.

Other Literary Forms. The Song contains several other forms, such as: (1) formula imposing an oath (2:7; 3:5; 5:8; 8:4), showing how strongly the woman's friends support her commitment, how love is so compelling that it should not be aroused prematurely, and how earnestly she wants freedom to be with her lover undisturbed; (2) teasing song (1:7f.), catching the banter between the lovers in their desire to be together (see 2:14f.; 5:2f.); (3) boasting song (6:8-10; 8:11f.), expressing the lover's delight in her uniqueness, a delight shared by the friends, who join in praising her (6:10); (4) invitation to love (2:5, 17; 4:16; 7:11-13; 8:14), offered by the woman, usually with the urgency of an imperative.

Apart from the lovers, the participants are identified only with great difficulty. Brief responses (1:8; 5:9; 6:1, etc.) have been credited to "daughters of Jerusalem," perhaps friends or "bridesmaids" (1:5; 2:7; 3:5; 5:8, etc.); citizens of Jerusalem, who describe the royal entourage as it approaches the city (3:6-11); and citizens of the woman's hometown (8:5). In this highly figurative poetry the central characters may be re-creating the speeches of others: the Shulammite[13] seems to be quoting her brothers in 8:8f. These short responses may be attributed, regardless of context, to a chorus. This simple approach is a welcome relief from attempts (especially in the last century) to treat the Song as a highly complex drama.

The book's impact lies in the intensity of the love depicted, especially in the rich and graphic imagery. These very qualities which are the poem's source of strength present problems to western tastes. The vividly detailed descriptions of the lovers' bodies and their frank, passionate desire seem too highly spiced. But they are the product of a distant time and place. They are vivid but not lurid. The open honesty of their approach elevates them above the innuendo sometimes found in their contemporary western counterparts. Frequently the similes or metaphors sound strange or even uncomplimentary:

> Your hair is like a flock of goats,
>   moving down the slopes of Gilead; (4:1)

or:

> Your neck is like the tower of David,
>   built in courses;
> on it hang a thousand bucklers,
>   all of them shields of warriors. (v. 4)

"Orientals fix the eye on one single striking point, which according to our conceptions is perhaps not characteristic."[14] Thus, in the wavelike motion of a flock of goats moving down a distant slope the poet finds an image of the grace and beauty of the beloved's tresses falling in gentle waves upon her shoulders. Similarly, the strength and erectness of her neck, ornamented with jewelry, remind him of David's tower-fortress bedecked with warriors' shields.[15] The metaphors serve a noble purpose: They form "an intricate series of connections between the beauty of the Lover or the Beloved and the world," made beautiful by the Creator's hand.[16]

Suggested Interpretations

Scholars have found it hard to agree about the origin, meaning, and purpose of the Song. Erotic lyrics, absence of a religious note, and opaqueness of plot baffle them and tempt their imaginative ingenuity. The resources of modern scholarship — archaeological discoveries, recovery of huge bodies of ancient literature, insights into oriental psychology and sociology — have produced no clear scholarly consensus.[17]

Allegorical. The earliest recorded Jewish interpretations (in the Mishnah, Talmud, and Targum) find in it a portrait of God's love for Israel. This accounts for the book's use at Passover, which celebrates God's covenant love. Not content with general allusions to God's relationship with Israel, the rabbis vied to discover specific references to Israel's history.

The Church Fathers baptized the Song, seeing in it Christ's love for the Church or the individual believer.[18] Christians also have contributed detailed and imaginative interpretations, as attested by headings tradition- ally found in the KJV containing such interpretative summaries as "The mutual love of Christ and his Church" or "The Church professeth her faith in Christ." The place of allegory is featured in some modern Roman Catholic commentaries.[19]

Typical. To avoid the subjectivity of the allegorical approach and honor the literal sense of the poem, this method stresses the major themes of love and devotion rather than the details of the story. In the warmth and strength of the lovers' mutual affection, typological interpreters hear overtones of the relationship between Christ and his Church. Justification for this view has been based on parallels with Arabic love poems, which may have esoteric or mystical meanings; on Christ's use of the story of Jonah (Matt. 12:40) or the serpent in the wilderness (John 3:14); and on the well-known biblical analogies of spiritual marriage (e.g., Jer. 2:2; 3:1ff.; Ezek. 16:6ff.; Hos. 1–3; Eph. 5:22-33; Rev. 19:9).

The devotional benefits from allegorical or typical approaches to the Song cannot be denied. The question, however, is what the author intended. Any allegorical reading is hazardous because the possibilities for variety in interpretation are limitless. One is more apt to find his or her own ideas than to discern the author's intent. Further, the text gives no hint that the Song is to be read in other than its natural sense.[20]

Dramatic. The presence of dialogue, soliloquy, and choruses (see above) has led students of literature, both ancient (e.g., Origen, *ca.* A.D. 240) and modern (e.g., Milton), to treat it as a drama. Two forms of dramatic analysis have held sway: (1) two main characters, Solomon and the Shulammite, identified by some scholars (quite incorrectly in the view of this survey) with Pharaoh's daughter, whom Solomon wed in a marriage of convenience (1 Kgs. 3:1),[21] (2) three characters including the maiden's shepherd lover as well as Solomon and the Shulammite.[22] The plot turns on the Shulammite's faithfulness to her rustic lover despite Solomon's luxurious attempts to woo and win her. Both views have weaknesses: the absence of any dramatic instructions, and the complexity introduced if the Shulammite responds to Solomon's overtures by reminiscing of her shepherd sweetheart. A major obstacle to all such interpretations is the paucity of evidence for formal drama among the Semites, particularly the Hebrews.

Nuptial Songs. A study of Syrian wedding rites fostered a fresh look at the Song at the end of the last century.[23] Some scholars found in such week-long festivities a number of parallels to elements within the Song: bride and groom are treated like king and queen; descriptions of the beauties and virtues of the lovers are sung; the bride performs a sword dance (see 6:13; 7:1); March is the preferred month (see 2:11); the couple are mounted on a beautifully decorated threshing table which becomes a royal throne (see 3:7-10).[24]

Even if the contention that similar wedding customs can be traced in Jewish antiquity is accepted,[25] problems remain: the Song as it stands cannot easily be divided into parts corresponding to the seven days, and the Shulammite is nowhere called a queen.

Liturgical Rites. A few scholars have sought to illuminate obscure Old Testament passages by comparison with the religious customs of Mesopotamia, Egypt, or Canaan. An example is the theory that Canticles is derived from liturgical rites of the cult of Tammuz (cf. Ezek. 8:14), Babylonian god of fertility.[26] These rites celebrated the sacred marriage (Gk. *hieros gamos*) of Tammuz and his consort Ishtar (Ashtarte) which produced the annual spring fertility.[27] Modern western culture shows that pagan religion may leave a legacy of terminology without influencing religious beliefs (e.g., names of days and months); still, it seems highly questionable that the Hebrews would have accepted a pagan liturgy, smacking of idolatry and immorality, without thorough revision in terms of Israel's distinctive faith.[28] Canticles bears the marks of no such revision.

Funeral Rituals. A theory that has attracted more interest than support views the Song as part of a Hebrew pattern of mourning. Feasts something like wakes are thought to have included sexual activities. Their purpose was to affirm the continuity of love and life in the face of the separation occasioned by death.[29]

Love Song. In recent decades some scholars have viewed the Song as a poem or collection of love poems, perhaps but not necessarily connected with wedding celebrations or other specific occasions.[30] Attempts are made to divide the Song into several independent poems. But an overriding air of unity[31] is heard in the continuity of theme, refrainlike repetitions (e.g., 2:7; 3:5; 8:4), chainlike structure binding one part to the preceding, preparations in chs. 1–3 for the consummation of the love relationship in 4:9–5:1, implications of that consummation in 5:2–8:14.

The chart on pages 518-19 tries to capture the unity, diversity, and movement within the Song.[32]

In the tone of the lyric poetry one can feel the Song's message. While movement is evident, there is only a shadowy sketch of a plot. The couple's love is as intense at the beginning as at the end; thus, the poem's power lies not in a lofty climax (though the scene of consummation is its center, 4:9–5:1) but in the creative and delicate repetitions of the themes of love — a love longed for when apart (e.g., 3:1-5) and enjoyed to the full when together (e.g., ch. 7), relished amid the splendor of the palace (e.g., 1:2-4) or in the serenity of the countryside (7:11ff.), and reserved exclusively for the covenant partner (2:16; 6:3; 7:10).[33] It is a love strong as death, which water cannot quench nor floods drown, a love freely given yet beyond price (8:6f.)

Purpose

What place does such love poetry have in Scripture, especially if not originally intended as an allegorical or typical message of God's love?

> The book is an object lesson, an extended proverb or parable (*māšāl*) illustrating the rich wonders of human love, itself a gift of God's love.

Though expressed in bold language, the Song provides a wholesome, biblical balance between the extremes of sexual excess or perversion and of

517

Section	Theme	Type of Song	Singer	Text
Title	Royal Relationship	Prose	Editor	1:1
Poem I	Longing & Discovery 1:2–2:7	Song of Yearning for absent lover	Woman	1:2-4
		Self-description of modesty	Woman	1:5-6
		Teasing Dialogue imaginatively seeking an encounter	Woman, Man	1:7-8
		Song admiring her worth and beauty	Man	1:9-11
		Song of Admiration in reply	Woman	1:12-14
		Song of Admiration in dialogue	Woman, Man, Woman, Man	1:15–2:4
		Song of Yearning for intimacy	Woman	2:5-6
		Call for patience with love's course	Woman	2:7
Poem II	Invitation, Suspense, Response 2:8–3:5	Description of the lover's approach and invitation	Woman	2:8-14
		Teasing Response turned serious by Affirmation of Mutual Possession	Woman	2:15-16
		Invitation to intimacy	Woman	2:17
		Description of frustration and fulfillment	Woman	3:1-4
		Call for patience with love's course	Woman	3:5
Poem III	Ceremony and Satisfaction 3:6–5:1	Dramatic and Admiring Description of the groom's arrival	Woman	3:6-11
		Description of the bride's beauty	Man	4:1-7
		Invitation Song to bride	Man	4:8
		Admiration Song to bride	Man	4:9-15
		Invitation Song to groom	Woman	4:16
		Song of Eager Response	Man	5:1a
		Song of Encouragement (Daughters of Jerusalem)	Daughters of Jerusalem	5:1b
Poem IV	Frustration and Delight 5:2–6:3	Report of a vexing dream	Woman	5:2-7
		Call for urgent help	Woman	5:8
		Teasing Questions	Daughters of Jerusalem	5:9
		Description of lover's beauty	Woman	5:10-16
		Teasing Question	Daughters of Jerusalem	6:1
		Response of delight and commitment	Woman	6:2-3

Section	Theme	Type of Song	Singer	Text
Poem V	Pomp and Celebration 6:4–8:4	Descriptive Song with touches of a boast	Man	6:4-10
		Fantasy of separation	Woman	6:11-12
		Plea to return	Daughters of Jerusalem	6:13a
		Teasing Reply in question form	Woman	6:13b
		Description of the dancing woman	Daughters of Jerusalem	7:1-5
		Yearning Song for intimacy	Man	7:6-9
		Invitation to fulfillment	Woman	7:10–8:3
		Call for patience with love's course	Woman	8:4
Poem VI	Passion and Commitment 8:5-14	Question signaling the couple's return	Daughters of Jerusalem	8:5a
		Seductive Reminder of love's continuity	Woman	8:5b
		Yearning Song of chastity	Woman	8:6-7
		Test of chastity	Woman, speaking for her brothers	8:8-10 (8-9)
		Boast of chastity	Woman	8:11-12
		Yearning Song to hear her voice	Man	8:13
		Invitation Song to take his fill of love	Woman	8:14

asceticism, too often taken as a Christian view of sex, which denies the essential goodness and rightness of physical love within the divinely prescribed framework of marriage. We may go a step further: "Not only does it speak of the purity of human love; but, by its very inclusion in the canon, it reminds us of a love that is purer than our own."[34]

CHAPTER 38

Ruth

The Old Testament has all kinds of illustrious heroes. But does God work through common people? This delightful little book tells of God's providence in the life of one ordinary Israelite family.

> Your people shall be my people, and your God my God. Ruth 1:10

Name and Contents

The book is named for its principal character, Ruth the Moabite.[1] Because of famine, Elimelech of Bethlehem takes his family to live in Moab. Sadly, he and his two sons die there, leaving his wife Naomi and the sons' Moabite wives, Ruth and Orpah. When the famine ends, Naomi heads back to Judah. She persuades Orpah to go back to Moab, but Ruth resolutely refuses. The two widows return to Bethlehem just as the harvest begins. Ruth goes out to glean grain and by chance arrives in the fields of Boaz, a kinsman of Elimelech. As a relative, Boaz has the duty to marry a widowed in-law. So Naomi sends Ruth to propose such a marriage. Boaz is willing, but a closer relative has prior legal right to her. In the story's climax, Boaz cleverly obtains the right, marries Ruth, and the two have a son. The book celebrates him as a "son . . . born to Naomi" (4:17a) for the child Obed preserves her family line. More important, he turns out to be the grandfather of David.

Date and Authorship

Like most Old Testament narratives, the book of Ruth does not identify its author. The Talmud credits the book to Samuel, but such an attribution cannot be correct. The book must originate after David's rule (4:17b), and he reigned some years after Samuel's death. Scholars disagree on the date, with estimates ranging from the early Monarchy to the postexilic era. In our view, the evidence favors a date in the period of the Monarchy (tenth-sixth centuries B.C.).[2]

Social Features

Two unfamiliar social customs make the story difficult for modern readers to understand. The first is the duty whereby a close relative marries the widow of a kinsman who has no son in order to produce one. Without that son, the dead man's family line would not survive. Formerly, scholars identified this custom as "levirate marriage," the duty taught in Deut. 25:5-10 (cf. also Gen. 38).[3] Like the levirate, the arrangement in Ruth is intended to provide an heir for a deceased relative. Unlike the levirate, however, Boaz is not Elimelech's brother nor is Ruth Elimelech's widow. Instead, the duty falls to Boaz because he is Elimelech's close relative, i.e., a "kinsman-redeemer" (Heb. gō'ēl; 2:20). By a kind of "legal fiction," Ruth substitutes for Naomi as Elimelech's widow. Hence, we prefer to describe the practice in Ruth as "levirate-like" or even as a "kinsman-marriage."[4]

This custom explains a key turning point in the book: Naomi's clever ploy to induce Boaz to accept this duty. Perhaps Boaz had assumed that he was not close enough to Elimelech to perform it. So Naomi sends the young and attractive Ruth to motivate him. A daring, exquisitely told episode — the scene at the threshing floor in ch. 3 — details how Ruth did it. But an unexpected complication denies success to Naomi's plan: Boaz defers to the prior right of a closer relative.[5] The next morning, he convenes a legal hearing at the city gate,[6] invites the other relative to join, and obtains the right to Ruth.

The second custom, the redemption of land, marks a surprising development in the story. At the gate, readers expect Boaz immediately to discuss Ruth's marriage proposal. Instead, he announces that Naomi is "selling the parcel of land which belonged to our kinsman Elimelech" (4:3). Boaz offers to buy it if the other fellow does not. This is the first inkling of property owned by Elimelech. Behind it stands an ancient Israelite custom: ownership of ancestral land always had to remain in the family. A family might mortgage it to fend off poverty. But the law required the nearest next of kin to buy it back into family ownership (cf. Lev. 25:25ff.). In this case, the other relative agreed to buy Elimelech's property from Naomi (4:4).

By springing a further surprise, however, Boaz prompts the kinsman to give up his rights. Boaz informs him that to own the land the man must also marry Ruth and provide Elimelech an heir (v. 5). Immediately, the relative withdraws, claiming the deal would hurt his own inheritance (v. 6). Financially, the prospective buyer could handle the redemption obligation were it his only responsibility. For, by reaping him profits, Elimelech's land would actually pay for itself. Also, the marriage alone would not jeopardize his own estate, since profit from the property would support any heir until he was old enough to inherit it. But the man cannot accept the dual duty. An heir born to Ruth and him would inherit Elimelech's land, and he would be out the money he paid Naomi for it.

Threshing floor such as the one where Ruth persuaded Boaz to fulfill his responsibility as next of kin (Ruth 3). *(Neal and Joel Bierling)*

Voluntarily, he cedes his rights in the matter to Boaz (v. 6). Apparently, Boaz was wealthy enough to handle the dual obligation. Better, the deal may have given Boaz the son which he, like Elimelech, lacked. The concluding genealogy lists him, not Mahlon and Elimelech, as David's ancestor (4:18-22). That may imply that Boaz was either unmarried (unlikely) or had no son of his own (perhaps). In any case, the child born of his marriage to Ruth actually continued *two* family lines, those of Boaz and Elimelech.

Literary Nature and Theology

Scholars generally agree that the genre of Ruth is a short story.[7] Its length falls between that of a brief "tale" and a long "novella." It has a simple plot which runs its course in a brief time span (about six weeks). It also has only three main characters. More important, rather than to trace their development, it aims to help readers understand them. That suits the purpose of a short story — to edify and instruct readers in an entertaining way. The story subtly induces readers to share the characters' experience of God's providential activity. Implicitly, it asks them to emulate or avoid the examples of its characters.[8] The book of Ruth, thus, compares favorably to other Old Testament short stories: the marriage of Isaac (Gen. 24), Dan. 1–6, and Jonah.

Though not tightly arranged, the book generally displays a mirror structure. That is, later elements in the story parallel and resolve earlier ones. The following somewhat simplified schema highlights the book's main structural and thematic parallels:

1:1-5	Introduction: the family of Elimelech
1:6-18	Naomi's concern: marriage of daughters-in-law
1:19-22	Naomi's grief, emptiness
2:1-2	Dialogue: Naomi and Ruth
2:3-17	Dialogue: Ruth and Boaz
2:18-23	Dialogue: Ruth and Naomi
3:1-5	Dialogue: Naomi and Ruth
3:6-15	Dialogue: Ruth and Boaz
3:16-18	Dialogue: Ruth and Naomi
4:1-2	Legal process: land, marriage, heir
4:13-17	Naomi's fullness in newborn son
4:18-22	Genealogy: the family of David

As is evident, ch. 1 generally parallels ch. 4, while chs. 2 and 3 correspond to each other. Chs. 2 and 3 show a kind of "sandwich" structure. Talks between Ruth and Naomi (2:2; 3:1-5) enclose the story's "meat" — crucial dialogues between Ruth and Boaz (2:3-17; 3:6-15). As for chs. 1 and 4, Naomi's outcry of emptiness (1:20-21) finds its happy solution in her friends' cry: "Naomi has a son!" (4:17a). Finally, the opening introduction of Elimelech's family (1:5) has its counterpart in the closing genealogy (4:18-22).

Without doubt, the short story of Ruth is a literary masterpiece.[9] The story features a highly artistic, almost poetic, rhythmic prose. Masterfully, the author uses dialogue to advance plot. The story's many conversations, not the author's narration, move events along. Again, the writer cleverly dispenses information like a card player wary of tipping his hand. For example, in ch. 2, a "flashback" gives facts withheld earlier (v. 7). Similarly, the narrator withholds mention of Elimelech's field until late in the story — to the surprise of readers (4:3).

Also, the story uses language in powerful ways. For example, words with sexual overtones (e.g., "know," "lie down") dominate the report of Ruth's secret visit to Boaz (ch. 3). The sensual language makes the scene seem daring and dangerous. Further, the narrator shrewdly repeats key words at crucial points. They knit the story together and signal its major thematic developments: (1) by repeating the word "child," the writer implies that the "child" Obed replaces Naomi's dead "children" (1:5b; 4:16); (2) the story twice mentions Ruth's "loyalty," a clue to one of the book's main themes (1:8; 3:10; cf. 2:20); (3) the repetition of "empty" shows that, with Boaz's help, Naomi's earlier emptiness is about to end (1:21; 3:17).

Theologically, the book stresses God's gracious guidance of this family's life.[10] The Lord intervenes directly at two key points, significantly shaping subsequent events — sending the famine, the event which draws Naomi back to Bethlehem (1:6), and causing Ruth to become pregnant, thereby finally giving Naomi her heir (4:13). But God's guidance becomes especially clear in relation to the prayers by the characters for divine blessing (1:8-9; 2:12, 20; 3:10). By the end, God has answered them all: Ruth has a home and child with Boaz. No wonder Naomi's friends give God the credit for the story's happy ending (4:14-15).

> In sum, the book teaches the "all-causality" of God — a continuous, sovereign guidance of everything.

Strikingly, however, in Ruth God's guidance takes a unique form.[11] In much of the Bible, God intervenes directly and supernaturally in human affairs to effect the purposes of redemption. But in Ruth no guidance comes through dreams, visions, angelic messengers, or voices from heaven. No prophet arises to announce "thus says the LORD." Instead, God "is everywhere — but totally hidden in purely human coincidences and schemes. . . ."[12] God's firm, loving providence lurks behind Ruth's "lucky" meeting with Boaz (2:3-4) and Naomi's risky plan (3:1-5). In short, the book stresses that God works behind the scenes *in* the deeds of faithful persons like Ruth, Naomi, and Boaz.[13]

Message

Something else is striking in the book: the author likes to identify Ruth as "the Moabite."[14] That label provides a clue to part of the message. The book stresses that God welcomes non-Israelites into the covenant.[15] If they show the devotion of Ruth (1:16-17), they will likewise enjoy protective "refuge" under God's wings (2:12). In extending God's mercy to foreigners Ruth reflects the same open attitude as other Old Testament books like Jonah.[16]

Further, the book promotes the practice of Israel's covenant ideal, the lifestyle of *hesed* or "loyalty." In essence, to do *hesed* is voluntarily to "go beyond the call of duty."[17] Ruth's stunning statement of love and devotion puts that lifestyle into words: "Where you go, I will go; where you lodge, I will lodge; your people shall be my people, and your God my God" (1:16). Also, the actions of the book's main characters personify it. The story, thus, beckons readers to practice similar sacrificial loyalty. It calls them to emulate the costly commitment of Ruth, the perseverance and cleverness of Naomi, and the generosity and integrity of Boaz. In so doing, they too will experience God's providential blessing.

Finally, the book teaches the divine providence which brought forth David (4:17b). The closing genealogy (4:18-22) sets the story of these ordinary folks from Bethlehem in a larger context. It shows the direct link between their lives and God's work in Israel as a nation. The son born to Naomi is more than just God's gift to continue her family line. He also begins the history of God's rule through the dynasty of David.[18] In this way the book ties in to the Bible's main theme of redemptive history. Thus, directed by God's hidden guidance, the faithfulness of Ruth, Naomi, and Boaz achieved more than they knew. From their family stemmed the great David and, many generations later, great David's greater Son.

CHAPTER 39

Lamentations

Born of a calamity, this little book has, for twenty-five centuries, poignantly voiced the pangs of God's people in times of suffering. Its title aptly describes its contents. The five chapters contain Judah's lamentations mourning the destruction of Jerusalem and its temple (586 B.C.). The historical narratives of 2 Kgs. 25 and Jer. 52 give the facts; the five poems of Lamentations capture the emotions.

> The LORD is like an enemy;
>   he has swallowed up Israel.
> He has swallowed up all her palaces
>   and destroyed her strongholds.
> He has multiplied mourning and lamentation
>   for the Daughter of Judah. Lam. 2:5, NIV

Title and Use. The LXX and Vulgate have a similar title: "Wailings" or "Dirges" (Gk. *Threnoi;* Lat. *Threni*). The Vulgate subtitle, *Id est Lamentationes Jeremiae Prophetae,* became the basis for the English name. The usual Hebrew name is *'êkâ* ("How!"), the typical word of lament with which chs. 1–2 and 4 begin.[1]

In the Hebrew Bible, Lamentations is usually third among the five scrolls (Megilloth) read during the Jewish annual feasts or fasts. On the Ninth of Ab (mid-July), Jews traditionally mourn the destruction of Solomon's temple by

Nebuchadnezzar and also of the second temple by the Roman Titus (A.D. 70). The reading of Lamentations as part of such observances seems to date to the early years of the Exile, immediately after the disasters which the book commemorates. Jeremiah describes a company of eighty men from Shechem, Shiloh, and Samaria that made a pilgrimage to the temple's site in 585 (Jer. 41:4f.). Also, Zechariah (518) mentions a seventy-year-old custom of fasting in the fifth (Ab) and seventh (Tishri) months (7:1-7). Christian liturgy and hymnody has sometimes heard in the descriptions of Jerusalem's agony phrases that anticipate Jesus' crucifixion.

Date and Authorship. Lamentations is a fruit of Judah's disastrous defeat and painful exile. Its contents establish the range of possible dating (586-530).[2] The vivid impressions of chs. 1–4 suggest that someone composed their woeful strains shortly after Jerusalem's fall. Ch. 5 may be from somewhat later in the Exile, when the sharp pains of defeat had dulled into the chronic ache of captivity.

Lamentations is anonymous, and the text itself says nothing of authorship. A tradition took form in pre-Christian times attributing the book to Jeremiah.[3] Perhaps that tradition developed from the Chronicler's report that Jeremiah uttered laments over Josiah's death (2 Chr. 35:25). Similarities in tone between the books of Lamentations and Jeremiah, especially sensitivity to Judah's suffering, support the traditional view. Also, Lamentations' profound theological insight, which combines the themes of judgment and grace, reminds one of Jeremiah. Again, one observes certain parallels in style (e.g., both describe Judah as a smitten virgin; Jer. 14:17; Lam. 1:15).

Arguments against Jeremiah's authorship usually follow these lines: (1) Would Jeremiah have led in lamentation rather than calling the survivors to repentance and pointing to God's new day? (2) Can one attribute to Jeremiah passages that speak of the failure of the prophetic vision (2:9) or seem to imply policies that Jeremiah had opposed (4:12, 17)? (3) Do the variations in poetic style and in the alphabetic order of the acrostic poems suggest multiple rather than single authorship?[4]

Since the book itself names no author, it seems best to regard it as anonymous. On the other hand, its contents point to the kind of person whom the Spirit inspired to write the book: (1) an eyewitness to the tragic events described in minute detail; (2) a profound theologian who grasped the deeper causes of the terrible judgment; (3) a poet of great skill; (4) a true patriot who mourned his country's passing and yet knew that such death was the only hope for new life. If it was not Jeremiah, Judah was blessed to have other persons of similar remarkable gifts. As Jeremiah had prepared Judah to expect great losses, so this individual helped Judah to deal with the harsh reality of them. In what follows, we use "author" to reflect our conclusion that Lamentations in its final form is not a collection of diverse materials but conveys the insight and skill of one person.

527

Poetic Style

Acrostic Form. An acrostic is a poetic device in which successive lines or stanzas begin with letters which, read downward, present a pattern. The ancient Near East shows examples of *name/sentence acrostics* in which the initial signs spell out a name or sentence. The Hebrew Bible features *alphabetic acrostics* in which successive lines or stanzas open with successive Hebrew letters (see Pss. 25; 34; 37; 119; Prov. 31:10-31).[5]

The first four chapters of Lamentations are alphabetic acrostics with stylistic variations. Chs. 1–2 contain twenty-two verses of three lines each, and the first word of each verse begins with the successive Hebrew letter. Ch. 4 does the same, but the verses are two lines each. Ch. 3 is the most tightly constructed, its sixty-six verses contain twenty-two clusters of three verses each, and each of the three begins with the appropriate letter. Though not in alphabetic form, ch. 5 even seems to reflect the influence of the acrostic pattern: it too has twenty-two verses of one line each.

Why the acrostic? It may be an aid to memory: remembering the order may help one to recall the content of each verse. This mnemonic purpose, however, probably does not account for the alphabetic structure of Lam. 1–4: the series of acrostics might confuse the memory more than help it. How would one know which verse beginning with *gimel* or *daledh* belonged in which chapter? As a piece of artistry the acrostic was an act of devotion by the poet.

In Lamentations the acrostic form seems to serve at least two other purposes: (1) it symbolizes completeness — i.e., that the poem covers its painful subject completely from *aleph* to *taw* (i.e., A to Z); (2) it places artistic constraints on the lament, thus keeping it from deteriorating to an uncontrolled wail, howl, or whine.[6]

Dirges. The opening exclamation "how!" (Heb. *'êkâ*) and the short, sobbing parallel lines identify parts of Lamentations as dirges or laments over a great tragedy.[7] Typically, Israel used dirges to lament the death of a loved one (2 Sam. 1:19-27). The dirge *(qînâ)* was also used to highlight any tragedy, particularly one that seemed difficult to reverse.[8]

The dirge form in Lamentations shows too much variety to be labeled strictly a funeral song. The city of Jerusalem is not described as a corpse, but a lonely widow (1:1). More important, the city itself at times joins in the lamenting (e.g., vv. 12-16, 18-22). At other times the poet addresses the city directly:

> What can I say for you, to what compare you,
> O daughter Jerusalem? (2:13)[9]

An effective device in the Hebrew dirge is the dramatic contrast, which describes the previous state of the deceased or bereaved in glowing terms (see 2 Sam. 1:19, 23). The stark contrast with the past makes the present tragedy all the more pathetic:

> How lonely sits the city
>> that once was full of people!
> How like a widow she has become,
>> she that was great among the nations!
> She that was a princess among the provinces
>> has become a vassal. (Lam. 1:1)

Individual and Communal Complaints. Alternating with the dirge forms are complaint patterns akin to those in Psalms and Jeremiah. Lamentations uses both an individual form (ch. 3), where one person (probably the poet) speaks on behalf of the community, and a communal form (ch. 5), where the whole congregation complains before the Lord of its suffering.[10]

The individual complaint in ch. 3 begins with a description of suffering. Instead of appealing to God directly, it describes divine judgment in the third person (vv. 1-18). Only toward the end does the poet consistently address God in the second person (vv. 55-66). Still, many standard elements of the complaint are present: (1) description of suffering in highly figurative terms: darkness, illness, chains, animal attack, assault with arrows (vv. 1-18); (2) plea for relief (v. 59); (3) expression of trust (vv. 21-36); (4) certainty of being heard (vv. 55-63); (5) plea for vengeance on the enemies who inflicted God's punishment on Judah (vv. 64-66).[11]

The communal complaint in ch. 5 focuses almost exclusively on the poignant description of suffering (vv. 2-18). It begins and ends with a plea for restoration (vv. 1, 20-22) and reflects a brief glint of hope (v. 19).

Use of the complaint form does more than merely give the book literary variety. It goes beyond the dirge by allowing the poet or congregation to address the Lord directly (the dirge, by contrast, is usually voiced to those present at the mourning rites). Also, while the dirge may only describe the sin that caused the calamity, the complaint provides opportunity for personal confession of sin (compare 3:40-42 with 1:18). Finally, the complaint makes room for hope by expressing trust and the certainty of being heard by God. The familiar hymn "Great Is Thy Faithfulness" borrows its theme and language from the heart of Lamentations (3:22-23).

Lamentations is a precise and delicate blend of form and content. Acrostics, dirges, complaints, hyperbolic emphasis, and vivid metaphorical descriptions of suffering all combine to voice in very memorable terms both the doom and the hope of a people for whom dire judgment was the necessary prelude to grace.

Theological Contribution

What Jeremiah prophesied, Lamentations portrayed — the destruction of Jerusalem and decimation of its populace. Beyond the physical suffering lay the spiritual torment of the question, "Why?" Those who strolled through Jerusalem's ashes did not regard the judgment as wrong. Indeed the poet holds God to be right in judging rebellion (1:18), punishing sin (vv. 5, 8f., 18, 22; 2:14; 3:40-42; 4:13, 22; 5:7), and revealing righteous wrath (1:12ff.; 2:1-9, 20-22; 3:1-18; 4:6, 11).

Yet the final disaster must have caused a crisis of faith, with which Lamentations' theology of doom and hope tries to come to terms. The people of Judah must have been thoroughly puzzled that the harsh hand of God had brushed aside Josiah's reforms so lightly. Within a mere score of years God allowed the righteous king to fall in battle (609) and the sacred city to be breached and defiled (586). Did not God's action in history violate the clear pattern taught in Deuteronomy and followed throughout the Monarchy — the righteousness of a ruler leads to blessing on God's people?[12]

The firm belief that Zion would never fall made Judah's crisis of faith even worse. While dynastic upheavals and Assyrian conquests rocked the northern kingdom, the Davidic monarchy survived for four centuries in Judah. Rooted in God's special covenant with David's son (2 Sam. 7), this stability led to a belief that no enemy attack could ever humble Jerusalem. After all, the

Lamentation scene, Eighteenth Dynasty (late fourteenth-century B.C.) relief from Memphis. *(Foto Marburg)*

one true God lived there — he would never let an enemy ransack that home. Sennacherib's mysterious defeat in the days of Hezekiah (701) only reinforced this sublime confidence.

Then Nebuchadnezzar shattered the illusion: he pierced the impregnable walls and burned the inviolable temple. What was God doing? What were God's people to believe? How could they handle this reversal of a policy they deemed unshakable?[13]

Lamentations was written to express these tensions of faith and doubt through the catharsis of confession, aided by the completeness symbolized in the acrostic form. It was written also to encourage acceptance of God's judgment while affirming hope beyond that judgment.[14]

> Though history, at God's hands, has trapped his people in tragic surprise, the book urges Israel not to doubt that divine sovereignty ultimately will do what is good for them and all creation.

The tragic plunge from height of favor to depth of despair dominates Lamentations as it does Job. In both, God's purposes are shrouded in mystery. Yet hope and faith are made possible by the revelation of the character of the God who has allowed such pain. After admitting her guilt, Judah's only cause for hope is in God's mercy and benevolence.[15]

The poet's strong faith must have heartened generations of fellow Jews. To find hope in the midst of disaster and lead others to do the same takes the deepest knowledge of God.

Lamentations weaves together the three great strands of Israel's literature and faith: the prophets' insights into the judgment and grace of the covenant Lord; the priests' liturgical expressions of contrition and hope; the wise teachers' wrestlings with the mysteries of suffering. The poet of Lamentations is heir to them all, but not as merely scribe or recorder. The texture and pattern of the weaving are his own, adding a subtlety and beauty that make the book a treasured tapestry of biblical revelation.

CHAPTER 40

The Scroll of Esther

The book of Esther both troubles and delights its readers.[1] Its events take place not in Israel but in Susa, Persia's winter capital. It never uses the word *God* or the name *Yahweh*, and its Jewish heroine marries an unbelieving Gentile king. Worse, her fellow Jews commit bloody acts of self-defense against their enemies.[2] Nevertheless, after long debate, Jewish scholars accepted the book as canonical, and readers through the ages have benefited from that decision.[3]

> These days should be remembered and kept throughout every generation, in every family, province, and city; and these days of Purim should never fall into disuse among the Jews, nor should the commemoration of these days cease among their descendants. Esth. 9:28

The Story and Its Background

Plot. The story of Esther has one of the Bible's most ingenious plots. (See the chart of the structure of the book on pp. 534-37.[4]) It begins at a magnificent banquet put on by the Persian king, Ahasuerus (probably Xerxes I, 485-465 B.C.). Tipsy with wine, the king orders Queen Vashti to display her beauty before the crowd. When she refuses, the king banishes her and seeks a replacement. The beauty of Hadassah (Esther), a Jewish orphan raised by her cousin Mordecai, leads Ahasuerus to make her queen.

Trouble arises when Mordecai refuses to honor Haman, a high Persian official. Rather than punish Mordecai alone, Haman plans a vendetta against all the Jews. At his suggestion, the king condemns all Jews to death on 13 Adar (the twelfth month), but Mordecai urges Esther to plead for their lives before the king. Curious twists of plot soon snare the unlucky Haman in his own conspiracy. When Ahasuerus finds Haman romancing Queen Esther, the king has him hanged on the very gallows Haman had erected to execute Mordecai.

Under Persian law even Ahasuerus himself cannot repeal his edict against the Jews. So, at Esther's urging, the king decrees that on 13 Adar the Jews may defend themselves. Later he extends the period an additional day. The Jews kill thousands of their enemies and celebrate the event by feasting and exchanging gifts. Mordecai decrees that Jews, henceforth, should celebrate Purim[5] every year. He also becomes "next in rank" to the king.

Historicity and Genre. Scholars have long discussed whether the book is history (see 10:2) or fiction. Most hold that a historical kernel, at least, lies behind its persecution theme.[6] But, against its historicity, they allege that some internal details conflict with known historical facts. For example, according to Herodotus, the name of Ahasuerus' queen during this period was Amestris, not Vashti or Esther (7.61, 114; 9.109). Further, all Persian queens were supposed to come from only seven noble families (3.84). If so, the Jewess Esther could not have become queen.[7]

Again, scholars deem certain story elements to be historically improbable. They doubt that a sane monarch would order a massacre like the one against the Jews. Also, they question the claim that the Jews killed 75,000 people in one day (9:16). Surely, they argue, such bloodshed would have found its way into historical records. Finally, some find the story's string of startling coincidences easier to believe as literary inventions than as historical reporting.[8]

But several lines of evidence suggest that the author based the story on history.[9] The story reflects an accurate knowledge of ancient Persia. The dates given for Ahasuerus' reign coincide with our knowledge of his life. The opening banquet in his "third year" (i.e., 483 B.C.; 1:3) fits just before his departure for war against Greece. Esther becomes queen in his seventh year (i.e., 479 B.C.; 2:16). The four-year interval corresponds to his campaign against the Greeks which ended in the disastrous naval battle of Salamis. Further, the book shows detailed knowledge of the Persian court and administrative system. The author knows of the council of seven nobles (1:14), the empire's excellent postal system (3:13; 8:10),[10] the belief in momentous days (3:7), and the keeping of royal records (2:23; 6:1).

Second, the alleged historical inaccuracies and improbabilities have ex-

THE STRUCTURE OF ESTHER

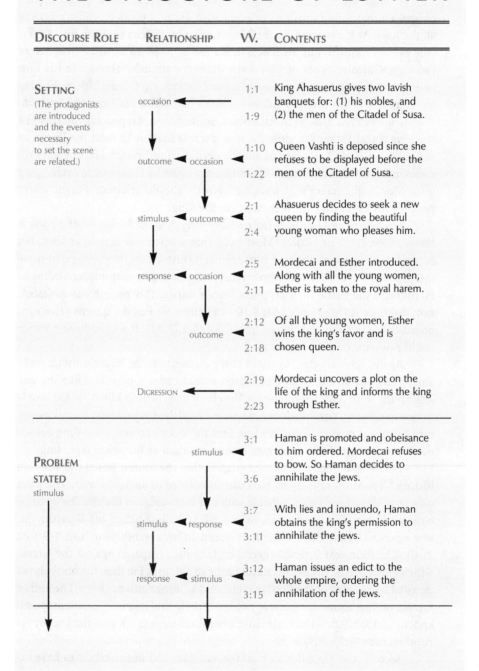

DISCOURSE ROLE	RELATIONSHIP	VV.	CONTENTS

SETTING
(The protagonists
are introduced
and the events
necessary
to set the scene
are related.)

occasion ◄

outcome ◄ occasion ◄

stimulus ◄ outcome ◄

response ◄ occasion ◄

outcome ◄

DIGRESSION ◄

1:1
1:9 — King Ahasuerus gives two lavish banquets for: (1) his nobles, and (2) the men of the Citadel of Susa.

1:10
1:22 — Queen Vashti is deposed since she refuses to be displayed before the men of the Citadel of Susa.

2:1
2:4 — Ahasuerus decides to seek a new queen by finding the beautiful young woman who pleases him.

2:5
2:11 — Mordecai and Esther introduced. Along with all the young women, Esther is taken to the royal harem.

2:12
2:18 — Of all the young women, Esther wins the king's favor and is chosen queen.

2:19
2:23 — Mordecai uncovers a plot on the life of the king and informs the king through Esther.

PROBLEM

STATED
stimulus

stimulus ◄

stimulus ◄ response ◄

response ◄ stimulus ◄

3:1
3:6 — Haman is promoted and obeisance to him ordered. Mordecai refuses to bow. So Haman decides to annihilate the Jews.

3:7
3:11 — With lies and innuendo, Haman obtains the king's permission to annihilate the jews.

3:12
3:15 — Haman issues an edict to the whole empire, ordering the annihilation of the Jews.

534

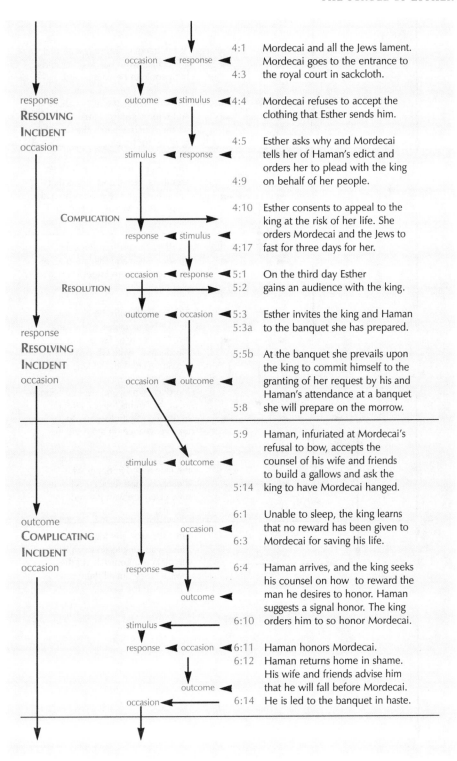

	occasion ◀ response ◀	4:1	Mordecai and all the Jews lament. Mordecai goes to the entrance to
		4:3	the royal court in sackcloth.
response	outcome ◀ stimulus ◀ 4:4		Mordecai refuses to accept the
RESOLVING			clothing that Esther sends him.
INCIDENT			
occasion		4:5	Esther asks why and Mordecai
	stimulus ◀ response ◀		tells her of Haman's edict and orders her to plead with the king
		4:9	on behalf of her people.
		4:10	Esther consents to appeal to the
COMPLICATION			king at the risk of her life. She orders Mordecai and the Jews to
	response ◀ stimulus ◀	4:17	fast for three days for her.
	occasion ◀ response ◀ 5:1		On the third day Esther
RESOLUTION		5:2	gains an audience with the king.
	outcome ◀ occasion ◀ 5:3		Esther invites the king and Haman
		5:3a	to the banquet she has prepared.
response		5:5b	At the banquet she prevails upon
RESOLVING			the king to commit himself to the
INCIDENT			granting of her request by his and
occasion	occasion ◀ outcome ◀		Haman's attendance at a banquet
		5:8	she will prepare on the morrow.
		5:9	Haman, infuriated at Mordecai's
			refusal to bow, accepts the
	stimulus ◀ outcome ◀		counsel of his wife and friends to build a gallows and ask the
		5:14	king to have Mordecai hanged.
		6:1	Unable to sleep, the king learns
outcome	occasion ◀		that no reward has been given to
COMPLICATING		6:3	Mordecai for saving his life.
INCIDENT			
occasion	response ◀	6:4	Haman arrives, and the king seeks his counsel on how to reward the
	outcome ◀		man he desires to honor. Haman suggests a signal honor. The king
	stimulus ◀	6:10	orders him to so honor Mordecai.
	response ◀ occasion ◀ 6:11		Haman honors Mordecai.
		6:12	Haman returns home in shame. His wife and friends advise him
	outcome ◀		that he will fall before Mordecai.
	occasion ◀	6:14	He is led to the banquet in haste.

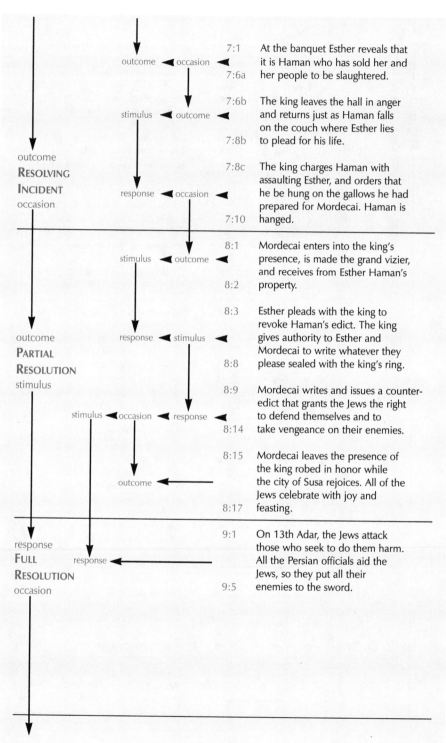

			7:1	At the banquet Esther reveals that
outcome	occasion			it is Haman who has sold her and
			7:6a	her people to be slaughtered.
			7:6b	The king leaves the hall in anger
stimulus	outcome			and returns just as Haman falls
				on the couch where Esther lies
			7:8b	to plead for his life.
outcome			7:8c	The king charges Haman with
RESOLVING				assaulting Esther, and orders that
INCIDENT				he be hung on the gallows he had
occasion	response	occasion		prepared for Mordecai. Haman is
			7:10	hanged.

			8:1	Mordecai enters into the king's
stimulus	outcome			presence, is made the grand vizier,
				and receives from Esther Haman's
			8:2	property.
			8:3	Esther pleads with the king to
				revoke Haman's edict. The king
outcome	response	stimulus		gives authority to Esther and
PARTIAL				Mordecai to write whatever they
RESOLUTION			8:8	please sealed with the king's ring.
stimulus			8:9	Mordecai writes and issues a counter-
				edict that grants the Jews the right
stimulus	occasion	response		to defend themselves and to
			8:14	take vengeance on their enemies.
			8:15	Mordecai leaves the presence of
				the king robed in honor while
outcome				the city of Susa rejoices. All of the
				Jews celebrate with joy and
			8:17	feasting.

			9:1	On 13th Adar, the Jews attack
response				those who seek to do them harm.
FULL	response			All the Persian officials aid the
RESOLUTION				Jews, so they put all their
occasion			9:5	enemies to the sword.

536

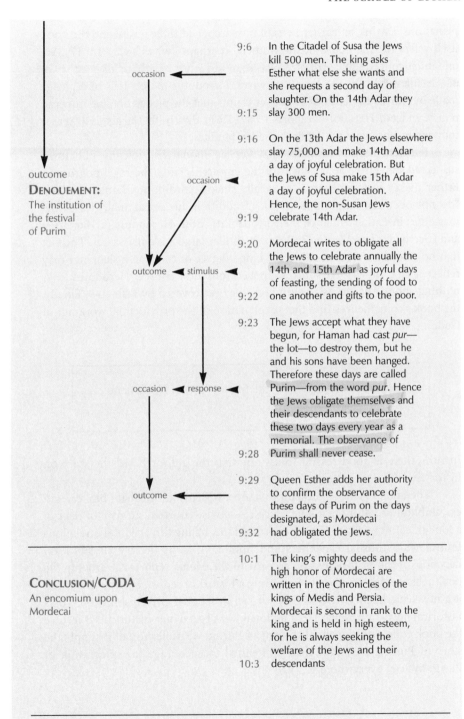

9:6   In the Citadel of Susa the Jews
kill 500 men. The king asks
occasion   Esther what else she wants and
she requests a second day of
slaughter. On the 14th Adar they
9:15   slay 300 men.

9:16   On the 13th Adar the Jews elsewhere
slay 75,000 and make 14th Adar
a day of joyful celebration. But
outcome   occasion   the Jews of Susa make 15th Adar
a day of joyful celebration.
Hence, the non-Susan Jews
9:19   celebrate 14th Adar.

9:20   Mordecai writes to obligate all
the Jews to celebrate annually the
outcome   stimulus   14th and 15th Adar as joyful days
of feasting, the sending of food to
9:22   one another and gifts to the poor.

9:23   The Jews accept what they have
begun, for Haman had cast *pur*—
the lot—to destroy them, but he
and his sons have been hanged.
Therefore these days are called
occasion   response   Purim—from the word *pur*. Hence
the Jews obligate themselves and
their descendants to celebrate
these two days every year as a
memorial. The observance of
9:28   Purim shall never cease.

9:29   Queen Esther adds her authority
to confirm the observance of
outcome   these days of Purim on the days
designated, as Mordecai
9:32   had obligated the Jews.

outcome

DENOUEMENT:
The institution of
the festival
of Purim

CONCLUSION/CODA

An encomium upon
Mordecai

10:1   The king's mighty deeds and the
high honor of Mordecai are
written in the Chronicles of the
kings of Medis and Persia.
Mordecai is second in rank to the
king and is held in high esteem,
for he is always seeking the
welfare of the Jews and their
10:3   descendants

planations. Darius, an earlier Persian monarch, had three wives, and the book itself refers to "the house of the women" (perhaps "wives"; cf. 2:14, 17). So, one must concede that Amestris, Vashti, and Esther may have all been wives of Ahasuerus. As for the source of wives, Herodotus merely tells of a pledge made by Darius to his allies but never claims that the pledge became imperial policy. Indeed, Herodotus reports (3.87; 7.61) that both Darius and Xerxes took wives who were not from the seven families.

Further, there is evidence that Persian monarchs violently put down suspected subversive activity within the empire.[11] Thus, the royal pogrom in Esther makes historical sense, especially since according to Haman the Jews "do not obey the king's laws" (3:8). In addition, historical analogies of the massacres in Esther enhance their probability. Both Herodotus (1.106; 3.79) and Cicero (*De lege Manilia* 3.7) report similar large-scale massacres. The fact that no record survives of either the king's decree or the Jewish slaughter may reflect a lack of written sources. Indeed, our best source, Herodotus, says nothing about Ahasuerus' twelfth year, the year covered by Esth. 3–9. Finally, the book's coincidences find their explanation in the providential workings of God.

> Coincidences in Esther are the fingerprints of God's hands at work.

In sum, there is good reason to assume that the author based the story on history.[12]

The book's genre is difficult to define. It shares motifs with biblical and extrabiblical literature (e.g., the success of a wise courtier, survival of Jews in a foreign country, etc.).[13] But it is also unique, telling the origin of a religious festival with unusual cleverness and humor. Also, its literary classification depends on the historicity one accords to the events reported. Certainly the book tells too good a story to be simply a historical report. So, one might call it a novelistic history (i.e., history told with fictional embellishments)[14] or a historical novel or novella (i.e., a fictional work based on a history).[15] But since the book ends with the establishment of Purim, we prefer to call it simply the story of Purim, since it is clearly intended to encourage the celebration of Purim by Jews everywhere.[16]

Religious Significance

To Authenticate Purim? Some scholars believe Esther was written in order to explain and authenticate retrospectively the feast of Purim.[17] Today (commemorated in the month Adar — Feb./March) Purim is a boisterous celebration, full of merriment and high spirits, in which the ordinary conventions of decorum and deportment are suspended and a spirit of satire and fun is given full sway. That this character began very early can be seen from the Talmudic instruction: "Drink wine until you can no longer distinguish between 'Blessed be Mordecai' and 'Cursed be Haman' " (*Meg.* 7b).[18] The Rabbis honored Esther as equal with or possibly above the Torah (Jer. Talmud *Meg.* 70b). According to the medieval scholar Maimonides, when the Messiah's coming does away with the Bible, Esther and Torah would remain.[19] But 9:11-16 describes how the Jews massacred their enemies for two days. One wonders, thus, whether the rabbinical hyperbole reflects respect for its religious and ethical teachings or the value of its promise of survival to a persecuted people. Certainly the Rabbis wrote to counter the many bitter criticisms leveled against Jews.

Which Came First — Purim or Esther? We challenge the view that Esther was written to give authority to an already extant feast of Purim.[20] The feast has no known origin in Persian, Babylonian, or other lore. If it did not originate in the historical events described, the (fictional) story of Esther must have given it birth. Scholars commonly date the book's origin to the second century because 2 Macc. 15:36, the first apparent reference to it, mentions "Mordecai's day."[21] Josephus offers the earliest extrabiblical report of the whole story of Esther.[22]

Several things make such a late date questionable. There is evidence that the Hebrew text originated at least before the second century B.C. The Greek additions — clearly not part of the original Hebrew text — were already in the LXX (second century at the latest). Also, the Hebrew of Esther is unlike that of the Dead Sea Scrolls (second century B.C. and later) and, hence, must represent a pre-second-century form of the language.[23] Further, Esther shows no traces of the somewhat legalistic Judaism of that period, e.g., regard for the Torah, prayer, Jewish feasts, etc. Finally, the book lacks the apocalyptic elements common in second-century Palestine and believed to reflect Persian influence (e.g., dualism, angelology, and satanology).

We conclude that the story of Esther and the observance of Purim came from the Persian Diaspora. Their arrival in Palestine may have been considerably later, depending on the interpretation of 9:20-22, 29-32.

Doctrine of Providence. Esther has no explicit reference to God, but it certainly proclaims faith in God's protection of his people.[24] Haman sought to destroy all Jews throughout the kingdom (3:6). Given the Persian empire's

Gold drinking vessel (fifth century B.C.), thought to be from Ecbatana (Hamadan). *(Metropolitan Museum of Art, Harris Brisbane Dick Fund, 1954)*

vastness (see map, p. 546), this meant extermination of almost all living Jews. When Mordecai learned of the edict, he put on sackcloth and ashes and wept publicly (4:1) at the very entrance of the king's gate. The Jews also mourned with fasting, weeping, and lamenting.

When Esther sought the reason, Mordecai sent her a copy of the decree (4:8). He also charged her to intercede with the king for her people. She had not told the king that she was a Jew (2:20).[25] But Mordecai knew that this fact would come out, and Esther could not hope to escape, even in the palace (4:13). At that point Mordecai expressed his firm faith in Providence: "For if you keep silence at such a time as this, relief and deliverance will rise for the Jews from another quarter, but you and your father's house will perish" (v. 14). He also pressed Esther to view her ascent to the throne as a pivotal act of that same

Providence: "Who knows? Perhaps you have come to royal dignity for just such a time as this?" (v. 14).

Anti-Semitism. Fully developed animosity toward Jews results in genocide. This diabolical scheme to exterminate Jews is probably much older than the time of Haman. In Moses' day, Pharaoh attempted to annihilate (or drastically limit the population growth) of the Hebrew slaves. Edom's centuries-long hostility toward Judah also probably reflects a kind of anti-Semitism. But the New Testament teaches that this is not merely anti-Jewish hostility, but hatred of the people of God (John 15:18). Its source is satanic: it represents the attempt to defeat God's redemptive purpose. It afflicts all of God's people, Christians as well as Jews, and in its final form it is anti-Messiah or anti-Christ (personified as "Antichrist"). In part Esther teaches: "Let my people alone. If you attempt to harm them, the harm will return on you" (see 9:1).

The Jews included the scroll of Esther in their canon. They regarded its message as ageless as the Torah itself, continuing even into the age of the Messiah. Christians also included it in their Scriptures, recognizing its divine authority.

> Esther instructs the Christian that God does not tolerate anti-Jewish hostility.

It also says that as God's people, Christians can and will become the object of the world's hatred and persecution (see John 15:18-20). Likewise, they can also have faith that "belief and deliverance" will arise, as it did for Mordecai and Esther and the Jews in the Persian empire.

Scripture does not commend the violence used by the Jews in ancient Persia. Later, a Jewish teacher would say: "All who take the sword will perish by the sword" (Matt. 26:52). Many avoid the problem of ch. 9 by saying that the event in Esther never happened. But such acts *do* happen — witness the horrors of the Crusades or the terror of the Holocaust — though they should not. Vengeance is a divine prerogative, and belongs to the Lord alone (Deut. 32:35; Rom. 12:19; Heb. 10:30).

CHAPTER 41

The Chronicler's Perspective

When turning in the English Bible from Kings to Chronicles,[1] one senses familiar terrain. It may seem curious that the narrative of redemptive history, progressing from Genesis through the Exodus, Conquest and Settlement, Monarchy, and Exile, should be sidetracked by a return to "Adam, Seth, Enosh" (1 Chr. 1:1) and a repetition of the familiar stories of David, Solomon, and their successors. Indeed, about one-half of the material in Chronicles[2] is repeated from earlier Old Testament books.

The viewpoint or perspective of the Chronicler is what sets this work off from that of his predecessors and justifies its inclusion in the canon. Far from being Samuel and Kings warmed over, Chronicles has a freshness and flavor all its own. When its purposes are understood, it furnishes rich nourishment for Christian faith, life, and ministry.

> Then David said to the whole assembly, "Bless the LORD your God." And all the assembly blessed the LORD, the God of their ancestors, and bowed their heads and prostrated themselves before the LORD and the king. On the next day they offered sacrifices and burnt offerings to the LORD, a thousand bulls, a thousand rams, and a thousand lambs, with their libations, and sacrifices in abundance for all Israel; and they ate and drank before the LORD on that day with great joy. 1 Chr. 29:20-22

Reconstruction of Herodian temple at Jerusalem. *(William Sanford LaSor)*

Continuity and selectivity are twin considerations for a historian. Continuity is necessary because of the interrelatedness of history. Each event bears a definite relationship to others, like a thread in a fabric, and cannot be understood in isolation. Selectivity is mandatory because no one could record (and who would want to read?) everything that happened in any given era. The historian, therefore, singles out and highlights what is significant. Both considerations involve subjectivity: the historian makes decisions on the basis of what seems important, influenced by personal interests, such as economics, sociology, politics, religion, or military encounters.

The Chronicler is not a historian in the strict western sense. To him Israel's history was pregnant with spiritual and moral lessons, which he brought to birth through a kind of historical midwifery. He is not concerned so much with the bare facts of Israel's history as with their meaning. If all valid historical writing is interpretative, the Chronicler's is highly interpretative. Above all, it is paradigmatic history. As a paradigm tells us how to frame the various tenses of a verb, Chronicles tells its readers how and how not to live, by presenting both positive and negative role models.

The Chronicler's main sources of information were the books of Samuel and Kings.[3] He usually follows them closely. In retelling the story of the coup against Athaliah (2 Kgs. 11) in 2 Chr. 23 he has openly and idealistically replaced the secular temple guards of the earlier narrative with Levite gate-keepers. It was his way of urging respect for the sanctity of the temple area.

Sometimes the Chronicler appears to rely on other literary traditions. The account of an overwhelming military invasion in Jehoshaphat's reign (2 Chr. 20) seems to be a literary reworking of an actual incursion on a smaller scale.[4] Behind Manasseh's temporary deportation to Babylon, to which the Chronicler attaches great theological significance (2 Chr. 33:11-20), there may lie the king's involvement in a western rebellion against Assyria.[5]

The numbers in Chronicles, particularly regarding the size of combating armies, sometimes seem inflated. According to 1 Chr. 21:5 the troops of the whole of Israel numbered 1,100,000 and of Judah, 470,000. But this is comparable with the numbers given in the parallel text in 2 Sam. 24:9, which attributes 800,000 to the northern tribes and 500,000 to Judah, a total of 1,300,000, so that the Chronicler is substantially following his source. However, in 2 Chr. 13:3, which has no biblical parallel, the 400,000 Judean troops over against 800,000 northern troops can hardly be taken literally; the same must be said of Jehoshaphat's million soldiers in 2 Chr. 14:9 (MT v. 8), another text without parallel. These numbers appear to be a deliberate part of the Chronicler's homiletical presentation, a resort to rhetorical mathematics in order to enhance the glory of the ancient narratives.[6]

Structure

Four main parts comprise the historical account of 1 and 2 Chronicles:

Genealogies from Adam to postexilic Judah	1 Chr. 1–9
The reigns of David and Solomon	1 Chr. 10–2 Chr. 9
Judean reigns during the divided kingdom	2 Chr. 10–28
Judean reigns in the sole kingdom	2 Chr. 29–36

It is clear that the book's focus is the reigns of two kings, David and Solomon, to whom no less than twenty-nine chapters are devoted. This period is set apart by divine turning points at the beginning and end, "The LORD . . . turned the kingdom over to David" (1 Chr. 10:14) and "it was a turn of affairs brought about by God" (2 Chr. 10:15). Both are endorsed by prophetic revelation: David's accession fulfilled "the word of the LORD by Samuel" (1 Chr. 11:3; cf. 12:23), while the division of Solomon's kingdom fulfilled the Lord's "word which he had spoken by Ahijah" (2 Chr. 10:15).

Throughout the book structural markers create sections that contain encouraging or challenging themes. David's coronation and its background (1 Chr. 11–12) focus on the help David received from others and from God (12:1, 17, 18, 21, and 22) and include names consisting of or compounded with *ûēzer* "help" (11:12, 28; 12:9). In 2 Chr. 13–16 the theme of faith during crisis is explored in three episodes via a key verb "rely" (13:18; 14:11; 16:7, 8). The account of Jehoshaphat's reign in 2 Chr. 17–20 counterpoints fellowship with the Lord or with the ungodly via the keyword "with" (17:3; 18:3; 19:6; 20:17, 35). Chs. 21–23 celebrate in three episodes the preservation of the threatened Davidic dynasty by polarizing the phrases "house/sons of David" and "house of Ahab" (21:6, 7, 13; 22:3, 4; 23:3, cf. v. 18).

In chs. 29–32 Hezekiah is presented as a model of moral obedience and ensuing blessing by the framework "he did what was right in the sight of/before the Lord" (29:2; 31:20) and "he prospered" (31:21; 32:30). In chs. 33–34 the reigns of Manasseh, Amon, and Josiah are portrayed in terms of two cases of turning from apostasy (33:1-9, 21-25) to obedient faith (33:10-20; 34:1-33).[7]

Historical Perspective

The Chronicler could not have compiled his work much before 400 B.C.,[8] especially if he is also responsible for the books of Ezra and Nehemiah.[9] Thus removed by more than a century from even the latest events that he records, the author singles out those episodes whose significance he finds of lasting value, particularly with regard to his contemporary circumstances. The Chronicler is keenly sensitive to the way the past illustrates the present. He seeks to teach his fellow Jews the weighty lessons of grace and judgment in Israel's history.

Those lessons were crucial to the survival and stability of the Chronicler's people. They had been battered by the displacement of the Exile and beleaguered by hard times back in the land.[10] The Chronicler's concern was to recount the history in such a way as to assure the people that Yahweh was ruling and to urge their full loyalty to him. He took them back to the reigns of David and Solomon, and challenged them to take seriously the present significance of God's revelation through those kings. He wanted to bring postexilic Judah to a proper self-understanding in the light of God's purposes.

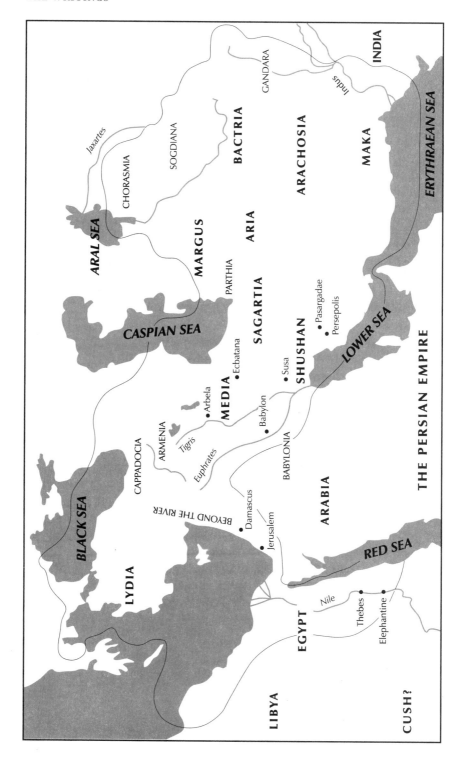

Theological and Pastoral Perspective

The message of this immense work may be reduced to two verses which sum it up, 1 Chr. 17:12 and 2 Chr. 7:14. Each is set in a context of divine revelation, to David and Solomon respectively.

> He shall build a house for me, and I will establish his throne forever. 1 Chr. 17:12

The first verse announces through the prophet Nathan a new era of divine revelation, centered in the founding of David's dynasty and Solomon's building of the temple. For the Chronicler that era continued to his own day, as the qualifying "forever" implies. What preceded in Israel's history was the old epoch of the law or Torah, established by Moses and Joshua, which regulated life in the land. It was now succeeded by the era launched through David and Solomon. The Chronicler throughout his work wrestled with the relation between the old era and the new, between the law and the prophets, and sought to show how the old word from God still had relevance, though partly superseded by the kingship and the temple. The old Mosaic covenant had been taken over into the new, royal covenant. Torah and temple were symbols of the complete revelation that God wanted his people to accept.

The span of the divine purpose stretched from the remote past to the present. But it did not stop there. It was to continue into the unseen future. The Davidic monarchy had not survived the cataclysm of exile. Yet the divine promise "forever," echoed in 2 Chr. 13:5; 21:7, called for faith and hope that it would be restored. So David's genealogy in 1 Chr. 3 is carefully traced down to the Chronicler's own time: the heirs to the ancient and future throne awaited God's summons. Meanwhile a crucial obligation for God's people was to maintain temple worship faithfully and meaningfully. In this respect David (1 Chr. 15:1–16:36), Solomon (2 Chr. 5–7), Hezekiah (2 Chr. 29–31), and Josiah (2 Chr. 35) were role models for postexilic Judah.

> If my people who are called by my name humble themselves, pray, seek my face, and turn from their wicked ways, then I will hear from heaven, and will forgive their sin and heal their land. 2 Chr. 7:14

This second verse characterizes the new temple era as an era of grace. The temple constituted not only a place of worship but a place where prayers were brought and found their answers, especially prayers of confession and repentance. Its very site commemorated forgiveness of David's sin in holding a census (1 Chr. 21:1–22:1). There was no room for consideration of David's adultery with Bathsheba and his murder of Uriah in the Chronicler's narrow perspective, but David's national sin in numbering the people is given full coverage because of its connection with the temple. David was both a negative and a positive example.

The temple was a monument to the grace of God, for God's last word was not the Torah but a gracious promise. The conditional blessings and curses of the Torah found a counterbalance in a temple-based promise of forgiveness to a remiss but repentant people. God's first word still stood as the divine standard for the covenant people. When the Torah was broken by human sin, dire sanctions came into operation, as the Chronicler is ever ready to insist. Only true repentance can avert this punishment.

The Chronicler constantly invokes the theme of individual responsibility and the consequences of one's own actions, taking a leaf out of Ezekiel's book (Ezek. 18), where the choice of death or life confronts each generation. For too long the postexilic community had lived under the long shadow of the Exile, which haunted the lives of generation after generation. The Chronicler offers a principle of each generation's accountability before God. This meant not only quick retribution but the opportunity of a fresh start with God (cf. Ezek. 18:21-24, 30-32).

For the repentant, God's grace was at hand to repair the damage and ensure the survival of the believing community. In the later chapters of 2 Chronicles this theology of grace is repeatedly emphasized by means of echoes of 2 Chr. 7:14 (30:6-9, 18-20; 32:25-26; 33:12-13, 18-19, 23; 34:27), with a final warning of a generation that willfully refused it (36:12-16).

Who was this group called "my people" in 2 Chr. 7:14? The Chronicler gave an insistent answer throughout his work. Many in postexilic Judah would have defined it narrowly, claiming, "We are the remnant, the elect people of God." The Chronicler challenges them to think in terms of the ancient ideal of an Israel made up of twelve tribes. Many who claimed descent from Jacob lived in the province of Samaria. Were they to be written off, these prodigal sons and daughters? A favorite phrase of the Chronicler is "all Israel," which carries his assertion that a divided fellowship falls short of the divine ideal.

The genealogies of the twelve tribes of Israel in 1 Chr. 2–9 define the people of God in broad terms. They follow the declaration of the special role of the people of Israel in God's sight, having been selected from all the nations of the world (1 Chr. 1:1–2:2). Certainly the northern tribes were apostate, having been led astray by their own kings. Yet Judah too had many skeletons in its closet. To both communities God offered a hand of reconciliation and fellowship. Judah needed to court its northern brothers and sisters, and win them back to God. The scenario of northerners and Judeans worshipping together at the Jerusalem temple (2 Chr. 30) is offered as an ideal for the Chronicler's contemporaries to embrace. In this respect he was calling them to honor the prophetic hope of the reunion of the two kingdoms of Judah and Israel under a Davidic king (Hos. 3:5; Mic. 5:2-4; Jer. 3:11-18; 31; Ezek. 37:15-25).

CHAPTER 42

Ezra-Nehemiah

Israel's return from exile in Babylon did not go well. The people had expected the dawn of the national resurrection predicted by Ezekiel (Ezek. 37:1-14). Instead, they faced a crisis which threatened to still the feeble heartbeat of nationhood. Happily, God provided two leaders, Ezra and Nehemiah, to nurse the state's health toward stability.

Now therefore, our God — the great and mighty and awesome God, keeping covenant and steadfast love — do not treat lightly all the hardship that has come upon us . . . since the time of the kings of Assyria until today. . . . Here we are, slaves to this day — slaves in the land that you gave to our ancestors to enjoy its fruit and its good gifts. Its rich yield goes to the kings whom you have set over us because of our sins; they have power also over our bodies and over our livestock . . . , and we are in great distress. Because of all this we make a firm agreement in writing, and on that sealed document are inscribed the names of our officials, our Levites, and our priests. Neh. 9:32, 36-38

Name and Canonical Location

Each of the two books is named for its respective principal character.[1] English Bibles place Ezra and Nehemiah with the "historical" books after 1-2 Chronicles, but in the Hebrew canon they form part of the third division, the Writings. Though their contents chronologically follow those of Chronicles, the MT places Ezra and Nehemiah before Chronicles.[2] Further, the Hebrew canon probably regarded the two books as a single work: the end of Ezra lacks the expected final Masoretic notes, the total verse-count at the end of Nehemiah is for both books, and the middle verse given assumes a combined work. The contents also support this assumption, for the "memoirs" of Ezra begun in Ezra 7–10 conclude in Neh. 8–10.

Their division in the Hebrew Bible into two books did not take place until the fifteenth century A.D., apparently in Christian circles.[3] However, the so-called "Nehemiah memoirs" (Neh. 1:1–7:73a; chs. 11–13) may originally have circulated as an independent work before their incorporation into the present book. The Nehemiah section bears the heading "The words of Nehemiah son of Hacaliah." Also, its literary style and form differ significantly from that of the Ezra section, and it duplicates at least one major section — the list of returning exiles (Neh. 7 = Ezra 2).

	1	2	3	4
MT	Ezra	Nehemiah	(lacking)	(lacking)
KJV, RSV	Ezra	Nehemiah	1 Esdras	2 Esdras*
LXX	Esdras B		Esdras A	(lacking)
Vulgate	1 Esdras	2 Esdras	3 Esdras	4 Esdras

1: Old Testament book of Ezra

2: Old Testament book of Nehemiah

3: Greek work containing 2 Chr. 35–36, Ezra, and Neh. 8:1-12, with some difference in order, plus an account not in the Old Testament

4: Composite apocalyptic work originally in Greek but now extant only in a Latin text

* The Ezra Apocalypse in English translation is sometimes called 4 Ezra.

Contents

Ezra-Nehemiah presents the events of two distinct periods of Israel's restoration to the land after the Exile: (1) the return of the exiles and rebuilding of the temple, 538-516 B.C. (Ezra 1–6); (2) the establishment of the community's religious life (Ezra) and physical surroundings (Nehemiah), 458–*ca.* 420 (Ezra 7–Neh. 13).

Return from Exile and Temple Rebuilding. A decree from Cyrus, king of Persia, authorized Jews to return home to rebuild the temple (Ezra 1:1-4). Sheshbazzar prince of Judah did so, bringing along the temple vessels taken by Nebuchadnezzar (chs. 1–2). Among the returnees were Zerubbabel and Jeshua the priest (2:2) who rebuilt the altar and reestablished regular sacrifices (3:1-6).[4] They also began to lay the temple's foundation and to rebuild its structure (vv. 7-13).

When the local populace offered help (4:1f.), Zerubbabel turned them down (v. 3). So, for spite they seriously hindered the project during the reigns of Cyrus and his successor, Darius (vv. 4f.). Ch. 4 summarizes their opposition not only to Zerubbabel's rebuilding of the temple but also to Nehemiah's rebuilding of the city walls in the middle of the next century. Most of the account is in Aramaic (4:8–6:18), and ch. 4 concludes by reporting that the work stopped "until the second year of the reign of King Darius of Persia" (v. 24). Chs. 5–6 tell of the final rebuilding of the temple under the leadership

Cyrus cylinder (536 B.C.), permitting release of the Jewish exiles and reconstruction of the temple. *(British Museum)*

of Zerubbabel and Jeshua and the constant prodding of the prophets Haggai and Zechariah (5:1f.). The account recalls the initial opposition of Tattenai, Persian governor (or satrap) of the district Beyond the River.[5] He wrote to Darius to verify the Jews' claim that their construction complied with an edict of Cyrus. Darius' staff found the decree in the royal archives, so he ordered Tattenai not only to permit the construction but to pay its cost in full from the royal revenues and to provide materials for sacrifices (5:3–6:12). The Jews finished the temple on the third of Adar in the sixth year of Darius (12 March 515; 6:15). They celebrated a festival of dedication (vv. 16-18), and on the fourteenth day of the following month (21 April 515) held a Passover feast.

Work of Ezra and Nehemiah. No record of events survives for the period between the completion of the temple and the time of Ezra fifty-seven years later. The only information is the brief notice in Ezra 4:4-6 that the "people of the land" wrote an accusation against the Jews early in the reign of Ahasuerus (486-465; better known by his Greek name Xerxes).[6]

(1) Return of Ezra; problem of mixed marriages (Ezra 7–10). In 458,[7] the priest Ezra (v. 11), a "scribe skilled in the law of Moses" (v. 6), returned from Babylonia to Jerusalem. The king had commissioned him to "make inquiries about Judah and Jerusalem according to the law of your God" (v. 14). He was also to appoint magistrates and judges to govern all who knew that law and to teach those who did not (v. 25). Ch. 8 details the story of the return in the first person, including a list of the families who accompanied Ezra. It concludes with a third-person summary of the offerings given by the returned exiles and the delivery of the king's commission to the Persian authorities (vv. 35f.). In ch. 9, the narrative resumes in the first person with the report of Jewish officials that many Jews — even priests and Levites — had intermarried with peoples of the land (vv. 1f.). After Ezra's fast (vv. 3-5) and long prayer (vv. 6-15), a large crowd surrounded him, in great remorse offering to divorce their non-Israelite wives under Ezra's supervision (10:1-5). By mutual agreement, Ezra appointed a commission of elders to investigate matters (vv. 13-17), and their two-month investigation produced a list of offenders (vv. 18-44).

(2) Return of Nehemiah (Neh. 1–2); building of the walls (chs. 3–7). Here the memoirs of Ezra break off and do not resume until 7:73b. Instead, the narrative takes up the story of Nehemiah's return. Since large portions are in the first person, they are called Nehemiah's memoirs. In December of 445,[8] Hanani, Nehemiah's brother, arrived in Susa, the Persian capital, from Jerusalem with a Judean delegation. They informed him that the inhabitants of Judea were in dire straits and the walls of Jerusalem still lay in ruins (vv. 4-11). Nehemiah, who was cupbearer (a high-ranking officer in the court) to the king (v. 11), wept at the distressing news and prayed fervently (vv. 4-11). Four months later,[9] as Nehemiah was serving Artaxerxes, he informed the king of the city's deplorable conditions and asked permission to return and rebuild it

(2:1-5). With royal authority to requisition timber for the walls (vv. 6-8), Nehemiah journeyed west (vv. 9-11).

During his first three days in Jerusalem, he secretly surveyed the ruined walls at night (vv. 11-16). Then, informing the Jews of his commission, he urged them to rebuild the walls (vv. 17f.). Ch. 2 concludes with the ridicule of Sanballat the Horonite, Tobiah the king's official in Ammon, and Geshem the Arabian (vv. 19f.).

Ch. 3 recounts the successful completion of the wall, listing the groups involved and the wall section each constructed (vv. 1-32). Again, Sanballat and Tobiah opposed the project, first with mockery (4:1-6 [MT 3:33-38]), then with the threat of armed attack (vv. 7-9 [MT 4:1-3]). In response, Nehemiah armed the workers and organized half the force to labor and half to stand guard (vv. 10-23 [MT 4:17]). Economic hardships plagued many Jews, hardships made worse by the additional burden of work on the walls (5:1-5). As emergency measures, Nehemiah pledged to take no interest or collateral for loans to needy Jews and required the same from rich citizens. They complied, returning all such previous transactions (vv. 6-13). Ch. 5 concludes with a summary of Nehemiah's generosity, as governor, in not drawing his share of local taxes to supply meals at his own common table (vv. 14-19). Opposition continued. His opponents tried to trick Nehemiah to leave the city so they might attack him (6:1-4) and threatened to tell the king that he planned to rebel (vv. 5-9). Finally the foes commissioned false prophecies to cause Nehemiah to barricade himself in the temple for fear of his life (vv. 10-14). He resisted these ploys, and the wall was completed on 25 Elul after fifty-two days' work (v. 15).[10]

Ch. 7 includes Nehemiah's ordinances for the safety of the city (vv. 1-3) and the observation that the population was very small (v. 4). This prompted Nehemiah to take a census, but he found the list of the first returnees (vv. 6-7a, a repetition of Ezra 2:2-70 except for minor differences). Finally, the resumption of Ezra's story interrupts Nehemiah's memoirs, which conclude in ch. 11.

(3) Ezra's reading of the law; feast of Booths, fast and covenant (Neh. 7:73b–10:39 [MT 40]). On the first day of the seventh month (8:2), by popular demand Ezra read aloud from the "book of the law of Moses, which the LORD had given Israel" (v. 1). He read from dawn until midday, standing on a wooden pulpit facing the square before the Water Gate (v. 3). At the same time, the Levites also read and explained the law "so that the people understood the reading" (v. 8). At first, the people grieved over their sins at hearing the law, but, led by Ezra, the leaders urged them to celebrate a joyous festival instead (vv. 9-12).

The next day, the reading concerned instructions about observing the feast of Booths in the seventh month. Since it was already that month, the people brought branches, built huts, and celebrated the festival for eight days (vv. 13-18).

On the twenty-fourth day, the people held a solemn fast and met for worship (9:1-5). Meanwhile, Ezra publicly offered a long prayer of confession (vv. 6-37), culminating in a decision to make a firm covenant (v. 38 [MT 10:1]). A literary interruption — a lengthy list in the third person of those who signed the covenant — follows (10:1-27 [MT 2-28]). Then Ezra's prayer resumes, stating the terms of the covenant: to keep the law, observe strict rules of marriage, keep the Sabbath, and pay tithes and temple dues regularly (vv. 28-39 [MT 29-40]).

(4) Repopulation of Jerusalem; dedication of the walls; Nehemiah's social and religious reforms during his second governorship; statistical lists (chs. 11–13). This section concludes the account of Nehemiah and very clearly continues the narrative broken off at 7:4. It begins with a brief summary of the repopulation of Jerusalem by lot (11:1f.). A series of lists follow: the residents of Jerusalem (vv. 3-24) and the villages of Judah and Benjamin (vv. 25-36); priests and Levites who returned with Zerubbabel (12:1-9); the genealogy of high priests from Jeshua to Jaddua (vv. 10f.); heads of priestly and levitical houses (vv. 12-26). Next comes the account of the dedication of the walls, celebrated by two processions around them in opposite directions, meeting at the temple (vv. 27-43). To conclude, the section details the appointment of officials to collect tithes and offerings (vv. 44-47) and the exclusion of foreigners from the community (13:1-3).

Brief summaries of reforms during Nehemiah's second governorship bring the book to an end.[11] These reforms include: the expulsion of Tobiah the Ammonite from his room in the temple (vv. 4-9); measures to provide the Levites their tithes (vv. 10-14), to prevent violation of the Sabbath (vv. 15-22), to preclude mixed marriages (vv. 23-29). The chapter ends with a summary of Nehemiah's good works (vv. 30f.).

Historical Background

During this restoration period, Judah was only a small part of a vast Persian province. Its political and religious fortunes depended on Persian power and policy. When Nebuchadnezzar, the conqueror of Jerusalem, died in 562, Babylonian power rapidly declined under ineffectual rulers.[12] Babylon's end came at the hands of Persia, a new power destined to dominate the ancient Near East for two centuries.[13] The founder of this empire was Cyrus, king of Anshan in southern Iran, who rebelled against his Median overlords and by 550 succeeded in conquering their immense empire.[14] He extended its domain from the Aegean Sea to the frontier of Afghanistan. Babylon then stood alone and in 539 fell to the Persians after a single battle on the border. Cyrus controlled all western Asia to the outskirts of Egypt.

Cyrus was an enlightened ruler whose general policy was to permit people deported by the Babylonians to return to their homelands. He also respected the religious beliefs of his subject peoples and governed by permitting considerable local autonomy. He kept firm control, however, through the Persian army and a complex governmental system. In keeping with his policy of repatriation, Cyrus permitted a group of Jewish exiles to return to Judah in 538 and even funded the rebuilding of the temple.

Judah remained relatively unaffected by the major historical events of the empire. The following table summarizes the rest of Persian history, particularly that period relevant to Ezra-Nehemiah:[15]

Ruler	Major Events
Cambyses (530-522)	Conquered Egypt in 525.
Darius I (522-486)	Defeated and executed the usurper Gaumata to regain the throne. Faced empire-wide revolt for two full years. Gave empire its definitive organization and greatest stability and extent. Only failure was the attack on Greece.
Xerxes I (Ahasuerus) (486-465)	Destroyed Babylon in 482. Invaded Greece but was repulsed and completely driven out in 466.
Artaxerxes I (Longimanus) (465-424)	Faced rebellion in Egypt for six years. Signed the peace of Callias (449), giving the Greek cities independence and banning the Persian fleet from the Aegean.
Darius II (Nothus) (423-404)	As a result of Peloponnesian War, gained firm control of Asia Minor.
Artaxerxes II (404-358)	Egypt gained independence in 401. Major western rebellion barely put down.
Artaxerxes III (Ochus) (358-338)	Ruthless ruler who reconquered Egypt.
Darius III (336-331)	Empire dissipated in gory intrigues and internal weakness, falling to Alexander the Great in 331.

This turbulent, momentous period in ancient Near Eastern history is the setting for the events of the return from exile and establishment of the Jewish community under Ezra and Nehemiah.

Literary Nature

Ezra-Nehemiah incorporates a wide variety of literary genres and written sources. Structurally, the book consists of three main narrative blocks: the Sheshbazzar and Zerubbabel narrative (Ezra 1–6), the primarily first-person Ezra narrative (Ezra 7:1–10:44; Neh. 7:73b–10:39), and the largely first-person Nehemiah narrative (Neh. 1:1–7:73a; 11:1–13:31).[16] These, in turn, draw on the following sources:

(1) Memoirs of Ezra and Nehemiah, both themselves doubtless taken from longer autobiographical accounts.[17]

(2) Documents and letters. Ezra 6:3-5 gives the edict of Cyrus in Aramaic allowing the exiles to go home, while 1:2-4 offers a Hebrew adaptation of it addressed to Jews in exile. Ezra 7:12-26 presents the letter of Artaxerxes authorizing Ezra's return, also adapted for the exiles. Other Aramaic letters between officials in Palestine and the Persian court include the letter from Rehum and Shimshai to Artaxerxes (4:8-22) and the exchange between Tattenai and Darius (5:7-17; 6:6-12). These ultimately must have come from the Persian state archives.

(3) Lists. For example: inventory of temple vessels returned to Sheshbazzar by the Persian court (1:9-11); list of exiles who returned with Zerubbabel (Ezra 2:1-70, repeated in Neh. 7:7-72a); list of heads of families who returned with Ezra (Ezra 8:1-14); list of those who married foreign wives (10:18-44); list of builders of the wall (Neh. 3:1-32). A series of lists also dominates the closing section of the account of Nehemiah's first governorship: the new inhabitants of Jerusalem (11:3-19); villages occupied by Jews (vv. 25-36); high priests from Jeshua to Jaddua (12:10f.); and heads of priestly and levitical families (vv. 12-26). All of these lists must have come from the temple archives or records of the Jewish governor's office.

A very striking literary features is the way the book divides the memoirs of Ezra and Nehemiah in half and then interleaves them with one another as follows:

(1) Ezra 7:1–10:4	First half of Ezra's memoirs: his arrival; problem of mixed marriages
(2) Neh. 1:1–7:73a	First half of Nehemiah's memoirs: his arrival; building of the wall
(3) 7:73b–10:39 [MT 40]	Second half of Ezra's memoirs: reading of the law; feast of Booths; covenant
(4) 11:1–13:31	Second half of Nehemiah's memoirs: dedication of the wall; second governorship

557

Ezra arrived in Artaxerxes' seventh year (458), Nehemiah in his twentieth year (445). Thus, Ezra spent thirteen years in Jerusalem (about which nothing is preserved) before tackling the major task for which the king had commissioned him: to establish the law.

The Sheshbazzar-Zerubbabel narrative (Ezra 4) also illustrates the author's literary methods. After reporting the exiles' refusal to allow the people of the land to help rebuild the temple (vv. 1-3), the narrator summarizes their opposition to (v. 4f.) and frustration of the rebuilding process from the reign of Cyrus (538-530) to that of Darius I (522-486). Then he briefly mentions an accusation against the Jews in the reign of Ahasuerus (Xerxes I, 486-465; v. 6) and an Aramaic letter to Artaxerxes I (465-424; v. 7). Finally, he gives the full text of another letter to Artaxerxes (vv. 8-16) along with his reply ordering the reconstruction to cease (vv. 17-22). So authorized, the project's enemies stopped the work by force (v. 23). Since the temple was completed in 515, the last three accounts must relate to the building of the walls. Obviously, the narrator did not intend to present a complete, chronological report. Rather, he organized his material around a topic — accusations against returning exiles.

Authorship and Date

Like many ancient writings, Ezra-Nehemiah preserves no direct indication of authorship. The Talmud attributes 1-2 Chronicles and Ezra-Nehemiah to Ezra, but adds that Nehemiah completed the work.[18] Most twentieth-century scholars have held a similar view, namely, that an author-compiler, traditionally identified as "the Chronicler," wrote everything except the Nehemiah memoirs.[19] Recent studies, however, have seriously challenged this conclusion by demonstrating the significant differences between Chronicles and Ezra-Nehemiah. They include differences in language and style,[20] purpose and ideology,[21] as well as literary and theological features.[22] While the issue remains unsettled, two recent influential commentators argue that Ezra-Nehemiah originated as a book independently of Chronicles and the so-called Chronicler.[23]

As for the book's date, those who believe a single author/compiler completed Chronicles-Ezra-Nehemiah date the work to 400 or shortly thereafter. They argue that the lists of Solomon's descendants (1 Chr. 3:10-24) and high priests (Neh. 12:10f., 22) carry down to that date at the latest.[24] Certainly, the book mentions no person or event later than 400. Among those who assume a separate origin for Ezra-Nehemiah and Chronicles, Williamson suggests a

Hasmonean tower built on a portion of Nehemiah's wall, traces of
which are seen in the lower courses of the tower and other parts of the wall.
(William Sanford LaSor)

date of 300, claiming that the book's intention was to discredit the Samaritan temple of that time.[25] In our view, a date in the early fourth century seems probable.

Historical and Chronological Considerations

Above we noted that the author/compiler organized the book around topics rather than strict chronology.[26] The book, thus, has raised several perplexing historical and chronological questions among modern readers.

Sheshbazzar and Zerubbabel. The first question concerns the relationship between Sheshbazzar and Zerubbabel. The book of Ezra clearly states that Sheshbazzar "the prince of Judah" (1:8) led the first return and brought back the temple vessels taken by Nebuchadnezzar (v. 11b).[27] Ezra 5:14 calls him governor, and v. 16 reports his laying of the temple's foundation. But the book gives no other information about Sheshbazzar, not even his ancestry. Also, ch. 2 seems to continue ch. 1 by listing the names of the exiles who returned, but Zerubbabel heads the list and Sheshbazzar does not appear at all!

The rest of the book credits Zerubbabel and Jeshua the priest with first setting up an altar and worship services (ch. 3), laying the temple foundation (v. 10), and leading the rebuilding of the temple itself (5:1f.).[28] The book of Haggai consistently designates Zerubbabel governor, but it is unclear whether he returned with the first group of exiles in 538 or sometime later. At any rate, inspired by the preaching of Haggai and Zechariah, he launched the rebuilding of the temple in 520.

Thus far, no satisfactory explanation as to how Zerubbabel succeeded Sheshbazzar commends itself. As for who laid the temple foundation, there are several ways to explain why the book gives the honor to both men. Perhaps Sheshbazzar started the project but made little progress, Zerubbabel actually finishing the job later. Or, Zerubbabel may have returned early enough to play a major role in laying the foundation under the authority of Sheshbazzar.[29] In any case, recent archaeological evidence tends to confirm the portrait in Ezra that Judah was an independent province with its own governor from Sheshbazzar to Nehemiah.[30] Bullae,[31] seals, and stamped jar handles found at Jerusalem and Ramat Rahel bear the names of Judah's governors and their officers in the late sixth century.[32] Several names may even represent members of Zerubbabel's immediate family.[33] This evidence undercuts the view common among earlier scholars that Judah was merely a district within the province of Samaria and had no governor of its own before Nehemiah.[34]

Ezra and Nehemiah: Who Came First? The second question concerns the date and order of the arrivals of Ezra and Nehemiah to Jerusalem. Clearly, the biblical picture is that Ezra preceded Nehemiah, arriving in 458 (Artaxerxes' seventh year; Ezra 7:7). Nehemiah arrived thirteen years later in 445 (Artaxerxes' twentieth year; Neh. 2:1), served as governor for twelve years, then returned to Persia in 433 (Artaxerxes' thirty-second year; 13:6). A short time later he came back to Judah for a second term of unknown length. The Elephantine texts establish that the Artaxerxes connected with Nehemiah is Artaxerxes I (Longimanus; 465-424),[35] but no extrabiblical correlation exists for any person or event mentioned in the Ezra material.

Despite the biblical order, many modern scholars believe that Nehemiah actually preceded Ezra.[36] Thus, they understand the Artaxerxes of Ezra to be Artaxerxes II (Mnemon; 404-358), dating his arrival to 398.[37] They claim that, by interleaving the memoirs of Ezra and Nehemiah, the author/compiler has presented a distorted, improbable picture of events. For example, they observe that, with three exceptions (Neh. 8:9; 12:26, 31-36), the memoirs of each never mention the two men together. It is as if they ignored each other even though their time in Jerusalem overlapped considerably.[38]

Further, it seems unlikely they would have served the Jewish community at the same time, since they enjoyed similar authority and responsibilities. More important, given Ezra's imperial mandate to read the law publicly, how likely is it that he would have waited thirteen years before executing it (Ezra 7:7; Neh. 2:1)?

Despite the problems, the present order of Ezra-Nehemiah remains the most plausible option.[39] That the memoirs of each fail to mention the other proves nothing about their relationship or contemporaneity. Neither Haggai nor Zechariah mentions the other, although they both preached in Jerusalem at the same time. That both Ezra and Nehemiah tackled similar responsibilities may in fact be due to the enormity of the problems addressed; the situation required a team effort. Also, though they enjoyed similar authority, the book clearly distinguishes their office (i.e., priest versus governor).

Finally, there is no ready explanation as to why Ezra waited thirteen years to read the law as his imperial commission required. But, in our view, that is not reason enough to set aside the book's clear dating of his arrival to 458, thirteen years before that of Nehemiah. In fact, a fifth-century (or early fourth-century) date for the book's composition puts its origin reasonably close to the time of the actual events. That assumption decreases the probability that the author/compiler could have misunderstood the order of Ezra and Ne-hemiah. Further, had he done so, it seems unlikely that the first audience, who may have known the sequence independently, would have accepted it.[40]

Achievements and Significance

An understanding of the historical background of the restoration period underscores the true greatness of Ezra and Nehemiah. The fall of Jerusalem and the Exile had brought Israel's hopes of great national destiny crashing cruelly to earth. It had also shaken Israel's confidence in two long-held theological truths — the security of Zion as God's permanent earthly home, and the promise to David of an unfailing dynasty. By appealing to the theology of covenant, however, the prophets had explained the tragedy to a confused Israel and given them hope. The prophets interpreted the disaster as God's judgment for Israel's dereliction of covenant duties and promised future restoration as the work of God's faithfulness to the ancient covenant. This theological insight, along with the beneficent decree of Cyrus in 538, gave birth to Israel's restoration as a people. By the late fifth century, Ezra and Nehemiah had firmly established a viable religious and political community in Palestine.

More importantly, to prevent Israel's assimilation by other nations, they gave Israel a new identity centered around the law and temple. Thus, law and temple worship replaced trust in Zion and the Davidic monarchy as the theological foundation of Israel's future.[41]

The Role of Ezra. Ezra the priest was the primary architect of Israel's new identity. He had prepared himself for the task by the rigorous studying and personal practicing of the law of God (Ezra 7:10). That is why the book portrays him as almost a second Moses. Significantly, his primary title is "scribe" (Heb. *sōpēr*, v. 6). In preexilic use, scribe designated a high-ranking state official — a minister of finance (2 Kgs. 22:3ff.), secretary of state (Isa. 36:3; cf. 22:15), or keeper of palace records (2 Kgs. 18:18; Jer. 36:12).

But in Ezra's day, the Torah or law had become the focal point of national identity, so scribe — the expert interpreter of the law — came to designate the community's primary spiritual leader.[42] For example, in the dramatic public reading of the law (Neh. 8), Ezra plays the leading role while his Levite associates assist him.[43] Unlike the preexilic practice, Ezra combined the roles of priest and scribe. Eventually a professional class of scribes was to emerge and displace the priesthood as the nation's spiritual leaders. In the New Testament, the scribes were the most influential leaders in religious matters.

Ezra's imperial commission authorized him to appoint magistrates and judges, to teach the "law of your God," and to punish those who failed to obey it (Ezra 7:25f.). It gave him an official Persian title, "scribe of the law of the God of heaven" (v. 12) — in modern terms, perhaps "secretary of state for Jewish affairs."[44] Thus Ezra arrived in Jerusalem with both the power and zeal to reorganize the Jewish community around the law.[45]

The Role of Nehemiah. If Ezra reestablished Israel spiritually, Nehemiah gave the fragile community physical stability. As cupbearer (a young, highly trusted official) to the Persian king, he had learned of "trouble and shame" in Judah (Neh. 1:3) and obtained appointment as governor there (ch. 2). With skill and daring, Nehemiah executed his imperial commission to rebuild the city. He surveyed the walls at night to avoid detection by possible opponents and organized a labor force. Under his expert supervision, the project remarkably was finished in only fifty-two days, despite determined opposition (2:19; 4:1-3 [MT 3:33-35], 7-12 [MT 4:1-5]; 6:1-9).

Nehemiah's prayers reveal a man of deep piety and strong conviction. With the wall in place, Nehemiah sought to repopulate Jerusalem and to correct social, economic, and religious abuses. Thus, Nehemiah enhanced both the physical security of the capital and the socio-economic stability of the entire religious community. In partnership with Ezra, he preserved the people of God from whom would come Jesus Christ, the fulfillment of all the old covenant's hopes and promises.[46]

Theological Themes

The author/compiler of Ezra-Nehemiah has woven several theological themes amid the seeming tangle of lists of names and personal memoirs. First, the book stresses the continuity of the postexilic religious community under Ezra and Nehemiah with Israel's ancient past. For example, at the outset the book interprets the temple rebuilding authorized by Cyrus as the fulfillment of Jeremiah's prophecy (Ezra 1:1). That interpretation immediately links events in Ezra-Nehemiah with Israel's preexilic period. Further, in his long prayer at the public reading of the law (Neh. 9), Ezra reviews redemptive history from Abraham's call through the Exodus to the conquest of Canaan (vv. 1-25). He views the restoration as a new exodus which continues that great history and bears similar testimony to God's saving power and covenant faithfulness.[47]

It is also no coincidence that Israel celebrates Passover once the temple is rebuilt (Ezra 6:19-22) and the feast of Booths after the law is read (Neh. 8:14-18). Both ceremonies commemorate Israel's wilderness experience, implying that the postexilic people of God had experienced a new exodus similar in redemptive meaning to that of their ancestors (see v. 17). This new Israel, however, understood itself as a covenant people, not a nation-state. Granted, harsh political realities involuntarily imposed this identity on the returnees. Yet this identity had ancient roots, for Israel was a "people of God" long before it became a nation. As von Rad notes:

> . . . Israel threw off the vestment of her statehood together with her monarchy with surprising ease and without apparent internal crisis. This must be connected with the fact that the state as such was somewhat of a borrowed garment for Israel; for long before she became a state, she had belonged to Jahweh.[48]

Certainly, this non-political, spiritual identity anticipated the New Testament's view of the New Israel, the Church, which transcends ethnic, national, and geographic barriers.

A second theme underscores the temple and the Torah as the twin bases of postexilic Israel's identity. At the outset, Ezra-Nehemiah signals the importance of the temple by quoting Cyrus' decree that it be rebuilt (Ezra 1:3-4). It then sketches the reconstruction project, underscoring its thematic importance by its ability to overcome obstacles. When the building is done, a suitable joyous celebration acclaims the process as divinely guided (6:14-22). But, most important, the temple symbolizes the renewed presence of Israel's God among his people.[49] By providing a place where Israel may commune with God regularly, God has signaled the desire for ongoing contact with the people.

This idea of divine presence also anticipates two New Testament concepts of God's presence: the Person who bodily revealed God's glory by living among his people (John 1:14), and the people in whom God now lives and whose lives glorify him (1 Cor. 3:16f.; 6:19f.). But Ezra and Nehemiah could hardly have imagined what John saw — that one day God and his people would live in the same city, the New Jerusalem, without a temple at all (Rev. 21–22).

Literarily, however, the temple is a preface to the emergence of Torah in the book. No sooner is the temple finished than Ezra the priest suddenly appears armed with his imperial commission to teach the law (Ezra 7). It is Torah that guides the postexilic community to divorce its foreign wives (10:3) and to banish certain aliens from Israel (Neh. 13:1ff.). Implicitly, the law also drives the reforms which Nehemiah undertakes at the book's conclusion (Neh. 13:4ff.). After the law is read publicly (Neh. 8), it also evokes the community's confession of sin and renewal of the covenant (Neh. 9–10). In sum, the law defined postexilic Judah's understanding of what behavior God required for them truly to be the people of God.[50]

Some readers, however, see the law's centrality in Ezra-Nehemiah as the root of an unattractive exclusivism and fear of foreigners. But fairness demands that one understand Israel's postexilic faith in its own context. The restored community was a tiny island in a vast, turbulent ocean of pagan peoples. That harsh reality called for the book's stern measures. The danger was that if Israel too easily accommodated their neighbors, the nations would eventually absorb Israel, thus extinguishing the community and its precious heritage. Of course, this does not excuse later Israelites who perpetuated these attitudes long after they were necessary. We may fault them for producing that prejudice against non-Jews which the New Testament exposes and with which the early Church contended. At the same time we must confess as evil the historic Christian propensity toward anti-Semitism.

The third theme derives from the importance of documents in the book.[51] The decree of Cyrus gets events rolling (ch. 1), and other decrees keep them moving. Significantly, Ezra 1:1 introduces the Cyrus decree as the fulfillment of the prophecy of Jeremiah. Further, Ezra 6:14b says that the temple reconstruction was finished "by the command of the God of Israel and by decree of Cyrus, Darius, and King Artaxerxes." In other words, theologically the book stresses that divine guidance stood behind everything, even the actions of human kings and Jewish leaders. The restoration was no stroke of luck caused by beneficent Persian political policy. Rather, it resulted from the intervention of Israel's God in the arena of human history. This intervention and the documentation that signaled it were taken seriously by the Jews. They responded in kind by a documentation of their own: they pledged their loyalty to the covenant in writing, an act unique in the Old Testament (Neh. 9:38–10:39).

The final theme points beyond the story of Ezra and Nehemiah to future divine interventions.[52] For example, Ezra's prayer strongly contrasts Israel's present slavery to foreign kings with their promised liberty in the land (Neh. 9:32ff.). The conflict creates an expectation that the God who brought the restoration may intervene in the future to restore fully Israel's freedom. Also, it is significant that, despite the community's new covenant with God (ch. 10), the book's closing chapter (Neh. 13) treats virtually all the abuses supposedly settled already. In other words, it leaves the impression that much remained to be done among God's postexilic people, again hinting at future divine work.

> Theologically, the book subtly nurtures aspirations of future divine intervention in Israel.

These aspirations would await the coming of one greater than Ezra and Nehemiah. Only the one who far excelled even giants like Moses and Elijah could turn those ancient aspirations into reality. In Christ the work done by Ezra and Nehemiah — the preservation of God's precious people — would reach its ultimate, eternal fruition.

CHAPTER 43

Daniel

The book of Daniel belongs to a genre of literature known as apocalyptic.[1] Through story and vision, it communicates the most mysterious message of the Old Testament: the kingdoms of this world are not beyond God's control; in fact they one day will be replaced by God's own kingdom. The prophets give glimpses of this future. In the text of Daniel, however, this message is sustained despite the arrogance of world empire after world empire. It is revealed in visions that convey the passionate intent of God to reign as sovereign over his creation. It seems pitiful that a work of such grandeur has sometimes been ridiculed as the record of fantasies of a people too much oppressed, or used merely as the vehicle for speculation about the end of the world and the setting of dates for end-time events. Better to grasp the colossal promise of God who governs world history than to design caricatures that belittle this noble prospect.

> And in the days of those kings the God of heaven will set up a kingdom that shall never be destroyed, nor shall this kingdom be left to another people. It shall crush all these kingdoms and bring them to an end, and it shall stand forever. Dan. 2:44

Daniel as Apocalyptic Prophecy

Apocalypse has been defined as "a genre of revelatory literature with a narrative framework, in which a revelation is mediated by an otherworldly being to a human recipient, disclosing a transcendent reality which is both temporal, insofar as it envisages eschatological salvation, and spatial insofar as it involves another, supernatural world."[2] Daniel is generally regarded as fitting this definition, yet many scholars insist that we treat it as though it intended us to read it as history. Some (e.g., E. J. Young, R. K. Harrison; see note 17) argue for the historicity of the sixth-century setting of the book and oppose a later authorship as a sheer deception. Others (e.g., H. H. Rowley, J. A. Montgomery), treating Daniel's name as a pseudonym, argue against a sixth-century origin and locate it in second-century Palestine.[3]

The question of historical basis is a complicated one. It is sufficient to say here that Daniel's main purpose is not to record detailed history but to use stories and symbols to demonstrate God's control of history. The Revelation (Apocalypse) of John has a similar purpose: to demonstrate how God's covenant promises will be kept in the face of all evil opposition; that promise-keeping is what history is all about. When Daniel gives its accounts of "Nebuchadnezzar,"[4] "Belshazzar," and "Darius the Mede," it intends to reveal the meaning of their destinies with God and the superiority of God's kingship to theirs. It will not do to read Daniel the same way we read the writing of the history of the Roman Empire. The grandeur of the book's vision and intent cannot be ignored. Its wisdom cannot be found either in brute facts or in the pride and spread of human empire. It must be found in the sovereign Lord's freedom to act in covenant relationship to protect the chosen people and to remind them of a supernatural power to whom ultimately the whole world must give account.

Prophecy. In the Hebrew canon Daniel is included not among the Prophets, but among the Writings *(keṯûḇîm)*. Some argue on the basis of its supposed second-century authorship that the prophetic section of the canon *(neḇî'îm)* was already closed, and Daniel had to find its place among the Writings. Others hold that the book does not have the marks of traditional prophecy: it does not directly condemn sinful behavior or commend the keeping of the law.

One basic purpose of the book is to depict events in such a way that God's promises to his covenant people are unfolded in the context of world history and the times of the end. God gave Daniel and his companions "knowledge and skill in every aspect of literature and wisdom; Daniel also had insight into all visions and dreams" (Dan. 1:17). When called to interpret Nebuchadnezzar's dream, he states that God "has disclosed to King Nebuchadnezzar what will happen at the end of days" (2:28; cf. vv. 44f.). Nebuchadnezzar's

Statue of shaggy male goat (Ur, ca. 2500 B.C.), which in Daniel's vision of ch. 8 represents "the king of Greece." (British Museum)

dream of the tree cut down foretells his lot until he recognizes "the Most High has sovereignty over the kingdom of mortals" (4:25 [MT 22]). The words Belshazzar saw written on the wall concern the end of his kingdom (5:26). Daniel's dream of the four beasts previews the end of all the kingdoms that oppose God and the coming of that kingdom which the saints of the Most High are to inherit (7:17, 27). The vision of the Ram and the He-goat is "for the time of the end" (8:17; cf. v. 19). The vision of the evenings and mornings is to be sealed up because "it refers to many days from now" (8:26). Daniel's concern over the seventy years of Jeremiah's prophecy is interpreted in terms of both the restoration of Jerusalem and also "the time of an anointed prince"

(9:25). The prophecy of conflict between Persia and Greece leads to "the man" who tells Daniel that he came "to help you understand what is to happen to your people at the end of days" (10:14).

Similarly we note the prophecy concerning future kings in Persia, the victory of Greece (a reasonable inference, but not specifically stated), and the breaking of that kingdom into four parts (an inference; cf. 11:3f.). The vision appears to detail the end of the Persian empire, Alexander's victory, the division of his kingdom among his generals ("successors" or *Diadochoi*), and the rise of the Ptolemies in Egypt and the Seleucids in Syria. All of this leads to "the abomination that makes desolate" (11:31; cf. 9:27; 12:11; see also Matt. 24:15; Mark 13:14). The prophecy climaxes when Michael arises, "the great prince, the protector of your people" (12:1). Then "your people shall be delivered" (12:1) and the resurrection of the dead will occur (v. 2 clearly indicates a still-distant future). When Daniel wants to know more at this point, he is reminded that "the words are to remain secret and sealed until the time of the end" (v. 9; cf. v. 4). There is no doubt the book of Daniel is prophetic, pointing its readers to their future with God.

Apocalyptic Prophecy. Daniel is, however, a very different kind of prophecy from that of most of the prophets. As indicated, the purpose of the prophets of Israel was to make known Yahweh's will, including the future of the world. Even in their punishment, the people of God were to cherish the hope of their restoration. So the dimension of foretelling is present in all of the prophetic tradition, even when it is secondary to God's call to covenant obedience. God's ultimate purpose (teleology), Daniel's main theme, was and is always a part of the full meaning of Israel's prophecy.

In apocalyptic prophecy, the stress is clearly on the future. The book of Daniel begins in the Babylonian court and recounts the actions of Babylonian or Persian kings. His visions there include Persia, Greece, kings of the north and south, rulers that make trouble for the people of God, an anointed one cut off, and the cessation of sacrifices. The readers seem encouraged to fit these prophecies into real historical situations. As the people of God, they are then both comforted in a historical need (as the stories stress) and pointed to a future bound up with God, a future displayed especially in the visions.

Apocalyptic prophecy is given in forms that are to be understood as both timely and timeless. Knowledge of the time of the end is sealed up, but the people of God are called into circumstances where they ask, as did Daniel: "How long shall it be till the end of these wonders?" (12:6); "What shall be the outcome of these things?" (v. 8). The message is perseverance and hope. Only when one loses a grip upon this purpose and attempts to unseal the book, or to fit apocalyptic visions into historical schemes (or vice versa), does the primary message become obscure. The book of Daniel was never intended to exhaust its meaning in the days of Antiochus Epiphanes (175-164 B.C.), or the

Roman destruction of Jerusalem, in A.D. 70, or in any calamity the world has yet known. It was intended "for the time of the end," and, for as long as time lasts, to proclaim to all who believe that their times are in God's hands, even in the midst of persecution. The twofold truth that Daniel announces is (1) the Most High rules, and (2) his saints will one day inherit a kingdom which shall never be destroyed.

Daniel and the Book

The Person. According to 1:6, Daniel was one of the youths taken from Jerusalem to Babylon by Nebuchadnezzar to be trained for service in the king's palace. The only known details of his life or lineage are those recorded in the book.

There is a Daniel[5] mentioned in Ezek. 14:14, 20; 28:3 as a model of wisdom and righteousness like Daniel and his friends in Babylon. Because this Daniel is linked with Noah and Job, some argue that Ezekiel must be referring to the Daniel of the apocalyptic prophecy. However, a "Dan'el" (written with the consonants *dn'l* as in Ezekiel) is mentioned in Ugaritic writings.[6] It can be argued that, since Daniel was only a boy at the time of Ezekiel, it was unlikely for Ezekiel to have grouped him with Noah and Job. It is conceivable, however, that Daniel's extraordinary experiences (as recorded in the book) may well have become known outside Babylon.[7] But such questions ought to be left open. The book of Daniel is not so much concerned with the biography of Daniel as with God's future for his people.

According to dates given in the book, Nebuchadnezzar took the youths to Babylon in 605 (probably on a campaign just before he succeeded to the throne).[8] His dream, which Daniel interpreted, was in 603. Daniel continued in royal service "until the first year of King Cyrus" (538; 1:21), and received a revelation in the third year of Cyrus (10:1; the date in v. 4 is equivalent to 23 April 536). If Daniel was in his early teens in 603,[9] he would have been about seventy-five in 536, the end of his ministry during both the Babylonian and Persian empires.

Contents. The book divides literally into two halves: stories (court-narratives, chs. 1–6) and visions (chs. 7–12). However, another way of structuring the book is possible based on language. From 2:4b to 7:28, the Hebrew Bible records in Aramaic the struggle of Daniel and his friends in the two world empires.[10] From 8:1 to the end the book returns to Hebrew. This use of languages cuts across the ready division of the book into stories and visions. This Aramaic bridge must be considered in discussions of the date, composition, and unity of the book.

Daniel may be outlined as follows:

Daniel's prayer for his people (vv. 3-19)

Gabriel's interpretation (vv. 20-27)

Angelic revelation by the Tigris (10:1–12:13; third year of Cyrus of Persia)

Angel's dramatic epiphany (10:1–11:1)

Angel's prophecy of Persia's defeat by Greece and the subsequent splintering of Greece's empire (11:2-4)

Angel's prophecy of war between king of the south and king of the north (11:5-28)

Angel's prophecy of profaning of temple by king of the north (11:29-35)

Angel's prophecy of pride and blasphemy of king of the north (11:36-39)

Angel's prophecy of the end of the king of the north (11:40-45)

Angel's prophecy of Michael's protection and a divine resurrection (12:1-4)

Angel's command to keep the words sealed and the time hidden (12:5-10)

Angel's beatitude on those who persevere (12:11-13)

Daniel and the Kings. The first six chapters are sometimes called the historical section. Without denying their historicity, we must ask in what sense they are intended to relate to history. Was the author's purpose to give a selective account of Babylonian life from 605 to 538? Or were historical names and places employed as the media through which the revelation of God's sovereignty was to be understood?

A clear pattern is evident in these chapters. An event takes place — a dream, a fiery furnace, the handwriting on the wall — and perhaps an interpretation is given. A reaction results: (1) the king expresses faith in Daniel's God as "God of gods" (2:47), "Most High" (4:34), "the living God, enduring forever" (6:26 [MT 27]); (2) he issues a decree that no one speak against this God (3:29); or (3) he orders everyone to tremble and fear "before the God of Daniel" (6:26). Insistently the pattern serves to point readers to God.

Questions arise about this structure. Why would God give a revelation concerning "what will happen at the end of days" (2:28) to these gentile (thus pagan) rulers rather than to the covenant people? Is it not more reasonable to assume that such revelations were directed to the Jews (Israelites) through this literary means? If the effect of the various events was so great on the kings, why have we found no evidence outside the Bible? In the case of "Darius the Mede," whose laws could not be altered, why was not his decree (6:26f. [MT 27f.]) carried out by succeeding kings? What kind of history are these stories and the visions they record?

It is not easy to understand the way apocalyptic is to be related to history. We seem to be observing here a watershed in God's revelatory and redemptive process. When the Medo-Persians defeated the Babylonians, the power of empire passed from the Semitic peoples to the Indo-Europeans.[11] Christians believe that with the first advent of Christ, the crucifixion and resurrection, and then the subsequent destruction of Jerusalem in A.D. 70, an era ended and a new one began. With the momentous decision of the Jerusalem conference of the Church (Acts 15), gentiles were admitted for the first time to a covenant relationship with God. The distinction between Jew and gentile in this sense ended (Rom. 9:24-26; cf. Hos. 2:23 [MT 25]; Eph. 2:11-15). Daniel's stories and visions are designed to herald these new manifestations of God's kingship. In a context of imperial arrogance and cruelty, God pictured the great rulers of the age yielding to his authority. Their condescension before — if not actual faith in — the God of Israel may be the visionary way of saying that an age is ending and another about to begin. From this age on, even gentiles must and will serve the God of Daniel. That God alone is worthy of the worship of the human race, for time and the times are in his hands. Kings and empires, so far as this apocalyptic declaration is concerned, are servants of the Almighty.

Daniel's Dreams. A distinct change occurs in the second section of the book. The events in chs. 1–6 are narrated in the third person. Beginning in ch. 7, they are told in the first person (with very few exceptions, e.g., 7:1; 10:1). The focus in chs. 1–6 is on historical kings: Nebuchadnezzar, Belshazzar, and Darius the Mede.[12] Though the visions are dated in the reigns of the kings, in chs. 7–12 the concern is symbolic figures or angels: "four great beasts" emerging from the sea (7:3), a human-like figure "with the clouds of heaven" (v. 13), another with ten horns on its head and "the other horn" (v. 20), a "ram" charging to the west, north, and south (8:3f), a he-goat from the west (v. 5) with a great horn that is broken and replaced by four horns, one of which "grows exceedingly great" (vv. 8f.); and two heavenly beings, "Gabriel" (v. 16; 9:21) and "Michael" (10:13, 21; 12:1). These chapters are marked as "apocalyptic" by their unnatural or even grotesque character. But both parts of Daniel have the same purpose: to reveal heavenly realities and events that are to come in the world. In this sense, both are apocalyptic, as the parallels between chs. 2 and 7 suggest.

According to the date formulas, the visions of chs. 7–12 are intermixed chronologically with the events of chs. 1–6. Nebuchadnezzar's first dream is dated in the second year of his reign (603/2; 2:1). Belshazzar's feast and the handwriting on the wall (5:30) must be dated to the day that Babylon fell to the Medo-Persian power, 12 October 539. His first year (7:1) is dated *ca.* 554, and the third year (8:1), *ca.* 552. The first year of Darius the Mede (see 9:1) — however the name is interpreted — is to be placed in the first year of the Persian hegemony (538). If he is taken to be Darius I in 11:1, the first year

573

would be 520. The third year of Cyrus (10:1) would be 536.[13] These dates are important clues to the unity of Daniel's message.

Date and Authorship

Probably no date of a biblical book has been so positively asserted or so stridently denied as that of Daniel. Traditionally, the work has been assigned to the end of the sixth century B.C. The unusually detailed prophecies of events in Palestinian history have led many to propose dates much later: (1) What seem to be accounts concerning the Persians and Greeks (chs. 10–11) — the "mighty king" (probably of Greece; 11:3) and the division of his kingdom into four parts "but not to his posterity" (taken to be Alexander the Great and his successors; v. 4); (2) the kings of the south and north (read as the Ptolemies and Seleucids; vv. 5f.); and (3) particularly the details of the profaning of the temple and "the abomination that makes desolate" (assumed to be the desecration of the temple by Antiochus IV Epiphanes in 168; v. 31). A large number of scholars (liberal and conservative)[14] now contend that Daniel was written *ca.* 164.[15] To some conservative scholars, such a date would make the prophecies "after the event" *(ex eventu)* and therefore fraudulent; the book would be deception, not divine revelation.[16] The discussion has been long and sometimes heated.[17]

Language. The linguistic evidence has not always been given its proper weight in dating the book. Scholars have long been aware that the language of Daniel is earlier than the second century.[18] The consensus was that the Hebrew resembled that of the Chronicler and was earlier than that of the Mishnah. It is, indeed, noticeably closer to Chronicles than to Qumran (second-first centuries). Similarly, the Aramaic (2:4b–7:28) is closer to that of Ezra and the fifth-century papyri than to that from Qumran. Thus, some scholars have tended to date chs. 1–6 earlier, and suggest that a later author built on this material for chs. 7–12. This does not explain two facts: (1) the Aramaic section continues through ch. 7, which is of the same age as the Aramaic of chs. 2–6; (2) the Hebrew of chs. 7–12 is identical with that of chs. 1–2.

The linguistic evidence, both Hebrew and Aramaic, suggests a date possibly in the fourth or even fifth century. The evidence of the LXX and Qumran[19] indicates that Daniel was in existence in its full form, and had been distributed over a relatively wide area, prior to the time of Antiochus Epiphanes. This raises questions for theories of a second-century authorship.

Author. Other than the statement that Daniel "wrote down the dream" (7:1), no claim of authorship is made in the book. The first six chapters, narrated in the third person, may well have been written by someone else about Daniel. The last six chapters, largely in the first person, may have been accounts told by Daniel to someone else, after which the words were written down to preserve the significance of his dreams and visions (see 7:1). It is sometimes argued, on the basis of Matt. 24:15, that Daniel himself wrote the book.[20] But Jesus says "spoken of by the prophet Daniel." This cannot be taken to assert that he himself necessarily recorded those words in writing. According to the Talmud, a Jewish tradition placed some sort of editorial responsibility for Daniel on the men of the Great Synagogue,[21] sometime between Ezra (ca. 450) and Simeon the Just (270). It is not unreasonable, then, to attribute the dreams and visions to Daniel, who passed them on (in written form or otherwise), and to understand that they were finally put into their canonical form in the fourth or third century. The role of a group of sages ("those who are wise," 12:3, 10) should not be overlooked.

Daniel is called a *prophet* in a Florilegium (collection of scriptural prooftexts) from Qumran (4QFlor), by Jesus (Matt. 24:15), and Josephus (Ant. x.11.4 249). Yet the book is included in the Writings of the canon, not in the Latter Prophets. Why? The suggestion has been made that Daniel was, strictly speaking, a seer (Heb. *ḥôzeh, rô'eh*), since he received revelations in dreams and visions and not words from the Lord. But this kind of distinction between prophet and seer cannot be sustained. The canonical prophets also received revelations in visions (see Isa. 1:1) with their words. Some have proposed that Daniel had the prophetic *gift* but did not occupy that *office*.[22] But this too appears to be a specious distinction, without biblical warrant. The view that Daniel was not sent to Israel but to the Babylonian court[23] and therefore a ministry appropriate to that empire seems more reasonable.

Even this suggestion is not compelling, however. Daniel, indeed, was sent to Israel. His message was intended primarily for the people of God, who canonized it. The empires can but listen in to it, and the book has served both synagogue and church without permanent effect on the gentiles. On the basis of the book's genre, it was understood that its message concerned the end time by all those who used it in the pre-Christian period (Enoch, the Sibylline Oracles, 1 Maccabees), by Jesus (see Matt. 24:5-21) and John of the Apocalypse (Rev. 13:1, 5, 7). It has no immediate reference to Israel or the Jews (except in Daniel's prayer for his people [ch. 9] and in accusations against them [3:8, 12]). It therefore stands in a unique category marked off even from the apocalyptic portions of such prophets as Isaiah, Ezekiel, and Zechariah. The unique genre and the long process of its assembly and completion are the most likely explanations for its inclusion in the Writings and not the Latter Prophets.

In sum, scarcely any biblical book calls for more humility and caution as to firm conclusions of its date and authorship. The traditional view that the revelations to Daniel are prophecies delivered well before the events is grounded in a confidence that God as the author of Scripture is perfectly able to announce future events in great detail. The more recent approaches that set the visions in the times of Antiochus Epiphanes serve to remind us how different chs. 7–12 are from most biblical prophecy. Furthermore, we need to learn more about the nature of apocalyptic literature in its relationship to history, to prophecy, and to wisdom literature. In the long run, the question of Daniel's genre and how God intends us to understand it may be the issue on which the book's future students should concentrate. Meanwhile we ponder the conclusion of a recent commentator:

> Whether the stories are history or fiction, the visions actual prophecy or quasi-prophecy, written by Daniel or someone else, in the sixth century B.C., the second, or somewhere in between, makes surprising little difference to the book's exegesis. One understands the book on the basis of what it says.[24]

Interpretation of the Prophecy

Interpretation of the dreams and visions in Daniel is most difficult. This may be partly because so many commentators begin with Antiochus Epiphanes and chs. 10–11, and force all other interpretation to conform to this point.[25] In other schools of interpretation, much of the problem derives from the attempt to convert the times, weeks (or heptads), and days into chronological systems that predict precise dates of future events. For all interpreters the difficulty lies largely in its use of forms and figures that appear intentionally obscure. The book is shut up and sealed "until the time of the end" (12:4), and must wait for complete understanding until that time. But this does not mean we are left utterly ignorant of its intention.

The Kingdoms and the Kingdom. In ch. 2, Daniel interprets Nebuchadnezzar's dream image of "what shall be hereafter" (v. 45). The four parts of the image represent four successive kingdoms, beginning with Nebuchadnezzar's (vv. 38-40). As the fourth kingdom deteriorates (vv. 41-43), a "stone . . . cut out not by human hands" (v. 34) smashes the whole of the image, so that no trace of it is left (v. 35). The stone "became a great mountain and filled the whole earth" (v. 35). It is interpreted by Daniel as signifying God's permanent reign, which shatters all other kingdoms (vv. 44f.).

This dream and its interpretation anticipate the vision of the four beasts in ch. 7. Even those who argue for two authors, or at least an earlier and a later part of the book, look upon ch. 7 as embellishing the theme of ch. 2. The two must be considered together. In ch. 7, four beasts rise from the sea (v. 3). They emerge successively (vv. 5-7). The fourth beast grows horns, the fourth of which speaks "arrogant words" (v. 11). But then the beast is slain, and Daniel sees in a vision "with the clouds of heaven . . . one like a human being" (v. 13). To him "dominion and glory and kingship" is given over "all peoples, nations, and languages" and its sovereignty would never pass away (v. 14). The beasts signify that "four kings shall arise out of the earth. But the holy ones of the Most High shall receive the kingdom," and ultimately possess it forever (vv. 17f.).

This is the heart of the theme of the book. The purpose is not to focus on the Hellenistic age, though these pictures surely brought comfort to God's persecuted and beleaguered people. The book's aim is to display the kingdom of God as victorious over all the ages. True, when Daniel wanted to know more about the "fourth beast" (8:15) — obviously, the last kingdom to exist before God's kingdom is to be established — the details that are given suggest that the period from the end of the Persian empire is in view (cf. v. 20), along with the time of Alexander (v. 21) and his four successors (v. 22), until that time when a king of great power and destruction (vv. 23, 25) shall be broken "and not by human hands" (v. 25). But prophecies that concern the future often have "prophetic perspective" (or compenetration), so that the near-at-hand and the distant future are merged in a mysterious manner. In Isa. 9, for example, what starts out as a message of brightness and joy for Zebulun and Naphtali (representative portions of the land taken captive by Assyria) moves on to "the latter time" (9:1 [MT 8:23]), and climaxes with the "Prince of Peace" on the throne of David. "His authority shall grow continually . . . from this time onward and forever more" (vv. 6f. [MT 5f.]). God gave new meaning to the house of David in its New Testament fulfillment (Luke 1:32). The remarkable promise was kept. Daniel's vision must be understood in just such a way.

No one claims that the kingdom "not made with hands" replaced that of Antiochus Epiphanes[26] with a historical reality. No one familiar with the prophets can interpret either the present Christian age or the preceding Maccabean period as the fulfillment of Daniel's vision of the everlasting kingdom, much less that described, for example, by Isaiah, Jeremiah, or Ezekiel.

The typical systems of interpretation of chs. 2 and 7 may be diagrammed as in the figure on page 578.[27]

No choice among these options is free of difficulties. It is hard to split the Persian empire into two successive kingdoms, as do those who make the second and third kingdoms the Medes and Persians. But it is equally difficult to find the Roman empire in Daniel's dreams and visions. Again, whatever system of interpretation is chosen, close reading of the text puts the spotlight on the kingdom of God which replaces all of these kingdoms.

Fourth Beast. In response to Daniel's desire to know more about the fourth beast (7:19), he is given a further vision. A beast with ten horns, and

Head of gold (First beast)	> Babylonian empire	Babylonian empire	Babylonian empire
Breast of silver (Second beast)	> Medo-Persian empire	Median kingdom	Medo-Persian empire
Belly of brass (Third beast)	> Greek empire	Persian empire	Alexander the Great
Legs of iron (Fourth beast)	> Roman empire	Greek empire	Alexander's successors

then another coming up, made war with the saints and prevailed over them "until the Ancient One came" (vv. 20-22). "One of the attendants" (v. 16; cf. v. 23) explains the vision: the fourth kingdom will be different from the others (v. 23), and will be exceedingly cruel and destructive. One of its kings is blasphemous, and persecutes "the holy ones of the Most High" (v. 27). This continues "for a time, two times, and half a time" (v. 25). Then his dominion is taken and given to the saints of the Most High (vv. 26f.).

We must not get lost in details here and miss the clear message. Is this time span three and one-half years, and is it half of the so-called Great Tribulation? Is this blasphemous king the Antichrist, or the 666 of the Revelation? Such mysteries are part of the book's sealing. When the final fulfillment takes place, the meaning will be clear. Meanwhile, the message is one of firm hope to all "the holy ones of the Most High." Whenever any earthly ruler persecutes the people of God, his times are limited and his destruction assured. Saints of every age have found true comfort in their interpretations of this message, and yet the vision retains its age-long message of hope and assurance only within the significance of its sealed nature.

Ram, He-goat, and Horn. The horn is symbolic of power (1 Kgs. 22:11; Zech. 1:18ff. [MT 2:1ff.]), particularly that of the reigning house (Ps. 132:17; Ezek. 29:21). In chs. 7–8 and Rev. 13 and 17, the horns symbolize rulers of empires. The ram with two horns standing on the banks of the river Ulai in Elam represents the Medo-Persian empire. A he-goat comes from the west with amazing speed (8:5), destroying the ram. It has a great horn, which is broken and replaced by four conspicuous horns (v. 8). This has usually been interpreted to signify Alexander the Great, who died (323 B.C.) shortly after conquering Persia and the east (332 B.C.), and was succeeded by four generals. Out of one horn emerges "a little horn" which grows influential (v. 11). This "little horn" is usually identified with Antiochus Epiphanes (*ca.* 215-163). He is known to have profaned the temple on 25 Chislev (27 Dec.) 168 (see 1 Macc. 1:54; 2 Macc. 6:2; Josephus, *Ant.* xii.5.4.248-256). Daniel asks how long the profanation will continue, and is told: "For two thousand three hundred evenings and mornings; then the sanctuary shall be restored to its rightful state" (v. 14).[28]

The interpretation given by Gabriel is a vision "for the time of the end" (v. 17), and supports the identifications of the kings of Media and Persia (v. 20), the king of Greece (v. 21), Alexander the Great, and his four successors (v. 22). At the end "a king of bold countenance" (v. 23) shall arise and cause fearful destruction (v. 24), "but, he shall be broken, and not by human hands" (v. 25). Here again one-on-one identification is hazardous. If Antiochus Epiphanes is intended, was he broken by no human hand? It is better to leave the message in a shape that appreciates its timeless form, that respects its sealing as the revelation of God. The ultimate fulfillment "refers to many days from now" (v. 26), but its purpose belongs to the people of God in any age. Their enemies are God's enemies, and God's kingdom belongs to a time when God's eternity is experienced forever. The present comfort it provides is not a stoic set of the face; the destiny it promises is sealed in God's own heart.

Daniel's Prayer for His People. Daniel believed, from his knowledge of Jeremiah's prophecy, that a period of seventy years was decreed for the desolation of Jerusalem (9:2; cf. Jer. 25:11f.). Aware that the time of the weeks was nearly up, Daniel prayed to God, confessing his sins and those of his people. He asked God to act without further delay (9:19). Once again, Gabriel (in Luke 1:26, an angel; in intertestamental literature, an archangel) speaks to Daniel of "the time of an anointed prince" (v. 25). The studies of vv. 25-27 are extensive. Calculations of the "seven weeks," "sixty-two weeks," and the remaining "one week," which is divided in half (v. 27), have concerned a whole spectrum of scholarship. Lack of a common result raises doubts about the methods used. No compelling consensus has ever been reached.

"An anointed prince" (vv. 25f.) is expressed by Heb. *māšiaḥ.* The KJV, NASB, and others translate "Messiah" here, although the definite article is lacking. Indeed, the term may not refer to a messianic prince (despite the NRSV reading) who is to rule over the coming kingdom. But later, "Messiah" became a technical term (see below, Ch. 51). Efforts to understand the seven weeks as forty-nine years and to demonstrate that this prophecy was fulfilled when the temple was rebuilt, or to calculate from the sixty-two weeks the date of the coming of the Christ or the Crucifixion (cf. v. 26), have yielded much confusion. The order in the passage is this: (1) the going forth of the word to restore Jerusalem; (2) the coming of an anointed one, a prince; (3) Jerusalem rebuilt "with streets and moat, but in a troubled time" (v. 25); (4) the anointed one cut off, city and sanctuary laid waste; and (5) the coming prince destroys the city and makes a covenant for "one week"; then for "half of the week" he halts sacrifice and offering (v. 27). Frankly, very grave difficulties arise in attempting to fit this order into most reconstructions posited by interpreters.[29]

Actually, Gabriel has taken Jeremiah's prophecy of seventy years, understood to apply to the period of the Exile, and turned it into an end-time prophecy of "seventy weeks of years" (v. 24). This complex transformation of the picture includes restoration of the city, a troubled time, the cutting off of an anointed prince (who seems to have ruled during the sixty-two "weeks"), a coming prince, and his troops, bent on destroying the city and sanctuary (v. 26). Those who, in any age, long for the restoration of Jerusalem find here a message of hope. Those who seek the messianic prince are assured that he will come. Those living in days of trouble, wars, and desolations know that this is only for "one week" and that in the end the "desolator" must meet his ordained end (v. 27). Truly, Gabriel's reply profoundly exceeds Daniel's original petition.

Desolating Abomination. In a precisely dated vision (23 Apr. 536; 10:4), Daniel is told what is to befall his people in the latter days (10:14). Michael, one of the chief princes (v. 13) also described as "your prince" (v. 21), and the speaker ("a man clothed in linen," v. 5; probably the Gabriel mentioned in 9:21) play central roles. This should indicate to the reader that the circumstances transcend what is usually considered historical. The ruler of Persia had withstood this speaker "twenty-one days." Then Michael came to aid the offensive (v. 13) and remained to do battle, all while the speaker left to tell Daniel of the events to come (v. 14). However, he would return "to fight against the prince of Persia" (v. 20).[30]

The message appears to continue in ch. 11.[31] "Three more kings" are to arise in Persia, and a fourth who moves against Greece (v. 2). Then "a warrior king shall arise" — not identified with Greece in the biblical text, although often so interpreted — who rules "with great dominion" (v. 3). His kingdom is divided "toward the four winds of heaven, but not to his posterity" (v. 4).

Interpreters take this mighty king to be Alexander the Great, who made no provision for a succession and who was followed by four generals who carved up his empire. Most commentators take the details of this vision quite specifically: the "king of the south" is the Lagide or Ptolemaic line, which ruled from Egypt *ca.* 323-30 B.C. The "king of the north" is the Seleucid line, which held sway from Syria for approximately the same period. However, such detailed exposition cannot be fitted into the events of the period with historical precision. The book of Daniel is neither "history written in advance" nor "prophecy after the event." It is apocalyptic, which is always in some sense trans-historical. It is rooted in history and springs from history, but its purpose takes history where it has never been before and provides a message in time that is bound up with God's eternity. For this reason, Daniel's prophecies have served God's people not only under the Ptolemies and Seleucids, but in the first century B.C., the first century A.D., and all succeeding periods.[32]

The king of the north, turning back (to Jerusalem) from a thwarted attack on the king of the south, pays court to "those who forsake the holy covenant" (v. 30). His forces profane the temple, take away the continual burnt offering, and set up "the abomination that makes desolate" (vv. 29-31; cf. 12:11; Matt. 24:15; Mark 13:14). Modern commentators have usually made this portion of Daniel little more than a review of history.[33] Jesus Christ, on the other hand, along with many Jews of his time, saw here a message that could apply to an indefinite future, whether the destruction of Jerusalem in A.D. 70 or the coming of the Son of Man (Matt. 24:15; cf. v. 3; Mark 13:2, 4). A great and powerful ruler would come to "seduce with flattery" those who claim to belong to the household of faith and "violate the covenant." This happened when the Hellenizers sought to turn Jews into gentiles in the pre-Maccabean period. It has happened many times since, and will happen to a much greater extent at the end of the age. "But the people who are loyal to their God shall stand firm and take action" (Dan. 11:32).

At that time, Michael will take charge (12:1). "A time of trouble" will ensue (see Matt. 24:21; Mark 13:19; Rev. 12:7; 16:18), but Daniel is assured "your people shall be delivered." Dan. 12:2 is a clear reference to the resurrection at the end of the age. Among those secrets that are "sealed until the time of the end" (v. 9) are the "times" (v. 7) and the "days" (vv. 11f.). Again, both real comfort and true hope shape the purpose of Daniel's vision.

One Like a Son of Man. In 7:13, when the beasts are slain, "one like a son of man" — note the contrast with beasts — comes "with the clouds of heaven." As the title of address used by Ezekiel (see above, pp. 360-61), the designation "son of man" simply means "human being" (so NRSV), "man." Jesus often referred to himself by this title. Some scholars claim that he was thus claiming to be the Messiah. But this seems quite unlikely.[34] Jesus was using a term that had come to have a deeper meaning and would in time come to possess an expanded significance to include the fulfillment of Daniel's prophecy (Matt. 24:30; 26:64 and par.; cf. Rev. 1:7, 13; 14:14).[35]

To understand this development, the history of the term needs investigation. Book II of Enoch, the "parables" or "similitudes," contains a rather full doctrine of the "son of man." He is depicted not as a human being, but as a preexistent heavenly being who rules over a universal kingdom. In early Judaism, two doctrines are separately developed: (1) the Messiah, a human king from the line of David, and (2) a divine or semidivine being, a "son of man," who comes from heaven to bring to a close this age and to inaugurate the "age to come." The Qumran community embraced a purely human messiah, as Son-of-David. No part of Enoch Book II has been found there, although many fragments of other parts of the book were recovered. Some would date book II as later, possibly after A.D. 100. At any rate, whereas in Judaism the ideas were kept distinct, the New Testament blends them into one doctrine (see Matt

26:63f.), in explanation of the uniqueness of Jesus. The term's range of meaning must be able to reflect this development.

> The Christian Church has always been intrigued by the book of Daniel. At times its scholars have ventured some fanciful interpretations. Especially painful have been the attempts to use Daniel's symbolic numbers as a guide to the exact timing of Christ's second coming. But most expositions have been a source of real hope in times of deep distress.[36]

Attempts either to establish historical details or to determine the times and seasons may, indeed, miss the book's capacity to deliver in the midst of time an eternal message. Yet if that message is sought first, the details need not be lost, for they will become clearer as the time of the end approaches. A healthy concern for biblical apocalyptic that seeks first to hear what Word the Spirit speaks, is greatly to be desired — particularly in times of trouble. "Let anyone who has an ear listen to what the Spirit is saying to the churches" (Rev. 3:22).

PART FOUR

THE BACKGROUND

CHAPTER 44

The Authority of the Old Testament for Christians

The Old Testament was the Bible used by Christ and the apostles. Almost uniformly (2 Pet. 3:16 is an exception) the words "Scripture" or "Scriptures" in the New Testament refer to the Old Testament (e.g., John 5:39; 10:35; Acts 8:32; Gal. 3:8; 2 Tim. 3:16). For about two decades after Christ the only parts of the New Testament in existence were fragmentary accounts of his life and teachings. During this period when a vital Church was extending its influence into Syria, Asia Minor, and North Africa, the basis for preaching and teaching was the Old Testament as reinterpreted by Jesus and his early followers.

Jesus and the Old Testament

> You search the scriptures . . . and it is they that testify on my behalf. John 5:39

Christ recognized the binding authority of Scripture while reserving for himself the right to be its true interpreter. Although Jesus crossed swords with Jewish leaders at many points, the New Testament records no quarrel over the inspiration or authority of the Old Testament. On the contrary, Christ frequently appealed to the Scriptures as the ground for his claims and teachings. This is illustrated in the triple use of "it is written" in the temptation story (Matt. 4:1-11). Furthermore, John's account of Jesus' argument with the Jewish leaders concerning the right to call himself God's Son (John 10:31-36) hinges on a commitment to the reliability of the Scriptures.

In this confidence in the Old Testament as the written word of God, Jesus followed his Jewish ancestors. Centuries before, God's words and acts of revelation had gripped them with such power and clarity that they treasured them in written record. Stage by stage a body of authoritative literature had grown among the Israelites: laws, narratives of their past, oracles of their prophets, teachings of their sages, and hymns and prayers of their worship. These documents shaped the understanding of their life, faith, and destiny. They recognized in them the word of the one Lord whom they knew to be the only true God.

Though sharing the attitude of many Jewish contemporaries toward the authority of the Old Testament, Jesus' interpretation of it differed sharply on at least two points. First, like the prophets, he sensed the emptiness of much of Jewish legalism, in which routine and ritual had become a worthless substitute for purity of heart, integrity, and social concern (e.g., Mark 7:1-13; Matt. 9:13; 12:7, which quote Hos. 6:6). As the true prophet, the new Moses, Jesus interpreted the law in the Sermon on the Mount (Matt. 5–7). Renouncing some prevalent misinterpretations of the law, Jesus emphasized love, forgiveness, and inward piety. He brought fresh import to major prophetic themes, which some Jewish teachers had neglected in magnifying the letter of the law.

Second, and more distinctively, Jesus insisted that he is the personal fulfillment of the Old Testament; he is its major theme. His declaration in the synagogue in his home town — "Today this scripture has been fulfilled in your hearing" (Luke 4:21) — may be seen as the epitome of his claim. This sense of fulfillment both sparked his conflict with the Jewish officialdom (John 5:46) and shaped his followers' attitude toward the Scriptures (Luke 24:44f.).

Christ transformed Old Testament interpretation by drawing together in himself various strands of teaching and braiding them into a single cord. He was the great prophet like Moses who taught the new law from the mountain; the peerless priest who made the whole temple system obsolete (cf. Matt. 12:6; John 2:13-15); the wise king, the "greater than Solomon" (Matt. 12:42); David's son and Lord, rightful heir to Israel's throne (Mark 12:35-37; 15:2); the triumphant Son of man (Dan. 7:13ff.; Mark 13:26); and the suffering servant (Isa. 53; Mark 10:45). The major themes of prophetic expectation found their consummation in him.

Compared to the viewpoint of many of his Jewish contemporaries, Christ's approach to the Old Testament was dynamic, not static. He looked upon the Scripture not as a catalogue of fixed principles regulating religious conduct, but as the inspired and authoritative record of God's activity in history, an activity which presses toward its climax in the kingdom which Jesus brought near. As Jesus' words are spirit and life (John 6:63), so the Old Testament when viewed with his insights becomes a guide to life (John 5:39).

In highlighting the prophets as legitimate interpreters of the *Torah* (the stories and laws of the Pentateuch) and in focusing the Old Testament revelation on himself, Christ shaped the patterns of biblical interpretation adopted by the apostolic writers. For example, Matthew's concern is the correspondence between events in his Messiah's life and Old Testament prophecy. Note his "to fulfill what had been spoken" (e.g., 1:22; 2:15, 17, 23; 4:14; 12:17; 13:35; 21:4; 27:9). John's Gospel makes frequent explicit and implicit comparisons of Moses and Christ (e.g., 1:17; 3:14; 5:45-47; 6:32; 7:19).

Paul and the Old Testament

As a Jew and a rabbi, Saul of Tarsus knew the Old Testament well; as a Christian and an apostle, Paul found the familiar text pregnant with fresh meaning. Like Jesus he accepted the full inspiration and authority of the Scripture (2 Tim. 3:16) and found its deepest significance in its anticipation of and preparation for the New Testament. The similarities between Christ's approach and Paul's are not accidental. Undoubtedly Christ singled out pertinent Old Testament passages and taught his disciples how to interpret them.[1]

In his four pillar epistles — Romans, 1-2 Corinthians, and Galatians — Paul's dependence on the Old Testament shows itself most clearly. A large percentage of his more than ninety quotations are found in them. And both his dominant theological themes and his means of argument are drawn from the Jewish Scriptures. Paul bowed to the authority of Scripture, he used it to clinch his cases. He respected its verdicts; he revered its holiness. In so doing, he set the pattern for all who handle the oracles of God.

The transformation of Paul's understanding of the Old Testament was drastic: the Christ whose followers he had doggedly vowed to stamp out became for him the very heart of Old Testament revelation:

> For Paul, Christ was not only a factor giving added meaning to the Old Testament but the only means whereby the Old Testament could be rightly understood; it was not merely that he saw Christ in the Old Testament but that he viewed the whole scope of Old Testament prophecy and history from the standpoint of the Messianic Age in which the Old Testament stood open, fulfilled in Jesus Christ and in His new creation.[2]

The extent to which Paul grounds his doctrinal instruction in Old Testament soil is indicated by a score of topics. These include the fall of Adam and Eve and its effects (Rom. 5:12-21), the universality of sin (3:10, 20), the obedience and sufferings of Christ (15:3), justification by faith (1:17; 4:1ff.; 10:5ff.), and the final salvation of the Jews (11:26).[3]

Typology plays a major part in the Pauline epistles.[4] Studies of New Testament typology[5] have stressed the continuity between Paul's and Christ's uses of Old Testament types and have contrasted both of them with the interpretative methods of Philo of Alexandria and Jewish rabbinical writers. The revival of interest in typology is kindled from two sparks: (1) a renewed regard for the unity of the Bible and (2) fresh study of the ways in which the New Testament writers depend upon the Old. The unity of the Bible is a dynamic one, based on the continuity of God's activity in both Testaments. This insight has helped explain the historical character of biblical typology.[6] For Paul the same God was working in both ages, so that the patterns of his past activity were prototypes of his present and future acts. In their use of God's past activity to illustrate God's present and future works, both Christ and Paul follow the example of the Old Testament itself. There, for instance, the Exodus from Egypt sets the pattern for the return from captivity — the New Exodus (cf. Isa. 43:16-20). The Old Testament is authoritative for Paul not primarily in its mystical, or allegorical message. What counted most for him was its inspired record of God's creative, elective, and redemptive activity. He saw this pattern consummated in the New Age ushered in by the Incarnation of Jesus Christ.

In putting emphasis on the historical continuity within the Bible we should not miss the moral or ethical relationship between the Testaments. The New Testament certainly transcends the Old in ethical insights. Yet the earlier revelation has much to say about themes featured in the teachings of Christ and the apostles: doing God's will is the highest good; immorality, idolatry, inhumanity, and spiritual rebellion are to be shunned; honesty, integrity, diligence are to be treasured; concern for the rights and needs of others is valued as a sterling quality (2 Tim. 3:16ff.; 1 Cor. 10:1, 11).

The freedom with which Paul and other New Testament writers (especially Matthew) sometimes handled the Old Testament has been puzzling. At times they followed no known Greek or Hebrew textual tradition. The apostolic authors sometimes wove interpretative strands into their quotations. However, these notes are usually not arbitrary or capricious. They should be classed as quotation expositions which neither follow the text with slavish literalism nor alter its meaning with arbitrary interpretation.[7] In interpreting the Scriptures, Paul paid close attention to their historical setting and their grammatical structure. Yet he interpreted historical events not so much according to their past significance as in terms of their meaning for later fulfillment. He moved beyond the obvious grammatical structure to a meaning which the grammar allows but which also fits an overall interpretation of the Old Testament revelation.[8]

Conclusion

This pattern of authority and these principles of interpretation could easily be applied to other New Testament writings such as Hebrews, James, and Revelation. Laced with Old Testament allusions and quotations, each has its own way of employing them. James, for instance, draws heavily upon Israel's wisdom tradition as it was manifest in both the teaching techniques and the thought of Christ, the Master Sage. The author of Hebrews employed Old Testament proof texts and types to demonstrate the marked superiority of Christ and his new covenant. John in the Revelation, convinced that Christ is the Alpha and Omega, constantly described the cosmic climax of history in terms borrowed from Old Testament descriptions of God's acts in mercy and judgment. His book suggests that this climax is what was spoken of and longed for by the prophets — the triumph of the kingdom of God.

Following their Lord's example in embracing the authority of the Scriptures, the New Testament writers found in them not the letter which kills but the Spirit-directed witness to God's life-giving activity. They read the Scriptures not as dreary collections of enslaving laws but as the earlier acts in a great drama of salvation. Its central actor was their Lord. Modern readers are no less in need of the earlier acts, for in them may still be seen the deeds of God and the various responses of surrender and rebellion which those deeds prompted. What was important, authoritative, and crucial to the Lord himself and subsequently to the early Church cannot be any less so today (1 Cor. 10:11).

In study as in worship, humankind needs the entire revelation, the whole Bible. The Old Testament belongs not to the Jewish people alone but to all. It is the account of the ways in which God has worked; it is the summary of what he has demanded; it is the record of his preparation for Christ's coming; it is the best canvas on which to catch the picture of his dealings with the human family through the centuries. In short, it is the indispensable foundation on which the New Testament is built.

To understand the Old Testament as Christian Scripture, one must see it through the eyes of Jesus and his apostles. They were especially inspired by God's Spirit to grasp the meaning of God's revelatory words and deeds and the directions in which they were moving.

Yet at the same time, the modern reader must try to see the Old Testament passages on their own terms. We must ask: "What was the Old Testament author saying to his own times?" We must sit with the hearers in the marketplace, city gate, temple, or synagogue and try to understand God's words as they heard them. We must see God through their eyes and discern God's purposes as they did.

In other words, we must be sensitive to the original context of an Old Testament passage. Why was it written and when? What problems called it into being? What question was it initially intended to answer? What did it tell people about God's will and ways or about their responsibilities that they would not otherwise have known? Only when we begin to understand the intent of a passage for the author's own times, can we seek the full significance of the passage for Christian faith and life. The Old Testament context will not tell us all we need to know about the meaning of the passage. But unless we start there, we can easily twist the Scriptures to our own purposes. The intention and meaning of the individual authors must be grasped if we are to capture the meaning put there by the overall Author, the Spirit of God. We hear God's voice through all of Scripture. That voice gives the whole Bible its authority for us as God's people.

CHAPTER 45

Revelation and Inspiration

The Bible is a unique book. On the one hand it is an outstanding piece of human literature; on the other it claims to owe its origin to God. The key theological terms that give expression to this uniqueness are revelation and inspiration. Revelation refers to the divine disclosure (lit. "uncovering") of truth in the Scriptures; inspiration relates to the initial human reception of that truth prompted by the divine Spirit. Both terms may only be understood properly as we listen to what the Bible itself has to say about them.

Revelation

> . . . instruction shall not perish from the priest, nor counsel from the wise, nor the word from the prophet. Jer. 18:18

Jeremiah lists three human channels of divine revelation in ancient Israel: (1) the *priests* who gave the people instruction *(torah)* on religious and ethical matters; (2) the *wise* who offered advice concerning life's problems to kings and commoners; (3) the *prophets* who delivered messages that expressed God's purposes for the people. All three groups basically had an oral ministry: the Old Testament is substantially the written record of their spoken traditions, in

Jebel Musa, traditionally identified with Mt. Sinai, where the Lord
spoke to Moses (Exod. 19:3). *(Neal and Joel Bierling)*

its three divisions of Law, Prophets, and Writings. Early Judaism and the New
Testament alike hailed this record as Scripture.

In Old Testament times the three groups were accepted as mediators of
God's will for the believing community. They were agents of the communication of divine truth. This is most obvious in the case of the prophets. The
whole gamut of the vocabulary of communication is used of their testimony,
succinctly summed up in terms of God's speaking "in many and various ways
by the prophets" (Heb. 1:1). A typical prophetic oracle begins with the so-called
messenger formula "thus says the LORD" and often ends with the divine saying
formula "says the LORD," for instance in Amos 5:16-17. In Jer. 1:9 there is a
divine assurance to the prophet, "Now I have put my words in your mouth."
Isa. 40–48 is especially rich in its references to God's oral revelation to the
exiles: through the prophet God *tells, declares* to the people so that they may
know, *proclaims* so they may hear, *announces,* and *speaks.*[1]

There are reflective statements in the Old Testament that invite the reader
to stand back and ponder this concept of divine revelation: "Surely the Lord
GOD does nothing, without revealing his secret to his servants the prophets"
(Amos 3:7). God, we are told, used the institution of prophecy to transmit to
Israel what would otherwise have taken them by surprise, a revelation of

coming events and their meaning. By such means the purposes of the Lord of Israel's history were disclosed.[2]

The ministry of the prophets was not the only means of divine revelation. There is a testimony to the Torah or Mosaic law in such terms in Deut. 29:29: "The secret things belong to the LORD our God, but the revealed things belong to us and to our children forever, to observe all the words of this law." Similarly, Ps. 147:19 celebrates Israel's unique privilege as recipient of the Torah: "He declares his word to Jacob, his statutes and ordinances to Israel." The wisdom tradition also had the function of revelation according to Prov. 2:6: "For the LORD gives wisdom; from his mouth come knowledge and understanding." The wisdom movement, for all its emphasis on discussion and reflection, traced its insights back to God. Its hard-won discoveries were ultimately the disclosures of the all-wise God.

This last text appears to have a canonical function. In its context of a theological introduction to written collections of proverbs, it makes a claim of revelation for the resultant book. Another such canonical claim is evident in Deut. 34:10: "Never since has there arisen a prophet in Israel like Moses, whom the LORD knew face to face." The Torah is celebrated at its close as the fruit of a uniquely intimate relationship between God and its human founder. Accordingly late Old Testament texts could call the Torah not only the law of Moses but "the law of the LORD"[3] and "the law of God."[4]

Likewise, the canonical book of Ps. is carefully provided with an introduction in Psalm 1, which commends the study of the book as the very *torah* ("law") of the Lord. Here *torah* refers to divine instruction and stamps the book of Psalms as revelation: "Because Israel continues to hear God's word through the voice of the psalmists' response, these prayers now function as the divine word itself."[5]

Similar evidence is afforded by the headings to the books of prophetic oracles: "The key vocabulary in the titles to the prophetic books is theological language which designates them as divine revelation" and "the fundamental intention of the superscriptions is to identify the prophetic books as the word of God."[6] At the beginning of five books, the formula originally applicable to a particular message, "the word of the LORD came to . . ." is inclusively applied to all the oracles found in written form.[7] The whole is characterized as written revelation. Other books open with the comprehensive term "vision" (Isa. 1:1; Obad. 1; Nah. 1:1), which here refers not to a visionary experience but to a series of oracles as revealed by God. Similarly the verb "saw" in Amos 1:1; Mic. 1:1; and Hab. 1:1 is applied to the divine revelation given through these prophets (cf. Isa. 1:1). The concept of revelation was extended from the oral form of a prophet's messages to the written form, and then applied to it as a literary whole. God was yet speaking to future generations of believers through the written word.

Inspiration

> All Scripture is inspired by God and is useful for teaching, for reproof, for correction, and for training in righteousness. 2 Tim. 3:16

The voices of chosen human mediators were used to convey the truths God intended to reveal to Israel. The positive interaction between divine revealer and human spokespersons required inspiration. Inspiration is primarily a quality that relates to persons, but it may also develop into a characteristic of books, as the product of inspired persons. The apostle Paul reflected on this quality of the Old Testament and its role in the purposes of God in building up Christian believers in their faith and ethical stance (2 Tim. 3:16).

The Old Testament, from which Timothy had been taught since childhood under the tuition of his mother and grandmother, is here said to be "inspired by God."[8] What this means may be adduced from a parallel statement concerning the oral stage of the prophetic section of the Old Testament: "men and women moved by the Holy Spirit spoke from God" (2 Pet. 1:21).[9] The term in 2 Tim. 3:16 rendered "inspired by God" may literally be rendered "God-spirited": it alludes to the work of God's Spirit as the medium of inspiration.[10]

The concept is borrowed from the Old Testament itself, where preexilic prophecy is described in such terms: "the words which the LORD of hosts had sent by his spirit through the former prophets" (Zech. 7:12); again, God is addressed in prayer as one who "warned [Israel] by your spirit through your prophets" (Neh. 9:30).[11] Sometimes the preexilic prophets themselves described their ministry in this way.[12] Such inspiration is the operation by which the prophets were enabled to utter God's word. The word was the content of their messages, while God's Spirit was the transcendent power that enabled them to perceive it and so proclaim it.[13]

This is clearly a prophetic model of inspiration. The prophets were acutely conscious of transmitting messages that emanated from God. It would not be helpful to define such inspiration in terms of dictation. The diverse evidence of personality and style shows how strong a role the humanness of the prophets played. Essentially a biblical doctrine of inspiration is concerned with the product rather than the processes; it does not deal in theories, psychological or otherwise, as to how inspiration was achieved.

Strictly speaking, one would need other models in order to understand the inspired quality of the laws of the Pentateuch,[14] of the various types of literature found in the Writings, and indeed of the history writing that pervades all three parts of the Old Testament canon. In the New Testament Luke consulted "eyewitnesses" and carefully researched the material for his canonical gospel (Luke 1:1-3). The same human processes of using secular sources and oral traditions are evident in the historiography of the Old Testament.[15]

Yet within the Old Testament there is evidence of a movement toward a simple prophetic model to describe what was actually produced by complex processes. The divine revelation that, according to the heading in Jer. 1:1-2, characterizes the book of Jeremiah includes the record of the prophet's career and even reproachful complaints such as he addressed to God in Jer. 20:7-18. It was at the literary stage that human words of all kinds could be recognized as revelation and so invested with a particular type of inspiration which was primarily a prophetic phenomenon.

In fact, the production of prophetic books was a much more prolonged and complex process than the inspiration of a speaking prophet. It is now recognized that behind prophetic literature lies the work of editors and arrangers and circles who preserved oral traditions and presented them to later generations of God's people. Even more complex must have been the development of the Pentateuch, where separate oral and written, narrative and legal traditions eventually coalesced into a single literary work after a period of centuries. To speak of inspiration, as one must to be true to the Bible, there has to be an acknowledgment of God's inspiring providence so that the written word eventually reflected the divine intention.

In the light of these literary processes, may one speak of the believing community as having been inspired?[16] Only with reservations: "Communities as such do not write books, individuals do."[17] Nevertheless, it was within the community of Israel and in response to its successive needs that the books of the Old Testament gradually grew to their present form. Neither a single prophetic author nor a final redactor may be credited with a monopoly on inspiration.

By the period of the New Testament, Judaism invested the Hebrew Bible as a whole with a prophetic quality of inspiration. All the biblical writers were regarded as prophets by Philo and Josephus.[18] The New Testament itself appears to reflect this viewpoint, encouraged by the eschatological conviction that "the ends of the ages have come on" its participants (1 Cor. 10:11; cf. Rom. 1:2; 4:23f.; 15:4). Those who heard the whole Old Testament as a word of predictive truth treasured it as the product of a prophetic model of interpretation, the legacy of the Holy Spirit, as 2 Tim. 3:16 implies.[19]

The Goal of Scripture

We need next to consider the purpose of the Old Testament, to seek to clarify the nature of its inspired revelation. The key Pauline text defines its purpose as twofold: it conveys both theological and ethical truth (2 Tim. 3:16). The Old Testament teaches what Christians should and should not believe ("for teaching, for reproof") and how they should and should not behave ("for correction, and for training in righteousness"). Paraphrasing this the Westminster Confession of 1647 described the books of the Old and New Testaments as "given by the inspiration of God to be the rule of faith and life." A little later it spoke of Scripture's "infallible truth," a phrase borrowed from Luke 1:4, where the evangelist's purpose is defined as teaching the "truth" or "infallibility" concerning early Christian traditions.[20] The Old Testament is trustworthy for the purposes for which God has inspired it and by no means liable to deceive in these areas. Correspondingly, one should not seek to derive from it truths not demanded by the biblical intention. It is possible to ask too much of Scripture and to project back into it ideal pictures of what the Bible ought to be, which do it no honor. The important question is not what kind of Bible God could have produced, but what kind God has produced.

In particular, it is not necessary to infer from the fact of inspiration a doctrine of inerrancy, which tends to build a fence of protective arguments around the Bible.[21]

> In order to discern Scripture's view of itself, one must take into account not only its doctrinal statements but also its data. One must respect the tension between separate traditions instead of rushing to harmonize them with clever ingenuity. Our task is to proclaim the message of the Bible rather than to bear the burden of a theological necessity to resolve all minutiae.

Divine revelation has been given in a particular historical and cultural context. At times it reflects the cultural limitations of God's people to whom it was first given.[22] Certainly we may not expect the technical standards or information to which our own culture has made us accustomed in matters of geography, history, or science. In the light of the cultural translation that the reader is sometimes required to make, should one speak of the Bible as containing, rather than itself being, the word of God? No, because the historical grounding of the word itself reflects the divine intent.

Particular passages are to be studied in the light of their literary format, contexts, and intention. They need to be understood within the stage of revelation they reflect. "Scripture is like mosaic. All pieces of it are important, fixed there by God himself. Yet only when the pieces are in place can we grasp the whole picture."[23] With such an understanding we turn eagerly to the theology and ethics of the Old Testament as sure guides to the fullness of revelation in Jesus Christ.

CHAPTER 46

The Concept of Canon

"People of the book" is the phrase often used to describe Jews, Christians, and Muslims. The two latter groups followed the lead of the Jews for whom the Scriptures were the record of their history, the documents of their law, the testimony of their uniqueness, the guide to their worship, and, above all, the revelation of the one true and living God. The Christian Church was born with a book in its hands; that book which Jesus and his first followers revered was the Hebrew Old Testament. Its documents comprise the first half of the Christian canon. "Canon" comes from a Greek word that means "measuring stick." Since the fourth century A.D. this term has been used in Christian circles to refer to the standard or official list of books that make up the Bible, as a rule of faith and practice for God's people.

> Then he said to them, "These are my words that I spoke to you while I was still with you — that everything written about me in the law of Moses, the prophets, and the psalms must be fulfilled." Luke 24:44

A Tripartite Canon

As the Old Testament portion of this canon, the Hebrew Bible has been traditionally divided into three parts, the Law, the Prophets, and the Writings.[1] Evidence for this arrangement is quite old. About 130 B.C., Ben Sira's grandson, who translated the apocryphal book of Ecclesiasticus, referred to it three times in his prologue. Along with the fixed names "the Law and the Prophets," he variously called the third section, "the other (books) that have followed in their steps," "the other ancestral books," and "the rest of the books." In the first half of the first century A.D. Philo referred to "the Laws and the oracles given by inspiration through the Prophets and the Psalms" (*On the Contemplative Life* 25). "Psalms" appears to be an abbreviated reference to the Writings, as its first book. Similarly, in Luke 24:44 the risen Jesus is reported as speaking of "the law of Moses, the Prophets and the Psalms." Mention may also be made of Matt. 23:35; Luke 11:51, where Jesus pointed to the first and last martyrs in the Old Testament canon: Abel in Genesis and Zechariah in 2 Chronicles (24:20), evidently the last book of the Writings.[2]

Canonical Seams

The Hebrew Bible contains clear markers of the divisions between its three parts.[3] The Pentateuch (Deut. 34:10-12) is rounded off by calling attention to Moses' uniqueness as a divinely authenticated prophet. The section of the Prophets which follows is thus regarded as a supplement to the Torah or Law, which is set on a higher level. On the other side of this division, in Josh. 1:7-8, there is a command to Joshua to study all the law of Moses. Mal. 4:4-6, at the end of the Prophets, endorses the law of Moses, while affirming the eschatological hope to which the Prophets point. In the introductory Ps. 1, at the beginning of the Writings, v. 2 commends the reading of "the law of the LORD." The phrase refers primarily to the psalms which follow, but canonically may have been interpreted in terms of the Pentateuch or indeed the whole of the written revelation in the Old Testament canon.

Two Misconceptions

Earlier scholarship drew two conclusions about the origin and extent of the canon, which more recent study has discarded. First, it was held that the Jewish canon was closed about A.D. 90 at the so-called council of Jabneh or Jamnia. There was a rabbinical school at Jabneh (a town near the Mediterranean coast west and slightly north of Jerusalem) which took over the legislative powers of the Sanhedrin after the fall of Jerusalem in A.D. 70. But the debate about the inspiration of Ecclesiastes and the Song of Songs attested at the meeting had no such official status: the debate continued in rabbinical circles into later times. Rather, the controversy gave evidence of an uneasiness in certain quarters about the presence of these books in an already generally recognized canon.[4] It should be noted that the phrase used in such debates for the inspiration of the canonical books was to "make the hands unclean." This rabbinic ruling, which reflected the value of the books, discouraged irreverent mishandling of them by insisting on the washing of hands after touching them.

The second misconception is the notion that there was a wider canon in Hellenistic Jewish or Alexandrian circles than in Palestine itself. This notion was based on the fact that the fourth and fifth century A.D. codices of the Septuagint variously include books of the Apocrypha, Tobit, Judith, Wisdom, Ecclesiasticus, and the books of Maccabees. However, Philo of Alexandria never cited the Apocrypha. The codices seem to reflect Christian reading habits, including not only canonical books but also what were later called "ecclesiastical" books used for edifying reading at church services.[5]

Canonization

In 2 Macc. 2:14-15 it is stated that, after the devastating war waged against the Jews by Antiochus IV (called Epiphanes) of Syria, Judas Maccabaeus, who led a Jewish revolt against the Syrians, collected together all the books scattered in the war. This activity, about 164 B.C., probably had a decisive role in the canonization of the Hebrew Bible, including an official listing of its canonical books. With this collection may be associated the depositing of the Jewish scriptures in an archive in the Jerusalem temple, which is attested by Josephus and early rabbinical literature.[6]

This official work of Judas Maccabaeus may also be responsible for the incorporation of the book of Daniel, which in its final form appears to reflect a slightly earlier dating in the second century B.C.[7] Appreciation of its valuable

Nash papyrus (first or second century B.C.), containing the Ten Commandments and the Shema (Deut. 6:4-5). *(Cambridge University Library)*

601

role in the recent crisis was thus affirmed. Doubtless the collection of biblical books also permitted the inclusion of the book of Esther, which commemorated earlier persecution and deliverance.[8]

As to earlier stages of canonization, the Pentateuch seems to have been officially recognized in Judah in the period of Ezra (cf. Ezra 7:10, 14, 26; Neh. 8:1-2), who brought the completed document from the exilic community in Babylonia and established its religious and legislative authority among the postexilic community.[9] The general acceptance of the prophetic section of the canon, which includes the history epic of Joshua, Samuel, and Kings (sometimes called Deuteronomistic History), depends on the dating of the relatively late Zech. 9–14.[10]

Twenty-Four or Twenty-Two Books

The earlier accounts of the number of books in the Old Testament canon in Jewish and Jewish-based tradition vary in featuring twenty-four or twenty-two books. The disparity in numbering does not seem to imply any difference in the overall size of the canon. It is probable that the smaller number was a subsequent artificial device, to compare the canon to the number of letters in the Hebrew alphabet. In so doing, the scribes celebrated the totality of the biblical revelation, embracing all God wanted the people to know from A to Z, as it were.[11]

4 Ezra (or 2 Esdras) 14:44-48, which is generally dated about A.D. 100, mentions twenty-four openly published inspired books, in addition to secret sectarian works. In the Babylonian Talmud (*Baba Bathra* 14b) a *baraitha* (or rabbinic tradition) dating from the period A.D. 70-200 cites, apart from the Pentateuch, eight prophetic books and eleven books of the Writings, which gives a total of twenty-four canonical books. The second section is enumerated in the order Joshua, Judges, Samuel, Kings, Jeremiah, Ezekiel, Isaiah, and the Twelve (or the Minor Prophets on one scroll). The order of the Writings is listed as follows: Ruth, Psalms, Job, Proverbs, Ecclesiastes, Song of Songs, Lamentations, Daniel, Esther, Ezra, Chronicles. Ruth was evidently put before Psalms, which was traditionally credited to David, because of its closing Davidic genealogy, while "Ezra" includes the book of Nehemiah.

As for the number twenty-two, it was apparently found first in the first century B.C., in the Greek translation of the book of Jubilees, no copies of which have survived. But quotations from it have been recovered in writings of the Church Fathers from the early Christian centuries.[12] In the last decade of the first century A.D., Josephus (*Against Apion* 1:8) wrote of a twenty-two-book canon, specifying the five books of the law, thirteen books of the prophets, and four books "containing hymns to God and precepts for the conduct of human life." His last section probably consisted of Psalms, Proverbs, Song of Songs, and Ecclesiastes. All of the books in the Writings which were regarded as historical were evidently pushed back into the second section. We do not know whether putting historical books together was due to his own bent as a historian or to a generally accepted view of prophecy as including all inspired historical works.[13] His second section of the canon was probably composed of Job, Joshua, Judges, Samuel, Kings, Isaiah, Jeremiah, Ezekiel, the Twelve, Daniel, Chronicles, Ezra-Nehemiah, and Esther. Ruth was appended to Judges, and Lamentations to Jeremiah. In the early third century A.D. Origen, who was in touch with Jewish tradition, mentioned twenty-two books as the canonical number. At the end of the fourth century Jerome, who received training from Jewish rabbis, also spoke of twenty-two canonical books, in his preface to his Latin translation of Samuel and Kings. He also mentioned an alternative tradition of twenty-four books that listed Ruth and Lamentations separately.

The Old Testament Canon in the Early Church

The Christian Church evidently carried out an important change of order, placing the books of prophetic oracles, from Isaiah onwards, at the end of the Old Testament. The purpose of this change was to pave the way for the added New Testament as the record of the fulfillment of the Old Testament prophecy. Thus about A.D. 170 Melito, bishop of Sardis, having visited Palestine to check the identity of "the books of the old covenant," listed the prophets last. In the early third century Origen gave the Old Testament books in the order that appears in the Christian codices of the Septuagint, namely the law, histories, poetry, and prophecies.

By the fourth century there appeared a rift between the popular custom in the churches of the west and the opinion of scholars like Jerome. The churches used the extra, apocryphal books in the Old Latin version, taken over from the Septuagint codices. Even the council of Hippo in A.D. 393, influenced by Augustine, later bishop of that North African city, did not choose to distinguish between canonical and ecclesiastical (or apocryphal) writings of the Old Testament. On the other hand, the eastern churches of Asia Minor, Palestine, and Egypt tended to keep to the narrower Jewish canon. It was this narrower canon that the Reformers opted for in the sixteenth century, while the Roman Catholic Church endorsed the wider view of the canon at the Council of Trent in 1546.

The Function of Canon

In recent years, a number of scholars have taken into consideration the *function* of the canon of Scripture. While *canon* has traditionally been defined in terms of a completed collection of biblical books, these scholars have been concerned to inquire how the concept of canon affects the reading of its various parts. Brevard S. Childs has emphasized the importance of the final literary form that each of the Old Testament books took when it was recognized as authoritative by the community of faith. In an endeavor to reclaim the Old Testament from academic scholarship for use by the Church, he has deprecated preoccupation with the presumed early stages of the literary text. He has insisted that the canonical shape of each book be respected, in order to establish its essential meaning.[14] Thus, for him it is important that the book associated with the northern prophet Hosea has come down to us in a form edited for Judean readers, as its heading hints (1:1). Likewise, in the Pentateuch he has stressed the final, canonical form of the text as the concern of exegesis, over against a rigid distinction between diverse literary sources.

On the other hand, James A. Sanders has pointed to the dynamic function of canon in terms of the application of its manifold truth to the life of the believing communities who have received it. Thus the Pentateuch in its final form, by being set outside the promised land, was designed to bring its primary message to the Jewish exiles in Babylonia. The Hebrew Bible provides both a stable text and a flexible capacity for adaptation in its interpretation. The same canonical word can address new situations in which God's people find themselves. It has a dual message of challenge and assurance which must be selectively applied. Whether its encouragement or call for repentance is brought to the fore depends on the particular situation of the congregation to whom the word comes.[15]

> The Old Testament speaks on, bringing relevant and indispensable illumination to all who read it as God's word. Failure to do so is to court tragedy — the tragedy of blocking the light without which the New Testament's message of Jesus who is the Christ cannot be clearly discerned.

Canon of the Old Testament

Hebrew Bible (24)	English Bible (Protestant) (39)	English Bible (Catholic) (46)
TORAH (5)	LAW (5)	LAW (5)
Genesis	Genesis	Genesis
Exodus	Exodus	Exodus
Leviticus	Leviticus	Leviticus
Numbers	Numbers	Numbers
Deuteronomy	Deuteronomy	Deuteronomy
PROPHETS (8)	HISTORY (12)	HISTORY (14)
Former Prophets (4)	Joshua	Josue (Joshua)*
Joshua	Judges	Judges
Judges	Ruth	Ruth
1-2 Samuel	1 Samuel	1 Kings (1 Samuel)
1-2 Kings	2 Samuel	2 Kings (2 Samuel)
Latter Prophets	1 Kings	3 Kings (1 Kings)
Isaiah	2 Kings	4 Kings (2 Kings)
Jeremiah	1 Chronicles	1 Paralipomenon (1 Chr.)
Ezekiel	2 Chronicles	2 Paralipomenon (2 Chr.)
The Twelve	Ezra	Esdras-Nehemias (Ezra, Neh.)
Hosea	Nehemiah	Tobias (Tobit)
Joel	Esther	Judith
Amos		Esther
Obadiah	POETRY (5)	
Jonah	Job	POETICAL AND WISDOM (7)
Micah	Psalms	Job
Nahum	Proverbs	Psalms
Habakkuk	Ecclesiastes	Proverbs
Zephaniah	Song of Solomon	Ecclesiastes
Haggai		Canticle of Canticles
Zechariah	MAJOR PROPHETS (5)	Wisdom of Solomon
Malachi	Isaiah	Ecclesiasticus (Sirach)
	Jeremiah	
WRITINGS (11)	Lamentations	PROPHETICAL LITERATURE (20)
'Emeth (Truth) (3)	Ezekiel	Isaias (Isaiah)
Psalms	Daniel	Jeremias (Jeremiah)
Proverbs		Lamentations
Job	MINOR PROPHETS (12)	Baruch
Megilloth (Scrolls) (5)	Hosea	Ezechiel (Ezekiel)
Song of Solomon	Joel	Daniel
Ruth	Amos	Osee (Hosea)
Lamentations	Obadiah	Joel
Ecclesiastes	Jonah	Amos
Esther	Micah	Abdias (Obadiah)
Daniel	Nahum	Jonas (Jonah)
Ezra-Nehemiah	Habakkuk	Micheas (Micah)
1-2 Chronicles	Zephaniah	Nahum
	Haggai	Habacuc (Habakkuk)
	Zechariah	Sophonias (Zephaniah)
	Malachi	Aggeus (Haggai)
		Zecharias (Zechariah)
		Malachias (Malachi)
		1 Machabees
		(1 Maccabees)
		2 Machabees
		(2 Maccabees)

*Recent editions of the Catholic Bible and some recent Roman Catholic writers have conformed to the names as used in the RSV.

CHAPTER 47

Formation of the Old Testament

The printed Old Testament has a lengthy history. A product of a distant time and place, it has come through a centuries-long process of editing, collecting, copying, and translating. Documents from dozens of authors spanning almost a millennium have been combined and transmitted by devoted but fallible hands. In what languages did the biblical writers speak and write? Are present Bibles accurate representations of the original documents? How important are the ancient translations in helping to recover the meaning of passages obscured by scores of copyists? On what basis were the Old Testament books chosen? Have recent discoveries like the Dead Sea Scrolls forced changes in attitudes toward the accuracy or authority of the Bible? These and many other questions arise as one considers the complex process through which God's providence allowed the Old Testament to pass before reaching the present.

> This word came to Jeremiah from the LORD: "Take a scroll and write on it all the words that I have spoken to you." . . . Then Jeremiah called Baruch son of Neriah, and Baruch wrote on a scroll at Jeremiah's dictation all the words of the LORD that he had spoken to him. Jer. 36:1-2, 4

Languages

The two languages of the Old Testament, Hebrew and Aramaic, are members of the family of kindred languages called "Semitic," a word derived from the name of Noah's son Shem.[1] Although any classification has its pitfalls, grouping them geographically is sometimes helpful:[2]

Northeast Semitic	Northwest Semitic	Southeast Semitic	Southwest Semitic
Babylonian	Aramaic	Old South Arabic	Arabic
Assyrian[3]	Amorite	Ethiopic	
Eblaite[4]	Moabite		
	Phoenician		
	Ugaritic		
	Hebrew		

The Olympian achievements among linguists and philologists of the past century or so have placed scholars today in a better position to interpret the Scriptures in terms of their language and cultural setting than any previous generation in the history of the Church.

Hebrew. The affinities between Hebrew and the other Canaanite languages are recognized by the Old Testament itself, for one of the names applied to it is literally "lip of Canaan" (Isa. 19:18). The patriarchal narratives in Genesis suggest that Abraham's family spoke Aramaic and that the patriarch and his descendants learned a Canaanite dialect when they settled in Canaan. For example, Jacob called the stone pile in Gen. 31:47 by a Hebrew name, while Laban used Aramaic. Particularly helpful for understanding the Hebrew language have been numerous Phoenician inscriptions from the time of the Hebrew monarchy (tenth to sixth centuries B.C.), the Moabite stone (an excellent illustration of the kinship between Hebrew and Moabite), and the Ugaritic tablets from Ras Shamra on the northern Syrian coast. Of the three, Ugaritic has made the most substantial contribution to the knowledge of Hebrew and of Old Testament life and literature because of both the quality and quantity of its literature. The importance of these kindred languages is heightened by the discouraging scarcity of Hebrew texts contemporary with the Old Testament.[5]

The earliest Hebrew texts were written in the Paleo-Hebrew script, which was borrowed and adapted from the Phoenicians. The forms of its letters are very similar to those of the Phoenician and Moabite inscriptions mentioned above. The Paleo-Hebrew script apparently gave way to the square type of writing more characteristic of Aramaic about 200 B.C., although the ancient

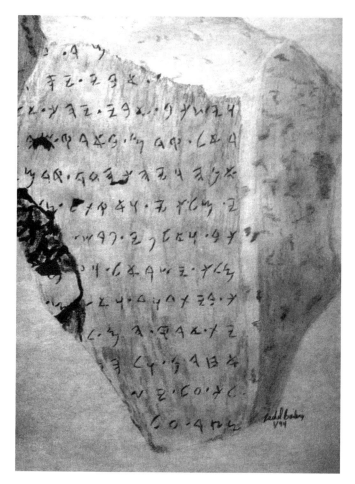

Inscription from Tel Dan stele (early ninth century B.C.)
which mentions "the king of Israel . . . of the
house of David." *(Rachel Bierling)*

style is found on occasion in the Dead Sea Scrolls, particularly in referring to
the divine name Yahweh. Early manuscripts contained consonants only, the
vocalic pronunciation being supplied by the reader.[6]

The written vowels (or vowel points) which appear in printed Hebrew
Bibles were added shortly after A.D. 500 by the Masoretes, a group of Jewish
scholars who were able to stabilize the pronunciation of biblical Hebrew as
they understood it.

However, ancient translations of the Old Testament, together with nonbiblical evidence such as Canaanite words in the Amarna letters,[7] suggest that
the traditional pronunciation of the Masoretes differs at many points from

608

that of the original biblical speakers. As a matter of fact, it is probable that dialect variations originally existed in biblical Hebrew but have been obscured by the Masoretic attempts at standardization. The work of the Masoretes has also made it difficult to track the ways in which Hebrew changed through the centuries during which the Bible was composed.

Hebrew words, like those of other Semitic languages, are usually based on roots containing three consonants. Various vowel patterns together with the addition of prefixes and suffixes determine the semantic significance of the word. For example, words based on the root *mlk* include *melek* "king," *malkâ* "queen," *malkût* "rulership," *mālak* "he ruled," and *mamlākâ* "kingdom."

The verbal system differs in some fundamental ways from other more familiar languages. For instance, there are two basic tenses, perfect and imperfect, which actually denote kind of action (i.e., whether completed or not completed) rather than time distinctions (usually determined from the context). Hebrew grammar tends to be direct and simple, especially in sentence structure. For instance, coordinate clauses are found far more commonly than the subordination familiar in English.

Aramaic. When the Assyrian empire began to push west in the middle of the eighth century, Aramaic was adopted as the official language of diplomacy and commerce. During the heyday of the Persian empire (*ca.* 500) it was the second, if not the first, tongue of the peoples of the Near East from Egypt to Persia. The Hellenizing conquests of Alexander spread Greek throughout this area, but it supplanted Aramaic only partially and gradually, as the New Testament suggests.[8]

Aramaic had a lengthy history before becoming the *lingua franca* of the Middle East. For this reason scholars have become increasingly cautious about branding passages in the Hebrew Bible as "late" on the basis of Aramaic words occurring in them. Indeed, some scholars point to an Aramaic word (i.e., the word translated "repeat" in the NRSV, Judg. 5:11) in one of the earliest poems in the Bible, the Song of Deborah (*ca.* 1150).

The book of Genesis testifies to the close relationship between Hebrew and Aramaic-speaking peoples early in the Old Testament (e.g., Gen. 31:47). Aramaic was known to Judah's court officers well before the Exile (note the conversation between Hezekiah's delegation and the Assyrian Rabshakeh, *ca.* 701; 2 Kgs. 18:17-37). Later it was adopted as the first language of many commoners during the Captivity and afterwards. Thus, the authors of Ezra and Daniel felt no need to furnish translations of the lengthy Aramaic passages in their writings.

Text

Materials and Methods of Writing. The scroll or roll was the standard form in which the Scriptures were preserved in Old Testament times.[9] The Dead Sea Scrolls are a good indication of the nature of ancient rolls and the methods of writing employed. Made of carefully prepared leather (parchment), the scrolls are composed of many pieces sewn together and carefully scraped. The Isaiah scroll (1QIsa[a]), for instance, comprises seventeen leaves sewn together to make a roll about 24 feet long. The scribe took pains to mark both horizontal and perpendicular lines on the leather to serve as guides for the lines and columns (cf. Jer. 36:23) and to assure neatness.

However, the earliest biblical documents were probably written on papyrus. It was used in Egypt as early as the third millennium and was exported to Phoenicia by 1100 at the latest. The material for these rolls was prepared by splitting the papyrus reeds and laying one layer of reeds on top of another at right angles. The natural gum of the papyrus served as glue for the crossed strips of each section and for the number of sections joined together to make a scroll. The scribes wrote only on the inside of the scroll, using the horizontal strips as guide lines. Although the Harris papyrus measures more than 120 feet, scrolls longer than about 30 feet were difficult to make and awkward to handle. This fact may help to account for the division of some Old Testament books into two parts (Samuel, Kings, Chronicles).

The more formal writing was on papyrus, but many other materials were used, generally for shorter messages: tablets of wood, wax, or clay, and fragments of broken pottery (ostraca; sing. ostracon). Papyrus is extremely perishable. This makes unlikely any substantial discoveries of papyrus scrolls in Israel or Jordan, where the climate, unlike Egypt's, is too moist to allow their survival.[10] The transition from papyrus to leather apparently took place in the late pre-Christian centuries. The use of codices (books) instead of scrolls dates from about the first century A.D. The introduction of book form greatly facilitated the circulation of the Scriptures because, for the first time, many documents could be contained in a manageable volume.

The instruments of writing in antiquity varied greatly and were determined largely by the system of writing employed. Cuneiform, for instance, was either carved in stone with a chisel (for many permanent or public documents) or inscribed on clay tablets with a stylus. The customary implements in Israel were apparently the reed pen, whose point probably was sharpened and split with a pen knife. Jeremiah, however, mentions an iron pen with a diamond point (17:1), which may have been used for writing on harder materials. The ink for the reed pens was made from the lampblack of olive oil lamps and, much later, from various metallic powders. The amazing durability of nonmetallic ink is demonstrated by the Qumran scrolls and, centuries earlier, by the Lachish letters.

Standardization of the Text. A chief problem of biblical scholarship is that none of the original writings (sometimes called the *autographa*) of Scripture has survived. All we possess are copies. For the most part scribes were attempting to copy the text accurately. Yet ancient manuscripts of the Old Testament in Hebrew and in translation indicate that a certain amount of freedom must have prevailed among the scribes who copied the biblical documents in the pre-Christian centuries. Moreover, as human beings they were bound to commit errors despite their concern and care. Centuries of copying and sometimes even editing have allowed changes, or variant readings, to be introduced into the text.

It is apparent why some mistakes were inevitable. Both the Paleo-Hebrew script and the later square alphabet contain letters which can be confused because they look alike. In addition, earlier manuscripts lacked vowels or punctuation. They did not have even verse or chapter markings. Without these things there are ambiguities which can spawn problems in transmission. A scribe might make a subjective judgment about the meaning and then supply an explanatory word or phrase, or perhaps rearrange elements to clarify the passage. Occasionally a copyist would substitute a more common word for an obscure one. Furthermore, as the Hebrew letters *yôd*, *wāw*, and *hē* gradually

Inkwells from the scriptorium at Qumran (first century A.D.).
(Israel Department of Antiquities)

were utilized as vowel markers, the possibility of errors in spelling increased. In cases where the scroll was read aloud to a room of scribes, auditory mistakes could arise.

The science (and art) of textual criticism is the task of spotting the errors and restoring the Hebrew and Aramaic texts to a form as close to the original as possible. Scholars carefully compare the available manuscripts to examine and evaluate the variant readings. How can a scholar know which reading is an error? Sometimes it is obvious that a scribe has unwittingly repeated a letter, word, or phrase. This is known as dittography. The opposite is haplography: failing to repeat something in the copy which is found twice in the source manuscript.[11] Brief sections may have been omitted by homoioteleuton (Greek for "similar ending"), when a scribe's eye skipped from one phrase to another with a similar ending, omitting the intervening material. When something is left out because of a similar beginning the error is called homoioarchton.

At times, as in the case of Jeremiah's book (see Ch. 24), two or more separate editions seem to have existed simultaneously. Explanatory notes or other marginal comments by one scribe may have been included within the text by another. Again, one scribe's textual omissions crowded into the margin or between the lines may have been regarded as glosses and left out by his successor. Theological prejudice accounts for a few changes, such as the substitution of *bōšet* ("shame") for the element *ba'al* ("Baal" or "lord") in some proper names in the books of Samuel.[12] Another possible source of variation is oral tradition. Sections of the text may have been transmitted orally in forms somewhat different from the written version. In other cases two or more oral forms may have been preserved in the text when reduced to writing.[13]

After the destruction of Jerusalem in A.D. 70, Judaism was threatened by decentralization associated with the loss of the temple and by Christian evangelism throughout the Mediterranean world. Rabbis and scribes took definite steps to standardize the text for study and worship. Christians began to use the LXX, the Septuagint or Greek Old Testament, cherished for years by Jews in the Diaspora. This sparked Jewish opposition to the LXX and increased Jewish loyalty to every word of the Hebrew text. A driving force behind the movement to standardize the text was Rabbi Akiba (died *ca.* A.D. 135), a vigorous opponent of Christianity and a meticulous scholar of the Hebrew scriptures. The exact results of Akiba's textual endeavors are shrouded in antiquity, but he likely established a text which, with considerable modification in details, has persisted until today. At the same time that the consonantal text of the Hebrew Bible was being established in the second century A.D., much effort was also being expended to revise and standardize the LXX.[14]

While the scribes edited and transmitted the text, the Masoretes (see above) ensured its careful preservation. Appearing about A.D. 500, they carried on the scribal practice of making textual notes in the manuscript margins. The letters, words, and verses of each book were counted carefully, and a note was added at the close of each book to summarize the totals for the book. This final masora (lit. "tradition") contained mnemonic devices by which each new copy of the scroll could be checked for accuracy.

In printed Hebrew Bibles the basic text is that of ben Asher, who flourished in Tiberias during the tenth century.[15] Thanks to the millennium-long process of standardization, the variations among the available manuscripts, including the Qumran scrolls, are often minor and have little bearing on the theological teachings of the Old Testament.

The Practice of Textual Criticism. Few disciplines in Old Testament studies call for as much discernment as textual criticism. More than with the New Testament, for which manuscripts are both more abundant and closer to the date of origin, the Old Testament presents severe problems to the textual scholar. The chief problem is to get behind the attempted standardization which began in the early Christian centuries.[16] Such efforts have been frustrated frequently by the scarcity of early manuscripts. Before the discovery of the Dead Sea Scrolls the earliest complete Hebrew manuscripts dated from the tenth century A.D. Adding to the problems are the difficulties which obscure Hebrew words and phrases posed for the early translators into Greek, Syriac, and Latin. Although these and other ancient translations offer considerable aid in reconstructing the earliest Hebrew text, they sometimes fail just at those points where help with an unclear passage is needed most. It seems that the ancient translators on occasion were as baffled as their modern counterparts by the Hebrew Bible.

How then does a textual critic recover the original reading where Hebrew manuscripts or ancient translations offer variant readings or where the Masoretic Text (MT) is itself puzzling? One must carefully weigh all the evidence to determine which is the earliest and best reading. It is important to determine each case on its own merits, for in one verse a certain Greek manuscript may be more reliable, while in another the scales may tip in favor of a Qumran reading. Other times the MT is superior.[17] It is very tedious and time-consuming to compare meticulously all the ancient versions; both church and synagogue owe a great debt of gratitude to those who have labored in the field of textual criticism.

Not all the ancient versions, however, carry the same weight. A version dependent on another (sometimes called a "secondary" or "daughter" version) is not of equal authority with the primary versions based on the Hebrew text. Furthermore, each version has its own textual problems: parts may have been translated more accurately or based on more reliable Hebrew manuscripts. When confronted with several reasonably reliable readings, one may employ certain rules of thumb. First, the more difficult reading is usually to be preferred because scribes and translators tend to smooth out rough passages.

Similarly, the shorter reading frequently is preferable, since copyists are more apt to add glosses to the text than omit authentic phrases or sentences. A third, and extremely important, principle is to accept that reading as authentic which best accounts for all the other variants.

One must assume that what the author of a given passage wrote originally made sense. If all attempts to restore the text based on the evidence of variant readings have led to an impasse, one may be justified in guessing what the text must have said. But then one must readily admit the high degree of tentativeness of such conjectures. Happily, the day is past when biblical scholars emended the text on a whim. Caution is more and more the watchword. Readings are adopted and emendations suggested only on the basis of careful textual and linguistic analyses.

A word of reassurance: at no point is the basic teaching of the Old Testament in question. Readers of the various Hebrew texts and the ancient versions heard and responded to the word of God just as we moderns do to our translations. The precise meanings of some words are in doubt (several hundred Hebrew words are difficult to define with confidence because they occur only once or twice in the Bible), and the exact form of the Hebrew text is questionable in many passages. Nevertheless, biblical scholars are able to reconstruct the probable meaning in a vast majority of the difficult passages, and the message of virtually every section of the Old Testament is clear. The Old Testament, which God has seen fit to preserve, can be relied upon as his word in all its truth and authenticity.

Ancient Versions

The term "ancient versions" refers to a number of translations of the Old Testament made during the late pre-Christian and early Christian centuries. The scarcity of ancient Hebrew manuscripts makes these versions highly important as witnesses to early textual traditions. Their historic roles in aiding the spread of the Jewish and Christian faiths should not be underestimated.

Samaritan Pentateuch. Though the details of the final breach between Jews and Samaritans are hazy, a complete cleavage certainly had developed by *ca.* 350 B.C. The hostility between them is well known from the New Testament (cf. John 4:7, 42). By about 100 B.C. the Samaritans had developed their own form of the Pentateuch. Their community never accepted the Prophets and Writings which have become parts of the Jewish and Christian canon.

Although not strictly a version, the Samaritan Pentateuch (which still is treasured by the tiny community at Nablus, near ancient Shechem) preserves an old form of the Hebrew text. How independent it is from the MT and how it relates to the LXX are matters of ongoing debate.[18] Most of the approximately six thousand variations from the MT are matters of spelling or grammar. Both Jews and Samaritans may have made slight alterations in the text to refute the claims of the other. For example, in Deut. 27:4 MT *Ebal* is, in the Samaritan, *Gerizim,* the sacred mountain of Samaria; cf. John 4:20. Similarly, in more than a score of passages in Deuteronomy (e.g., 12:5, 11, 14, 18; 14:23, 25), MT "the place which the LORD your God *will choose*" is altered to *"has chosen"* to show that the sacred mountain is Gerizim, not Zion (which did not fall into Israelite hands until David's time).

Although no really accurate critical edition survives, the Samaritan text is useful as a confirmation of certain ancient readings in the versions, notably the LXX, with which it agrees against the MT in nearly two thousand instances. Many of these involve a correction in spelling. For example, MT *Dodanim* should be *Rodanim* in Gen. 10:4; cf. LXX and 1 Chr. 1:7. In Gen. 22:13, MT "and behold a ram behind" should read "and behold one ram"; cf. LXX. These alterations involve a change in one Hebrew word from *r* to *d,* in letters which resemble each other closely in both the Phoenician and the square script. Others imply the omission of a word. For example, Gen. 15:21, with LXX, probably should be read "and the Girgashite, *and the Hivite,* and the Jebusite." Occasionally an entire phrase may have been omitted from the MT and may be restored from the Samaritan and the LXX, as with Cain's statement "Let us go out to the field" in Gen. 4:8, NRSV.[19]

Aramaic Targums. The inroads which Aramaic made on Hebrew as the spoken language after the return from exile made necessary an Aramaic translation to accompany the synagogue readings. Originally oral, these targums (Heb. *targumîm*) probably began to assume written form shortly before the Christian era. Their history is difficult to trace, but the major problems that impede use of the written targums in textual studies are the lack of good critical editions and their tendency to become paraphrases or commentaries rather than translations.[20]

The most important and most faithful translation is the Targum of Onkelos,[21] the official synagogue rendering of the Pentateuch. Of some use in textual criticism in corroborating other versions, Onkelos is more important as a witness to the Jewish attitude toward the Old Testament. Its lengthy history (portions from Palestine as early as the beginning of the Christian period, final editing probably in fourth or fifth century A.D. Babylonia) has permitted insertion of brief comments or interpretative glosses, which illuminate the growth of Judaism but are of little value in textual criticism.

Contrasted with Onkelos is the Jerusalem Targum I, sometimes called "Pseudo-Jonathan." It was written in a Palestinian dialect of Aramaic and completed about the seventh century A.D. Though it contains some earlier material, its translation of the Law is cluttered with Jewish traditions and legal instructions. It is therefore even less useful to the textual critic than Targum Onkelos.[22]

The main Aramaic translation of the prophets, the Targum of Jonathan,[23] took shape in Babylonia in about the fifth century A.D., adapted from a Palestinian version. It takes greater liberties with the text than Onkelos, particularly in the Latter Prophets where the poetry required extended paraphrase.

The targums to the Writings are many and varied. Most are paraphrases rather than translations, and their late date (seventh century A.D. and after) curtails their usefulness for textual studies.

The Samaritans also produced a targum to their Pentateuch. Its survival in several different forms, with no official edition yet discovered, is a witness to the fluidity of ancient texts and to the freedom with which early translators sometimes handled biblical materials.[24]

Septuagint (LXX). The history of the LXX is not only shrouded in antiquity but also clouded by Jewish and Christian legends which stress its miraculous origin. According to these legends the translators worked in isolation from each other and yet produced translations which agreed verbatim. Named after the traditional number of translators (Lat. *septuaginta* "seventy," thus LXX), it seems to have originated among the Jewish community in Alexandria between 250 and 100 B.C. The largest single question among LXX scholars has been whether an authoritative translation that gave rise to many revisions ever existed. Some have argued the negative and likened its development to that of the targums: various unofficial translations were made as the need arose, with the text somewhat standardized in early Christian times, when it became the Church's authoritative Old Testament. Others, who now seem to be in the majority, find in the multitude of revisions evidence of an original translation.[25]

The LXX exhibits considerable variety in theological outlook and in literalness and accuracy of translation, so its readings cannot be accepted haphazardly. Nevertheless, it is of crucial significance in textual studies, since it represents a form of the Hebrew text prior to the standardizing which took place in the early Christian centuries. In connection with the Samaritan Pentateuch and the Dead Sea manuscripts, it is the most valuable witness to the pre-Masoretic forms of the Hebrew text.

Other Greek Versions. As Christians used the LXX more and more, Jewish communities in the Diaspora turned to other Greek translations. Early in the second century A.D., Aquila, a gentile convert to Judaism and perhaps a disciple of Rabbi Akiba, produced a wooden, literal rendering which rigidly adhered to the text and so was rapidly and avidly embraced by many Jews. Unfortunately, only fragments of his work have survived.

Toward the end of the same century, Theodotion, apparently also a proselyte, revised an older translation, producing a version which proved more popular with Christians than with Jews. Apart from his translation of Daniel, which has virtually replaced the LXX, only fragments remain. These works, as well as Symmachus' superior translation (also late second century A.D.), are known through the surviving fragments of Origen's *Hexapla* (*ca.* A.D. 220), a monumental attempt at textual criticism in which the Hebrew text and various versions were recorded carefully in parallel columns for comparison.

Syriac Version. Usually called Peshitta (or Peshitto; interpreted as "simple," i.e., like *koiné* or *Vulgate,* the accepted version of the "common" people), the translation into Syriac (a dialect of Aramaic) apparently took place in the early centuries of the Christian era. Its value for textual studies is limited by several factors. First, parts of the Pentateuch seem to be dependent on the Palestinian targum. Also, the influence of the LXX is apparent in some passages, so agreements between the two sometimes may be considered only a single witness to an ancient reading. Our ability to assess the Peshitta's contribution to Old Testament studies has been considerably enhanced by the publication of a critical edition now underway.[26]

Latin Versions. Latin translations were first necessary not in Rome (where the learned used Greek) but in North Africa and southern Gaul. Based on the LXX, the Old Latin translations (*ca.* A.D. 150) are more valuable as witnesses to the Greek text than as aids in clarifying the Hebrew. Knowledge of the Old Latin tradition is limited to quotations by the Latin Church Fathers, brief manuscripts, and some medieval liturgical books and Bibles.[27]

The variety of the many Old Latin translations posed for the Latin Church the problem of which text to use in liturgy and theological conversation. Pope Damasus I (*ca.* A.D. 382) commissioned the gifted scholar Jerome to produce an authoritative version. Substantial parts of Jerome's translation are based on the Hebrew text, although other sections, notably the Psalms, rely on the Greek versions. His use of the Hebrew made his translation suspect for some time, even by his friend Augustine, but the suspicion was ill-founded. Jerome worked cautiously and, in perplexing passages, leaned heavily upon the LXX, Aquila, Theodotion, and especially Symmachus, as well as the accepted Old Latin.

The composite origin of Jerome's "Vulgate" ("accepted by the common people" or "popular") limits it for textual criticism. Its readings are usually dependent on the MT or on one of the principle versions. In other words, it rarely preserves an independent witness to a more pristine form of the text. Furthermore, because Jerome's version was not accepted as authoritative for centuries (not officially until the Council of Trent in 1546) it was susceptible to editorial alteration influenced by the other Latin translations. So the Vulgate — still the authorized Roman Catholic version[28] — requires a great deal of caution when one uses its readings to correct the MT.

Other Secondary Versions. The other main Old Testament translations are important testimonies to the widespread outreach of Christianity and the zeal of missionaries to transmit the word of God in the vernacular. All of these secondary versions are more important for reconstructing the histories of the texts on which they were based than in correcting the Hebrew text.

Based on the LXX, the *Coptic translations* were produced in about the third and fourth centuries A.D. for the peasant population of Egypt. Though written in a form of the Greek alphabet and employing many Greek loan-words, Coptic is the latest stage of the Egyptian language. The diverse dialects called for several translations, particularly Sahidic ("Upper," i.e., Southern Egyptian), Akhmimic, and Bohairic ("Lower," i.e., Northern Egyptian), which became the dominant dialect still in liturgical use today in the Coptic Orthodox churches. Many fourth- and fifth-century manuscripts have been preserved by the dry Egyptian climate.

By contrast, manuscripts of the *Ethiopic translation* date from the thirteenth century and later, although translating may have begun by the end of the fourth century. Most extant manuscripts seem to depend on the LXX but have been altered under the influence of medieval Arabic versions. Apart from individual books or sections, no reliable critical edition exists.

Even later are the *Armenian and Arabic versions.* The Armenian dates from the fifth century and seems to be based on both the Peshitta and the LXX. Rather than one standard translation, the Arabic represents a rash of versions which sprang up in Egypt, Babylon, and Palestine, drawn from an assortment of accessible versions — Hebrew or Samaritan, LXX, Peshitta, and Coptic. The earliest may be pre-Islamic (*ca.* A.D. 600), but most are later by several centuries.[29]

CHAPTER 48

Geography

Because God's revelation took place in space and time, hundreds of place names appear in Scripture. The primary stage of the drama of human salvation was Canaan, "the Promised Land," with scenes occurring in Mesopotamia (modern Iraq), Persia (Iran), Syria, Lebanon, and Egypt. Awareness of the geography of this area is essential for an understanding of the biblical message.

The Bible World

Palestine is the land bridge connecting Europe, Asia, and Africa. "The Fertile Crescent" is one name of the arable strip of land bordering the Syrian desert, i.e., the lands along the Tigris-Euphrates rivers in Mesopotamia and the coastal lands of the eastern Mediterranean (the Levant). The southwestern end of this crescent included Palestine. Palestine, though, was historically the poorest part of the Fertile Crescent. Its territory was very narrow, lacking any major navigable rivers. The overland routes which connected these three continents, nevertheless, made Palestine a hub of commerce and marching armies. Thus ancient Israel's history took place on center stage in the Near East.

From the Atlantic Ocean to southeastern Asia runs an almost continuous belt of mountains — the Pyrenees, Alps, Balkans, Caucasus, Elburz, Hindu Kush, and Himalayan ranges. These mountains held back the cold winter winds and gave the lands to the south a pleasant climate. They also deterred invasions from the north. To the south the deserts (the Sahara,

Syrian, and Arabian deserts) served as a barrier to invaders. As a result, the Mediterranean world, the Mesopotamian region, the foothills of the Iranian plateau, and the Indus river valley became the "cradle of civilization" — the area in which the human family progressed from savage hunter-fishers to civilized food producers.

Palestine

Name. Palestine gets its name from the tribe *Pelishtim* (Philistines), a tribe numbered among the Sea Peoples. They settled along the southern coast in the twelfth century B.C. In the fifth century Herodotus referred to the area as "Philistine Syria."[1] This name, however, is not used in the Old Testament,[2] which prefers "the land of Canaan" from its principal inhabitants, the Canaanites. With the Israelite settlement, it began to be called "Israel" or "the land of Israel" (1 Sam. 13:19, etc.). The term Holy Land (cf. Zech. 2:12) came into common use in the Middle Ages in connection with the Crusades.

Extent and Significance. The advantage of using the name Palestine over Israel or Canaan is that it includes the land on both sides of the Jordan River, i.e., Cisjordan (west) and Transjordan (east).[3] Palestine extends from the southern slopes of Mt. Hermon, the highest mountain in the area (9,230 ft. [2,814 m.]), to the edge of the southern desert (the Negeb), bounded on the west by the Mediterranean (or Western) Sea and on the east by the Arabian steppe. This is the land "from Dan to Beersheba" (Judg. 20:1; 1 Sam. 3:20).

God's promise to Abraham, however, included an area larger than Palestine. Gen. 17:8 mentions simply "all the land of Canaan," but in other places the land of promise extends north as far as "the entrance of Hamath" (in modern Syria) and south to "the river of Egypt" (Wâdī el-ʿArîsh in northern Sinai; Wâdī is a watercourse that is dry except in the rainy season; cf. Num. 34:1-12). Under David and Solomon, Israel reached its greatest extent, occupying most of this territory plus much of Transjordan, even though the promise did not include it (Num. 34:12).

North-South Divisions. Geographers have shown that the geological structure of this Levantine region is mainly northeast-southwest.[4] It is more important here to note the more obvious north-south features. These four features are from west to east: (1) the coastal plain, (2) the western (or "central") mountain range, (3) the rift valley system, and (4) the Transjordan mountain range or plateau which gradually slopes east to the Syrian and Arabian deserts. Palestine is considerably wider (from east to west) at its southern end,[5] so some variations in this general pattern may be expected.

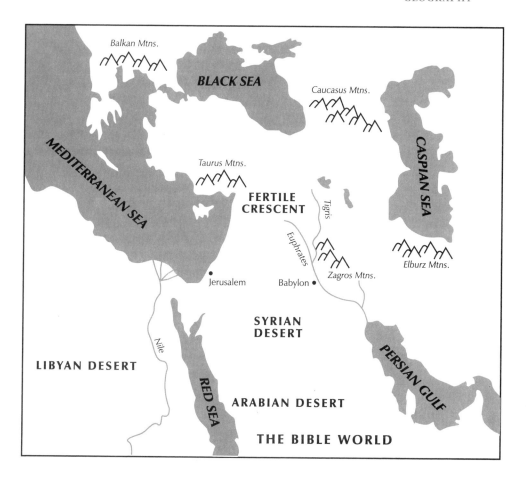

Balkan Mtns.

BLACK SEA

Caucasus Mtns.

MEDITERRANEAN SEA

CASPIAN SEA

Taurus Mtns.

**FERTILE
CRESCENT**

Tigris

Euphrates

Elburz Mtns.

Zagros Mtns.

• Jerusalem

Babylon •

**SYRIAN
DESERT**

Nile

LIBYAN DESERT

PERSIAN GULF

RED SEA

ARABIAN DESERT

THE BIBLE WORLD

621

1. *The coastal plain* is narrow in the north, becoming nonexistent at the Ladder of Tyre (the present Israeli-Lebanese boundary) and at the foot of Mt. Carmel (Haifa). In the south, the coastal plain is broad and divided into three regions: (1) the Plain of Asher (between the Ladder of Tyre and Mt. Carmel), (2) the Plain of Sharon (south of Mt. Carmel to Joppa or Tel Aviv), and (3) the Philistine plain (Joppa to Gaza). There were few natural seaports along the coastal plain. Acco (Acre), Dor, and Joppa were the principal ones in antiquity.

With limited access to the sea during much of its history, Israel never became a maritime power. Mediterranean shipping in the Levant was dominated by the Phoenicians, who lived on the coast of Lebanon, and the best ports were from Acco north — Tyre and Sidon being the most famous. Israel's major maritime adventures were joint efforts with the Phoenicians. The southern port at Ezion-geber on the Gulf of Aqaba served as a gateway to harbors on the Red Sea and possibly the east coast of Africa (1 Kgs. 10:26-28).

In the coastal plain a major north-south highway from Egypt to Damascus and on to Mesopotamia followed the coast. Often it was located several miles inland because of numerous marshes and sand dunes. It is called the Via Maris, "the Way of the Sea" (cf. Isa. 9:1).

2. *The central mountain range* forms the backbone of the land. It is broken only at the Plain of Jezreel (or Esdraelon) in lower Galilee. A spur of the central range juts northwest to the sea to form the beautiful Carmel range. Before the Carmel range the Via Maris turned inland traversing through the narrow pass of Wâdî ʿAra. It was guarded at its entrance into the plain of Jezreel by the town of Megiddo. At Megiddo a spur turned north to the Phoenician cities. Several shorter, but more difficult, roads crossed the north-south ridge of the central range.

The Plain of Jezreel, the widest and most fertile valley in Palestine, separates the hilly region to the north from the mountains to the south. The northern region is best known as Galilee. The region to the south does not have a clear-cut natural boundary before the steppe or Negeb. Following political division of the land during the Israelite kingdom, the southern region may be divided into Samaria and Judea. South of the Negeb is the Sinai peninsula.

(a) *Galilee.* The natural boundary north of Galilee is the gorge of the Litani River to the northwest and Mt. Hermon to the northeast. The southern boundary is formed by the Carmel range to the southwest and Gilboa, a hill-cluster, to the southeast. Upper Galilee is mountainous, with elevations often above 3,000 ft. (914 m.). Lower Galilee to the south is composed of rolling hills and broad valleys, sloping south to the broad Esdraelon plain. Galilee comes from a Hebrew word meaning "the region of," and clearly is only part of a phrase, so the original name may have been "the region of the Gentiles" (Isa. 9:1).

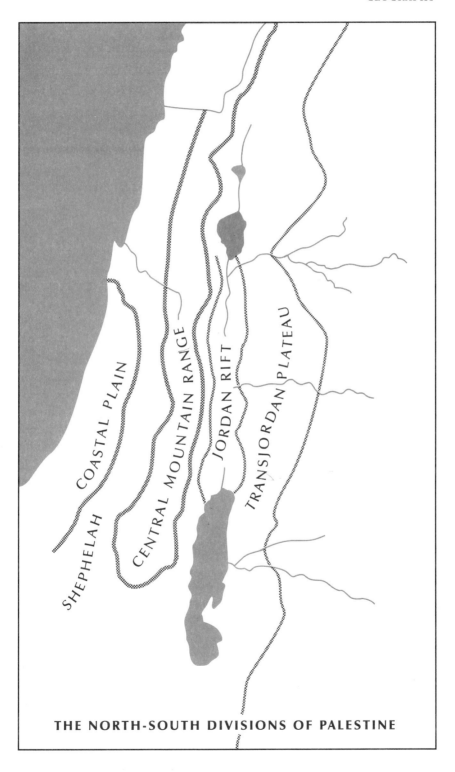

THE NORTH-SOUTH DIVISIONS OF PALESTINE

(b) *Samaria.* The northern boundary of Samaria is the Plain of Esdraelon. The eastern boundary is the Jordan, and the Mediterranean forms the western limits. Samaria has no clear natural southern boundary, but the town of Bethel is known to have been near the southern limits (1 Kgs. 12:29f.). Most of Samaria is mountainous; the general elevation is around 2,000 ft. (610 m.), with a few mountains reaching to some 3,000 ft. (915 m.). Western Samaria sloped down to the maritime plain. The arid eastern part drops quickly to the Jordan. The hills produce fruits such as olives, grapes, and pomegranates and provide grazing for flocks. Interspersed among the hills are wide, fertile valleys, which are excellent for growing grain. The land is watered principally by the seasonal rains.

The name Samaria comes from the capital city, which was built by Omri (1 Kgs. 16:24). Before the building of Samaria, Shechem was the most important city. After the Assyrians conquered Samaria (722 B.C.), they deported the Israelites most likely to revolt — the religious and political leaders — while at the same time settling captives from other nations in Samaria. From the intermingling of these captives with the indigenous Israelites came the mixed population known as the Samaritans (cf. 2 Kgs. 17:6, 24; Neh. 4:2; John 4:9).

(c) *Judah.* The region from the lower border of Samaria south to the Negeb is generally called Judea. This name properly belongs to the New Testament period. It is derived from Judah, the principal tribe. Jerusalem to the north and Hebron to the south were the key cities. The mountainous area is somewhat higher and more rocky than Samaria. The valleys are narrow, stoney, and often arid. Judea is much less fertile than Samaria. Olive trees and vineyards grow in terraced areas, and grain can be raised in some valleys and on the plateau around Bethlehem.

To the east, the land drops off suddenly to the Dead Sea; this area is "the wilderness of Judah." The wilderness is from 10 to 15 miles wide (16-23 km.). Rainfall is limited. It is not strictly desert, for in the spring, with adequate rain, the hills offer good grazing to the flocks. To the west is a gradual slope of piedmont, the Shephelah. It consists of low hills interspersed with valleys that supply fruit, vegetables, and grains. Under the Judges and the early Monarchy this area was the center of contention between the Israelites (in the mountain range) and the Philistines (along the coastal plain).

(d) *The Negeb.* The term Negeb is used in Scripture for the region around and south of Beersheba.[6] It is a high steppe, receiving scarcely enough rainfall to support any vegetation. Spring rains may provide pasture for flocks during the spring. By digging wells and by careful rock-mulching, people (especially the Nabateans, *ca.* fifth century B.C.–second century A.D.) did settle in the Negeb.[7]

(e) *Sinai.* The peninsula, with its great, barren wilderness and its massive mountains in the south, was never considered part of Palestine. Because it is

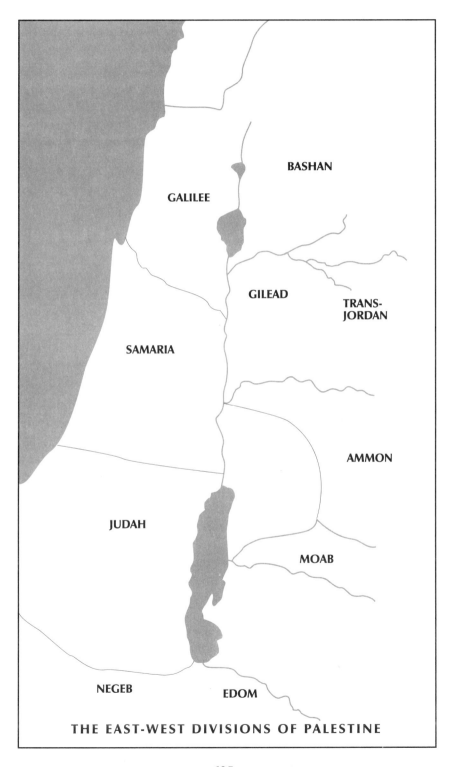

BASHAN

GALILEE

GILEAD

TRANS-
JORDAN

SAMARIA

AMMON

JUDAH

MOAB

NEGEB

EDOM

THE EAST-WEST DIVISIONS OF PALESTINE

One of the four sources of the Jordan river: the Nahr Ḥasbânî.
(William Sanford LaSor)

prominent in the early narratives three features deserve mention: (1) The "wilderness of Zin" is a barren region in northern Sinai. Its most important sites are Khirbet el-Qudeirât and ʿAin Qedeis. Both have been suggested as the location of Kadesh-barnea, where the Israelites encamped for much of their thirty-eight years in the wilderness (cf. Deut. 1:19; Num. 13:26; 14:26-35). (2) The "river of Egypt" is Wâdī el-ʿArîsh (not the Nile), formed by the drainage of the Sinai mountains. It flows approximately north and enters the Mediterranean at modern el-ʿArîsh. (3) The great mountain massif in the southern end of the peninsula, where Sinai (or Horeb) was most likely located, is a region of rugged peaks rising to more than 7,000 ft. (2,134 m.).

3. *The Jordan rift* is part of the Great Rift, which extends from the Kara Su valley in Turkey to Victoria Falls at the southern end of Zambia. This area has experienced great seismic activity (cf. Amos 1:1). Its deepest part is the Dead Sea. The Jordan rift includes the tributaries of the Upper Jordan, the Sea of Galilee, the Jordan River, the Dead Sea, and the Arabah.

(a) *Upper Jordan.* Copious springs gush from the slopes of Mt. Hermon to form the tributaries of the Upper Jordan. In biblical times, they formed a marshy region which drained into Lake Huleh, a turnip-shaped lake about 4 mi. (6.4 km.) long. Today, the marshes and lake have been drained. The Upper Jordan continues in the "Middle Jordan," a gorge about 10 mi. (16 km.) as the

626

river drops from about 200 ft. (70 m.) above sea level to empty into the Sea of Galilee, 686 ft. (209 m.) below sea level.

(b) *Sea of Galilee.* In Scripture the Sea of Galilee has various names: Chinnereth ("harp"; Num. 34:11), Gennesaret (Luke 5:1), and Tiberias (John 21:1). The harp-shaped lake is 13 mi. (21 km.) long and 8 mi. (13 km.) wide. Being below sea level and situated between the hills of Galilee and the Golan Heights, it enjoys a subtropical climate. The sea is subject to sudden and severe storms. The northwestern shore, the plain of Gennesaret, was very fertile.

(c) *Jordan River.* From the Sea of Galilee to the Dead Sea, about 60 mi. (97 km.) by air, the river meanders for about 200 mi. (325 km.). Due to the saline soil in the Jordan valley, the river carries a considerable quantity of salt into the Dead Sea.

A cross section of the Jordan valley shows that it is actually a valley within a valley. The largest valley, which extends from the hills of Samaria to the edge of the Transjordan plateau, is known by the Arabic name *Ghôr.* The Ghôr is about 5 mi. (8 km.) wide just south of the Sea of Galilee, but more than 12 mi. (20 km.) wide at Jericho. Within the Ghôr is the Zôr, the "jungle" or "pride" (NSRV "thicket") of the Jordan (Zech. 11:31; Jer. 12:5), a valley 10 or 20 ft. (3 or 6 m.) deep and as much as 150 ft. (50 m.) wide. The banks are almost perpendicular. Within the Zôr lies the actual Jordan watercourse, a river 15 to 25 ft. (5 to 8 m.) wide. Because the Jordan overflows its banks in flood season and spreads out in the Zôr, dense vegetation grows there (see diagram). Some scholars have suggested that the stopping-up of the Jordan as the Israelites were to cross from Moab to Gilgal resulted when an earthquake tumbled the steep marl banks into the Zôr at Adam (modern Damiyeh; cf. Josh. 3:13, 16). This did happen in A.D. 1267, when the Jordan was dammed for several hours, and again in connection with the 1927 earthquake.[8]

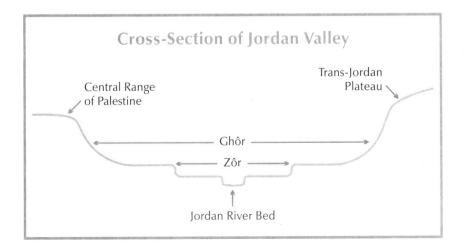

Cross-Section of Jordan Valley

Central Range of Palestine

Trans-Jordan Plateau

Ghôr

Zôr

Jordan River Bed

(d) *Dead Sea.* The lowest body of water on earth is the Dead Sea, about 1,290 ft. (395 m.) below sea level; its bottom at the deepest point is about 2,500 ft. (765 m.) below sea level. The sea is 48 mi. (77 km.) long and 9 mi. (14 km.) wide at its widest point. It is called the "salt sea" (Gen. 14:3), "sea of the Arabah" (Josh. 3:16), and "east sea" (Zech. 14:8). Josephus called it the "sea of asphalt" (*War* 4.8.4. §476), and the Arabs today call it the "Sea of Lot." It is not mentioned in the New Testament. Because evaporation is the only means of escape for the tons of water the Jordan pours into the Dead Sea each day, its concentration of salts is about 26 percent. Nothing can live in it, hence the name given to it by the Greeks.

(e) *Arabah.* South of the Dead Sea, an arid valley, rising to 656 ft. (200 m.) above sea level and then descending to the sea, stretches to the Gulf of Aqaba, 185 mi. (298 km.) south. In the Old Testament the name Arabah is used also for the valley of the Dead Sea and for the Jordan river valley.

(f) *Gulf of Aqaba.* The extension of the Jordan rift toward the Red Sea is known as the Gulf of Aqaba. In antiquity, "Red Sea" meant not only that body of water but also the Gulf of Aqaba, Gulf of Suez, and even the Arabian Sea and Indian Ocean. The Red Sea through which the Israelites passed in the Exodus (Exod. 13:18; 15:22) is probably none of these.[9]

4. *Transjordan* is a high plateau. It rises suddenly from the Jordan rift to 2,000-3,000 ft. (610-915 m.) or so above sea level, then slopes gently to the Syrian and Arabian deserts. As one goes to the south the land rises, reaching some 5,000 ft. (1524 m.) in Edom. Well watered by a complex system of rivers and streams, it has long been noted for its produce. The drainage systems form a number of rivers that have cut deep gorges as they flow toward the Jordan valley. These gorges form natural boundaries. A major north-south road called the King's Highway traversed this area.

Regions of Transjordan. (a) North of the Yarmuk gorge and east of the Upper Jordan and Sea of Galilee was *Bashan,* a region formed largely by decomposed volcanic rock and, therefore, exceptionally fertile. In Roman times the area was known as Gaulanitis (the modern Golan heights). It was an important source of wheat and it was one of the best places in ancient Israel for the raising of cattle (cf. Amos 4:1).

(b) *Gilead,* south of the Yarmuk, was a land of numerous valleys with good grazing land, and rugged hills with forests of oak and other trees. The proverbial "balm of Gilead" (Jer. 8:22; 46:11), noted for medicinal and cosmetic properties, was a valuable export. The southern boundary of Gilead is not clearly specified. Some scholars believe it was the Arnon (Wâdī el-Môjib), but the Jabbok gorge (Wâdī Zerqa) is more commonly accepted.

(c) *Ammon* was situated roughly between the Jabbok and the Arnon gorges, more specifically on the tributaries of the Jabbok, well east of the Jordan. The major city was Rabbath-ammon, modern Amman, the capital of the Hashemite Kingdom of Jordan. The kingdom of Sihon (thirteenth century) lay between Ammon and the Jordan.

(d) *Moab* was situated mostly between the Arnon and the Zered (Wâdî el-Hesâ), but at times it extended north beyond the Arnon. The "plains of Moab," between Wâdî Nimrîn and the Dead Sea, stretch up the gentle slope toward Heshbon (Ḥesbân) and Madeba.

(e) *Edom* is generally identified with the region east of the Arabah between the Zered and the head of the Gulf of Aqaba. During most of the Old Testament period Edom spread across both sides of the Arabah. The high mountain range called Mt. Seir was the center of the Edomites' territory, whose capital was at Sela (Greek Petra; 2 Kgs. 14:7).

(f) *Midian,* not included in the Transjordan, lay south of Edom, east of the Gulf of Aqaba and opposite Sinai.

Climate

The entire eastern Mediterranean is influenced largely by the Etesian ("annual") winds, which in the winter bring moisture generally from the northwest, and in the summer dry weather mainly from the southwest. As a result, there are two seasons: rainy (approximately December to March) and dry (May to September). At the turn of season, the hot desert ("east") wind, known as *ḥamsîn*[10] or the sirocco, may blow between April and the middle of June and from the middle of September to the end of October for several days at a time. The sirocco raises temperatures greatly, making life unbearable. These hot winds quickly wither trees and plants.

Along the coast there is not much extreme variety in temperature, either during a day or from season to season. In the central mountain range the summer days are hot, but the nights are pleasant. Rainy days in winter can be very cold. In the Jordan River Valley, being below sea level, the winters are very pleasant (around 70° F), but the summer heat is intense (often over 110° F). Overall, though, because of the wide diversity of the terrain in Palestine, local climates vary greatly.

Rainfall. Since the winds blow mainly from the west, any moisture they bring is deposited as rain on the coastal plain, on the western slopes of both the central mountain range, and the Transjordan plateau. Rainfall is very erratic. The amount that falls varies widely from year to year. As a result there can be years of severe drought or years of plenty.

Showers may begin at the end of the dry season about November; they are called "the former rains." In some years rains may not start until as late as

Aerial view of Jerusalem looking east toward the Kidron Valley and the Mount of Olives. In the foreground the Dome of the Rock marks the site of the ancient temple. *(Neal and Joel Bierling)*

January. Nevertheless, if they are plentiful enough, the harvest will be good. The rainy season may extend into April; these rains are called "latter rains."[11] The early and late rains were viewed as special blessings.

The rains are heaviest in the north and the mountains (e.g., 26 in. [650 mm.] in Haifa and Nazareth; 25.5 in. [555 mm.] in Jerusalem), tapering off sharply in the Negeb. The eastern slopes of the central mountain range, by contrast, are arid. During the dry summer, heavy dew supports the vegetation.

In the Transjordan where the elevation is higher than Cisjordan, the summer days are hotter and the nights cooler. Winters are also chillier. The rain clouds that cross the Cisjordan re-form over these mountains, often dropping more rain. Greater amounts of rain fall in the north; as one travels south through Moab to Edom the amount of rainfall diminishes dramatically.

Climatic Change. According to one theory, the climate has changed significantly between patriarchal times and the present, drying up much of the land, and causing deforestation and other results. But available records do not appear to support this theory. The amount of rainfall, average temperature, and other climatic matters seem to have remained relatively constant in Palestine and the surrounding regions for the past six thousand years. Changes in the amount of vegetation are probably better explained as the result of two common elements unusually hostile to a region's ecology: people and goats. Between them, hills have been stripped of trees and soil eroded by rains, to give the appearance of a change of climate.

Significance of Geography

Given Palestine's strategic location it became the crossroads for merchants and armies. Major battles determining which nation extended its control into another continent were fought here. Palestine was often under the military control of a major power, whether Egyptian, Mesopotamian, Hittite, Persian, Greek, or Roman. But during periods when there were no great empires, Palestine served as a buffer zone. Such was the state of affairs when the Israelites entered Canaan after the Exodus, and this continued during much of the monarchy and until the rise of the Assyrian empire.

Physical characteristics account for the isolation of the Israelites settled in the central mountains. The principal north-south highways that armies and merchants traveled lay either along the coastal plain to the west (Via Maris) or on the edge of the Transjordan plateau to the east (King's Highway). A foreign ruler might mock Israel's God as "a god of the mountains but not of the valleys" (1 Kgs. 20:28), but this only indicates that the Israelites were relatively secure in their "mountain fastness." Such a situation was in fact far truer of Judah than of Samaria. Thus Jerusalem both resisted capture until David's day and survived the fall of Samaria by over 130 years.

But physical features also contributed to frequent Israelite disunity. The land was designed more for tribal possessions or city-states than for a strongly unified nation.

631

CHAPTER 49

The Chronological Puzzle

The Old Testament teems with chronological data. Books dealing with earlier periods usually express dates only in years, and they cannot be coordinated with any extrabiblical data.[1] Other books (e.g., Kings and Chronicles, Jeremiah, Ezekiel, Daniel, Haggai, Zechariah, Ezra, and Nehemiah) contain a wealth of chronological material. Some of their dates can quite readily be converted to our present system of calendration. But others offer seemingly insoluble problems. Before discussing these, we need some idea of the ancient systems of counting time and building calendars.

> The time that the Israelites lived in Egypt was four hundred thirty years. At the end of four hundred thirty years, on that very day, all the companies of the LORD went out from the land of Egypt. Exod. 12:40-41

> In the four hundred and eightieth year after the Israelites came out of Egypt, in the fourth year of Solomon's reign over Israel, in the month of Ziv, which is the second month, he began to build the house of the LORD. 1 Kgs. 6:1

The Year and Its Divisions

The Bible reports that Methuselah lived 969 years (Gen. 5:27) and that Abraham was 100 years old when Isaac was born (21:5). These startlingly high figures raise a question: did the ancients count time the way moderns do? Basically, the answer is "yes." Ancient time divisions were derived from the observation of celestial phenomena just as modern ones are.

Day. In the Semitic world the day began at sunset or, more specifically, with the appearance of the first star. Later, when the day was divided into hours, it began at 6 p.m. (the hour does not appear in the Old Testament).[2] Since a "day" runs from evening to the following period of daylight, it actually encompasses part of two "days" in the modern sense. Hence, to ensure accuracy, scholars customarily use a double date, e.g., "6/7 June," i.e., the day that begins the evening of the sixth and ends at sundown on the seventh.[3]

Month. As the sun's apparent movement determined the day, so the moon determined the month. Earliest records show that it began with the new moon (the first appearance of the thin crescent in the western sky at sunset). The moon's cycle is 29.5 days, hence months were alternately 29 and 30 days.[4]

The lunar month only occasionally coincides with the modern calendar month. The equivalent is customarily represented by a compound, e.g., "Nisan = March/April." But this is not always precise. For example, in 1992 Nisan began on 4 April, and Nisan was April/May. In a year requiring an intercalary month (see below), the normal equivalents as a rule will not hold.

Year. According to the earliest records, ancient peoples reckoned the year by the change in seasons, occasioned in turn by the solar cycle of 365.25 days. Thus, since months derived from the lunar cycle and years from the solar cycle, they could not be synchronized exactly. Suppose that in year *x*, the new moon of Nisan coincided with the spring equinox so both solar and lunar cycles began at the same time. Twelve months later (i.e., $12 \times 29.5 = 354$ days), the first of Nisan would be about eleven days before the spring equinox. The year of twelve lunar months is a *lunar year;* that of approximately 365 days is a *solar year.*

The lunar year is satisfactory for nomads, who move their flocks with the seasons and need not know when to plow and plant. But the farmers of Palestine needed a calendar keyed to the solar year. Likewise in Egypt, where the annual flooding of the Nile dictated the phases of agricultural production, a solar calendar was necessary. In Mesopotamia, approximate correlation of the lunar and solar years was achieved by intercalation (i.e., the addition of an extra month) when necessary. In Egypt, an approximate solar calendar prevailed by counting twelve months of thirty days each (hence, not a lunar calendar), plus five extra days each year.[5]

Egyptian zodiac, reckoning time by the movement of heavenly bodies;
Pharaonic village, Cairo. *(Neal and Joel Bierling)*

Intercalation. The Babylonians added an intercalary month when needed to align the lunar year with the solar year. Such intercalation is necessary seven times in nineteen years and was probably decreed by the priest or king. It aimed either to bring the month Nisan into phase with the spring equinox or to bring Tishri into phase with the fall equinox. Though biblical evidence is scarce, scholars believe that the Hebrews patterned their calendar after Babylonian practices at least by the time of the Exile (sixth century).[6]

Civil Year and Sacred Year. In addition to these confusing practices, the Hebrews had two ways of marking the new year. According to Exod. 12:2, Yahweh told Moses that Nisan was to be the first month.[7] But the Jewish New Year, Rosh Hashanah ("the head of the year"), is in the fall, in Tishri. Accordingly, there was a civil year, which began with Tishri (around the autumnal equinox) and paralleled the agricultural year, and a religious year, which began with Nisan (in the spring). Different kings and nations alternated between the two.[8]

Calendar. Using names derived from Babylonian, the Hebrew year was as follows:

Hebrew	Babylonian	Approximate Equivalent	Sacred Year and Name	Order in Civil Year
Nisan	Nisanu	Mar./Apr.	1st	7th
Iyyar	Ayaru	Apr./May	2nd	8th
Sivan	Siwanu (Simanu)	May/Jun.	3rd	9th
Tammuz	Du'uzu	Jun./Jul.	4th	10th
Ab	Abu	Jul./Aug.	5th	11th
Elul	Elulu/Ululu	Aug./Sep.	6th	12th
Tishri	Tisritu	Sep./Oct.	7th	1st
(Mar)hesvan	(W)arah-samnu	Oct./Nov.	8th	2nd
Kislev	Kisliwu (Kislimu)	Nov./Dec.	9th	3rd
Tebet	Tebitu	Dec./Jan.	10th	4th
Sh^{e}bat	Sabatu	Jan./Feb.	11th	5th
Adar	Addaru	Feb./Mar.	12th	6th
(Veadar)		(intercalary month)		

Regardless of when the year began, "first month" refers to Nisan, "second month" to Iyyar, etc. Thus in Jer. 36:22, where a Tishri-Tishri year applies, the "ninth month" was in the winter, i.e., Kislev (November/December), not Sivan (May/June).[9]

Accession Years and Nonaccession Years. Modern calendars designate years by numbers attached to a known event. Thus, A.D. 1993 means 1,993 years "in the year of the Lord," counting from the presumed year of the birth of Jesus. But in Bible times events were often dated according to the year of a king's reign, as in the formula "in the second year of Darius" (Hag. 1:1).

Kings, however, were not considerate enough to die at the end of a year so the new king could start his reign on New Year's Day. What, then, should the new king call the portion of the old year that was left? For example, suppose that King Z died on 19 August, and his son succeeded him on 20 August, but the New Year began in Tishri (hypothetically here, 20 September). Sometimes the new king would call the period from 20 August to 19 September the "first year" of his reign. But if he reckoned the "first year" as the period beginning 20 September, then the new king might call the time from his accession to the next New Year the "accession year." If so, his "first year" would start the next New Year's Day.

The two methods of counting are called the accession-year system and the nonaccession-year system. Obviously, the total number of years of a succession of kings using one system differs from that calculated by the other system. To give the modern equivalent for the formula "In the second year of

635

Darius the king, in the sixth month, on the first day of the month," one must first know whether Darius used the accession-year or nonaccession-year method. The sixth month would be Elul, regardless of whether he used the Tishri-Tishri or the Nisan-Nisan year (see above), and the first day would be the day of the new moon — which, if the year can be determined, can be calculated by astronomical tables.

The Chronological Puzzle in Kings and Chronicles

Basis of the Puzzle. 1-2 Kings and 1-2 Chronicles abound in chronological details. They tell the length of reign of every king of Judah and Israel, the relationship of their respective reigns to each other (called "synchronisms"), and the age of the kings of Judah at their accession. Furthermore, they sometimes synchronize important events with the year of the king's rule. Especially important are chronological references to events also recorded in secular history — e.g., the invasion of Shishak (1 Kgs. 14:25), Sennacherib's assault on Jerusalem (2 Kgs. 18:13). On occasion biblical writers even synchronized an event with a year in the reign of a foreign king. For example, Jer. 25:1 identifies the fourth year of Jehoiakim with the first of Nebuchadnezzar, while 32:1 connects the tenth year of Zedekiah with Nebuchadnezzar's eighteenth.

The trouble is, however, that much of this lavish information appears at first glance self-contradictory. For instance, 2 Kgs. 1:17 records that Joram, son of Ahab, began to reign in the second year of Jehoram, son of Jehoshaphat of Judah, while 3:1 puts it in the eighteenth year of Jehoshaphat. Similarly, some puzzling results emerge when one totals the years of the reigns. For example, consider the time from the division of the kingdom under Rehoboam and Jeroboam (1 Kgs. 12), who began to rule about the same time, to the reigns of Joram of Israel and Ahaziah of Judah, who died at the same time (2 Kgs. 9:24, 27). One would expect the total years of rule to be the same for each kingdom, but in fact the span is ninety-eight years and seven days for Israel and ninety-five years for Judah.

The figures for the next period are even more puzzling. Jehu of Israel and Athaliah of Judah rose to power at the same time, so the totals of the years from their accession to the fall of Samaria (placed in the ninth year of Hoshea and the sixth of Hezekiah; 18:10) should agree. But for Israel the total is 143 years, seven months; for Judah, 166 years. The situation is further complicated by Assyrian chronological information which allows about 120 years for the same events.[10]

Even more vexing are attempts to harmonize the synchronisms given for some kings. For instance, Jeroboam II ruled Israel for forty-one years (14:23). Simple subtraction would suggest that his son Zechariah succeeded him in the fourteenth year of Azariah (Uzziah), who had ascended the throne of Judah in Jeroboam's twenty-seventh year (15:1). The text, however, dates Zechariah's accession to Azariah's thirty-eighth year (v. 8), leaving twenty-four years unaccounted for. Until recently attempts to make sense of the numbers as they stand have encountered almost insurmountable difficulties. By far the most significant breakthrough has been the detailed system worked out by E. R. Thiele.[11] The strength of Thiele's solutions to these perplexing puzzles is that they make sense of the biblical data without recourse to undue emendation or drastic adjustments. But some scholars fault Thiele for assuming, without (in their view) adequate biblical evidence, that Israel had coregencies (see below). They also question his somewhat arbitrary shifting of the basis for his dates (e.g., by appealing to changes in the method of reckoning royal reigns or in the date of New Year's Day).

Recently Hayes and Hooker proposed an entirely new chronology for the monarchy period,[12] but it suffers a weakness similar to that of Thiele's: rather than coregencies, it assumes that five kings voluntarily abdicated the throne but does not offer (in our view) adequate biblical evidence.[13] So, despite its weaknesses, we still retain Thiele's view as the most credible answer to the chronological puzzle of Kings. Since the problems vary for different historical periods, we will survey each period, briefly presenting Thiele's suggested solutions with some modifications.

From the Division of the Kingdom to the Accession of Pekah (ca. 931-740). During the biblical period, Assyria, Babylonia, and Persia generally used the accession-year system of reckoning discussed above. Thus, the first problem is to determine which method each kingdom of Israel used. Also, one must ask in what month the regnal years of each began. Did both kingdoms use the same month, and was each kingdom consistent? This question is important because, as we noted above, the Hebrews sometimes reckoned Nisan (March/April) as the first month of the year and sometimes Tishri (September/October). A further question is, how would a scribe refer to dates of a kingdom which used another method — merely reproduce the alien system or transpose it into familiar terms?

Again, one must consider the possibility of coregencies, where one king begins to rule before another dies. This overlap would mean that actual reigns were not so long as the individual years of rule added together might indicate. Another factor is the possibility of interregnal periods when no king was on the throne.

Thiele carefully checked the various possible answers to the above questions to see which approaches best satisfied all the numerical data in Kings and Chronicles. While scholars question some of his conclusions, his methods offer a credible working theory. First, during the first sixty years or so after the schism under Jeroboam I and Rehoboam, royal scribes in Judah used the accession-year system, and those in Israel, the nonaccession-year. Furthermore, whenever data are given about a king of Judah, the accession-year method is used both for his figures and the synchronism with Israel's king. Similarly, for a northern king the nonaccession-year scheme is followed not only for his reign but for his contemporary in the south.

Again, Thiele argues that Judah's regnal year ran from Tishri to Tishri throughout the Monarchy and beyond (see Neh. 1:1 and 2:1). Israel, however, perhaps to be different from Judah and perhaps in imitation of Egypt and Assyria, followed a Nisan-Nisan regnal calendar.[14] Further, Thiele explains some numerical discrepancies as due to coregencies, particularly in Judah, but concludes that neither kingdom shows evidence of interregnal periods.[15] Also, he marshals evidence that Judah switched from an accession-year to a nonaccession year method for the fifty-two-year period between Jehoram and Joash (*ca.* 848-796). During that period, Judah's kings enjoyed a close alliance with Ahab's descendants, and Thiele suggests that the pagan queen mother Athaliah brought this innovation.[16]

Political pressures by powerful Assyria evidently forced both kingdoms to an accession-year system early in the eighth century (under Jehoash in Israel [*ca.* 798] and Amaziah in Judah [*ca.* 796]).[17] Both kingdoms used the accession-year scheme until the close of their histories.

How can dates in antiquity be established with any assurance of accuracy? Archaeological findings such as pottery or other ancient ruins can only give dates in broad, round figures. Similarly, the margin of error for dating organic materials by testing their carbon 14 remains about ten percent. How can one say that the battle of Qarqar was fought in 853 or that Nebuchadnezzar destroyed Jerusalem in 586?

Actually, Israel's enemies, the Assyrians, have given the most help in placing the relative chronology of the Bible against an absolute chronology in ancient history. The Assyrians followed a solar year corresponding to the modern year. More important, they established an office of eponym (Assyrian *limmu*) to which they appointed annually a high official, governor, or king. By keeping lists of these eponyms, they provided a system of reference to every year from 891 to 648. Furthermore, one text mentions an eclipse which astronomers fix at 15 June 763. When compared with

Assyrian king lists, the eponym lists provide the means of establishing the Assyrian royal chronology. The importance of the Assyrian texts for biblical chronology can scarcely be exaggerated because they concentrate on the most significant period for biblical chronology — the Divided Monarchy.[18]

Fixed points in biblical chronology can be determined on the basis of synchronisms between Assyrian and Israelite history. The reign of Shalmaneser III, who fought Ahab at Qarqar in 853 and took tribute from Jehu in 841, provides an excellent opportunity to correlate Israel's history with the absolute Assyrian chronology. The campaigns of Tiglath-pileser III, Shalmaneser V, Sargon II, and Sennacherib afford further cross-references.

Accession of Pekah to Death of Ahaz (ca. 740-715). This brief period is one of the most frustrating chronologically, so scholars often question the accuracy of Kings here. While 2 Kgs. 15:30 says that Hoshea of Israel came to power in the twentieth year of Jotham, v. 33 notes that Jotham reigned just sixteen years! Even more startling are the problems involving Pekah of Israel. Hebrew chronology suggests that his reign began in 740, while Assyrian records of Tiglath-pileser suggest that it closed in 732. However, v. 27, which gives the synchronism for Pekah's succession, also states that he reigned twenty years! The difficulties become more disturbing in the reigns of Ahaz and Hezekiah. Comparison of 15:27, 30; 16:1f.; 18:1 leads to the impossible conclusion that Ahaz was twenty-six when his twenty-five-year-old son, Hezekiah, began to reign! As Thiele points out, the synchronism of 18:1, which brings Hezekiah to the throne in Hoshea's third year, cannot be correct.[19]

Plausibly, however, Thiele argues that Pekah apparently reckoned his reign as beginning in 752, even though this was actually the year of Menahem's accession. A possible explanation is that Pekah ruled a rival kingdom centered in Gilead at the same time as Menahem ruled in Samaria. In 740 when Pekah, in turn, disposed of Pekahiah, Menahem's son, he apparently decided to take credit for the twelve years of the combined reigns of Menahem and Pekahiah. When Pekah's accession is reckoned from 752, the entire chronology of the period begins to take shape.[20]

As for the puzzling synchronisms involving Ahaz and Hezekiah (2 Kgs. 17:1; 18:1, 9f.), Thiele's explanation seems credible: long after the events a scribe or editor, who failed to understand Pekah's "twenty" years, assumed that Pekah had died in 720 and incorrectly synchronized Hoshea's accession in 720, which he knew to be the twelfth year of Ahaz. This was done despite the correct synchronization of Hoshea's reign in 15:30 ("the twentieth year of Jotham").

Knowing that Hezekiah came to the throne in the sixteenth year of Ahaz, the scribe or editor incorrectly synchronized events in Hezekiah's reign with Hoshea's and vice versa. In other words, one may disregard the synchronisms of 17:1; 18:1, 9f., since Hoshea had been carried into captivity by the Assyrians several years before Hezekiah was crowned. The reviser misunderstood the twelve-year coregency of Jotham (his father, Uzziah, had contracted leprosy) and Pekah's crediting himself with the twelve years of Menahem and Pekahiah. He, thus, inaccurately correlated the reigns of Jotham and Ahaz so they overlapped by about twelve years.[21]

Conclusion. Thiele's painstakingly thorough research has provided ground-breaking new solutions to one of the great riddles of Old Testament history. He substantiates the accuracy of the Scripture and shows how it harmonizes with Assyrian chronological records. At the same time, he has isolated a source of several faulty synchronisms. Nevertheless, the topic of chronology continues to evoke lively scholarly discussion, and many problems await final solutions. Despite the unsettled problems, however, one should not miss the theological implication of the chronology of Kings. It implies that the material is historical and reminds Bible readers that God was at work in Israel's history during this period.[22]

CHAPTER 50

Archaeology

Archaeology is both science and art. It aims for the discovery and evaluation of ancient material remains in order to ascertain the identity, nature, and extent of past civilizations and cultures. As a science, archaeology is an adjunct to anthropology. The objects of such study may be found in museums all over the world. The types of artifacts found during archaeological excavations range from stone tools from the earliest periods of human history to fine glazed pottery of much later eras. In short, "people are the main interest of archaeology, and the objects they have created are the means through which archaeology seeks to learn about them."[1]

For some two centuries archaeologists have probed the lands specifically related to the Old Testament. Truly amazing discoveries have been made which illuminate Old Testament backgrounds and life from the Stone Age to modern times. And more is yet to come. As William G. Dever has said, "Archaeology is one of the fastest-moving of all the social science disciplines today, both in theoretical reformulations and in the astonishing type and array of new data that it is turning up."[2]

The Biblical Beginnings

In the early days of archaeological expeditions, the great attraction of the Near East for westerners related to treasure-hunting. Museums would pay handsomely for exquisite art objects and stunning artifacts. Then came excavators such as Sir Flinders Petrie and William F. Albright who sought to put archaeology on a more scientific footing. Since they were Bible scholars, their investigations in Palestine particularly took on the flavor of biblical research. The efforts of a pioneer like Albright were immensely valuable: his approach was a vast improvement over the treasure-hunting mentality that preceded him, and he and others worked out a chronological matrix that was foundational for Near Eastern studies.

Traditional Case for Biblical Archaeology

One of Albright's students, G. Ernest Wright, argued for a specifically *biblical* archaeology:

> Biblical archaeology is a special "armchair" variety of general archaeology. The biblical archaeologist may or may not be an excavator himself, but he studies the discoveries of the excavations in order to glean from them every fact that throws a direct, indirect or even diffused light upon the Bible. He must be intelligently concerned with stratigraphy and typology, upon which the methodology of modern archaeology rests. . . . Yet his chief concern is not with methods or pots or weapons in themselves alone. His central and absorbing interest is the understanding and exposition of the Scriptures.[3]

Such an attitude will persist among "armchair" archaeologists as long as there is an archaeological enterprise in the ancient Near East, indeed, as long as there is an interest in the Bible itself.

Wright goes on to say:

> The Bible, unlike the other religious literature of the world, is not centered in a series of moral, spiritual and liturgical teachings, but in the story of a people who lived at a certain time and place.[4]

It is precisely the degree of certitude attaching to the Old Testament *as history* that has occasioned the long-standing (and perhaps widening) divide between historians and literary critics of the Bible. While some would insist on the historical dependability of the Bible, others argue that the Bible cannot be relied upon as sober history. Or some affirm that it does not matter, that the "point" is in the spiritually uplifting aspect of Scripture. We should not be forced to a choice: each discipline has a unique contribution to make to biblical studies.

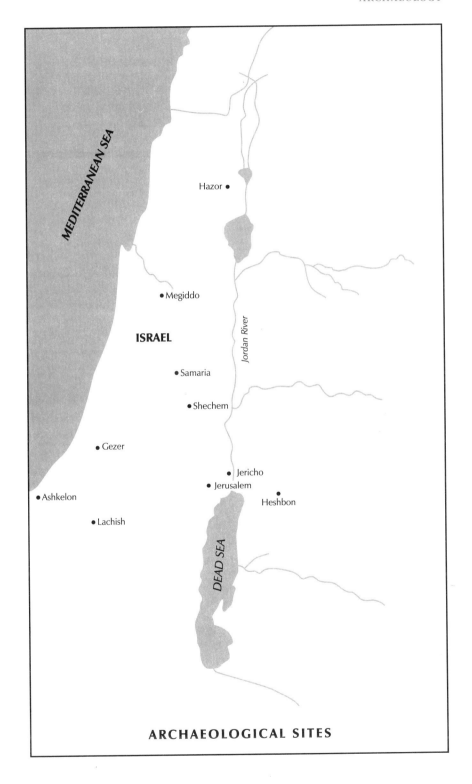

MEDITERRANEAN SEA

Hazor ●

● Megiddo

ISRAEL

Jordan River

● Samaria

● Shechem

● Gezer

● Jericho
● Jerusalem
Heshbon ●

● Ashkelon

● Lachish

DEAD SEA

ARCHAEOLOGICAL SITES

Contemporary Debate about the Role of Archaeology

The current debate, however, no longer centers in the polarization between historians and literary critics but reflects an intramural contest among historians themselves. The core issue is the nature of historiography, the approach to the study and writing of history. To what extent can the biblical narratives be regarded as historical without clear support from external evidence in archaeological findings or extrabiblical texts? Part of the impact of the quest for a purely objective practice of history-finding has been a redefinition of the role of archaeology.

The Advent of Syro-Palestinian Archaeology

In the last decades of the twentieth century there has been a reaction against the biblical archaeology of the past. The chief scholar associated with a trend to redesignate the discipline as "Syro-Palestinian" archaeology is William G. Dever.[5] He has decried the term "biblical archaeology," because he believes, and rightly so, that archaeology in the Near East has to keep pace with New World archaeology, the "New Archaeology" of the Americas, and its methods.

How did this "new" approach begin? Archaeologists began to sense the shortcomings of past approaches. For the prehistoric period, where there are no written sources, earlier archaeologists tended to create a sort of counterfeit history of the past, which imagined what ancient people might have thought or believed. Such an approach was often undisciplined, speculative. As a more scientific corrective, the New Archaeology was born.[6] With it came some striking changes.

The Outlook of the New Archaeology

Theory. Theory in archaeology is fundamental. Syro-Palestinian or biblical archaeology is really the construct of professional practitioners, people who spend great amounts of time and energy "in the dirt." Theory is constantly being molded by the desires of and limits on the director of an excavation: the need to excavate in minimal time, with perhaps minimal staff, certainly with minimal living conditions, and limited resources, especially money. Money

Volunteers at Tel Miqne-Ekron excavation measuring the
locations of distinctive features in the balk while making
a section drawing. *(Neal and Joel Bierling)*

typically dictates the direction and emphasis in the field. The tendency is
generally to award support to dig-proposals with the widest multidisciplinary
base.[7]

A Multidisciplinary Practice. The typical roster of job descriptions on a
dig reflect its multidisciplinary character. Under the administrative responsibility of the dig director, the chief archaeologist is assisted by field supervisors
with dig experience who oversee square supervisors in the field. These leaders
have a background, not in archaeology alone, but in anthropology or some

645

other specialty. The main burden of digging is borne by the square supervisors, their volunteers, and local workers. The ceramicist or pottery expert reads the pottery. A conservator seeks to protect fragile artifacts through chemistry. An epigrapher deciphers and interprets any inscriptions. In the newer framework, one can also find a survey team that works off the tell. Included in this segment of the expedition are an ethnographer, a geologist, an osteologist (who studies bone material), a geographer, and possibly an artist, who attempts through drawing to capture some sense of how the ancients lived. The survey team is concerned not just with mapping the region, but studying its ecology. A paleoethnobotanist may be taking samples of froth flotation to study the ancient horizon of cereal crops and the flora of the site.

One of the camp administrators may double as the lead computer programmer for recording the mass of data that accumulates so rapidly on a dig. And people are always needed to clean and count things. Washing the pottery is often a daily necessity. If the dig is large enough, cooks, a doctor, and a camp manager are also much needed and appreciated. The order of the day, therefore, is multidisciplinary cooperation, much as in the multidisciplinary study programs gaining popularity in our universities. The "New Archaeology" has brought this approach to the study of the Old Testament. And this is all to the good. Information should be welcomed, no matter who contributes it.

Environmentalism, Ecosystems, and Archaeology. Study of the region surrounding an ancient Near Eastern city mound is now valued by archaeologists. Geography and climate, geology and hydrography, are all relevant.[8] How does hillside terracing help in dry farming areas? What is the relationship of two sites that share the same watershed? What food systems and strategies can be detected through time in, e.g., the Madaba Plains of Jordan? One must study the regional and historical fluctuations between sedentarization and bedouinization from Heshbon south to Jalul, and northeast to Tell el-'Umeiri and Tell Jawa. The region today is devoted to the raising of wheat and barley.[9] What was the region like environmentally in the Iron II period? Questions of this type receive careful attention.

Special care is paid to ecosystems having the same microclimate and topographic, geochemical, and biotic characteristics. "Ecosystem" is defined as the interaction of organisms within such an area.[10] In searching for significant information about ecological units, one must consider such features as topography, the presence or absence of surface and subsurface water, soils, cultivation, and the species and distribution of the flora.[11] Much can be learned in archaeology from studies *off* the tell (the mound being excavated).

The Underlying Assumptions of Archaeology

Archaeology *as a discipline* is unique in that it retrieves its raw data from the earth. According to Lawrence E. Toombs, it is a rather humble enterprise that should not masquerade in grandiose fashion as a branch of history, linguistics, or anthropology. Yet archaeologists need to be conversant in many related areas, in order to interpret their finds intelligently.[12]

Information and Its Recovery. First, archaeology begins with the intentions of the excavators. What kinds of information do the excavators aim to recover? This will determine what they do with and to the earth. Secondly, what digging method should be utilized? This calls for control in both the horizontal and the vertical dimensions, i.e., the dimensions of space and time. Since digging is three-dimensional, the digger must establish stratigraphic control over every feature (soil layer, wall, pit, floor surface, and more) in the excavation square. Technique and supervision are essential in order to maintain this control. A third factor buttressing control is the system of recording employed in the field.[13] The excavator is continually torn by the need to "get on with it" in the dirt under his trowel, and the equal necessity of maintaining his recording processes. Control is enhanced by the daily top plan, usually begun on-site, and completed back at camp. Such a picture is truly worth a thousand words. The plan shows the progress of excavation every twenty-four hours, and acts as a file for the excavator. A host of questions fill the mind during the course of a dig season. Pottery reading, managing one's photographs taken in the field, keeping tabs on the objects found in one's square or area, monitoring registration numbers for finds, searching the literature for comparisons to artifacts found in current digging — these are the kinds of tasks that occupy the excavator's waking (and sleeping) hours.

Kinds of Data to be Gathered. Archaeologists cannot save everything. But they are now saving far more than they once did in the digging process. A large quantity of pottery is kept, usually sherds (fragments), and many, many objects of stone, bone, clay, and metal. The recording process, including sorting, classifying, bagging, tagging, and packing for shipping a large amount of material, is not completed during a few weeks' time. It may take years, and many hands are involved.

Publishing the Work. Here many a good Palestinian stratigrapher has faltered. How to separate on paper the facts gleaned from digging and the interpretation of their significance? Sites must be compared to other sites for relative chronology as a basis for understanding historical problems and, eventually, cultural horizons. It is very significant, for example, for a team to know that their Stratum A is equivalent to Megiddo Stratum B. Other archaeologists will come along and reevaluate such a connection. Toombs has asked:

647

"Should the final publication try to do it all or leave loose ends for others to work on and to criticize the authors for failing to do so? It is undoubtedly the magnitude of these problems, rather than laziness or unconcern, that accounts for the abysmally poor publication record of Palestinian archeologists."[14] Some critics of this neglect are not so charitable.

Archaeological Field Methods

How does the digging team begin? Preliminary surveying, like laying out the course of a new roadway, marks off the areas for digging.

Surveying on the Tell. One of the first tasks on arriving at the site in the early light of morning is to set up the theodolite, an instrument which combines the functions of a transit and a level. It is used for measuring elevations (in meters above sea level), and, like a camera, rests on a tripod. Normally the theodolite is set up on reasonably level ground and the points are shot; that is, one sights a hand-held meter stick with its base resting on the point to be measured, the corner of a wall, or a big flagstone. Then one swings the device to sight a known point of elevation and computations are made. For electronic long-distance measuring a low-intensity laser beam is used today, reflecting a hand-held mirror over distances up to about 200 m.

Use of a Magnetometer. A magnetometer is another electronic improvement on a surveyor's transit. It makes possible the detection of irregularities in the earth's magnetic field. When something like pottery has been brought to a temperature above 600 degrees centigrade, its magnetic particles are disturbed. After cooling there is an alignment of particles according to the day of cooling.[15] So an anomaly may be detected underground. Anything that had been burned in antiquity would show up in the numbers of the computer that the magnetometer operator wears strapped to himself. Occasionally the operator must return to the position where he took his reading to begin his series of measurements. Sunspot activity might throw off his work for a day, and he might have to cancel operations and try again the next day. In this manner any burn layers, or similar anomalies, may be detected. This method can be used for preliminary survey on a sight. (The writer was part of a team that measured Tell Mozan, Syria, in this manner utilizing a grid of 50-meter squares.) Ground Penetrating Radar affords similar results.

Ground Penetrating Radar. Another method of subsurface survey is a ground probing radar system. A pulse of electromagnetic energy is transmitted downward into the soil, where it is reflected back by any subsurface obstacles, to the receiving antenna, which passes the signal to a recording device. The operator may view the transmission on a color monitor, like a television screen, and "read" underground. These methods are expensive, but save many man-hours of digging "blind" in the field.

Field Drawing. A further result of surveying and measuring is the preparation of scale drawings in the field. These follow closely the progress of excavation and correlate with the huge number of photographs generated on a dig. Some kind of drawing board with a metal clip paper holder at the margin is necessary, because one is always fighting the wind. The present writer used polyethylene film rather than plain meter paper, and drew sections and top plans of architecture in the Petra church (1991-92) at 1:20 scale. Field drawings eventually become printed illustrations in site reports.

Stratigraphy. Despite technical and multidisciplinary advances, the standard method of archaeological excavation is still founded on two bases: stratigraphy and pottery typology. Stratigraphy is the study of the sequential deposition of layers of human occupation at an ancient site. Each stratum is analyzed and dated by its contents, whether pottery, coins, tools, or other objects. Soil samples are taken from each stratum for analysis. Archaeologists know what kinds of crops the ancients cultivated and ate. Stratigraphy is a major aid in reconstructing the occupational history of an archaeological site.

Wheeler-Kenyon Stratigraphic Methods. The Wheeler-Kenyon stratigraphic method of digging is named for Sir Mortimer Wheeler, and for Dame Kathleen Kenyon, who refined and established it among archaeologists. The real innovator behind such field techniques was actually General Augustus Lane-Fox Pitt-Rivers (1827-1900), who, far ahead of his time, brought "precision to impeccably organized excavations on his estates in southern England,"[16] including plans and sections that located every object, no matter how ordinary.

With the expectation today that archaeology should be exhaustively digitized, one still must deal with the basic soil layers of a site and read its pottery. Once the surveying team has located the necessary benchmarks at the site, and laid out the squares, the chief archaeologist gives the order to begin. As mentioned above, a field supervisor, next in command, may have about four squares to oversee at the same time. A square supervisor may also have an assistant.

They start at the highest corner in any 5.0- or 6.0-meter square, using a big pick on the knotted topsoil and roots. Even in the top few centimeters of pickwork something noteworthy may come to light, so the digger is always vigilant. Once the topsoil is disposed of, control is established over the square horizontally. Are there any separable areas, colors, or textures that might be given different locus numbers? A locus is any separable feature in the square: a soil layer, a floor, at least three stones in alignment that may prove to be a wall, a hearth, a pit, or its lining. The rule is that several loci may be combined

Archaeological Periods

Prepottery Neolithic	8000–6000 B.C.
Pottery Neolithic	6000–4000 B.C.
Chalcolithic	4000–3200 B.C.
(Introduction of copper tools)	
Early Bronze	3200–2000 B.C.
(Copper tools are dominant)	
Middle Bronze	2000–1550 B.C.
Late Bronze	1550–1200 B.C.
Iron I (Early Iron)	1200–900 B.C.
(Introduction of iron tools)	
Iron II (Middle Iron)	900–586 B.C.
Iron III (Late Iron or Persian)	586–330 B.C.
Hellenistic	330–63 B.C.
Roman	63 B.C.–A.D. 323
Byzantine	A.D. 323–636

[handwritten annotation: copper + stone]

later, but once designated, it is impossible to separate loci on paper after they have been destroyed in the dirt, so, as in most endeavors, the initial steps are all important.

In a shallow deposit, bedrock may be encountered too soon, in a matter of hours. If so, one moves on, that is, "jumps" to an adjoining square that may be more fruitful. On the other hand, there may, after several meters, be no finds, no architecture, and no buoyant spirits left among the excavators; even though this is not treasure hunting, one still entertains the hope of discovery as a reward for all the perspiration! At other times, however, with each scrape of the trowel, pottery fragments leap to the first light they have "seen" in thousands of years. The square supervisor is kept busy, particularly if local workmen are digging, just filling out pottery tags and writing notes in the journal. Pails and pails of pottery can come out of one square in a day. Everyone is involved in carrying pails, about ⅔ to ¾ full, to the bus at the end of the dig day. These must not be spilled. If they are, the contents will be contaminated and of no use to the pottery registrar back at camp. There can be no mixing of pail contents. The dating of a layer could be thrown off entirely by such a mishap.

Stratigraphic excavation is reasonable in soil layers, but is probably less important in excavating, say, the inside of a temple with its debris. If an earthquake brought down the temple and there was subsequent looting from the debris, there may be little meaningful layering. Even in something as mundane as a town wall, the archaeologist is seeking to determine if there are any use surfaces, like a kitchen floor, in association with the wall, abutting it, for example. In analyzing the floor surface, the questions should be: when was the construction phase of this floor, when was its use phase, and when was the destruction or abandonment phase? It would be nice if coins were left in the construction debris, footprints and kitchen utensils were left whole or gently crushed on the kitchen floor (mendable!), and a nice burn layer were thick and clearly discernible, indicating the destruction. But the occupational debris can be scant and interpretation much more subtle.

The early morning light is best for reading layers; in the high Syrian sun of midday it is difficult to see, given the brightness (that also plays havoc with the dig photographers' efforts). Shadows cast by stones in the balk further complicate the eyestrain. But as the layers are uncovered, the pottery and small finds of all descriptions, including bone, bead, and stone, are bagged and tagged. The balks (four sides of the ideal excavated square) are also marked with locus numbers. And everything is swept clean each sunup for the photographer to record not only the progress of excavation, but also the most important features fresh out of the dirt.

"Oh, you went to the Holy Land on a dig. What did you find?" When people ask excavators that polite but sincere question, the diggers typically look rather dumbfounded. On hearing that familiar question, their minds flash back across several months, perhaps years, of recording, including computerized recording, of all kinds of "finds." Stone mortar and pestles for grinding grain; a Middle Bronze goblet; a large, nearly complete Late Bronze storage jar that must have held grain for the village; a terra-cotta figurine of a goddess from some family's idol shelf in Palestine; a bronze needle about 10 centimeters long, used to repair clothing; a pocket-sized cuneiform tablet in Akkadian or Ugaritic, evidently a business document of everyday use (or someone's tax receipt); a small household lamp, with a nozzle pinched in the rim of one side (by someone who was right-handed!), with a lighted wick lying in oil, emitting enough light to enable the family to get to bed at night; fragments from a large cooking pot, well fired, and nicely burnished, over which the mother of the household prepared family meals — these are the common artifacts that tell a poignant story all their own to those who take the time to *observe* the dynamics of an ancient culture.

Pottery Typology. At camp, pottery takes precedence over people! The pails must be filled with water and allowed to sit during lunch and nap times: on the Madaba Plains Project and Tell Jawa systems the present writer worked with, we washed today's pottery after about 4:00 P.M. and read yesterday's, which has been dried. Pottery is read by the ceramics expert and, advisably, a knowledgeable helper.

To the expert, pottery reading is something like looking at a pile of wristwatches: the diagnostic shapes of rims, bases, and handles; inclusions of any sort (stone grits, straw) in the clay matrix itself; burnishing or slip; incising and decoration, glazing and the type and quality of the firing of the clay — all tell their story, permitting one to date the potsherd and, ultimately, the layers of occupational debris at the site.

Burials. Bodies are preserved in various ways: they can be naturally desiccated, freeze-dried, or soaked in peat.[17] In the Bronze and Iron ages, burials were accomplished by means of shaft tombs. Bodies were lowered vertically into what was often a bell-shaped vault. Grave objects accompanied the dead. An excellent example of this practice may be seen in the Bronze Age necropolis at Bab edh-Dhra' in Jordan, on the east side of the Dead Sea. By the time of the Romans, rock-cut tombs were common; steps led down to a central chamber with loculi (grave spaces) radiating off in three or four directions. Bodies were placed feet first in a space while the family of the deceased stood in the middle of the chamber to pay their last respects. Grave objects of all types are prizes to study, revealing much about ancient culture generally and, in particular, about attitudes concerning death and the hereafter, attitudes that sometimes are strikingly like our own.

Israeli Refinements in Method

There are many excellent archaeologists in Israel, perhaps too many for a country about the size of New Jersey. Since the 1950s there have been several main lines of activity. Renewed excavation at previously excavated sites has been primarily the domain of Americans, such as Wright at Shechem. New excavations, such as the very important work of Yigael Yadin at Hazor, have typically been undertaken by Israelis. From these distinct endeavors have emerged "American" and "Israeli" schools and methods of research.[18] By 1982, a new generation of Israeli archaeologists had begun to test previous assumptions. Although a variety of methods and priorities are represented among their ranks, the methodological recommendations of David Ussishkin provide the basis of a useful summary.[19]

Digging Techniques. 1. Israeli archaeologists focus on *quality*. The approach they favor is *slow* and *limited* excavation. Dig only part of the mound, they argue, one-half at most, so archaeologists of the future can check the work, with better methods. 2. Anson Rainey says "reveal as much as possible" (laterally). But a care for the vertical is now also in vogue. It is helpful to take the best from several methods: some principles from the Wheeler-Kenyon method (at Samaria, Jerusalem, Jericho, later at Shechem and Gezer, and still later at Hesban and Tell el-ʿUmeiri), working with an eye to the vertical as well as the horizontal. Making plans of the sections is *increasingly* a significant factor in determining a dig strategy, interpreting the finds, and publishing the results.

Architectural Method. A lot of the new approach stems from "architectural method," developed in Israel since the work of Yadin at Hazor in the 1950s. The idea is to study complete architectural units, the whole room, not just a portion of it. In the restoration process, one stresses whole pottery vessels retrieved from destruction levels. A good recent example of architectural method is the excavation of the Byzantine Church at Petra, Jordan, during 1992-93, under the directorship of Pierre and Patricia Bikai. The field supervisor, Z. Fiema, left one "standing balk," a partial square for tourists to view, showing the dirt that had fallen/eroded into the church after destruction. Interior walls of the church were preserved to a height of about 2.0 meters. A triple-apse basilica, with bema, nave, and atrium, features beautiful mosaics of floral and faunal motifs in both side aisles.[20] A similar, though massive, undertaking is that of Martha Joukowsky at the South Temple at Petra. A huge amount of very interesting data is expected to emerge at this Nabataean temple complex, presently under excavation.

Sorting pottery by style and composition is invaluable in dating archaeological materials. *(J. R. Kautz)*

653

3. With respect to pottery and artifacts, Ussishkin argues, stress should be on typological study and publication of complete vessel forms rather than on random small sherds.

Regional Approach. Another tendency in Israeli archaeology is to excavate one central mound in combination with the study of its surroundings. This regional approach prolongs the work, potentially for many years. Examples are the work done at Beer-Sheva, Yokneam, Tel Michal, Tel Aphek, and Tel Lachish (and in Jordan at Tell Heshbon, Tell el-'Umeiri, Tell Jawa, and elsewhere).

It is difficult to imagine archaeology in the Holy Land in the biblical period without connections to the Old Testament and historical records and sources, in short, "biblical backgrounds," the subject matter that attracted many to this field in the first place. Ussishkin himself cannot picture working at Lachish without engaging the strong historical and biblical connections of the site. These connections are understandably emotional, and constitute a large part of the motivation of Israeli archaeologists, despite the movement away from older forms of "biblical" archaeology. Special interest in the biblical period does not, of course, mean that the digger would neglect Chalcolithic (prebiblical) and Islamic (postbiblical) finds. Israeli archaeologists are trying to develop field work technically and professionally. But they are inescapably affected by historical and biblical interest.[21]

Modern Techniques of Dating

Radiochronometry. What was once familiar as "Carbon-14 dating" is known today as "radiochronometry." This is a dating technique based on the fact that radioactive isotopes disintegrate with the passage of time. The isotopes used in archaeology have a half-life (the time necessary for the amount of the isotope in question to be reduced by half) of from several thousand years to more than one million. The best known, Carbon 14 (C-14), has a half-life of 5,730 years. The amount of radioactivity still remaining will establish the time elapsed since the death of the object being dated. However, the rate of production of C-14 has not always been uniform, as seen in comparisons with dates based on, say, tree-ring dating (dendrochronology). Nevertheless, the method (first proposed in 1946 by William F. Libby) has enabled a solid chronological framework to be formed in numerous cases, thus making an important breakthrough in archaeological technique.[22]

Potassium-argon (K/Ar) Dating. This method of dating can be used on minerals in rocks. Potassium 40 (K-40) decomposes into argon (A-40), the half-life of the K-40 isotope being 1300 million years. Uniform conditions through time are presupposed in using the method. Potassium-argon dating is used in anthropology to date the surroundings of early hominid fossils.[23]

Thermoluminescence. Provided they have been subjected to heat, pottery, flint, and glass can be dated by thermoluminescence. Heated in the laboratory, these materials emit light which varies in intensity according to the amount of radioactivity to which they have been exposed since they were last heated. This method is widely used for dating ceramics and pieces of flint.[24]

The Uses of Archaeology

Archaeology's Limitations. Archaeology does not and cannot prove the Bible to be accurate. Most archaeologists will be the first to acknowledge that. In the majority of cases, archaeology itself is too imprecise a science to afford confirmation of the biblical record. The fact that virtually all the archaeologist's conclusions are inferential and therefore tentative means that one should lean upon them with great care. Archaeological assertions are subject to change with new evidence. The relevant objects of investigation are ancient, distant, silent, and usually fragmentary. Our best techniques, carefully applied, can reconstruct only a fraction of the material world and even less of the mind, spirit, and ethos of the people whose habitats we invade with pick and trowel.

Several factors indicate that archaeology alone is an inadequate base on which to build our reconstructions of history.[25] First, unless inscriptions or texts of some kind are discovered, it is impossible to garner specific information about events and people. Artifacts and strata can yield general evidence of the kind of life lived in a given site, but very little more.[26] And the soil of Palestine, in contrast to the palaces and tombs of Mesopotamia and Egypt, has been notoriously stingy in yielding inscriptional materials, with the single exception of the Dead Sea Scrolls, which are dated too late to give a helping hand to historians of earlier periods.

Second, since few inscriptions have survived, all evidence recovered has to be interpreted. Pottery fragments do not sort themselves out or announce their own typology. Strata do not come with labels. Archaeologists have to organize these data and suggest their meaning. This task is not entirely objective and may be handled quite differently by various interpreters, depending on their theoretical concerns, including their views of the biblical records. One archaeologist speaks of the experience of touching, seeing, even tasting an ash layer. The experience, he notes, is "not history until I talk about it or write about it to someone else." Yet those steps involve interpretation. Is the ash layer "destructive debris" or "burnt debris"? Does it represent a site-wide destruction, or someone's courtyard hearth or dump? Such categorization transforms specific data into "general concepts" and begins the "creative process of historiography."[27]

Third, the data available through archaeology are both partial and changing. Not all sites have been identified, and some may have been identified wrongly. Furthermore, no site has been completely excavated, and even when excavation has been thorough, most of its material remains have not survived. New data constantly change the picture, with the result that most conclusions drawn at any given time must be held tentatively, awaiting further information.

As far as biblical studies are concerned, archaeology plays a valuable but only partial role in the task of interpretation. It serves best as an adjunct to literary and theological studies. It keeps them down to earth and can contribute immense amounts of detailed insight to their research.

Archaeology's Contributions. Biblical scholars do well to let the Syro-Palestinian archaeologists pursue their work without the pressure of having to relate their findings to Scripture. Since insights from archaeology have to be interwoven with other biblical disciplines, it may be best to view biblical archaeology as a biblical rather than a strictly archaeological enterprise. "It is the responsibility of Biblical scholars, not archaeologists, to ferret out pertinent material evidence and apply it to the Bible."[28]

What archaeology can contribute to biblical studies will vary from period to period in the narratives of Scripture. (1) In the Primeval History of Genesis 1–11, the major contributions to date have been the discovery of Mesopotamian texts that refer to the creation and a great flood, along with the architectural ties between Babylonian ziggurats and the Tower of Babel. (2) The backgrounds of the Patriarchal stories have been somewhat illuminated by our knowlege of life in Mesopotamia and Egypt during the Early and Middle Bronze ages.[29] The social and religious practices of Abraham, Isaac, and Jacob can be read against the known backgrounds of the period, including the picture of city-states in Canaan. (3) As Chapter 4 has indicated, there is considerable correlation between the Exodus account and what we know of the Rameside period in Egypt, though there is much more that we do not and perhaps cannot know. (4) The periods of the Conquest under Joshua and the settlement under the judges have yielded substantial information but with mixed results. Excavations at some sites have been viewed as supportive of the biblical accounts while others have raised questions.[30]

(5) In these periods as well as the early decades of the Monarchy under Saul, David, and Solomon, two interrelated strategies seem necessary. First, we need to encourage further archaeological explorations and research. There is much yet to be learned. The eager, able crew of Israeli archaeologists will undoubtedly lead the way in these endeavors, including the delicate task of

excavating the pertinent levels in Jerusalem. Second, and equally important, biblical scholars need to use all possible methods of biblical interpretation to try to shed new light on the way history was written in Scripture. Conflicts and contradictions may arise from either side. Some scholars may misread the dirt and its contents while others misinterpret the text in its style, genre, and intent. Light needs to shine from both ends of the tunnel for us to read the past aright.

(6) The periods of the Divided Monarchy and Judah's last fling at independence (9th to 6th centuries) are undoubtedly the best documented in Old Testament history. The abundance of Assyrian and Babylonian records bring clarity to scores of details in the books of Kings and the prophets from Amos to Jeremiah. At the same time the archaeological evidence from Israel and Judah, Ammon and Moab teems with information not available for the earlier periods. A glance at the two important studies by Philip King will spark joy and kindle curiosity in the mind of all who love Scripture and want to understand it from within its own time and setting.[31] Even champions of the New Archaeology have saluted King's work as a signal example of how text and archaeological remains ought to be brought together. Dever's comment may be a fit way to close this discussion: "The 'real life setting' that King establishes so persuasively for many difficult or enigmatic passages in Jeremiah makes text after text more credible. . . . This is what the much-debated 'Biblical archaeology' movement should have been all along: an *informed dialogue* between artifact and text."[32]

In the following pages we survey ten key archaeological sites, summarizing for each one its importance, special features, and important excavations undertaken.

ASHKELON

Importance

- Mentioned in Egyptian Execration Texts, major city in MBII.
- Suffered destruction at time of "Hyksos expulsion."
- During LB under Egyptian rule (cf. Amarna Texts, 320-326, 370).
- Rebelled against Merneptah *ca.* 1207, as recounted in Israel Stele.
- Philistines arrived *ca.* 1175.
- Listed in OT as one of Philistine Pentapolis (Josh. 13:3; 1 Sam. 6:4, 17).
- Also mentioned in David's elegy over death of Saul and Jonathan (2 Sam. 1:20).
- From Tiglath-pileser's invasion of Philistia in 734, Ashkelon was tributary to Assyria until late in 8th century. Its rebellion and alliance with Hezekiah of Judah was put down by Sennacherib in 701, succeeded by Esarhaddon and Ashurbanipal.

Ashkelon, as early as Middle Bronze II-A an important Mediterranean port also located along the Way of the Sea. *(Neal and Joel Bierling)*

- After Assyria, Egypt, then Babylonians under Nebuchadrezzar gained control in 604.
- Under the Persians Ashkelon became a Tyrian city.[1]

Archaeological Features

- Evidence of occupation from Chalcolithic to Mameluke times.
- Enormous fortification system consisted of earthwork, 1.2 mi. in length around city.
- MB IIA-C glacis (rampart) constructed to protect city. It grew to *ca.* 150 acres in MB period, one of largest cities in Canaan and Syria.
- Limited excavations for LB period, but Iron I Philistine domination from *ca.* 1175-604 is well documented in ceramic shift from monochrome Mycenean IIIC:1 style to Philistine bichrome ware. Iron II Phoenician pottery was part of continuous occupational sequence from 10th to 7th centuries.
- Persian period one of best preserved down to wide destruction *ca.* 300 B.C.

Location

- On Mediterranean coast, some 39 mi. S of Tel Aviv, and 10 mi. N of Gaza.
- Has good soil and groundwater.
- Good location for agriculture by irrigation and sea trade.

Important Excavations

1921-22 J. Garstang and W. J. Pythian-Adams.
- P-A discovered Bronze and Iron Age Ashkelon, and stratified evidence of Philistine culture.

1985-present L. Stager for the Harvard Semitic Museum.
- Cultural sequences from 4th millennium B.C. through the 13th century A.D.

For Further Reading

Dothan, T. *The Philistines and Their Material Culture.* New Haven: 1982.
Esse, D. L. "Ashkelon." *ABD.* Vol. 1.
Stager, L. E. "Ashkelon." *NEAEHL.* Vol. 1.

Note

1. L. E. Stager, "Ashkelon," *NEAEHL,* 1:103-4.

GEZER

Importance

- First mention of Gezer on walls of Great Temple of Amon at Karnak during reign of Thutmose III (*ca.* 1490-1436).
- Prominent in Amarna period; ten letters attested from three Gezer kings.
- Famous Merneptah Stele (*ca.* 1207) states Israel destroyed, Gezer seized.
- Mentioned in Battle of Makkedah in Aijalon Valley (Josh. 10:33; 12:12).
- Allotted to Ephraim (Josh. 16:3, 10; Judg. 1:29; 1 Chr. 6:67; 7:28).
- Levitical city (Josh. 21:21).
- Referred to in David's campaigns against Philistines (2 Sam. 5:25; 1 Chr. 14:16; 20:4).
- Given to Solomon, part of marriage to daughter of pharaoh (1 Kgs. 9:15-17).
- Fortified by Solomon like Megiddo, Hazor, and Jerusalem.
- Relief of Tiglath-pileser III (*ca.* 745-728) at Nimrud depicts siege of city called *Ga-az-ru,* undoubtedly Gezer, during Assyria's campaign in Philistia, 734-733.
- Important in Maccabean period (1 Macc. 9:52; 13:43-48, 53).

Middle Bronze tower at Gezer in the Judean foothills. (*Neal and Joel Bierling*)

Archaeological Features

- 34th century, Chalcolithic ceramics, lithics.
- City not fortified in EBI and II, indicating relative obscurity.
- Greatest expansion in MBII.
- City still not fortified, but domestic housing well planned with fine plaster floors.
- Rock-hewn cisterns abounded, filled with natural runoff water.
- Zenith of power in MBIIIB-C period, first fortifications.
- Inner Wall traceable for some 400 m. around tell.
- Possibly as many as 25 defense towers.
- Large Inner Wall was 4.0 m. thick and preserved to a height of 4.5 m.
- Glacis, or rampart, added, alternating closely packed fills of debris from mound and freshly quarried chalk topped with thick plaster coating.
- Remarkable high place discovered by Macalister included row of ten monoliths, some over 3.0 m. high, erected in north-south line just inside Inner Wall in north-central area of the tell. Now known to be from MBIIC.
- Cultic or diplomatic interpretation debated, perhaps in connection with covenant renewal ceremony or a tribal/city-state league (cf. Exod. 24:1-11).
- LBI scarcely represented; partial abandonment may have followed Thutmose's destruction.
- Gezer experienced rebirth at beginning of LBIIA (*ca.* 14th century), undoubtedly associated with Amarna period, when Canaan was under Egyptian domination.
- Macalister cut water shaft off from its context, so it cannot be dated.
- With sloping tunnel 45.0 m. long, it may belong to Iron II like Hazor, Megiddo, and Gibeon.
- Partial hiatus in occupation at very end of 13th and beginning of 12th centuries. Tempting to relate this to destruction claimed by Pharaoh Merneptah, *ca.* 1207.
- Site may have been partially destroyed and deserted before coming of Sea Peoples in early 12th century.
- In Iron I, Philistine period at Gezer well attested (Strata XIII to XI).
- Architecture after Philistine strata became much poorer.
- Site came to violent end that may be synchronized with campaigns of Egyptian pharaoh who, according to 1 Kgs. 9:15-17, had "taken Gezer and burnt it with fire" before ceding it to Solomon, probably in *ca.* 950. (Suggested that this pharaoh was Siamun, of 21st Dynasty, but uncertain on present evidence).
- Iron II: first Israelite level at Gezer is Stratum VIII.

- Upper gate was exceptionally well built, with foundations in guardrooms going some 2.0 m. below surface and with fine masonry at jambs.
- Gezer under Solomon may have been only a token administrative center.
- A destruction, heavy in gateway area, brought Stratum VIII to an end, probably the work of Shishak (Sheshonq), *ca.* 924.
- In Stratum VII Solomonic gate rebuilt, but destroyed by Stratum VI, probably by Tiglath-pileser III in Assyrian campaigns of 733-732.
- Royal jar handles from *ca.* the time of Josiah (640-609) are attested, when Gezer was part of the Kingdom of Judah. Gate was badly destroyed in what must have been Babylonian invasion of 587-586.
- Gezer was burned and a significant historical gap ensued through most of Persian period, which takes history to end of canonical Old Testament.
- Hellenistic period saw considerable activity at Gezer.
- Roman boundary stones were set up by owner of area.

Location

- Tell Jezer, 33-acre mound, 5 mi. SSE of Ramleh. C. Clermont-Ganneau first made identification of site in 1871.
- Located on last of foothills in Judean Range, sloping down to meet northern Shephelah. Nearly 360 degrees of lookout view possible.
- Lies at juncture of trunk road leading to Jerusalem branching off from Via Maris.
- Good underground springs and fertile agricultural fields.

Important Excavations

1902-9 R. A. S. Macalister
- During period of primitive notions about stratigraphy.
- Dug trenches to bedrock, all the while dumping debris from each trench into one just cleared out.
- Material published by categories, for example, all burials together, rather than by chronological periods, so few objects can be related to strata.

1964-90 Hebrew Union College Biblical and Archaeological School, later the Nelson Glueck School of Biblical Archaeology, under directors: 1964-65 G. Ernest Wright; 1966-71 W. G. Dever; 1972-74 J. D. Seger; 1984, 1990 W. G. Dever.
- Clarified much of mound, redating Macalister.
- Exposed walls, gates, other architecture.
- Clarified ceramic horizon, incorporating new methods.[1]

For Further Reading

Dever, William G. "Gezer." *NEAEHL.* Vol. 2, pp. 496-506.

———— et al. *Gezer 1: Preliminary Report of the 1964-66 Seasons.* Vol. 1. Jerusalem: 1970.

————. *Gezer 2: Report of the 1967-70 Seasons in Fields I and II.* Jerusalem: 1974.

————. *Gezer 4: The 1969-71 Seasons in Field IV, "The Acropolis" 1-2.* Jerusalem: 1986.

Gitin, S. *Gezer 3: A Ceramic Typology of the Late Iron II, Persian, and Hellenistic Periods at Tell Gezer 1-2.* Jerusalem: 1990.

Mazar, A. *Archaeology of the Land of the Bible 10,000-586 B.C.E.* New York: 1990.

Note

1. W. G. Dever, "Gezer," *NEAEHL,* 2:496-505.

HAZOR

Importance

- Egyptian Execration texts of 19th-18th centuries contain earliest mention of Hazor, a major trade center.
- Babylonian Amarna texts of 14th century speak of ʿAbdi-Tirshi, king of Hazor, embroiled in political controversy and planning to join Habiru. These latter were socio-political outcasts and nomads who marauded sedentary villages.[1]
- "King Jabin of Canaan, who reigned in Hazor" (Judg. 4:2), was leader of confederation of Canaanite city-states who fought against Joshua at "the waters of Merom" (Josh. 11:7). Joshua reportedly "burned Hazor with fire," and only Hazor (11:10-13).
- Other sites in Central Hill country do not have similar destruction layers for LB period, however, leaving Hazor an isolated example.
- Main interest in these passages is compiler's, or editor's, gloss, which

Area A in the center of the upper city at Hazor, with the Solomonic gate and wall and a pillared storehouse dating to the ninth century B.C.
(Israel Department of Antiquities)

seeks to explain why Hazor alone was target of Joshua's attack.[2] The whole long-standing controversy over lack of agreement between Joshua and Judges on Conquest is ameliorated somewhat by archaeological conclusions that whatever conquest there was spanned some 100 years. See excavations by Usshishkin at Lachish.[3]

- 1 Kgs. 9:15 states: "This is the account of the forced labor that King Solomon conscripted to build the house of the Lord and his own house, the Millo and the wall of Jerusalem, Hazor, Megiddo, Gezer. . . ." Yadin comments: "In the whole saga of biblical archaeology, there are few cases in which so many owe so much to so few words, and one of the most exciting subjects dealt with in the following chapters is how this verse from Kings helped us in our excavations at Hazor, as well as at Megiddo and Gezer."[4]
- Solomon rebuilt or refortified Gezer, Megiddo, Hazor, and other locations.
- Destroyed by Tiglath-pileser III of Assyria *ca.* 733, during the reign of Pekah (2 Kgs. 15:29).

Archaeological Features

- The Lower City. Huge 170-acre area occupied from 18th to 13th centuries. Area C here yielded the "stelae temple," an edifice that contained, among others, a basalt stele depicting two hands raised in prayer toward a crescent and a circle. This area was destroyed in the 13th century, about the time of the Israelite settlement, and not rebuilt.[5]
- The Upper City mound. About 25 acres in size, the tell itself yielded 21 strata from Early Bronze II to Hellenistic Period of 3rd-2nd century.

Location

- Large city from Canaanite and Israelite times in Upper Galilee. Bears the Arabic names of Tell el-Qedah and Tell Waqqas.
- It is about 13 km. N of Sea of Galilee.

Important Excavations

1928 Garstang
- Trial soundings, not published in detail.
- Dated a destruction to 1400.

1955-58, 1966-69 J. A. de Rothschild Expedition, directed by Y. Yadin.
- Yadin reported that not much was known about *northern* Israel when he

started at Hazor; it was rather like initiating a new field. His attention was drawn to Hazor because of important role played by city in the history of the country in biblical times. He was in a position to reconstruct history of Hazor from historical documents and then confront his theories with results of excavations, an exciting situation in archaeological practice.[6]

For Further Reading

Aharoni, Y. "New Aspects of the Israelite Occupation in the North." In *Near Eastern Archaeology in the Twentieth Century.* Ed. J. A. Sanders. Garden City: 1970.
Fritz, V. "Conquest or Settlement?" *BA* 50 (1987): 84-100.
Hamilton, J. M. "Hazor." *ABD.* Vol. 3, pp. 87-88.
Yadin, Y. *Hazor: The Rediscovery of a Great Citadel of the Bible.* New York: 1975.
————, and A. Ben-Tor. "Hazor." *NEAEHL.* Vol. 2, pp. 594-605.

Notes

1. Y. Yadin and A. Ben-Tor, "Hazor," *NEAEHL*, 2:594.
2. Y. Yadin, *Hazor: The Rediscovery of a Great Citadel of the Bible* (New York: 1975), p. 12.
3. D. Ussishkin states: "[Lachish] may have been the largest city in Canaan after Hazor was destroyed in the thirteenth century BCE" ("Lachish," *NEAEHL*, 3:899).
4. Yadin, *Hazor*, p. 13.
5. J. M. Hamilton, "Hazor," *ABD*, 3:87-88.
6. Yadin, *Hazor*, p. 11.

HESHBON

Importance

- Traditionally identified with modern Tell Hesban on the Jordanian Mishor (Plateau).
- First biblical reference in Num. 21:21-30 (cf. Deut. 2:16-37) to city of Sihon, king of the Amorites, with a kingdom stretching from the Jabbok River south to the Arnon (Josh. 12:2). Border with Moabites changed frequently, complicating interpretation of geographical allusions (cf. Judg. 11:12-28).
- No occupation before 1200; therefore no help on early date of Exodus. Questions remain. Did site name move? Were Amorites in time of Exodus semi-nomadic and left no material remains? Is story anachronistic?

Archaeologists preparing to lift mosaic from the apse of a sixth-century A.D. church at Heshbon. *(Avery Dick, Heshbon Expedition)*

- City allotted to Reuben in the conquest of Canaan; later to Gad (cf. Num. 32:1-5; Josh. 21:34-40).
- Moabite Stone of 9th century mentions Medeba, Nebo, and Jahaz as Moabite; Heshbon must have been included in King Mesha's territory.
- Locale seems to belong to Moab in Isa. 15:4; 16:8-9; Jer. 48:2, 34-35, but must be back in Ammonite hands by Jer. 49:3.
- Site important in Hellenistic, Roman, and Byzantine times.[1]

Archaeological Features

- 19 separable strata discovered, dating from 1200 B.C. to 1500 A.D.
- Iron Age remains fragmentary due to wholesale removal of top of mound by later inhabitants. Pottery dated to Iron II/Persian period dumped into a plaster-lined reservoir, 17.5 m. on E side, 7.0 m. deep, which might be a "Pool of Heshbon," mentioned in Song of Sol. 7:4.
- Ammonite ostraca found in reservoir fill point to Ammonite control of site in 7th-6th centuries, for example, ostracon #4, a document for distributing supplies and money to court officials.[2]
- Iron II/Persian town had central government planning (judging from presence of the reservoir), in an area of mixed farming, including small tree and vineyard farming.[3]

Location

- 15-acre mound at elevation of *ca.* 900 m., with good defensive visibility.
- On edge of Jordanian plateau, overlooking Madaba Plains farming region, with Jordan Valley and Dead Sea to W and desert to E.
- About 37 mi. E of Jerusalem, 12 mi. SW of Amman, 5 mi. NE of Mt. Nebo.
- Along "King's Highway," a 4,000-year-old transportation artery NS through Jordan (cf. Num. 20:17).

Important Excavations

1968-1976 Andrews University Heshbon Expedition, directed by S. H. Horn (1968-73) and L. T. Geraty (1974-76)
- Discovered Iron I village.
- Unearthed possible Iron II fort, reservoir, perhaps Mesha's attempt to fortify his border against Israel.
- Found SW cemetery with Roman tombs.
- Conducted important regional survey project (D. Waterhouse, R. Ibach).[4]

For Further Reading

Geraty, L. T. "Heshbon." *NEAEHL.* Vol. 2, pp. 626-630.

————, and L. G. Herr, eds. *The Archaeology of Jordan and Other Studies. (S. H. Horn Fs.).* Berrien Springs: 1986.

Ibach, R. D., Jr. *Hesban 5: Archaeological Survey of the Hesban Region.* Berrien Springs: 1987.

LaBianca, Ø. S., and L. Lacelle. *Hesban 2: Environmental Foundations.* Berrien Springs: 1986.

Merling, D., and L. T. Geraty, eds. *Hesban after 25 Years.* Berrien Springs: 1994.

Sauer, J. A. *Heshbon Pottery 1971.* (Andrews University Monographs 7). Berrien Springs: 1973.

Notes

1. L. T. Geraty, "Heshbon," *NEAEHL,* 2:626-27.

2. F. M. Cross, "Ammonite Ostraca from Heshbon," *Andrews University Seminary Studies* 13 (1975): 1-20.

3. Geraty, "Heshbon," pp. 627-28.

4. Cf. R. D. Ibach, Jr., *Hesban 5: Archaeological Survey of the Hesban Region* (Berrien Springs: 1987).

669

JERICHO

Importance

- Mound called Tell es-Sultan, badly eroded today, was OT Jericho.
- Joshua sent spies to city (Josh. 2).
- Israelites marched around Jericho until walls fell (Josh. 5:13–6:23).
- Became Benjaminite city (Josh. 16 and 18).
- Held by Moabites under Eglon (Judg. 3).
- Home of a school of the prophets (2 Kgs. 2:4-5, 15).

Archaeological Features

- Fascinating, very important Neolithic site.
- Last MB buildings destroyed by fire, possibly work of Hyksos returning from Egypt, *ca.* 1560.
- LB site abandoned through most of 15th century, reoccupied soon after 1400, and abandoned again in 2nd half of 14th century (so no support for 1445 date for Exodus).

Neolithic stone tower at Jericho (ca. 8000-7000 B.C.), the world's oldest walled city. *(Neal and Joel Bierling)*

670

- LB pottery certainly later than 1400-1380.
- Site then destroyed again, but not as late as 13th century (so no support for 1290 or 1234 dates for Exodus.[1]

Location

- Tell el-Sultan, OT Jericho, *ca.* 1.2 mi. from modern oasis er-Riha, just NW of the Dead Sea.

Important Excavations

1907-9, 1911 Sellin and Watsinger
- Interpreted large portion of revetment glacis as Iron II. Now known to be MB.
- Dated houses on SE of tell from 11th to 9th centuries.

1932-1936 John Garstang
- Reported finding walls of Joshua's destruction.
- Dating partially unreliable due to poor excavation techniques at the time.

1952-1958 Kathleen Kenyon
- Used improved Wheeler-Kenyon, 3-dimensional digging methods.
- Opened tombs from EB to Roman times.
- Sunk three main trenches.
- Showed that so-called LB walls in Garstang's City D, which he associated with Joshua's destruction of Jericho (Josh. 6:24), were misdated; later shown by Kenyon to be two successive phases of EB town wall.
- Canaan poor, mostly unwalled, in LB, due to strength of Egyptian 18th Dynasty, and expulsion of Hyksos.[2]

For Further Reading

Holland, T. A., and E. Netzer. "Jericho." *ABD.* Vol. 3, pp. 723-740.
Kenyon, K. "Jericho (Tell es-Sultan)." *NEAEHL.* Vol. 2, pp. 674-681.

Notes

1. K. Kenyon, "Jericho (Tell es-Sultan)," *NEAEHL*, 2:680.
2. T. A. Holland and E. Netzer, "Jericho," *ABD*, 3:736.

JERUSALEM

Importance

- Egyptian Execration texts (20th-19th centuries), Amarna Letters (14th century), and Sennacherib inscriptions (7th century) mention Jerusalem. Shortened form *Salem* in Gen. 14:18 and Ps. 76:2 seems also early.[1]
- Difficult to trace history of Jerusalem before David, partly because area is so built up, hindering excavation. City began on SE spur below the location of later Temple Mount.
- Bronze Age pottery found in various areas. Amarna Letters speak of Egyptian rule over indigenous Canaanites. "The Land of Jerusalem" at this mid-14th-century juncture probably more a region than a pinpoint on map.
- "Jebusites"[2] inhabited Jerusalem before David (cf. Ezek. 16:3).
- Term "the Araunah" also pertinent. Basic may be a Hurrian word *ewrine* ("lord"), found in Hittite, Ugaritic. Related to Hittites, Jebusites controlled land of Jerusalem during 12th-11th centuries B.C.[3]
- City of David and Temple Mount: David took Jerusalem from Jebusites early in his reign (2 Sam. 5:6-9), although 1 Chr. 11:4-7 credits Joab. Jebusites lived with people of Benjamin in Jerusalem (Judg. 1:21). David transferred seat of government from Hebron to Jerusalem, to City of David. David "built the city round about from the Millo in complete circuit" (1 Chr. 11:8; 2 Sam. 5:9). "Millo" may refer to terraces on E slope of SE spur that formed retaining walls for structures above. Finds from period have been published by K. M. Kenyon and Y. Shiloh. David brought Ark to Jerusalem, when city became capital, but Jerusalem sacred before David. Mount Moriah, where Abraham built his altar (Gen. 22), was place nicknamed "the LORD provides." Here David purchased the "threshing floor of Araunah the Jebusite" and built his altar, later to become locale for Solomon's Temple, at the place of Abraham's altar. In Christian times, one might note that the Church of the Holy Sepulchre, a location where the Lord also "provided," is in easy line-of-sight proximity to this sacred place.
- Royal Temple and the Royal Palace: Construction of acropolis of Jerusalem, including Temple and royal palace, began after death of David. Style was Tyrian, and plan was typical of Neo-Hittite and Aramean royal cities. Whole project took some twenty years' effort. Temple was built during first seven years of work. Palace buildings included palace itself, House of Pharaoh's Daughter, throne room, Hall of Columns, and House of the Forest of Lebanon; these latter were built over balance of thirteen

Walls of the Middle Bronze Age city on Mount Ophel (2000-1500 B.C.);
remains from the Hasmonean era (141-137 B.C.) can be
seen on top. *(Neal and Joel Bierling)*

years. There were also international trade markets nearby, as are crammed into Old City today.

- City of Judah: Temple continued to be center of national and religious feelings of people throughout Divided Monarchy. Foreign influences — Phoenician, then Aramean, then Assyrian — made impact on Jerusalem's life. Attention was given to Temple area by kings of Judah, notably by Jehoshaphat, who set up "certain Levites and priests and heads of families of Israel" (2 Chr. 19:8) in a kind of high court in Jerusalem. Joash made repairs on Temple and city's fortifications. Uzziah and Joram reinforced defenses of city against Assyrian threat. Ophel, built between royal palace and City of David, constituted a new citadel. After the shattering of Northern Kingdom of Israel, Hezekiah of Judah gains a measure of strength between Assyria on north and Egypt on south, culminating in his notable project involving diversion of Gihon Spring waters underground, south to Pool of Siloam (2 Chr. 32:30).
- Even "wicked" King Manasseh was instrumental in refortifying Jerusalem. Greater heights achieved by Josiah in withstanding Assyria.
- Under Josiah the walled city of Jerusalem included the Makhtesh (apparently in Tyropoeon Valley), and the Mishneh on the western hill. It was Josiah who emphasized worship at the central sanctuary in Jerusalem.
- Temple was destroyed in 586 B.C. by Babylonians, yet Jerusalem continued to be focal point of Jews, both inside and outside the borders of the country.

- Cyrus of Persia in 538 B.C. allowed Jews to return to their homeland, and they began to build a new, Second Temple.

Archaeological Features

- Y. Shiloh traced stratified history of Jerusalem from Chalcolithic Period in second half of fourth millennium B.C. to present day. He reported that "there is little archaeological evidence for the Jebusite town of the twelfth and eleventh centuries BCE."[4] But Shiloh could reconstruct contours of the city in 10th century B.C. from Stratum 14, found in his areas D1 and E, on eastern slope of City of David spur.
- It was Macalister who first uncovered a "stepped stone structure," which he thought belonged to Jebusite times. Most recently, Shiloh has shown that structure was part of southeastern corner of David's citadel/stronghold, which stood between his Lower City and the Temple Mount.
- Question of City of David's western defenses has yet to be settled. The Western Gate or Valley Gate was excavated by Crowfoot in 1927-1928. Together with an associated wall it may date to tenth to eighth centuries B.C., before city spread further to west.
- David's citadel or Ophel (the biblical equivalent of "acropolis," Isa. 32:14; 2 Chr. 27:3; 33:14) was built on top of remains of the Canaanite city fortress.
- "No excavation in Jerusalem has yet produced finds relating to the Temple itself; all reconstructions of it and of its environs rely on the details in the biblical description, as well as on comparative studies of construction techniques and architectural constituents known from other, contemporary administrative centers in this country and Syria."[5]
- In 8th century B.C. Jerusalem reached greatest development. After fall of Samaria in 722 B.C., Israel prepared for Assyrian attack. Jerusalem's swollen population spread to western hill. Fortifications were redone, and Hezekiah's Tunnel was added to Warren's Shaft and the Siloam Tunnel for a supply of water for city.
- Seventh-century edifices include so-called "House of Ahiel," a house with four rooms in City of David (Shiloh's area G), with name Ahiel appearing on two ostraca near the house. There is also the "Burnt Room," which demonstrates severity of conflagration of 586 B.C. in Babylonian destruction of Jerusalem. Of particular interest is the City of David's "House of the Bullae," which contained fifty-one bullae with seal impressions listing Hebrew names. Most noteworthy of these, found on a plastered floor near Shiloh in 1982, mentions a person in Bible, "[Belonging to] Gemaryahu son of Shaphan" (Jer. 36:10-12). This Gemariah was strong supporter of Jeremiah at court of King Jehoiakim (Jer. 36:26).[6]

- Over 250 clay bullae in Hebrew from same period have appeared on antiquities market. These seem to be genuine. Baruch the son of Neriah (Jer. 36:4) and Jerahme'el the son of the king (Jer. 36:26) are among the names. Baruch was indeed Jeremiah's secretary, and the scribe after whom deuterocanonical Book of Baruch is named (Bar. 1:1, 2).[7] Rounding out list of some published seals of this type and time, there is one of unknown provenience mentioning "Ishmael son of Nethaniah" (Jer. 40:14; 41:1), an Ammonite "hit man" who was to kill Gedaliah governor of Judah, and, from Tell el-'Umeiri in Central Jordan, an Ammonite seal impression was found in 1984 which reads "[Belonging to] Milkom-'Or, servant of Ba'al-Yasha'." This Baal-Yasha' is called Baalis in Jer. 40:14, and it was he that sent Ishmael to kill Gedaliah.[8]
- Eighth to sixth centuries were most important historically and biblically in nation's history. We have "an unambiguous stratigraphical and chronological sequence: stratum 12 must be assigned to late eighth century BCE, stratum 11 to early seventh century BCE, and stratum 10 to late seventh and mainly sixth centuries BCE. A gap begins with destruction of Jerusalem in 586 BCE" (cf. 2 Kgs. 25:8-10; 2 Chr. 36:18-19).[9] The wholesale burning, destruction, and collapse left dramatic evidence.
- Jerusalem's water systems, including Gihon Spring, which is situated in the Kidron Valley at the foot of the eastern slope of the City of David. Unusual, intermittent spring, gushing forth several times a day. There are three notable underground water systems in the City of David spur. These will be described in turn:
- Warren's Shaft. In 1867 C. Warren discovered the water shaft that has been named after him. Y. Shiloh cleared the shaft. A long horizontal tunnel leads to the top of the shaft, then the shaft itself proceeds vertically for some 12.3 m. down to the level of the Gihon Spring. Water was pumped up to the top of the shaft by the people.[10] The popular notion that David/Joab climbed up this shaft to take the city from the Jebusites (2 Sam. 5:6-8; 1 Chr. 11:4-7) is unsubstantiated by any clear archaeological evidence. In that scenario, the Jebusites would have been the builders of Warren's Shaft, rather than the Israelites of the 10th century B.C., the more likely builders. Other such sites at Megiddo, Hazor, Gezer, Gibeon, and Ibleam show that this kind of water supply system was common to Israelite construction throughout the country.
- The Siloam Tunnel. This famous tunnel was built to solve a particular problem associated with the Gihon Spring. It carried water some 400 m. paralleling the Kidron Valley, now underground, now open to the valley, and finally ending at the Pool of Siloam.
- Hezekiah's Tunnel. The Gihon system was unprotected from enemy attack, however, and required a shrewd piece of ancient engineering,

675

combined with favorable openings in the underground rock, allowing the opening of Hezekiah's Tunnel. Archaeology confirms the biblical record at 2 Kgs. 20:20; 2 Chr. 32:3, 4, 30), showing that Hezekiah's Tunnel supplanted the Siloam Tunnel and brought water into regulated reservoirs that were protected by city walls. Most likely these three systems, Warren's, Siloam, and Hezekiah's, functioned simultaneously until the fall of Jerusalem in 586 B.C.

For Further Reading

Avigad, N. *Discovering Jerusalem.* Nashville: 1983.

Bahat, D. "Jerusalem Down Under: Tunneling along Herod's Temple Mount Wall." *BARev* 21/6 (1995): 30-47.

Boling, R. G., and G. E. Wright. *Joshua.* AB. Garden City: 1982.

Busink, T. A. *Der Tempel von Jerusalem.* Band I: *Der Tempel Salomos.* Leiden: 1970.

Geraty, L. T., et al. "The Madaba Plains Project: A Preliminary Report on the First Season [1984] at Tell el-'Umeiri and Vicinity." *ADAJ* 31 (1987): 187-199; 569-577.

Kenyon, K. *Royal Cities of the Old Testament.* New York: 1971.

————. *Digging Up Jerusalem.* London: 1974.

King, P. J. *Jeremiah: An Archaeological Companion.* Louisville: 1993.

Mazar, B., and Y. Shiloh. "Jerusalem: The Early Periods and the First Temple Period." *NEAEHL.* Vol. 2, pp. 698-701.

Simons, J. *The Geographical and Topographical Texts of the Old Testament.* Leiden: 1959.

————. *Jerusalem in the Old Testament.* Leiden: 1952.

Yadin, Y., et al., eds. *Jerusalem Revealed: Archaeology in the Holy City, 1968-1974.* Jerusalem: 1975.

Notes

1. B. Mazar and Y. Shiloh, "Jerusalem: The Early Periods and the First Temple Period," *NEAEHL,* 2:698.

2. On the name, see J. Simons, *The Geographical and Topographical Texts of the Old Testament* (Leiden: 1959).

3. Mazar and Shiloh, p. 699.

4. *Ibid.,* p. 702.

5. *Ibid.,* p. 704.

6. P. J. King, *Jeremiah: An Archaeological Companion* (Louisville: 1993), p. 94.

7. Cf. H. Shanks, "Fingerprint of Jeremiah's Scribe," *BARev* 22/2 (1996): 36-38.

8. Cf. L. T. Geraty et al., "The Madaba Plains Project: A Preliminary Report on the First Season at Tell el-'Umeiri and Vicinity," *ADAJ* 31 (1987): 196.

9. Mazar and Shiloh, p. 708.

10. *Ibid.,* p. 710.

LACHISH

Importance

- Identified at Tell ed-Duweir by W. F. Albright in 1929 from Eusebius's *Onomastikon,* 120:20.
- 31-acre site figured strongly in biblical accounts.
- Greatest prosperity toward end of LB; may have been largest city in Canaan after destruction of Hazor in 13th century.
- Mentioned in Hermitage Papyrus 1116A and Amarna Letters.
- Canaanite city under Egyptian domination, down to about 1130.
- Level VI possibly destroyed by Israelites (cf. Josh. 10:31-32).
- City second only to Jerusalem in Judean Kingdom period.
- Some believe Lachish fortified by Rehoboam (2 Chr. 11:5-12, 23).
- Death of Amaziah in 769 took place here (2 Kgs. 14:19; 2 Chr. 25:27).
- Sennacherib's army set up command post from which to attack Jerusalem (2 Kgs. 18:14; cf. wall reliefs in palace at Nineveh).
- City destroyed by Nebuchadnezzar in 587/586.
- Exiles from Babylon occupied site in Persian period (Neh. 11:30).

Approach road at Lachish, leading to the gate complex. *(Neal and Joel Bierling)*

Archaeological Features

- Earliest occupational remains from EBII.
- MBIIB-C fortifications, palace, cult place, and many tombs.
- Impressive glacis/rampart of horizontal fill and lime plaster around city.
- "Fosse" temple built in moat at bottom of glacis in LB period.
- LB Acropolis Temple built for Canaanite cult with Egyptian accessories.
- Monarchic period city gate largest in Israel (25.0 × 25.0 m.).
- Palace-fort at greatest extent in Level III, destroyed by Assyrians.
- Assyrian siege-ramp, Judean counter-ramp, military weaponry attest to Sennacherib's attack in 701 at SW corner of mound.
- Royal Judean storage jars and their stamps made during reign of Hezekiah.[1]
- Settlement rebuilt after time of Josiah.
- Famed "Lachish Letters" found by Starkey in room near outer gate, Babylonian period.
- Level II destroyed by Nebuchadrezzar/Babylonians during conquest of Judah, 587, as shown by ostraca, bullae, seals (cf. Jer. 34:7).
- Level I datable to Babylonian, Persian, and Early Hellenistic times.

Location

- On edge of Nahal Lachish (Wadi Ghafr) in Shephelah lowlands, where road from Hebron passed by site to Mediterranean coast.
- Good wells, fertile lands made city viable.

Important Excavations

1932-38 Wellcome-Marston Expedition (J. L. Starkey, L. G. Harding, O. Tufnell)
- Found city gates, levels II and I.
- Discovered outer revetment wall.
- Uncovered Solar Shrine, Great Shaft, the palace-fort, and the Fosse Temple.
- Found famous Lachish Ostraca, 1935ff.
- Excellent dig in its time; Starkey, disciple of Petrie, used his methods.

1966 Aharoni, for Hebrew University; 1968 for Tel Aviv University
- Clarified plans of temples at Lachish and Arad.

1973 Ussishkin for Tel Aviv University
- Worked on areas opened by Starkey.

• Clarified city gates from Judean Kingdom at time of Assyrian invasion.

For Further Reading

Tufnell, O. *Lachish III, The Iron Age.* London: 1953.
———. *Lachish IV, The Bronze Age.* London: 1958.
Ussishkin, D. "Lachish." *ABD.* Vol. 4.
———. "Lachish." *NEAEHL.* Vol. 3, p. 909.

Note

1. D. Ussishkin, "Lachish," *NEAEHL,* 3:909; cf. O. Tufnell, *Lachish III: The Iron Age (Text)* (London: 1953), pp. 315-316.

MEGIDDO

Importance

- Identified as Tell el-Mutesellim in Arabic.
- Scene of battle in Judg. 5:19; cf. Josh. 12:21.
- Manassites unable to take some strong Canaanite towns, notably Megiddo (Josh. 17:11-13; Judg. 1:27-28; 1 Chr. 7:29).
- One of Solomon's fortified cities in 5th administrative district (1 Kgs. 4:12; 9:15).[1]
- Pharaoh Sheshonq (Shishak) conquered Megiddo in Rehoboam's 5th year (*ca.* 925, not mentioned in Bible).
- Ahaziah (2 Kgs. 9:27), Josiah (2 Kgs. 23:29; 2 Chr. 35:22) died near Megiddo. Judah felt defeat sorely: "the mourning for Hadad-rimmon in the plain of Megiddo" (Zech. 12:11), evident reference to Josiah's death.

Archaeological Features

- 20 strata, beginning in 4th millennium.
- Canaanite temples of great interest.
- Gate complexes at Megiddo, Hazor, and Gezer afford corpus for comparative study. Area AA city gate from Stratum VIII, 15th-14th centuries B.C.[2]

Model of Tell el-Mutesellim, site of ancient Megiddo, showing many of the twenty strata of occupation. *(Neal and Joel Bierling)*

- "Megiddo Ivories" a trademark at site, esp. LBII example depicting ruler on his throne receiving victory procession after battle.[3]
- Stratum VB marks beginning of 10th century, time of David.
- Strata VA-IVB are from 10th century as well, time of Solomon and Shishak.
- Northern stable area (debated among experts), gate area, also on north, and spectacular subterranean water tunnel system have all been reevaluated and dated to Iron Age.
- Level IVA belongs to 9th-8th centuries, from Omri and Ahab to Assyrian conquest in 732 B.C. Level III is from time of Assyrian rule, or 780-650 B.C., and Stratum II is from time of Josiah.

Location

- Sits astride the SE extent of Carmel Range.
- Near international trade route, linking Mesopotamia with Egypt along the Via Maris.
- Supreme military, economic, mercantile, and cultural center.
- Famous Valley of Armageddon to N.

Important Excavations

1903-5 German Society for the Study of Palestine
- Schumacher dug 20-25 m. trench through whole mound, datable from MBII to Iron Age.

1925-39 Oriental Institute of the University of Chicago under Fisher, Guy, and Loud.
- Northern city gate, temple area to E singled out for investigation from 1935 on.

1960, 1970, 1972 Hebrew University
- Y. Yadin excavated on a small scale in NE part of site, and on W to clarify stratigraphy in temples in area BB.[4]

For Further Reading

Aharoni, Y. "Megiddo." *NEAEHL*. Vol. 3, pp. 1003-24.
Davies, G. I. "Solomonic Stables at Megiddo after All?" *PEQ* 120 (1988): 130-141.
Kenyon, K. *Royal Cities of the Old Testament*. New York: 1971.
Lamon, R. S. *The Megiddo Water System*. Chicago: 1935.
May, H. G. *Material Remains of the Megiddo Cult*. Chicago: 1935.

Rendsburg, G. A. "The Date of the Exodus and the Conquest/Settlement: The Case for the 1100s." *VT* 42/4 (1992): 510-527.

Ussishkin, D. "Megiddo." *ABD.* Vol. 4, pp. 666-79.

Notes

1. Y. Aharoni and Y. Shiloh, "Megiddo," *NEAEHL*, 3:1004.
2. *Ibid.,* p. 1010.
3. *Ibid.,* p. 1012.
4. D. Ussishkin, "Megiddo," *ABD,* 4:668.

SAMARIA

Importance

- Capital of Israel, the Northern Kingdom, from Omri's time (884-874; 1 Kgs. 16:23, 24) until Assyrian conquest (722).
- Fortified heavily by Ahab (874-853; 1 Kgs. 22:39) and probably embellished by Jeroboam II (793-753; 2 Kgs. 14:23-29).
- Served as capital of the Assyrian province of Samaria in 7th century.
- Retained some importance under Persians (539-332), though headquarters of the Samaritan community shifted south to Shechem.

Archaeological Features

- Acropolis of 4 acres, made level on hilltop by a huge platform supported by retaining walls.
- Fortress/palace built by Omri and expanded by Ahab. Stones carefully cut and erected without mortar. Probably a Phoenician technique adopted by Ahab.
- Outer casemate wall (1.8 m.), inner wall (1.0 m.) with 7 m. of space between, made installation 10.0 m. thick. Survived Assyrian attack and remained useful for centuries.[1]

Palace of Omri and Ahab at Samaria. *(Neal and Joel Bierling)*

683

- "Ivory house," a section of palace that contained numbers of carved ivory plaques, apparently inlays for furniture or wall paneling. Note "beds of ivory" (Amos 6:4).
- Storehouse in which were found 63 ostraca, on which were recorded transactions of wine and grain.
- A multilevel city with royal acropolis above and house of the people on slopes and at base of hill.

Location

- Central hill country, 10 km. NW of Shechem.
- Strategically placed by Omri at junction of north-south road and two other main thoroughfares W to coast at Sharon; route N to Phoenicia.
- Hilltop setting (430 m. above sea level) provided wide view in all directions.
- Fertile neighboring lands.

Important Excavations

1908-10 Harvard University
- Unearthed west part of fortress from 9th century.
- Discovered treasure trove of ostraca.

1931-35 Consortium of 5 institutions (Harvard, Palestine Exploration Fund, British Academy, British School of Archaeology in Jerusalem, Hebrew University).[2]
- Extended clearing of royal fortress.
- Uncovered ivory carvings from Ahab's day.
- Confronted serious obstacles to their planned stratigraphy in jumbled state of construction remains from various levels.

For Further Reading

Avigad, N. "Samaria (City)." *NEAEHL*. Vol. 4.
Kenyon, K. *Royal Cities of the Old Testament*. New York: 1971.
Oppenheim, A. L. "Babylonian and Assyrian Historical Texts." *ANET*. Pp. 265-317.
Purvis, J. D. "Samaria (City)." *ABD*. Vol. 5, pp. 914-921.
Wright, G. E. "Israelite Samaria and Iron Age Chronology." *BASOR* 155 (1959): 13-29.

Notes

1. N. Avigad, "Samaria (City)," *NEAEHL*, 4:1303.
2. *Ibid.*, p. 1302.

SHECHEM

Importance

- Attested in Execration Texts and Amarna Letters.
- Mentioned in Bible in connection with Abraham (Gen. 12:6), Jacob (Gen. 33:18-20; 35:1-4), Jacob's family (Gen. 34), and Joseph (Gen. 37:12-17). Also in Deuteronomic history: Deut. 27; Josh. 8:30-35; Judg. 9; Josh. 24:1, 32; and 1 Kgs. 12.
- Location of sanctuary and covenant renewal ceremonies.
- First town in MB period.
- Destroyed, reoccupied in 16th century; important LB city as proven by Amarna Letters.
- A city of refuge (Josh. 20:7), part of Levitical allotment.
- Abimelech, Rehoboam, and Jeroboam came here to establish sovereignty over region (Judg. 9; 1 Kgs. 12). Biblical accounts in Judges can be synchronized with material remains.
- One of districts that provisioned Samaria in Samaria Ostraca, presumably from first half of 8th century (cf. Josh. 17:2).[1]

Archaeological Features

- Underneath Migdal Temple on NW quadrant of mound, evidence of EBI was found. There was no EB II-III pottery, however.
- Resettled, but unfortified, in about 1900.
- MBIIC city expanded, NW gate built; cp. Megiddo, Hazor, Gezer. On acropolis now was fortress temple, or *migdal*.
- Another abandonment period, 1540-1450.
- Shechem a prominent city-state from 1750-1540.
- LB Age and Iron I: *ca.* 1450, NW and E gates both rebuilt. *Migdal* rebuilt, altar and huge *masseba* (sacred pillar) put in forecourt. City prominent in period of Lab'ayu.
- Major destruction brought city to an end about 1350-1300.
- Monarchic Period: third abandonment surprising. From 1150/1125 to 975 city virtually unpopulated.
- Recovery, then destruction, presumably in connection with Pharaoh Shishak's raid in about 918.[2]
- Jeroboam I's rebuilding (1 Kgs. 12:25); Shechem again a city.[3]
- Fine example of typical "four-room" house destroyed about 724 by Assyrians.

Fortress temple at Shechem, rebuilt ca. 1450 B.C. with large standing
stone in forecourt. *(Neal and Joel Bierling)*

- Assyrian Occupation and Persian Period. Scanty remains. Attic (Greek)
  black-glazed ware is found in the potsherds.

Location

- Several names attach to this Central Hill Country site: ancient Shechem,
  Tell Balâtah, is nestled between Mt. Gerizim and Mt. Ebal in territory of
  Ephraim. From nearby Roman Neapolis is derived modern Arabic name
  Nablus.
- From Shechem to Jerusalem is distance of just 40 mi. (67 km.). With
  abundant water still, modern village covers part of southern half of tell.
- Sites along main route to N are Samaria and Dothan.
- Both "Jacob's Well" (John 4) and "Joseph's Tomb" are in the vicinity.
- There is a well-known Samaritan religious enclave atop Mt. Gerizim.

Important Excavations

1913-14; 1926-27; 1934 Austro-German Expedition
- E. Sellin opened up areas that later have been redefined as Hellenistic,
  Late Israelite (Late Iron Age), Early Israelite (Early Iron Age), Canaanite
  (Bronze Age), and earlier, back to Chalcolithic Period.

686

- After World War I Sellin returned (1926-27) and found fortification system at Shechem would be a complex puzzle to work out.
- Sellin dug at Shechem again in 1934, working on his final report until 1943. His records were destroyed in Berlin during World War II.

1956-73 Drew-McCormick Expedition
- Harvard's G. Ernest Wright used opportunity at Shechem to arrange a training dig for American, Canadian, and European scholars. They used the Wheeler-Kenyon method, then developing, and based their ceramics on advances made by the 1950s by Albright.
- Their mission was to tie the loose ends that Sellin had left and make sense of stratigraphy of site.
- Wright was first to introduce cross-disciplinary research, including an association with R. Bullard, a geologist.
- Digging by Americans spanned period from 1956 to salvage and clean-up done by W. G. Dever in 1972 and 1973.
- 24 distinct strata were uncovered and analyzed.[4]
- Shechem has enjoyed the attention of some of the best American archaeologists ever.

For Further Reading

Campbell, E. F. "Shechem (Tell Balâtah)." *NEAEHL.* Vol. 4, pp. 1345-1354.

Hunt, M. "Moreh." *ABD.* Vol. 4, p. 904.

Toombs, L. E. "Shechem (Place)." *ABD.* Vol. 5, pp. 1174-1186.

————. "The Stratigraphy of Tell Balatah (Ancient Shechem)." *ADAJ* 17 (1972): 99-110, pls. I-XI.

Wright, G. E. *Shechem: The Biography of a Biblical City.* London: 1965.

Notes

1. E. F. Campbell, "Shechem," *NEAEHL,* 4:1347.

2. L. E. Toombs, "The Stratigraphy of Tell Balatah (Ancient Shechem)," *ADAJ* 17 (1972): 101.

3. Campbell, "Shechem," p. 1353.

4. *Ibid.,* p. 1347; Toombs, "Shechem (Place)," *ABD* 5:1177.

CHAPTER 51

Messianic Prophecy

"Messianic," as a technical term, does not occur in the Old Testament. How then can one speak of "messianic prophecy"?

Because Christians are principally concerned with Christ, they have a special interest in looking for prophecies of Christ in the Old Testament. This quest, in fact, has traditionally shaped much of the attention Christians have paid to the Old Testament. Some have been tempted to deal with these themes apart from the context in which they were developed. We have made it our aim to treat the prophetic messages largely in terms of their own historical setting. It seems, therefore, appropriate to conclude our survey with a sketch of the subject of messianic prophecy which has held and must hold much fascination for thoughtful Christians.

> Bartimaeus . . . a blind beggar, was sitting by the roadside. When he heard that it was Jesus of Nazareth, he began to shout . . . "Jesus, Son of David, have mercy on me." Mark 10:46-49

Messianic Prophecy and Prophecy in General

Like biblical prophecy in general (see Ch. 16, above), messianic prophecy is not simply "history written in advance." However much it relates to the coming Messiah, it also had force that applied to the times in which it was given. We cannot, therefore, treat biblical prophecy as if it were a "timeless" prediction of the time of Messiah.

The Word "Messiah." The English word derives from Heb. *māšîaḥ* (sometimes written *mashiach*), a common adjective meaning "anointed." It was translated into Greek as *christos* "anointed," from which come "Christ" and "christen." The words "Messiah" and "Christ" have the same basic meaning. With reference to Jesus as the "Christ," the New Testament writers identified him absolutely as the Jewish Messiah. As the terms develop in usage, "Christ" takes on additional meanings. The Christian connotations become broader than those assigned to the historic Jewish "Messiah."

We must be careful, therefore, not to begin with a concept of the New Testament Christ. We must appreciate the historical preparation in Israel for the coming of Messiah. Otherwise, we work backwards in time without a true grasp of the real significance of time. We should first ask what the people of Israel heard when they developed their understanding of the Hebrew term. It was typically used as an adjective meaning "anointed," often with respect to "the anointed priest" (Lev. 4:3, 5, 16) and several times with reference to kings (Pss. 2:2; 18:50 [MT 51], etc.). Sometimes it is used as a substantive, "anointed one," applied even to the Persian king Cyrus (Isa. 45:1). But nowhere in the Old Testament does the word occur with the technical meaning of "Messiah."[1]

Only after the formation of the Old Testament canon and before the time of Jesus, in the intertestamental period, did the word come to be used as a technical term, usually with the article, "the Anointed" (Pss. Sol. 17:36; 18:8; cf. 1 Enoch 48:10; 52:4). By the time of Jesus, Messiah was in common use as a title of the One who was to hold a divinely appointed office.[2] When the rulers sent priests and Levites to interrogate John the Baptist, he replied: "I am not the Messiah" (John 1:20). His reply was understood perfectly, for they asked next: "Are you Elijah?" According to Jewish teaching, Elijah was to come just prior to the advent of the Messiah (Mal. 4:5 [MT 3:24]). Likewise, when Jesus asked the apostles: "Who do men say that I am?" Peter replied: "The Christ . . ." (Matt. 16:15f.). The early Church adopted this title for Jesus (see Acts 2:36). Then "Jesus the Christ (Messiah)," was simplified to "Jesus Christ," virtually a proper name.

Messianic Prophecy without Messiah? To answer this question we must first understand that prophecy is a message from God (see Ch. 16), a message that links its present situation to God's ongoing redemptive activity in the history of Israel. This passionate program of divine rescue culminates in Jesus Christ. Therefore, we can acknowledge as "messianic" any prophecy which ties the present with God's ultimate purposes. We may best understand, then, the term "messianic prophecy" in this broad sense and sharpen our definition of it by noting several distinctions.

(1) Soteriological prophecy. Many prophetic passages express the general idea that God is working to save his people. The time is surely coming when this purpose will be achieved. Such hope is to be found in the story of the Fall, where God tells the serpent that the seed of the woman will crush the serpent's head — i.e., that the adversary of God's plan for the human race will be defeated in the long run (see Gen. 3:15). Although often called "messianic prophecy," this passage might better be placed in the category of soteriological prophecy, prophecy which proclaims God's ultimate victory over everything opposed to his saving purpose for his creation.

(2) Eschatological prophecy. Quite a number of prophecies, especially in books later than 722 b.c. when Samaria fell, relate to the days to come or the end of the age. As early as Amos,[3] we find statements like this:

> "In that day I will raise up
>> the booth of David that is fallen
>> and repair its breaches,
>>> and raise up its ruins,
>>> and rebuild it as in the days of old." (Amos 9:11)

> "The time is surely coming," says the LORD,
>> "when the one who plows shall overtake the one who reaps,
>> and the treader of grapes the one who sows the seed. . . .
> I will restore the fortunes of my people Israel,
>> and they shall rebuild the ruined cities and inhabit them." (vv. 13f.)

These passages we take as referring to the "messianic age" (see below). Still, they mention no messianic person; God himself is central. Since such texts concern the end time, they may be classified as eschatological prophecy.

(3) Apocalyptic prophecy. In a few prophecies, particularly exilic and postexilic, divine intervention brings about the final victory over the enemies of God's people. Sometimes this is connected with the "day of Yahweh," an expression already in use by the time of Amos (see Amos 5:18). The day of Yahweh, or day of the Lord, is a day of judgment (Isa. 2:12-22), wrath (Zeph. 1:7-18), and salvation or victory (3:8-20). When Gog of the land of Magog comes against Israel "in the latter years," it is God in person, using earthquake, pestilence, torrential rains, and every kind of terror, who defeats Gog and saves his people and their land (Ezek. 38:1–39:29). This dramatic invasion of God into the historical chain of events and the prophecies that depict it may be called "apocalyptic."

(4) Messianic prophecy. Only when the Messiah is clearly in view, or when the messianic reign is described, should prophecy technically be called messianic. Otherwise, great confusion arises.[4] But if the term "Messiah" does not as such occur in the Old Testament, how then may we best learn about the person and kingdom of the Messiah?

Messianic Person and Office

Son of David. According to Jewish usage in the intertestamental and New Testament periods (*ca.* 300 B.C.–A.D. 300), "Messiah" meant specifically that Son of David who was to appear as the messianic king according to God's ancient promise to the House of David (2 Sam. 7). The New Testament uses it precisely in this sense. Thus Jesus asked the Pharisees: "What do you think of the Messiah? Whose son is he?" and they replied, "The son of David" (Matt. 22:42). When Jesus rode into Jerusalem in a manner recalling Solomon's coronation (1 Kgs. 1:38) and suggesting the fulfillment of Zechariah's prophecy (Matt. 21:5; cf. Zech. 9:9), the crowds shouted, "Hosanna to the Son of David!" (Matt. 21:9). When the apostles were concerned with establishing Jesus' messianic claims, they centered on Old Testament passages that mentioned David (Acts 1:16; 2:25), and argued that it was actually the Messiah who was intended (see Acts 2:29-31, 34-36, substituting "Messiah" for "Christ").[5]

Davidic Dynasty. When David was planning to build a temple (or "house") for Yahweh, the prophet Nathan was sent, first to veto that plan, and then to promise "the Lord will make you a house" (2 Sam. 7:11). The following words are from the "Davidic covenant":

> I will raise up your offspring after you, who shall come forth from your body. . . . I will establish the throne of his kingdom forever. . . . Your house and your kingdom shall be made sure forever before me; your throne shall be established forever. (vv. 12-16).

On the basis of this covenant the terms "house of David," "throne of David," and "son of David" assume a large role in Old Testament prophecy (see discussion of the prophecy from the Chronicler's perspective (Ch. 41).

In reviewing Samuel and Kings (see Chs. 12–15), we noted that the Davidic dynasty contined until the fall of the southern kingdom. The postexilic prophets and the writings (Ezra and Nehemiah) demonstrate that the Davidic line was established once more in the person of Zerubbabel. In the New Testament genealogies of Jesus (Matt. 1; Luke 3), Jesus was of the line of David.

Tomb of King David, from whose line would spring
"a righteous Branch" (Jer. 33:15). *(Garo Nalbandian)*

The centrality of the Davidic dynasty for the messianic hope becomes vitally important.

Isaiah proclaimed a hope concerning the "latter time" (Isa. 9:1). A child would be born and would take upon himself the burden of government, "to establish it, and to uphold it with justice and with righteousness from this time forth and for evermore." The authority of this government was to be "upon the throne of David" (vv. 6f.). Isaiah also mentioned "a shoot . . . from the stump of Jesse, and a branch . . . out of his roots" (11:1). The reference is to David as the son of Jesse; even though cut down, the Davidic line would spring up again from the same roots. Jeremiah too, features the Davidic covenant (Jer. 33:17, 20f.), citing "a righteous branch" and "a shoot of righteousness to spring up for David" (Jer. 23:5f.; 33:14-16). He even announces that "they shall serve . . . David their king, whom I will raise up for them" (30:9). Ezekiel says: "I will set up over them one shepherd, my servant David," who "shall be prince

692

among them" (34:23f.). Similar statements are found in other prophets (Hos. 3:5; cf. Mic. 5:2 where "Bethlehem" is to be the hometown of a new ruler). The prophetic tradition and the hope it would create in Israel is profoundly bound up with the Davidic dynasty.

Royal Psalms.[6] A number of psalms deal with the king, enthroned in Jerusalem. Yet they contain expressions that indicate One who is greater than the ruling monarch. For example, Ps. 2 refers to the king on Zion (the portion of Jerusalem where the palace was located), but it addresses him as Yahweh's "son" (v. 7). It promises that God will give him the nations for a heritage and the ends of the earth for a possession (v. 8). This affirmation seems to look forward to a time when the king will not only rule over Israel but even over the gentiles. A wedding song, Ps. 45 is also addressed "to the king" (v. 1 [MT 2]), and celebrates the glory of his kingship. But it goes on to say: "Your throne, O God, endures forever and ever" (v. 6 [MT 7])[7] and concludes: "I will cause your name to be celebrated in all generations; therefore the peoples will praise you forever and ever" (v. 17 [MT 18]). This certainly looks beyond the reign of the incumbent king! Ps. 110 opens: "Yahweh says to my lord: 'Sit at my right hand, until I make your enemies your footstool' " (v. 1). Other expressions are used that elsewhere are connected with the end of the age, such as "the day of his wrath" (v. 5) and "execute judgment among the nations" (v. 6). These few examples show that the king who sat on the throne of David was a symbol of something greater in space and time than himself and his reign, and could even in some way signify Yahweh as a commissioned, anointed representative. Psalms like these that express faith in God's promise to establish his eternal kingdom, and that also refer to the king or throne in Jerusalem, can properly be called messianic psalms. They are closely related to messianic prophecy and may have contributed to its themes and motifs.

Messianic Kingdom. In the messianic prophecies we discern that the writers envisaged more than simply the continuity of the Davidic dynasty. "Son of David" comes to suggest a broader, deeper idea. While individual kings are called "son of Jeroboam," "son of Nebat," or "son of Ahaz," the prophetic passages title the future ruler "son of David."

> Thus, the original covenant with David is constantly called to mind. Also in view is the permanent kingdom to be established in the latter days and to exist "forever and ever."[8] It includes the nations (or gentiles) and extends to the ends of the earth. But it is more than a mere extension in space and time of the kingdom of Judah. It differs in its shape and

> substance, being founded on a total righteousness and perfect peace never known in the history of Israel nor anywhere else. The Spirit of the Lord Jesus rests upon the messianic king who judges with righteousness and equity in a new epoch, in the age to come. Isa. 11:2-4.

Even changes in the natural order are part of the prophetic picture of this messianic kingdom:

> The wolf shall live with the lamb,
> the leopard shall lie down with the kid,
> the calf and the lion and the fatling together,
> and a little child shall lead them.
> . . . . . .
> They will not hurt or destroy in all my holy mountain;
> for the earth shall be full of the knowledge of the LORD,
> as the waters cover the sea. (vv. 6-9)

The focus of this chapter has been on the kingly aspects of messianism. But the subject as featured in the New Testament is considerably broader. Jesus is pictured there not only as the fulfillment of the royal ideal as Son of David but of many other Old Testament themes as well: as wise man he is greater than Solomon (Matt. 12:42); as Son of Man he fulfills Daniel's vision (Dan. 7:13ff.); as prophet and lawgiver he is a second Moses (Matt. 5–7); as priest he outranks Aaron (Heb. 5–7); as Servant of Yahweh he gives his life a ransom for many (Mark 10:45). Strands, including the royal one, that were originally separate or distinguished in the Old Testament, were braided together by Jesus himself. They reflect his consciousness of being God's Anointed and Chosen One.

Abbreviations

AASOR	*Annual of the American Schools of Oriental Research*
AB	Anchor Bible
ABD	*Anchor Bible Dictionary*
ABRL	Anchor Bible Reference Library
ADAJ	*Annual of the Department of Antiquities of Jordan*
AJA	*American Journal of Archaeology*
AJSL	*American Journal of Semitic Languages and Literature*
ANEP	J. B. Pritchard, *The Ancient Near East in Pictures,* 2nd ed. (Princeton: 1969)
ANET	J. B. Pritchard, *Ancient Near Eastern Texts,* 3rd ed. (Princeton: 1969)
AOAT	Alter Orient und Altes Testament
Ant.	Josephus, *Antiquities of the Jews*
ARAB	D. D. Luckenbill, ed., *Ancient Records of Assyria and Babylonia,* 2 vols. (Chicago: 1926-1927)
BA	*Biblical Archaeologist*
BANE	G. E. Wright, ed., *The Bible and the Ancient Near East* (1961; repr. Winona Lake: 1979)
BARev	*Biblical Archaeology Review*
BASOR	*Bulletin of the American Schools of Oriental Research*
BDB	F. Brown, S. R. Driver, and C. A. Briggs, *A Hebrew and English Lexicon of the Old Testament* (Oxford: 1907)
BDPT	R. G. Turnbull, *Baker's Dictionary of Practical Theology* (Grand Rapids: 1967)
BHS	*Biblia Hebraica Stuttgartensia*

Bibl	*Biblica*
BJRL	*Bulletin of the John Rylands Library*
BKAT	M. Noth and H. W. Wolff, eds., Biblischer Kommentar: Altes Testament (Neukirchen)
BST	J. A. Motyer and J. R. W. Stott, eds., The Bible Speaks Today
BWANT	Beiträge zur Wissenschaft von Alten und Neuen Testament
BZAW	Beihefte zur Zeitschrift für die alttestamentliche Wissenschaft
CAH	I. E. S. Edwards et al., eds., *Cambridge Ancient History,* 3rd ed., 2 vols. in 4 parts (Cambridge: 1970–)
CBC	Cambridge Bible Commentary
CBQ	*Catholic Biblical Quarterly*
CC	Communicator's Commentary
CCHS	B. Orchard, ed., *A Catholic Commentary on Holy Scripture* (New York: 1953)
ConB	Coniectanea biblica
CTM	*Concordia Theological Monthly*
DJD	Discoveries in the Judaean Desert of Jordan (Oxford: 1955–)
DOTT	D. W. Thomas, ed., *Documents from New Testament Times* (New York: 1961)
FOTL	The Forms of the Old Testament Literature (Grand Rapids)
FRLANT	Forschungen zur religion und Literatur des Neuen und Alten Testament
HAT	O. Eissfeldt, ed., Handbuch zum Alten Testament (Tübingen)
HDB	J. Hastings, ed., *Dictionary of the Bible,* 4 vols. (New York: 1898-1902); supplement (1904); rev. ed., 1 vol. (1963)
HKAT	Handkommentar zum Alten Testament (Göttingen)
HSAT	E. Kautzsch and A. Bertholet, eds., *Die Heilige Schrift des Alten Testament,* 4th ed. (Tübingen: 1922-1923)
HSM	Harvard Semitic Monographs
HTR	*Harvard Theological Review*
HUCA	*Hebrew Union College Annual*
IB	G. A. Buttrick, ed., *The Interpreter's Bible,* 12 vols. (Nashville: 1952-1957)
IBD	N. Hillyer, ed., *The Illustrated Bible Dictionary* (Wheaton: 1980)
ICC	The International Critical Commentary (Edinburgh)
IDB	G. A. Buttrick, ed., *The Interpreter's Dictionary of the Bible,* 4 vols. (Nashville: 1962)
IDBSup	K. Crim, ed., *The Interpreter's Dictionary of the Bible, Supplement* (Nashville: 1976)
IEJ	*Israel Exploration Journal*
Interp	*Interpretation*
ISBE	J. Orr, ed., *International Standard Bible Encyclopedia,* 5 vols.

(Grand Rapids: 1939); rev. ed., 4 vols., G. W. Bromiley et al., eds. (1979-1988)

ITC	International Theological Commentary (Grand Rapids)
JAOS	*Journal of the American Oriental Society*
JB	The Jerusalem Bible
JBL	*Journal of Biblical Literature*
JJS	*Journal of Jewish Studies*
JNES	*Journal of Near Eastern Studies*
JPOS	*Journal of the Palestine Oriental Society*
JPS	Jewish Publication Society
JQR	*Jewish Quarterly Review*
JSNTSup	Journal for the Study of the New Testament, Supplement Series
JSOT	*Journal for the Study of the Old Testament*
JSOTSup	Journal for the Study of the Old Testament, Supplement Series
JSS	*Journal of Semitic Studies*
KAT	E. Sellin and J. Herrmann, eds., Kommentar zum Alten Testament (Leipzig, Gütersloh)
KJV	King James Version
LGB	R. Alter and F. Kermode, eds., *The Literary Guide to the Bible* (Cambridge, Mass.: 1987)
LXX	Septuagint
MT	Masoretic Text
NASB	New American Standard Bible
NBC	D. Guthrie and J. A. Motyer, eds., *The New Bible Commentary Revised* (Grand Rapids: 1970)
NCBC	R. E. Clements and M. Black, eds., The New Century Bible Commentary (Grand Rapids)
NEAEHL	*New Encyclopedia of Archaeological Excavations of the Holy Land*
NEB	New English Bible
NICOT	R. L. Hubbard, ed., The New International Commentary on the New Testament (Grand Rapids)
NIV	New International Version
NRSV	New Revised Standard Version
OBS	J. J. Finkelstein and M. Greenberg, eds., *Oriental and Biblical Studies* (Philadelphia: 1967)
OTL	The Old Testament Library (Philadelphia)
OTMS	H. H. Rowley, ed., *The Old Testament and Modern Study* (Oxford: 1951)
OTS	*Oudtestamentische Studiën*
PEQ	*Palestine Exploration Quarterly*

POTT	D. J. Wiseman, ed., *Peoples of Old Testament Times* (Oxford: 1973)
RB	*Revue biblique*
RSV	Revised Standard Version
RV	Revised Version
SBLDS	Society for Biblical Literature Dissertation Series
SBLMS	Society for Biblical Literature Monograph Series
SBT	Studies in Biblical Theology
SJLA	Studies in Judaism in Late Antiquity
SJT	*Scottish Journal of Theology*
SOTS	The Society for Old Testament Study
TCERK	L. Loetscher, ed., *Twentieth-Century Encyclopedia of Religious Knowledge,* 2 vols. (Grand Rapids: 1949)
TDNT	G. Kittel and G. Friedrich, eds., *Theological Dictionary of the New Testament,* 10 vols. (Grand Rapids: 1964-1976)
TOTC	Tyndale Old Testament Commentary
USQR	*Union Seminary Quarterly Review*
UUÅ	*Uppsala Universitets Årsskrift*
VSAT	Verbum Salutis Ancien Testament
VT	*Vetus Testamentum*
VTSup	*Vetus Testamentum, Supplements*
WBC	Word Biblical Commentary
WMANT	Wissenschaftliche Monographien zum Alten und Neuen Testament
WTJ	*Westminster Theological Journal*
WUNT	Wissenschaftliche Untersuchungen zum Neuen Testament
ZAW	*Zeitschrift für die alttestamentliche Wissenschaft*
ZB	Zürcher Bibelkommentare
ZNW	*Zeitschrift für die neutestamentliche Wissenschaft*
ZPBD	M. C. Tenney, ed., *The Zondervan Pictorial Bible Dictionary* (Grand Rapids: 1963)
ZPEB	M. C. Tenney, ed., *The Zondervan Pictorial Encyclopedia of the Bible,* 5 vols. (Grand Rapids: 1975)

For Further Reading

Chapter 1 — The Pentateuch

Alter, R. *The Art of Biblical Narrative.* New York: 1981. (The application of literary principles to the interpretation of ancient narratives leads to an analysis different from that of the documentary hypothesis.)

Blenkinsopp, J. *The Pentateuch: An Introduction to the First Five Books of the Bible.* ABRL. New York: 1992. (A scholarly summary of contents and message), based on a highly modified view of the traditional description of the composition).

Bright, J. *Early Israel in Recent History Writing.* Naperville: 1956.

———. "Modern Study of Old Testament Literature." Pp. 13-31 in *BANE.* (Argues for new approach)

Cassuto, U. *Documentary Hypothesis.* Trans. I. Abrahams. Jerusalem: 1961. (Challenge to documentary hypothesis)

Childs, B. S. *Introduction to the Old Testament as Scripture.* Philadelphia: 1979. (Esp. pp. 109-135)

Clements, R. E. "Pentateuchal Problems." Pp. 96-124 in G. W. Anderson, ed., *Tradition and Interpretation.* Oxford: 1979. (Thorough survey of recent trends)

Clines, D. J. A. *The Theme of the Pentateuch.* JSOTSup 10. Sheffield: 1978. (Identifies *posterity, relationship,* and *land* as three major components of the theme, while showing how they are prepared for in Gen. 1–11 and played out in Gen. 12–Deuteronomy.)

Driver, S. R. *Introduction to the Literature of the Old Testament.* 9th ed. 1913; repr. Magnolia, Mass.: 1972. (Esp. pp. 1-159; still indispensable for the older viewpoint)

Eissfeldt, O. *The Old Testament: An Introduction.* Trans. P. R. Ackroyd. New York: 1965. (Comprehensive survey of scholarship, thorough bibliography)

Knierim, R. "Criticism of Literary Features, Form, Tradition, and Redaction." Pp. 123-166 in D. A. Knight and G. M. Tucker, eds., *The Hebrew Bible and Its Modern Interpreters.* Philadelphia: 1985. (A scintillating review of various critical methods being employed in Old Testament studies since World War II with a call to reconceptualize and integrate these methods for proper historical exegesis)

Knight, D. A. "The Pentateuch." Pp. 263-296 in D. A. Knight and G. M. Tucker, eds., *The Hebrew Bible and Its Modern Interpreters.* Philadelphia: 1985. (A description of the present state of disagreement in Pentateuchal studies)

Livingston, G. H. *The Pentateuch in Its Cultural Environment.* Grand Rapids: 1974. (Esp. pp. 184-283; applies archaeological and manuscript discoveries)

McEvenue, S. *Interpreting the Pentateuch.* Collegeville, Minn.: 1990.

Mann, T. *The Book of the Torah.* Atlanta: 1988.

Rendtorff, R. *The Old Testament: An Introduction.* Trans. J. Bowden. Philadelphia: 1986.

———. *The Problem of the Process of Transmission in the Pentateuch.* Trans. J. J. Scullion. Sheffield: 1990. (Critical evaluation of the documentary hypothesis and a call for the study of the larger complexes of the tradition)

Sawyer, J. F. A. *From Moses to Patmos: New Perspective in Old Testament Study.* London: 1977.

Whybray, R. N. *The Making of the Pentateuch.* Sheffield: 1987. (A thorough evaluation of the methods used by those who support the documentary hypothesis; the weaknesses of these methods are underscored. Less persuasive is Whybray's late dating and historical skepticism in his attempt to view the Pentateuch as a "national history," parallel to that of Herodotus [5th cent. B.C.].)

Wright, G. E. *The Old Testament against Its Environment.* Naperville: 1950.

Chapter 2 — Genesis: Primeval Prologue

Anderson, B., ed., *Creation in the Old Testament.* London: 1984.

Clines, D. J. A. *The Theme of the Pentateuch.* Sheffield: 1978. Pp. 61-79.

Hamilton, V. *The Book of Genesis 1–17.* NICOT. Grand Rapids: 1990.

McKenzie, J. L. *Myths and Realities: Studies in Biblical Theology.* Milwaukee: 1963.

Renckens, H. *Israel's Concept of the Beginning. The Theology of Genesis 1–3.* New York: 1964.

Richardson, A. *Genesis I–XI.* 3rd ed. Torch Bible Commentary. London: 1959.

Rogerson, J. *Genesis 1–11.* JSOT Old Testament Guides. Sheffield: 1991.

Thielicke, H. *How the World Began: Man in the First Chapters of the Bible.* Philadelphia: 1961.

Wenham, G. *Genesis 1–15.* WBC 1. Waco: 1987.

Westermann, C. *The Genesis Accounts of Creation.* Trans. N. E. Wagner. Philadelphia: 1964.

————. *Genesis 1–11.* Minneapolis: 1984.

Chapter 3 — Genesis: Patriarchal History

Bailey, L. *The Pentateuch.* Nashville: 1981.

Delitzsch, F. *A New Commentary on Genesis.* 2 vols. 5th ed. Edinburgh: 1899. (Outdated in literary treatment and Near Eastern background, but a profound theological study)

Dumbrell, W. J. *Creation and Covenant.* Nashville: 1984. (The covenants from Noah to David are studied in detail; the various aspects of the covenant with Abraham in chs. 12; 15; 17 are carefully treated.)

Hendel, R. S. "Genesis, Book of." *ABD* 2:933-941. (A summary of the research on the contents, composition, historical and literary background, and religious practices)

Hess, R., P. Satterthwaite, and G. Wenham, eds., *He Swore an Oath: Biblical Themes from Genesis 12–50.* Cambridge, U.K.: 1993. (A remarkable set of essays on the historical background and theological meaning of the Patriarchal narratives)

Hillers, D. R. *Covenant: The History of a Biblical Idea.* Baltimore: 1969. (Contrasts and compares Abrahamic and Mosaic covenants)

Kidner, D. *Genesis: An Introduction and Commentary.* Chicago: 1967.

LaSor, W. S. "Egypt." *ISBE* 2 (1982): 29-47. (Succinct presentation of historical background)

Millard, A. R., and D. J. Wiseman, eds., *Essays on the Patriarchal Narratives.* 2nd ed. Leicester: 1983. (Helpful discussion of recent issues relative to historicity, literary nature, and interpretation)

Moberly, R. W. L. *The Old Testament of the Old Testament.* Overtures to Biblical Theology. Minneapolis: 1992. (Ch. 3, "The Religion of the Patriarchs," presents a detailed analysis of the faith of the patriarchs, distinguishing it from that of Israel after Sinai.)

————. *Genesis 12–50.* JSOT Old Testament Guides. Sheffield: 1992. (Thoughtful interaction with recent scholarship)

Sarna, N. *Genesis.* The JPS Commentary. Philadelphia: 1989. (An excellent commentary from a Jewish perspective)

Scullion, J. J. "Genesis, the Narrative of." *ABD* 2:941-962. (A helpful analysis of the literary structure and stylistic devices)

Thompson, J. Arthur. "Covenant (OT)." *ISBE* 1 (1979): 790-793.

von Rad, G. *Genesis.* OTL. Philadelphia: 1972.

Wenham, G. *Genesis 16–50.* WBC. Dallas: 1994. (A fine analysis of the form, meaning, and background of the text)

Westermann, C. *Genesis 12–36* and *Genesis 37–50.* Trans. J. Scullion. Minneapolis:

1985 and 1986. (A thorough commentary on Genesis that emphasizes the form-critical approach)

Wiseman, D. J. "Assyria." *ISBE* 1 (1979): 332-341. (Succinct presentation of historical background)

———. "Babylonia." *ISBE* 1 (1979): 391-402. (Succinct presentation of historical background)

Chapters 4–5 — Exodus

Cassuto, U. *A Commentary on the Book of Exodus.* Trans. I. Abrahams. Jerusalem: 1967. (A stimulating treatment that avoids the standard literary critical views)

Childs, B. S. *The Book of Exodus.* OTL. Philadelphia: 1974.

Durham, J. I. *Exodus.* WBC. Waco: 1987. (A fine interpretative translation with notes and comments)

Ellison, H. L. *Exodus.* The Daily Study Bible Series. Philadelphia: 1982. (Clear, devout exposition of the text)

Gowan, D. E. *Theology in Exodus: Biblical Theology in the Form of a Commentary.* Louisville: 1995. (Exposition of theological themes of Exodus and their contribution to the rest of the Bible)

Hoffmeier, J. K. "Moses." *ISBE* 3 (1986): 415-425.

Johnstone, W. *Exodus.* JSOT Old Testament Guides. Sheffield: 1990. (Survey of recent scholarship, with special attention to the purported impact of P and D on Exodus)

Moberly, R. L. *At the Mountain of God.* JSOTSup 22. Sheffield: 1983.

Sarna, N. M. "Exodus, Book of." *ABD* 2:688-700.

———. *Exodus.* The JPS Torah Commentary. Philadelphia: 1991. (An excellent commentary from an outstanding Jewish scholar; presents brief comments in a verse-by-verse format)

Stamm, J. J., and M. E. Andrew. *The Ten Commandments in Recent Research.* London: 1967. (Full discussion of interpretation)

Westerholm, S. "Tabernacle." *ISBE* 4 (1988): 698-706. (Good bibliography)

Widengren, G. "What Do We Know about Moses?" Pp. 21-47 in J. I. Durham and J. R. Porter, eds., *Proclamation and Presence.* Richmond: 1970. (Defends basic historicity from a critical evaluation of the literary sources)

Zimmerli, W. *The Law and the Prophets.* Oxford: 1965. (Insightful treatment of the role of law in the Old Testament structure of faith and history)

Chapter 6 — Leviticus

Anderson, G. A. *Sacrifices and Offerings in Ancient Israel: Studies in Their Social and Political Importance.* HSM 41. Atlanta: 1987.

Cross, F. M., Jr. *Canaanite Myth and Hebrew Epic.* Cambridge, Mass.: 1973. (Essays on Israel's early priesthood, pp. 195-215; and the "Priestly Work," pp. 293-325)

de Vaux, R. *Studies in Old Testament Sacrifice.* Cardiff: 1964.

Douglas, M. *Purity and Danger.* London: 1966.

Grabbe, L. L. *Leviticus.* JSOT Old Testament Guides. Sheffield: 1993. (A survey of recent research with particular attention to insights from cultural anthropology)

Haran, H. *Temples and Temple-Service in Ancient Israel.* Winona Lake: 1985.

Harris, R. L. "Leviticus." In *The Expositor's Bible Commentary with the New International Version of the Holy Bible.* Grand Rapids: 1990. Vol. 2, pp. 499-654.

Harrison, R. K. *Leviticus.* TOTC. Leicester, U.K.; Downers Grove, Ill.: 1980.

Hartley, J. E. *Leviticus.* WBC 4. Dallas: 1992.

Knight, G. A. F. *Leviticus.* Daily Bible Study Series. Edinburgh; Philadelphia: 1981. (Devout and straightforward reading of the text)

Kuichi, N. *The Purification Offering in the Priestly Literature.* JSOTSup 56. Sheffield: 1987.

Levine, B. A. *Leviticus/Wayyiqrā'.* The JPS Torah Commentary. Philadelphia: 1989. (A fine commentary on the JPS translation for the Jewish community)

Milgrom, J. *Studies in Cultic Terminology and Theology.* SJLA 36. Leiden: 1983.

Noordtzij, A. *Leviticus.* Bible Student's Commentary. Trans. R. Togtman. Grand Rapids: 1982. (A solid evangelical interpretation)

Noth, M. *Leviticus.* Trans. J. E. Anderson. OTL. Philadelphia: 1965. (Literary- and historical-critical)

Snaith, N. H. *Leviticus and Numbers.* Rev. ed. Century Bible. London: 1967. (Text and notes)

Wenham, G. J. *The Book of Leviticus.* NICOT. Grand Rapids: 1979.

Wright, C. J. H. *God's People in God's Land.* Grand Rapids: 1990. (Study of relationship of land, family, and property in ancient Israel)

Chapter 7 — Numbers

Albright, W. F. "The Oracles of Balaam." *JBL* 63 (1944): 207-233. (Text and notes; supports historicity)

Blenkinsopp, J. *The Pentateuch.* ABRL. New York: 1992. (Good analysis of major themes)

Budd, P. J. *Numbers.* WBC 5. Waco: 1984. (Full exposition and introduction)

Carpenter, E. E. "Numbers, Book of." *ISBE* 3 (1986): 561-567. (Fine survey of contents, scholarly discussions, and theological message)

Fish, S. *The Book of Numbers.* Soncino Books of the Bible. London: 1950. (Text and translation, with notes; oriented toward Jewish reader)

Marsh, J. "Introduction and Exegesis of Numbers." *IB* 2:137-308.

Milgrom, J. "Numbers, Book of." *ABD* 4:1146-1155.

Noth, M. *Numbers.* Trans. J. D. Martin. OTL. Philadelphia: 1968. (Stresses use of various traditions and literary sources in the composition of Numbers)

Olson, Dennis T. *The Death of the Old and the Birth of the New: The Framework of the Book of Numbers and the Pentateuch.* Chico, Calif.: 1985.

Wenham, G. J. *Numbers.* Downers Grove: 1981. (Strong emphasis on the historicity of the book)

Chapter 8 — Deuteronomy

Brown, R. *The Message of Deuteronomy.* BST. Leicester: 1993. (Exposition with theological and pastoral insights)

Carmichael, C. M. *The Laws of Deuteronomy.* Ithaca, N.Y.: 1974. (Examines literary and historical problems)

Christensen, D. L. *Deuteronomy 1–11.* WBC. Dallas: 1991. (Translation and commentary with emphasis on liturgical use in Israel)

Clements, R. E. *God's Chosen People.* London: 1968. (Theological interpretation of Deuteronomy)

———. *Prophecy and Covenant.* London: 1965.

———. *Deuteronomy.* JSOT Old Testament Guides. Sheffield: 1989.

Craigie, P. C. *The Book of Deuteronomy.* NICOT. Grand Rapids: 1976. (Espouses conservative position regarding date and unity)

Daane, J. *The Freedom of God.* Grand Rapids: 1973. (Contrasts biblical view of election with that of Reformed scholastic theology)

Kaufman, S. A. "The Structure of the Deuteronomic Law," *Maarav* 1/2 (1978-79): 105-158.

McBride, S. D., Jr. "Polity of the Covenant People: The Book of Deuteronomy," *Interp* 41(1987): 229-244.

McCarthy, D. J. *The Old Testament Covenant.* Oxford: 1972. (Expansion of *CBQ* 27 [1965]: 217-240)

———. *Treaty and Covenant.* Analecta Biblica 21 (1965). (Form-critical study of ancient Near Eastern documents and the Old Testament; esp. pp. 109-140)

McConville, J. G. *Law and Theology in Deuteronomy.* JSOTSup 33. Sheffield: 1984.

Miller, P. D. *Deuteronomy — Interpretation.* Louisville: 1990. (Solid combination of literary analysis, theological significance, and pastoral use)

Nicholson, E. W. *Deuteronomy and Tradition.* Philadelphia: 1967. (Literary and historical problems)

Phillips, A. *Deuteronomy.* Cambridge Bible Commentary. Cambridge: 1973. (Commentary on NEB)

Polzin, R. "Deuteronomy." *LGB*, pp. 92-101. (Analysis of the forms and flow of the speeches)

Rowley, H. H. *The Faith of Israel.* London: 1956. (Includes essay on Israelite equation of the good life with obedience to the will of God)

Weinfeld, M. *Deuteronomy and the Deuteronomic School.* Oxford: 1972. (Studies sermonic composition, relationship to wisdom, and the law as rationalistic ideology)

———. "Deuteronomy, Book of." *ABD* 2:168-183.

Zimmerli, W. *The Law and the Prophets*. Trans. R. E. Clements. Oxford: 1965. (Esp. pp. 31-45 on Law and Covenant)

Chapter 9 — The Former Prophets

Fretheim, T. M. *Deuteronomic History*. Interpreting Biblical Texts. Nashville: 1983. (An introduction and a study of key texts, concerned with both basic and contemporary meaning)

Noth, M. *The Deuteronomistic History*. JSOTSup 15. Sheffield: 1981. (A translation of the ground-breaking work on the Deuteronomistic History, which has won widespread acceptance)

Porter, J. R. "Old Testament Historiography." Pp. 125-162 in G. W. Anderson, ed., *Tradition and Interpretation*. Oxford: 1979. (Pp. 132-152 on the Deuteronomistic historical work)

Provan, I. W. *1 and 2 Kings*. New International Biblical Commentary. Peabody, Mass.: 1995. (Valuable introduction outlining the importance of both the historical content and the literary-theological perspective of the authors of Kings)

————. "Ideologies, Literary and Critical: Reflections on Recent Writings on the History of Israel," *JBL* 114 (1995): 585-606. (Cogent criticisms of recent scholars' attempts to downplay the historical value of the biblical accounts)

Rast, W. E. *Joshua, Judges, Samuel, Kings*. Proclamation Commentaries. Philadelphia: 1978. (An overview and a detailed study of leading theological themes)

Weinfeld, M. *Deuteronomy and the Deuteronomic School*. Oxford: 1972. (Suggests a lengthy development in Deuteronomistic tradition beginning in Hezekiah's day and continuing to the Exile)

Chapter 10 — Joshua

Albright, W. F. *Yahweh and the Gods of Canaan*. New York: 1968. (A strong argument for the uniqueness of the biblical God)

Butler, T. C. *Joshua*. WBC 7. Waco: 1983. (A detailed, technical commentary featuring the theological emphasis of the book)

Childs, B. S. *Biblical Theology of the Old and New Testaments*. Minneapolis: 1993. (An exposition of the thematic ties between the two halves of the Christian Bible)

Clinton, J. R. *The Joshua Portrait*. Altadena, Calif.: 1990. (Lessons about Christian leadership from Joshua's example)

Craigie, P. C., and G. H. Wilson. "Religions of the Biblical World: Canaanite." *ISBE* 4 (1988): 95-101.

Freedman, D. N. "Hexateuch." *IDB* 2:597f. (Useful bibliography)

Gray, J. *Joshua, Judges, Ruth*. Grand Rapids: 1986.

Hamlin, E. J. *Joshua*. Grand Rapids: 1983.

705

Kaufmann, Y. *The Biblical Account of the Conquest of Palestine.* Trans. M. B. Dagut. Jerusalem: 1953. (Former Prophets not a "Deuteronomistic historical work")

LaSor, W. S. "Archeology of Egypt." *ISBE* 1 (1979): 253-255, esp. III.F, G; IV.E.

————. "Egypt." *ISBE* 2 (1982): 40-44, VIII.F-H.

Liverani, M. "Ugarit; Ugaritic." *ISBE* 4 (1988): 937-941.

McCarthy, D. J. "The Theology of Leadership in Joshua 1–9." *Bibl* 52 (1971): 165-175.

Miller, J. M., and G. M. Tucker. *The Book of Joshua.* CBC. New York: 1974. (Literary, historical, theological study)

Soggin, J. A. *Joshua: A Commentary.* Trans. R. A. Wilson. OTL. Philadelphia: 1972. (Supports hypothesis of a "Deuteronomistic" school)

Waltke, B. K. "Israel, Religion of." *ISBE* 2 (1982): 929-932, esp. II.B. Name, D. Covenant, III.a Gift of the Land, B. Holy War.

————. "Joshua, Book of." *ISBE* 2 (1982): 1134-1138. (Influenced by Kaufmann's picture of the conquest)

Weippert, M. *The Settlement of the Israelite Tribes in Palestine.* Trans. J. D. Martin. SBT 21. Naperville: 1971. (Critical survey of "classical" hypotheses)

Wood, B. G. "Did the Israelites Conquer Jericho?" A New Look at the Archaeological Evidence," *BARev* 16 (1990): 44-58.

————. "Dating Jericho's Destruction: Bienkowski Is Wrong on All Counts," *BARev* 16 (1990): 45-49, 69. (Defends an Israelite conquest of Jericho *ca.* 1400 B.C.E. against P. Bienkowski's view that Jericho was destroyed in the Middle not Late Bronze Age)

Woudstra, M. H. *The Book of Joshua.* NICOT. Grand Rapids: 1981. (Stresses the ways in which the Hebrew narrative anticipates later developments in Israel's life)

Yamauchi, E. M. "Archeology of Palestine and Syria." *ISBE* 1 (1979): 276-278, esp. II.D, E, F.

Yeivin, S. *The Israelite Conquest of Canaan.* Istanbul: 1971. (Successive waves of incoming Israelites)

Youngblood, R. F. "Amarna Tablets." *ISBE* 1 (1979): 105-108.

Chapter 11 — Judges

Alt, A. "The Settlement of the Israelites in Palestine." In *Essays on Old Testament History and Religion.* Trans. R. A. Wilson. Oxford: 1966, pp. 135-69; Garden City: 1968, pp. 175-221.

Blenkinsopp, J. "Structure and Style in Judges 13–16." *JBL* 82 (1963): 67-76.

Boling, R. G. *Judges.* AB 6A. Garden City: 1975. (Form critical; applies recent archaeological finds)

Crenshaw, J. L. *Samson: A Secret Betrayed, a Vow Ignored.* Atlanta: 1978. (Applies "aesthetic criticism" to Samson "saga")

Fensham, F. C. "Judges, Book of." *ISBE* 2 (1982): 1156-1159.

Grohman, E. D. "Moab." *IDB* 3:412-415. (Rise of Iron Age civilization)

Hamlin, E. J. *Judges*. Grand Rapids: 1990.

Hildebrand, D. R. "Samson." *ISBE* 4 (1988): 309-311.

Jobling, D. *The Sense of Biblical Narrative: Structural Analyses in the Hebrew Bible II*. JSOTSup 39. Sheffield: 1986. Pp. 47-87. (Relationship between literary structure and political theory in Judges and 1 Sam. 1–12)

Levertoff, P. "Judge." *ISBE* 2 (1982): 156.

Lind, M. C. *Yahweh Is a Warrior*. Scottdale, Pa.: 1980. (Esp. ch. 4, "The Conquest as Yahweh's War")

McKenzie, J. L. *The World of the Judges*. Englewood Cliffs, N.J.: 1966. (Thorough study, emphasizing cultural, religious, and historical background)

Martin, J. D. *The Book of Judges*. CBC. New York: 1975.

Mayes, A. D. H. *Israel in the Period of the Judges*. SBT. Naperville: 1974. (Argues against amphictyony hypothesis, favoring community whose members acknowledge Yahweh as God and whose unity was founded at Kadesh)

———. *Judges*. JSOT Old Testament Guides. Sheffield: 1985.

Noth, M. "The Background of Judges 17–18." Pp. 68-85 in B. W. Anderson and W. Harrelson, eds., *Israel's Prophetic Heritage*. New York: 1962. (Sees book as pro-monarchical)

———. *Das System der zwölf Stämme Israels*. Stuttgart: 1930. (Classic reconstruction of premonarchical history of Israel, stressing twelve-tribe amphictyony)

Rogers, M. G. "Book of Judges." *IDBS*, pp. 509-514.

Smend, R. *Yahweh War and Tribal Confederation*. Trans. M. G. Rogers. Nashville: 1970. (Esp. pp. 43-75, "Major and Minor Judges")

Soggin, J. *Judges*. OTL. London: 1987.

Wharton, J. A. "The Secret of Yahweh: Story and Affirmation in Judges 13–16." *Interp* 27 (1973): 48-66.

Williams, J. G. "The Structure of Judges 2:6–16:31." *JSOT* 49 (1991): 77-86.

Chapter 12 — Birth of the Monarchy

Ackroyd, P. R. *The First Book of Samuel*. CBC. New York: 1971.

———. *The Second Book of Samuel*. CBC. New York: 1977.

Albright, W. F. "Reconstructing Samuel's Role in History." Pp. 42-65 in *Archaeology, Historical Analogy, and Early Biblical Tradition*. Baton Rouge: 1966.

Anderson, A. A. *2 Samuel*. WBC 2. Dallas: 1989. (Thorough exposition of Hebrew text)

Baldwin, J. G. *1 and 2 Samuel*. TOTC. Leicester, U.K.; Downers Grove, Ill.: 1988.

Brueggemann, W. "Samuel, Book of 1-2." *ABD* 5:965-973. (Summary of narrative and theology)

Campbell, A. F. *The Ark Narrative*. SBLDS. Missoula: 1975. (Form-critical, traditio-historical study of 1 Sam. 4–6; 2 Sam. 6)

Eslinger, L. M. *Kingship of God in Crisis: A Close Reading of 1 Samuel 1–12*. Sheffield: 1985.

Flanagan, J. W. "Samuel, Book of 1-2." *ABD* 5:957-965. (Summary of text, composition, and content)

Gordon, R. P. "David's Rise and Saul's Demise: Narrative Analogy in 1 Samuel 24–26." *Tyndale Bulletin* 31 (1980): 37-64.

———. *1 and 2 Samuel*. JSOT Old Testament Guides. Sheffield: 1984. (Concise summary of main contemporary approaches)

Gunn, D. *The Fate of King Saul*. JSOTSup 14. Sheffield: 1980.

Hertzberg, H. W. *I and II Samuel*. Trans. J. S. Bowden. OTL. Philadelphia: 1964.

Hoffner, H. A., Jr. "A Hittite Analogue to the David and Goliath Contest of Champions?" *CBQ* 30 (1968): 220-225.

Klein, R. W. *1 Samuel*. WBC 10. Waco: 1983. (Detailed commentary showing the role of 1 Samuel in the Deuteronomic history)

McCarter, P. K., Jr. *I Samuel*. AB. Garden City: 1980. (Comprehensive)

Miller, P. D., and J. J. M. Roberts. *The Hand of the Lord*. Baltimore: 1977. (Literary and historical reassessment of ark narrative, including comparative and structural studies)

Payne, D. F. *Kingdoms of the Lord: A History of the Hebrew Kingdoms from Saul to the Fall of Jerusalem*. Grand Rapids: 1981. (An excellent account of the history of this period and its impact on Israel's faith)

Petersen, D. L. *The Role of Israel's Prophets*. JSOTS 17. Sheffield: 1981. (Analysis of meaning and function of various prophetic titles: Seer, Man of God, etc.)

Rosenberg, J. "1 and 2 Samuel." *LGB*, pp. 122-143. (Examines literary symmetries, roles of David, and overall argument of 1-2 Samuel)

Segal, M. H. "The Composition of the Books of Samuel." *JQR* 55 (1964): 318-339; 56 (1965): 32-50, 137-157. (Sees later compilation including stories of the ark, Saul, Samuel, first and second stories of David)

Tsevat, M. "Studies in the Book of Samuel." *HUCA* 32 (1961): 191-216; 33 (1962): 107-118; 34 (1963): 71-82; 36 (1965): 49-58.

———. "Ishbosheth and Congeners, the Names and Their Study." *HUCA* 46 (1975): 71-87.

Vannoy, J. R. *Covenant Renewal at Gilgal*. Cherry Hill, N.J.: 1977. (Study of 1 Sam. 11:14–12:25)

Chapter 13 — Israel's Golden Age: David and Solomon

Alt, A. "The Formation of the Israelite State." In *Essays on Old Testament History and Religion*. Trans. R. A. Wilson. Oxford: 1966; Garden City: 1968. (Esp. pp. 171-237 [1966]; 223-309 [1968] on David and Solomon)

Anderson, A. A. *2 Samuel*. WBC. Dallas: 1989. (Solid introduction and exposition of Hebrew text)

Bright, J. "The Organization and Administration of the Israelite Empire." Pp. 193-208 in F. M. Cross, Jr., W. E. Lemke, and P. D. Miller, Jr., eds., *Magnalia Dei: The Mighty Acts of God*. Festschrift G. E. Wright. Garden City: 1976. (Role of David's personality, development of central administration)

Brueggemann, W. *First and Second Samuel.* Interpretation. Louisville: 1990. (Exposition for teaching and preaching grounded in strong scholarship)

Carlson, R. A. *David, the Chosen King.* Trans. E. J. Sharpe and S. Rudman. Stockholm: 1964. (Traditio-historical approach to 2 Samuel)

Cross, F. M., Jr. "The Ideologies of Kingship in the Era of the Empire: Conditional Covenant and Eternal Decree." Pp. 219-273 in *Canaanite Myth and Hebrew Epic.* Cambridge, Mass.: 1973.

Davey, C. J. "Temples of the Levant and the Buildings of Solomon." *Tyndale Bulletin* 31 (1980): 107-146.

Gordon, R. P. *1 and 2 Samuel.* JSOT Old Testament Guides. Sheffield: 1984.

Gray, J. *I and II Kings.* 2nd ed. OTL. Philadelphia: 1970. (Extensive bibliography)

Gunn, D. M. *The Story of King David: Genre and Interpretation.* JSOTSup 6. Sheffield: 1978.

Ishida, T. "Solomon." *ABD* 6:105-112.

———, ed. *Studies in the Period of David and Solomon and Other Essays.* Tokyo: 1982.

Long, B. O. *1 Kings, with an Introduction to Historical Literature.* FOTL 9. Grand Rapids: 1984. (Analysis of entire book in terms of structure, genre, setting, and intentions)

Malamat, A. "Aspects of the Foreign Policies of David and Solomon." *JNES* 22 (1963): 1-17. (Examines kingdom of Hadad-ezer, Hamath, David's and Solomon's foreign marriages)

McCarter, P. K., Jr. *II Samuel.* AB 9. Garden City: 1984. (Detailed exposition with careful attention to historical, philological, theological, and literary issues)

Mendenhall, G. E. "The Monarchy." *Interp* 29 (1975): 155-170. (Israel followed model of Syro-Hittite state, introducing a paganization with fateful social and political consequences.)

Ollenburger, B. C. *Zion the City of the Great King.* JSOTSup 41. Sheffield: 1987.

Porten, B. "The Structure and Theme of the Solomon Narrative (1 Kings 3–11)." *HUCA* 38 (1967): 93-128. (Argues for structured, unified account)

Provan, I. W. *1 and 2 Kings.* New International Biblical Commentary. Peabody, Mass.: 1995. (Exposition with balanced attention to historical, literary, and theological concerns)

Robinson, J. *I Kings.* CBC. New York: 1972.

———. *2 Kings.* CBC. New York: 1976.

Thornton, T. C. G. "Solomonic Apologetic in Samuel and Kings." *Church Quarterly Review* 169 (1968): 159-166. (Much of 2 Samuel and 1 Kgs. 1–2 was composed in latter part of Solomon's reign to justify his accession and actions.)

Tsevat, M. "Ishbosheth and Congeners, the Names and Their Study." *HUCA* 46 (1975): 71-87.

Wiseman, D. J. *1 and 2 Kings.* TOTC. Leicester and Downers Grove: 1993. (Excellent study of historical and cultural setting of Israel's monarchy)

Chapter 14 — Divided Monarchy

Battenfield, J. A. "YHWH's Refutation of the Baal Myth through the Actions of Elijah and Elisha." Pp. 19-34 in A. Gileadi, ed., *Israel's Apostasy and Restoration*. Grand Rapids: 1988.

DeVries, S. J. *1 Kings*. WBC. Waco: 1985.

Hauser, A. J., and R. Gregory. *From Carmel to Horeb: Elijah in Crisis*. Sheffield: 1990. (Fine literary analysis of the Elijah narratives)

Hayes, J. H., and J. M. Miller. *A History of Ancient Israel and Judah*. Philadelphia: 1986. Pp. 218-339. (Recent historical treatment of this period)

Hobbs, T. R. *2 Kings*. WBC. Waco: 1985.

Hubbard, R. L., Jr. *First and Second Kings*. Everyman's Bible Commentary. Chicago: 1991. (Clear and devout exposition)

LaSor, W. S. "1 and 2 Kings." In D. Guthrie, ed., *The New Bible Commentary: Revised*. Grand Rapids: 1970.

Long, B. O. *1 Kings*. Grand Rapids: 1984; *2 Kings*. Grand Rapids: 1991. (Excellent commentaries focusing on literary forms)

McConville, J. G. "Narrative and Meaning in the Books of Kings." *Bibl* 70 (1989): 31-49. (Useful overview of the book's message)

Moore, R. D. *God Saves: Lessons from the Elisha Stories*. Sheffield: 1990. (Fine literary treatment of 2 Kgs. 5; 6:8-23; and 6:24–7:20)

Rofé, A. *The Prophetical Stories*. Jerusalem: 1988. (Thorough study of literary types of stories about prophets)

Savran, G. "1 and 2 Kings." *ADB*, pp. 146-163. (A sensitive study of the literary structure and techniques with notes on their relationship to the theological themes and prophetic influences of Kings)

Smith, M. S. *The Early History of God: Yahweh and the Other Deities in Ancient Israel*. New York: 1990.

Woods, F. E. *Water and Storm: Polemics against Baalism in the Deuteronomic History*. New York: 1993.

Chapter 15 — Judah Alone

Clements, R. A. *Isaiah and the Deliverance of Jerusalem. A Study of the Interpretation of Prophecy in the Old Testament*. Sheffield: 1980. (Argues that the narratives are theological and derive from the royal Zion theology of Josiah's day)

Fewell, D. N. "Sennacherib's Defeat: Words at War in 2 Kings 18:13–19:37." *JSOT* 34 (1986): 79-90. (Literally, the text is an ironic story showing that Yahweh, not Assyria, enjoys autonomy.)

Hayes, J. H., and J. M. Miller, eds. *A History of Ancient Israel and Judah*. Philadelphia: 1986. Pp. 346-436.

Hobbs, T. R. *2 Kings*. WBC 13. Waco: 1985. (A full-scale commentary on the Hebrew text)

Holladay, J. S. "Religion in Israel and Judah under the Monarchy: An Explicitly

Archaeological Approach." Pp. 249-299 in P. D. Miller et al., eds., *Ancient Israelite Religion: Essays in Honor of Frank Moore Cross.* Philadelphia: 1987. (Surveys and interprets archaeological evidence about Israel's religion)

Lowery, R. H. *The Reforming Kings. Cults and Society in First Temple Judah.* Sheffield: 1991. (Argues that Assyrian imperialism made Josiah's reform radically different from earlier ones)

Millard, A. R. "Sennacherib's Attack on Hezekiah." *Tyndale Bulletin* 36 (1985): 61-77. (Defends the text's historicity in light of ancient Near Eastern evidences)

Nelson, R. D. *First and Second Kings.* Louisville: 1987. Pp. 235-269. (An insightful literary and theological interpretation of Kings)

————. "Realpolitik in Judah (687-609 B.C.E.)." Pp. 177-189 in W. W. Hallo et al., eds., *Scripture in Context II.* Winona Lake: 1983.

Provan, I. *Hezekiah and the Book of Kings.* BZAW 172. Berlin/New York: 1988. (Recent rigorous study of the composition of the book of Kings)

Wiseman, D. J. *Chronicles of the Chaldean Kings (626-556 B.C.).* London: 1956. (Translation of Neo-Babylonian texts plus commentary)

Chapter 16 — Prophets and Prophecy

Albrektson, B. *History and the Gods.* Lund: 1967. (Historical events as divine manifestations in the ancient Near East and Israel)

Blenkinsopp, J. *A History of Prophecy in Israel.* Philadelphia: 1983. (Traces the development of prophetic ministry from the Settlement to the Hellenistic period)

Coggins, R., A. Phillips, and M. Knibb, eds., *Israel's Prophetic Tradition: Essays in Honor of Peter Ackroyd.* Cambridge, U.K.: 1982. (Outstanding essays on prophetic periods and themes)

Crenshaw, J. L. *Prophetic Conflict.* BZAW 124 (1971). (Effect on Israelite religion)

Davies, E. W. *Prophecy and Ethics: Isaiah and the Ethical Traditions of Israel.* JSOTS 16. Sheffield: 1981. (Analysis of the traditions that influenced the prophetic message)

Fohrer, G. "Remarks on Modern Interpretation of the Prophets." *JBL* 80 (1960): 309-319. (Critique of form-critical approach)

Freeman, H. E. *An Introduction to the Old Testament Prophets.* Chicago: 1968. (Conservative introduction to each book)

Heschel, A. *The Prophets.* New York: 1962. (Classical Jewish interpretation of the prophetic messages)

Interpretation 32/1 (January 1978). (Review articles suggesting revision of standard views: R. R. Wilson, "Early Israelite Prophecy," pp. 3-16; H. W. Wolff, "Prophecy from the Eighth through the Fifth Century," pp. 17-30; G. M. Tucker, "Prophetic Speech," pp. 31-45; B. S. Childs, "The Canonical Shape of the Prophetic Literature," pp. 46-55; J. Limberg, "The Prophets in Recent Study: 1967-1977," pp. 56-68)

Johnson, A. R. *The Cultic Prophet in Ancient Israel.* 2nd ed. Cardiff: 1962.

Koch, K. *The Prophets.* Trans. M. Kohl. Philadelphia: 1983 (Assyrian Period), 1984 (Babylonian and Persian Periods). (Thorough review of the prophets from Amos to Jonah in the light of modern scholarship)

Lindblom, J. *Prophecy in Ancient Israel.* Oxford: 1962. (Standard summary of prophetic experience and thought, with emphasis on "ecstasy")

Petersen, D. L. *The Roles of Israel's Prophets.* JSOTS 17. Sheffield: 1981. (Study of the nature of prophecy and the meaning of terms that describe the prophets)

Rowley, H. H., ed. *Studies in Old Testament Prophecy.* Edinburgh: 1950.

Synave, P., and P. Benoit. *Prophecy and Inspiration.* Trans. A. R. Dulles and T. L. Sheridan. New York: 1961. (Stimulating collection of Roman Catholic scholars' views)

Wilson, R. R. "Prophecy and Ecstasy: A Reexamination." *JBL* 98 (1979): 321-337.

Winward, S. F. *A Guide to the Prophets.* Richmond: 1968. (Emphasis on teachings)

Chapter 17 — Hebrew Poetry

Alter, R. *The Art of Biblical Poetry.* New York: 1985. (Influential, ground-breaking treatment of biblical poetry)

Berlin, A. *The Dynamics of Biblical Parallelism.* Bloomington: 1985. (Best recent study of biblical parallelism)

Dahood, M. "Hebrew Poetry." *IDBS,* pp. 669-672. (Summary of literary techniques detected through comparison with Ugaritic poetry)

Klein, W. W., C. L. Blomberg, and R. L. Hubbard, Jr. "General Rules of Hermeneutics." Pp. 215-255 in *Introduction to Biblical Interpretation.* Dallas: 1993. (Thorough introduction to Hebrew poetry with an eye to proper interpretation)

Kugel, J. L. *The Idea of Biblical Poetry.* New Haven: 1981. (A new approach to the meaning of parallelism)

Miller, P. D., Jr. "Poetry and Interpretation." Pp. 29-47 in *Interpreting the Psalms.* Philadelphia: 1986. (Survey of the interpretation of poetry)

O'Connor, M. P. *Hebrew Verse Structure.* Winona Lake: 1980. (Reassessment based on comparative poetic study, linguistics, literary criticism)

Pardee, D. *Ugaritic and Hebrew Poetic Parallelism: A Trial Cut ('nt I and Proverbs 2).* VTSup 39. Leiden: 1988. (Explores parallelism by comparing Hebrew and Ugaritic literary samples)

Petersen, D. L., and K. H. Richards. *Interpreting Hebrew Poetry.* Guides to Biblical Scholarship. Minneapolis: 1992. (Excellent general introduction to biblical poetry)

Watson, W. G. E. *Classical Hebrew Poetry: A Guide to Its Techniques.* JSOTS 26. Sheffield: 1986. (Most comprehensive volume on Hebrew poetry available today)

Chapter 18 — Amos

Andersen, F. I., and D. N. Freedmen. *Amos.* AB 24A. Garden City: 1989. (Comprehensive study with emphasis on structure and language)

Barton, J. *Amos' Oracles against the Nations.* SOTS Monograph. Sheffield: 1980.

Brueggemann, W. "Amos IV 4-13 and Israel's Covenant Worship." *VT* 15 (1965): 1-15. (Shows prophetic dependence on older traditions)

Carroll, R., M.D. *Contexts for Amos: Prophetic Poetics in Latin American Perspective.* JSOTS 132. Sheffield: 1992. (Emphasis on social background of Amos and its parallels in third world settings)

Clements, R. *When God's Patience Runs Out.* Downers Grove: 1988.

Coote, R. B. *Amos among the Prophets: Composition and Theology.* Philadelphia: 1981. (Attempts to trace in the composition of the book three distinct stages from Amos' day to the Exile)

Hammershaimb, E. *The Book of Amos.* Trans. J. Sturdy. Oxford: 1970. (Exegetical)

Hayes, J. H. *Amos, Eighth Century Prophet.* Nashville: 1988. (Credits most of the book to Amos)

Hubbard, D. A. *Joel and Amos.* Downers Grove: 1989. (Emphasis on literary forms and structure)

Mays, J. L. *Amos.* OTL. Philadelphia: 1969. (A thorough yet readable study)

McComiskey, T. E. *Amos.* Expositor's Bible 7. Grand Rapids: 1985. (Good historical and philological insights)

Niehaus, J. *Amos.* In *The Minor Prophets,* ed. T. E. McComiskey. Grand Rapids: 1992. (Covenant law-suits as background for Amos' mission)

Paul, S. M. *Amos.* Hermeneia. Minneapolis: 1991. (Thorough study by a Jewish scholar; excellent bibliography)

Polley, M. B. *Amos and the Davidic Empire.* Oxford: 1989.

Robertson, J., and C. Armerding. "Amos." *ISBE* 1 (1979): 114-117.

Smith, G. A. *The Book of the Twelve Prophets.* Expositor's Bible 4. Rev. ed. Grand Rapids: 1956. Pp. 456-549. (Classical exposition, artfully expressed)

Stuart, D. *Hosea-Jonah.* WBC. Waco: 1987. (Amos' judgment speeches seen as covenant curses)

Wolff, H. W. *Joel and Amos.* Trans. W. Janzen, S. D. McBride, Jr., and C. A. Muenchow. Hermeneia. Philadelphia: 1977. (An analytic commentary, with strong emphases on form criticism and clan wisdom in Amos' background)

Chapter 19 — Hosea

Andersen, F. I., and D. N. Freedman. *Hosea.* AB 24. Garden City: 1980. (A monumental and devout work that will influence future study of Hosea)

Ball, E. "Hosea." *ISBE* 2 (1982): 761-767.

Beeby, H. D. *Hosea: Grace Abounding.* ITC. Grand Rapids: 1989. (An exposition filled with insights drawn from an Asian perspective)

Daniels, D. *Hosea and Salvation History: The Early Traditions of Israel in the Prophecy of Hosea.* New York: 1990.

Emmerson, G. I. *Hosea: An Israelite Prophet in Judean Perspective.* JSOTS 28. Sheffield: 1984. (A discussion of frequent references to Judah in Hosea)

Hubbard, D. A. *Hosea.* TOTC 22A. Leicester, U.K.; Downers Grove, Ill.: 1989. (A more detailed account of the approaches taken in this chapter)

McComiskey, Thomas. *Hosea.* In *The Minor Prophets: An Exegetical and Expository Commentary.* Grand Rapids: 1992. (A solid work that separates technical notes from general comments on each page)

Östborn, G. *Yahwe and Baal: Studies in the Book of Hosea and Related Documents.* Lund: 1956.

Rowley, H. H. "The Marriage of Hosea." In *Men of God.* London: 1963. Pp. 66-97.

Snaith, N. H. *Mercy and Sacrifice: A Study of the Book of Hosea.* London: 1953.

Stuart, Douglas. *Hosea–Jonah.* WBC 31. Waco: 1987. Pp. 2-220.

Yee, G. A. *Composition and Tradition in the Book of Hosea.* SBLDS. Atlanta: 1987.

Chapter 20 — Micah

Alfaro, J. J. *Justice and Loyalty: A Commentary on the Book of Micah.* ITC. Grand Rapids: 1989. (A concern for social justice)

Allen, L. C. *The Books of Joel, Obadiah, Jonah and Micah.* NICOT. Grand Rapids: 1976. (An exegetical and expository commentary that takes structure and editing into account)

Clark, D. J., and N. Mundhenk. *A Translator's Handbook on the Books of Obadiah and Micah.* Helps for Translators. London, New York, Stuttgart: 1982. (A clear, concise exposition)

Hagstrom, D. G. *The Coherence of the Book of Micah.* SBLDS 89. Atlanta: 1988. (A literary analysis by a student of Mays)

Hillers, D. R. *Micah.* Hermeneia. Philadelphia: 1984. (A synchronic treatment of the book)

Mason, R. *Micah, Nahum, Obadiah.* JSOT Old Testament Guides. Sheffield: 1991, pp. 8-53. (A survey of recent study on the background, composition, and message)

Mays, J. L. *Micah.* OTL. Philadelphia: 1976. (An emphasis on redaction criticism whereby most of the book is attributed to the late exilic and postexilic periods)

Waltke, B. K. *Micah.* TOTC 23a. Leicester, U.K.; Downers Grove, Ill.: 1988. Pp. 135-207. (An exegetical commentary that attributes the whole book to the mouth and pen of Micah)

Wolff, H. W. *Micah.* Trans. Gary Stansel. Minneapolis: 1990. (A thorough commentary that posits a lengthy history of the development of the book)

Chapters 21–22 — Isaiah

Childs, B. S. *Isaiah and the Assyrian Crisis.* SBT, 2nd ser. 3. London: 1967.

Clements, R. E. *Isaiah 1–39.* NCBC. Grand Rapids: 1981. (Sees chs. 36–39 as early link between 1–35 and 40–55)

Conrad, E. W. *Reading Isaiah.* Minneapolis: 1991.

Emmerson, Grace I. *Isaiah 56–66.* JSOT Old Testament Guides. Sheffield: 1992. (Review of recent debate, especially on problems of postexilic community)

Hanson, P. D. *Isaiah 40–66.* Interpretation. Louisville: 1995. (Exposition of themes and their setting for use of preachers and teachers)

Hayes, J. H., and S. A. Irvine. *Isaiah, the Eighth-Century Prophet: His Times and His Preaching.* Nashville: 1987.

Kaufmann, Y. *The Babylonian Captivity and Deutero-Isaiah.* Trans. C. W. Efroymson. New York: 1970. (Challenges view that Israel first accepted monotheism only in postexilic period)

Kissane, E. J. *The Book of Isaiah,* 2 vols. Rev. ed. Dublin: 1960. (Fine study by Roman Catholic author)

Knight, G. A. F. *Deutero-Isaiah: A Theological Commentary on Isaiah 40–55.* Nashville: 1965.

————. *The New Israel: Isaiah 56–66.* Grand Rapids: 1985.

Kruse, C. G. "The Servant Songs: Interpretive Trends Since C. R. North." *Studia Biblica et Theologica* 8 (1978): 3-27.

Motyer, J. A. *The Prophecy of Isaiah.* Downers Grove, Ill.: 1993. (Thorough exposition of the book as a unity preexilic in date)

Muilenburg, J. "Introduction to Isaiah 40–66." *IB* 5:381-414.

North, C. R. *The Suffering Servant in Deutero-Isaiah.* 2nd ed. London: 1956. (Thorough treatment with exhaustive bibliography)

Power, E. "Isaias." *CCHS* §§419a-451s. (Thorough bibliography; interesting development of prophet's message)

Skinner, J. *The Book of the Prophet Isaiah.* 2 vols. Cambridge Bible. Cambridge: 1897-1898. (A classic)

Smart, J. D. *History and Theology of Second Isaiah.* Philadelphia: 1965.

Ward, J. M. *Amos and Isaiah.* Nashville: 1969. (Pp. 143-279; sees literary and theological affinity between "First Isaiah" and Amos)

Watts, J. D. W. *Isaiah 1–33.* WBC 24. Waco: 1985.

————. *Isaiah 34–66.* WBC 25. Waco: 1985. (Treats the work as a drama that interprets Israel's history chronologically from the eighth to fifth century)

Westermann, C. *Isaiah 40–66.* Trans. D. M. G. Stalker. OTL. Philadelphia: 1967.

Whybray, R. N. *Isaiah 40–66.* NCBC. Grand Rapids: 1981.

————. *The Second Isaiah.* JSOT Old Testament Guides. Sheffield: 1983. (A good summary of recent scholarship)

Wildberger, H. *Isaiah 1–12.* Trans. T. H. Trapp. Minneapolis: 1991. (A technical study of the first section of the book)

Young, E. J. *The Book of Isaiah.* 3 vols. Grand Rapids: 1965-1972. (Conservative, careful exegesis, defending the unity of book and authorship)

Chapter 23 — Zephaniah, Nahum, and Habakkuk

Achtemeier, E. R. *Nahum-Malachi*. Interpretation. Atlanta: 1986. (A concise exposition, particularly helpful to preachers and teachers)

Baker, D. W., *Nahum, Habakkuk, Zephaniah*. TOTC. Leicester and Downers Grove: 1988. (Sensitive to literary forms, historical background, and theological implications)

Roberts, J. J. M. *Nahum, Habakkuk, and Zephaniah*. OTL. Louisville: 1991. (Balanced commentary with eye to textual, grammatical, and semantic matters)

Robertson, O. P. *The Books of Nahum, Habakkuk, and Zephaniah*. NICOT. Grand Rapids: 1990. (Thorough, reliable commentary)

Smith, R. L. *Micah-Malachi*. WBC 32. Waco: 1984. (Useful, concise exposition of Hebrew text)

Wal, A. van der. *Nahum, Habakkuk: A Classified Bibliography*. Amsterdam: 1988.

Watts, J. D. W. *The Books of Joel, Obadiah, Jonah, Nahum, Habakkuk, and Zephaniah*. CBC. New York: 1978. (Brief yet balanced exposition)

Zephaniah

Ball, I. J., Jr. *A Rhetorical Study of Zephaniah*. Berkeley: 1988.

Christensen, D. L. "Zephaniah 2:4-15: A Theological Basis for Josiah's Program of Political Expansion." *CBQ* 46 (1984): 669-682. (Suggests close connection between Zephaniah's foreign oracles and events in Josiah's reign)

Kapelrud, A. S. *The Message of the Prophet Zephaniah*. Oslo: 1975.

Kselman, J. S. "Zephaniah, Book of." *ABD* 6:1077-1080.

Mason, R. *Zephaniah, Habakkuk, Joel*. JSOT Old Testament Guides. Sheffield: 1994. (Thorough review of modern study)

Nahum

Cathcart, K. J. *Nahum in the Light of Northwest Semitic*. Biblica et orientalia 26. Rome: 1973.

Coggins, R. "An Alternate Prophetic Tradition." Pp. 77-94 in R. Coggins, A. Phillips, and M. Knibb, eds. *Israel's Prophetic Tradition*. Cambridge: 1982. (Emphasizes Nahum's picture of God's universal sovereignty)

Haldar, A. O. *Studies in the Book of Nahum*. UUÅ 46-47. Uppsala: 1947.

Maier, W. A. *The Book of Nahum: A Commentary*. Grand Rapids: 1959. (Conservative Lutheran)

Mihelic, J. L. "The Concept of God in the Book of Nahum." *Interp* 2 (1948): 199-207.

van der Woude, A. S. "The Book of Nahum: A Letter Written in Exile." *OTS* 20 (1977): 108-126. (Dates book 660-630; Nahum is from northern Galilee.)

Habakkuk

Brownlee, W. H. *The Midrash Pesher of Habakkuk.* SBLMS 24. Missoula: 1979.

Eaton, J. H. "The Origin and Meaning of Habakkuk 3." *ZAW* 76 (1964): 144-171. (Philological, mythological analysis)

Gowan, D. E. *The Triumph of Faith in Habakkuk.* Atlanta: 1976. (Exegetical and expository)

Hiebert, T. *God of My Victory: The Ancient Hymn in Habakkuk 3.* HSM 38. Decatur, Ga.: 1986.

Lloyd-Jones, D. M. *From Fear to Faith: Studies in the Book of Habakkuk.* London: 1972. (Conservative exposition)

Mason, R. *Zephaniah, Habakkuk, Joel.* JSOT Old Testament Guides. Sheffield: 1994. (Thorough review of recent research)

Peckham, B. "The Vision of Habakkuk." *CBQ* 48 (1986): 617-636.

Sweeney, M. A. "Habakkuk, Book of." *ABD* 3:1-6.

Chapter 24 — Jeremiah

Carroll, R. P. *From Chaos to Covenant: Prophecy in the Book of Jeremiah.* New York: 1981. (Takes view that Jeremiah is the product of the community rather than of the lone prophet)

————. *Jeremiah, A Commentary.* OTL. Philadelphia: 1986.

Craigie, P. C., P. H. Kelley, and J. F. Drinkard, Jr. *Jeremiah 1–25.* WBC 26. Dallas: 1991.

Crenshaw, J. L. "A Living Tradition: The Book of Jeremiah in Current Research." Pp. 100-112 in J. L. Mayes and P. J. Achtemeier, eds., *Interpreting the Prophets.* Philadelphia: 1987. (Excellent survey of research on the origin and structure of the book)

Holladay, W. L. *Jeremiah.* 2 vols. Hermeneia. Minneapolis: 1986. Philadelphia: 1989. (Outstanding technical commentary)

————. *Jeremiah: A Fresh Reading.* New York: 1990. (Excellent survey of the book's message, with applications)

Keown, G. L., P. J. Scalise, and T. G. Smothers. *Jeremiah 26–52.* WBC 27. Dallas: 1995.

King, P. J. *Jeremiah: An Archaeological Companion.* Louisville: 1993. (Archaeological insights on the history, geography, and culture of Jeremiah's time)

McConville, J. G. *Judgment and Promise: An Interpretation of the Book of Jeremiah.* Winona Lake: 1993. (Argues against the theory of a deuteronomistic editing of the book)

Perdue, L., and B. W. Kovacs. *A Prophet to the Nations: Essays in Jeremiah Studies.* Winona Lake: 1984. (An anthology of articles on aspects of Jeremiah's ministry and message by a team of internationally known scholars)

Soderlund, S. *The Greek Text of Jeremiah: A Revised Hypothesis.* Sheffield: 1985.

(Argues that the shorter LXX text goes back to a Hebrew text shorter and superior to MT)

Thompson, J. A. *The Book of Jeremiah*. NICOT. Grand Rapids: 1980. (A major conservative interpretation of the book)

Unterman, J. *From Repentance to Redemption: Jeremiah's Thought in Transition.* Sheffield: 1987. (Argues for a shift in Jeremiah's thought from a focus on repentance to one on New Covenant)

Chapter 25 — Ezekiel

Allen, L. C. *Ezekiel 1–19, Ezekiel 20–48*. WBC 28-29. Dallas: 1994, 1990. (A detailed commentary that takes seriously historical perspective and literary growth)

Blenkinsopp, J. *Ezekiel*. Interpretation. Louisville: 1990. (A fine expository commentary)

Boadt, L. "Ezekiel, Book of." *ABD* 2:711-722.

Bodi, D. *The Book of Ezekiel and the Poem of Erra*. Freiburg: 1991. (Suggests links with contemporary Babylonian literature)

Craigie, P. C. *Ezekiel*. Daily Study Bible Series. Philadelphia: 1983. (A commentary with devotional application)

Greenberg, M. *Ezekiel 1–20*. AB. New York: 1983. (A "holistic" treatment of the book that explores literary structure)

Hals, R. M. *Ezekiel*. Forms of Old Testament Literature. Grand Rapids: 1989. (A form-critical study, including the intention and theology of each pericope)

Klein, R. W. *Ezekiel: The Prophet and His Message*. Columbia, S.C.: 1988. (A helpful study of the main topics of the book)

Levenson, J. D. *Theology of the Program of Restoration of Ezekiel 40–48*. Missoula: 1976. (A study of theological themes and their links with other Old Testament traditions)

McKeating, H. *Ezekiel*. JSOT Old Testament Guides. Sheffield: 1993. (Excellent survey of research, with attention to both literary and theological features)

Matties, G. H. *Ezekiel 18 and the Rhetoric of Moral Discourse*. Atlanta: 1990. (A thorough study of an important chapter)

Taylor, J. B. *Ezekiel: An Introduction and Commentary*. TOTC. Downers Grove: 1969. (Still a good basic commentary)

Vawter, B., and L. J. Hoppe. *A New Heart: A Commentary on the Book of Ezekiel*. ITC. Grand Rapids: 1991. (A straightforward commentary that places some emphasis on theology)

Zimmerli, W. *Ezekiel 1, Ezekiel 2*. Hermeneia. Philadelphia: 1979, 1983. (A classic, detailed commentary that seeks to uncover the layers of Ezekiel's own contributions and later amplifications)

Chapter 26 — Obadiah and Joel

Obadiah

Ackroyd, P. R. "Obadiah, Book of." *ABD* 5:2-4. (Review of recent study)

Allen, L. C. *The Books of Joel, Obadiah, Jonah, and Micah.* NICOT. Grand Rapids: 1976. (Good survey and analysis of the critical problems)

Baker, D. W. *Obadiah.* TOTC. Leicester: 1988. (Concise and helpful commentary)

Coggins, R. *Obadiah.* ITC. Grand Rapids: 1985.

Lillie, J. R. "Obadiah — A Celebration of God's Kingdom." *Currents in Theology and Mission* 6 (1969): 18-22.

Stuart, D. *Hosea-Jonah.* WBC 31. Waco: 1987.

Thompson, J. A. "Introduction and Exegesis of Obadiah." *IB* 6:857-867.

———. "Obadiah, Book of." *IBD,* pp. 1106-1107. (Good survey)

Watts, J. D. W. *Obadiah: A Critical and Exegetical Commentary.* Grand Rapids: 1969.

Wolff, H. W. *Obadiah and Jonah: A Commentary.* Trans. M. Kohl. Minneapolis: 1986. (Thorough study with Christian applications)

Joel

Ahlström, G. W. *Joel and the Temple Cult of Jerusalem.* VTSup 21 (1971).

Allen, L. C. *The Books of Joel, Obadiah, Jonah, and Micah.* NICOT. Grand Rapids: 1976. Pp. 19-126. (Excellent commentary, devout and thorough)

Hubbard, D. A. *Joel and Amos.* TOTC. Leicester and Downers Grove: 1989. (Commentary on which the approach of this chapter is based)

Kapelrud, A. S. *Joel Studies.* UUÅ 4. Uppsala: 1948. (Reflects Scandinavian school; thorough criticism of previous scholarship)

Prinsloo, W. S. *The Theology of the Book of Joel.* BZAW 163. Berlin and New York: 1985.

Stuart, D. *Hosea-Jonah.* WBC 33 (1987). Pp. 222-271. (A solid commentary with strong Christian applications)

Thompson, J. A. "Joel's Locusts in the Light of Near Eastern Parallels." *JNES* 14 (1955): 52-55.

Wolff, H. W. *Joel and Amos.* Hermeneia. Philadelphia: 1977. (Includes valuable digressions on locusts, day of Yahweh, teacher of righteousness)

Chapter 27 — Jonah

Aalders, G. C. *The Problem of the Book of Jonah.* London: 1948. (A classic defense of the historical interpretation)

Ackerman, S. "Jonah." *LGB,* pp. 234-243. (A literary interpretation highlighting the use of irony)

Alexander, T. D. *Jonah*. TOTC. Leicester and Downers Grove: 1988. (An introduction and commentary based on an interpretation as "didactic history")

Allen, L. C. *The Books of Joel, Obadiah, Jonah, and Micah*. NICOT. Grand Rapids: 1976. (An exposition in terms of a postexilic parable)

Carlisle, T. J., *You! Jonah!* Grand Rapids: 1968. (A striking collection of poems and illustrations on the experience of Jonah)

LaCoque, A., and P.-E. Lacoque. *Jonah: A Psycho-Religious Approach to the Prophet*. Columbia, S.C.: 1990. (A psychological interpretation)

Salters, R. B. *Jonah and Lamentations*. JSOT Old Testament Guides. Sheffield: 1994. (A balanced survey of the literary and theological themes)

Sasson, J. M. *Jonah*. AB 24B. New York: 1990. (A detailed commentary with a literary approach, refraining from conclusions about date, genre, or purpose)

Stuart, D. *Hosea-Jonah*. WBC 31. Waco: 1987. (A theological commentary based on an historical interpretation)

Watts, J. W. "Jonah's Psalm (Jonah 2:3-10)." Pp. 132-144 in *Psalm and Story: Inset Hymns in Hebrew Narrative*. Sheffield: 1992. (Discusses the Song of Thanksgiving in terms of its context in the book and its role in leading the reader to identify with Jonah)

Wolff, H. W. *Obadiah and Jonah: A Commentary*. Minneapolis: 1986. Pp. 75-191. (Treats the book as an "ironically didactic novella" posing the question about Israel's attitude toward God's unlimited mercy for the whole world)

Chapter 28 — Haggai

Achtemeier, E. R. *Nahum-Malachi*. Interpretation. Atlanta: 1986.

Ackroyd, P. R. *Exile and Restoration*. Philadelphia: 1968.

Baldwin, J. G. *Haggai, Zechariah, Malachi*. TOTC. Downers Grove: 1972.

Coggins, R. J. *Haggai, Zechariah, Malachi*. JSOT Old Testament Guides. Sheffield: 1987.

Mason, R. *The Books of Haggai, Zechariah and Malachi*. CBC. Cambridge: 1977.

———. "The Prophets of the Restoration." Pp.137-154 in R. Coggins, A. Phillips, and M. Knibb, eds., *Israel's Prophetic Tradition*. Festschrift P. R. Ackroyd (Cambridge: 1982).

———. "The Purpose of the 'Editorial Framework' of the Book of Haggai." *VT* 27 (1977): 413-421.

Meyers, C. L., and E. M. Meyers. *Haggai, Zechariah 1–8*. AB 25B. Garden City: 1987.

Petersen, D. L. *Haggai and Zechariah 1–8*. OTL. Philadelphia: 1984.

———. "Zerubbabel and Jerusalem Temple Restoration." *CBQ* 36 (1974): 366-372.

Smith, R. L. *Micah-Malachi*. WBC 32. Waco: 1984.

Verhoef, P. A. *The Books of Haggai and Malachi*. NICOT. Grand Rapids: 1987.

Wolff, H. W. *Haggai*. Minneapolis: 1988.

Chapter 29 — Zechariah

Achtemeier, E. R. *Nahum-Malachi.* Interpretation. Atlanta: 1986.

Baldwin, J. G. *Haggai, Zechariah, Malachi.* TOTC. London: 1972.

Carroll, R. P. "Twilight of Prophecy or Dawn of Apocalyptic?" *JSOT* 14 (1979): 3-33.

Coggins, R. J. *Haggai, Zechariah, Malachi.* JSOT Old Testament Guides. Sheffield: 1987.

Halpern, B. "The Ritual Background of Zechariah's Temple Song." *CBQ* 40 (1978): 167-190. (1:7–6:15 in light of extrabiblical literature)

Hanson, P. D. *The Dawn of Apocalyptic.* Philadelphia: 1975.

———. "Zechariah, Book of." *IDBS*, pp. 982-983.

Mason, R. A. *The Books of Haggai, Zechariah and Malachi.* CBC. Cambridge: 1977.

———. "The Relation of Zechariah 9–14 to Proto-Zechariah." *ZAW* 88 (1976): 227-239.

Meyers, C. L., and E. M. Meyers. *Haggai, Zechariah 1–8.* AB 25B. Garden City: 1987.

———. "Zechariah, Book of: Zechariah 1–8." *ABD* 6:1061-1065.

Neil, W. "Zechariah, Book of." *IDB* 4:943-947.

Petersen, D. L. *Haggai and Zechariah 1–8.* OTL. Philadelphia: 1984.

———. "Zechariah, Book of: Zechariah 9–14." *ABD* 6:1065-1068.

———. *Zechariah 9–14 and Malachi.* OTL. Louisville: 1995.

Smith, R. L. *Micah-Malachi.* WBC 32. Waco: 1984.

Chapter 30 — Malachi

Achtemeier, E. R. *Nahum-Malachi.* Interpretation. Atlanta: 1986.

Baldwin, J. G. *Haggai, Zechariah, Malachi.* TOTC. Downers Grove: 1972.

Braun, R. "Malachi — A Catechism for Times of Disappointment." *Currents in Theology and Mission* 4 (1977): 297-303. (Commentary on oracles and their format)

Coggins, R. J. *Haggai, Zechariah, Malachi.* JSOT Old Testament Guides. Sheffield: 1987.

Glazier-McDonald, B. *Malachi: The Divine Messenger.* SBLDS 98. Atlanta: 1987.

Hill, A. E. "Malachi, Book of." *ABD* 4:478-485.

Kaiser, W. C., Jr. *Malachi: God's Unchanging Love.* Grand Rapids: 1984.

Mason, R. A. *The Books of Haggai, Zechariah and Malachi.* Cambridge, U.K.: 1977. (Pp. 135-162 argue that book is basically a unity, by levitical author closer to Haggai and Zech. 1–8 than to Zech. 9–14.)

McKenzie, S. L., and H. N. Wallace. "Covenant Themes in Malachi." *CBQ* 45 (1983): 549-563.

Neil, W. "Malachi." *IDB* 3:228-232. (A full discussion)

Petersen, D. L. *Zechariah 9–14 and Malachi.* OTL. Louisville: 1995. (An excellent full-scale commentary based on "three oracles" approach)

Smith, G. A. *The Book of the Twelve Prophets. Expositor's Bible* (1956) 4:640-651. (Very helpful; classic of biblical interpretation)

Smith, R. L. *Micah-Malachi.* WBC 32 (1984). Pp. 296-342.

Sutcliffe, E. F. "Malachias." *CCHS* §§555a-558g. (Some good material)

Verhoef, P. A. *The Books of Haggai and Malachi.* NICOT. Grand Rapids: 1987.

Chapter 31 — Introduction to the Writings

Henshaw, T. *The Writings: The Third Division of the Old Testament Canon.* London: 1963. (Historical background, summary, and analysis of individual books)

Morgan, D. F. *Between Text and Community: The "Writings" in Canonical Interpretation.* Minneapolis: 1990. (Traces the Writings to diverse communal needs they sought to answer)

Chapter 32 — Psalms

Allen, L. C. *Psalms 101–150.* WBC 21. Waco: 1983. (A detailed commentary that majors in form, structure, and exegesis)

———. *Psalms.* Word Biblical Themes. Waco: 1987. (A discussion of theological themes in the Psalms)

Anderson, B. W. *Out of the Depths: The Psalms Speak to Us Today.* Rev. ed. Philadelphia: 1983. (A good introduction to the Psalms)

Brueggemann, W. *The Message of the Psalms.* Minneapolis: 1984. (A study of selected psalms that relates their forms to human experience)

Craigie, P. C. *Psalms 1–50.* WBC 19. Waco: 1983. (A detailed commentary that makes full use of the author's expertise in Canaanite studies)

Day, J. *Psalms.* JSOT Old Testament Guides. Sheffield: 1990. (Genre-based survey of recent scholarship)

Gerstenberger, E. S. *Psalms, Part 1, with an Introduction to Cultic Poetry.* Forms of the Old Testament Literature. Grand Rapids: 1988. (A form-critical study of Pss. 1–60)

Kidner, D. *Psalms 1–72, Psalms 73–150.* TOTC. Downers Grove: 1975. (A basic commentary with the Christian reader in mind)

Kraus, H.-J. *Psalms 1–59, Psalms 60–150.* Trans. H. C. Oswald. Minneapolis: 1988, 1989. (A detailed textual and form-critical commentary that makes full use of Gunkel's insights)

———. *Theology of the Psalms.* Trans. K. Crim. Minneapolis: 1986. (The best volume on this subject)

Longman, T. III. *How to Read the Psalms.* Downers Grove, Ill.; Leicester, U.K.: 1988. (Popular study of genres, artistry, and messages)

Mays, J. L. *The Lord Reigns: A Theological Handbook to the Psalms.* Louisville: 1994.

Miller, P. D., Jr. *Interpreting the Psalms.* Philadelphia: 1986. (A helpful study of laments and hymns and their contemporary significance)

Tate, M. E. *Psalms 51–100.* WBC 20. Dallas: 1990. (A detailed and thorough commentary, one of the best in the series)

Westermann, C. *The Psalms: Structure, Content, Message.* Trans. R. D. Gehrke. Minneapolis: 1980. (A study of the forms of the Psalms, written by an expert in the field)

————. *Praise and Lament in the Psalms.* Trans. K. R. Crim and R. N. Soulen. Edinburgh: 1981. (A specialist study of laments, thanksgiving songs, and hymns)

Chapter 33 — Wisdom Literature

Crenshaw, J. L. *Old Testament Wisdom: An Introduction.* Atlanta: 1981. (A fine survey of the whole field)

Emerton, J. A. "Wisdom." Pp. 214-237 in G. W. Anderson, ed., *Tradition and Interpretation.* Oxford: 1979. (Esp. pp. 221-231, "The Wisdom Literature and Other Parts of the Old Testament")

Gammie, J. G. et al., eds. *Israelite Wisdom.* Festschrift S. L. Terrien. New York: 1978. (Theological and literary essays)

Gammie, J. G., and L. Perdue, eds. *The Sage in Israel and the Ancient Near East.* Winona Lake: 1990. (The most comprehensive set of essays on this subject)

Hubbard, D. A. "Wisdom." *IBD*, pp. 1650f. (Parts of the preceding discussion were adapted from this article.)

————. "Wisdom Literature." *IBD*, pp. 1651f. (Parts of the preceding discussion were adapted from this article.)

Mack, B. L. "Wisdom Myth and Mythology." *Interp* 24 (1970): 46-60. (Depicts creativity of wisdom schools in interpreting postexilic situation)

Morgan, D. F. *Wisdom in the Old Testament Traditions.* Atlanta: 1981. (A review of the role of wisdom in the various periods of biblical literature)

Murphy, R. E. *Wisdom Literature.* Forms of the Old Testament Literature 13. Grand Rapids: 1981.

————. *The Tree of Life: An Exploration of Biblical Wisdom Literature.* ABRL. New York: 1990. (Discussion of the contents, techniques, and issues of wisdom literature including the apocryphal works)

O'Connor, Kathleen M. *The Wisdom Literature.* Message of Biblical Spirituality 5. Collegeville, Minn.: 1988. (Survey of wisdom corpus from the scholarly perspective of a Roman Catholic woman)

Scott, R. B. Y. *The Way of Wisdom in the Old Testament.* New York: 1971. (Particularly insightful on differences between Old Testament and ancient Near Eastern wisdom)

Sheppard, G. T. "Wisdom." *ISBE* 4 (1988): 1074-1082.

Von Rad, G. *Wisdom in Israel.* Trans. J. D. Martin. Nashville and New York: 1972. (A classic study of the methods and thought of Israel's wisdom teachers)

Wilken, R. L. *Aspects of Wisdom in Judaism and Early Christianity.* Notre Dame: 1975. (Cross-cultural essays on wisdom in late antiquity)

Chapter 34 — Proverbs

Alden, R. L. *Proverbs: A Commentary on an Ancient Book of Timeless Advice.* Grand Rapids: 1983. (Verse-by-verse exposition)

Crenshaw, J. L. "Proverbs, Book of." *ABD* 5:513-520.

Fox, M. V. "Aspects of the Religion of the Book of Proverbs." *HUCA* 39 (1968): 55-69. (*ḥokmâ*, in the sense of ethical-religious wisdom, viewed as a bridge to Hellenistic thought)

Hubbard, D. A. "Proverbs, Book of." *ISBE* 3 (1986): 1015-1020.

———. "Proverbs, Book of." *IBD*, pp. 1290f. (Parts of the preceding discussion were adapted from this article.)

———. *Proverbs.* CC 15a. Dallas: 1989. (An exposition of Proverbs which features the central topics of the book)

Kitchen, K. A. "Proverbs and Wisdom Books of the Ancient Near East: The Factual History of a Literary Form." *Tyndale Bulletin* 28 (1977): 69-114. (Prov. 1–24 is of second millennium origin, formed into literary unity in early first millennium.)

Leeuwen, R. C. van. *Context and Meaning in Proverbs 25–27.* SBLDS 96. Atlanta: 1988.

Murphy, R. E. *Wisdom Literature: Job, Proverbs, Ecclesiastes, Ruth, Canticles, Ecclesiasticus, Esther.* FOTL 13. Grand Rapids: 1981. (Analysis of literary forms)

———. "Wisdom and Creation." *JBL* 104 (1985): 3-11. (Wisdom in Proverbs and later writings as revelation of God)

Nels, P. J. *The Structure and Ethos of the Wisdom Admonitions in Proverbs.* BZAW 158. Berlin and New York: 1982.

Parker, K. I. "Solomon as Philosopher King? The Nexus of Law and Wisdom in 1 Kings 1–11." *JSOT* 53 (1992): 75-91. (Solomon's wisdom nullified when he failed to keep the law)

Perdue, L. G. *Wisdom and Creation: The Theology of Wisdom Literature.* Nashville: 1994. (See esp. ch. 3.)

Perry, T. A. *Wisdom Literature and the Structure of Proverbs.* University Park, Pa.: 1993. (Technical analysis of the structure of proverbs as a key to grasping their deeper meaning)

Scott, R. B. Y. *Proverbs-Ecclesiastes.* AB 18. Garden City: 1965.

Thompson, J. M. *The Form and Function of Proverbs in Ancient Israel.* Hague: 1974. (Includes examination of skeptical element in Hebrew wisdom)

Westermann, C. *Roots of Wisdom: The Oldest Proverbs of Israel and Other Peoples.* Trans. J. Daryl Charles. Louisville: 1995. (Masterful study of the background, form, and meaning of proverbs in the Old Testament)

Whybray, R. N. *The Book of Proverbs.* CBC. New York: 1972. (Standard commentary by wisdom expert)

Williams, J. G. *Those Who Ponder Proverbs: Aphoristic Thinking and Biblical Literature.* Sheffield: 1981. (The use of proverbial forms and themes throughout the Bible)

Chapter 35 — Job

Andersen, F. I. *Job.* Downers Grove: 1976. (Excellent concise commentary)

Atkinson, D. *The Message of Job.* Leicester: 1991. (The message of Job from the perspective of a pastoral-counselor)

Clines, D. J. A. *Job 1–20.* Dallas: 1989. (A superior commentary that makes insightful suggestions for interpreting the difficult lines in the book of Job)

Dhorme, E. *A Commentary on the Book of Job.* Trans. H. Knight. London: 1967. (Classic commentary, strong on philology and grammar)

Glatzer, N. "The Book of Job and Its Interpreters." Pp. 197-221 in A. Altmann, ed., *Biblical Motifs.* Cambridge, Mass.: 1966. (Survey of rabbinic interpretation through Middle Ages)

Guillaume, A. *Studies in the Book of Job.* Leiden: 1968. (Sees book as product of "Arabian milieu")

Habel, N. C. *The Book of Job.* Philadelphia: 1985. (An excellent commentary that discusses the meaning of the text from perspective of the wording and the structure)

Hartley, J. E. *The Book of Job.* NICOT. Grand Rapids: 1988. (Sensitive and insightful focus on exegesis and the theology of the major blocks of the text)

Gutiérrez, G. *On Job: God-Talk and the Suffering of the Innocent.* Trans. M. J. O'Connell. Maryknoll, N.Y.: 1987. (A fine discussion of the message, with emphasis on the hard lot of the disenfranchised in the third world)

Janzen, J. G. *Job.* Interpretation. Atlanta: 1985. (Geared to preachers and teachers)

MacKenzie, R. A. F. "The Transformation of Job." *Biblical Theology Bulletin* 9 (1979): 51-57. (Identifies "transformation theme" akin to that in classical Greek tragedies)

Perdue, L. G. *Wisdom in Revolt: Metaphorical Theology in the Book of Job.* JSOTS 112. Sheffield: 1991. (Innovative analysis of Job in terms of various metaphors describing divine-human relationships)

Perdue, L. G., and W. C. Gilpin, eds. *The Voice from the Whirlwind.* Nashville: 1992. (Several essays from symposium on the book of Job)

Polzin, R. *Biblical Structuralism; Method and Subjectivity in the Study of Ancient Texts.* Philadelphia: 1977. (Includes study of the framework, code, and message of Job, pp. 54-121)

Rowley, H. H. *Job.* NCBC. London: 1970. (Thoughtful, thorough exposition with good theological insight)

Sanders, P., ed. *Twentieth Century Interpretations of the Book of Job.* Englewood Cliffs: 1968. (Reprinted essays on meaning, method by G. B. Gray, A. S. Peake, A. Toynbee, G. Murray, K. Rexroth, and others)

Terrien, S. L. *Job: Poet of Existence.* Indianapolis: 1957. (Christian-existentialist interpretation)

Wolfers, D. *Deep Things out of Darkness: The Book of Job. Essays and a New English Translation.* Grand Rapids: 1995. (A fascinating study that reads Job as a debate prompted by the Assyrian invasion of Judah during Hezekiah's righteous reign in the late eighth century and the resulting questions of divine providence)

Zerafa, P. P. *The Wisdom of God in the Book of Job*. Rome: 1978. (A national interpretation: restoration from Exile is an act of God's mercy, not result of human obedience to wisdom)

Zuck, R. B., ed. *Sitting with Job*. Grand Rapids: 1992. (Contains a variety of articles from many perspectives on the book of Job)

Chapter 36 — Ecclesiastes

Crenshaw, J. *Ecclesiastes*. OTL. Philadelphia: 1987. (A competent if at times skeptical commentary)

Eaton, M. *Ecclesiastes*. TOTC. Leicester: 1983. (A handy, thoughtful exposition)

Fox, M. V. *Qohelet and His Contradictions*. Sheffield: 1989. (Scholarly, thought provoking, yet overly pessimistic)

Ginsberg, H. L. *Studies in Koheleth*. New York: 1950.

Gordis, R. *Koheleth — The Man and His World*. New York: 1968. (A master work on language, message, and meaning)

Hubbard, D. *Ecclesiastes, Song of Solomon*. CC 15B. Dallas: 1991. (Applies to the whole text the interpretative approaches sketched in this chapter)

Loader, J. A. *Polar Structures in the Book of Qoheleth*. BZAW 152 (1979). (Form-critical analysis finding "intended polar structures" rather than "contradictions")

———. *Ecclesiastes: A Practical Commentary*. Trans. J. Vriend. Grand Rapids: 1986. (A popular exposition based on *Polar Structures* [see above])

Murphy, R. E. *Ecclesiastes*. WBC 23A. Dallas: 1993. (Clear, succinct, balanced, and thorough study)

Ogden, G. S. "The 'Better'-Proverb (Tôb-Spruch), Rhetorical Criticism, and Qoheleth." *JBL* 96 (1977): 489-505.

———. *Qoheleth*. Sheffield: 1987. (Excellent study of structure, argument, and word meanings)

Whitley, C. F. *Koheleth*. BZAW 148 (1979). (Detailed study of the language; argues for post-Maccabean composition)

Whybray, R. N. *Ecclesiastes*. NCBC. Grand Rapids: 1989. (A solid, useful guidebook)

Chapter 37 — The Song of Songs

Albright, W. F. "Archaic Survivals in the Text of Canticles." Pp. 1-7 in D. W. Thomas and W. D. McHardy, eds., *Hebrew and Semitic Studies Presented to Godfrey Rolles Driver*. Oxford: 1963. (Alleged Canaanite elements)

Brenner, Athalya. *The Song of Songs*. JSOT Old Testament Guides. Sheffield: 1989. (Survey of research on background, literary qualities, and interpretation, including feminist readings)

Carr, G. Lloyd. *The Song of Solomon*. TOTC. Leicester: 1984.

Fox, Michael V. *The Song of Songs and the Ancient Egyptian Love-Songs*. Madison: 1985.

Gollwitzer, H. *Song of Love: A Biblical Understanding of Sex*. Trans. K. Crim. Philadelphia: 1979. (An affirmation of a positive approach to sex in the Bible)

Hubbard, D. A. "Song of Solomon." *IBD*, pp. 1472-1474. (Parts of the preceding discussion were adapted from this article.)

————. *Ecclesiastes, Song of Solomon*. CC 15B. Dallas: 1991.

Keel, O. *The Song of Songs*. A Continental Commentary. Trans. F. J. Gaiser. Minneapolis: 1994. (A thorough commentary, beautifully illustrated with ancient Near Eastern art)

Kessler, R. *Some Poetical and Structural Features of the Song of Songs*. Ed. J. Macdonald. Leeds University Oriental Society Monograph 8. Leeds: 1957.

Landy, F. "Beauty and the Enigma: An Inquiry into Some Interrelated Episodes of the Song of Songs." *JSOT* 17 (1980): 55-106. (Examines 1:5f., 7f.; 8:8-10, 11f.)

————. *Paradoxes of Paradise: Identity and Difference in the Song of Songs*. Sheffield: 1983. (Artful discussion of the love relationships)

Murphy, R. E. *The Song of Songs*. Hermeneia. Minneapolis: 1990. (A masterful commentary which catches both the literary qualities and the pictures of human love as reflections of the divine)

Chapter 38 — Ruth

Anderson, A. A. "The Marriage of Ruth." *JSS* 23 (1978): 171-183. (Disputes identification of levirate union in Ruth)

Berlin, A. "Poetics in the Book of Ruth." Pp. 83-110 in her *Poetics and Interpretation of Biblical Narrative*. Sheffield: 1983. (Studies the story's literary techniques)

Bush, F. W. *Ruth, Esther*. WBC 9. Dallas: 1996. (Detailed analysis of the story and background with commentary on Hebrew text)

Davies, E. W. "Inheritance Rights and the Hebrew Levirate Marriage." *VT* 31 (1981): 138-144, 257-268. (Surveys the book's legal background)

Fewell, D. N., and D. M. Gunn. *Compromising Redemption*. Louisville: 1990. (Focuses on the literary roles of the story's main characters)

Fisch, H. "Ruth and the Structure of Covenant History." *VT* 32 (1982): 425-437.

Gow, M. D. *The Book of Ruth: Its Structure, Theme and Purpose*. Leicester: 1992. (Thorough recent analysis of the book)

Hubbard, R. L., Jr. *The Book of Ruth*. NICOT. Grand Rapids: 1988. (Full-scale commentary)

Niditch, S. "Legends of Wise Heroes and Heroines." Pp. 451-456 in D. A. Knight and G. M. Tucker, eds., *The Hebrew Bible and Its Modern Interpreters*. Philadelphia/Chico: 1985. (Surveys current scholarly discussion)

Prinsloo, W. S. "The Theology of the Book of Ruth." *VT* 30 (1980): 330-341.

Rauber, D. F. "Literary Values in the Bible: The Book of Ruth." *JBL* 89 (1970): 27-37. (Analysis by specialist in literary studies)

Sasson, J. M. *Ruth: A New Translation with a Philological Commentary and a Formalist-Folklorist Interpretation.* 2nd ed. Sheffield: 1989.

Chapter 39 — Lamentations

Ackroyd, P. R. *Exile and Restoration: A Study of Hebrew Thought of the Sixth Century B.C.* OTL. Philadelphia: 1968.

Gordis, R. *The Song of Songs and Lamentations.* 3rd ed. New York: 1974.

Gwaltney, W. C., Jr. "The Biblical Book of Lamentations in the Context of Near Eastern Lament Literature." Pp. 191-211 in W. W. Hallo et al., eds., *Scripture in Context* II. Winona Lake: 1983.

Hillers, D. R. *Lamentations.* Rev. ed. AB 7A. Garden City: 1992. (Excellent translation and philological study)

Hubbard, D. A. "Lamentations, Book of," *IDB*, pp. 861-871. (Parts of the preceding discussion were adapted from this article.)

Krašovec, J. "The Source of Hope in the Book of Lamentations." *VT* 42 (1992): 223-233.

McDaniel, T. F. "The Alleged Sumerian Influence upon Lamentations." *VT* 18 (1968): 198-209.

Provan, I. W. *Lamentations.* NCBC. Grand Rapids: 1991.

Renkema, J. "The Literary Structure of Lamentations (I–IV)." Pp. 294-396 in W. van der Meer and J. C. de Moor, eds., *The Structural Analysis of Biblical and Canaanite Poetry.* Sheffield: 1988. (Detailed analysis of various kinds of structural elements in the book)

Salters, R. B. *Jonah and Lamentations.* JSOT Old Testament Guides. Sheffield: 1994. (Recent research on the contents, genre, and theology)

Shea, W. H. "The *qinah* Structure of the Book of Lamentations." *Bibl* 60 (1979): 103-107. (Acrostics define precise structure of the work as a whole.)

Westermann, C. *Lamentations: Issues and Interpretation.* Trans. C. Muenchow. Minneapolis: 1994. (A welcome study of recent research and interpretation with the author's usual balanced conclusions)

Chapter 40 — The Scroll of Esther

Baldwin, J. G. *Esther.* TOTC. Downers Grove, Ill.: 1984.

Berg, S. B. *The Book of Esther: Motifs, Themes and Structure.* SBLDS 44. Missoula: 1979. (Jewish people share with Yahweh responsibility for their fate.)

Bergquist, J. L. *Judaism in Persia's Shadow: A Social and Historical Approach.* Minneapolis: 1995.

Bush, F. W. *Ruth, Esther.* WBC 9. Dallas: 1996. (Full exegetical treatment and literary and theological exposition)

Fox, M. V. *Character and Ideology in the Book of Esther.* Columbia, S.C.: 1991. (In-depth study of the book's characters)

Humphreys, W. L. "The Story of Esther and Mordecai: An Early Jewish Novella."
Pp. 97-113 in G. W. Coats, ed., *Saga, Legend, Tale, Novella, Fable. Narrative
Genres in Old Testament Literature*. Sheffield: 1985. (Excellent literary analy-
sis)

Jones, B. W. "Two Misconceptions about the Book of Esther." *CBQ* 39 (1977):
171-181. (Intent is to reconcile Jews to their status as a minority; cites
humorous aspects of book)

Loader, J. A. "Esther as a Novel with Different Levels of Meaning." *ZAW* 90 (1978):
417-421.

Moore, C. A. *Esther*. AB 7B. Garden City: 1971. (Comprehensive commentary)

———. "Esther Revisited Again." *Hebrew Annual Review* 7 (1983): 169-186. (Surveys recent studies of the book)

Niditch, S. *Underdogs and Tricksters: A Prelude to Biblical Folklore*. San Francisco:
1987. Pp. 126-152.

Yamauchi, E. A. *Persia and the Bible*. Grand Rapids: 1990. (Valuable historical and
cultural background on the Persian empire)

Chapter 41 — The Chronicler's Perspective

Allen, L. C. *1, 2 Chronicles*. CC 10. Waco: 1987. (A Christian interpretation of the
Chronicler's concerns)

Braun, R. L. *1 Chronicles*. WBC 14. Waco: 1986. (A detailed exegetical commentary)

———. *Understanding the Basic Themes of 1, 2 Chronicles*. Dallas: 1991. (A helpful
study of key topics)

De Vries, S. J. *1 Chronicles, 2 Chronicles*. FOTL 11. Grand Rapids: 1989. (Detailed
examination of literary forms accompanied by insightful exposition)

Dillard, R. B. *2 Chronicles*. WBC 15. Waco: 1987. (A detailed exegetical commentary)

Jones, G. H. *1 and 2 Chronicles*. JSOT Old Testament Guides. Sheffield: 1993.
(Thorough account of recent research)

McConville, J. G. *I and II Chronicles*. Daily Study Bible. Philadelphia: 1984. (An
introductory exegetical and expository treatment)

Myers, J. M. *I Chronicles, II Chronicles*. AB 12, 13. New York: 1965. (Standard work
of lasting value)

Selman, M. J. *1 Chronicles, 2 Chronicles*. TOTC 10a, 10b. Leicester, U.K., Downers
Grove, Ill.: 1994. (Both scholarly and devout)

Williamson, H. G. M. *Israel in the Books of Chronicles*. Cambridge: 1977. (Differ-
entiates between Chronicles and Ezra-Nehemiah in terms of authorship;
demonstrates the Chronicler's anti-exclusiveness)

———. *1 and 2 Chronicles*. New Century Bible. Grand Rapids: 1982. (A detailed
commentary of distinction)

Chapter 42 — Ezra-Nehemiah

Bossman, D. "Ezra's Marriage Reform: Israel Redefined." *Biblical Theology Bulletin* 9 (1979): 32-38. (Purification of the cultic community)

Clines, D. J. A. *Ezra, Nehemiah, Esther.* NCBC. Grand Rapids: 1984.

Eskenazi, T. C. *In an Age of Prose. A Literary Approach to EzraNehemiah.* SBLMS 36. Atlanta: 1988. (Excellent, thorough literary study of Ezra-Nehemiah)

Holmgren, F. C. *Ezra and Nehemiah: Israel Alive Again.* ITC. Grand Rapids: 1987. (Clear comments and useful theological observations)

Kidner, D. *Ezra and Nehemiah: An Introduction and Commentary.* TOTC. Downers Grove: 1979. (Evangelical and strongly apologetic, yet aware of larger scholarly discussion)

Klein, R. W. "Ezra-Nehemiah, Books of." *ABD* 2:731-742. (Most recent overview of the book and its critical problems)

———. *Israel in Exile: A Theological Interpretation.* Overtures to Biblical Theology 6. Philadelphia: 1979.

Mason, R. *Preaching the Tradition: Homily and Hermeneutics after the Exile.* Cambridge, U.K.: 1990. Pp. 147-183. (A form-critical study of the addresses in Ezra-Nehemiah in the context of other postexilic speeches)

Shaver, J. R. *Torah and the Chronicler's History Work.* Brown Judaic Studies 196. Atlanta: 1989. (Argues that the Chronicler's Torah was not the present Pentateuch since it included laws absent from it)

Williamson, H. G. M. "The Composition of Ezra i–vi." *JTS* 34 (1983): 1-30. (Claims that a single author wrote Ezra 1–6 to justify the primacy of the Jerusalem temple against a rival one on Mt. Gerizim)

———. *Ezra, Nehemiah.* WBC 16. Waco: 1985. (Most comprehensive commentary study available)

Chapter 43 — Daniel

Baldwin, J. G. *Daniel.* Downers Grove: 1978. (Helpful exposition with thoughtful arguments for the unity of the book and the historical bases of the stories)

Borsch, F. H. *The Son of Man in Myth and History.* Philadelphia: 1967. (Background and influence of "Son of Man" vision in Dan. 7)

Brekelmans, C. H. W. "The Saints of the Most High and Their Kingdom." *OTS* 14 (1965): 309-329.

Clifford, R. J. "History and Myth in Daniel 10–12." *BASOR* 220 (1975): 23-26. (Ultimate enemy is Death)

Collins, J. J. *The Apocalyptic Vision of the Book of Daniel.* HSM 16. Missoula: 1977. (Book is collection of traditional writings; difficulties of apocalyptic imagery)

———. *Daniel with an Introduction to Apocalyptic Literature.* FOTL 20. Grand Rapids: 1984. (Detailed study of structure, genre, and literary forms; careful attention is paid to the *intention* of each section)

Davies, P. R. "Eschatology in the Book of Daniel." *JSOT* 17 (1980): 33-53. (Opposes apocalyptic interpretation)

————. *Daniel*. JSOT Old Testament Guides. Sheffield: 1985. (Analysis of background, contents, and message; Daniel is a unique combination of sources, not merely an apocalypse)

Goldingay, J. E. *Daniel*. Dallas: 1989. (A good survey of recent scholarship, capped by an outstanding summary-conclusion)

————. *Daniel*. Word Biblical Themes. Dallas: 1989. (Clear summary of the main components of the book and its message)

Hartman, L. F., and A. A. Di Lella. *The Book of Daniel*. AB 23. Garden City: 1978. (Sees Daniel as edited in Maccabean period)

Jones, B. W. "The Prayer of Daniel IX." *VT* 18 (1968): 488-493. (Apocalyptic used to answer problem of suffering)

Lacocque, A. *The Book of Daniel*. Trans. D. Pellauer. Atlanta: 1979. (Chs. 1–6 are midrashim; 8–12, apocalypses; 7, both.)

Millard, A. R. "Daniel 1–6 and History." *Evangelical Quarterly* 49 (1977): 67-73. ("Probably accurate as to its details")

Nicholson, E. W. "Apocalyptic." Pp. 189-213 in G. W. Anderson, ed., *Tradition and Interpretation*. Oxford: 1979. (Survey of modern opinion on nature and purpose of apocalyptic literature)

Rowley, H. H. *Darius the Mede and the Four World Empires in the Book of Daniel*. 2nd ed. Cardiff: 1959.

Saydon, P.-P. "Daniel." *CCHS* 494a-513r.

Wallace, R. S. *The Lord Is King: The Message of Daniel*. Downers Grove, Ill.: 1979. (Contemporary applications)

Whitcomb, J. C. *Darius the Mede: A Study in Historical Identification*. Grand Rapids: 1959.

Wilson, R. D. *Studies in the Book of Daniel: A Classic Defense of the Historicity and Integrity of Daniel's Prophecies*. 1917; repr. Grand Rapids: 1979.

Wood, L. *Commentary of Daniel*. Grand Rapids: 1973. (Dispensationalist)

Chapter 44 — The Authority of the Old Testament for Christians

Barr, J. *The Scope and Authority of the Bible*. Philadelphia: 1980. (Challenges some accepted conservative approaches to the Scripture)

Bright, J. *The Authority of the Old Testament*. Nashville: 1967. (Focuses on interpretation for preaching)

Bruce, F. F. *This Is That: The New Testament Development of Some Old Testament Themes*. Exeter: 1958. (A thematic exposition of the unity of the Bible)

Carson, D. A., and H. G. M. Williamson, eds. *It Is Written: Scripture Citing Scripture*. Cambridge: 1988. (Collection of essays on the topic)

Coats, G. W., and B. O. Long, eds. *Canon and Authority*. Philadelphia: 1977. (Esp. essays by Long on prophetic authority, W. S. Towner on wisdom)

Dodd, C. H. *The Authority of the Bible.* Rev. ed. New York: 1938.

France, R. T. *Jesus and the Old Testament.* London: 1971. (Fine summary of Jesus' citations of Old Testament texts)

Forstman, H. J. *Word and Spirit: Calvin's Doctrine of Biblical Authority.* Stanford: 1962.

Goldingay, J. *Approaches to Old Testament Interpretation.* Rev. ed. Downers Grove: 1990. (Especially "The Old Testament as Scripture," pp. 123-199)

Gowan, D. E. *Reclaiming the Old Testament for the Christian Pulpit.* Atlanta: 1980. (Demonstrations of use of Old Testament materials as basic for Christian preaching)

Hesse, F. "The Evaluation and the Authority of Old Testament Texts." Trans. J. A. Wharton. Pp. 285-313 in C. Westermann, ed., *Essays on Old Testament Hermeneutics.* Richmond: 1963.

Johnson, R. C. *Authority in Protestant Theology.* Philadelphia: 1959.

Lohfink, N. *The Inerrancy of Scripture and Other Essays.* Berkeley: 1992. (Esp. ch. 2 with its argument on the "organic" inspiration and authority of the Bible as a whole)

Marsh, J. "Authority." *IDB* 1:319f.

Kelsey, D. H. *The Uses of Scripture in Recent Theology.* Philadelphia: 1975.

Ramm, B. L. *Protestant Biblical Interpretation.* 3rd ed. Grand Rapids: 1970. (Textbook of hermeneutics for conservative Protestants)

Chapter 45 — Revelation and Inspiration

Achtemeier, P. J. *The Inspiration of Scripture: Problems and Proposals.* Philadelphia: 1980. (A reverent grappling with the problems a modern mind finds in inspiration)

Berkouwer, G. C. *Holy Scripture.* Trans. and ed. J. B. Rogers. Grand Rapids: 1975. (A theological treatment by a Reformed scholar who rejects inerrancy in favor of infallibility)

Davis, S. T. *The Debate about the Bible: Inerrancy versus Infallibility.* Philadelphia: 1977. (A discussion that is grounded in a high view of Scripture)

Marshall, I. H. *Biblical Inspiration.* Grand Rapids: 1982. (A clearly written contribution from an evangelical New Testament scholar)

Orr, J. *Revelation and Inspiration.* New York: 1910. (A classic theological treatment)

Vawter, B. *Biblical Inspiration.* Philadelphia: 1972. (A survey and critique of Roman Catholic conceptions of inspiration, written by an Old Testament scholar)

Chapter 46 — The Concept of Canon

Barton, J. *Oracles of God: Perceptions of Ancient Prophecy in Israel after the Exile.* New York: 1986. (Argues for a relatively late process of canonization)

Beckwith, R. *The Old Testament Canon of the New Testament and Its Background*

732

in Early Judaism. Grand Rapids: 1985. (An exposition of an early view of canonization)

Blenkinsopp, J. *Prophecy and Canon*. Notre Dame: 1977. (A study of the religious forces underlying canonization)

Bruce, F. F. *The Canon of Scripture*. Downers Grove, Ill.: 1988. (Covers the canon of both the Old and New Testaments)

Childs, B. S. *Introduction to the Old Testament as Scripture*. Philadelphia: 1979. (The classic exposition of his canonical approach)

Morgan, D. F. *Between Text and Community: The "Writings" in Canonical Perspective*. Minneapolis: 1990. (Applies Childs' and Sanders' methodologies to the Writings)

Sanders, J. A. *Torah and Canon*. Philadelphia: 1972. (A basic statement of his canonical criticism)

———. *Canon and Community: A Guide to Canonical Criticism*. Philadelphia: 1984. (A developed form of his position)

———. "Canon: Hebrew Bible." *ABD* 1:837-852. (A summary of his own position and a critique of Beckwith's approach)

Chapter 47 — Formation of the Old Testament

Bruce, F. F. *The Books and the Parchments*. 3rd ed. Westwood, N.J.: 1963. (Esp. pp. 114-162; includes examples in English of versional differences)

Cross, F. M., and S. Talmon, eds. *Qumran and the History of the Biblical Text*. Cambridge: 1975.

Deist, F. E. *Towards the Text of the Old Testament*. Trans. W. K. Winckler. Pretoria: 1978.

Driver, G. R. "Hebrew Language"; "Semitic Language." *Encyclopaedia Britannica*. Chicago: 1970.

Klein, R. W. *Textual Criticism of the Old Testament*. Philadelphia: 1974.

McCarter, P. K. *Textual Criticism: Recovering the Text of the Hebrew Bible*. Philadelphia: 1986.

Roberts, B. J. *The Old Testament Text and Versions*. Cardiff: 1951. (Good bibliography)

Tov, E. *Textual Criticism of the Hebrew Bible*. Minneapolis: 1992.

Waltke, B. K. "Old Testament Textual Criticism." Pp. 156-186 in D. S. Dockery, K. A. Mathews, and R. B. Sloan, eds., *Foundations for Interpretation: A Complete Library of Tools and Resources*. Nashville: 1994.

Chapter 48 — Geography

Aharoni, Y. *The Land of the Bible*. 2nd ed. Philadelphia: 1979. (This volume focuses on the location of place names)

Aharoni, Y., and M. Avi-Yonah. *Macmillan Bible Atlas*. Rev. ed. New York: 1977.

(264 maps of biblical events, showing geographical influences and historical processes)

Baly, D. *The Geography of the Bible.* 2nd ed. New York: 1974. (A very clear and accurate description of the land of the Bible)

Eichholz, G. *Landscapes of the Bible.* Trans. J. W. Doberstein. New York: 1963.

Frank, H. T. *Discovering the Biblical World.* Maplewood, N.J.: 1975. (Stereographic physical maps; illustrated)

Glueck, N. *The River Jordan.* New York: 1968. (Exploration and descriptions of the geography and culture of the Jordan valley)

Hopkins, D. C. *The Highlands of Canaan.* Sheffield: 1985. (Treats agricultural activity in the early iron age)

Pritchard, J. B., ed. *The Harper Atlas of the Bible.* New York: 1987. (Magnificent combination of maps, charts, illustrations, and explanations of Bible lands and sites)

Smith, G. A. *Historical Geography of the Holy Land.* 25th ed. New York: 1931. (A classic; descriptive aspects particularly useful)

Van Der Woude, A. S., ed. *The World of the Bible.* Trans. S. Woudstra. Grand Rapids: 1986 (Beginning section has concise summary of biblical geography)

Zohary, M. *Plants of the Bible.* Cambridge, U.K.: 1982. (Survey of geography and climate as introduction to descriptions and photos of the flora of Palestine)

ISBE Articles

Buehler, W. W. "Galilee, Sea of." *ISBE* 2 (1982): 391-392.

Harrison, R. K. "Arabah." *ISBE* 1 (1979): 218-220.

Harrison, R. K., and J. K. Hoffmeier. "Sinai." *ISBE* 4 (1988): 525-528.

Kautz, J. R. "Moab." *ISBE* 3 (1986): 389-396.

LaSor, W. S. "Bashan." *ISBE* 1 (1979): 436-437.

———. "Galilee." *ISBE* 2 (1982): 386-391.

———. "Gilead." *ISBE* 2 (1982): 468-470.

———. "Judah, Territory of." *ISBE* 2 (1982): 1148-1150.

———. "Palestine." *ISBE* 3 (1986): 632-649.

———. "Perea." *ISBE* 3 (1986): 762-763.

———. "Samaria, Country of." *ISBE* 4 (1988): 298-303.

Macdonald, B. "Edom." *ISBE* 2 (1982): 18-21.

Rainey, A. F. "Negeb." *ISBE* 3 (1986): 511-513.

———. "Shephelah." *ISBE* 4 (1988): 473-474.

Thompson, J. A. "Ammon." *ISBE* 1 (1979): 111-112.

Van Selms, A. "Samaria." *ISBE* 4 (1988): 295-298.

Vogel, E. K. "Jordan." *ISBE* 2 (1982): 1119-1125.

Chapter 49 — The Chronological Puzzle

Campbell, E. F. "The Ancient Near East: Chronological Bibliography and Charts." *BANE,* pp. 281-293.

Cogan, M. "Chronology: Hebrew Bible." *ABD* 1:1002-1011.

DeVries, S. J. *Yesterday, Today and Tomorrow.* Grand Rapids: 1975. (Important study of Israelite concept of time)

Green, A. R. "Regnal Formulas in the Hebrew and Greek Texts of the Books of Kings." *JNES* 42 (1983): 167-180.

Hayes, J. H., and P. K. Hooker. *A New Chronology for the Kings of Israel and Judah and Its Implications for Biblical History and Literature.* Atlanta: 1988. (Recent detailed chronology)

Hughes, J. *Secrets of the Times: Myth and History in Biblical Chronology.* Sheffield: 1990. (Argues that the chronology in Kings is a schematic revision of an earlier historical chronology)

Na'aman, N. "Historical and Chronological Notes on the Kingdoms of Israel and Judah in the Eighth Century B.C." *VT* 36 (1986): 71-92. (Attempts to solve some of this century's most difficult chronological questions)

Tadmor, H. "The Chronology of the First Temple Period." B. Mazar, ed. *The World History of the Jewish People.* Jerusalem: 1979. Vol. 4/1, pp. 44-60, 318-320. (Offers an influential alternate chronology to that of Thiele)

Thiele, E. R. *The Mysterious Numbers of the Hebrew Kings.* New rev. ed. Grand Rapids: 1983. (Masterful, conservative work on the chronological problems of Kings)

Chapter 50 — Archaeology

Abujaber, R. S. *Pioneers over Jordan.* London: 1989.

Aharoni, Y. *The Archaeology of the Land of Israel.* Trans. A. F. Rainey. Philadelphia: 1982.

————. *The Land of the Bible: A Historical Geography.* Trans. A. F. Rainey. Philadelphia: 1967.

Albright, W. F. *The Archaeology of Palestine.* Gloucester, Mass.: repr. 1971.

Ahlström, G. W. *The History of Ancient Palestine.* Minneapolis: 1993.

Amiran, R. *Ancient Pottery of the Holy Land.* Jerusalem and Ramat Gan: 1969.

Baly, D. *The Geography of the Bible.* Rev. ed. New York: 1974.

Ben-Tor, A., ed. *The Archaeology of Ancient Israel.* New Haven and London: 1992.

Binford, S. R., and R. Lewis, eds. *New Perspectives in Archeology.* Chicago: 1968.

Biran, A. *Biblical Dan.* Jerusalem: 1994.

Blakely, J. A., and L. E. Toombs. *The Tell el-Hesi Field Manual: The Joint Archaeological Expedition to Tell el-Hesi, Vol. I.* Cambridge, Mass.: 1980.

Bright, J. *A History of Israel.* 3rd ed. Philadelphia: 1981.

Bunimovitz, S. "How Mute Stones Speak: Interpreting What We Dig Up." *BARev* 21/2 (1995): 58-67, 96-100.

Butzer, K. W. *Archaeology as Human Ecology: Method and Theory for a Contextual Approach.* Cambridge, U.K.: 1982.

Dever, W. G. "The Death of a Discipline." *BARev* 21/5 (1995): 50-55, 70.

————. "Palestine, Archaeology of (Bronze-Iron Ages)." *ABD.* New York: 1992. Vol. 5, pp. 109-114.

————. *Recent Archaeological Discoveries and Biblical Research.* Seattle and London: 1990.

————. "Syro-Palestinian and Biblical Archaeology." *ABD.* New York: 1992. Vol. 1, pp. 354-367.

————, and H. D. Lance, eds. *A Manual of Field Excavation.* Cincinnati: repr. 1982.

Dornemann, R. H. *The Archaeology of the Transjordan.* Milwaukee: 1983.

Finkelstein, I. *The Archaeology of the Israelite Settlement.* Jerusalem: 1988.

————, and N. Na'aman, eds. *From Nomadism to Monarchy: Archaeological and Historical Aspects of Early Israel.* Jerusalem: 1994.

Harding, G. L. *The Antiquities of Jordan.* London: 1959.

Kenyon, K. M. *Archaeology in the Holy Land.* 4th ed. London: 1979.

————. *The Bible and Recent Archaeology.* Rev. ed. by P. R. S. Moorey. Atlanta: 1987.

King, P. J. *American Archaeology in the Mideast: A History of the American Schools of Oriental Research.* Philadelphia: 1983.

————. *Amos, Hosea, Micah — An Archaeological Commentary.* Philadelphia: 1988.

————. *Jeremiah: An Archaeological Companion.* Louisville: 1993.

Kitchen, K. A. "The Patriarchal Age: Myth or History?" *BARev* 21/2 (1995): 48-57, 88-95.

LaBianca, Ø. S., and L. Lacelle. *Hesban 2. Environmental Foundations: Studies of Climatical, Geological, Hydrological, and Phytological Conditions in Hesban and Vicinity.* Berrien Springs, Mich.: 1986.

Libby, W. F. *Radiocarbon Dating.* 2nd ed. Chicago: 1955.

Mazar, A. *Archaeology of the Land of the Bible, 10,000-586 B.C.E.* New York: 1990.

Miller, J. M. "Approaches to the Bible through History and Archaeology: Biblical History as a Discipline." *BA* 44 (1982): 211-223.

————, and J. H. Hayes. *A History of Ancient Israel and Judah.* Philadelphia: 1986.

Renfrew, C., and P. Bahr. *Archaeology: Theories, Methods and Practice.* New York: 1991.

Sauer, J. A. "Syro-Palestinian Archaeology, History, and Biblical Studies." *BA* 45 (1982): 201-209.

Schick, R., Z. T. Fiema, and K. 'Amr. "The Petra Church Project, 1992-93: A Preliminary Report." *ADAJ* 37 (1993): 55-66.

Simms, S. "The Petra Ethnoarchaeological Project." *American Center of Oriental Research Newsletter* 7.1 (Summer 1995), 1-3.

Stern, E., ed. *NEAEHL.* 4 vols. Jerusalem: 1993.

Toombs, L. E. "The Development of Palestinian Archaeology as a Discipline." *BA* 45 (1982): 89-91.

Ussishkin, D. "Where Is Israeli Archaeology Going?" *BA* 45 (1982): 93-95.

World Atlas of Archaeology. Ed. C. Flon et al. New York: 1988.

Wright, G. E. *Biblical Archaeology.* Rev. ed. Philadelphia: 1962.

Chapter 51 — Messianic Prophecy

Bentzen, A. *King and Messiah.* London: 1954. (Expounds Scandinavian viewpoint)

de Jonge, M. "Messiah." *ABD* 4:777-788.

Groningen, G. van. *Messianic Revelation in the Old Testament.* Grand Rapids: 1990. (A somewhat formalistic but very informative treatment)

Kaiser, W. C. *The Messiah in the Old Testament.* Grand Rapids: 1995. (A catalogue of all the passages purported to speak of the Messianic Age)

Klausner, J. *The Messianic Idea in Israel.* Trans. W. F. Stinespring. New York; 1955. (From time of Moses to third century A.D.)

Landianan, L. *Messianism in the Talmudic Era.* New York: 1979. (Essays on origins, natural and supernatural aspects of Jewish and Christian messianic phenomena)

Motyer, J. A. "Messiah." *IBD*, pp. 987-994.

Mowinckel, S. *He That Cometh.* Trans. G. W. Anderson. Nashville: 1956. (Includes discussion of "Son of Man")

O'Doherty, E. "The Organic Development of Messianic Revelation." *CBQ* 19 (1957): 16-24.

Ringgren, H. *The Messiah in the Old Testament.* SBT 18. London: 1956. (Supports traditional interpretation, using historical exegesis)

Rivkin, E. "The Meaning of Messiah in Jewish Thought." *USQR* 26 (1971): 383-406. (Addresses problems of Judaism in Greco-Roman world)

Scholem, G. *The Messianic Idea in Judaism.* Trans. M. A. Meyet and H. Halkin. New York: 1971. (Essays stressing complex relationship between Jewish mysticism and messianism)

Teeple, H. M. *The Mosaic Eschatological Prophet.* JBL Monograph. Philadelphia: 1957. (Examines views of return of Moses or a prophet like him in the eschatological age)

Wright, C. J. H. *Knowing Jesus through the Old Testament.* Downers Grove, Ill.: 1995. (Survey of Old Testament themes and the ways that Jesus fulfills them)

General Bibliography

In the "For Further Reading" section, beginning on page 699, a bibliography appears for each chapter of *Old Testament Survey*. In addition to those, the following bibliography is included as a representative (but not exhaustive) list of additional resources for the study of the message, form, and background of the Old Testament. For the most part the texts included are intended for nonspecialists (though the subjects and individual texts included may sometimes be challenging).

Bibliographical Sources for OT Study

Book List. Sheffield, Eng.: Society for Old Testament Study. (Annual review of books on the OT.)

Childs, B. *Old Testament Books for Pastor and Teacher*. Philadelphia, 1977.

Elenchus bibliographicus biblicus. Rome; Pontifical Biblical Institute. (A classified bibliography of periodical literature on theological subjects and the books of the Bible.)

Fitzmyer, J. *An Introductory Bibliography for the Study of Scripture*. Rev. ed. Rome, 1981.

Goldingay, J. *Old Testament Commentary Survey*. 2nd ed. Madison, Wisc., 1981

International Review of Biblical Studies. Düsseldorf: Patmos Verlag. (A classified bibliography of the periodical literature.)

Langevin, P., ed. *Biblical Bibliography*.

Longman, T. *Old Testament Commentary Survey*. Grand Rapids, 1991.

Old Testament Abstracts. Catholic Biblical Association. (Bibliography of periodical literature classified by topic and book, issued thrice yearly.)

Concordances, Dictionaries, and Encyclopedias

(See Bailey, L. "What a Concordance Can Do for You: The Bible Word by Word," *BARev* 10 [1984] 60-67; Harrelson W., "What is a Good Bible Dictionary?" *BARev* 12 [1986] 54-61.)

Botterweck, G., and H. Ringgren, eds. *Theological Dictionary of the Old Testament,* 7 vols. Grand Rapids, 1974-95.

Bromiley, G., ed. *The International Standard Bible Encyclopedia,* 4 vols. Grand Rapids, 1979.

Buttrick, G., ed. *The Interpreter's Dictionary of the Bible: An Illustrated Encyclopedia.* 5 vols. Nashville, Tenn., 1962, 1976.

Encyclopaedia Judaica. Jerusalem, 1971-72.

Freedman, D., ed. *Anchor Bible Dictionary.* 6 vols. New York, 1992.

Goodrick, E., and J. Kohlenberger, eds. *The NIV Exhaustive Concordance.* Grand Rapids, 1990.

Kohlenberger, J., ed. *The NRSV Concordance Unabridged Including the Apocryphal/Deuterocanonical Books.* Grand Rapids, 1991.

Metzger, B., and M. Coogan, eds. *The Oxford Companion to the Bible.* New York, 1993.

Strong, J., ed. *Strong's Exhaustive Concordance of the Bible: With brief dictionaries of the Hebrew and Greek words of the original with references to the English Words.* Nashville, Tenn., 1890; repr. 1977.

Thomas, R., ed. *New American Standard Exhaustive Concordance of the Bible,* Nashville, Tenn., 1981.

Computer Resources for OT Study

Bible Windows. Cedar Hill, Tex.: Silver Mountain Software. (KJV, RSV; Heb. OT; Greek NT; LXX; and Vulg. for IBM-PC)

BibleWorks for Windows. Seattle, Wash.: Hermeneutika (Includes KJV, ASV, and RSV for IBM-PC)

BibleSource. (Available for both DOS and Windows) Grand Rapids: Zondervan. (Includes NIV, KJV, NASB; Heb. OT and Greek NT available; for IBM-PC)

Logos Bible Study Software for Windows. Oak Harbor, Wash.: Logos Research Systems. (KJV with Strong's numbers, NIV, NKJV, NRSV; Heb. OT; Greek NT available; for IBM-PC)

macBible. Grand Rapids: Zondervan. (KJV, NASB, NIV, NRSV; Heb. OT; Greek NT; and LXX available; for Apple Macintosh)

TheWORD. Dallas, Tex.: Wordsoft Software. (KJV, NKJV, NRSV; Heb. OT; Greek NT; plus various search programs; for IBM-PC)

Archaeological and Geographical Resources for OT Study

Aharoni, Y. *The Land of the Bible.* 2nd ed. Philadelphia, 1979.

———— and M. Avi-Yonah. *The Macmillan Bible Atlas.* 3rd rev. ed. New York, 1993.

Baly, D. *The Geography of the Bible*. Rev. ed. New York, 1974.

Beitzel, B. *The Moody Atlas of Bible Lands*. Chicago, 1987.

Mazar, A. *Archaeology of the Land of the Bible, 10,000-586 B.C.E.* New York, 1993.

Smith, G. *Historical Geography of the Holy Land*. 25th ed. New York, 1931.

Stern, E., ed. *The New Encyclopedia of Archeological Excavations in the Holy Land*, 4 vols. New York, 1993.

The Cultural and Historical Setting of the OT

Albright, W. F. *Yahweh and the Gods of Canaan*. 1968; repr. Winona Lake, 1978.

Anderson, G. W., ed. *Tradition and Interpretation*. Oxford: 1979.

Beyerlin, W. *Near Eastern Religious Texts Relating to the Old Testament*. Philadelphia, 1978.

Bright, J. *A History of Israel*. 3rd. ed. Philadelphia, 1981.

Cross, F. *Canaanite Myth and Hebrew Epic*. Cambridge, 1973.

Foster, B. *Before the Muses: An Anthology of Akkadian Literature*. 2 vols. Bethesda, Md., 1993.

Frankfort, H., et al. *Before Philosophy. The Intellectual Adventure of Ancient Man*. Baltimore, 1949.

Hallo, W., and W. Simpson. *The Ancient Near East: A History*. New York, 1971.

Hayes, J., and J. Miller. *A History of Ancient Israel and Judah*. Philadelphia, 1986.

Hoerth, A., et. al., eds. *Peoples of the Old Testament World*. Grand Rapids, 1994.

Jacobsen, T. *The Treasures of Darkness: A History of Mesopotamian Religion*. New Haven, Conn., 1976.

Kitchen, K. *Ancient Orient and Old Testament*. Chicago, 1966.

Millard, A., et al., eds. *Faith, Tradition, and History. Old Testament Historiography in Its Near Eastern Context*. Winona Lake, 1994.

Miller, J. *The Old Testament and the Historian*. Philadelphia, 1976.

Pritchard, J., ed. *Ancient Near Eastern Texts Relating to the Old Testament*. 3rd ed. Princeton, N.J., 1969.

Roaf, M., and N. Postgate, eds. *Cultural Atlas of Mesopotamia and the Ancient Near East*. New York, 1990.

Shanks, H., ed. *Ancient Israel: A Short History from Abraham to the Roman Destruction of the Temple*. Washington, D.C., 1988.

Simpson, W. *The Literature of Ancient Egypt: An Anthology of Stories, Instructions, and Poetry*. New Haven, Conn., 1972.

Smelik, K. *Writings from Ancient Israel: A Handbook of Historical and Religious Documents*. Louisville, Ky., 1991.

von Soden, W. *Introduction to the Ancient World. The Background of the Ancient Orient*. Grand Rapids, 1993.

de Vaux, R. *Ancient Israel*. Trans. J. McHugh. 2 vols. Philadelphia, 1978.

Wiseman, D. *Peoples of Old Testament Times*. Oxford, 1973.

Wright, G. *The Bible and the Ancient Near East*. Festschrift W. F. Albright. 1961; repr. Winona Lake, 1979.

The Literary and Historical Criticism of the OT

Note: the term "literary criticism" has undergone a significant shift in meaning in recent years. In the older sense the term referred to the delineation of the sources lying behind the biblical texts, a study now more properly termed "source criticism" (cf. Habel). In the newer sense the term refers to the literary art of the biblical texts, such as literary artifice, plot, structure, characterization, etc. (cf. Alter).

Alter, R. *The Art of Biblical Narrative.* New York, 1981.

———— and F. Kermode, eds. *The Literary Guide to the Bible.* Cambridge, 1987.

Barr, J. *Holy Scripture: Canon, Authority, Criticism.* Philadelphia, 1983.

Barton, J. *Reading the Old Testament: Method in Biblical Study.* Philadelphia, 1984.

Berlin, A. *Poetics and Interpretation of Biblical Narrative.* Sheffield, Eng., 1983.

Childs, B. *Biblical Theology in Crisis.* Philadelphia, 1970.

Coggins, R., and J. Holden. *Dictionary of Biblical Interpretation.* Philadelphia, 1990.

Goldingay, J. *Approaches to Old Testament Interpretation.* Rev. ed. Downers Grove, Ill., 1990.

Habel, N. *Literary Criticism of the Old Testament.* Philadelphia, 1971.

Hayes, J. *Old Testament Form Criticism.* San Antonio, 1974.

Jeppesen, K., and B. Otzen, eds. *The Productions of Time, Tradition History in Old Testament Scholarship.* Sheffield, Eng., 1984.

Kirkpatrick, P. *The Old Testament and Folklore Study.* JSOTSup 62. Sheffield, Eng., 1988.

Klein, R. *Textual Criticism of the Old Testament.* Philadelphia, 1974.

Knight, D., and G. Tucker, eds. *The Hebrew Bible and Its Modern Interpreters.* Philadelphia, 1985.

Longman, T. *Literary Approaches to Biblical Interpretation.* Grand Rapids, 1987.

McKnight, E. *What Is Form Criticism?* Philadelphia, 1969.

Patte, D. *What Is Structural Exegesis?* Philadelphia, 1976.

Powell, M. *The Bible and Modern Literary Criticism: A Critical Assessment and Annotated Bibliography.* New York, 1992.

Ryken, L., and T. Longman, eds. *A Complete Literary Guide to the Bible.* Grand Rapids, 1993.

Sanders, J. *From Sacred Story to Sacred Text.* Philadelphia, 1987.

Soulen, R. *Handbook of Biblical Criticism.* 2nd ed. Atlanta, 1971.

Sternberg, M. *The Poetics of Biblical Narrative. Ideological Literature and the Drama of Reading.* Bloomington, Ind., 1985.

Tucker, G. *Form Criticism of the Old Testament.* Philadelphia, 1971.

————, D. Petersen, and R. Wilson, eds. *Canon, Theology, and Old Testament Interpretation.* Philadelphia, 1988.

Wilson, R. *Sociological Approaches to the Old Testament.* Philadelphia, 1984.

Introductions to the OT

Bentzen, A. *Introduction to the Old Testament.* 2 vols. Copenhagen, 1948.

Childs, B. *Introduction to the Old Testament as Scripture.* Philadelphia, 1979.

Craigie, P. *The Old Testament: Its Background, Growth, and Content.* Nashville, Tenn., 1986.

Dillard, R., and T. Longman. *An Introduction to the Old Testament.* Grand Rapids, 1994.

Driver, S. *Introduction to the Literature of the Old Testament.* 9th ed.; repr. Magnolia, Mass., 1973.

Eissfeldt, O. *The Old Testament: An Introduction.* Trans. P. Ackroyd. New York, 1965.

Fohrer, G. *Introduction to the Old Testament.* Trans. D. Green. New York, 1968.

Gottwald, N. *The Hebrew Bible — A Socio-Literary Introduction.* Philadelphia, 1985.

Harrison, R. *Introduction to the Old Testament.* Grand Rapids, 1979.

Rendtorff, R. *The Old Testament. An Introduction.* Trans. J. Bowden. Philadelphia, 1986.

Soggin, A. *Introduction to the Old Testament.* 3rd ed. Trans. J. Bowden. OTL. Louisville, Ky., 1989.

The Interpretation and Theology of the OT

Caird, G. *The Language and Imagery of the Bible.* Philadelphia, 1980.

Childs, B. *Old Testament Theology in a Canonical Context.* Philadelphia, 1985.

———. *Biblical Theology of the Old and New Testaments: Theological Reflection on the Christian Bible.* Minneapolis, 1993.

Dyrness, W. *Themes of the Old Testament.* Downers Grove, Ill., 1979.

Eichrodt, W. *Theology of the Old Testament.* Trans. J. Baker. 2 vols. OTL. Philadelphia, 1961.

Hasel, G. *Old Testament Theology: Basic Issues in the Current Debate.* 3rd ed. Grand Rapids, 1982.

Hayes, J., and F. Prussner. *Old Testament Theology: Its History and Development.* Atlanta, 1985.

Kaiser, W. *Toward an Old Testament Theology.* Grand Rapids, 1981.

Martens, E. *God's Design: A Focus on Old Testament Theology.* Grand Rapids, 1981.

Ollenburger, B., E. Martens, and G. Hasel, eds. *The Flowering of Old Testament Theology: A Reader in Twentieth-Century Old Testament Theology, 1930-1990.* Winona Lake, 1992.

von Rad, G. *Old Testament Theology.* Trans. D. Stalker. 2 vols. New York, 1962-65.

Rogerson, J., ed. *Beginning Old Testament Study.* Philadelphia, 1982.

Zimmerli, W. *The Law and the Prophets. A Study of the Meaning of the Old Testament.* New York, 1965.

———. *Old Testament Theology in Outline.* Trans. D. Green. Atlanta, 1978.

Endnotes

CHAPTER 1 — THE PENTATEUCH

1. This analysis of the promise follows that of D. J. A. Clines, *The Theme of the Pentateuch,* JSOTSup 10 (Sheffield: 1978), pp. 25-43.

2. This relationship is set forth by G. von Rad in *Genesis,* trans. J. Marks, OTL (Philadelphia: 1972), pp. 152-155, to which the following exposition is indebted. For a more carefully nuanced discussion, see Clines, *The Theme of the Pentateuch,* pp. 61-79.

3. *Prolegomena to the History of Ancient Israel,* trans. J. S. Black and A. Menzies (1885; repr. Magnolia, Mass.: 1973), p. 1.

4. Note that it is in the genre of the suzerain-vassal treaty form, whose comparison with the Mosaic covenant has been so fruitful (see pp. 73-75), that one finds precisely this combination of history (in the historical prologue) and law (in the stipulations). Surely the correlation between this striking feature of the Pentateuch's form and the structure of one of its most important constituents, the Mosaic covenant, cannot be accidental!

5. E.g., it is often claimed that Gen. 37:27, 28a differ as to who bought Joseph — Ishmaelites (v. 27) or Midianites (v. 28a) — and who sold him to Egypt — Ishmaelites (v. 28b; 39:1) or Midianites (37:36). When this ambiguity is combined with the similar roles of Reuben in 37:21f., 29f. and Judah in vv. 26f., it often is alleged that duplicate stories are conflated here: in one Judah rescues Joseph by arranging his sale to Ishmaelites who take him to Egypt; in the other Reuben saves him from death by having him cast into the pit from which, unknown to the brothers, Midianites draw him out and take him to Egypt. However, comparison of Judg. 6:1-3 and 8:24 shows "Ishmaelites" and "Midianites" as overlapping terms; Ishmaelites means something like "nomads" or "Bedouin," and Midianites, a particular tribe, as the Amalekites and "people of the East" (Judg. 6:3). With this in mind, the roles of Reuben and Judah can be fitted into a consistent narrative.

6. In all the many thousands of Akkadian literary compositions, only three (two Akkadian and one Sumerian) incorporate explicit references to authorship. Even in these references and others found in lists of literary compositions, the term "author" is not to

be taken in the modern sense; it is expressed with the formula *sȧ pi* "in (of) the mouth of," which identifies either the oral source or the redactor. Thus, the "author" built on earlier versions and was in part simply an adaptor. See W. W. Hallo, "New Viewpoints on Cuneiform Literature," *IEJ* 12 (1962): 14f.

7. For this analysis, see R. J. Thompson, *Moses and the Law in a Century of Criticism Since Graf* (Leiden: 1970), pp. 2ff.

8. Thompson, *ibid.*, p. 3, notes that the process can be observed in a comparison between Kings and Chronicles, where "the book of the law of Moses" in 2 Kgs. 14:6 becomes "the law, in the book of Moses" in 2 Chr. 25:4. Further evidence can be drawn from the frequency of the mention of Moses: twice each in 1 Samuel and Daniel; 5 times in the prophets; 8 in Psalms; 10 in 1-2 Kings; but 31 in Ezra-Nehemiah-Chronicles. Cf. J. L. McKenzie, "Moses," pp. 589f. in *Dictionary of the Bible* (Milwaukee: 1965).

9. W. F. Albright, *The Archeology of Palestine,* rev. ed. (Baltimore: 1960), p. 225.

10. The actual statement is that Ezra copied the Scriptures in "Assyrian" (Syrian) characters, i.e., the square Hebrew or "Aramaic" script, not the Old Hebrew characters; Talmud *Sanh.* 21b-22a. He presided over the Great Synagogue, to whom is ascribed the final collection of sacred books; *B. Bat.* 15a.

11. Albright, *Archeology of Palestine,* p. 225.

12. A number of excellent surveys and studies, from various points of view, are available. Noteworthy are the following: (1) short summaries: D. A. Hubbard, "Penta-teuch," *IBD,* pp. 1181-1187; D. N. Freedman, "Pentateuch," *IDB* 3:711-726; (2) longer treatments: R. K. Harrison, *Introduction to the Old Testament* (Grand Rapids: 1969), pp. 3-82; Thompson, *Moses and the Law;* A. Robert and A. Feuillet, *Introduction to the Old Testament* (New York: 1968), pp. 67-128; and especially B. S. Childs, *Introduction to the Old Testament as Scripture* (Philadelphia: 1979), pp. 112-127.

13. F. M. Cross, *Canaanite Myth and Hebrew Epic* (Cambridge, Mass.: 1973), pp. 293-325.

14. Y. Kaufmann, *The Religion of Israel,* trans. M. Greenberg (Chicago: 1960), pp. 166-211.

15. For an excellent introduction to the subject, see G. M. Tucker, *Form Criticism of the Old Testament* (Philadelphia: 1971). For a comprehensive treatment, see K. Koch, *The Growth of the Biblical Tradition,* trans. S. M. Cupitt (New York: 1969).

16. R. Rendtorff, *The Old Testament: An Introduction,* pp. 157-163 and especially *The Problem of the Process of Transmission in the Pentateuch.* Furthermore, Whybray in *The Making of the Pentateuch* has subjected the assumptions and methodologies used by sup-porters of the documentary hypothesis to a thorough critical analysis. He has found that the tenets used to support this hypothesis are untenable in light of current knowledge.

17. See Childs, *Old Testament as Scripture,* pp. 109-135. For use of a similar method see J. A. Sanders, *Torah and Canon* (Philadelphia: 1972).

18. The phrase is that of Childs, *Old Testament as Scripture,* p. 127.

19. *Ibid.,* pp. 131ff.

CHAPTER 2 — GENESIS: PRIMEVAL PROLOGUE

1. See A. Robert and A. Tricot, eds., *Guide to the Bible,* 2nd. ed., trans. E. P. Arbez and M. R. P. McGuire (New York: 1960), pp. 480f.

2. Heb. *'āḏām* means "man, humankind," not man the individual. To indicate the individual, Hebrew uses other formulations, such as *ben-'āḏām* "son of *'āḏām,*" or "one

belonging to the category *'ādām*," or an entirely different word, such as *'îš*, "man (not woman)."

3. The connection between *ḥawwâ* "Eve" and the verbal root *ḥāyâ* "to live" is, linguistically speaking, obscure. It is a form of popular etymology in which similarity of sound suggests similarity of meaning.

4. See A. Heidel, *Babylonian Genesis,* 2nd ed. (Chicago: 1963), for a full discussion and balanced, judicious conclusions.

5. In 2:8, as well as 2:10; 4:16, "Eden" is a geographical location, not a proper name as elsewhere (2:15; 3:23; cf. Isa. 51:3; Ezek. 31:9).

6. For a detailed study of these similarities, see Heidel, *Gilgamesh Epic and Old Testament Parallels,* 2nd ed. (Chicago: 1949), pp. 244-260.

7. Cf. B. S. Childs, *Introduction to the Old Testament as Scripture* (Philadelphia: 1979), p. 158.

> "The Genesis material is unique because of an understanding of reality which has subordinated common mythopoeic tradition to a theology of absolute divine sovereignty. . . . Regardless of terminology — whether myth, history, or saga — the canonical shape of Genesis serves the community of faith and practice as a truthful witness to God's activity on its behalf in creation and blessing, judgment and forgiveness, redemption and promise."

8. See H. Frankfort et al., *Intellectual Adventure of Ancient Man* (Baltimore: 1949), pp. 11-36.

9. See J. Daniélou, *In the Beginning . . . Genesis* I-III (Baltimore: 1965), pp. 30ff.

10. This follows also from the fact that the phrase *nepeš ḥayyâ* "living being" does *not* mean "living soul," as is usually understood in English. In fact, in no other place is the expression used of man; everywhere else it refers to the animals (Gen. 1:20, 24, 30; 2:19; 9:12, 15f.). See G. von Rad, *Genesis,* trans. J. H. Marks, OTL, 2nd ed. (Philadelphia: 1972), p. 77.

11. The following analysis is indebted to H. Renckens, *Israel's Concept of the Beginning* (New York: 1964), pp. 156ff.

12. D. Kidner, *Genesis,* Tyndale Old Testament Commentaries (Downers Grove: 1967), p. 68.

13. G. Wenham, *Genesis,* WBC (Dallas: 1987), pp. 139-140.

14. Kidner, *ibid.,* p. 84.

15. D. J. A. Clines, *JSOT* 13 (1979): 35.

16. D. J. A. Clines, *The Theme of the Pentateuch* (Sheffield: 1978), pp. 68f.

17. G. von Rad, *Genesis,* p. 153.

CHAPTER 3 — GENESIS: PATRIARCHAL HISTORY

1. Each of the major cycles of patriarchal stories is introduced by a *toledoth* formula naming the *father* of the principal character of that section. Terah (11:27) introduces the Abraham cycle, Isaac (25:19) introduces the cycle about Esau and Jacob, while the Joseph cycle is introduced by an abrupt reference to Jacob (37:2). The reference to Terah is easily explained because it actually introduces the short expanded genealogy in 11:27-32, linking the primeval prologue to the story of Abraham.

2. The important textual finds relevant to the patriarchal period are (1) the Mari documents, eighteenth century (*ANET,* pp. 482f.); (2) Nuzi texts, fifteenth century (*ANET,*

pp. 219f.); (3) Cappadocian texts, nineteenth century; (4) Alalakh tablets, seventeenth and fifteenth centuries; (5) various legal documents: e.g., the Code of Hammurabi (eighteenth century), Middle Assyrian laws (thirteenth century), Hittite laws (fifteenth century); (6) documents from the First Dynasty of Babylon, nineteenth-sixteenth centuries; (7) Ugaritic texts, fourteenth century (*ANET*, pp. 129-149); (8) Egyptian Execration texts, nineteenth-eighteenth centuries (*ANET*, pp. 328f.); (9) Amarna tablets, fourteenth century (*ANET*, pp. 483-490).

3. For a thorough treatment with full bibliography, see J. Bright, *A History of Israel*, 3rd ed. (Philadelphia: 1981), pp. 23-66. For an excellent one-volume general history of the ancient Near East, see W. W. Hallo and W. K. Simpson, *The Ancient Near East: A History* (New York: 1971). Splendid summary articles are found in *ABD* 4:714-777 ("Mesopotamia, History of") and 2:321-374 ("Egypt, History of").

4. "Sumer, Sumerians," *ISBE* 4 (1988): 662. See also H. J. Nissen, *The Early History of the Ancient Near East: 9000-2000 B.C.* (Chicago and London: 1988).

5. The almost incredible discoveries at Tell Mardikh in northwestern Syria will force additions to and revisions of many statements about this period. It has been claimed that Ibrum, king of Ebla (the site's ancient name), was contemporary with Sargon of Akkad (however, the epigrapher, G. Pettinato, has since claimed that the name "Sargon" was misread in the texts) and controlled a large empire in the area. City-states as far away as Palestine (including Jerusalem) were tributary to him. The local culture was highly developed, including bilingual dictionaries giving the meanings of Sumerian words in the local language (presently termed Eblaic or Eblaite). Portions of a law code have been found, antedating the code of Ur-nammu by at least four hundred years. For a status report on the discoveries at Ebla and the difficulties of interpreting the language, see R. D. Biggs, *ABD* 2:263-270.

6. *ANET*, pp. 405-410.

7. Students of Egyptian history differ slightly among themselves about dates in the early periods. These rough summaries are based on K. Kitchen's article on Egypt's chronology in *ABD* 2:322-331.

8. W. LaSor, "Tell Mardikh," *ISBE* 4 (1988): 750-758.

9. See M. Liverani in *POTT*, pp. 100-133. Also, G. E. Mendenhall, *ABD* 1:199-202.

10. "The Patriarchal Traditions," in J. H. Hayes and J. M. Miller, eds., *Israelite and Judaean History*, OTL (Philadelphia: 1977), pp. 74f.

11. MB I is one of the most debated periods archaeologically in the whole era of early Palestine. Not even the nomenclature for the period is fixed. W. F. Albright's designation MB I indicates that he understood the period as separate from EB and connected to MB II which followed. On the basis of her excavations at Jericho, however, K. M. Kenyon posited a complete cultural break between "MB I" and both the preceding EB and succeeding MB II periods, and thus posited an "Intermediate EB/MB period." Others demurred and opted for a designation "EB IV" since the closest connections seemed to be with the preceding period. For a detailed discussion of the period, interpreting the evidence as suggesting a more sedentary than nomadic culture that arose from developments within Palestine itself rather than invasions from Syria, see T. L. Thompson, *The Historicity of the Patriarchal Narratives: The Quest for the Historical Abraham*, BZAW 133 (1974): 144-171.

12. The designation MB II B-C is given to accommodate a break in the period suggested by the ceramics and stratigraphy of certain excavations.

13. These dates follow Dever in *Israelite and Judaean History*, esp. p. 89, and R. de Vaux, *The Early History of Israel*, trans. D. Smith (Philadelphia: 1978), p. 68.

14. This is the view widely disseminated by J. Bright, *History*, pp. 55f., 96.

15. It is fair to say that the very choice of the term "Amorite" for these peoples has tended to foster a much more unified view of their history and ethnic identity than the evidence warrants. A far better, less prejudicial term would be "Early West Semites." In addition, the only ethnic migrations that the texts thus far support are (1) from the northern Syro-Arabian desert east and south into Babylonia in the Ur III period (2060-1950) and (2) from the same area north across the Euphrates into northwest Mesopotamia in the Old Babylonian period about two centuries later. See Thompson, *Historicity*, pp. 67-165.

16. This relationship is based on the apparent similarity of the two name fonts (see, for example, W. F. Albright, *From the Stone Age to Christianity*, 2nd ed. [Garden City: 1957], p. 164), which has not been substantiated by further study. See W. L. Moran, "The Hebrew Language in Its Northwest Semitic Background," *BANE*, p. 78 note 29; and esp. Thompson, *Historicity*, pp. 91-97.

17. Geographical names are notoriously conservative and usually preserve an ethnic picture far older than the period in which they occur.

18. So also de Vaux, *Early History*, p. 68.

19. For a discussion of the Hurrian penetration of Syria and Palestine, see F. W. Bush, "Hurrians," *IDBS*, pp. 423f. For a more detailed treatment of the date and extent of their penetration of Palestine, see de Vaux, "Les Hurrites de l'histoire et les Horites de la Bible," *Revue biblique* 74 (1967): 481-503.

20. On this point see D. J. Wiseman, "Abraham Reassessed," pp. 149ff. in A. R. Millard and Wiseman, eds., *Essays on the Patriarchal Narratives*, 2nd ed. (Leicester: 1983).

21. His most important treatment has been the chapter "Hebrew Beginnings," pp. 1-9 in *The Biblical Period from Abraham to Ezra* (New York: 1963). Others are "The Hebrew Background of Israelite Origins," pp. 236-249 in *From the Stone Age to Christianity*; "Abram the Hebrew: A New Archaeological Interpretation," *BASOR* 163 (1961): 36-54; "The Patriarchal Backgrounds of Israel's Faith," pp. 53-110 in *Yahweh and the Gods of Canaan* (1968; repr. Winona Lake: 1978); and, published shortly after his death, "From the Patriarchs to Moses: 1. From Abraham to Joseph," *BA* 36 (1973): 5-33.

22. *History*, pp. 77-103.

23. In Germany A. Alt and M. Noth espoused a much less positive assessment of the historical worth of Gen. 12–50. Alt and Noth, of course, while not ignoring the results of archaeology, were interested primarily in the study of the preliterary history of the narratives, and of the oral traditions from which they emerged, using the literary techniques of *Gattungsgeschichte* (investigation of literary categories) and *Redaktionsgeschichte* (investigation of the process of composition and editing). Albright and his followers, while not eschewing the methodology and results of literary criticism, laid far greater weight on the parallels between the biblical texts and the nonbiblical materials. The two approaches came into open conflict in a series of journal articles and reviews. In *Early Israel in Recent History Writing*, Bright criticized Noth's methodology, in particular his negative conclusions regarding the validity of the traditions, his disregard for the archaeological evidence, and the inability of his views to explain adequately either the birth of Israel or its faith. Noth addressed the use of archaeology more directly in "Hat die Bible doch recht?" pp. 7-22 in *Festschrift für Günther Dehn* (Neukirchen: 1957); and "Der Beitrag der Archäologie zur Geschichte Israels," *VTS* 7 (1960): 262-282; cf. *Die Ursprünge des alten Israel im Lichte neuer Quellen* (Cologne: 1961).

These exchanges led to some moderation of the two positions, as de Vaux has summarized: "Method in the Study of Early Hebrew History," pp. 15-29 in J. P Hyatt, ed. *The Bible in Modern Scholarship* (Nashville: 1965); *The Bible and the Ancient Near East*, pp. 111-121; and "On Right and Wrong Uses of Archaeology," pp. 64-80 in J. A. Sanders, ed.,

Near Eastern Archaeology in the Twentieth Century (Garden City: 1970). See also J. A. Soggin, "Ancient Biblical Traditions and Modern Archaeological Discoveries," *BA* 23 (1960): 95-100.

24. *Biblical Period*, p. 5.

25. This was predicated on his view of this period as a nomadic interlude between the urban cultures of EB III and MB II, and on his dating of it as late as 1800. Both contentions have been given up. See above, note 13; also Thompson, *Historicity*, pp. 144-186; and esp. Dever, *Israelite and Judaean History*, pp. 82f., 93-95.

26. E.g., Bright, *History*, p. 85; E. A. Speiser, "The Patriarchs and Their Social Background," in B. Mazar, ed., *The Patriarchs and Judges*, The World History of the Jewish People, 1st ser. 2 (Brunswick, N.J.: 1971); S. Yeivin, "The Patriarchs in the Land of Canaan," *ibid;* G. E. Mendenhall, "Biblical History in Transition," pp. 36-38 in *BANE;* D. N. Freedman, "Archaeology and the Future of Biblical Studies: The Biblical Languages," p. 297 in Hyatt, *The Bible in Modern Scholarship*. For a very helpful summary of the major positions, see de Vaux, *Early History*, pp. 259-263.

27. *Early History*, pp. 257-266.

28. Although there had always been scholars who had dissented from the majority position (e.g., Mazar, "The Historical Background of the Book of Genesis," *JNES* 28 [1969]: 73-83), the major assault has been that of Thompson, *Historicity*, and J. Van Seters, *Abraham in History and Tradition* (New Haven: 1975). Both volumes seek to show that the majority consensus has no validity. Thompson observes: "The results of my own investigations, if they are for the most part acceptable, seem sufficient to require a complete reappraisal of the current position on the historical character of the patriarchal narratives. These results support the minority position that the text of Genesis is not a historical document"; *Historicity*, p. 2.

Although Thompson's primary judgment as to the historicity of the patriarchs is based on the literary judgment that the texts do not purport to be historiographical (p. 3), the bulk of the book attempts to demonstrate that the major lines of argumentation from the archaeological, epigraphical, and socio-juridical data for the historicity of the patriarchal narratives are not valid. He dates the traditions they contain to the ninth-eighth century.

29. For helpful discussions of the historical nature of the patriarchal narratives, see M. J. Selman, in Millard and Wiseman, eds., *Essays on the Patriarchal Narratives*, pp. 103-105; K. A. Kitchen, *The Bible in Its World* (London: 1978), pp. 61-65; J. T. Luke, *JSOT* (1977): 35-38; and W. W. Hallo, "Biblical History in Its Near Eastern Setting: The Contextual Approach," pp. 1-26 in C. D. Evans, Hallo, and J. B. White, eds., *Scripture in Context: Essays on the Comparative Method* (Pittsburgh: 1980).

30. See Bright, *History*, pp. 75f.

31. See Kitchen, *Bible in Its World*, pp. 61ff.

32. Gen. 15:13; Exod. 12:40.

33. The Merneptah stele dates to the fifth year of that Pharaoh; this year must date between 1220 and 1209; see Kitchen, *Bible in Its World*, p. 144 note 46.

34. This latest acceptable date of 1700 assumes that the Israel mentioned in the Merneptah stele refers to the Israelite tribes that came out of Egypt. This of course cannot be demonstrated, but it provides the latest viable date for the end of the patriarchal period based on the biblical data. If the 480 years of 2 Kgs. 6:1 is taken literally, then the biblical data places the Exodus *ca.* 1450 and the end of the patriarchal period is *ca.* 1850. (But see discussion of the 480 years in Chapter 4, below.) In any case the date in question belongs to the early centuries of the second millennium.

35. See Bright, *History,* pp. 77ff.; de Vaux, *Early History,* pp. 193-200, 264; Kitchen, *Bible in Its World,* p. 68.

36. Names similar to Abram, Israel, and Jacob can be exampled from the Mari texts (eighteenth century) to the Ahiram sarcophagus (thirteenth/tenth century). A careful analysis of Thompson's study will show that for the name Abram after *ca.* 1000 he can refer to only four formally similar names from Assyrian texts of the late eighth and early seventh centuries (pp. 30-35); for the names Israel and Jacob, he can only note examples of similar names from the Aramaic dialects of Palmyra and Elephantine, from Epigraphic South Arabic, and from Jewish names in texts from Babylon, dating to the fifth century, taken from Noth, *Die israelitischen Personennamen.* See also de Vaux, *Early History,* p. 206.

37. The evidence makes it very difficult to date them to the period which Thompson posits, the Iron Age, more specifically, the end of the tenth or during the ninth century; see *Historicity,* pp. 316, 324-326.

38. For a detailed review of the archaeological evidence and a suggestion from the lack of occupation of the Negeb in MB II that Abraham should be dated to the end of MB I and Jacob to MB II, see J. J. Bimson, "Archaeological Data and the Dating of the Patriarchs," pp. 59-92 in Millard and Wiseman, eds., *Essays on the Patriarchal Narratives.*

39. Gen. 12:1 reads: "Leave your country, your kindred [i.e., the tribal or subtribal group, related by blood], and your father's house [i.e., the extended family]. . . ."

40. Arab Bedouin nomadism is based upon the camel, which alone can survive and traverse the Nefud, the central Syro-Arabian desert. The widespread domestication of the camel did not take place in the ancient Near East earlier than *ca.* 1200; see J. T. Luke, *Pastoralism and Politics in the Mari Period* (Ph.D. diss., University of Michigan, 1965), pp. 42f. Recent archaeological and pictographic evidence has reopened the question: "If we hold that the patriarchal stories are essentially historical in outlook, we would not be totally amiss in suggesting that domestic camels may have been known to the inhabitants of Syria-Palestine as early as the turn of the 3d millenium B.C." J. Zarins, *ABD* 1:826.

41. In Mesopotamia, Syria, and Palestine, this zone of about 4-10 in. of annual rainfall lies between the desert and the cultivable regions with a higher rainfall and moves in a great semicircle up the Mesopotamian valley, across south-central Syria, and down the Palestinian coastal area. See the map in Dever, *Israelite and Judaean History,* p. 728.

42. The view that nomadism and village agriculturalism are mutually exclusive lifestyles must be corrected. In point of fact, archaeological evidence from prehistoric ages strongly suggests that the cultural evolution of the village proceeded from general food-collecting to incipient cultivation to primary village farming communities without nomadic interludes. It is also likely that sheep and goats were domesticated in the village agricultural setting and that pastoralism developed from the village. See R. J. Braidwood, *Prehistoric Investigations in Iraqi Kurdestan,* Studies in Ancient Oriental Civilization 31 (Chicago: 1960), pp. 170-184; and J. T. Luke, *Pastoralism and Politics,* pp. 22ff.

43. See Dever, *Israelite and Judaean History,* pp. 112-117; de Vaux, *Early History,* pp. 229-233; and N. K. Gottwald, "Were the Early Israelites Pastoral Nomads?" pp. 223-225 in J. J. Jackson and M. Kessler, eds., *Rhetorical Criticism* (Pittsburgh: 1974).

44. De Vaux, *Early History,* pp. 230f.; Dever, *Israelite and Judaean History,* pp. 115f.

45. See especially M. J. Selman, "The Social Environment of the Patriarchs," *Tyndale Bulletin* 27 (1976): 114-136; de Vaux, *Early History,* pp. 241-256; and Thompson, *Historicity,* pp. 196-297.

46. See Selman, "Social Environment," p. 116.

47. For a list of such customs based on sound comparative methodology, see Selman,

in Millard and Wiseman, eds., *Essays on the Patriarchal Narratives,* pp. 125-129. See also A. R. Millard, *ABD* 1:35-41.

48. A. R. Millard's summary of the evidence is apt: "To place Abraham at the beginning of the 2d millennium B.C. is, therefore, sustainable. While the extra-biblical information is not all limited to that era, for much of ancient life followed similar lines for centuries and does not demand such a date, it certainly allows it, in accord with the biblical data" (*ABD* 1:40).

49. The only passage in Gen. 12–50 that could possibly relate to general world history is the account of the attack of the four kings in ch. 14. Although no connections with known events have been found, the kings' names fit the nomenclature of the second millennium well. Amraphel can be plausibly interpreted as Amorite; Arioch is very possibly Hurrian (*Arriyuk* or *Arriwuk* at Nuzi); Tidal is the Hebrew form of *Tudhalias,* the name of four Hittite kings; and Chedorlaomer clearly contains two Elamite name elements not yet found together elsewhere. On the "proto-Aramean" background of the patriarchal narratives and the vexed question of their relationship to the Hapiru/Apiru, see Bright, *History,* pp. 90-95; de Vaux, *Early History,* pp. 200-209.

50. To others with differing purposes, it may seem at times as if they have distorted their accounts, but this is a matter of viewpoint. See further J. R. Porter, "Old Testament Historiography," pp. 125ff. in G. W. Anderson, ed., *Tradition and Interpretation* (Oxford: 1979).

51. There seems to be nothing against the hypothesis that these traditions were first put into writing in Moses' time (and likely at his instigation). In view of the fact that various contracts, particularly marriage contracts, are of great antiquity, it is not unreasonable to suppose some written documents. Further, the widespread use of patronymics (Abram ben Terah, etc.) makes the recording of genealogical lists relatively easy.

52. On the tenacity of oral tradition, see Albright, *From the Stone Age to Christianity,* pp. 64-76, esp. 72ff. For a less positive evaluation of oral tradition, see R. N. Whybray, *The Making of the Pentateuch: A Methodological Study* (Sheffield: 1987), pp. 138-185.

53. See Bright, *History,* p. 98. The phrase also occurs in the Amarna letters (fourteenth century); see de Vaux, "El et Baal, le dieu des pères et Yahweh," *Ugaritica VI* (1969): 504.

54. Another measure of this personal relationship can be seen in a class of "sentence names" where kinship terms, such as *ʾāḇ* "father" and *ʾaḥ* "brother," serve as epithets for the divine being (e.g., *Abiram* equals "My [Divine] Father is Exalted"). See Bright, *History,* p. 99.

55. See the parallel passage in Jer. 34:19ff. The literal meaning of the Hebrew phrase "to make a covenant" is "to cut a covenant." The same idiom is found in a fifteenth-century text from Qatna. Slaying an animal to effect a covenant was common among the Amorites from Mari, where "to slay a donkey" was idiomatic for "to enter into a covenant."

56. The translation is that of Speiser, *Genesis;* the strophic structure follows that of J. Muilenburg, "Abraham and the Nations," *Interp* 19 (1965): 391.

57. A favorite phrase for the land is "the land of your sojourning," Gen. 17:8; 28:4; 37:1; 47:9. The verb translated "sojourning" comes from the same root as *ger* "resident alien"; hence the NRSV "land where you live as an alien."

58. Westerners, who live in a mobile society where the bonds of family and family residence are broken so easily, need to recall that such mobility was almost impossible for ancient peoples, firmly rooted in a patriarchal and patrilocal culture. A text at Nuzi tells of a man who totally disinherits two of his sons because they moved to another town!

59. See G. W. Coats, "Abraham's Sacrifice of Faith," *Interp* 27 (1973): 387-400. For

further Christian insights to this story, see R. Moberly, "Christ as the Key to Scripture: Genesis 22 Reconsidered," in R. Hess, P. E. Satterthwaite, and G. Wenham, eds., *He Swore an Oath: Biblical Themes from Genesis 12–50* (Cambridge, U.K.: 1993), pp. 143-173.

60. On the concept of righteousness, see G. von Rad, *Old Testament Theology,* trans. D. M. G. Stalker (New York: 1962), 1:370ff.

61. *Ibid.,* 1:171.

62. The biblical account indicates that Jacob "prevailed" (32:28). It is clear, however, that God really prevailed, not only in the change in Jacob's life, but in the very name "Israel" — "God shall prevail."

63. See M. G. Kline, *By Oath Consigned* (Grand Rapids: 1968), pp. 16ff.

64. On the Abrahamic and Mosaic covenants and their relationship, stressing their similarity, see F. W. Bush, "Images of Israel: The People of God in the Torah," pp. 99-111 in R. L. Hubbard et al, eds., *Studies in Old Testament Theology* (Dallas: 1992).

CHAPTER 4 — EXODUS: HISTORICAL BACKGROUND

1. Except for occasional mention in the Bible of their cultural (if not racial) survivors in North Syria, they were lost to historical memory until excavations by the Deutsche Orient-Gesellschaft early in this century.

2. As indicated, the Sea Peoples were of Aegeo-Cretan origin. Tentative identification of their names with ethnic groups or places known elsewhere gives tantalizing evidence of their migration and/or origin. Thus, Hittite and Egyptian sources for the battle of Kadesh list *Luka,* who may be equated with the Lycians, a people in south-central Asia Minor, and the *Sherden,* who perhaps later gave their name to Sardinia. Merneptah and Rameses III mention the *Aqiwasha,* probably the Achaeans, known from Homer and called the Ahhi-yawa in Hittite sources; the *Turusha,* connected with the Tyrsenians (or Etruscans) of Italy; and the *Tsikal,* who perhaps gave their name to Sicily. This invasion of Aegean peoples is very likely related to events connected with the end of the Mycenaean period in Greece, reflected in part in the Trojan war of Homer's *Iliad.* See W. F. Albright, "Some Oriental Glosses on the Homeric Problem," *AJA* 54 (1950): 162-176. On the origin of the Philistines and the course of their occupation of Palestine see Albright, "Syria, the Philistines and Phoenicia," in *CAH* II/1 (1971): 24-33. Cf. also K. Kitchen, "The Philistines," *POTT*, pp. 53-78.

3. In Amarna letter 23, Tushratta the Indo-European king of Hurrian Mitanni announces his intention to send Ishtar of Nineveh, an Assyrian deity famous for her healing powers, to Egypt to Amenophis III, who is apparently ill.

4. See E. A. Speiser, "The Hurrian Participation in the Civilization of Mesopotamia, Syria and Palestine," pp. 244-269 in J. J. Finkelstein and M. Greenberg, eds., *Oriental and Biblical Studies* (Philadelphia: 1967).

5. On the extent and transmission of this cultural diffusion, including widespread evidence of contact with the Aegean world as well, see C. H. Gordon, *Before the Bible* (New York: 1962), esp. pp. 22-46.

6. See Albright, *The Proto-Sinaitic Inscriptions and Their Decipherment* (Cambridge, MA: 1969).

7. For a thorough review of earlier views, replete with bibliography, see H. H. Rowley, *From Joseph to Joshua* (London: 1950). More general is J. Bright, *History,* 118-130. Also helpful for the student are C. deWit, *The Date and Route of the Exodus* (London: 1960) and K. A. Kitchen, *Ancient Orient and Old Testament* (Chicago: 1966), pp. 57-75. See also

T. Briscoe, "Exodus, Route of," *ISBE* 2 (1982): 238-241 and J. M. Miller, "The Israelite Occupation of Canaan," pp. 213-284 in J. H. Hayes and Miller, eds., *Israelite and Judean History*, OTL (Philadelphia: 1977).

8. In the nature of the case probably none will be found. The Israelites in Egypt were despised state slaves. Ancient rulers either did not record their defeats or else reported them as victories (e.g., Rameses II's account of the battle of Kadesh), and the escape of a group of state slaves is unlikely to have been recorded in any form that would be preserved for posterity.

9. See, for example, the treatment of this evidence by Albright, *Yahweh and the Gods of Canaan*, pp. 35-52, 153-182. See also N. Sarna, "Exodus, Book of," *ABD* 2:696-698; K. Kitchen, "Exodus," *ABD* 2:700-708.

10. See the presentation by G. E. Wright, *Biblical Archaeology* (Philadelphia: 1962), pp. 54-58.

11. See Albright, *Yahweh and the Gods of Canaan*, pp. 89ff., and R. de Vaux, *The Early History of Israel*, trans. D. Smith (Philadelphia: 1978), 325-327.

12. Albright, *Yahweh and the Gods of Canaan*, pp. 165ff.

13. See Kitchen, "Exodus," *IBD*, p. 489. For a striking parallel in modern times, see de Vaux, *Early History*, p. 374.

14. As Kitchen points out, numerous Near Eastern chronological problems are just as impossible to solve definitively in the present state of knowledge as is the date of the Exodus, despite evidence contemporaneous with the events in question. An example is the vexed problem of the date of Hammurabi; *Ancient Orient and Old Testament*, p. 75 n. 64.

15. How much prior is an open question. The stele gives no indication when Merneptah clashed with Israelite forces (conceivably in Sinai). It is often noted that on the stele "Israel" is written with the determinative for "people" rather than for "country," indicating that Israel was not yet sedentary. However, Egyptologists have observed that the stele is written carelessly, not always using determinatives with precision. Hence, this argument carries little weight in the absence of other evidence. It should further be noted that this view tacitly assumes that the group Merneptah met was the same group that had been in Egypt. Although it is a natural assumption, there is no evidence that such is the case.

16. See Kitchen, *Ancient Orient and Old Testament*, pp. 57ff. and de Vaux, *Early History*, p. 325.

17. A precise date is not possible, since there is an uncertainty of some fourteen years in the date of Rameses' accession. See K. Kitchen, *The Bible in Its World*, p. 144 n. 46, and "Exodus," *ABD* 2:701, 703.

18. This complexity is clearly presented in I. Finkelstein, *The Archaeology of the Israelite Settlement* (Jerusalem: 1988) and V. Fritz, "Conquest or Settlement," *BA* 50 (1987): 84-100. Also see A. Mazar, *Archaeology of the Land of the Bible: 10,000-586 B.C.* (New York: 1990), pp. 328-338, 353-355. For a concise and clear review of the views over the last century see W. G. Dever, *Recent Archaeological Discoveries and Biblical Research* (Seattle: 1990), pp. 39-84. In addition, questions have arisen about the claim from N. Glueck's survey of the TransJordan plateau (*The Other Side of the Jordan* (1940; repr. Cambridge, Mass.: 1970), pp. 114-125) that because the kingdoms associated with this region did not exist before *ca.* 1300, Israel's need to detour around Edom and Moab (Num. 20:14-21) thus had to take place after that date. An exploration of new sites, together with a re-examination of a number that Glueck explored, undertaken in 1978, gives evidence that there was no occupational gap in the central Moab plateau in the Late Bronze (1550/1500-1200) or Iron I (1200-1000) periods. Therefore, no argument for any specific Exodus date can be supported

by the pottery evidence from the Moabite plateau. See J. R. Kautz, "Tracking the Ancient Moabites," *BA* 44 (1981): 27-35 and J. J. Bimson, *Redating the Exodus and Conquest,* *JSOTSup* 5 (1978): 70-74.

19. G. E. Wright, *Biblical Archaeology* (Philadelphia: 1962), pp. 80-83. Tell Beit Mirsim is usually identified with biblical Debir, but a much more suitable candidate for Debir is now Khirbet Rabud; see M. Kochavi, "Khirbet Rabud = Debir," *Tel Aviv* 1 (1974): 2-33. Tell el-Ḥesi is usually identified with biblical Eglon. On the difficult question of the destruction of Jericho and Ai, see Kitchen, *Ancient Orient and Old Testament,* pp. 62-64.

20. Finkelstein, *Archaeology of the Israelite Settlement,* p. 299.

21. Kitchen, *ABD* 2:702.

22. Finkelstein, *Archaeology of the Israelite Settlement,* pp. 348-351.

23. Kitchen, *ABD* 2:702-703.

24. Cf. N. M. Sarna, *Exploring Exodus* (New York: 1986), pp. 15-26; reprinted as "Exploring Exodus: The Oppression," *BA* 49 (1986): 68-80.

25. Gen. 15:16 states that the Israelites would return to Canaan in the fourth *dôr,* usually translated "generation." Heb. *dôr* means lit. "cycle of time," i.e., "age, period." Ugaritic and Assyrian evidence now shows that the word indicated a span of eighty years or more. Kitchen, *Ancient Orient and Old Testament,* p. 54, esp. note 99.

26. See D. N. Freedman, "The Chronology of Israel and the Ancient Near East," in *BANE,* pp. 271 and esp. 295 note 16. The three hundred years of Judg. 11:26 must be understood in the same way.

27. For discussions that present cogent arguments for a date in the fifteenth century, see Bimson, *Redating the Exodus and Conquest,* and W. H. Shea, "Exodus, Date of," *ISBE* 2 (1981): 230-238.

28. See I. Beit-Arieh, "The Route through Sinai," *BARev* 15 (May/June 1988): 28-37.

29. DeWit, *Date and Route,* pp. 13-20. See also de Vaux, *Early History,* pp. 378f.

30. The Hebrew word is *sûp,* "reeds," generally admitted to be a borrowing of Eg. *twf(y)* "papyrus." It is so used in Exod. 2:3, 5, referring to the reeds in the Nile in which Moses was hidden. Elsewhere *yam sûp,* lit. "Sea of Reeds," also refers to the Gulf of Aqaba on the other side of the Sinai peninsula (e.g., 1 Kgs. 9:26), and to the Gulf of Suez, south of the region of the Exodus (e.g., Num. 33:10). The latter is an extension of the name of the reedy lakes lining the route of the Suez canal to the two northern arms of the Red Sea. Kitchen, "Red Sea," *IBD,* p. 1323.

31. Albright, "Baal-Zephon," pp. 1-14 in W. Baumgärtner et al., eds., *Festschrift für A. Bertholet* (Tübingen: 1950).

32. Presented in detail in J. Finegan, *Let My People Go* (New York: 1963), pp. 77-89 and regarded as more probable by DeWit, *Date and Route,* pp. 13-20.

33. View adopted by Wright, *Biblical Archaeology,* pp. 60-62.

CHAPTER 5 — EXODUS: MESSAGE

1. A not infrequent position in more extreme modern criticism. See the study of the treatment of Moses by M. Noth in J. Bright, *Early Israel in Recent History Writing* (London: 1959), pp. 51ff.

2. R. de Vaux, *The Early History of Israel,* trans. D. Smith (Philadelphia: 1978), pp. 327-330; Bright, *A History of Israel,* 3rd ed. (Philadelphia: 1981), p. 124.

3. See K. A. Kitchen, "Moses," *IBD,* pp. 1026-1030.

4. The question is difficult, however. In defense of the Egyptian origin, see J. G.

Griffiths, "The Egyptian Derivation of the Name Moses," *JNES* 12 (1953): 225-231. For some cautions, see Kitchen, *IBD*, p. 1026.

5. Further evidence is the fact that four generations from Levi to Moses does not accord with the 400 years of Gen. 15:13 and the 430 years of Exod. 12:40f. for the period between the patriarchs and the Exodus, which other evidence suggests should be understood literally.

6. Midian proper was south of Edom and east of the Gulf of Aqaba, in the northern Hejaz of modern Saudi Arabia; but the nomadic Midianites ranged far and wide. In the Old Testament they are found in Moab (Gen. 36:35), Palestine (37:28), and especially raiding the valley of Jezreel in the time of Gideon (Judg. 6:1-6). In the Exodus period they apparently had occupied western and southern Sinai (Num. 10:29-32; note also that this is where Moses saw the burning bush; Exod. 3:1ff.).

7. The force of "name" is but a special example of how the Israelites, as many ancient and modern peoples, attached a power to the word which now has been largely lost. In many ways their conception has a deeper and truer sense of reality. See the excellent study by J. L. McKenzie, "The Word of God in the Old Testament," pp. 37-58 in *Myths and Reality* (Milwaukee: 1963).

8. See esp. W. Eichrodt, *Theology of the Old Testament,* trans. J. A. Baker, OTL (Philadelphia: 1961), 1:206ff.

9. A number of interpreters contend that God here refuses to reveal the mystery of his being: he is the Unnameable, the Ineffable, the Incomprehensible.

10. See the excellent study by de Vaux, "The Revelation of the Divine Name YHWH," pp. 48-75, esp. 67ff., in J. I. Durham and J. R. Porter, eds., *Proclamation and Presence* (Richmond: 1970). Emphasis or intensity is expressed by repetition of the same verb in the predicate (somewhat like the Hebrew cognate accusative).

11. This statement is immensely interesting here, since it immediately follows God's promise to proclaim his name (v. 18). In fulfillment of the promise in 34:5-7, when God does proclaim his name, the identical two verbs are used: "Yahweh, Yahweh, a God merciful and gracious. . . ." In ch. 33 the revelation is connected with the fact that God above all is merciful and gracious, reflected in the striking connection of his name, revealed in 3:13-15, with the dramatic redemption from slavery in Egypt.

12. Recently a very forceful attempt has been made to understand both "I am who I am" in v. 13 and "Yahweh" in v. 15 as derived from the causative rather than the basic stem of the Hebrew verb. This would yield some such meaning as "I am he who creates" or "I create what comes into being." This position, however, appears to bring other ideas to this text. See de Vaux, "Revelation of the Divine Name," pp. 64f. For a full discussion of the arguments for the interpretation as well as its weaknesses, see B. S. Childs, *The Book of Exodus,* OTL (Philadelphia: 1974), pp. 62ff.

13. "The four-lettered word," referring to the Hebrew consonants of the divine name. Throughout its long history, until centuries after the New Testament period, Hebrew was written without vowels. When vowels were added to the consonantal text to preserve the received tradition, the vowels of 'adōnay were written on the name *YHWH*, since Jews read Heb. 'adōnay "Lord" for *YHWH*. This is the source of the name "Jehovah." The pronunciation Yahweh comes from the grammatical requirements of the name's interpretation given in 3:13-15.

14. For the significance and role of the prophet as messenger, see C. Westermann, *Basic Forms of Prophetic Speech,* trans. H. C. Waite (Philadelphia: 1967), pp. 90-114.

15. De Vaux, *Early History,* pp. 361-365.

16. E.g., J. C. Rylaarsdam, "Introduction and Exegesis of Exodus," *IB* 1:839.

17. G. Hort, "The Plagues of Egypt," *ZAW* 69 (1957): 84-103; 70 (1958): 48-59. The editors note that this article, which differs so markedly from prevailing opinions, has been assured by those competent in the natural sciences to be geologically and microbiologically accurate.

18. The desert "sandstorm" which begins to strike Egypt from the south in late February or early March and usually lasts two or three days.

19. As with the mosquitoes, flies, hail, and locusts under any interpretation.

20. The inundation of the Nile reaches the Delta region in late July or August. The tenth plague would have had to take place in March-April (Nisan) to provide the basis for the date of Passover.

21. Hence the aptness of the English translation "passover." The meaning of the verb is determined from context, with little likelihood that it is related to the similar sounding verb *pāsaḥ* "to limp, to dance."

22. Thus, for example, in the description of the Passover in Lev. 23, the feast of Unleavened Bread is connected with the offering of the first sheaf of the spring barley harvest (vv. 10ff.).

23. The view which sees the original setting as a springtime festival of nomadic and "semi-nomadic" shepherds does have the most to commend it. In this view the sacrifice and festival were originally a rite to ensure the safety and fecundity of the flocks, especially at the point of embarking upon the annual journey to spring and summer pasturage. All elements of the Passover ritual fit this setting. For a clearer discussion, see de Vaux, *Ancient Israel*, trans. J. McHugh (New York: 1965), 2:488-493. On this view, Moses imaginatively reinterpreted this festival, providing the communal symbolic act which would unite the Israelites for their perilous journey.

24. The question is much disputed. One of the best studies is J. Jeremias, *The Eucharistic Words of Jesus*, trans. A. Ehrhardt (Oxford: 1955). Whether or not it took place on the actual date of Passover is one of the difficult problems. See John 13:1 and J. Jocz, "Passover," *Zondervan Pictorial Encyclopedia of the Bible* (Grand Rapids: 1975), 4:608f. Cf. also W. S. LaSor, *The Dead Sea Scrolls and the New Testament* (Grand Rapids: 1972), pp. 201-205.

25. See I. H. Marshall, *Last Supper and Lord's Supper* (Grand Rapids: 1981).

26. Note Childs, *Old Testament as Scripture*, p. 176: "The canonical effect of Ex. 15 in rehearsing the same event is to actualize the victory in the form of a liturgical celebration, concluding with the response, 'Yahweh will reign for ever and ever.' An event in past history has been extended into present time and freed for every successive generation to encounter."

27. Comparisons with Ugaritic texts show that the poem is considerably earlier than the prose accounts that surround it. On this basis, W. F. Albright and others have dated the poem as early as the thirteenth or twelfth century. Parallels in poetic structure are so close that some have suggested that actual verses of Canaanite poetry have been borrowed and adapted to suit the needs of Israelite religion. The evidence extends to such prosaic literary features as the use of verb tenses and archaic spelling. See W. F. Albright, *The Archaeology of Palestine*, rev. ed. (Baltimore: 1960), pp. 232f.; F. M. Cross, Jr., and D. N. Freedman, "The Song of Miriam," *JNES* 14 (1955): 237-250; and Cross, *Canaanite Myth and Hebrew Epic* (Cambridge, Mass.: 1973), pp. 112-144.

28. The manna is presented as a miraculous provision, though a partial analogy is a sweet substance exuded by an insect which infests a species of tamarisk tree in southern Sinai. See F. S. Bodenheimer, "The Manna of Sinai," pp. 76-80 in G. E. Wright and D. N. Freedman, eds., *The Biblical Archaeologist Reader* 1 (repr. Grand Rapids: 1981).

29. The thunderstorm is often the scene of God's self-manifestation; see Pss. 18:7-14; 29. The cloud and fire are symbols of God's presence. See G. E. Mendenhall, "The Mask of Yahweh," pp. 32-66 in *The Tenth Generation* (Baltimore: 1973).

30. Childs, *Exodus,* p. 367.

31. For a discussion of these two covenants that takes into account both their similarities and their differences, see F. W. Bush, "Images of Israel: The People of God in the Torah," pp. 99-109 in R. L. Hubbard et al, eds., *Studies in Old Testament Theology* (Dallas: 1992).

32. Initially set forth by G. Mendenhall, "Ancient Oriental and Biblical Law," *BA* 17 (1954): 25-46; and "Covenant Forms in Israelite Tradition," *idem,* 59-76; both repr. in E. F. Campbell and D. N. Freedman, eds., *The Biblical Archaeologist Reader* 3 (Grand Rapids: 1981): 3-53. For numerous biblical and extrabiblical examples see J. Arthur Thompson, *The Ancient Near Eastern Treaties and the Old Testament* (London: 1964).

33. The only one explicitly missing, and for obvious reasons, is the list of divine witnesses to and guarantors of the treaty. Yet Joshua used both the people as witnesses against themselves and a great stone which he set up in the sanctuary at Shechem; see Josh. 24:22-27.

34. This concept of the Decalogue as "legal policy" is set forth in detail in D. R. Hillers, *Covenant: The History of a Biblical Idea* (Baltimore: 1969), pp. 88ff.

35. These laws sometimes are regarded as stemming from centuries later in Israel's life. Granted, they may have been supplemented and reshaped by Israel's subsequent experience; no system of laws can remain static as the life and circumstances of the people they regulate change. Nonetheless, there is every reason to believe that their original core goes back to Moses. Moses is seen as administering justice and appointing judges when the task became too great (18:13-26). It is inconceivable that Moses did not begin the process of organizing the various laws into a form that could guide the community and also of interpreting the covenant stipulations.

36. The Hebrew word most frequently translated "tabernacle" is *miškān,* which, it would appear, originally simply meant "a dwelling," specifically a tent. In Old Testament usage, however, it is almost totally restricted to the tent shrine that preceded the temple.

37. This literary device, which seems repetitive and unnecessary, is characteristic of that period. In the Keret epic from Ugarit, El reveals to King Keret in exhaustive detail how to conduct the military campaign to recapture his destined bride from her father's house. Later Keret carries out these commands, and the passage is repeated verbatim.

38. Scholars frequently have regarded the description of the tabernacle as unhistorical, a projection into the past of the later temple and its theology. Some features of the tradition indeed seem to have been embellished in light of later development. E.g., the silver required (38:25) would have weighed approximately 3.8 tons! However, many features in the tradition, together with extrabiblical examples, demonstrate that the core of the tradition goes back to the Mosaic period. See Cross, "The Priestly Tabernacle," in Wright and Freedman, eds., *The Biblical Archaeologist Reader* 1:201-228; Kitchen, "Some Egyptian Background to the Old Testament," *Tyndale House Bulletin* 5-6 (1960): 7-13.

39. On the significance of the tabernacle sacrifices, see pp. 95-97.

40. The JB notes that the literal translation reads "pitched his tent among us." The Greek *skēnē,* "tent" or "tabernacle," is used also of the mode of God's permanent presence with his people (Rev. 21:3; NRSV "home").

41. From a literary standpoint these chapters seem to be a complex composite of various accounts. Cf. R. W. L. Moberly, *At the Mountain of God: Story and Theology in Exodus 32–34,* JSOTS 22 (Sheffield: 1983).

42. For other instances where Yahweh seemed headed on one course and then "changed his mind" (NRSV; "repented" is the traditional translation), see the regret God expressed over his decision to let Saul be king ("was sorry"; 1 Sam. 15:35). Also God's decision not to trigger the announced judgment on Israel, after Amos begged God not to (Amos 7:3, 6).

43. N. M. Sarna, *Exodus,* The JPS Torah Commentary (Philadelphia: 1991), p. 208.

44. T. E. Fretheim, *Exodus, Interpretation* (Louisville: 1991), p. 296.

45. For a full exposition of this passage that well captures its remarkable theology of grace see Moberly, *At the Mountain of God.* For a succinct treatment see Bush, "Images of Israel: The People of God in the Torah," in R. L. Hubbard et al., eds., *Studies in Old Testament Theology* pp. 107-9.

46. Num. 14:18; Ps. 86:15; 103:8; 145:8; Joel 2:13; Jon. 4:2; Neh. 9:17, 31; cf. Deut. 4:31; 5:9-10; Ps. 111:4; 112:4; Jer. 32:18-19; Nah. 1:3; Lam. 3:32; Dan. 9:4.

47. J. I. Durham, *Exodus,* WBC (Dallas: 1987), p. 459.

48. Cf. B. Childs, *The Book of Exodus,* OTL (Philadelphia: 1974), pp. 607-609.

49. Durham, *Exodus,* p. 466.

50. Fretheim, *Exodus,* p. 311.

CHAPTER 6 — LEVITICUS

1. The primary meaning of "cult" (or cultus) is "worship" or "the rites and ceremonies of a religion."

2. See R. Abba, "Priests and Levites," *IDB* 3:876-889, for a careful study. According to the classical Wellhausenian theory, the distinction between priests and Levites was postexilic, and the entire cult as described in Leviticus was a construction of postexilic Judaism. However, Abba shows that the Priestly Code was both preexilic and pre-Deuteronomic and thus of far greater historical value than previously thought. For further evaluation of Wellhausen's reconstruction, see D. A. Hubbard, "Priests and Levites," *IBD,* pp. 1266-1273.

3. For an overview of the role of Israel as a "kingdom of priests," see A. Lacocque, *But As for Me* (Atlanta: 1979).

4. A. Rainey, "The Order of Sacrifices in Old Testament Ritual Texts," *Bibl* 51 (1970): 486-498.

5. The terminology, as translated from Hebrew, is not always uniform. The "whole burnt offering" or "burnt offering" sometimes is called a "holocaust," from a Greek word meaning "wholly burned."

6. Only later is there evidence that the offerer could purchase at the temple precincts an offering which had cost him no personal effort.

7. Cf. R. Rendtorff, *Studien zur Geschichte des Opfers im Alten Israel,* WMANT 24 (1967): 89-111; *Die Gesetze in der Priesterschrift,* FRLANT 62, 2nd ed. (Göttingen: 1963), pp. 5-7, 11-12.

8. J. Milgrom, "Two Kinds of *Ḥaṭṭā't,*" *VT* 26 (1976): 333-337 and "Israel's Sanctuary: The Priestly 'Picture of Dorian Grey,'" *RB* 83 (1976): 390-399; both articles are in *Studies in Cultic Terminology and Theology,* SJLA 36 (Leiden: 1983), pp. 70-74, 75-84.

9. J. Milgrom, *Cult and Conscience,* SJLA 18 (Leiden: 1976).

10. M. Douglas, *Purity and Danger* (London: 1966), pp. 51, 57.

11. M. P. Carroll, "One More Time: Leviticus Revisited," in *Anthropological Approaches to the Old Testament,* ed. B. Lang (Philadelphia: 1985), pp. 120-126.

12. Cf. J. Milgrom, "Ethics and Ritual: The Foundations of the Biblical Dietary Laws," in *Religion and Law: Biblical-Judaic and Islamic Perspectives*, ed. E. Firmage et al. (Winona Lake: 1990), pp. 159-198.

13. Cf. W. Zimmerli, "I Am Yahweh," in *I Am Yahweh*, trans. D. Stott (Atlanta: 1982), pp. 1-28.

14. H. T. C. Sun, "An Investigation into the Compositional Integrity of the So-Called Holiness Code (Leviticus 17–26)," dissertation (Claremont: 1990).

15. Cf. B. Z. Wacholder, "The Calendar of Sabbatical Cycles during the Second Temple and the Early Rabbinic Period," *HUCA* 44 (1973): 153-196, and N. Sarna, "Zedekiah's Emancipation of Slaves and the Sabbatical Year," in *Orient and Occident*, ed. H. Hoffner, Jr., AOAT 22 (Kevelaer: 1973), pp. 143-149.

16. R. Hubbard, Jr., "The Go'el in Ancient Israel," *Bulletin for Biblical Research* 1 (1991): 3-19.

17. E. Leach, *Culture and Communication* (Cambridge: 1976), pp. 84-88; J. Hartley, *Leviticus*, WBC 4 (Dallas: 1992), pp. lvii-lviii.

18. E. Feldman, *Biblical and Post-Biblical Defilement and Mourning: Law as Theology*, The Library of Jewish Law and Ethics (New York: 1977), pp. 31-76.

19. Cf. P. Garnet, "Atonement Constructions in the Old Testament and the Qumran Scrolls," *EvQ* 46 (1974): 131-163, and L. Morris, *Apostolic Preaching of the Cross* (London: 1956), pp. 144-213.

20. Translation of Lev. 17:11 adapted from Hartley, *Leviticus*, p. 261.

21. A. Schenker, "Das Zeichen des Blutes . . . ," *Münchener Theologische Zeitschrift* 34 (1983): 197-198.

22. N. Füglister, "Sühne durch Blut — Zur Bedeutung von Leviticus 17,11," in *Studien zum Pentateuch*, ed. G. Bravlik and F. S. W. Kornfeld (Wien: 1977), pp. 143-164. Cf. D. McCarthy, "The Symbolism of Blood and Sacrifice," *JBL* 88 (1969): 166-176; "Further Notes on the Symbolism of Blood and Sacrifice," *JBL* 92 (1973): 205-210. Also H. Gese, *Essays on Biblical Theology*, trans. K. Green (Minneapolis: 1981), pp. 107-108.

23. Rabbinic passages can be found in C. G. Montefiore and H. Loewe, *A Rabbinic Anthology* (New York: 1974), ch. 3. Prayers are from *Siddur Avodat Israel*, but similar ones can be found in any of the prayer books. The reference to "our daily testimony" is to the Shema (Deut. 6:4f.), recited daily by religious Jews.

CHAPTER 7 — NUMBERS

1. No effort should be made to press these date formulas, for Numbers attributes no theological significance to them other than a general reference to the "forty years" in the wilderness (cf. 14:33f.). However, it is highly unlikely that the dates were mere fictions of postexilic editors. It is not unreasonable to suppose that, in addition to the written log of the stages of the journeying (33:2), Moses and his helpers also kept a record of the dates — at least those preserved in the account.

2. Y. Aharoni, *The Holy Land*, Antiquity and Survival 2/2-3 (1957), pp. 289f.

3. Comparison of Num. 33:38f. with Deut. 1:3 shows that the journey from Mt. Hor, where Aaron died, to Moab took six months.

4. However, if Moses was in fact "very humble, more so than anyone else on the face of the earth" (12:3), he could hardly have written such a statement!

5. Comparison of Num. 15:22-31 with Lev. 4:2-12 indicates some examples of this

problem. In general it is difficult to harmonize all the details of the offerings in Lev. 1–7 with the sporadic references in Numbers.

6. J. A. Thompson, "Numbers," *NBC*, p. 169.

7. See C. R. Krahmalkov, "Exodus Itinerary Confirmed by Egyptian Evidence," *BARev* 20:5 (1994): 56-62, 79.

8. J. Milgrom, "Numbers, Book of," *ABD* 4:1148-1150. His conclusion is noteworthy: "In sum, we have 26 strong reasons and 23 supportive ones for affirming the antiquity of the Priestly material in the book of Numbers" (p. 1150).

9. A second census, taken on the Plains of Moab in the next generation, numbered 601,730.

10. Several scholars have attempted to demonstrate the mathematical possibility of this figure. E.g., T. Whitelaw shows that if fifty-one of Jacob's fifty-three grandsons had four male decendants each, the total in seven generations would amount to 835,584; "Numbers, Book of," *ISBE* (1939): 4:2166. Others have pointed out that the figures are unreasonable, particularly in view of the fact that out of the male population that included over 600,000 above the age of twenty, there were only 22,273 firstborn males over the age of one month (3:43) — which would require forty or forty-five males in every household. Little is gained from such discussions.

11. Some who take the numbers literally feel the problem is probably to be explained by supposing that at one time the numbers were written as numerals and not in words, as in the present Hebrew text. Hebrew letters do have numerical value, so *aleph* is used for 1 and also for 1000, *beth* equals 2 and also 2000, etc. However, there are no extant biblical texts in Hebrew where the numbers are so written.

12. Shalmaneser's figures are significant:

Hadadezer of Damascus	1200 chariots	1200 cavalry	20,000 men
Irḫuleni of Hamath	700	700	10,000
Ahab the Israelite	2000	—	10,000
From Que	—	—	500
From Musri	—	—	1,000
From Irqanata	10	—	10,000
Matinu-Ba'lu of Arvad	—	—	200
From Usanata	—	—	200
Adunu-ba'lu of Shian	30	—	1,000?
From Gindibu in Arabia	—	100 Camel Riders	—
Basa' ben Ruhubi of Ammon	—	—	000?

He speaks of "these twelve kings," although only eleven people are mentioned, and claims to have killed 14,000; *ARAB* 1 §611, *ANET*, p. 279.

13. *ARAB* 2 §55; *ANET*, pp. 284f. For the problem of who actually captured Samaria, see pp. 211, 280, above.

14. *ARAB* 2 §240; *ANET*, p. 288.

15. W. F. Albright, *From the Stone Age to Christianity,* 2nd ed. (Garden City: 1957), p. 291.

16. Heb. *'elep,* pl. *'elāpîm,* means either "one thousand" or a large group or family; cf. Mic. 5:2 (MT 5:1; "thousands," KJV; "clans," RSV). The same consonants could be pointed to read *'allûpîm* "chiefs, chieftains." The vowel points were not added until sometime between the sixth and ninth centuries A.D., but many scholars believe that the oral tradition on which this pointing was based was highly reliable.

17. W. M. F. Petrie, *Egypt and Israel,* rev. ed. (London: 1911), pp. 42ff.

18. G. E. Mendenhall, "The Census Lists of Numbers 1 and 26," *JBL* 77 (1958): 52-66; cf. B. S. Childs, *Introduction to the Old Testament as Scripture* (Philadelphia: 1979), p. 200.

19. It would, however, require rejecting the totals in Num. 1:46 and 26:51, among other details.

20. The 74 "thousands" of Judah would number 600 fighting men, whereas the 62 of Dan would number 700, and 41 of Asher, 500. Between the first and second census, the "thousands" of Simeon dropped from 59 to 22, but the "hundreds" only from 300 to 200.

21. One in the first census ends in fifty, and one in the second, in thirty.

22. The difference between the 22,273 firstborn males and the 22,000 Levites is accounted for by the levy of five shekels on each of the 273; cf. 3:46-48.

23. R. K. Harrison, *Introduction to the Old Testament* (Grand Rapids: 1969), pp. 631ff.

24. J. A. Thompson, "Numbers," p. 169. It may be illuminating that the Qumran community, almost certainly comprising no more than 250 to 300 people at a time, uses the same terminology. The regulation concerning the annual census reads: "The priests shall pass over first in order, according to their spirits, one after another; and the Levites shall pass over after them, and all the people shall pass over third in order, one after another, by thousands and hundreds and fifties and tens, so that every man of Israel may know his appointed position . . ." (1QS 2:21).

25. See G. B. Gray, *Numbers,* ICC (New York: 1903), pp. 11-15; J. Garstang, *Joshua, Judges* (New York: 1931), p. 120; R. E. D. Clark, "The Large Numbers of the Old Testament," *Journal of the Transactions of the Victoria Institute* 87 (1955): 82ff.; J. W. Wenham, "Large Numbers in the Old Testament," *Tyndale Bulletin* 18 (1967): 19-53.

26. The theme of *presence* is developed in a way that embraces the message of the Old Testament by S. Terrien, *The Elusive Presence: Toward a New Biblical Theology* (San Francisco: 1978).

27. Many scholars believe the manna was the honeylike excretion of certain insects on tamarisk branches that drops to the ground during the night. See F. Bodenheimer, "Manna," *BA* 10 (1947): 1-6. This identification fails to explain why the manna ceased on Sabbaths; why, regardless of the amount gathered, there was enough and only enough; and why the phenomenon started when the Israelites entered Sinai and ceased when they left Moab for Canaan.

28. The technical term is "anthropopathism" where God manifests human feelings. To describe him as if he had a human form is "anthropomorphism."

29. See the discussion on Hosea, below. See also Josh. 22:17.

30. See W. S. LaSor, *The Dead Sea Scrolls and the New Testament* (Grand Rapids: 1972), p. 111.

31. Fresh light on the Balaam story may come from a plaster text discovered in 1969 at Deir 'Alla on the east side of the Jordan valley. Originally part of a wall, the text was inscribed in black and red ink and badly shattered by an earthquake. Now dated about 800 B.C.E., it tells the story of a message of doom conveyed to Balaam, son of Beor, by divine messengers from El, the Canaanite high-god. For some preliminary observations on its biblical significance see Jo Ann Hackett, "Balaam," *ABD* 1:569-572; M. Dijkstra, "Is Balaam Also among the Prophets?" *JBL* 114 (1955):43-64.

CHAPTER 8 — DEUTERONOMY

1. G. von Rad, *Deuteronomy,* trans. D. Barton, OTL (Philadelphia: 1966), pp. 19f.

2. M. G. Kline, *Treaty of the Great King* (Grand Rapids: 1963), p. 48. For the

"constitutional" understanding of Deuteronomy see S. D. McBride, Jr., "Polity of the Covenant People," *Interp* 41 (1987): 229-244; for the "interpretation of Decalogue" approach see S. A. Kaufman, "The Structure of the Deuteronomic Law," *Maarav* 1/2 (1978-1979): 105-158.

3. Among other scholarly works, see G. E. Mendenhall, *BA* 17 (1954), repr., pp. 25-43 in E. F. Campbell, Jr., and D. N. Freedman, eds., *The Biblical Archeologist Reader* 3; *Law and Covenant in Israel and the Ancient Near East* (Pittsburgh: 1955); and "Covenant," *IDB* 1:714-723, esp. 716. See also D. J. Wiseman, "The Vassal-Treaties of Esarhaddon," *Iraq* 20 (1958): 23ff.; J. Muilenburg, "The Form and Structure of the Covenantal Formulations," *VT* 9 (1959): 347-365; M. Tsevat, "The Neo-Assyrian and Neo-Babylonian Vassal Oaths and the Prophet Ezekiel," *JBL* 78 (1959): 199-204. For the proposed dependence of Deuteronomy on the suzerain-vassal treaties of Esarhaddon, see M. Weinfeld, "Deuteronomy, Book of," *ABD* 2:169-171.

4. P. C. Craigie, *The Book of Deuteronomy*, NICOT (Grand Rapids: 1976), pp. 79-83. Such documents may have used "covenant" (Heb. and Egyptian both use *brt* as the consonants in the word) to describe a labor agreement between the Pharaoh and the Israelites. The Sinai Covenant and its expansion in Deuteronomy may have used familiar terms and conditions to describe the new relationship between the sovereign Lord and the chosen people.

5. The term "pious fraud" was used on occasion with reference to this book. See J. Wellhausen, *Prolegomena to the History of Ancient Israel,* trans. J. S. Smith and C. A. Menzies (repr. Magnolia, Mass.: 1973), pp. 25-28.

6. According to M. Noth, there never was a "Hexateuch" (Genesis-Joshua), *Überlieferungsgeschichtliche Studien* 1, 3rd ed. (Tübingen: 1967): 180-182.

7. G. von Rad, *Studies in Deuteronomy,* trans. D. M. G. Stalker (London: 1953), p. 68.

8. A. C. Welch, *The Code of Deuteronomy* (London: 1924).

9. See von Rad, *Deuteronomy*, p. 26.

10. T. Oestreicher, *Das deuteronomische Grundgesetz,* Beiträge zur Förderung christlicher Theologie 27/4 (1923).

11. G. E. Wright, "Introduction and Exegesis of Deuteronomy," *IB* 2:321, mentions especially R. H. Kennett, G. Hölscher, F. Horst, and J. Pedersen.

12. Wright, *ibid.,* p. 326; cf. S. R. Driver, *Deuteronomy,* ICC (New York: 1895), p. lxi. For a summary of recent discussion on the background of Deuteronomy, see R. E. Clements, "Pentateuchal Problems," pp. 117f. in G. W. Anderson, ed., *Tradition and Interpretation* (Oxford: 1979). Also Clements, *Deuteronomy,* JSOT Old Testament Guides (Sheffield: 1989).

13. See D. L. Christensen, *Deuteronomy 1–11,* WBC 6 A (Dallas: 1991), pp. l-li.

14. For a summary of these three possible influences, see P. D. Miller, *Deuteronomy — Interpretation* (Louisville: 1990), pp. 5-8.

15. Christensen, *Deuteronomy 1-11,* p. lxii.

16. B. S. Childs, *Introduction to the Old Testament as Scripture* (Philadelphia: 1979), p. 212, stresses the homiletical style which belongs to the present shape of the book as an essential part of the explanation of the law: "The new interpretation seeks to actualize the traditions of the past for the new generation in such a way as to evoke a response of the will in a fresh commitment of the covenant."

17. P. D. Miller, *Deuteronomy,* pp. 2-5, views the book in terms of these three perspectives. See also R. Polzin, "Deuteronomy," in *LGB,* p. 92.

18. Because the word translated "one" appears to be a predicative adjective and not an attributive adjective, the translation "one Lord" is rejected here.

761

19. Heb. *bāḥar* occurs 30 times in Deuteronomy, 20 each in Isaiah and 1-2 Samuel, and 15 in 1-2 Kings.

20. On the concept of election, see H. H. Rowley, *The Biblical Doctrine of Election*, 2nd ed. (Naperville: 1965), p. 210.

21. The Hebrew word *bᵉrît* occurs 285 times throughout the Old Testament, including 26 in Deuteronomy, 24 in Genesis, 23 each in Joshua and 1-2 Kings, 20 in Psalms, 19 in Jeremiah, and 17 in Ezekiel.

22. The United Bible Societies' *Greek New Testament*, notes that Deuteronomy is quoted or cited 195 times in the New Testament. Only Psalms, Isaiah, Genesis, and Exodus are used more frequently.

23. Thus far, 27 manuscripts are of Psalms, 24 of Deuteronomy, 18 of Isaiah, and 15 each of Genesis and Exodus. See D. L. Christensen, *Deuteronomy 1–11*, pp. xlv-xlix, for a recent tabulation of citations from Deuteronomy in the Dead Sea Scrolls.

CHAPTER 9 — THE FORMER PROPHETS

1. For the order of books in the Christian Old Testament see "Canon of the OT," *ISBE* 1 (1979): 591-601; F. F. Bruce, *The Canon of Scripture* (Downers Grove: 1988), pp. 47-48, 68-114.

2. The person responsible for such works was probably the *sôpēr* or royal secretary. See T. N. D. Mettinger, *Solomonic State Officials*, ConB, OT series 5 (Lund: 1971), pp. 40-42.

3. See the annals of Assur-nasir-pal (*ARAB* 1 §§437-483) or Shalmaneser III (*ANET*, pp. 276-281). See also the account of the campaigns of Thutmose III (*ANET*, pp. 234-241). Several editions of Herodotus and Josephus are available.

4. For instance, exactly the same historical data are available to writers of "Black history" as to any other historian. They select data that are important to African Americans, believing justifiably that previous historians tended to omit data they judged irrelevant for Anglo-Americans. Future historians, seeking to present a more balanced picture, will doubtless select data of concern to both groups.

5. Herodotus dates to the fifth century B.C.; *History of the Persian Wars*, trans. A. D. Godley, Loeb Classical Library (London: 1921-1924).

6. See W. F. Albright, *History, Archaeology, and Christian Humanism* (New York: 1964); E. Yamauchi, *The Stones and the Scriptures* (Philadelphia: 1972); J. Arthur Thompson, *The Bible and Archaeology*, 3rd ed. (Grand Rapids: 1982); W. S. LaSor, "Archeology," *ISBE* 1 (1979): 243f. Recent archaeological interpretations have posed significant questions about the accuracy of biblical data, especially in the book of Joshua. See Chs. 10 and 50 for further discussion.

7. See H. G. M. Williamson, *1 and 2 Chronicles* (Grand Rapids: 1982), pp. 18-19.

8. See M. Noth, *The Deuteronomistic History*, JSOTS 15 (Sheffield: 1981), pp. 12-17. Most proponents of a Deuteronomistic History begin the work with the book of Joshua.

9. These are not to be confused with the biblical books of Chronicles. 1-2 Chronicles had not yet been written, and "the rest of the acts" of such named kings are not found in them. As further evidence, the same references occur in Chronicles; cf. 2 Chr. 20:34.

10. There is no clear agreement among scholars as to whether the "Deuteronomistic history" was the product of one individual, a series of editors, or a "school" of interpreters influenced by the prophets and the rediscovered book of Deuteronomy. For a summary of recent research, see S. L. McKenzie, "Deuteronomistic History," *ABD* 2:160-168.

11. M. Weinfeld, *Deuteronomy and the Deuteronomic School* (Oxford: 1972).

12. G. W. Coats, *CBQ* 47 (1985): 53.

13. B. S. Childs, *Introduction to the Old Testament as Scripture* (Philadelphia: 1979), p. 238.

14. See G. von Rad, *Old Testament Theology*, trans. D. M. G. Stalker, 2 vols. (New York: 1962-1965) 1:342-143; H. W. Wolff, "The Kerygma of the Deuteronomic Historical Work," in *The Vitality of Old Testament Traditions*, ed. W. Brueggemann and H. W. Wolff (Atlanta: 1975), pp. 83-100.

CHAPTER 10 — JOSHUA

1. According to 3:15 "the Jordan overflows all its banks throughout the time of harvest," that is, springtime, when the Jordan waters flowed over the narrow bed of the river into the Zor. See p. 627.

2. Israel sometimes is referred to in the singular ("he" or "she") and sometimes the plural ("they"). In this sentence both occur.

3. This meant to destroy utterly a person, possessions, or a city. See pp. 147-149.

4. According to a number of scholars, a distinct contradiction appears in the accounts of the conquest. But J. Bright says: "No essential contradiction therefore exists between the various conquest narratives. Chapters 1–12 schematize the story under three phases; they do not declare that nothing remained to be done"; *IB* 2:547. See also W. F. Albright, "The Israelite Conquest of Canaan in the Light of Archaeology," *BASOR* 74 (1939): 11-23; and G. E. Wright, "The Literary and Historical Problem of Joshua 10 and Judges 1," *JNES* 5 (1946): 105-114. Cf. B. K. Waltke, "Joshua," *ISBE* 2 (1982): 1135, III.

5. The title of the book probably stems from this fact and does not imply that he wrote it. The book gives no such indication, and very few scholars today accept the Jewish tradition (cf. *b. (Talm.) B.Bat.* 15a).

6. J. Bright, *IB* 2:545.

7. Bright notes, "No doubt by the same hand"; *IB* 2:545.

8. E. M. Good says: ". . . it seems justifiable to doubt that the Pentateuchal documents continue into Joshua. . . . In its present form Joshua is thoroughly Deuteronomic"; "Joshua, Book of," *IDB* 2:990.

9. For example: (1) the chief Phoenician city was Sidon (13:4-7; 19:28), but later, Tyre; (2) Rahab was still alive (6:25); (3) the sanctuary was not yet permanently located (9:27); (4) the Gibeonites were still menial servants in the sanctuary (v. 27; cf. 2 Sam. 21:1-6); (5) the Jebusites still occupied Jerusalem (15:8; cf. 2 Sam. 5:6-10); (6) the Canaanites were still in Gezer (16:10; cf. 1 Kgs. 9:16); and (7) old place names are used and must be interpreted (15:9f.).

10. Later material includes: (1) Joshua's death (24:29-32); (2) relocation of Dan (19:40; cf. Judg. 18:27ff.); (3) reference to the "hill country of Judah" and "of Israel" (11:21), which seems to presuppose the division of the kingdom after Solomon's death; (4) passages which summarize the life of Joshua (4:14) or later Israelite history (10:14); (5) reference to the book of Jashar (10:13; cf. 2 Sam. 1:18); (6) reference to Jair (13:30; see Judg. 10:3-5); and (7) expansion of the territory of Caleb (15:13-19; see Judg. 1:8-15).

11. "The Walls of Jericho," *Palestine Exploration Fund Quarterly Statement* (1931): 192-194.

12. K. M. Kenyon, *Digging Up Jericho* (New York: 1957). See also Miss Kenyon's article in *ISBE* 2 (1982): 993-995.

13. See J. A. Callaway, *ABD* 1:125-130. For four suggested explanations arising from the account of the conquest of Ai, see H. J. Blair, "Joshua," in *NBC*, p. 240. See also R. K. Harrison in *ISBE* 1 (1979): 81-84.

14. See H. H. Rowley, *From Joseph to Joshua* (London: 1950), pp. 1-56.

15. See M. Noth, *History of Israel*, trans. P. R. Ackroyd, 2nd ed. (New York: 1960), pp. 68-84.

16. See Rowley, *From Joseph to Joshua*, pp. 109-163.

17. See Bright, *Early Israel in Recent History Writing*, pp. 39f.

18. For an excellent survey of the theory of two invasions of Canaan, see Rowley, *From Joseph to Joshua.*

19. G. E. Mendenhall, *The Tenth Generation: The Origins of the Biblical Tradition* (Baltimore: 1973).

20. N. K. Gottwald, *The Tribes of Yahweh: A Sociology of the Religion of Liberated Israel, 1250-1050 B.C.E.* (Maryknoll, N.Y.: 1979).

21. B. S. Childs, *Biblical Theology of the Old and New Testaments* (Minneapolis: 1993), pp. 143-148; see pp. 196-207 for a survey of scholarship on the problems. See also W. G. Dever, *ABD* 3:545-58.

22. This analysis is greatly simplified. Actually there are more biblical data — the number of generations between certain persons, and figures about years or generations between persons or events — some of which support the earlier date, some the later. See *NBC*, pp. 232f.

23. Popularly known as "Tell el-Amarna" (although there is no tell). Approximately 348 letters formed part of the diplomatic correspondence of Amenophis III and Amenophis IV (Akhenaten) with vassal kings in Palestine and Syria and others:

13	with Kadasman-enlil and Burnaburias of Babylon
2	from Assur-uballit of Assyria
13	with Tusratta of Mitanni
8	with king of Alasia (Cyprus?)
1	with the Hittite Suppululiuma
1	from Zita, probably brother of Suppululiuma

See E. F. Campbell, Jr., "The Amarna Letters and the Amarna Period," *BA* 23 (1960): 2-22; repr. in *The Biblical Archaeologist Reader* 3:54-75.

24. The Hittite campaign was led by Muwatallis (*ca.* 1306-1282) and the battle is dated in Rameses' fifth year, *ca.* 1286. Rameses apparently withdrew, and the struggle continued for about a decade. Hattusilis, brother of Muwatallis, had seized the throne from Muwatallis' son. Copies of the treaty have been found in Egypt and the Hittite capital, Boghazköy. The latter part of the reign of Rameses II was a time of peace and much building activity in Egypt.

25. S. H. Langdon, "Letter of Ramesses II to a King of Mirā," *Journal of Egyptian Archaeology* 6 (1919): 179ff.; J. H. Breasted, *The Battle of Kadesh* (Chicago: 1903); *ANET*, p. 319.

26. J. A. Knudtzon, *Die El-Amarna-Tafeln*, 2 vols., Vorderasiatische Bibliothek (Leipzig: 1907, 1915); S. A. B. Mercer, *The Tell el-Amarna Tablets*, 2 vols. (Toronto: 1939). For the most recent collection of all the letters, see W. L. Moran, *Les Lettres d'El-Amarna*, Litteratures Ancienne du Proche-Orient 13 (1987). Selections in *ANET*, pp. 482-490, include correspondence with the Hittites, Mitanni, Assyria, city-states in Palestine and Phoenicia, and Babylon. See also N. Na'aman, *ABD* 1:174-181.

27. *Yašuya* occurs only once, in tablet EA 256:18; Mercer, *The Tell el-Amarna*

Tablets, 2:664. However, it is not the philological equivalent of Joshua. In the same tablet, *Ayab* (Job) and *Benenima* (Benjamin?) also occur, but there is no basis to suppose that these are the biblical figures. Tablet EA 256 refers to a revolt, but hardly conquest by a foreign power.

28. Oriental Institute, *The Assyrian Dictionary* (Chicago: 1956) 6:84f., cites usage and variant spellings.

29. *ANET,* p. 247.

30. Assyriologists who met in a world congress at Paris in 1953 to discuss the problem in depth came to varying conclusions. See M. Greenberg, *The Ḫab/piru,* American Oriental Series 39 (New Haven: 1955); J. Bottéro, *Le Problème des Ḫabiru à la 4ième rencontre assyriologique internationle,* Cahiers de la Société asiatique 12 (1954). Cf. B. J. Beitzel, "Habiru," *ISBE* 2 (1982): 586-590, who documents references to the Habiru from the twenty-first to the twelfth centuries, and shows conclusively that the identification of Hebrews with Habiru is impossible.

31. For further reading, see G. L. Archer, Jr., *A Survey of Old Testament Introduction* (Chicago: 1964), pp. 253-259; Albright, *Yahweh and the Gods of Canaan* (repr. Winona Lake: 1978), pp. 73-91; A. Haldar, "Habiru, Hapiru," *IDB* 2:506; T. O. Lambdin, "Tell el-Amarna," *IDB* 4:529-533; N. P. Lemche, *ABD* 3:6-10.

32. W. F. Albright, *Yahweh and the Gods of Canaan,* p. 152, notes: "We are as yet in no position to say that the Northwestern Semites were more 'depraved' (from a Yahwist point of view) than the Egyptians, Mesopotamians and Hittites, but it is certainly true that human sacrifice lasted much longer among the Canaanites and their congeners than in either Egypt or Mesopotamia. The same situation seems to hold for sexual abuses in the service of religion, for both Egypt and — on the whole — Mesopotamia seem to have raised the standards in this area at a much earlier date than was true in Canaan."

33. While the exact location of Joshua and his forces is impossible to determine, the verse indicates that the sun was in the east, and the moon in the west. This would suggest a time just before or after sunrise when the moon was waning. Joshua had made an all-night march (v. 9), and may have been asking not for more sunlight but more darkness. Blair (*NBC,* p. 244) adopts this interpretation and suggests that the verb "to go" may here mean "to rise," although this is contrary to its common use with reference to the sun; it usually refers to the setting of the sun.

34. For a sensitive handling of the story, see T. Butler, *Joshua,* WBC 7 (Waco: 1983), pp. 116-117.

35. A stimulating summary of the role of the land in Israel's faith is found in W. Brueggemann, *The Land* (Philadelphia: 1977). See also, E. A. Martens, *God's Design: A Focus on Old Testament Theology* (Grand Rapids: 1981), pp. 97-115.

CHAPTER 11 — JUDGES

1. For the problems arising from the seeming differences in Joshua and Judges, see G. E. Wright, *JNES* 5 (1946): 105-114; H. H. Rowley, *From Joseph to Joshua* (London: 1950), pp. 100-104; Y. Kaufmann, *The Biblical Account of the Conquest of Palestine,* trans. M. B. Dagut (Jerusalem: 1953), pp. 65ff. See also F. C. Fensham, "Judges, Period of," *ISBE* 2 (1982): 1159-1161.

2. Heb. *šôpēṭ,* usually translated "judge," is related to Phoenician (Punic) and Ugaritic words that help clarify its meaning. The Romans referred to the civil rulers of Carthage as *sufes* or *sufetes,* which Z. S. Harris takes as Phoen. *špt;* see *A Grammar of the Phoenician*

Language, American Oriental Series (New Haven: 1936), p. 153. The Ugaritic story of Anat has this couplet:

> *mlkn. aliyn b'l*
> *tptn. win d'lh*
> Our king is Aliyan Ba'al,
> Our judge, there is none who is above him (51.iv.43f.)

See R. G. Boling, *ABD* 3:1107-1117.

3. Cf. J. F. Strange, "Greece," *ISBE* 2 (1982): 557-567, esp. III. Early Civilizations (6100-1200 B.C.), B. Minoan, C. Mycenaean and IV. The Great Migrations (1200-850 B.C.). See also F. F. Bruce, "Hittites," *ISBE* 2 (1982): 720-723, esp. II. Neo-Hittite City-States, p. 722; R. A. Crossland and A. Birchall, eds., *Bronze Age Migrations in the Aegean* (Park Ridge, N.J.: 1974), pp. 189-197.

4. See K. A. Kitchen, "The Philistines," *POTT*, pp. 53-78. On the power void caused by their invasions, see S. Moscati, *The Face of the Ancient Orient* (Chicago: 1960), p. 204. See also W. S. LaSor, "Philistines," *ISBE* 3 (1986): 841-846; *CAH* 3d ed., II/1 (1973), pp. 359-378.

5. Cf. T. V. Brisco, "Midian, Midianites," *ISBE* 3 (1986): 349-351.

6. The reduction of iron ore and the use of nonmeteoric iron implements now is known to have been considerably earlier than the 1200 B.C. date for the beginning of the Iron Age. See N. K. Gottwald, *The Tribes of Yahweh: A Sociology of the Religion of Liberated Israel, 1250-1050 B. C. E.* (Maryknoll, N.Y.: 1979), pp. 656-658 and notes 335, 584-586. In fact, nonmeteoric iron artifacts have been found in Egypt dating from the 4th Dynasty (*ca.* 2500 B.C.), in Iraq from *ca.* 2800, and in Syria-Palestine *ca.* 1825; cf. G. F. Hasel, "Iron," *ISBE* 2 (1982): 880f.

7. J. Gray, *The Canaanites* (New York: 1964); D. Harden, *The Phoenicians* (New York: 1962); S. Moscati, *Ancient Semitic Civilizations* (New York: 1957), pp. 99-123; C. G. Libolt, "Canaan, Canaanites," *ISBE* 1 (1979): 585-591; A. R. Millard, "The Canaanites," *POTT*, pp. 29-52; P. M. Bikai et al., "The Phoenicians," *Archaeology* 43/2 (Mar.-Apr. 1990): 22-35.

8. K. M. Kenyon, *Amorites and Canaanites* (New York: 1966), p. 76. Recent discoveries at Tell Mardikh (Ebla) may cause revision of theories about the early Canaanites.

9. According to K. M. Kenyon, the biblical evidence suggests that the Amorites lived in the hill country (central mountain range), while the Canaanites lived in the coastal plain, Valley of Esdraelon, and Jordan valley; *Amorites and Canaanites,* p. 3. Cf. A. H. Sayce and J. A. Soggin, "Amorites," *ISBE* 1 (1979): 113-114. See also G. E. Mendenhall, "Amorites," *ABD* 1:199-203.

10. Cf. *CAH* 3d ed. II/1 (1973): 659-682; II/2 (1975): 1-20, 117-129, 252-273; extensive bibliography in II/1, pp. 809-811; II/2, pp. 912f., 951-954, 991f.

11. W. G. Dever, *ABD* 3:550.

12. Cf. "Amphictyony," *ISBE* 1 (1979): 118; M. Noth, *History of Israel* (1960), pp. 85-109.

13. J. Garstang has given a remarkably close parallel between the history of Egypt in Palestine and the details of Judges based on this system of chronology; *Joshua Judges,* pp. 51-66, esp. 65. However, he has handled the biblical figures rather loosely, for if taken as found, the Exodus has to occur at least one hundred years earlier, between 1554 and 1544. In that case, his correlation between Israelite and Egyptian history breaks down.

14. F. C. Fensham makes the attractive observation that "480" in 1 Kgs. 6:1 results from multiplying twelve generations by the figure 40, the assumed number of years in a

generation. However, the length of a generation is more nearly 25 (based on figures in the Bible, as well as extrabiblical), and 12 × 25 = 300 (Fensham gets "280," probably figuring the "fourth year of Solomon's reign" as part of the twelfth generation; he does not explain the basis of the twelve generations), and this is more nearly compatible with the later date for the Exodus.

15. Early elements: Song of Deborah (ch. 5); Jebusites in Jerusalem (1:21); Sidon still the chief city of the Phoenicians (3:3); Canaanites still in Gezer (1:29). Late elements: destruction of Shiloh had occurred (18:31); "in those days there was no king in Israel" (17:6; 18:1), implying a date in the Monarchy; "until the captivity of the land" (v. 30), suggesting a date after Assyrian invasions had begun, unless *hā'āreṣ* "the land" was a corruption of *ha'arôn* "the ark" — a very simple confusion; see J. E. Steinmueller, *Companion to Scripture Studies* (New York: 1941), 1:79; E. J. Young, *An Introduction to the Old Testament* (Grand Rapids: 1958), p. 180.

16. See D. N. Freedman, *Pottery, Poetry, and Prophecy* (Winona Lake: 1980), pp. 167-178.

17. See R. G. Boling, "Judges, Book of," *ABD* 3:1107-1117.

18. J. M. Myers ("Introduction and Exegesis of Judges," *IB* 2:678f.) and C. F. Kraft ("Judges, Book of," *IDB* 2:1019f.) seek to reconstruct the history of composition, putting the final stage after the Exile.

19. See C. F. Burney, *The Book of Judges*, 2nd ed. (repr. New York: 1970), pp. 391-409; G. F. Moore, *Judges*, ICC (New York: 1910), pp. 364f. Most scholars today have abandoned the view that Samson was a solar-hero, cf. J. L. Crenshaw, *Samson: A Secret Betrayed, a Vow Ignored* (Atlanta: 1978), pp. 15-22.

20. The word used (*sᵉrānîm*) is peculiar to the Philistines and has been compared to the Greek "tyrant," a name used for rulers in the region from which the Philistines are thought to have originated.

21. C. F. Kraft, "Samson," *IDB* 4:200.

22. Y. Kaufmann, in the light of the early and later portions of Judges, holds that we must distinguish between an earlier Deuteronomist and a later one (*apud* "Judges, Book of," *ISBE* 2 [1982]: 1158). He ascribes the framework of Judges to the earlier one.

CHAPTER 12 — BIRTH OF THE MONARCHY

1. 1-2 Samuel, 1-2 Kings are called 1-2-3-4 Kingdoms. Jerome, in the Vulgate, followed the same pattern but called the books 1-2-3-4 Kings.

2. Talmud *B. Bat.* 14b. But 1 Sam. 25:1; 28:3 go beyond Samuel's death.

3. The Chronicles of Samuel, Nathan, and Gad have not been identified, but sections from them and other sources are possibly included in Samuel, Kings, and Chronicles.

4. K. Budde, *Die Bücher Richter und Samuel, ihre Quellen und ihr Aufbau* (Giessen: 1890), was apparently the first to apply the documentary approach systematically to Samuel.

5. E.g., J. Mauchline, *I and II Samuel*, New Century Bible (Greenwood, S.C.: 1971), pp. 16-30; R. W. Klein, *1 Samuel*, WBC (Waco: 1983), pp. xxviii-xxxii.

6. See W. Brueggemann, "Samuel, Book of 1-2: Narrative and Theology," *ABD* 5:968-971; C. Kuhl, *The Old Testament, Its Origins and Composition*, trans. C. T. M. Herriott (Richmond: 1961), p. 134; O. Kaiser, *Introduction to the Old Testament*, trans. J. Sturdy (Minneapolis: 1975), p. 160: the way opened up by L. Rost (*Überlieferung von der Thronnachfolge Davids, Beiträge zur Wissenschaft vom Alten [und Neuen] Testament* iii [1926]) of looking for older, originally independent single works, is winning the day.

7. The framework of Judges and Kings is usually credited to a late seventh- to early sixth-century "Deuteronomist" editor who gave these books their final form under the influence of the newly discovered "book of the law" (2 Kgs. 22:8ff.), Deuteronomy (see Ch. 8). Such a theory frequently, but not always, dates Deuteronomy in the seventh century. The reservations expressed by Y. Kaufmann should not be overlooked. He has shown that many of the chief emphases of Deuteronomy, including the pattern of judgment for sin and reward for righteousness, are detectable as early as the Judges; *The Biblical Account of the Conquest of Palestine,* trans. M. B. Dagut (Jerusalem: 1953), pp. 5-7. He finds no Deuteronomistic influence in Samuel. This verdict receives some support, though for different reasons, in E. Sellin and G. Fohrer, *Introduction to the Old Testament,* trans. D. E. Green (Nashville: 1968), pp. 194f. P. K. McCarter, Jr., *1 Samuel,* AB (Garden City: 1980), pp. 14-23, argues that much of Samuel had already been assembled in a form that contributed to the deuteronomistic history more than it derived from it.

8. The Hebrew text of Samuel apparently has suffered much and is among the poorest preserved of Old Testament writings. The monumental studies of S. R. Driver (*Notes on the Topography and Text of the Books of Samuel,* 2nd ed. [Oxford: 1918]), along with the inquiries of P. A. H. de Boer (*Research into the Text of I Samuel I–XVI* [Amsterdam: 1938]; "I Samuel XVII," *Oudtestamentische Studien* 1 [1942]: 79-103; "Research into the Text of I Samuel XVIII–XXXI," *Oudtestamentische Studien* 6 [1949]: 1-100), have helped clarify the text. A major contribution comes from the Qumran scrolls, which include three Hebrew fragments of Samuel akin to the Hebrew prototype of the Septuagint, especially the Lucianic tradition.

9. In his summary of the textual situation in Samuel, McCarter, *1 Samuel,* pp. 4-11, lists eleven ancient witnesses that need consideration in reconstructing the text. They range from three LXX traditions, through Old Latin, Targum Jonathan and Syriac, to the Qumran scrolls and Josephus.

10. For a sketch of the various contemporary critical approaches, see J. W. Flanagan, "Samuel, Book of 1-2," *ABD* 5:960-961.

11. P. K. McCarter, Jr., *1-2 Samuel,* 2 vols., AB (Garden City: 1980, 1984); R. W. Klein, *1 Samuel,* WBC (Waco: 1983); A. A. Anderson, *2 Samuel,* WBC (Dallas: 1989). We must be careful not to impose on biblical historical accounts the definitions and criteria of modern historians (Anderson, p. xxxiv).

12. D. Gunn, *The Story of King David,* JSOTSup 6 (Sheffield: 1978, repr. 1982); also his *The Fate of King Saul,* JSOTS 14 (Sheffield: 1980); J. P. Fokkelman, *Narrative Art and Poetry in the Book of Samuel,* vol. 1; *King David* (Assen, the Netherlands: 1981); L. M. Eslinger, *Kingship of God in Crisis: A Close Reading of 1 Samuel 1–12* (Sheffield: 1985).

13. Gunn, *Story of King David,* pp. 37-38.

14. Flanagan, "Samuel, Book of 1-2."

15. Cf. L. T. Dolphin, "Shiloh," *ISBE* 4 (1988): 477-478 for biblical and archaeological information.

16. Deut. 16:16 enjoins attendance at the central sanctuary three times a year: the feasts of Unleavened Bread, Weeks, and Booths. This law, however, like much Pentateuchal legislation, may represent an ideal not systematically carried out. Practical considerations may have limited the pilgrimages to one per year.

17. E.g., J. Wellhausen, *Prolegomena to the History of Ancient Israel,* trans. J. S. Smith and C. A. Menzies (1885; repr. Magnolia, Mass.: 1973), pp. 130, 135f.; R. H. Pfeiffer, *Religion in the Old Testament,* ed. C. C. Forman (New York: 1961), pp. 78f.

18. J. Bright suggests that such occasions also may have involved a recital of God's gracious deeds and a renewal of allegiance to him; *A History of Israel,* 3rd ed. (Philadelphia:

1981), p. 171. Deut. 31:9-13 provides for such ceremonies during the feast of Booths at least every seven years. Thus, Hannah's despair may have been deepened by memory of God's past blessings, which seem to have passed her by. Psalms of complaint frequently rehearse God's past redemptive acts so as to make the prayer for rescue more poignant (Pss. 22:4f.; 44:1-3).

19. Num. 6:1-21 describes these vows, including avoidance of contact with a corpse. Note also Samson in Judg. 13:4ff.; Amos 2:11-12.

20. Regarding those Nazirites called Rechabites (descendants of Jonadab ben Rechab; 2 Kgs. 10:15-17), Bright observes: "[abstinence from wine and refusal to live settled lives] was rather a symbolic renunciation of the agrarian life and all that it entailed. It moved from the feeling that God was to be found in the ancient, pure ways of the desert, and that Israel had departed from her destiny the moment she came into contact with the contaminating culture of Canaan"; *The Kingdom of God* (Nashville: 1953), pp. 55f.

21. Samuel probably means "El is his name," "name of El," or "name of God." Hannah's explanation (1:20) is a popular etymology. Perhaps she connected Samuel (*šᵉmû'ēl*) with the phrase "asked of God" (*šā'ûl mē'ēl*) because of the similar sound.

22. R. Patai (*Sex and Family in the Bible and the Middle East* [Garden City: 1959], pp. 192-195) cites other biblical passages to show that sucklings or children just weaned could walk, talk, and comprehend (see Isa. 11:8; 28:9; Ps. 8:2). 2 Macc. 7:27 mentions a three-year suckling period. This custom still prevails in parts of Jordan, where a case is known of a child being nursed until his tenth year.

23. Luke's description of the growth of the boy Jesus (2:25) reflects 1 Sam. 2:26, just as his version of the Magnificat, Mary's song of triumph (1:46-55), closely resembles Hannah's song.

24. The precise relationship between Samuel and the tribe of Levi is hard to determine. 1:1 suggests that Elkanah, Samuel's father, is an Ephraimite, while 1 Chr. 6:28 lists Samuel among the descendants of Levi. Samuel's family may have been Levites dwelling in Ephraim, or Samuel may have been an adopted member of the tribe because of his priestly activities.

25. H. H. Rowley has stressed the importance of this sense of vocation: ". . . It is clearly held that what made him a genuine prophet was not parental dedication, but the fact that when he was still a child the word of God came to him by divine initiative"; *The Servant of the Lord and Other Essays on the Old Testament,* 2nd ed. (Oxford: 1965), pp. 112ff.

26. T. Dothan, "Philistines," *ABD* 5:333: "It is very likely that these new settlers [Philistines] brought with them a knowledge of iron-working which acted as a stimulus to local industry."

27. Some have interpreted Dagon as a fish god (Heb. *dāg* "fish"), but he was more likely a grain god (Heb. *dāgān* "grain"). His name is found also in Ugaritic, Phoenician, and Babylonian texts. Whichever explanation is correct, the Philistines clearly adopted a Semitic name for their chief god. Philistine proper names were often of Semitic derivation. This and other linguistic data would indicate a cultural interchange between the Philistines and the Canaanites. See Gordon, *The World of the Old Testament* (Garden City: 1958), pp. 121f.

28. See A. F. Campbell, *The Ark Narrative,* SBLDS 16 (Missoula: 1975). See the balanced discussion of the narrative and its present role in the text in R. Klein, *1 Samuel,* pp. 38-40.

29. See I. Finkelstein, "Seilan, Khirbet," *ABD* 5:1069-1072.

30. No evidence exists that Samuel had anything to do with the ark at Kiriath-jearim.

His activity as Judge took him throughout the land (1 Sam. 7:15f.), but Ramah, where he built an altar, seems to have been the center of his religious activity.

31. The external Philistine threat may have been augmented with internal struggles that encouraged the establishment of the monarchy. Affluent families may have joined the call for a king in order to protect and enhance their economic power in a time when others were lobbying for traditional egalitarian values. See N. K. Gottwald, *The Hebrew Bible: A Socio-Literary Introduction* (Philadelphia: 1985), p. 319. Also W. Brueggemann, *ABD* 5:969.

32. Typical of this approach is the analysis of A. R. S. Kennedy, who holds that the source favorable to the monarchy, which he labels M, is the older source and included most of 1 Sam. 13–2 Sam. 6. The source which opposes the monarchy he identifies as Deuteronomic (D) and associates with the framework of Judges, in that it depicts Samuel as Judge of all Israel, *Samuel*, rev. ed., Century Bible (New York: 1905). Kennedy's view probably is more widely received now than when first formulated. See Snaith, *OTMS*, p. 101; G. W. Anderson, *A Critical Introduction to the Old Testament*, 2nd ed. (Naperville: 1960), pp. 74ff.

33. W. Brueggemann, *ABD* 5:969. See also J. Bright, *History*, p. 188.

34. C. R. North, *The Old Testament Interpretation of History* (London: 1946), p. 98, argues that theocracy and monarchy are viewed in the text as complementary:

> It is going beyond the evidence to argue that the author of 1 Samuel 7:2–8:22, 10:17–24:12, was inveterately hostile to the monarchy as such. . . . Theocracy was his ideal; but even so Yahweh would need a vicegerent, either a judge or a king, through whom He could act.

35. Isa. 14:4ff. and Ezek. 28:1ff. accurately reflect the attitude of true Israelites toward the sacral kingship of their neighbors. See further H. Cazelles, "The History of Israel in the Pre-Exilic Period," in G. W. Anderson, ed., *Tradition and Interpretation*, pp. 293-295.

36. *Nāgîd* (lit. "one put first or foremost"; "ruler" or "prince" in the NRSV) is the term used in the accounts of the selection of the leader (9:16; 10:1; 13:14; 2 Sam. 5:2; 6:21; 7:8). It is variously translated, "prince," "king-elect," or "chief." Its use in those stories may be to distinguish the human leader from Yahweh the king. See R. Klein, *1 Samuel*, pp. 88-90; J. W. Flanagan, *ABD* 5:962, for discussion of the nuances of *na-gîd*.

37. Yet even the successive failure of the kings prepared the way for hope in "David's greater son," who fulfilled Israel's messianic longings. See Chapter 51.

38. At least four models of leadership have been proposed to describe Saul's role: (1) permanent judge; (2) self-appointed protector; (3) chieftain; (4) state-builder. See D. Edelman, "Saul," *ABD* 5:991-992. Saul probably combined facets of (3) and (4).

39. As by Weiser, *The Old Testament*, p. 163.

40. D. Edelman, *ABD* 5:997 (map).

41. This is not the only instance of Saul's ecstatic activity. An even more startling description of ecstatic behavior is found in 1 Sam. 19:24: "And he too stripped off his clothes, and he too fell into a frenzy before Samuel. He lay naked all that day and all that night."

42. See H. H. Rowley, *The Servant of the Lord*, pp. 99ff., for a discussion of 9:9. The verse is an explanatory gloss on the term "seer," inserted into the narrative by an editor whose readers apparently were more familiar with the office of prophet. D. L. Petersen, *The Roles of Israel's Prophets* (Sheffield: 1981), pp. 38-40, sketches the "role label *rô'eh*" with emphasis on the prediction of information in exchange for payment from the enquirer.

43. See Bright, *History*, pp. 188-191, for an excellent summation of Saul's military feats and the structure of his government.

44. For summaries and analyses of this account see W. Brueggemann, *ABD* 5:970;

D. M. Howard, Jr., "David," *ABD* 2:41-44; R. P. Gordon, *1 and 2 Samuel,* JSOT Old Testament Guides (Sheffield: 1984), pp. 60-70.

45. Many have connected this name with *dawidum,* apparently "leader" or "chieftain" in the Akkadian letters found at Mari. Recent interpretation, however, understands the word in the Mari texts to mean "defeat" and renders the connection with David most improbable. See H. Tadmor, "Historical Implications of the Current Rendering of Akkadian *daku,*" *JNES* 17 (1958): 129-141.

46. The Goliath story is found in at least three separate accounts. While 1 Sam. 17 (see also 19:5; 21:9; 22:10, 13) credits the slaying to David, 2 Sam. 21:19 mentions an Elhanan as conqueror of Goliath. 1 Chr. 20:5 states that it was Lahmi, brother of Goliath, whom Elhanan slew. One thing is certain: the text of 1-2 Samuel contains numerous difficulties and frequently must be amended, especially with the aid of the LXX. E. J. Young has suggested two possible reconstructions in this case, both naming Elhanan as slayer of Goliath's brother; *An Introduction to the Old Testament,* rev. ed. (Grand Rapids: 1958), p. 182. Another possibility is to view Elhanan as another name for David. Ancient kings frequently assumed throne names, as do modern monarchs and popes. Elhanan would be the given name and David the regnal or throne name. See A. M. Honeyman, "The Evidence for Regnal Names among the Hebrews," *JBL* 67 (1948): 23-25; J. N. Schofield, "Some Archaeological Sites and the Old Testament," *Expository Times* 66 (1954-55): 250-252. The troublesome name of Elhanan's father, Jaare-oregim (2 Sam. 21:19), may actually be a garbled version of "Jesse"; *'ōreḡîm* obviously has been miscopied from the end of the verse, where it is translated "weavers."

47. Though severed heads or hands were customary evidences of the number of battle victims, foreskins were requested because the Philistines did not practice circumcision; C. H. Gordon, *The World of the Old Testament,* p. 161 note 20. Similarly, Egyptians often cut off the male genitals of the uncircumcised Libyans they had slain.

48. We know almost nothing about how the Urim and Thummin worked. They may have been flat disks with "yes" and "no" sides. When both agreed the answer was clear. When they disagreed, further guidance was sought. For alternative explanations involving some special use of light, perhaps reflected from the facets of a gem, see C. Van Dam, "Urim and Thummin," *ISBE* 4 (1988): 957-959.

49. For fuller discussion of the Qinah (dirge) form and its use of dramatic contrast, particularly with the exclamation "how!" (see vv. 19, 25), see Chapter 39 on Lamentations. (It might be noted that the "Qinah meter" (3 + 2), proffered by some scholars, is not found as a rule in Lamentations. Cf. W. S. LaSor, "An Approach to Hebrew Poetry through the Masoretic Accents," *Essays on the Occasion of the Seventieth Anniversary of the Dropsie University,* ed. A. I. Katsh and L. Nemoy [Philadelphia: 1979], pp. 327-353, esp. p. 332.)

50. Eshbaal ("Man of Baal" or, more probably, "Baal exists") is used in 1 Chr. 8:33; 9:39. Scribal resentment toward Baal has in 2 Samuel resulted in the change of *ba'al* to *bōšeṯ* "shame."

51. See J. D. Levenson and B. Halpern, "The Political Import of David's Marriages," *JBL* 99 (1981): 507-518.

52. Only the context can determine whether the entire people or the northern tribes are meant by the term "Israel."

53. The identity of Salem and Jerusalem seems to be confirmed by Ps. 76:2.

54. Cf. W. S. LaSor, "Jerusalem," *ISBE* 2 (1982): 1001-1007.

55. *Ibid.,* p. 1006.

56. W. Brueggemann, *First and Second Samuel,* Interpretation (Louisville: 1990), p. 119.

CHAPTER 13 — ISRAEL'S GOLDEN AGE: DAVID AND SOLOMON

1. The accounts of wars with the Philistines in 21:15-22 may be summaries of battles early in David's reign rather than at the end, as their place in the narrative might be taken to indicate.

2. For a detailed discussion of its uniqueness and possible relationships with the Abrahamic covenant of Gen. 15, see R. E. Clements, *Abraham and David* (Naperville: 1967), pp. 47-60.

3. The genealogies, however (1 Chr. 6:4-8; 24:1-3), are not without problems. Many attempts have been made to disassociate the line of Zadok from that of Aaron. Though the precise connection may not be clear (the genealogies may skip generations or include names adopted but not born into the line), the reasons usually given for disassociating the two lines are not compelling.

4. C. H. Gordon observes: "Foreign mercenaries have no [family or local loyalties] and tend to be well disciplined, loyal to their commander and interested in his personal welfare, for on him depends their professional welfare"; *The World of the Old Testament* (Garden City: 1958), p. 170.

5. J. Bright (*A History of Israel,* 3rd ed. [Philadelphia: 1981], pp. 205f.) points out that David's administration is patterned, in part at least, on Egyptian models.

6. See W. Brueggemann's summary (*First and Second Samuel* [Louisville: 1990], p. 245) adapted from J. W. Flanagan's "Social Transformation and Ritual in 2 Samuel 6," in Carol Meyers and M. O'Connor, eds., *The Word of the Lord Shall Go Forth* (Winona Lake: 1983), pp. 361-372.

7. A. Weiser, *Introduction to the Old Testament* (New York: 1961), p. 165. For a thorough study of the literary style and intent, see R. N. Whybray, *The Succession Narrative,* SBT (Naperville: 1968). A survey of recent discussions on this section is found in J. R. Porter, "Old Testament Historiography," pp. 151f. in G. W. Anderson, ed., *Tradition and Interpretation* (Oxford: 1979). The label "Succession Narrative" has less scholarly support than it had when Whybray wrote. Debate on where it begins (ch. 2, 6, or 9?) and ends (ch. 20 or 1 Kgs. 2?) is still in process. The "succession" theme is thought to be more marked than the point and counterpoint of David's weakness and Yahweh's persistent commitment to the promises of ch. 7.

8. His name, like Ishbosheth's, stems from scribes who altered its original form, Meribbaal (1 Chr. 8:34; 9:40), to show their contempt for the Canaanite fertility god Baal. The Israelites referred sometimes to their covenant Lord as Baal ("master"). Hosea, however, rejected this title for Yahweh because of its pagan connotations (Hos. 2:16f.).

9. Jewish tradition appropriately connects the prayer for forgiveness in Ps. 51 and the thanksgiving for forgiveness in Ps. 32 with this episode.

10. One of Absalom's activities was to associate publicly with David's concubines (16:20-22), a political (as well as sexual) move that would help Absalom tighten his grip on the crown.

11. Hushai and Ahithophel seem to be early examples of the wise men or counselors who played major roles in determining policy in Israel (see Jer. 18:18). Later these wise ones were instrumental in shaping the biblical wisdom literature. Hushai's simile (2 Sam. 17:8) is a familiar wisdom device. For background on these sages, see W. McKane, *Prophets and Wise Men,* SBT 44 (Naperville: 1965), pp. 13-62.

12. On the importance of name-lists, whether of family or administrators, for the structure of 1-2 Samuel, see J. W. Flanagan, *ABD* 5:962. He calls them "patronage networks" and includes 1 Sam. 14:49-51; 2 Sam. 2:2-3; 3:2-5; 5:13-16; 8:15-18; 20:23-26.

13. This pattern has been noted by many commentators, e.g., J. Baldwin, *1 and 2 Samuel*, TOTC, pp. 282-283; A. A. Anderson, *2 Samuel*, WBC (Dallas: 1989), p. 248.

14. See W. Brueggemann's comments on the frame of the narrative in *ABD* 5:967-968.

15. Brueggemann, p. 968. J. Rosenberg, in "1 and 2 Samuel," *LGB*, points with admiration to the many themes and aspects of life that are interwoven in 1-2 Samuel: "Both structurally and artistically, Samuel is the centerpiece of the Hebrew Bible's continuous historical account" (p. 143).

16. The influential women in David's court (e.g., Michal and Bathsheba) seem to have set the pattern for other queen mothers of Judah. Note that the author of Kings records without fail the name of each king's mother (e.g., 15:2-10).

17. The chief archaeologist of the dig at Tel Dan, A. Biran, has tentatively dated the inscription in the first half of the ninth century B.C. It may stem from King Baasha's war with Ben Hadad I *ca.* 885 B.C. (1 Kgs. 15:16-22). For text and background of its discovery, see *BARev* 20/2 (March/April 1994): 26-39.

18. Jehoiachin's release from prison (*ca.* 560) described in 2 Kgs. 25:27-30 sets the earliest possible date for completion of the book. However, most of it was probably compiled and edited two or three decades earlier. See Chapter 9, "The Former Prophets."

19. This work, like the two named in the next clause, as well as several others mentioned in the Old Testament, has not been found, and is probably not extant.

20. Materials from official records of the northern kingdom probably were brought south by refugees after the fall of Samaria in 721. See further B. S. Childs, *Introduction to the Old Testament as Scripture* (Philadelphia: 1979), pp. 287-289. For a detailed list of the source materials of the compiler together with some suggestions of later annotation and comments, see S. DeVries, *1 Kings*, WBC 12 (1985), pp. xlix-lii. On the literary forms employed, see B. O. Long, *1 Kings*, FOTL 9 (Grand Rapids: 1984).

21. J. A. Montgomery and H. S. Gehman, *The Book of Kings*, ICC (Edinburgh: 1951), pp. 44f. For a cluster of arguments strongly supportive of the historical character of the work, see D. J. Wiseman, *1 and 2 Kings*, TOTC (Leicester and Downers Grove: 1993).

22. The request of administrative wisdom parallels accounts in Egyptian royal literature: kings are described as especially equipped to make innovations in the life and culture of their people. See T. Ishida, "Solomon," *ABD* 6:111.

23. The term "temple" in English is also used of the Temple Mount ("Mountain of the House [of the Lord]"). Visitors sometimes mistakenly think the remains of the walls (on the east, south, and west) are remains of the temple. Cf. S. Westerholm, "Temple," *ISBE* 4 (1988): 739-776.

24. For a thorough discussion of the temple, including drawings and diagrams, see Carol Meyers, "Temple, Jerusalem," *ABD* 6:330-369. See also J. Gutmann, ed., *The Temple of Solomon* (Tallahassee: 1976).

25. Cf. A. F. Rainey, "Gezer," *ISBE* 2 (1982): 458-460.

26. Cf. M. Liverani, "Phoenicia; Phoenicians," *ISBE* 3 (1986): 853-862.

27. 40,000 is apparently a scribal error; cf. 2 Chr. 9:25.

28. For a survey of archaeological findings from Solomon's era (Iron Age IIA), see A. Mazar, *Archaeology of the Land of the Bible* (New York: 1990), pp. 375-402. The Megiddo stables, previously attributed to him, more recently have been credited to Ahab; Y. Yadin, "New Light on Solomon's Megiddo," *BA* 23 (1960): 62-68. Whether the large buildings were actually stables is now open to question. See J. B. Pritchard, "The Megiddo Stables: A Reassessment," pp. 268-276 in J. A. Sanders, ed., *Near Eastern Archaeology in the Twentieth Century;* Yadin, "The Megiddo Stables," pp. 249-252 in F. M. Cross, Jr., W. E. Lemke,

and P. D. Miller, Jr., eds., *Magnalia Dei: The Mighty Acts of God,* Festschrift G. E. Wright (Garden City: 1976).

29. See D. A. Hubbard, "Queen of Sheba," *ISBE* 4 (1988): 8-11.

30. For an assessment of the way in which Solomon's power contributed to the deterioration of Israel's ideals, see W. Brueggemann, *The Prophetic Imagination* (Philadelphia: 1978), pp. 28-43. An analysis of the role of Israel's kings in the administration of justice is found in K. W. Whitelam, *The Just King: Monarchical Judicial Authority in Ancient Israel,* JSOTSup 12 (Sheffield: 1979).

31. S. W. Holloway, "Kings, Book of 1-2." *ABD* 4:77.

CHAPTER 14 — DIVIDED MONARCHY

1. The "one tribe" left of the house of David was Benjamin (11:32, 36). Ahijah did not mention Judah because he assumed that they would remain loyal to their own king. Actually, Benjamin, the border area between north and south, was a bone of contention throughout the Divided Monarchy. The LXX account of Jeroboam's career differs slightly from that of the Hebrew text.

2. According to Hayes and Miller, two different but related groups made up the northern participants: representatives of old, large cities (e.g., Shechem, Megiddo, and Tirzah), and members of the Ephraim/Israel tribal group; cf. J. H. Hayes and J. M. Miller, *A History of Ancient Israel and Judah* (Philadelphia: 1986), pp. 230-231.

3. See the illuminating literary analysis by R. L. Cohn, "Literary Technique in the Jeroboam Narrative," *ZAW* 97 (1985): 23-35. According to Cohn, the narrative has a chiastic structure centered around what he calls the "Man of God interlude" (13:1-32), the turning point which heads Jeroboam toward disaster.

4. G. H. Jones, *1 and 2 Kings* (Grand Rapids: 1984), vol. 1, p. 258. The calves were analogous to the ark of the covenant, which the Bible describes as Yahweh's throne or footstool (cf. Ps. 132:6-8).

5. Many scholars regard the mention of Josiah (13:2) as "prophecy after the event," but other explanations merit consideration. It may be a rare biblical example of specific prediction, or the name may be a symbolic name ("he whom Yahweh supports") rather than a reference to Josiah; see C. F. Keil and F. Delitzsch, *Commentary on the Old Testament,* repr. 10 vols. (Grand Rapids: 1973). Again, the editors may have added the name later to show that Josiah's reforms (2 Kgs. 23) fulfilled the prophecy.

6. The Asherim (1 Kgs. 14:15) took their name from the Canaanite goddess Asherah, consort of El or Baal. Customarily they were sacred trees or posts planted or erected at sacred shrines. Evidently worship of the golden calves opened the door for other acts of idolatry. For the provocative thesis that official Israelite religion originally regarded Asherah as a consort of Yahweh, not Baal, see S. M. Olyan, *Asherah and the Cult of Yahweh in Israel* (Atlanta: 1988); cf. the more traditional view of K. G. Jung, "Asherah," *ISBE* 1 (1979): 317f.

7. Sheshonk had come to power by toppling Egypt's weak Twenty-first Dynasty; cf. K. A. Kitchen, "Shishak," *ISBE* 4 (1988): 489. Earlier he had shown disdain for Judah by harboring the fugitive Jeroboam (11:40).

8. The text seems to say that Abijam and Asa have the same mother, Maacah (15:2, 10). They may indeed have been brothers, so "son" (v. 8) would be a scribal error. More likely, the queen mother was such a powerful figure that she continued to wield influence under her grandson Asa and overshadowed his mother. Biblical terms of relationship often

describe wider relationships than their literal meanings suggest (cf. Matt. 1:1). In this case, Heb. "son" could also mean "grandson."

9. Though similar, the introductory formula for northern kings omits the mother's name (cf. vv. 33f.). More important, it always evaluates the king negatively, normally with the verdict, "He did what was evil in the sight of the Lord, and walked in the way of Jeroboam and in his sin which he made Israel to sin." The concluding regnal formula is also stereotyped, e.g., v. 31: "Now the rest of the acts of Nadab, and all that he did, are they not written in the Book of the Chronicles of the Kings of Israel?" (This is not the biblical book but the official court records from which the editors of Kings drew.)

10. 2 Kgs. 18–20; 22–23:30; R. H. Lowery, *The Reforming Kings. Cults and Society in First Temple Judah* (Sheffield: 1991), pp. 88-99.

11. The stories in Kings were written down after the northern kingdom fell and, thus, reflect the perspective of historical hindsight. Actually, Jeroboam himself may have been a devout worshipper of Yahweh, but his zeal for his religious innovations proved ultimately destructive to Israel's historic faith.

12. K. M. Kenyon, *Archaeology in the Holy Land* (New York: 1960), p. 262.

13. See Kenyon, *ibid.*, pp. 260-269, and esp. A. Parrot, *Samaria, the Capital of the Kingdom of Israel* (London: 1958), for the archaeological findings.

14. Cf. M. Liverani, "Tyre," *ISBE* 4 (1988): 933-935.

15. Cf. J. H. Stek, "Elijah," *ISBE* 2 (1982): 64-68.

16. See G. Savran in *LGB*, pp. 146-163, and S. W. Holloway in *ABD* 4:76-77.

17. Jezebel's pivotal role in Ahab's policies is summarized: ". . . Ahab, who sold himself to do what is evil in the sight of the Lord, urged on by his wife Jezebel" (1 Kgs. 21:25). Recent studies have suggested that Jezebel may have been a high priestess of Baal in Tyre as well as a seasoned participant in its politics. See Gale A. Yee, *ABD* 3:848-849.

18. A. Rofé, *The Prophetical Stories: The Narratives about the Prophets in the Hebrew Bible, Their Literary Types and History* (Jerusalem: 1988), p. 196.

19. Ben-hadad of Syria dedicated a monument "for his Lord Melqart," showing that he was worshipped beyond Israel and Tyre. Ahab and Ben-hadad may have had more in common than their fear of Assyria. For text and comments on the Melqart stele, see M. Black, *DOTT*, pp. 239-241. For the identification of Baal and Melqart, see R. de Vaux, *The Bible and the Ancient Near East* (Garden City: 1971), pp. 238-251.

20. The phrase is that of Rofé, *Prophetical Stories*, p. 194. See the excellent literary analysis in R. L. Cohn, "The Literary Logic of 1 Kings 17–19," *JBL* 101 (1983): 333-350; D. D. Herr, "Variations of a Pattern: 1 Kings 19," *JBL* 104 (1985): 292-294; and J. A. Todd, "The Pre-Deuteronomistic Elijah Cycle," pp. 11-27 in R. B. Coote, *Elijah and Elisha in Socioliterary Perspective*, Semeia Studies (Atlanta: 1992).

21. J. R. Battenfield, "YHWH's Refutation of the Baal Myth through the Actions of Elijah and Elisha," in A. Gileadi, ed., *Israel's Apostasy and Restoration: Essays in Honor of Roland K. Harrison* (Grand Rapids: 1988), pp. 19-37.

22. Hauser argues that the central motif of 1 Kgs. 17–19 is Yahweh's battle with death; cf. A. J. Hauser, "Yahweh versus Death — The Real Struggle in 1 Kings 17–19," pp. 9-89 in A. J. Hauser and R. Gregory, *From Carmel to Horeb: Elijah in Crisis* (Sheffield: 1990).

23. Some scholars consider the mention of 400 prophets of Asherah to be a later gloss since the text never refers to them again (e.g., vv. 22, 25, 40; so MT editor; de Vaux, *The Bible and the Ancient Near East*, p. 239 note 6). But Jones (*1 and 2 Kings*, 2:317) makes a good case for the text's originality.

24. R. D. Nelson (*First and Second Kings* [Louisville: 1987], p. 117) observes how the repetition of a Hebrew verbal root underscores this point: "To limp along undecided [Heb.

psḥ qal; v. 21] is in effect to choose to dance [Heb. *psḥ piel*] with Baal's prophets (v. 26)." To use fire as evidence of deity put Baal on the spot since Ugaritic reliefs portray Baal as a storm-god whose hands hold a lightning bolt (so Battenfield, "YHWH's Refutation," pp. 24-25).

25. So NRSV; cf. NIV "a gentle whisper." Perhaps James had in mind this gloomy episode: "Elijah was a man of like nature with ourselves . . ." (5:17). For a fine literary analysis, see Hauser, *From Carmel to Horeb*, pp. 60-82.

26. For the literary parallels, see B. O. Long, *1 Kings* (Grand Rapids: 1984), pp. 201-202. We suggest that the point of the "sound of sheer silence" may be that Yahweh is overwhelmingly superior to Baal because he can also make his presence known without dramatic visual display (similarly, Todd, "Pre-Deuteronomistic Elijah Cycle," p. 23; contrast Hauser, *From Carmel to Horeb*, p. 70).

27. Similarly, Hauser, *From Carmel to Horeb*, pp. 73-74.

28. According to v. 42, Ahab had violated the "ban" (Heb. *ḥerem*) — the divinely sanctioned annihilation of an enemy (cf. Josh. 6–7; 1 Sam. 15).

29. See the fine literary study by D. Robertson, "Michaiah ben Imlah: A Literary View," pp. 139-146 in *The Biblical Mosaic*, ed. R. M. Polzin and E. Rothman (Philadelphia: 1982).

30. For the gruesome details of Jezebel's death, see 2 Kgs. 9:30-37.

31. C. H. Gordon (*The World of the Old Testament* [Garden City: 1958], p. 200) suggests that the Hebrew idiom indicates a fraction. If so, the request would be for two-thirds of Elijah's spirit.

32. Gordon notes that even recently in Arab Palestine some villages had reputations for generous hospitality, while others were known for disrespectful and even harmful treatment of strangers. Perhaps the taunting of Elisha was the latest of a number of incidents which revealed that the lads of Bethel were really lawless young hoodlums. Such disregard for ancient ideals of hospitality and respect for age is unsurprising in a society where the elders also were casual toward the standards of the past.

33. Elisha may have been more ecstatic in his prophetic activity and, therefore, more at home with the prophetic guilds than Elijah (see 3:15; see also 1 Sam. 10:5-12).

34. See the fine literary treatment of this text by R. D. Moore, *God Saves: Lessons from the Elisha Stories* (Sheffield: 1990), pp. 71-84. According to Moore (pp. 83, 84), its lesson is that "Yahweh is showing Israel a radically different way of salvation," one that "consists in servanthood 'before the Lord.' "

35. The strong ties between Israel and Judah, forged by Omri, remained binding for several generations. Intermarriage between the ruling houses was a contributing factor (e.g., Jehoshaphat's son, Jehoram of Judah, was married to a daughter of Ahab; 8:18).

36. Mesha boasts of this and subsequent victories in the Moabite stone (cf. *ANET*, pp. 320-321). He dated his revolt against Israel at the midpoint of the reign of Omri's son. While no record of Moabite revolt against Ahab survives, the slackening of Israel's hold upon Moab may have begun during his reign and been completed during that of Jehoram, Ahab's son. Another means of correlating the inscription with the biblical account is to interpret "son" as "grandson," i.e., Jehoram.

37. Cf. Moore, *God Saves*, p. 94 (his full literary treatment, pp. 84-94, is worthy of note).

38. Moore, *God Saves*, pp. 103-104 (cf. pp. 95-104).

39. Sensing the contradictory nature of Elisha's statement, Hebrew scribes changed "to him" *(lô)* in the first statement to "not" *(lô')* so both statements would agree in announcing that Ben-hadad would not recover but would die. The NRSV rendering, however, seems to represent the original idea.

40. An Assyrian inscription of Shalmaneser IV confirms the biblical account: "Adadidri [Ben-hadad] forsook his land [i.e., died an unnatural death]. Hazael, son of a nobody, seized the throne . . ." (cf. *ANET*, p. 280). See Unger, *Israel and the Arameans of Damascus*, p. 75; M. Burrows, *What Mean These Stones?* (Baltimore: 1941), p. 281.

41. Jehoram of Israel and his relative, Ahaziah (*ca.* 841) of Judah, took advantage of the momentary political chaos in Damascus to recapture Ramoth-gilead from the Syrians (vv. 25-29). Although Jehoram was wounded and withdrew from the front to recover, the venture succeeded.

42. The loss of Edom probably carried with it the loss of access to the copper mines and harbor facilities at Ezion-geber on the Gulf of Aqabah.

43. "House of Omri" became standard Assyrian nomenclature for Samaria for a century or more after Omri's death, eloquent testimony to the prestige he enjoyed and brought to his nation. For a picture and relevant excerpts of the Black Obelisk, see Hayes and Miller, *A History of Ancient Israel and Judah*, pp. 261, 287-288.

44. Israel's fortunes took a slight turn for the better under Jehoahaz's son Jehoash, who defeated Hazael's son Ben-hadad II three times, as Elisha had prophesied just before his death (vv. 14-25). According to T. E. Mullen, "The Royal Dynastic Grant to Jehu and the Structure of the Books of Kings," *JBL* 107 (1988): 193-206, the editors of Kings explain the survival of Jehu's dynasty through four generations in terms of a royal dynastic grant to Jehu by Yahweh (2 Kgs. 10:28-31) similar to that given David (2 Sam. 7:8-16).

45. See Jotham's fable, which also involves a conversation among plants (Judg. 9:7-15). The interchange between Ahab and Ben-hadad also illustrates the use of witty or proverbial expressions between enemy rulers: "Ben-hadad . . . said, 'The gods do so to me, and more also, if the dust of Samaria will provide a handful for each of the people who follow me.' The king of Israel answered . . . 'One who puts on armor should not brag like one who takes it off' " (1 Kgs. 20:10f.).

46. 2 Chr. 25:5-13 supplies the motive for the conflict. The Judean king had hired Israelite mercenaries to aid in his conquest of Edom, but in obedience to a prophet he sent them north without allowing them to take part in his southern campaign. The embittered mercenaries raided Judean cities, thus provoking Amaziah to challenge Israel.

47. The clause "And . . . slept with his fathers" (e.g., 15:22) seems to indicate a natural death. The only apparent exception in Kings is Ahab, who died in battle (1 Kgs. 22:34-37, 40).

48. For more on the Assyrian king, cf. W. S. LaSor, "Tiglath-pileser," *ISBE* 4 (1988): 849ff. See Chapter 16, below, for a discussion of Pekah's dates and the problems raised by them.

49. Counting coregencies at both ends, Uzziah's reign (15:1-7) stretched some fifty-two years (*ca.* 790-739), although leprosy curtailed his public activities much of this time. Only Manasseh (*ca.* 695-642) ruled longer.

50. This alliance and the war it waged often is named for the two countries, Syro-Ephraimite. Ephraim was the name of the northern kingdom's most powerful tribe and was used to describe the kingdom and especially the hill-country around Samaria.

51. Recent explorations in the Gulf of Elat seeking to identify with accuracy have centered on an island called *Jezîrat Far'ôn*, "Island of Pharaoh," which possesses the only natural harbor in the area. See M. Lubetski, "Ezion-geber," *ABD* 2:724-725.

52. At this juncture, with Ahaz harassed from north and south, Isaiah brought hope and comfort in his famous Immanuel prophecy (Isa. 7:1-17). The Chronicler indicates that the Edomites and the Philistines joined in by pressuring Judah's southern and western frontiers (2 Chr. 28:18).

53. Cf. W. S. LaSor, "Shalmaneser," *ISBE* 4 (1988): 444-447, esp. 446f.; and "Sargon," *ISBE* 4 (1988): 338ff.

CHAPTER 15 — JUDAH ALONE

1. Cf. W. S. LaSor, "Sennacherib," *ISBE* 4 (1988): 394-397.

2. Today the spring is known as the Virgin's Fountain. In 1880 a Hebrew inscription was discovered that describes the tunnel's completion, when crews digging from each end met in the middle. For the text of the Siloam inscription, see N. H. Snaith, *DOTT*, pp. 209-211. Both 2 Chr. 32:30 and Ecclus. 48:17 also mention Hezekiah's water project. See W. S. LaSor, "Jerusalem," *ISBE* 2 (1982): 1011.

3. Sennacherib's invasion enjoys more documentation than any in Israel's history. Several references from Sennacherib himself supplement data from the Siloam inscription. The Taylor prism gives the fullest account, detailing the tribute that Hezekiah paid: thirty talents of gold, three hundred talents of silver, plus other valuable objects and numerous slaves (18:14-16). The Bull inscription and the Nineveh Slab inscription both contain summary references to Hezekiah's submission. For full translations, see D. J. Wiseman, in *DOTT*, pp. 64-69.

4. Wiseman in *DOTT*, p. 67.

5. Herodotus ii.141 reports that an invasion of field mice devoured the quivers, bows, and shield straps so the Assyrians were unable to fight effectively or defend themselves. For more than a century, scholars have debated whether 2 Kgs. 18–19 and Isa. 36–37 telescope two Assyrian invasions under Sennacherib — one in 701, the other some years later. Recent studies tend to support the two-invasion theory, but no firm consensus has emerged. For a discussion of the two-invasion theory, cf. J. Bright, *A History of Israel*, 3rd ed. (Philadelphia: 1981), pp. 298-309; LaSor, "Sennacherib," p. 396; W. H. Shea, "Sennacherib's Second Palestinian Campaign," *JBL* 104 (1985): 401-418.

6. *ANEP*, pp. 371-374.

7. The Tartan (*tartannu* "second") was apparently the highest military officer of Assyria; the Rabsaris (lit. "chief of the eunuchs"), a high administrative official in the palace bureaucracy; and the Rabshakeh, probably not the chief cupbearer as once thought, but chief of the nobles (lit. "high ones" from *šaqu* "to be high"). As spokesman for the emissary, the Rabshakeh seems to be the ranking diplomatic official. That such senior officials were sent shows how seriously Sennacherib viewed the mission. For a thoughtful meditation on Rabshakeh, see J. Ellul, *The Politics of God and the Politics of Man*, trans. G. W. Bromiley (Grand Rapids: 1972), pp. 143-161.

8. See the illuminating literary study by D. N. Fewell, "Sennacherib's Defeat: Words at War in 2 Kings 18:13–19:37," *JSOT* 34 (1986): 79-90.

9. Hezekiah's recovery from seemingly terminal illness also evidenced God's miraculous care. The sign given by Isaiah — the shadow that moved back ten steps on the sundial — is as puzzling astronomically as Joshua's sun that stood still. No obvious correlation with an eclipse seems possible given the date of the healing — at least fifteen years before Hezekiah's death in 687 and probably before Merodach-baladan's expulsion from Babylon in 703. Franz Delitzsch's theory of a miracle in the form of an optical illusion may be as good as any; C. F. Keil and F. Delitzsch, *Commentary on the Old Testament*, repr. 10 vols. (Grand Rapids: 1973), at 2 Kgs. 20:11.

10. Prisms of Esarhaddon and Ashurbanipal mention Manasseh as paying tribute to Assyria; *ANET*, pp. 291, 294.

11. Kings is silent about Manasseh's captivity in Babylon and his subsequent repentance (2 Chr. 33:10-17). Whatever reformation may have resulted was both superficial and short-lived. The major purpose of Kings was to show that divine judgment on Manasseh's wicked rule was inevitable. Any mention of modest reform would have been a digression. See F. F. Bruce, *Israel and the Nations* (Grand Rapids: 1969), p. 75, for the circumstances (probably some conspiracy with Egypt against Assyria) leading to Manasseh's captivity.

12. See Bright, *History*, p. 316. T. R. Hobb, *2 Kings*, WBC 13 (Waco: 1985), pp. 142-143 argues that "people of the land" describes the aroused populace in general and not any particular stratum of society.

13. Since the historical and political events from Josiah to the fall of Judah under Zedekiah are essential to understanding Jeremiah, they will be treated more thoroughly there (Ch. 24).

14. Cf. the recent treatment by R. H. Lowery, *The Reforming Kings. Cults and Society in First Temple Judah* (Sheffield: 1991), pp. 190-209.

15. Cf. W. S. LaSor, "Ashurbanipal," *ISBE* 1 (1979): 321f.; R. K. Harrison, "Nabopolassar," *ISBE* 3 (1986): 470. The role of the Scythians (a West Siberian people who settled in the Black Sea–Caspian area *ca.* 2000 and later invaded northern Persia and Urartu) is not well understood. Some scholars following Herodotus 1.104-106 (e.g., Bruce, *Israel and the Nations*, p. 77) believe that a Scythian invasion hastened Assyria's undoing. Others (Bright, *History*, p. 315) leave the question open. Cf. A. R. Millard, "Scythians," *ISBE* 4 (1988): 364ff.

16. Since Jerome (Commentary on Ezekiel, 1:1), scholars have identified this scroll with Deuteronomy, esp. chs. 12–26. For theories of the date of Deuteronomy see pp. 114-116.

17. See K. A. Kitchen, "Neco," *ISBE* 3 (1986): 510.

18. See A. R. Millard, "Medes, Media," *ISBE* 3 (1986): 297ff.

19. See K. A. D. Smelik, *Writings from Ancient Israel* (Louisville: 1991), pp. 116-131, for poignant evidence of the terror of this era from the Lachish ostraca (potsherds) found at Tell ed-Duweir, a fortified city that guarded Judah's southwestern borders against Philistine invasion.

20. See W. S. LaSor, "Evil-Merodach," *ISBE* 2 (1982): 211.

21. For other interpretations of this episode, see J. D. Levenson, "The Last Four Verses in Kings," *JBL* 103 (1984): 353-361 (despite Judah's disaster, David still has a living descendant); and C. T. Begg, "The Significance of Jehoiachin's Release: A New Proposal," *JSOT* 36 (1986): 49-56. (The people of Judah need not fear Babylon if they serve it.)

CHAPTER 16 — PROPHETS AND PROPHECY

1. For a helpful summary of recent studies, see W. McKane, "Prophecy and the Prophetic Literature," pp. 163-188 in G. W. Anderson, ed., *Tradition and Interpretation* (Oxford: 1979); D. L. Petersen, *The Role of Israel's Prophets*, JSOTS 17 (Sheffield: 1981); J. Blenkinsopp, *A History of Prophecy in Israel* (Philadelphia: 1983).

2. H. G. Liddell and R. Scott, *A Greek-English Lexicon*, ed. H. S. Jones, 9th ed. (New York: 1940) 2:1540a.

3. *TDNT* 6 (1968): 783f.

4. For the derivation see Akk. *nabû* "to call"; cf. Hammurabi i.17. For the morphology or word formation, see W. S. LaSor, *Handbook of Biblical Hebrew* (Grand Rapids: 1979), §§24.2441. See also W. F. Albright, *From the Stone Age to Christianity*, 2nd ed. (Garden City: 1957), pp. 231f.

5. It will become clear that this description does not imply that the prophet is *only* God's mouth, i.e. that the prophet is passive and acts somewhat like a robot or recording machine, giving forth God's message.

6. See H. H. Rowley, *The Servant of the Lord and Other Essays on the Old Testament*, 2nd ed. (Oxford: 1965), pp. 105-108. D. L. Petersen has sought to make a case for a regional difference in the two terms: "seer" being the typical title in Judah, and "prophet" in Israel (*The Role of Israel's Prophets*, p. 63).

7. T. H. Robinson, *Prophecy and the Prophets in Ancient Israel* (London: 1923), p. 50. An earlier expression of the "ecstatic" nature of prophecy was voiced by G. Hölscher, *Die Propheten* (Leipzig: 1914).

8. W. Robertson Smith, *The Old Testament in the Jewish Church*, 2nd ed. (London: 1908), quoted by H. H. Rowley, *The Servant of the Lord*, p. 100.

9. Note accounts of the call in Isa. 6:1-13; Jer. 1:4-10; Ezek. 1:1-3; Hos. 1:2-9; Amos 3:1-8; 7:12-15. The similarities in literary pattern show that there may have been a "call/commissioning report" as a recognized genre. At the same time the differences suggest that each account was adapted to the specifics and peculiarities of the circumstances.

10. See J. Lindblom, *Prophecy in Ancient Israel* (Philadelphia: 1962), pp. 182-197.

11. 2 Pet. 1:21 (NRSV mg.). However, manuscript evidence for "saints"/holy men or simply "men and women" seems about evenly divided.

12. For a survey of the beginnings and growth of prophecy, see J. Blenkinsopp, *A History of Prophecy in Israel*.

13. The various relationships between the prophets and the political and religious establishments of their day have been explored thoroughly by R. R. Wilson, *Prophecy and Society in Ancient Israel* (Philadelphia: 1980).

14. It is helpful to remember that the greatest of all prophets, Jesus Christ, did not write his prophecies; they were written down by others and preserved in the Gospels.

15. Cf. W. S. LaSor, "The Prophets during the Monarchy: Turning Points in Israel's Decline," in *Israel's Apostasy and Restoration*, Festschrift R. K. Harrison, ed. A. Gileadi (Grand Rapids: 1988), pp. 59-70.

CHAPTER 17 — HEBREW POETRY

1. Consider these powerful images from the prophet Hosea: "Ephraim is joined to idols" (4:17); "Ephraim is a cake not turned" (7:8); "Ephraim is like a dove, silly and without sense" (v. 11); "Ephraim was a trained heifer that loved to thresh" (10:11); "It was I who taught Ephraim to walk" (11:3); "Ephraim herds the wind" (12:1).

2. See the proposed emendation in *BHS* of Joel 1:4.

3. E.g., Amos 6:12 reads: "Do horses run upon rocks?/Does one plow with oxen?" Clearly, the second line should be as incredible as the first, hence it is sometimes emended to read: "Does one plow *there* with oxen?" or "Does one plow *the sea* with oxen?" For a proposed emendation of the Heb. text, cf. *BHS in loc.*

4. See the useful discussion of poetic language in W. W. Klein, C. L. Blomberg, and R. L. Hubbard, Jr., *Introduction to Biblical Interpretation* (Dallas: 1993), pp. 241-252.

5. The Jewish scholar Ibn Ezra (A.D. 1093-1168) anticipated the idea, but the foundational work on the subject is R. Lowth, *De sacra poesi Hebraeorum* (London: 1753). Among contemporary scholars, A. Berlin, *The Dynamics of Biblical Parallelism* (Bloomington: 1985), represents the approach which contemporary scholars favor.

6. A. Berlin, "Parallelism," *ABD* 5:155. See the rest of her fine article (pp. 155-162).

7. D. L. Petersen and K. H. Richards, *Interpreting Hebrew Poetry* (Minneapolis: 1992), p. 27, who also survey the recent lively discussion of parallelism (pp. 21-35).

8. A. Berlin, *Dynamics,* p. 99. For the recent emerging consensus concerning parallelism, see J. L. Kugel, *The Idea of Biblical Poetry* (New Haven: 1981); and R. Alter, *The Art of Biblical Poetry* (New York: 1985), pp. 10-26.

9. Berlin, *Dynamics,* pp. 29, 31-126; and her convenient summary, "Parallelism," pp. 158-160.

10. For other examples, see Klein, Blomberg, and Hubbard, *Biblical Interpretation,* pp. 230-236.

11. In Hebrew, the grammar of "deal with us" and "repay us" features a verb followed by a prepositional phrase.

12. The "/" sign means "parallels" or "is parallel to." Likewise *a''* is read "a double prime," and *a'''* is read "a triple prime." *Stich* means "poetic line," and poetic passages may have one line (monostich), two lines (distichs), three lines (tristichs), or even four lines (tetrastichs). Cf. W. S. LaSor, "Samples of Early Semitic Poetry," pp. 99-121 in G. Rendsburg et al., eds., *The Bible World,* Festschrift C. H. Gordon (New York: 1980).

13. To make the verse's basic structure obvious, this example and others to follow present an exact, literal translation. The hyphenated words render a single Hebrew word.

14. Actually, "father" and "mother" are both opposites (i.e., contrary genders) and synonyms (i.e., subtypes of parents). They are synonyms because they derive from the common word-pair "father and mother," i.e., "parents." Here the poet has split the word-pair, using "father" in one stich and "mother" in the other. See the helpful discussion of word-pairs in Berlin, "Parallelism," p. 157, and our discussion below.

15. E.g., the four lines of Isa. 33:22 end with the same sound *-nû/-ēnû,* while Isa. 22:5 strings together three similar sounds in a row *(mehûmâ, mebûsâ, mebûkâ).*

16. By contrast, a reader can "scan" Greek and Latin poetry, identifying the rhythm of short and long syllables (we SING thy PRAISE, o LORD our GOD). The rhythms are so regular that one can even categorize them, e.g., "iambic pentameter" (five measures, each an iamb or combination of an unaccented and an accented syllable [we SING]).

17. See conveniently Petersen and Richards, *Hebrew Poetry,* pp. 37-47.

18. For more details, see Klein, Blomberg, and Hubbard, *Biblical Interpretation,* pp. 219-220.

19. Ugarit was a city along the Mediterranean coast (modern Lebanon) destroyed in the fourteenth century B.C. Excavations there have unearthed numerous written clay tablets which attest the close ties of language and culture which Ugarit shared with Israel. Thus, it seems indisputable that Hebrew poetry would follow the poetic practices of its Ugaritic counterpart. See the evidence in W. S. LaSor, "An Approach to Hebrew Poetry through the Masoretic Accents," pp. 327-353 in A. I. Katsh and L. Nemoy, eds., *Essays on the Occasion of the Seventieth Anniversary of the Dropsie University* (Philadelphia: 1979); *idem,* "Samples of Early Semitic Poetry."

20. Cf. S. Gevirtz, *Patterns in the Early Poetry of Israel* (Chicago: 1963), pp. 7-10 and *passim.*

21. For more examples, see Klein, Blomberg, and Hubbard, *Biblical Interpretation,* pp. 239-240.

22. For a thorough study of figurative speech, see G. B. Caird, *The Language and Imagery of the Bible* (Philadelphia: 1980).

23. Klein, Blomberg, and Hubbard, pp. 221-225, 236-241, provide an excellent survey.

CHAPTER 18 — AMOS

1. Heb. *bōqēr* is a general word for "tender of cattle." The more technical term is Heb. *nōqēd* (1:1). Though NRSV has "among the shepherds," the word is better translated "rancher" to picture Amos as a wealthy owner of many small cattle (sheep and goats), not a simple shepherd (Heb. *rō'ēh*). The sycamore figs probably served as fodder for his sheep. See B. E. Willoughby, "Amos, Book of," *ABD* 1:205.

2. See also 1 Chr. 27:28; R. K. Harrison, "Sycamore; Sycamore Tree," *ISBE* 4 (1988): 674.

3. **Hinnābē'* (niphal), lit. "make yourself a prophet" or "act the part of a prophet."

4. See H. H. Rowley, "The Nature of Old Testament Prophecy," *The Servant of the Lord and Other Essays on the Old Testament,* 2nd ed. (Oxford: 1965), p. 120, for a discussion of the problem and valuable bibliography. For a fuller study, see his article, "Was Amos a Nabi?" in J. W. Fück, ed., *Festschrift Otto Eissfeldt* (Halle: 1947), p. 191. See also D. L. Petersen, *The Roles of Israel's Prophets* (Sheffield: 1981), for the view that the term "prophet" was the characteristic term for this office in Israel, while in Judah "seer" would have been used more commonly.

5. See 2 Kgs. 14:23-29. Jeroboam was apparently coregent from 793-782, for the fifteenth year of Amaziah would be 782, and the forty-one years of Jeroboam's reign must be dated so as to end in 753; see W. S. LaSor, "1 and 2 Kings," *NBC,* p. 358.

6. For Amaziah of Judah, see 2 Kgs. 14:1-22; for Azariah (Uzziah), 15:1-7. Azariah must have been coregent 790-767. For detailed chronology, see LaSor, *NBC,* p. 323; see also p. 358 on 14:17-22.

7. P. J. King, *Amos, Hosea, Micah — An Archaeological Commentary* (Philadelphia: 1988), pp. 21, 38.

8. Cf. A. R. Millard, "Urartu," *ISBE* 4 (1988): 955. Urartu was a region in eastern Asia Minor between Lake Van (in modern Turkey) and Lake Urmia (in modern Iran). Urartu was at the peak of its power in the latter portion of the ninth century and the beginning of the eighth which overlaps Amos' period of prophetic activity.

9. Cf. W. S. LaSor, "Syria," *ISBE* 4 (1988): esp. pp. 690-692.

10. According to 2 Kgs. 14:25, this had been foretold by the prophet Jonah ben Amittai; cf. Jon. 1:1.

11. The buildings, of course, were not of ivory. Syrian craftsmen had achieved a high level of skill in crafting ivory pieces, especially ivory inlays, many of which have been found in archaeological excavations.

12. See D. A. Hubbard, *Joel and Amos* (Downers Grove: 1989), for a discussion of the use of form and content in the book of Amos.

13. See Ps. 62:11 (MT 12): "Once God has spoken; twice have I heard this"; Prov. 30:15: "Three things are never satisfied; four never say 'Enough'" [see Ugaritic "with thee thy seven lads, thine eight swine" (67:5, 8f.); "Behold, a day and a second day the fire eats into the house, the flame into the palace" (51:6, 24-26)]. This feature of Hebrew (and Semitic) poetry has been discussed briefly in the Chapter on Hebrew poetry, above. Often the "x + 1" item is elaborated upon and considered most significant; see Prov. 6:16-19.

14. H. Marks, "The Twelve Prophets," *LGB,* p. 223.

15. See J. Wellhausen, *Prolegomena to the History of Ancient Israel,* trans. J. S. Smith and C. A. Menzies (repr. Magnolia, Mass.: 1973), p. 474. See also C. F. Whitley, *The Prophetic Achievement* (Leiden: 1963), pp. 93ff. The theory that Amos introduced ethical monotheism was discussed in connection with the theory that J (eighth century) was the

earliest source of the "Hexateuch" (p. 114, above). The two theories were used in what is basically a circular argument.

16. See R. E. Clements, *Prophecy and Covenant* (London: 1965), pp. 14-17; H. H. Rowley, *The Faith of Israel* (London: 1956), p. 71.

17. For example, the law of Yahweh (2:4), prophets and Nazirites (v. 11), sacrifices, tithes (4:4), leaven (v. 5), offerings (5:22), songs, harps (v. 23), new moon and sabbath (8:5), Sheol (9:2), destruction of the Amorite (2:9), the Exodus (v. 10; 3:1), pestilence as in Egypt (4:10), Sodom and Gomorrah (v. 11), day of Yahweh (5:18), David (6:5), Joseph (v. 6), and the temple (8:3). To remove any of these because they belong to a "later" tradition is circular reasoning; see R. H. Pfeiffer, *Introduction to the Old Testament*, rev. ed. (New York: 1948), pp. 582f.

18. In Amos "Yahweh" is named fifty-two times; "the Lord Yahweh," nineteen; and "Yahweh God of Hosts," six.

19. Y. Kaufmann, *The Religion of Israel*, ed. and trans. M. Greenberg (Chicago: 1960), p. 365; see also J. Lindblom, *Prophecy in Ancient Israel* (Oxford: 1962), pp. 311f.

20. A handy summary of prophetic teaching on social justice is found in J. Limburg, *The Prophets and the Powerless* (Atlanta: 1977). See also B. C. Birch, *Let Justice Roll Down: The Old Testament Ethics and Christian Life* (Louisville: 1991).

21. Note, for instance, Eissfeldt's acceptance of the view of Wellhausen; *The Old Testament: An Introduction*, trans. P. R. Ackroyd (New York: 1965), p. 401, citing *Die Kleinen Propheten*, 4th ed. (Berlin: 1963), p. 96. But cf. Clements, *Prophecy and Covenant*, pp. 49 note 1, 111f. For an assessment of this matter in terms of the canonical function of ch. 9, see B. S. Childs, *Introduction to the Old Testament as Scripture* (Philadelphia: 1979), pp. 405-408.

22. See also G. von Rad, *Old Testament Theology*, trans. D. M. G. Stalker, 2 vols. (New York: 1962-1965) 2:138.

23. See H. H. Rowley, *Worship in Ancient Israel* (Philadelphia: 1967), pp. 144-175. See also H. Graf Reventlow, *Das Amt des Propheten bei Amos*, Forschungen zur Religion und Literatur des Alten und Neuen Testaments 80 (1962).

24. "Turn, return, turn back, repent," etc., all translate one Hebrew verb *(šûḇ)*, used many times in the prophets. Unfortunately, the English translations obscure this. The KJV, for example, translates *šûḇ* 123 different ways!

25. A common expression in Amos is *neʾûm yhwh*, variously translated in English: "says the Lord" (RSV), "it is Yahweh who speaks" (JB), "declares the Lord" (NASB). It occurs many times in nearly all the prophets. Yahweh, the covenant name of the God of Israel, appears to be used almost exclusively when the covenant relationship lies behind a situation or statement.

CHAPTER 19 — HOSEA

1. See A. Weiser, The Old Testament: Its Formation and Development, trans. D. M. Barton (New York: 1961), p. 233.

2. It is uncertain whether Hosea directly mentions the Syro-Ephraimitic coalition between Pekah of Israel and Rezin of Damascus. Isaiah described the threat this alliance presented to Ahaz of Judah (see Isa. 7) and its downfall at the hands of Tiglath-pileser (*ca.* 733). Possibly the battle call of Hos. 5:8 refers to conflict between Israel and Judah in the border towns of Benjamin:

Blow the horn in Gibeah,
the trumpet in Ramah.
Sound the alarm at Beth-aven [a derogatory name for Bethel, meaning "house
of nothing" instead of "house of God"];
look behind you, Benjamin!

3. Those who take these chapters as parallel accounts would call attention to the difference in literary form. Ch. 1 is prose narrative written in the third person and sometimes is thought to have been composed by disciples of the prophet. Ch. 3 is a prose narrative in the form of a first person memoir, usually thought to have come from the prophet himself.

4. H. W. Wolff, *Hosea*, trans. G. Stansell, Hermeneia (Philadelphia: 1974), pp. 14f.

5. See W. Rudolph, "Präparierte jungfrauen?" *ZAW* 75 (1963): 65-73; also J. L. Mays, *Hosea*, OTL (Philadelphia: 1969), p. 26.

6. The prophets did not always enjoy obeying God's commands. Walking "naked and barefoot for three years as a sign and a portent against Egypt and Ethiopia" was certainly not a task that Isaiah relished (Isa. 20:2f.).

7. See H. H. Rowley, "The Marriage of Hosea," *BJRL* 39 (1956-1957): 233: "Like Another, he learned obedience by the things that he suffered, and because he was not broken by an experience that has broken so many others, but triumphed over it and in triumphing perhaps won back his wife, he received through the vehicle of his very pain an enduring message for Israel and for the world."

8. Note the formal tone of this indictment, using literary forms which probably originated in the legal sphere; see Mic. 6:1-16. On the literary forms used in Hosea, see D. A. Hubbard, *Hosea*, TOTC 22A (Leicester, U.K.; Downers Grove, Ill.: 1989), pp. 34-38.

9. Heb. *ḥesed*, a favorite word of Hosea, blends the ideas of loyalty and love. Used of God, it means "covenant love" or "steadfast love"; for persons, as here, "kindness" or "charity" is implied.

10. T. C. Vriezen, *An Outline of Old Testament Theology*, 2nd ed. (Newton Centre, Mass.: 1970), p. 154. The relationship between knowledge and communion is illustrated in the use of "to know" (*yāda'*) for sexual intercourse (e.g., Gen. 4:1).

11. Citing H. B. Huffmon, "The Treaty Background of Hebrew Yada'," *BASOR* 181 (1966): 31-37; and with S. B. Parker, "A Further Note on the Treaty Background of Hebrew *Yāda'*," *BASOR* 184 (1966): 36-38, Brueggemann concludes: "It is now beyond dispute that 'know' means to acknowledge covenant loyalty and the accompanying demands"; *The Land* (Philadelphia: 1977), p. 105 note 21.

12. His book abounds with references to Israel's antiquity: Jacob's exploits (12:3ff.); idolatry at Baal-peor (9:10; cf. Num. 25); terrible debauchery at Gibeah (9:9; 10:9; see Judg. 19:24-26); destruction of the cities of the plain (11:8; cf. Gen. 19:23-25); Achan's sin at Achor (2:15; cf. Josh. 7:24-26).

13. A helpful resume of the attitudes of Amos and Hosea to the cult is R. Vuilleumier, *La tradition cultuelle d'Israël dans la prophétie d'Amos et d'Osée*, Cahiers Théologiques 45 (1960).

14. "In wrath" is based on a textual emendation. A literal reading is "unto the city." The text of Hosea apparently has suffered more than any other Old Testament book in editing and copying through the centuries. The classic textual study is H. S. Nyberg, *Studien zum Hoseabuche*, UUÅ (1935); see also Wolff, *Hosea*.

15. W. Eichrodt, *Theology of the Old Testament*, trans. J. A. Baker, OTL (Philadelphia: 1961) 1:251.

16. *Ibid.*, 1:251f.

17. *Ibid.*, 1:252.

18. J. M. Ward, *Hosea: A Theological Commentary* (New York: 1966), pp. 191-206, captures the power and poignancy of that struggle.

19. Sometimes called prophetic symbolism; the prophet demonstrates or acts out his message, and God uses the demonstration to fulfill the message. See also B. S. Childs, *Introduction to the Old Testament as Scripture* (Philadelphia: 1979), pp. 381f.

CHAPTER 20 — MICAH

1. See L. C. Allen, *The Books of Joel, Obadiah, Jonah and Micah*, NICOT (Grand Rapids: 1976), pp. 241-253, who, apart from 7:8-20, finds only 4:1-8 to be non-Mican.

2. J. L. Mays finds Micah's sayings only in portions of the first three chapters; *Micah*, OTL (Philadelphia: 1976), p. 13. Note, by contrast the cautious conclusion of G. W. Anderson: "When we consider the variety of denunciation and promise found in the teaching of other prophets, such as Micah's contemporaries, Hosea and Isaiah, it is unrealistic to claim that a prophet could not predict severe punishment . . . and also, at some other stage in his ministry, promise restoration"; see *A Critical Introduction to the Old Testament*, 2nd ed. (Naperville, 1960), p. 156. For a thorough discussion see K. Jeppesen, "New Aspects of Micah Research," *JSOT* 8 (1978): 3-32.

3. H. W. Wolff, *Micah the Prophet* (Philadelphia: 1981), p. 40, attempts to illustrate Micah's technique of punning in 1:10: "In Dustville *(bēt l'ap^e râ)* roll yourselves in the dust *('āpār)*." He compares this to a threat that "Portland will lose its port."

4. Hittite legal documents, especially treaties, begin with summoning the gods as witnesses. Rejecting this polytheism, Old Testament court scenes typically call on elements of creation (cf. Isa. 1:2).

CHAPTER 21 — ISAIAH: BACKGROUND

1. As a means of comparison, these quotations account for 9¾ columns in the United Bible Societies' *Greek New Testament*, compared to 9½ columns for quotations from the Psalms and 5¾ each for Genesis and Exodus.

2. O. Eissfeldt, *The Old Testament: An Introduction*, trans. P. R. Ackroyd (New York: 1965), p. 305.

3. The verbs are imperatives and not imperfects, as in NRSV mg. "The spoil speeds, the prey hastes."

4. See R. K. Harrison, *IBD*, p. 1417; G. V. Smith, *ISBE* 4 (1988): 410-411.

5. Eissfeldt, *Old Testament*, p. 310.

6. See W. S. LaSor, *Great Personalities of the Old Testament* (Westwood, N.J.: 1959), pp. 136-143; C. R. North, *IDB* 2:733.

7. Eissfeldt, *Old Testament*, p. 305.

8. Others understand in this a reference to the city-state of Ya'ud (Sam'al) in the Kara-su valley of northern Syria. It is most difficult to see how it could have been Judah, as M. Noth admits; *The History of Israel*, trans. P. R. Ackroyd, 2nd ed. (New York: 1960), p. 257 note 3.

9. The chronology of this period is puzzling. J. H. Hayes and S. A. Irvine (*Isaiah, the*

Eighth Century Prophet: His Times and His Preaching [Nashville: 1987], p. 236) place Ahaz's death in the same year as Tiglath-pileser's — 728-727.

10. Whether this was in 701 or 687 has been much debated; see L. L. Honor, *Sennacherib's Invasion of Palestine* (New York: 1926); J. Bright, *A History of Israel*, 3rd ed. (Philadelphia: 1981), pp. 298-309. The Assyrian record may have compressed two campaigns, one in 701 B.C., another about 687 which involved the siege of Lachish. See A. K. Grayson, "Sennacherib," *ABD* 5:1088-1089.

11. *ARAB* 2:240; *ANET*, p. 288.

12. Eissfeldt, *Old Testament*, p. 305; cf. Noth, *History*, pp. 257-269. For further background on the key figures of the period see W. S. LaSor, "Tiglath-pileser," *ISBE* 4 (1988): 849-851; "Sennacherib," *ISBE* 4 (1988): 394-397; "Sargon," *ISBE* 4 (1988): III. Sargon II, pp. 338-340; "Merodach-baladan," *ISBE* 3 (1986): 325-326; S. J. Schultz, "Uzziah," *ISBE* 4 (1988): 960f.; "Jothan," *ISBE* 2 (1982): 1140; "Ahaz" *ISBE* 1 (1979): 76-78 (with W. S. Caldecott); "Hezekiah," *ISBE* 2 (1982): 703-705; W. H. Shea, "Menahem," *ISBE* 3 (1986): 317f.; K. A. Kitchen, "Tirhaka," *ISBE* 4 (1988): 859; J. K. Hoffmeier, "So," *ISBE* 4 (1988): 558.

13. For the history of critical study of Isaiah, see G. L. Archer, Jr., *A Survey of Old Testament Introduction* (Chicago: 1964), pp. 318-339; *CCHS* §§421f.; B. S. Childs, *Introduction to the Old Testament as Scripture* (Philadelphia: 1979), pp. 316-338; Eissfeldt, *Old Testament*, pp. 303-346; North, *IDB* 2:737-743; E. J. Young, *An Introduction to the Old Testament* (Grand Rapids: 1958), pp. 199-207; R. K. Harrison, *ISBE* 3 (1986): 893-895; C. R. Seitz and R. J. Clifford, *ABD* 3:472-507.

14. S. R. Driver's analyses, though dated, may still serve as a prototype; *Introduction to the Literature of the Old Testament*, 9th ed. (repr. Magnolia, Mass.: 1972).

15. *Ibid.*, pp. 236-243.

16. *Ibid.*, pp. 238-240.

17. *Ibid*, p. 243.

18. A. Weiser, *The Old Testament: Its Formation and Devlopment*, trans. D. M. Barton (New York: 1961), p. 206.

19. See also T. Henshaw, *The Later Prophets* (London: 1958), p. 255.

20. See J. Gray, *I and II Kings*, OTL (Philadelphia: 1975), p. 325.

21. *Old Testament Theology* trans. D. M. G. Stalker, 2 vols. (New York: 1962-1965) 2:242, with a footnote to 41:25ff.; 48:14.

22. See R. K. Harrison, *Introduction to the Old Testament* (Grand Rapids: 1969), p. 794; also *ISBE* 2 (1982): 904.

23. O. T. Allis, *The Unity of Isaiah* (Philadelphia: 1950), pp. 51-61. Josephus (*Ant.* 2.1.102 §§1-7) writes that Cyrus was so impressed with finding his name in a book "140 years before the temple was destroyed" that he gave the Jews leave to go back to their own land and rebuild the temple. Most scholars today would read this note in Josephus as legend, without relevance in validating either Isaiah's authorship of the prophecy of Cyrus or the reason for Cyrus' action.

24. J. L. McKenzie, *Second Isaiah*, AB 20 (Garden City: 1968), p. xxi. McKenzie also reports an in-depth study of style by J. Reinken using modern statistical methods: "This study simply does not support the thesis of different authorship nor does it support the thesis of unity of authorship. This is to say that the vocabulary alone is not decisive. Nor is the style alone any more decisive"; p. xvi.

25. R. K. Harrison, *ISBE* 2 (1982): 896.

26. Henshaw, *Latter Prophets*, p. 256.

27. *Ibid.*, p. 265.

28. See D. N. Freedman, "The Structure of Isaiah 40:1-11," in *Perspective on Language and Text*, ed. E. W. Conrad and E. G. Newing (Eisenbrauns: 1987), pp. 167-194.

29. Often called by the German term *Sitz im Leben*.

30. See Driver, *Introduction*, p. 237.

31. *Das Buch Jesaja*, 4th ed., HKAT (Göttingen: 1922), generally considered the landmark commentary in developing the approach to triple authorship.

32. C. C. Torrey, who held the strange view that there never was a Babylonian exile, pointed out that if the few references to Babylon and Cyrus could be eliminated as later glosses, almost all of chs. 40–66 could be assigned to a Palestinian situation; *The Second Isaiah: A New Interpretation* (New York: 1928), pp. vii-viii. The word "Babylon" occurs thirteen times in Isaiah: once each in chs. 21; 43; 47; twice each in chs. 13; 14; 48; and four times in ch. 39.

33. E. M. Curtis, *ABD* 3:379.

34. The verbs *ṣôr* and *ḥᵃtōm* are imperative forms as pointed — but who is speaking? If Yahweh, then "my disciples" seems out of place, and "your disciples" (Isaiah's) would make better sense. If Isaiah, then to whom is he giving the command? If to his disciples, then "my disciples" is again difficult, and "yourselves" would seem preferable. Scholars, therefore, are inclined to emend the pointing and read the words as infinitives absolute, read as finite verbs — thus "I have bound up, etc." or "I will bind up, etc.," indicating a conclusion to which Isaiah has come.

35. The verb *ṣārar* "to bind up" means to shut in, confine, hold together, and *ḥtm* "to seal" means to authenticate with a seal, to protect, to seal up; see Dan. 12:4. The intent is not to keep anyone from seeing or knowing the contents — in fact, the contents of Isaiah's prophecy (and also Daniel's) were known to every generation. The idea of safeguarding and authenticating the message for a future time, both in Isaiah and in Daniel, is clear from the contexts.

36. "Disciples" and "school" must not be viewed as representing some kind of formal systematization. It is highly likely that a great and influential religious leader could gather a cadre of followers, some of whom would continue his work and ideas after his death. A possible comparison would be the "disciples" and "schools" of great critical and theological scholars in Germany in the past few centuries. Some hint of such a school may be found in Talmud *B. Bat.* 15a: "Hezekiah and his company wrote Isaiah, Proverbs, the Song of Songs, and Ecclesiastes" — which, in the light of other Talmudic tradition, seems to imply the gathering, editing, and publishing of sayings; of. Prov. 25:1.

37. See G. A. F. Knight, *Isaiah 40–55 and Isaiah 56–66*, ITC (Grand Rapids; Edinburgh: 1984/5), for this argument.

38. See, e.g., J. H. Hayes and S. A. Irvine, *Isaiah*, p. 13: "With the exception of Isaiah 34–35, practically all of the prophetic speech material in what is traditionally called First Isaiah — that is Isaiah 1–39 — derives from the eighth-century B.C.E. prophet."

39. *Old Testament as Scripture*, p. 324.

40. *Ibid.*, p. 333.

41. *Ibid.*, p. 329.

CHAPTER 22 — ISAIAH: MESSAGE

1. *Introduction to the Old Testament* (Grand Rapids: 1969), p. 764; *ISBE* 2 (1982): 900-901. Harrison has followed the lead of W. H. Brownlee (*Meaning of the Qumran Scrolls for the Bible*, 1964), who divided each half of the book into seven parallel sections:

Subject	1–33	34–66
Ruin and restoration	1–5	34–35
Biographical material	6–8	36–40
Agents of divine blessing and judgment	9–12	41–45
Oracles against foreign powers	13–23	46–48
Universal redemption and deliverance of Israel	24–27	49–55
Ethical sermons	38–31	56–59
Restoration of the nation	32–33	60–66

2. J. D. W. Watts, *Isaiah 1–33 and Isaiah 34–66,* WBC. Waco: 1985/7.

3. E. W. Conrad, *Reading Isaiah* (Minneapolis: 1991).

4. So central is the Hezekiah narrative to Isaiah's message and mission that it has been adapted and included in the books of Kings (2 Kgs. 18–20). Most scholars now hold to the priority of the Isaiah account, whereas earlier scholarship tended to view the King's record as primary and Isaiah's as derivative. See C. R. Seitz, *ABD* 3:483; J. H. Hayes and S. A. Irvine, *Isaiah, the Eighth-Century Prophet: His Times and His Preaching* (Nashville: 1987), pp. 372-373.

5. On the "Zion Tradition" see J. D. Levenson, *ABD* 6:1098-1102; on the term of endearment "Daughter of Zion (Isa. 37:22)," see E. R. Follis, *ABD* 6:1103.

6. On this central message as summarized in the vision of the heavenly council (40:1-10; cf. ch. 6), see R. N. Whybray, *The Second Isaiah,* JSOT Old Testament Guides (Sheffield: 1983), p. 45.

7. R. J. Clifford, *ABD* 3:498-499, has grouped many of these arguments into five strong contrasts he calls "polarities": (1) first and last things; (2) Babylon and Zion; (3) Yahweh and the gods; (4) Israel and the nations; (5) The Servant and Israel. These polarities highlight the uniqueness of Israel's Lord and the new work being done, as well as the continuity between what God has done in the past and what he is now doing.

8. See C. Westermann, *Prophetic Oracles of Salvation in the Old Testament* (Louisville: 1991), for a thorough discussion of this category, with special attention to both halves of the book of Isaiah.

9. For more detail on the literary forms, see Whybray, *Second Isaiah,* pp. 20-42; R. J. Clifford, *ABD* 3:495-497; C. Westermann, *Isaiah 40–66,* OTL (Philadelphia: 1969), pp. 11-21.

10. For comments on the division, see C. Westermann, *Isaiah 40–66,* pp. 302-304. P. Hanson, *The People Called: The Growth of Community in the Bible* (San Francisco: 1986), pp. 253-76, identifies the two hostile parties as the "Zadokites" or priests responsible for regulation of public worship and the Visionary Followers of Second Isaiah who believed that exclusive priesthood should be abolished since in the restoration all God's people were to be priests and ministers (61:6). For a critique of Hanson's views, see C. R. Seitz, *ABD* 3:502-507.

11. The expression occurs in the following passages: 1:4; 5:19, 24; 10:20; 12:6; 17:7; 29:19; 30:11f., 15; 31:1; 37:23; 41:14, 16, 20; 43:3, 14; 45:11; 47:4; 48:17; 49:7; 54:5; 55:5; 60:9, 14. Note "the Holy One of Jacob" (29:23); "God the Holy One" (5:16); "your holy One" (43:15); "his holy One" (10:17; 49:7); "whose name is Holy" (57:15). In 40:25 "Holy One" (Heb. *qādôs*) stands alone; also Hab. 3:3; Job 6:10; Prov. 9:10; 30:3 (footnote in NRSV).

12. N. H. Snaith, *The Distinctive Ideas of the Old Testament* (London: 1944), pp. 30f.

13. See H. H. Rowley, *Worship in Ancient Israel* (Philadelphia: 1967), pp. 37-70.

14. See *BDB,* pp. 379f., for a detailed study of the word *ṭāmēʾ.*

15. Greatly misunderstanding this effort, some scholars have insisted that the prophets were anticultic and antipriesthood. A much-needed corrective was supplied by R. E. Clements, *Prophecy and Covenant* (London: 1965), esp. chs. 4–5.

16. For further reading, see Snaith, *Distinctive Ideas*, pp. 21-50; J. Muilenburg, "Holiness," *IDB* 2:616-625; W. Eichrodt, *Theology of the Old Testament*, trans. J. A. Baker, 2 vols., OTL (Philadelphia: 1961) 1:270-282.

17. See Muilenburg, "Holiness."

18. Taking all the forms of the root *yšʿ* together, nouns and verbs, of some 342 occurrences in the Old Testament, 122 are found in Psalms, and about 50 in Isaiah (15 each in chs. 1–39 and 56–66, 20 in chs. 40–55).

19. Of the name Savior, N. Snaith says: "this appellation is by no means confined to Second-Isaiah, for it is the theme of many Psalms and of most of the prophets. The name Saviour is, however, so frequent in Second-Isaiah as to be a marked feature of his vocabulary"; *Distinctive Ideas*, p. 86. The word counts simply will not support this statement. "Salvation" may be the "theme" of most of the prophets, but the word itself is a hallmark of Isaiah.

20. The Hebrew root in its various forms occurs some 122 times in the Old Testament, of which about 26 occurrences are in Isaiah (1 in chs. 1–39, 18 in chs. 40–55, and 7 in chs. 56–66). Otherwise the bulk of its occurrences will be found in Leviticus (21 times in chs. 25 and 27), Ruth (19 times in chs. 3–4), and Numbers (6 times). Two other words are used to convey the idea of redemption, namely *pādâ*, "ransom," and forms of *kippēr*, "covering," "atonement," "propitiation."

21. See W. S. LaSor, *Daily Life in Bible Times* (Cincinnati: 1966), pp. 45-47.

22. See further R. C. Dentan, "Redeem, Redeemer, Redemption," *IDB* 4:21f.

23. For the meaning of *qinʾâ* "zeal, jealousy," see BDB, p. 888; G. A. Smith, *The Book of Isaiah,* Expositor's Bible, rev. ed. (1927; repr. Grand Rapids: 1956) 3:649; A. Stumpff, *"zelos," TDNT* 2:878-880.

24. The basic difficulty lies in the Hebrew word *rûaḥ*, which may mean "wind" as well as "spirit." In addition, there is a problem of interpretation, for a passage may refer to the "Spirit (of Yahweh)" or to the "spirit (of man)." Furthermore, "spirit" may be a quality or an attribute, even when used of God. For example, is "a spirit of justice" in 28:6 a human attribute or a gift of the divine Spirit (see 30:1, RSV)? In 37:7 is Yahweh intending to put some evil or perverse spirit in the king of Assyria, or is it the Spirit of Yahweh who will give the king the false rumor?

25. E. J. Kissane, *The Book of Isaiah*, rev. ed. (Dublin: 1960) 1:135.

26. While this interpretation could be a *sensus plenior* ("fuller sense"), it can hardly be derived from the passage in its context. See LaSor, "Interpretation of Prophecy," *BDPT*, pp. 128, 135; "The *Sensus Plenior* and Biblical Interpretation," pp. 260-277 in W. W. Gasque and LaSor, eds., *Scripture, Tradition, and Interpretation*, Festschrift E. F. Harrison (Grand Rapids: 1978).

27. It is important to recognize that Isa. 61:1 stands on its own, apart from any New Testament claim that it has been fulfilled. The passage, without any such interpretation, had to make sense to those who first heard or read it, and to all who read it prior to its "fulfillment." This is not to deny fulfillment of Scripture, but to insist on putting prophecy and fulfillment in their proper order.

28. N. H. Snaith, *Distinctive Ideas*, pp. 72f.

29. See E. R. Achtemeier, "Righteousness in the Old Testament," *IDB* 4:80.

30. "Every relationship brings with it certain claims upon conduct, and the satisfaction of these claims, which issue from the relationship and in which alone the relationship

can persist, is described by our term *ṣdq*"; H. Cremer, *Biblisch-theologisches Wörterbuch,* 7th ed. (Gotha: 1893), p. 233, quoted in G. von Rad, *Old Testament Theology,* trans. D. M. G. Stalker, 2 vols. (New York: 1962-1965) 1:371; see von Rad's own treatment, pp. 370-383.

31. Snaith, *Distinctive Ideas,* pp. 68-78.

32. Eichrodt, *Theology of the Old Testament* 1:240.

33. *Ibid.,* 1:245.

34. *Ibid.,* 1:247. Heb. *ṣidqat yhwh* is used of the saving acts of Yahweh, often in the Psalms; cf. BDB, p. 842, 6.a.

35. See Matt. 6:1f.; W. Bauer, *A Greek-English Lexicon of the New Testament,* trans. and rev. W. F. Arndt and F. W. Danker (Chicago: 1979), p. 196; G. Schrenk, *"dikaiosynē," TDNT* 2:192-210.

36. For further reading, see Snaith, *Distinctive Ideas,* pp. 51-78, 87-93; Eichrodt, *Theology* 1:244-47; Schrenk, *TDNT* 2:182, 210; Achtemeier, *IDB* 4:80-85.

37. Snaith, *Distinctive Ideas,* p. 74. See also Isa. 40:14; L. Morris, *The Biblical Doctrine of Judgment* (Grand Rapids: 1960), pp. 7f.

38. Snaith, *Distinctive Ideas,* p. 76.

39. While the Old Testament is concerned with the rights of all people, it expresses particular concern for the rights of those who cannot normally obtain justice, i.e., the widows and fatherless, the poor and the resident alien.

40. *Das Buch Jesaja,* HKAT (Göttingen: 1892).

41. J. A. Soggin, *Introduction,* p. 313: "They are marked out not only by a special theme, independent from that of the rest of the work, but also by the fact that they have evidently been interpolated in their present context, from which they can be removed without any resultant damage or interruption."

42. For specifics, see the very detailed note in H. H. Rowley, *The Servant of the Lord and Other Essays on the Old Testament,* 2nd ed. (Oxford: 1965), p. 6 note 1. For brief summaries of contemporary interpretation, see Whybray, *Second Isaiah,* pp. 65-78. Also, R. J. Clifford, *ABD* 3:499f.

43. After having accepted the theory of the Servant Songs for about forty years, W. S. LaSor, on the basis of continuing study of the text, came to a different conclusion: "a careful reading of the entire section, extending from chapter 41 (not 42) through chapter 53, will show that it is *all* about the Servant of the Lord"; *Israel: A Biblical View* (Grand Rapids: 1976), p. 16. P.-E. Bonnard, independently, came to much the same conclusion. Calling those who isolate the poems "victims of prejudice," he says: "Isaiah 40–55 constitutes rather a symphony on the Servant Israel"; *Le Second Isaie: son disciple et leurs éditeurs,* Etudes Bibliques (Paris: 1972), p. 7; see his discussion, pp. 37-56, and table, pp. 39f.

44. See D. J. A. Clines, *I, He, We, and They: A Literary Approach to Isaiah 53,* JSOTSup 1 (Sheffield: 1976).

45. LaSor, "Interpretation of Prophecy," p. 135.

CHAPTER 23 — ZEPHANIAH, NAHUM, AND HABAKKUK

1. For a full discussion of the geography, see W. S. LaSor, "Jerusalem," *ISBE* 2 (1982): 1013ff., D.5; also Y. Aharoni and M. Avi-Yonah, eds., *The Macmillan Bible Atlas,* map 114, p. 74. In contrast, H. Cazelles seems to identify the Mishneh of 2 Kgs. 22:14 with Zephaniah's Maktesh; "The History of Israel in the Pre-exilic Period," p. 311 in G. W. Anderson, ed., *Tradition and Interpretation* (Oxford: 1979).

2. E.g., A. Bentzen, *Introduction to the Old Testament*, 2 vols. (Copenhagen: 1948) 2:153. See A. R. Johnson, *The Cultic Prophet in Ancient Israel; The Cultic Prophet and Israel's Psalmody* (Cardiff: 1979); cf. W. McKane, "Prophecy and the Prophetic Literature," p. 166 in Anderson, ed., *Tradition and Interpretation.*

3. D. W. Baker, *Nahum, Habakkuk, Zephaniah*, TOTC (Leicester and Downers Grove: 1988), p. 84.

4. Note the famous medieval Latin hymn, *Dies irae, dies illa.*

5. *History* 1.104-106.

6. The difficult phrase "who leaps over the threshold" may refer to the eagerness with which the servants of the rich descended upon the hovels of the poor to loot their scanty goods. An alternate interpretation sees a reflection of pagan superstition; see Hyatt, *JNES* 7 (1948): 25f.: "mount the podium" of an idol (see 1 Sam. 5:5), J. J. M. Roberts, *Nahum, Habakkuk, and Zephaniah*, OTL (Louisville: 1991), p. 179.

7. P. R. House, *Zephaniah: A Prophetic Drama*, JSOTSup 69 (Sheffield: 1988), has outlined the whole book as a drama. For a critique of House's analysis, see Roberts, *Nahum, Habakkuk, and Zephaniah*, pp. 161-162.

8. See Baker, *Nahum, Habakkuk, Zephaniah*, p. 87.

9. English translations are unable to convey the striking puns used in Zephaniah's incisive denunciation (v. 4).

10. Ethiopia may stand here in lieu of Egypt. In the decades just prior Egypt had been under the sway of Ethiopian rulers (Twenty-fifth Dynasty); see Nah. 3:9.

11. The day is past when scholars could relegate all such passages of hope to the postexilic period; see F. C. Fensham, "Book of Zephaniah," *IDBS*, p. 984. Increasing appreciation of the nature of Israel's covenant-keeping God has confirmed that hand in hand with an emphasis on judgment was the hopeful expectation that the God who wounded would heal, or better, that he healed by wounding. His faithfulness, not Israel's response, is what shapes the future. The judgment speeches against the foreign nations are one way of conveying hope: the nations' doom meant Judah's welfare *(shalôm)*. See W. McKane, "Prophecy and the Prophetic Literature," in Anderson, ed., *Tradition and Interpretation*, pp. 172-175.

12. On the possible origins and meaning of the day of the Lord, see A. S. Kapelrud, *The Message of the Prophet Zephaniah* (Oslo: 1975), pp. 80-87; G. von Rad, *Old Testament Theology*, trans. D. M. G. Stalker, 2 vols. (New York: 1962-1965) 2:119-125. See also W. S. LaSor, *The Truth about Armageddon* (San Francisco: 1982), pp. 136-137.

13. On the positive aspects of judgment see L. Morris, *The Biblical Doctrine of Judgment* (Grand Rapids: 1960), pp. 22-24; W. S. LaSor, *Armageddon*, pp. 180-190.

14. G. A. Smith, *Book of the Twelve Prophets*, Expositor's Bible (repr. 1956) 4:573.

15. Even his hometown, Elkosh (1:1), has defied identification, although sites in Assyria (north of Mosul), Galilee, and Judah have been suggested.

16. Cf. W. S. LaSor, "Sennacherib," *ISBE* 4 (1988): 394-397; "Esarhaddon," *ISBE* 2 (1982): 128f.; "Ashurbanipal," *ISBE* 1 (1979): 321f.

17. C. J. Gadd, *The Fall of Nineveh* (London: 1923).

18. Further evidence of Nahum's conscious literary technique has allegedly been found in the imperfect acrostic pattern of 1:2-11. However, attempts to restore the original acrostic have not been successful. See D. L. Christensen, "The Acrostic of Nahum Reconsidered," *ZAW* 87 (1975): 17-30, and "The Acrostic of Nahum Once Again: A Prosodic Analysis of Nahum 1:1-10," *ZAW* 99 (1987): 409-414.

19. O. Kaiser, *Introduction to the Old Testament*, trans. J. Sturdy (Minneapolis: 1975), pp. 231f. However, B. S. Childs, *Introduction to the Old Testament as Scripture* (Philadelphia:

791

1979), pp. 441f., notes that the view that the book was intended for liturgical use after Nineveh's fall rather than a prophecy before that fall lacks solid scholarly support.

20. A. Parrot calls this "a remarkable touch of local color," since in the region of Nineveh all walls were built of sun-dried brick; *Nineveh and the Old Testament*, trans. B. E. Hooke (New York: 1955), p. 84.

21. Parrot refers this to the nearby fortresses of Tarbisu and Asshur, which fell before Nineveh and without as much resistance; *ibid.*, p. 79.

22. These two images accord well with the fact that Nineveh was dedicated to Ishtar, goddess of war and love; see Parrot, *ibid.*, p. 26.

23. Bentzen (*Introduction* 2:150) numbers Nahum among the nationalistic prophets condemned by Jeremiah. See also G. Fohrer, *Introduction to the Old Testament*, trans. D. E. Green (New York: 1968), p. 451. But Nahum's sense of moral outrage differs considerably from the easy optimism of the false prophets.

24. Von Rad, *Old Testament Theology* 2:189.

25. E. R. Achtemeier, *Nahum-Malachi*, Interpretation (Atlanta: 1986), pp. 5-6. See Childs, *Old Testament as Scripture*, pp. 443f., on how the hymn (psalm) sets the theological tone for the book.

26. *Reflections on the Psalms* (New York: 1958), p. 30; his chapter on "The Cursings" contains many helpful observations.

27. On Nahum's picture of Yahweh as God of war, see K. J. Cathcart, *ABD*, 4:1000.

28. R. Calkins, *The Modern Message of the Minor Prophets* (New York: 1947), p. 86. For observations on Nahum's belief in the "moral cohesiveness of history" and God's "righteous judgment of a morally offensive and inhuman empire," see N. K. Gottwald, *All the Kingdoms of the Earth* (New York, Evanston, London: 1964), pp. 231f.

29. A tradition preserved in the apocryphal Bel and the Dragon speaks of Ambakom (the Greek form of Habakkuk's name), son of Jesus of the tribe of Levi. No means exist either to substantiate or refute this tradition, which is not found in Theodotion's translation.

30. Habakkuk's interest in public worship is shown by the psalmlike nature of ch. 3 and its musical notation (v. 1). Whether he was a temple prophet, as Mowinckel and others have argued (see Bentzen, *Introduction* 2:151), is uncertain.

31. M. A. Sweeney, "Habakkuk, Book of," *ABD* 3:3.

32. For a full study of "oracle" = "burden," see R. D. Weis, *A Definition of the Genre Maśśā' in the Hebrew Bible*, Ph.D. dissertation (Claremont, Calif.: 1986).

33. Some interpret the circumstances as the external pressure of the Assyrians, soon to be supplanted by the Babylonians. This view usually involves drastic rearrangement of the text (esp. 1:13); see Childs, *Old Testament as Scripture*, pp. 448-450, for various interpretations of the historical situation.

34. Habakkuk's plea has many parallels in the Psalms, particularly those of individual and communal complaint (e.g., 7:9 [MT 10]; 13:1-4 [MT 2-5]; 22:1-5 [MT 2-6]; 44:23-26 [MT 24-27]; note especially the outcries of "how long?", "why?" See Lewis, *Reflections on the Psalms*, pp. 9-19, for some apt observations on judgment.

35. See, e.g., Ps. 12: complaint (vv. 1-4 [MT 2-5]); salvation speech (v. 5 [MT 6]); word of assurance (v. 6 [MT 7]); prayer for protection (vv. 7f. [MT 8f.]).

36. In one Assyrian inscription Esarhaddon speaks of catching a king of Sidon like a fish and cutting off his head, while a stele found at Zinjirli in northern Syria depicts him holding Tirhakah of Egypt and an unnamed ruler on a leash with a ring through their lips; see Parrot, *Nineveh*, pp. 64f.

37. For a summary of the structure and proposed backgrounds of the woe oracles,

see W. E. March, "Prophecy," pp. 164f. in J. H. Hayes, ed., *Old Testament Form Criticism* (San Antonio: 1974).

38. Commentators frequently suggest that v. 19 may originally have preceded v. 18, so that the *woe* cry, as usual, begins the oracle.

39. R. H. Pfeiffer (*Introduction to the Old Testament,* rev. ed. [New York: 1948], p. 597) and many others view ch. 3 as an appendix taken from an ancient hymnal. The mention of Shigionoth (v. 1), probably a hymn tune (cf. Ps. 7:1), the occurrences of "Selah" (vv. 3, 9, 13), and the musical notations in v. 19 support such a theory. Though perhaps not connected with the prophecy originally, this hymn makes a fitting climax in its appeal for God's intervention and confidence in his righteousness. The title in v. 1, attributing the hymn to Habakkuk, need not be discredited; in fact, it would be difficult to discover reasons for adding this chapter if it were not his work. W. F. Albright finds "no valid reason why this book should not be treated as a substantial unit and dated between 605 and 589 B.C. . . ."; see his "The Psalm of Habakkuk," p. 2, in H. H. Rowley, ed., *Studies in Old Testament Prophecy* (Edinburgh: 1950). J. J. M. Roberts describes the flow of the book as "a coherent, sequentially developed argument that extends through the whole book" (*Nahum, Habakkuk, and Zephaniah,* p. 81).

CHAPTER 24 — JEREMIAH

1. See A. Bentzen: ". . . a book on prophecy will always be, to a great extent, a book on Jeremiah"; *Introduction to the Old Testament,* 2 vols. (Copenhagen: 1948) 2:116.

2. See J. Skinner, *Prophecy and Religion: Studies in the Life of Jeremiah* (Cambridge: 1922), p. 19: "There was no family in Israel whose fortunes had been so closely bound up with the national religion as that into which Jeremiah was born. And nowhere would the best traditions and the purest *ethos* of the religion of Yahweh be likely to find a surer repository than in a household whose forbears had for so many generations guarded the most sacred symbol of its imageless worship, the Ark of God."

3. W. L. Holladay takes 627 to be the year of Jeremiah's birth (so J. P. Hyatt, *IB,* p. 779), but this proposal has not been widely accepted; cf. *Jeremiah,* Hermeneia (Philadelphia: 1989) 2:25-26.

4. See H. Cunliffe-Jones, *The Book of Jeremiah,* Torch Bible Commentary (Naperville: 1960), pp. 32ff. Concerning our knowledge of Jeremiah the person, we do not share the skepticism of R. P. Carroll, *Jeremiah.* JSOT Old Testament Guides (Sheffield: 1989), p. 12: "We should treat the character of Jeremiah as a work of fiction and recognize the impossibility of moving from the book to the real 'historical' Jeremiah, given our complete lack of knowledge independent of the book itself." For a defense of Carroll's view, see his *From Chaos to Covenant: Uses of Prophecy in the Book of Jeremiah* (New York: 1981). In contrast to Carroll's skepticism is W. Holladay's strong affirmation (*Jeremiah* 2:25): "I submit, then, that the data of the book can be used to build up a credible portrayal of the prophet, a portrayal against which there are no opposing data."

5. Cf. the insight of J. Steinmann: "Jeremiah was truly the genius of torment and discord, the Euripides, the Pascal or the Dostoyevsky of the Old Testament." Quoted in Carroll, *Jeremiah,* p. 75.

6. Cunliffe-Jones, *Book of Jeremiah,* p. 34, lists several passages which reflect Jeremiah's intimate knowledge of and concern for his land: e.g., 1:11; 2:23, 31; 4:7, 11; 5:6; 6:29; 7:11, 18, 34; 8:7; 12:5; 14:6; 17:8, 11; 18:3f.; 22:6. See also E. F. F. Bishop, *Prophets of Palestine: The Local Background to the Preparation of the Way* (London: 1962), pp. 115ff.

7. The national god of the Ammonites. He is also called Molech or Moloch (see 32:35; Lev. 18:21), whose name probably means "king." The *-ôm* ending is probably an elative: "*the* king."

8. Capital of Ammon, modern Amman.

9. For discussion of Jeremiah's salvation speeches, see C. Westermann, *Prophetic Oracles of Salvation in the Old Testament* (Louisville: 1991), pp. 137-167.

10. For their interpretation, see our discussion below under Composition.

11. Jer. 17:11 seems to be a proverb in the form of a familiar "like-so" comparison between animal and human behavior.

12. Perhaps ʿAin Kârim (ʾEn Kerem), west of Jerusalem, but more probably Ramat Rahel about two miles south of the capital; P. C. Craigie, P. H. Kelley, and J. F. Drinkard, *Jeremiah 1–25*, WBC 26 (Dallas: 1991), p. 100.

13. For additional genres and examples, see J. R. Lundbom, "Jeremiah (Prophet)," *ABD* 3:690-698.

14. For example, the episode in ch. 24 takes place sometime after 597, that of ch. 25 in 605 (i.e., Jehoiakim's fourth year), and that of ch. 26 "at the beginning of the reign of King Jehoiakim" (i.e., *ca.* 608).

15. See the convenient summary of the discussion in J. R. Lundbom, "Jeremiah, Book of," *ABD* 3:709-710, 712-716. For a more detailed treatment, see R. P. Carroll, *Jeremiah, A Commentary*, OTL (Philadelphia: 1986), pp. 38-50.

16. Chief exceptions are the poetry in chs. 30–31, which form part of the Book of Comfort (chs. 30–33), and the oracles against the nations (chs. 46–51).

17. Lundbom, "Jeremiah, Book of," p. 710; Holladay, pp. 22-24. For a contrary view, see Carroll, *Jeremiah, A Commentary*, pp. 44-45, 61. According to W. McKane, *Jeremiah*, ICC (Edinburgh: 1986), the book originated as a "rolling corpus" (i.e., by small pieces of text triggering commentary which together became the final book). McKane does not address the matter directly (he covers only chs. 1–25), but his theory seems to exclude Baruch from any role in the book's composition (see pp. l-lxxxviii). McKane's second volume was not available when this *Survey* went to press.

18. The book may also allude to other collections of Jeremiah's work which the present form has incorporated. In context, 25:13 seems to refer to a collection of oracles against nations, 30:2 to a collection of oracles of hope. Thus, one may rightly regard the book of Jeremiah as a "collection of collections." Cf. also 46:1, which introduces the oracles against the nations (chs. 46–51).

19. See L. Stulman, *The Prose Sermons of the Book of Jeremiah*, SBLDS 83 (Atlanta: 1986), who summarizes the discussion (pp. 7-31) and gives a catalog of so-called "deutero-nomistic" words and phrases (pp. 31-48).

20. Among recent commentators, Carroll (*Jeremiah, A Commentary*, pp. 38-50, 65-82) and McKane (pp. xlvii-l, lxxxvi) exemplify this influential approach. E. W. Nicholson suggested that the texts represented preaching during the Babylonian exile which both drew from and developed Jeremiah's teaching; see his *Preaching to the Exiles: A Study of the Prose Tradition in the Book of Jeremiah* (New York: 1971).

21. See Lundbom, "Jeremiah, Book of," 709; Holladay, 12-13. J. G. McConville even argues that, by intermixing prose and poetry, Jeremiah merely followed the practice of earlier prophets like Hosea; see *Judgment and Promise: An Interpretation of the Book of Jeremiah* (Winona Lake: 1993), pp. 152-155. This argument forms part of his case that the entire book originated in Jeremiah's lifetime rather than from the hands of later Deuteronomists (p. 181).

22. For an overview of the evidence, see Lundbom, "Jeremiah, Book of," pp. 707-709.

Cf. also J. G. Janzen, *Studies in the Text of Jeremiah*, HSM 6 (Cambridge, Mass.: 1973); and S. Soderlund, *The Greek Text of Jeremiah: A Revised Hypothesis* (Sheffield: 1985).

23. E. Tov favors the latter view, deriving both LXX and MT (his "edition II") from a hypothetical "edition I" (the "Final Deuteronomic edition of Jeremiah"); cf. "The Literary History of the Book of Jeremiah in the Light of Its Textual History," pp. 211-237 in J. H. Tigay, ed., *Empirical Models for Biblical Criticism* (Philadelphia: 1985). On the other hand, if two versions originated independently, the shorter version might be connected with Jeremiah's period in Egypt, the longer one with editors in either Babylon or Palestine.

24. See C. R. Seitz, "The Prophet Moses and the Canonical Shape of Jeremiah," *ZAW* 101 (1989): 18-27. If MT preserves the original order, the LXX probably followed the pattern of other prophetic books like Isaiah 1–39 and Ezekiel (i.e., oracles of doom against Judah, oracles of doom against nations, and oracles of hope for Judah).

25. In our view, McConville, *Judgment and Promise*, offers the best overview of the book of Jeremiah to date, and we acknowledge our debt to his treatment for some of what follows.

26. The term "legacy" suggested by Lundbom ("Jeremiah, Book of," p. 706) seems appropriate since the Hebrew word *dibrê* (1:1; 51:64) covers both "words" and "acts." For an alternative approach to the book's structure, see J. Rosenberg, "Jeremiah and Ezekiel," *LGB*, pp. 190-194.

27. J. Rosenberg, "Jeremiah and Ezekiel," p. 185.

28. Both this and the following cycle derive their names from their respective main subjects. Apparently, whoever edited these collections did so around their themes.

29. I.e., Israel's enemies who attacked her.

30. Passages which treat Judah's idolatry as spiritual prostitution show clearly the influence of Hosea's message on Jeremiah. For details, see McConville, pp. 152-163.

31. Scholars used to think the northern enemy was the Scythians (see Ch. 23 above, concerning Zephaniah). But the main evidence for that view — Herodotus' description of their exploits in Syria, Palestine, and Egypt (*History* 1.103-6) — has received little confirmation. Instead, Jeremiah probably refers either to foreign enemies in general (they usually invaded Judah from the north) or to the Babylonians, who rose to power during Jeremiah's early ministry.

32. The "house" here is the temple in Jerusalem. Shiloh was site of an early Israelite temple served by Eli and Samuel (see 1 Sam. 1–4). It was probably destroyed by the Philistines about three centuries before Jeremiah.

33. See K. M. O'Connor, *The Confessions of Jeremiah: Their Interpretation and Role in Chapters 1–25*, SBLDS 94 (Atlanta: 1988), p. 157. O'Connor (pp. 156, 158) concludes that the "Prose Writer" (i.e., the author of the prose in chs. 1–20) incorporated the Confessions into chs. 1–25. We are inclined to identify that writer as Jeremiah's secretary, Baruch. See also M. S. Smith, *The Laments of Jeremiah and their Contexts*, SBLMS 42 (Atlanta: 1990); and A. R. Diamond, *The Confessions of Jeremiah in Context; Scenes of Prophetic Drama*, JSOTSup 45 (Sheffield: 1987).

34. An important minor theme in chs. 1–25 also confirms that judgment is inevitable. One function of a prophet was to intercede with Yahweh on behalf of Israel (e.g., chs. 21; 37), but on several occasions God forbids Jeremiah to do so (7:16; 11:14; 14:11; cf. 15:1). Apparently, the die of disaster for Judah had already been cast.

35. See McConville, pp. 61-78, who believes that in the Confessions Jeremiah represents Judah, so his hopeful fate raises Judah's hopes for a similar future.

36. The Hebrew (*yhwh ṣidqēnû*) suggests a pun on Zedekiah (*ṣidqîyāhû*). God's new king would be all that Zedekiah should have been and was not.

37. See McConville, p. 132. Probably for the same reason, the book also includes God's assurances to Ebed-melech, who once rescued Jeremiah (38:7ff.), and Baruch that each would have his "life as a prize of war" (39:18; 45:5).

38. For their literary background and interpretation, see conveniently McConville, pp. 135-148, and Seitz, "The Prophet Moses and the Canonical Shape of Jeremiah," pp. 18-27, to whom we owe some of what follows.

39. As noted earlier, the LXX has the oracles in a different order (e.g., the oracles of Babylon fall third). The other nations addressed include the Philistines, Moab, the Ammonites, Edom, Damascus, and Elam.

40. What Num. 14:34 views as judgment, Jeremiah sees as part of Israel's devout past. Perhaps when compared with Judah's rejection of the Lord in Jeremiah's day and the strong judgment yet to come, the wilderness wanderings could be seen as a period of grace.

41. "Worthless things" is equivalent to "idols." The wording shows the emptiness of idolatry and its impact — people become what they worship.

42. The mention of both Israel and Judah (v. 31) reflects Jeremiah's idealism. He looked to a time when God would repair the rupture of Jeroboam's division and the ravage of Assyrian invasion. Like the other great prophets, Jeremiah could not picture a future that did not involve the unity of the whole house of Jacob.

43. Jesus and the early Church seized upon this radical newness as a means of describing the transformation brought about by the Christian gospel (Mark 14:24; Heb. 8).

44. Though Jeremiah did not use the term, the new king is the "Messiah." The combination of a new covenant and a return to the land, without mention of a messianic king, is found in 32:36-41.

45. See J. G. S. S. Thomson, *The Word of the Lord in Jeremiah* (London: 1959).

46. See B. S. Childs, *Introduction to the Old Testament as Scripture* (Philadelphia: 1979), p. 347: "The memory of his proclamation was treasured by a community of faith and consciously shaped by theological forces to serve as a witness for future Israel."

47. See the alternate scheme which assumes that Jeremiah responded to the public reading of the law every seven years in Holladay, *Jeremiah* 1:1-10.

CHAPTER 25 — EZEKIEL

1. Several other interpretations of the "thirtieth year" have been given: (1) the time when all of Ezekiel's prophecies were written down much later; (2) thirty years after some landmark event like Josiah's recovery of the law book (622 B.C.; 2 Kgs. 22:8), Jehoiachin's exile (598 B.C.), or Ezekiel's call (563 B.C.). See L. Boadt, *ABD* 2:713.

2. B. Bron, a psychiatrist, in an article "Zur Psychopathologie und Verkündigung des Propheten Ezechiel. Zum Phänomenon der prophetischen Ekstase" (*Schweizer Archiv für Neurologie, Neurochirurgie und Psychiatrie* 128 [1981]: 21-31), has judged that, while Ezekiel had ecstatic experiences, the way he is described in the book shows no psychotic or schizophrenic symptoms.

3. For historical details see J. Bright, *A History of Israel*, 3rd ed. (Philadelphia: 1981), pp. 324-354; J. M. Miller and J. H. Hayes, *A History of Ancient Israel and Judah* (Philadelphia: 1986), pp. 385-435.

4. J. Lindblom, *Prophecy in Ancient Israel* (Oxford: 1962), pp. 386f.

5. G. F. Moore, *Judaism in the First Centuries of the Christian Era* (Cambridge, Mass.: 1927) 1:247.

6. *Ibid.*, pp. 246f.; Talmud *Shab.* 13b, *Hag.* 13a, *Men.* 45a.

7. S. R. Driver, *Introduction to the Literature of the Old Testament,* 9th ed. (repr. Magnolia, Mass.: 1972), p. 297.

8. G. Hölscher, *Hesekiel: Der Dichter und das Buch,* BZAW 39 (Giessen: 1924).

9. *Ezekiel 1,* trans. R. E. Clements, Hermeneia (Philadelphia: 1979), pp. 69-74. The translator renders *Nachinterpretation* as "updating of tradition."

10. *Ezekiel 1–20. AB* 22 (New York: 1983).

11. Calculated from tables in R. A. Parker and W. H. Dubberstein, *Babylonian Chronology 626 B.C.–A.D. 75* (Providence, R.I.: 1971), pp. 27f.

12. Heb. *ben 'ādām.* The plural *bᵉnê hā'ādām* "sons of man, human beings," occurs elsewhere; *ben 'ādām* is found in parallel with *'ĕnôš* in Job 25:6; Ps. 8:4 (MT 5). According to Eichrodt (*Ezekiel,* p. 61), the expression in Dan. 8:17 is derived from Ezekiel.

13. See R. W. Klein, *Ezekiel: The Prophet and His Message* (Columbia, S.C.: 1988), pp. 16-28.

14. See L. C. Allen, "The Structure and Intention of Ezekiel 1," *VT* 43 (1993): 145-161.

15. Cf. 37:26. Accordingly the Qumran community, in their Temple Scroll, envisioned an eschatological temple that Yahweh would "create" (G. Vermes, *The Dead Sea Scrolls in English,* 3rd ed. [London: 1987], p. 138).

16. See W. A. Van Gemeren, *Interpreting the Prophetic Word* (Grand Rapids: 1990), pp. 186-187, 208-209.

CHAPTER 26 — OBADIAH AND JOEL

1. See K. A. D. Smelik, *Writings of Ancient Israel* (Louisville: 1991), pp. 143, 158.

2. Parallels:

Obadiah	Jer. 49	Obadiah	Joel
v. 1	v. 14	v. 10	3:19 [MT 4:19]
v. 2	v. 15	v. 11	3:3 [MT 4:3]
v. 3a	v. 16a	v. 15	3:4, 7 [MT 4:4, 7]
v. 4	v. 16b	v. 15	1:15; 2:1; 3:14 [MT 4:14]
v. 6	v. 9	v. 17	2:32 [MT 3:5]
v. 6	v. 10a	v. 17	3:17 [MT 4:17]
v. 8	v. 7	v. 18	3:8f. [MT 4:8f.]
v. 9a	v. 22b		
v. 16	v. 12		

The parallels between vv. 1-9 and Jer. 49:7-22 are much closer than those with Joel. Jer. 49:14-16 is remarkably similar to vv. 1-4. Jer. 49:7-11 contains much of the same material as vv. 5-9, but the portions do not seem to represent direct quotations, either of one another or both of an earlier source. The parallels with Joel simply involve similarity of expression, with no evidence of the use of a longer quotation. These parallels raise the question whether such materials were used in public worship and thus became part of common quotation.

3. J. A. Soggin, *Introduction to the Old Testament,* trans. J. Bowden, OTL (Philadelphia: 1976), p. 341.

4. H. W. Wolff, *Obadiah and Jonah: A Commentary,* trans. M. Kohl (Minneapolis: 1986), p. 18.

5. G. E. Wright and F. V. Filson, eds., *Westminster Historical Atlas to the Bible*, rev. ed. (Philadelphia: 1956), pl. X; Y. Aharoni and M. Avi-Yonah, *Macmillan Bible Atlas*, maps 52, 155; L. H. Grollenberg, *Shorter Atlas of the Bible*, puts Teman north of Petra; p. 164. But see P. C. Hammond, "Sela," *ISBE* 4 (1988): 383f., and E. A. Knauf, "Teman," *ABD* 6:347-348. Note "God came from Teman" (Hab. 3:3) and "YHWH of Teman" in a blessing found in one of the inscriptions at Kuntillet Ajrud, ruins about 50 kilometers south of Kadesh Barnea. See K. A. D. Smelik, *Writings from Ancient Israel* (Louisville: 1991), pp. 155-160.

6. Soggin, *Introduction*, p. 341.

7. E.g., A. F. Kirkpatrick, *The Doctrine of the Prophets*, 3rd ed. (London: 1901), pp. 57ff. M. Bic has dated the book of Joel as the earliest of the Minor Prophets because it supposedly reflects the struggle of Yahweh with Baalism, which goes back as far as Elijah; *Das Buch Joel* (Berlin: 1960), pp. 106-109.

8. E.g., S. R. Driver, *The Books of Joel and Amos*, 2nd ed., Cambridge Bible (Cambridge: 1915). R. H. Pfeiffer suggests a date *ca.* 350; *Introduction to the Old Testament*, rev. ed. (New York: 1948), p. 575. A. Robert and A. Feuillet vote for a date *ca.* 400; *Introduction to the Old Testament* (New York: 1968), p. 359. See also H. W. Wolff, *Joel and Amos*, Hermeneia (Philadelphia: 1977), pp. 4-6.

9. *Joel Studies* (Uppsala: 1948), pp. 191f. Kapelrud stresses the oral transmission of prophetic messages, making the actual writing of the book some years (perhaps centuries) later. On somewhat different grounds, C. A. Keller (*Joël, Abdias, Jonas*, Commentaire de l'Ancien Testament 11a [Neuchatel: 1965], p. 103) and W. Rudolph (*Joel*, KAT 13/2 [1975]) have argued strongly for a late preexilic date: 630-600 and 597-587, respectively.

For exilic dates, see B. Reicke, "Joel und seine Zeit," in H. J. Stoebe, J. J. Stamm, and E. Jenni, eds., *Wort-Gebot-Glaube*, Festschrift W. Eichrodt, Abhandlungen zur Theologie des Alten und Neuen Testaments 59 (1970): 133-141. J. Myers suggests a date *ca.* 520, making Joel a contemporary of Haggai and Zechariah; "Some Considerations Bearing on the Date of Joel," *ZAW* 74 (1962): 177-195. G. W. Ahlström dates the book 515-500; *Joel and the Temple Cult of Jerusalem*, VTSup 21 (1971). R. Dillard, "Joel," *The Minor Prophets* (Grand Rapids: 1992) 1:243, calls this early post-exilic dating "the best handling of the evidence."

10. For further discussion of Joel's date see L. C. Allen, *The Books of Joel, Obadiah, Jonah, and Micah*, NICOT (Grand Rapids: 1976), pp. 19-25, and D. A. Hubbard, *Joel and Amos*, TOTC (Leicester and Downers Grove: 1989), pp. 23-27.

11. E. B. Pusey went so far as to equate the four types of locusts with the successive invasions of Assyria, Babylonia, Macedonia, and Rome; *The Minor Prophets* (1886; repr. Grand Rapids: 1950) 1:160. D. Stuart, *Hosea-Jonah*, WBC (Waco: 1987), p. 226, lists three possible invasions as the backdrop of Joel: Assyria in 701, Babylonia in 598 or 588 B.C. For Stuart, both chs. 1 and 2 describe military attacks for which the locusts are imaginative figures of speech.

12. The outstanding advocate of this approach was A. Merx, *Die Prophetice des Joel und ihre Auslegen* (Halle: 1879). J. A. Bewer, *Joel*, ICC (Edinburgh: 1911), and Pfeiffer, *Introduction*, combine the literal and apocalyptic interpretations by finding actual insects in ch. 1 and apocalyptic creatures in ch. 2.

13. E.g., Driver, *Joel and Amos;* G. W. Wade, *Joel*, Westminster Commentaries (London: 1925); J. A. Thompson, *IB;* R. Dillard, "Joel," in *The Minor Prophets* 1 (Grand Rapids: 1992).

14. B. S. Childs, *Introduction to the Old Testament as Scripture* (Philadelphia: 1979), p. 391.

15. Elements characteristic of salvation speeches abound here: (1) God's promises are uttered in the first person; (2) God's creatures are commanded "fear not" (2:21f.) and "be glad" (vv. 21, 23); (3) specific damages will be repaired (e.g., vv. 19f., 24-26); (4) the net result will be enlarged awareness of God's presence and uniqueness (v. 27), for which the people will praise the Lord (v. 26).

16. See Ps. 22. The psalmist sees in his rescue cosmic significance: "All the ends of the earth shall remember and turn to the LORD" (v. 27 [MT 28]). Even generations yet unborn will feel the effects of what God has done for him (v. 30).

17. Actually, the Old Testament has no word for *nature* as a principle or order of reality; it sees the universe as *creation,* under God's direct and immediate control.

18. "The northerner" (v. 20) apparently describes the locust army, which on this occasion may have invaded from the north. In general, the term is synonymous with enemy, since at this time the major military threats to Judah were posed by nations marching from the north or northeast (see Jer. 1:13-15; Zeph. 2:13). It may also connote Israel's apprehension about the north, where their neighbors thought their gods lived (see Isa. 14:13).

CHAPTER 27 — JONAH

1. Sometimes the message is addressed to a foreign nation (e.g., Obadiah's words concerning Edom), but it is unlikely that it was delivered to, or even directly intended for, any other than Yahweh's people Israel.

2. To state that the story is told about an eighth-century prophet neither affirms not denies its historicity (see below), not does it establish an eighth-century date for its writing.

3. The location of Tarshish is uncertain. See D. W. Baker, *ABD* 6:331-333. A location in Spain would suit the story.

4. Jonah's description of Yahweh's compassion is phrased in terms frequently used in Israel's liturgy (Pss. 86:15; 103:8; Exod. 34:6; Joel 2:13). It is as though he cites a portion of a creed to defend his position.

5. The ignorant 120,000 have been interpreted as children. More likely they represent the whole population of Nineveh and their lack of true knowledge of God and his demands of human life. D. J. Wiseman ("Jonah's Nineveh," *Tyndale Bulletin* 30 [1979]: 39-40) points out that "right hand and left hand" in Babylonian texts can mean "truth and justice" or "law and order."

6. R. B. Dillard and T. Longman III, *An Introduction to the Old Testament* (Grand Rapids: 1995), p. 293, agree that "the question of the intention of historicity is totally without effect on the interpretation of the book's theological message or even the exegesis of individual passages."

7. Sadly, people "have been looking so hard at the great fish that they have failed to see the great God"; G. Campbell Morgan, *The Minor Prophets* (Westwood: 1960), p. 69.

8. "Three days' journey in breadth" seems to refer to the distance across the city. A day's journey can be calculated at about twenty miles.

9. Jonah 3:3, *hāyetâ.* In such a clause, the verb "to be" is usually omitted unless necessary to give the tense.

10. See for instance the commentaries of D. Stuart, D. Alexander, and the summary article by W. C. Williams in *ISBE* 2 (1982): 1112-1116.

11. G. A. Aalders, *The Problem of the Book of Jonah* (London: 1948), p. 12.

12. The seriousness with which Jewish tradition took Jonah's story is attested in its

use in the synagogue on Yom Kippur (the day of atonement), the most solemn of the high holidays.

13. See D. F. Payne, "Jonah from the Perspective of the Audience," *JSOT* 13 (1979): 3-12, esp. pp. 11-12; J. Day, "Problems in the Interpretation of the Book of Jonah," *OTS* 26 (1990): 32-47, esp. p. 47.

14. T. J. Carlisle, *You! Jonah!* (Grand Rapids: 1968), p. 64.

CHAPTER 28 — HAGGAI

1. See W. S. LaSor, *Great Personalities of the Old Testament* (Westwood, N.J.: 1959), p. 171.

2. *ANET*, p. 315.

3. See R. P. Dougherty, *Nabonidus and Belshazzar*, Yale Oriental Series (New Haven: 1929), pp. 170, 176. Cf. *ANET*, p. 315.

4. *ANET*, p. 316.

5. *DOTT*, p. 93.

6. It is sometimes objected that 538 was not "the first year of Cyrus," as Ezra dates it; see L. W. Batten, *Ezra and Nehemiah*, ICC (Edinburgh: 1949). However, Cyrus dates his reign from his conquest of Babylon. "From the seventh month of Cyrus' accession year (539) business texts dated to him continue without break to the twenty-seventh day of the fourth month *(Du'uzu)* of his ninth year, July, 530 B.C."; W. H. Dubberstein, "The Chronology of Cyrus and Cambyses," *AJSL* 55 (1938): 417.

7. Others date this return to the days of Artaxerxes II (404-358) or Artaxerxes III (358-338) or by emending Ezra 7:7 to read "thirty-seven" (thus in the year 428). See Chapter 42.

8. Passages such as Isa. 48:20-21 and 51:9-11 must therefore be somewhat figurative. Yet it is easy to see how the Jews might describe their release in such lofty terms, viewing it as a miracle surpassing the Exodus, given their lengthy captivity.

9. This assumes an identification of Sheshbazzar with the Shenazzar of 1 Chr. 3:16-18.

10. Although Zedekiah reigned in Jerusalem after Jehoiachin was exiled to Babylon, the ending to the book of Kings emphasizes the release of Jehoiachin from prison (2 Kgs. 25:27-29). This may indicate that Jehoiachin was the last surviving king (Jer. 52:11) or the last legitimate king (since Zedekiah was appointed by the Babylonians he may have been considered a puppet).

11. Although the date is unclear it must have been during or before 520 since Haggai's prophecies to Zerubbabel begin in that year. According to R. D. Wilson, Sheshbazzar was the Babylonian name equivalent to Zerubbabel; "Sheshbazzar," *ISBE* (1939): 4:2766. Few scholars have accepted this identification. Comparison of Ezra 5:14-16 with 5:2 suggests that Sheshbazzar no longer was alive when Zerubbabel began his work. See R. L. Pratt, Jr., "Sheshbazzar," *ISBE* 4 (1988): 475.

12. See 1 Chr. 3:16-19. It cannot be resolved whether his father was Pediah (1 Chr. 3:19) or Shealtiel (Ezra 3:2; 8; 5:2; Neh. 12:1; Hag. 1:1, 12, 14; 2:2, 23; Matt. 1:12; Luke 3:27), but both were sons of Jehoiachin.

13. Based on the tables in R. A. Parker and W. H. Dubberstein, *Babylonian Chronology 626 B.C.–A.D. 75* (Chicago: 1956), pp. 28-29.

14. Doubt has been cast on this theory by R. J. Coggins, *Samaritans and Jews* (Oxford: 1975).

15. For a clear, detailed, yet succinct presentation of this view, see O. Eissfeldt, *The Old Testament* (New York: 1976), pp. 427-428. He gives credit to J. W. Rothstein, *Juden und Samaritaner: Die grundlegende Scheidung von Judentum und Heidentum,* BWANT 3 (Leipzig: 1908), pp. 5-41.

16. Ezra 3:6, which states that the foundation of the temple was not yet laid when Zerubbabel arose, and 3:10, which credits him with laying it, do not necessarily contradict 5:16, which gives the credit to Sheshbazzar. It may be that (a) some or all of the foundation stones had been removed in the interim between the two governors or (b) "laying the foundation" was partly ceremonial and had to be repeated with the new efforts of Zerubbabel. See C. L. Meyers and E. M. Meyers, *Haggai, Zechariah 1-8,* AB 25B (Garden City: 1987), pp. 63-64, 244-255.

17. Though singular, this term occurs with a plural verb, and could be revocalized as a plural; hence the NAB translates "treasures." The NIV follows the KJV with "desired." This has been interpreted by some to mean a messiah who is the desired one of all the nations. However, it is unlikely that Haggai was in this term pointing to an individual. Compare Isa. 45:14 and 60:10-12 where it is also promised that the wealth of the nations will flow to Jerusalem.

18. Ezekiel predicted that after the restoration of the temple, the glory of Yahweh would reenter it, inaugurating a return to paradise-like conditions (Ezek. 43; 47). Given Haggai's strong assurances that God would fill the rebuilt temple with glory and shake all the nations, it is no wonder the people thought that the messianic age was about to dawn.

19. The problem with this passage is that construction had apparently been going on for several months, yet one stone had not been placed upon another (2:15). Meyers and Meyers (*Haggai, Zechariah 1-8,* pp. 80-82) explain that the text probably refers to a foundation dedication ceremony. Some parts of the earlier foundation would have been intact and new stones would have been laid, but it was necessary for Zerubbabel to lay the foundation symbolically by ritually placing some stones in the ground, according to the proper custom, in order to ensure the fertility of the land.

20. Isaiah spoke of a chosen servant who would bring justice to the earth (Isa. 42:1-4). God calls King David "my servant" (2 Sam. 7:5) and David likewise speaks of God's choosing of him (2 Sam. 6:21). Cf. Ps. 78:70. See Ch. 5.

21. The temple which Herod the Great rebuilt in the days of Jesus was considered to be simply a refurbishing.

22. Based on the fact that it took about four months to make the nine-hundred mile journey (see Ezra 7:8f; see also Ezek. 33:21, where news of Jerusalem's fall reached Babylon a little less than five months after the event).

23. See Isa. 1:12-17; Amos 5:21-24; Hos. 6:6; Mic. 6:6-8; Jer. 7:21-23.

24. This does not make Haggai a false prophet. Zerubbabel was indeed God's servant and chosen, but chosen to build the temple, not to usher in the kingdom of God. He also fulfilled the figure of the "signet ring" by administering Yahweh's plans, thereby putting the ratifying stamp on them. In addition, as a Davidic scion he ruled as governor, though not as king.

25. According to Christian thought, God delayed the advent of the Messiah for about 500 years from the completion of the second temple. According to Jewish belief, the delay still continues.

26. While Christians do see many aspects of fulfillment of biblical hope in Jesus' first coming (inaugurated eschatology), other aspects await his return (see 1 Cor. 15:24-27).

27. See Y. Yadin, "Bar Kochba," *IDBS,* pp. 89-92.

28. Cf. W. S. LaSor and T. C. Eskenazi, "Synagogue," *ISBE* 4 (1988): 676-684.

29. See G. F. Moore, *Judaism in the First Centuries of the Christian Era* (Cambridge, Mass.: 1927) 1:29-47. W. S. LaSor has suggested the term "nascent Judaism" since some Jews have rejected the term "normative" ("Religions of the Biblical World: Judaism," *ISBE* 4 [1988]: 117-123).

30. See especially H. Danby, *The Mishnah* (Oxford: 1933).

31. For background on the Apocrypha see B. Metzger, *An Introduction to the Apocrypha* (New York: 1957); and O. Eissfeldt, *The Old Testament: An Introduction,* trans. P. R. Ackroyd (New York: 1965), pp. 571-603; for the text of the books, see *JB; The New English Bible, with the Apocrypha* (Oxford and Cambridge: 1970); B. Metzger and R. Murphy, *The New Oxford Annotated Bible with the Apocrypha/Deuterocanonical Books* (New York: 1991), NRSV text.

32. For background on the Pseudepigrapha (Greek for books falsely ascribed to ancient writers), see Eissfeldt, *Old Testament,* pp. 603-637; for texts, see J. H. Charlesworth, ed., *The Old Testament Pseudepigraphia,* 2 vols. (Garden City: 1983).

33. For background and text of the Qumran literature (Dead Sea Scrolls), see A. Dupont-Sommer, *The Essene Writings from Qumran,* trans. G. Vermes (Gloucester, Mass.: 1973); G. Vermes, *The Dead Sea Scrolls in English* (Baltimore: 1962). For helpful summaries of the discoveries and their importance see E. M. Cook, *Solving the Mysteries of the Dead Sea Scrolls: New Light on the Bible* (Grand Rapids: 1994), and J. C. VanderKam, *The Dead Sea Scrolls Today* (Grand Rapids: 1994).

1. Month 8 of Year of Darius (YD) 2 began 27 Oct. 520 (1:1); the date in 1:7 converts to 15 Feb. 519, and that in 7:1 to 7 Dec. 518.

2. Zechariah was a very common name. T. M. Mouch distinguishes thirty-three persons so named ("Zechariah," *IDB* 4:941-943). Matt. 23:35 provides an example of how they could become confused. It refers to the martyrdom of Zechariah the son of Barachiah. However, there is no evidence for the martyrdom of the prophet whose book we are discussing. Surely, the intended Zechariah is the son of Jehoiada, whose martyrdom is recorded in 2 Chr. 24:20-22. Such an identification makes the Matthew passage much clearer. Jesus bracketed the whole period of the Old Testament by mentioning the first martyr: Abel (in Genesis, the first book); and the last: Zechariah, the son of Jehoiada (in Chronicles, the final book in the Hebrew Bible).

3. T. Henshaw, *The Latter Prophets* (London: 1963), pp. 246f.

4. O. Eissfeldt, *The Old Testament: An Introduction,* trans. P. R. Ackroyd (New York: 1965), pp. 429, 434-437.

5. W. Neil, "Zechariah, Book of," *IDB* 4:944. Cf. F. C. Fensham, "Zechariah, Book of," *ISBE* 4 (1988): 1183-1186.

6. For a survey of the views, see Eissfeldt, *Old Testament,* pp. 434-440.

7. We shall occasionally use these terms in a neutral fashion — not to indicate a position on authorship but as a way of distinguishing chs. 1–8 from 9–14.

8. For surveys of various views see Eissfeldt, *Old Testament,* pp. 435-440; D. L. Peterson, "Zechariah 9–14," *ABD* 6:1065-1066; R. B. Dillard and T. Longman III, *An Introduction to the Old Testament* (Grand Rapids: 1995), pp. 427-436.

9. A. Bentzen, *Introduction to the Old Testament,* 2 vols. (Copenhagen: 1948) 2:161.

10. The words of W. Neil are typical: "The latter part of the book of Zechariah presents vast, and in part, insoluble problems in respect of authorship, date, and interpre-

tation. While it is not possible to establish beyond dispute whether one, two, three, or a variety of authors were responsible for chs. 9–14, it is almost universally agreed that on linguistic and stylistic grounds, as well as in theological ideas and historical background, the author of these chapters cannot be the prophet Zechariah" ("Zechariah, Book of," *IDB* 4:945). For the opinion that the whole book was written by Zechariah, see R. K. Harrison, *Introduction to the Old Testament* (Grand Rapids: 1969), pp. 953-956; J. S. Wright, *IBD*, pp. 1677-1679; G. L. Robinson, "Zechariah, Book of," *ISBE* 5 (1939): 3139f.; G. L. Archer, Jr., *A Survey of Old Testament Introduction* (Chicago: 1964), pp. 415f.; and S. Bullough, "Zacharias," *CCHS*, §545k.

11. The date formulae are common to Zechariah and Haggai. This may indicate that the two books were edited together. See chart in Chapter 28.

12. The Fourth Vision is different from the other seven. Its introduction is unique, omitting the stock expressions of the rest. There is no angel and hence no exchange of question and answer between messenger and prophet. Consequently, some consider ch. 3 to be secondary. However, since it is a vision and since it does fit the chiastic pattern, we include it in our discussion. If it were removed, the structural analysis would remain the same for the other pairs of visions. And the content would change little, for the central theme is the double (dyarchic) leadership whether expressed in one vision or two.

13. C. L. Meyers and E. M. Meyers, *Haggai, Zechariah 1–8*, AB 25B (Garden City: 1987), pp. l-lxiii.

14. *Ibid.*, pp. 80-82. See also note 19 in Chapter 28.

15. The Heb. word for "branch" is *ṣemaḥ* except for Isa. 11:1 which has *nēṣer*. By a process that is not strange in Judaism and rabbinical exegesis, Matthew cites this passage to prove that the Messiah "shall be called a Nazarene" (Matt. 2:23). These exact words cannot be found in the canonical prophets. See J. G. Baldwin, "*Ṣemaḥ* as a Technical Term in the Prophets," *VT* 14 (1964): 93-97.

16. The term for "anointed" is not the customary Heb. *māšiaḥ* "messiah" but *bᵉnê-hayyiṣhar* "sons of (anointing) oil."

17. See Gen. 10:10; 11:2; Isa. 11:11; BDB, p. 1042.

18. Some compare the portrayal of four horsemen in Rev. 6:2-8. However, Zechariah's vision is of chariots, not horsemen (but cf. 1:8). Moreover, while Zechariah may be the source of figures used in Revelation, Revelation is not the source of Zechariah's figures. Therefore, the meaning of Revelation must not be imposed on Zechariah.

19. Meyers and Meyers, *Haggai, Zechariah 1–8*, p. 331.

20. Hebrew has the plural "crowns" in 6:11 and 14.

21. Neil, *IDB* 4:945.

22. P. D. Hanson, *The Dawn of Apocalyptic* (Philadelphia: 1979), p. 256.

23. Reconstructions can be speculative and the text of this oracle is poorly preserved. It may be preferable to see any confusion here as resulting from errors in copying rather than deliberate editing.

24. P. D. Hanson, "Zechariah, the Book of," *Harper's Bible Dictionary* (San Francisco: 1985), p. 1159.

25. See chart in Chapter 28.

26. Not all scholars agree. Paul Lamarche has offered a complex if somewhat contrived structural analysis (*Zacharie IX–XIV, Structure littéraire et messianisme* [Paris: 1961]). His views are accessible in English in J. G. Baldwin, *Haggai, Zechariah, Malachi* (London: 1972), pp. 75-81.

27. For more information see Hanson, "Apocalypse, Genre," *IDBS*, pp. 27-28, and "Apocalypticism," *IDBS*, pp. 28-34.

28. Even apocalyptists may envision history continuing or starting over, as in Isa. 66:22-24 and Rev. 21:1-27 with the creation of new heavens and earth. But this is only after the old world has passed away. And the new world will bear little resemblance to the old. Thus the eschaton is much more of a severe cataclysmic rupture in apocalyptic than in prophecy.

29. It is possible that they stem from the same time, recording the voice of a party of political outcasts — "visionaries" — who opposed the leadership of Zerubbabel and Joshua — the "hierocratic party" (Hanson, "Zechariah, Book of," *IDBS*, pp. 982-983). If so the two voices must be kept in dynamic tension. It will not do to dissolve the dialectic in favor of the visionaries. Ezra, Haggai, and Zech. 1–8 contain no condemnations of the leaders; on the contrary the leaders are highly exalted. Both voices in Scripture must be heard: the pragmatic side which builds structures and the visionary side which shows the frailties of those structures and points to a new and better world to come.

30. Haggai spoke of the shaking of the nations (Hag. 2:7, 21-22) and Zechariah of the casting down of the horns of the nations (Zech. 1:21) and both clearly understood this to be God's doing. God's kingdom would not be wholly a human achievement. Nevertheless, there is a difference of degree. There is more continuity between the old world and the new in Haggai and Zech. 1–8 and more discontinuity in Zech. 9–14. There is more human instrumentality in the former; less in the latter.

31. Jesus was humble, but the donkey was not necessarily a symbol of that humility, as some readers think. The mule, which was a cross between a donkey and a horse, was a royal animal in Israel. By riding on a donkey, Jesus not only fulfilled the prophecy in Zech. 9; he may also have been laying claim to the throne of his father David just as Solomon did by having his coronation on a mule (1 Kgs. 1:32-40; cf. 2 Sam. 18:9).

32. In Heb. the poetic parallelism clearly indicates one animal: "a donkey"/"a colt, the foal of a donkey" (Zech. 9:9). Apparently, this came to be understood more prosaically because Matthew has Jesus riding on two animals (Matt. 21:5-7). John's account is preferable, with one beast (John 12:14-15).

33. Matthew cites Jeremiah (Matt. 27:9-10), but Judas' actions and the quotation in Matthew most closely resemble Zech. 11:12-13.

CHAPTER 30 — MALACHI

1. It has been suggested that these three "burdens" were originally written by one person (R. C. Dentan, "Introduction and Exegesis of Malachi," *IB* 6:1117). Others disagree because Malachi and the passages in Zechariah differ markedly in style and structure (B. S. Childs, *Introduction to the Old Testament as Scripture* [Philadelphia: 1979], pp. 491f.).

2. Targum on Mal. 1:1; see 3:1; see also Talmud *Meg.* 15a.

3. G. L. Robinson, "Malachi," *ISBE* (1939) 3:1969.

4. Another possibility is that 2:11b-13a is secondary (O. Eissfeldt, *The Old Testament: An Introduction*, trans. P. R. Ackroyd [New York: 1965], p. 442). Removing these verses makes for a more unified passage. Could they have been added by a scribe siding with Ezra, who wanted the people to divorce their foreign wives (Ezra 10:10-11, 19, 44), against Malachi, who strongly opposed divorce (Mal. 2:14-16)?

5. Admittedly, it is possible that this verse is only saying that God is father of both Israel and Judah.

6. On the metaphor of "king" in Mal. 1:11, see Åke Viberg in *Tyndale Bulletin* 45/2 (1994): 297-319.

7. R. J. Coggins is dubious about efforts to use the content of the book for arriving at a specific date. He concludes that "Malachi is to be placed within the Persian period, some time between 515 and 330 B.C.; but that greater precision than that is scarcely available" (*Haggai, Zechariah, Malachi*, JSOT Old Testament Guides [Sheffield: 1987], p. 75). On the other hand, A. E. Hill, "Malachi, Book of," *ABD* 4:480-481, uses L. Polzin's "typological" method of comparing texts linguistically as a guide to dating them. He locates Malachi in the forty-year period between 515 and 475 B.C., thanks to the close affinity in style to Haggai and Zech. 1–8. D. L. Petersen, *Zechariah 9–14 and Malachi*, OTL (Louisville: 1995), p. 3, seems to agree with Hill: "Malachi . . . derives from the early-middle Persian period."

8. When one noun is bound to a following noun such that the second is in a genitival relationship to the first, the first is said to be in the construct with the second. Normally, proper names such as "Yahweh" cannot stand in construct with another noun.

9. In this view Sabaoth would be understood as the name of a pre-Israelite deity which was taken over by the Israelites and applied to their God, Yahweh. Sabaoth does occur as a name in the LXX.

10. This is found in numerous places, such as 2 Sam. 5:10; 1 Kgs. 19:10, 14, and is translated "the LORD God of hosts" in most English Bibles.

11. See E. Kautzsch and A. E. Cowley, eds., *Gesenius' Hebrew Grammar* (Oxford: Oxford, 1974), §125h, p. 403.

12. F. M. Cross, *Canaanite Myth and Hebrew Epic* (Cambridge: 1980), pp. 68-71 (esp. p. 71).

13. The expression occurs 267 times in the Old Testament, mostly in the prophets; B. W. Anderson, "Lord of Hosts," *IDB* 3:151. According to one count, it is found 63 times in Isaiah (57 in chs. 1–39), 83 in Jeremiah, 14 in Haggai, 53 in Zechariah (44 in chs. 1–8), and 24 in Malachi. It occurs only 5 times in all the rest of the prophets, and not at all in Ezekiel. Considering the relative sizes of the books, the term was used more frequently by the postexilic prophets, with remarkable "density" (i.e., the number of times it is used per page) in Malachi.

14. S. R. Driver, "Lord of Hosts," *HDB* 3 (1900): 137f. See also B. W. Anderson, "Hosts, Host of Heaven," *IDB* 2:654-656; BDB, p. 839.

15. See G. P. Hugenberger, *Marriage as a Covenant: A Study of Biblical Law and Ethics concerning Marriage Developed from the Perspective of Malachi*, VTSup 52 (1994).

16. Esarhaddon settled foreigners in the territory of the former kingdom of Israel in the seventh century B.C. If they remained distinct, then at least they borrowed their Yahwistic faith from the local populace. However, it is quite likely that they also intermarried with the remnant of the Israelites.

17. For a fuller discussion of this view see Paul D. Hanson, *The Dawn of Apocalyptic: The Historical and Sociological Roots of Jewish Apocalyptic Eschatology* (Philadelphia: 1979), and "Apocalypticism," *IDBS*, pp. 28-34. For a different view and for a survey of the various positions see J. M. O'Brien, *Priest and Levite in Malachi*, SBLDS 121 (Atlanta: 1990).

18. In the Passover Seder, "Elijah's cup" remains untouched throughout the service. Toward the end of the service the door is opened to see if Elijah has come. If he has not, the service concludes with the hope that the fulfillment will occur before the next year. The epilogues, which feature Moses and Elijah, serve not only as a fit closing to "Malachi" but may also aim to link "Malachi" and the Book of the Twelve, which it completes, to other main portions of the canon: *Torah* (Moses) and *Former Prophets* (Elijah). See D. L. Petersen, *Zechariah 9–14 and Malachi*, pp. 232-233.

19. John, however, seems to be unaware of his role in this regard, for he denies that he is Elijah when asked (John 1:21).

20. This does not necessarily mean it was the last prophetic work to be written. Daniel, which is placed in the Writings, may have been completed at a later period.

CHAPTER 31 — INTRODUCTION TO THE WRITINGS

1. The debate was not whether these books should be added to the canon, but whether they should be withdrawn from the canon.

2. O. Eissfeldt, *The Old Testament: An Introduction,* trans. P. R. Ackroyd (New York: 1965), p. 570.

3. *Ibid.,* p. 443. At times Ruth came just before Psalms to give the genealogy of David, the psalmist (see Talmud *B. Bat.* 14b).

4. Though many biblical books have an extended history of composition before being put in final form, in the case of Psalms and Proverbs one must consider the process of collection as well as that of composition of the various songs and sayings.

CHAPTER 32 — PSALMS

1. The use of that title is at least as old as Philo (*ca.* A.D. 40), who uses the literal Greek equivalent *hymnoi.*

2. Luke 24:44 acknowledges the book's priority among the Writings and employs the title Psalms to describe the whole collection.

3. Cf. W. S. LaSor and T. C. Eskenazi, "Synagogue," *ISBE* 4 (1988): 681-684, V. Worship Service.

4. Qumran Cave 2 has yielded a Hebrew copy of Ps. 151. See J. A. Sanders, *The Psalms Scroll of Qumran Cave II,* Discoveries in the Judean Desert 4 (London: 1965), pp. 54-64.

5. J. Muilenburg, introduction to H. Gunkel, *The Psalms: A Form-Critical Introduction,* trans. T. M. Homer (Philadelphia: 1967), p. iv.

6. In addition to the work cited in note 5, see Gunkel, *Einleitung in die Psalmen,* 3rd ed. HAT (Göttingen: 1975) [completed in 1933 by J. Begrich after Gunkel's death], as a ready source for his massive contribution to the study of the Psalms.

7. For an analysis of the philosophical and cultural influences which prompted this shift from historical and literary criticism to form criticism, see E. Gerstenberger, "Psalms," pp. 179-183 in J. H. Hayes, ed., *Old Testament Form Criticism* (San Antonio: 1974).

8. With this cf. the Introduction to cultic poetry in E. S. Gerstenberger, *Psalms; Part 1,* Forms of the Old Testament Literature (Grand Rapids: 1988), pp. 5-22, for a survey of recent developments.

9. This central section typically is expressed either (1) with Hebrew participles describing God's activity; usually translated as relative clauses (e.g., "who forgives all your iniquity, who heals all your diseases," 103:3), or (2) with "for" (Heb. *ki*) to introduce the reasons for praise (e.g., "For the Lord is good; his steadfast love endures forever . . . ," 100:5).

10. *The Psalms in Israel's Worship,* trans. D. R. Ap-Thomas (Nashville: 1967) 1:106-192; see esp. pp. 129f.

11. Mowinckel rejected the contrast: "To the Israelite way of thinking there is no

contradiction between [becoming king] and that he is king for ever; such a contradistinction is modern and rationalistic" (*The Psalms* 1:115).

12. *Worship in Israel*, trans. G. Boswell (Richmond: 1966), pp. 205-207.

13. C. Westermann strongly supports Kraus, arguing that the eschatological hope expressed is the dominant characteristic (*The Praise of God in the Psalms*, trans. K. R. Crim [Richmond: 1961], pp. 145-151).

14. The term complaint is preferred to lament to describe the prayers for help in the Psalms. Lament better fits the *qînâ*, the funeral dirge used in 2 Sam. 1:17-27, where the tragedy is irreversible.

15. This schema of elements is adapted from Westermann's analysis in *The Praise of God in the Psalms*, pp. 53f.

16. Ps. 89 begins like a solo hymn, with an account of God's might and majesty, and a reminder of God's covenant with David (89:1-37). Vv. 38-51 are clearly a complaint, asking relief from enemy invasion. The references to "David," "your servant," and "your anointed" clearly mark the king as speaker (vv. 49-51).

17. E.g., 3; 5–7; 13; 17; 22; 25–28; 31; 35; 36; 38–40; 42–43; 51; 54–57; 59; 61; 64; 69–71; 86; 88; 102, 108–109; 120–130; 139–143.

18. Westermann calls these "motifs designed to move God to intervene" (*The Praise of God in the Psalms*, p. 64).

19. See R. de Vaux, *Ancient Israel*, trans. J. McHugh, 2 vols. (New York: 1965), pp. 417f.

20. D. J. A. Clines, *Theological Students Fellowship Bulletin* 71 (1975): 1-8. The weakness of most other views of kingship is their imposing on the Scriptures patterns found elsewhere in Near Eastern societies.

21. For instance, 2:1f. is cited in Acts 4:25f.; 45:6f. in Heb. 1:8f.; 110:1 in Matt. 22:44; Acts 2:34f.; 110:4 in Heb. 5:6, 10.

22. J. K. Kuntz, "The Canonical Wisdom Psalms of Ancient Israel — Their Rhetorical, Thematic, and Formal Dimensions," in J. J. Jackson and M. Kessler, eds., *Rhetorical Criticism* (Pittsburgh: 1974), pp. 186-222.

23. R. E. Murphy, "A Consideration of the Classification, 'Wisdom Psalms,'" *VTSup* 9 (1962): 165-167.

24. See G. H. Wilson, *The Editing of the Hebrew Psalter* (Chico: 1985), pp. 204-207.

25. For descriptions of the feasts and discussions of their history, development, and meaning, see de Vaux, *Ancient Israel*, pp. 71-110; Kraus, *Worship in Israel*, pp. 26-69.

26. *The Psalms*, trans. H. Hartwell, OTL (Philadelphia: 1962), pp. 35-52.

27. H. H. Guthrie, *Israel's Sacred Songs* (New York: 1966), p. 19.

28. Kraus, *Worship in Israel*, pp. 131f., 136-141, 179-188.

29. *Ibid.*, pp. 208-218. For further comments on the "blessing of departure," see Westermann, "Book of Psalms," *IDBS*, p. 708.

30. See M. Dahood, *Psalms*, AB 1 (Garden City: 1965), pp. xxix-xxx; AB 3 (Garden City: 1970), pp. xxxiv-xxxvii. This massive work is distinguished by its use of Ugaritic and other Northwest Semitic texts to clarify the meaning of the psalms. Many of Dahood's parallels are dubious, but an impressive number remain.

31. A. A. Anderson, *Psalms*, NCB (London: 1972) 1:43-51.

32. See E. Slomovic, "Toward an Understanding of the Formation of Historical Titles in the Book of Psalms," *ZAW* 91 (1979): 350-380; B. S. Childs, *Introduction to the Old Testament as Scripture* (Philadelphia: 1979), pp. 520-522.

33. C. S. Lewis, *Reflections on the Psalms* (New York: 1958), pp. 20-33, has helpful comments on these cursings.

34. Trans. D. M. Stalker, 2 vols. (New York: 1962-1965) 1:355-459.

CHAPTER 33 — WISDOM LITERATURE

1. This document shows the intensely religious form that wisdom could take in the First Intermediate Period: "Do not trust in length of years, for they regard a lifetime as (but) an hour. A man remains over after death, and his deeds are placed beside him in heaps. However, existence yonder is for eternity, and he who complains of it is a fool. (But) as for him who reaches it without wrongdoing, he shall exist yonder like a god, stepping out freely like the lords of eternity" (*ANET*, p. 415).

2. "Sumerian Wisdom Literature: A Preliminary Survey," *BASOR* 122 (1951): 28-31. See W. McKane, *Proverbs: A New Approach*, OTL (Philadelphia: 1970), pp. 51-208, for a very useful survey of Egyptian and Mesopotamian wisdom. See also R. J. Williams, "Wisdom in the Ancient Near East," *IDBS*, pp. 949-952.

3. L. R. Mac-Fisher, "A Survey and Reading Guide to the Didactic Literature of Ugarit: Prolegomenon to a Study on the Sage," *The Sage in Israel and the Ancient Near East*, ed. J. G. Gammie and L. Perdue (Winona Lake: 1990), pp. 67-81; and "The Scribe (and Sage) in the Royal Court at Ugarit," *ibid.*, pp. 109-115.

4. W. G. Lambert, *Babylonian Wisdom Literature* (London: 1960), p. 1.

5. See A. Bentzen, *Introduction to the Old Testament*, 2 vols. (Copenhagen: 1948) 1: 174-177. On the importance of "observation and experience," see also C. Westermann, *Roots of Wisdom* (Louisville: 1995), pp. 6-38.

6. J. A. Wilson in *ANET*, p. 412.

7. Lambert, *Babylonian Wisdom Literature*, pp. 96-107.

8. *Ibid.*

9. *Ibid.*, p. 220. The point seems to be that people sometimes trip on snares they lay for others — a familiar motif in Proverbs (12:13; 29:6).

10. *Ibid.*, pp. 217, 219.

11. See R. H. Pfeiffer in *ANET*, pp. 410f.; note Jotham's tale in Judg. 9:7-15, where the trees debate which of them should be king.

12. Lambert, *Babylonian Wisdom Literature*, pp. 230, 232. The latter anticipates the modern saying: "With friends like these, who needs enemies?"

13. *Ibid.*, p. 232; a favorite biblical analogy (e.g., Ezek. 34:5; Zech. 10:2; Matt. 9:36).

14. *Ibid.*, p. 235.

15. *Ibid.*, p. 247. This cause-and-effect proverb, a rhetorical question expecting the answer "of course not," is reminiscent of the sayings in Amos 3:3-6.

16. *Ibid.*, p. 249; cf. "you reap what you sow" or "your sins will find you out."

17. J. Paterson, *The Book That Is Alive* (New York: 1954), pp. 12ff.

18. R. C. Trench, *From Proverbs, and Their Lessons*, 7th ed. (London: 1857), summarized by Paterson, *Book That Is Alive*, p. 47. For a thorough study of proverbs in antiquity, see J. M. Thompson, *The Form and Function of Proverbs in Ancient Israel* (Hague: 1974).

19. Excerpts are from Lambert, *Babylonian Wisdom Literature*, pp. 33-61.

20. These couplets illustrate the use of synonymous parallelism in Akkadian poetry. As in Hebrew writings, this parallelism marks off poetry from prose.

21. Lambert, *Babylonian Wisdom Literature*, pp. 63-91.

22. This analysis follows the more serious interpretation of the text rather than Speiser's satirical interpretation, evaluated by Lambert, *Babylonian Wisdom Literature*, pp.

139-141; the quotations are from pp. 145-149. See also T. Jacobsen in H. Frankfort et al., *The Intellectual Adventure of Ancient Man* (Chicago: 1946), pp. 216-218, and W. S. LaSor, pp. 104-106 in G. Rendsburg et al., eds., *The Bible World*, Festschrift C. H. Gordon (New York: 1980).

23. The use of other wisdom techniques, like fables (e.g., Judg. 9:8-15) and riddles (e.g., 14:12-19), is further evidence of the role of the wise in Israel. See E. Jones, *Proverbs and Ecclesiastes*, Torch Bible Commentary (Naperville: 1961), pp. 28-31; G. von Rad, *Wisdom in Israel*, trans. J. D. Martin (Nashville: 1972), pp. 24-50.

24. On clan life as a setting for the development of both wisdom and legal sayings, see E. Gerstenberger, "The Woe-Oracles of the Prophets," *JBL* 81 (1962): 249-263; and H. W. Wolff, *Amos the Prophet: The Man and His Background*, trans. F. McCorley, ed. J. Reumann (Philadelphia: 1973). Carol R. Fontaine, "The Sage in Family and Tribe," *Sage in Israel*, p. 155.

25. For a recent interpretation of Solomon's role, see W. A. Brueggeman, "The Social Significance of Solomon as a Patron of Wisdom," *Sage in Ancient Israel*, pp. 117-132.

26. For negative answers to both these questions see R. N. Whybray, *The Intellectual Tradition in the Old Testament*, BZAW 135 (1974), and "The Sage in the Royal Court," *Sage in Ancient Israel*, pp. 133-139, who argues for an understanding of the wise as members of the intelligentsia who may have followed other vocations or professions. He is skeptical of the view that formal schools existed in the monarchic period. For a more positive approach to the question of school and office, see A. Lemaire, "The Sage in School and Temple," *Sage in Ancient Israel*, pp. 165-181.

27. See J. Lindblom, "Wisdom in the Old Testament Prophets," in M. Noth and D. W. Thomas, eds., *Wisdom in Israel and in the Ancient Near East*, VTSup 3 (1955): 192-204; also Wolff, *Amos the Prophet*; J. W. Whedbee, *Isaiah and Wisdom* (Nashville: 1970); R. C. van Leeuwen, "The Sage in the Prophetic Literature," *Sage in Ancient Israel*, pp. 298-306.

28. The role of the wise as statesmen has been stressed, perhaps too much, by McKane, *Prophets and Wise Men* (Naperville, Ill.: 1965).

29. See D. A. Hubbard, "The Wisdom Movement and Israel's Covenant Faith," *Tyndale Bulletin* 17 (1966): 3-33.

30. On *order* as foundational to wisdom thinking, see W. Zimmerli, "Concerning the Structure of Old Testament Wisdom," pp. 175-199 in J. L. Crenshaw, ed., *Studies in Ancient Israelite Wisdom* (New York: 1976): "God's claims need not be called into conflict with those of man. Rather, it is his belief that man's requirements in life are best cared for within the divine order of the world, and that man's real claim on advantage will be entirely satisfied through willing participation in the world's divine ordering" (p. 198); von Rad, *Wisdom in Israel*: "One becomes competent and expert as far as the orders in life are concerned only if one begins from knowledge about God" (p. 67); H. H. Schmid, *Wesen und Geschichte der Weisheit*, BZAW 101 (1966): 21. For a thorough analysis of the theological roots and fruits of Old Testament wisdom, see Leo G. Perdue, *Wisdom and Creation: The Theology of Wisdom Literature* (Nashville: 1994).

31. For the contribution of wisdom literature to the New Testament, see H. Conzelmann, "Wisdom in the New Testament," *IDBS*, pp. 956-960. Also B. Witherington III, *Jesus the Sage: The Pilgrimage of Wisdom* (Minneapolis: 1994).

CHAPTER 34 — PROVERBS

1. Carole R. Fontaine, *Traditional Sayings in the Old Testament: A Contextual Study* (Sheffield: 1982).

2. See A. R. Johnson, "לb℮m," *VTSup* 3 (1955): 162-169. See W. McKane, *Proverbs: A New Approach,* OTL (Philadelphia: 1970), p. 26, for the assumption that *māšāl* has a meaning such as "model," "exemplar," "paradigm."

3. B. S. Childs, *Introduction to the Old Testament as Scripture* (Philadelphia: 1979), pp. 551f.

4. M. Weinfeld, "The Origins of the Humanism in Deuteronomy," *JBL* 80 (1961): 241-247.

5. G. von Rad (*Wisdom in Israel,* trans. J. D. Martin [Nashville and New York: 1972], p. 153) observes that Wisdom in Prov. 8 "has no divine status, nor is it a hypostatized attribute of Yahweh; it is, rather, something created by Yahweh and assigned to its proper function."

6. C. H. Dodd, *The Interpretation of the Fourth Gospel* (Cambridge: 1953), p. 275: "It is difficult to resist the conclusion that, while the Logos . . . has many of the traits of the Word of God in the Old Testament, it is on the other side a concept closely similar to that of Wisdom, that is to say, the hypostatized thought of God projected in creation, and remaining as an immanent power within the world and in man." See H. Ringgren, *Word and Wisdom* (Lund: 1947), for a survey of the personification of wisdom in the ancient Near East; also J. A. Emerton, "Wisdom," in *Tradition and Interpretation,* ed. G. W. Anderson (Oxford: 1979), pp. 231-233.

7. See W. D. Davies, "The Old and the New Torah: Christ the Wisdom of God," pp. 147-176 in *Paul and Rabbinic Judaism* (New York: 1967); R. G. Hamerton-Kelly, *Preexistence, Wisdom, and the Son of Man,* Society for New Testament Studies Monograph 21 (Cambridge: 1973); R. L. Wilken, ed., *Aspects of Wisdom in Judaism and Early Christianity* (Notre Dame: 1975); E. J. Schnabel, *Law and Wisdom from Ben Sira to Paul,* WUNT 2 (Tübingen: 1985): 16; Celia Deutsch, *Hidden Wisdom and the Easy Yoke,* JSNTS 18 (Sheffield: 1987); B. Witherington III, *Jesus the Sage: The Pilgrimage of Wisdom* (Minneapolis: 1994).

8. W. F. Albright, *VTSup* 3 (1955): 5.

9. See O. Kaiser, *Introduction to the Old Testament,* trans. J. Sturdy (Minneapolis: 1975), p. 379.

10. R. N. Whybray, "Book of Proverbs," *IDBS,* p. 702.

11. For example, J. Goldingay, "The Arrangement of Sayings in Proverbs 10–15," *JSOT* 61 (1994): 75-83. Also T. Hildebrandt, "Proverbial Pairs: Compositional Units in Proverbs 10–29," *JBL* 107 (1988): 207-224.

12. J. Crenshaw, "Wisdom," p. 231 in J. H. Hayes, ed., *Old Testament Form Criticism* (San Antonio: 1974).

13. Von Rad, *Wisdom in Israel,* p. 120.

14. See N. K. Gottwald, *A Light to the Nations* (New York: 1959), p. 472. Von Rad is much more positive in judging the quality of the proverbs.

15. How that doctrine of reward and retribution worked has been the subject of sharp debate. K. Koch sees the punishment meted out to the foolish as not the work of God directly but the inevitable result of their wicked acts — an almost automatic form of retribution (26:27), only occasionally aided by Yahweh. H. Gese also affirms a connection between an act and its consequences but allows for a greater degree of divine freedom and intervention (cf. 21:31). For a summary of these arguments, see Emerton, "Wisdom," pp. 216-218.

16. Von Rad, *Wisdom in Israel,* p. 50.

17. G. E. Bryce, *A Legacy of Wisdom: The Egyptian Contribution to the Wisdom of Israel* (Lewisburg, Pa.: 1979). C. Westermann, *Roots of Wisdom: The Oldest Proverbs of Israel and Other Peoples* (Louisville: 1995), pp. 86-91, 155-159.

18. Trans. J. Wilson, *ANET,* pp. 421-425.

19. See C. H. Gordon, *Ugaritic Textbook,* Analecta Orientalia 38 (Rome: 1965), §§7.7, 17.3.

20. On the numerical form, see von Rad, *Wisdom in Israel,* pp. 36f., 122f.; Crenshaw, "Wisdom," pp. 236-238. See also Chapter 17, above.

21. See von Rad, *Wisdom in Israel,* pp. 97-110; also W. Zimmerli, "The Place and Limit of Wisdom in the Framework of the Old Testament Theology," *SJT* 17 (1964): 146-158.

22. McKane, *Proverbs,* pp. 17-21.

23. Von Rad, *Wisdom in Israel,* p. 62; see Kaiser, *Introduction,* p. 383.

24. See C. T. Fritsch, "The Gospel in the Book of Proverbs," *Theology Today* 7 (1950): 169-183; R. E. Murphy, "The Kerygma of the Book of Proverbs," *Interp* 20 (1966): 3-14. A list of "subject-studies" has been compiled by D. Kidner, *The Proverbs,* TOTC (Chicago: 1964), pp. 31-56. See especially B. Witherington III, *Jesus the Sage,* pp. 212-380.

CHAPTER 35 — JOB

1. M. H. Pope, *Job,* AB, 3rd ed. (Garden City: 1979), pp. 5f. Parallels have been found in Akkadian texts from Mari, Alalakh, and Ugarit. See W. F. Albright, "Northwest-Semitic Names in a List of Egyptian Slaves from the Eighteenth Century B.C.," *JAOS* 74 (1954): 222-233.

2. Daniel or Danel here is usually considered the Ugaritic hero Dan'el rather than the biblical figure whose book is included among the Major Prophets. The Aqht legend describes Dan'el as a king who dispenses justice to the widow and fatherless. See S. B. Frost, "Daniel," *IDB* 1:761.

3. Cf. N. Sarna, "Epic Substratum in the Prose of Job," *JBL* 76 (1957): 13-25.

4. J. Hartley, *The Book of Job* (Grand Rapids: 1988), pp. 13-15.

5. R. Gordis, *The Book of God and Man* (Chicago: 1965), p. 53.

6. The differences in theology, ethics, tone, and mood between Job and alleged parallels (e.g., the Indian legend of Hariscandra, *Sumerian Man and His God,* Akkadian Ludlul Bel Nemeqi, Babylonian Theodicy, Babylonian Poem of the Righteous Sufferer, Egyptian Protests of the Eloquent Peasant, or Admonitions of Ipu-wer) are so striking as to highlight not Job's dependence on earlier documents but the uniqueness of the work. For summaries, see Pope, *Job,* pp. lvii–lxxi; F. I. Andersen, *Job,* TOTC (Downers Grove, Ill.: 1976), pp. 23-32.

7. Andersen, *ibid.,* p. 32.

8. O. Kaiser, *Introduction to the Old Testament,* trans. J. Sturdy (Minneapolis: 1975), p. 391, citing K. Budde.

9. G. von Rad, *Old Testament Theology,* trans. D. M. G. Stalker, 2 vols. (New York: 1962-1965) 1:412.

10. D. Robertson, *The Old Testament and the Literary Critic* (Philadelphia: 1977), p. 41.

11. For a survey of wisdom forms in Job and elsewhere, see J. L. Crenshaw, "Wisdom," pp. 225-264 in J. H. Hayes, ed., *Old Testament Form Criticism* (San Antonio: 1974).

12. N. C. Habel, *The Book of Job,* OTL (Philadelphia: 1985), pp. 275-276.

13. This sarcastic interpretation of ch. 28 is developed by Robertson, *Old Testament and the Literary Critic,* p. 46.

14. A. Weiser, *Das Buch Hiob* (Göttingen: 1974), p. 214.

15. Gordis, *The Book of God and Man,* p. 105, notes that Job's major complaints against God — innocent suffering, unjust persecution, and refusal to hear — are answered in reverse order: refusal to hear (vv. 11-30), unjust persecution (34:1-30), innocent suffering (vv. 31-37).

16. Inclusion of daughters in the inheritance seems remarkable in view of Israelite law (Num. 27:8), where a daughter inherited her father's property only if no son existed to serve as heir.

17. The twofold restoration of Job's possessions, especially his livestock (vv. 10, 12), may show wry humor — Israelite law required thieves to pay double for stealing an ox, ass, or sheep (Exod. 22:4 [MT 3]). Some versions, following the Qumran Targum (11 QtgJob), read *šibʿānâ* (42:13) as a dual form ("twice seven") and credit Job with fourteen sons in the restoration (cf. Dhorme, Gordis).

18. Furthermore, recent studies on nomadism in the ancient Near East have modified the older view which was based largely on Arabic models of camel nomadism. New theories posit a villager-pastoralist symbiosis between the settled agricultural community and the pastoralists moving seasonally into the steppe with the flocks seeking pasturage. Villagers and pastoralists were integrated parts of one tribal community. For a brief but thorough resume of the theory and its evidence, see W. G. Dever, "The Patriarchal Traditions," pp. 102-117 in J. H. Hayes and J. M. Miller, eds., *Israelite and Judaean History,* OTL (Philadelphia: 1966).

19. Another possibility is that the text of this book became damaged during the centuries of transmission. This would explain the abbreviated and disjointed nature of Bildad's and Job's last speeches as well as the absence of a speech from Zophar.

20. E.g., A. Robert and A. Feuillet, *Introduction to the Old Testament* (New York: 1968), pp. 425f.: "The invocation of wisdom seems to be an interpolation. . . . One might even say that the theme does not seem to be occasioned at all by the statements of Job and his friends." See H. H. Rowley, *Job,* NCBC (Grand Rapids: 1980), pp. 13f.

21. P. Skehan, "Job's Final Plea (Job 29–31) and the Lord's Reply (Job 38–41)," *Bibl* 45 (1964): 51-62.

22. R. Gordis, *The Book of Job* (New York: 1978), p. 558.

23. O. Eissfeldt, *The Old Testament: An Introduction,* trans. P. R. Ackroyd (New York: 1965), p. 457.

24. Elihu's youth, 32:6-10, may explain why he is not mentioned in the prologue; perhaps he tagged along as a student of the others and was treated as part of the entourage not worthy of being named.

25. The prologue indicates that the three friends came from a distance and had to set a time and place (2:11) of rendezvous before they visited Job.

26. R. Gordis, *The Book of Job,* p. 581.

27. H. Gese, *Lehre und Wirtlichkeit in der alten Weisheit* (Tübingen: 1958). N. H. Snaith has also used this pattern to reconstruct the development of the text in three stages: (a) prologue and epilogue (without mention of friends), Job's monologues (chs. 3; 29–31) and apology (40:3-5), and Yahweh's speeches (chs. 38–41); (b) account of the friends (2:10-13; 42:7-10) and dialogue (chs. 4–28); and (c) Elihu's speeches (chs. 32–37); see *The Book of Job: Its Origin and Purpose,* SBT, 2nd ser. 11 (Naperville, Ill.: 1968).

28. C. Westermann, *The Structure of the Book of Job: A Form-Critical Analysis,* trans. C. A. Muenchow (Philadelphia: 1981).

29. G. von Rad finds the dialogues not "contentious debates" but "complaints from the one side and pastoral words of comfort from the other"; *Wisdom in Israel,* p. 209. Note J. A. Soggin: "As well as being a piece of wisdom literature, the book of Job is a dramatic representation of the literary genre of the 'individual lament' in a dramatic form"; *Introduction to the Old Testament,* trans. J. Bowden, OTL (Philadelphia: 1976), p. 389.

30. See G. Fohrer, review of Westermann, *Der Aufbau des Buches Hiob,* VT 7 (1957): 107-111.

31. B. Gemser, "The *Rib-* or Controversy-Pattern in Hebrew Mentality," *VTSup* 3 (1955): 135. This view is based in part on L. Köhler, *Hebrew Man,* trans. P. R. Ackroyd (Nashville: 1956), which reconstructs ancient Israelite court procedures partly on the basis of Job.

32. M. B. Crook, *The Cruel God: Job's Search for the Meaning of Suffering* (Boston: 1959), p. 5.

33. E.g., C. Fries, *Das philosophische Gesprach vom Hiob bis Platon* (Tübingen: 1904).

34. H. M. Kallen, *The Book of Job as a Greek Tragedy Restored* (New York: 1918); cf. R. B. Sewall, *The Vision of Tragedy,* 2nd ed. (New Haven: 1980), pp. 9-24.

35. J. W. Whedbee, "The Comedy of Job," *Semeia* 7 (1977): 1; see J. A. Holland, "On the Form of the Book of Job," *Australian Journal of Biblical Archaeology* 2 (1972): 160-177. For a view akin to this but denying the happy ending, see Robertson: "Irony pervades the entire book and provides the decisive key to understanding its complicated theme"; *The Old Testament and the Literary Critic,* p. 34.

36. Midrash *Gen. Rab.* 67; Talmud *B. Bat.* 15a.

37. For the possible range of meaning for *māšāl,* see D. A. Hubbard, "Proverb," *ISBE* 3 (1986): 1013. Also Chapter 34 above.

38. Andersen, *Job,* pp. 36-37.

39. So also Pope: "The book viewed as a unit is *sui generis* and no single term or combination of terms is adequate to describe it"; *Job,* p. xxxi.

40. Gordis, *The Book of God and Man,* pp. 174-189; see also *Poets, Prophets and Sages* (Bloomington: 1971), pp. 104-159.

41. Gordis, *The Book of Job,* p. 20, reviews various interpretations and settles on this: "a man will give anyone else's skin on behalf of, i.e., to save his own skin."

42. Translation from Gordis, *The Book of God and Man,* p. 179.

43. *Ibid.,* p. 181. Gordis extends the quotation to include vv. 3f.

44. *Ibid.,* p. 184. Illustrations of these last two uses of quotations also can be found in Ecclesiastes (see above, pp. 503, 505), suggesting that this was a standard technique of unconventional wisdom.

45. On ch. 21, see *ibid.,* pp. 185f.

46. Andersen, *Job,* p. 33.

47. Von Rad, "Job XXXVIII and Ancient Egyptian Wisdom," pp. 281-291 in *The Problem of the Hexateuch,* trans. E. W. T. Dicken (Edinburgh: 1966); cf. A. H. Gardiner, *Ancient Egyptian Onomastica,* 3 vols. (London: 1947).

48. G. E. Bryce, *A Legacy of Wisdom: The Egyptian Contribution to the Wisdom of Israel* (Lewisberg, Pa.: 1979), pp. 164f. Similarly perhaps the detailed descriptions of Behemoth (40:15-24) and Leviathan (ch. 41) reflect forms in which sages set their scientific study of the animal world.

49. *ANET,* pp. 477f.

50. Similar in form is 27:13, actually an "introductory appraisal" because it precedes the section it summarizes (vv. 14-23).

51. Note B. S. Childs: "The present shape of the book seeks to address a wide range

of different questions about wisdom which vary in accordance with the battle being fought. The contours of both the outer and inner limits of wisdom are carefully drawn, and any attempt to cut the tension is to sacrifice the specific canonical role of this remarkable book"; *Introduction to the Old Testament as Scripture* (Philadelphia: 1979), p. 543; see also p. 544 on the book's function with respect to the larger canon, particularly in supplying "a critical corrective to the reading of the other wisdom books, especially Proverbs and Ecclesiastes."

52. Robert and Feuillet, *Introduction*, p. 425.

53. For further background on a biblical approach to suffering, see H. W. Robinson, *The Cross in the Old Testament* (London: 1955); E. S. Gerstenberger and W. Schrage, *Suffering*, trans. J. E. Steely (Nashville: 1980).

CHAPTER 36 — ECCLESIASTES

1. *Qôheleṭ* (1:1f., 12; 7:27; 12:8-10) is a feminine participle of a verb derived from *qāhāl* "congregation" or "assembly." This form apparently denoted an office and secondarily was used to describe the one who held the office. Ezra 2:55-57 contains similar cases of feminine participles which once designated offices but became proper names: Hassophereth "scribe" and Pochereth-hazzebaim "tender of gazelles." Cf. English names like Penman and Fowler.

2. The Talmud (*B. Bat.* 15a) also included the opinion that these books, along with Isaiah, were put in written form by King Hezekiah and his colleagues; see Prov. 25:1.

3. The Mishnah ("second law") contains the earliest rabbinic commentary on various biblical commandments, organized by subjects. It was compiled early in the Christian era. Cf. J. Neusner, "Talmud," *ISBE* 4 (1988): 717-724, esp. p. 718.

4. Though W. F. Albright posited a slightly earlier (fifth century) date *(Yahweh and the Gods of Canaan)*, Franz Delitzsch's verdict still stands: "If the Book of Koheleth were of old Solomonic origin, then there is no history of the Hebrew language. . . . the Book of Koheleth bears the stamp of the postexilian form of the language"; C. F. Keil and Delitzsch, *Commentary on the Old Testament*, repr. 10 vols. (Grand Rapids: 1973) 6:190. D. C. Fredericks, *Qoheleth's Language: Reevaluating Its Nature and Date*, ANETS 3 (Lewiston, N.Y.: 1988), has argued that a preexilic date is not ruled out by Qoheleth's language.

5. J. Muilenburg had dated these fragments late in the second century B.C.; see "A Qoheleth Scroll from Qumran," *BASOR* 135 (1954): 20-28.

6. See R. E. Murphy, *The Tree of Life*, ABRL (New York: 1990), pp. 172-173, for a helpful summary of the debate over possible foreign influences. Murphy's conclusion is similar to that of O. Eissfeldt, who acknowledges that Qoheleth's Hellenistic environment may have made a modest contribution in thought and language, but "there is nothing more than casual contact" with any particular Greek school or writings; *The Old Testament: An Introduction*, trans. P. R. Ackroyd (New York: 1965), pp. 498f.

7. Albright, *VTSup* 3 (1955): 15. M. Dahood's arguments for a Phoenician linguistic background have not carried the day; "Canaanite-Phoenician Influence in Qoheleth," *Bibl* 33 (1952): 30-52, 191-221; "The Phoenician Background of Qoheleth," *Bibl* 47 (1966): 264-282. A. Weiser, citing supposed Egyptian influence on thought and Greek impact on language, argues for an Alexandrian origin; *The Old Testament: Its Formation and Development*, trans. D. M. Barton (New York: 1961), pp. 309f.

8. Qoheleth's context and audience must have been affluent. Otherwise his denunciations of wealth, pleasure, and fame would have fallen on deaf ears. See R. Gordis, "The Social Background of Wisdom Literature," pp. 196f. in *Poets, Prophets and Sages* (Bloomington: 1971).

9. For the development of these themes and their role in the book's structure, see A. G. Wright, "The Riddle of the Sphinx: The Structure of the Book of Qoheleth," *CBQ* 30 (1968): 313-334.

10. For a discussion of possible meanings for *hebel*, see E. M. Good, *Irony in the Old Testament* (Philadelphia: 1965), pp. 176-183; Murphy, *The Tree of Life*, pp. 53-54, 62; D. A. Hubbard, *Ecclesiastes, Song of Solomon*, CC 15B (Dallas: 1991), pp. 46-47.

11. Good, *Irony in the Old Testament*, p. 171. Murphy's comment is apt (*The Tree of Life*, p. 50): "The work . . . lies somewhere between a treatise and a collection of sayings and thoughts." Tremper Longman III, *Fictional Akkadian Autobiography: A Generic and Comparative Study* (Winona Lake: 1991), pp. 120-123, notes comparisons in overall structure between Qoheleth and Akkadian documents which combine first person narrative with didactic sections.

12. The variety of contemporary analyses is noted by Wright, "Riddle of the Sphinx," 314-320. Wright's own construction offers a commendable alternative which has the merit of pointing out the book's subtle inner unity.

13. Adapted from an outline privately circulated by R. B. Laurin; see Laurin, *The Layman's Introduction to the Old Testament* (Valley Forge: 1970), pp. 104f. The adaptation highlights the conclusions about enjoying life now. A pioneer in the study of Ecclesiastes, C. D. Ginsburg recognized their importance as boundary markers for the book's major divisions; *Coheleth* (London: 1861).

14. G. A. Barton, *The Book of Ecclesiastes*, ICC (Edinburgh: 1908), pp. 43-46. As Wisdom glosses, Barton listed 4:5; 5:3, 7a; 7:1a, 3, 5-9, 11f., 19; 8:1; 9:17f.; 10:1-3, 8-14a, 15, 18f. Among the alleged pious additions were, e.g., 2:26; 3:17; 7:18b, 26b, 29; 8:2b, 3a, 5-6a, 11-13; 11:9b; 12:1a, 13f. Decades later still, E. Jones took an almost identical approach; *Proverbs and Ecclesiastes*, Torch Bible Commentary (Naperville: 1961), pp. 259-262.

15. For outlines that feature the book's unity, see H. L. Ginsberg, "The Structure and Contents of the Book of Koheleth," *VTSup* 3 (1955): 138-149, and Wright, "Riddle of the Sphinx," p. 313f.

16. Murphy, *The Tree of Life*, p. 52: "it seems better to take the book [except for the epilogue, 12:9-14] as all of one piece despite the difficulties. This allows for tensions . . . within the author himself. . . ."

17. R. Gordis, *Koheleth — the Man and his World* (New York: 1968), p. 110. For a summary of the efforts of W. Zimmerli, K. Galling, and F. Ellermeier to divide the book into literary units (usually more than thirty), virtually all attributed to Qoheleth, see O. Kaiser, *Introduction to the Old Testament*, trans. J. Sturdy (Minneapolis: 1975), p. 398.

18. *Wisdom in Israel*, trans. J. D. Martin (Nashville and New York: 1972), p. 227.

19. *Die Weisheit des Predigers Salomo* (Berlin: 1936), p. 26. J. L. Crenshaw cites the stylistic affinity of these confessions to the Egyptian royal confessions (German *Bekenntnis*); "Wisdom," p. 257 in J. H. Hayes, ed., *Old Testament Form Criticism* (San Antonio: 1974).

20. "What Does It Profit a Man? The Wisdom of Koheleth," *Judaism* 20 (1971): 179.

21. Ellermeier finds three subgroups: (1) unitary critical reflection: the observation begins with a negative and consistently criticizes an optimistic understanding of life (3:16-22; 6:1-6); (2) critical broken reflection: the starting observation is positive, then criticizes false optimism (3:1-15; 4:13-16); and (3) critical reverse broken reflection: the thought begins negatively, then progresses to something of value, though the initial reservation remains (4:4-6; 5:13-20 [MT 12-19]); *Qohelet* 1 (Herzberg: 1967): 88ff. For a summary of Ellermeier's analysis, which is based on the direction of the argument more than the precise literary form, see Kaiser, *Introduction*, p. 399.

22. Ampler treatment of the use of proverbs in various forms of argumentation may

be found in R. Gordis, *Koheleth*, pp. 95-108; and in his "Quotations in Biblical, Oriental, and Rabbinic Literature," pp. 104-159 in *Poets, Prophets and Sages*.

23. Other rhetorical questions are found in 1:3; 2:2, 12, 15, 19, 25; 3:21; 5:6, 11 [MT 5, 10]; 6:6, 8, 11f.; 7:16f.; 8:1, 4, 7. The answers they insist on are almost always negative: "nothing," "none," "no one."

24. For the "funeral" interpretation of this language see G. Ogden, *Qoheleth* (Sheffield: 1987) and especially M. Fox, *Qohelet and His Contradictions* (Sheffield: 1985). For "aging" as the meaning see J. Crenshaw, "Wisdom," in Hayes, ed., *Old Testament Form Criticism*, pp. 246ff.

25. The opposites "born-die," "plant-pluck," etc. are examples of merismus, a literary device in which extremes are mentioned to cover everything in between.

26. See 1:3, 9, 14; 2:11, 17-20, 22; 3:16; 4:1, 3, 7, 15; 5:13, 18 [MT 12, 17]; 6:1, 12; 8:9, 15, 17; 9:3, 6, 9, 11, 13; 10:5.

27. W. J. Fuerst, *The Books of Ruth, Esther, Ecclesiastes, The Song of Songs, Lamentations*, CBC (Cambridge: 1975), p. 103.

28. See von Rad, "The Doctrine of the Proper Time," pp. 138-143 in *Wisdom in Israel*.

29. "Eternity" is probably the best translation of *'ôlām* here, provided it is not taken in quantitative terms alone, the mere extension of time into the distant future. In this context, it must stand for "God's ways in the world," "the course of worldly events as God alone shapes and understands them." He has granted the consciousness that he is at work but not the power to grasp what he is doing. See Gordis, *Koheleth*, pp. 221f.; Williams, *Judaism* 20 (1971): 182-185.

30. Wright, "Riddle of the Sphinx," pp. 325f.

31. Von Rad, *Wisdom in Israel*, pp. 226-237.

32. W. Zimmerli, *SJT* 17 (1964): 158.

33. *Ibid.*

34. See Williams, *Judaism* 10 (1971): 185-190, on these terms.

35. Note Zimmerli's summation, *SJT* 17 (1964): 156: "In a manner hitherto unheard-of in the Old Testament, Ecclesiastes sees death as the power that takes away the power of the whole creation and even of man's Wisdom."

36. See 2:10, 21, 24; 3:13; 4:4, 6, 8f.; 5:15, 19 [MT 14, 18]; 6:7; 8:15; 10:15; verb form *'āmal*: 1:3; 2:11, 19f.; 5:16 [MT 15]; 8:17.

37. See 2:24f.; 3:12, 22; 5:18-20 [MT 17-19]; 7:14; 8:15; 9:7-9; 11:8f.

38. M. Dahood notes the frequency of commercial terms like *(yitrôn, môtar)*, toil *('āmāl)*, business *('inyān)*, money *(kesep)*, portion *(ḥeleq)*, success *(kišrôn)*, riches *('ōšer)*, owner *(ba'al)*, and deficit *(ḥesrôn)*.

39. J. S. Wright has captured well this dominant note of joy; "The Interpretation of Ecclesiastes," *Evangelical Quarterly* 18 (1946): 18-34. See also R. E. Murphy, "Qohélet le sceptique," *Concilium* 119 (1976): 60; R. K. Johnston, " 'Confessions of a Workaholic': A Reappraisal of Qoheleth," *CBQ* 38 (1976): 14-28.

40. Note B. S. Childs: "By being set in the eschatological framework of a coming divine judgment, Koheleth's message is not only limited to present human activity, but sharply relativized in the light of the new and fuller dimension of divine wisdom. When later Jews and Christians contrasted the wisdom of this world (1 Cor. 1:20) with the wisdom of God, they were interpreting the Hebrew scriptures according to their canonical shaping"; *Old Testament as Scripture*, pp. 588f.

41. For a Christian application of Qoheleth's main themes, see D. A. Hubbard, *Ecclesiastes, Song of Solomon*, CC 15B (Dallas: 1991). The "Epilogues" to each section try to capture these Christian insights.

CHAPTER 37 — THE SONG OF SONGS

1. Mishnah *Yad.* 3:5.

2. B. S. Childs, *Introduction to Old Testament as Scripture* (Philadelphia: 1979), p. 578.

3. Talmud *B. Bat.* 15a attributes the song to Hezekiah and his scribes, undoubtedly following Prov. 25:1.

4. *Pardēs* "orchard," 4:13; *appiryôn*, from Greek *phoreíon*, AV "chariot," but better NRSV "palanquin," 3:9.

5. *še* instead of *ʾašer*, except in 1:1, though early uses of *še* show that this evidence is suggestive more than conclusive.

6. See S. R. Driver, *Introduction to the Literature of the Old Testament*, 9th ed., repr. (Magnolia, Mass.: 1972), p. 448.

7. Mention of Tirzah (6:4) may argue against an exilic or postexilic date for at least this part of the Song. This ancient Canaanite city (Josh. 12:24), the first capital of the northern kingdom (1 Kgs. 14:17; 15:21; 16:6ff.), is not mentioned after *ca.* 750 (2 Kgs. 15:14, 16). A strong case for an early date for at least some of the poetry may be made from its obvious similarities with the Egyptian love poetry of the Eighteenth Dynasty (*ca.* 1250); see J. B. White, *A Study of the Language of Love in the Song of Songs and Ancient Egyptian Poetry*, SBL Dissertation Series 38 (Missoula: 1978), pp. 91-159; R. E. Murphy, "Song of Songs," *IDBS*, p. 837.

8. H. J. Schonfield, *The Song of Songs* (New York: 1959), pp. 75-83.

9. O. Kaiser, *Introduction to the Old Testament*, trans. J. Sturdy (Minneapolis: 1975), p. 366: "It should be assumed then that in Canticles we have a later collection of wedding and love songs from different periods."

10. Murphy, "Song of Songs."

11. Childs, *Old Testament as Scripture*, pp. 574-578.

12. See White, *Language of Love*, pp. 50-55, which combines the insights of F. Horst, "Die Formen des althebräischen Liebesliedes," pp. 176-187 in H. W. Wolff, ed., *Gottes Recht* (Munich: 1961), with those of W. Staerk, *Lyrik*, Die Schriften das Alten Testaments 3/1 (Göttingen: 1920), and E. Würthwein, *Die fünf Megilloth*, 2nd ed., HAT 18 (Tübingen: 1969). These literary analyses have been refined by R. Murphy, FOTL 13 (1981): 98-124.

13. The only name given the heroine (6:13; MT 7:1), its derivation and meaning are problematic. It has been linked to an unknown town of Shulam or considered a variant of Shunammite. Some identify her as Abishag, the Shunammite (1 Kgs. 1:3ff.). H. H. Rowley rejects these views, contending that the term is a feminine form of Solomon, "the Solomoness"; "The Meaning of the Shulammite," *AJSL* 56 (1939): 84-91.

14. A. Bentzen, *Introduction to the Old Testament*, 2 vols. (Copenhagen: 1948) 1:130. T. Boman offers useful insights regarding the figures of speech: e.g., comparisons between the maiden and a tower (4:4; 7:4f.), a wall (8:10), or Mt. Carmel (7:5) are expressions of her purity, her inaccessibility as a chaste and sheltered virgin aloof from the temptations of those who would seek to defile her. References to the dovelike qualities of the Shulammite (1:15; 2:14; 4:1) are also descriptive of her purity; *Hebrew Thought Compared with Greek*, trans. J. L. Moreau (Philadelphia: 1960), pp. 77-89.

15. Some passages are illuminated by an understanding of Semitic custom. E.g., the Shulammite's wish that her lover were her brother "that nursed at my mother's breast" in order that they might have ready access to each other probably refers not to a uterine brother (from the same womb) but a "milk brother," nursed by her mother. Rather than incest, such love could be enjoyed without shame or the normal social restrictions which

prevented easy access between lovers. See R. Patai, *Sex and Family in the Bible and the Middle East* (Garden City: 1959), pp. 194f.

16. F. Landry, "The Song of Songs," in *LGB*, p. 309.

17. This section is heavily indebted to H. H. Rowley, "The Interpretation of the Song of Songs," pp. 195-245 in *The Servant of the Lord and Other Essays on the Old Testament*, 2nd ed. (Oxford: 1965). For a massive compendium on the history of interpretation, see M. Pope, *Song of Songs*, AB 7C (Garden City: 1977), pp. 89-229.

18. In the beauty and purity of the Shulammite, some of the patristic interpreters (e.g., St. Ambrose) find the Virgin Mary; see F. X. Curley, "The Lady of the Canticle," *American Ecclesiastical Review* 133 (1955): 289-299. See also E. Ann Matter, *The Voice of My Beloved: The Song of Songs in Western Medieval Christianity* (Philadelphia: 1990).

19. A. Robert, R. Tournay, A. Feuillet, *Le Cantique des Cantiques*, Etudes Bibliques (Paris: 1973). See also R. J. Tournay, *Word of God, Song of Love*, trans. J. E. Crowley (New York: 1988).

20. The works of J. Fischer (*Das Hohe Lied*, Echter Bibel 10 [Würzburg: 1950]) and of L. Krinetski (*Das Hohe Lied*, Kommentare und Beiträge zum Alten und Neuen Testament [Düsseldorf: 1964]) illustrate the strengths and weaknesses of a typological approach; cf. White, *Language of Love*, pp. 20f. A variation is the "parabolic" interpretation ventured by T. R. D. Buzy, *Le Cantique des Cantiques*, 3rd ed. (Paris: 1953), and H. Schneider, *Das Hohelied*, Herders Bibel Kommentar 7/1 (Freiburg im Breisgau: 1962); both find in the Song a parable of a renewed covenant between Israel and Yahweh.

21. Franz Delitzsch in C. F. Keil and Delitzsch, *Commentary on the Old Testament*, repr. 10 vols. (Grand Rapids: 1973).

22. S. R. Driver, *An Introduction to the Literature of the Old Testament*, 9th ed. (Edinburgh: 1913).

23. J. G. Wettstein, Appendix to Keil-Delitzsch, *Commentary* 6, trans. M. G. Easton (repr. 1976), pp. 162-176.

24. K. Budde, *Das Hohelied*, HSAT (Tübingen: 1923).

25. Schonfield, *The Song of Songs*, pp. 32-34. See also Würthwein, *Die Fünf Megilloth*, pp. 25-71, and J.-P. Andet, "The Meaning of the Canticle of Canticles," *Theology Digest* 5 (1957): 88-92.

26. T. S. Meek, "The Song of Songs," *IB* 5:98-148.

27. See H. Schmökel, *Heilige Hochzeit und Hoheslied*, Abhandlungen fur die Künde des Morgenlandes 32/1 (Wiesbaden: 1956); S. N. Kramer, *The Sacred Marriage Rite* (Bloomington: 1969). White, *Language of Love*, p. 24, notes the imprecise nature of the supposed parallels and the vast differences in tone from the Song.

28. See White, *ibid.*, p. 24: "It is difficult to believe that sacred marriage could have been deeply rooted in Israel to the extent that a part of the ritual could have achieved inclusion into the Hebrew canon."

29. Pope, *Song of Songs*, pp. 210-229.

30. E.g., W. Rudolph, *Das Hohelied*, KAT 17/2 (Gütersloh: 1962); G. Gerlemann, *Das Hohelied*, BKAT 18 (Neukirchen: 1965).

31. See Rowley, *The Servant of the Lord*, p. 212. For a strong argument that the Song is an anthology rather than a unified poem, see White, *Language of Love*, pp. 28-34; also R. Gordis, *The Song of Songs and Lamentations*, rev. ed. (New York: 1974), p. 16: "If the Song of Songs be approached without any preconceptions, it reveals itself as a collection of lyrics."

32. This analysis is adapted from D. Hubbard, *Ecclesiastes, Song of Solomon*, CC 15B (Dallas: 1991), pp. 265-266. For another approach that stresses catchwords that cannot be

poems, see F. Landsberger, "Poetic Units within the Song of Songs," *JBL* 73 (1954): 203-216. For a similar scheme of several poems unified by repetition of key terms, see J. C. Exum, "A Literary and Structural Analysis of the Song of Songs," *ZAW* 85 (1973): 47-79. D. A. Dorsey, "Literary Structuring in the Song of Songs," *JSOT* 46 (1990), 81-96, argues well for a seven-poem pattern in which poem IV (3:6–5:1) is the center. It is wrapped in a symmetrical envelope with I (1:2–2:7) corresponding to VII (8:5-14), II (2:8-17) to VI (7:11–8:4), and III (3:1-5) to V (5:2–7:10).

33. See White, *Language of Love,* p. 27: "Although the Israelite social ethos did not exclude eroticism, the social morality did exclude adultery and emphasized the necessity of virginity before marriage. The Song . . . cannot, therefore, be understood as a tract justifying premarital sexual intercourse." S. C. Glickman stresses both the Song's unity and its marital setting by noting a chronological sequence from courtship (1:1–3:5), to wedding procession (3:6-11), to consummation (4:1–5:1), and beyond; *A Song for Lovers* (Downers Grove, Ill.: 1976).

34. E. J. Young, *An Introduction to the Old Testament,* rev. ed. (Grand Rapids: 1958), p. 354.

CHAPTER 38 — RUTH

1. Jewish tradition places the book of Ruth among the Writings. But the English Bible, following the LXX, the Vulgate, and some early Jewish tradition, places it immediately after Judges, since both books are set in the same time. For discussion see F. W. Bush, *Ruth, Esther.* WBC 9 (Dallas: 1990).

2. For alternatives, see R. L. Hubbard, Jr., *The Book of Ruth* (Grand Rapids: 1988), pp. 23-35 (Solomonic period); and Bush, *Ruth, Esther* (early postexilic era).

3. From Latin *levir* "brother-in-law," thus "marriage with the brother-in-law." For excellent summaries of the main arguments and problems, see H. H. Rowley, "The Marriage of Ruth," pp. 169-194 in *The Servant of the Lord and Other Essays on the Old Testament,* 2nd ed. (Oxford: 1965); also T. and D. Thompson, "Some Legal Problems in the Book of Ruth," *VT* 18 (1968): 79-99.

4. For a discussion of the issues involved, see Bush, *Ruth, Esther.*

5. Clearly, the closer the relationship to the deceased, the greater was the kinsman's duty to carry out the custom. One may, thus, hypothesize that the kinsman duty followed an order of obligation similar to those for inheritance (Num. 27:8-11) and enslaved relatives (Lev. 25:47-55), i.e., brother, paternal uncle, paternal uncle's son, and "the member of his clan who is most nearly related" (Num. 27:11).

6. The gate is where business and legal transactions were carried on in ancient cities. For its broader significance, see E. A. Speiser, " 'Coming' and 'Going' at the 'City' Gate," *BASOR* 144 (1956): 20-23.

7. They follow the foundational article of H. Gunkel, "Ruth," pp. 65-92 in *Reden und Aufsätze* (Göttingen: 1913). For the distinction between "novella" (Gunkel's term) and "short story," see W. L. Humphreys, "Novella," pp. 82-96 in G. Coats, ed., *Saga, Legend, Tale, Novella, Fable. Narrative Forms in Old Testament Literature* (Sheffield: 1985).

8. For an earlier study of the genre *short story,* see E. F. Campbell, "The Hebrew Short Story: Its Form, Style and Provenance," pp. 83-101 in H. N. Bream, R. D. Heim, and C. A. Moore, eds., *A Light unto My Path* (Philadelphia: 1974). On the genre of Ruth, see Bush, *Ruth, Esther.*

9. For the literary devices with which the author skillfully crafts the story, see the introduction to E. F. Campbell, Jr., *Ruth,* AB 7 (Garden City: 1975), pp. 10-18.

10. See B. S. Childs, *Introduction to the Old Testament as Scripture* (Philadelphia: 1979), p. 565.

11. See R. Hals, *The Theology of the Book of Ruth* (Philadelphia: 1969), pp. 18f.

12. Hals, "Book of Ruth," *IDBS,* p. 759.

13. This theology of absolute but hidden causality also undergirds the Court History of David (2 Sam. 9–20) and the story of Joseph (Gen. 37; 39–50).

14. 1:22; 2:2; 4:5, 10; in addition, her foreign origin is stressed in 2:6, 10.

15. Sensing this theme, some earlier scholars even thought the book was a postexilic polemic against the exclusivism of Ezra and Nehemiah. For bibliography, see Rowley, *The Servant of the Lord,* p. 173.

16. While a strong separation existed in Israelite society and faith (and so also in Judaism), Ruth and Jonah show that a significant segment of Old Testament society recognized the genuinely universal element in the nation's life and purpose.

17. K. Sakenfeld, *The Meaning of Hesed in the Hebrew Bible: A New Inquiry* (Missoula: 1978), pp. 233-234; in more popular form, see *idem, Faithfulness in Action* (Philadelphia: 1985), pp. 39-42.

18. See Childs, *Old Testament as Scripture,* p. 566. Hubbard (*The Book of Ruth,* pp. 39-42) suggests that the book has a political purpose, i.e., to show that God's providence brought about the rule of David.

CHAPTER 39 — LAMENTATIONS

1. Some rabbis also used the name *Qînôt,* meaning "funeral dirges" or "lamentations."

2. Suggestions that the poems echo the cruelty of Antiochus Epiphanus and his Syrian troops of the second century B.C. have not received general scholarly support. They may, however, have been used to mourn those tragic events.

3. Targum at Jer. 1:1; Talmud *B. Bat.* 15a; LXX and Vulgate headings. Note the LXX introduction: "And it came to pass after Israel was taken captive and Jerusalem laid waste that Jeremiah sat weeping and raised this lament over Jerusalem. . . ." During the intertestamental period, originally anonymous books commonly came to be attributed to prominent historical figures.

4. On acrostics, see below. The question here concerns the order of *'ayin* and *pe:* ch. 1 has *'ayin* before *pe;* chs. 2–4 have *pe* before *'ayin.* On alphabetic order in biblical acrostics, see R. Gordis, *Poets, Prophets and Sages* (Bloomington: 1971), pp. 82f. The reversal of *'ayin* and *pe* is found in the alphabet from 'Isbet Sartah (twelfth century B.C.) but may simply be a schoolboy's mistake; see D. R. Hillers, "Lamentations, Book of," *ABD* 4:139.

5. The acrostic is found in Babylonian poetry at least as early as 1000 B.C. Using a cuneiform syllabary, the author begins each line of the eleven-line stanza with the same character, and carries out this scheme for twenty-seven stanzas. Cf. W. S. LaSor, "Samples of Early Semitic Poetry," *The Bible World,* ed. G. Rendsburg et al., Festschrift C. H. Gordon (New York: 1980), esp. pp. 104-106; and W. Soll, *Psalm 119: Matrix, Form, and Meaning* (Washington, D.C.: 1991), pp. 5-34.

6. For the conceptual meaning of the acrostic pattern, see N. K. Gottwald, *Studies in the Book of Lamentations,* 2nd ed., SBT 14 (London: 1962), pp. 23-32; and Soll, *Psalm 119,* pp. 25-34.

7. See esp. sections of chs. 1–2; 4. For a brief discussion of rhythmic patterns that the dirge may use, see Gordis, *Poets, Prophets and Sages,* p. 68.

8. Sumerians used a lament form to mourn the loss of a city to a foreign invader. Apparent parallels with the book of Lamentations have raised questions about possible Sumerian influence. Direct influence seems unlikely, so it is safer to say that Lamentations is an example of a literary-liturgical pattern with early antecedents in Mesopotamia. For an account of the supposed parallels, see W. C. Gwaltney, Jr., "The Biblical Book of Lamentations in the Context of Near Eastern Lament Literature," in W. W. Hallo et al., eds., *Scripture in Context* II (Winona Lake: 1983), pp. 191-211.

9. The Hebrew construction is an appositive, to be understood as "daughter which is Jerusalem" (likewise the frequent "daughter of Zion," e.g., 2:8, 10, 13). "Daughter" is a term of endearment, and the phrases could be translated "Cherished Jerusalem" or "Fair Zion." For possible broader connotations, see E. R. Follis, "The Holy City as Daughter," pp. 173-184 in Follis, ed., *Directions in Biblical Hebrew Poetry,* JSOTSup (Sheffield: 1987).

10. Sometimes the word "lament" describes these prayers. But it seems less confusing to reserve that term for the dirge, with its description of a virtually hopeless situation like death, and to use "complaint" for the prayers which plead for God's rescue from unhappy circumstances. Cf. Job's complaints discussed above (p. 477).

11. The poet's flair for variety led him to use elements of a communal complaint in the middle of the chapter (vv. 40-47). For more on dirges, laments, and complaints, see E. S. Gerstenberger, *Psalms 1,* FOTL 14 (Grand Rapids: 1988), pp. 10-14.

12. N. Gottwald points up the sharp tension between Deuteronomic faith and historical adversity; *Studies in the Book of Lamentations,* pp. 47-53. Cf. Childs, *Old Testament as Scripture,* p. 593.

13. For a detailed presentation of this tension, see B. Albrektson, *Studies in the Text and Theology of the Book of Lamentations* (Lund: 1963), pp. 219ff.; cf. also M. S. Moore, "Human Suffering in Lamentations," *Revue biblique* 90 (1983): 534-555.

14. "One of the results of incorporating the events of the city's destruction into Israel's traditional terminology of worship was to establish a semantic bridge between the historical situation of the early sixth century and the language of faith which struggles with divine judgment. For this reason the book of Lamentations serves every successive generation of the suffering faithful for whom history has become unbearable"; Childs, *Old Testament as Scripture,* p. 596. See also I. Provan, *Lamentations,* NCBC, p. 23, for a summary of J. Renkema's discussion of faith and doubt in tension. For an exposition of hope as the dominant theme see S. P. Re'emi, "The Theology of Hope: A Commentary on the Book of Lamentations," in R. Martin-Achard and S. P. Re'emi, *God's People in Crisis,* ITC (Grand Rapids: 1984), pp. 73-134.

15. J. Krašovec, "The Source of Hope in the Book of Lamentations," *VT* 42 (1992): 223-233.

CHAPTER 40 — THE SCROLL OF ESTHER

1. Heb. *mᵉgillat 'ester,* often referred to simply as *Megillah* or "Scroll." Its use at the Jewish festival of Purim makes it the most widely published Old Testament book.

2. The LXX text contains 107 additional verses, "Additions to Esther." These occur before 1:1, after 3:13; 4:17; 8:12, and at the end. They make the book sound more religious,

perhaps attempting to promote its canonicity. For the book's textual history, see D. J. A. Clines, *The Esther Scroll: The Story of the Story* (Sheffield: 1984); and M. Fox, *The Redaction of the Books of Esther* (Atlanta: 1996).

3. Attacks on the book have been strong and sometimes bitter. Luther wished it "did not exist at all"; nos. 3391f., *Tischreden* (Weimar: 1914) 3:302. The rabbis challenged its canonicity (Jer. Talmud *Meg.* 70d) chiefly because it inaugurated a new feast, thus implying that the rule of Moses was incomplete. In response, some proposed the theory that the story of Esther was revealed to Moses at Sinai but was not to be put into writing until the Persian period; see G. F. Moore, *Judaism* 1:245. Among Christians the book did not receive official recognition as Scripture until the council of Carthage in A.D. 397.

4. See F. W. Bush, *Ruth, Esther.* WBC 9 (Dallas: 1996).

5. From *pur* (in Akkadian, a four-sided die), the lot which Haman cast (3:7). According to one interpretation, it was cast until it indicated the day on which the pogrom was to be carried out. If so, the casting took place in Nisan (April/May) of Ahasuerus's twelfth year, and the date selected was the thirteenth of Adar (March/April), eleven months later (cf. v. 13). For examples of ancient dice and their use, see W. H. Hallo, "The First Purim," *BA* 46 (1983): 19-26.

6. So S. Niditch, "Legends of Wise Heroes and Heroines," in D. A. Knight and G. M. Tucker, eds., *The Hebrew Bible and Its Modern Interpreters* (Philadelphia/Chico, Calif.: 1985), p. 446. What follows draws on the even-handed discussion in D. J. A. Clines, *Ezra, Nehemiah, Esther* (Grand Rapids: 1984), pp. 256-261; and J. G. Baldwin, *Esther,* TOTC (Downers Grove, Ill.: 1984), pp. 16-24.

7. Scholars also frequently claim that 2:5f. implies that Mordecai was more than 120 years old at the time — a very unlikely possibility. The problem goes away if one takes the pronoun "who" (v. 6) as referring not to Mordecai but to Kish, his great-grandfather (so NRSV). One need not take "Agagite" (3:1) as a reference to Agag (cf. 1 Sam. 15:8) and link Mordecai (a descendant of Kish, hence supposedly related to Saul) and Haman with the Saul-Agag story. Haman may be a Persian or Elamite name (J. Wiebe, *ABD,* Vol. 3, p. 33). Susa was in the southern portion of Persia that was originally Elam (see map of Persian empire, p. 546).

8. So Clines, *Ezra, Nehemiah, Esther,* pp. 259, 260.

9. Even Fox, who doubts the book's historicity, concedes that the author intended it to be read as history; cf. M. V. Fox, *Character and Ideology in the Book of Esther* (Columbia, S.C.: 1991), pp. 148-150. Elsewhere (p. 11) he says, "Although I doubt the historicity of the Esther story, . . . every year at Purim when I hear the Scroll read in the synagogue, I know it is *true.* . . . Indeed, I relive its truth and know its actuality."

10. The familiar saying regarding the U.S. mail being delivered in all kinds of weather was borrowed from the Persians. Darius I (522-486 B.C.) had it engraved on a mountainside at Behistun on the caravan road between Ecbatana and Babylon. Darius' boast was accurate: his system of relay riders traversed the 1,200 miles between Persia and the Aegean coast in six days, a feat unmatched until the Pony Express linked St. Joseph, Missouri, and Sacramento, California, more than two millennia later.

11. Baldwin, *Esther,* pp. 18-19; cf. A. Kuhrt, "The Cyrus Cylinder and Achaemenid Imperial Policy," *JSOT* 25 (1983): 94-95.

12. Persian sources attest several Persian court officials from Susa by the name Mardukâ (i.e., Mordecai). One may be the biblical figure, but we cannot be certain; cf. D. J. A. Clines, "In Quest of the Historical Mordecai," *VT* 41 (1991): 129-136; E. M. Yamauchi, "Mordecai, the Persepolis Tablets, and the Susa Excavations," *VT* 42 (1992): 272-275. Yamauchi (pp. 273-274) lists other Persian names which parallel those in Esther.

13. Cf. the Joseph story, Dan. 2–6, Judith, and the Tale of Ahikar (*ANET*, pp. 427-430).

14. Cf. Clines, *Ezra, Nehemiah, Esther*, pp. 256-257.

15. Cf. Niditch, "Legends of Wise Heroes and Heroines," pp. 446-448, who provides a convenient survey of other recent proposals; and W. L. Humphreys, "The Story of Esther and Mordecai: An Early Jewish Novella," pp. 97-113 in G. W. Coats, ed., *Saga, Legend, Tale, Novella, Fable. Narrative Genres in Old Testament Literature* (Sheffield: 1985).

16. On the genre of the book see Bush, *Ruth, Esther*.

17. See J. A. Soggin, *Introduction to the Old Testament*, trans. J. Bowden, OTL (Philadelphia: 1976), p. 403.

18. See G. F. Moore, *Judaism* 2:53.

19. Cited in B. W. Anderson, "Introduction and Exegesis of Esther," IB 3:830.

20. On the connection of Esther and Purim see Bush, *Ruth, Esther*.

21. See R. H. Pfeiffer, *Introduction to the Old Testament*, rev. ed. (New York: 1948), pp. 740f.

22. *Apion* i.8 40; *Ant.* xi.6 §§184-296. Josephus identifies Ahasuerus as Artaxerxes (successor to Xerxes) and follows rabbinic tradition in making Haman a descendant of King Agag and the destruction of the Amalekites the basis of Haman's hatred of the Jews. Josephus seems to have used the LXX text.

23. Esther is the only canonical book not found at Qumran. The book's Hebrew is typical of Late Biblical Hebrew, a stage of the language distinguishable from the Hebrew of Qumran; cf. R. Bergey, "Late Linguistic Features in Esther," *JQR* 75 (1984): 66-78.

24. For an exposition of the book's implicit but clear conception of the providence of God, see D. J. A. Clives, *The Esther Scroll: The Story of the Story*, pp. 154-158; and Bush, *Ruth, Esther*.

25. Perhaps at the time Persia practiced the custom of *kitmân* "guarded secret" or *taqiyyä* "piety," acceptance of a pretension to be of a race, culture, or religious belief for the sake of peaceful coexistence; see W. S. LaSor, *Handbook of Biblical Hebrew* (Grand Rapids: 1979) 1:66f. In modern times, this custom has made it possible for Sunni and Shi'ite Muslims, normally bitter enemies, to make the pilgrimage to Mecca together.

CHAPTER 41 — THE CHRONICLER'S PERSPECTIVE

1. The name Chronicles stems from Jerome's suggestion (*ca.* A.D. 400) that the book be called a "chronicle of the entire sacred history." The Hebrew title (*dibrê hayyāmîm*) means "the days' events" and so a historical journal. The LXX calls it *Paraleipomena* "what was omitted," returning to material omitted from 1-2 Samuel and 1-2 Kings and identifying the book with the unused source material to which the literary formula used in Kings, from 1 Kgs. 14:19 onwards, alludes, "the rest of the acts of. . . ." In the Hebrew canon Chronicles is the last book of the Writings, following Ezra and Nehemiah.

2. The division into 1-2 Chronicles is found in the LXX but not in Hebrew manuscripts before the Middle Ages. It was dictated by the extra space required by the Greek language. Therefore, the term Chronicles refers to both books as a whole, and their writer is called the Chronicler. Recent research has differentiated between Chronicles and Ezra-Nehemiah and tended to view them as separate works. See H. G. M. Williamson, *1 and 2 Chronicles*, New Century Bible (Grand Rapids: 1982), pp. 5-11.

3. He seems to have worked from an old Palestinian text different at points from the MT and preserved in part in the Qumran edition of Samuel (4QSam^a). See J. R. Porter,

"Old Testament Historiography," p. 156, in G. W. Anderson, ed., *Tradition and Interpretation* (Oxford: 1979); S. L. McKenzie, *The Chronicler's Use of the Deuteronomistic History* (Atlanta: 1985). The Chronicler mentions a number of writings credited to prophets, e.g., Samuel, Nathan, Gad (1 Chr. 29:29), Ahijah, Iddo (2 Chr. 9:29), Shemaiah (12:15), Jehu (20:34), Isaiah (32:32). Twice these bear the name "midrash," which here means "story" or "commentary" (13:22; 24:27). These writings appear to refer to the books of Samuel and Kings, according them a prophetic value such as the later title "Former Prophets" given to the Deuteronomistic History in the Hebrew canon attested (cf. 2 Chr. 20:34; 32:32; see Williamson, *1 and 2 Chronicles*, pp. 17-19).

4. See Williamson, *1 and 2 Chronicles*, pp. 291-294.

5. *Ibid.*, pp. 391-393; Dillard, *2 Chronicles*, WBC 15 (Waco: 1987), pp. 264-266.

6. See further G. F. Hasel, *ISBE* 1 (1979): 668-669.

7. See L. C. Allen, "Kerygmatic Units in 1 and 2 Chronicles," *JSOT* 41 (1983): 21-36.

8. D. N. Freedman dates the Chronicler's work *ca.* 515 and connects it with the ministries of Haggai and Zechariah; he attributes the memoirs of Ezra and Nehemiah to a later hand which stressed the religious patterns of Moses rather than the religious contributions of David as stressed in Chronicles ("The Chronicler's Purpose," *CBQ* 23 [1961]: 441). However, some point in the fourth century B.C. is more likely, especially in the light of the length of the Davidic genealogy in 1 Chr. 3:10-24; see Williamson, *1 and 2 Chronicles*, pp. 15-17.

9. R. W. Klein, *ABD* 1:993, summarizes three of the prevailing views of the Chronicler's relationship to the other postexilic histories in the books of Ezra-Nehemiah: (1) the Chronicler included Ezra-Nehemiah along with Chronicles in his work; (2) Chronicles and Ezra-Nehemiah are separate works, each with its own author; (3) the Chronicler wrote both Chronicles and Ezra-Nehemiah but as separate works. Klein recognizes the supporting reasons for each of these options but leans heavily toward the second.

10. Specifics about the Chronicler's historical and social circumstances are difficult to determine, especially if his work is dated to the late fifth or early fourth century, since few details of the historical period have been preserved.

CHAPTER 42 — EZRA-NEHEMIAH

1. Observe, however, that Ezra is the main character of Neh. 7:73b–10:39, the second half of his so-called memoirs. The LXX and Vulgate title the books inconsistently, and two apocryphal books are entitled Ezra or use the Greek form Esdras. For the more common names, see Table.

2. This is by far the most common order, but the famous Aleppo codex (tenth century) and several later texts place Chronicles at the beginning of the Writings with Ezra-Nehemiah at the end.

3. It is first attested in Origen (third century).

4. Jeshua apparently is one Hebrew form of the New Testament name Jesus.

5. Aram. *ʿabar-nahărâ*, lit. "the other side of the river," a technical term for the administrative district (or satrapy) of the Persian empire west of the Euphrates along the Syrian and Palestinian coast to the borders of Egypt. Obviously the name assumes a westward orientation from Persia and Mesopotamia.

6. Apparently, the vague "they" (v. 6) are the "people of the land" (v. 4), who effectively stopped work on the temple until the days of Darius. These were descendants of the intermarriage between Israel's northern tribes and the other peoples whom the

Assyrians settled in Palestine. Ch. 4 mentions two such settlements, one under Esarhaddon (681-669; v. 2) and one under "the great and noble Osnappar" (v. 10), usually identified with Assurbanipal (668-627).

7. I.e., the fifth month of the seventh year of Artaxerxes (7:8).

8. I.e., the month of Chislev in the twentieth year of Artaxerxes (1:1; 2:1).

9. Apparently, Ezra and Nehemiah followed the calendrical practice of preexilic Israel which began the year in the autumn with Tishri. Thus, Chislev of Artaxerxes' twentieth year (1:1) would be December 445–January 444, while Nisan (2:1) would be April-May 444. Since both omit mention of a specific day, they probably refer to the first day of the respective month. For a summary of the Hebrew calendar, see Chapter 49, below.

10. Many consider this figure, which represents about nine weeks (assuming no work on the Sabbath), as far too short a time for so monumental a task. They prefer the figure given by Josephus (*Ant.* 11.5.8) of two years and four months (e.g., J. Bright, *A History of Israel,* 3rd ed. [Philadelphia: 1981], p. 381). But recent excavations in the Jewish Quarter of the Old City suggest that the city of Nehemiah's time consisted only of the area along the Ophel ridge south of the Temple Mount. There is no evidence that the western hill was occupied during the Persian and early Hellenistic periods. See N. Avigad, "Excavations in the Jewish Quarter of the Old City, 1969-1971," pp. 41-51 in Y. Yadin, ed., *Jerusalem Revealed* (New Haven: 1976). Further, in this period, the city's eastern wall above the Kidron valley ran along the ridge crest rather than farther down the slope as did the preexilic wall. Thus, Nehemiah's city was far smaller than its preexilic predecessor; see K. M. Kenyon, *Jerusalem* (New York: 1967), pp. 107-111. For a succinct statement and a map, see B. Mazar, *The Mountain of the Lord* (Garden City: 1975), p. 193. For a persuasive and detailed defense of the contrary position, see W. S. LaSor, "Jerusalem," *ISBE* 2 (1982): 1017-1020, III.F.2. Possibly Nehemiah found significant sections of the wall extant, so part of the work involved filling in the breaches and completing the height, rather than starting anew.

11. The text records that Nehemiah returned briefly to Persia in Artaxerxes' thirty-second year (433; 13:6). Thus, his second governorship began *ca.* 432.

12. See W. S. LaSor, "Nebuchadrezzar," *ISBE* 3 (1986): 506ff.

13. Cf. R. E. Hayden, "Persia," *ISBE* 3 (1986): 776-780, esp. 778.

14. Cf. D. J. A. Clines, "Cyrus," *ISBE* 1 (1979): 845-849.

15. For an excellent overview, see Bright, *History,* pp. 360-375. See also J. M. Miller and J. H. Hayes, *A History of Ancient Israel and Judah* (Philadelphia: 1986), pp. 437-475.

16. S. Talmon, "Ezra and Nehemiah," pp. 358-359 in *LGB.*

17. Of the Ezra material, Ezra 7:27–9:15 is in the first person (except 8:35f.), the rest in third person narrative, except the covenant section (Neh. 9:38–10:39 [MT 10:1-40]). Of the Nehemiah material, Neh. 1:1–7:5 and 12:31–13:31 are first-person narrative.

18. *B. Bat.* 15a.

19. The most persuasive case has been argued by C. C. Torrey, *Ezra Studies* (1910; repr. New York: 1970); and A. S. Kapelrud, *The Question of Authorship in the Ezra-Narrative* (Oslo: 1944). More recently, see D. J. A. Clines, *Ezra, Nehemiah, Esther,* NCBC (Grand Rapids: 1984), pp. 2-12; and Bright, *History,* p. 395. Several scholars have even argued that the Chronicler was Ezra himself or a close disciple; cf. W. F. Albright, *JBL* 40 (1921): 104-124; J. M. Myers, *Ezra-Nehemiah,* AB (Garden City: 1965), p. lxviii; Bright, *History,* p. 398.

20. S. Japhet, *VT* 18 (1968): 330-371. But see the critique of Japhet by R. W. Klein, "Ezra and Nehemiah in Recent Studies," p. 375 note 34 in F. M. Cross, W. E. Lemke, and P. D. Miller, Jr., eds., *Magnalia Dei: The Mighty Acts of God,* Festschrift G. E. Wright (Garden City: 1976).

21. D. N. Freedman, *CBQ* 22 (1961): 436-442. To account for both the differences and similarities, F. M. Cross, Jr., proposed a theory of three successive editors behind the composite work Chronicles-Ezra-Nehemiah. The first worked in the time of Zerubbabel (*ca.* 520), supporting the temple reconstruction and emphasizing royal Davidic ideology; the second lived after the work of Ezra (i.e., post-458); and the third, who incorporated Nehemiah's memoirs, worked *ca.* 400; "A Reconstruction of the Judean Restoration," *JBL* 34 (1975): 4-18, esp. 14f.

22. J. D. Newsome, Jr., "Toward a New Understanding of the Chronicler and His Purpose," *JBL* 94 (1975): 201-217.

23. H. G. M. Williamson, *Ezra, Nehemiah,* WBC 16 (Waco: 1985), pp. xxi-xxiii; T. C. Eskenazi, *In an Age of Prose: A Literary Approach to Ezra-Nehemiah,* SBLMS 36 (Atlanta: 1988), pp. 14-36.

24. See Bright, *History,* pp. 396ff.; Myers, *Ezra-Nehemiah,* pp. lxviiiff.; Clines, *Ezra, Nehemiah, Esther,* pp. 12-13. Cf. the influential study by W. F. Albright, *JBL* 40 (1921): 104-124. The LXX of 1 Chr. 3:10-24 extends the list of Davidides to eleven generations instead of seven.

25. Williamson, *Ezra-Nehemiah,* p. xxxvi; cf. S. Japhet, *ZAW* 94 (1982): 89 note 55 (first quarter of the fourth century). For criticism of Williamson's Samaritan assumption, see Clines, *Ezra, Nehemiah, Esther,* p. 13.

26. The term "author/compiler" assumes that the author both wrote material himself (e.g., the third-person introduction to the Ezra section, Ezra 7:1-10) and used a variety of source materials (see above).

27. Hiphil *he'ᵉlâ* must mean "took up" rather than "sent up," since 5:15f. clearly states that Sheshbazzar returned to Jerusalem.

28. Zerubbabel is the son of Shealtiel (3:2, 8; 5:2; cf. Hag. 1:1, 12), who, according to 1 Chr. 3:17, was the eldest son of Jehoiachin (the last king of Judah, exiled in 597). But 1 Chr. 3:19 gives the father of Zerubbabel as Pedaiah, a younger son of Shealtiel.

29. Both harmonizations, however, must contend with the claim of Ezra 3:6 that, when Zerubbabel built an altar and instituted sacrifices, the foundations of the temple were not yet laid. One also wonders why, if Sheshbazzar returned earlier, he had not taken those steps.

30. Note the title "governor" given to Sheshbazzar and Zerubbabel (Ezra 5:14; Hag. 1:1, 14), the reference to "the province of Judah" (Ezra 5:8), "governor of the Jews" (6:7), and Nehemiah's statement about "the former governors who were before me" (Neh. 5:15).

31. Small lumps of clay pressed on the cord tying a scroll to seal it. The document's writer often stamped the clay with his own official or personal seal which survives as a kind of inscription when the cord and attached document disintegrate.

32. See J. H. Hayes and J. M. Miller, eds., *Israelite and Judaean History,* OTL (Philadelphia: 1977), pp. 460-462, 490-491 (bibliography); G. Widengren, "The Persian Period," pp. 510f. in Hayes and Miller, *History.* One cannot determine, however, whether these governors preceded or followed Nehemiah.

33. So S. Talmon, "Ezra and Nehemiah," *IDBS,* p. 321. One seal is that of "Shelomit, the 'maidservant' of the governor," and one is tempted to identify her with Shelomith, Zerubbabel's daughter (1 Chr. 3:19); cf. N. Avigad, *Bullae and Seals from a Post-Exilic Judean Archive,* Qedem 4 (Jerusalem: 1976), pp. 11-13, 31f.

34. E.g., Myers, *Ezra-Nehemiah,* p. 133; Bright, *History,* p. 363.

35. See *ANET,* pp. 491f. These business documents and letters come from a Jewish military colony on the island of Elephantine, north of the first waterfall of the Nile and opposite Aswan, established as early as the fall of Jerusalem in 586. The texts throw brilliant

light on the affairs of the Jewish colony in Upper Egypt, especially for the period 425-400. In 410 these Jews wrote a letter to Johanan, high priest at Jerusalem (Neh. 12:22), regarding the rebuilding of their temple. In 407 they sent a long appeal on the same matter to Bagoas, governor of Judah, mentioning also a similar letter to "Delaiah and Shelemiah, the sons of Sanballat the governor of Samaria." If this is the same Sanballat who staunchly opposed Nehemiah (2:19; 4:1 [MT 3:33]), the Artaxerxes to which 2:1 refers must be Artaxerxes I.

36. See the helpful discussion in R. W. Klein, "Ezra-Nehemiah, Books of," *ABD* 2:735-737; and Clines, *Ezra, Nehemiah, Esther,* pp. 16-24.

37. Most recently, Miller and Hayes, *History,* pp. 465-469. Alternatively, Bright (*History,* pp. 391-402) proposed a date of 428 by emending Ezra 7:7-8 to read the "thirty-seventh" year of Artaxerxes instead of his "seventh" year. There is, however, no textual evidence to support this emendation.

38. Scholars who hold this view discard the references to Ezra and Nehemiah together as unreliable later additions to the text.

39. Klein, "Ezra-Nehemiah, Books of," p. 737; Williamson, *Ezra, Nehemiah,* pp. xliii-xliv; and Clines, *Ezra, Nehemiah, Esther,* pp. 14-24, adopt this date for Ezra, but conclude that the present arrangement of the text is not determined by chronological concerns but by thematic ones. Chronologically, Neh. 8 and 9, Ezra's reading of the law, belongs after Ezra 8, and hence Ezra's reforms actually took a little more than a year (Klein, "Ezra, Nehemiah, Books of," p. 735; Williamson, *Ezra, Nehemiah,* pp. xlviii-l).

40. Talmon, "Ezra and Nehemiah," pp. 363-364 in *LGB.* For further discussion, see E. M. Yamauchi, "The Reverse Order of Ezra/Nehemiah Reconsidered," *Themelios* 5 (1980): 7-13.

41. Early in the restoration period, Israel may have looked to Sheshbazzar and Zerubbabel to restore the Davidic monarchy and the old order. Both were descendants of David, and Haggai and Zechariah spoke of Zerubbabel in messianic terms. The shakiness of the Persian empire during the early years of Darius I may also have fueled such hopes. But eventually such hopes lost their spark.

42. The discovery of "the book of the law" in 621 (Josiah's eighteenth year) illustrates how peripheral the law actually was to Israel's life before the Exile. Workers renovating the temple found it, as if it had not been used in ages. Such disuse would have been utterly impossible in the postexilic period.

43. The precise role played by the Levites in "reading" the law here remains uncertain. The ambiguous Heb. *mᵉpōrāš* (lit., "divided, split up"; v. 8) may mean (1) "clearly," (2) "paragraph by paragraph," or (3) "in (Aramaic) translation." For options, see Clines, *Ezra, Nehemiah, Esther,* pp. 184-185.

44. J. Blenkinsopp, "The Sage, Scribe, and Scribalism in the Chronicler's Work," pp. 307-315 in J. G. Gammie and L. G. Perdue, eds., *The Sage in Israel and the Ancient Near East* (Winona Lake: 1990). This Persian terminology may also have influenced the description of Ezra as "scribe" discussed above (Ezra 7:6). The imperial Aramaic equivalent *sâpᵉrâ* was a common term for a Persian imperial official, usually followed by a genitive as here. However, as we argued, within Israel itself the term took on larger leadership connotations.

45. Most scholars feel that the law was our Pentateuch which Ezra probably collected and edited; cf. Williamson, *Ezra, Nehemiah,* p. xxxix ("similar to, if not yet fully identical with, our Pentateuch"). For the recent view that Ezra's Torah went beyond the canonical Pentateuch, see J. R. Shaver, *Torah and the Chronicler's History Work,* Brown Judaic Studies 196 (Atlanta: 1989).

46. According to Eskenazi's fine literary study (*Age of Prose,* pp. 127-154), the book portrays Ezra and Nehemiah as opposites — Ezra the "self-effacing teacher of Torah,"

Nehemiah the "self-glorifying entrepreneur." Their work complements each other, and the contrast between them symbolizes postexilic Judah's incorporation of diversity into its community.

47. The concepts of Isa. 40–66 also lie behind Ezra's words. Again and again these chapters portray the "new thing" which Yahweh will do (42:9; 43:19; 48:3) as a new exodus, e.g., a highway through the desert that blossoms and flows with water (40:3-5; 41:18f.; 49:9-11). For other illustrations of continuity, see Clines, *Ezra, Nehemiah, Esther,* pp. 25-26; Eskenazi, *Age of Prose,* pp. 40-41.

48. *Old Testament Theology,* trans. D. M. G. Stalker, 2 vols. (New York: 1962-1965) 1:90.

49. P. R. Ackroyd, *Exile and Restoration* (Philadelphia: 1968), p. 248.

50. As Ackroyd observes (*Exile and Restoration,* p. 255), the true purpose of the law was to promote "the recognition that there is no part of life which is outside the concern of God, and that the completely fit community is one in which all life is brought under control."

51. See Eskenazi, *In An Age of Prose,* p. 42: ". . . all that transpires from Ezra 1:1 to Neh. 13:31 is unified by the command of Israel's God coupled with the command of the three kings."

52. See Williamson, *Ezra, Nehemiah,* pp. li-lii.

CHAPTER 43 — DANIEL

1. See discussion of Zechariah, pp. 409, 411 above.

2. *Semeia* 14, p. 9; quoted in J. J. Collins, *Daniel,* FOTL 20 (Grand Rapids: 1984; repr. 1989), p. 4.

3. See P. D. Hanson, *IDBS,* p. 27; and p. 567 above.

4. The form Nebuchadnezzar occurs regularly in Daniel, as in all other places in the Bible except Jeremiah (Nebuchadnezzar 10 times, Nebuchadrezzar 27) and Ezekiel. BDB has no more reason to say that the spelling Nebuchadnezzar is used "incorrectly" (p. 613) than does an American to say that "colour" is incorrect. The spelling differences are regional or dialectal. For recent discussion of the historical backgrounds of these stories, see J. G. Baldwin, *Daniel* (Downers Grove, Ill.: 1978), pp. 19-29.

5. The Hebrew consonants of the name in Daniel are *dny'l*; in Ezekiel *dn'l*; hence some would read "Danel" (NRSV footnote).

6. E.g., 1 Aqht 19; see C. H. Gordon, *Ugaritic Textbook* 1:245-250; *ANET,* pp. 149-155, with bibliography; J. Day, "The Daniel of Ugarit and Ezekiel and the Hero of the Book of Daniel," *VT* 30 (1980): 174-184. S. B. Frost's thesis that the biblical story was built on stories of the Ugaritic (Phoenician) Daniel is without foundation; as Frost concedes: "The older traditions make no reference to the other outstanding characteristics of the hero of the book of Daniel"; *IDB* 1:762. These characteristics are wisdom and righteousness (p. 761), which relate to Dan'el of Ezekiel and not the Ugaritic Dan'il.

7. Nippur, in the vicinity of Tel Abib, where Ezekiel lived, was only about 80 km. (50 mi.) from Babylon.

8. In May/June 605 Nebuchadnezzar "conquered the whole area of the Hatti-country" (which would include Palestine). Nabopolassar died on 8 Ab of his twenty-first year (15 Aug. 605) and on 1 Elul (7 Sept.) Nebuchadnezzar "sat on the royal throne in Babylon," but did not "take the hands of Bel" until the month of Nisan (2 Apr. 604). The preceding period he called his "accession year," in which he returned to Hatti-land until Shebat (Feb. 604) and

"took the heavy tribute of the Hatti-territory to Babylon." See D. J. Wiseman, *Chronicles of the Chaldean Kings (626-556 B.C.)* (London: 1956), p. 69. Dates are calculated from R. A. Parker and W. H. Dubberstein, *Babylonian Chronology 626 B.C.–A.D. 75* (Providence: 1971), p. 27. The "third year of the reign of Jehoiakim" (1:1) would end on 6 Oct. 605 (using a Tishri-Tishri year), which would fit Nebuchadnezzar's invasion of summer 605.

9. The royal captives are called Heb. *yᵉlādîm* "children" (1:4), which can be used for "offspring" of any age. Since these captives were to be trained for court service, they must have been quite young.

10. Arguments concerning the date of the Aramaic in R. D. Wilson, *The Aramaic of Daniel* (New York: 1912), and esp. H. H. Rowley, *The Aramaic of the Old Testament* (London: 1929), are linguistically outdated. See now J. A. Fitzmyer, *The Aramaic Inscriptions of Sefire* (Rome: 1967); *A Wandering Aramean* (Missoula: 1979); "The Aramaic Language and the Study of the New Testament," *JBL* 99 (1980): 5-21; D. W. Gooding, "The Literary Structure of the Book of Daniel and Its Implications," *Tyndale Bulletin* 32 (1981): 43-79; J. Greenfield, "Aramaic," *IDBS*, pp. 39-44; W. S. LaSor, "Aramaic," *ISBE* 1 (1979): 229-233.

11. See LaSor, *Great Personalities of the Old Testament* (Westwood, N.J.: 1959), pp. 171f.

12. For problems of identification, see D. J. A. Clines, "Belshazzar," *ISBE* 1 (1979): 455f.; "Darius," *ibid.*, pp. 867f.; R. P. Dougherty, *Nabonidus and Belshazzar,* Yale Oriental Series 15 (New Haven: 1929); Wiseman, *Notes on Some Problems in the Book of Daniel* (London: 1965), pp. 9-16.

13. The date in v. 4 converts to 23 April 536. In spite of charges that the Scripture writers were ignorant of the fact that Cyrus had reigned already since 559, all extant documents of Cyrus date his reign from the capture of Babylon. See Chapter 28 note 6 above.

14. F. F. Bruce, *Israel and the Nations,* while not specifically dating Daniel, seems to indicate that the writing was after the events; see pp. 124, 133, 141 note 1.

15. Frost dates it "between December 17 (?), 167 (1 Macc. 1:54), and the corresponding date in 164 (1 Macc. 4:52)," and narrows this to "*ca.* 166-165 B.C."; *IDB* 1:767.

16. Cf. J. J. Collins, *Daniel*, pp. 11-14. It should be noted that in apocalyptic literature, an *ex eventu* prophecy, i.e., based on an event that had already occurred, could still be a prophecy of a future event.

17. See R. K. Harrison, *Introduction to the Old Testament* (Grand Rapids: 1969), pp. 1105-1134; "Daniel, Book of," *ISBE* 1 (1979): 861-865; R. D. Wilson, "Daniel, Book of," *ISBE* (1939) 2:783-787; C. Boutflower, *In and around the Book of Daniel* (1923; repr. Grand Rapids: 1963), pp. 1-12; E. J. Young, *The Prophecy of Daniel* (Grand Rapids: 1949), pp. 15-26, 223-253; E. B. Pusey, *Daniel the Prophet* (New York: 1885), pp. 1-57, 232-461; B. S. Childs, *Introduction to the Old Testament as Scripture* (Philadelphia: 1979), pp. 611-621 and bibliography, pp. 608, 611; O. Eissfeldt, *The Old Testament: An Introduction,* trans. P. R. Ackroyd (New York: 1965), pp. 517-529 and bibliography, pp. 512f.; A. Jeffrey, "Introduction and Exegesis of Daniel," *IB* 6: 341-352; G. L. Archer, Jr., *A Survey of Old Testament Introduction* (Chicago: 1964), pp. 365-388; J. G. Baldwin, *Daniel,* TOTC (Downers Grove: 1978). J. B. Payne calls late date views "a deception and a fraud"; "Daniel, Book of," *ZPBD*, p. 199. R. Dillard and T. Longman, *Introduction to the Old Testament* (Grand Rapids: 1995), pp. 329-352, offer a wise and balanced conservative interpretation.

18. See F. Delitzsch, "Daniel," in J. J. Herzog, ed., *Realenzyklopedie für protestantische Theologie und Kirche* 3 (Hamburg: 1855): 273; J. A. Montgomery, *The Book of Daniel,* ICC (Edinburgh: 1927), pp. 13-22.

19. Fragments of Daniel from Qumran indicate that the Aramaic section at that date began and ended where it does in the Hebrew Bible.

20. See E. J. Young, *The Prophecy of Daniel* (Grand Rapids: 1949), pp. 19f.

21. *B. Bat.* 15a; see note 10 above.

22. Young, *The Prophecy of Daniel*, p. 20.

23. *Ibid.*

24. J. E. Goldingay, *Daniel*, WBC 30 (Dallas: 1989), p. xl.

25. See Montgomery: "The historical objective of the book, whether it is understood as contemporaneous to the writer or as prophetically foreseen, is the Hellenistic age"; *Daniel*, p. 59. He supports this position using chs. 10–12.

26. Some who follow the Antiochus Epiphanes interpretation simply say that the author of this part of the book was mistaken; see Frost, *IDB* 1:768.

27. See Boutflower, *In and around the Book of Daniel*, pp. 13-23; Young, *The Prophecy of Daniel*, pp. 274-294; Montgomery, *Daniel*, pp. 59-62; Jeffrey, *IB* 6:382-390, 452-467; G. F. Hasel, "The Four World Empires of Daniel 2 against Its Near Eastern Environment," *JSOT* 12 (1979): 17-30.

28. Often taken to mean 2,300 evening and morning sacrifices, hence 1,150 days. But Jeffrey observes that "from data in 1 Maccabees, the actual number of days between the defilement of the altar in 168 B.C. and its rededication in 165 was, on any calculation, somewhat less than 1,150 days" (*IB* 6:476) — actually 1,094 days.

29. For careful exegesis, see Montgomery, *Daniel*, pp. 377-401; Young, *The Prophecy of Daniel*, pp. 191-221. Goldingay, *Daniel*, pp. 257-268.

30. Apparently the beginning of doctrines and theories about angelic Princes of the nations; see Montgomery, *Daniel*, pp. 419f.

31. The date formula in v. 1 seems to be a gloss, added to clarify the chronological sequence, but it may be a "flashback" spoken by the same speaker in ch. 10.

32. This view is supported by the use of Daniel in Enoch; the Qumran literature; the New Testament, especially Revelation; and other writings.

33. See Montgomery, *Daniel*, pp. 420-468: "There appears to be an utter lack of allusion to this chapter in early Jewish and Christian literature. And subsequently the Jewish commentators, with their characteristic lack of historical sense, make the chapter a phantasmagoria of fanciful allusions . . ."; p. 468. Perhaps early Jewish and Christian commentators better understood the nature of apocalyptic.

34. H. H. Rowley points out that it would have been meaningless for Jesus to charge his disciples to tell no one that he was the Christ if "son of man" was an equivalent term; *The Relevance of Apocalyptic*, 2nd ed. (London: 1947), pp. 30f. See M. Casey, "The Corporate Interpretation of 'One like a Son of Man' (Dan. VII 13) at the Time of Jesus," *Novum Testamentum* 18 (1976): 167-180. See also D. Aune, "Son of Man," *ISBE* 4 (1988): 574-581.

35. See W. S. LaSor, *Great Personalities*, p. 42.

36. See Goldingay's commentary, pp. xxx-xxxviii, for a summary of Christian interpretation of Daniel through the centuries. Times of persecution or threat of conquest by pagan powers sparked keen interest in the book time and again.

CHAPTER 44 — THE AUTHORITY OF THE OLD TESTAMENT FOR CHRISTIANS

1. So, among others, C. H. Dodd, *According to the Scriptures* (London: 1952), pp. 108ff. Cf. E. E. Ellis, *Paul's Use of the Old Testament* (Grand Rapids: 1957), p. 113.

2. Ellis, *ibid.,* pp. 115f.

3. *Ibid.,* p. 116.

4. Typology has been defined as "the establishment of historical connections between certain events, persons or things in the Old Testament and similar events, persons or things in the New Testament." See G. W. H. Lampe and K. J. Woollcombe, *Essays in Typology* (London: 1957), pp. 147ff.

5. E.g., Lampe and Woollcombe.

6. *Ibid.,* pp. 147ff.

7. F. F. Bruce compares the arbitrary interpretations of a passage from Amos in the Zadokite Admonition and Stephen's sympathetic, sensitive rendering of another prophetic passage in Amos 7:42f.; *Biblical Exegesis in the Qumran Texts* (Grand Rapids: 1959), p. 73.

8. Ellis, *Paul's Use of the Old Testament,* pp. 147f.

CHAPTER 45 — REVELATION AND INSPIRATION

1. See Isa. 41:22f., 26; 43:12; 44:7f.; 45:21; 48:3, 5f., 8, 14-16.

2. In the Biblical Theology movement of the 1950s there was an emphasis on God's revelation of himself in history only by divine acts. This approach skews the Old Testament evidence. The interpretation of those acts in words plays a key role in the divine revelation, as James Barr has observed in *Old and New in Interpretation* (London: 1966), p. 21: "The progression of the story is given not only by what God does but also by what he says."

3. 1 Chr. 16:40; 2 Chr. 12:1; 17:9; 31:3f.; 34:14; 35:26; Ezra 7:10; Neh. 9:3.

4. Neh. 8:8, 18; 10:29. Cf. in prayers "your law" in Neh. 9:26, 29, 34; Dan. 9:11.

5. B. S. Childs, *Introduction to the Old Testament as Scripture* (Philadelphia: 1979), p. 513. For a discussion of the means whereby human responses to God in prayer and praise became regarded as divine revelation, see L. C. Allen, *Psalms,* Word Biblical Themes (Waco: 1987), pp. 117-122.

6. G. M. Tucker, "Prophetic Superscriptions and the Growth of a Canon," *Canon and Authority,* ed. G. W. Coats and B. O. Long (Philadelphia: 1977), pp. 65, 68.

7. Jer. 1:2; Hos. 1:1; Joel 1:1; Mic. 1:1; Zeph. 1:1; cf. Mal. 1:1. This introductory rubric is usually called "message-reception formula."

8. The syntax is ambiguous: the NRSV gives as an alternative "Every scripture inspired by God is also . . . ," which sounds tautologous. Actually, the options seem to depend on the meaning of the Greek *graphē,* whether "writing" or "scripture." So the alternative translation is, "Every writing inspired by God is also . . ." (F. F. Bruce, *The Canon of Scripture* [Downers Grove, Ill.: 1988], p. 29 note 2). Readers of the English Bible can be reassured by the fact that Timothy would have been taught from the Greek version of the Old Testament, which, for all its deficiencies, let the inspiration of the original shine through. The New Testament does not, however, acknowledge a single "inspired" version.

9. Switching from the written stage ("prophecy of scripture," 2 Pet. 1:20) to the oral stage would not have been so noticeable in a cultural setting where the Old Testament was known from being read aloud and heard by the congregation.

10. The Greek *theopneustos,* often understood as "God-breathed," in its thematic context appears to be a compound adjective developed from the phrase *to pneuma tou theou* "the Spirit of God." The adjective "inspired" which the RSV imported into Matt. 22:43; Mark 12:36; Luke 2:27; 1 Cor. 12:6, 11; 1 Tim. 1:18 has been wisely removed in the NRSV. The example in 1 Thess. 1:6 could also have been removed.

11. In the Old Testament God's "spirit" (with a small "s"), like the hand of God, is an extension of the divine being and a means of God's self-revelation to humanity.

12. See Isa. 30:1, where "will" is literally "spirit"; Hos. 9:7; Mic. 3:8; cf. Num. 11:29; 1 Kgs. 22:24; Joel 2:28-29.

13. One can hardly object to the concept of verbal inspiration, since thoughts must be expressed in words.

14. "In what sense is it revelation when the Bible has a text containing a law which is ancient customary law only mildly differing from the law of a neighboring social group?" asked Barr (*Old and New in Interpretation,* p. 98). On different models of inspiration see B. Vawter, *Biblical Inspiration* (Philadelphia, 1972), pp. 162-168.

15. Cf. Ps. 78:1-4 and the "Annals" of 1 Kgs. 14:29, etc.

16. See especially J. L. McKenzie, "The Social Character of Inspiration," *CBQ* 24 (1962): 115-124, reprinted in *Myths and Realities* (Milwaukee: 1963), pp. 37-58. There is, of course, another sense in which the community is sometimes said to be inspired, in hearing and reading the Scriptures. By means of this usage one may proceed to speak of the Bible becoming, rather than being, the word of God. However, this subjective use of the term "inspiration" is confusing and better replaced by the more traditional term "illumination" (cf. Ps. 119:18).

17. P. Achtemeier, *The Inspiration of Scripture* (Philadelphia: 1980), p. 133.

18. See R. Beckwith, *The Old Testament Canon of the New Testament Church* (Grand Rapids: 1985), pp. 70, 79, 95 note 32, 126.

19. Cf. Mark 12:36, where Ps. 110:1 is attributed to "David . . . by the Holy Spirit." Cf. too Heb. 9:8. In Heb. 1:1 God's Old Testament revelation through "the prophets" consists not only of the books of the prophets proper but also of the Psalms and Deuteronomy, according to the citations in Heb. 1:5–2:13.

20. The Greek *asphaleia* "truth, reliability" is etymologically parallel to the late Latin *infallibilitas.* Both denote the quality of not being liable to stumble or fall.

21. R. K. Johnston, *Evangelicals at an Impasse: Biblical Authority in Practice* (Atlanta: 1978), p. 36: " 'Inerrant,' when qualified hermeneutically, seems to die the death of a thousand qualifications."

22. Theologians have traditionally spoken of the Bible's historical relatedness in terms of divine condescension or accommodation. As an example of the cultural conditioning or "time-boundness" of the Bible G. C. Berkouwer has adduced some of Paul's statements regarding womanhood and marriage, which indeed echo Old Testament standards (*Holy Scripture* [Grand Rapids: 1975], pp. 186-187).

23. D. A. Hubbard, *What We Evangelicals Believe* (Pasadena: 1979), p. 61.

CHAPTER 46 — THE CONCEPT OF CANON

1. It is often referred to as Tanakh, an acronym of Torah (Law), Nebi'im (Prophets), and Kethubim (Writings).

2. For the description of Zechariah as "son of Barachiah" in Matt. 23:35 see R. Beckwith, *The Old Testament Canon in the New Testament Church* (Grand Rapids: 1985), pp. 212-220.

3. Cf. J. Blenkinsopp, *Prophecy and Canon* (Notre Dame: 1977), pp. 85-95, 120-123.

4. See the classic article of J. P. Lewis, "What Do We Mean by Jabneh?" *Journal of Bible and Religion* 32 (1964): 125-132, reprinted in *The Canon and Masorah of the Hebrew Bible: An Introductory Reader,* ed. S. Z. Leiman (New York: 1974), pp. 254-261.

5. See especially A. C. Sundberg, *The Old Testament of the Early Church* (Cambridge, Mass.: 1964), pp. 3-79.

6. See Beckwith, *Old Testament Canon,* pp. 152-153.

7. See S. Z. Leiman, *The Canonization of Hebrew Scripture* (Hamden: 1976), pp. 26, 29-30.

8. The book of Esther has not been found among the Qumran scrolls. The Qumran community may have rejected it because it did not align with its own calendar. Cf. Beckwith, *Old Testament Canon,* p. 312.

9. However, the older view that a fifth-century schism between Jews and Samaritans supports canonization at this time is no longer viable. The Samaritans regarded only the Pentateuch as canonical scripture. However, the division seems to have occurred much later, about 120 B.C. The Samaritan Pentateuch reflects in its script, spelling, and text (apart from sectarian deviations) the period 150-50 B.C., as Qumran parallels have shown. Presumably the Samaritans rejected the other Jewish scriptures because of the recognition of the Jerusalem temple and the denunciation of the sins of Ephraim that appear in them. See Beckwith, *Old Testament Canon,* p. 131, with reference to the work of J. D. Purvis, *The Samaritan Pentateuch and the Origin of the Samaritan Sect* (Cambridge, Mass.: 1968).

10. Beckwith (*Old Testament Canon,* pp. 138-152) envisages a bipartite canon that did not have the Prophets and Writings differentiated until about 164 B.C. Probably, however, the distinctive prophetic books, including the historical epic so imbued with prophetic traditions, had been recognized as a separate entity at an earlier stage.

11. See Beckwith, *Old Testament Canon,* pp. 250-251, 256, 260-262.

12. See Beckwith's discussion in *Old Testament Canon,* pp. 235-240.

13. See Beckwith, *Old Testament Canon,* pp. 124-125; J. Barton, *Oracles of God* (New York: 1986), p. 34.

14. In his more recent writing he has been more prepared to recognize the value of studying earlier stages in the writing process. See *The New Testament as Canon: An Introduction* (Philadelphia: 1984), pp. 35-37.

15. In a similar vein W. Brueggemann, *The Creative Word: Canon as a Model for Christian Formation* (Philadelphia: 1982), pp. 10-13, has differentiated the tripartite canon in terms of established order, disruptive challenge, and human potential under God.

CHAPTER 47 — FORMATION OF THE OLD TESTAMENT

1. Not all of Shem's descendants spoke Semitic languages. Elam and Lud, for instance, used non-Semitic languages (Gen. 10:22), while a few descendants of Ham (e.g., Canaan, v. 6, and the sons of Cush mentioned in v. 7) spoke Semitic rather than Hamitic languages.

2. Thomas O. Lambdin, *Introduction to Biblical Hebrew* (New York: 1971), p. xiii. For a more detailed chart, see J. Huehnergard, "Languages (Introductory)," *ABD* 4:157. Arabic ("Arabian") is classified as "central."

3. Babylonian and Assyrian are called collectively "Akkadian."

4. The language of the Ebla Tablets has not yet been classified with certainty. Some scholars consider it closest to Akkadian. See R. D. Biggs, "Ebla Texts," *ABD* 2:264.

5. The Gezer calendar, apparently a schoolboy's exercise tablet (*ca.* 1000); the Samaritan ostraca, about seventy-five brief inscriptions on potsherds (*ca.* 750); the Siloam inscription telling of the completion of Hezekiah's water tunnel (*ca.* 700); and the Lachish letters, about one hundred lines of legible Hebrew (*ca.* 589) are the most important of the

nonbiblical Hebrew documents dating from the Old Testament period. For a more complete inventory, see K. A. D. Smelik, *Writings from Ancient Israel: A Handbook of Historical and Religious Documents* (Louisville: 1991).

6. Vowels in postbiblical Hebrew are written above or below the consonants by a system of dots and dashes called points. "Unpointed" Hebrew is the consonantal text without these vowel indications.

7. Akkadian diplomatic correspondences between officials in Canaan (among others) and their Egyptian superiors, dating from the fourteenth century and discovered at Tel el-Amarna in Egypt.

8. Aramaic was possibly the native tongue of Jesus and most New Testament authors (e.g., the evangelists, except Luke). Note Jesus' use of *mammon* (Matt. 6:24), *Raca* (5:22; RSV mg.), *Ephphatha* (Mark 7:34), *Talitha cumi* (Mark 5:41), *Eloi, lama sabachthani* (Mark 15:34), and *Abba* (Mark 14:36), all of which seem to represent Aramaic originals. For Aramaic influence on the Gospels and Acts, particularly on the Greek sentence structure, see M. Black, *An Aramaic Approach to the Gospels and Acts*, 3rd ed. (London: 1967). However, see also the references in Chapter 43 regarding the book of Daniel.

9. See Ps. 40:7 (MT 6); Jer. 36:2ff. (the best OT account of methods of writing Scripture); Ezek 2:9-3:3; Zech. 5:1f.

10. Papyrus fragments were found at Qumran, Wadi Murabbaat, Nahal Hever, and Wadi ed-Daliyeh.

11. Some text critics use the term *haplography* in a wider sense, when anything has been omitted from a text.

12. Ishbosheth in 2 Sam. 2:8 is Eshbaal in 1 Chr. 8:33; Jerubbesheth of 2 Sam. 11:21 is Jerubbaal in Judg. 6:32; Mephibosheth in 2 Sam. 4:4 is Meribaal in 1 Chr. 8:34; 9:40. In the time of Saul, "Baal," i.e., "Lord," could be used of Yahweh, the Lord of Israel. Perhaps these changes can be dated after the time of Hosea, in whose day God called for an end to this practice (Hos. 2:16-17).

13. Some of the duplication among the proverbs and psalms may be accounted for in this fashion. E.g., Pss. 14; 53 are well known to be identical except that Ps. 14 uses the divine name Yahweh and 53 uses Elohim. See also Pss. 40:13-17; 70.

14. Ralph W. Klein, *Textual Criticism of the Old Testament: From the Septuagint to Qumran* (Philadelphia: 1974), pp. 5-10.

15. R. Kittel's *Biblia Hebraica,* revised by K. Elliger and W. Rudolph as *Biblia Hebraica Stuttgartensia* (Stuttgart: 1968-1977), gives an accurate reproduction of ben Asher's text, even though the variant readings in the critical apparatus are not always accurate and the suggested emendations are not always happily chosen; see B. J. Roberts, "The Textual Transmission of the Old Testament," pp. 1-30 in G. W. Anderson, ed., *Tradition and Interpretation* (Oxford: 1979).

16. This is because the standardized text in certain instances is inferior. Ancient people sometimes made choices based on tradition or prejudice rather than upon scientific evidence. Hence, superior manuscripts or readings might have been discarded unknowingly.

17. There used to be a prejudice for the MT against the LXX because the former is in Hebrew while the latter is in Greek and is a translation. It was thought that when the LXX differed from the MT, it was due to the creativity of the translators. Some scholars would not even consider the ancient translations unless the MT was incomprehensible (as at times it is) or unless there was massive support for the non-MT reading. However, since the discovery of the Dead Sea Scrolls at Qumran, which sometimes agree with the LXX against the MT, it is now indisputable that the LXX at times preserves better readings than

the MT and must be taken seriously as an ancient witness. Although it is in Greek, it was translated from an ancient Hebrew manuscript. By retroverting the LXX back into Hebrew, one can often get a better picture of development of the text. For more information, see F. M. Cross, Jr., "The History of the Biblical Text in the Light of Discoveries in the Judaean Desert," *Qumran and the History of the Biblical Text* (Cambridge: 1975), pp. 177-195; R. W. Klein, *Textual Criticism of the Old Testament*, pp. 11-15.

18. See B. Waltke, "Samaritan Pentateuch," *ABD* 5:934-938 for the view that the Samaritans began with a text quite like the MT ("Proto-MT") and gradually altered it by scribal mistakes, simplifications, additions, and theological adaptations.

19. Recent scholars have tended to revise the older views about the nature of the links between the Samaritan Pentateuch and the LXX. See B. Waltke, "Samaritan Pentateuch," and J. E. Sanderson, *An Exodus Scroll from Qumran: 4Q Paleo-Exod and the Samaritan Tradition* (Atlanta: 1986).

20. The need for a reliable critical text is being met currently by A. Sperber, ed., *The Bible in Aramaic*, 4 vols. (Leiden: 1959-1973).

21. Perhaps a Babylonian corruption of "Aquila," whose name also graces an ancient Greek version of the Bible. For a summary of the history and pilgrimage of Onkelos (also spelled Onqelos) see P. S. Alexander, "Targum, Targumim," *ABD* 6:321-322.

22. Two ancient targums found only in fragmentary form, the Palestinian targum on the Pentateuch and the Jerusalem II targum (or Fragment Targum), are witnesses to the didactic and interpretative nature of the targums, which contain lavish extrabiblical commentary.

23. Jewish tradition attributes this targum to Jonathan ben Uzziel, a pupil of the famous Rabbi Hillel in the first century A.D. Some modern scholars, however, associate the name with its Greek equivalent "Theodotion," the name of the person responsible for one of the Greek versions. However, the official targum texts were hardly the work of individuals, but more probably were derived by groups of scholars from the numerous targumic traditions in circulation. On these and related matters, see Alexander, "Targum, Targumin," *ABD* 6:320-323.

24. On the Samaritan Targums, see B. Waltke, "Samaritan Pentateuch," *ABD* 5:935. He cites research indicating that (1) the various manuscripts represent independent translations, ranging from about 100 B.C. to A.D. 1000; (2) their textual tradition is the same as the manuscripts we have for the Samaritan Pentateuch; (3) the Samaritan Targums were evidently influenced by the Targum of Onkelos during the years between A.D. 800 and 1000.

25. P. Kahle (*The Cairo Genizah*, 2nd ed. [London: 1959]) and others (e.g., A. Bentzen, *Introduction* 1:80-85; E. Würthwein, *The Text of the Old Testament*, trans. E. F. Rhodes [Grand Rapids: 1979]) hold the former view. H. S. Gehman ("Septuagint," *TCERK* 2:1015-1017) and H. M. Orlinsky ("On the Present State of Proto-Septuagint Studies," *JAOS* 61 [1941]: 81-91) favor an archetypal or original LXX which developed in various ways through editors and copyists. More recently, see Klein, *Textual Criticism of the Old Testament*, and especially M. K. H. Peters, "Septuagint," *ABD* 5:1093-1104. Peters' essay and bibliography call particular attention to the work of E. Tov and J. W. Wevers.

26. P. A. H. de Boer, ed., *Vetus Testamentum Syriace iuxta simplicem Syrorum versionem 1* (Leiden: 1972). Called the "Leiden Peshitta Institute" editions, about a dozen of the twenty-four Old Testament books have appeared, together with the bulk of the Apocryphal writings. For recent discussion of the Peshitta and other Syriac versions, see S. P. Brock, "Versions, Ancient (Syriac)," *ABD* 6:794-799.

27. A modern edition of the Old Latin texts is in process: B. Fischer, ed., *Vetus Latina: Die Reste der Altlateinischen Bibel* (Freiburg: 1949-). Progress on the Old Testament has

been slow. *Genesis* (Fischer, 1951-54) and *Isaiah* (R. Gryson, 1987) have been published, along with several deutero-canonical books (W. Thiele, *Sirach* and *Wisdom of Solomon*, 1977-87).

28. Modern Catholic scholars, nevertheless, are avidly and productively studying the Scriptures in Hebrew, Aramaic, and Greek, as shown by the *JB* and *NJB*. For an up-to-date discussion of the Latin versions, see P.-M. Bogaert, *ABD* 6:799-803.

29. For other versions, e.g., Gothic, Georgian, Old Slavic, Anglo-Saxon, consult J. D. Douglas, ed., *The New International Dictionary of the Christian Church* (Grand Rapids: 1974) and *ABD* 6:803-813. For Coptic see W. E. Mills, *ABD* 6:803; for Gothic and Georgian see J. N. Birdsall, *ABD* 6:803-805; 810-813; for Ethiopic, R. Zuurmond, *ABD* 6:808-810; for Armenian, J. M. Alexanian, *ABD* 6:805-808.

CHAPTER 48 — GEOGRAPHY

1. Herodotus 1.105, *en tē Palaistinē Suriē*.

2. "Palestine" occurs in Joel 3:4 of the KJV, and "Palestina" in Exod. 15:14 and Isa. 14:29, but this is an accident of translation. The RSV correctly renders the word "Philistia."

3. "Palestine" does not occur in the New Testament. Transjordan is called "Perea," a name with approximately the same meaning (Greek for "[the land] over there").

4. D. Baly, *Geography of the Bible*, 2nd ed. (New York: 1974), pp. 28-41.

5. Palestine at its northern end, from the sea to the Upper Jordan, is about 32 mi. (52 km.) wide; at its southern end, from Gaza to Sodom, about 65 mi. (105 km.).

6. The traditional southern boundary of Judah was Beersheba, although the tribal boundary was considerably further south (Josh. 15:1-4). In the Old Testament the Negeb is generally of little significance and considered outside the land.

7. See N. Glueck, *Rivers in the Desert*, rev. ed. (Philadelphia: 1968).

8. N. Glueck, *The River Jordan* (Philadelphia: 1946), p. 118.

9. "Sea of Reeds," the literal rendering of the Hebrew phrase usually translated "Red Sea," describes neither the Gulf of Suez nor the Red Sea, and most likely applies to reed-filled marshes in the vicinity of Lake Timsah or the Bitter lakes.

10. Arabic "fifty." About fifty days of such weather occur each year — but not a seven-week season, for the *hamsîn* rarely lasts more than three or four days at a time.

11. The occasional statement that Palestine had two rainy seasons arises from a misunderstanding of these terms.

CHAPTER 49 — THE CHRONOLOGICAL PUZZLE

1. E.g., Gen. 5:3, 5f., etc. An exception is the Flood account where even the month and day are given; cf. 7:11; 8:13.

2. The Sumerians marked a "double hour" (i.e., *ca.* 120 minutes) by first dividing the sky into halves and thirds and then marking the sun's position approximately with respect to those reference points. Sundials were in use by the eighth century B.C., and the Greeks and Romans used the hour as a unit. Where "hour" occurs in the Old Testament, it simply means "time, occasion"; cf. Dan. 3:6.

3. R. de Vaux (*Ancient Israel*, trans. J. McHugh, 2 vols. [New York: 1965], p. 181) cites evidence that the Hebrews originally had a morning-to-morning day, but his theory has not found general acceptance.

4. The earliest Semitic words for "month" were derived from the word for "moon" (cf. English "month," essentially "moonth"). Later, the common Hebrew word *ḥōdeš* "newness" replaced the earlier word.

5. The Egyptians anchored their calendration to the heliacal rising of the star Sothis or Sirius (the Dog Star), but failed to adjust for leap year. As a result, their calendar fell short one day in four years, or one year in 1,460 (the "Sothic cycle"). Nevertheless, they did keep careful records of the amount the calendar year diverged from the rising of Sothis. For more on Mesopotamian and Egyptian calendars, see F. Rochberg-Halton, "Calendars: Ancient Near East," *ABD* 1:810-814.

6. The time of intercalation appears to have been somewhat arbitrary at first. Later, a system was developed ("Metonic cycle," adopted *ca.* 432) in which intercalary months were added to the third, sixth, eighth, eleventh, fourteenth, seventeenth, and nineteenth years. The Babylonians had no uniform time for intercalation, for the intercalary month was sometimes added between Ululu and Tašritu (in the fall) and sometimes between Addaru and Nisanu (in the spring). The Hebrews finally decided to add the month after Adar, even though their year began in the fall. See Rochberg-Halton, pp. 810-813; J. C. VanderKam, "Calendars: Ancient Israelite and Early Jewish," *ABD* 1:814, 816-817.

7. Nisan is not mentioned, for at that time the month was called Abib, possibly a Canaanite name (Exod. 13:4). Later the Babylonian name was adopted.

8. De Vaux (*Ancient Israel*, p. 191) argues that the autumnal year was original, since the first month was called in Akkadian *Tišritu* "beginning." But he apparently failed to note that the next month was *Warah-samnu* "eighth month."

9. A similar phenomenon is evident in modern calendar names. Originally September meant "seventh month" (from Lat. *septem* "seven"); October "eighth month" (from *octo*); November "ninth month" (from *novem*); and December "tenth month" (from *decem*). When the year was changed, these names were retained.

10. Jehu, at the outset of his reign, paid tribute to Shalmaneser III *ca.* 841. Samaria fell to Sargon II *ca.* 721. An additional complication arises from the different chronological data in the LXX, especially the Old Greek and Lucianic rescensions. For alternative assessments of the LXX text, see G. H. Jones, *1 and 2 Kings*, 2 vols. (Grand Rapids: 1984), pp. 19-21; and A. R. Green, "Regnal Formulas in the Hebrew and Greek Texts of the Books of Kings," *JNES* 42 (1983): 167-180.

11. E. R. Thiele, *The Mysterious Numbers of the Hebrew Kings*, new rev. ed. (Grand Rapids: 1983). The authors are deeply indebted to Thiele's work for the material in this section. For an excellent summary of approaches to the chronological problems and the canonical function of this material, see B. S. Childs, *Introduction to the Old Testament as Scripture* (Philadelphia: 1979), pp. 294-300.

12. J. H. Hayes and P. K. Hooker, *A New Chronology for the Kings of Israel and Judah and Its Implications for Biblical History and Literature* (Atlanta: 1988). See also J. Hughes, *Secrets of the Times: Myth and History in Biblical Chronology* (Sheffield: 1990), who argues that the chronology of Kings is schematic, not literal, though "based on an originally historical chronology" (p. 3).

13. The authors (p. 23) appeal to the phrase "Baasha and his house" (1 Kgs. 16:3, 7) to suggest that Baasha was still alive when Zimri killed Elah, his son and successor. While one might read the text that way, the narrative strongly implies that Baasha died before Zimri killed his surviving family and, thus, offers doubtful evidence of Baasha's abdication.

14. Thiele, *Mysterious Numbers*, pp. 43-56; so also Jones, *1 and 2 Kings*, p. 17. For the opposite view, see M. Cogan, "Chronology: Hebrew Bible," *ABD* 1:1006.

15. Contrast Hayes and Hooker, *A New Chronology*, pp. 12, 13, who reject coregen-

cies and assume an empty throne at three transitions of power: (1) the struggle between Zechariah, Shallum, and Menaham (2 Kgs. 15); (2) the succession of Jehoahaz by Jehoiakim; (3) the succession of Jehoiachin by Zedekiah (2 Kgs. 23; 24).

16. *Mysterious Numbers*, pp. 56-60. Apparently Athaliah encouraged the royal scribes to make the change retroactive to include the reign of Jehoram.

17. Many scholars share this assumption (so Jones, p. 17), but Hayes and Hooker (pp. 13-14, 86-88) date the change to Josiah's eighteenth year (624 B.C.).

18. Also important is the Canon of Ptolemy (*ca.* A.D. 70-161), which traces the rulers of Babylon from 747 B.C. onward, the Persian kings, Alexander and his successors in Egypt, and the Roman kings to Ptolemy's own day. His knowledge of astronomy as well as geography and history makes his work all the more valuable, with more than eighty observations on solar, lunar, or planetary positions. His mention of the accession of Sargon II of Assyria to the throne of Babylon in 722/21 provides an important cross-check with the Assyrian eponym lists.

19. *Mysterious Numbers*, pp. 199-204.

20. *Ibid.*, pp. 120, 124-131. In fairness to Thiele's critics (notably Cogan, "Chronology," p. 1007) we need mention that this scenario assumes an early rather than a late date (i.e., 742 vice 738) for an episode in Assyrian records involving Menaham. The date is a matter of dispute, and those who accept the late dating reject Thiele's solution.

21. *Mysterious Numbers*, pp. 134-138. Alternatively, Cogan (p. 1008) believes that the date in 2 Kgs. 18:13 should head the prophetic story in 2 Kgs. 20. See also the recent explanations based on assumed coregencies; cf. N. Na'aman, "Historical and Chronological Notes on the Kingdoms of Israel and Judah in the Eighth Century B.C.," *VT* 36 (1986): 83-91; and L. McFall, "Some Missing Coregencies in Thiele's Chronology," *Andrews University Seminary Studies* 30 (1992): 48-52.

22. Cf. the insightful discussion in Childs, *Old Testament as Scripture*, pp. 297-300.

CHAPTER 50 — ARCHAEOLOGY

1. A. Ben-Tor, *The Archaeology of Ancient Israel* (New Haven: 1992), p. 1.

2. W. G. Dever, "Archaeology, Syro-Palestinian and Biblical, *ABD* 1:366.

3. G. E. Wright, *Biblical Archaeology* (Philadelphia: 1962), p. 17.

4. *Ibid.*

5. Cf. Dever's assessments of the debate, *Recent Archaeological Discoveries and Biblical Research* (Seattle: 1990); cf. "The Death of a Discipline," *BARev* 21/5 (1995): 50-55, 70.

6. C. Renfrew and P. Bahn, *Archaeology: Theories, Methods, and Practice* (New York: 1991), p. 339.

7. Dever, *ABD*, 1:355.

8. Cf. Ø. LaBianca and L. Lacelle, *Environmental Foundations. Hesban 2* (Berrien Springs, Mich.: 1986).

9. R. S. Abujaber, *Pioneers over Jordan* (London: 1989), p. 8.

10. *World Atlas of Archaeology*, ed. Christine Flon et al. (New York: 1988), p. 408.

11. LaBianca and Lacelle, p. 110.

12. L. E. Toombs, "The Development of Palestinian Archeology as a Discipline," *BA* 45 (1982): 89.

13. *Ibid.*

14. *Ibid.*, p. 90.

15. *World Atlas of Archaeology*, p. 412.

16. Renfrew and Bahn, *Archaeology*, p. 29.

17. *Ibid.*, p. 372.

18. Ben-Tor, *The Archaeology of Ancient Israel*, pp. 5-6.

19. D. Ussishkin, "Where Is Israeli Archeology Going?" *BA* 45 (1982): 93-95.

20. R. Schick, Z. T. Fiema, and K. ʿAmr, "The Petra Church Project: A Preliminary Report," *ADAJ* 37 (1993): 55-66, esp. pl. I.

21. Ussishkin, p. 95.

22. *World Atlas of Archaeology*, p. 414; W. F. Libby, *Radiocarbon Dating*, 2nd ed. (Chicago: 1955).

23. *Ibid.*

24. *Ibid.*, p. 417.

25. Cf. W. P. Long, *The Art of Biblical History. Foundations of Contemporary Interpretation* 5 (Grand Rapids: 1994), pp. 142-149, for the discussion on which some of the following paragraphs are based.

26. Cf. J. M. Miller, "Old Testament History and Archaeology," *BA* 50 (1987): 59.

27. F. Brandfon, "The Limits of Evidence: Archaeology and Objectivity," *Maarav* 4/1 (1987): 30.

28. P. J. King, "The *Marzeah* Amos Denounces," *BARev* 14/4 (1988): 34.

29. Cf. recently K. A. Kitchen, "The Patriarchal Age: Myth or History?" *BARev* 21/2 (1995): 48-57, 88, 90, 92, 94-96, 98-100.

30. Cf. the excellent study by I. Finkelstein, *The Archaeology of the Israelite Settlement* (Jerusalem: 1988).

31. P. J. King, *Amos, Hosea, Micah — An Archaeological Commentary* (Philadelphia: 1988); *idem, Jeremiah: An Archaeological Companion* (Louisville: 1993).

32. W. G. Dever, cited on jacket of King's *Jeremiah — An Archaeological Companion.*

CHAPTER 51 — MESSIANIC PROPHECY

1. Some scholars read "Messiah" in Dan. 9:25f., but there it lacks the article and is translated better "an anointed prince" (NRSV).

2. For a fuller discussion, see W. S. LaSor, "The Messianic Idea in Qumram," pp. 344-351 in Ben-Horin, B. D. Weinryb, and S. Zeitlin, eds., *Studies and Essays in Honor of Abraham A. Neuman* (Leiden: 1962); "The Messiah: An Evangelical Christian View," pp. 76-95 in M. Tanenbaum, M. R. Wilson, and A. J. Rodin, eds., *Evangelicals and Jews in Conversation on Scripture, Theology, and History* (Grand Rapids: 1973); *The Truth about Armageddon: What the Bible Says about the End Times* (San Francisco: 1982, repr. 1986): 330-338, esp. 330-333.

3. For the authenticity of these verses, see p. 250. See also G. von Rad, *Old Testament Theology*, trans. D. M. G. Stalker, 2 vols. (New York: 1962-1965) 2:138; R. E. Clements, *Prophecy and Covenant* (London: 1965), pp. 111f.; D. A. Hubbard, *Joel and Amos*, TOTC (Leicester, U.K.; Downers Grove, Ill.: 1989), pp. 100-102, 239-242.

4. For a strong protest against this confusion of terms and a fine contribution to the clarification, see J. Coppens, "Les origines du messianisme: Le dernier essai: de synthäse historique," pp. 35-38 in *L'Attente du Messie*, Recherches bibliques (Bruges: 1954).

5. Although "Messiah" and "Christ" were practically interchangeable terms at first, New Testament uses are frequently taken as referring exclusively to Jesus. The apostles were arguing that Jesus was the Messiah and that the Messiah was David's son.

6. For a balanced study, see J. L. McKenzie, "Royal Messianism," *CBQ* 19 (1957):

25-52. See also D. J. A. Clines, "The Psalms and the King," *Theological Students Fellowship Bulletin* 11 (1975): 1-8.

7. The Hebrew also could be translated "Your throne is God," but not "your divine throne," as in the RSV.

8. The Hebrew language did not possess the Greek idea of infinity. The expression "forever and ever" probably conveyed in Hebrew something like "for a long time and then some."

Index of Names

Aaron, 65, 67, 77, 86, 102, 106-109, 184, 222
Abaddon, 471
Abel (place), 456
Abel (son of Adam), 26-27, 249, 599
Abiathar, 178, 184, 187, 191-192, 329
Abigail, 179
Abihu, 86, 91
Abijah. *See* Abijam
Abijam, 135, 199
Abimelech, 8, 177
Abishag, 191
Abner, 180
Abraham, 4-5, 8, 31, 41-42, 44-45, 48-50, 65, 177, 224, 633; call of, 1-15, 32-35, 47-48, 120-121
Abrahamic covenant, 46, 50, 66, 73, 97, 119, 151, 184, 227, 249-250, 374, 751n.64, 772n.2
Absalom, 187-193, 772n.10
Absalom, pillar of, 377
Abyssinian rains, 70
Acco, 215, 622
Achan, 140, 175
Acre. *See* Acco
Acts of Solomon, 134, 193
Adad-nirari III, 245
Adam (city), 627
Adam (first man), 19, 24-26, 32, 63, 588
Adonijah, 191-193
Adoniram/Adoram, 190, 194, 198

Aegean, 156, 555
Aegeo-Cretan tribes. *See* Sea Peoples
Afghanistan, 555
Africa: east coast of, 622; North, 56, 617
Agur, 468-469
Ahab, 105, 135, 201-208, 216, 250, 275, 545, 636, 639
Ahasuerus, 391, 532-538, 553, 558
Ahaz, 210, 212, 256, 271, 277-298 passim, 639
Ahaziah (son of Ahab), 204
Ahaziah (son of Jehoshaphat), 207, 636
Ahijah, 135, 198, 225, 544
Ahikam, 330, 334
Ahimaaz, 187
Ahimelech, 178, 184
Ahinoam, 179
Ahithophel, 189, 456, 772n.11
Ahmosis, 38, 53, 65
Ai, 132, 140-141, 147
Aijalon, valley of, 149
'Ain Qedeis, 626
Akhenaten, 53-54, 146, 764n.23
Akhetaten, 146
Akhmimic dialect, 618
Akiba, Rabbi, 510-511, 612, 616
Akkad, 34
Akkadians, 34-35; dialect of, 57, 743n.6; literature of, 19, 36, 102, 112, 450, 811n.1
Alalakh, 37; tablets of, 746n.2

Index of Authors

855